THE ROLLING STONES
ALL THE SONGS

THE ROLLING STONES
ALL THE SONGS

The Story Behind Every Track

Philippe Margotin and Jean-Michel Guesdon

TABLE OF CONTENTS

6_ Foreword

8_ A Band is Born

13_ Ian Stewart, the Sixth Stone

14_ *Come On / I Want To Be Loved*

18_ Andrew Loog Oldham, Inventor of the Rolling Stones

20_ *I Wanna Be Your Man / Stoned*

24 · THE ROLLING STONES

44 · THE ROLLING STONES

56 · FIVE BY FIVE

68 · THE ROLLING STONES NO.2

134 · AFTERMATH

176 · GOT LIVE IF YOU WANT IT!

184 · BETWEEN THE BUTTONS

204 · FLOWERS

312 · GET YER YA-YA'S OUT!

324 · STONE AGE

330 · STICKY FINGERS

360 · EXILE ON MAIN ST.

454 · BLACK AND BLUE

470 · SOME GIRLS

492 · EMOTIONAL RESCUE

510 · TATTOO YOU

594 · FLASHPOINT

600 · VOODOO LOUNGE

628 · BRIDGES TO BABYLON

648 · FORTY LICKS

90 OUT OF OUR HEADS

114 GOT LIVE IF YOU WANT IT!

128 DECEMBER'S CHILDREN (AND EVERYBODY)

212 THEIR SATANIC MAJESTIES REQUEST

246 BEGGARS BANQUET

280 LET IT BLEED

394 GOATS HEAD SOUP

416 IT'S ONLY ROCK' N' ROLL

436 META-MORPHOSIS

532 UNDER-COVER

552 DIRTY WORK

570 STEEL WHEELS

656 RARITIES 1971 - 2003

664 A BIGGER BANG

690 GRRR!

696_ Glossary
698_ Index
702_ Bibliography

FOREWORD

April 7, 1962. Onstage at the Ealing Club in London, a young, blond-haired guitarist launches into the intro of "Dust My Broom," a blues number from the depths of the Mississippi Delta. His bottleneck glides up and down the strings of his Hofner Committee guitar, producing an unfamiliar, mesmerizing sound. His name is Brian Jones. Among the audience in the packed, smoky room are two young musicians who appreciate his performance even more than most: Mick Jagger and Keith Richards. The three of them share a passion for the blues of Muddy Waters, Howlin' Wolf, Jimmy Reed, and Lightnin' Hopkins, and decide to throw in their musical lot together. Over the following months they are joined by Ian Stewart, a pianist well-versed in the dynamic rhythms of boogie-woogie, Bill Wyman, and finally Charlie Watts. The Rolling Stones are born, and with them one of the most extraordinary and exciting musical stories of the twentieth century.

May 1963. A few months before John F. Kennedy's assassination. Harold MacMillan is Prime Minister of the United Kingdom and General de Gaulle is President of France. Pouring forth from the radio are the Beatles with "From Me To You," Gerry and the Pacemakers with "How Do You Do It?" and Billy J. Kramer and the Dakotas with "Do You Want To Know A Secret." In London, five disenchanted-looking musicians with dark circles under their eyes from spending night after night practicing the magical chords and riffs of those eternal Chicago blues are getting ready to record their first single, "Come On." And their dedication pays off, for this debut release will seal their destiny and kick-start the career of the greatest rock 'n' roll band in the world!

Ever since that auspicious spring of 1963, the Rolling Stones have been a glittering star in the rock 'n' roll firmament, and the concert given by the London band in 2016 to a captivated crowd in Cuba demonstrates that the legend is far from over. Where does this Rolling Stones magic come from? Without doubt from their rebelliousness, their love of provocation, and their black humor and acerbic wit. But most of all it derives from their music—that special cocktail of blues and rock 'n' roll, country and gospel that sums up half a century of good vibrations and cool sounds. A music born of the incredible bond between Mick Jagger and Keith Richards, two songwriters who have forged a route to success by spurning fashion and holding critics in utter contempt. The music of the Stones comes across as authentic because it is the music of a never-ending party, of a categorical refusal to grow old.

Because the Stones are an English band, *The Rolling Stones All the Songs* is based on their British discography. Where the track listing of the US version of an album differs from the UK release, we have indicated this and made a point of including any songs that are not on the UK album. In the case of the live albums, we have covered all the songs that have never been recorded in the studio. Finally, in order to be absolutely straight with the reader, wherever it has proved impossible to be sure about a date or a musician's name, we have inserted a (?).

The Stones have been rolling for more than half a century. The most extraordinary thing is not that they have discovered the elixir of eternal youth for themselves; it is that they have chosen to share it with their fans, both onstage and on disc. May *The Rolling Stones All the Songs* be an enduring contribution to their alchemy!

The blond angel from Cheltenham who started the Rolling Stones.

A BAND IS BORN

In 1962, during the early days of spring, English rock history was about to be made under London's foggy skies. It all started with a chance encounter, when Mick Jagger and Keith Richards met Brian Jones, a blond angel who played the guitar so well he might have hailed from Chicago. The stones had not yet begun to roll. But they were already well formed.

It All Started at the Ealing Club

"Ealing Broadway Station. Turn left, cross at Zebra and go down steps between ABC Teashop and Jewellers. Saturday at 7.30 P.M." This brief notice published in the March 17, 1962—Saint Patrick's Day—issue of the *New Musical Express* gave directions to the Ealing Club and the opening gig by Alexis Korner's band Blues Incorporated, "the most exciting event of this year," as the magazine put it. Located at 42A The Broadway, in Ealing, London W5, a district hitherto known for its moving picture studios, the Ealing Club had recently been born out of the ashes of the Ealing Jazz Club at the instigation of Alexis Korner and Cyril Davies. Their aim was to promote the blues to a London music scene that was still somewhat conformist and that could hardly see past jazz (traditional or modern) and skiffle.

Korner and Davies played guitar and harmonica, respectively. Members of Chris Barber's jazz band at the end of the forties, they then performed as a duo in the Soho clubs, drawing on the repertoire of the black bluesmen of the United States. Later, their paths would diverge. After forming the band Blues Incorporated together, Davies abandoned it in 1963 for a more traditional form of blues, starting the Cyril Davies R&B All-Stars. As of May 1962, the Blues Incorporated lineup consisted of (in addition to its two founding members) the singer Long John Baldry, the pianist Keith Scott, the saxophonist Dick Heckstall-Smith, the bassist Jack Bruce, (the future bassist for Cream, who played double bass back then), and a certain Charlie Watts on drums.

Brian "Elmo Lewis" Jones

Over the course of the days, the band attracted a growing number of blues enthusiasts to the Ealing Club. Among them was one Brian Jones. Born in Cheltenham, Gloucestershire, on February 28, 1942, Lewis Brian Hopkin Jones was the son of an aeronautical engineer and a piano teacher. Possessing an IQ of 133, Jones was a hyperintelligent child who showed a particular talent on the saxophone and the guitar. He was resistant to all forms of discipline, however, and in 1959, to the great displeasure of his parents, he abandoned his studies to go traveling in Scandinavia. The fact that he had got two girls pregnant within a matter of months of each other, a schoolgirl of fourteen and a married Cheltenham woman (Angeline), no doubt played a part in his sudden infatuation with the lands of northern Europe. Upon his return to England, Brian played alto saxophone for a time with the local band the Ramrods, before leaving Cheltenham for good in 1961 to set up home in London with the mother of his third child, Pat Andrews, a girl of just fifteen years of age. There, he started to frequent the blues scene, which was still in its infancy, and played from time to time with Alexis Korner.

On April 7, 1962, Brian Jones had just teamed up with Blues Incorporated again for a performance under the alias Elmo Lewis ("Elmo" in homage to one of his idols, the bluesman Elmore James). When he launched into "Dust My Broom" with a killer slide intro played on his Hofner Committee, the reaction was one of general stupefaction. In the audience, three young musicians in particular were awed. Their names were Mick Jagger, Keith Richards, and Dick Taylor. "He was the first person I ever heard playing slide electric guitar," recalls Keith. "Mick and I both thought he was incredible."[1]

Mick, Keith, Dick . . .

Michael Philip Jagger and Keith Richards were born in 1943, five months apart, in Dartford, Kent, some fifteen miles

Alexis Korner (guitar) and Cyril Davies, with Charlie Watts in the background.

(twenty-five kilometers) from London—the former on July 26, the latter on December 18. Mick was the son of Eva and Basil "Joe" Jagger, a gym teacher at a school in Dartford, and the elder brother of Christopher, who would also become a singer. The family belonged to the middle class, conservative with a small *c*, in which traditions such as saying grace before a meal were observed and strict discipline prevailed. The Jaggers initially lived at 39 Denver Road before moving in 1954 to a road named The Close in a far more "respectable" district.

Keith's father, Herbert William Richards, was an electrician and later, after sustaining a severe leg injury during the Normandy landings, a foreman in a London power station. His mother Doris demonstrated washing machines while bringing up her one and only son. The Richards family lived in a small house on Chastilian Road, not far from Denver Road, and later moved to Temple Hill, some distance from the center of Dartford.

Mick Jagger and Keith Richards both attended Wentworth Primary School, but went on to follow different academic paths—the London School of Economics for Mick, Sidcup Art College for Keith. On the morning of October 17, 1961, both of them found themselves by chance at Dartford train station. The future Stones singer was holding two precious items that immediately sparked Richards's interest. The latter recalls this decisive moment: "Did we hit it off? You get in a carriage with a guy that's got *Rockin' at the Hops* by Chuck Berry on Chess Records, and *The Best of Muddy Waters* also under his arm, you are gonna hit it off."[2] In addition to their shared taste in music, Mick Jagger and Keith Richards discovered that they also, by coincidence, had a friend in common: Dick Taylor. Born in Dartford on January 28, 1943, this former Sidcup Art College student was a guitarist in the same group as Mick: Little Boy Blue and the Blue Boys. Shortly after their encounter, Keith joined the lineup, whose other members were Bob Beckwith on guitar and Alan Etherington (Mick

Jagger's best friend in those days) on percussion. A strong bond developed between Keith and Mick as Little Boy Blue and the Blue Boys recorded their first songs on a makeshift tape recorder and sent the tape to Alexis Korner . . .

. . . and the Others

After Brian Jones's slide guitar demonstration onstage at the Ealing Club, Mick Jagger, Keith Richards, and Dick Taylor exchanged a few words with him. "I think Mick was the first one to go up and talk to him, and discovered that he had his own band, most of whom deserted him in the next few weeks,"[2] recalls Keith Richards. Later, on May 2, 1962, to be precise, Brian Jones put an advertisement in *Jazz News* for new musicians, specifically a harmonica player and/or tenor saxophonist, a pianist, a bassist, and a drummer. Ian "Stu" Stewart, a pianist well versed in the percussive rhythms of boogie-woogie, but also a great admirer of Duke Ellington and Ella Fitzgerald, was the first to respond. Brian then recruited the guitarist Geoff Bradford. "I formed a band called Blues By Six," recalls Bradford. "We played the Marquee Jazz Club. This fellow came up to me and said, 'My name's Brian Jones and I'm thinking of forming a band. Do you want to be in it?'"[1] Bradford agreed to do a trial, as did Brian Knight, the singer–harmonica player with Blues By Six, who pulled out soon after. During the course of June 1962, Ian Stewart invited the new vocalist with Blues Incorporated, one Mick Jagger (who had just joined Alexis Korner's band), to come along to a rehearsal, and Jagger turned up with Keith Richards and Dick Taylor in tow. This led to a reunion with Brian. Bradford, who didn't have the same passion for Chuck Berry, also ended up leaving the group.

The Rollin' Stones: Bluesmen at Eighteen

The Rollin' Stones (the name was Brian's idea, in homage to Muddy Waters) were born. Or the band's first incarnation, at any rate, consisting of Brian Jones (guitar, harmonica), Mick

Giorgio Gomelsky, who ran the Crawdaddy Club and was the Stones' first manager.

Jagger (vocals, harmonica), Keith Richards (guitar), Dick Taylor (bass), and Ian Stewart (piano). They gave their first concert at the Marquee on July 12, 1962, with Mick Avory (who was later to join the Kinks) on drums. Soon after this, following an advertisement in the *Melody Maker*, Tony Chapman, previously drummer with the Cliftons, took Avory's place.

At the end of the summer of 1962, Brian Jones, Mick Jagger, and Keith Richards moved into a small flat at 102 Edith Grove in Chelsea with a certain James Phelge. "The place would have been perfect as a replica of a World War Two battlefront,"[3] Phelge would later say of the modest apartment. At this time the young musicians were living hand to mouth: Brian had just been fired from the store Whiteleys of Bayswater, having been caught with his hand in the cash register, and Keith was reselling deposit bottles, while Mick was in receipt of a modest grant as a student at the London School of Economics. What did it matter if there was no more money at the beginning of the month than there was at the end? There was always music—blues and rock 'n' roll. Having managed to scrape together a few pounds, the Rollin' Stones, minus Dick Taylor, who had chosen to return to his studies, booked Curly Clayton Sound Studios in Highbury for October 27 (or October 26, according to Bill Wyman). There they recorded three numbers: "You Can't Judge a Book by the Cover" by Willie Dixon, "Soon Forgotten" by St. Louis Jimmy, and "Close Together" by Jimmy Reed. The demo was sent off to two record companies with no success.

Day after day passed in the same manner: rehearsals in the afternoon at 102 Edith Grove and gigs at the Ealing Club in the evening. Ever since Taylor had walked out, the Stones had an urgent need for a new bassist. Another advertisement was placed. At the beginning of December, on the recommendation of Tony Chapman, with whom he had played in the Cliftons, Bill Wyman agreed to go and meet one of the Stones, Ian Stewart, at the Red Lion.

Born William George Perks in London on October 24, 1936, Bill Wyman was one of the five children of William Perks, a bricklayer, and his wife Molly. He assumed the name Bill Wyman in memory of a friend with whom he had completed his national service in the Royal Air Force. Mad about music, Bill played guitar before switching to the bass upon joining the Cliftons in 1961. Ian Stewart was interested. He invited Bill Wyman along for an audition on December 7. This audition was all the more successful for the superb Vox AC30 guitar amp the bassist had brought along with him. Bill: "I was wearing a suit and a tie, as I thought a band should dress smartly. It did not impress them, but my equipment did."[1] Seven days later, on December 14, Wyman played his first concert with the Stones at the Ricky Tick Club at the Star and Garter Hotel in Windsor. However, this did not prevent Brian Jones from placing another advertisement for a new bassist in the *Jazz News* of December 27 . . . an ad that fortunately went unanswered.

On January 11, 1963, Tony Chapman played with the group for the last time at the Ricky Tick in Windsor. The reason? He did not fit. Brian Jones, who for a long time had wanted the former Blues Incorporated drummer, who had gone on to join Blues By Six, by his side, was eventually rewarded for his patience. Charlie Watts, born in London on June 2, 1941, a graphic design student and jazz enthusiast, officially became a member of the Rollin' Stones on January 11, 1963. Now the lineup was complete.

Giorgio Gomelsky's Crawdaddy Club

Two months later, Brian Jones, Mick Jagger, Keith Richards, Ian Stewart, Bill Wyman, and Charlie Watts returned to the recording studio, this time the International Broadcasting Company (IBC) Studios at 35 Portland Place, London. The studios had just been bought by Eric Robinson (an eminent figure at the BBC), whose sound engineer was Glyn Johns. On

Mick Jagger, Keith Richards, and Brian Jones at Studio 51, a club on Great Newport Street in London, on April 14, 1963.

March 11, 1963, the Rolling Stones recorded Bo Diddley's "Diddley Daddy" and "Road Runner," Willie Dixon's "I Want to Be Loved," and two songs by Jimmy Reed: "Honey, What's Wrong?" (alias "Baby, What's Wrong?") and "Bright Lights, Big City." "I thought the results were tremendous," recalls Glyn Johns. "I had finally got to record the music that had inspired me so much on my American pal Pat's Jimmy Reed album. They sounded like the real deal. I remember being particularly impressed by Brian Jones's harmonica playing, and the extraordinary feel and sound that Charlie and Bill got, and it goes without saying, Stu's piano playing."[4]

At the time the Rollin' Stones crossed the threshold of IBC Studios, they had just become the resident band at the Crawdaddy Club at the Station Hotel in the suburb of Richmond in southwest London. This establishment, which took its name from a Bo Diddley song ("Doing the Craw-Daddy"), was run by Giorgio Gomelsky, a highly cultured man who, after developing an interest in jazz, started to believe in the future of English blues. This "Russian émigré, a great bear of a man, with incredible drive and enthusiasm,"[2] in the words of Keith Richards, acted in a sense as the group's first (unofficial) manager. It was he who got the group its initial press coverage, in the *Richmond and Twickenham Times* of April 13, 1963, and it was he who produced the April 20 session at the RG Jones Studio in Morden, Surrey, during which Bo Diddley's "Pretty Thing" and "It's All Right Babe" were recorded. Finally, and most importantly, it was Gomelsky who got various musicians and insiders of the music world who were in a position to help his protégés, to come to Richmond. Thus on April 14, the Beatles turned up at the Crawdaddy for a performance by the Stones. Two weeks later it was Andrew Loog Oldham and Eric Easton's turn to sit down at a table in the club.

The Decca A&R man Dick Rowe.

The "Dynamite and the Detonator"

Eric Easton, who ran a small artists' agency on London's Regent Street, was a moneyman. Oldham was a visionary publicist who had worked with Brian Epstein, the Beatles' manager, and understood the key role the media could play in the success of a band. It took him no more than a few seconds to grasp the potential of the Rollin' Stones when he heard them for the first time at the Station Hotel in Richmond. "I'd never seen anything like it,"[5] he would write in his memoirs, ". . . I heard the anthem of a national sound, I heard the sound of a national anthem. I heard what I always wanted to hear. I wanted it; it already belonged to me. Everything I'd done up until now was a preparation for this moment. I saw and heard what my life, thus far, had been for."[5] Keith Richards would sum up the decisive encounter on this April evening in 1963 in the following pithy statement: "We were the dynamite, Andy Oldham the detonator."[2]

From that moment, things started to move very quickly. On April 29, Oldham and Easton set up the company Impact Sound, whose precise object was to oversee both the image and the recordings of the Rolling Stones. Ian Stewart saw himself relegated to the role of supplementary musician and road manager—owing to his general appearance, which was out of keeping with the look expected of a rock star in those days—and the tape recorded at IBC was bought back for £90. Oldham even went as far as to ask Keith to remove the s in his name, on the grounds that it was more hip (an orthographical change that has not been taken into account in this book for reasons of consistency). Regarding Oldham's role, Bill Wyman has commented: "We went with him (Andrew) on the morning of May 4, 1963, to Carnaby Street, where he bought us all tight black jeans, black roll-neck sweaters and highly fashionable Anello & Davide black Spanish boots with Cuban heels."[6]

Perfect Timing

On May 5, Oldham persuaded Dick Rowe, the A&R man at Decca, to attend a Stones gig at the Crawdaddy. This man, famous in the music world for having turned down an opportunity to sign the Beatles in March 1962, did not want to make the same mistake again and followed George Harrison's advice to "sign the Rollin' Stones."[7] Thus on May 8 (or 9), Brian Jones, in his capacity as leader, signed a three-year management contract with Impact Sound, which led a few days later to a recording contract with Decca.

On becoming manager (and producer) of the Rollin' Stones in spring 1963, Andrew Loog Oldham, already adept at working the media, soon abandoned the idea of making Mick, Brian, Keith, Bill, and Charlie the London equivalents of Liverpool's Fab Four. Uniforms and neatly combed hair were not for them. The Stones were more disillusioned sulk, vacant expression, derisive stare. To put it in a nutshell, and to quote the title of one of their as-yet-unwritten songs, their image was that of five middle-class adolescents who had "Grown Up Wrong." The band members saw themselves, however, not as bad boys, but simply as lads who had grown up listening to the blues of Muddy Waters and Jimmy Reed, as eighteen-year-old bluesmen who had seen their dream come true. "'We've done Mississippi, been through Chicago.' You kid yourself. But it was really flying into the face of it. And of course the timing was dead right."[2]

To put the finishing touches to this image of a "group your parents love to hate," Oldham made the band members change their look, excluded Ian Stewart, whose overly conventional appearance—in reality he perhaps may not have been the best-looking man in the world—clashed with Oldham's media plans, and added a small g to the end of *Rollin* . . . Now the curtain could rise on one of the most exciting bands in the history of rock 'n' roll.

The pianist Ian Stewart (far left), at this time still a member of the Rolling Stones.

IAN STEWART, THE SIXTH STONE

After placing an advertisement in the *Jazz News* of May 2, 1962, Brian Jones installed himself on the second floor of the Bricklayers Arms, a pub on Broadwick Street where the auditions were to be held. The first person to come through the doors was a strapping fellow in his twenties.

"Stu," Piano Virtuoso

Born on July 18, 1938, in Pittenweem, a small fishing village on the eastern coast of Scotland, Ian Stewart grew up in Cheam, in the London Borough of Sutton. From the age of six, he learned the piano and the banjo, and later started to play in amateur groups. Blues and boogie-woogie were his two musical passions. "I'd always wanted to play this style of piano," said Ian Stewart, "cause I'd always been potty on Albert Ammons. The BBC used to have jazz programs every night, and one night many years ago my ears were opened. I'd thought boogie was piano solo stuff, and they had this program called 'Chicago Blues.' I don't remember any records, all I can remember is that they had this style of piano playing with guitars, harmonicas, and a guy singing. So when a little advert appeared in *Jazz News*—a character named Brian Jones wanted to form a R&B group—I went along and saw him."[8] And he continues: "I'll never forget, he had this Howlin' Wolf album goin', I'd never heard anything like it. I thought, Right, this is it. He said, 'We're gonna have a rehearsal.'"[8]

Ian Stewart was thus the first musician hired by Brian Jones. Because of his maturity and virtuosity on the piano, Stu, as he was known, quickly came to exert a real influence over the other members of the group. Keith Richards describes his first meeting with Ian Stewart at the Bricklayers Arms: "And I can hear this boogie-woogie piano, this unbelievable Meade Lux Lewis and Albert Ammons stuff. I'm suddenly transported in a way. I feel like a musician and I haven't even got there!"[2]

The Wrong Kind of Face

The problem was that Ian Stewart was a few years older than Brian, Mick, and Keith, and above all was infinitely less eccentric than them. For Andrew Oldham, who was in control of the Rolling Stones' destinies, he did not look the part. Using the inevitable failure of a group of six musicians as a pretext, Oldham ousted Stewart, who had to content himself with playing piano on future recording sessions and carrying the equipment of the other five when they were on tour. For the pianist, it was a snub, a humiliation. But he loved the Stones too much—and believed in them too much—to rebel. He therefore consented. "I'd probably have said, 'Well, fuck you,'" admits Keith Richards, "but he said 'OK, I'll just drive you around.' That takes a big heart, but Stu had one of the largest hearts around."[9] And this is how things remained until the middle of the eighties. However, as Cynthia Stewart Dillane (who became his wife in 1967) would later attest, he took this exclusion very badly: "Stu was deeply hurt, because he wasn't good-looking in the genre of the day. I don't think he felt anything except hurt."[5] No doubt a deep resentment too, as this remark quoted by Oldham himself in his memoirs suggests: "Andrew Oldham? I wouldn't piss on him if he was on fire."[5]

Present on all the Rolling Stones' albums released between 1964 and 1986 except *Their Satanic Majesties Request* (1967) and *Beggars Banquet* (1968), Ian Stewart began to suffer from respiratory problems in the mid-eighties. On December 11, 1985, he was nevertheless onstage in Nottingham with Rocket 88—the boogie-woogie group he had formed at the end of the seventies with Charlie Watts, Alexis Korner, and Dick Morrissey. The next day he suffered a fatal heart attack in the waiting room of a medical specialist.

Two months later, at the 100 Club in London, the Stones took to the stage alongside Rocket 88 for a tribute gig in honor of the "sixth" Rolling Stone. Finally, in 1986, the quintet succeeded in getting Stewart's name added to their own with his induction into the Rock and Roll Hall of Fame. To close with praise from Keith Richards: "Ian Stewart. I'm still working for him. To me the Rolling Stones is his band. Without his knowledge and organization, without the leap he made from where he was coming from, to take a chance on playing with this bunch of kids, we'd be nowhere."[2]

The Stones perform "Come On" during their first appearance on *Ready Steady Go!* on August 23, 1963.

SIDE A
1963

COME ON

Chuck Berry / 1:50

SINGLE
Come On / I Want to Be Loved
RELEASE DATE
United Kingdom: June 7, 1963
Label: Decca
RECORD NUMBER: F 11675

Musicians
Mick Jagger: vocals
Keith Richards: rhythm guitar
Brian Jones: harmonica, backing vocals
Bill Wyman: bass, backing vocals (?)
Charlie Watts: drums
Recorded
Olympic Sound Studios, Carlton Street, London: May 10, 1963
Technical Team
Producers: Andrew Oldham, Eric Easton
Sound Engineer: Roger Savage

Mick Jagger altered the lyrics of "Come On" slightly, replacing the phrase *Some stupid jerk* in Chuck Berry's version with the words *Some stupid guy.*

Genesis

In early May 1963, Eric Easton and Andrew Oldham reached an agreement with Brian Jones, as leader of the group, for a three-year management contract. On May 10, the London gang entered Olympic Sound Studios in Carlton Street, at the heart of the capital's West End, for their first official recording session. Oldham had had the studio booked since May 2: £40 for three short hours. The sound engineer, Roger Savage, would retain a memory of having worked free of charge, although he was actually paid £5 per hour: "I agreed to record them one night without payment, because he didn't have any money, so we sorta crept into Olympic late one night. . . . We set up and did four songs quite quickly."[5] A number of songs were thus recorded on May 10. In her book about Brian Jones, the journalist Laura Jackson[10] mentions a superb version of "Dust My Blues" (by Elmore James), with Brian Jones on slide guitar. But the number chosen as the A-side for this first single was "Come On."

"Come On" is a Chuck Berry song that was released by the rock 'n' roll pioneer in October 1961 but failed to chart (unlike the B-side, "Go Go Go," which climbed to number 38). *Everything is wrong since me and my baby parted*, sings Mick Jagger. This is a world away from the dark and brooding image the Rolling Stones had already started to cultivate, and equally far removed from the low-down blues, the "music of the devil" they had been voraciously imbibing since first setting foot in the clubs of Soho.

Why "Come On," then? By all accounts, because this song had the potential to hook the widest possible audience. "The idea was Andrew's—to get a strong single so they'd let

Mick Jagger in 1964. Job: lead singer of the Rolling Stones!

us make an album, which back then was a privilege,"[11] confides Keith Richards. One thing is certain: Jagger and the other members of the group have always hated this song, and it was under duress that they performed it (lip-synching) on the occasion of their first appearance on the television show *Thank Your Lucky Stars* (what's more, dressed in black-and-white houndstooth jackets with a black velvet collar) on July 7, 1963. The Stones subsequently refused to include the number in their set list. When Oldham became aware of this at the Scene Club in Soho, he flew into a rage: "He went crazy when we didn't play "Come On" and we had a row about it. He insisted we play it at every show."[1]

Production

It is not difficult to see why the Stones did not particularly like their version of "Come On," which they considered to be too pop. Compared to Chuck Berry's version, it lacked groove and the group seems static, devoid of any sense of fun and indeed of any hint of their own real sound . . . Nevertheless, their cover has a certain charm. The framework is laid down by the Charlie Watts–Bill Wyman combination, with Wyman launching into the introduction with an excellent bass line, extremely precise and percussive, on his Dallas Tuxedo. Keith Richards provides a good rhythmic structure with ample reverb on his Harmony H70 Meteor. The sound and phrasing of Brian Jones's contributions on his Hohner harmonica are reminiscent to a certain degree of John Lennon, and Mick Jagger delivers the lyrics with an assurance and a texture of voice ultimately not unlike those he still possesses today. His vocal is double-tracked by means of overdub, with backing vocals by Bill and Brian. Only

Ian Stewart failed to perform on the song, acknowledging later that he didn't play because he didn't like the piece.

At the end of the May 10 session, John Savage turned to Andrew Oldham and asked him to do the mixing. Oldham, undergoing his baptism by fire as a producer, exclaimed: "I don't know a damn thing about recording, or music for that matter."[12] It was therefore Savage who set to work. Listening to the band, Dick Rowe and various other managers at Decca, somewhat taken aback by the results, consulted on what was to be done. "Dick Rowe suggested to Eric [Easton] that the Stones go back into the studio with a 'perhaps more qualified producer'"[5] This was a slap in the face for the ambitious Oldham, then barely nineteen years old. The five Stones had to rerecord the whole thing, this time at Decca's West Hampstead studios. This session is believed to have taken place on May 16 or 18. After the recording, Mick Jagger called Oldham and said: "It didn't go well, in fact it's worse than the Olympic session." Rowe eventually decided to bring out the first version, thereby ratifying a recording contract with the Stones via Impact Sound.

The first Rolling Stones single hit the United Kingdom's record stores on June 7, 1963. By July 31 it had reached the promising position of number 21 on the charts. So perhaps Oldham had been right after all.

Oldham had no compunction about buying copies of "Come On" in order to propel the single up the charts.

Muddy Waters, the Rolling Stones' mentor, at the Newport Jazz Festival.

SIDE B
1963

I WANT TO BE LOVED

Willie Dixon / 1:52

SINGLE
Come On / I Want to Be Loved
RELEASE DATE
United Kingdom: June 7, 1963
Label: Decca
RECORD NUMBER: F 11675

Musicians
Mick Jagger: vocals
Keith Richards: rhythm guitar
Brian Jones: harmonica
Bill Wyman: bass
Charlie Watts: drums
Recorded
Olympic Studios: May 10, 1963
Technical Team
Producers: Andrew Oldham, Eric Easton
Sound Engineer: Roger Savage

Genesis
While it may come as something of a surprise to learn that the Rolling Stones recorded one of Chuck Berry's most pop-like compositions (that is to say, one of those least imbued with the spirit of blues/rock 'n' roll) for the A-side of their first single, logic reasserted itself with the B-side. "I Want to Be Loved" had, after all, been written by Willie Dixon and performed by Muddy Waters, two emblematic figures of Chicago electric blues and mainstays of Chess Records. In other words, two major points of reference for the five young Londoners whose group took its name from a Muddy Waters blues number: "Rollin' Stone."

Muddy Waters recorded "I Want to Be Loved" in 1955, with "My Eyes (Keep Me in Trouble)" on the B-side. Eight years later, the Rolling Stones put their name to a more up-tempo version. This blues number had already been in the group's repertoire for several months and had even been recorded by them during the session at IBC Studios, with Glyn Johns as producer and sound engineer.

Production
The most striking aspect of "I Want to Be Loved" is Jagger's voice. Unlike the way it sounds on "Come On," there is a youthful, fragile quality about it. This time, however, the Stones are in their element. They are playing the blues, and Brian Jones underlines this with his excellent harmonica playing, with reverb, redolent of Big Walter Horton. Charlie Watts, playing a Sonor Chicago Star kit (with very prominent snare drum) is solidly supported by Bill Wyman's bass and Keith Richards's rhythm guitar. It is possible to hear the

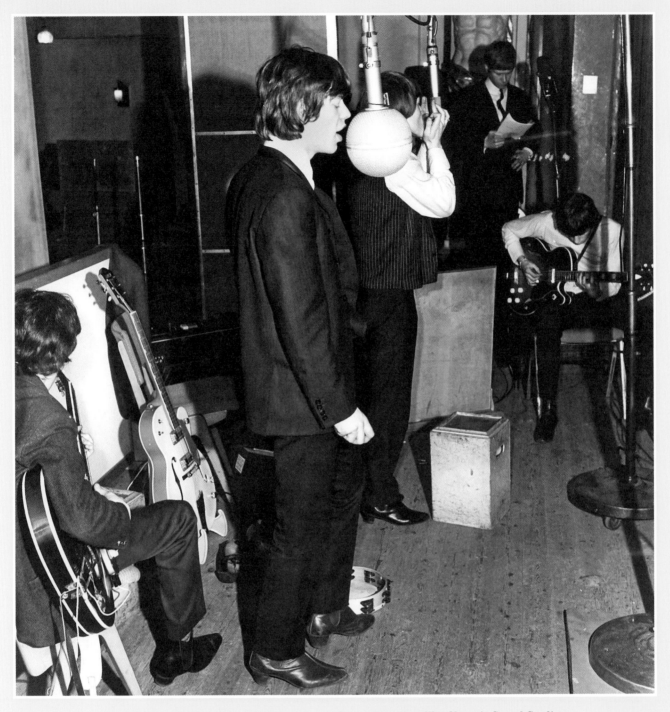

The Stones at Regent Sound Studios in a configuration not unlike Olympic Sound Studios.

latter speeding up slightly during the harmonica solo (around 1:10), however. Finally, although present at the recording, and by contrast with the March 11 version realized by Glyn Johns (which was, moreover, closer to Muddy Waters's version), Ian Stewart's piano is totally inaudible. Roger Savage, the sound engineer, provides an explanation: "The main thing I remember was that Andrew told me to turn Ian Stewart's piano microphone off; he obviously didn't want him in the band because he didn't look the part . . . When they came up the stairs to the control room to play back there was no piano! Nobody said anything."[5]

FOR STONES ADDICTS

The other songs recorded on May 10, 1963, may have been "Dust My Blues" and either Jerry Leiber and Mike Stoller's "Love Potion No. 9" or Willie Dixon's "Pretty Thing."

ANDREW LOOG OLDHAM, INVENTOR OF THE ROLLING STONES

April 21, 1963. When *Record Mirror* journalist Pete Jones convinced him to travel to the Crawdaddy Club in Richmond to attend a gig by a group of six musicians who had christened themselves the Rollin' Stones, Andrew Oldham may only have been nineteen years old, but he had already cut a swath through the field of British pop. Born in London on January 29, 1944, Andrew never knew his father Andrew Loog, a Texas lieutenant in the United States Army Air Corps who was shot down over the English Channel on June 13, 1943. Brought up by his mother, Celia Oldham, an Australian from New South Wales who settled in England (where she practiced the noble profession of nursing) in 1948, he attended a number of different educational establishments, including Aylesbury School for Boys (Buckinghamshire), Cokethorpe School at Hardwick (Oxfordshire), and subsequently Wellingborough School (Northamptonshire). At a certain point he developed a strong interest in cinema. After seeing Nicholas Ray's *Rebel Without a Cause* (1955) he began to identify with James Dean, and also had a special affinity for the Free Cinema of Tony Richardson and Lindsay Anderson and the *Nouvelle Vague* of Jean-Luc Godard, Claude Chabrol, and François Truffaut.

Initial Foray into the World of Music

At the end of the fifties, music and fashion also entered Andrew Loog Oldham's life. This was a double passion that soon became all-consuming. As he began to frequent the clubs of Soho, such as the 2i's, the Flamingo, and Ronnie Scott's, Oldham started to develop more and more of a taste for jazz and subsequently rock 'n' roll. Before long he set up his first public relations company, in collaboration with Peter Meaden (the future manager of the Who), and then, with various agencies, worked for a number of musicians from Chris Montez to Little Richard via Bob Dylan (during the singer's first visit to London in November 1962) and the Beatles (for whom he obtained an article in the columns of *Vogue*), this time as Brian Epstein's assistant at North End Music Stores (NEMS). His experience in the world of fashion, meanwhile, was marked by close relationships with John Stephen, who had already acquired the sobriquet "King of Carnaby Street," and then Mary Quant, who was in the process of emancipating young women of the baby-boomer generation with the miniskirt.

After the Crawdaddy gig, Oldham phoned Epstein: "I informed him I was resigning from NEMS, that I'd seen this group called the Rollin' Stones and wanted to devote myself to them, try and become their manager."[5] He nevertheless proposed a deal to the Beatles' manager in order to benefit from his experience. "Perhaps because Brian was already frantic from working the Beatles, Gerry & the Pacemakers, Billy J. Kramer and Cilla Black, he didn't really hear me; perhaps I wasn't that loud. Whatever—Epstein chose to pass on the offer."[5] In fact, this gave Andrew Oldham the opportunity he had dreamed of to take charge of his destiny.

The Great Architect of the Stones

With Eric Easton, a London artists' agent who presided over the fortunes of, among other artists, the guitarist Bert Weedon and Brian Matthew, the presenter of *Thank Your Lucky Stars*, Oldham founded Impact Sound and, immediately after seeing the Rollin' Stones at Richmond, became the group's official manager (Giorgio Gomelsky having only acted as their manager on an informal basis).

Oldham's mission was twofold: to get his protégés new club bookings and a record deal—which was achieved with Decca in the first few days of May 1963, and to work on their image. This would prove to be the work of a true genius, of "the great architect of the Stones' public persona,"[2] to borrow the words of Keith Richards. For Oldham, it was a question of intriguing, of shocking, of focusing teenage rebelliousness and frustrations—in other words of presenting an image substantially more anti-establishment than that of the Beatles. After expelling Ian Stewart under the pretext that a group of six musicians would not sell and replacing the apostrophe in *Rollin'* with a *g*—for the sake of better comprehension—Oldham focused all his efforts on the media, which were continually on the lookout for a quote with a whiff of scandal about

Andrew Loog Oldham. With his media savvy, it was Oldham who created the Rolling Stones' dark and brooding image.

it. He must have loved that on February 28, 1964, the day after a concert by the Rolling Stones in Cardiff, Judith Simons wrote in the *Daily Express*: "They look like boys whom any self-respecting mum would lock in the bathroom! But the Rolling Stones, five tough young London-based music makers with doorstep mouths, pallid cheeks, and unkempt hair are not worried what mums think!"[35] Furthermore *Melody Maker* published the question, "Would you let your sister go with a Rolling Stone?," which appeared in the music paper on March 14. He was also the author of the following slogan on the back of their first opus: "The Rolling Stones are more than just a group—they are a way of life." This could be summed up in another phrase attributable to Oldham: "the group parents love to hate."

The Midwife of the "Glimmer Twins"

Andrew Oldham was not merely the ingenious orchestrator of the "anti-Beatles" image or of the "Stones bashing" that worked like a dream from 1964 onward and got the London gang on the front pages of the newspapers. Most importantly, it was he who forced Mick Jagger and Keith Richards to write. Keith's initial reaction is telling: "Who do you think I am, John Lennon?"[36] "It had never crossed my mind to be a songwriter until Andrew came to me and Mick and said, 'Look, how many good records are you going to keep on making if you can't get new material? You can only cover as many songs as there are, and I think you're capable of more.' We had never thought of that. He locked us up in a room about the size of a kitchen and said, 'You've got a day off, I want to hear a song when you come out.' 'Who does he think he is? He's got to be joking,' Mick and I said. But in his own way Andrew was right. We walked out of there with a couple of songs."[37] It was thanks to Oldham, therefore, that Jagger and Richards—soon to be nicknamed the Glimmer Twins—would go on to become one of the most gifted songwriting partnerships in the history of rock.

Though the manager and producer of the Rolling Stones, Andrew Oldham also had other irons in the fire. In 1965 he

founded Immediate Records, one of the premier independent British labels, which would later produce artists such as Chris Farlowe, the Small Faces, and The Nice, and also, some time later, created The Andrew Oldham Orchestra, a band that was not exactly an orchestra, but rather a random and never definitive grouping of session musicians and stars (including the Stones) with whom Oldham made records.

The Decline of the Oldham Empire

But this well-oiled piece of machinery ground to a halt in 1967, when Brian, Mick, and Keith became prime targets of the authorities for the possession and consumption of narcotics. Oldham left for California, where he helped Lou Adler and John Phillips organize the Monterey Pop Festival (June 16–18, 1967). Out of sight, out of mind: as of September 20, 1967, Oldham ceased to be the manager of the Stones. He no longer recognized himself in the new direction taken by the group (notably at the time of *Their Satanic Majesties Request*), who reproached him with not putting enough effort into the production of their records. In reality, the Stones no longer had any need for a manager by this time. The dismissed Oldham subsequently poured all his energy into Immediate Records, the label he had created two years before, which would be declared bankrupt in 1970. After enduring a rough patch, he moved to Colombia. According to Sheila, his first wife: "He was devastated by the whole thing, and I don't think he's recovered."[38] Andrew Loog Oldham still lives in Bogotá, where he writes, presents radio shows, and gets involved with the occasional music project.

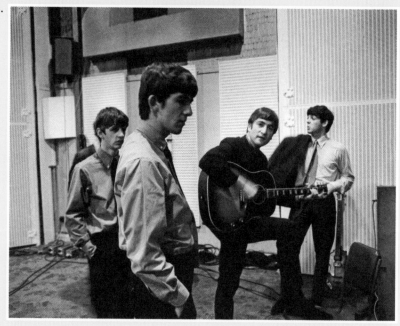

The Beatles at Abbey Road in 1963. The Stones owed their first hit, "I Wanna Be Your Man," to the Liverpool boys.

I WANNA BE YOUR MAN

Lennon-McCartney / 1:44

SINGLE
I Wanna Be Your Man / Stoned
RELEASE DATE
United Kingdom: November 1, 1963
Label: Decca
RECORD NUMBER: F 11764

Musicians
Mick Jagger: vocals
Keith Richards: rhythm guitar
Brian Jones: slide guitar, backing vocals
Bill Wyman: bass
Charlie Watts: drums
Recorded
De Lane Lea Music Recording Studios (Kingsway Sound Studios), Kingsway, London: October 7, 1963
Technical Team
Producers: Andrew Oldham, Eric Easton
Sound Engineer: (?)

"I Wanna Be Your Man" is not on any of the Rolling Stones' original albums. It is included in the compilations *Milestones* (1972), *Rolled Gold: The Very Best of the Rolling Stones* (1975), *Singles Collection: The London Years* (1989), and *GRRR!* (2012).

Genesis

Excited as they may have been to hear "Come On" playing on the British airwaves, Mick, Brian, Keith, Bill, and Charlie shared the opinion of certain critics that their first single failed to convey the energy they generated onstage, let alone reflect the music that really excited them. Andrew Oldham was acutely aware of this too, all the more so as the group's repertoire at that time contained nothing that could be thought of as a potential hit. Yet it was hoped that this putative second single would enable the Rolling Stones to make a decisive leap forward, to present themselves as the Beatles' most serious challenger. They recorded a version of "Poison Ivy" by the Coasters and "Putty in Your Hands" by the Shirelles, but the results were unanimously rejected on the grounds of inadequate quality. Where, then, to look for the successor to "Come On"?

As things turned out, it was the Lennon-McCartney songwriting duo that was to set them on the right track. On September 10, 1963, while walking along Charing Cross Road, Andrew Oldham spotted John Lennon and Paul McCartney. The manager of the Stones mentioned that he was having trouble finding a sufficiently catchy number for his protégés to record as their second single. Magnanimously, the young Liverpudlian songwriters, then in the process of recording their second album, *With the Beatles*, offered to come to the aid of the London quintet. They suggested that the Stones record one of their own compositions, an impassioned, direct love song—and potential hit—that they were getting ready to record the following day for their new album. Its title? "I Wanna Be Your Man."

The Stones perform "I Wanna Be Your Man" on the television program *Top of the Pops* on January 1, 1964.

Andrew Oldham took Lennon and McCartney straight to Studio 51, Ken Colyer's jazz club on Great Newport Street, not far from Charing Cross Road, where the Stones were rehearsing. The two Beatles showed them the chords and the words, and then, as a few ideas began to be exchanged, took themselves off into a corner for a moment—to everyone's astonishment—to finish the song off. "Paul, being left-handed, amazed me by playing my bass backwards,"[1] recalls Bill Wyman. In barely twenty minutes, it was as good as done. Keith Richards also recalls this key incident: "They played it through with us. Brian put on some nice slide guitar; we turned it into an unmistakably Stones rather than Beatles song. It was clear that we had a hit almost before they'd left the studio."[2] Oldham was suddenly able to see his protégés' future in a different light: "They gave us a real tutorial in the reality they were forging for themselves."[5] Lennon maintained that from this day on, the Stones started to write their own songs. He would later acknowledge with some amusement that the song they had offered the Londoners was not one of their best: "It was a throwaway,"[13] he told David Sheff in 1980. "That shows how much importance we put on them. We weren't going to give them anything great, right?"[13]

Production

Three weeks later, on Monday, October 7, the Stones recorded "I Wanna Be Your Man." Brian Jones sets the tone with his slide riffs and the solo played on his Gretsch Anniversary. Plugged into his Vox AC30 amplifier, this instrument possesses what was, for the time, an unusually saturated sound. Bill Wyman also plays an important part in the overall sound with his brand-new Framus Star F5/150 bass played with a plectrum. (He seems to have been using a second model, with a slightly different pickguard, that day.) The contributions of Keith and Charlie are more discreet, despite the latter's new drum kit, the Ludwig Super Classic he started playing around this time. As on "Come On," Ian Stewart is conspicuous by his absence. Jagger, for his part, makes the lyrics of the Liverpudlian duo his own, demonstrating considerable self-assurance. Compared to the Beatles' version, the group sounds more direct, more rough-edged, and more aggressive, with an entirely appropriate "garage band" feel. The Stones' version is without doubt more effective than the Fab Four's. In spite of everything, the critics remained lukewarm. Released on November 1, 1963, the Rolling Stones' second single nevertheless peaked at number 12 on the British charts on November 14.

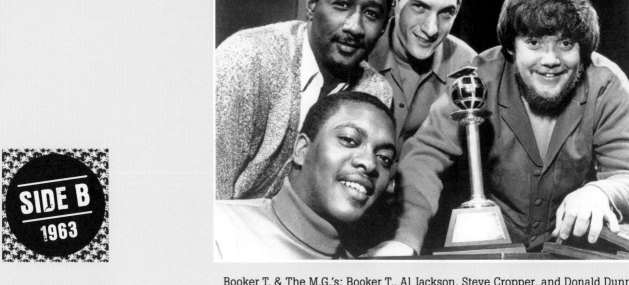

Booker T. & The M.G.'s: Booker T., Al Jackson, Steve Cropper, and Donald Dunn.

SIDE B
1963

STONED

Nanker Phelge / 2:09

SINGLE
I Wanna Be Your Man / Stoned
RELEASE DATE
United Kingdom: November 1, 1963
Label: Decca
RECORD NUMBER: F 11764

Musicians
Mick Jagger: vocals
Keith Richards: lead guitar
Brian Jones: harmonica
Bill Wyman: bass
Charlie Watts: drums
Ian Stewart: piano
Recorded
De Lane Lea Music Recording Studios (Kingsway Sound Studios), Kingsway, London: October 7, 1963
Technical Team
Producers: Andrew Oldham, Eric Easton
Sound Engineer: (?)

Genesis

"Stoned" occupies a special place in the career of the Rolling Stones, which was still in its infancy. It is neither a cover nor, properly speaking, an original composition, but more of an improvisation on "Green Onions" by Booker T. & The M.G.'s, "an inversion,"[1] as Bill Wyman puts it, which reached number 3 on the *Billboard* pop chart in September 1962.

The track is credited to Nanker Phelge, a pseudonym used for those songs "written" or developed collaboratively by the various members of the group between 1963 and 1965. *Nanker* was the name of one of Brian Jones and Keith Richards's favorite "funny faces" (fingers in the nostrils, drooping eyelids . . .), while *Phelge* refers to their roommate at Edith Grove, James Phelge.

James describes his surprise when he saw his name on the Stones' second single: "I took my eyes from the record and saw the three of them standing there watching me intently, their faces lit with broad smiles. . . .'I hope you don't mind us using your name?' Brian asked. 'We wanted to put it on the records.' 'No, that's great,' I said and read the label one more time. 'What is *Stoned* anyway?' 'Just something we made up in the studio,' said Keith, 'an instrumental.'"[3]

The recording of "Stoned" would provide an opportunity for the revelation of another facet of Eric Easton's character. With the session barely over, Oldham flew off in haste to Paris in order to deal with the early symptoms of manic depression that were beginning to affect him, a condition he would struggle with for the next thirty years of his life. In his absence, Easton, his associate, took it upon himself to explain to the Stones that their number was an original composition and that

"Stoned" was credited to Nanker (after the grotesque faces Brian and Keith enjoyed making) and Phelge (the name of their Edith Grove housemate).

it was time to find a publisher in order to collect the future royalties. He told them about Southern Music, a company he recommended wholeheartedly, neglecting to inform them that he was co-publisher with that enterprise, specifically through South-Eastern Music. Upon Oldham's return from Paris, he neglected to notify the manager of this "minor" detail. It was only at the beginning of 1964, after attempts were made to find the Stones a publisher for other songs that the deception came to light. From that point on, relations became more and more strained until they reached the breaking point in 1965, when Easton would be replaced by a certain Allen Klein . . .

Production

"Stoned" is an instrumental that was made in barely thirty minutes; Mick Jagger does no more than repeat the phrases *stoned* and *outta my mind* from time to time, with plenty of reverb on the voice as well as on the harmonica, played, it is presumed, by Brian Jones. This time Ian Stewart, playing for the first time on a release by the group, is given pride of place with a very prominent boogie-woogie piano part. The sixth Stone gives the impression of giving vent to his frustrations; one senses that he is pounding the keyboard in rage.

This number is obviously derived from "Green Onions": the riff resembles the original, there is the same ride cymbal from Charlie, Keith's—highly effective—solo is in a similar vein to the original, and Mick's interventions are not without some resemblance to those of Booker T. Jones himself. In his memoirs, Oldham describes "Stoned" as a "constructive plagiarism."[5] Nevertheless, the Stones had just recorded their first self-penned number, the highly promising first in a long succession. And *Beat Monthly* described the number as a "groovy instrumental."[1] An encouraging start.

FOR STONES ADDICTS

On a few hundred copies of the Stones' second single, the title of the B-side was printed as *Stones* rather than *Stoned*. This is a highly sought-after collector's item.

(Get Your Kicks On) Route 66
I Just Want To Make Love To You
Honest I Do
I Need You Baby (Mona)
Now I've Got A Witness
   (Like Uncle Phil And Uncle Gene)
Little By Little
I'm A King Bee
Carol
Tell Me (You're Coming Back)
Can I Get A Witness
You Can Make It If You Try
Walking The Dog

ALBUM

RELEASE DATE

United Kingdom: April 17, 1964

Label: Decca

RECORD NUMBER: LK 4605

Number 1 for 12 weeks

THE ROLLING STONES

THE ROLLING STONES, ON VINYL AND ONSTAGE

The Album

By the time the Rolling Stones entered the studio to record their first album, the Beatles had already released *Please Please Me* (March 22, 1963) and *With the Beatles* (November 22, 1963). Lennon and McCartney had demonstrated that they were extremely gifted songwriters, with, in particular, "All My Loving," "She Loves You," and "I Want to Hold Your Hand" opening up the United States and preparing the way for the British Invasion. The same cannot be said of the London quintet. Writing songs was not yet really their cup of tea. Their trump card was the blues—whether from the Mississippi Delta or the smoke-filled clubs of Chicago, which they were becoming more adept at playing each evening, above all Brian, who was sliding his bottleneck along the guitar strings as if his life depended on it.

This first album consisted of twelve tracks, recorded in five sessions between January 3 and February 25. It comprised nine cover versions, a debut credit for the Jagger-Richards songwriting duo ("Tell Me"), a group collaboration ("Now I've Got a Witness"), and finally a song (titled "Little by Little") co-written by the group with Phil Spector, the inventor of the famous "wall of sound." The track listing is entirely representative of the Stones' stage repertoire at that time. Keith Richards: "The entire record was virtually our stage act apart from one or two dubs thrown in it. 80 per cent of it was straight what we played at Studio 51 or Richmond."[14] And this is precisely what won over the press from day one. A number of journalists expressed appreciation for the raw sound and the "immediate" character of the music, and went as far as to draw a parallel with the first few recordings made by Elvis Presley for Sun.

The general public did not wait for the enthusiastic comments of the music press before welcoming the Rolling Stones to the world of the LP in the most fitting way. Ten thousand fans preordered the first album, surpassing the Beatles and *Please Please Me* (a mere 6,000!). *The Rolling Stones* would remain at the top of the charts for twelve weeks and achieve the distinction of being one of the biggest-selling albums of 1964. Furthermore, in terms of albums released that year, the Rolling Stones were the only group to share the top spot on the charts with the Beatles (*A Hard Day's Night* twenty-one weeks and *Beatles for Sale* seven weeks). Stonemania had finally gotten under way . . .

The Recording

Founded by Ralph Elman in the fifties, Regent Sound Studios, located at Denmark Street in London,[4] had, since 1961, belonged to James Baring, an aristocrat and Old Etonian with a passion for rock 'n' roll. Regent Sound Studios was oriented more toward commercial work and was used for recording voices for advertisements, although in terms of equipment and size, the facilities remained extremely modest. The studio itself was "no larger than an average good-sized hotel room," notes Oldham, "with the control room the size of the hotel room's bathroom."[5] It was, however, exactly what the young producer was looking for: an inexpensive studio of compact

One of the rare photographs of the Rolling Stones wearing suits.

dimensions that would produce a compressed sound, a space in which each musician would interfere and react with the others—the very opposite of the usual criteria, in other words. Another major advantage was that the studio was mono only, which was ideal for producing the grainy, textured sound they all cherished: "Mono had the element we needed," says Oldham, "what you hear is what you get."[5] Regent Sound Studios was also somewhere that allowed musicians to work without pressure in a reasonably relaxed atmosphere. Oldham: "I have no doubt the feel of those early Stones records was due in no small part to avoiding the major studios."[5]

The Rolling Stones and Ian Stewart entered the studio on January 2, 1964, the day after their first appearance on *Top of the Pops*. Keith Richards recalls the available equipment: "a two-track Revox [Grundig according to a different interview] in a room insulated with egg cartons."[14] That Thursday in January, however, the six Stones were to serve as sidemen, with each of them paid £2 to accompany Oldham's new protégée, the singer (and actress) Cleo Sylvestre in the recording of "To Know Him Is to Love Him" (by Phil Spector), the A-side of a single Oldham was producing, and after that the Andrew Loog Oldham Orchestra, directed by Mike Leander, in a recording of "There Are But Five Rolling Stones" (by Mike Leander and Andrew Oldham), which was destined for the B-side (with a few wrong notes from Stu [for example at 0:16]!).

The sessions for the group's first album started properly on January 3 with Bill Farley, the in-house engineer who knew how to capture the sound they wanted to hear. "When they first arrived," Farley later recalled, "no one had thought about arrangements. They just busked it until they got the feeling of the number. There was no dubbing [Keith Richards would later claim that there had been one or two overdubs]. They just told me exactly what they wanted as soon as the number had been worked out. How it turned out so well in the

end I never really knew."[15] The resulting sound is direct, rough-edged, and typical of their stage performances.

The session dates vary from source to source. The following is what those involved can remember. On January 3, the Rolling Stones recorded three numbers: "Carol," "Mona," and "Route 66" (some say it was January 4 and add "You Can Make It If You Try" to the list). On January 10, the day of release of the EP *The Rolling Stones* (featuring "You Better Move On," "Poison Ivy," "Bye Bye Johnny," and "Money," although the 16, 17, and 18 of that month are also put forward as the release date), they returned to Regent Sound Studios to record "Not Fade Away" ("Honest I Do" and "I'm a King Bee" are also mentioned). There was then a gap of three weeks, during which the group played a gig to a packed house each evening. The album sessions resumed on February 4 with "Andrew's Blues" (not used), "Can I Get a Witness," "Little by Little," and "Mr. Spector and Mr. Pitney Came Too" (not used).

On that particular day, four distinguished guests were present in addition to the Stones: the composer and producer Phil Spector; the founding members of the Hollies, Graham Nash and Allan Clarke; and the singer Gene Pitney, who had come straight from the airport armed with a good supply of cognac. Bill Wyman recalls: "Pitney played piano while Spector and the Hollies played tambourine and maracas and banged coins on empty bottles. We recorded three songs, 'Little by Little,' 'Can I Get a Witness' and 'Now I've Got a Witness,' which we invented on the spot. The session then degenerated into silliness, but everybody had a great time cutting 'Andrew's Blues' and 'Spector and Pitney Came Too'—both of which were very rude."[6] Finally, on February 24 and 25, "I Just Want to Make Love to You," "Walking the Dog," "You Can Make It If You Try," "Honest I Do," "I'm a King Bee," and "Tell Me," were recorded for the album as well as "Good Times, Bad Times" (and probably "Over You" by Allen Toussaint).

A Gretsch G6118 Anniversary, similar to the one owned by Brian Jones, which was green.

The Album Cover

The Rolling Stones' first album was released on April 17, 1964. The cover photograph was taken by Nicholas Wright. From left to right can be seen Brian, Keith, Bill, Charlie, and Mick, photographed from the side, against a dark background, with their faces turned toward the lens in a halo of light—neither the name of the group nor the title of the album appear on it. The tone is nevertheless set by a few words on the back of the cover: "The Rolling Stones are more than just a group—they are a way of life." Another masterstroke from Oldham, who had found a way of dispelling Decca's misgivings!

Technical Details

At the beginning of 1964, Regent Sound Studios were probably equipped with a Revox G36 tape recorder, which was a model produced in 1963. By comparison with the usual criteria of the professional studios of the day, this might seem somewhat inadequate. However, as Oldham has explained, this equipment, along with the small size of the studio, was responsible for the authentic and direct sound obtained on the Stones' early records. Nevertheless, it had its limits. Keith Richards: "It was easy to make that kind of sound but hard to make a much better one."[14]

The Instruments

As for their previous recordings ("I Wanna Be Your Man" and "Stoned"), the guitarists remained true to their instruments. Keith played his Harmony Meteor H70 and Brian played the green Gretsch G6118 Anniversary he had bought in May 1963, each plugged into his Vox AC30 guitar amp. Keith also used a Harmony 1270 12-string acoustic. Bill alternated between his very first fretless bass (the Dallas Tuxedo that can be heard on "Come On"), and his recently purchased Framus Star. His amplification consisted of a Vox AC30 amp head and a Vox T60 bass cabinet. Charlie had also been playing a new acquisition since May 1963, a superb Ludwig Super Classic drum kit, the "Oyster Blue Pearl." As for Ian Stewart, the keyboard player can be heard on upright piano and organ (presumed to be a Vox Continental MK1). The other instruments present on the record include harmonicas, hand claps, tambourines, and even a cognac bottle struck with a coin!

(GET YOUR KICKS ON) ROUTE 66

Bobby Troup / 2:22

Musicians
Mick Jagger: vocals, hand claps (?)
Keith Richards: rhythm guitar, lead guitar
Brian Jones: rhythm guitar
Bill Wyman: bass, hand claps (?)
Charlie Watts: drums, hand claps (?)
Recorded
Regent Sound Studios: January 3, 1964
Technical Team
Producer: Andrew Loog Oldham
Sound Engineer: Bill Farley

Bobby Troup was an actor and pianist and the composer of "Route 66," which the Stones recorded in 1964.

Genesis

Bobby Troup is familiar to television viewers from his role acting in *Emergency!*, a popular seventies television series in the United States. Most importantly, he is known to rock 'n' roll and rhythm 'n' blues enthusiasts as the composer of "Route 66." Based on the twelve-bar blues structure, this song, composed in 1946, takes its name from the famous road that connects Chicago and Santa Monica. In a certain sense it represents a glorification of travel as a symbol of freedom (several years before the writers of the Beat generation). *Get your kicks on Route 66*: the refrain says it all!

The song was first recorded by Nat King Cole in 1946 and became an enormous hit. Since then, numerous singers, from Chuck Berry to Brian Setzer and from Natalie Cole to the Cramps, have incorporated it into their repertoires. It even became a hymn for the bands of the British Invasion, with covers by the Rolling Stones, and later Them.

Production

The Rolling Stones recorded their version on January 3, 1964. They had already honed the number to such a point onstage, notably at the Crawdaddy Club in Richmond the previous year, that by this point they were performing it like a well-oiled machine. Compared to the Nat King Cole or Chuck Berry versions, the Stones revisit the route west with a great deal more adrenaline, which no doubt explains the substantial increase in tempo as they play. Having started at around 160 bpm, they finish at approximately 170 bpm! In fact, one cannot help wondering whether there was an edit at 0:10, just after *motor west*, so suddenly does the tempo change. But the energy is infectious and the five musicians play as one: the guitars deliver a solid, efficient pulse in an emphatically "Chuck Berry" mode, with a perfectly judged solo from Keith. Bill lays down a nice groove and even attempts a walking bass line that seems to delight Charlie. The drummer has clearly neglected to oil his bass drum pedal, which squeaks noticeably from the beginning of the track. Mick has gained in assurance since "Come On," and his voice, with reverb and a slight delay, now has the effect of truly bringing the song to life and focusing the listener's attention. Finally, hand claps have been added, no doubt by means of overdub. The Stones are rolling freely on their version of "Route 66."

I JUST WANT TO MAKE LOVE TO YOU

Willie Dixon / 2:19

FOR STONES ADDICTS

"I Just Want to Make Love to You" was chosen as the B-side of the single "Tell Me," released on June 13, 1964. A live version, recorded at Wembley on July 6, 1990, can be found on the album *Rarities 1971–2003* (2005).

Musicians
Mick Jagger: vocals, tambourine (?), hand claps (?)
Keith Richards: rhythm guitar, lead guitar
Brian Jones: harmonica
Bill Wyman: bass, hand claps (?)
Charlie Watts: drums, hand claps (?)
Recorded
Regent Sound Studios: February 24–25, 1964
Technical Team
Producer: Andrew Loog Oldham
Sound Engineer: Bill Farley

The Stones have changed Willie Dixon's lyrics slightly, with the phrase *I don't want 'cause I'm sad and blue* replacing *I don't want you to be true.*

Willie Dixon, the legendary songwriter of modern Chicago blues.

Genesis

"I Just Want to Make Love to You" is a blues number in the purest tradition of Chess Records, the label that epitomizes modern Chicago blues. It was written by Willie Dixon and recorded in 1954 by Muddy Waters (vocal) with the best lineup he ever had: Dixon himself on double bass, Jimmy Rogers on guitar, Little Walter on harmonica, Otis Spann on piano, and Fred Below on drums. The song was released as a single with the title "Just Make Love to Me" (with "Oh Yeh" as the B-side) and reached number 4 on the rhythm 'n' blues chart of the day.

Although Etta James put her name to a superb adaptation in 1961, and Muddy Waters recorded a new version in 1968 for the album *Electric Mud*, the task of bringing "I Just Want to Make Love to You" (whose words have the merit of being extremely unambiguous) to the attention of their generation fell to the Rolling Stones. If there is any need to point out one more difference between the Stones and the Beatles, this is it: while the Fab Four were singing "I Want to Hold Your Hand," the Stones were extolling the virtues of a far more raunchy form of intimacy!

Production

Musically, the London quintet has considerably upped the tempo relative to the original recording. The result is more Bo Diddley than Muddy Waters, even if Brian, on harmonica, remains true to the magic created back in the day by Little Walter. The number possesses a strong rhythmic foundation sustained with verve by Keith, Bill, and Charlie. It is a shame about the quality of production though: Mick's reverbed vocal is saturated from start to finish, as are some of Charlie's breaks (1:01). Brian's solo harmonica is not really given enough prominence, but is instead dominated by Keith's rhythm guitar, which is far too loud and regrettably forces the tempo. Hand claps have been added, no doubt by means of overdub, as well as a tambourine, which comes in after 1:56, presumably played by Mick. The sound is roots and almost "garage band," and is certainly less successful than "Route 66."

HONEST I DO

Ewart Abner / Jimmy Reed / 2:11

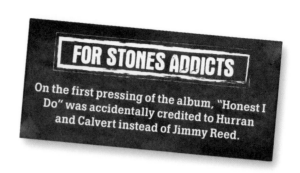
Musicians
Mick Jagger: vocals, harmonica
Keith Richards: guitar
Brian Jones: guitar
Bill Wyman: bass
Charlie Watts: drums
Recorded
Regent Sound Studios: February 24–25, 1964
(January 10, according to other sources)
Technical Team
Producer: Andrew Loog Oldham
Sound Engineer: Bill Farley

Genesis

Jimmy Reed is one of the many guitarists from the state of Mississippi who subsequently gave modern Chicago blues its stamp of credibility. The Rolling Stones, who were playing "Ain't That Lovin' You Baby," "The Sun Is Shining," and "Bright Lights, Big City" well before they signed with Decca, cite the "big boss man" as one of their biggest influences. "Jimmy Reed was a very big model for us," writes Keith Richards. "That was always two-guitar stuff. Almost a study in monotony in many ways, unless you got in there. . . . We were fascinated by it, Brian and I. We would spend every spare moment trying to get down Jimmy Reed's guitar sounds."[2]

Production

Jimmy Reed recorded "Honest I Do" in 1957 and went on to reach number 4 with it on the US R&B chart. Seven years later, it was the Rolling Stones' turn to record it, with Brian Jones and Keith Richards conscientiously applying the technique of weaving two (not especially well-tuned) guitars, as practiced by the master. The harmonica part is played—extremely well—by Mick Jagger. By contrast with his penetrating voice, his harmonica playing is drenched in a long and deep reverb whose effect is to accentuate the plaintive character of the lyrics. Once again, the production is not as careful as it might have been, and the sound borders on—and, in the case of Charlie's tom breaks, exceeds—the saturation point. Ultimately the Stones' version adheres fairly closely to Reed's, with the same prominent snare drum, a reasonably slow tempo, and a bluesy harmonica.

Jimmy Reed, the guitarist and harmonica player who played a relaxed, rural Louisiana blues, not least on "Honest I Do."

🎧 IN YOUR HEADPHONES

At the very end of the track, during the fade-out at precisely 2:07, one of the two guitars finds itself alone, the other instruments having suddenly dropped out!

I NEED YOU BABY (MONA)

Ellas McDaniel / 3:33

Musicians
Mick Jagger: vocals, maracas
Keith Richards: rhythm guitar, lead guitar (?)
Brian Jones: rhythm guitar
Bill Wyman: bass
Charlie Watts: drums
Unidentified: hand claps, tambourine
Recorded
Regent Sound Studios: January 3, 1964
Technical Team
Producer: Andrew Loog Oldham
Sound Engineer: Bill Farley

Genesis

Better known as Bo Diddley, Ellas McDaniel was a major source of inspiration for young British and US groups at the beginning of the sixties. A syncopated rhythm that had its origins in the depths of the Mississippi Delta before being revisited in the Chess Records canon of electric blues was the source at which the Rolling Stones drank—even before the Pretty Things, who took their name from a song by the rock 'n' roll pioneer. "I Need You Baby (Mona)" was released in 1957 as the B-side of "Hey! Bo Diddley."

Production

The London gang cut their own version of "Mona" during the session of January 3, 1964. The original spirit of the song derives from that hypnotic "Bo Diddley beat" that can also be found in "Not Fade Away," released by Buddy Holly in October 1957 and later by the Rolling Stones themselves, for their third British single, on January 10, 1964.

The version of "Mona" offered up by the five English boys is distinctly more aggressive and more tribal than the original. This impression is reinforced by the drumming, with Charlie playing mainly on the toms. Unfortunately, Bill's bass is lost in the sea of noise and provides the drummer with only limited support. It is the two guitars that play the most prominent part, heavily colored by the vibrato delivered by their Vox AC30 guitar amps, creating an authentic "Bo Diddley" sound. One of the two—Keith seems the most likely candidate—plays a solo that adheres closely to the original. The maracas played by Mick, who takes his cue from the master Jerome Green on the original recording, are another element in common with Diddley. Jagger delivers the lyrics brilliantly, the particular quality of his voice bringing a feline character to the number. On top of all this, added no doubt by means of overdub, are a tambourine part and hand claps, both highly effective.

Bo Diddley, bluesman, rock 'n' roll pioneer, and . . . major influence on the London quintet.

NOW I'VE GOT A WITNESS (LIKE UNCLE PHIL AND UNCLE GENE)

Nanker Phelge / 2:32

Musicians
Mick Jagger: tambourine
Keith Richards: rhythm guitar, lead guitar
Brian Jones: harmonica
Bill Wyman: bass
Charlie Watts: drums
Ian Stewart: organ
Recorded
Regent Sound Studios: February 4, 1964
Technical Team
Producer: Andrew Loog Oldham
Sound Engineer: Bill Farley

FOR STONES ADDICTS

"Now I've Got a Witness" is said to have been added at the last moment in order to complete the album.

"Now I've Got a Witness" was one of the first songs credited to Nanker Phelge.

Genesis

"Now I've Got a Witness" is a number conceived by the whole group, hence the Nanker Phelge credit. The Rolling Stones also had the support of various handpicked guests, however, hence the subtitle "Like Uncle Phil and Uncle Gene"—more specifically, "Uncle" Phil Spector and "Uncle" Gene Pitney, who attended some of the recording sessions for this debut album. Ian Stewart also plays for the first time on the record. Credited on the sleeve with guest status in exactly the same way as Spector and Pitney, Stewart was nevertheless a full-fledged member of the Rolling Stones.

Production

"*We* used to put out instrumentals from the very first album—'Now I've Got a Witness'—just let a band have a blow once in a while,"[11] reveals Keith Richards. This instrumental was recorded on February 4, following "Can I Get a Witness." This explains a number of things, not least the shared tempo and keyboard part—this time played not by Gene Pitney on the piano but by Ian Stewart on the organ. Brian Jones again plays a wonderful harmonica, as if straight out of Chess Studios. It is just a shame that it has been mixed down. Keith Richards, for his part, slots a pleasant but not exactly unforgettable solo on his Harmony Meteor H70 into this classic blues framework. Mick Jagger abandons his role as singer for once, modestly picking up a tambourine instead. However, it is the rhythm section that really shines, with Charlie Watts and Bill Wyman complementing each other to great effect, the latter choosing to support the drums on the upper reaches of his fingerboard. "Now I've Got a Witness" is the first original, group-credited number on the album and benefits from good production. A fact perhaps not unconnected with Phil Spector's presence at the session . . .

🎧 **IN YOUR HEADPHONES**
Mick Jagger seems to have a few problems with his tambourine between 1:14 and 1:17!

LITTLE BY LITTLE

Nanker Phelge / Phil Spector / 2:41

Musicians
Mick Jagger: vocals, harmonica
Keith Richards: rhythm guitar, lead guitar
Brian Jones: rhythm guitar
Bill Wyman: bass
Charlie Watts: drums
Gene Pitney: piano
Phil Spector: percussion, maracas (?)
Musician(s) not identified: hand claps, tambourine
Recorded
Regent Sound Studios: February 4, 1964
Technical Team
Producer: Andrew Loog Oldham
Sound Engineer: Bill Farley

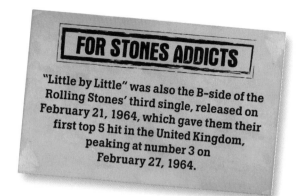

FOR STONES ADDICTS

"Little by Little" was also the B-side of the Rolling Stones' third single, released on February 21, 1964, which gave them their first top 5 hit in the United Kingdom, peaking at number 3 on February 27, 1964.

Genesis

While British rhythm 'n' blues of the early sixties was essentially a reworking of Chicago blues, differing from the original in nuance only, the pillars of this black American music scene were not always given the credit they deserved. In the case of "Little by Little," for example, the Rolling Stones used the title of a blues number recorded in 1959 by Junior Wells and Earl Hooker and the laid-back rhythm characteristic of Jimmy Reed—in this instance "Shame, Shame, Shame" (dating from 1963)—without crediting any bluesman. The lyrics, on the other hand, are original. The song tells of a love that is dying little by little because the narrator of the song has discovered that his lover has been untrue.

Production

The main aim of the session of February 4, 1964, was to record the B-side of "Not Fade Away" so that the single could be released as soon as possible—as Decca was urging. The Rolling Stones, however, were fighting and had stopped speaking to one another. Andrew Oldham appealed for help to Phil Spector and Gene Pitney, who were stopping over in London after a brief trip to Paris. Pitney came up with the idea of pretending it was his birthday and that family tradition demanded the occasion be celebrated with cognac. The ploy worked! The newly restored harmony fostered a collaborative relationship between Spector and Jagger, who wrote the number in a few minutes in a corridor at Regent Sound Studios. One thing is for sure: with Phil Spector in charge, Gene Pitney at the piano, and Graham Nash and Allan Clarke of the Hollies also lending their support, the Rolling Stones were able to make a fine homage to the blues . . . and it only took them twenty minutes or so. For this reworking of "Shame, Shame, Shame," the Stones and their guests let it rip, dispensing with any strict setup and allowing Jagger to send Richards off on a nicely executed guitar solo ("All right, Keith, come on!") before himself launching into an impassioned harmonica break ("My turn!"), with Wyman going off on a kind of supercharged chorus on his bass (between 1:29 and 1:37). Pitney would later reveal that although credited with playing the maracas on the album, Spector actually contributed by striking an empty cognac bottle with a United States half-dollar!

The Stones with Phil Spector (left) and Gene Pitney (seated), their bandmates on "Little by Little."

I'M A KING BEE

Slim Harpo / 2:38

Musicians
Mick Jagger: vocals, harmonica
Keith Richards: rhythm guitar
Brian Jones: lead guitar
Bill Wyman: bass
Charlie Watts: drums
Recorded
Regent Sound Studios: February 24–25, 1964
(January 10, according to some sources)
Technical Team
Producer: Andrew Loog Oldham
Sound Engineer: Bill Farley

Slim Harpo, master of swamp blues and the composer of "I'm a King Bee," in 1957.

Genesis

"I'm a King Bee" is one of the most famous songs by Slim Harpo (the archetypal proponent of Louisiana or swamp blues). Slim recorded it in 1957 for the Excello label at the famous studio of J. D. Miller in Crowley, Louisiana, taking inspiration from the rhythm of "Rockin' and Rollin'" by the Texan bluesman Melvin "Lil' Son" Jackson. "I'm a King Bee" might not have been an immediate success on the hit parades, but a few years later it would become an essential number for British and US rock groups from Pink Floyd to the Doors and from the Grateful Dead to Led Zeppelin. Its insistent, hypnotic rhythm played an important part in this, as did the lyrics with their strong erotic charge: *Well I'm a king bee, buzzing around your hive/Yeah I can make honey baby, let me come inside.*

Production

Listening to the Rolling Stones' version provides an insight into the work performed by Brian and Keith on guitar, and by Mick on vocal to penetrate the secrets of this "devil's music" born in the bayous of Louisiana. Their adaptation differs from Slim Harpo's original in the substantially greater rock 'n' roll energy and the significantly more suggestive drive with which they endow the song. Jagger interprets the text with his customary talent, a defining mix of sensuality and insolence. He even indulges in a very good harmonica solo that seems to hold the attention of his bandmates to such an extent that they forget to change chord (at 2:01)! For the first time on the record, Richards plays an acoustic guitar, probably his Harmony 1270 12-string. But the track's real interest derives from the combination of the slide executed by Wyman on his fretless Dallas Tuxedo bass and the brief response delivered by Jones on the downbeats. The effect is awesome, and worthy of the most skilled proponents of the genre. Jones also performs a brief solo imitating a bee in response to Jagger's instruction to buzz (*Well, buzz a while!*) before taking up his bottleneck and executing a few heartfelt slides on his green Gretsch Anniversary. As for the drums, in an interview published soon after the release of the record, Charlie revealed that he had wrapped his bass drum in his £60 coat in order to obtain the sound he was after!

1964

CAROL

Chuck Berry / 2:35

Musicians
Mick Jagger: vocals
Keith Richards: guitar
Brian Jones: guitar
Bill Wyman: bass, backing vocals (?)
Charlie Watts: drums
Unidentified musician(s): hand claps
Recorded
Regent Sound Studios: January 3, 1964
Technical Team
Producer: Andrew Loog Oldham
Sound Engineer: Bill Farley

Genesis

Like many Chuck Berry songs, "Carol" is an ode to adolescence, with the inevitable sleek automobiles, rock 'n' roll dancing joints, and, of course, the exaltation of female sensuality. To put it in a nutshell, it is a song on which the Chuck Berry legend was founded. It was released as a single in August 1958 (with "Hey Pedro" as the B-side) and reached number 18 on the charts.

Production

Following "Come On" and various other numbers they had performed onstage, the Rolling Stones now dipped into the Chuck Berry repertoire again for their first album. In fact "Carol," recorded on January 3, 1964, was, along with "Route 66," one of the first tracks they completed for it. They imbue it with the same energy as "Route 66," moreover, and one can only admire the way Keith and Brian complement each other. Compared to Chuck Berry's version, the Stones' seems to have been given a shot of adrenaline. Carried along by an excellent rhythm section consisting of Charlie (whose bass drum pedal is still squeaking!), Bill, and Brian, Keith, on his Harmony, plays jubilant guitar licks that, it has to be said, closely resemble those of the inventor of the duckwalk—including the actual solo. Mick, who sings with a slight delay, plays his part with assurance and sets the whole thing alight. The only thing lacking is Ian Stewart's piano, an instrument that is nevertheless present on Berry's version. Finally, prominent and indispensable hand claps have been overdubbed. One thing to note is the very poor fade-out, which begins in the wrong place and continues for too long.

Jimmy Page, who attended some of the Stones' early gigs, remembers this Chuck Berry cover in particular: "They did Carol and it sounds raw as fuck, they were really spitting it out. The whole vibe of it was just great. Carol was the sort of thing we'd been listening to for a number of years, and all of a sudden there's a band of guys doing it in your living room. Amazing."[17]

For a period of several years, "Carol" was to become one of the group's bravura stage numbers, One of their best versions can be found on the album *Get Yer Ya-Ya's Out!* (1970).

Chuck Berry and Keith Richards on *Hail! Hail! Rock and Roll* in 1986.

TELL ME (YOU'RE COMING BACK)

Mick Jagger / Keith Richards / 4:05

Musicians
Mick Jagger: vocals
Keith Richards: 12-string rhythm, backing vocals
Brian Jones: rhythm guitar, tambourine, backing vocals
Bill Wyman: bass, backing vocals
Charlie Watts: drums
Ian Stewart: piano
Recorded
Regent Sound Studios: February 24–25, 1964
Technical Team
Producer: Andrew Loog Oldham
Sound Engineer: Bill Farley

Black Sabbath in 1973. The hard rock group took its inspiration for "Laguna Sunrise" from the intro to "Tell Me."

Genesis

As the first recorded number credited to Mick Jagger–Keith Richards, "Tell Me (You're Coming Back)," marked an important turning point for the pair. It also marked their ascendancy over the group and, as a consequence, the end of Brian Jones's leadership, at least on a musical level. According to the legend, it was Oldham who essentially forced Jagger and Richards to shut themselves away in a room and stay there until they had written their first song or two. Wyman, however, contests this legend: "Andrew had been encouraging them to write their own songs for some time, although the story that he locked them in the flat until they wrote some material is just another Rolling Stones myth."[1] Whatever the facts of the matter, the duo had embarked on a highly promising path and started to write more and more songs. These include "My Only Girl," recorded by Gene Pitney with the title "That Girl Belongs to Yesterday" in early 1964.

The first official Jagger-Richards composition comes as something of a surprise in that it is a pop ballad rather than a blues number, thereby confirming the growing influence of Andrew Oldham, who sees this as a way of reaching a wider audience—at the expense of Jones, who was a purist of the Chicago twelve-bar blues. The lyrics are somewhat sentimental: *I want you back again/I want your love again*. This is far closer to the sweet love songs of the beat groups than to the torrid "I Just Want to Make Love to You" and covers of Motown soul numbers, and the black rock 'n' roll music of Chuck Berry and Bo Diddley. Jagger explains in 1968: "We didn't want to do blues forever, we just wanted to turn people on to other people who were very good and not carry on doing it ourselves."[18]

Production

The recording took place on February 24 and 25, 1964. Mick Jagger recalls: "Keith was playing 12-string and singing harmonies into the same microphone as the 12-string. We recorded it in this tiny studio in the West End of London called Regent Sound, which was a demo studio."[19] And according to Keith, there was nothing finished about the version of "Tell Me" that eventually made it onto the record: "Yeah, and that was a demo. Andrew stuck it on the album because we needed another track. It was cut as a demo and Andrew was gonna try

Keith Richards and Mick Jagger: the first of their own compositions that they recorded was a ballad entitled "Tell Me (You're Coming Back)."

and flog it off to somebody."[11] In other words, Oldham wanted to find another artist to record it in order to generate royalties. Although no major artist has ever covered it, there have, to date, been fifty or so versions of the song. Keith opens the number with chords on his 12-string Harmony 1270, supported by Charlie on toms and Bill on bass (mixed down). Mick then launches into his vocal, aiming at breaking the hearts of the teenage girls he addresses both earnestly and in a tone of pained emotion. To say the least, "Tell Me" is not the Stones' greatest masterpiece—either in terms of style (it is simply a pretty little song in the manner of the Merseybeat bands or the Dave Clark Five) or production (the ensemble is pretty untidy, particularly the vocal harmonies sung simultaneously by Keith, Brian, and Bill, which are not equal to those of the Beatles or even the Hollies, who attended some of the recording sessions for the album). Brian plays rhythm on his Gretsch, whose sound is curiously saturated through his Vox AC30. He also delivers a not particularly unforgettable solo based on arpeggios, whose reverb level gets progressively stronger (see his performance on the *Mike Douglas Show* in June 1964). It is also Brian who plays the overdubbed tambourine. In his excellent book *Rolling with the Stones,*[1] Bill mentions that Stu was on piano, as the liner notes also make clear. But to hear his contribution requires some careful listening. Nevertheless, the Stones are unique, and despite being an early piece of work, this song possesses a charm that was soon to produce an effect, for "Tell Me" was released

as a single in the United States (with "I Just Want to Make Love to You" [spelled "I Just Wanna Make Love to You"] on the B-side) on June 13, 1964, a week after the start of their first US tour. The release was a success, and it was with this song that the group entered the *Billboard* charts for the first time. It peaked at number 24 on August 8, 1964, and spent a total of ten weeks in the hit parade. This song was never released as a single in the United Kingdom. It is interesting to note that a number of years later, someone pointed out to Oldham that the English version was longer on the fade-out than the US version. Oldham, surprised, replies that he had not noticed at the time because he had been too busy, adding: "By the time I wasn't too busy, I really didn't care!"[20]

FOR STONES ADDICTS

There is a version of "Tell Me" with piano (although the piano part is almost inaudible) and another without. This second version was included by mistake on the very first copies of *The Rolling Stones.* It is interesting to note that the album version runs to 4:05, whereas the single only plays for 2:40, the guitar solo having totally disappeared.

CAN I GET A WITNESS

Brian Holland / Lamont Dozier / Eddie Holland / 2:58

Musicians
Mick Jagger: vocals
Keith Richards: acoustic rhythm guitar, backing vocals
Brian Jones: tambourine, backing vocals
Bill Wyman: bass, backing vocals
Ian Stewart: piano
Unidentified musician(s): hand claps
Recorded
Regent Sound Studios: February 4, 1964
Technical Team
Producer: Andrew Loog Oldham
Sound Engineer: Bill Farley

Brian Holland, Lamont Dozier, and Eddie Holland, Motown's leading songwriting trio.

Genesis

"Can I Get a Witness" is a number by the trio Brian Holland–Lamont Dozier–Eddie Holland (H.D.H.), who were inspired purveyors of hits to Berry Gordy's record company Motown. The number was written for Marvin Gaye, who recorded it on July 17, 1963, with the Supremes, and with the Holland brothers and Lamont Dozier, no less, on backing vocals. The title of the song refers to the ritual in black churches whereby the preacher poses the question *Can I get a witness?* and the congregation devoutly and contemplatively responds with an *Amen.*

Production

In addition to its religious dimension and the enormous subtlety and sensitivity of Marvin Gaye's voice, the success of "Can I Get a Witness," which peaked at number 22 on the *Billboard* pop chart in December 1963, rests on the boogie-woogie piano of Earl Van Dyke (a member of the famous Funk Brothers). Ian Stewart was one of Britain's most faithful proponents of this style of piano playing. His role is therefore key to the Rolling Stones' version, in which Mick Jagger is recast in the role of a preacher for the good cause. In fact, the Stones' version relies even more heavily on the piano than Marvin Gaye's. This gives it something of a Ray Charles flavor, despite being fundamentally more rock 'n' roll. Jagger adopted a more rasping, bluesy voice with a rapid-fire delivery that makes him almost unrecognizable. Oldham explains why. He suggested that the Stones do a version of "Can I Get a Witness," but Jagger did not know the words very well. "I called Freddy Bienstock, who published the song," recalls Oldham, "and Mick ran from Regent Sound to pick up the sheet music left in reception at Freddy's Savile Row office." Upon his return, Mick rushed straight to the mic "and that's the reason the vocal on our 'Can I Get a Witness' sounds so breathless."[5] The bass-drums duo lay down the perfect groove, and Keith plays rhythm on his Harmony 1270 12-string. Brian has abandoned his Gretsch and makes do (at least it is presumed to be Brian) with the tambourine. Yet Oldham, in his memoirs, mentions guitar overdubs. Does he mean Brian or Keith? Finally, the vocal harmonies are sung by Keith, Brian, and Bill. Hand claps can also be heard, no doubt overdubbed.

YOU CAN MAKE IT IF YOU TRY

Ted Jarrett / 2:03

Musicians
Mick Jagger: vocals, tambourine (?)
Keith Richards: acoustic guitar, backing vocals
Brian Jones: rhythm guitar, backing vocals
Bill Wyman: bass, backing vocals
Charlie Watts: drums
Ian Stewart: organ
Recorded
Regent Sound Studios: February 24–25, 1964
(January 3 or 4, according to some sources)
Technical Team
Producer: Andrew Loog Oldham
Sound Engineer: Bill Farley

Brian Jones with his superb green Gretsch Anniversary.

Genesis

Born in Nashville in 1925, Ted Jarrett wrote his first songs as a teenager. But it was not until after the Second World War that his career really got under way, first of all as a disc jockey on the Nashville radio station WSOK, and then as the writer of "It's Love Baby (24 Hours a Day)," which became a number 2 on the R&B charts for Louis Brooks and his Hi-Toppers. Jarrett subsequently put his name to two more hits: "Love, Love, Love" for the honky-tonk singer Webb Pierce (1955) and "You Can Make It If You Try" for the rhythm 'n' blues singer Gene Allison (1957).

Production

Acclaimed by the public (reaching numbers 3 and 36 on the black and pop charts, respectively, in 1958), "You Can Make It If You Try" came into being after Jarrett was abandoned by his girlfriend. The Rolling Stones express this heartache extremely well, with Jagger's vocals and Stewart's keyboard both strongly gospel-tinged. This effect is reinforced by Stu, accompanying the group on what is apparently a Vox Continental. And without really departing from the gospel idiom, the Stones bring a rock 'n' roll flavor to the number that is absent from Gene Allison's—slower—version. Once again, Keith is on acoustic guitar while Brian carves out a doo-wop counterpoint on his Gretsch Anniversary, accompanied by a backing vocal in similar mode (and more successful than the backing on "Tell Me") from Bill, Brian, and Keith. "You Can Make It If You Try" provides the Rolling Stones with a new palette: after rock, blues, rhythm 'n' blues, and the pop ballad, here they try their hand at gospel. Oldham wanted to reach the widest possible audience, and it looks as though he succeeded.

FOR STONES ADDICTS

On the first few copies of the album, the *If* is missing from the title, yielding: "You Can Make It You Try"! So to all collectors out there . . .

WALKING THE DOG

Rufus Thomas / 3:09

Musicians
Mick Jagger: vocals
Keith Richards: lead guitar
Brian Jones: vocal harmonies, rhythm guitar, whistling
Bill Wyman: bass
Charlie Watts: drums
Unidentified musician(s): hand claps
Recorded
Regent Sound Studios: February 24–25, (January 3–4, according to some sources)
Technical Team
Producer: Andrew Loog Oldham
Sound Engineer: Bill Farley

The Rolling Stones performed "Walking the Dog" on the Australian show *Big Beat '65* on January 29, 1965. The two guitarists have changed their instruments: Brian Jones is playing his famous Vox "Teardrop" and Keith is on his Gibson Les Paul Standard.

FOR STONES ADDICTS

"Walking the Dog" was released in Australia in 1965 as the B-side of the single "Under the Boardwalk," the Rolling Stones' first number 1 in that country (for three consecutive weeks!).

Genesis

The name Rufus Thomas inevitably evokes the Memphis scene. After starting out as a singer at Elks Club on Beale Street, Thomas joined Sam Phillips's Sun stable before moving to Jim Stewart and Estelle Axton's Stax (originally called Satellite), where he recorded "Cause I Love You" with his daughter Carla in 1960. He even provided this record company with one of its first resounding hits with "Walking the Dog," which reached number 10 on the *Billboard* pop chart in December 1963.

As with so many blues and rhythm 'n' blues numbers, double entendre plays an important part. As well as its obvious meaning, *walking the dog* has overtones of masturbation and oral sex. *If you don't know how to do it/I'll show you how to walk the dog*, sings Mick Jagger in the role of a connoisseur . . .

Production

"Walking the Dog" is a song steeped in the soul of the Southern states, in which the Rolling Stones are perfectly at home. In their brilliant version they give the impression of being entirely at ease. In an extremely rare instance in their recording history, Brian Jones provides the vocal harmonies for Mick Jagger and whistles at the end of the refrains, causing Keith Richards to comment drily: "I always knew he had talent!"[21] It is interesting, moreover, to note the very husky quality of his voice. Keith again, on the subject of Brian: "Brian at that time is the leader of the band. He pulled us all together, he's playing good guitar, but his love is the harmonica. On top of that, he's got the pop star hangup—he wants to sing, with Mick, like 'Walking The Dog.'"[11] Brian also plays rhythm on his green Gretsch Anniversary, while Keith Richards plays lead on his Harmony Meteor H70, delivering extremely good blues-rock licks throughout as well as an excellent solo—without doubt the best on the album. Bill Wyman and Charlie Watts lay down the necessary groove, supported by overdubbed hand claps that are both very prominent in the mix and fearsomely efficient. As for Mick Jagger, the singer does not have to try too hard to bring out the secondary meaning of the lyrics. Compared to the Rufus Thomas version, the British quintet's possesses a more aggressive and ostensibly rock 'n' roll dynamic. All in all, one of the best tracks on the album.

Bye Bye Johnny
Money
You Better Move On
Poison Ivy

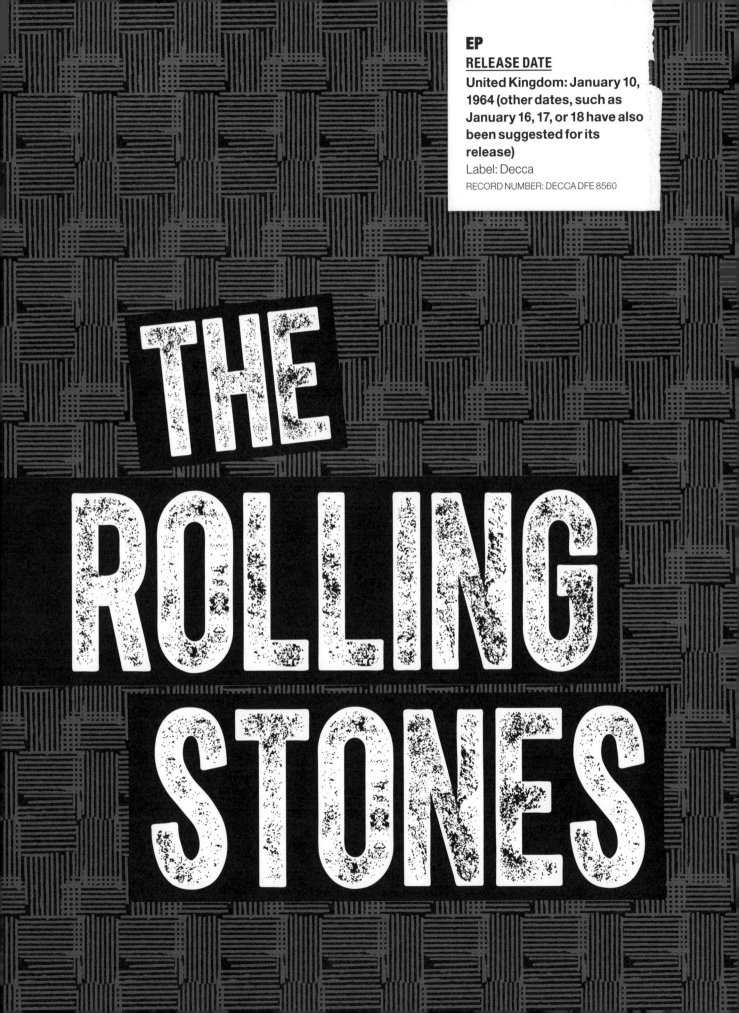

EP
RELEASE DATE
**United Kingdom: January 10,
1964 (other dates, such as
January 16, 17, or 18 have also
been suggested for its
release)**
Label: Decca
RECORD NUMBER: DECCA DFE 8560

THE ROLLING STONES

BYE BYE JOHNNY

Chuck Berry / 2:11

Musicians
Mick Jagger: vocals
Keith Richards: guitar lead, backing vocals
Brian Jones: rhythm guitar, backing vocals
Bill Wyman: bass
Charlie Watts: drums
Recorded
Decca Recording Studios, West
Hampstead, London: August 8, 1963
Technical Team
Producer: Andrew Loog Oldham
Sound engineer(s): not identified

Genesis

After the success of "I Wanna Be Your Man," which reached number 12 on the British charts, Decca and Andrew Loog Oldham wanted to test the Rolling Stones' popularity. To this end they had the band record a four-track EP that they named *The Rolling Stones.* The first number was "Bye Bye Johnny" by Chuck Berry, recorded in 1960 for Berry's album *Rockin' at the Hops* and also released as a single with "Worried Life Blues" as the B-side. "Bye Bye Johnny" is a sequel to the celebrated "Johnny B. Goode," which tells the story of a country boy and brilliant guitarist whose mother predicts he will be a star. In "Bye Bye Johnny," the guitarist's mother is the heroine. She is described putting her son on a Greyhound bus heading west, where he is to make motion pictures in Hollywood. She later receives a letter from Johnny, telling her that he has fallen in love and will return to the Southern states as soon as he has got married . . .

Production

The Stones' version is far more dynamic than Chuck Berry's. Keith launches right in, re-creating the original introduction note for note on his Harmony Meteor. His sound is pretty saturated, resulting no doubt from the Top Boost function on his new Vox AC30 guitar amp. He also plays the solo in the style of his American idol, acquitting himself extremely well. Brian, who had also recently acquired a Vox AC30, plays rhythm on his Gretsch. Unfortunately, he is too loud, impairing the overall balance to some degree. Bill is as nimble as ever on his fretless Dallas Tuxedo and combines with Charlie to form the same rock-solid rhythm section. Mick has no difficulty with the lead vocal and is supported by a highly enthusiastic, although unfortunately totally saturated, backing vocal. It should be said that Oldham, who was in charge of production, had not succeeded in mastering the art during the three months since he assumed the role for "Come On" on May 10. Hence the rather unmethodical ensemble and accelerations in tempo. During the first refrain, between 0:22 and 0:29, the group can be heard suddenly stepping on the gas.

Chuck Berry, a pioneer of rock 'n' roll. The Stones repeatedly drew on his catalog.

1964

MONEY

Berry Gordy / Janie Bradford / Barrett Strong / 2:33

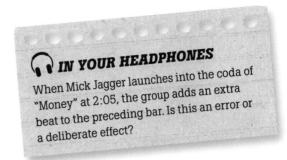

🎧 **IN YOUR HEADPHONES**
When Mick Jagger launches into the coda of "Money" at 2:05, the group adds an extra beat to the preceding bar. Is this an error or a deliberate effect?

Musicians
Mick Jagger: vocals, tambourine
Keith Richards: guitar, backing vocals
Brian Jones: harmonica, backing vocals
Bill Wyman: bass
Charlie Watts: drums
Recorded
De Lane Lea Studios, Kingsway, London: November 14, 1963
Technical Team
Producer: Eric Easton
Sound engineer(s): not identified

"Money" marked the start of a big Motown adventure for Barrett Strong, one of the song's co-writers.

Genesis

From the time of Tamla Motown's creation in 1959, Berry Gordy was able to rely on a solid team that included Smokey Robinson, Marvin Gaye, Barrett Strong, and Janie Bradford. The first hit for the Detroit record company was penned by Berry Gordy himself with Janie Bradford and Barrett Strong. This was the aptly named "Money (That's What I Want)." It was recorded by Barrett Strong and released on the Tamla label in August 1959. The song rose to numbers 2 and 23 on the R&B and pop charts, respectively.

Long before entering the *Rolling Stone* list of 500 Greatest Songs of All Time (at number 288), there had already been numerous cover versions of "Money (That's What I Want)." The Beatles recorded the song during the sessions for their second album, *With the Beatles*. Over the weeks that followed, it was the Rolling Stones' turn to add it to their repertoire. This was at the instigation of Mick Jagger, who had purchased the single bearing the Motown name a little while before: "I can remember buying Barrett Strong's Money, which was [a] really big R&B hit in America, but didn't happen when it came out in England. When we saw that those things were popular, we said, 'well, let's do that.' So we did."[24]

Production

After attempting an initial version at the Decca Recording Studios on August 8, the Stones recorded another take on November 14, this time at De Lane Lea Studios. In the absence of Andrew Oldham, it was Eric Easton who looked after the production. The best that can be said of it is that the results leave something to be desired, especially in terms of recording quality. The sound is saturated, the instruments are difficult to distinguish, and Mick Jagger would have benefited from some adjusting in the coda. The Stones did not want to bring in Ian Stewart, who would have been able to play the riff on the piano, following Barrett Strong's example, so Keith Richards plays it on the guitar, supported by Bill Wyman on bass. Brian Jones is on harmonica but his contribution is drowned out by the general noise. Jagger pulls out all the stops to bring the number off, but there is no getting around the fact that his performance is not up to the standard of Strong or Lennon. Easton was perhaps aiming for a "garage band" sound, but all the evidence is that he failed.

YOU BETTER MOVE ON

Arthur Alexander / 2:41

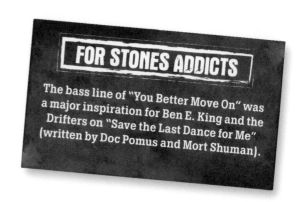

Musicians
Mick Jagger: vocals
Keith Richards: rhythm guitar
Brian Jones: acoustic guitar, backing vocals
Bill Wyman: bass, backing vocals
Charlie Watts: drums
Recorded
Decca Recording Studios, West
Hampstead, London: August 8, 1963
Technical Team
Producer: Andrew Loog Oldham
Sound engineer(s): not identified

Genesis

The third number on the EP is titled "You Better Move On." It was composed in 1961 by Arthur Alexander, and recorded in a modest shack rented by Rick Hall in Alabama that was to become the prestigious Fame Studios of Muscle Shoals. This song has inspired numerous cover versions, notably by the Hollies in the United Kingdom. The song's protagonist refuses to heed the advice of "kind souls" who would have him believe that the woman he loves is not for him and that he ought to leave—the fruit of bitter personal experience for Arthur Alexander.

Production

By the time they recorded it during the session on August 8, 1963, the Rolling Stones had been performing "You Better Move On" for over a year. This was one of the first ballads to be cut by the group. It was also for this number that Brian got out his Harmony 6-string acoustic for the first time in the Stones' recording history. Mick takes hold of Alexander's lyrics and delivers a sensitive interpretation, intended to move the group's audience of teenage girls. His voice is clearly doubled-tracked in the bridge, between 1:19 and 1:50. Bill takes it upon himself to play a lilting bass line but joins Brian, with plenty of reverb, on backing vocals, which are on the whole, pretty successful. An imperturbable Charlie marks the tempo on his ride cymbal while Keith plays rhythm on his Harmony Meteor. The result hit the mark in the United States. Oldham would never tire of congratulating himself on the successful marriage between his ideas and those of the group: "For a second time, the collision between my pop opportunism and the Stones' R'n'B purity had ended amicably in a hit."[5] According to Roy Carr, a future contributor to the *New Musical Express*, if the number had been marketed as a single rather than as an EP, "It could have been their first UK No. 1."[1] "You Better Move On" was included in the album *December's Children (And Everybody's)* that was released in the United States on December 4, 1965.

"You Better Move On" was the song with which disc jockeys chose to promote the Stones' EP.

Arthur Alexander, the composer of "You Better Move On," a bluesy ballad covered by the Stones.

1964

POISON IVY

Jerry Leiber / Mike Stoller / 2:06

Musicians
Mick Jagger: vocals, tambourine
Keith Richards: rhythm guitar
Brian Jones: rhythm guitar, backing vocals
Bill Wyman: bass, backing vocals
Charlie Watts: drums
Recorded
Decca Recording Studios, West Hampstead,
London (first version): July 9 (or 15, according to some sources) / De Lane Lea Studios, Kingsway, London (definitive version): November 14, 1963
Technical Team
Producer: Eric Easton
Sound Engineer: not identified

Charlie Watts, excellent from beginning to end of "Poison Ivy," on his Ludwig Super Classic kit.

Genesis

From "Hound Dog" to "Stand by Me," Jerry Leiber and Mike Stoller's songs have been performed by a huge number of artists, at the forefront of whom are Elvis Presley and doo-wop bands the Drifters and the Coasters. "Poison Ivy" was written by Leiber and Stoller in 1958. Recorded the following year by the Coasters, it climbed to number 1 on the R&B charts and number 7 on the pop charts. The heroine, Poison Ivy, is apparently the embodiment of the femme fatale. She is as attractive as she is dangerous: *She's pretty as a daisy*, but *late at night when you're sleeping/Poison ivy comes a creeping all around*. Jerry Leiber would later tell David Ritz that he had made Poison Ivy "a metaphor for a sexually transmitted disease."[22]

Production

The "Poison Ivy" recording session on November 14, 1963, was not the group's first experience with the song. They had already worked it up four months earlier, on July 9, 1963, for the B-side of a single that never saw the light of day. Dick Rowe of Decca asked Michael Barclay to "assist" Andrew Oldham. Barclay was an experienced producer who had been responsible, among other things, for the success of the doo-wop version of "What Do You Want to Make Those Eyes at Me For?" by Emile Ford & The Checkmates (1959–1960). According to Rowe, the recording was a disaster: "The Stones thought Mick was a fuddy-duddy; he thought they were mad."[23] The results were unsatisfactory. A few copies of the single were pressed, but were withdrawn from sale by Decca not long after.

Four months later, "Poison Ivy" was back on the menu. The Rolling Stones rerecorded it during the November 14 session, making a far better version than the first time around. The result was extremely well crafted, and Eric Easton's production was in a different league than his work on "Money." Brian and Keith's guitars complement each other perfectly, Bill and Charlie provide extremely good rhythmic support—with Charlie wrapping up the number with a drum break on his Ludwig Super Classic—and Mick is in fine form (with plenty of reverb), carrying off this second version with conviction while at the same time playing a not particularly audible tambourine. He is supported by Bill and Brian's backing vocals, which to some extent recalls the Beatles of the day.

Inspired by Bo Diddley, "Not Fade Away" was created by Buddy Holly & The Crickets, shown here on The *Ed Sullivan Show* in 1957.

NOT FADE AWAY

Charles Hardin / Norman Petty / 1:48

SINGLE

*Not Fade Away / Little by Little**

RELEASE DATE

United Kingdom: February 21, 1964

Label: Decca

RECORD NUMBER: DECCA F 11845

* LITTLE BY LITTLE: SEE THE ALBUM *THE ROLLING STONES*

Musicians

Mick Jagger: vocals, hand claps, tambourine, maracas
Keith Richards: 12-string acoustic guitar, guitar solo
Brian Jones: harmonica
Bill Wyman: bass
Charlie Watts: drums

Recorded

Regent Sound Studios: January 10, 1964 (January 28 and February 4, according to some sources)

Technical Team

Producer: Andrew Loog Oldham
Sound Engineer: Bill Farley

Genesis

Recorded by Buddy Holly at the Norman Petty Studios in Clovis, New Mexico, on May 27, 1957, "Not Fade Away" was released the following October as the B-side of his single "Oh, Boy!" The song takes its rhythm from Bo Diddley—the logically named "Bo Diddley Beat," or "Bo Diddley Sound"—that is a modern version of African American religious chants, the *shouts* that had their origins in the folk culture of West Africa. There is also a certain rhythmic affinity with the Cuban dance known as the habanera. A syncopated, hypnotic rhythm that corresponds perfectly to the idea of a love that "never dies."

Although a cover, Andrew Loog Oldham has always considered "Not Fade Away" to be a Rolling Stones song, indeed the first by the Jagger-Richards songwriting partnership, for their arrangement. The A-side of their third single in the United Kingdom (with "Little by Little" as the B-side), "Not Fade Away" reached number 3 on the UK charts on February 27, 1964. It also opens side one of the American LP *The Rolling Stones, England's Newest Hit Makers* (displacing "Mona," track four on the British LP), which was released in April 1964.

Production

After listening to the Buddy Holly recording, Keith Richards immediately saw that "Not Fade Away" fit the Stones' repertoire perfectly and that he would be able to transcend the original with a more aggressive, more accentuated riff. In truth, however, the person who really identified the number as a potential next single for the group was none other than Oldham himself. He explains in his memoirs: "[I] found Keith

Mick Jagger gives one of his first great vocal performances on "Not Fade Away" (1964).

exactly where I'd left him that morning—fag in mouth, guitar on knee, singing bits of Buddy Holly's 'Not Fade Away.'"[5] Suddenly, hearing Keith incorporate a riff that was far more "Bo Diddley" than anything on the original version, things fell into place for Oldham: "I heard our next record. I could actually hear the record in the room. The way he played it—you could hear the whole record. It was less pop more rock. It was a magical moment for me."[5]

The recording took place at Regent Sound Studios on January 10. Other dates have also been mentioned by various sources, such as January 28 and February 4, when Phil Spector was present in the studio, but neither of these is confirmed by Bill Wyman, least of all the second: "It's often said that we recorded 'Not Fade Away' at this session, with Phil Spector playing maracas, but Andrew used this as publicity, although he was more impressed than the media were."[1]

According to Oldham, the take used as the basis for overdubbing took just twenty-five minutes. Keith, who had played the song numerous times at the apartment he shared with Mick and Oldham in Willesden, launches into the introduction on his Harmony 1270 12-string acoustic. The result is instant magic, providing a glimpse of the art of the riff that Richards would continue to hone throughout his career. Bill answers almost immediately with an E on his bass (at 0:05), which is the group's signal. The machine lurches into action, and it could be said that "Not Fade Away" defines the true sound of the Rolling Stones for the very first time: the energy, the aggression, and the sensuality. Their version is far superior to Buddy Holly's; the five English boys take hold of the number and give it an irresistible drive. Bill Wyman: "Buddy played it very lightly.

We just got into it and put the Diddley beat up-front."[1] Charlie further accentuates the tribal aspect with his heavy, aggressive use of the toms. Brian contributes to the success of the number with an excellent harmonica accompaniment that shows off his exceptional mastery of the instrument. Mick, who double-tracks his own voice, gives one of his best vocal performances of 1964, delivering the lyrics perfectly. According to Bill Wyman, he also performs the hand claps and played the tambourine and maracas (again overdubbed). Finally, Keith adds an extremely successful overdubbed solo on his Harmony Meteor, which he shares with Brian on harmonica. One could almost view "Not Fade Away" as the real birth of the Stones, as the beginning of their true artistry.

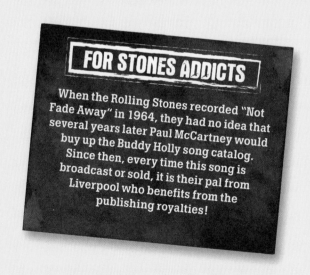

FOR STONES ADDICTS

When the Rolling Stones recorded "Not Fade Away" in 1964, they had no idea that several years later Paul McCartney would buy up the Buddy Holly song catalog. Since then, every time this song is broadcast or sold, it is their pal from Liverpool who benefits from the publishing royalties!

IT'S ALL OVER NOW

Bobby Womack / Shirley Womack / 3:30

SINGLE

It's All Over Now / Good Times, Bad Times

RELEASE DATE

United Kingdom: June 26, 1964

Label: Decca
RECORD NUMBER: DECCA F 11934

Musicians

Mick Jagger: vocals, tambourine
Keith Richards: lead guitar, backing vocals
Brian Jones: rhythm guitar, backing vocals
Bill Wyman: bass
Charlie Watts: drums

Recorded

Chess Studios, Chicago: June 10, 1964

Technical Team

Producer: Andrew Loog Oldham
Sound Engineer: Ron Malo

Genesis

In the mid-sixties, Murray the K was one of the most famous disc jockeys on the East Coast of the United States. Hosting a show on the New York radio station WINS (Ten-Ten WINS), he played a major role in the British Invasion. While referring to himself somewhat self-flatteringly as the "fifth Beatle," he was also a fan of the Rolling Stones. Thus on June 1, the day the group arrived in New York, he played the five Londoners "It's All Over Now," which had been recorded some time previously by Bobby Womack's group the Valentinos for SAR Records, the label founded by Sam Cooke (a producer as well as a singer-songwriter). Furthermore, Murray the K convinced the group to record the song themselves in order to widen their repertoire. It tells of a man who has stopped loving a woman because she has made him cry, a woman who has *run around with every man in town.*

"It's All Over Now" was released in the United Kingdom (with "Good Times, Bad Times" as the B-side) on June 26, 1964, and reached number 1 on the charts on July 2. It was the Londoners' first number 1 in their native country. The single was released in the United States on July 25, a little more than a month after they completed their first tour. "It's All Over Now" peaked at number 26 on the *Billboard* charts on September 19.

Production

The session took place on June 10, 1964, in the studios of Chess Records, a veritable place of pilgrimage for the Rolling Stones, who had been invoking the names of Muddy Waters, Willie Dixon, and Howlin' Wolf since the group's earliest days.

Brian Jones plays his guitar of choice, the Gretsch Anniversary, in a gig at Alexandra Palace, London, on June 26, 1964, the day the single "It's All Over Now" was released.

Keith recalls: "2120 South Michigan Avenue was hallowed ground—the headquarters of Chess Records in Chicago. We got there on a last-minute arrangement made by Andrew Oldham, at a moment when the first half of our first US tour seemed like a semidisaster."[2]

In charge of the session was Ron Malo, Chess's revered sound engineer, who had been responsible for the success of Bo Diddley, Chuck Berry, Muddy Waters, Howlin' Wolf, and Etta James . . .

It is immediately apparent that the recording quality has been raised to a new level. All the instruments can be heard, and in particular Jagger's voice sounds like never before. His delivery of the lyrics and the texture of his voice are finally shown off to their best advantage. Compared to the Valentinos' version, that of the British band sounds determinedly both more blues and more rock, but also with a country feel that did not go unnoticed in the US. "We didn't think it sounded country & western until we read it,"[1] states Bill Wyman. The two-guitar introduction immediately commands attention. Keith, who was now playing his new Epiphone Casino, and Brian, faithful to his Gretsch Anniversary, obtain a swampy sound thanks to the reverb added by the studio's fender amps. This introduction with its weaving guitars is typical of the Stones' sound. Charlie used the studio's Ludwig drum kit (his

bass drum can be heard clearly for the first time!) and he is supported by Bill with his Framus Star bass plugged directly into the console (no distortion in the bass). Mick taps out the beat on a tambourine (no doubt overdubbed) and is accompanied in the refrains by Keith and Brian on backing vocals, with Mick and Keith sharing a refrain for the first time. It is Keith who delivers the solo, which John Lennon told Keith he didn't like: "John could be quite direct. The only rude thing I remember him saying to me was about my solo in the middle of 'It's All Over Now.' He thought it was a crap. Maybe he got out the wrong side of the bed that day. OK, it certainly could have been better."[2] Finally, in the coda, Brian can be heard marking the rhythm with thunderous chords on the guitar, still with plenty of reverb. The result is a triumph.

Bobby Womack is said to have asked his manager to intervene to get the Stones to record "It's All Over Now." He subsequently claimed to hate their version before coming to appreciate—and to greatly appreciate—the level of royalties.

Keith, Charlie, Bill, Mick, and Brian enjoy a moment of relaxation in a London coffee shop. Good times . . .

SIDE B 1964

GOOD TIMES, BAD TIMES

Mick Jagger / Keith Richards / 2:30

SINGLE

It's All Over Now / Good Times, Bad Times

RELEASE DATE

United Kingdom: June 26, 1964

Label: Decca
RECORD NUMBER: F 11934

Musicians
Mick Jagger: vocals
Keith Richards: 12-string acoustic guitar
Brian Jones: harmonica
Bill Wyman: bass (?)
Charlie Watts: drums

Recorded
Regent Sound Studios: February 24–25, 1964

Technical Team
Producer: Andrew Loog Oldham
Sound Engineer: Bill Farley

Led Zeppelin open their eponymous first album with a track titled "Good Times, Bad Times" but this is credited to Page, Jones, and Bonham, and has nothing to do with the Stones number of the same name.

Genesis

"Good Times, Bad Times" is one of the first songs to be written by Mick Jagger and Keith Richards—at Andrew Oldham's urging. In terms of both the lyrics and the music, it was written under the influence of the black American bluesmen. A love affair is made up of good and bad times, sings Jagger, adding that in spite of the *hard times . . . there's gotta be trust in this world.*

Production

This stripped-down ballad, dominated by Keith Richards's Harmony 1270 12-string, has a strong acoustic blues feel. The use of this instrument works well, with great licks that are reminiscent of Blind Willie McTell and Leadbelly. Keith is accompanied on the harmonica by Brian Jones, who plays with his customary excellence. It is difficult to hear the bass, but this is possibly because Bill Wyman is playing with deliberate understatement. Charlie Watts has chosen to confine himself to the bass drum, but occasionally lacks a certain precision in his placing of the beat (listen from 0:54). Finally, Mick Jagger delivers the lyrics with a combination of feeling and restraint, and the ample reverb on his voice reinforces the blues side of the ballad. It is a good number, and an homage to the musicians the writers especially admire. "Good Times, Bad Times" figures on various albums, notably *12x5* (October 1964). It is a shame the song has virtually never been covered by other artists.

Keith Richards on his 12-string acoustic, the Harmony 1270.

If You Need Me
Empty Heart
2120 South Michigan Avenue
Confessin' The Blues
Around And Around

EP

RELEASE DATE

United Kingdom: August 14, 1964

Label: Decca

RECORD NUMBER: DECCA DFE 8590

FIVE BY FIVE

IF YOU NEED ME

Wilson Pickett / Robert Bateman / Sonny Sanders / 2:05

Musicians
Mick Jagger: vocals, tambourine
Keith Richards: rhythm guitar, backing vocals (?)
Brian Jones: rhythm guitar, backing vocals (?)
Bill Wyman: bass, backing vocals (?)
Charlie Watts: drums
Ian Stewart: organ
Recorded
Chess Studios, Chicago: June 11, 1964
Technical Team
Producer: Andrew Loog Oldham
Sound Engineer: Ron Malo

Solomon Burke, the incredible singer of "If You Need Me," whose solemn gospel vibe the Stones respected.

Genesis

"If You Need Me" is a song written in 1963 by Wilson Pickett, the producer Robert Bateman (co-writer of the Marvelettes' "Please Mr. Postman"), and Sonny Sanders. After recording a demo, Pickett sent it to Jerry Wexler, the charismatic producer at Atlantic Records. Wexler instantly fell for the melody and characteristic rhythm of the soul ballad and asked Solomon Burke to record it. The "King of Rock 'n' Soul," as he was later nicknamed, transformed it into one of the biggest hits of his career, taking it to number 2 on the R&B charts. There was nothing Wilson Pickett could do but weep. Or almost nothing . . . what he actually did was record his own version of the song, which was the first release by Lloyd Price's label, Double L Records, although he was not able to progress beyond number 30 on the R&B charts with his own song!

Production

In June 1964, it was the Rolling Stones' turn to record "If You Need Me"—at the prestigious Chess Studios in Chicago. The cover by the six Brits is substantially more energetic than the versions by either Solomon Burke or even Wilson Pickett. It is Ian Stewart who sets the tone on a Hammond B-3 organ with a sound and style of playing that are simultaneously blues and gospel. He is supported by the guitars of Keith Richards and Brian Jones: the one arpeggiating the chords as in any self-respecting ballad, the other strumming more discreetly. Mick Jagger's vocals respect the gospel feel of the number, and he also incorporates the "sermon" (between 1:00 and 1:28) that is an indispensable component of the gospel genre, while at the same time infusing the song with a rock 'n' roll drive that brings the whole thing alive. Jagger is supported by a second voice, probably Keith, who in turn is joined in the vocal harmonies (during the sermon) by Brian or Bill. Finally, Charlie's drumming is impeccable, laying down a discreetly swinging groove while at the same time providing Bill with a platform for a solid bass line. The overall sound is concise, direct, and entrancing, thanks to the magic of Chess and Ron Malo.

1964

EMPTY HEART

Nanker Phelge / 2:39

Musicians
Mick Jagger: vocals, tambourine
Keith Richards: lead guitar, backing vocals
Brian Jones: rhythm guitar, harmonica, backing vocals (?)
Bill Wyman: bass
Charlie Watts: drums
Ian Stewart: organ
Recorded
Chess Studios, Chicago: June 11, 1964
Technical Team
Producer: Andrew Loog Oldham
Sound engineer: Ron Malo

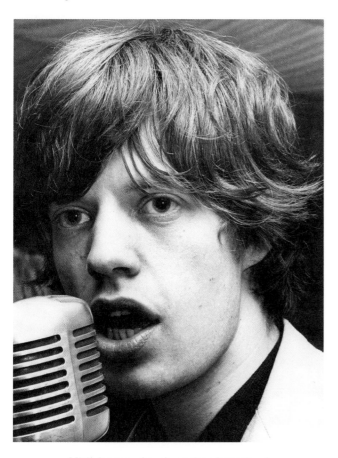

Mick Jagger, already at the pinnacle of his art with Empty Heart."

FOR STONES ADDICTS

The Rolling Stones played "Empty Heart" live throughout 1964 before removing it from their set lists.

Genesis

Whereas "If You Need Me" is infused with the soul of the South, "Empty Heart" has the unmistakable feel of modern blues, in particular the kind created at Chess Studios. Mick Jagger plays the role of a tenderhearted romantic for whom life without love is meaningless: *Well you've been my lover for a long long time/Well you left me all alone and end my time,* he sings.

Production

"Empty Heart" was recorded during the Rolling Stones' second session at Chess Studios, the day after "It's All Over Now." The song was created by the six members of the group, which explains why it is credited to Nanker Phelge. It is more of an improvisation than a number with well-defined refrains and verses. But the results are explosive. The atmosphere of "Empty Heart" derives first and foremost from Brian Jones's (probably overdubbed) harmonica with ample reverb. This too is reminiscent of the great names who worked with Chess Records, in particular Sonny Boy Williamson (Alex Miller), who was responsible for dozens of hits for the Chicago label (including "Don't Start Me Talkin'," "Your Funeral & My Trial," and "Let Your Conscience Be Your Guide") before going on to record with the Yardbirds and the Animals. Brian is also responsible for the superb introduction, in which he gives his Gretsch ample vibrato in true Bo Diddley style. Keith plays lead on his Epiphone, delivering distinctly blues-rock licks that literally electrify the number. Significant character is added by an unusual drum part from Charlie in which the ride cymbal plays a very prominent role and the snare drum marks the fourth beat of the bar. Supported by Bill's bass, the rhythm section is nothing other than a metronomically precise locomotive. Ian has again been called upon to make a discreet but indispensable contribution on the Hammond organ. And Mick delivers an excellent vocal performance, seconded by the incredible Keith (and probably Brian too), who launches into a distinctly gospel falsetto (at 0:41 and 1:42). All in all, "Empty Heart" is a very good, impressively produced number that shows the Stones progressing in leaps and bounds since their arrival in the United States. The song went on to be covered many times, notably by MC5 in 1972 and by the Grateful Dead in 1966.

2120 SOUTH MICHIGAN AVENUE

Nanker Phelge / 2:10

Musicians
Mick Jagger: tambourine
Keith Richards: guitar
Brian Jones: harmonica
Bill Wyman: bass
Charlie Watts: drums
Ian Stewart: organ

Recorded
Chess Studios, Chicago: June 11, 1964

Technical Team
Producer: Andrew Loog Oldham
Sound Engineer: Ron Malo

COVER
2120 South Michigan Avenue is also the name of an album released by George Thorogood & The Destroyers in 2011, which includes a very good cover of the Stones' number.

The legendary Chess Studios in Chicago, the cradle of modern electric blues.

Genesis
"2120 South Michigan Avenue" clearly refers to the address of Chess Studios and Chess Records in Chicago, founded by Leonard Chess in 1947 as Aristocrat before being renamed in 1950, when Phil joined his brother Leonard in the crazy enterprise. It must surely have taken an inordinate love of the blues on the part of these two Jews from Poland, as well as a distinctly reckless streak, for them to commit themselves to the promotion of a musical style that up to that time had been of sole interest to the African American community, a community that was poor, despite its overwhelming majority, and subject to the implacable laws of racial segregation. Who could have imagined that a decade later, Muddy Waters, Willie Dixon, Howlin' Wolf, and Chuck Berry would have become the mentors of the baby boomers of aged, prudish England, the architects of an incredible musical revolution?

Production
"I played the bass riff for 2120 South Michigan Avenue and then everyone picked up on it. It was credited to Nanker Phelge."[1] The number was effectively structured around this very good bass line played by Bill on his Framus Star, whose sound is mildly saturated (probably through the mixing desk because he was not using a guitar amp). "2120 South Michigan Avenue" is an instrumental in which Mick contents himself with playing the tambourine. Keith plays rhythm guitar on his Epiphone Casino, and Brian gives an excellent harmonica solo with abundant reverb. It has to be acknowledged that this harmonica provides the number with all its interest (other than the riff). Stu is again part of the setup, showing what he is capable of on the B-3 and thereby contributing that very particular sound which was so characteristic of the sixties. Ron Malo remembers that they recorded quickly because Muddy Waters had just stopped by at the studio: "So Muddy came in and they did a couple of his things. So they did this tune they wanted to dedicate to Muddy and for lack of a better title, the tune became *2120 South Michigan Avenue—Muddy Waters Was There* and dedicated it to Muddy Waters."[25] Bill Wyman denies the rumor that Muddy Waters took part in the session: "It has been said that he played guitar towards the end of the track. Not true. He did not play with us in the Chess Studios— not that we would have minded."[1]

CONFESSIN' THE BLUES

Jay McShann / Walter Brown / 2:51

Musicians
Mick Jagger: vocals, harmonica
Keith Richards: lead guitar
Brian Jones: rhythm guitar
Bill Wyman: bass
Charlie Watts: drums
Ian Stewart: piano
Recorded
Chess Studios, Chicago: June 11, 1964
Technical Team
Producer: Andrew Loog Oldham
Sound Engineer: Ron Malo

The Stones in the studio with Ian Stewart (in the back) in 1964.

Genesis

The pianist and singer Jay McShann was one of the mainstays of the musical scene in Kansas City, where a form of swing jazz developed in the thirties that had its roots firmly in the blues tradition. His band is also famous for numbering Charlie Parker, the inaugurator of the bebop aesthetic, as well as tenor saxophonist Ben Webster and the singer Walter Brown among its musicians. The latter was the archetypal blues shouter. He recorded "Confessin' the Blues" with Jay McShann's band in Dallas, Texas, on April 30, 1941, and this went on to become one of the great blues standards.

Production

For their recording of "Confessin' the Blues" (the fourth number on the EP) at Chess Studios, the Rolling Stones took their inspiration not so much from the original version by Jay McShann and Walter Brown, or even from Chuck Berry's version, as from Little Walter's 1958 recording of the song for the Checker label (a subsidiary of Chess). The British group have slowed the tempo considerably, resulting in a wonderful blues number whose impact has been augmented by the talented Ron Malo, the sound engineer who provided the Stones with access to the sound of their idols. The two guitars launch straight in. The sound is raucous, with Keith, on lead, carving out weighty phrases on his Epiphone while Brian provides a steady rhythm on his Gretsch. As well as singing, Mick also (almost certainly) plays the harmonica, the true heart of the song, his playing skillfully bathed in reverb by Ron Malo. This time, Stu plays an excellent boogie-woogie piano that has perhaps been mixed down a little too much. With this cover of "Confessin' the Blues," which they had been playing since the early days, the Stones manage to get close to the sound and caliber of all the great names that preceded them at this place. Chess was a key stage in the group's development, and "Confessin' the Blues" was included on the album *12x5*, released in the United States in October 1964.

AROUND AND AROUND

Chuck Berry / 3:05

Musicians
Mick Jagger: vocals
Keith Richards: lead guitar
Brian Jones: rhythm guitar
Bill Wyman: bass
Charlie Watts: drums
Ian Stewart: piano
Recorded
Chess Studios, Chicago: June 11, 1964
Technical Team
Producer: Andrew Loog Oldham
Sound Engineer: Ron Malo

FOR STONES ADDICTS

On October 28 and 29, 1964, the Stones took part in the *Teen Age Music International (TAMI) Show* alongside the likes of James Brown, the Supremes, the Beach Boys, Chuck Berry, and Gerry and the Pacemakers. They opened their performance with . . . "Around and Around." Incidentally, Chuck Berry did extremely well, with no less than six of his songs performed during the course of *TAMI*.

Chuck Berry, master of the mind-blowing intro and the *duckwalk*.

Genesis

In his autobiography,[16] Chuck Berry explains that "Around and Around" came to him during a jam session during a final rehearsal before going onstage: "One of the riffs we struck upon never left my memory and I waxed in the tune with words about a dance hall that stayed open a little overtime." And the music pioneer explains how he preferred to use the phrase *'til the moon went down* to *'til the early morning.* "Around and Around" was chosen as the B-side for "Johnny B. Goode," released by Chess Records in March 1958.

Production

What else could the Rolling Stones do at Chess Studios but pay homage to Chuck Berry, whose mantle they claimed to be taking up? There was nothing random about their choice of "Around and Around." The number had been part of the Little Boy Blue and the Blue Boys' repertoire since 1962. Mick Jagger, Keith Richards, Dick Taylor, Bob Beckwith, and Allen Etherington had even recorded it (the very first recording in the career of the Rolling Stones!) and sent the tape to Alexis Korner.

In barely two years, the Stones had achieved the feat of recording "Around and Around" in the very same studios where its creator had made so many immortal masterpieces. Keith Richards leads in with Berry's unforgettable riff. The Stones are at ease and self-assured. Their version is nothing less than a lesson in rock 'n' roll, in which each band member dedicates himself to rocking to the max. Keith Richards carves out the lion's share for himself with a superb guitar part that clearly resembles the original, while at the same time allowing his own unmistakable style to shine through. He is utterly at one with his Epiphone Casino. Keith is supported by Brian Jones—of whom it can never be overstated what an extraordinary rhythm guitarist he was—on his Gretsch. Ian Stewart plays a superb piano part that demonstrates how essential he was to the group, while Bill Wyman and Charlie Watts work as a veritable rhythm machine. Finally Mick Jagger, in magnificent form, puts the icing on the cake with a highly controlled performance (perhaps even a little too controlled). Chuck Berry, who was present in the studios, is supposed to have said: "Swing on, gentlemen, you are sounding most well, if I may say so."[1] History does not record whether he was talking about "Around and Around" or some other number . . .

Brian Jones, still loyal to his Gretsch during the recording of "Congratulations."

SIDE B
1964

CONGRATULATIONS

Mick Jagger / Keith Richards / 2:28

SINGLE (US)
Time Is on My Side* / Congratulations
RELEASE DATE
United States: September 26, 1964
Label: London Records
RECORD NUMBER: LONDON RECORDS 45-LON9708* (SEE P. 80)

Musicians
Mick Jagger: vocals
Keith Richards: 12-string acoustic guitar, backing vocals
Brian Jones: rhythm guitar, backing vocals (?)
Bill Wyman: bass
Charlie Watts: drums
Recorded
Regent Sound Studios: May 12, 1964
Technical Team
Producer: Andrew Loog Oldham
Sound Engineer: Bill Farley

The word "Congratulations" was misspelled on the album *12x5,* where it was printed as "Congradulations." It was not until the album was released on CD that the mistake was corrected.

Genesis
"Congratulations" was one of the first ballads written by Mick Jagger and Keith Richards, possibly during the session on May 12, 1964, at Regent Sound Studios. Although it lacks the emotional power of the future "Play with Fire" and "Lady Jane," it gives a hint of the duo's taste for mockery and even cynicism. The congratulations in question are addressed by the songwriters to a master in the art of breaking hearts who sows nothing but sadness around him.

Production
"Congratulations" is thus a ballad whose tone is pretty bleak, and this is possibly why Decca and Oldham did not feel it was appropriate to offer it to the British public. With its somewhat muddled and untidy sound, the production cannot be counted among Oldham's finest. Charlie Watts introduces the number with a tom break. Keith Richards immediately joins him on his Harmony 1270 12-string that gives the number its color. He even plays a solo, albeit not a particularly unforgettable one, on this instrument (1:38). Brian Jones accompanies him with distinctly fifties-sounding licks on his Gretsch (and a wrong note at 2:07!). Indeed the whole feel is reminiscent of the fifties, with Bill Wyman using a plectrum on his bass (no doubt his Framus), which is given plenty of reverb, as are Charlie's drums. Mick Jagger whispers the ballad with emotion but a certain lack of conviction, while Keith (and possibly Brian?) provide vocal harmonies. "Congratulations" gives the impression of being a demo rather than a final version; the rhythmic ensemble is no more than average and the bridge is too predictable. This song is another surprising demonstration of

Bill Wyman and his famous Framus Star F5/150 bass.

the emphatically pop flavor and ballad style of the early Jagger-Richards compositions. The blues comes to the fore in their writing no more than rock.

Forming the B-side of the single "Time Is on My Side," which was released in the United States on September 26, 1964, "Congratulations" can also be found between "Under the Boardwalk" and "Grown Up Wrong" on the album *12x5*, released in the United States on October 17, 1964. It was another nine years before "Congratulations" appeared on an album in the UK, and then only on the compilation *No Stone Unturned*, which was released in the United Kingdom in October 1973.

COVERS

Denied the opportunity to listen to a recording of "Congratulations" by the Rolling Stones, the British public were nonetheless able to fall back on a pop cover of the Jagger-Richards composition recorded by the little-known group West Five in 1965.

The Stones with a memorable performance of Willie Dixon's "Little Red Rooster" on *Ready Steady Go!* in 1964.

SIDE A
1964

LITTLE RED ROOSTER

Willie Dixon / 3:06

SINGLE
Little Red Rooster / Off the Hook
RELEASE DATE
United Kingdom: November 13, 1964*
Label: Decca
RECORD NUMBER: DECCA F 12014* *OFF THE HOOK* [(SEE P. 88)

Musicians
Mick Jagger: vocals
Keith Richards: acoustic rhythm guitar
Brian Jones: slide guitar, harmonica
Bill Wyman: bass
Charlie Watts: drums
Recorded
Regent Sound Studios: September 2–3 (?), 1964
Technical Team
Producers: Andrew Loog Oldham
Sound Engineer: Bill Farley

Genesis
When writing "Little Red Rooster," Willie Dixon drew on the work of the pioneers of country blues such as Charley Patton and Memphis Minnie, who had recorded "Banty Rooster Blues" (1929) and "If You See My Rooster" (1936), respectively, and even Blind Lemon Jefferson, who gave the world the provocative "Black Snake Moan" in 1927. Like his illustrious predecessors, Dixon handles the double entendre with consummate skill: *I am the little red rooster . . . Keep everything in the farm yard upset in every way . . . Ain't had no peace in the farm yard/Since my little red rooster's been gone.* The sexual metaphor is clear . . .

"Little Red Rooster" was recorded by Howlin' Wolf, accompanied by Hubert Sumlin (guitar), Johnny Jones (piano), Willie Dixon (double bass), Sam Lay (drums), and possibly Jimmy Rogers (guitar), in June 1961. It was released as a single with "Shake for Me" in October 1961 and appeared on the album *Howlin' Wolf* the following year. Although it failed to chart, this did not prevent it from becoming a modern blues standard covered by legions of performers from Sam Cooke to . . . the Rolling Stones.

Production
Andrew Loog Oldham was not keen on the idea of recording "Little Red Rooster" at the very moment his protégés were starting to free themselves from the hold of Chicago blues with singles such as "Tell Me" and "It's All Over Now." "Andrew didn't want us to do it. He wanted us to do some more pop-oriented song,"[26] claimed Bill Wyman in 1978. The Stones, however, held their ground—and were right to do so.

Andrew Loog Oldham, always ready with some advice . . .

"We were getting no-no's from the record company, management, everyone else," writes Keith Richards, "but we felt we were on a crest of a wave and we could push it. It was almost in defiance of pop."[2]

The Rolling Stones' version is a masterpiece. It is sometimes said that Mick, Keith, Bill, and Charlie recorded their parts on September 2, 1964, and that Brian Jones overdubbed his guitar the following day. But photographs taken during the session prove that Brian Jones was very much present in the studio and recording with his friends that day. Moreover, it was nothing short of a veritable bravura moment for the founder of the Rolling Stones, the sensuality of whose slide guitar playing admirably underscores Jagger's vocals (*The dogs begin to bark, hounds begin to howl*), while at the same time expressing his profound attachment to the African American idiom. Brian plays one of Keith's brand-new guitars, a superb white Fender Telecaster, not, as some people suggest, with open G tuning, but with standard tuning, as demonstrated by various videos from the time. Furthermore, in 1964 open tuning was not very common in the United Kingdom, and the Stones did not start to use it until the album *Beggars Banquet* (1968). With the bottleneck on his little finger, Brian delivers an excellent slide guitar, doubtless one of his best. He is accompanied by Keith on rhythm, who is using his new 6-string acoustic for the first time, a Framus Jumbo that has replaced his Harmony. It is noticeable that Bill's bass sounds like a double bass. It seems that Keith is doubling it on his guitar, his bottom E string no doubt tuned down several tones for the purpose. Charlie's snare drum sound is curious too. He is definitely using brushes, but the result sounds

as if it is being doubled by Latin percussion. Credit for the (overdubbed) harmonica part also goes to Brian, even though television broadcasts of the day show Jagger on harmonica. Either way, the quality of the playing is beyond dispute. Moreover, the production lives up to the group's performance, with excellent sound engineering by Bill Farley.

By the time the Stones' cover of "Little Red Rooster" (with "Off the Hook" as the B-side) was released on November 13, 1964, some 200,000 fans had preordered the single. By December 9, it had reached number 1 on the UK singles chart, their second top placing following "It's All Over Now" in July. Brian Jones had thus achieved his objective of getting the blues to the summit of the British hit parade. Moreover, "Little Red Rooster" was one of the Rolling Stones recordings best loved by the Stones themselves. In the United States, by contrast, it was decided not to release the single because the earlier versions of "Little Red Rooster" had been banned from the airwaves on account of their strong sexual connotations. The group nevertheless took every opportunity that came along to perform it on television, notably in May 1965 on *The Ed Sullivan Show*, *Shindig!* (with Howlin' Wolf on as well!), and *Shivaree*. Between 1964 and 2003, "Little Red Rooster" was regularly included in the band's set lists for its world tours. In his autobiography *Life*, Keith Richards would later describe the impact the record had on the US public: " . . . suddenly Muddy and Howlin' Wolf and Buddy Guy are getting gigs and working. It was a breakthrough. And the record got to number one. And I'm absolutely sure what we were doing made Berry Gordy at Motown capable of pushing his stuff elsewhere, and it certainly rejuvenated Chicago blues as well."[2]

Everybody Needs Somebody To Love
Down Home Girl
You Can't Catch Me
Time Is On My Side
What A Shame
Grown Up Wrong

Down The Road Apiece
Under The Boardwalk
I Can't Be Satisfied
Pain In My Heart
Off The Hook
Susie Q

UNITED STATES RELEASE: (FEBRUARY 13, 1965)

Everybody Needs Somebody To Love / Down Home Girl / You Can't Catch Me / Heart Of Stone / What A Shame / I Need You Baby (Mona) / Down The Road Apiece / Off The Hook / Pain In My Heart / Oh Baby (We Got A Good Thing Goin') / Little Red Rooster / Surprise, Surprise.

UNITED STATES RELEASE: (OCTOBER 17, 1964)

Around And Around / Confessin' The Blues / Empty Heart / Time Is On My Side (Mono Version 1, Organ Intro) / Good Times, Bad Times / It's All Over Now / 2120 South Michigan Avenue / Under The Boardwalk / Congratulations / Grown Up Wrong / If You Need Me / Susie Q.

THE ROLLING STONES

NO.2

ALBUM
RELEASE DATE
United Kingdom:
January 15, 1965
Label: Decca
RECORD NUMBER: LK 4661
Number 1 for 10 weeks

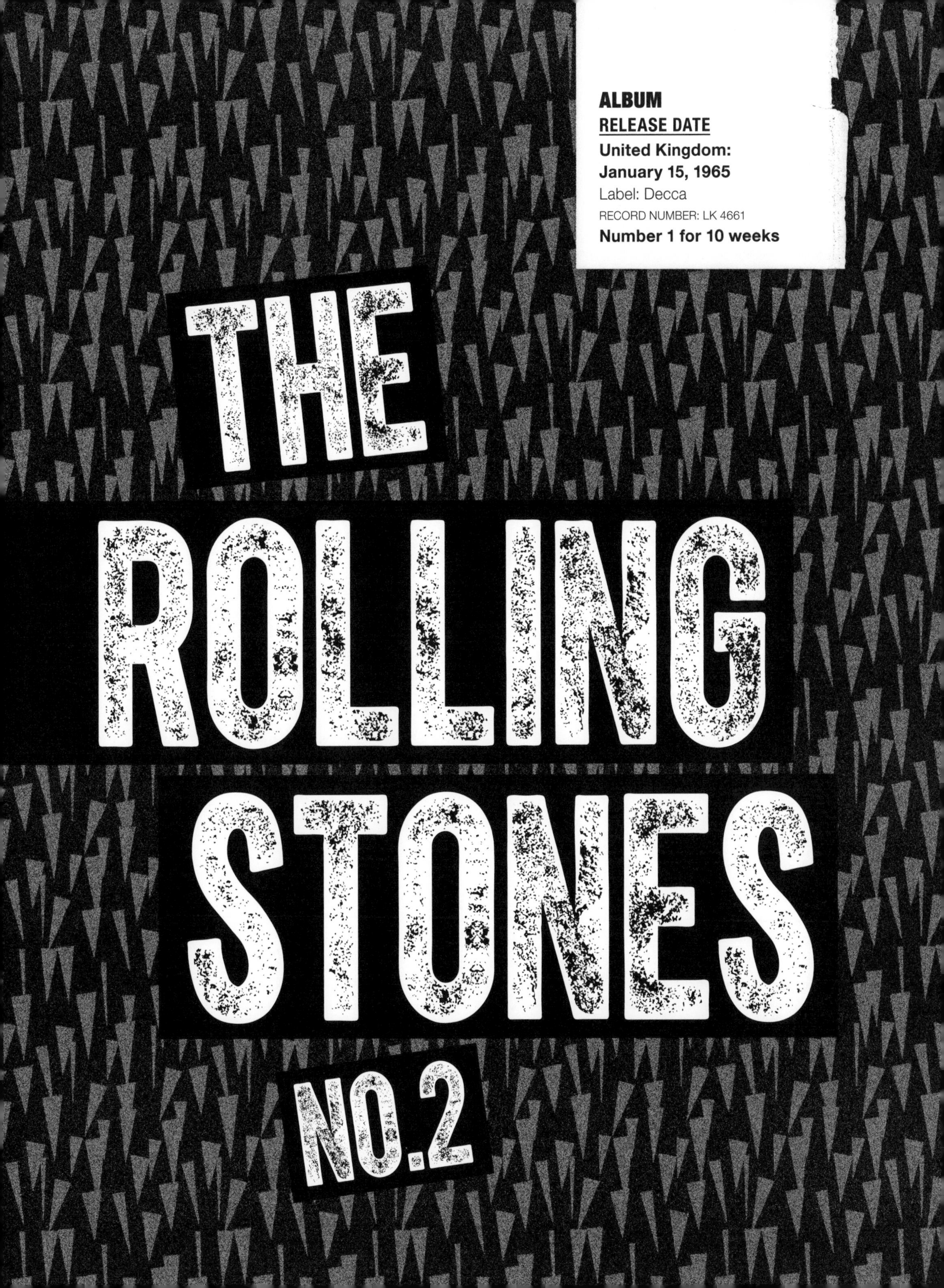

1965

THE ROLLING STONES NO. 2: THE SECOND ALBUM FROM THE MOST AMERICAN OF BRITISH GROUPS

On June 1, 1964, the Rolling Stones took off from London for their first tour of the United States. If the "bad boy" image skillfully cultivated by Andrew Oldham had intrigued or seduced the several hundred fans who greeted them at John F. Kennedy Airport, the establishment and certain sections of the entertainment world seemed little disposed to extend a warm welcome to the group. During their appearance on the *Hollywood Palace* TV show on June 3, for example, Dean Martin treated them to his usual pithy turn of phrase aimed at raising a laugh among the crowds, joking about their hair not being long: "They just have low foreheads and high eyebrows."[27] He then added: "That's the father of the Rolling Stones. He's been trying to kill himself ever since,"[27] referring to a trampoline artiste who was also a guest on the show.

Organized from London by Eric Easton, the tour that kicked off in San Bernardino, California, on June 5 and ended with two shows at Carnegie Hall in New York on June 20 was a partial success: the band triumphed on the West and East Coasts, but flopped completely in San Antonio, Texas, where the audience reserved their applause for the local groups and loudly booed the five Londoners.

The Rolling Stones would nevertheless return to the United States a few months later for a second tour: thirteen dates and eleven cities including Sacramento, California, and Chicago, Illinois, between October 24 and November 15. According to Charlie Watts, "America was a joke when we arrived, but by the time we left we had an audience and by the time we came back we had made a hit record. It was all uphill, but the audience grew every time."[9]

The Album

Produced by Andrew Loog Oldham, *The Rolling Stones No. 2* was released in the United Kingdom on January 15, 1965, in other words three months after *12x5* (October 16, 1964—or October 24 according to some sources) and a month before *The Rolling Stones, Now!* (February 13, 1965), two LPs that were aimed exclusively at the US market. It marked a distinct development from the Stones' previous album in that it includes three of the early songs composed by Mick Jagger and Keith Richards, who were pushed into writing by Andrew Oldham: "What a Shame," "Grown Up Wrong," and "Off the Hook." Musically, this LP nevertheless sounds like a logical follow-up to the previous one. Like its predecessor, it is another reworking of modern blues and black rock 'n' roll, and in particular of Muddy Waters and Chuck Berry (Chess Studios having played a not insignificant role in this). At the same time, however, it is possible to detect, on the part of the five Londoners, a desire to explore new musical avenues: soul in "Everybody Needs Somebody to Love," "Time Is on My Side," and "Pain in My Heart," and swamp blues in "Susie Q." Furthermore, with this second album, Mick Jagger confirmed that he was capable of adapting to any style, and Brian Jones and Keith Richards, supported by a rhythm section of rare efficiency, revealed themselves to be truly complementary

Bobby Keys (shown here in 1971). A happy encounter.

and compatible guitarists, the alchemists of a blues rock of outstanding sensual intensity.

The Rolling Stones No. 2 was an enormous success from day one in the United Kingdom. It was number 1 for ten weeks and remained on the charts for thirty-seven consecutive weeks. The critics were also enthusiastic, even in Liverpool, where the *Mersey Beat* announced on January 16, 1965: "It's a very fine LP, with the Stones well into their rootsy, true R&B style, with no concessions made to commercialism or the hit-parade. There's a fantastic atmosphere to most tracks and this helps the group to sound more live than on any previous record."[1] Half a million copies were sold throughout the world, 400,000 in the United Kingdom alone.

The Album Cover

The cover photograph is identical to that used for the US album *12x5*, with the only difference that neither the name of the group nor the title of the album (an idea that began with the first LP) appears on it. This photograph takes the form of a close-up of the five members of the group against a blue background that grows progressively darker from left to right. Charlie Watts at the center and Brian Jones on the right are both wearing ties, which comes as something of a surprise. Keith Richards is in the foreground and Bill Wyman is on the left. Mick Jagger, with his collar unbuttoned, is at the back on the left. The photo was taken by David Bailey, a photographer who came to attention through his work in *Vogue* magazine and made a name for himself immortalizing "swinging London." He was already a close friend of Mick Jagger by this time and explains that he positioned Mick deliberately because he did not want the others to think he had received special treatment as a personal friend.[9] On the back are black-and-white portraits of the five Rolling Stones accompanied by a long and controversial text by Andrew Loog Oldham. Constantly on the lookout for new ways of attracting publicity, the group's manager

encourages potential buyers who are too hard up to buy the record to go and knock a blind man on the head and steal his wallet. In January 1965, a certain Mrs. Gwen Matthews, secretary of the Bournemouth Blind Aid Association, made a complaint. The matter was debated two months later in the House of Lords. Decca, sensing that trouble lay ahead, took preemptive action by removing the incriminating text from subsequent pressings and stickered the copies awaiting sale. Bill Wyman observes that "When you read Oldham's sleeve notes you certainly realize that he was on another planet."[1]

The Recording

Seven of the twelve tracks on the second album by the Rolling Stones—as well as their first number 1 hit "It's All Over Now"—were recorded in the United States during their US tours. This was unprecedented for a British group. They completed the record in seven sessions: three at the legendary Chess Studios in Chicago (June 10–11 and November 8), one at the prestigious RCA Studios in Hollywood (November 2), and three at the Regent Sound Studios in London (September 2 and 28–29), which they now knew like the back of their hands. The group's sound is rich and diverse, and, paradoxically, this varied sound quality enabled them to discover their sonic identity.

The first sessions were held in Chicago on June 10 and 11, 1964. Chess Studios enjoyed a mythical status among blues lovers, and Keith Richards recalls: "There in the perfect sound studio, in the room where everything we'd listened to was made, perhaps out of relief or just the fact that people like Buddy Guy, Chuck Berry and Willie Dixon were wandering in and out, we recorded fourteen tracks in two days."[2] These fourteen numbers included the single "It's All Over Now" (released in the UK on June 26 and in the US on July 25), and two songs that were included on *The Rolling Stones No. 2*: "I Can't Be Satisfied" and "Down the Road Apiece."

1965

Mick, Keith, Charlie, Brian, and Bill set off to discover the United States.

Chuck Berry is supposed to have taken refuge in the echo chamber at Chess Studios for two months while undergoing a difficult period in his life.

The London quintet returned to Chess during their second US tour of 1964, on November 8, and recorded another seven numbers including, it has been claimed, a version of "Little Red Rooster" in the presence of Willie Dixon himself (although this story has never been confirmed), "Time Is on My Side," and "What a Shame." Chess is also a particular sound, one of whose architects was Ron Malo, the extraordinary sound engineer who would work with numerous artists during his career including Buddy Rich, Ahmad Jamal, Bo Diddley, Muddy Waters, Chuck Berry. Ron Malo provided the Rolling Stones with the opportunity to sound like their idols. Malo would later maintain that he had no difficulty getting things right: "I didn't have to work to get a sound. It was simple to set up, very simple microphoning."[28] And he was the de facto producer of the record in collaboration with the group. Mick Jagger confirmed this in 1968: "[Andrew] didn't know anything about blues. The cat who really got it together was Ron Malo."[29] All the more so as Oldham, according to Ian Stewart, was reluctant to record at Chess. "It was done very much against Andrew's wishes,"[1] he would later claim.

A few days earlier, on November 2, the Stones had cut six numbers in the enormous Studio A at the RCA Studios in Hollywood. Of these, "Everybody Needs Somebody to Love," "Down Home Girl," and "Pain in My Heart" were also selected for the second album. It was through Phil Spector's favorite arranger, Jack Nitzsche, that the British band came to work with David Hassinger, one of RCA's best sound engineers. Hassinger went on to record numerous artists during the course of his career, notably Jefferson Airplane, Sam Cooke, and the Byrds. In 1969 he bought the studios of a small label called Moonglow Records. Renamed the Sound Factory, these studios eventually became one of the most renowned recording venues in the United States. For his part, Jack Nitzsche, who had taken a liking to the Stones at the TAMI Show in October 1964 (he was directing the house band), contributed piano parts to the album recordings made during the RCA sessions. He was the very first musician from outside the band to do this, although there would be many more over the coming years.

As for the other five tracks on the album, they were all recorded at Regent Sound Studios in London with the faithful Bill Farley at the controls: "Off the Hook" and "Under the Boardwalk" on September 2, and "Grown Up Wrong," "You Can't Catch Me," and "Susie Q" on September 28–29.

The Rolling Stones onstage. And soon to be on top of the world.

Technical Details

Due to the rarity of studio photographs and eyewitness accounts, the equipment used to record the Rolling Stones in 1964 is relatively difficult to identify. What is known is that Bill Farley used an AKD C12 microphone to capture Mick Jagger's voice and Neumann U67s for the guitar amps. Ron Malo is thought to have used a Universal Audio 610 console at Chess while also benefiting from an amazing echo chamber made by Putnam & Co. (one of the jewels in the Chess Studios crown), while David Hassinger used a Neve console and Neumann M49, RCA 77-DX, RCA 44-BX, and Shure mics.

The Instruments

The Rolling Stones invested in some new musical instruments in order to make this second album. Richards abandoned his Harmony Meteor H70 in favor of an Epiphone Casino, a Gibson Les Paul dating from 1959, a white Fender Telecaster (that only Brian would use while recording), and a Framus Jumbo 5/97 6-string acoustic. Brian Jones retained his Gretsch G6118 Anniversary, but at the beginning of July acquired a superb Vox MKIII, a model that was immediately nicknamed the "Teardrop." The guitarists plugged into Fender Showman

and Fender Concert amps. Bill Wyman continued to play his Framus Star bass, occasionally using a Fender 6-string bass at the RCA Studios. He used Vox Foundation and Fender Bassman amps and occasionally plugged directly into the console. Charlie Watts used a house Ludwig drum kit at Chess, while remaining faithful to his own Ludwig "Oyster Blue Pearl" for the other sessions. Mick Jagger and Brian Jones used Hohner Echo Super Vamper harmonicas. As for Ian Stewart, the Stones' keyboardist played a Hammond B-3 organ and a Steinway piano. Finally, numerous percussion instruments including tambourine, güiro, castanets, and triangle were also used on the recordings.

Keith Richards[2] remembers seeing Muddy Waters in the middle of painting the ceiling at Chess, while Bill Wyman[1] specifically refutes this. The Stones' bassist does, however, claim that Muddy helped them carry their equipment into the studio.

The Vox MK III "Teardrop," which would become one of Brian Jones's emblematic guitars.

The 1959 Gibson Les Paul, a model identical to the one Keith Richards owned.

EVERYBODY NEEDS SOMEBODY TO LOVE

Solomon Burke / Bert Berns / Jerry Wexler / 5:05

Musicians
Mick Jagger: vocals, tambourine
Keith Richards: lead guitar, backing vocals
Brian Jones: rhythm guitar, backing vocals (?)
Bill Wyman: bass, backing vocals (?)
Charlie Watts: drums
Ian Stewart: piano
Recorded
RCA Studios, Hollywood: November 2, 1964
Technical Team
Producer: Andrew Loog Oldham
Sound engineer: Dave Hassinger

Among the most outstanding covers of this song are those by Wilson Pickett, Dusty Springfield, the 13th Floor Elevators, the Jerry Garcia Band, and, of course, the Blues Brothers.

The Soul Clan. Joe Tex, Ben E. King, Wilson Pickett, Solomon Burke, and Don Covay surrounding the singer Peter Wolf.

Genesis

Although this number is credited to "Solomon Burke–Bert Berns–Jerry Wexler," Burke has always protested that he was the sole writer, claiming that he used to sing it in church as a child. He claims to have sung it to Jerry Wexler and Bert Berns during a recording session at Atlantic on May 28, 1964, but that they judged the tempo to be far too fast for the song to be a hit. Wexler, meanwhile, has always claimed that the song resulted from a three-way collaboration. Whatever the truth may be, "Everybody Needs Somebody to Love" was only a modest success for Solomon Burke on the 1964 R&B charts. It did, however, spawn a vast number of cover versions and entered the *Rolling Stone* list of Greatest Songs of All Time at number 429. The Stones recorded it on November 2, 1964. There are two studio versions. The first, which opens the second British album, has a running time of 5:05; the second, which opens *The Rolling Stones, Now!*, destined for a US audience, plays for only 2:58.

Production

The version of this number on the UK album offers the listener a taste of the RCA studio sound with David Hassinger at the controls. It is a rich, well-defined, mellow sound that in no way adulterates the rock 'n' roll essence of the Rolling Stones. As such it differs from the rawer, more direct sound of Regent Sound Studios. At 5:05, this was the longest number recorded by the six British musicians to date. John Lennon had the following to say about this: "The album's great, but I don't like five-minute numbers."[1] Jagger and his group transform the song into a rhythm 'n' blues epic, a hypnotic odyssey based around Bill's bass riff (which differs slightly from the Solomon Burke version) and Charlie's drums. Brian plays rhythm on his superb Vox Teardrop, with Keith playing lead on his 1959 Gibson Les Paul, both plugged into Fender Showman amps. There seem to be two solo guitar parts, notably from 3:10 (easier to identify on the stereo version), in all probability overdubbed by Keith. The vocal counterpoint and harmonies, sung, it is presumed, by Keith and no doubt supported by Bill and Brian, never cease to surprise the listener, who is regaled with a falsetto (2:35) and various other vocal extravagances that are effective on the whole. Ian is on piano, although his highly rhythmic playing could perhaps be more

1965

Solomon Burke in 2001, at the Sixteenth Annual
Rock and Roll Hall of Fame Induction Ceremony.

prominent. Mick's vocals border on gospel-like preaching,
while at the same time remaining undeniably rock 'n' roll.
Also featuring tambourine and hand claps (overdubbed), this
long version emphasizes the considerable progress made by
the group since their first album, in terms of both sound and
interpretation.

The second, "short" version, which was available exclusively in the United States (on the album *The Rolling Stones,
Now!*) is quite different. The tempo is roughly the same but
the approach differs. The atmosphere is more soul, the backing vocal is more prominent, and there is more reverb on the
overall sound. The hand claps are prominent and accentuate
the somewhat Motown feel. The Stones give the impression
of letting themselves go, in particular in the vocal harmonies,
which, if the truth be told, are not always precisely in tune (for
example at 1:37) but the ensemble is nevertheless successful.
How did this version come to be released at all, the long version having initially been earmarked for the album? Clearly a
wrong turn was taken somewhere along the line.

On November 2, 2002, during their *Licks
World Tour*, the Stones joined Solomon Burke
onstage at the Wiltern Theatre in
Los Angeles to perform "Everybody Needs
Somebody to Love." The recording is
available on the *Live Licks* album, which
was released in November 2004.

FOR STONES ADDICTS

Mick Jagger performed "Everybody Needs
Somebody to Love" at the 2011 Grammy
Awards in homage to Solomon Burke, who
died on October 10, 2010.

DOWN HOME GIRL

Jerry Leiber / Arthur Butler / 4:15

Musicians
Mick Jagger: vocals, harmonica
Keith Richards: lead guitar
Brian Jones: rhythm guitar
Bill Wyman: 6-string bass
Charlie Watts: drums
Jack Nitzsche: piano
Recorded
RCA Studios, Hollywood: November 2, 1964
Technical Team
Producer: Andrew Loog Oldham
Sound engineer: Dave Hassinger

Songwriters Jerry Leiber (right) and
Mike Stoller in the studio, 1965.

Genesis

"Down Home Girl" was written by Jerry Leiber and Arthur Butler, two great shapers of the musical revolution of the fifties and sixties. The first collaborated with Mike Stoller on a number of hits for Elvis Presley, the Drifters, and the Coasters, while Butler was the singer with the Impressions (with Curtis Mayfield) as well as a renowned songwriter.

The expression *down home* is used to describe a person with qualities associated with the rural Southern states. The heroine of the song, a "natural girl," comes from the Deep South, New Orleans to be precise. She may smell of turnip greens but she is a fine-looking woman who moves in such a sensual way that men *gotta get down and pray* and *go to Sunday mass*.

Alvin Robinson was the first to record a version of "Down Home Girl," just a few months before the Stones. Keith Richards remembers how the group came to choose this song: "Andrew and I walked into the Brill Building, the Tin Pan Alley of US song, to try and see the great Jerry Leiber, but Jerry Leiber wouldn't see us. Someone recognized us and took us in and played us all these songs, and we walked out with 'Down Home Girl.'"[2] As simple as that.

Production

The Stones' version is pure gold. In terms of feel, it is halfway between Motown and the blues. Brian executes a very good guitar intro on his "Teardrop" before launching into a rhythm part with ample reverb. Keith plays lead on his Les Paul, delivering an insistent three-note lick at the end of every other line (played by the trumpet on the original version). Bill, trying out for the first time a Fender 6-string that he picked up in the studio, delivers an excellent bass line, explaining later that this instrument: "gives a fantastic treble effect."[1] The piano part is played not by Ian Stewart but, at the request of the group, by Jack Nitzsche, who at that time was Phil Spector's valued collaborator and as such the co-creator of the famous "wall of sound." Finally, not only is Mick's delivery of the lyrics excellent, he also seems to be responsible for the harmonica part. "Down Home Girl" is one of the most commercial, though sadly underestimated, numbers of the Stones' early career, one that perhaps deserved to be released as a single.

1965

YOU CAN'T CATCH ME

Chuck Berry / 3:38

Musicians
Mick Jagger: vocals
Keith Richards: lead guitar
Brian Jones: rhythm guitar
Bill Wyman: bass
Charlie Watts: drums
Recorded
Regent Sound Studios, London: September 28–29, 1964
Technical Team
Producer: Andrew Loog Oldham
Sound engineer: Bill Farley

Bill Wyman with a rocking, swinging style of play on his Framus Star bass.

Genesis

In "You Can't Catch Me," Chuck Berry draws on a real-life experience. While returning from a concert in New York at the wheel of his Buick, a number of convertibles drew up and tried to race him on the New Jersey Turnpike. Before long a patrol car arrived on the scene. Everything turned out all right in the end, however, and all that remained was for Chuck Berry to transform the incident into a song—and embellish it with a highly attentive girlfriend and a radio playing rock 'n' roll.

"You Can't Catch Me" was the third song that Chuck Berry recorded at Chess Studios—on May 21, 1955 to be released the following year (with "Havana Moon" as the B-side), it failed to chart. On the other hand, it was featured on the original soundtrack of *Rock, Rock, Rock* (1956), a movie by Will Price glorifying the pioneers of rock 'n' roll.

The Rolling Stones incorporated "You Can't Catch Me" into their playlist a mere twelve years after originally recording the song. An initial cut was made on June 24–26, 1964, at Regent Sound Studios, while the version on the album dates from September 28 to 29.

Production

For this third cover on the album, the group opted for a more fifties sound. Brian Jones, most probably playing his Gretsch Anniversary, employs a characteristic slap-back echo. Charlie Watts, perfectly at ease with this type of groove, overdubs himself playing the rim of his snare drum, supported by Bill Wyman, on his Framus Star bass, who swings incessantly up and down the fingerboard. Keith Richards, less faithful than usual to the Chuck Berry guitar part (except in the intro), plays short licks on his Epiphone Casino and delivers a solo that is more blues rock than rockabilly. As for Mick Jagger, he delivers the lyrics without any real spark, for this is not one of the best Chuck Berry covers the Stones have ever made. Slower than the original, it lacks conviction and may seem a little repetitive toward the end. No doubt the group was not on form that day. The track may be well made, but one expects better of the Stones . . . Nevertheless, Keith names "You Can't Catch Me" as his favorite number on the album: "It has a fantastic heavy beat which builds up like a locomotive coming up behind you."[1]

TIME IS ON MY SIDE

Norman Meade / 2:58

For the first few pressings of the album, in both its UK and US versions, "Time Is on My Side" was credited to "Norman, Meade" as if these were the names of two co-writers rather than the pseudonym of a single person. To avoid confusion, the writer's real name, *Jerry Ragovoy*, is used today.

Musicians
Mick Jagger: vocals, tambourine
Keith Richards: rhythm guitar, lead guitar, backing vocals
Brian Jones: rhythm guitar
Bill Wyman: bass, backing vocals
Charlie Watts: drums
Ian Stewart: organ
Recorded
Chess Studios, Chicago: November 8, 1964
Technical Team
Producer: Andrew Loog Oldham
Sound engineer: Ron Malo

Irma Thomas, nicknamed the Soul Queen of New Orleans. One of her biggest hits? "Time Is on My Side."

Genesis

Using the pseudonym Norman Meade, Jordan "Jerry" Ragovoy wrote "Time Is on My Side" at the request of the arranger Garry Sherman. Sherman wanted the trombonist Kai Winding, whose sessions he was supervising, to extend his appeal beyond his usual jazz audience. Although this first version, dating from October 3, 1963, failed to achieve chart success (despite superb vocals from the Gospelaires, in other words Dionne and Dee Dee Warwick and Cissy Houston), it inspired two highly successful covers the following year. The first was by Irma Thomas, the "Soul Queen of New Orleans" (as the B-side of "Anyone Who Knows What Love Is [Will Understand]"), and the second was by the Rolling Stones, sung by Mick Jagger. *Time is on my side, yes it is/Now you always say/That you want to be free/But you'll come running back*, he sings with all the confidence of the true soul singer.

Production

The Rolling Stones decided to record "Time Is on My Side" after buying the sheet music in Los Angeles. They actually released two versions of the song on disc. The first was recorded during their session on June 10, 1964, at Chess (or during the sessions on June 24–26, 1964, in London according to other sources). With a running time of 2:50, it starts with an organ intro played by Ian Stewart on a Hammond B-3 in pure gospel style. There is abundant reverb on the overall sound, and Jagger attacks the lyrics with a plaintive voice and his characteristic vocal mannerisms. He is supported by Bill and Keith with backing vocals that are not always precisely in tune (for example, the "Time, time, time" at 2:14). It is a shame these harmonies were not better crafted. Keith plays rhythm and lead (on his Epiphone Casino) and his solo in the bridge is reasonably close in spirit to that on the Irma Thomas version. However, it is not always any more rhythmically successful (for example, in the coda from 2:14) than Mick's very prominent tambourine, no doubt overdubbed. The number nevertheless possesses an undeniable charm, and the Stones make a virtue out of these small defects, which lend their cover a certain touching appeal. This version can be found on the album *12x5*, which was destined for the US market. It was even released as a single, peaking at number 6 on the

Billboard charts on December 5, 1964 (the Stones' first top 10 hit in the United States).

The second version, cut on November 8 at Chess Studios in Chicago, was used for the British album, *The Rolling Stones No. 2*. This time Keith accompanies Ian's organ on the intro. The tempo is slightly slower, and Keith, playing his 1959 Gibson Les Paul, delivers a very good solo with a very clear sound obtained from his Fender Showman amp. The track sounds far drier than the June 10 version thanks to greater discretion in the use of the famous Chess echo chamber. Jagger is no longer as prominent in the mix. His voice is more recessed but at the same time more rock 'n' roll. Despite a number of slips (for example "To me" at around 1:23), the backing vocals are considerably more in tune than before. Bill provides a very good bass line on his Framus Star bass, plugged directly into the console, which he plays with a pick. Charlie supports his colleagues with aplomb, ensuring that this version is less untidy than the earlier one. The only fly in the ointment is the tambourine part, again overdubbed, which is clearly not in time, particularly at the beginning of the number (listen at around 0:35). Brian, who played his arpeggios on his Gretsch Anniversary on the first recording, now uses his Vox "Teardrop." This second version of "Time Is on My Side" exemplifies the very good work done by the Stones to make a song their own, that is to say to distance themselves from the original version. Also worth noting is the proper ending, which can be heard distinctly despite the rapid fade-out.

From left to right: Bill on his Framus Star bass, Brian on his Vox "Teardrop," Charlie on his Ludwig kit, Mick on vocals, and Keith on his Gibson Les Paul.

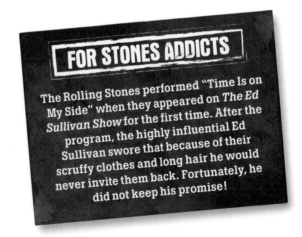

FOR STONES ADDICTS

The Rolling Stones performed "Time Is on My Side" when they appeared on *The Ed Sullivan Show* for the first time. After the program, the highly influential Ed Sullivan swore that because of their scruffy clothes and long hair he would never invite them back. Fortunately, he did not keep his promise!

WHAT A SHAME

Mick Jagger / Keith Richards / 3:03

Musicians
Mick Jagger: vocals
Keith Richards: rhythm guitar
Brian Jones: slide and lead guitar, harmonica
Bill Wyman: bass
Charlie Watts: drums
Ian Stewart: piano
Recorded
Chess Studios, Chicago: November 8, 1964
Technical Team
Producer: Andrew Loog Oldham
Sound engineer: Ron Malo

FOR STONES ADDICTS

In 1966 the group Love released an eponymous album featuring a song called "Can't Explain," whose lyrics are based on those of "What a Shame."

Genesis

"What a Shame" testifies to the Rolling Stones' visceral attachment to modern blues of the Willie Dixon, Muddy Waters, and Howlin' Wolf kind, and it is tempting to wonder whether the London group was still under the thumb of Brian Jones. Although a Jagger-Richards composition—admittedly one of their first—the lyrics have something of that darkness or sadness that is characteristic of the blues: *What a shame/Nothing seems to be going right . . . You might wake up in the morning/And find your poor self dead*. The fact that this number was recorded in the temple of Chicago blues also explains a thing or two. Mick Jagger had begun to see himself as Sonny Boy Williamson II—and by this stage he was not far from wrong. Neither had the other members of the group much more to learn from their mentors, least of all Ian Stewart, whose playing sounds as if he might have spent his childhood in a juke joint somewhere between Memphis and New Orleans. However, Jagger would explain in the *Melody Maker* of November 28, 1964, that the lugubrious aspect of the lyrics reflected the atmosphere at Chess: "Sunday in Chicago is like Sunday in Scotland—dead."

"What a Shame" was released as the B-side of "Heart of Stone," which climbed to a perfectly respectable number 19 in the United States on February 20, 1965. This is the first time both sides of a 45 were credited to Jagger-Richards.

Production

With a very good introduction from both guitars, Keith playing his Les Paul in a kind of blues picking style and Brian playing slide on his Vox "Teardrop," the Stones launch into this electric blues headfirst, providing a framework for Mick's excellent vocal performance. Credit should also be given to the Watts-Wyman duo for laying down an infectious groove, and to Stu for his superb piano (sadly mixed down). It is Brian, however, who takes the number to a new level with a brilliant harmonica solo (most likely overdubbed) underneath which Bill indulges in a somewhat unusual bass line. One of the first attempts by Mick Jagger and Keith Richards to write something other than a ballad, "What a Shame" can perhaps be faulted at a compositional level as the writing does not distinguish itself sufficiently from the standards of the blues genre, but it is a very good number nevertheless.

The Stones perform on *Ready Steady Go!* on June 26, 1964, with Brian Jones in his role of blues harmonica virtuoso.

1965

GROWN UP WRONG

Mick Jagger / Keith Richards / 2:06

Musicians
Mick Jagger: vocals, harmonica
Keith Richards: rhythm guitar, backing vocals
Brian Jones: slide and lead guitar
Bill Wyman: bass
Charlie Watts: drums
Unidentified musician(s): hand claps

Recorded
Regent Sound Studios: September 28–29, 1964

Technical Team
Producer: Andrew Loog Oldham
Sound engineer: Bill Farley

Genesis

When writing this song, Mick Jagger put himself in the shoes of a teenager who sees his girlfriend drifting away from him: *you've grown up all wrong*, he tells her. By this he means: you've become an adult without me realizing it, you've grown up too quickly. And as a result, *I'm through with you*.

For many fans, and also for the establishment—though for quite different reasons—this song is highly symbolic. Its title sums up perfectly the image the Rolling Stones wanted to convey of themselves to the media—using Andrew Oldham's extensive PR know-how—as "the band that has grown up all wrong." Indeed it is possible to see the group as one big symbol. Mick, Brian, Keith, Bill, and Charlie took delight in demolishing the last remaining vestiges of the previous era with hooks that reflected teenage fantasies and chord progressions that had originated in the studios and frenetic clubs of Chicago and Detroit. "Grown Up Wrong" is a bit like Howlin' Wolf's "Smokestack Lightning" or John Lee Hooker's "Boogie Chillen'"—a song with a hypnotic beat that hits listeners in the guts.

Production

With an excellent slide guitar intro played by Brian Jones (probably on his Gretsch), this is the second Jagger-Richards number (after "What a Shame") that ventures into blues territory. Ballads like "Tell Me" and "Congratulations" had become a thing of the past, and from now on the blues would shine through in the Stones' own songs. "Grown Up Wrong" is constructed around Brian's riff and supported by Bill's drone bass. Charlie plays a heavy, vehement beat on his Ludwig drum kit with the hi-hat half-open. Hand claps that are not particularly convincing in terms of either the way they are recorded or their execution double the snare drum and reinforce the insistent rhythm. Brian plays a solo, mainly without bottleneck, that never really leaves the ground. Mick shares the refrains with Keith, who provides backing vocals with plenty of reverb—mainly to good effect. And it is again Mick who plays harmonica in the coda, with very good blues phrasing. Although attractive, "Grown Up Wrong" is not one of the Stones' best songs nor one of their finest productions. However, the Jagger-Richards songwriting partnership was gradually finding its groove and before long would yield what made it unique.

Mick Jagger: symbol of a youth that had turned out badly? "Grown Up Wrong" sounds like a slogan of the sixties.

DOWN THE ROAD APIECE

Don Raye / 2:55

Musicians
Mick Jagger: vocals
Keith Richards: lead guitar
Brian Jones: rhythm guitar
Bill Wyman: bass
Charlie Watts: drums
Ian Stewart: piano
Recorded
Chess Studios, Chicago: June 11, 1964
Technical Team
Producer: Andrew Loog Oldham
Sound engineer: Ron Malo

The bass line of "Down the Road Apiece" on the version by the Will Bradley Trio may have been Henry Mancini's inspiration for his extremely well-known "Peter Gunn Theme" (1959).

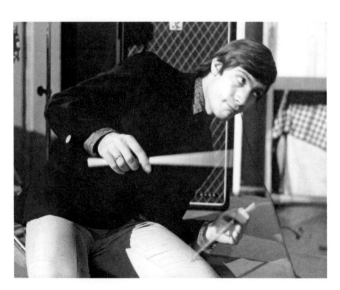

Charlie Watts plays with metronomic rigor, as always, on "Down the Road Apiece."

Genesis

Don Raye, a vaudeville artist and songwriter, wrote "Down the Road Apiece" for the musicians of the Will Bradley/Ray McKinley Orchestra, who recorded it with some success in 1940 as the Will Bradley Trio. This typical boogie-woogie number praising the talent of a group of phenomenal musicians and a club that is *open every night about twelve to six* was subsequently covered by many other artists including Amos Milburn in 1946 and Chuck Berry, who transformed it into a rock 'n' roll anthem, in 1960.

And it is from the Chuck Berry version that the Rolling Stones (after Manfred Mann before them) took their inspiration during the recording session in Chicago on June 11, 1964. Keith Richards in particular demonstrates that he has already learned everything there is to know about the guitar style of Chuck "Johnny B. Goode" Berry, while Ian Stewart remains true to the older boogie-woogie tradition.

Production

The Stones had been playing "Down the Road Apiece" since 1962, before Bill Wyman and Charlie Watts had even joined the group. Right from the introduction, played by Keith Richards on his Epiphone Casino, the group sounds very much in its element. The groove is extraordinary and indeed far superior to the Chuck Berry version, the six Britons demonstrating that they were unrivaled at making a song their own. From the moment Richards launches into the opening notes of "Down the Road Apiece" with that archetypal Chicago blues sound, he shows that he has become an excellent lead guitarist. This is without a doubt one of his best guitar performances from this stage of his career. Stewart also takes pride of place with his utterly irresistible boogie-woogie piano, which is nothing less than a work of art. Jagger is not to be outdone with a very good delivery of the lyrics. And if the number works this well, it is thanks in no small part to the veritable swing machine made up of the excellent Wyman and Watts. With Jones on his Gretsch Anniversary, "Down the Road Apiece" is one of the most successful tracks on the album. Were the Stones motivated by the presence of Chuck Berry at the June 11 recording session? Bill Wyman recalls: "He was the nicest I can remember him ever being, but don't forget, we were recording his songs!"[1]

1965

UNDER THE BOARDWALK

Arthur Resnick / Kenny Young / 2:48

Musicians
Mick Jagger: vocals
Keith Richards: acoustic guitar, backing vocals
Brian Jones: rhythm guitar
Bill Wyman: bass, backing vocals (?)
Charlie Watts: drums
Unidentified musician(s): güiro, triangle

Recorded
Regent Sound Studios: September 2, 1964

Technical Team
Producer: Andrew Loog Oldham
Sound engineer: Bill Farley

"Under the Boardwalk" has been covered by a wide range of artists from the Beach Boys to Rickie Lee Jones to John Mellencamp and the Undertones.

The Drifters on the stage of *Thank Your Lucky Stars* in March 1965. The vocal group was an inspiration for the Stones.

Genesis

Boardwalks tend to run along the shore of beach resorts, particularly on the East Coast. Arthur Resnick and Kenny Young, who wrote "Under the Boardwalk," have made it the meeting place of a couple who are deeply in love. This apparently innocuous love story has tragic associations in real life, however. The Drifters recorded the song on May 21, 1964, the day after their lead singer Rudy Lewis (who had taken over from Ben E. King) died from an overdose. Rather than cancel the session, Jerry Wexler of Atlantic asked Johnny Moore to sing lead vocal in his place, which explains the mood of sadness and nostalgia. It also no doubt explains the success of the single, which peaked at number 4 on the *Billboard* charts on August 22, 1964.

The Rolling Stones recorded the song on September 2, 1964, just two months after the release of the Drifters' single.

Production

There is no escaping the fact that in covering what was a huge hit for the Drifters, the Stones were taking on a masterpiece. The British group performs creditably, however, and although a comparison would not necessarily be in their favor, the Stones' version is nevertheless well made. Originally realized by a vocal group with a tremendous lead singer in the figure of Johnny Moore, "Under the Boardwalk" forced Mick Jagger to change his approach. He acquits himself very well, striking the right tone and compensating for his different vocal qualities with a timbre of astonishing freshness. Where Moore is perfectly at ease singing falsetto, Jagger prefers a more fragile and expressive delivery. Where the Drifters excel in the vocal harmonies, Keith Richards and probably Bill Wyman support their lead singer with discreet, efficient harmonies. A güiro (with delay) and a triangle can be heard on the recording (a first for a Stones record) as can Keith's new 6-string acoustic, a Framus Jumbo 5/97, over which the guitarist double-tracks a solo that has something of a "mariachi" flavor.

I CAN'T BE SATISFIED

McKinley Morganfield / 3:26

Musicians
Mick Jagger: vocals
Keith Richards: rhythm guitar
Brian Jones: slide guitar
Bill Wyman: bass
Charlie Watts: drums
Recorded
Chess Studios, Chicago: June 10, 1964
Technical Team
Producer: Andrew Loog Oldham
Sound engineer: Ron Malo

Blues great Muddy Waters (shown here in 1978), composer of "I Can't Be Satisfied," which the Stones covered in 1964.

Genesis

"I Can't Be Satisfied" is the A-side of the third single recorded by Muddy Waters—alias McKinley Morganfield—for the Aristocrat label (soon to be renamed Chess) in 1948 with "I Feel Like Going Home" as the B-side. In this sprightly blues number, the founder of modern blues expresses what a good number of African Americans from the Southern states felt after making the big move to the industrial cities of the North: bitter disenchantment. Gradually, this disenchantment took a more personal turn: *Woman I'm troubled/I be all worried in mind/ Well baby I just can't be satisfied/And I just can't keep from cryin'.* Clearly, it is a question here of frustration—sexual frustration, it goes without saying. And this is exactly what interested the Rolling Stones, who recorded "I Can't Be Satisfied" at Chess Studios on June 10, 1964.

Production

To say that the Stones' version is better than that of Muddy Waters would be incorrect. The master of Chicago blues remains the master. But it is admittedly just as good. "I Can't Be Satisfied" is a little gem as far as both production and performance are concerned. Mick Jagger is in supreme form and knows how to make the most of the effects at his disposal. With the brilliant Ron Malo at the controls, Mick starts off almost drowning in reverb (for the first three lines) before moving back into the foreground with a drier sound. The effect is remarkable, and typical of the records produced at Chess. Charlie Watts plays a ternary rhythm, striking the rim of his snare drum and giving the number an almost rockabilly drive. Bill Wyman, playing his Framus Star bass (no doubt plugged into his Fender Bassman amp) is doubled almost throughout by Keith Richards on his Epiphone Casino. The effect is as successful as it is unexpected. Most importantly, however, "I Can't Be Satisfied" allows Brian Jones to demonstrate his mastery of the slide guitar. His playing reveals just how much he loved the blues. He plays with a finesse with which few white guitarists have been able to compete. Brian acknowledged the quality of his own playing in 1965: "'I Can't Be Satisfied' is my favorite track. I played bottleneck guitar on it and it has one of the best guitar solos I've ever managed."[31] Who could possibly disagree, Brian?

1965

PAIN IN MY HEART

Allen Toussaint / 2:12

Musicians
Mick Jagger: vocals
Keith Richards: lead guitar
Brian Jones: rhythm guitar
Bill Wyman: bass
Charlie Watts: drums
Jack Nitzsche: toy piano
Recorded
RCA Studios, Hollywood: November 2, 1964
Technical Team
Producer: Andrew Loog Oldham
Sound engineer: Dave Hassinger

Allen Toussaint, composer of "Pain in My Heart" and architect of the influential New Orleans sound.

Genesis

"Pain in My Heart" is the song from which Otis Redding's first album, released on the Atco label (a subsidiary of Atlantic) on January 1, 1964, took its name. The singer from the state of Georgia was already at the peak of his emotional power, to such an extent that this song influenced most of the composers of soul ballads in the sixties. It was written by Allen Toussaint, one of the masters of the New Orleans sound (who often used his wife's maiden name, Naomi Neville, as a pseudonym). A disciple of Professor Longhair, Toussaint, after serving as the artistic director at Minit Records, set up the Tou-Sea label with Marshall Sehorn and went on to make a name for himself as one of the very best producers of New Orleans rhythm 'n' blues, directing sessions for Ernie K-Doe ("Mother-In-Law"), Lee Dorsey ("Do-Re-Mi," "Ride Your Pony," "Working in the Coalmine"), and Irma Thomas ("Ruler of My Heart"). "Pain in My Heart" is actually an adaptation of "Ruler of My Heart." Although Otis Redding's version of "Pain in My Heart" only reached number 61 on the US charts, it seduced the Rolling Stones into cutting their own version of it at the RCA Studios in Hollywood on November 2, 1964.

Production

The Stones' cover of this ballad is more pop than soul, with Mick Jagger's voice, somewhere between blues and rock, lending the number a more hard-edged and less plaintive feel. The production, entrusted to David Hassinger, has a sound that is immediate and perfectly defined, possessing the inimitable "texture" that characterizes the majority of "made in the USA" productions dating from this period. Immediately noticeable is the distortion on Bill Wyman's bass, which sounds almost like a euphonium. According to Wyman, this distortion was added afterward by Hassinger. Wyman is playing a 6-string bass for the second time, the famous Fender Bass VI. Hence the equally rich sound in the treble range. Brian Jones plays rhythm on his Vox "Teardrop" with vibrato from his amp. Keith Richards, who plays lead on his Les Paul, maintains a reasonably discreet presence. Once again Jack Nitzsche is on piano, this time a toy piano, nicknamed the "Nitzsche-phone," but in truth fairly recessed in the mix. One other thing to note is Charlie's bass drum pedal, which does not stop squeaking throughout the entire track!

OFF THE HOOK

Mick Jagger/Keith Richards / 2:34

Musicians
Mick Jagger: vocals, backing vocals (?)
Keith Richards: rhythm and lead guitar, backing vocals (?)
Brian Jones: rhythm guitar
Bill Wyman: bass
Charlie Watts: drums
Recorded
Regent Sound Studios, London: September 2, 1964
Technical Team
Producer: Andrew Loog Oldham
Sound engineer: Bill Farley

The most original cover of "Off the Hook" was recorded by Pete Best, the Beatles' first drummer.

To date, "Off the Hook" has been covered by around twenty different artists, the most interesting of which is the Pete Best Combo, whose leader, Pete Best, was none other than the Beatles' very first drummer. Best was cast adrift in August 1962. That version was released on the album *Rebirth* in 1981. Could this song mark the end of the Beatles versus Stones rivalry?

Genesis

The blues greats had made such a deep impression on the Rolling Stones that when Mick Jagger and Keith Richards started writing their own songs, there was no escaping the Chicago influence. This is especially true of "Off the Hook," which is actually a more or less obvious copy of "Off the Wall," a song recorded by Little Walter for Checker Records (a subsidiary of Chess) in 1953 that reached number 8 on the R&B charts. The main difference is that "Off the Wall" is an instrumental, whereas "Off the Hook" recounts the trials and tribulations of a lover who wants to talk to his girlfriend—whose line is constantly busy. Chess Records wanted to bring a lawsuit for plagiarism but in the end a compromise was reached whereby the Chicago record company was offered fifty percent of the royalties. Furthermore, when Little Walter's "Off the Wall" was released, Big Walter Horton, who had recorded it in Memphis for Sun Records, claimed to be the sole composer!

"Off the Hook" was recorded on September 2 at Regent Sound Studios, although, according to some sources, it had been worked on during the June 24–26 sessions. This number was chosen as the B-side of the single "Little Red Rooster," released on November 13, 1964.

Production

Keith Richards opens "Off the Hook" with an introduction that is half-country, half–Chuck Berry. He is playing his new 1959 Gibson Les Paul, plugged into a Vox AC30. His sound is clear and precise, and he can be heard changing the position of his guitar mics immediately before launching into the rhythm part (at 0:08). "Off the Hook" is based on a moderately heavy beat sustained by Charlie Watts on his ride cymbal and by Bill Wyman on bass, playing a riff that has nothing in common with the bass line of Little Walter's version. Brian Jones plays rhythm, though not particularly audibly, on his Vox "Teardrop," and Mick Jagger, disconsolate at being ignored by his girlfriend, double-tracks his singing to give his voice greater weight, a doubling that, it has to be said, is not always fully successful. It also seems to be Jagger (rather than Keith Richards) singing harmony on some of the choruses, as can be heard at 1:15. It may not be a major number in the Rolling Stones' catalog, but "Off the Hook" possesses an engaging catchiness.

1965

SUSIE Q

Dale Hawkins / Stan Lewis / Eleanor Broadwater / 1:51

Musicians
Mick Jagger: vocals
Keith Richards: lead guitar
Brian Jones: rhythm guitar
Bill Wyman: bass
Charlie Watts: drums
Unidentified musician(s): hand claps
Recorded
Regent Sound Studios: September 28–29, 1964
Technical Team
Producer: Andrew Loog Oldham
Sound engineer: Bill Farley

The California band Creedence Clearwater Revival recorded "Susie Q" with a thoroughly swamp blues vibe.

Genesis

A familiar face in the clubs of Shreveport, Louisiana, from the second half of the fifties, the singer and guitarist Dale Hawkins went down in history as the musician who combined the rockabilly of Elvis Presley/Scotty Moore with the swamp blues of Slim Harpo and Lightnin' Slim. Hence his sobriquet "the architect of swamp rock boogie."

Hawkins owes this flattering reputation to one song in particular, Susie Q, which he recorded in 1957 at the KWKH radio station in Shreveport with the wonderful James Burton (the guitarist of Ricky Nelson and subsequently Elvis Presley) on lead guitar. Released as a single by Checker Records in May 1957, it reached number 27 on the *Billboard* charts on July 1, 1957, to the enormous delight of Hawkins, of course, but also of Stan Lewis (the owner of Jewel/Paula Records, whose records were at that time distributed by Chess/Checker) and Eleanor Broadwater, who had taken the precaution of having themselves credited as co-writers.

I like the way you walk/I like the way you talk: Susie Q inspired a huge number of singers and groups and went on to enter the list of 500 Songs That Shaped Rock and Roll. In addition to the Rolling Stones, these artists have included Johnny Rivers, Creedence Clearwater Revival, José Feliciano, and Suzi Quatro, to name just a few.

Production

The Stones recorded this song during the session on September 28–29, 1964. Their version is both faster and significantly harder-edged than Dale Hawkins's, which was already forceful enough by the standards of the day. The guitar sound is close to distortion even though the renowned fuzz tone would not make an appearance in the Stones' world for another few months. Led in by Charlie on his Ludwig toms, the group makes its version of "Susie Q" a formidable vehicle for the great blues-rock energy that it alone truly possessed in 1964. Mick's singing is excellent, Bill glides smoothly up and down the neck of his bass, Brian provides a rhythmic backdrop on his Vox "Teardrop," and Keith plays superb licks on his Les Paul before concluding the number with a frenetic solo that ends all too soon. While Creedence Clearwater Revival made what is probably the definitive version of this song, the Rolling Stones need in no way be ashamed of theirs.

She Said Yeah
Mercy Mercy
Hitch Hike
That's How Strong My Love Is
Good Times
Gotta Get Away
Talkin' About You
Cry to Me
Oh, Baby (We Got A Good Thing Going')
Heart Of Stone
The Under Assistant West Coast
Promotion Man
I'm Free

ALBUM
RELEASE DATE
United Kingdom:
September 24, 1965
Label: Decca
RECORD NUMBERS: LK 4733 (MONO),
DECCA SKL 4733 (STEREO)
On charts for 24 weeks,
peaked at number 2

OUT OF OUR HEADS

OUT OF OUR HEADS, THE ALBUM THAT SET THE STONES FREE

Five young Englishmen at the heart of black American rhythm 'n' blues: this was the concept behind the Stones' third (British) studio album.

The Album

As *Out of Our Heads* was flooding out of record stores on either side of the Atlantic, Andrew Oldham hired a business manager. Allen Klein immediately renegotiated the Rolling Stones' record contract with Decca, obtaining a far more attractive deal for the band. This new album and the singles "(I Can't Get No) Satisfaction" and "Get Off of My Cloud," recorded during the same period, marked a decisive leap forward. No longer were Mick, Brian, Keith, Bill, and Charlie merely five artists united by a shared passion for blues and rock 'n' roll; they were five internationally acclaimed musicians, the spearheads, along with the Beatles, of the British Invasion. However, while the months preceding the release of this album saw the Stones performing all over the world—including one Northern American tour and three epic shows at the Paris Olympia (April 16–18, 1965)—unleashing "Stonemania" wherever they went, a rift was developing at the heart of the group. Brian Jones, who felt his leadership ebbing away in favor of Mick Jagger and Keith Richards, started to become unpredictable, showing signs of depressive and occasionally aggressive behavior. He wanted to continue along the sanctified path of the blues, but his two bandmates did not see things the same way. Acutely sensitive and somewhat paranoid by nature, he tried LSD for the first time on May 16 in Long Beach, California. From this point forward, the Stones increasingly had to balance recording with drugs.

Musically, this third studio album (from a British perspective) differed little from the preceding one. It was another journey into the heart of rhythm 'n' blues, which the London band had reworked and made their own to the extent that numbers such as "She Said 'Yeah,'" "Mercy, Mercy," and "Hitch Hike," recorded by Larry Williams, Don Covay, and Marvin Gaye, respectively, sound like Rolling Stones originals (due mainly to Mick's vocal qualities and Brian and Keith's weaving guitars). Again there is a Chuck Berry cover, "Talkin' About You," as part of their ongoing homage to the master.

On the other hand, there is a discernible development in terms of the Stones' own compositions and the messages that Jagger and Richards were addressing to their audience. With his disenchanted pout, his wayward lock of hair, and his derisive glance, the Rolling Stones' lead singer was no longer in a mood to be taken in by women. "Gotta Get Away," which implies that it is impossible to have a happy love affair, and above all "Heart of Stone," whose "hero" is a nonchalant, cynical seducer, contain the seeds of the misogyny that lay at the heart of the Rolling Stones myth. "The Under Assistant West Coast Promotion Man" tackles a different subject. This is a contemptuous indictment of the record industry as symbolized by an extremely strange and insipid PR assistant from London Records who accompanied the Rolling Stones on their first US tour. And "I'm Free," is an appeal for immediate gratification, a hymn to individual liberty (perhaps in response to the protest movements of the time). Ultimately, this new album (UK version) includes only four original songs, of which three are credited to Jagger-Richards and one to the group ("The Under Assistant West Coast Promotion Man").

The "brains" of the Rolling Stones: Allen Klein (left) and Andrew Loog Oldham.

Barely one more, then, than the preceding album. But the songwriting duo would soon make an impact with songs of a completely new caliber that would propel them into the major league of songwriters.

Out of Our Heads was released initially in the United States, on July 30, 1965, and then in the United Kingdom, on September 24. There are some differences in the track listing. The numbers "She Said Yeah," "Gotta Get Away," "Talkin' About You," "Oh, Baby (We Got a Good Thing Going)," "Heart of Stone," and "I'm Free" were replaced on the US version by "The Last Time," "I'm Alright" (from the EP *Got Live If You Want It!*), "(I Can't Get No) Satisfaction," "Play with Fire," "The Spider and the Fly," and "One More Try." It is interesting to note that this was also the track listing chosen for the countries of continental Europe, with an emphasis on the singles, both A- and B-sides (following the enormous impact of "Satisfaction"). The album was a hit in both its versions, becoming the Stones' first number 1 in the United States (where it was eventually certified platinum) and achieving second place in the United Kingdom behind the Beatles' *Help!*, and remaining on the charts for twenty-four weeks.

The UK Sleeve

While the US version of *Out of Our Heads* recycles the David Bailey photograph used on the cover of *The Rolling Stones No. 2*, the British version is far more enigmatic. It shows Brian kneeling in the foreground, with Keith, Charlie, Bill, and Mick standing behind him. All five give the impression of being caught in a trap between two dumpsters. Does this perhaps symbolize the snare laid by the record industry? And there is another innovation: Why has an asterisk been added to the end of the band's name (which, incidentally, is featured on the cover, along with the title of the album, for the first time)?

This black-and-white photograph was taken at Andrew Oldham's request by Gered Mankowitz. After working for Camera Press, Mankowitz opened his own studio at 9 Masons Yard in 1963. The sleeve of *Out of Our Heads* (UK version) was the photographer's first masterstroke in the world of rock 'n' roll. Mankowitz recalls the historic moment: "This image became my first cover for the band, and was the fulfillment of a dream for me at the age of 18!"[32] Unfortunately he lost the negative a few years later, probably during a break-in at his studio.

To his great surprise, it was recently restored to him after having been discovered in a warehouse in West London. A print of the image now hangs in the National Portrait Gallery in London.

The Recording

The album sessions extended from November 2, 1964, to September 6, 1965, a period of ten months. The Stones only spent six sessions in the studios, however: five at the RCA Studios in Hollywood, under the aegis of Dave Hassinger, and one at Chess Studios in Chicago in the care of Ron Malo. These magical locations were responsible in part for the "American-style" productions. They were mythical places that by this time the group had come to know well, having recorded there before. And *Out of Our Heads* confirmed the Rolling Stones as the most American of British bands.

In keeping with Decca policy (following Brian Epstein's practice for the Beatles), and unlike the US version, the twelve tracks on the British album (in the case of the North American and continental European album, eleven studio recordings and one live recording, "I'm Alright," from a concert given in England) included none of the group's singles dating from this period.

Three numbers for the second album date from the session of November 2, 1964: "Heart of Stone," "Hitch Hike," and "Oh, Baby (We Got a Good Thing Going)." The sessions at Chess took place in May 1965 during the US tour. Between May 10 and 12, "Mercy, Mercy," "The Under Assistant West Coast Promotion Man," and "That's How Strong My Love Is" were cut for the UK album as well as James Brown's "Try Me," (not included on the album) and an initial version of "(I Can't Get No) Satisfaction."

The sessions continued from May 12 at the RCA Studios in Hollywood: "(I Can't Get No) Satisfaction" was recorded on May 12–13, followed by, for the UK album, "Good Times" and "Cry to Me," and for the US (and European) album, "The Spider and the Fly" and "One More Try," plus (for neither album) "I've Been Loving You Too Long" (included on the compilations *The Rest of the Best* and *More Hot Rocks [Big Hits & Fazed Cookies]*) and "My Girl" (included on *Flowers* and the compilation *The Rest of the Best*). The recordings concluded in Hollywood on September 5 and 6 with, first of all, the single "Get Off of My Cloud" and "Blue Turns to Grey" (included on the US

Anita Pallenberg, the first muse of
Brian Jones . . . and the Stones.

LP *December's Children [And Everybody's]* and the compilations *Stone Age* and *The Rest of the Best*), and then, for *Out of Our Heads*, "She Said Yeah," "Gotta Get Away," "Talkin' About You," and "I'm Free" followed by "Looking Tired" (not included on the album) and "The Singer Not the Song."

Dave Hassinger would later reveal that, contrary to the legend, the Stones did not, during this period, record throughout the night: "No, never. I'd say twelve to fourteen hours might have been the longest. They'd usually start at about 2:00 in the afternoon and go to midnight or 2:00 or 3:00 in the morning."[33] After all, as Keith Richards would later claim: "We were basically working 350 days a year. You'd have 10 days off the tour to go to L.A. and record."[34] While various substances might have been used to help them stay alert, a certain freshness was inevitably needed in the studio, including when the Rolling Stones recorded *Out of Our Heads*.

The Instruments

For the first numbers recorded during the initial session at the RCA Studios on November 2, 1964, the Stones played the same instruments that they used for the previous album, that is to say the 1959 Gibson Les Paul (Keith Richards), the Vox "Teardrop" (Brian Jones), the Framus Star bass (Bill Wyman) and the Ludwig Super Classic (Charlie Watts). For the remaining sessions, between May and September 1965, new instruments made an appearance: superb Gibson Firebird VIIs and Gibson Heritage 6-string acoustics for Keith and Brian, an extraordinary Rickenbacker "1993" 12-string for Brian, and a Framus Star Bass De Luxe, nicknamed "Humbug" for Bill. In addition to the usual harmonicas, pianos, organs, and tambourines, marimbas can also be heard on the album, played in all likelihood by Ian Stewart ("Good Times").

The famous Gibson "reverse" Firebird VII, another iconic Stones guitar.

SHE SAID YEAH

Sonny Bono / Roddy Jackson / 1:34

Musicians
Mick Jagger: vocals
Keith Richards: rhythm guitar, lead guitar, backing vocals
Brian Jones: rhythm guitar, lead guitar
Bill Wyman: bass, backing vocals
Charlie Watts: drums

Recorded
RCA Studios, Hollywood: September 5 or 6, 1965

Technical Team
Producer: Andrew Loog Oldham
Sound engineer: Dave Hassinger

Larry Williams was an important influence on the bands of the British Invasion. Before "She Said 'Yeah,'" the Beatles had already covered "Bad Boy" and "Dizzy Miss Lizzy."

Larry Williams, on whose repertoire the young pioneers of English rock 'n' roll would draw at the beginning of the sixties.

Genesis

"She Said 'Yeah'" was recorded by Larry Williams in August 1958 as the B-side of his single "Bad Boy." It was written by Sonny Bono and Roddy Jackson. Bono, who had started his career as a songwriter at Specialty Records before joining Phil Spector's team, is best known as half of the Sonny and Cher duo, of "I Got You Babe" and "The Beat Goes On" fame, formed in 1964. Roddy Jackson was a rockabilly singer and songwriter who signed with Specialty at Sonny Bono's instigation. It may not have achieved success in the US charts, but "She Said 'Yeah'" made a mark on British groups of the early sixties, as did various other Larry Williams numbers. The Rolling Stones recorded the song on either September 5 or 6, 1965. Based on the song's communicative energy, it is tempting to consider the Stones' version of "She Said 'Yeah'" as one of the first ever examples of hard or even punk rock (a dozen or so years before the term was coined).

Production

The Stones chose this pepped-up version of "She Said 'Yeah'" as the opener for their third album. The honor of introducing the piece goes to Brian Jones and Keith Richards and a knockout combination of their two guitars, the superb Gibson Firebird VIIs that have their first outing on this album. Brian plays the riff, with effervescent distortion courtesy of Gibson's famous Maestro Fuzz-Tone, while Keith takes on the roles of both rhythm and solo guitarist (with a small timing problem between 1:02 and 1:06). Bill Wyman is not to be outdone, doubling his bandmates with a very fast and fluid bass line on his new Framus Humbug, played high up the fingerboard. Charlie Watts, remaining faithful to his Ludwig, marks the beat with power and energy, bringing an uncustomary weight to his playing. "She Said 'Yeah'" would not, however, have the feel it does without Mick Jagger's supercharged delivery of the words and the rasping quality of his voice, which contributes a new vitality to the band's sound. Compared to Larry Williams's excellent, more R&B, version, the Stones' extensively reworked cover represents an explosion of adrenaline that would soon catch on among the bands of the British Invasion.

1965

MERCY MERCY

Don Covay / Ronald Dean Miller / 2:45

Musicians
Mick Jagger: vocals
Keith Richards: rhythm guitar, backing vocals
Brian Jones: rhythm guitar
Bill Wyman: bass
Charlie Watts: drums
Recorded
Chess Studios, Chicago: May 10, 1965
Technical Team
Producer: Andrew Loog Oldham
Sound engineer: Ron Malo

Some twenty years after this number was recorded, Don Covay joined the Stones in the studio, providing backing vocals, with Bobby Womack on the song "Harlem Shuffle," on the album *Dirty Works* (1986).

Before revolutionizing the rock world, Jimi Hendrix played on Don Covay's "Mercy, Mercy."

Genesis

The son of a preacher from South Carolina, Don Covay cut his teeth as a singer with his family's gospel group, the Cherry Keys. He then joined the Rainbows, singing occasionally alongside Marvin Gaye and Billy Stewart, before becoming Little Richard's chauffeur. The rock 'n' roll pioneer is thought to have encouraged him to try his hand as a songwriter, a successful initiative that would give Chubby Checker, Solomon Burke, and Wilson Pickett their route to the charts, notably with "I'm Gonna Cry (Cry Baby)," which also provided Atlantic with its first hit. Songs by Ronald Dean Miller, meanwhile, have been covered by many artists including Aretha Franklin, Stevie Wonder, and Wilson Pickett.

Don Covay had his biggest hit, in the role of both writer and performer, in 1964 with a song called "Mercy, Mercy." The recording session, financed by the disc jockey Nathaniel "Magnificent" Montague (of the New York radio station WWRL) and Herb Abramson, the co-founder of Atlantic, took place in mid-May 1964 at the A-1 Recording Studio in New York with a group called the Goodtimers (and a twenty-two-year-old guitarist named Jimi Hendrix). "Mercy, Mercy" was released the following August under the name Don Covay & the Goodtimers and climbed to number 1 on the Cashbox R&B chart and number 35 on the *Billboard* pop chart.

Production

"Mercy, Mercy" is the first song the Rolling Stones recorded at Chess Studios the day after performing at the Arie Crown Theater in Chicago as part of their third US tour. With Ron Malo at the controls, they rediscovered a rich, sensual sound. Keith Richards plays the introduction on his Gibson Les Paul in a style not too far removed from the original version played by the incomparable Jimi Hendrix. Brian supports Keith on his Vox "Teardrop" with a sound distorted, it is presumed, through the amp, before launching into the guitar riffs, leaving the rhythm part (and also the vocal harmonies) to Keith. Charlie's bass drum has never before been as prominent as it is here. Supported by Bill Wyman on his Framus Star bass, it contributes a very R&B feel, reinforced by Mick Jagger's excellent vocal delivery. Entirely in keeping with the spirit of the song, Mick passes from a full-on soul sound to a Smokey Robinson–style falsetto.

HITCH HIKE

Marvin Gaye / Clarence Paul / William "Mickey" Stevenson / 2:26

Musicians
Mick Jagger: vocals, backing vocals (?)
Keith Richards: lead guitar, backing vocals
Brian Jones: rhythm guitar
Bill Wyman: bass, backing vocals (?)
Charlie Watts: drums
Unidentified musician(s): hand claps

Recorded
RCA Studios, Hollywood: November 2, 1964

Technical Team
Producer: Andrew Loog Oldham
Sound engineer: Dave Hassinger

Genesis
The song's narrator is getting ready to hitchhike his way around the United States, from Chicago to St. Louis to Los Angeles, in search of the woman he loves. "Hitch Hike" was the result of a collaboration between Marvin Gaye, Mickey Stevenson, and Clarence Paul. Released as a single in December 1962 (with "Hello There Angel" as the B-side), it was a hit for Marvin Gaye, achieving a promising number 30 on the *Billboard* charts on March 16, 1963. Motown's emblematic singer would later perform it at the *TAMI Show* (a concert recorded on October 28 and 29, 1964, and broadcast on December 29) in which the Rolling Stones also took part.

Production
The Rolling Stones likely decided to include "Hitch Hike" in their repertoire after hearing and enjoying Marvin Gaye's performance of it at the recording of the show. This session, at which the Stones recorded various other numbers for inclusion on their second album, such as "Everybody Needs Somebody to Love" and "Down Home Girl," took place at the RCA Studios in Hollywood on November 2. The "Hitch Hike" intro is played by Keith and Brian on their Les Paul and Vox "Teardrop" guitars, respectively, whereas on the original it is introduced by horns. The result is more effective and the intro is seemingly better suited to guitar, particularly when reinforced by plenty of reverb. Charlie and Bill lay down their customary solid rhythmic foundation, enabling Mick to assure the listener that he will find his beloved even if he has to hitchhike around the world. Other than the highly effective intro, however, the Stones' version does not live up to Marvin Gaye's. The backing vocals, sung presumably by Keith and Bill (or overdubbed by Mick?) hardly bear comparison with those of Martha & The Vandellas. Ultimately, the Englishmen are not entirely convincing, which is a shame given the promising introduction. They had been more successful with their cover of another Marvin Gaye song, "Can I Get a Witness," on their first album.

Marvin Gaye, star of the *TAMI Show*, with Martha & The Vandellas in October 1964.

1965

THAT'S HOW STRONG MY LOVE IS

Roosevelt Jamison / 2:23

Musicians
Mick Jagger: vocals
Keith Richards: rhythm guitar
Brian Jones: organ (?)
Bill Wyman: bass
Charlie Watts: drums
Ian Stewart: piano
Recorded
Chess Studios, Chicago: May 10, 1965
Technical Team
Producer: Andrew Loog Oldham
Sound engineer: Ron Malo

The blues and gospel singer O. V. Wright recorded "That's How Strong My Love Is" in 1964.

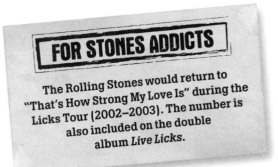

Genesis

Born in the state of Mississippi, Roosevelt Jamison later settled in Memphis, Tennessee, becoming one of the celebrities of the local music scene, both as a songwriter and as a manager. It was he who discovered O. V. Wright in the Beale Street district. He persuaded the blues and gospel singer to record "That's How Strong My Love Is" for Quinton Claunch's label Goldwax Records in 1964. The song enabled O. V. Wright to widen his audience, but it was Otis Redding who would transform it into a hymn of Southern soul: *I'll be the weeping willow drowning in my tears/And you can go swimming when you're here/And I'll be the rainbow after the tears are gone/Wrap you in my colors and keep you warm*. Otis Redding released the single "Mr. Pitiful" in December 1964 with "That's How Strong My Love Is" as the B-side.

Production

This declaration of passionate love in ballad form suits Mick Jagger's voice to a T. By now the singer had complete control of his tone, with the ability to alternate between raucous and more gentle phrasing. This is one of his best performances on the album and he was obviously inspired by Otis Redding to rise to this level. Their version is more spirited, a quality sustained throughout by Charlie Watts on the ride cymbal. Jagger even allows himself some freedom with the melody of the verses, making the song more or less unrecognizable other than in the refrains. Keith Richards alone plays rhythm on his Gibson Les Paul. Brian Jones seems to be playing the organ (inaudibly, other than perhaps on the bridge between 1:08 and 1:19). Although there is some room for doubt, he can certainly be seen playing it on the *Ready Steady Go!* show broadcast on September 10, 1965 (recorded on September 2). The piano is audible but discreet (around 1:19), marking Ian Stewart's return after being absent from the Stones' recordings for a little while.

GOOD TIMES

Sam Cooke / 1:59

TWIST OF FATE

Soon after this session, the Rolling Stones signed a contract with the very same manager who presided over the career of Sam Cooke: a certain Allen Klein.

IN YOUR HEADPHONES

At precisely 0:30 Jagger can be heard singing the beginning of the phrase *It could take all night long*, that has been clumsily erased.

Musicians
Mick Jagger: vocals
Keith Richards: lead guitar, backing vocals
Brian Jones: acoustic guitar
Bill Wyman: bass
Charlie Watts: drums
Ian Stewart: marimbas
Recorded
RCA Studios, Hollywood: May 13, 1965
Technical Team
Producer: Andrew Loog Oldham
Sound engineer: Dave Hassinger

Genesis

On December 11, 1964, Sam Cooke was found dead in the bedroom of a motel located at 9137 South Figueroa Street, Los Angeles. The manager of the establishment, Bertha Franklin, confessed to the police that she had shot the singer after being attacked by him. Just thirty-three years of age, Sam Cooke left behind a handful of songs that had catapulted him to the very summit of soul music and made him a model for Otis Redding and Marvin Gaye.

Although "Good Times" did not experience the same chart success as "You Send Me" or "Chain Gang," the song nevertheless reached number 11 on the pop charts in 1964. *I got my plans, I don't know about you/I'll tell you exactly what I'm gonna do*: there was no hint here of the tragic and premature fate that was to befall Sam Cooke.

Production

Five months after Sam Cooke's death, the Rolling Stones recorded "Good Times" in the RCA Studios on Sunset Boulevard with the talented Dave Hassinger as sound engineer. This was the famous session at which they were to record the legendary "(I Can't Get No) Satisfaction." The group nevertheless devoted sufficient attention to "Good Times" to do it justice. Charlie Watts introduces the number with a break on the toms. The atmosphere is so relaxed, it is easy to imagine the Stones by the side of a swimming pool, glasses in hand. This exotic flavor is reinforced by the marimbas (on the original version) played by Ian Stewart, even though their presence is discerned rather than properly heard. Brian Jones strums his new Gibson Heritage 6-string acoustic. Keith Richards plays the riffs on his Les Paul (or possibly his Firebird), while Bill Wyman supports his bandmates on his Framus (Star? Humbug?), perhaps more placidly than usual. Mick Jagger, meanwhile, adopts a nonchalant vocal style that perfectly suits the atmosphere of the number—something of a rarity for the Stones.

Sam Cooke's last hit during his lifetime was "Good Times." And his manager was Allen Klein.

GOTTA GET AWAY

Mick Jagger / Keith Richards / 2:06

Musicians
Mick Jagger: vocals
Keith Richards: lead guitar, 12-string (?)
acoustic guitar, backing vocals
Brian Jones: rhythm guitar
Bill Wyman: bass
Charlie Watts: drums
James W. Alexander: tambourine
Unidentified musician(s): hand claps
Recorded
RCA Studios, Hollywood: September 5 or 6, 1965
Technical Team
Producer: Andrew Loog Oldham
Sound engineer: Dave Hassinger

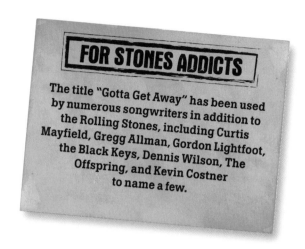

A sixties icon with his Gibson Firebird, a legendary guitar of the . . . sixties.

Genesis

"Gotta Get Away" is the only Jagger-Richards song on the first side of the LP *Out of Our Heads*. Its narrator has had enough of his girlfriend as a result of all her lies. He can no longer *stand to see [her] face*, even in pictures of her on his wall. In short, he has decided: *I got to get away*. Mick Jagger sings the song in a tone of justified reproachfulness. The Stones' singer is thus lifting the curtain on the nature of love: dishonesty in an affair of the heart can only end badly. This can perhaps be seen as a foretaste of the sexism displayed (or cultivated?) by the London gang.

"Gotta Get Away" is definitely not the best song written by the duo during this early stage of their career. This has led some people to suggest that it was mere filler. Be that as it may, it nevertheless possesses a particular atmosphere that enabled the Stones to stray off the path of blues, rock 'n' roll, and soul and try something new. Could this explain why it was excluded from the track listing of the US version of the album and instead released as a single?

Production

This is the third time the Stones had recorded for their new album at the RCA Studios. During early September 1965 they worked on a number of self-penned songs including "Gotta Get Away." The feel of the song immediately brings to mind a combination of the Beatles and the Byrds. Jagger does not give his best vocal performance, with some passages lacking a certain assurance despite Keith Richards providing a helping hand with the harmonies. "Gotta Get Away" is actually dominated by the guitars. There seems to a 12-string acoustic on the recording, no doubt Keith's Harmony 1270, as well as a rhythm part presumably played by Brian on his Gibson Firebird VII and an overdubbed lead guitar, also played by Keith on his Epiphone Casino. Charlie Watts, who is completely at ease in this type of groove, is supported by hand claps and tambourine provided by James W. Alexander (a talented musician, producer, and composer and a former producer of the Soul Stirrers and Sam Cooke). Bill Wyman also lends his support with a very pop-rock bass line, but overall, this number, likable though it may be, lacks conviction. Moreover, tighter timing would have helped. "Gotta Get Away" was selected for the B-side of "As Tears Go By," which was released in the United States on December 18, 1965.

TALKIN' ABOUT YOU

Chuck Berry / 2:31

Musicians
Mick Jagger: vocals
Keith Richards: lead guitar, backing vocals
Brian Jones: rhythm guitar
Bill Wyman: bass
Charlie Watts: drums
Ian Stewart (?): piano
Jack Nitzsche (?): piano
Recorded
RCA Studios, Hollywood: September 5 or 6, 1965
Technical Team
Producer: Andrew Loog Oldham
Sound engineer: Dave Hassinger

Bill Wyman's Framus Humbug bass is prominent on
"Talkin' About You," written by Chuck Berry.

Genesis

The narrator of this song is talking to a young woman. He tells her he has seen a girl uptown who is *so fine* and has *such lovely skin* that she *oughta be somewhere in Hollywood.* He then reveals that this girl, whom he wants to be his girlfriend, is the person sitting by his side. The song is a pretty declaration of love with a rock 'n' roll accompaniment that is pure Chuck Berry, and was released as a single in 1961 (with "Little Star" as the B-side). It is not to be confused with "Talkin' About You" by Ray Charles, which was released in 1958.

Production

Chuck Berry was a major source of inspiration for British groups of the early sixties, and many are the guitarists who have lifted the rock 'n' roll pioneer's guitar sequences for "Johnny B. Goode," "Carol," and "Roll Over Beethoven." The Beatles had been performing "I'm Talking About You" at the Star Club in Hamburg as early as 1962. Three years later the Rolling Stones came to record it, having likewise honed it onstage, in their case since the beginning of 1964. Paradoxically, although the Stones were continually improving from concert to concert and from recording to recording, "Talkin' About You" is definitely not their best version of a Chuck Berry song!

They have chosen to considerably slow down the tempo (from 148 to 120 bpm) in order to give the number a heavier, more insistent groove. The effect brings Bill Wyman to the fore with a big sound obtained from his Framus Humbug plugged into a Fender Bassman amp. Charlie Watts avoids stressing the beat even further by opting for an excellent funky, airy style. Keith Richards performs the intro exactly as Chuck Berry does, before switching to rhythm and later playing a solo. Brian Jones supports him with a second (discreet but efficient) rhythm part, which he seems to play in power chords on his Gibson Firebird VII. Jagger fulfills his role as front man with a good vocal performance, assisted by Richards on backing vocals. A piano part attributable to either Ian Stewart or Jack Nitzsche can also be made out. The Stones' version is more rhythm 'n' blues than rock 'n' roll, but although well put together, it is a long way from matching Chuck Berry's.

CRY TO ME

Bert Russell / 3:09

Musicians
Mick Jagger: vocals
Keith Richards: lead guitar, backing vocals
Brian Jones: rhythm guitar
Bill Wyman: bass, backing vocals (?)
Charlie Watts: drums
Ian Stewart: piano (or organ)
Jack Nitzsche: organ (or piano)
Recorded
RCA Studios, Hollywood: May 13, 1965
Technical Team
Producer: Andrew Loog Oldham
Sound engineer: Dave Hassinger

FOR STONES ADDICTS

Two months after the Rolling Stones recorded this number, the Pretty Things reached number 28 on the British charts with "Cry to Me."

The Pretty Things. From left to right: ex–Stone Dick Taylor, Viv Prince, Phil May, and Brian Pendleton.

Claus Ogerman, who arranged the Solomon Burke version, collaborated with numerous artists such as Billie Holiday, Stan Getz, Antônio Carlos Jobim, Bill Evans, Wes Montgomery, Frank Sinatra, Diana Krall, but also the Shadows and Ben E. King. A busy life indeed!

Genesis

After coming to attention with "Twist and Shout," Bert Russell, better known by the name Bert Berns, immediately became one of the pillars of Atlantic. A few months earlier, he had written "Cry to Me" for Solomon Burke. The recording place took place on December 6, 1961, with Berns as producer and Claus Ogerman as arranger and conductor. The song was released as a single (with "I Almost Lost My Mind") at the beginning of 1962 and climbed to numbers 5 and 44, respectively, on the *Billboard* R&B and pop charts.

A song about solitude, located musically at the point where rhythm 'n' blues meets gospel, "Cry to Me" can almost be said to sum up Southern soul, which would be highly successful during the sixties. After Solomon Burke, and then Betty Harris in 1963, the Rolling Stones were the next to be seduced by this superb song. This was the second Bert Berns number they had covered, the first being "Everybody Needs Somebody to Love," which opened their second LP.

Production

Once again, Mick Jagger displays all his virtues as a soul singer. He also takes liberties with the tune, and in the first few bars it is difficult to recognize the song as the same one sung by Solomon Burke. Mick shows his skill at bringing different vocal colors to bear, alternating a gentle tone and a rock-style delivery. His performance is excellent and demonstrates that within barely two years, he has attained a level of vocal skill equal to his later reputation. The Stones have chosen once again to reduce the tempo of the original version (see "Talkin' About You"). This produces a different feel, with a sound that is more like Otis Redding in "A Change Is Gonna Come." Brian Jones's rhythm guitar (Vox "Teardrop"?) with plenty of vibrato suits the mood well. Keith Richards plays a very good lead guitar with well-executed blues licks and phrasing, and his solo in the coda (around 2:33) is a triumph. He also provides backing vocals in the coda, most likely supported by Bill Wyman. The latter gets a big sound from his bass, which he plays with a pick, and gives his part even greater prominence, by only coming in after the intro. Ian Stewart is back at the keyboard, most likely on piano, while Jack Nitzsche (probably) accompanies him on the organ, not particularly audibly. The last time the Stones played "Cry to Me" was on the television show *Ready, Steady, Go!* on October 22, 1965.

1965

OH, BABY (WE GOT A GOOD THING GOING')

Barbara Lynn Ozen / 2:08

Mick Jagger and Keith Richards (with his Gibson Les Paul) had already become the Glimmer Twins.

Another Barbara Lynn Ozen song, "I'm a Good Woman," was sampled in 2002 by Moby.

Musicians
Mick Jagger: vocals
Keith Richards: lead guitar
Brian Jones: rhythm guitar
Bill Wyman: bass
Charlie Watts: drums
Ian Stewart (?): piano
Recorded
RCA Studios, Hollywood: November 2, 1964
Technical Team
Producer: Andrew Loog Oldham
Sound engineer: Dave Hassinger

"Oh Baby" was one of singer and rhythm 'n' blues guitarist Barbara Lynn Ozen's biggest hits.

Genesis

Barbara Lynn Ozen is a singer and guitarist from Beaumont, Texas, who spent a lot of time listening to the bluesmen of the South, such as Jimmy Reed, Guitar Slim, and Brenda Lee. Under the aegis of the renowned New Orleans producer Huey P. Meaux, she recorded "You'll Lose a Good Thing" at Cosimo Matassa's J&M Studios (with Dr. John on piano), which climbed to number 1 on the R&B chart and number 8 on the *Billboard* pop chart. This song, covered not long after by Aretha Franklin, was to propel her to the forefront of the rhythm 'n' blues scene. "Oh, Baby (We Got a Good Thing Going)" is one of Barbara Lynn Ozen's most important songs.

The Rolling Stones recorded it on November 2, 1964. Their version is striking. Originally a rhythm 'n' blues song with horns, they transform it into a rock 'n' roll number carried by Keith and Brian's guitars while Mick sings: *You may talk all about me/And scandalize my name/But deep down inside me/I know I'm the only man.*

Production

Recorded during the Stones' first session at the RCA Studios in the presence of Dave Hassinger, who would stick with the group until *Between the Buttons* (1967), "Oh, Baby (We Got a Good Thing Going)" is one of a number of songs the group learned on the spot in the studio. Of such tracks Keith Richards would later say: "we'd do 'em as quickly as possible."[39] The result is of good quality, however, with the Stones imparting a very Chuck Berry feel to the Barbara Lynn song, thanks not least to Keith generously firing out guitar licks on his 1959 Gibson Les Paul. It is also the lead guitarist who opens the number with a very good intro that is quite different from the horn opening of the original version, and from the very moment the group launches into the first bar, the Stones seem perfectly in control. Brian Jones delivers a solid rhythm part in pure rock 'n' roll tradition on his Vox "Teardrop," supported by Bill Wyman's purring bass, a boogie-woogie piano part played most definitely this time by Ian Stewart, and the incomparable swing obtained by Charlie Watts from his Ludwig drum kit. As for Mick, he is completely in his element. The result is convincing, although perhaps lacking a touch of passion that would enable "Oh, Baby (We Got a Good Thing Going)" to really catch fire.

HEART OF STONE

Mick Jagger / Keith Richards / 2:51

Musicians
Mick Jagger: vocals
Keith Richards: rhythm guitar and solo, backing vocals
Brian Jones: lead and rhythm (?) guitar
Bill Wyman: bass
Charlie Watts: drums
Jack Nitzsche: piano, tambourine
Recorded
RCA Studios, Hollywood: November 2, 1964
Technical Team
Producer: Andrew Loog Oldham
Sound engineer: Dave Hassinger

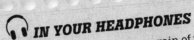

IN YOUR HEADPHONES

Charlie Watts is guilty once again of failing to adequately grease his bass drum pedal. Listening carefully, it can be heard squeaking throughout the number, most noticeably between 0:59 and 1:03 and between 1:41 and 1:43.

Genesis

Can "Heart of Stone" be regarded as the true birth of the Jagger-Richards songwriting partnership? Yes or no, this song is indicative of the maturity acquired by the group during the period between the first and second singles composed by the duo from Dartford. Whereas "Tell Me" can be classed as a pleasant enough little pop song in which a lover pines for his girlfriend, the first person in "Heart of Stone" is someone who takes a sadistic pleasure in making girls cry, someone who prides himself on having a *heart of stone* that none of them will ever be able to break. To put it bluntly, this person *ain't the kind to meet.*

After a number of carefully orchestrated media coups by Andrew Oldham—starting with the well-known headline "Would you let your sister go with a Rolling Stone?" in *Melody Maker*, the London quintet were now propagating a dark, misogynistic image of themselves in their own songs. *I ain't got no love*: clearly, this phrase from "Heart of Stone," should not be taken literally, but it nevertheless has a slogan-like quality and confirms the Stones' desire to be somewhat different.

Production

The Rolling Stones recorded "Heart of Stone" at the RCA Studios in Hollywood during their second United States tour of 1964. Dave Hassinger recalls: "I really don't know the Stones, or any of them that well. I didn't socialize with them, but we were friends in the studio . . . The first record I did was 'Heart Of Stone' . . . "[40] Contrary to their habit of entering the studio and working up numbers on the spot, some time had already been spent on "Heart of Stone" prior to the November 2 session. A demo exists (included on the 1975 album *Metamorphosis*) that had been recorded on July 21 at Regent Sound Studios in London with Bill Farley at the controls, Mick Jagger as the only representative of the Stones, a certain Jimmy Page on guitar, and Clem Cattini on drums. The words are the same (both verses and refrain). The arrangement, however, has changed. Whereas the number was originally a country-folk ballad with pedal steel guitar and vocal harmonies, at the RCA Studios "Heart of Stone" was transformed into a soul ballad in the spirit of those recorded by Otis Redding or Bobby Blue Bland.

"Heart of Stone," one of the first big Jagger-Richards hits, carried by Watts's drumming.

The Allman Brothers Band. The band from the South on their way to another hit with "Heart of Stone."

Unusually, the intro is strummed by Keith Richards on his Gibson Les Paul. He is immediately joined by Brian Jones, who comes in with the main riff, identical to that created by Jimmy Page on the Regent Sound demo. Two other guitar parts are overdubbed: a second rhythm part with plenty of vibrato (no doubt Brian on his Vox "Teardrop"), and a very good solo played with some passion by Keith. Bill Wyman provides a good bass line, supporting some excellent drumming from Charlie Watts. Based on the recollections of our esteemed bassist, it would seem that Ian Stewart is on piano. However, he is completely inaudible. On the other hand, Jack Nitzsche's tambourine is very prominent, enriched by some reasonably emphatic delay and reverb. Mick Jagger's performance is immaculate. He works the words to perfection, at times nonchalant, at times arrogant and almost fragile, but always with a rock and soul flavor to his delivery. He also double-tracks himself on the first phrase of the refrain (*'Cause you'll never break, never break, never break, never break*) in order to bring out the meaning of the words. The task of harmonizing with the singer falls to Keith alone, in a voice that would have benefited from some support by Bill or Brian. Under the aegis of Dave Hassinger and Andrew Oldham, the Stones have finally produced a truly successful creation of their own.

"Heart of Stone," which is one of the best songs on *Out of Our Heads*, was released as a single in the United States (with "What a Shame" as the B-side) on December 19, 1964. The Jagger-Richards number did well, reaching number 19 on the *Billboard* charts on February 20, 1965.

THE UNDER ASSISTANT WEST COAST PROMOTION MAN

Nanker Phelge / 3:07

Musicians
Mick Jagger: vocals
Keith Richards: lead guitar, acoustic guitar (?)
Brian Jones: harmonica, acoustic guitar (?)
Bill Wyman: bass
Charlie Watts: drums
Ian Stewart: piano
Recorded
Chess Studios, Chicago: May 10, 1965
Technical Team
Producer: Andrew Loog Oldham
Sound engineer: Ron Malo

FOR STONES ADDICTS

Does "The Under Assistant West Coast Promotion Man" reveal the influence of Bob Dylan? The long title reflects the type of song only Dylan was doing at this time.

Brian Jones with Bob Dylan in a New York City club in 1965.

Genesis

With a pen dipped in vitriol, Mick Jagger wrote the words to "The Under Assistant West Coast Promotion Man." This all-out attack on the record industry was launched by the Stones' singer at a moment when relations between Andrew Oldham and Eric Easton had reached a point of no return and Allen Klein was getting ready to enter the scene as the new manager of the London group. A tirade both skillfully ironic and cynical enables it to hit home all the more lethally, for behind this figure of the under assistant West Coast promotion man lurked a real person. During their first US tour, the Stones were accompanied by a "promo man" from London Records, a certain George Raymond Sherlock, who, according to Bill Janovitz,[15] "was a nervous guy with a George Hamilton perma-tan and teased hair." *Well I promo groups when they come into town/Well they laugh at my toupee, they sure do put me down.* Knowing they refer to a specific individual gives lines such as these all the more of an edge. It is worth pointing out that George Sherlock would later work with the Doors, Pink Floyd, and Janis Joplin . . . With this song the Rolling Stones provide a dazzling demonstration of their ability to create their own material on the basis of personal experience. Hence Jagger's use of the first person singular!

Production

Recorded at Chess Studios, "The Under Assistant West Coast Promotion Man" is a twelve-bar blues-rock number based on "Fannie Mae" by Buster Brown. Driven by the excellent rhythm machine of Charlie and Bill, it provides a good demonstration of an archetypal Stones groove. With a shuffle on the hi-hat and the bass marking every beat of the bar, Keith enters, picking a riff on his Les Paul with a plectrum. A second guitar, presumably acoustic (possibly Keith's Framus Jumbo 5/97) can also be distinguished. But is Keith or Brian responsible for the overdub? There can be no such doubt about the excellent harmonica accompaniment, which, it has to be said, gives the number all its color. It is a talented performance in which Brian goes back to his roots. Other than toward the end, Mick's performance is pretty one-dimensional and Stu's piano is not easy to hear. Finally, the group gets a chord change wrong at 2:41, trimming the blues to ten bars! This number was chosen as the B-side of the single "(I Can't Get No) Satisfaction."

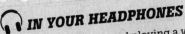
I'M FREE

Mick Jagger, Keith Richards / 2:24

Musicians
Mick Jagger: vocals, vocal harmonies
Keith Richards: lead guitar, rhythm guitar
Brian Jones: rhythm guitar (?), organ
Bill Wyman: bass
Charlie Watts: drums
James W. Alexander: tambourine

Recorded
RCA Studios, Hollywood: September 6, 1965

Technical Team
Producer: Andrew Loog Oldham
Sound engineer: Dave Hassinger

Chris Farlowe recorded a cover of "I'm Free" a year after the Stones recorded their version.

Genesis

This manifesto for freedom tells of the countercultural byways that the Rolling Stones liked to take. Whereas the civil rights movement and intellectuals in the United States were advocating an end to discrimination—in other words, freedom for all, regardless of skin color or social status—the London six were extolling individual liberty. *So love me, hold me, love me, hold me/I'm free to get what I want any old time*, sings Jagger. "I'm Free" may well have been triggered by the exhausting tours, long, restrictive recording sessions, and groupies determined to pursue the members of the band right up to their hotel rooms. However, what Jim Morrison of the Doors was saying in "When the Music's Over" was not so very different: *We want the world and we want it now.*

Production

This Jagger-Richards song recorded on September 6, 1965, is in the same vein as "Gotta Get Away." It reveals a threefold influence: the Don Covay–style folk ballad, the folk rock of the Byrds, and the Beatles, particularly in the writing and harmonization of the refrains (the words *hold me, love me* recall "Eight Days a Week." As far as the verses are concerned, the song is structured around alternating C and F chords with a bass in the key of C, a formula used in numerous songs, particularly of the country-folk type. The Stones differ by intelligently weaving three guitars, one strummed (Brian's Rickenbacker 12-string?), another played with emphatic vibrato, and a third that delivers a distinctly Byrds-like riff. In the refrains, Charlie adopts a style similar to Ringo Starr, supported by, once again, a contribution from James W. Alexander on tambourine. Brian also plays the organ (efficiently, though not very audibly), while Mick sings and double-tracks a falsetto over his vocal line. Finally, Keith overdubs a clear-sounding solo (on his Epiphone Casino?) that cannot exactly be described as inspired.

Released as the B-side of the US single "Get Off of My Cloud" on September 25, 1965, the Stones performed "I'm Free" live until the end of the sixties. They later recorded an acoustic version for the album *Stripped* (1995) and later still performed the number in front of Martin Scorsese's cameras at the Beacon Theater in New York (for the film *Shine a Light*, 2008).

THE LAST TIME

Mick Jagger / Keith Richards / 3:42

SINGLE
The Last Time / Play with Fire
RELEASE DATE
United Kingdom: February 26, 1965
Label: Decca
RECORD NUMBER: F 12104

Musicians
Mick Jagger: vocals, backing vocals (?)
Keith Richards: acoustic guitar, rhythm
guitar and guitar solo, backing vocals
Brian Jones: lead guitar
Bill Wyman: bass
Charlie Watts: drums
Jack Nitzsche: tambourine
Recorded
RCA Studios, Hollywood: January 18, February 18, 1965
Technical Team
Producer: Andrew Loog Oldham
Sound engineer: Dave Hassinger

🎧 **IN YOUR HEADPHONES**
At 1:30, Brian Jones can be heard botching a
note in his riff.

In 1967, The Who recorded "The Last Time" in order to support Mick and Keith when the two Stones found themselves in trouble with the law.

Genesis

"The Last Time" is the first out-and-out rock 'n' roll composition by Mick Jagger and Keith Richards to be used as the A-side of a single. Keith Richards: "It took us eight, nine months before we came up with 'The Last Time,' which is the first one that we felt we could give to the rest of the guys without being sent out the room. If I'd gone to the Rolling Stones with 'As Tears Go By,' it would have been 'Get out and don't come back.'"[2]

Mick and Keith wrote "The Last Time" in their London flat at 10a Holly Hill in the tranquil district of Hampstead at the end of 1964. The refrain was inspired by the Staple Singers' version of the gospel number "This May Be the Last Time," recorded for Vee-Jay in 1955. Keith Richards explains: "I think I was trying to learn it on guitar just to get the chords, sitting there playing along with the record."[9] And by dint of working away at it, he eventually came up with a song that was completely different from the original gospel number—other than the title and a good portion of the words, that is. "Mick and I played around with it for days because we weren't happy with the first title we thought up, which was The Last Time,"[1] confided Keith Richards, not without a touch of humor, to *Beat Instrumental* (April 1965). In the end, after failing to come up with anything better, they retained it. Most of the song, however, is pure Rolling Stones. It even contains the first riff that truly bears the stamp of the London group! The words, meanwhile, are addressed to a young woman who has evidently been giving her boyfriend a hard time, with the result that he has decided to leave. "The Last Time" was released as a single in the United Kingdom on February 26, 1965. By March

The Verve sampled United States Release: "The Last Time" in their hit "Bitter Sweet Symphony."

4 it had climbed to number 1, where it remained for three of its thirteen-week stay in the charts. This was the third consecutive number 1 by the group in its home country, but the first to be credited to Jagger-Richards.

"The Last Time" is not just another Rolling Stones song. It marked a decisive moment in their career. Jagger and Richards had finally established themselves as songwriters capable of getting to the top of the charts. "It gave us a level of confidence; a pathway of how to do it," admits Keith Richards, "and once we had done that, we were in the game."[9] Over the course of the following months, they demonstrated this confidence time and time again.

Production

An initial session took place at De Lane Lea Studios in London on January 11–12, 1965, but no one was happy with the results. The definitive recording followed at RCA Studios in Hollywood on January 18 with Dave Hassinger at the controls. It is Brian Jones who opens the number and brands it with the heady riff that is so emblematic of the Stones. The British group had found their musical signature, and in the future their songs would be recognizable from riffs like this, which differentiated them from any other band. Brian plays it in the middle register on his Vox "Teardrop," with reverb and probably a light vibrato courtesy of his amp. Keith accompanies him on his Framus Jumbo 5/97 acoustic and plays the solo on his Gibson Les Paul. In terms of its form, this is an unusual solo, with Keith alternating chords and licks and interweaving with Brian's riff (he has apparently doubled his solo part with another rhythm guitar). Charlie lays down a very

rock 'n' roll groove, playing his cymbal throughout the number, and Bill supports him with a bass that unfortunately gets buried in the mix. Jack Nitzsche is given a tambourine to play, which enters with the first notes of the riff, and Mick Jagger delivers a very good vocal performance, skillfully bringing out the threats he sees implied in the lyrics. He recorded this part on February 18, having decided he was unhappy with his first version, cut a month earlier to the day. To do this he returned to RCA Studios in Hollywood (without Brian Jones, Bill Wyman, and Charlie Watts) after the band returned from its Australia/New Zealand/Far East tour.

Phil Spector (standing) and Jack Nitzsche were present at the "Play with Fire" session.

SIDE B
1965

PLAY WITH FIRE

Nanker Phelge / 2:14

SINGLE

The Last Time / Play with Fire

RELEASE DATE

United Kingdom: February, 26 1965

Label: Decca
RECORD NUMBER: F 12104

Musicians

Mick Jagger: vocals, tambourine
Keith Richards: acoustic guitar
Phil Spector: bass guitar
Jack Nitzsche: harpsichord
Unidentified musician(s): percussion (bongos?)

Recorded

RCA Studios, Hollywood: January 18, 1965

Technical Team

Producer: Andrew Loog Oldham
Sound engineer: Dave Hassinger

FOR STONES ADDICTS

The film *The Darjeeling Limited* (2007) by Wes Anderson provides a very rare opportunity to hear "Play with Fire" in its entirety.

Genesis

Who is this young woman with her *diamonds* and *pretty clothes*, the daughter of an *heiress* who *owns a block in Saint John's Wood* but who gets her kicks in the poor district of Stepney? No one knows, but there is no doubt that the members of the Rolling Stones encountered characters like this in the fashionable London clubs they frequented. Was Mick Jagger writing about a three-way relationship, that is to say a man having an affair with a daughter and her mother? "Ah, the imagination of teenagers!"[1] replied Jagger when asked this question by *Rolling Stone* magazine in 1968. Either way, the Stones' singer provides a very good description in this song of the classless society that London seemed to have become in the mid-sixties that owed nothing to lineage and everything to talent.

Production

The version that can be heard on the single was cut during the night of January 18, following the recording of "The Last Time," which proved so trying. By the time they finished, it was seven o'clock in the morning. Brian, Bill, and Charlie had either fallen asleep or were already on a flight back to London. Mick and Keith were therefore the only members of the Rolling Stones to perform on "Play with Fire." They were assisted by Phil Spector (who had come to hear the group recording at Andrew Oldham's request) and Jack Nitzsche. An end-of-session atmosphere prevailed . . . "*Play with Fire* is like that," Keith Richards told Robert Greenfield in August 1971, "with Phil Spector on tune-down electric guitar [he would talk about Bill Wyman's bass in *Life* in 2010], me on acoustic, Jack Nitzsche on harpsichord, and Mick on tambourine with

Mick Jagger and Chrissie Shrimpton.

echo chamber."[11] This "medieval blues"–style number demonstrates that the Jagger-Richards duo had made considerable progress in their songwriting. It can also be seen as a prelude to other songs in the same vein, such as "Lady Jane" on the album *Aftermath* (1966). Its strength is derived in part from the unintended paring back of the instrumentation, with a very good acoustic part played by Richards on his Framus Jumbo, Nitzsche's harpsichord, and Spector's almost inaudible bass. Despite his tired-sounding voice, Jagger gives a very good performance while at the same time playing the tambourine (not always strictly in time). It is interesting to note that the percussion part (bongos?) is almost impossible to make out other than at the end of the number (2:09).

We Want The Stones ******
Everybody Needs Somebody To Love
Pain In My Heart
(Get Your Kicks On) Route 66
I'm Moving On ***
I'm Alright ***

* "We Want the Stones" is not a song but a chant uttered by an audience on the verge of hysteria, moments before its heroes Mick, Brian, Keith, Bill, and Charlie appear onstage.

** The studio recordings of "Everybody Needs Somebody to Love" and "Pain in My Heart" were released on *The Rolling Stones No. 2*, while "Route 66" is on the group's first album. The other numbers on the EP, "I'm Moving On" and "I'm Alright" have not been officially recorded by the Stones in the studio.

EP
RELEASE DATE
United Kingdom: June 11, 1965
Label: Decca
RECORD NUMBER: DFE 8620

GOT LIVE IF YOU WANT IT!

I'M MOVING ON

Hank Snow / 2:13

1965

Musicians
Mick Jagger: vocals, harmonica
Keith Richards: rhythm guitar, backing vocals (?)
Brian Jones: slide guitar
Bill Wyman: bass
Charlie Watts: drums
Recorded
Live at the Regal Theatre in Edmonton (London) on March 5 or at the Empire Theatre in Liverpool on March 6, or possibly at the Palace Theatre in Manchester on March 7
Technical Team
Producer: Andrew Loog Oldham
Sound engineer: Glyn Johns

Hank Snow, an icon of Canadian country music and composer of "I'm Moving On."

Genesis

Having recorded around 140 albums and scored more than 80 chart hits between the fifties and the seventies, Hank Snow is Canada's best-known country singer and songwriter. In March 1950 he recorded "I'm Movin' On" in Nashville. This is the story of a man who has tired of his mistress and decides to return to Tennessee to his wife. Released as a single in May 1950 (with "With This Ring, I Thee Wed" as the B-side), the song was a phenomenal success, remaining at number 1 on the country chart for twenty-one weeks (a record equaled only by "I'll Hold You in My Heart [Till I Can Hold You in My Arms]" by Eddy Arnold in 1947 and "In the Jailhouse Now" by Webb Pierce in 1957) and spending a total of forty-four weeks on the *Billboard* pop chart. The Rolling Stones have never recorded it in the studio, but it has been part of their repertoire ever since they first started to perform live.

Production

"I'm Movin' On" (along with the rest of the EP) was recorded by the IBC Mobile Unit with Glyn Johns as sound engineer. The Stones had already recorded with Johns on March 11, 1963, before signing with Decca. Before long, Johns would become one of the most important recording engineers in their career. For the time being, this live recording enabled him to discover what the group sounded like in performance. The energy is palpable as the Londoners electrify their audience. This version differs considerably from Hank Snow's, bearing more of a resemblance to Ray Charles's. The Stones opt for a blues-rock feel in which Brian's slide guitar (played on Keith's Epiphone Casino) re-creates the Chicago blues flavor that Brian had mastered to perfection. Charlie delivers some powerful drumming, supported by an excellent bass line from Bill, who zips up and down the neck of his Framus with a velocity that belies his impassive image. Keith seems to be on rhythm, and at the beginning of the number he can be heard doubling Bill's bass with a guitar sound with amp distortion. Mick is in fine form as the front man and also demonstrates his skill on the harmonica. It is most likely Keith who can be heard supporting him on backing vocals. "I'm Movin' On" is a very good number that the Stones successfully made their own.

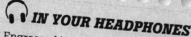
I'M ALRIGHT

Ellas McDaniel / Nanker Phelge / 2:21

Musicians
Mick Jagger: vocals, maracas
Keith Richards: lead guitar, backing vocals
Brian Jones: rhythm guitar
Bill Wyman: bass
Charlie Watts: drums
Ian Stewart: piano (?)

Recorded
Live at the Regal Theatre in Edmonton (London) on March 5 or at the Empire Theatre in Liverpool on March 6, or possibly at the Palace Theatre in Manchester on March 7

Technical Team
Producer: Andrew Loog Oldham
Sound engineer: Glyn Johns

Mick Jagger, on maracas, gives a highly energetic performance of the aptly named "I'm Alright."

Genesis

In 1963, in Myrtle Beach, South Carolina, Bo Diddley (real name Ellas McDaniel) recorded one of the most famous live albums of the entire rock 'n' roll era: *Bo Diddley's Beach Party*, with "I'm Alright" prominently featured. The Rolling Stones incorporated it into their repertoire in 1963, a time when they were on the rise. Their version is an anthem to happiness and love: . . . *it's alright all night long/It's alright all day too/Yeah it's alright, it's alright.* The number came to occupy an important place in their set list, and they gave a particularly exuberant performance of it for the recording of the EP, which took place in early March 1965. Curiously, this song copyrighted by Bo Diddley in 1963, in other words two years earlier, is credited to the Stones (Nanker Phelge). It should be pointed out that while the music is clearly Bo Diddley's, the Stones considerably reworked the words. No doubt this unusual case resulted in some kind of accommodation between the parties concerned.

Production

Energy. That is the only way to describe the Stones live. Keith opens the number with Bo Diddley's riff on his Gibson Les Paul, distorted through the amp. He is joined by Brian on his Vox "Teardrop" and soon after by Bill on his Framus. During the introduction, it is also possible to hear what sounds like bongo-style percussion, but is most probably Charlie on his medium toms. As the master of ceremonies, Mick works his audience to fan the flames into an almighty blaze. He is supported by equally unbridled backing vocals from Keith. Different pairs of maracas, played by Mick, can also be heard, sounding at times like Pete Townshend sliding down the neck of his guitar while powering the strings with a pick and at full volume. The Stones are definitely a live act.

"(I Can't Get No) Satisfaction" has been covered countless times. Among the successful versions are those by Otis Redding (with horns!), Aretha Franklin, and Devo (in cold wave style). There are also many others that it would be better to forget, however.

Frank Zappa borrowed heavily from the "Satisfaction" riff (complete with distorted sound) for the track "Hungry Freaks, Daddy," on his first album *Freak Out!* Released in 1966, this record was produced by Tom Wilson, Bob Dylan's second producer.

SIDE A 1965

(I CAN'T GET NO) SATISFACTION

Mick Jagger / Keith Richards / 3:43

SINGLE

(I Can't Get No) Satisfaction / The Spider and the Fly

RELEASE DATE

United Kingdom: August 20, 1965

Label: Decca
RECORD NUMBER: F 12220

Musicians

Mick Jagger: vocals
Keith Richards: lead guitar, rhythm guitar, acoustic guitar, backing vocals
Brian Jones (?): rhythm guitar
Bill Wyman: bass
Charlie Watts: drums
Jack Nitzsche: tambourine, piano (?)

Recorded

RCA Studios, Hollywood: May 12, 1965

Technical Team

Producer: Andrew Loog Oldham
Sound engineer: Dave Hassinger

Genesis

The Rolling Stones toured Canada and the United States between April 23 and May 29, 1965. On May 6 they were in Clearwater, Florida, for the ninth show of their North American tour. Keith Richards recalls: "I wrote 'Satisfaction' in my sleep. I had no idea I'd written it, it's only thank God for the little Philips cassette player. The miracle being that I looked at the cassette player that morning and I knew I'd put a brand-new tape in the previous night, and I saw it was at the end. Then I pushed rewind and there was Satisfaction. It was just a rough idea . . . and forty minutes of me snoring."[2]

Richards had thus sketched out what was to become the most emblematic song in the Rolling Stones' catalog. He had the riff and the phrase *I don't get no satisfaction*, which came straight from "30 Days" by his mentor Chuck Berry, complete with its grammatically dubious double negative (*If I don't get no satisfaction from the judge*). He then played it for Mick Jagger, who, by the side of the swimming pool of the Jack Tar Harrison Hotel (now the Fort Harrison Hotel) in Florida, provided the lyrics—a relentless indictment of the establishment, of the society that had developed on either side of the Atlantic since the fifties, of media disinformation, and of advertising; it is also made clear that sexual frustration is the source of much of the trouble. Mick Jagger assumes the role of chronicler of his times and, following Bob Dylan's example, his social and societal criticism is all the more effective for the derision—and a certain sense of alienation—that it contains: *But he can't be a man 'cause he doesn't smoke/ The same cigarettes as me* and *I'm tryin' to make some girl/ Who tells me baby better come back later next week/'Cause*

you see I'm on a losing streak. Jagger completed the words four days before the group entered the studio.

After undergoing a startling transformation—from acoustic folk song with harmonica to electric rock number with fuzz pedal—"(I Can't Get No) Satisfaction" was released as a single on June 6, 1965, in the United States (with "The Under Assistant West Coast Promotion Man" as the B-side) and on August 20 in the United Kingdom (with "The Spider and the Fly" as the B-side). The song was a resounding success. In the United States the single entered the charts as soon as it was released and on July 10 knocked the Four Tops' "I Can't Help Myself" off the number 1 position. In the United Kingdom, it reached number 1 on August 26 (for two weeks!) and remained on the charts for twelve weeks. It also topped the charts in West Germany, Austria, and the Netherlands, and got to number 3 in France.

Today, "(I Can't Get No) Satisfaction" is number 2 on *Rolling Stone* magazine's list of Greatest Songs of All Time. This is a verdict shared by Rickie Lee Jones: "I grew up listening to the Stones in a climate of Stones-versus-Beatles. I was a Beatle girl. The Stones were tough. Mick danced funny and had big lips. Brian was beautiful but seemed out of his mind. If I am going to pick up one song, though, I am going back to the source: Satisfaction. The guitar line has become part of our rock 'n' roll vocabulary." [41]

Production

In an interview with *Rolling Stone* magazine, Mick Jagger explains: "It sounded like a folk song when we first started working on it and Keith didn't like it much, he didn't want it

to be a single, he didn't think it would do very well. That's the only time we have had a disagreement." [42] This initial version was recorded by the Rolling Stones at Chess Studios in Chicago on May 10–11, 1965. Scott Ross, a disc jockey and a friend of the Rolling Stones, remembers listening to the song before the fuzz tone was added: "It had a harmonica track on it—Brian on harmonica. I bet Mick, Keith and Brian that it was going to be the biggest record the Stones had ever had, and that was before the fuzz-tone was put on." [6] After this session, the Rolling Stones took off for Los Angeles to record at the RCA Studios. During the course of their May 12 session, they reworked "(I Can't Get No) Satisfaction" in various different arrangements. Keith had intended to have the song's riff played by horns in the style of Otis Redding. But however much he distorted the sound through his amps, he was unable to achieve a satisfactory effect. It was then that Ian Stewart inadvertently came up with a solution when he went and bought a little magic box, the latest novelty from Gibson, otherwise known as the legendary Maestro Fuzz-Tone. Keith recalls: "And then Ian Stewart went around the corner to Wallach's Music City or something and came around with a distortion box: 'Try this.'" [11] And the result was indeed magic. With this distorted sound and the acoustic-electric arrangement, the riff's few notes took on an enormous emotional power. All that remained was to record the piece. Dave Hassinger found the sound of the riff a little slender and gave it more body by simply suppressing some of the frequencies in the middle register. Keith Richards has overdubbed the riff, with reverb, on his Gibson Firebird VII. He alternates this with the "unfuzzy" sound of his 6-string for the recording of the counterpoint

Keith Richards, the composer of "Satisfaction," one of the most famous songs in the history of rock music, written in his sleep . . .

FOR STONES ADDICTS

Although officially credited with rhythm guitar, it is thought that Brian Jones may not have been present at the recording of "(I Can't Get No) Satisfaction" at the RCA Studios, possibly because his health was already declining. What can be said for sure is that he amused himself on a few occasions by playing the notes of "Popeye the Sailorman" as Keith was launching into his famous riff. This can surely be seen as a sign of things to come!

phrases, and enriches the rhythm part by overdubbing his Gibson Heritage acoustic. Bill Wyman plays an excellent bass part that underscores the riff not identically, but at an interval of a fourth, thereby endowing the piece with an additional energy and color. Charlie Watts plays, as always, with metronomic regularity. He would later describe how, after trying out various accompaniments, he borrowed a rhythm from Roy Orbison's "Pretty Woman." Amusingly, Stevie Wonder would in turn borrow Charlie's drum motif for his November 1965 hit "Uptight (Everything's Alright)." Jack Nitzsche adds real value on the tambourine. According to Oldham, Nitzsche also plays piano, but sadly his part is completely inaudible. Finally, Mick Jagger, in a single take, adds a classic vocal part that would establish him as one of the leading rock 'n' roll singers of all time.

An Unexpected Hit

The new version of "(I Can't Get No) Satisfaction," failed to meet with unanimous approval, however. "After we listened to the master, we discussed whether or not it should be the new single. Andrew and Dave Hassinger were very positive about it, so we put it to the vote. Andrew, Dave, Stu, Brian, Charlie and I voted yes, while Mick and Keith voted no. It became the next single by majority vote."[1] Keith does not seem to have taken this vote seriously, however. Astonishingly, he did not believe that the group had just recorded a hit; quite the contrary, in fact. For him, "Satisfaction" was merely a demo in the style of Otis Redding, and the riff played through the fuzz box was no more than a stand-in for a horn line. As the Stones got back on the road after leaving the RCA Studios, they were convinced they would be recording a definitive version upon their return. But Oldham took no notice, and instead followed his own instincts. He called them up ten days or so later to announce: "The last thing you did, 'Satisfaction,' that's the single." Keith's reaction? "Suddenly I was hearing it on the radio on every station and I thought, 'I'm not going to complain,' although I never considered it to be the finished article."[9] The guitarist rightly points out that " . . . the fuzz tone had never been heard before anywhere, and that's the sound that caught everybody's imagination."[2] Strangely enough, Keith was not a fan of this sound effect, which he would use relatively little throughout his career, "(I Can't Get No) Satisfaction," one of the biggest hits in the history of rock 'n' roll, remains the property of Allen Klein's company ABKCO.

🎧 IN YOUR HEADPHONES

Keith can be heard turning on his Fuzz-Tone before the first refrain (0:35) and again for the second, where he comes in slightly late (1:35), and finally for the last, when he turns it on too early and distorts a note prior to the beginning of the riff (2:33).

Brian Jones during the Stones set at the NME Poll Winners concert. With his Vox MK III "Teardrop" slung over his shoulder.

THE SPIDER AND THE FLY

Mick Jagger / Keith Richards / 3:38

SINGLE
(I Can't Get No) Satisfaction / The Spider and the Fly
RELEASE DATE
United Kingdom: August 20, 1965
Label: Decca
RECORD NUMBER: F 12220

Musicians
Mick Jagger: vocals, harmonica
Keith Richards: lead guitar
Brian Jones: rhythm guitar
Bill Wyman: bass
Charlie Watts: drums
Recorded
RCA Studios, Hollywood: May 12, 1965
Technical Team
Producer: Andrew Loog Oldham
Sound engineer: Dave Hassinger

FOR STONES ADDICTS

An unplugged version of "The Spider and the Fly" can be found on the compilation album *Stripped*, which was released in 1995. The rinsed-out blonde is no longer thirty years old but. . . fifty.

Genesis

The nineteenth-century British poet Mary Howitt is known primarily as the author of the fable "The Spider and the Fly," published in 1829. In it she tells of the misfortunes of a fly who is seduced by the flatteries of a deceitful, manipulative spider. Were Mick Jagger and Keith Richards inspired by this dark story? Indirectly, no doubt.

From a musical point of view, "The Spider and the Fly" is a twelve-bar blues very much in the Chess tradition. Interviewed by *Rolling Stone* in 1995, Mick Jagger explains: "It's a Jimmy Reed blues with British pop-group words, which is an interesting combination: a song somewhat stuck in a time warp."

Production

The sound of the "The Spider and the Fly" resembles the Chess sound to such an extent that it could well have been recorded at the legendary studios. Furthermore, Bill Wyman, in his book *Rolling with the Stones*,[1] dates the recording to May 10, when the Stones were indeed working under Ron Malo's supervision. But Dave Hassinger was also capable of such an achievement, and a degree of doubt is therefore permissible. Keith and Brian open the number with a very good intro in which their two guitars interweave and enter into a dialogue with one another. Keith then takes up the lead, most likely on his Gibson Les Paul, and Brian launches into the rhythm part, presumably on his Vox "Teardrop." In addition to delivering a fine vocal performance, Mick also plays harmonica. Here, the Stones demonstrate once again their perfect mastery of the genre.

A SHARK
NAMED ALLEN KLEIN

"(I Can't Get No) Satisfaction" reached number 1 on the US pop chart at the beginning of July 1965, not long after the contract expired between the Rolling Stones on the one hand and Decca Records and Impact Sound on the other (May 1965). Andrew Loog Oldham, who was less a financier than a public relations man, wanted to be able to defend the interests of his group from a position of strength during the forthcoming negotiations with the bosses at Decca. The right person to support him in this delicate task was no longer Eric Easton (alongside whom he had negotiated the Stones' first contract with the major label), but Allen Klein. Keith Richards recalls that Easton was tired: "My attitude at the time was that Eric Easton, Andrew's partner and our agent, was just too tired. In fact he was ill. Onward. Whatever happened later with Allen Klein, he was brilliant at generating cash."[2] In reality, Oldham had wanted to split from Easton ever since he had discovered that Easton had unscrupulously and secretively taken control of the Stones' early songs in 1963 through the agency of South-Eastern Music, a publishing company in which he had an active interest.

A Businessman Through and Through

By 1965, the formidable reputation of Allen Klein as a businessman had already crossed the Atlantic. After studying at Upsala College in New Jersey, this son of Jewish immigrants from Budapest, born in Newark in 1931, passionately wanted to work in the recording industry, which was then experiencing an unprecedented boom in the United States. Taken on by the Harry Fox Agency as adviser to Joe Fenton, Klein was responsible for collecting mechanical rights (those of Dot Records in particular) and redistributing them to the music publishers. Luck was apparently on his side, for he bumped into a former Upsala student named Don Kirshner, who had just founded the music publisher Aldon Music (1958) in partnership with Al Nevins. Kirshner knew everyone in the New York music business, from Jerry Leiber and Mike Stoller to Carole King, Gerry Goffin, and Phil Spector. This was the break Klein had been looking for. In 1960, he set up Allen

Klein and Company, renaming it ABKCO Industries (an acronym of Allen & Betty Klein and Company) a few months later. Although Bobby Darin was one of the first singers and composers whose career he managed, it was as the business manager of Sam Cooke, whose contract with RCA he completely revised, both financially and artistically, that he acquired his reputation as a fearsome businessman.

One Contract May Conceal Another

Andrew Oldham therefore got in touch with Allen Klein during the period following the phenomenal success of "(I Can't Get No) Satisfaction." The US businessman assured him that he could force Decca to revise the clauses in the contract for both the United States and the United Kingdom, but that he could not do it without the agreement of the Rolling Stones themselves. The two men agreed to meet at the Columbia Records convention in Miami. Mick Jagger, who happened to be on vacation in the United States at the time, also attended this meeting. Soon afterward, Oldham sent Klein a letter in which he officially agreed to the negotiation of a new recording contract and undertook to inform Eric Easton and the members of the Rolling Stones immediately. A second letter followed, setting out that even after expiration of the contract, Klein would continue to receive twenty percent of the group's royalties in the United States and Canada (but not in Europe).

On July 26, 1965 Allen Klein met the five members of the Rolling Stones for the first time at the Hilton Hotel in London and revealed the strategy he was planning to employ with Decca. The next day, the Stones learned to their amazement of the initial contract between Impact Sound and Decca, whereby Andrew Oldham and Eric Easton received fourteen percent of royalties from all the Stones' discs, while passing on a mere six percent to the members of the group, a percentage from which they deducted a further twenty-five percent as a management fee. This gave Allen Klein a free hand to act.

On July 29, 1965, Klein, supported by his attorney Marty Machat, succeeded in obtaining a far more attractive contract

Allen Klein becomes the Stones' business manager. For better at first, for worse later on . . .

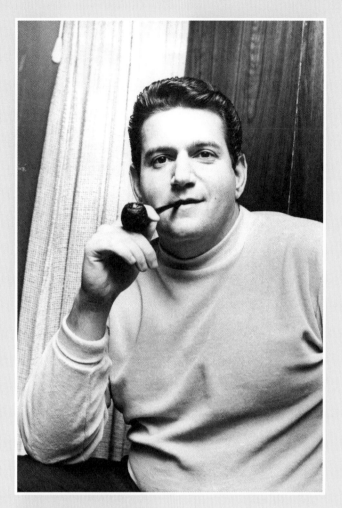

from Sir Edward Lewis, the chairman of Decca: an advance on royalties of $600,000 for the first year, followed by $700,000 per annum for the next ten years, from July 30, 1965, to July 1, 1974 (after the definitive removal of Eric Easton, that is). "[Sir Edward Lewis] was on his last legs, let's face it," remembers Keith Richards. "We just stood there with shades on. It was really the old guard and the new. They crumbled and we walked out of there with a deal bigger than the Beatles'. And this is where you've got to take your hat off to Allen."[2]

Setting a Wolf to Mind the Sheep

Not everyone in the group shared his enthusiasm. Bill Wyman was not particularly impressed with Klein's verve and came to regret that none of the Stones had been able to have their contract read by an attorney before signing: "My fears about Allen Klein proved to be well-founded."[1] Allen Klein was far from acting solely in the interests of the Rolling Stones. First and foremost, he was acting in his own. Over the course of the months that followed, the Stones' initial faith in him gave way to mistrust. After the financial expert and friend of the group Prince Rupert Loewenstein read the various contracts carefully and went over the accounts with a fine-tooth comb in 1970, it would be no exaggeration to describe the situation as open conflict. Not only did Mick, Keith, Bill, and Charlie discover that Klein had not paid their tax for several years (a colossal sum in Britain during the second half of the sixties and one that threatened to ruin them), they also, more seriously, found out that after paying them a million dollars in the form of a minimum guarantee, he was able to exploit the Jagger-Richards catalog as he saw fit via his company ABKCO. On July 20, 1971, when their contract with Decca expired, the Rolling Stones removed Allen Klein and replaced him with Prince Loewenstein. The following year they instituted legal proceedings against Klein, and also against Andrew Oldham and Eric Easton, for the recovery of several million dollars. Despite this, Jagger and Richards would never regain possession of the songs they had written in the sixties!

History Repeats Itself

The Rolling Stones were not the only group to have had difficulties with Allen Klein. So too did the Beatles. After the death of Brian Epstein in August 1967, the four members of the Liverpudlian band started to look after their own affairs, but without possessing any real business acumen. Two years later, Apple's finances were in urgent need of attention, and the Beatles needed a business manager they could trust. John proposed Allen Klein, whose aggressive, direct style suited him perfectly. George and Ringo agreed, and Klein was duly engaged by the majority of the Beatles on February 3, 1969. Paul, however, steadfastly refused to sign the slightest contract with the new business manager (which did not prevent the latter from renegotiating the Beatles' contract with EMI). Furthermore, on December 31, 1970, he brought an action against John, George, Ringo, and the management of Apple, aiming to bring about the end of the Beatles as a legal entity. His motive was to prevent Klein from appropriating the Beatles' back catalog as he had the Stones' songs from the sixties. Soon afterward, following the misappropriation of funds from the humanitarian Concert for Bangladesh (1971), organized by George Harrison, the latter would sever all ties with Allen Klein, as would John Lennon and Ringo Starr. George Harrison had made his feelings clear in the song "Beware of Darkness" on the album *All Things Must Pass*, which was released in 1970. Allen Klein died in New York on July 4, 2009.

SIDE A
1965

The five Rolling Stones in the back of a van. The only way to avoid the rampaging fans.

GET OFF OF MY CLOUD

Mick Jagger / Keith Richards / 2:55

SINGLE
Get Off of My Cloud / The Singer Not the Song
RELEASE DATE
United Kingdom: October 22, 1965
Label: Decca
RECORD NUMBER: F 12263

Musicians
Mick Jagger: vocals
Keith Richards: rhythm guitar, backing vocals
Brian Jones: lead guitar, acoustic guitar (?)
Bill Wyman: bass, backing vocals (?)
Charlie Watts: drums
Ian Stewart: piano
Unidentified musician(s): hand claps
Recorded
RCA Studios, Hollywood: September 5, 1965
Technical Team
Producer: Andrew Loog Oldham
Sound engineer: Dave Hassinger

Genesis

"(I Can't Get No) Satisfaction" was still on the charts and still being given plenty of airtime when Andrew Oldham asked the Rolling Stones where their next single was. The five had not exactly been idle since the release of their worldwide hit. They had appeared on one television program after another in the United Kingdom (*Ready, Steady Go!*, *Live*, *Scene at 6.30*, and *Thank Your Lucky Stars*) and had performed in Dublin and Belfast on September 3 and 4. In short there was no let-up in the pace of their lives . . . And this was to be the subject of their new song.

With words by Mick Jagger and music by Keith Richards, "Get Off of My Cloud" is a raw, energetic reflection on what it is to be a rock star, a life that is not without its good side, but which can also be a living hell. Keith Richards would later describe it as "basically a response to people knocking on our door asking us for the follow-up to 'Satisfaction.'"[9] By "people," the musician means not just fans but also professionals in the recording industry including, of course, Oldham himself.

"Get Off of My Cloud" is a song about alienation and not, as some people would have it, drugs, a claim that led some radio stations to ban the song. In fact, it is a song about alienation that Mick Jagger, the lyricist, would turn into a protest song against Middle America: "The grown-up world was a very ordered society in the early '60s, and I was coming out of it. America was even more ordered than anywhere else. I found it was a very restrictive society in thought and behavior and dress."[19] The singer added: " . . . New York was wonderful and so on, and L.A. was also kind of interesting. But outside of that we found it the most repressive society, very prejudiced in

Screaming Lord Sutch, who plays a key role in the video for "Get Off of My Cloud."

every way. There was still segregation. And the attitudes were fantastically old-fashioned. Americans shocked me by their behavior and their narrow-mindedness."[19] Jagger was laying into a narrow-minded United States that had exalted advertising to the status of supreme value, and was shouting a warning: *Get off of my cloud*. This warning would become number 1 in the United States and the United Kingdom on November 6 and October 28, respectively.

Production

Recorded on September 5, 1965, "Get Off of My Cloud" opens with Charlie playing his Ludwig Super Classic Blue Pearl kit in a spirit not so far removed from the break he plays with abundant reverb on "Satisfaction." The guitars then enter with a three-chord sequence (intro and verses) that features in hundreds of rock numbers, including, to name just a few, "La Bamba" by Ritchie Valens, "Twist and Shout" by the Isley Brothers, and "Louie Louie" by the Kingsmen. Brian applies himself to playing a short and extremely insistent phrase on his Rickenbacker "1993" 12-string, while Keith plays rhythm on his Gibson Firebird. He refrains from using his Maestro Fuzz-Tone this time, not wishing to overexploit the phenomenal success of the "Satisfaction" riff. He nevertheless obtains a weighty, highly charged sound (with the Firebird plugged into a Fender Showman) that is ideal for this number. It is just

about possible to make out an acoustic guitar, presumably played by Brian, and another electric guitar part providing support in the refrain. (Listen to the stereo version of the song.) Bill is not to be outdone, providing a very good bass line that travels up and down the length of the neck of his Framus Humbug. As in numerous television programs from this time, he also seems to be sharing the backing vocals with Keith. Stu is on piano, but his playing is barely audible. Keith reports that the group solicited his help whenever the sound needed padding out: "Stu, this sounds a bit thin. Can you just play a little piano under it?"[34] And Stu would make his usual discreet but indispensable contribution. Finally, Mick sings his words with a certain aggression, but his voice gets somewhat buried in the mix and is not always particularly intelligible. Keith would later describe Oldham's work on the track as being one of his "worst productions."[11] He also claims that he never cared for the finished recording. In 1971 he confided to Robert Greenfield that "The chorus was a nice idea,"[11] but he regretted that the production had been rushed in order to follow up on the success of "Satisfaction," and also that the initial tempo had been sped up at Oldham's request: "Actually, what I wanted was to do it slow like a Lee Dorsey thing."[11] Was he thinking here of "Ya Ya," the Dorsey hit from 1961? The fact remains that "Get Off of My Cloud" rose to the top of the charts on both sides of the Atlantic as soon as it was released.

The Beatles seem to have inspired the melody of "The Singer Not the Song."

SIDE B
1965

THE SINGER NOT THE SONG

Mick Jagger / Keith Richards / 2:22

SINGLE
Get Off of My Cloud / The Singer Not the Song
RELEASE DATE
United Kingdom: October 22, 1965
Label: Decca
RECORD NUMBER: F 12263

Musicians
Mick Jagger: vocals
Keith Richards: 6-string and 12-string acoustic guitar, backing vocals
Brian Jones: 12-string electric guitar
Bill Wyman: bass
Charlie Watts: drums
Recorded
RCA Studios, Hollywood: September 5 or 6, 1965
Technical Team
Producer: Andrew Loog Oldham
Sound engineer: Dave Hassinger

Genesis

Mick Jagger and Keith Richards borrowed the title for the B-side of the British single "Get Off of My Cloud" from a 1961 feature film directed by Roy Ward Baker. This film created something of a stir upon its release because it deals with the love of a seductive young woman for a Catholic priest, and the ambiguous relationship between the priest and a criminal. The latter is an atheist and although he accepts the priest (the singer), he does not accept his religion (the song). Mick Jagger adapts this idea by transposing it to the relationship between a man and a woman. What he wants to get across is no doubt that the important thing for the man is not simply to be with a woman, but to choose one who understands him. The last verse reveals that for the narrator *There's something wrong.* Has he chosen an unsuitable companion after all?

Production

"The Singer Not the Song" is not for the squeamish! The number fails on account of its poor recording and is frightfully out of tune. Who is to blame? Brian with his Rickenbacker 12-string or Keith with his Harmony 12-string or possibly his 6-string acoustic? It is difficult to say. Possibly both. Moreover, the harmonies in the choruses are far from perfect. And if, on top of all this, one also takes into account the songwriters' significant borrowings from the Beatles' number "Not a Second Time" (on the album *With the Beatles*, 1963), the verdict cannot be altogether positive. Why none of the members of the group, nor Jack Nitzsche, Dave Hassinger, or Andrew Loog Oldham expressed any misgivings about the results is a mystery. Fortunately, not everything about the song is bad: Mick delivers a

Bill Wyman, his attention keenly focused on the daily lives of the Stones.

good vocal performance (double-tracked) although he sometimes seems to lack any point of reference against which to adjust his voice. Bill's bass and Charlie's drumming are beyond reproach, and the concluding harmonies, still very Beatles in style, and pretty ambitious, work reasonably well in spite of everything. The falsetto part, which comes as something of a surprise on a Stones record, seems to be sung by Keith. The final outcome is disappointing, and it is a shame that greater care was not taken with the production.

The punk singer Patti Palladin covered "The Singer Not the Song," which was released on the compilation album *Destination Bomp* in 1994.

She Said Yeah
Talkin' About You
You Better Move On
Look What You've Done *
The Singer, Not The Song
(Get Your Kicks On) Route 66
Get Off Of My Cloud
I'm Free
As Tears Go By
Gotta Get Away
Blue Turns To Grey *
I'm Moving On

* Seules ces chansons sont des inédits
et seront traitées dans ce cha...

ALBUM
RELEASE DATE
United States:
December 4, 1965
Label: London Records
RECORD NUMBER: LONDON LL 3451
Number 4, thirty-three
weeks on the charts

DECEMBER'S CHILDREN (AND EVERYBODY)

1965

DECEMBER'S CHILDREN, THE BEAT ALBUM OF THE STONES

The Album

This album can be seen as a kind of end-of-year gift from London Records to US fans of the Rolling Stones. This "made in the USA" opus brings together twelve numbers recorded between August 1963 and October 1965 in different places and for different records. "She Said Yeah," "Talkin' About You," "I'm Free," and "Gotta Get Away" are from the British version of *Out of Our Heads*. "You Better Move On" is taken from the EP *The Rolling Stones*. "Get Off of My Cloud" and "The Singer Not the Song" had previously been released as a single, as had "As Tears Go By." "Route 66" and "I'm Moving On" are from the EP *Got Live If You Want It!* Only "Look What You've Done" and "Blue Turns to Grey" had not previously been released.

December's Children (and Everybody's) reuses the cover image, Gered Mankowitz's superb black-and-white photograph, from the British version of *Out of Our Heads*. The title was chosen by Oldham, who was looking for a fashionable idea inspired by "beat poetry,"[19] as Mick Jagger would later put it. The album reached number 4 on the charts.

The superb
Rickenbacker
12-string that Brian
Jones uses on "Blue
Turns to Grey."

LOOK WHAT YOU'VE DONE

McKinley Morganfield / 2:16

Musicians
Mick Jagger: vocals
Keith Richards: rhythm guitar
Brian Jones: harmonica
Bill Wyman: bass
Charlie Watts: drums
Ian Stewart: piano
Recorded
Chess Studios, Chicago: June 11, 1964
Technical Team
Producer: Andrew Loog Oldham
Sound engineer: Ron Malo

Genesis

This song, released as a single in 1960 (with "Love Affair" as the A-side), was originally recorded by Muddy Waters, the bluesman whose influence helped the Rolling Stones to become the number one British blues-rock group. In it the guitarist from Rolling Fork, Mississippi, confides his troubles. His wife or girlfriend has left him, leaving him all alone with a permanently broken heart. Left with nothing but memories, he hears a bird crying in the distance as night falls . . . Ray Manzarek, the future keyboard player with the Doors, said that "Look What You've Done" was actually written not by Muddy Waters but by a pair of young songwriters, one of whom was himself, who supposedly sent a demo of their song to Chess in Chicago only to discover some time later, to their enormous delight, that it had been recorded by none other than Muddy Waters. The only problem is that it was credited not to them but to a certain McKinley Morganfield . . .

Production

The Rolling Stones recorded this version of "Look What You've Done" during a two-day spell (June 10 and 11, 1964) at Chess Studios, the fief of Muddy Waters. Once again it is Brian Jones who lends the number its distinctive color, with harmonica playing that soulfully evokes a person carrying all the troubles of the world on his shoulders. It is worth stressing again just how good Jones was on this instrument. As if further proof were necessary, he plays an absolutely superb solo (1:05). The group's gradual abandoning of the blues, a genre that Brian Jones so loved, and for which he had a passion that he was so good at transmitting, is without a doubt a cause for regret. On this number he shares the glory with Ian Stewart, who plays an excellent boogie-woogie piano, likewise demonstrating his love of the genre. Keith, playing rhythm on his Epiphone Casino, is the only guitar. He is supported by Bill and Charlie, who play their parts with the utmost serenity, providing Mick with a solid foundation for the lyrics, which the singer nevertheless delivers with a certain restraint. The result of the supposed presence of Muddy Waters at the recording? The Stones' version is in no way unworthy of the original. On the contrary, they contribute a subtly British feel to the number that differentiates them from their US elder.

The Doors' keyboard player Ray Manzarek claims to have co-written "Look What You've Done."

1965

BLUE TURNS TO GREY

Mick Jagger / Keith Richards / 2:30

Musicians
Mick Jagger: vocals
Keith Richards: rhythm guitar, backing vocals
Brian Jones: 12-string guitar
Bill Wyman: bass
Charlie Watts: drums
Recorded
RCA Studios, Hollywood: September 5 or 6, 1965
Technical Team
Producer: Andrew Loog Oldham
Sound engineer: Dave Hassinger

Genesis

Mick Jagger and Keith Richards were clearly in a poetic frame of mind when they started to write songs together. "Blue Turns to Grey" tells the story of a pitiful romantic youth who is abandoned to his sad fate by his girlfriend. While waiting to find her again, or for another girl to come along and make him forget his pain, *blue turns to grey. I feel so down,* sings Mick Jagger.

In February 1965, this song by the Dartford duo was recorded more or less simultaneously by the Mighty Avengers, a vocal group produced by Oldham, and Dick & Dee Dee, a US pop duo (also produced by Oldham, who met the pair at the *TAMI. Show* in 1964). However, it was Cliff Richard & The Shadows who made the song a hit in the United Kingdom, taking their version, which they recorded at Abbey Road studios, to number 15 on the charts in March 1966. The Stones' recording, meanwhile, dates from September 5 or 6, 1965.

Production

"Blue Turns to Grey" demonstrates just how far the Jagger-Richards songwriting partnership had developed since "Tell Me." "Mick and I were still learning how to write material for the Stones,"[11] Keith Richards would later claim. Nevertheless, this number reveals a certain mastery in the composition of both music and words. It is a ballad, which Brian Jones gives a Byrds-like electric folk flavor with his Rickenbacker "1993" 12-string played with abundant vibrato. Keith also uses plenty of vibrato on his 6-string electric (Gibson Firebird VII or Epiphone Casino) which both harmonizes with, and provides the perfect support for, Brian's playing. The combination of the two guitars is brilliant. The bass and drums provide a highly successful pop rhythm, and Mick Jagger delivers a very good performance of his lyrics. He is accompanied in the choruses by Keith, while also apparently double-tracking his own voice. "Blue Turns to Grey" is a very good song (that bears some resemblance to "Mercy, Mercy" in its soft version), and if the Stones did not record it for *Out of Our Heads*, this must be because they thought its Byrds-like character was better suited to their US audience.

With "Blue Turns to Grey," Keith Richards demonstrated that he had made considerable progress in the writing of ballads.

Mother's Little Helper
Stupid Girl
Lady Jane
Under My Thumb
Doncha Bother Me
Goin' Home
Flight 505
High And Dry
Out Of Time
It's Not Easy
I Am Waiting
Take It Or Leave It
Think
What To Do

ALBUM
RELEASE DATE
United Kingdom: April 15, 1966
Label: Decca
RECORD NUMBERS: LK 4786 (MONO), DECCA SKL 4786 (STEREO)
Number 1 for 8 weeks

AFTER-MATH

1966

AFTERMATH:
THE SOUNDTRACK OF SWINGING LONDON

Aftermath marked the end of the Rolling Stones' apprenticeship and the beginning of a golden age for the band that would continue into the first half of the seventies. *Aftermath*, *Between the Buttons* (1967), *Their Satanic Majesties Request* (1967), *Beggars Banquet* (1968), *Let It Bleed* (1969), *Sticky Fingers* (1971), *Exile on Main St.* (1972): the Stones' output during these years constitutes a brilliant body of work virtually unrivaled in the musical history of the twentieth century (one exception, no doubt, being the Beatles). What had become apparent from listening to the singles "(I Can't Get No) Satisfaction" and "Get Off of My Cloud" was now confirmed by the Stones' fourth (British) album: liberated from various overwhelming influences, notably that of the Chicago bluesmen, the Rolling Stones were now creating their own music. From "Mother's Little Helper" to "What to Do," *Aftermath* was, in a sense, the soundtrack of Swinging London, a gift to hip young people. *Aftermath* was one of the brightest stars of the new culture (or counterculture) that was to reach its zenith the following year in the Summer of Love.

The Album

Aftermath therefore represents a very clear departure in the career of the Rolling Stones. "That was a big landmark record for me,"[19] confesses Mick Jagger. It was the first album made up entirely of original compositions, all credited to Jagger-Richards. The styles are varied and numerous: rock, blues, Baroque, classical, pop, country, world music, R&B.

The LP is even infused with traces of Phil Spector, Smokey Robinson, and Otis Redding. "It was the period where everything—songwriting, recording, performing—stepped into a new league," writes Keith, "and the time when Brian started going off the rails."[2] Indeed, as the Glimmer Twins were gaining a greater influence over the artistic choices of the group, Brian saw his status as leader slipping away for good. Feeling progressively more excluded, his behavior started to become increasingly erratic and problematic.

However, Brian was not the only fly in the ointment. *Aftermath* would also reveal an initial rift between the band members and Oldham. On the subject of their manager, Keith revealed to a journalist in the *New Musical Express* in February 1966 that "The Stones have practically become a projection of his own ego."[1] The presence on the scene of Allen Klein, and the various activities he was forcing the band to undertake, was also starting to become a strain.

Throughout that year, however, Oldham continued to retain firm control of their destinies, managing the band with skill and efficiency. And for the first time, he encouraged the Stones to prioritize the LP over singles. When the producer (still as formidable a public relations man as ever) declared on April 16, 1966, in *Disc* magazine that "Their songs reflect the world around them. I think it's better than anything they've done before,"[30] he was not exaggerating. In spite of the infernal pace of their touring in 1965, which extended virtually without interruption from January 6 (Belfast) to December 5 (San Diego and Los Angeles), Mick and Keith progressed

Blond and glamorous: Brian and Anita, the sixties couple par excellence.

Brian Jones derived a newfound confidence from his role during the *Aftermath* sessions. In his private life, he was enjoying a great romance with Anita Pallenberg.

FOR STONES ADDICTS

Bill Wyman describes how *Aftermath* was supposed to have been used as the soundtrack for a Nicholas Ray movie *Back, Behind and in Front*. The project never got off the ground because Mick failed to see eye to eye with the director.

enormously as songwriters. Comparisons were already being made with Lennon and McCartney, and with Bob Dylan.

Settling Scores

What is clear is that the Dartford duo were positioning themselves firmly on the fringes of society. For these two there was no question of sharing some generalized, openmouthed optimism, and this they made very clear. As a lyricist, Mick Jagger was indulging in some score settling, not infrequently through language and imagery that had the power to hurt. Already accused of misogyny, the Stones' singer was now going a step further by demonstrating an Oscar Wildean disdain for the apparently weaker sex. In "Stupid Girl," which may well have been intended as an indirect attack on his first (official!) girlfriend, Chrissie Shrimpton, his targets are the supposed greed and facile certitudes of women. In "Under My Thumb," "Out of Time," and even "Think," a man's revenge on his mistress (or perhaps wife) becomes a source of real pleasure, while in "High and Dry," the cynicism of a former lover is almost a work of art. On the other hand, Jagger was also capable of showing compassion toward women. In "Mother's Little Helper," he evokes the daily existence of a model wife who has to swallow countless little yellow pills in order to cope with her life, while in "Lady Jane" he assumes the guise of a troubadour in what is effectively a paean to courtly love.

Women, that is to say lovers and wives, are not the only targets of Mick and Keith's invective. In the aforementioned "Mother's Little Helper," as in "What to Do," modern society stands accused of being the source of everyone's woes. The duo's criticisms are also leveled at their own lives as rock stars: the never-ending tours in "Goin' Home" and the fans who copy their idols to the point of mimicry in "Doncha Bother Me." All in all, *Aftermath* is a somber album in which desolation, paranoia, despair, and frustration are echoed as track succeeds track.

A "Brian Jones" Sound

The darker themes make for a stark contrast with the music. With the exception of "Doncha Bother Me" and "It's Not Easy"—the first being very Chicago blues and the second very Chuck Berry in tone—the tracks on *Aftermath* resemble nothing the London group had previously recorded. With this record the Rolling Stones style of art rock came into being, one that the band would pursue on the albums *Between the Buttons* and *Their Satanic Majesties Request*. Although Mick Jagger and Keith Richards were the creators of this new musical aesthetic—after all, it was exclusively to them that Oldham entrusted the task of songwriting—Brian Jones was the conductor or, more accurately, the architect. The new sound of the Stones was most definitely Brian. At this time he was the best musician of the five, but he did not write. He sought to overcome this frustration by playing numerous different instruments. Brian was already known as an excellent harmonica player and inspired slide guitarist. During the course of *Aftermath* he reveals other aspects of his artistic curiosity: the dulcimer on "Lady Jane" and "I Am Waiting," the electric 12-string on "Mother's Little Helper," the marimba on "Under My Thumb" and "Out of Time," the harpsichord and bells on "Take It or Leave It." It is from this experimentation that the album derives its musical diversity. The photographer Gered Mankowitz explains: "He was amazing. He could literally play any musical instrument you put into his hands, regardless of whether he'd ever seen it before. He must be remembered for that."[42] In this sense, *Aftermath* was definitely Brian Jones's album!

Could You Walk on the Water?

The Rolling Stones' fourth studio album was released in the United Kingdom on April 15, 1966, a month before Bob Dylan's *Blonde on Blonde* and the Beach Boys' *Pet Sounds* (which were issued on the same day, May 16, 1966), and three

A new sonority for the Stones' fourth (British) album. Brian Jones plays the dulcimer.

months before the Beatles' *Revolver*. Andrew Loog Oldham initially dreamed of calling the album *Could You Walk on the Water*, provoking an agitated response form the directors of London Records in the United States, who did not want to incite the wrath of the Christians. Thus the choice eventually fell on *Aftermath*. The album was received rapturously by the press. In the *NME*, Keith Altman wrote: "Those masterminds behind the electric machines—The Rolling Stones—have produced the finest value for money ever on their new LP."[44] The public also gave the album the reception it deserved: in the United Kingdom, *Aftermath* was number 1 for eight consecutive weeks, toppling from the top spot the soundtrack to *The Sound of Music*, and remained on the charts for twenty-eight weeks.

In the United States, the new Stones album went on sale on June 20, 1966 (July 2 according to Bill Wyman), and featured just eleven tracks. "Mother's Little Helper" (which was released as a single with "Lady Jane" as the B-side, reaching number 8 on August 13, 1966), "Out of Time," "Take It or Leave It," and "What to Do" had mysteriously disappeared, while "Paint It Black" (released as a single in the United Kingdom on May 13, 1966) had been added. The album nevertheless reached number 2 on the *Billboard* chart and was certified platinum.

The Album Cover

The musical change of *Aftermath* was not accompanied by any revolutionary graphic design for the sleeve of the British album. The cover image is a close-up of the faces of the five Rolling Stones aligned diagonally against a background that veers from pale pink to black. The album title is split over two lines. The photograph was taken by Guy Webster, who was also responsible for the sleeve of the first Doors album (*The Doors*, 1967). The cover design is credited to Sandy Beach, in reality none other than Andrew Loog Oldham. Brian was not happy with it and made this clear to *Melody Maker* in April 1966: "I don't like the album cover Andrew did."[1] The black-and-white photographs on the reverse of the album were taken, most probably at the recording session on December 8, 1965, by Jerry Schatzberg (who was also the photographer for Dylan's *Blonde on Blonde*, before becoming a celebrated filmmaker).

The photograph adorning the cover of the US LP, credited to David Bailey, corresponds better to the Stones' new artistic direction. It shows Brian and Keith in the foreground with Mick, Charlie, and Bill behind. It is a color photo with a black background, deliberately blurred in an allusion to the psychedelic movement.

Production

The Rolling Stones brought their 1965 US tour to a close with two concerts in California on December 5: the first at Golden Hall in San Diego, the second in the Los Angeles Memorial Sports Arena. Three days later, they entered the RCA Studios in Hollywood, with which they were by now extremely familiar. The sound engineer Dave Hassinger was

The Rolling Stones
at the Olympia in
Paris, March 1966.

waiting for them. "It's been great working with the Stones, who, contrary to the countless jibes of mediocre comedians all over the world, are real professionals, and a gas to work with,"[45] he writes on the back of the album sleeve. This was the first time since their debut LP that they would record an entire album in the same studio with the same sound engineer. They would only spend two sessions cutting the tracks, the first between December 8 and 10, 1965, and the second between March 6 and 9, 1966. The album, along with various other tracks that were to appear on different compilations and singles, would take just seven days to record. Hassinger later spoke of this speed of execution: "Whereas today, we might spend as much as six months on a contemporary project. But the Stones . . . they really knew what they were after and they really knew when they had it. They never went for perfection. They went for total feel. You could have a little mistake, as long as it didn't disturb the feel or if it wasn't distracting."[33]

"19th Nervous Breakdown," which was released as a single, came into being on December 8, 1965. Between December 8 and 10, 1965 the Stones recorded "Mother's Little Helper," "Doncha Bother Me," "Take It or Leave It," "Think," "Ride On Baby" (included on the compilations Flowers [1967] and The Rest of the Best [1983]), "Sittin' on the Fence" (on the compilations Flowers, Through the Past Darkly [1969], More Hot Rocks [Big Hits & Fazed Cookies] [1972], and The Rest of the Best), and "Sad Day" (B-side of the US single "19th Nervous Breakdown," and included on the compilations No Stone Unturned, The Rest of the Best, The Rolling Stones Singles—The London Years [1989]).

At the end of these three days of recording, Charlie voiced his enthusiasm: "We recorded 10 numbers, I think that musically they are the best thing that we've ever done."[1] After appearing on various television shows in the United Kingdom and the United States, and then touring Australia and

New Zealand (between February 18 and March 1), the group returned to the RCA Studios, where between March 6 and 9, 1966, they recorded "Out of Time," "Lady Jane," "It's Not Easy," and "Stupid Girl," plus "Paint It Black" and "Long Long While," which were released as the two sides of a single in the United Kingdom (and separately included on the compilations More Hot Rocks [Big Hits & Fazed Cookie], No Stone Unturned, The Rest of the Best, The Rolling Stones Singles—The London Years), and then "Under My Thumb," "High and Dry," "Flight 505," "I Am Waiting," and "What to Do."

Keith Richards reflects on the recording of the LP: "On albums like December's Children and Aftermath, I did the parts that Brian normally would have done. Sometimes I'd overlay eight guitars and then just maybe use one bar of the takes here and there in the mixing, so at the end of it, it sounds like it's two or three guitars and you're not even counting anymore. But there's actually eight in there, and they're just in and out, in the mix."[2] The final result is an unmitigated success. The Stones took a little longer in the studio, and this shows in the individual tracks. "Our previous sessions have always been rush jobs," explains Keith. "This time we were able to relax a little, take our time."[1] The studios were surrounded night and day by increasing numbers of fans who indulged in ever more intrusive behavior. However, nothing really interfered with the recording process as everyone was determined to benefit from this period of relative calm to throw themselves into the making of the new album. Even Brian Jones, who was repeatedly found taking a nap during the sessions . . .

The Instruments
Numerous new musical instruments made their appearance on Aftermath. Most of them, including the marimba, the dulcimer, and the sitar, were played by Brian Jones. He also added to his collection of guitars, starting with a superb

Multi-instrumentalist Brian Jones plays the sitar in a performance of "Paint It Black."

The 6-string Gibson Hummingbird would become one of Keith's favorite acoustic guitars.

Rickenbacker 360/12 (the same model that George Harrison and Roger McGuinn played), after his Rickenbacker "1993" 12-string was stolen during the group's fourth North American tour (October 29–December 5, 1965). Like Keith Richards, he also acquired a Gibson Firebird "non-reverse" (their previous model being a "reverse") and a Gibson Hummingbird 6-string acoustic. Keith also treated himself to a Guild M-65 Freshman. Bill Wyman, although remaining faithful to his Framus Humbug, recorded with a Vox Wyman bass designed especially for him. As for Charlie Watts, in addition to his Ludwig Super Classic, the drummer also plays xylophone, bongos, and finger cymbals on the album. Other instruments, such as harpsichord, organ, and piano, were also used during the sessions but have not all been identified.

In 1967, the Stones, who had been captivated by the sublime Brigitte Bardot, were offered a role in the French star's next movie, *Two Weeks in September*, directed by Serge Bourguignon. They declined in the belief that they would soon be making their own full-length movie, although this never came to fruition. What a shame!

MOTHER'S LITTLE HELPER

Mick Jagger / Keith Richards / 2:45

Musicians
Mick Jagger: vocals
Keith Richards: 12-string electric guitar, 6-string acoustic guitar, backing vocals
Brian Jones: 12-string electric guitar
Bill Wyman: bass
Charlie Watts: drums
Recorded
RCA Studios, Hollywood: December 8–10, 1965
Technical Team
Producer: Andrew Loog Oldham
Sound engineer: Dave Hassinger

Bill Wyman with his Framus Humbug bass, on which he performs the prominent glissandos on "Mother's Little Helper."

Genesis

Keith Richards probably composed this number during the Stones' sixth British tour (September 24 to October 17, 1965) or else during their fourth North American tour (October 29 to December 5, 1965). Mick Jagger wrote the words. *What a drag it is getting old*: the first line encapsulates the theme of the song. Jagger turns the spotlight on wives and mothers who have not noticed the passing of the years, but suddenly find themselves exhausted, yet still having to take care of all the household chores. In order to get through their dreary daily routine, and more importantly to help them cope with the lack of understanding, or indifference even, of their husband and the incessant boisterousness of their children, they turn to little yellow pills, the tranquilizers they hope their doctors will prescribe.

As always with the Stones, and with Mick Jagger in particular, there is no shortage of mockery and cynicism. Or of audacity, because to deal with the subject of drugs and the frustration of housewives and mothers in such an explicit way was still, at the time, unusual, even in Swinging London. "Mother's Little Helper" does, however, bear a resemblance to the topical songs written by Bob Dylan during the same period. It is a reasonably realistic description of Western society during the mid-sixties, in this case focusing on the immoderate consumption by British housewives of a tranquilizer called diazepam (nicknamed "blues" or "vallies"). *They just helped you on your way, through your busy dying day*, sings Jagger in the last line of the song.

Dave Hassinger would later reveal that the lyrics were inspired by his wife Marie: " . . . Jack or somebody wanted some downers, not real downers, just something mild . . . She brought down these little pills, I forget exactly what they were, Valiums I think . . . But this song was written for her. I heard that through Jack."[28]

Production

In terms of musical genre, "Mother's Little Helper" is folk rock, which is not so very different from what the Kinks were doing at this time ("A Well Respected Man"). The uniqueness of this track derives primarily from its overall sonority, which is somewhat oriental in feel: "'a very strange disc,' . . . 'like a music-hall number, with an electric twelve-string on it which

Keith and Brian are responsible for the superb guitars on this track.

made it very distinctive,'"[46] explains Mick Jagger. The very individual color of the riff derives from a combination of Brian Jones's brand new 12-string electric (his superb Rickenbacker 360/12) and another 12-string in the hands of Keith Richards (both played slide). "The track just needed something to make it twang,"[34] Keith would tell Alan Di Parma in 2002. He explains that somebody in the studio lent him an unnamed 12-string electric: "God knows where it came from. Or where it went. But I put it together with a bottleneck. Then we had a riff that tied the whole thing together. And I think we over-dubbed onto that."[34] The sonority of this riff is reminiscent of "Paint It Black," in spirit at least. Keith would later speak of "semigypsy melodies. I don't know where they came from. Must be in the blood somewhere."[34] He was also responsible for the acoustic rhythm part played on his Gibson Hummingbird (overdubbed). An electric guitar chord, played either with volume pedal or by means of the technique known as *violining*, can be heard on the intro, at 0:30 to be precise. The effect is powerful and leads into the riff perfectly.

"Mother's Little Helper" owes much of its success to Charlie Watts, who sets a groove for the group on his Ludwig Super Classic kit, but also to Bill Wyman's excellent bass part, with "Memphis, Tennessee"–style glissandos (played most likely on his Framus Humbug), that lend the track a "creeping" quality. He also seems to be playing a bass with distortion courtesy of the Maestro Fuzz-Tone (from 1:22). Alternatively, this could be an electric guitar played by either of the two guitarists. As for Mick Jagger, the singer's performance is on a par with that of his bandmates. Oldham would later describe his delivery of the lyrics (which is double-tracked and supported by Keith on vocal harmonies) as "near-cockney,"[5] implying at the same time that this was just one aspect of his range. "Mother's Little Helper" ends somewhat unexpectedly on a G major chord despite its underlying tonality of E minor. Although responsible for the overall composition, Keith would later acknowledge that this was not his doing: "It might have been Bill Wyman who came up with that ending."[34]

As the opening track, "Mother's Little Helper" offers a spectacular demonstration of the group's development, not only in terms of composition, but also in terms of lyrics, recording, and performance. The Rolling Stones had crossed a threshold and over the following years would work ceaselessly to achieve new heights.

This song was left off the US version of *Aftermath*. Instead it was released in the United States as a single (with "Lady Jane" as the B-side) on July 2, 1966, peaking at number 8 on August 13.

JACK NITZSCHE:
A FIRST-CLASS ARRANGER

The Rolling Stones' connection with Jack Nitzsche begins on October 28 and 29, 1964, at the Santa Monica Civic Auditorium. They met during the filming of the *T.A.M.I. Show*, of which the American arranger was musical director. Impressed by the British group, Nitzsche saw the Stones as future "leaders of change."[28] Jack was a friend of Dave Hassinger, one of the best recording engineers at the RCA Studios in Hollywood, and went to considerable lengths to organize a meeting between them. As a result of his efforts, Mick, Brian, Keith, Bill, Charlie, and Stu walked through the doors of the legendary Los Angeles studios for the first time on November 2, 1964. They recorded six numbers for their second album, with Hassinger at the controls and Nitzsche accompanying the group.

An American Brian Jones

Although Nitzsche was initially surprised by the Stones' working method—more specifically by the total absence of any structured approach—a firm friendship and profound artistic understanding developed between him and the group. The American arranger supported the British quintet throughout the sixties and seventies, bringing his considerable musical creativity to bear in key numbers such as "Paint It Black," "Let's Spend the Night Together," and "You Can't Always Get What You Want," and even occasionally playing keyboards. Keith Richards was the first to recognize Jack Nitzsche's contribution to the group, describing him as a "beautiful . . . freak . . . an American Brian Jones if you like."[14] It could perhaps be said that the brilliant arranger provided the Stones with a support and musical direction comparable to that lavished on the Beatles by George Martin. Keith portrays Nitzsche in his book *Life* as follows: " . . . Jack Nitzsche was an almost silent—and unpaid for reasons still not clear except he did it for fun [fifty dollars to arrange titles like "Da Doo Ron Ron" or "Be My Baby"!]—arranger, musician, gluer-together of the talent, a man of enormous importance for us in that period."[2]

Phil Spector's Right-Hand Man

Born in Chicago, Illinois, on April 22, 1937, Bernard Alfred " Jack" Nitzsche was the son of German immigrants. In 1955, he settled in Los Angeles in the hope of becoming a jazz saxophonist but took a job as a copyist at Specialty Records, where he made the acquaintance of Sonny Bono. It was with the latter that he wrote the song "Needles and Pins," which was successfully recorded by Jackie DeShannon and then by the Searchers. By this time, Nitzsche had already started arranging for Phil Spector, with whom he created the famous "wall of sound" that would make a permanent impact on the history of rock with numbers such as "Be My Baby" (1963) for the Ronettes and "River Deep—Mountain High" (1966) for Ike & Tina Turner. "Jack was the Genius, not Phil,"[2] writes Keith Richards, adding elsewhere that: "Personally I've always felt he was never given enough credit for his work with Phil Spector."[14]

Jack Nitzsche, one of the architects of the Rolling Stones' sound during the mid-sixties, was, for the band, more of a guide and adviser than an arranger as such. That he was a talented musician was corroborated by his work with many other artists. After completing the string arrangement for "Expecting to Fly," on the album *Buffalo Springfield Again* (1967), he made a key contribution to Neil Young's international success to say nothing of his role as pianist with Crazy Horse.

Music for the Big Screen

In the eighties, Jack Nitzsche threw himself into writing music for the movies. Most prominently, he was responsible for the soundtrack for *An Officer and a Gentleman* (directed by Taylor Hackford, 1982) whose song "Up Where We Belong," which Nitzsche co-wrote with his then wife Buffy Sainte-Marie and Will Jennings, was performed by Joe Cocker and Jennifer Warnes, and went on to win both a Grammy Award and the Academy Award for Best Original Song. Other soundtracks include *One Flew Over the Cuckoo's Nest* (Milos Forman, 1975) and *9½ Weeks* (Adrian Lyne, 1986).

Jack Nitzsche died of a heart attack on August 25, 2000.

FOR STONES ADDICTS

Growing estranged from Mick, Chrissie Shrimpton tried to commit suicide by swallowing sleeping pills. When she checked out of St. George's Hospital, she discovered that he had left her for Marianne Faithfull.

STUPID GIRL

Mick Jagger / Keith Richards / 2:56

Musicians
Mick Jagger: vocals
Keith Richards: lead guitar, acoustic guitar, backing vocals
Brian Jones: rhythm guitar (?)
Bill Wyman: bass
Charlie Watts: drums
Ian Stewart: organ
Jack Nitzsche: tambourine (?)
Recorded
RCA Studios, Hollywood: March 6–9, 1966
Technical Team
Producer: Andrew Loog Oldham
Sound engineer: Dave Hassinger

Mick Jagger with Chrissie Shrimpton, to whom "Stupid Girl" is perhaps addressed.

Genesis

Mick Jagger's obsessive misogyny reached a climax in "Stupid Girl." Everything about the young woman in the song is subjected to mockery. And the attack becomes increasingly vicious from verse to verse. This *stupid girl* is grasping, critical of people without knowing them, and bitches about things she has never seen. In short, despite purring *like a pussycat*, this lady is *the sickest thing in this world*.

A more explicit condemnation of the opposite sex is difficult to imagine. Is this diatribe directed against all women? It is not impossible that the Rolling Stones' singer was targeting his girlfriend of the time, Chrissie Shrimpton, the younger sister of the top model and sixties muse Jean Shrimpton. Mick and Chrissie met in 1962 at the London School of Economics. She was still a secretary in Covent Garden (her modeling career had not yet started) when their relationship ended abruptly in 1966. Mick then started to make eyes at Marianne Faithfull. In December 1995, Jagger acknowledged that he was going through a difficult period at that time: "Obviously, I was having a bit of trouble. I wasn't in a good relationship. Or I was in too many bad relationships. I had so many girlfriends at that point. None of them seemed to care they weren't pleasing me very much."[19] "Stupid Girl" is the favorite Stones song of Scottish folksinger Jackie Leven: "The song has this kind of football chant rhythm and I like the fact that the playing's awkward and sounds like they could only just play it. And they [Mick and Keith] never attempt to blend harmonies like everyone else, they still sound like two geezers shouting in a pub. It's really hopeless and very exciting."[47]

Production

Charlie Watts leads in with a tom break. "Stupid Girl" is a medium-pace rock number whose rhythm owes something to Stevie Wonder's "Uptight (Everything's Alright)." Mick Jagger delivers his lyrics in a sarcastic tone bordering on invective, with the occasional childish overtone. Keith Richards plays lead guitar and acoustic guitar, most probably leaving the second, electric, rhythm guitar part to Brian Jones. Ian Stewart is on the organ, and his playing is the key element on the track, despite a number of wrong notes (for example at 0:29). Bill Wyman supports his bandmates with a solid bass line, and it is probably the loyal Nitzsche on tambourine.

LADY JANE

Mick Jagger / Keith Richards / 3:08

Musicians
Mick Jagger: vocals
Keith Richards: acoustic guitar
Brian Jones: dulcimer
Bill Wyman: bass
Charlie Watts: xylophone (?)
Jack Nitzsche: harpsichord

Recorded
RCA Studios, Hollywood: March 6–9, 1966

Technical Team
Producer: Andrew Loog Oldham
Sound engineer: Dave Hassinger

FOR STONES ADDICTS

The Neil Young track "Borrowed Tune," on the album *Tonight's the Night* (1975), is an exact replica of "Lady Jane." In the fourth verse the singer even confides: *I'm singin' this borrowed tune/I took from the Rolling Stones.* It is interesting to note the contribution of a certain Jack Nitzsche to various tracks on this album.

Neil Young in London around 1970. His aptly named "Borrowed Tune" was heavily inspired by "Lady Jane."

Genesis

The identity of the heroine of "Lady Jane" has given rise to much speculation. For some, she is Jane Seymour, the third wife of King Henry VIII of England, who died twelve days after giving birth to the future Edward VI. According to this version, the song was inspired by a letter addressed by Henry VIII to Jane in which he assures her of his love and reveals his decision not to delay in executing of his second wife, Anne Boleyn, by decapitation. For others, the song is about Jane Ormsby-Gore, the daughter of David Ormsby-Gore (the fifth Baron Harlech) and, most importantly, the emblematic designer of Swinging London, with whom the Stones' singer had an affair. Or again, perhaps the name of the heroine should be seen as another example of the licentious double entendre of which the singer of the Rolling Stones was so fond: this song was written by Mick Jagger at the beginning of 1966, after he had read *Lady Chatterley's Lover* by D. H. Lawrence, in which the sex organs of the woman are christened . . . Lady Jane.

Nothing can be less certain, of course. During an interview with Jonathan Cott,[18] Mick Jagger confided: "'Lady Jane' is a complete sort of very weird song. I don't really know what that's all about myself. All the names are historical but it was really unconscious that they should fit together from the same period." For Keith Richards, the ballad presents an image of the England of times gone by: "To me, 'Lady Jane' is very Elizabethan. There are a few places in England where people still speak that way, Chaucer English."[11]

If "Lady Jane" reveals a new facet of Mick Jagger as a writer, the medieval, or Baroque, atmosphere of the number owes a great deal to the talent of Brian Jones, and more specifically to his subtle performance on the dulcimer. "Brian was getting into dulcimer then, because he dug Richard Farina," explains Keith Richards. "It has to do with what you listen to. Like I'll just listen to old blues cats for months and not want to hear anything else, and then I just want to hear what's happening and collect it all and listen to it. We were also listening to a lot of Appalachian music then too."[18]

"Lady Jane" was released as a single in the United States (as the B-side of "Mother's Little Helper") on July 2, 1966. It reached number 24 on the *Billboard* chart on August 13.

The instrument that lends "Lady Jane" its quasi-medieval, quasi-Baroque atmosphere is the dulcimer. Here Brian Jones plays the Vox Bijou electric dulcimer, which he used in concert.

Production

"Lady Jane" can be regarded as one of the most important songs on *Aftermath*. It presents such an unexpected image of the Stones, so far removed from their blues-rock reputation, that one could perhaps be forgiven for wondering whether it really was written by them. The maturity of the writing is undeniable, a maturity the songwriters were perhaps not aware of at the time. What gives "Lady Jane" its distinctive musical color is the dulcimer part played by Brian Jones, the talented multi-instrumentalist who, inspired by the playing of Richard Fariña, had purchased an acoustic Appalachian dulcimer during the recording sessions. He played his new acquisition with a goose quill, thereby bestowing a highly unusual and individual sound on the song. Vox later built an electric dulcimer for him to use when touring, the Vox Bijou dulcimer, which he played with a pick. (This can be heard during the Stones' appearance on *The Ed Sullivan Show* on September 11, 1966.) Brian is not the only member of the band to distinguish himself on this track, however, for Keith plays an excellent acoustic guitar part (no doubt on his Gibson Hummingbird), picking out arpeggios with a plectrum. Another key element on "Lady Jane" is Jack Nitzsche's harpsichord, which makes its entrance at 1:41 during the instrumental section, substantially reinforcing the Baroque feel of the song. Although discreet, Bill Wyman plays his Vox Wyman bass during each of the three last lines of each verse, which serve as a chorus. Charlie Watts also makes a contribution, this time using sticks to strike not drums, but what seems to be a xylophone (listen at 1:24), as is also attested by the band's appearance on *The Ed Sullivan Show*. The effect is subtle and introduces an ethereal note. That leaves Mick Jagger, who sings, as Keith describes, in the English of Geoffrey Chaucer, with well-articulated words and precise diction—entirely in keeping with the general atmosphere. "Lady Jane" is a success in terms of both its writing and its recording, and the talent of Dave Hassinger no doubt had more than a little to do with the latter.

Richard Fariña formed a folk duo with Margarita Mimi Baez, the younger sister of Joan Baez. He died in a motorcycle accident on April 30, 1966.

UNDER MY THUMB

Mick Jagger / Keith Richards / 3:41

Musicians
Mick Jagger: vocals
Keith Richards: acoustic guitar, lead guitar, fuzz bass
Brian Jones: marimba
Bill Wyman: bass
Charlie Watts: drums
Ian Stewart: piano
Unidentified musician(s): finger snaps, hand claps

Recorded
RCA Studios, Hollywood: March 6–9, 1966

Technical Team
Producer: Andrew Loog Oldham
Sound engineer: Dave Hassinger

Mick Jagger hounded by fans. The trials and tribulations of being a rock star . . .

Genesis

The criticisms that rained down on the shoulders of the Rolling Stones when they started singing their misogynist and antifeminist diatribes assumed a new dimension with "Under My Thumb." This time, the central character is not leaving his girlfriend. She has made his life a misery, and he is staying with her in order to finally indulge in some role reversal. He will no longer be the plaything of this diabolical creature, but will instead be a kind of domineering Pygmalion. The first verse has a certain startling clarity to it: *Under my thumb/The girl who once had me down/ Under my thumb/The girl who once pushed me around.* The narrator—Jagger himself?—is relishing his revenge, and throughout the song it is this sense of delight that dominates; the pleasure of seeing this *squirmin' dog* turn into the sweetest *pet in the world*, of ruling with a rod of iron a girl who has had the upper hand (in the bedroom as well?) for far too long!

This thirst for revenge on women expressed by Mick Jagger and Keith Richards in "Under My Thumb" would anger even the most inured feminists. The song has to be seen as yet another in a sequence of provocations, and certainly also as a desire to take up a contrary stance to the politically correct, to the progressive movements. Mick Jagger: "But if you really listen to the lyrics closely—not too closely—'under my thumb, a girl who once had me down'—you see? It's not so unfair. Why should it apply to *every girl*? But I think it was really true. It's funny to think about it—it was very adolescent, those songs, about adolescent experiences."[48] And the Rolling Stones' singer would pursue this conciliatory line two years later, again in *Rolling Stone*: "That's going back to my teenage years!"[29] and claim that the *squirmin' dog* thing was a matter of being deliberately provocative: "Well, that was a joke. I've never felt in that position vis-à-vis a person—I'd never want to really hurt someone."[29] So Chrissie Shrimpton was not in his sights after all? Keith would take a more self-justifying approach, blaming the pressure from fans who pursued the band members as far as their hotel rooms, and the fatigue engendered by incessant touring, concluding that "that's how one got."[11]

Brian Jones played the marimba on "Under My Thumb."

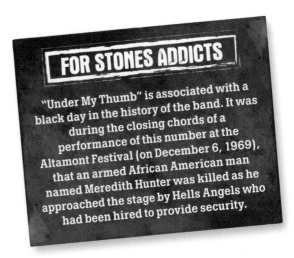

Production

Since the days of "Satisfaction," when the group had experienced extraordinary international success, Brian Jones had been playing the guitar less and less. Keith Richards explains: "I don't know if he lost interest because he got on a star trip, but it seemed to coincide anyway with his lack of interest in the guitar."[11] Brian's enthusiasm for all kinds of other instruments also dates from this time. On "Under My Thumb" he plays a marimba rented by Dave Hassinger specially for that session. It was this new sonority that gives the number its true identity, just as the dulcimer had done for "Lady Jane." Keith Richards deplored Brian's ever more frequent absences, but would later acknowledge his great value when he did turn up: "When he was there and came to life, he was incredibly nimble. He could pick up any instruments that were lying around and come up with something. Sitar on 'Paint It Black.' The marimbas on 'Under My Thumb.' But for the next five days we won't see the motherfucker, and we've still got a record to make."[2] As a result, it is Keith who provides all the guitar parts on the number: lead guitar, acoustic guitar, and even a fuzz bass (using the Maestro Fuzz-Tone) played on Bill's Vox Wyman (from 0:32). For his part, Bill plays a very good bass guitar along the lines of Brian's marimba part, with a superb sound obtained from one of his two basses, the Framus Humbug or the Vox Wyman. In doing so he supports Charlie's brilliant, Motown-like groove. Ian Stewart accompanies his bandmates on the piano, fleshing out Keith's guitar playing with discreet but efficient chords. Finally, Mick Jagger delivers his lyrics with a voice that is simultaneously sardonic, aggressive, and sensual, and enhanced by an ever-present reverb. It would seem that Mick is also responsible for the finger snaps in the intro and the hand claps throughout the track (no doubt assisted by Jack Nitzsche).

FOR STONES ADDICTS

"Under My Thumb" is associated with a black day in the history of the band. It was during the closing chords of a performance of this number at the Altamont Festival (on December 6, 1969), that an armed African American man named Meredith Hunter was killed as he approached the stage by Hells Angels who had been hired to provide security.

DONCHA BOTHER ME

Mick Jagger / Keith Richards / 2:41

Musicians
Mick Jagger: vocals, harmonica
Keith Richards: rhythm guitars, acoustic guitar
Brian Jones: slide guitar
Bill Wyman: bass
Charlie Watts: drums
Ian Stewart: piano
Recorded
RCA Studios, Hollywood: December 8–10, 1965
Technical Team
Producer: Andrew Loog Oldham
Sound engineer: Dave Hassinger

Charlie Watts in action. His drumming plays a key role in "Doncha Bother Me."

Genesis

A strange paradox can be observed on this album: the member of the Rolling Stones quickest to claim the legacy of the blues pioneers also did the most to widen their musical horizons by turning his hand to a vast array of musical instruments. In "Doncha Bother Me," the Brian Jones who comes to the fore, with his mastery of the bottleneck, once again returns to his roots, in a sense.

Credited to Jagger-Richards, "Doncha Bother Me" (working title: "Don't Ya Follow Me") is a blues number like those the Rolling Stones had been playing from the outset. And would play again, notably during the recording of the legendary *Exile on Main St.* This time, Mick Jagger inveighs against all those people who copy others, who have no personality of their own. *I said "Oh no, doncha follow me no more,"* he sings at the start of each verse. This is no doubt to be interpreted as a reproach aimed at the fans. With a line that Ray Davies would have been proud of, *Well the lines around my eyes/Are protected by a copyright law,* the song can be seen as the Stones' equivalent of the Kinks' "Dedicated Follower of Fashion" (released as a single the same year as *Aftermath*).

Production

As on "Stupid Girl" and "Under My Thumb," it is Charlie Watts who opens "Doncha Bother Me." This time, he innovates by apparently playing a bass tom with reverb, muffled with towels and equalized in the treble. He is immediately joined on honky-tonk piano by Ian Stewart and on guitar, his Gibson Firebird VII, by the band's slide specialist, Brian Jones. The other guitars are almost certainly played by Keith Richards: two rhythm guitars (left and right on the stereo version) and a 6-string acoustic. Bill Wyman's bass is unfortunately pretty recessed in the mix and does not provide its usual support. Mick Jagger's delivery of the lyrics is excellent, and it is also the singer who plays the short harmonica solo with abundant reverb. "Doncha Bother Me" is perhaps not one of the Stones' best numbers, but it possesses a particular harmonic structure that makes it strangely memorable: it is difficult to distinguish whether the initial phrases of the verses (*Oh no, doncha follow me no more*) are in the minor or the major, and this immediately grabs the listener's attention. Is this intentional or a mistake? Either way, the number works well.

GOIN' HOME

Mick Jagger / Keith Richards / 11:13

Musicians
Mick Jagger: vocals
Keith Richards: lead guitar and rhythm guitar
Brian Jones: harmonica
Bill Wyman: bass
Charlie Watts: drums
Ian Stewart: piano
Jack Nitzsche: tambourine
Recorded
RCA Studios, Hollywood: December 8–10, 1965
Technical Team
Producer: Andrew Loog Oldham
Sound engineer: Dave Hassinger

Genesis

Keith Richards came up with the riff for "Goin' Home," and Mick Jagger wrote the words during the Stones' second US tour, shortly before the band entered the RCA Studios. The lyrics describe a man who has been away from home for far too long. He has just one wish: to hold his love in his arms once again.

The number then develops into a long improvisation. Keith Richards: "It was the first long rock and roll cut. It broke that two-minute barrier. We tried to make singles as long as we could do then because we just like to let things roll on. Dylan was used to building a song for 20 minutes because of the folk thing he came from. . . . That was another thing. No one sat down to make an 11-minute track. I mean 'Goin' Home,' the song was written just the first two and a half minutes. We just happened to keep the tape rolling, me on guitar, Brian on harp, Bill and Charlie and Mick. If there's a piano, it's Stew."[50]

Production

There are two parts to "Goin' Home": the first is more or less country rock, while the second, beginning around 3:06, is a long improvisation over the same E major chord. Dave Hassinger recalls that after six takes, each lasting around 2:30, Oldham encouraged everyone to carry on: "So we just kept going," he explains. "It was totally cut live. There were no overdubs on it. It was all extemporaneous. It was hypnotic."[33] However, the talented sound engineer's memory seems to have let him down, because Keith can be heard playing two electric guitars, a rhythm part with vibrato and a solo, so there must have been some overdubbing (on the right in the stereo version), while Brian plays a harmonica part that is a little drowned out in the mix. Mick also overdubs vocal harmonies (again on the right). From 3:10, though, there are no more overdubs, and the track has a peculiar stereo configuration in which Mick's voice is heard in the middle with the group on the left and nothing on the right! And this goes on for eight minutes! Another peculiarity is that Charlie uses brushes not on his snare drum, but on the head of his bass drum, which he has turned onto its side! Bill plays an excellent bass line that he varies throughout the track, and Stu comes in on piano around 3:09.

Brian, Bill, and Mick on the set of *Ready Steady Go!* in October 1966.

FLIGHT 505

Mick Jagger / Keith Richards / 3:27

Musicians
Mick Jagger: vocals
Keith Richards: lead guitar, acoustic guitar, backing vocals
Brian Jones: rhythm guitar (?)
Bill Wyman: bass
Charlie Watts: drums
Ian Stewart: piano
Recorded
RCA Studios, Hollywood: March 6–9, 1966
Technical Team
Producer: Andrew Loog Oldham
Sound engineer: Dave Hassinger

FOR STONES ADDICTS

The Stones take Flight 505 to the United States, while the Beatles, for their part, return from the Soviet Union on a British Overseas Airways Corporation (BOAC) plane in the song *"Back in the USSR."*

Genesis

This song, written by Mick Jagger at the Beverly Hills Hotel shortly before the band entered the studio, tells of an unfortunate man who takes a flight in order to embark on a new life. He jumps into a taxi and asks the airline ticket agent to get him on flight number 505. The passenger has a glass in his hand and the world at his feet, and things could not be better. Until the airplane crashes into the ocean, that is. This is another example of black humor from Mick Jagger, a chronicler, in his own way, of lost illusions.

Some people have suggested that "Flight 505" refers to the plane crash that took the lives of Buddy Holly, The Big Bopper, and Ritchie Valens on February 3, 1959 ("The Day the Music Died"). There is no truth in this, however. Not only did the plane that was to take the three rock 'n' roll pioneers to Fargo, North Dakota, come down on dry land, near Clear Lake, Iowa, Bill Wyman himself, in his book *Stone Alone*, states that this flight 505 was the number of the British Airways flight that carried the Rolling Stones across the Atlantic for their first US tour in June 1964.[6]

Production

Ian Stewart opens this track for a change with some very good boogie-woogie piano, a style at which he excelled. He also injects a touch of humor, concluding his piano intro with an allusion to "(I Can't Get No) Satisfaction" (0:19)! The band responds by launching into this rock 'n' roll number that is not unlike many others the Stones had been playing since their earliest days. There is nothing mind-blowing about it, with each member of the band performing his part conscientiously but without sparkle. Mick Jagger sings of the hero's misfortunes, but there is something a little puerile about the lyrics, which are in a different league than what a certain Bob Dylan was capable of at this time. Keith Richards provides the vocal harmonies and plays both rhythm and lead guitar, supported, it would seem, by Brian Jones on second rhythm guitar. No doubt seduced by the fuzz bass used by Paul McCartney on "Think for Yourself" on the album *Rubber Soul* (released at the end of 1965), Keith adds some of the same to various tracks on *Aftermath*. On "Flight 505" he doubles sections of Bill Wyman's bass line with fuzz bass, but this is not exactly indispensable to the overall effect.

1966. The Stones take off for their fifth North American tour.

HIGH AND DRY

Mick Jagger / Keith Richards / 3:08

Musicians
Mick Jagger: vocals
Keith Richards: 6-string and 12-string acoustic guitar
Brian Jones: harmonica
Bill Wyman: bass
Charlie Watts: drums
Recorded
RCA Studios, Hollywood: March 6–9, 1966
Technical Team
Producer: Andrew Loog Oldham
Sound engineer: Dave Hassinger

FOR STONES ADDICTS

In addition to the Stones, countless other writers would also use "High and Dry" as a title for their songs, including Radiohead, Lalo Schifrin, Poco, the Ventures, and Jamie Cullum.

Brian Jones backstage, taking a well-deserved few minutes' break . . .

Genesis

As the title suggests, "High and Dry" is another song about breaking up. Its chief delight, one might say, is the cynicism displayed by the rejected lover. *I think she found it was* [her] *money I was after*, sings Jagger, before adding: *It's lucky that I didn't have any love towards her/Next time I'll make sure that the girl'll be much poorer.*

Musically, "High and Dry" is without doubt the fruit of the Rolling Stones' travels to the heart of the United States. Keith Richards in particular developed an interest in the country music traditions. This song was the first proper incursion by the London group into hillbilly, with Mick Jagger affecting the characteristic accent of the country-and-western singer and Brian Jones playing a very low-down harmonica.

Production

Barely back from their second tour to Australia and New Zealand (February 18 to March 1, 1966), the Rolling Stones lost no time in returning to Hollywood and the RCA team to lay down "High and Dry" during their second session at the studios, between March 6 and 9, 1966. In this track, Mick and his deluxe jug band present the very first Stones composition influenced by hillbilly and bluegrass. Keith launches into the intro on a 6-string acoustic (his Gibson Hummingbird?) and can also be heard playing a 12-string acoustic, probably his Harmony 1270 (overdubbed). Brian accompanies him throughout with a very good harmonica part and highly successful solo (1:34). Charlie confines himself to bass drum and hi-hat. Bill supports him with a pumping bass line that is not up to his usual standards of accuracy as far as the notes are concerned, giving rise to a suspicion that he is not totally in his element in this number. Mick can be imagined singing "High and Dry" leaning on the bar of a saloon with a Stetson on his head, cowboy boots on his feet, and a Jack Daniel's in his hand. In this number the Stones do country Leadbelly-style, and to great effect.

OUT OF TIME

Mick Jagger / Keith Richards / 5:37

Musicians
Mick Jagger: vocals, finger snaps
Keith Richards: rhythm guitar, acoustic guitar, backing vocals
Brian Jones: marimba, vibraphone (?)
Bill Wyman: bass
Charlie Watts: drums
Ian Stewart: organ
Jack Nitzsche: piano
Recorded
RCA Studios, Hollywood: March 6–9, 1966
Technical Team
Producer: Andrew Loog Oldham
Sound engineer: Dave Hassinger

Mick Jagger next to Chris Farlowe, who recorded "Out of Time" in the spring of 1966.

FOR STONES ADDICTS

"Out of Time" was selected for the album *Metamorphosis* (1975). This version is actually the backing track of the Chris Farlowe cover over which Mick Jagger has added his voice. It reached number 44 on the British charts in September 1975!

Genesis

The subject of "Out of Time" is not so different from that of "Under My Thumb." A young woman decides to go back to the boyfriend she has abandoned and been unfaithful to. But several years have passed, and it is too late. Her time is up, and her former lover has no hesitation in telling her so: *You're obsolete my baby/My poor old-fashioned baby.* In short, he is taking his revenge by lambasting her with cruel words in order to make her suffer the way he suffered when she deserted him.

"Out of Time" is a pop song with a great tune that reveals a Motown influence on its authors Jagger and Richards. It exists in various different versions. The recording used on the British album *Aftermath* is the RCA Studios version, dating from March 6–9, 1966, with Brian Jones on marimba. The song was left off the US album, but the same version was included on the compilation *Flowers* with the only difference that it has been cut from 5:37 to 3:42. There is also the Chris Farlowe version, recorded on April 27–30 and May 6, 1966, in Pye Studios in London with the pianist and arranger Arthur Greenslade and the guitarist Jimmy Page. This version, produced by Mick Jagger and released on Oldham's label Immediate Records, reached number 1 in the United Kingdom on August 3, 1966, and remained on the charts for thirteen weeks. It also entered the hit parade again in September 1975 (reaching number 44).

Production

Based on the opening notes from Ian Stewart on the Hammond organ and Brian Jones on the marimba, one almost expects to hear the voice of Marvin Gaye or the Supremes, so fully had the London band assimilated US musical culture, from Chicago blues to the R&B of Detroit. And when Mick launches into the melody in his plaintive, vindictive, impassioned voice, it has to be acknowledged that the contrast between the cynical lyrics and the sugary music is nothing less than magical. Keith plays rhythm electric and rhythm acoustic and also delivers a solo on acoustic (which is not always perfectly in time). Brian seems to divide himself between the marimba and a vibraphone (or a metallophone) that can be heard in the refrains (listen at 0:36). Bill and Charlie form an excellent rhythm team, and Jack Nitzsche plays the piano.

IT'S NOT EASY

Mick Jagger / Keith Richards / 2:56

Musicians
Mick Jagger: vocals
Keith Richards: lead guitar, backing vocals
Brian Jones: rhythm guitar
Bill Wyman: bass
Charlie Watts: drums
Ian Stewart: organ
Recorded
RCA Studios, Hollywood: March 6–9, 1966
Technical Team
Producer: Andrew Loog Oldham
Sound engineer: Dave Hassinger

"It's Not Easy" has not given rise to very many covers, although Blue Öyster Cult used to perform a supercharged version of the song in concerts between 1970 and 1973.

Marianne Faithfull in 1966. Was it she who got Mick Jagger *running like a cat in a thunderstorm*?

Genesis

After pointing his finger at all the defects he can find in the female sex, might Mick Jagger now be showing signs of making amends? This is certainly suggested by the narrator's admission that *It's not easy living on your own* and that *It seems a big failing in a man/To take his girl for granted if he can.* However, no sooner has he recognized the error of his ways than he pleads extenuating circumstances: *Got me running like a cat in a thunderstorm*, he sings, before lifting the curtain a little on this girlfriend when he fantasizes about the *glow of her long clean hair/As she goes to sit on her own high chair.* Might this mysterious creature be a "honky-tonk woman"?

Production

This track marks a return to a Chuck Berry–influenced style of rock 'n' roll. "It's Not Easy" (an allusion, perhaps, to "It's So Easy!" by Buddy Holly and his Crickets?) may not be the best track on the album, but it provides Keith Richards with an opportunity to demonstrate his skills as a guitarist by opening the number with a short blues-jazz-style intro on his 6-string electric (probably his Guild M-65 Freshman) with the treble rolled off. He plays this instrument throughout, improvising highly effective blues licks. He also plays lead guitar and a solo (both overdubbed), no doubt on his Gibson Firebird. Brian plays rhythm, also on his Firebird, and Ian delivers a very good organ part. The bass is a fuzz bass that would generally be played by Bill, but since Keith has already played fuzz bass on "Flight 505" and "Under My Thumb," he may well be responsible here too. This was no doubt an innovative effect in 1966, but today the sound comes across as somewhat strident and provides little real support. This does not in the slightest trouble Charlie Watts, who really rocks as he works his Ludwig with gusto. Mick Jagger does not give the impression of being at all distressed by the solitude described in the lyrics. He sings with a degree of detachment and does not seem unduly concerned by the subject matter. But, hey, this is rock 'n' roll!

I AM WAITING

Mick Jagger / Keith Richards / 3:11

Musicians
Mick Jagger: vocals
Keith Richards: acoustic guitar
Brian Jones: dulcimer
Bill Wyman: bass
Charlie Watts: drums
Jack Nitzsche (?): tambourine
Recorded
RCA Studios, Hollywood: March 6–9, 1966
Technical Team
Producer: Andrew Loog Oldham
Sound engineer: Dave Hassinger

Brian Jones playing the dulcimer during the Stones' appearance on *Ready Steady Go!* in 1966.

Genesis

The lyrics Mick Jagger wrote for this song are somewhat enigmatic, and inevitably recall the Dylan of *Highway 61 Revisited* and *Blonde on Blonde*. The narrator is *Waiting for someone to come out of somewhere*, and then evokes *escalation fears*. This waiting, this thing much feared, could refer to death, which can strike at any moment and whose existence human beings try to banish from their thoughts.

The musical atmosphere of "I Am Waiting" is comparable to that of "Lady Jane," due mainly to Brian Jones's use of the dulcimer. It also hints at an imminent plunge into psychedelic rock.

Production

"I Am Waiting" is without a doubt one of the Rolling Stones' underestimated gems—of the kind that pepper the discographies of great artists. After a superb intro with half-folk, half-Baroque sonorities, played by Keith Richards on his Hummingbird acoustic, Brian Jones comes in on the dulcimer, contributing a unique character all his own, a character that is, moreover, far removed from the usual color of this instrument. Bill Wyman would rightly claim that "It was Brian's musical abilities that make those recordings sound so much better than they might otherwise have done."[1] And this is certainly true. But his bandmates were not exactly idle: Bill plays (with pick) a very good, highly melodic bass line with a perfectly rounded, precise tone, almost certainly on his Vox Wyman bass (see *Ready, Steady Go!*), Charlie Watts provides a sober accompaniment to the verses, playing his toms gently, before letting go on his Ludwig kit during the choruses, Jack Nitzsche is apparently on tambourine (which gets slightly out of time between 0:55 and 1:00), and Mick Jagger gives a nuanced delivery of the words, thereby accentuating the mystery in which they are shrouded. He also, apparently, harmonizes with his own voice by means of overdub. "I Am Waiting" is one of the triumphs of the album. It featured in the Wes Anderson movie *Rushmore*, which came out in 1998, enabling it to be discovered by a new audience.

TAKE IT OR LEAVE IT

Mick Jagger / Keith Richards / 2:47

Musicians
Mick Jagger: vocals
Keith Richards: acoustic guitar, backing vocals
Brian Jones: organ
Bill Wyman: bass
Charlie Watts: drums, finger cymbals
Jack Nitzsche: harpsichord
Recorded
RCA Studios, Hollywood: December 8–10, 1965
Technical Team
Producer: Andrew Loog Oldham
Sound engineer: Dave Hassinger

"Take It or Leave It" was recorded by the Searchers and released as a single on April 13, 1966. Their cover of the Jagger-Richards song was the penultimate chart hit by the Merseybeat band (number 31 on April 11, 1966).

Mick Jagger deep in conversation with Andrew Loog Oldham.

Genesis

"Take It or Leave It" resembles the earliest songs by Mick Jagger and Keith Richards, composed not so much at the request of, but rather on the orders of Andrew Loog Oldham. An unpretentious song, it nevertheless attests to Mick's feel for a telling phrase and to Keith's ability to write memorable melodies.

The lyrics once again concern the difficult relations between men and women. To what is the narrator referring with *Just take it or leave it*? Quite simply his status as a lover, and he has no shortage of grievances with which to reproach his former girlfriend: *When you want you're bad/But you can be so kind*. And then: *There've been times when you tried/ Makin' eyes at all my so-called friends*.

Production

"Take It or Leave It" may indeed have been suggested by Andrew Loog Oldham, who was an unconditional admirer of Phil Spector. It certainly has to be acknowledged that the Stones were navigating what were, for them, uncharted waters, far from their blues-rock roots. This track never ceases to surprise, and even, perhaps, disconcert, above all when Mick and Keith start singing their somewhat indigestible *oh la la la ta ta tas*. In the intro, Keith strikes up martial-sounding chords on his acoustic (which he double-tracks), supported by Charlie's snare drum sounding like a firing squad. The latter can also be heard playing finger cymbals, very much in the Spector spirit. Only castanets could give the track any more color than it already has. Brian Jones plays organ throughout, while Jack Nitzsche plays harpsichord in the refrains and during the *oh la las*. Bill's is very recessed and offers little real support. One may well wonder what exactly was going through Mick's head as he performed his song in a resigned voice. Was it his groupies he was targeting? Might he have been trying to move or unsettle them? At Oldham's suggestion? He double-tracks his own voice in the refrains and is backed by Keith on harmonies. The results are somewhat strange, and ultimately it is not easy to reach an objective opinion on this song. The Stones are full of surprises!

THINK

Mick Jagger / Keith Richards / 3:09

Musicians
Mick Jagger: vocals
Keith Richards: lead guitar, acoustic guitar, backing vocals
Brian Jones: rhythm guitar
Bill Wyman: bass
Charlie Watts: drums
Recorded
RCA Studios, Hollywood: December 8–10, 1965
Technical Team
Producer: Andrew Loog Oldham
Sound engineer: Dave Hassinger

Keith Richards with his Epiphone Casino,
the guitar he plays on "Think."

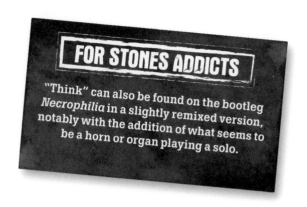

Genesis

Mick Jagger is once again settling scores with women, at any rate those who have caused him to suffer (presumably before he achieved his spectacular double status as rock star and sex symbol). The scenario: the male half of a couple that has been separated for a year is addressing his former partner. Who was responsible for the breakup? He asks her to be mature and, most importantly, to think about the past. *Take a look and you will find/You're gettin' old before your time*: it is a cruel assessment, all the more so as the former lover is accused of not keeping her promises.

In addition to Marianne Faithfull, another important ambassador of the music of the Rolling Stones in the mid-sixties was Chris Farlowe. Seduced by the melody of "Think," the singer from Islington asked Mick Jagger, Keith Richards, and Andrew Loog Oldham to produce his cover of the song. "Think" was his first single to enter the British charts: initially on January 2, 1966 (number 49), and for a second time on February 16 (number 37).

Production

It is interesting to note Keith's use of his Maestro Fuzz-Tone, which gives his Epiphone Casino its distorted sound throughout. Paradoxically, the musician who popularized fuzz guitar in rock music employed it rarely, and then only as a substitute for the horn section he had in his head . . . He had already done this on "(I Can't Get No) Satisfaction," and on "Think" his use of it as a horn stand-in is even clearer. In addition to fuzz guitar, Keith seems to be playing a 6-string acoustic that launches the intro (whose first four notes are the same as the riff of George Harrison's "Wah-Wah" [1970]) and lead guitar, taking a solo at around 1:50. This leaves Brian Jones on rhythm (on his Gibson Firebird). Bill Wyman plays an excellent bass line on his Framus Humbug, and Charlie Watts sets a good groove on his Ludwig kit. Mick Jagger is entirely at ease in this type of song halfway between pop and R&B. He is supported by good vocal harmonies from Keith. However, the results are not truly satisfying. The production is good, the number well written, and the tune catchy, but "Think" lacks that extra dimension that is needed to raise it to the level of "Mother's Little Helper" or "Paint It Black."

WHAT TO DO

Mick Jagger / Keith Richards / 2:32

Musicians
Mick Jagger: vocals
Keith Richards: rhythm electric guitar,
acoustic guitar, backing vocals
Brian Jones: guitar (?)
Bill Wyman: bass
Charlie Watts: drums
Ian Stewart (?): piano
Recorded
RCA Studios, Hollywood: March 6–9, 1966
Technical Team
Producer: Andrew Loog Oldham
Sound engineer: Dave Hassinger

There is a completely offbeat cover of "What to Do" by the Meat Puppets, who unveil an astonishing vision of the song (1999).

Bill Wyman and Charlie Watts: the
Rolling Stones' rhythm section . . .

Genesis

Aftermath concludes with an evocation of boredom—the boredom one feels watching TV or spending one's money on drinking and dancing until dawn. The narrator then addresses his contemporaries getting into a train, worrying about being late for work while he is getting ready to go to bed. Although predating punk by some ten years, this is not so very different from the "No future," "Blank Generation" idea.

The music, on the other hand, is not at all similar to that of the Sex Pistols or the Clash, groups that would rouse rock music from its lethargy during the second half of the seventies. It is a pop song that combines acoustic and electric instruments, adopting the same approach as beat bands such as the Searchers and the Hollies.

Production

Once again, a drum break from Charlie Watts launches this number in a style reminiscent of the doo-wop groups of the fifties. "What to Do" is certainly not the jewel in the *Aftermath* crown; it is more of a filler. There is nothing exceptional about the writing, which gives the impression that the Jagger-Richards duo were simply going through the motions. Mick sings this ode to boredom with a certain casualness and Beach Boys–style backing vocals overdubbed by himself and Keith. Fortunately, he rediscovers his soul-rock style of delivery in the verses and bridges, particularly the last (1:54), in which he excels, no doubt under the influence of Otis Redding. At 1:33 there is a slight hiccup in his voice! It is doubtful whether Brian Jones played any part in the recording as both the acoustic guitar and rhythm electric (with vibrato) bear the stamp of Keith Richards. Bill Wyman and Charlie Watts fulfill their roles with their usual assurance and efficiency. Finally, it seems to be Ian Stewart on piano. "What to Do" was not included on the US version of *Aftermath*, only on the UK album.

Brian Jones, the unwitting hero of "19th Nervous Breakdown."

SIDE A
1966

19TH NERVOUS BREAKDOWN

Mick Jagger / Keith Richards /3:58

SINGLE

19th Nervous Breakdown / As Tears Go By

RELEASE DATE

United Kingdom: February 4, 1966

RECORD NUMBER: DECCA F 12331

Musicians

Mick Jagger: vocals

Keith Richards: guitar, backing vocals

Brian Jones: guitar

Bill Wyman: bass

Charlie Watts: drums

Ian Stewart: piano

Recorded

RCA Studios, Hollywood: December 8–10, 1965

Technical Team

Producer: Andrew Loog Oldham

Sound engineer: Dave Hassinger

At Oldham's request, Glyn Johns, the band's erstwhile (and future) sound engineer, remixed "19th Nervous Breakdown," giving greater prominence to Jagger's voice. Unfortunately, this mix was rejected by the Stones' manager.

Genesis

The Rolling Stones were in Los Angeles at the end of their second US tour of 1965, when the phrase "19th Nervous Breakdown" occurred to Mick Jagger. The verses then came to him almost as a matter of course. "19th Nervous Breakdown" . . . the words sound good, they sound right, above all because they describe the state of extreme fatigue in which the five musicians found themselves by the end of the year. The screaming crowds, the fans trying to climb onto the stage, security staff who were overwhelmed by events, outbreaks of violence . . . the nervous tension was at its peak when the Stones were performing live. Brian Jones in particular found it harder and harder to live up to the demands of his rock star status, and his consumption of various substances did nothing to help matters. "He had been pushing himself too far, too fast and too long,"[42] writes biographer Laura Jackson.

Mick Jagger was no doubt thinking of Brian Jones's increasingly erratic behavior when he wrote "19th Nervous Breakdown." Beyond this, and as always (one might say), the song was another tirade against women—an "anti-girl" song just like "Stupid Girl," as Keith Richards would later write in *Life*.[2] This time the Stones' singer had in his sights the spoiled children of the well-to-do—girls who have everything and care for nothing, the type whose mothers *owe a million dollars tax*. But perhaps there are extenuating circumstances in the life of this egocentric young girl who talks far too loudly, not least a father who has failed to notice that the times have changed, to the extent that he is still manufacturing *sealing wax*. The narrator wanted to help her—but to no avail: *On our first trip I tried so hard to rearrange your mind/But after a*

The Rolling Stones on *The Ed Sullivan Show*, February 13, 1966.

while I realized you were disarranging mine. Should this be seen as a reference to hallucinogenic, consciousness-heightening drugs?

"19th Nervous Breakdown" was released as a single in the United Kingdom (with "As Tears Go By" as the B-side) on February 4, 1966, and in the United States (with "Sad Day" as the B-side) on February 12. It shot to number 2 in both countries, and left a permanent impression on the singer Alice Cooper: " . . . '19th Nervous Breakdown' was a modern rock song. It didn't sound like Chuck Berry or an old blues. It sounded like something brand new, fresh and exciting."[50]

Production

Alice Cooper would not be the only one to sing the praises of "19th Nervous Breakdown." Pete Townshend, the guitarist and songwriter of the Who, was inspired by it to write one of his most famous songs: "'Substitute' began as a homage to Smokey Robinson by way of the Rolling Stones' '19th Nervous Breakdown,'"[51] he writes in his autobiography (2012). The musical color of this number is unique and bears the inimitable stamp of the Rolling Stones. Keith Richards is, of course, largely responsible for this with the highly characteristic riff played on his Epiphone Casino (he can also be seen playing it on his Guild M-65 Freshman on *The Ed Sullivan Show* of February 13, 1966), but Brian's rhythm guitar (Gibson Firebird VII with vibrato), with which Keith sets up a pattern of alternating octaves borrowed directly from Bo Diddley's "Diddley Daddy" (1955) should not be overlooked either. The result is magnificent, a perfect symbiosis between the two guitarists. It is worth noting that Keith inserts a distorted guitar phrase before each refrain (on *look around*). Nor would "19th Nervous Breakdown" be what it is without Bill Wyman's superb bass line, which travels up and down the neck of his Framus Humbug, and it was at the request of his bandmates that he comes up with the brilliant descending slide in the coda (3:29), which was also, according to the bassist, inspired by Bo Diddley. "Why don't you do something at the end there," they suggested, "some kind of a lick that will fill up the space between the vocals and the band."[28] At their urging, Bill plays a long glissando, with pick, which sounds like a bomb in a nosedive, an effect known to guitarists as the *dive bomb*. Charlie Watts plays a very good drum part with an appropriately high-strung feel. Finally, Mick Jagger, who is never as convincing and effective as when he is delivering lyrics written with vitriol, gives an exemplary performance. During the Stones' performance of this number on *The Ed Sullivan Show* on February 13, 1966, Brian Jones can be seen in a pretty bad state, barely moving, pale-faced, with dark rings under his eyes, and wearing a forced smile. He seems isolated from the others, somewhat lost, holding his Gibson awkwardly, and behind the tempo on certain chord changes. It is a sorry sight, and one cannot help wondering whether the song was indirectly addressed to him.

Mick singing and Keith playing his Gibson Heritage on *The Ed Sullivan Show* in 1966. In "As Tears Go By," they had written one of the most beautiful ballads in their catalog.

The Rolling Stones recorded an Italian version of "As Tears Go By" titled "Con Le Mie Lacrime."

FOR STONES ADDICTS

This Jagger-Richards number was originally titled "As Time Goes By," which was also the title of the song sung by Dooley Wilson in *Casablanca* (1942) by Michael Curtiz. Oldham therefore substituted *tears* for *time*, which no doubt explains why he is credited as co-author.

SIDE B
1966

AS TEARS GO BY

Mick Jagger / Keith Richards / Andrew Loog Oldham / 2:46

SINGLE
19th Nervous Breakdown / As Tears Go By
RELEASE DATE
United Kingdom: February 4, 1966
RECORD NUMBER: DECCA F 12331

Musicians
Mick Jagger: vocals
Keith Richards: 12-string acoustic guitar
Mike Leander: arranger and conductor
Unidentified orchestral players
Recorded
IBC Studios, London: October 26, 1965
Technical Team
Producer: Andrew Loog Oldham
Sound engineer: Glyn Johns

Genesis

Keith Richards: "I knew what Andrew wanted: don't come out with a blues, don't do some parody or copy, come out with something of your own. A good pop song is not really that easy to write. It was a shock, this fresh world of writing our own material, this discovery that I had a gift I had no idea existed. It was Blake-like, a revelation, an epiphany."[2]

Paradoxically, one of the very first songs penned by the Rolling Stones was a romantic ballad, light-years away from anything the Dartford duo would subsequently write. The narrator of this melancholy-filled number is moved by the sight of children playing, by their smiling faces—the simple things of life that are worth more than all the riches in the world. Behind all this there is great sadness, as the title suggests. For the taciturn Charlie Watts, ". . . that music was the very, very beginning of flower power."[9] Mick Jagger recalls: "I wrote the lyrics, and Keith wrote the melody. But in some rock, you know, there's no melody until the singer starts to sing it. Sometimes there's a definite melody, but quite often it's your job as the singer to invent the melody. I start with one melody, and I make it another melody, over the same chord sequence."[19] The music may well have been written by Keith Richards, but the gifted songwriter Lionel Bart remembers ". . . helping out with the lyrics of 'As Tears Go By' with Mick, and on 'Satisfaction.'"[5] Fact or fantasy?

After listening carefully to "As Tears Go By," originally titled "As Time Goes By," Andrew Loog Oldham liked it but did not regard it as an appropriate song for the Rolling Stones. He therefore offered it to a young singer named Marianne Faithfull, whom he had just met. She had not yet recorded

SINGLE

anything, but Oldham saw in her a talent waiting to be discovered. "As Tears Go By," which was thus favored over a song by the same Lionel Bart ("I Don't Know How"), was released as a single in June 1964 (with "Greensleeves" as its B-side) and climbed to a very respectable ninth place in the UK charts on September 16, 1964, before reaching number 6 on the *Billboard* chart on January 29, 1966. Marianne Faithfull's career was launched . . . Amusingly, Faithfull would later explain that she felt "'As Tears Go By' was like a Françoise Hardy song," adding that "Maybe that's what Mick picked up from me when we met."[5] Who is to say?

Production

There is an earlier version of this nostalgic ballad recorded at De Lane Lea Studios in London during the sessions of March 8–14, 1964. Mick Jagger seems to have been the only member of the Rolling Stones present. He was accompanied by Jim Sullivan on 12-string guitar and Eric Ford on bass. The song was titled "As Time Goes By." The version used on the single (which is also included on *December's Children* and various compilations), now renamed "As Tears Go By," was recorded at the IBC Studios in London on October 26, 1965. This provided the Stones with an opportunity to hook up with their erstwhile accomplice, the sound engineer Glyn Johns, who was soon to play a key role in their output. In actual fact, it is only Mick Jagger and Keith Richards who were involved in the recording. Keith plays the one guitar on the number,

his old friend the Harmony 1270 12-string acoustic. His picking (with plectrum) is very effective, despite some dubious tuning. Mick delivers his lyrics extremely well, with an uncustomary sensitivity and fragility. The string arrangements are by Mike Leander, who also conducts the players, and one cannot help comparing "As Tears Goes By" to the Beatles' "Yesterday," from the album *Help!* (August 1965), both performed by a singer, a guitar, and strings. As fate would have it, Mike Leander was called to Paul McCartney's rescue in 1967 to orchestrate "She's Leaving Home," George Martin being unavailable on that occasion. The final result is a success, although it is understandable that this number, which falls outside the group's usual musical orbit, should not be included on any official album in the United Kingdom, but instead used as the B-side of a single. It was a question of image. Compared to Marianne Faithfull's recording, the Stones' comes across as more convincing and less "manufactured." It was nevertheless thanks to her cover that Mick and Keith hit the jackpot for the first time: "The first real cash I ever saw came from selling 'As Tears Go By,'" recalls Keith Richards, " . . . For the first time in my life, I'd got money"[2] And to think that this was even before "(I Can't Get No) Satisfaction."

"As Tears Go By" was released as a single in the United States on December 18, 1965 (with "Gotta Get Away" as the B-side) and reached number 6 on the *Billboard* chart on January 29, 1966.

MARIANNE FAITHFULL:
JAGGER'S MUSE

When "As Tears Go By" entered the UK hit parade in August 1964, Marianne Faithfull was just seventeen years old. A few months later (March 1965), she accompanied her boyfriend John Dunbar to a party for the release of a single by Adrienne Posta, which Andrew Loog Oldham had produced. Paul McCartney, Jane Asher, and Jane's brother Peter were present, as were various members of the Rolling Stones, including Mick Jagger. "I wouldn't even have known he was there if he hadn't had a flaming row with his girlfriend, Chrissie Shrimpton,"[52] she would later write. Oldham, on the other hand, made an enormous impression on her. "I'd never met anyone like Andrew before,"[52] she confides. For his part, the producer was absolutely fascinated by the young woman, whom he immediately suspected of having artistic potential. "The moment I caught sight of Marianne I recognized my next adventure, a true star," he writes. "In another century you'd have set sail for her; in 1964 you'd record her."[5] And this he duly did, getting her to cut one of the first songs ever written by Mick Jagger and Keith Richards, and simultaneously flinging her into the hermetic world of the Stones.

A Venus in Furs

Marianne Evelyn Faithfull was born in London on December 29, 1946. She was the daughter of an Austro-Hungarian aristocrat, Eva von Sacher-Masoch, Baroness Erisso, and the great-great-niece of the writer Leopold von Sacher-Masoch (whose novel *Venus in Furs* gave rise to the term *masochism*). Her father, Glynn Faithfull, was an officer with the British Army during the Second World War, during which troubled time he met Eva in Vienna.

During her school years, Marianne developed an interest in the theater (she joined the Progress Theatre troupe at thirteen years of age) and music, including the folk of Joan Baez and the rock 'n' roll of Chuck Berry. John Dunbar, whom she met in Cambridge in 1963, was her first great love. The son of the filmmaker Robert Dunbar, John was a leading counterculture figure in the United Kingdom. He mixed with writers of the Beat generation such as Allen Ginsberg, Lawrence

Ferlinghetti, and Gregory Corso, and was an early experimenter with hallucinogenic drugs. In 1965 he opened the Indica Gallery with Barry Miles and Peter Asher.

In May of that year, Marianne Faithfull and John Dunbar married, and Marianne gave birth to a son, Nicholas. In the meantime, she had released her first two albums (produced by Tony Calder) and joined the intimate circle of Brian Jones and Anita Pallenberg, who lived at Courtfield Road, where all sorts of experimentation with psychedelic drugs went on.

It was at this time that Mick Jagger came into her life. Marianne embarked on her romance with the singer after attending a Rolling Stones show in Bristol (October 7, 1966). He broke up with Chrissie Shrimpton, and Mick and Marianne came to be feted as one of Swinging London's most glamorous couples, along with Brian and Anita (before long Keith and Anita). At the same time, they embarked on a downward spiral of sex, drugs, and rock 'n' roll, that infernal trio, which culminated in a police raid on Redlands, Keith's Sussex home, on February 12, 1967. Heroin, pills of one kind or another, cannabis resin . . . the drug squad had certainly not been wasting its time. Richards, Jagger, and their friend Robert Fraser, an art dealer, were hauled into court. And Marianne Faithfull, utterly

naked beneath a fur rug when the police showed up, kept the tabloid headline writers busy.

"Sister Morphine"

However, there was more to the relationship between Marianne Faithfull and Mick Jagger than the snippets of scandal in which the press took such delight. The young woman also helped to widen the singer's intellectual and spiritual horizons. She guided him in the choice of his reading material, from Mikhail Bulgakov to William Blake (Allen Ginsberg having already suggested setting the poem "The Grey Monk" to music). "He was insatiably curious," she writes. "He read Eliphas Levi, the 1870s French hermetic magician who had influenced Rimbaud and later the filmmaker Harry Smith."[52] Furthermore, a number of major Rolling Stones songs were directly or indirectly influenced by Marianne, such as "Sympathy for the Devil," "You Can't Always Get What You Want," "Wild Horses," and "Sister Morphine." Marianne also recorded two fine albums of her own during this time, *North Country Maid* (1966) and *Love in a Mist* (1967) as well as taking a number of movie roles, in *Made in U.S.A.* (1966) by Jean-Luc Godard (in which she sings "As Tears Go By"), *The Girl on a Motorcycle* (1968)

by Jack Cardiff, and as Ophelia in Tony Richardson's *Hamlet* (1969) among others.

The split between Marianne and Mick occurred in May 1970 after the Rolling Stones had signed a new contract with Atlantic Records. Ahmet Ertegun (the boss of Atlantic) feared that Marianne would jeopardize the deal (which was, after all, worth some thirty million dollars) with her drug addiction. "When the Stones' money manager Prince Rupert Loewenstein came into the picture, I knew my days were numbered,"[52] writes Marianne Faithfull. In any case, she had no desire to follow Jagger to the South of France—not least because of her son, custody of whom she was still hoping—in vain—to be awarded.

For Marianne, who finally divorced John Dunbar in 1970, there would be life after Mick Jagger and the Rolling Stones. This is confirmed by some fifteen albums, including the remarkable *Broken English* (1979), *Strange Weather* (1987), and *Give My Love to London* (2014), as well as her acting roles on stage and screen. And, in any case, her interest went beyond Mick: "My first move was to get a Rolling Stone as a boyfriend. I slept with three [Mick, Brian, and Keith] and decided the lead singer was the best bet."[52]

SAD DAY

Mick Jagger / Keith Richards / 3:02

SINGLE
19th Nervous Breakdown* / Sad Day
RELEASE DATE
United States: February 12, 1966
RECORD NUMBER: LONDON RECORDS 45 LON 9823* *19TH NERVOUS BREAKDOWN* (SEE P. 160)

Musicians
Mick Jagger: vocals
Keith Richards: lead guitar, acoustic guitar (?), backing vocals (?)
Brian Jones: acoustic guitar (?)
Bill Wyman: bass
Charlie Watts: drums
Jack Nitzsche: electric piano
Recorded
RCA Studios, Hollywood: December 9, 1965
Technical Team
Producer: Andrew Loog Oldham
Sound engineer: Dave Hassinger

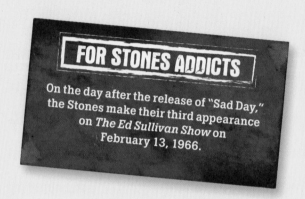

FOR STONES ADDICTS

On the day after the release of "Sad Day," the Stones make their third appearance on *The Ed Sullivan Show* on February 13, 1966.

Genesis

A dreadful start of a day for the character in the song, who has a painful awakening. He remembers the argument he has had with his girlfriend, who has finally left him. Where has she gone? He phones her to find out, but she is not there. The moral of this story of a breakup—yet another in the Stones' catalog—is that *There is only one thing in this world/That I can't understand, that's a girl.*

As another song about the emotional ups and downs of women, and how this is a source of stress and despair for their partners, "Sad Day" would certainly not have been out of place on *Aftermath*. And as a folk-rock number enhanced with Baroque arrangements, it would have fitted in musically too. Recorded at the same session as "Mother's Little Helper," "Take It or Leave It," and "Goin' Home," it was left out of the final selection for the album. Indeed, it can only be assumed that neither the Stones nor Oldham were overly taken with it, as it was not included on any LP until the compilation *No Stone Unturned* in 1973. Although it was chosen as the B-side of the US single "19th Nervous Breakdown," it failed to set the world alight.

Production

This underestimated little song has never assumed its proper place in the Stones' discography. "Sad Day" is a harmonically somewhat curious blues-rock-pop number with some dissonance in the chord structure. It is the kind of song that goes round and round for hours after getting into one's head. The overdubbed intro, on 6-string acoustic, is interesting and innovative, but it is difficult to know whether it is played by Brian

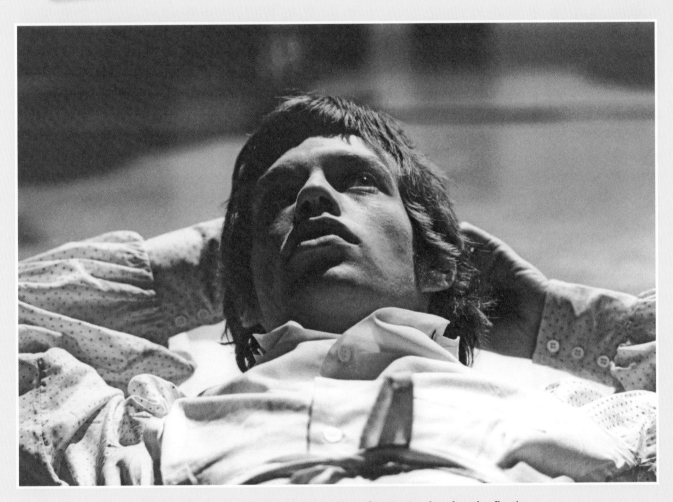

Mick Jagger between two television takes. A moment of profound reflection.

or Keith. Keith is almost certainly on lead, with a little counterpoint lick that he plays throughout the number. The effect is highly successful, as is the interplay between the two guitars. Charlie Watts sets an excellent groove on his Ludwig kit, while Bill Wyman's bass is difficult to hear. It is presumably Jack Nitzsche on electric piano, most likely a Wurlitzer, contributing a sonority hitherto little employed by the Stones. Mick performs his vocal part well, doubling himself on the harmonies. Without being a masterpiece, "Sad Day" is a very good song that offers an insight into the Stones' future musical direction.

Brian (left) tuning his sitar and Bill his Vox Wyman bass prior to a performance of "Paint It Black" on *Ready Steady Go!* on October 7, 1966.

PAINT IT BLACK

Mick Jagger / Keith Richards / 3:46

FOR STONES ADDICTS

Andrew Oldham's obsession with punctuation explains why the Rolling Stones' song is sometimes written "Paint It, Black" and sometimes "Paint It Black," each version yielding a different meaning. The first provoked the anger of the antiracist movements of the day. Keith Richards provides an alternative explanation: "Don't ask me what the comma in the title is for—that's Decca's."

SINGLE

Paint It Black / Long Long While

RELEASE DATE

United Kingdom: May 13, 1966

RECORD NUMBER: DECCA F 12395

Musicians

Mick Jagger: vocals
Keith Richards: acoustic guitar, lead guitar, backing vocals
Brian Jones: sitar, acoustic guitar (?)
Bill Wyman: bass, organ
Charlie Watts: drums, percussion
Jack Nitzsche: piano
Unidentified musicians: tambourine, bongos, castanets

Recorded

RCA Studios, Hollywood: March 6–9, 1966

Technical Team

Producer: Andrew Loog Oldham
Sound engineer: Dave Hassinger

Genesis

"Paint It Black" has given rise to many a commentary and (often far-fetched) interpretation. Contrary to what has been claimed, this Stones song is not about either Vietnam or Mick Jagger's breakup with Chrissie Shrimpton, or his budding relationship with Marianne Faithfull. On the other hand, it is possible to see in it a reference to a bad trip under the influence of hallucinogenic substances, particularly in the red/black, light/dark contrasts.

More probably, it is a metaphor of death. The very first line of the first verse brings to mind a devastated lover attending the funeral of his girlfriend. The *red door* is his bleeding heart, a door he wants *painted black*. A lover who feels he is to blame (*I could not foresee this thing happening to you*) and destined to lead a solitary existence (*I see people turn their heads and quickly look away*). The funeral cortege is also described: *I see a line of cars and they're all painted black*. "Paint It Black" could also be an expression of disenchantment—the end of illusions, of utopias that came into being with the countercultural movements (even if we are still only in 1966 at this point!). The melody in turn comes from Keith Richards: "It was a different style to everything I'd done before. Maybe it was the Jew in me. It's more to me like 'Hava Nagila' or some Gypsy lick. Maybe I picked it up from my granddad."[2]

"Paint It Black" was released as a single in the United States on May 7, 1966 (with "Stupid Girl" as the B-side) and on May 13 in the United Kingdom (with "Long Long While" as the B-side). It soared to number 1 on both sides of the Atlantic. In Britain, where some 200,000 people

had preordered, the press could not help comparing it to the Beatles, in particular regarding the use of the sitar. This attracted a scathing response from Brian Jones in the magazine *Beat Instrumental*: "What utter rubbish. You might as well say that we copy all the other groups by playing guitar. Also, everyone asks if it's going to be the new trend. Well, personally, I wouldn't like it to be. You don't have to get that weird Indian sound from a sitar." But he immediately added: "Take 'Norwegian Wood.' Atmospherically, it's my favorite track by the Beatles. George made simple use of the sitar and it was very effective."[1]

Production

The Stones got "Paint It Black" in the can during their second session in the studio working on *Aftermath*, between March 6 and 9, 1966. Once again, Brian Jones gives a brilliant demonstration of his gifts as a multi-instrumentalist, thereby putting an extraordinary personal stamp on the song. This time, as we have seen, his choice falls on the sitar. Although he defended himself against the accusations of the press, it is obvious that the Beatles' "Norwegian Wood" was a major influence. An influence, that is, in the sense that the Liverpudlian band had opened the way to an experimentation

When the Stones appeared on the show *Ready Steady Go!* (October 7, 1966), Mick Jagger's mic stopped working in the coda to "Paint It Black," leaving him voiceless.

Mick Jagger singing "Paint It Black," which hit number 1 on both sides of the Atlantic in 1966, on *Ready Steady Go!*

with new sounds in which almost the entire rock community indulged during the sixties. Other than this, Brian Jones owes nobody anything for his indispensable contribution to "Paint It Black." According to Bill Wyman, Brian acquired the instrument during the first *Aftermath* sessions at the RCA Studios, between December 8 and 10, 1965: "Stu was kept very busy throughout the sessions, as he always was . . . He got me a six-string bass that I played on one number, as well as a sitar for Brian."[1] It was a certain Hari (and this is not a diminutive of Harrison!), a pupil of Ravi Shankar (the master of the sitar who would achieve great renown in the West as a result of his collaboration and friendship with George Harrison), who taught Brian the basics of the instrument. And during the recording of the number in March 1966, Hari was by his side to coach him. The production of "Paint It Black" was laborious. While the band were rehearsing to little effect—"That song was going nowhere," Andrew Loog Oldham would later write[15]—Bill Wyman sat down at the organ and came up with an inspired idea: "Bill was playing an organ," explains Keith Richards, "doing a takeoff of our first manager who started his career in show business as an organist in a cinema pit. We'd been doing it with funky rhythms and it hadn't worked and he started playing it like this and everybody got behind it. It's a two-beat, very strange."[11] Bill in turn recalls having played the Hammond organ in imitation of Easton. "Charlie immediately took up the rhythm and Brian played the melody line on sitar," he explained in 2002, "I played normal bass on the record and on listening back to it, I suggested Hammond organ pedals. I lay on the floor under the organ and played a second bass riff on the pedals with my fists, at double-time." The bassist concludes with a note of regret: "Funnily enough it was never credited as a Nanker Phelge composition. I can't think why."[1]

Another key element is Charlie Watts's drumming, with his dominant toms and cymbals driving the song. Charlie

explains: "On 'Paint It Black' the drum pattern might have been suggested by Mick and I'd try it that way, or we'd be listening to a certain record at the time—it could have been anything like 'Going to a Go-Go.'"[9] It is certainly true that the Smokey Robinson & The Miracles hit had influenced Charlie, who rearranged it and sped up the tempo. The results are effective and make an important contribution to the success of the number. Keith, who would not neglect to stress that ". . . the musical riff is mostly coming from me. I'm the riff master,"[2] is most likely playing his Gibson Hummingbird acoustic (presumably doubled by Brian) and his Guild M-65 Freshman. Mick gives one of his best performances, alternating gentleness and aggression; his delivery of the lyrics is utterly masterful. He seems to overdub the vocal harmonies, before eventually being supported by Keith in the coda with hummed harmonies that contribute a Slavic feel. Keith overdoes it slightly by playing a bolero-type rhythm on his acoustic guitar (from 2:15), no doubt in an allusion to Ravel, which is supported by Charlie on percussion (castanets?). Bill adds to the general tension by playing glissandos on his Vox Wyman bass, producing a very effective "pumping" effect. The piano part seems to be played by Jack Nitzsche, but is unfortunately barely audible. By contrast, tambourine and what may be bongos can be heard well.

"Paint It Black" is one of the Rolling Stones' greatest songs, and Andrew Loog Oldham's production one of his best. (It was also to be one of his last with the group.) The contribution of each musician is essential to the whole, and the overall effect is of a strain of rock music strongly tinged with exoticism. Mick Jagger would later refer to "this kind of Turkish song."[19] And why not? Although "Paint It Black" does not in any way deal with Vietnam, for many GIs it would be ineradicably associated with a youth spent in Asia.

LONG LONG WHILE

Mick Jagger / Keith Richards /3:01

SINGLE
Paint It Black / Long Long While
RELEASE DATE
United Kingdom: May 13, 1966
RECORD NUMBER: DECCA F 12395

Musicians
Mick Jagger: vocals, maracas (?)
Keith Richards: lead guitar, rhythm guitar
Brian Jones: acoustic rhythm guitar
Bill Wyman: bass
Charlie Watts: drums
Ian Stewart (?): organ
Jack Nitzsche (?): piano
Recorded
RCA Studios, Hollywood: March 6–9, 1966
Technical Team
Producer: Andrew Loog Oldham
Sound engineer: Dave Hassinger

Genesis

The theme of this song is sufficiently rare in the Mick Jagger canon to be worth drawing attention to: in "Long Long While" the male half of a couple acknowledges the error of his ways (even if it has taken him a long time to get around to it). He wants to be forgiven at all costs, and hopes to get the one he still loves to change her mind. This is all said without any ulterior motive, and Mick Jagger delivers his lyrics with all the passion of the eternal . . . romantic. Or rather of the soul singer, for "Long Long While" is a ballad in that heartbreaking style—by which we mean the songs of Otis Redding, Wilson Pickett, and Solomon Burke. This number was a logical choice as the B-side for the single "Paint It Black," released in the United Kingdom on May 13, 1966.

Production

With a piano intro played most likely by Jack Nitzsche and directly inspired by that of "You Really Got a Hold on Me" by Smokey Robinson & The Miracles (1962), "Long Long While" was recorded between March 6 and 9, 1966, while the Stones were still working on *Aftermath*. Dave Hassinger endeavored to make the group sound like its US counterparts, and the results are highly convincing. Once again, Mick Jagger demonstrates that he has been an assiduous student of the masters of soul. Brian Jones plays arpeggios on his Gibson Hummingbird acoustic. In this he is assisted by Keith Richards, who doubles him on his Guild M-65 Freshman (not very well tuned), before launching into some very good blues-rock licks. Keith apparently uses another, distorted, rhythm guitar (his Gibson Firebird VII?) to boost the choruses. In addition to Jack Nitzsche's piano, a Hammond organ can also be heard, no doubt played by Ian Stewart, whose strongly Otis Redding–influenced sound is an important element in "Long Long While." Bill Wyman and Charlie Watts provide their bandmates with unwavering rhythmic support, and Mick Jagger (in all likelihood) plays the maracas in the coda (from 2:15). It may be a little lacking in originality, but "Long Long While" is a very good song performed masterfully by the Stones (despite the timing in the coda leaving something to be desired), a song that deserved better than to be used as a B-side.

SIDE A
1966

HAVE YOU SEEN YOUR MOTHER, BABY, STANDING IN THE SHADOW?

Mick Jagger / Keith Richards / 2:36

SINGLE

Have You Seen Your Mother, Baby, Standing in the Shadow? / Who's Driving Your Plane?

RELEASE DATE

United Kingdom: September 23, 1966

RECORD NUMBER: DECCA F 12497

Musicians

Mick Jagger: vocals
Keith Richards: lead guitar, acoustic guitar, backing vocals
Brian Jones: rhythm guitar
Bill Wyman: bass
Charlie Watts: drums
Jack Nitzsche: piano, tambourine (?)
Mike Leander: orchestration (trumpets)
Mike Leander Orchestra: trumpets
Andrew Loog Oldham: backing vocals

Recorded

RCA Studios, Hollywood: August 3–11, September 8, 1966
IBC Studios, London: August 31, 1966

Technical Team

Producer: Andrew Loog Oldham
Sound engineers: Dave Hassinger, Glyn Johns

Genesis

Have you seen your mother, baby, standing in the shadow? Mick Jagger has said that the words just came to him like that and that no particular significance should be attached to them. This may well be so. Nevertheless, one cannot help wondering whether the singer of the Rolling Stones, whose pout was assuming a more sardonic air from one day to the next, was getting his kicks from playing with double meanings and pursuing a private mission to rid the masses of their inhibitions. *Shadow* is no doubt intended in the sense of "a double life." A double life that the brother and the lover may also be leading. Is there a moralizing sense to the last line of the song? To live in the *brave old world* or to experience the *slide to the depths of decline* is the classic dilemma facing the adolescent in the song!

"Have You Seen Your Mother, Baby, Standing in the Shadow?" (coupled with "Who's Driving Your Plane") was apparently written by Keith at the piano. This was the first single by the Rolling Stones to be released on both sides of the Atlantic simultaneously, that is to say on September 23, 1966. "Another fantastic disc from the Stones, with such a complexity of startling sounds that it'll leave you breathless"[53] was the verdict of the *NME*; "It's only justice that sound engineer Dave Hassinger should get a credit,"[54] opined the *Record Mirror*. Despite the general enthusiasm in the music press, this song only made it to number 5 in the United Kingdom (on October 19, 1966) and number 9 in the United States (on October 29, 1966).

Role-playing and glitzy outfits for a performance of "Have You Seen . . ." on *The Ed Sullivan Show*.

During the band's performance of this song on *The Ed Sullivan Show* on September 11, 1966, Keith can be seen playing piano for the first time. Clearly, Mick alone is performing live, so Keith's piano was actually prerecorded on an instrumental track.

Production

The Rolling Stones were innovating in this song. It was the first time they used horns, and the combination of trumpets, guitars, keyboards, bass, drums, and percussion creates a sonic magma comparable to the wall of sound developed by Phil Spector and Jack Nitzsche (who was, of course, present during the recording).

However, before arriving at its final form, the song gave the entire team a considerable amount of trouble and still failed to meet everybody's expectations in the end, especially those of Keith Richards. Nevertheless, the sessions started well. The RCA Studios had been booked for the period August 3–11, 1966. Dave Hassinger was at the controls, although this was to be his last collaboration with the Stones. RCA would later accuse him of producing the Electric Prunes hit "I Had Too Much to Dream (Last Night)" on his own account and of using the studios in his free time without authorization. This brought to a close an extremely important era in the career of the Stones. In the meantime, however, he did everything he could to help the British band realize its next single. Keith would subsequently explain that he liked the song, but not the record: "It was cut badly. It was mastered badly. It was mixed badly."[11] Everyone, however, believed that the song had potential: "The only reason we were so hot on it was that the track blew our heads off, everything else was rushed too quickly."[11]

The intro begins with a combination of the two guitars, both with plentiful reverb, one distorted and the other giving the impression of being played with a wah-wah pedal (soon to be popularized by Jimi Hendrix and Eric Clapton). The horns, or more specifically trumpets, then come in. There was nothing random about this choice of instrument, explains Keith: "We tried trombones, saxes and every permutation of brass, before the trumpets. Everything else dragged."[1]

The score was written in London by Mike Leander, who then recorded it with the Mike Leander Orchestra at IBC

Studios in the presence of Jagger, Richards, and Oldham, with Glyn Johns as sound engineer. The session took place on August 31. Keith, who had been dreaming of horns ever since "Satisfaction," was finally happy. A week later, on September 8, they returned to the RCA Studios to insert the results and mix the song. In spite of this new sound color, the number still did not work. The rhythmic foundation recorded at the beginning of August was not up to scratch: the bass and drums were bogged down in a morass of sound; the Vox Wyman bass seemed to be distorted entering the console, and lacking in dynamism; and the acoustic, rhythm, and lead guitars were barely emerging from the ensemble. Only Jack Nitzsche's piano was prominent in the mix. A tambourine can be heard (Jack Nitzsche?), as can Mick Jagger's finger snaps in the bridge (1:03). Once again, Mick is very good, and his voice is no doubt the element that comes over best. He overdubs backing vocals with the help of Keith and, for the first and last time on a Stones record, Andrew Loog Oldham. The number ends with Keith's guitar, the same one he plays in the intro, this time alone.

Nightmare in the Studio

"Have You Seen Your Mother, Baby, Standing in the Shadow?" was the archetypal nightmare for any sound engineer or producer: everything is in place, there's a catchy tune, the musicians have put their all into it, but it just won't gel. The sound is small and the number just doesn't take off. Keith Richards has repeatedly claimed that the initial mix was "fantastic." Unfortunately, it is the second mix that was used in the end. This is because a shortened version was needed for the group's appearance on *The Ed Sullivan Show* on September 11, 1966. Bill Wyman: "The rhythm section is buried in the mix and it failed to create as much excitement as we all felt it should have done. Although we took longer to record and mix this single than any of our previous releases, Keith always felt it needed more."[1] And Mick Jagger would later describe the song as "not very good."[9]

"Who's Driving Your Plane?": Mick Jagger launches another attack on his real or imagined girlfriend.

WHO'S DRIVING YOUR PLANE?

Mick Jagger / Keith Richards / 3:14

SINGLE

Have You Seen Your Mother, Baby, Standing in the Shadow? / Who's Driving Your Plane?

RELEASE DATE

United Kingdom: September 23, 1966

RECORD NUMBER: DECCA F 12497

Musicians

Mick Jagger: vocals
Keith Richards: lead guitars
Brian Jones: rhythm guitar, harmonica
Bill Wyman: bass
Charlie Watts: drums
Ian Stewart (?): piano
Jack Nitzsche (?): piano

Recorded

RCA Studios, Hollywood / IBC Studios, London: August 3–11, 1966

Technical Team

Producer : Andrew Loog Oldham
Sound engineer: Dave Hassinger

Genesis

"Who's Driving Your Plane" is an electric blues number of the kind the Rolling Stones had enjoyed playing since day one. An ideal musical context for Mick Jagger, who uses the lyrics to lay into his girlfriend (real or imagined). What does he reproach her for? Not so much for being trained by her father or for submitting to the incessant psychological pressure of her mother, but rather for not knowing how to (or not wanting to) cut the umbilical cord. *Who's driving your plane?* is a turn of phrase typical of Jagger, on a par with "Get Off of My Cloud." *Are you in control or is it driving you insane?* The lover asks the question knowing, and fearing, the answer.

Production

It is interesting to note that "Who's Driving Your Plane?," the B-side of "Have You Seen Your Mother, Baby, Standing in the Shadow?" is the second title of the single to pose a question. Does this mean that Mick Jagger was going through a period of reflection? Setting aside this similarity, "Who's Driving Your Plane?" is an excellent blues track of a kind only the Stones could make. It reveals the influence of a boogie-woogie-tinged Chicago blues, a genre the band had well and truly mastered, and it is clear that they are enjoying themselves. There is nothing innovative about the track, but that was hardly the aim. Keith launches into the intro with a first, distorted, lead guitar, only to be joined by Brian Jones on harmonica. This is followed by a heavy rhythm set by Charlie Watts, with a shuffle beat in which the hi-hat features prominently, and Bill Wyman with an imposing bass line. Brian provides additional rhythmic support on his Gibson Firebird VII and Keith

The Rolling Stones. Five London bluesmen embark on their umpteenth flight bound for success.

adds a second lead guitar, this time with a clear sound, no doubt his Guild M-65 Freshman. According to the notes provided by Bill Wyman in his book *Rolling with the Stones*,[1] it is Jack Nitzsche on piano, but the playing sounds more like that of the boogie-woogie specialist Ian Stewart. Mick Jagger does not hold back on the lyrics. He is simply excellent, with a vocal texture that would not have disgraced the masters of the genre. To round off the roots atmosphere of the number, Mick sings with a prominent and relatively long delay, creating something really hard-hitting. Despite a slightly untidy mix, "Who's Driving Your Plane?" is a master class in the blues given by the Rolling Stones, although it is a shame that Brian's harmonica is somewhat buried in the ensemble. Another number that deserves something better than B-side status.

FOR STONES ADDICTS

A cover of "Who's Driving Your Plane?" was recorded in 1991 by the alternative rock band Honeymoon Killers (Jerry Teel and Cristina Martinez, a future member of Boss Hog).

Under My Thumb
Get Off Of My Cloud
Lady Jane
Not Fade Away
I've Been Loving You Too Long *
Fortune Teller *
The Last Time

19th Nervous Breakdown
Time Is On My Side
I'm Alright
Have You Seen Your Mother, Baby,
  Standing In The Shadow?
(I Can't Get No) Satisfaction

ALBUM
RELEASE DATE
United States: December 3, 1966
Label: London Records
RECORD NUMBER: LL 3493

GOT LIVE IF YOU WANT IT!

Mick Jagger and Brian Jones
onstage at the Royal Albert Hall in
London, September 23, 1966.

GOT LIVE IF YOU WANT IT!:
A LIVE ALBUM AS STOPGAP...

The Album

The success of the album *Aftermath* and the singles "Paint
It Black" and "Have You Seen Your Mother, Baby, Standing in the Shadow?" confirmed the extraordinary impact the
music of the Rolling Stones had in the United States. Similarly, during the 1966 tour of the United States and Canada, which started in Lynn, Massachusetts, on June 24 and
ended in Honolulu, Hawaii, on July 28, the Rolling Stones
were able to witness the electric effect, beyond their wild-
est hopes, they had on the crowds, often to the great displeasure of their elders. In his book *Rolling with the Stones*,[1]
Bill Wyman quotes the not exactly friendly comments made
by Inspector F. C. Errington of the Vancouver police on July
20, 1966: "This was the most prolonged demand of physical
endurance I have ever seen police confronted with during my
33 years of service. Sixty police officers were hampered by
the Stones themselves, who made offensive remarks and rude
gestures at them. Proportionately, the trouble was a lot worse
than the Beatles' show three years ago." And he adds: "It is
not only vulgar, it is disgusting. It's a tribal dance. Its purpose
is to get the youngsters sexually excited. The Stones would not
be welcome in the city in future."[1]

The reputation of the Stones among the authorities and
the establishment seems to have been inversely proportional
to their popularity among young people. London Records
understood this. Because there were several months until the
scheduled release of the next album of original compositions
by the London quintet (*Between the Buttons*, released on

January 20, 1967, in the United Kingdom and on February 11
in the United States), the Stones' US record company decided
to market an album for the end of the year.

This was titled *Got Live If You Want It!* With the exception of two songs recorded in the studio, it is a live album that
reached number 6 on the *Billboard* album chart. An EP version containing five tracks had been made available to the
British public the previous year (released June 11, 1965). In
reality, however, the LP version, although intended exclusively
for North America, was also pressed for the European market
(other than the UK) and a certain number of copies apparently
sold in German and Scandinavia (Decca record numbers LK
4838 [mono] and SKL 4838 [stereo], end of 1966/beginning
of 1967). Because of the modest volume of sales, this is one of
the Stones LPs most sought after by collectors.

The Recording

The original idea for this live album was to record the Rolling Stones in concert at the Royal Albert Hall in London on
September 23, 1966, which was their first show in the UK
for a year. However, in light of the collective hysteria generated by the group, especially among teenagers, which
threatened to degenerate into rioting, Andrew Loog Oldham decided to revise his plans. Although the record was
presented upon release as having been recorded live at the
Royal Albert Hall (the initial US pressings at least), in reality,
"Under My Thumb," "Get Off of My Cloud," "The Last Time,"
and "19th Nervous Breakdown" were recorded at City Hall,

Onstage at the Royal Albert Hall, September 23, 1966. The Stones, with Mick Jagger in the vanguard, electrify the crowd like messiahs of rock 'n' roll . . .

Newcastle, on October 1, 1966, while "Lady Jane," "Not Fade Away," "Have You Seen Your Mother, Baby, Standing in the Shadow?" and "(I Can't Get No) Satisfaction" were captured at Colston Hall in Bristol on October 7. To these eight numbers, two more should be added, "Time Is on My Side" and "I'm Alright," that were recorded between March 5 and 7, 1965, at either the Regal Theatre in London, the Empire Theatre in Liverpool, or the Palace Theatre in Manchester (and included on the EP by the same name destined for the UK public). This leaves two numbers, "I've Been Loving You Too Long" and "Fortune Teller," which were not recorded live at all, but entirely in the studio, the first between May 11 and 12, 1965, at the RCA Studios in Hollywood, and the second on July 9, 1963, at the Decca Studios in West Hampstead. Bill Wyman describes the subterfuge: "Both these songs had crowd atmosphere added . . . 'Lady Jane,' 'I'm Alright,' 'Have You Seen Your Mother,' and 'Satisfaction' all benefited from various amounts of overdubs at Olympic Studios in mid-October."[1] Was this, then, marketing "Oldham-style"?

Got Live If You Want It! is of little interest for its sound quality. The recording engineer Glyn Johns would later describe how he suspended microphones from the balcony in order to capture as well as possible the energy of the performance and the atmosphere—or perhaps it would be more accurate to say *as least badly* as possible, for the Stones played without really being able to hear themselves above the screaming that blocked out the music. For the recording, Johns used the IBC Mobile Unit, whose technical capacities were not yet really suited to rock concerts. On the other hand, the album is a terrific document of the times, of the extraordinary, adrenaline-fueled, and often erotically charged relationship between the Stones and their fans.

The Album Cover

The cover presents a selection of photographs of the Rolling Stones in action. These were taken by Gered Mankowitz, whom the group had asked to accompany them on their two North American tours in 1965.

The fans, mainly teenagers on the verge of hysteria, went so wild that the organizers and Andrew Loog Oldham feared the show would degenerate into a riot . . .

FOR STONES ADDICTS

The album opens with an impassioned introduction of the band by Long John Baldry, one of the singers with Alexis Korner's Blues Incorporated, which saw three young novices pass through its ranks in 1962: Charlie Watts, Brian Jones, and Mick Jagger.

1966

I'VE BEEN LOVING YOU TOO LONG

Otis Redding / Jerry Butler / 2:53

Musicians
Mick Jagger: vocals
Keith Richards: lead guitars, acoustic guitar
Brian Jones: rhythm guitar
Bill Wyman: bass
Charlie Watts: drums
Ian Stewart: organ
Jack Nitzsche (?): piano

Recorded
RCA Studios, Hollywood: May 11–12, 1965
IBC Studios, London: mid-October, 1966

Technical Team
Producer: Andrew Loog Oldham
Sound engineers: Dave Hassinger, Glyn Johns

Otis Redding, one of the great voices of southern soul, recorded "I've Been Loving You Too Long" in 1965.

Genesis

During the sixties, the songs of Otis Redding transformed black American music and also exerted a major influence on white singers in the world of rock 'n' roll. "I've Been Loving You Too Long," was one of the biggest hits of this singer from Georgia. Written with Jerry Butler in a hotel room in Buffalo, New York, the song was recorded more or less immediately. There are two versions: the first (mono), which dates from April 1965, was released as a single in April of that year and reached number 21 on the *Billboard* pop chart on June 19. The second (stereo) was one of eleven numbers recorded with Booker T. & The M.G.'s, the Mar-Keys, and the Memphis Horns at Stax Studios in Memphis during their July 9–10 sessions, and was subsequently released on the masterly album *Otis Blue/Otis Redding Sings Soul.*

A little more than a month after the release of the single, the Rolling Stones, enthralled by Otis Redding's performance, recorded their own version of this superb, moving love song: *My love is growing stronger as you become a habit to me/I've been loving you a little too long, I can't stop now.*

Production

The Stones appeared to be in a little too much of a hurry to cover this sublime number by Otis Redding. Recorded not live, but at the RCA Studios between May 11 and 12, 1965, with Dave Hassinger at the controls, it sounds as if the British band needed to properly hone their version of the song before recording it, particularly Mick Jagger. The singer flirts with disaster by trying to reach notes that are too high for him (between 0:19 and 0:35, and 1:14 and 1:27) and his performance is completely lacking in assurance. The bass-drums duo is not particularly convincing, and the horns on the original version have been replaced by Keith's fuzz guitar, which sounds anemic (despite the extraordinary riff for "Satisfaction" being recorded [courtesy of the Maestro Fuzz-Tone] at the same session). Keith also plays a number of lead guitar licks (1:02) as well as acoustic guitar (his Gibson Heritage). Brian plays arpeggios on his Gibson Firebird VII, and Jack Nitzsche (most likely) can be heard on piano. Toward mid-October 1966, a decision was made to insert an organ part played by Ian Stewart, as well as (barely credible) crowd noises in order to transform the number into a live recording.

FORTUNE TELLER

Allen Toussaint / 1:57

Musicians
Mick Jagger: vocals, tambourine (?)
Keith Richards: rhythm guitar, backing vocals
Brian Jones: rhythm guitar
Bill Wyman: bass
Charlie Watts: drums
Recorded
Decca Studios, West Hampstead, London: July 9, 1963
IBC Studios, London: mid-October, 1966
Technical Team
Producer: Andrew Loog Oldham
Sound engineers: Michael Barclay, Glyn Johns

FOR STONES ADDICTS

The version of "Fortune Teller" on the BBC album can be found on the compilation *More Hot Rocks (Big Hits & Fazed Cookies),* released in 1972 (now on CD).

Genesis

The New Orleans songwriter Allen Toussaint (writing under the pseudonym Naomi Neville), displays a lively sense of humor in this song. A young man visits a clairvoyant who predicts that he will fall in love with the next girl he meets. The following day, disappointed not to have encountered any girl to whom he can give his heart, he returns to the fortune teller and realizes that it is with her that he has fallen madly in love.

"Fortune Teller" was recorded in 1962 by the rhythm 'n' blues singer Benny Spellman, but met with no real success on the charts. The Rolling Stones recorded it a few months later. There seem to have been at least two versions: the first, initially chosen as the B-side of "Poison Ivy" (ultimately never released as a single), was brought to the awareness of fans through the BBC-issued album *Saturday Club*; the second is the version included on the album *Got Live If You Want It!*

Production

This was another number recorded not live, as advertised, but in the studio. The session dates back almost three years, to July 9, 1963, to be precise, under the supervision of Michael Barclay. Compared to the Benny Spellman version, the Stones' is significantly faster and has far more of a rock feel, this time giving the impression that the band is fully in control of its material. Mick Jagger's voice, supported by Keith Richards on backing vocals, sounds assured. Charlie Watts and Bill Wyman drive the number forward, the drummer on his brand-new Ludwig Super Classic Blue Pearl kit and Bill on his Dallas Tuxedo. Keith Richards, on his Harmony H70, shares rhythm guitar with Brian Jones, who plays his green Gretsch Anniversary. As with "I've Been Loving You Too Long," in mid-October 1966, Glyn Johns added a crowd atmosphere in order to make the recording "live." It would seem that the tambourine (played by Jagger?) was also recorded at this session, as it has a different color and presence than the rest of the number. It was most likely on this occasion too that Mick double-tracked his vocal and added additional backing vocals with Keith.

Mick Jagger in the studio (circa 1963) for the recording of "Fortune Teller," which was chosen for the album.

Yesterday's Papers
My Obsession
Back Street Girl
Connection
She Smiled Sweetly
Cool, Calm And Collected
All Sold Out

Please Go Home
Who's Been Sleeping Here?
Complicated
Miss Amanda Jones
Something Happened
To Me Yesterday

ALBUM
RELEASE DATE
United Kingdom: January
20, 1967
RECORD NUMBERS: DECCA LK 4852
[MONO]; SKL 4852 [STEREO])
Peaked at number 3, on the
charts for 22 weeks

BETWEEN THE BUTTONS

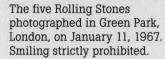
The five Rolling Stones photographed in Green Park, London, on January 11, 1967. Smiling strictly prohibited.

BETWEEN THE BUTTONS: THE EMBLEMATIC ALBUM OF THE COUNTERCULTURE

September 1966: the neuropsychologist Timothy Leary announces the creation of a new religion called the League of Spiritual Discovery, based on the taking of LSD. October 1966: the first sit-in takes place on the lawns of Golden Gate Park in San Francisco, marking an explosion of hippie counterculture that would reach its zenith the following year during the radiant Summer of Love. Also in 1966, the Beach Boys issue *Pet Sounds* and Bob Dylan *Blonde on Blonde* in May, while June sees the release of Frank Zappa's *Freak Out!*, July the Byrds' *Fifth Dimension*, and August the Beatles' *Revolver* and Jefferson Airplane's *Takes Off*. As for the Rolling Stones, they enter a decisive new artistic era with *Aftermath*, which goes on sale in the United Kingdom in April.

Aftermath and the single "Paint It Black" enabled the London rockers to emancipate themselves from their roots in blues and soul. Mick Jagger and Keith Richards were now writing their own songs, while Brian Jones, thanks to his talent as a multi-instrumentalist, brought color and enormous diversity to this repertoire. At a time when a new culture was bursting into life in the West, the next album from the Rolling Stones was to be the flamboyant expression of this movement while, of course, retaining the distinctive character of the group.

The Album

"I think it's better than *Aftermath*. We just want to go on making records that we like rather than worry about where we are going,"[55] confessed Mick Jagger in an interview with *Melody* *Maker* in January 1967. Is *Between the Buttons* superior to *Aftermath*? Not necessarily (a few years later, the singer of the Rolling Stones would revise his opinion). What is certain, however, is that it sounds like a logical follow-up to *Aftermath*, while also paving the way for *Their Satanic Majesties Request*. "*Between the Buttons* was the first record we made when we hadn't been on the road and weren't shit-hot from playing gigs every night," recalls Keith Richards. "Plus, everyone was stoned out of their brains. . . . So in a way, to us it felt like a bit of a new beginning."[34]

Between the Buttons is predominantly psychedelic in mood. Like Alice, the five Stones had passed through the looking glass and were exploring a new musical world. Brian Jones once more plays a vast array of instruments, notably the saxophone, while Mick Jagger and Keith Richards, as songwriters, reveal new inspiration (albeit influenced here and there by the Bob Dylan of *Blonde on Blonde*). The album also includes the first song to be written entirely by Jagger alone: "Yesterday's Papers." As for Bill Wyman and Charlie Watts, they are in their usual good form, providing an unfailingly solid rhythmic foundation. What comes through clearly, by contrast, is the less and less decisive role played by Andrew Loog Oldham, even if it is the Stones' manager who came up with the title for the LP (*between the buttons* presumably in the sense of something not yet decided). Charlie Watts would later reveal that the title sprang from a misunderstanding between the drummer and his producer: "Andrew told me to do the drawings for the LP and he told me the title

A psychedelic portrait of the Stones taken in 1966.

was between the buttons. I thought he meant the title was 'Between the Buttons,' so it stayed."[56]

Despite his evident continued involvement, Oldham was living his last few hours among the Rolling Stones. "Andrew's influence was on the wane and this was his production swan song with us," writes Bill Wyman, who had always had a difficult relationship with the manager. "He still had dreams of being an English Phil Spector, if only by cranking up the reverb to 11. Production subtlety was not Andrew's bag."[1] *Between the Buttons* was indeed to be the last official album produced by Oldham.

First Steps toward a Psychedelic Rock

With this album, the Rolling Stones were widening their musical horizons just as hallucinogenic substances are supposed to heighten consciousness (and allow people to "look God in the face," to borrow the title of a book by the French sociologist Michel Lancelot). Blues rock has given way to psychedelic rock, and also, in places, to a vaudeville style of music inspired by the Kinks. There are also, as always, some very attractive ballads, this time with more of a folk feel. As for the subject matter, this remains largely unchanged. Mick takes unabated

delight in his indictment of women. In "Yesterday's Papers," he hints at his fading relationship with Chrissie Shrimpton, and in "Complicated" at his budding liaison with Marianne Faithfull, while in "Cool, Calm and Collected" and "Who's Been Sleeping Here?" the powerful woman and the unfaithful woman, respectively, come under fire. Only "She Smiled Sweetly," which is comparable to the tender and inoffensive "As Tears Go By," escapes the bitterness.

Mick Jagger also tackles social criticism in "Back Street Girl," spotlighting the utter cynicism of a rich and respectable man having an affair with a woman from the wrong side of the tracks, and in "Something Happened to Me Yesterday," describes the day after an acid trip. Finally, in "Connection," Keith Richards describes the dehumanized decor of airports and, changing focus somewhat, the problems the Rolling Stones had with the authorities whenever they wanted to pass from one country to another.

Between the Buttons was released in the United Kingdom on January 20, 1967. This UK version comprises twelve tracks but no hits (in other words a number released as a single). In the United States, the album appeared in the record stores on February 11. The management of London Records

Glyn Johns, one of the sound engineers who played a decisive role in the Stones' career (shown here in 1975 taking part in an album session).

opted to play it safe, replacing "Back Street Girl" and "Please Go Home" with "Let's Spend the Night Together" and "Ruby Tuesday" (released together as a single on January 14 in the United States). Praise was heaped on the album on both sides of the Atlantic: "It is an eccentric album to say the least, with self-conscious undercurrents of sex, drugs, alcohol and excessive English whimsy," noted the renowned British music journalist Roy Carr. Meanwhile in the *Billboard* of February 11, 1967, it was judged that "'Miss Amanda Jones' and 'Cool, Calm and Collected' are outstanding in this winning package." Reaching numbers 3 and 2, respectively, in the United Kingdom and the United States, *Between the Buttons* today lies at number 357 on the *Rolling Stone* list of 500 Greatest Albums of All Time.

The Album Cover

The cover consists of a photograph by Gered Mankowitz. This shows, from left to right, Keith, Mick, Brian, Charlie, and Bill, their faces sallow and frozen-looking, with a few frail and leafless trees in the background. The photo was taken on Primrose Hill (north of Regent's Park) in London at five thirty in the morning after the band had spent the night recording at Olympic Studios. On the face of it, there is nothing particularly new about the picture, other than the blurring. "The whole point of the *Between the Buttons* pictures is that we were consciously trying to get an image of a band that had a vagueness to it, where you didn't have to be presented with everything in detail. And I was experimenting by putting Vaseline on the lens and using strange, distorted colours,"[6] explains Mankowitz. Brian Jones seems to be in a trance, which his fans were not exactly happy about. The photographer explains why: "During the *Between the Buttons* session he continuously tried to screw the pictures up; he was hiding behind his collar; he'd bought himself a newspaper and buried himself in it; he was just not cooperating."[6]

On the reverse is a cartoon by Charlie Watts explaining how the Rolling Stones achieved their popularity after overcoming numerous obstacles. There is also a short poem: *To understand this little rhyme/You first must tap your foot in time/Then the buttons come much nearer/And the Stones you see more clearer.* The *Record Mirror* of January 28, 1967 would declare: "The Stones' sleeves never seem to look very much different, but this one is more clever and more subtle than the rest."[1]

The Recording

The sessions for *Between the Buttons* were held in two stages. The twelve songs on the UK album plus "Have You Seen Your Mother, Baby, Standing in the Shadow?" were recorded at the RCA Studios in Hollywood between August 3 and 11, 1966, with Dave Hassinger engineering and, according to the credits, Jack Nitzsche on keyboards. This was to be the very last time the Stones would work with the talented sound engineer, who had enabled them to access an American sound and recorded the group's anthem "(I Can't Get No) Satisfaction."

The second stage took place between November 8 and December 6, this time at Olympic Sound Studios in London, which had recently been converted to music recording after having previously been used for cinema and television. At the controls was Glyn Johns, seconded by a certain Eddie Kramer, then an assistant sound engineer, who would go on to enjoy a high-profile career working with the likes of Jimi Hendrix and Led Zeppelin. The Stones were among the earliest clientele of Olympic Sound Studios, which soon became one of the recording venues for the bands of the sixties (including the Beatles, the Who, Led Zeppelin, and Jimi Hendrix). "Dandelion" (released as the B-side of the single "We Love You" and included on the compilation *Through the Past, Darkly [Big Hits Vol. 2]*), "Ruby Tuesday," and "Let's Spend the Night Together" (on the

The Rolling Stones, rock musicians and leading lights of Swinging London.

US album) were recorded there, and probably "If You Let Me" (on the album *Metamorphosis*). Olympic Sound Studios is also where the vocals, and overdubs of various instruments, were added to the tracks recorded at RCA Studios.

Nocturnal Sessions

Glyn Johns recalls that the sessions very soon became nocturnal: "By now it was quite normal to have sessions go all night, a habit started with the Stones in 1966 while we were making *Between the Buttons*, with almost every session starting at 8:00 p.m. and going till 7:30 or 8:00 the following morning."[4] Marianne Faithfull seems to have enjoyed the Stones' sessions more than those of other artists: "Stones sessions were less tiresome than most because they were social events as well, with lots of people hanging out. The studio was the Stones' court. Robert Fraser and Michael Cooper [the photographer] would be there, maybe Tara Browne [heir to the Guinness family fortune who died in a car accident in December 1966 and the inspiration for John Lennon's "Day in the Life"], Anita, of course, and any odd musicians who were in town or whom Mick and Keith happened to run into that day," she notes, nevertheless adding: "The longueurs of the studio

would frequently drive me into the street. I'd go round to David Courts', take a Mandrax and, if available, some LSD and then go back to the session. I'd sit in a corner and quietly vibrate."[52]

An Overproduced Album

From a technical point of view, the results are not on a par with *Aftermath* and this would give rise to some regrets. It is clear that the perception of the Stones and their entourage was altered by hallucinogenic substances, at least in some cases. Keith wrote: "Nobody was in great shape. Brian was starting to be wonky at the time."[34] Hence a record that is overproduced, psychedelic, and untidily mixed, in which the musical message is often obstructed by too many instruments. However, this yielded a tone that some people appreciated. "Frank Zappa used to say he really liked it," Mick Jagger explained to Jann S. Wenner in 1995. "It's a good record, but it was unfortunately rather spoiled. We recorded it in London on four-track machines. We bounced it back [mixed it on two tracks] to do overdubs so many times, we lost the sound of a lot of it."[19] Glyn Johns offers an unvarnished insight into the recording sessions of the time: "Typically, Keith might have a few bars of a chord sequence that he would sit and play over

Keith Richards's Gibson Les Paul Black Beauty. This is a 1957 model (reintroduced in 1994).

and over again for hours on end, with Bill and Charlie playing along, providing invaluable support with an extraordinary degree of patience." When the moment came for the other musicians, such as Brian and Stu, to get involved, and as the song was taking shape, Mick, who had been watching everything from the control room, would then join in, trying out a melody that he would sing in nonsense words. "This process would have been fascinating to be part of if it hadn't taken so long. Very often the adrenaline rush and excitement of what they were creating had long since evaporated by the time we arrived at a take that was acceptable to Keith."[4]

Between the Buttons also saw the arrival on the scene of Nicky Hopkins, an exceptional pianist who went on to have a remarkable career. His work with the Stones on "Let's Spend the Night Together" marked the beginning of a fifteen-year collaboration with the band.

The Instruments

As with *Aftermath*, the Rolling Stones used a vast array of musical instruments on the album. Brian Jones, who seems to have developed a mental block as far as the guitar was concerned, left the guitar playing to Keith Richards on most of the tracks. Keith made various new acquisitions during the course of 1966: a 1952 Gibson "Gold Top" Les Paul, a Gibson Les Paul Custom Black Beauty, a Guild F-212 12-string acoustic, and a "Fiesta Red" Fender Precision bass. Although moving away from the guitar, Brian took pleasure in mastering new instruments, such as a saxophone, vibes, a recorder, and a kazoo. He also used his Vox Bijou electric dulcimer. Bill remained loyal to his Wyman bass and Charlie to his Ludwig kit. Jack Nitzsche played the piano and shared the other keyboard playing with Ian Stewart and Nicky Hopkins. Additional instruments would also be used, such as various types of percussion and even a theremin, although not all of them have been identified.

YESTERDAY'S PAPERS

Mick Jagger / Keith Richards / 2:07

Musicians
Mick Jagger: vocals, tambourine
Keith Richards: lead guitar, backing vocals
Brian Jones: vibraphone, backing vocals
Bill Wyman: bass, backing vocals
Charlie Watts: drums
Jack Nitzsche: harpsichord
Recorded
RCA Studios, Hollywood: August 3–11, 1966 (?)
Olympic Sound Studios, London:
November 8–December 6, 1966
Technical Team
Producer: Andrew Loog Oldham
Sound engineers: Dave Hassinger (?), Glyn Johns
Assistant sound engineer: Eddie Kramer

The Stones' singer settles scores with women in "Yesterday's Papers."

Genesis

"Yesterday's Papers" was written and composed exclusively by Mick Jagger. Once again, the singer levels a relentless indictment against women, or rather against one woman in particular. The girl he is comparing to yesterday's papers could well be ex-girlfriend Chrissie Shrimpton. *Yesterday's papers are such bad news/Same thing applies to me and you*: the words may possess the virtue of clarity, but they are undeniably cruel. Marianne Faithfull would recognize the lyrics as a "horrible public humiliation"[57] for Chrissie Shrimpton. In this respect, "Yesterday's Papers" can be compared to "Under My Thumb" and "Stupid Girl" on *Aftermath*. Keith Richards has his own individual take on these songs that could be described as misogynistic: "Maybe we were winding them up . . . But I think the Beatles and the Stones particularly did release chicks from the fact of 'I'm just a little chick' . . . When you've got three thousand chicks in front of you that are ripping their panties and throwing them at you, you realize what an awesome power you have unleashed."[2]

Musically, too, this song follows logically from various numbers on *Aftermath*. The Stones had already entered the psychedelic era.

Production

The opening number, "Yesterday's Papers," immediately reveals a new and hitherto unknown dimension. As Mick Jagger's first musical composition, the harmonies differ from those of Keith Richards. It is a pop song halfway between the Beach Boys and the Beatles, with harmonies and chords that were new for the Stones. Divided into a number of sequences, it leaves room for a rich and different-sounding orchestration, even in the introduction. Charlie Watts chooses to play mainly his toms, supported by Mick on tambourine. Two basses can also be heard: the first is Bill Wyman on his Vox Wyman, the second is Keith, who doubles him on his new Fender Precision. The track then acquires a distinctly light and airy feel thanks to Brian Jones's vibes and Jack Nitzsche's harpsichord. Keith Richards follows his bandmates on fuzz guitar with emphatic vibrato (replacing the originally intended rhythm guitar). Another surprise is the very *Pet Sounds*–style harmonies sung most probably by Keith, Bill, and Brian. But the end result is extremely successful.

MY OBSESSION

Mick Jagger / Keith Richards / 3:18

Musicians
Mick Jagger: vocals
Keith Richards: lead guitar, backing vocals
Bill Wyman: bass, backing vocals (?)
Charlie Watts: drums
Ian Stewart: piano
Unidentified musician(s): hand claps
Recorded
RCA Studios, Hollywood: August 3–11, 1966
Olympic Sound Studios, London:
November 8–December 6, 1966
Technical Team
Producer: Andrew Loog Oldham
Sound engineers: Dave Hassinger, Glyn Johns
Assistant sound engineer: Eddie Kramer

During a concert at the Waldorf Theater, San Francisco, in September 1977, Blondie performed "My Obsession" (as well as the Doors' "Moonlight Drive").

Brian Wilson, the brilliant leader of the Beach Boys, was highly impressed by "My Obsession."

Genesis

The narrator is a man obsessed. He is madly in love with the girl right in front of him and wants her to be his, to belong to him alone. He wants to be her teacher, that is to say to introduce her to the pleasures of lovemaking, and makes this absolutely plain to her: *You'd be better off with me/And you'll know it when you lost it.* And then: *One* [possession] *that you should give away/Give it to me now I've no objection.* From obsession to madness is but a small step, and the delusional would-be lover takes this step at the end of the song: *Didn't see you were so young/I could almost be your son.* "A song like 'My Obsession' could just as well have been titled 'My Unbridled Lust,' but Jagger/Richards had at least a modicum of subtlety,"[58] writes Eric V. D. Luft. Mick Jagger's own opinion of this number would change over time: "'My Obsession,' that's a good one. They [this and 'Connection'] sounded so great, but then, later on, I was really disappointed with it."[19]

Production

"My Obsession" is a curious combination of R&B, Phil Spector, and psychedelia. As on so many Stones songs, Charlie Watts leads in with a heavy, hypnotic beat. Brian Jones probably did not play any part in the recording. A fuzz guitar played by Keith Richards (his Gibson "Gold Top" Les Paul?) then enters, and revolves around a particular hook throughout the number. Bill Wyman also plays fuzz on his Vox Wyman bass, but it is Ian Stewart who gives the number its musical color with a superb, occasionally dissonant, boogie-woogie piano part. During the session at the RCA Studios, Brian Wilson was brought to see the Stones, whom he did not yet know, by Lou Adler. Mick offered a joint, which he could not possibly refuse. And then he sat down on a sofa to watch: "Influenced by the pot, I thought 'My Obsession' was the best fucking rock and roll song I've ever heard in my life, and by the time I managed to make it home, a good several hours after spacing at the studio, I felt as if the Stones had knocked me on my ass. I just didn't see how the Beach Boys were going to compete. I canceled on Tony and stayed in bed for two straight days, smoking pot and licking my wounds."[59] However, this did not prevent him from writing "Good Vibrations" when he eventually got up. What is immediately obvious about "My Obsession" is the quality of the vocal harmonies. Might Mr. Wilson have lent the band a helping hand?

BACK STREET GIRL

Mick Jagger / Keith Richards / 3:28

Musicians
Mick Jagger: vocals
Keith Richards: acoustic guitar
Brian Jones: keyboards (?)
Bill Wyman: bass
Charlie Watts: percussion
Jack Nitzsche: harpsichord (?)
Nick De Caro: accordion
Recorded
RCA Studios, Hollywood: August 3–11, 1966 (?)
Olympic Sound Studios, London:
November 8–December 6, 1966
Technical Team
Producer: Andrew Loog Oldham
Sound engineers: Dave Hassinger (?), Glyn Johns
Assistant sound engineer: Eddie Kramer

The accordionist Nick De Caro (shown here around 1970), accompanies the Stones on "Back Street Girl."

Genesis

This song is a Rolling Stones–style treatment of social concerns. The subject of "Back Street Girl" is not a love affair but a purely physical relationship between a man—perhaps a wealthy aristocrat and valued member of society—and a girl from a lowly part of town. *Don't want you out in my world . . . Please don't be part of my life, Please don't you bother my wife*, sings Mick Jagger, before delivering the final blow to this young woman from the working class: *You're rather common and coarse anyway . . . Curtsy and look nonchalant, just for me.*

On the face of it, the cynicism of the Rolling Stones appears to be in overdrive here. But this is actually a social criticism of England in the sixties, and more specifically an attack on middle- or upper-class attitudes, a portrait of a privileged Englishman who, unable to obtain the pleasures he is looking for at home, goes in search of a *back street girl*. The words come across all the more harshly in conjunction with the gentle melody.

Production

In the lovely "Back Street Girl," which would have made Donovan proud, the Rolling Stones embrace another aspect of their production. The excellent 6-string acoustic guitar part played by Keith Richards (presumably on his Gibson Hummingbird) lends this song a very effective folklike character. Mick Jagger's performance is full of gentleness and subtlety, while at the same time bringing out the cynicism inherent in his lyrics. A touch of "world" charm is added by the half-French-, half-Cajun-style accordion playing of the talented Nick De Caro. It is difficult to know whether Brian Jones took part in the session, but it could be the multi-instrumentalist on harpsichord (or alternatively it might be Jack Nitzsche). It is also possible that Brian is responsible for the flute-like sound that can be heard in the distance, drowned in reverb. This sound is pretty indefinable, but it seems to emanate from either a Mellotron-type synthesizer or an organ. Bill plays a simple bass line, while Charlie has moved out from behind his Ludwig kit to play various percussion instruments, including small bells (right from the introduction) and castanets (listen at 0:38 and 1:50). The mix is one of the most successful on the album.

CONNECTION

Mick Jagger / Keith Richards / 2:09

Musicians
Mick Jagger: vocals (second voice), tambourine, bass drum
Keith Richards: vocals (lead vocals), lead guitar, bass (?)
Bill Wyman: bass (?)
Charlie Watts: drums, snare drum
Ian Stewart: piano, organ

Recorded
RCA Studios, Hollywood: August 3–11, 1966 (?)
Olympic Sound Studios, London:
November 8–December 6, 1966

Technical Team
Producer: Andrew Loog Oldham
Sound engineers: Dave Hassinger (?), Glyn Johns
Assistant sound engineer: Eddie Kramer

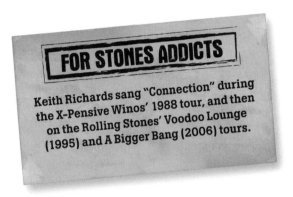

Genesis
"Connection" is essentially a Keith Richards song, almost certainly written late at night, between two concerts, in a hotel room. The subject explores the harsh realities of touring, not least plane changes and the dehumanized atmosphere of airport waiting rooms.

However, as so often with the Rolling Stones, there is probably a hidden meaning. *Everything is going in the wrong direction/The doctor wants to give me more injections/Giving me shots for a thousand rare infections*: does this refer to all the vaccinations the Rolling Stones were required to have before setting off to conquer the world, or to various illicit substances? Similarly, the phrase *My bags they get a very close inspection/I wonder why it is that they suspect 'em* clearly alludes to the zeal of the customs officers when the Stones arrive in town. Furthermore, it is interesting to note that in the imagery-laden parlance of drug dealers, *connection* means *dealer*.

Production
"Connection" was almost certainly recorded not at the RCA Studios, but rather in London, between November 8 and December 6, 1966. The sound is very English, and it was no doubt Glyn Jones who supervised the entire recording. For the first time ever on a Rolling Stones record, it is Keith Richards who sings the lead vocal, albeit supported throughout by Mick Jagger singing harmony. The king of the riff performs respectably, evidently acquiring a taste for the role of lead singer, which he would take up again in future. Despite the quality of the song, the production lacks a certain dynamism. In addition to singing, Keith also plays lead guitar (his Gibson Les Paul Black Beauty?) with a sound distorted through his new Vox UL760 amplifier. It also seems to be him on bass (Fender Precision?), as the playing is very different from Bill Wyman's and closer to that of a guitarist. Mick Jagger would explain to *NME* in January 1967: "That's me beating the bass drum with my hands. Stu on the piano and organ pedals."[44] This is pretty astonishing, all the more so as Charlie confines himself to the snare drum. However, the bass drum lacks power, and the track suffers as a result. Stu delivers a good piano part and makes an effective contribution on the organ pedals, which provide good bass support in the verses. Finally, there are also hand claps, but only in the intro.

The Stones, bound for New York City in September 1967, with the photographer Michael Cooper (at left).

🎧 IN YOUR HEADPHONES

At 1:19, the volume of Mick Jagger's singing falls away but then comes back rather abruptly and his voice is suddenly more present (at the beginning of *And says don't worry*).

SHE SMILED SWEETLY

Mick Jagger / Keith Richards / 2:44

Musicians
Mick Jagger: vocals, tambourine
Keith Richards: organ, bass, piano (?)
Charlie Watts: drums
Jack Nitzsche: piano (?)
Recorded
Olympic Sound Studios, London:
November 8–December 6, 1966
Technical Team
Producer: Andrew Loog Oldham
Sound engineer: Glyn Johns
Assistant sound engineer: Eddie Kramer

The romantic smile of Marianne Faithfull, the presumed subject of "She Smiled Sweetly."

Genesis

Here, Mick Jagger significantly tones down his approach to women. In this respect, "She Smiled Sweetly" is far closer to "As Tears Go By" than "Yesterday's Papers." There is no misogynistic double meaning. Instead, he wallows in romance: *She smiled sweetly/And says don't worry*. Did Mick Jagger really write the words? Or perhaps he had finally discovered that rare creature *That keeps her peace most every day* and *won't disappear [when] my hair's turning grey*. An ode to Marianne Faithfull? Perhaps, although he has said that the song was originally titled "'He Smiled Sweetly,' but someone (Andrew I think) changed it."[44]

Production

"She Smiled Sweetly" has a unique claim to fame within the Rolling Stones' discography: it is the first song in which no guitar can be heard. The reason? Keith Richards explains: "We did it in two takes and I played bass, organ, guitar, and piano on it. Charlie played drums and Mick sang it. It was just the three of us."[60] As far as the guitar is concerned, his memory must be playing tricks on him, because there is no guitar (unless it was left out in the mix). What this demonstrates, however, is that he now had the confidence to play most of the instruments himself. Was this due to a loss of interest on the part of Brian and Bill? Or were they unavailable? Whatever the reason, the end result gives us an opportunity to hear Keith on the organ, probably a Hammond B3. His playing is simple but effective. He also plays bass, no doubt his Fender Precision, which is unfortunately distorted on the recording and out of tune on certain notes (the neck is badly adjusted). Charlie Watts drums with great subtlety, playing a kind of up-tempo shuffle that literally drives the number forward. Mick Jagger is excellent on vocal and also overdubs the harmonies. In January 1967 he stated that "Jack Nitzsche [is] on piano,"[44] contradicting Keith's assertion above. However, the simplicity of the playing seems to lend weight to the guitarist's claim. A lightly played tambourine (or small bells) can also be heard, no doubt added by Mick. "She Smiled Sweetly" is a good, very English, pop song, light-years away from the blues the group played in their early days.

COOL, CALM AND COLLECTED

Mick Jagger / Keith Richards / 4:14

Musicians
Mick Jagger: vocals
Keith Richards: rhythm guitar, backing vocals
Brian Jones: electric dulcimer, kazoo, harmonica
Bill Wyman: bass
Charlie Watts: drums
Nicky Hopkins: piano
Recorded
RCA Studios, Hollywood: August 3–11, 1966
Olympic Sound Studios, London:
November 8–December 6, 1966
Technical Team
Producer: Andrew Loog Oldham
Sound engineers: Dave Hassinger, Glyn Johns
Assistant sound engineer: Eddie Kramer

FOR STONES ADDICTS

If "Cool, Calm and Collected" is reminiscent of the Kinks' Face to Face, there is perhaps a link in the figure of Nicky Hopkins, who took part in the recording of one of the tracks on the album, the sublime "Sunny Afternoon."

Genesis

Cool, calm, and collected. The girl described by Mick Jagger possesses many assets. And on top of everything else, she is *wealthy, knows who to smile to, and knows all the right games to play.* Can we detect some heavy irony here? A line such as *And her teeth ready, sharpened to bite* hints at, if not contempt, at least a certain ridiculing of this powerful woman who uses and abuses people in order to get what she wants.

Production

In "Cool, Calm and Collected," the Rolling Stones conspicuously embrace a music-hall or vaudeville style. This song is reminiscent of the Kinks, in particular the tracks "Party Line" and "Little Miss Queen of Darkness" on the album *Face to Face*, released in October 1966. Once again, Brian Jones seems to take great pleasure in bestowing a unique character on the number. Having abandoned his guitars, he now returns to the dulcimer (see "Lady Jane"), this time his Vox Bijou electric model. His playing is not exactly faultless, but even with the mediocre timing and tuning, he makes an essential contribution to the track. He would also seem to be responsible for the kazoo solo (1:13) a first on any Stones record, and the harmonica solo in the coda. Keith is on rhythm guitar, no doubt his Guild M-65 Freshman, and also uses his Fender Precision to shadow Bill in some of the refrains. Wyman delivers an excellent picked bass line, providing Charlie with support in setting an impeccable groove. Mick, not always at ease on the high notes, compensates with a performance that is halfway between rock and Broadway musical. Above all, "Cool, Calm and Collected" gives the listener an opportunity to discover Nicky Hopkins, whose excellent ragtime-style piano contributes a quirky, vaudeville character to the number. The piano also plays the intro, which bears a certain resemblance to Billy Preston's "Nothing from Nothing" (1974). Another unusual aspect of "Cool, Calm and Collected" is the tempo, which suddenly begins to speed up from 3:08. The sound is drowned in reverb from around 3:45, with a panoramic left/right stereo effect that grows frantic at 4:07. Laughter can be heard at the end (4:12), no doubt as a result of the hellish tempo arrived at by the group.

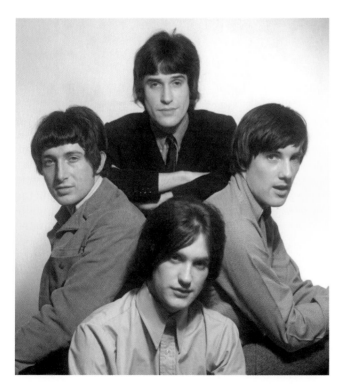

The Kinks, another English band influential in the sixties. The spirit of Ray Davies hovers over "Cool, Calm and Collected."

ALL SOLD OUT

Mick Jagger / Keith Richards / 2:17

Musicians
Mick Jagger: vocals
Keith Richards: rhythm guitar, lead guitar, backing vocals
Brian Jones: recorder, backing vocals
Bill Wyman: bass, organ (?), backing vocals
Charlie Watts: drums
Ian Stewart (?): organ
Jack Nitzsche (?): piano
Recorded
RCA Studios, Hollywood: August 3–11, 1966
Olympic Sound Studios, London:
November 8–December 6, 1966
Technical Team
Producer: Andrew Loog Oldham
Sound engineers: Dave Hassinger, Glyn Johns
Assistant sound engineer: Eddie Kramer

> There have not been many covers of "All Sold Out." Toward the end of the nineties, however, various artists included the song in their repertoires, including the Spinanes, who recorded a very good version of it in 1999.

Genesis

After the mockery of "Cool, Calm and Collected," the prevailing sentiment in "All Sold Out" (originally named "All Part of the Act") is anger. The narrator effectively indulges in a litany of reproaches. The song opens with the line: *Why put this sadness inside of me?* But there is worse to come. He feels betrayed by his girlfriend, or more precisely, suffers as a result of falling into the trap she has laid for him: *I hope that you're having fun with me/There's not much left to attack.*

Production

With "All Sold Out," the band turns back to rock music. Charlie Watts opens the number on his bass drum before launching into a heavy rhythm that, curiously, resembles a mixture of the Small Faces, Cream, and the Yardbirds. The same goes for the general sound of the number, in which it is difficult to hear the usual distinctive Stones take on rock 'n' roll. Keith Richards seems to be playing both guitars, the first rhythm (his Gibson Firebird VII?) and the second lead (his Gibson Les Paul Custom Black Beauty?). Both are distorted, no doubt through his amplifier, the Vox UL760. Bill's Vox Wyman bass is hardly recognizable in the overall sound, which may be Keith's doing. Mick is supported by very prominent backing vocals (Keith, Bill, and Brian?) and delivers his lyrics with a degree of aggression. Jack Nitzsche seems to be on piano and Ian Stewart or Bill Wyman on organ. Brian Jones, unexpectedly adds the recorder, which he plays on the two bridges (*All sold out . . . just like that*). One has to listen carefully to hear it (from 0:41 and 1:31) because the sound is pretty small and does not sit happily with the two distorted guitars. The tuning of the recorder leaves something to be desired in places, giving rise to a suspicion that he added it more in order to participate in some way than to really benefit the track. An instrumental take exists (on the bootleg *Have You Heard the Outtakes, Baby, Recorded in the Shadow?*) that was probably recorded at the RCA Studios in August 1966 and is superior to the version on the album. With greater cohesion and no backing vocals, the song is powerful and effective. The London overdubs do not really do it justice. Most importantly, the stereo version is to be avoided at all costs. "All Sold Out" should be listened to in mono. And preferably on vinyl.

Brian Jones, who plays the recorder and most likely sings backing vocals on "All Sold Out."

PLEASE GO HOME

Mick Jagger / Keith Richards / 3:17

Musicians
Mick Jagger: vocals, maracas
Keith Richards: lead guitar, rhythm guitar, backing vocals
Brian Jones: rhythm guitar (?), oscillator (theremin) (?)
Bill Wyman: bass (?), theremin (?)
Charlie Watts: drums
Recorded
RCA Studios, Hollywood: August 3–11, 1966 (?)
Olympic Sound Studios, London:
November 8–December 6, 1966
Technical Team
Producer: Andrew Loog Oldham
Sound engineers: Dave Hassinger (?), Glyn Johns
Assistant sound engineer: Eddie Kramer

Leon Theremin in 1919. His invention would be adopted by avant-garde rock musicians.

Genesis

Regrets and more regrets . . . The central character in this song is apparently having great difficulty recovering from his relationship with a woman who possesses *every* fault in the book. In any case, a mistake has been made and he asks, or rather orders, her to go home. *I don't have to ask what you do/I just have to look to get you.* And then, in the fourth verse: *You were told of the devious ways/That you thought you could get without pay.* To what is Mick Jagger referring here? To the route that leads into the psychedelic world, or simply to the selfishness of a former girlfriend?

Production

This song of rejection is a wink to Bo Diddley's "Diddley beat," which also features in two numbers previously recorded by the Stones: "Mona" and "Not Fade Away. The band's particular innovation here is to subject the beat to a psychedelic treatment. Accompanied by introductory feedback, no doubt obtained on his Gibson Firebird VII, Keith launches, into this famous rhythm created by the creator of the Diddley sound, possibly on his Gibson Les Paul Black Beauty, with distortion and an emphatic vibrato. Throughout the number, he also creates distortion effects—a sure way to create a psychedelic ambiance—on his Firebird. Charlie works the toms and cymbals of his Ludwig kit with some power, sustaining a highly convincing jungle beat supplemented by Mick on the maracas. Unfortunately, virtually no bass can be heard, begging the question of whether there actually is any on the track. Audible from the intro is a fairly high-pitched sound apparently emanating from an oscillator, a kind of frequency generator that can be freely modulated and which is available on most synthesizers. It is often thought to be a theremin, immortalized in the refrain of "Good Vibrations" by the Beach Boys. Many people believe it is played by that brilliant jack-of-all-trades Brian Jones, but it could equally be Bill Wyman. In his book *Rolling with the Stones*,[1] Wyman describes using a synthesizer during the album sessions. Is he referring to an oscillator, a theremin, or a Mellotron? Moreover, Brian seems to be playing a rhythm guitar part that can be heard at the back of the mix. Finally, Mick, assisted by Keith on the harmonies, produces a vocal effect at the end of the refrains resembling an electronic loop, an effect much used in the dub (no doubt Glyn Johns's idea).

WHO'S BEEN SLEEPING HERE?

Mick Jagger / Keith Richards / 3:57

Musicians
Mick Jagger: vocals, tambourine
Keith Richards: acoustic guitar, lead guitar
Brian Jones: harmonica (?), rhythm guitar (?)
Bill Wyman: bass
Charlie Watts: drums
Nicky Hopkins (?): piano
Recorded
RCA Studios, Hollywood: August 3–11, 1966 (?)
Olympic Sound Studios, London:
November 8–December 6, 1966
Technical Team
Producer: Andrew Loog Oldham
Sound engineers: Dave Hassinger (?), Glyn Johns
Assistant sound engineer: Eddie Kramer

The pianist Nicky Hopkins, whose lyrical playing is immediately recognizable.

Genesis

Upon returning home from a (business?) trip, the narrator has the decidedly unpleasant impression that someone has been visiting his girl during his absence: *Who's been eating off my plate?* and, infinitely worse, *Who's been sleeping here?* His loved one seems reluctant to tell him, leaving the unfortunate soul to imagine that the most improbable types have been there, from the baker to the laughing cavalier.

If there is one song that reveals the influence of Bob Dylan on the Rolling Stones during the second half of the sixties, it is "Who's Been Sleeping Here?" with its cast of characters worthy of the American songwriter's imagination: in addition to the aforementioned laughing cavalier, a butler, a sailor, the three musketeers, and the *cruel old grenadier*, recalling *Highway 61 Revisited* and *Blonde on Blonde*. There is even an attack on the media in the figure of the *noseless old newsboy*. The music, in turn, is very much in the folk-rock spirit, again following the example of the songs on these two Dylan albums.

Production

From the very first bars, the die is cast: in this song the Stones are venturing into Duluth territory, home of the heir to Woody Guthrie. Keith plays a very good intro on his Gibson Hummingbird. It is probably Brian on the harp, playing in a style closely copied from Dylan. The allusion is clear. Mick retains this identity, giving an excellent performance without any overdub or backing vocals to support him. Is this so that he can get closer to the folksinger? The rhythm section of Charlie and Bill inevitably recalls *Highway 61 Revisited*; indeed, one almost expects to hear Mike Bloomfield come in on guitar. Keith plays lead, delivering a number of well-executed solo phrases, while Brian plays rhythm on his Gibson Firebird VII. Finally, the very good piano part seems to have been played by Nicky Hopkins, in a style simultaneously rock and romantic. The only instrumental color that defies the folk-rock label is the guitar effect heard in the first verse, which may have been created on distorted slide guitar drowned in reverb with a volume pedal, or else a guitar recorded normally and then reversed. "Who's Been Sleeping Here?" is a very good song that at the same time pays tribute to Robert Zimmerman.

COMPLICATED

Mick Jagger / Keith Richards / 3:13

Musicians
Mick Jagger: vocals, tambourine
Keith Richards: acoustic guitar, lead
guitar (?), bass, backing vocals
Brian Jones: organ (?), rhythm guitar (?)
Bill Wyman: bass
Charlie Watts: drums
Jack Nitzsche (?): piano
Recorded
RCA Studios, Hollywood: August 3–11, 1966
Olympic Sound Studios, London:
November 8–December 6, 1966
Technical Team
Producer: Andrew Loog Oldham
Sound engineers: Dave Hassinger, Glyn Johns
Assistant sound engineer: Eddie Kramer

Marianne Faithfull, who took the place of Chrissie
Shrimpton in the affections of the Stones singer.

Genesis

She's educated/Doesn't give a damn, she's underrated. She treats me oh so kind, [She] does the same thing every day/ But she's dedicated/To having her own way/She's very complicated: these lines, sung with spirit by Mick Jagger in "Complicated," are no doubt addressed to Marianne Faithfull, who succeeded Chrissie Shrimpton as the object of the singer's affection. Strongly attracted to Marianne, Jagger was nevertheless aware that she could be a threat both to him and the other members of the group because of her continual run-ins with the authorities. "Mick obviously holds me responsible for a lot of what subsequently happened," writes Marianne Faithfull in her autobiography. "He used to say that I talked too much and the things I said were dangerous."[52] Marianne was nothing if not complicated.

Production

And the song itself is far from straightforward. The instrumental track was initially recorded at RCA with Dave Hassinger. Made up of numerous instrumental breaks, it gives the impression of being a strange, not fully finished composition, split into distinct sections and not properly mastered by the Stones. Charlie Watts takes a prominent role, playing the intro and no less than two other solo breaks with plenty of reverb. He is assisted by Mick Jagger (or possibly Jack Nitzsche?) on the tambourine, added in London in November. "Complicated" also gives Keith Richards plenty to do. He can be heard on his Fender Precision bass in the intro (from 0:03), thereafter doubling Bill's Vox Wyman. He also plays acoustic rhythm on his Gibson Hummingbird, and fuzz guitar to accompany the harmonies he shares with Mick, which, incidentally, are not always perfectly in tune (listen at 1:47). The most that can be said for these is that they are reasonably quirky, with a flower power feel that is nevertheless a little out of place in this context. Brian Jones seems to play electric rhythm guitar (Gibson Firebird VII) as well as the organ part, probably on a Vox Continental. Also present at the RCA sessions was Jack Nitzsche, whose touch can be recognized on the piano. "Complicated" gives the impression of having been difficult to record as a result of being too ambitious or too far removed from the musical world of the group. It nevertheless possesses a certain charm.

MISS AMANDA JONES

Mick Jagger / Keith Richards / 2:44

Musicians
Mick Jagger: vocals
Keith Richards: rhythm guitar, lead guitars, backing vocals
Bill Wyman: bass
Charlie Watts: drums
Ian Stewart: piano
Jack Nitzsche: organ
Recorded
RCA Studios, Hollywood: August 3–11, 1966 (?)
Olympic Sound Studios, London:
November 8–December 6, 1966
Technical Team
Producer: Andrew Loog Oldham
Sound engineers: Dave Hassinger (?), Glyn Johns
Assistant sound engineer: Eddie Kramer

Amanda Lear, Salvador Dalí's muse and the friend of Brian Jones, may have been "Miss Amanda Jones."

Genesis

A new muse has appeared in the world of the Rolling Stones. *She looks quite delightfully stoned/She's the darling of the discothèque crowd*: a remarkable and exciting young woman, this Miss Amanda Jones. Mick Jagger gives an insight into his thought process: although the heroine of the song is *of her lineage . . . she's rightfully proud, she's losing her nobility.* This is the price Amanda has to pay, the Stones' singer seems to be saying, for living happily ever after. But who is this Miss Amanda Jones? The song may be referring to Amanda Lear, who, before becoming Salvador Dalí's muse, was thought to have had a brief affair with Brian Jones. Or perhaps it is none other than Anita Pallenberg herself.

Production

"Miss Amanda Jones" can be regarded as the prototype of the sound the Stones adopted at the beginning of the seventies, with the characteristic combination of Keith Richards and Mick Jagger's voices (as found on numbers such as "Rip This Joint" and "Happy" from 1972). The same goes for the rhythm riff that Richards, the undisputed "riff master" would later develop into the group's unmistakable and immediately recognizable signature. The intro of "Miss Amanda Jones" is a success in the sense that Keith manages to find a new tone on his Gibson Les Paul Black Beauty, plugged most certainly into his Vox UL760 amplifier. This time he uses the amp distortion differently, creating a sound closer to the one he would later make. As well as the introductory riff (which recalls T-Rex "Get It On" from 1971), he also strings together an excellent rhythm part. In addition, he plays a second guitar with a clearer sound, delivering licks that correspond perfectly to his Les Paul, plus two other lead guitars. All of which seems to indicate that Brian Jones played no part in the recording. On the piano is Ian Stewart, and on the organ most probably Jack Nitzsche. Meanwhile, Bill and Charlie provide their usual precise rhythmic support. Mick Jagger finds a new way of delivering his lyrics, with his voice far freer and more adventurous than before. The only minus is that his doubling of his vocal in the bridges (0:55 and 1:40) has the effect of emphatically foregrounding his voice, out of keeping with the rest of the song. The same could be said of some of Keith's entries on lead guitar, which are suddenly excessively bright (0:54 and 1:39).

SOMETHING HAPPENED TO ME YESTERDAY

Mick Jagger / Keith Richards / 4:54

Musicians
Mick Jagger: vocals
Keith Richards: vocals, acoustic guitar,
rhythm electric guitar, bass (?)
Brian Jones: saxophone, tuba (?), clarinet (?)
Bill Wyman: bass
Charlie Watts: drums
Jack Nitzsche: piano
Unidentified musicians: trumpet, trombone, violin

Recorded
RCA Studios, Hollywood: August 3–11, 1966
Olympic Sound Studios, London:
November 8–December 6, 1966

Technical Team
Producer: Andrew Loog Oldham
Sound engineers: Dave Hassinger, Glyn Johns
Assistant sound engineer: Eddie Kramer

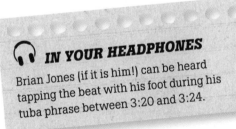

🎧 **IN YOUR HEADPHONES**
Brian Jones (if it is him!) can be heard
tapping the beat with his foot during his
tuba phrase between 3:20 and 3:24.

From 4:17, Mick Jagger can be heard talking.
This is a parody of the British television
series *Dixon of Dock Green*, which was
extremely popular between 1955 and 1976.
The main character is George Dixon, a bobby
at an East End police station who is often at
a loss to know whether something is legal
or not. Moreover, he is fond of whistling.

Genesis
This number probably refers to an experience with LSD or mescaline. The narrator is describing his feelings not during the trip, but afterward. He feels the need to confide in someone totally integrated into traditional society: *Something happened to me yesterday*, he tells him. Is it legal or illegal? He doesn't know. What he does know is that it was so *groovy*, something very strange . . . that really threw him. A memory, nonetheless: *Someone's singing loud across the bay/Sittin' on a mat about to pray.*

Had Mick Jagger and Keith Richards become Jesus freaks, by any chance?

Production
"Something Happened to Me Yesterday" is one of the Stones' contributions to the counterculture of the sixties—the equivalent, to some degree, of Bob Dylan's "Rainy Day Women #12 and 35." The message is expressed through music that skillfully combines vaudeville and Dixieland. As with "Cool, Calm and Collected," the atmosphere seems to be heavily inspired by the Kinks. The number opens with a New Orleans–style fanfare played by trumpet, trombone, and tuba. Mick Jagger, in his role of ringmaster, launches into this strange song with a serene, amused voice. He sings the verses and—for the first time ever—leaves the choruses to Keith. This alternation of the two singers is excellent and plays up the farcical side of the lyrics. Keith is also on acoustic and rhythm electric guitars, and apparently plays bass too, doubling Bill on his. Charlie comes across as relaxed and completely in his element, while Jack Nitzsche, on piano, is also having a ball. But what is Brian doing? Various brass instruments can be heard throughout the track (trumpet, trombone, and tuba) as well as a saxophone, a clarinet, and a violin. It is customary to attribute them all to him, but he cannot possibly have played, or mastered, all of these instruments. This would have required a lot of overdubs at a time when four-track recording was the norm, eight-track not having properly been introduced until a few months down the line. All the same, Brian definitely plays the saxophone, and possibly the tuba and the clarinet as well. The arrangements, however, are expertly done, no doubt by Jack Nitzsche. The closing track on the album is a triumph, and something of an unexpected digression for the Stones.

Ruby Tuesday
Have You Seen Your Mother, Baby,
   Standing In The Shadow?
Let's Spend The Night Together
Lady Jane
Out Of Time
My Girl *
Back Street Girl
Please Go Home
Mother's Little Helper
Take It Or Leave It
Ride On, Baby *
Sittin' On A Fence

* Only the released songs will be
discussed in this chapter.

ALBUM

RELEASE DATE

United States: June 26, 1967

Europe (not UK): July 15, 1967

Peaked at number 3, on the charts for 35 weeks

Record label: London Records (US, Japan)

RECORD NUMBER: LONDON RECORDS PS 509

Label: Decca (Europe, not UK)

RECORD NUMBERS: DECCA LK 4888 [MONO]; SKL 4888 [STEREO]

FLOWERS

FLOWERS: AN INVIGORATING COMPILATION

A Compilation

Eight days after the Monterey International Pop Music Festival (June 16–18, 1967), London Records launched the compilation *Flowers* in the North American market. (This album went on sale in Europe on July 15, 1967, but would not be made available in the United Kingdom until the mid-seventies.) If the Rolling Stones' US record company was celebrating the Summer of Love with this LP, it was also providing many fans with a catch-up opportunity, for the compilation brings together several songs that had been left off the US versions of *Aftermath* and *Between the Buttons*: "Mother's Little Helper," "Out of Time," and "Take It or Leave It" from the former, and "Back Street Girl" and "Please Go Home" from the latter. In addition to these five numbers, *Flowers* also includes "Ruby Tuesday," "Let's Spend the Night Together" (from the US version of *Between the Buttons*), "Have You Seen Your Mother, Baby, Standing in the Shadow?" (single), and "Lady Jane" (single) as well as three previously unreleased tracks: "My Girl," "Ride On, Baby," and "Sittin' on a Fence."

The Cover

The sleeve image of the compilation is a symbol in itself. The word *Flowers*, out of which grow five stems, each terminating in a portrait of a Rolling Stone in the guise of a flower, is psychedelic in terms of both its color scheme and its graphic design. Brian Jones's stem is apparently heavy with symbolism; according to Bill Wyman, this was a joke on the part of Mick and Keith: "Mick and Keith's idea of a joke was that Brian's flower should have no leaves on the stem."[1] The five photographs were taken by Guy Webster during the *Aftermath* session. The title concept is by Lou Adler and the graphics by Tom Wilkes, who was also the artistic director of the Monterey Festival and who would later work on another Stones record sleeve (*Beggars Banquet*). It has to be said that the graphic design for *Flowers* bears an uncanny resemblance to that of the first (and eponymous) album of Big Brother & the Holding Company, featuring Janis Joplin, which was released in August 1967.

MY GIRL

Smokey Robinson / Ronald White / 2:38

Musicians
Mick Jagger: vocals, percussion (?)
Keith Richards: lead guitar, rhythm guitar, backing vocals (?)
Brian Jones: rhythm guitar, backing vocals (?)
Bill Wyman: bass, backing vocals (?)
Charlie Watts: drums
Jack Nitzsche (?): piano
Mike Leander Orchestra: strings and flutes

Recorded
RCA Studios, Hollywood (?): May 12–13, 1965, September 8, 1966
IBC Studios, London (?): August 31–September 2, 1966

Technical Team
Producer: Andrew Loog Oldham
Sound engineer: Dave Hassinger
Assistant sound engineer: Glyn Johns

Smokey Robinson & The Miracles. "My Girl" was one of the vocal group's biggest hits.

Genesis

"My Girl" was written in 1964 by two members of the Miracles, Smokey Robinson and Ronald White, as a tribute to Smokey's wife, Claudette Rogers. Recorded by the Temptations, with David Ruffin singing lead vocals, the song was released as a single (with "[Talking 'bout] Nobody But My Baby" as the B-side) on December 21, 1964. It reached number 1 on the *Billboard* pop chart on March 6, 1965 (and the same position on the R&B chart). This was the Temptations' first number 1 and one of the biggest hits in Motown's history.

Production

At the same time as Otis Redding (on the album *Otis Blue/ Otis Redding Sings Soul*, July 1965) and two years before the Mamas & the Papas (on the album *Deliver*, 1967), the Rolling Stones recorded their own version of "My Girl" in 1965, most likely during the May 12–13 session at the RCA Studios in Hollywood with Dave Hassinger at the controls. Marginally faster than the original, this cover by the London band is well made, even if it follows the Temptations' orchestral arrangements too closely. The Stones, seem to get a little bogged down without ever managing to unstick themselves. Mick Jagger is no David Ruffin, and he seems ill at ease on the high notes (listen at 0:43). The singer may also be playing a percussion instrument, possibly the claves, with abundant reverb. Brian Jones is on rhythm guitar (Firebird?) and Keith plays the main riff, possibly on his Les Paul. Keith also seems to play a second rhythm guitar with distortion and vibrato (from 1:27). Bill Wyman leads into "My Girl" with an enormous bass sound obtained no doubt on his Framus Star bass, played with the fingers and plugged into his Vox Foundation amp. Charlie Watts sets a good groove that is perhaps a little too close to the original version. A piano can also be heard (Jack Nitzsche?). In *Rolling with the Stones*,[1] Bill Wyman dates the sessions to between August 31 and September 2, 1966, the period when Mick, Keith, and Oldham were back in London to record the horns for "Have You Seen Your Mother, Baby, Standing in the Shadow?" with the Mike Leander Orchestra at the IBC Studios. It is therefore undoubtedly Leander who orchestrated the strings and flutes for "My Girl." The final mixing presumably took place at the RCA Studios in Hollywood on September 8.

RIDE ON, BABY

Mick Jagger / Keith Richards / 2:52

Musicians
Mick Jagger: vocals
Keith Richards: lead guitar, autoharp, backing vocals
Brian Jones: rhythm guitar, harpsichord, marimba
Bill Wyman: bass
Charlie Watts: drums, bongos (?)
Jack Nitzsche (?): piano

Recorded
RCA Studios, Hollywood: December 8–10, 1965

Technical Team
Producer: Andrew Loog Oldham
Sound engineer: Dave Hassinger

Genesis

Any feminists who thought that Mick Jagger and Keith Richards had softened their stance, would have had their illusions shattered by "Ride On, Baby." The song is effectively a new attack on women: those who play their cards close to the vest and take a certain pleasure in making their partner suffer; those who possess a dream physique but are not very bright. *You walk up to me/And try to look shy/The red round your eyes/Says that you ain't a child . . . Well I've seen your face in a trashy magazine/You know where you're going but I don't like the places you've been*: Mick Jagger is not exactly subtle, least of all when he throws out the line: *By the time you're thirty gonna look sixty-five.*

"Ride On, Baby" was recorded at the RCA Studios in Hollywood during the *Aftermath* sessions of December 3–10, 1965, during which the Stones also cut the numbers "Mother's Little Helper," "Doncha Bother Me," and "Goin' Home." It did not feature in the final track listing of the band's fourth album, appearing for the first time on the compilation *Flowers*.

Production

"Ride On, Baby" is first and foremost a very good pop-rock song that bears a distant resemblance to Pachelbel's famous canon. The use of the harpsichord, thought to be played here by Brian, is therefore not out of place. Brian gave a further demonstration of his talent as a multi-instrumentalist by introducing an excellent marimba part, as he would again on "Under My Thumb" in March 1966. He is also said to be playing the koto on this track, but in all truth this Japanese instrument is completely inaudible. Instead, Keith is the innovative one with his autoharp, a chorded zither of German origin that was very popular in Appalachian music. According to Andy Babiuk,[28] this instrument was given to Keith as a present by Charlie. Keith also plays lead guitar, leaving the arpeggiated rhythm guitar with reasonably emphatic vibrato to Brian. Charlie, who introduces the track with a tom roll, is excellent, and is supported by some very good bass playing (with pick) from Bill Wyman on his Framus. Charlie also seems to be playing the bongos, but not very convincingly (around 1:21). Jack Nitzsche is apparently on piano, and Mick Jagger excels with a performance dipped in vitriol.

Bill Wyman, an enigmatic individual and a key contributor, on bass, to the Stones sound.

SITTIN' ON A FENCE

Mick Jagger / Keith Richards / 3:03

In December 1965, a duo named Twice as Much recorded a version of "Sittin' on a Fence" produced by Andrew Loog Oldham with the help of Jimmy Page on guitar. Released on the Immediate label, the single peaked at number 25 on the UK charts on August 3, 1966.

Musicians
Mick Jagger: vocals
Keith Richards: lead acoustic guitar, backing vocals
Brian Jones: rhythm acoustic guitar, harpsichord (?)
Bill Wyman: bass
Charlie Watts (?): tambourine
Jack Nitzsche (?): harpsichord
Recorded
RCA Studios, Hollywood: December 8–10, 1965
Technical Team
Producer: Andrew Loog Oldham
Sound engineer: Dave Hassinger

Keith Richards came up with a superb melody for Mick Jagger's dark-hued lyrics.

Genesis

Sitting on the fence, in other words being indecisive, is the precise situation in which the main character in this song has found himself ever since childhood. He finds it impossible to *know wrong from right*, to such an extent in fact that he feels very different from his former schoolmates, who *grew up and settled down*—although he does question their true motivation: might they not have gotten married simply because they had nothing better to do? And of course the narrator does not neglect to take a sideswipe at women: *But there is one thing I could never understand/Some of the sick things that a girl does to a man.* One of the distinctive characteristics of the Rolling Stones in the second half of the sixties, and of the Jagger-Richards duo in particular, was to come up with lyrics of utter darkness, of absolute nihilism, set to superb, often melancholy tunes. "Sittin' on a Fence" is one such number.

Production

This very good song, most probably composed by Keith alone, can be put into the same category as numbers like "Lady Jane" and "As Tears Go By," all of which are influenced by a classical aesthetic far removed from Robert Johnson and Bo Diddley. "Sittin' on a Fence" is a kind of Baroque folk song in which the role of honor is taken by an excellent solo guitar part that would not have offended that great master of the classical guitar, Andrés Segovia. Keith is most likely playing his new Gibson Hummingbird, and displays a surprising ability to make the leap from Chuck Berry to Vivaldi or Bach. It is interesting to note that his guitar seems to be fitted with nylon, rather than metal, strings. Two solo guitars can be heard in the intro, both played in a similar way. Is Brian the second guitarist? It is more likely to be Keith again (overdubbed), as Brian is playing the strummed acoustic rhythm guitar part. A harpsichord comes in at 2:08. Brian is often thought to be responsible, but it is more likely Jack Nitzsche, who has always performed this role for the Stones. Bill delivers a barely audible bass line, while Charlie plays tambourine. Finally, Mick double-tracks his vocals and is joined on the harmonies by Keith.

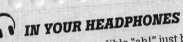

IN YOUR HEADPHONES

At 2:08 there is an audible "ah!" just before the harpsichord entry. And at 2:51, Keith fluffs a note during his solo.

Portrait of the band in 1965. Were the Stones on the "stairway to heaven"?

Sing This All Together
Citadel
In Another Land
2000 Man
Sing This All Together
(See What Happens)

She's A Rainbow
The Lantern
Gomper
2000 Light Years
From Home
On With The Show

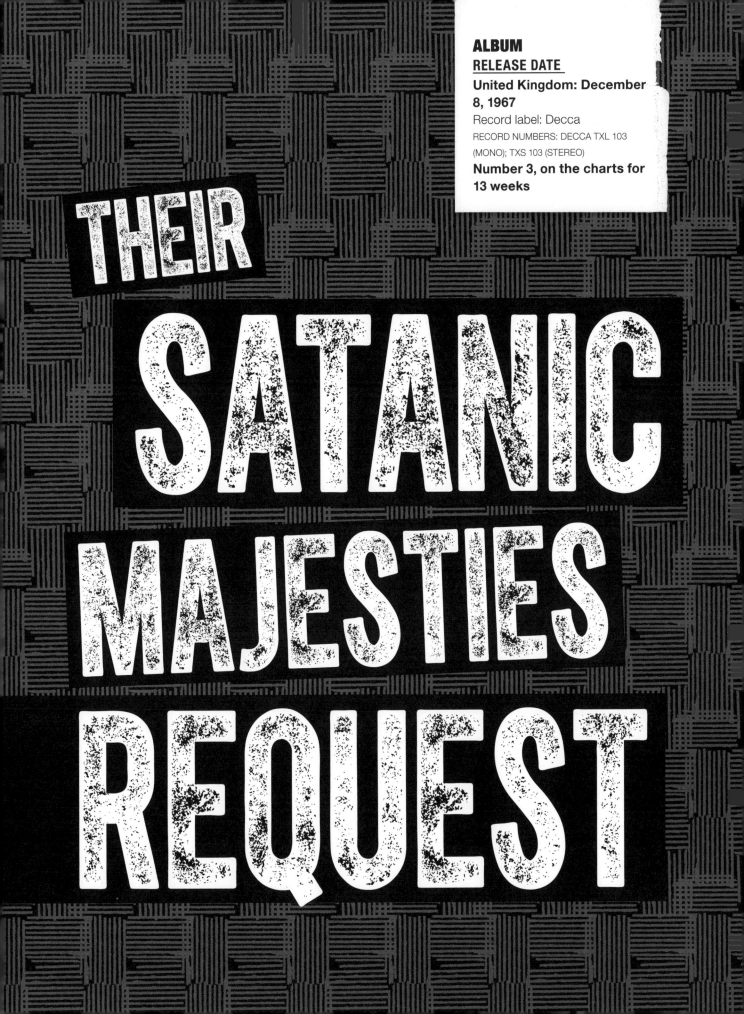

ALBUM
RELEASE DATE
United Kingdom: December 8, 1967
Record label: Decca
RECORD NUMBERS: DECCA TXL 103 (MONO); TXS 103 (STEREO)
Number 3, on the charts for 13 weeks

THEIR SATANIC MAJESTIES REQUEST

THEIR SATANIC MAJESTIES REQUEST: MADE UNDER THE INFLUENCE OF HALLUCINOGENS

1967 was a year of scandal and danger for the Rolling Stones. It all started on February 12 with a well-planned police raid on Redlands, Keith Richards's property in Sussex. A small party had been in progress there. Among the guests were George Harrison and his wife Pattie. The authorities waited for the couple to leave the premises before making their presence known, as the Beatles were not yet in the sights of the British justice system. More than a dozen police officers, armed with a search warrant under the Dangerous Drugs Act, frisked Keith Richards and Mick Jagger as well as their friend Robert Fraser. Marianne Faithfull, still under the influence of acid, was wrapped in a fur rug and nothing else, causing a sensation in the press. Various substances were found: amphetamines, heroin, and cannabis resin. Three months later, on May 10 to be precise, the two Rolling Stones and Fraser appeared in court in Chichester, Sussex. They were remanded on £100 bail until the trial, which was set for June. That same day, Brian Jones and Prince Stash Klossowski de Rola were arrested for possession of cocaine and hashish. They were immediately released upon payment of £250 bail.

The Stones in Court

The trial of Mick Jagger, Keith Richards, and Robert Fraser began on June 27. Hundreds of fans wearing T-shirts printed with ardent messages of support for the two Stones had gathered outside the courthouse. Keith and Mick were represented by the criminal law barrister Michael Havers (the future attorney general under Margaret Thatcher). The Rolling Stones' singer was also able to count on the assistance of Dr. Dixon Firth, called as a witness for the defense, who testified before Judge Leslie Block that the amphetamines found on Mick Jagger had been legally acquired in Italy as a remedy for seasickness. On June 29 it was Keith Richards's turn to explain the events at Redlands. He opted for a different line of defense, claiming that there had been a conspiracy against the defendants.

After a deliberation, all three were found guilty. Robert Fraser (having pleaded guilty) was sentenced to six months in prison and fined £200; Mick Jagger was sentenced to three months' imprisonment and ordered to pay £100 in costs; Keith Richards was given a year in jail and ordered to pay £500. Keith Richards and Robert Fraser were immediately taken to Wormwood Scrubs, while Mick Jagger was escorted to Brixton Prison.

The Butterfly Effect

The sentences provoked an outcry from the group's fans and from radio disc jockeys, who devoted entire programs to Rolling Stones songs, but also, more surprisingly, from the establishment, as represented by the *Times* (London). No less a figure than the editor of the venerable newspaper, the highly influential William Rees-Mogg, wrote a resounding editorial titled "Who Breaks a Butterfly on a Wheel," after a poem by Alexander Pope. In this piece, published in the July 1 edition, Rees-Mogg called for facts, not personalities, to be judged.

Keith Richards and Mick Jagger in the garden of Keith's house Redlands, which went down in history in February 1967 . . .

This editorial probably played a key role in the eventual outcome of the affair.

On July 31, Keith's conviction was quashed (due to lack of evidence) and Mick's commuted to a one-year conditional discharge. As for Brian, his prison sentence was eventually annulled on December 12 after multiple psychiatrists testified that the musician was subject to irrational fears. Although freed, he was required to undergo treatment and was placed on probation. However, something infinitely worse had happened to him. At the end of February, on the way to Morocco with Anita and Keith, Brian had been rushed to the hospital in Albi, in the department of Tarn, France, where the doctors diagnosed pneumonia. While he was in the hospital in Toulouse, Keith and Anita continued on their way. A liaison developed in the back of Keith's Bentley, leading to the inevitable breakup of Anita and Brian and a humiliation that was taken very badly by the founder of the Stones.

The Album

The Rolling Stones' sixth UK album is unlike any other they had previously released, even *Between the Buttons*. It can be seen as a strange anomaly in the career of the British group. The LP was originally going to be named *Cosmic Christmas* (or *The Rolling Stones' Cosmic Christmas*), which corresponds pretty well to the music on both sides of the album. Under the influence of psychotropic substances (some of the

band at least), the Rolling Stones recorded not exactly a concept album, but at any rate a homogeneous "space opera" of an album that was very much in keeping with the countercultural effervescence of the times, in a sense the translation into music of Timothy Leary's *The Politics of Ecstasy*, one of the founding texts of the psychedelic revolution. In this respect, *Their Satanic Majesties Request* is not so much a response to the Beatles' brilliant *Sgt. Pepper's Lonely Hearts Club Band*, released six months earlier, on June 1, 1967, but rather the British equivalent of the early acid rock albums, such as the Byrds' *Fifth Dimension* (July 1966) or Jefferson Airplane's *Surrealistic Pillow* (February 1967), which explains the interest it aroused among musicians on the California scene. "I thought it was a good album," said Marty Balin. "It was the psychedelic era, so that album was right on me."[61]

Their Satanic Majesties Request can therefore be seen as the Rolling Stones' contribution to the hippie movement and the Summer of Love, indeed to the flower power generation as a whole. Some of the improvisations on the album are reasonably lengthy, such as "Sing This All Together (See What Happens)" and "Gomper," and the range of instruments used is extremely wide, from the Mellotron to the electric dulcimer to the sitar and the tabla.

Some of the tracks on the album confirm the artistic compatibility of Mick Jagger and Keith Richards, who around this time assumed the appropriate moniker the Glimmer Twins.

Pete Townshend of the Who

The Who recorded "Under My Thumb" and "The Last Time" in 1967 in solidarity.

Charged with the possession of cannabis, Brian Jones leaves court under the affectionate gaze of his fans.

"She's a Rainbow" (for its melody) and "2000 Light Years from Home" (for its arrangements) can be ranked among the duo's best songs, while "In Another Land" demonstrated that Bill Wyman was also capable of writing songs. Furthermore—and this is another key element of the work—Mick Jagger provides further proof of his considerable talent as a lyricist. The Stones' sixth album gave him an opportunity to explore new themes. Misogyny and a taste for cynicism, which had provoked fury from some quarters, gave way to an inspired vision of the Rolling Stones' singer's world—for example in "Citadel," which could be seen a criticism of the materialism of the United States and the West and a reference to the louche world of Andy Warhol's Factory. Or "2000 Man," in which a man living at the turn of the twenty-first century has a relationship with a computer. Jagger also demonstrates a real interest in heroic fantasy in "She's a Rainbow" and "Gomper," and even for the dark fantasy of Edgar Allan Poe in "The Lantern." Clearly this was a new departure for the songwriter from Dartford.

Farewell to Oldham

The Rolling Stones' psychedelic offering went on sale on December 8, 1967, in the UK and Europe, and on December 9 in the United States. It was the first album to be produced by the band itself, without Andrew Loog Oldham, who was officially relieved of his duties as of September 20. Oldham no longer understood the direction his protégés were taking: " . . . it was the first time I'd been in the studio when I didn't understand what they were doing . . . I looked at it and said,

'Well, what the fuck am I doing here?'"[28] Jagger would later explain that the split was inevitable. Why? Oldham's lack of commitment: "The reason Andrew Oldham left was because he thought that we weren't concentrating and that we were being childish."[9] But there was also the disruptive intrusion into their daily lives of hallucinogenic substances. "Andrew did kind of disappear around the time of the drug bust,"[9] comments Keith Richards. After having managed and produced the Stones for almost five years, Oldham, as a result of all this, threw in the towel in order to focus on Immediate Records and look after the Small Faces. Charlie Watts puts it in a nutshell: "I don't think we really needed a manager, to be honest."[9]

Their Satanic Majesties Request was also the first Stones album on which the track listing was the same in every sales territory . . . and it was released to virtually blanket incomprehension by rock critics, especially to those who compared it to *Sgt. Pepper's Lonely Hearts Club Band*. Richard Corliss, in the *New York Times* April 28 edition, wrote: " . . . their imagination seems to have dried up when it comes to some of the arrangements." Keith Richards recalls that the album had a difficult birth: "Much of that year we struggled haphazardly to make *Their Satanic Majesties Request*," he writes in *Life*. "None of us wanted to make it, but it was time for another Stones album, and *Sgt. Pepper's* was coming out, so we thought basically we were doing a put-on."[2] In another interview, the guitarist would qualify this view: "In retrospect, I find some very interesting things on there. Soundwise, we could have done a better job on it."[11] Mick Jagger would later defend the band's change of artistic direction: "*Their Satanic*

Mick Jagger and John Lennon. Lennon, along with Paul McCartney, would lend the Stones a hand on a number of the album's recording sessions.

Majesties Request was a really fun moment, and there were some good songs on it: 'She's a Rainbow' was very pretty. Nicky Hopkins on piano was very much in evidence on that record. '2000 Light Years From Home' was a good track; we performed that live quite a lot, but the studio version was actually a bit too long and not focused enough."[9]

Despite the best efforts of the critics, the album reached number 3 in the United Kingdom and number 2 in the United States. It was therefore a very nice Christmas present—not just for the fans, but for the Rolling Stones themselves.

With a Little Help from Our Friends

Throughout their careers, the paths of the Stones and the Beatles were constantly crossing, and the two bands continually influenced one other, no more so than in 1967. *Their Satanic Majesties Request* is the proof. John Lennon reacted to the album's release by saying that if the Beatles were bringing something out, the Stones would follow suit a couple of months later. While defending the band against this charge, Keith could not deny the Beatles' influence: "Maybe we were doing it a little bit after them. Anyway, we were following them through so many scenes. We're only just mirrors ourselves of that whole thing. It took us much longer to get a record out for us, our stuff was always coming out later anyway."[11] Exchanges of personnel and references to each other can be found in a number of the

two bands' productions. It is well known, for instance, that the words *Welcome the Rolling Stones* can be read on the cover of *Sgt. Pepper* and that during the live broadcast of "All You Need Is Love," Mick, Keith, and Brian can be seen in the crowd adding their voice in the refrains. Similarly, Mick is supposed to have contributed backing vocals to "Baby You're a Rich Man," while Brian Jones played soprano saxophone on "You Know My Name (Look Up the Number)," the B-side of "Let It Be." In July 1967 two of the Beatles (John and Paul) would come along to sing harmony on "We Love You." In reality, and contrary to the image conveyed in the media, relations between the two bands were extremely amicable. To such a degree, in fact, that Mick Jagger and Paul McCartney envisioned setting up a communal recording studio for the two groups. This did not prevent Keith from airing his opinion of the Beatles' masterpiece *Sgt. Pepper* in 2015: "Some people think it's a genius album, but I think it's a mishmash of rubbish, kind of like *Satanic Majesties*—'Oh, if you can make a load of shit, so can we!'"[62]

The Album Cover

Even the fiercest critics of the music of *Their Majesties Satanic Request* nevertheless agree that the album cover is one of the most successful in the history of rock music. Charlie, Keith, Mick, Brian, and Bill (from left to right) are dressed

1967

Mick Jagger and sound engineer Glyn Johns during the recording of "We Love You."

as troubadours or fairy-tale characters in an extremely color-ful setting with the dome of a minaret and mountains visible in the background and two planets hanging in a blue sky.

All the same, the originality of the design relies mainly on the particular technique employed: lenticular print-ing, which creates a 3-D effect, giving the impression that four of the five Stones are turning their heads toward one another (the exception being Mick, who also has his arms crossed in front of him). The photograph was taken by Michael Cooper (who had been used by the Beatles for *Sgt. Pepper's*) at the request of Mick, who was adamant that the Stones' cover should cost more than the Beatles', created a few months earlier. "We went to New York, put ourselves in the hands of this Japanese bloke with the only camera in the world that could do the 3-D,"[2] recalls Keith Richards. "Bits of paint and saws, bits of Styrofoam. We need some plants! OK, we'll go down to the flower district!"[2] Mick Jag-ger: "We were on acid doing the cover picture. I always remember doing that. It was like being at school, you know, sticking on the bits of colored paper and things. It was really silly. But we enjoyed it."[19] The illustration on the back of the album cover is credited to Tony Meeviwiffen.

The Recording

There are three main reasons the album turned out to be relatively disappointing. To start with, the ongoing legal tribulations of Mick Jagger, Keith Richards, and Brian Jones inevitably led to the disruption and postponing of recording sessions. Secondly, there was the excessive consumption of narcotics. "I can remember virtually nothing of those ses-sions," Keith Richards would later confess. "It's a total blank. We were pretty much the way we look on the cover!"[9] Finally—and crucially—there was Andrew Loog Oldham's resignation. Although claiming at the time that the band no longer needed one, Jagger would later regret that there had been " . . . no producer to tell us, 'Enough already, thank you very much, now can we just get on with this song?'"[9]

As a result, the recording of *Their Satanic Majesties Request* took place at Olympic Studios over a period of more than nine months (from February to October 1967), with Glyn Johns engineering, assisted by Eddie Kramer,and Andy, Glyn's younger brother, in the role of tape operator (under assistant). Andy Johns went on to enjoy as prestigious a career as his brother, notably working alongside Glyn on *Sticky Fingers* in 1971 and engineering the greater part of Led Zeppelin's discography.

The first phase seems to have taken place between Feb-ruary 9 and 11, 1967 (the day before the dramatic events at Redlands), when the initial takes of "2000 Light Years from Home" were cut. Recording resumed in mid-May, when the Rolling Stones began work on "She's a Rainbow," "Telstar II," and "Manhole Cover" (the second and third takes of which

Mick Jagger and Keith Richards during a session at Olympic Sound
Studios in London for *Their Satanic Majesties Request.*

were not used in the end). The third phase took place in June and saw the recording of "Citadel" for the album and "We Love You" for the single. In July the Stones worked initially on "She's Doing Her Thing," "Blow Me Mama," and "Bathroom," all of which have vanished without trace, and subsequently on "In Another Land," "Sing This All Together," "Sing This All Together (See What Happens)," "2000 Man," "The Lantern," "Gomper," and "On with the Show"—to which should also be added "Child of the Moon" (the future B-side of "Jumpin' Jack Flash") and various other tracks that failed to make the final selection.

A Lack of Direction

There would be more sessions in August and September, and then again in October, when the finishing touches were put on the ten tracks selected for the album. Glyn Johns: "Mick Jagger arrived at the studios when they were working on *Their Satanic Majesties* and said he wanted a load of unusual sounds that had never been done before. I had a nosh and finally thought of something using echo. I plugged it all in and finally got it to work. I got Mick to listen and he said, 'Great, half-a-dozen more like that and we're okay.'"[1]

The tracks on the album are in the spirit of *Between the Buttons,* only crazier and more psychedelic. The Stones lack any points of reference and try to cover up the absence of any guiding principle with effects that are not always justified, and

by splitting up numbers into separate sequences. This time the break with their blues-rock roots is total. As a result, Ian Stewart hated what they were doing to such an extent that he played virtually no part in the sessions. Curiously, and contrary to all expectations, this album was to reawaken the interest of Brian Jones: "The only time Brian looked like coming into his own," recalled Stu, "was when they did that awful *Satanic Majesties,* where he got the chance to dabble with the mellotron. It was a terrible shame. He'd do anything."[1] Brian no longer touched the guitar. Instead he turned his attention once again to a multitude of other instruments, ranging from the saxophone to the concert harmonica. Despite his best efforts, however, Brian's contribution would not be able to compensate for the album's shortcomings in terms of production. Mick Jagger would later admit to feeling a sense of relief once the mixing of the album was over. This was a complicated process (performed at Olympic Studios and Bell Sound Studios in New York) that Glyn Jones would find exhausting: "Both Mick and Keith would take an active part in the mixing process and drove me nuts making me mix a track for hours when I felt I had got it in the first couple of passes . . . There were a couple of occasions when finally putting the album together I would play back earlier mixes that I had done on my own, to compare with the one they had chosen after hours of farting around, and in the cold light of day they would agree that mine were better."[4] Finally, *Their Satanic Majesties*

1967

The recording of this album, which lacked any guiding principle, would extend over more than nine months.

Request gave the Stones an opportunity to innovate by running one track into the next without a break.

The Instruments

Credit should be given to Brian Jones, who capitalized on his gifts as a multi-instrumentalist by mastering the Mellotron, which he used on many of the tracks to produce the sound of horns, flutes, mandolin, and strings. In addition, he found a concert harmonica lying in a corner of the studio, sat down at the Hammond B-3 organ, took out his electric dulcimer again, and played a number of percussion instruments. During the sessions he also purchased an electric guitar-mandolin, the Vox Mando-Guitar, which he does not, however, seem to have used. Keith remained loyal to his Gibson Les Paul Black Beauty, his Firebird VII, and his Hummingbird. He can also be seen in some photographs playing his blue Fender Telecaster. Bill and Charlie stuck to their regular instruments, and everyone played a wide assortment of percussion instruments as required by the different tracks.

FOR STONES ADDICTS

Her Britannic Majesty's Secretary of State for Requests and Requires . . . Reading these words inside his passport gave Mick the idea for an alternative to *Cosmic Christmas* as the title of the album they were preparing to release. In memory of his recent troubles with the authorities (who nearly confiscated his passport), the singer wanted to call the album *Her Satanic Majesty Requests and Requires.* This idea was categorically rejected by Decca, hence the less provocative title *Their Satanic Majesties Request.*

SING THIS ALL TOGETHER

Mick Jagger / Keith Richards / 3:47

Musicians
Mick Jagger: vocals
Keith Richards: rhythm guitar, lead guitar, bass (?)
Brian Jones: Mellotron, saxophone
Bill Wyman: bass (?)
Charlie Watts: drums
Nicky Hopkins: piano
Unidentified musicians: backing vocals, assorted percussion

Recorded
Olympic Sound Studios, London:
July, August–September 1967

Technical Team
Producers: the Rolling Stones
Sound engineer: Glyn Johns
Assistant sound engineer: Eddie Kramer

Keith Richards in the studio with Ian Stewart.

 IN YOUR HEADPHONES
After the instrumental bridge, the reprise of the chorus is slower (listen at 2:46). Is this the result of two parts recorded separately at differing speeds being edited together?

Genesis

In September 1967, the *NME* journalist Keith Altham went to Olympic Sound Studios during the recording of *Their Satanic Majesties Request*. He describes listening, at Brian Jones's instigation, to a take that lasted some fifteen minutes. This was the recording that would later be divided, giving rise to the two parts of "Sing This All Together." The track in question was an instrumental to which Mick then added words in the studio. Although the Stones had previously shown no more than a passing interest in the tender utopia of flower power, things seemed to have changed with *Their Satanic Majesties Request*, and above all with "Sing This All Together." *Why don't we sing this song all together/Open our heads let the pictures come.* The message leaves little room for misunderstanding: let us be guided by our imagination, it seems to be saying. There is a distinct resemblance to the Beatles' "All You Need Is Love" and the hippie anthems of the West Coast, such as those by the Grateful Dead and Jefferson Airplane. Indeed so strong is the resemblance that the listener could be forgiven for wondering whether this really is a Stones song at all.

Production

This opening track, whose working title was "God Bless You," plunges us into the world of psychedelia Rolling Stones–style, that is to say the musical equivalent of a painting by Hieronymus Bosch. Nicky Hopkins begins the intro on a heavily compressed piano before being joined by Brian Jones, who delightedly throws in some horn breaks on his Mellotron. A bass can be heard, most probably Keith Richards on his Fender Precision (played with pick). It is interesting to note that no other bass is audible on the track, probably a consequence of the highly (overly?) worked mix. The vocal line then begins, with an appealing melody taken up by a chorus of voices dominated by Mick Jagger's. The verses are equally pleasing, with Mick fairly recessed in the mix. The track includes an instrumental bridge dominated by plentiful percussion including a güiro, congas, maracas, a tambourine, vibes, a xylophone, and a marimba. Charlie Watts marks the beat on his bass drum with breaks on his cymbals and toms. Keith plays rhythm guitar and distorted lead, while Brian punctuates the number with the sound of horns and flutes on the Mellotron and a real saxophone that he plays himself (1:29).

1967

Keith's riff from "Citadel" was recycled by Roxy Music on their 1973 single "Street Life," from the album *Stranded*.

CITADEL

Mick Jagger / Keith Richards / 2:51

Musicians
Mick Jagger: vocals, maracas
Keith Richards: lead guitar, rhythm guitar, bass (?)
Brian Jones: Mellotron, saxophone (?)
Bill Wyman: bass
Charlie Watts: drums
Unidentified musicians: glockenspiel or vibraphone (?)
Recorded
Olympic Sound Studios, London: June–October, 1967,
De Lane Dea Studios, London: October 2–5, 1967
Technical Team
Producers: the Rolling Stones
Sound engineer: Glyn Johns
Assistant sound engineer: Eddie Kramer

The transgender actress Candy Darling may be a protagonist in "Citadel."

Genesis

The great minds of rock music think alike. Mick Jagger wrote the lyrics of "Citadel" in September 1967, that is to say a month before Bob Dylan recorded "All Along the Watchtower" for the album *John Wesley Harding. Men are armed shout who goes there?/We have journeyed far from here, armed with bibles make us swear.*

How should this song be interpreted? The citadel of the title may be intended as the symbol of a megalopolis—and more specifically of the frantic, oppressive, decadent life of the big city—a metaphor suggesting that the Stones' lyricist had been inspired by Fritz Lang's *Metropolis* (1927) and the heroic fantasy tales of Robert E. Howard. If so, the citadel may well represent New York, a city in which money is king, where *Flags are flying, dollar bills/Round the heights of concrete hills.* No doubt there is also a reference here to the Warholian world of the Factory. Moreover, one of the characters goes by the name of Candy, perhaps a reference to Warhol actress Candy Darling, whom Mick Jagger had met a short time before.

Production

"After Five," better known as "Citadel," follows directly from "Sing This All Together" without a break; indeed, each of the tracks on the album runs straight into the next one. This number is significantly punchier than the previous one. Keith plays the intro, delivering a very good riff in chords, probably on his Gibson Les Paul Black Beauty, with distortion, reverb, and plenty of vibrato. Charlie sets a heavy beat, supporting the guitarist's work admirably, while in turn underpinned by Bill's excellent bass, which is doubled by fuzz bass (Keith?) around 1:21. It is also Keith who reinforces the main riff with rhythm guitar and plays the lead guitar lick at around 2:28. From the intro onward an intermittent sound can be heard that resembles that of underwater sonar. This is probably a glockenspiel or vibraphone (Mellotron?) on which the same note (B) is repeated over and over again. The Mellotron is almost certainly played by Brian, producing a mandolin-like sound and also, in this case, a saxophone-like tone rather than the wind instrument itself (1:25 and 1:56). Meanwhile, Mick delivers an excellent performance and double-tracks his own vocal. The singer also plays the maracas. All in all, "Citadel" is a very good number.

IN ANOTHER LAND

Bill Wyman / 3:15

Musicians
Mick Jagger: backing vocals
Keith Richards: acoustic guitar, backing vocals
Brian Jones: Mellotron
Bill Wyman: lead vocal, bass, organ (?)
Charlie Watts: drums
Nicky Hopkins: harpsichord, piano
Steve Marriott: backing vocals, guitar (?)
Ronnie Lane (?): backing vocals

Recorded
Olympic Sound Studios, London: July 13–?, 1967

Technical Team
Producers: the Rolling Stones
Sound engineer: Glyn Johns
Assistant sound engineer: Eddie Kramer

FOR STONES ADDICTS

The single "In Another Land" was released in December 1967 under Bill Wyman's name, rather than that of the Rolling Stones, and with no promotion. This clearly did not help sales, and to this day Bill does not really understand the reason. Allen Klein is supposed to have suggested that it was a love song and as such was incompatible with the band's image . . .

Genesis

"In Another Land" occupies a special place in the catalog of the London quintet. This is because it is officially credited to Bill Wyman. The Rolling Stones bassist wrote the number at the beginning of July 1967 on a Thomas organ and then made a demo. Probably it would have progressed no further but for a lucky coincidence that he recounts in his memoirs: "Astrid [Lundström] and I drove to Barnes on 13 July to attend a recording session with the Stones at Olympic with Glyn Johns as engineer. Nobody else turned up except Charlie and pianist Nicky Hopkins. We were thinking of leaving when Glyn said to me, 'Do you have a song to do?' I sat at the piano and played 'In Another Land' and they all liked it."[6]

Science fiction meets psychedelia: Bill Wyman's song is highly characteristic of the second half of the sixties, in particular the summer of 1967. The story is of a man who wakes up from a dream only to find himself living another dream—a kind of dream within a dream. "In Another Land" was chosen as the A-side of a single released on December 2, 1967 (with "The Lantern" as the B-side), a few days before the album went on sale. It failed to chart in the United Kingdom, and in the United States it got no higher than number 87 on the *Billboard* pop chart.

Production

Right from the intro, Bill plunges the listener into a medieval, dreamlike world. The track starts with a harpsichord played by Nicky Hopkins and a cello sound possibly created on the Mellotron (Brian Jones?). The surrealistic atmosphere is reinforced by wind effects, in all likelihood obtained from the Olympic Studios sound bank. Bill plays bass and is probably on the organ too, combining perfectly with Nicky's harpsichord. The choruses give Charlie Watts an opportunity to let rip with an excellent drum part supported by Bill's melodic and distinctly pop bass line played on his Vox Wyman. They also provide Nicky with scope for some superb rock piano (overdubbed). Having got the rhythmic foundation down, Bill now had to turn his attention to the vocals. Not particularly used to singing, he employed a trick to make himself feel more at ease. His voice can be heard sounding not particularly assured and somewhat somber, but masked by a studio effect. He explains: "It then came time to add the vocals, which

Bill Wyman in the studio, working on the one and only song he would write for the band.

worried me. In the end I suggested tremolo on my voice." This is what gives his vocal (though not on the choruses) its curious quasi-aquatic, quasi-psychedelic timbre. Bill continues: "The Small Faces were recording next door, and Glyn asked Steve Marriott to come in and help me. We sang it together and it worked well. The track was given the working title 'Acid in the Grass.'" Steve Marriott sang a few lines of counterpoint and added a vocal part in the refrains. (It is sometimes claimed that Ronnie Lane, another member of the Small Faces, was also involved, but this has not been confirmed.) The number was then ready to be submitted to the Glimmer Twins for a verdict: "Next night Glyn told Mick and Keith about the session and played them what we'd done. They liked it, agreeing

it was compatible with the rest of the tracks. I'd finally broken the 'songwriting' stranglehold of Mick and Keith."[6] The Twins nevertheless insisted on adding some backing vocals of their own in the refrains. Keith also contributed some acoustic guitar on his Gibson Hummingbird and Brian adds his inimitable touch on the Mellotron, selecting what is probably a mandolin sound. All in all, "In Another Land" is a very good number, not far from the sound world of Syd Barrett, who had released "Arnold Layne" with Pink Floyd at the beginning of the year. It lacks a proper ending, however: from 2:54 twenty seconds of loud snoring can be heard! Legend has it that this was Bill, who had grown weary of waiting for Mick and Keith to return and had fallen asleep . . . Can Bill please confirm this?

2000 MAN

Mick Jagger / Keith Richards / 3:08

Musicians
Mick Jagger: vocals
Keith Richards: acoustic guitar, rhythm
electric guitar, lead guitar
Brian Jones: electric dulcimer (?)
Bill Wyman: bass
Charlie Watts: drums
Nicky Hopkins: organ, piano (?)
Recorded
Olympic Sound Studios, London: October 1967
Technical Team
Producers: the Rolling Stones
Sound engineer: Glyn Johns
Assistant sound engineer: Eddie Kramer

Kiss recorded "2000 Man" during the sessions for the album *Dynasty* (1979), a version that takes one's breath away

Brian takes a cigarette break during the *Satanic* recording sessions.

Genesis
What if history were to constantly repeat itself? This is the essence of what Mick Jagger seems to be saying in "2000 Man." The man of the year 2000 will be no better understood by his children than the man of yesterday or today. For the Stones' singer, the future does not seem to be synonymous with progress, and technical advances do not necessarily lead to personal fulfillment: *Well, my name is a number, a piece of plastic film/And I'm growin funny flowers in my little window sill.* Neither does the way in which morals have evolved provide grounds for any great enthusiasm: *Well my wife still respects me, I really misused her/I am having an affair with a random computer.*

Production
According to Mick Jagger in 1968, the album sessions "just got freakier as we went along."[18] "2000 Man," recorded in October toward the end of work on the album, is the proof. The track consists of three sections. The first opens with a very good acoustic intro played by Keith Richards on his Hummingbird, somewhat in the spirit of "Sittin' on a Fence." Brian Jones supports him on what sounds like his electric dulcimer, while Nicky Hopkins plays the piano. Unfortunately, this section is spoiled by the drumming. Seized by an overwhelming desire to complicate things, Charlie attempts to play a completely inappropriate rhythm. On top of this, a delay is applied to his snare drum, which has the effect of muddying his playing. The musicians probably did not have terribly clear ideas when it came to the mixing. What is essentially a charming folk sequence gives way to a second section, from 1:19, that is both livelier and in time. And when the track develops into an even more energetic rock number (1:37), the groove machine is in business again. Keith plays both lead and electric rhythm, and Nicky plays a prominent part with some excellent work on the Hammond B-3. After a short, slightly jazzy interlude (2:12), there is a return to the first section, but with a coherent rhythm and ensemble. Mick Jagger launches into his vocal part in a pretty high register before finding his feet in the rock section. He also overdubs the vocal harmonies. Nevertheless, "2000 Man" is far too complicated and confused to really work.

SING THIS ALL TOGETHER (SEE WHAT HAPPENS)

Mick Jagger / Keith Richards / 8:34

Musicians
Mick Jagger: vocals
Keith Richards: rhythm guitar, lead guitar
Brian Jones: Mellotron, flute, vibraphone, Jew's harp (?)
Bill Wyman: bass (?)
Charlie Watts: drums
Nicky Hopkins: piano
Unidentified musicians: assorted percussion (güiro, maracas, tambourine, toms, etc.), backing vocals

Recorded
Olympic Sound Studios, London: July 1967

Technical Team
Producers: the Rolling Stones
Sound engineer: Glyn Johns
Assistant sound engineer: Eddie Kramer

Keith Richards outside Mick Jagger's home on Marylebone Road, London.

Genesis

The closing track on side one of *Their Satanic Majesties Request* in a sense takes up where the first number on the album leaves off. The singing starts by reprising the closing lines from the opening track, as well as the music of the refrain: *Why don't we sing this song all together?/Open our minds let the pictures come.* The second part of the text is more abstruse: *Pictures of us in the circling sun/Pictures of the show that we're all one.* It is possible that Mick Jagger found his inspiration in *The Secret of the Golden Flower* or that he had read psychoanalyst Carl Jung's study of the Taoist treatise on inner alchemy.

Production

This track takes the form of a long improvisation, evidently recorded under the influence of hallucinogens: "I probably started to take too many drugs,"[19] Mick would later reveal when describing the context of this album. Having originally lasted for more than fourteen minutes, the number has been cut to 8:34. In the intro we find Brian trying his hand at a flute sound on the Mellotron, the same sound used by the Beatles on "Strawberry Fields Forever." A distant conversation, apparently on the subject of flower power, emerges from the background. Keith then comes out of nowhere, having taken it upon himself to rouse the listeners with some pretty abstract guitar chords. He is followed by an avalanche of percussion, more or less the same instruments that were used on "Sing This All Together." The track evolves as voices, screams, laughter, and choral chanting of the Tibetan *Om* are heard. Instruments surge into the foreground, their playing totally improvised, above all Brian on the Mellotron, alternating the sound of horns, flutes (in addition to the real flute in the ensemble), and the mandolin. Also, a piano is played by Nicky, a Jew's harp (0:39), vibraphone, and constant percussion, all led by Charlie's bass drum, which acts as a veritable psychedelic Ariadne's thread. At 7:02, there is a return of the refrain: Mick's voice is drowned in reverb before finding a drier tone. Keith plays electric rhythm guitar; Brian the vibraphone and then the Mellotron. Finally, the Stones bring their sound epic to a close with a final abstract sequence (7:53). This is constructed around a kind of white noise emanating from a frenzied oscilloscope and the sound of a gong drenched in reverb. The journey is over.

SHE'S A RAINBOW

Mick Jagger / Keith Richards / 4:35

Musicians
Mick Jagger: vocals, tambourine
Keith Richards: acoustic guitar, lead guitar
Brian Jones: Mellotron
Bill Wyman: bass
Charlie Watts: drums
Nicky Hopkins: piano, harpsichord
John Paul Jones: string arrangement
Unidentified musicians: backing vocals, percussion, harpsicord (?)

Recorded
Olympic Sound Studios, London:
February, May, and October 1967

Technical Team
Producers: the Rolling Stones
Sound engineer: Glyn Johns
Assistant sound engineer: Eddie Kramer

The string arrangements for "She's a Rainbow" were written by John Paul Jones, a future member of Led Zeppelin.

Genesis

"She's a Rainbow" sounds like a logical follow-up to "Lady Jane" or "Ruby Tuesday." It is a sort of musical fairy tale with not a trace of the legendary misogyny of Mick Jagger and Keith Richards. Indeed the heroine is endowed with almost supernatural virtues. *She's like a rainbow* and *like a queen in days of old, she shoots her colors all around.* Could this female figure perhaps be a fairy inspired by Arthurian legend or a short story by Lord Dunsany?

"She's a Rainbow" is without a doubt one of the songs most influenced by the festive optimism of flower power and therefore one of the most atypical in the catalog of the Dartford songwriting duo, which acquired a certain consistency from this time forward. This psychedelic pop song, carried by a subtle melody, somewhat makes a transition between the blues and rhythm 'n' blues of the band's beginnings and its triumphant return to blues rock in the upcoming single "Jumpin' Jack Flash" and the album *Beggars Banquet*. Billy Childish (a British poet, painter, and musician): "'She's a Rainbow' is a very pretty tune. I love how poetic it is, like a calibration of love and beauty in a Tudor garden. And then there's a little sadness there too, portending the end of the Stones' vitality as they ceased to be fans of Muddy Waters and became fans of themselves."[63]

"She's a Rainbow" was released as a single in the United States (but not in the United Kingdom), with "2000 Light Years from Home" as its B-side, on December 23, 1967. It reached number 25 on the *Billboard* pop chart on January 27, 1968.

Production

"She's a Rainbow" begins with twenty seconds of sound effects (on the album track but not on the single) re-creating the atmosphere of a carnival in which a fairground barker can be heard inviting the public to try their luck at some kind of ball game. The number then kicks off properly with a (lightly compressed) piano played by the highly talented Nicky Hopkins, accompanied by cello and tambourine. The orchestration then increases in volume, thanks to Charlie Watts's highly effective drumming, which literally drives the song forward, supported by Bill Wyman's imposing bass and Keith Richards's strummed acoustic (Gibson Hummingbird). Brian Jones

Keith, Bill, and Mick at work at Olympic Sound Studios.

again plays the Mellotron, contributing essential color to the song with a trumpet-dominated horn sound.

"She's a Rainbow" would not be what it is without its incredible string arrangements. Quite unorthodox in places, particularly in the closing stages (around 3:24), these could almost be an allusion to Bartók, with their strong dissonance reminding us that it is the Stones we are listening to, and that behind this subtle pop song lurks an element of derision. These arrangements were written by John Paul Jones, the future bassist and keyboard player of Led Zeppelin. The combination of the strings and Nicky Hopkins's piano is a triumph, and a touch of Mozart can almost be heard (in the instrumental section around 1:24) in addition to Bartók.

Another important, and unexpected, element is the handling of the backing vocals. The *oh la la las* are extremely kitsch and come as something of a surprise on a record by the rock band from London. However, these vocals seem to have been recorded at a slower speed in order to create a sound with a higher pitch and with a somewhat nasal, somewhat Mickey Mouse–like timbre when played back at normal speed. This is a technique put to good use by the Beatles on *Sgt. Pepper*. Mick Jagger seems perfectly at ease in this flower power context far removed from the world of Muddy Waters or Chuck Berry, offering abundant proof of his talent for adapting to the good vibrations of the day. Mick also

overdubs the vocal harmonies. From 2:45, percussion instruments can be heard that sound like bongos played with drumsticks, or perhaps Cuban timbales. For a few seconds only, the sound of a harpsichord can also be made out (at 3:30), probably played by Hopkins. Finally, and as if to exorcise too many intrusive colors and remind listeners of the fact of rock music, Keith concludes "She's a Rainbow" with a raging, distorted chord, probably played on his Gibson Les Paul Black Beauty.

FOR STONES ADDICTS

John Paul Jones, who was responsible for the string arrangement, joined Decca as a studio musician in 1964. Two years after playing on *Their Satanic Majesties Request*, he founded Led Zeppelin with Jimmy Page, Robert Plant, and John Bonham.

NICKY HOPKINS:
THE ECLECTIC DREAMER

As an individual he may have been unassuming, but as a musician he occupies a place of honor in the rock music of the sixties and seventies. Throughout these two decades, the name of Nicky Hopkins was to become indissolubly linked with that of the Rolling Stones. The happy encounter between the band and the pianist goes back to January 10, 1963, to the first gig given by the London quintet at the Marquee Club. "We were second on the bill to the highly rated Cyril Davies All-Star R&B Group, a twelve-piece band that included the highly respected pianist Nicky Hopkins . . . " [6] writes Bill Wyman. However, Hopkins would not begin to record regularly with the Stones until four years later, starting with *Between the Buttons*. Until then, Mick, Brian, Keith, Bill, and Charlie relied exclusively on Ian Stewart, who was brilliant when it came to blues and rock 'n' roll. The arrival on the scene of Nicky Hopkins coincided with a change of style from the Rolling Stones.

A Truly Gifted Pianist

By the time he took part in the *Between the Buttons* sessions (playing a major role on "Something Happened to Me Yesterday"), Nicky Hopkins had been an established pianist for a number of years. Born on February 24, 1944, in the London suburb of Perivale, he was the youngest of the four children of Freda and Alfred Hopkins. His father worked as an accountant at the famous Guinness brewery. From the age of three, Nicky displayed an aptitude for the piano and started taking lessons, which were eventually to lead him to the Royal Academy of Music in London. At sixteen he abandoned his study of the great classical composers and quit school, answering the call of Chuck Berry and the other rock 'n' roll pioneers. He became a member of Screaming Lord Sutch and the Savages, a trailblazing rock 'n' roll (and horror rock) band in Britain. Charlie Watts recalls his style at the time: "Nicky used to play with Screaming Lord Sutch and sounded like a cross between Jerry Lee Lewis and Otis Spann, lovely blues, all top end stuff." [9] Hopkins remained with the Savages for two years before leaving with other members of the group (the bassist Rick Brown and the drummer Carlo Little) to join the

harmonica player Cyril Davies in his newly formed band, the All-Stars.

The reputation of Nicky Hopkins grew with each gig given by the Cyril Davies All-Stars R&B Group at the Marquee. In 1963, however, the young pianist had to undergo surgery, which was followed by nineteen months of convalescence. Just as he felt ready to resume his role as pianist in the group, Cyril Davies died of endocarditis (January 7, 1964).

In the Studio with the Greatest Stars of Rock 'n' Roll

Hopkins therefore had to explore new avenues. Under the aegis of the producer Shel Talmy, he became a studio pianist, notably for the Who (*My Generation* [1965]), the Kinks (*Kink Kontroversy* [1965], *Face to Face* [1966]), and David Bowie ("Love You Till Tuesday" [1967]). In 1966 he recorded the album *The Revolutionary Piano of Nicky Hopkins*, and, most importantly, embarked on his collaboration with the Rolling Stones, making his first contribution to the Stones' aesthetic on "Cool, Calmed and Collected." This was to be the first of many. As things turned out, he continued to work with the biggest rock 'n' roll band in the world until *Tattoo You* in 1981—in other words throughout the Stones' most glorious period, which included *Their Satanic Majesties Request* (1967), *Beggars Banquet* (1968), *Let It Bleed* (1969), *Sticky Fingers* (1971), *Exile on Main St.* (1972), and *Goats Head Soup* (1973) and gave rise to such gems as "She's a Rainbow," "Sympathy for the Devil," "Loving Cup," and "Angie." Another great achievement was his contribution (on electric piano) in July 1968 to the recording of "Revolution" by the Beatles, who discovered him while they were singing backing vocals on the Stones' "We Love You."

Nicky Hopkins was always keen to widen his range of musical experiences. Although declining to join Led Zeppelin, he was happy to join the Jeff Beck Group, with whom he went on tour in the United States and recorded the albums *Truth* (1968) and *Beck-Ola* (1969). He also took part in Donovan's *Barabajagal* (1969) sessions and, on the West Coast,

Nicky Hopkins, one of the Rolling Stones' most loyal session musicians.

contributed to *Brave New World* (1969) and *Your Saving Grace* (1969) by the Steve Miller Band as well as *Volunteers* (1969) by Jefferson Airplane, with whom he appeared at Woodstock. That same year, 1969, he joined up with another emblematic acid rock band, the Quicksilver Messenger Service, to work on its albums *Shady Grove* (1969), *Just for Love* (1970), and *What About Me* (1970). He then hooked up with ex-Beatles John Lennon on *Imagine* (1971) and *Walls & Bridges* (1974), George Harrison on *Living in a Material World* (1973) and *Dark Horse* (1974), Ringo Starr on *Ringo* (1973) and *Goodnight Vienna* (1974), and Paul McCartney on *Flowers in the Dirt* (1989). Also from the seventies, it is worth mentioning his contributions to *I Can Stand a Little Rain* (1974) and *Jamaica Say You Will* (1975) by Joe Cocker,

Reflections (1976) by Jerry Garcia, and *Breakaway* (1975) by Art Garfunkel.

The seventies and eighties were marked by excesses of all kinds. After undergoing detox, Nicky Hopkins resumed his career as a studio musician and, taking up residence in Hollywood, even expanded it to include television and cinema. Health issues recurred, however. While working on a musical project with Joe Walsh and Frankie Miller, Nicky Hopkins died in Nashville, Tennessee, on September 6, 1994, at the age of fifty. He left behind hundreds of recordings made for and with the greatest names in rock 'n' roll as well as a number of solo albums, including the aptly named *The Tin Man Was a Dreamer* (1973). In the words of Nils Lofgren: "Nicky wrote the book on rock 'n' roll piano."[69]

THE LANTERN

Mick Jagger / Keith Richards / 4:24

Musicians
Mick Jagger: vocals
Keith Richards: acoustic guitar, lead guitar, backing vocals
Brian Jones: Mellotron, organ (?)
Bill Wyman: bass
Charlie Watts: drums
Nicky Hopkins: piano
Recorded
Olympic Sound Studios, London: July 1967
Technical Team
Producers: the Rolling Stones
Sound engineer: Glyn Johns
Assistant sound engineer: Eddie Kramer

FOR STONES ADDICTS

The song begins with the chiming of bells. Did this inspire John Lennon when he was making "Mother"?

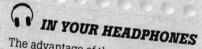 **IN YOUR HEADPHONES**

The advantage of the stereo version is that it is easy to isolate the left and right channels. On the right it is possible to hear that Keith's lead guitar has been eliminated from the mix, only to be picked up again as a result of leakage from the singers' headphones when they recorded their vocal parts.

Genesis

After the blaze of color of "She's a Rainbow," Mick Jagger plunges the listener into a somber, even horrific world in "The Lantern." *My face it turns a deathly pale/You're talking to me through your veil, The servants sleep/The doors are barred*: it is no longer Lord Dunsany who comes to mind, but Edgar Allan Poe, or even the pioneers of the Gothic novel, such as Horace Walpole and Sheridan Le Fanu. There is, however, a glimmer of hope: *So, please, carry the lantern high*, sings Jagger in the refrain. The narrator is addressing the one he loved and loves still—who has passed over to the other world. And the lantern is what unites the pair across the divide, or perhaps represents the light that will enable him to join her.

In terms of its lyrics, "The Lantern" is one of the most fascinating songs on the album, or indeed on any Rolling Stones album. This is probably why it was chosen for the B-side of the single "In Another Land," which was released in the United States.

Production

Neither is the song uninteresting musically, combining different styles: blues, boogie, pop, rock, folk, and dreamlike elements. Keith is the real architect of this number, firstly on his Hummingbird, developing a very good acoustic part with excellent blues licks, and then with his inspired lead guitar, which is simultaneously melodic and rock. He is almost certainly playing his Les Paul Black Beauty, with heavy, emphatic vibrato and distortion from the amp. Another important element is Nicky's boogie-woogie piano, which complements Keith's guitar playing brilliantly while also providing a point of reference for Bill and Charlie, both of whom deliver effective rhythmic support. Brian makes the occasional contribution on the Mellotron with horn and saxophone sounds. He also seems to be playing the Hammond organ in the intro and at around 2:30, although in the early versions of the song the organ is played throughout. Mick delivers his lyrics well and is supported by harmonies from Keith, with whom he shares the backing vocals. "The Lantern" is a song that deserves to be rediscovered, but it is important to get hold of the mono version, as the stereo version is a catastrophe, mixed by someone with tired ears.

GOMPER

Mick Jagger / Keith Richards / 5:09

Musicians
Mick Jagger: vocals, percussion (?)
Keith Richards: lead guitar, backing vocals
Brian Jones: electric dulcimer, recorder
Bill Wyman: bass (?)
Charlie Watts: tabla
Nicky Hopkins: organ
Recorded
Olympic Sound Studios, London: August–October 1967
Technical Team
Producers: the Rolling Stones
Sound engineer: Glyn Johns
Assistant sound engineer: Eddie Kramer

FOR STONES ADDICTS

There are various alternative takes of "Gomper." Rumor has it that one of them is a jam involving Brian Jones and Jimi Hendrix.

Charlie Watts plays tabla on "Gomper."

Genesis

This song again shows Mick Jagger in the guise of the heroic fantasy author. Is it a dream? Is it a fantasy? Is it the effect of a mind-altering substance? The narrator observes a young woman *by the lake with lily flowers* during *the evening hours*. *She swims to the side* and *the sun sees her dried.* The man is moved to tears when she starts to moan. "Gomper" is both the glorification of the beauty of a mysterious heroine and a manifesto of sorts for a "return to nature," for flower power. This is borne out by the succession of titles ("Flowers in Your Hair," "The Ladies, the Lilies and the Lake") by which the song was known before acquiring its final, enigmatic one.

Production

"Gomper" is the second song of extended duration on the album after "Sing This All Together (See What Happens)." Evidently, it is clearly the Stones' "Indian" sequence, just as "Within You Without You" on *Sgt. Pepper* was the Beatles'. As such it is a track that enables Brian Jones to be omnipresent, first of all in recording two electric dulcimer parts, which make the instrument sound almost like a sitar, and second with his performance on the recorder. Based for the most part around a D-major chord, "Gomper" enables Mick to assume a mystical, otherworldly singing style. Keith assists with backing vocals and also plays lead guitar, probably Brian's Rickenbacker 360/12 12-string. Bill seems to be accompanying the guitarist on bass, although it is possible that Keith is doubling himself on the lower strings of his guitar. The second section of the track begins at around 1:50 and takes the form of a pseudo-Indian improvisation that builds in volume for three minutes, during which Brian plays his recorder with conviction. Brian is probably also responsible for the cries of enthusiasm that can be heard from 4:37. An organ plays from the beginning to the end of the recording, probably Nicky on a Vox Continental. There is also a second organ that enters around 1:50 in order join in with the general improvisation. The tabla, the final important element in the instrumentation, are played by Charlie, as various photographs from the sessions attest. He seems not to have fully mastered the Indian drums, but this should perhaps not be held against him. "Gomper" may not be the best track on the album, but it is without a doubt the most psychedelic in the whole of the Stones catalog.

2000 LIGHT YEARS FROM HOME

Mick Jagger / Keith Richards / 4:45

<u>Musicians</u>
Mick Jagger: vocals, maracas
Keith Richards: lead guitar, bass (?) backing vocals
Brian Jones: Mellotron, electric dulcimer
Bill Wyman: bass, oscillator
Charlie Watts: drums
Nicky Hopkins: piano
Eddie Kramer (?): claves
<u>Recorded</u>
Olympic Sound Studios, London: July–September 1967
<u>Technical Team</u>
Producers: the Rolling Stones
Sound engineer: Glyn Johns
Assistant sound engineer: Eddie Kramer

Timothy Leary, enlightened intellectual, apologist of the counterculture, and apostle of LSD.

Genesis

Mick Jagger wrote "2000 Light Years from Home" in his cell in Brixton Prison during the night of June 29–30, 1967. Found guilty of the illegal possession of Benzedrine, he had been sentenced to three months in jail. Naturally, he did not know that he would be released on bail the following day, and was seized by a feeling of terrible loneliness, hence these superb lyrics. The author displays great subtlety in expressing his anxiety through metaphor. The personal situation of the Stones' singer is cleverly transformed into that of an astronaut whose sense of isolation grows as he approaches his final destination, the star Aldebaran. Here he is, one hundred light-years from home, then six hundred, then one thousand, and finally two thousand. The scenario is reminiscent of Ray Bradbury or Arthur C. Clarke, whose short story "The Sentinel" was made into a film by Stanley Kubrick (*2001: A Space Odyssey*) and released the following year.

"2000 Light Years from Home" could also be interpreted as the allegory of an LSD trip, the realization, in a certain sense, of the "politics of ecstasy" propounded by Timothy Leary. It would start with a *soft explosion, bound for a star with fiery oceans*, where energy is present *in every part*. A metaphor, Rolling Stones–style, for the Summer of Love. Musically, the song admittedly bears something of a resemblance to what the California bands were doing at the same time (for instance "Eight Miles High" by the Byrds and "White Rabbit" by Jefferson Airplane). It would, however, exert a profound influence on the British progressive scene.

"2000 Light Years from Home" was released as a single in several countries, notably the United States and the Federal Republic of Germany. In Germany it reached number 5 on January 5, 1968 (with "She's a Rainbow" as the B-side).

Production

This superb song, another highly ambitious one, hints at the sound worlds that bands such as Genesis, Yes, King Crimson, and even the Moody Blues would later create. Of the British bands, it could only have been influenced by Pink Floyd, who had just released their first album (*The Piper at the Gates of Dawn*, August 1967). This begs the question: did the Stones have a hand in the birth of British progressive rock music!?

Brian Jones playing the Mellotron, on which he makes a crucial contribution to "2000 Light Years from Home."

"2000 Light Years from Home" opens with an electro-acoustic sequence that includes sound effects created by playing tapes backward and by Nicky Hopkins plucking and striking his piano strings in the style of John Cage and his prepared pianos. Keith Richards then launches into a superb riff probably supported by a bass. However, what ultimately lends the texture of the song its enormous originality are the string sounds created by Brian Jones on the Mellotron, which bring a unique tone to the general atmosphere. Glyn Jones stresses this crucial contribution: "It was a nice track that anything could have been done to, but the whole conception of what Brian played changed the mood of the track from chalk to cheese and made it into what I regard as a fantastic track."[64]

A Hypnotic Rhythm

Charlie Watts, accompanied by Bill Wyman, creates a hypnotic rock rhythm over which can be heard Mick Jagger's very prominent maracas and Keith's distorted guitar. In places, Keith seems to support Bill's bass with his own fuzz bass. Mick, highly credible in his new, psychedelic guise, gives an

excellent vocal performance. Numerous sound effects have been integrated in order to evoke the interstellar ambiance of the lyrics: reversed tapes, echo at the end of the refrain (1:27), electronic patches, including an oscillator operated, according to Andy Babiuk,[28] by none other than Bill Wyman (2:31). As with several tracks on the album, "2000 Light Years from Home" is made up of a number of distinct sequences, allowing various instrumental breaks to initiate changes in ambiance and rhythm. This is the case at 2:44 and 3:59, with Charlie on toms and Brian on his electric dulcimer, which intones a few limpid notes while Keith plays distorted electric chords. The number then draws to a close with the sound of the Mellotron. Finally, on two of the refrains (2:36 and 3:49), Mick and Keith's vocals are accompanied by female voices that may perhaps be those of Marianne and Anita. "It's a sound experience, really," Mick would say about the album in 1995, "rather than a song experience."[19] He would also admit that "2000 Light Years from Home" was one of the two songs on the album that he actually likes, the other being "She's a Rainbow": "The rest of them are nonsense."[19]

On this album Brian Jones demonstrates his talent as a multi-instrumentalist. As such he makes an indispensable contribution to the sound of the band.

ON WITH THE SHOW

Mick Jagger / Keith Richards / 3:39

Musicians
Mick Jagger: vocals, maracas
Keith Richards: lead guitar, bass
Brian Jones: Mellotron, concert harmonica, organ (?)
Bill Wyman: bass
Charlie Watts: drums
Nicky Hopkins: piano
Unidentified musician(s): percussion
Recorded
Olympic Sound Studios, London: July 1967
Technical Team
Producers: the Rolling Stones
Sound engineer: Glyn Johns
Assistant sound engineer: Eddie Kramer

On with the Show was also the title of an American movie of 1929 directed by Alan Crosland. This was the first moving picture to be filmed entirely in Technicolor.

FOR STONES ADDICTS

In "On with the Show," Mick Jagger refers to two great standards of American popular music: "Old Man River" by Oscar Hammerstein II and Jerome Kern and "Stormy Weather" by Ted Koehler and Harold Arlen, immortalized in 1933 by Ethel Waters on record and performed onstage at the Cotton Club in Harlem.

Genesis

To conclude the album, Mick Jagger metamorphoses for a little more than three minutes into the master of ceremonies of a lowly strip joint. *It's non-stop, it's a continuous show* and *there's a bar downstairs.* Furthermore, for those wishing to escape the humdrum of everyday life, there are hostesses willing to satisfy the guest's every whim. *Your wife will never know that you're not really working late/Your hostess here is Wendy, you'll find her very friendly*, sings Jagger with a knowing air.

Originally titled "Surprise Me," "On with the Show" represents a complete break with the other songs on the album. There is no psychedelic atmosphere, but instead there are overtones of the Baroque pop and music hall of *Between the Buttons.*

Production

"On with the Show" begins with twelve seconds of sound effects recorded live, so the legend goes, on the corner of the road outside Olympic Studios. For this final trip to the land of *Their Satanic Majesties Request*, Keith strings together a fifties-sounding guitar riff. The atmosphere is welcoming and friendly, with Mick spreading the good word through a megaphone, in actual fact a sound effect obtained most probably by means of equalization during mixing. The bass/drums duo lay down a workable rhythm, and Keith can be heard shadowing Bill on fuzz bass. As with various other tracks on the album, a number of percussion instruments can be heard, including maracas, tambourine, claves, and cowbells. Nicky Hopkins plays an excellent and highly dynamic piano, while Brian, it would seem, is on organ. "On with the Show" also comprises two astonishing instrumental sections. At a certain point, the rhythm and atmosphere of the number change, giving way to a kind of polka strongly influenced by the traditional Paraguayan tune "Guyra Campana," in which Brian can be heard playing a concert harmonica and doubling himself with a mandolin sound from the Mellotron. Nicky accompanies him on piano, Bill on bass (possibly inspiring Paul McCartney's bass line on "Ob-La-Di, Ob-La-Da"), and the beat is marked on a güiro. All of this unfolds within the ambiance of a fashionable cocktail party. Finally, at the end of the track, Nicky Hopkins lets himself go with an off-the-wall ragtime to wrap up the album. "On with the Show" is a winner.

SIDE A
1967

FOR STONES ADDICTS

There are various covers of "Let's Spend the Night Together," including a version by Muddy Waters on his album *Electric Mud* (1968) and another by Tina Turner on her album *Acid Queen* (1975). The most dazzling, however, is David Bowie's, which was released as a single and is also on the album *Aladdin Sane* (1973).

LET'S SPEND THE NIGHT TOGETHER

Mick Jagger / Keith Richards / 3:27

SINGLE

Let's Spend the Night Together / Ruby Tuesday

RELEASE DATE

United Kingdom: January 13, 1967

Record label: Decca
RECORD NUMBER: DECCA F 12546

Musicians

Mick Jagger: vocals, percussion (?)
Keith Richards: rhythm guitar, bass, piano, backing vocals
Brian Jones: organ
Charlie Watts: drums
Jack Nitzsche: piano
Unidentified musician(s): hand claps

Recorded

Olympic Sound Studios, London: November 8–26, 1966

Technical Team

Producer: Andrew Loog Oldham
Sound engineer: Glyn Johns
Assistant sound engineer: Eddie Kramer

Genesis

Marianne Faithfull is categorical: "'Let's Spend the Night Together' was Mick's. It came out of that night we spent in the motel in Bristol."[52] The character in the song certainly seems impatient to demonstrate to his girlfriend all the love he feels for her—a love which is by no means exclusively cerebral. However, in an interview given to the *Melody Maker*, Mick Jagger claimed that "Let's Spend the Night Together" did not have to be seen as an invitation to indulge in physical lovemaking: "I always say 'Let's spend the night together' to any young lady I'm taking out. What it means is: shall we spend the evening together? If people have warped, twisted, dirty minds, I suppose it could have sexual overtones. The song isn't really very rude. When you hear it, you'll realise this."[55]

Despite Mick Jagger's protestations, "Let's Spend the Night Together" caused a tremendous scandal when the single was released (on January 13, 1967, in the United Kingdom and the following day in the United States). Some radio stations censored it, preferring to play the other side of the single, "Ruby Tuesday." The prize for caution (or maybe hypocrisy) goes to Ed Sullivan. On January 15, 1967, while the Rolling Stones were promoting their single, the charismatic presenter of *The Ed Sullivan Show* asked Mick not to sing the fateful phrase but instead to replace it with the line *let's spend some time together* in order to avoid offending the prudish ears of the young American television audience watching the show. After initially refusing, Mick in the end consented—but not without rolling his eyes in disapproval during the (taped) refrain. On the other hand, after appearing on *The London Palladium Show* on the British television

The Stones performed "Let's Spend the Night Together" on the television show *Sunday Night at the Palladium* on January 22, 1967.

station ITV a week later, the Stones refused to take part in the procession of stars that rounded off each show, enraging the producer Albert Locke: "Who do the Stones think they are?" Jagger's response: "That revolving stage isn't an altar. It's a drag ... Anyone who thought we were changing our image to suit a family audience was mistaken."[27]

Despite the ban imposed by various broadcasters, "Let's Spend the Night Together" became a big hit, peaking at number 3 in the United Kingdom on February 15, 1967.

Production

Although the words are credited to Mick Jagger, the music is by Keith Richards, who composed it at the piano, hence the importance of this instrument throughout the number. This song marked a turning point for the Rolling Stones because it was one of the first tracks they recorded at Olympic Studios (according to certain sources, the recording was begun at the RCA Studios).

Glyn Johns was the sound engineer. This was one session he would never forget: "On a Sunday afternoon in studio one at Olympic, we were recording Mick Jagger's vocal on 'Let's Spend the Night Together.' The track has already been recorded, so there was just Mick, Andrew Oldham, his driver Eddie, me, and my assistant in the studio. . . . We had been working for about twenty minutes and Mick was getting close to the take that we would eventually use. He had lit up a joint, so there was a haze of blue smoke hanging above him. We were in the middle of a take when much to our surprise the main door into the studio opened and two uniformed policemen gingerly entered."[4] Oldham's chauffeur hurriedly left the

studio, taking the illegal substances with him, while the two policemen apologized for having entered in such a fashion (they had anticipated catching some burglars red-handed). Glyn Johns: "After a brief polite conversation, [Mick] asked if they had their nightsticks with them. . . . Fascinated and somewhat overawed by Mick Jagger's presence, they readily agreed. Andrew passed them to Mick, saying that we needed some percussion on the bridge of the song. The two nightsticks sounded similar to claves when banged together."[4] As a result, two police officers can be said to have contributed to the recording of one of the Stones' most controversial songs!

The number begins with piano, bass, and backing vocals. The pianist is Jack, joined in various places by Keith, who would later recall playing his part with one finger. Keith is also on bass, as Bill was absent. He is probably using a pick on the Vox Wyman bass, as the sound is somewhat metallic, and he double-tracks the result to get a fatter sound. The effect is powerful and really helps to shape the number. Over this bass line Charlie develops a very Tamla Motown-style rhythm. Hand claps can be heard, albeit buried in the mix. Keith also plays rhythm guitar, but that too is barely audible. The backing vocals, sung by Mick and Keith, have a kitschy, even juvenile ring to them. It is interesting to observe a growing sophistication in the vocal harmonies as the duo's compositions develop. This is borne out in this number too, particularly in the bridge, which clearly alludes to the Beach Boys. Brian makes a contribution on the organ, which comes in during the same bridge (1:39). Finally, Mick excels in his ambivalent performance, singing this made-to-measure role with a kind of false modesty. Although a very good song, it is perhaps marred by the rather untidy mix.

Linda Keith, daughter of a Alan Keith, a radio broadcaster at the BBC and girlfriend of Keith Richards.

SIDE B
1967

RUBY TUESDAY

Mick Jagger / Keith Richards / 3:13

SINGLE
Let's Spend the Night Together / Ruby Tuesday
RELEASE DATE
United Kingdom: January 13, 1967
Record label: Decca
RECORD NUMBER: DECCA F 12546

Musicians
Mick Jagger: vocals, tambourine (?)
Keith Richards: acoustic guitar, double bass, backing vocals
Brian Jones: flute, piano or harpsichord (?)
Bill Wyman: double bass, bass
Charlie Watts: drums
Jack Nitzsche: piano
Recorded
Olympic Sound Studios, Pye Studios,
London: November 16, 1966
Technical Team
Producer: Andrew Loog Oldham
Sound engineer: Glyn Johns
Assistant sound engineer: Eddie Kramer

Genesis
Brian Jones is supposed to have had a hand in "Ruby Tuesday," which was destined to become one of the Stones most celebrated ballads. This, at least, is what Marianne Faithfull claims in her autobiography.[52] She recalls Brian playing a folk ballad that immediately caught Keith's attention: "'Yeah, nice, man,' said Keith and went over to the piano to bang it out. Brian was beaming. 'It's a cross between Thomas Dowland's *Air on the Late Lord Essex* and a Skip James blues, actually.' Keith was not interested in Lord Essex or Skip James for that matter. He had heard a riff and went at it like a dog with a bone. For ages 'Ruby Tuesday' had no lyrics . . . It was Brian and Keith's song."[52] It is certainly true that Mick Jagger played no part in the writing of the song: "It's just a nice melody, really. And a lovely lyric. Neither of which I wrote, but I always enjoy singing it."[1] Some time later, Keith shaped the song on the piano of his apartment in St. Johns Wood and also wrote the words, which speak very clearly of disappointment in love—his own after Linda Keith left him for a "so-called" poet. Of Bill Chenail, Keith writes: "He was a hip little bugger at the time because he came on with the Dylanesque bit. Couldn't play anything. Ersatz hip, as it's called." He adds, "That's the first time I felt the deep cut."[2]

A Second A-side
Who could hang a name on you?/When you change with every new day, still I'm gonna miss you: "Ruby Tuesday" may also be addressed to other women that the Stones had allowed to enter their circle, in particular Anita Pallenberg and Marianne Faithfull. It is also possible to see the song as an evocation

Bill Wyman plays upright bass on "Ruby Tuesday."

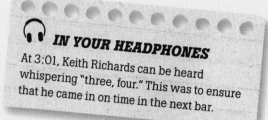
of the counterculture that was flourishing in London during the second half of the 1960s: *Catch your dreams before they slip away . . . Lose your dreams and you will lose your mind*.

Released on the same single as "Let's Spend the Night Together"—a double A-side—"Ruby Tuesday" was even more of a hit than it might otherwise have been as disc jockeys in the United States preferred to play the tender ballad rather than the other, more controversial, side. The song was the fourth Rolling Stones number 1 on the *Billboard* chart (after "[I Can't Get No] Satisfaction," "Get Off of My Cloud," and "Paint It Black").

Production

The recording of "Ruby Tuesday" (working title: "Title 8") took place during the sessions at Olympic Studios between November 16 and December 6, 1966. During this time, Brian Jones was working with the arranger Mike Leander on the soundtrack of the movie *A Degree of Murder* (original German title *Mord Und Totschlag*, 1967), a crime drama directed by Volker Schlöndorff and starring Anita Pallenberg (her first screen role). The Rolling Stone made use of a wide range of musical instruments, including the recorder, which dominates this number and gives it its particular, highly romantic, tone. Once again, the blond magician excels with a very good accompaniment on this instrument, which is endowed with emphatic delay and reverb.

"Ruby Tuesday" has no introduction but opens directly with the first verse. Jack Nitzsche contributes an excellent piano part, and Mick Jagger adopts a fragile, highly nostalgic voice supported by very good vocal harmonies from Keith Richards. Mick masters his tessitura extremely well, especially on the bass notes, but is less at ease in the refrains, which are perhaps a little high for him. From the very first bars, a double bass can be heard, played with the bow. Bill Wyman, who was not used to the instrument, was having some difficulty playing it and asked Keith to handle the bow. Glyn Jones recalls: "Bill couldn't manage it, he's very thin and he just couldn't hold the strings down and play as well, so he marked the notes on the neck of the bass in white pencil. He wasn't very sure, anyway, and he held the strings down with both hands while Keith plucked it [in reality bowed it]. It was really beautiful!"[64] The resulting sound considerably heightens the romantic feel of the song. Nevertheless, Bill returns to his electric bass in each of the refrains. The overall effect is highly poetic, at once pastoral, Baroque, and pop. It is probably Brian who adds a few phrases on the harpsichord (or possibly a honky-tonk piano) in the refrains. Keith, meanwhile, plays the only guitar on the number, his Gibson Hummingbird acoustic. Charlie Watts, accompanied by a very bright tambourine, sets an efficient rhythm, but perhaps overdoes his tom breaks. "Ruby Tuesday" is one of the Stones' most beautiful songs—and is well produced, in the bargain.

Summer 1967, Mick Jagger and Keith Richards at Olympic Sound Studios to record "We Love You."

In the promotional movie for "We Love You," Brian Jones can be seen playing a sitar and Mick Jagger the congas, instruments that played no part in the recording of the song. What is most striking is the deplorable state in which a completely wrecked Brian finds himself, while Keith seems to be in fine form by his side.

SIDE A
1967

FOR STONES ADDICTS

The sound of a cell door slamming at the beginning of the song is taken from an episode of *The Goon Show* (a BBC radio comedy program with Peter Sellers, Spike Milligan, and Harry Secombe). It was Bill Wyman who came up with this idea.

WE LOVE YOU

Mick Jagger / Keith Richards / 4:38

SINGLE
We Love You / Dandelion
RELEASE DATE
United Kingdom: August 18, 1967
Record label: Decca
RECORD NUMBER: DECCA F 12654

Musicians
Mick Jagger: vocals
Keith Richards: rhythm guitar, lead guitar, backing vocals
Brian Jones: Mellotron
Bill Wyman: bass
Charlie Watts: drums
Nicky Hopkins: piano
John Lennon, Paul McCartney: backing vocals
Recorded
Olympic Sound Studios, London: June 13 and 21, July 2 and 19, 1967
Technical Team
Producer: Andrew Loog Oldham
Sound engineers: Glyn Johns
Assistant engineer: Eddie Kramer

"We Love You" marks the end of the collaboration between Andrew Loog Oldham and the Stones.

Genesis
What with the trials and repeated scandals, spring and early summer 1967 were particularly tough times for Mick, Keith, and Brian. It was in this oppressive, anxious atmosphere, after Mick and Keith had been released on bail but before their appeal was upheld, that "We Love You" was composed.

You will never win/Your uniforms don't fit/We forget the place we're in/Because we love you, we love you. "We Love You" is more than just the Rolling Stones' contribution to the Summer of Love and the new hippie culture. Above all, it sounds like a hymn of thanks and love from the group to their fans, and is perhaps also, a plea for tolerance. It was released as a single (with "Dandelion" as the B-side) on August 18 in the United Kingdom and on September 2 in the United States, climbing to number 8 and number 50, respectively on the charts. This was a relative flop that would surprise the group.

Production
"'We Love You' was a case of creating the music in the studio, although Mick and Keith had had the basic idea for some time,"[1] writes Bill Wyman. The recording of the song was begun at Olympic Studios in London on June 13, with Mick, Keith, Brian, and Bill, but not Charlie, who was absent. It resumed on June 21, now with the drummer, and July 2, and concluded on July 19. Brian Jones, who had been hospitalized after suffering a nervous breakdown (upon returning from the Monterey Festival), joined the others in the studio for the final session. Like several of the tracks on *Their Satanic Majesties Request*, "We Love You" opens with sound effects, in this case footsteps in a prison corridor and the slamming

of a cell door, not so very far away from "House of the Rising Sun" territory. These sounds are followed by a superb piano intro played by Nicky Hopkins—a fantastic riff that the pianist had had in his head for some time, and in truth the backbone of the number. Bill immediately lends his support with fearsomely efficient glissandos on his Wyman bass. More steps can then be heard climbing a staircase, before flower-power-style backing vocals emerge from the tense atmosphere. But not just any backing vocals!

On July 19, after arriving back from Paris in the late afternoon, Keith Richards headed for the studios. Arriving in the early evening, he found the other Stones there as well as John Lennon, Paul McCartney, and Allen Ginsberg. The Beat poet was in London to take part in a demonstration in Hyde Park for the legalization of marijuana. A few days earlier, at McCartney's house, he had met Mick Jagger, who invited him, as well as John and Paul, to the session. Allen Ginsberg (who was present but did not sing) would later say: "They looked like little angels, like Botticelli Graces singing together for the first time."[65] John and Paul thus lent the Stones a helping hand with the backing vocals, in part to thank them for having participated in "All You Need Is Love" on June 25. And the Stones-Beatles combination worked wonderfully well. *We don't care if you only love "we,"* they proclaimed with one voice. A unique moment in the history of rock music.

Another important element in "We Love You" is Brian Jones's contribution on the Mellotron. George Chkiantz, who was present at the recording, recalls: "You try playing a Mellotron . . . Just try. There's a horrible time lag, depending on how many notes you push down, and most people, even great musicians, screwed it up. A terrible instrument—dreadful, very hard to play, impossible to maintain tempo—unless you were Brian Jones. Nobody else could have gotten anything like that."[66] Not only did Brian get it, he excelled at it, on this occasion choosing a horn sound. He also used the instrument to create an oriental flavor in the coda, probably in remembrance of Morocco. The effect is powerful and very "Summer of Love." The rhythm component on the track, comprising Keith's guitar (barely audible), Bill's bass, and Charlie's drumming, endows the number with a hypnotic drive, at least during the first half. Following a piano break, the tempo speeds up a little (2:03). Charlie then plays a different rhythmic pattern dominated by the toms, creating an effect reminiscent of Nick Mason on *The Piper at the Gates of Dawn*, above all in Brian's oriental-sounding section (from 3:46). Charlie's drumming is excellent, powerfully supported by Bill's bass. Keith, playing a somewhat discrete rhythm guitar, plays some short solo phrases on his Les Paul Black Beauty at around 3:05. Mick, meanwhile, supported by his Beatle friends, gives a magisterial performance. Finally, as a bonus, immediately after the last notes of the track (4:23), a few bars of "Dandelion" can be heard, slowed down and drowning in reverb.

"We Love You" is a very good single. Its lack of success can perhaps be attributed to its arguably overloaded production, but also to the dichotomy between the flower-power message of the lyrics and the scandals in which the Stones were implicated at the time.

Keith Richards and Anita Pallenberg with their two children, Marlon and Dandelion (on the left) in Cannes in 1973.

FOR STONES ADDICTS

Dandelion is the first name of the daughter born to Keith Richards and Anita Pallenberg on April 17, 1972. "She was only given the added name Angela because she was born in a Catholic hospital where they insisted that a 'proper' name be added," explains Keith. When she was older, Angela preferred to use this second name, for obvious reasons, saying "'Never again do you call me Dandy'"!

SIDE B
1967

DANDELION

Mick Jagger / Keith Richards / 3:48

SINGLE

We Love You / Dandelion

RELEASE DATE

United Kingdom: August 18, 1967
Record label: Decca
RECORD NUMBER: DECCA F 12654

<u>Musicians</u>
Mick Jagger: vocals, maracas
Keith Richards: acoustic guitar, backing vocals
Brian Jones: Mellotron, saxophone
Bill Wyman: bass
Charlie Watts: drums
Nicky Hopkins: harpsichord
John Lennon, Paul McCartney (?): backing vocals
<u>Recorded</u>
Olympic Sound Studios, London: June 12 and 13 and July 2, 1967
<u>Technical Team</u>
Producer: Andrew Loog Oldham
Sound engineer: Glyn Johns
Assistant engineer: Eddie Kramer

Genesis

Initially titled "Sometimes Happy, Sometimes Blue" (or "Fairground"), "Dandelion" takes its inspiration from British counting or nursery rhymes. The pauper, the beggar man, the thief, the tailor, the soldier, the rich man, the sailor, and the tinker that crop up throughout this song are characters from a counting game and nursery rhyme called "Tinker, Tailor" that dates from the end of the seventeenth century.

This song, then, is a nursery rhyme, albeit a psychedelic one: *One o'clock, two o'clock, three o'clock, four o'clock chimes/Dandelions don't care about the time/Dandelions don't tell no lies/Dandelion will make you wise . . .* At the time this song was released (as the B-side of "We Love You"), it was not difficult to imagine that Mick Jagger and Keith Richards were thinking of a quite different plant.

Production

There is a demo of "Dandelion" recorded during the sessions of November 8 to December 6, 1966. This version has Keith on electric rhythm guitar and singing guide vocal, Charlie on drums, and Mick on tambourine. Finalized six months later, the definitive version is a superb, radiant pop song influenced by the sound of the Beatles. Moreover, it would seem that Lennon and McCartney may have contributed to the backing vocals on this song too—to such an extent do the vocal arrangements resemble their work. This has never been confirmed, however. The dominant element in the song is the harpsichord part played by Nicky Hopkins, who was nevertheless not as at ease on the instrument as Jack Nitzsche could be. Keith plays his Hummingbird acoustic, Charlie is excellent

on his Ludwig kit, and Bill delivers a bass line that is simultaneously highly melodic and rhythmic.

Mick supports his bandmates on the maracas and gives a jubilant vocal performance. At around 2:01 Brian (presumably) plays a solo on the Mellotron with a sound closer to an oboe than a horn (although the Mellotron Mark II did not possess this particular sound), and he can also be heard playing a few brief phrases on his sax at 3:05. Charlie lets rip in the coda with some off-the-wall tom breaks, and as at the end of "We Love You," the Stones conclude "Dandelion" with a reprise of the riff, played on the piano, from the other side of the single. "Dandelion" was selected as the A-side in the United States and reached number 14 on the charts, performing significantly better than "We Love You," which progressed no higher than number 50.

A Promotional Movie Castigates the Establishment . . .

To promote the "We Love You" / "Dandelion" single, the Rolling Stones (Mick Jagger and Andrew Loog Oldham, in reality) decided to commission a promotional movie (the forerunner of the video). They turned to the director Peter Whitehead, who had developed a fascination with the Rolling Stones. The London quintet were already indebted to Whitehead for the 1966 documentary *Charlie Is My Darling* about the band's second Irish tour (September 3 and 4, 1965) as well as the promos for "Have You Seen Your Mother, Baby, Standing in the Shadow?," "Lady Jane," and "Let's Spend the Night Together."

For "We Love You," Peter Whitehead wanted to stick to topical events, and decided to draw a parallel between the prosecution of Oscar Wilde for homosexuality in 1895 and the trials recently undergone by Mick, Keith, and Brian. Accordingly, Mick Jagger, Marianne Faithfull, and Keith Richards played the parts of Oscar Wilde, Lord Alfred "Bosie" Douglas (himself a poet and the lover of the famous Irish author) and the Marquess of Queensberry (Bosie's father), with the director adding archival images (in particular of Brian Jones). Once the four-minute movie was finished, Peter Whitehead offered it to *Top of the Pops*. It was rejected out of hand by the show's producer, Johnnie Stewart, in the belief that such images should not be seen by young television viewers. The director responded as follows: "Pop music today is a socially committed form and the BBC are being irresponsible to ignore what is happening in the whole of the pop business today. I'm very annoyed at the decision. Pop is not all sweetness and light, as the programme would like to see it, and my film is a valid social comment."[6] The United States and West Germany revealed themselves to be far more tolerant than the United Kingdom, however, and in those countries Whitehead's film was able to be shown without any censorship.

Sympathy For The Devil
No Expectations
Dear Doctor
Parachute Woman
Jigsaw Puzzle
Street Fighting Man
Prodigal Son
Stray Cat Blues
Factory Girl
Salt Of The Earth

ALBUM
RELEASE DATE
United Kingdom: December 6, 1968
Record label: Decca
RECORD NUMBERS: DECCA LK 4955 (MONO); SKL 4955 (STEREO)
Number 5, on the U.S. charts for 32 weeks

BEGGARS
BANQUET

BEGGARS BANQUET: THE WILD MEN GORGE THEMSELVES

Where were the Rolling Stones in 1968? For four of the five members of the band, the months following the release of *Their Satanic Majesties Request* in December 1967 were relatively peaceful. Bill Wyman was recharging his batteries in his newly purchased manor house, Gedding Hall in Suffolk, while Charlie Watts (soon to become a father with the birth of his daughter Seraphina on March 18) was doing the same at his home in Lewes, Sussex. Keith Richards was dividing his time between his flat in London (3 Cheyne Walk, Chelsea) and Redlands, his Elizabethan manor house in Sussex, while Mick Jagger was living with Marianne Faithfull at his new flat at 48 Cheyne Walk and his country refuge Stargroves in the county of Hampshire.

The only Stone who had no share in this tranquility was Brian Jones. Deeply affected by his breakup with Anita Pallenberg, who was now in the midst of a great romance with Keith, he was edging closer to disaster every day as a result of the omnipresent narcotics and the ensuing wrath of the law. Arrested again on May 21 and charged with possession of cannabis, Brian appeared before Marlborough Street Magistrates Court. He was released on bail.

However, something potentially worse was happening. As his health declined, Brian Jones ceased to believe in the future of the group he himself had founded. Not only did he not compose—or at least not manage to get his compositions accepted by the others—he was no longer interested in the new musical directions being taken by the Jagger-Richards partnership or by rock music as a whole.

"He was by now completely disenchanted with the general pop scene, and told everyone he was hung up on electronic and experimental sounds,"[6] writes Bill Wyman. For Charlie Watts, the soul of the group had already, in his head, split with the other band members: "I think Brian lost interest and was more interested in being a pop star than a player—a lot of people are. It was also a phase when a lot of people were leaving bands and starting their own. Brian was the first of us to meet Bob Dylan and Jimi Hendrix and all those people; he was moving in that circle of people—he went to New York and met Allen Ginsberg and that crowd."[9] Another manifestation of the growing divide between Brian and the others was when he pleaded in vain for "Child of the Moon" to be the A-side of their latest single, rather than "Jumpin' Jack Flash."

The Album

Like a perfectly synchronized screenplay, it was just as the band's founder seemed to be distancing himself from his bandmates that the Rolling Stones recorded what was perhaps the most coherent album in their career and without a doubt one of their seminal works. The subjects covered on *Beggars Banquet* differ radically from those on the group's previous two LPs. The spirit of flower power had dissipated with the last fine days of the Summer of Love. Martin Luther King Jr. and Robert Kennedy were assassinated. Vietnam continued to claim lives. In France, in Mexico, in Japan, the old order was shaken by student protests, and in Czechoslovakia, Soviet forces crushed

On January 21, 1968, before the *Beggars Banquet* sessions had gotten under way, Brian Jones took part in the recording of a cover of Bob Dylan's "All Along the Watchtower" by the brilliant Jimi Hendrix. After trying his hand at the piano (not retained), it was ultimately his contribution on percussion that was immortalized.

any hope of liberalization in the Prague Spring. In short, 1968 was not 1967.

The band's seventh (British) studio album encapsulates this large-scale turmoil—as interpreted by the Rolling Stones in ten tracks in which there is barely a glimmer of optimism. This dark but fascinating album opens with "Sympathy for the Devil," which was destined to become a Stones classic. Mick Jagger dons Lucifer's dark robes to describe a world whose every value has been inverted. After a reference to Christ's torments, he sifts through the twentieth century, picking out the instigators of chaos from the Bolsheviks of the October Revolution to the Nazi troops who marched through Europe in the closing years of the thirties, to all those responsible for the death of the Kennedys, that is to say *you and me.* "Street Fighting Man," which opens the second side of the album, represents another high point on *Beggars Banquet.* The hour of revolution seems to have sounded everywhere except in Britain, where, in *sleepy London town,* the only option available to a teenager is to *sing for a rock 'n' roll band.* As for "Salt of the Earth," which concludes the album, this number exhibits an appalling cynicism but at the same time a relentlessly clear message: power has never belonged to the people—the *salt of the earth,* compared by the singer to *a faceless crowd,* a *swirling mass of gray and black and white*—and never will.

And the remaining songs on *Beggars Banquet* are very much in keeping with either "Sympathy for the Devil" or "Salt of the Earth." "Jigsaw Puzzle" confirms Mick Jagger's interest in social issues, with the *twenty thousand grandmas . . . all burning up their pensions,* as does "Factory Girl" with its *factory girl* who *wears scarves instead of hats,* while "Stray Cat Blues" and "Parachute Woman" take an unflinching look at male urges—those of a rock star perhaps?—through the

characters of, respectively, a fifteen-year-old groupie and a woman of apparently boundless erotic power. Finally, "Dear Doctor" tells of the misfortunes of a young man who has to marry a woman for whom he feels nothing but revulsion, and his deliverance when he is stood up by her on the day of the wedding, while "Prodigal Son" transplants the parable told by Christ to the southern United States.

A Radical Departure

As with the subject matter that inspired the Glimmer Twins on *Beggars Banquet,* the music also represents a radical departure from that of *Between the Buttons* and *Their Satanic Majesties Request.* Although the British underground scene was buzzing with excitement at this time, in particular generating great interest among students, not least with Pink Floyd's *A Saucerful of Secrets* and Soft Machine's eponymous first album, the Rolling Stones had drawn a line under their psychedelic interlude and shelved the ambient sound, horns, and miscellaneous instruments in favor of good old guitar, piano, and harmonica. "When we first started out we wanted to be a blues band and then we became more pop-oriented—because we wanted to be popular and to get played on the radio,"[9] explains Keith Richards. In this respect, *Beggars Banquet* restores a certain natural order. It is a return to the past—or more accurately a rereading of country blues and folk traditions by five musicians who had come a very long way and who were able to count on the virtuosity of the pianist Nicky Hopkins and the creativity of the producer Jimmy Miller. Hence the sonority based on the natural marriage of acoustic guitar and piano. Keith Richards again: "There was a lot of country and blues on *Beggars Banquet.* . . . By then we were thinking, hey, give us a good song, we can do it. We've got the sound and we know

1968

A medieval feast for the launch of *Beggars Banquet* at Kensington Gore Hotel on December 5, 1968.

we can find it one way or another if we've got the song—we'll chase the damn thing all around the room, up to the ceiling. We know we've got it and we'll lock on to it and find it."[2]

Beggars Banquet was the last record to be released by the Rolling Stones during Brian Jones's lifetime, although he was conspicuous mostly by his absence from the recording sessions, even leaving for Morocco with his new girlfriend Suki Potier prior to completion of the album. "We were quite happy that Brian wasn't around on *Beggars Banquet*, because when he wasn't there we could really get on with our work,"[9] explains Keith without beating around the bush. On the other hand, when he was present—and got involved—he literally lit up the recording with his musical genius, for example his slide guitar on "No Expectations."

Beggars Banquet went out into the world on December 6, 1968. One day before, in order to celebrate the event, the Rolling Stones had given a great "medieval" party to which some 120 journalists, disc jockeys, and celebrities had been invited (appropriate dress required!). Unable to get hold of the Tower of London, the band opted for the Elizabethan Room of the Gore Hotel in Kensington. This was the setting for a spectacular and memorable cream pie battle. Among those present that evening was David Ormsby-Gore, the fifth Baron Harlech and former ambassador to the United States, who summed up the evening as follows: "Not quite the sort of party I'm accustomed to, but thoroughly enjoyable."[6]

The album garnered universal praise. *Rolling Stone* made the following declaration: "The Stones have returned

The Stones at the *Beggars Banquet* sessions at Olympic Sound Studios.

and they are bringing back rock 'n' roll with them."[1] The *Sunday Mirror* wrote: ". . . the mixed bag of topics put to music include the Bible, Satan, street riots and, of course, sex. I find it the best Stones disc to date,"[67] and the *Chicago Sun-Times*: "The Stones have unleashed their rawest, lewdest, most arrogant, most savage record yet. And it's beautiful."[68] *Beggars Banquet* occupies fifty-eighth in the *Rolling Stone* list of 500 Greatest Albums of All Time but only made it to number 3 on the British charts, behind the Beatles' *White Album*, which had been released two weeks earlier (November 22), and the *Best of the Seekers*. Did it not deserve better?

The Album Cover

First of all, the title. Was *Beggars Banquet* intended as an allusion to the *Beggar's Opera* by Johann Christoph Pepusch and John Gay? The idea is more likely to have come from Christopher Gibbs, who was decorating Mick Jagger's Chelsea flat. It then led to a photo session at Sarum Chase, a neo-Tudor manor house located at 23 West Heath Road, Hampstead (London), in June 1968. One of the photographs taken by Michael Joseph that day was used for the inner sleeve.

As for the cover, that was a different matter entirely . . . The Rolling Stones had wanted a photograph with the power

to shock. While in Los Angeles, Mick and Keith (and Anita) had come across some particularly filthy lavatories attached to a graffiti-covered wall. They immediately got in touch with Barry Feinstein, a photographer who had started his career at *Life* magazine, before immortalizing various Hollywood stars and then turning his attention to the world of rock (Bob Dylan, Janis Joplin, George Harrison). Feinstein added a few inscriptions of his own before taking the photograph on July 26. Back in London, Mick and Keith showed the photograph to the managers of their record companies Decca and London. The response was one of general stupefaction! While London Records insisted that the name of the band be added to the cover, Sir Edward Lewis of Decca rejected the image out of hand, on the grounds that it was in poor taste. Mick Jagger replied: "Decca has put out a sleeve with an atom bomb exploding on the cover (*A-Tom-Ic Jones*). I find that more upsetting." He added some time later: "We have tried to keep it within the bounds of good taste. I mean, we haven't shown the whole lavatory."[6]

To no avail; even the singer's humor did not work. Sir Edward Lewis was implacable. *Beggars Banquet* was therefore released with an extremely sober-looking cover in the form of an invitation card featuring the words *Rolling Stones* and *Beggars Banquet* and the letters *R.S.V.P.* in black italics

Jean-Luc Godard with Bill Wyman and Mick Jagger holding a Gibson Hummingbird during the shooting of *One Plus One*.

A few copies were printed of the infamous *Beggars Banquet* lavatory cover rejected by Decca, the only beneficiaries of which were a number of Decca employees and a few close service partners. Today the record is extremely rare and no doubt the most sought after of all the Rolling Stones albums. Readers are advised to search their attics for copies!

Among the graffiti on the original cover of *Beggars Banquet* are the phrases: "Lyndon loves Mao," "John loves Yoko," "Bob Dylans dream," and "God rolls his own."

on a white background. The back of the cover lists the ten track names with the same white background. In this respect the cover design bears a resemblance to the Beatles' *White Album*. The originally intended cover would not be made available until the reissue of the album (as a remastered SACD/CD) in 2002.

The Recording

The production of *Beggars Banquet* extended from February until July 1968; the recording proper from March until June. The Rolling Stones initially got together in February in order to start preproduction work on their seventh UK studio album. Rehearsals began on February 21 and continued until March 14 at the RG Jones Studios in Morden, Surrey (with Brian Jones and Bill Wyman absent from some sessions). Accompanied by Jimmy Miller, their new producer, the Stones recorded numerous demos, all with Mick Jagger on acoustic guitar (which would not be the case on the album).

Work started in earnest at Olympic Sound Studios in London in mid-March. Jimmy Miller had succeeded Andrew Loog Oldham as producer on the recommendation of Glyn Johns, who appreciated Miller's modesty, self-effacement, and talent, three qualities that swung things in the American's favor. Mick said: "We chose Jimmy because, unlike so many other record producers, he does not have an ego problem. He will do what we want and not just what he wants."[1] Another, by no means negligible, consideration was that he was an accomplished musician himself, in particular an excellent drummer.

During the second half of March, they recorded "Jumpin' Jack Flash" (for the single), "Natural Magic" (for the soundtrack of *Performance*), and "No Expectations," "Stray Cat Blues," "Jigsaw Puzzle," and "Parachute Woman" for the album, plus "Highway Child" (not released).

The sessions resumed in May, when the band recorded "Salt of the Earth," "Street Fighting Man" (with Dave Mason),

"Dear Doctor," "Prodigal Son," "Factory Girl," plus a number of songs that were left off the album (such as "Sister Morphine" [included on *Sticky Fingers*] and "Blood Red Wine"). It is interesting to note that on May 12, the Rolling Stones made a surprise appearance at the New Musical Express Poll Winners' concert at the Empire Pool in Wembley, performing "Jumpin' Jack Flash" and "[I Can't Get No] Satisfaction" to an audience of ten thousand. This was to be Brian Jones's last concert with the band (not including *The Rolling Stones Rock and Roll Circus*).

The next sessions were held between June 4 and 10 and were devoted to recording "Sympathy for the Devil," which was also filmed by Jean-Luc Godard for his movie *One + One* (later renamed *Sympathy for the Devil*). At 4:15 one morning, a lighting rig set fire to the studio. It was a close shave. "Everyone was rushing around trying to put it out, while Jimmy Miller and I ran to save master tapes and put them in his car," recalls Bill Wyman. "Fortunately, the fire brigade soon had the situation under control and the sessions did not become the great lost Stones album."[1] The Rolling Stones then returned to Olympic Studios to add the final touches to "Sympathy for the Devil." The tracks destined for *Beggars Banquet* were then mixed (with some overdubs added at the last minute) by Glyn and Jimmy at the famous Sunset Sound Studios in Los Angeles between July 6 and 20.

The new album also brought some new musicians onto the scene. Ry Cooder, the highly talented slide guitar specialist, joined the Stones' private circle, Keith's in particular. He was present at one of the final sessions for the album (and apparently plays on "Prodigal Son"). Dave Mason from the band Traffic (produced by Jimmy Miller), another excellent guitarist, took part in the sessions, as did Ric Grech, the future bass player of Blind Faith (also produced by Jimmy Miller), the percussionist Rocky Dijon, an outstanding session musician who recorded with Nick Drake, Ginger Baker, Stevie

Keith Richards and Mick Jagger
rehearsing in the studio in front of
the cameras of Jean-Luc Godard, the
master of French New Wave cinema.

Brian Jones
borrowed Keith
Richards's Gibson
ES 330TD for
some of the tracks
on the album.

Wonder, etc.), and last, but by no means least, the Watts Street
Gospel Choir.

Technical Details

In the spring of 1968, Olympic Sound Studios acquired an
Ampex eight-track, which represented a technological revolution at the time. Glyn Johns and Eddie Kramer shared the
position of sound engineer, with Phill Brown, who went on to
have a prestigious career recording with Jimi Hendrix, David
Bowie, Led Zeppelin, Roxy Music, and many others, as assistant engineer. The main mic employed was the Neumann
U67, although the AKG C12A was used for the bass amp and
the Hammond organ, and the AKG D12 for the bass drum
and the Hammond. In addition to the Neumann U67, it seems
that an AKG D224 and a Shure SM57 were used for Mick's
voice. Reverb was provided by an EMT Echo Plate, and Tan-
noy/Lockwood monitors were used.

The Instruments

Judging from how much he had been playing it, Keith seemed
to have found his ideal guitar in the Gibson Les Paul Black
Beauty. He even went to the trouble of decorating this instrument with a psychedelic painting depicting a landscape and
prominent moon in the style of The Fool design team, the two
Dutch artists commissioned by the Beatles to repaint their guitars, automobiles, and before long the façade of the Apple
Boutique in London. In addition to his other guitars, which he
kept with him in the studio, Keith also uses a Fender Precision
bass, as can be seen on One + One. Although less prominent
at the sessions, Brian plays the Mellotron, the sitar, the tambura, and the harmonica, and also, in a number of places, picks
up the guitar—in particular a Gibson ES 330TD lent to him by
Keith, who acquired it in March 1967. Brian also treated himself to a very fine 6-string acoustic, a Gibson SJ-200 similar
to the one Bob Dylan is shown holding on the cover of Nashville Skyline. Bill goes back to his Dallas Tuxedo bass, which
he had more or less abandoned in 1964, in a few places, and
again tries his hand at the double bass. In June a drumming revolution took place when Charlie switched to a new drum kit, a
black Gretsch. As for the sidemen, Dave Mason excels on the

mandolin and the shehnai, Ric Grech on the violin, and Rocky Dijon on the congas. A wide range of other percussion instruments would also be used during the sessions, while Nicky Hopkins plays piano and Ian Stewart the organ. The Stones remained faithful to Vox amps, although in places Bill uses a new Hiwatt and Keith a Triumph Silicon 100.

Keith and Open Tuning

Beggars Banquet also marks a major change in Keith's approach to the 6-string: it was with this album that he adopted the open tuning so beloved of bluesmen. This involves replacing the traditional E-A-D-G-B-E guitar tuning with a tuning in (mostly) major keys, D (D-A-D-F#-A-D) or E (E-B-E-G#-B-E) being two of the most common. Playing the open strings of the instrument therefore yields a major chord. But what is it that led Keith to revolutionize his tuning? "I don't know," he would later explain. "Maybe it was because around that time, '67, we started having time off that we didn't know what to do with."[34] In actual fact, a number of musicians encouraged him to reexamine his guitar playing. One of these was Taj Mahal, who set him on this track in 1967. "He showed me a couple of things,"[11] acknowledges Keith. Another guitarist who prompted him to rethink his technique was Gram Parsons. There were others too: "And then Ry Cooder popped in, who had the tunings down. He had the open G."[11] Keith immediately adopted this tuning system (D-G-D-G-B-D), cherishing it above all the others. Finally, the last major influence was that of Don Everly: "And I realized that one of the best rhythm guitars in the world ever is Don Everly who always used open tuning . . . he was the one that turned me on to all of that."[11]

The great originality of the creator of "Satisfaction" lay in the fact that he did not use open tuning to play bottleneck, unlike the majority of guitarists. He used it when playing rhythm to introduce new and powerful sonorities. For example, the riffs of "Jumpin' Jack Flash," "Start Me Up," "Honky Tonk Women," "Brown Sugar" and many others. However, this change in the way he played was not brought about by external influences alone. "When I was locked into regular, I thought, 'The guitar is capable of more than this—or is it? Let's find out.'"[11]

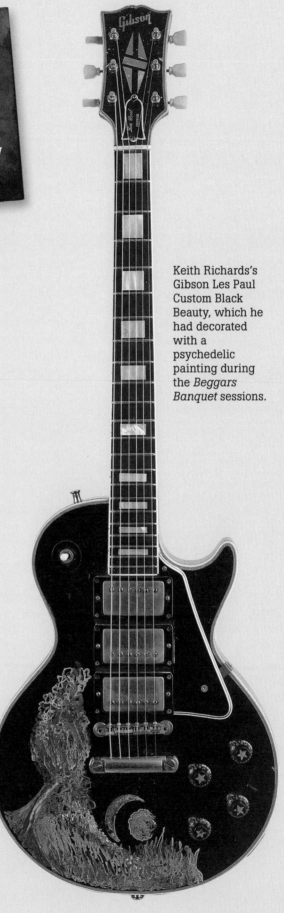

Keith Richards's Gibson Les Paul Custom Black Beauty, which he had decorated with a psychedelic painting during the *Beggars Banquet* sessions.

SYMPATHY FOR THE DEVIL

Mick Jagger / Keith Richards / 6:19

Musicians
Mick Jagger: vocals, maracas (?)
Keith Richards: lead guitar, bass, backing vocals
Brian Jones: acoustic guitar (?), backing vocals
Bill Wyman: shekere, backing vocals
Charlie Watts: drums, backing vocals
Nicky Hopkins: piano, backing vocals
Rocky Dijon: congas, cowbell (?)
Anita Pallenberg, Marianne Faithfull,
Suki Potier, Glyn Johns: backing vocals
Recorded
Olympic Sound Studios, London: June 4–10, 1968
Technical Team
Producer: Jimmy Miller
Sound engineer: Glyn Johns
Assistant sound engineer: Phill Brown

In the initial version of the song, Mick Jagger refers only to JFK. However, Robert Kennedy was assassinated on June 6, 1968, while the Stones were recording in the studio. Is this why the line was changed to *Who killed the Kennedys?*

There have been several covers of "Sympathy for the Devil." Worthy of a special mention is the Guns N' Roses version that can be heard at the end of the movie *Interview with the Vampire* (1994), directed by Neil Jordan and starring Tom Cruise and Brad Pitt.

Genesis

Did Mick Jagger's inspiration for "Sympathy for the Devil" really come from Baudelaire or some other French writer, as he implied in an interview with *Rolling Stone*[19] in 1995? It seems more likely that he wrote the lyrics to the song after having read *The Master and Margarita* by Mikhail Bulgakov (apparently at the instigation of Marianne Faithfull). In this novel, which went through four different versions prior to its publication in Western Europe in 1966, the great Russian writer skillfully blends fantasy and social satire. In turn inspired by Goethe's *Faust*, Bulgakov compares the life of Christ to that of an artist in Soviet Russia, against the backdrop of arbitrary arrest and internment in psychiatric hospitals.

There are two big ideas in Bulgakov's novel that recur in the words of the song (which was initially titled "The Devil Is My Name"): the reversal of values and the confusion of reality and appearance. The devil is presented as a man of taste, whereas *every cop is a criminal* and *all the sinners saints*. Christ himself is remembered for his *pain* but also for his *moments of doubt*. "My God, my God, wherefore hast thou forsaken me?" one can almost hear him crying.

Has evil triumphed over good? This is what Mick Jagger seems to be saying. The almost apocalyptic picture he paints of civilization is no mere fantasy, however. Having described the torments of Christ, he turns the spotlight on the twentieth century: the October Revolution, the assassination of the *Tsar and his ministers*, the Second World War, and finally the sixties and the assassination of the Kennedy brothers. The message is bleak, even terrifying: evil was the victor at Armageddon. Evil is Lenin and the Bolsheviks, who massacred without restraint, it is National Socialism, it is those who had John F. Kennedy assassinated in 1963, followed by his brother Robert five years later. In this respect, the message of "Sympathy for the Devil" hardly differs from that of "Jumpin' Jack Flash": the ideal of peace and love and the spirit of "All You Need Is Love" is dead almost before it has lived; the reality of the sixties is the Vietnam War, it is the Prague Spring crushed by Warsaw Pact troops, it is violence—everywhere. The same message is found here, then, but expressed with a Dylanesque poetic verve. "Mick wrote it almost as a Dylan song,"[11] Keith would later say. In this regard, one phrase in

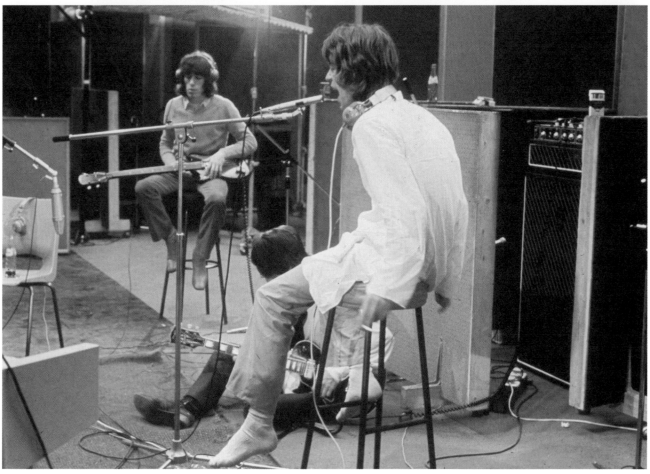

The Stones in the studio trying to find the perfect groove before recording.

the fourth verse is heavy with meaning: *And I laid traps for troubadours who get killed before they reached Bombay*: this is apparently a reference to the hippies for whom the road to India was littered with hazards and dramas.

Autopsy of a Song

"The first time I ever heard the song was when Mick was playing it at the front door of a house I lived in in Sussex. It was at dinner; he played it entirely on his own, the sun was going down—and it was fantastic,"[9] recalls Charlie Watts. For Mick did not just write the lyrics of this song, he also wrote the music. Keith would merely help him to find the right rhythm: "I was just trying to figure out whether it should be a samba or a goddam folk song."[9] For his very avant-garde full-length movie *Sympathy for the Devil*, Jean-Luc Godard filmed the Rolling Stones at Olympic Studios. Thanks to the cameras of the master of New Wave cinema, it is possible to witness the spectacular development of the number from a simple folk song, through several transformations, to rock 'n' roll samba—a kind of black mass à la Jagger-Richards. Godard's

movie is a unique document in the sense that it allows for a better understanding of the work of the Stones in the studio, in particular their way of capturing the quintessence of a song, in this case "Sympathy for the Devil." "The thing with a good band is not to put them in a studio and say 'It goes like this,'" explains Keith. "Put them in there and see what they come up with."[34] *Sympathy for the Devil* affords an insight into the division of roles among the various musicians. Mick provides the vocals, and, keen to communicate effectively with everyone, uses diplomacy to make himself understood; Keith, the de facto bandleader, instills his ideas in his troops with some subtlety and is constantly on the lookout for ways of achieving his objectives; Bill, more taciturn than ever, seems to submit to the wishes of the Glimmer Twins out of weariness; Charlie, barely any more cheerful than Bill, and totally impassive, does what is asked of him to the letter; Brian, isolated by three acoustic panels, seems miserable and alone as he applies himself to his guitar; finally, Nicky, no more jovial than the others, repeats his organ part tirelessly, without batting an eyelid. The atmosphere is not one of schoolboy

1968

Brian Jones and Suki Potier.

In 1966, Brian's new girlfriend Suki Potier had been going out with the Guinness heir Tara Browne. She was with him on December 18, 1966, when they were in the car crash in which Tara lost his life. This is the accident referred to by John Lennon in "A Day in the Life."

FOR STONES ADDICTS

Although it was during a performance of "Under My Thumb," rather than "Sympathy for the Devil," that Meredith Hunter was stabbed to death by a member of the Hells Angels at the Altamont concert on December 6, 1969, the Rolling Stones would not perform this song live for seven years after the appalling incident.

tomfoolery; it is serious, with everyone doing his best to contribute to the creation of the song. And this atmosphere is not exactly helped by the presence of Godard, with his somewhat inscrutable character. But Jimmy Miller sees to it that magic is made. Little by little, the definitive version of "Sympathy for the Devil," without doubt one of the Rolling Stones' most important songs, emerges.

Production

Charlie leads in on his Ludwig kit: " . . . I just played a jazz Latin feel in the style that Kenny Clarke would have played on "A Night In Tunisia"—not the actual rhythm he played, but the same styling."[9] Bill accompanies him on a shekere, an African percussion instrument similar to the maracas, and Rocky Dijon plays an excellent conga part, without a doubt one of the defining tones on the track. Other maracas join the ensemble, and Mick emits a number of shrieks boosted by delay. Before the start of the first verse, female voices (Anita and Marianne?) can be heard laughing and talking. Keith then comes in on his Fender Precision bass

plugged into Bill's Vox Foundation amp. His immaculate playing is accompanied by the piano of the outstanding Nicky Hopkins. In Godard's film, Brian can be seen playing his new Gibson acoustic, the famous J-200, but there is no escaping the fact that his guitar has been either suppressed from the mix or else recessed far behind the other instruments. Keith plays some very good solo phrases on his Les Paul Black Beauty. From around 3:29, another percussion instrument can be heard, probably a cowbell played by Rocky Dijon. Another characteristic feature of "Sympathy for the Devil" is its famous backing vocals (most likely Jimmy Miller's idea), the repeated woo woos sung from 1:56 by Anita Pallenberg, Marianne Faithfull, Suki Potier (Brian's new girlfriend), Glyn, Keith, Brian, Bill, Nicky, and Charlie, who nevertheless seems to have vowed not to unclench his teeth for a single moment. Finally, Mick, performing one of his best songs, is simply outstanding. His talent lights up the whole band. As the opening number of Beggars Banquet, "Sympathy for the Devil" augurs an exceptional album. And that proves to be the case.

JIMMY MILLER AND THE GOLDEN AGE OF THE STONES' SOUND

The first contact between Jimmy Miller and the Rolling Stones occurred at the beginning of 1968 at Olympic Studios in London. The producer was in the process of working with Dave Mason (at that time guitarist with Traffic) on the production of various tracks for the album *Music in a Doll's House* by Family when he received a phone call from Mick Jagger. The Stones' singer asked him to produce the band's next single, "Jumpin' Jack Flash" / "Child of the Moon." "I glided over to his house on a cloud,"[70] recalls Miller. It was Glyn Johns who had put the two men in touch with each other, and they immediately connected. In truth, the Stones were capable of producing themselves, as they had acquired enough experience by now, but they still needed an outside pair of ears. "We'd tried to do it ourselves," explains Keith Richards, "but it's a drag not to have someone to bounce off of. Someone who knows what you want and what he wants."[11] Richards would also offer a very precise definition of the role of producer: " . . . it's a close friend, someone you dig to work with, that translates for you. Eventually we found Jimmy Miller, after all those years."[11] The collaboration between the American producer and the London quintet immediately bore fruit: "Jumpin' Jack Flash" was an enormous hit all over planet rock. "They'd already written 'Jumping Jack Flash'. They were already quite willing to go back to R&B. But the chemistry worked. Being a drummer I was very rhythm minded."[11]

First Steps at Island Records

Jimmy Miller was born in Brooklyn, New York, on March 23, 1942. His father was Bill Miller, an entertainment promoter whose professional achievements included getting Elvis Presley back onto the stage. Steeped in the world of rock 'n' roll since his youngest days, Jimmy learned to play the drums and developed an interest in record production. In 1963 he met Chris Blackwell, the founder of Island Records (1959), who asked him to come to London to supervise sessions with his artists. The first two masterstrokes Miller pulled off were for Steve Winwood's band the Spencer Davis Group. "Gimme Some Lovin'" and "I'm a Man" (of which he was co-writer)

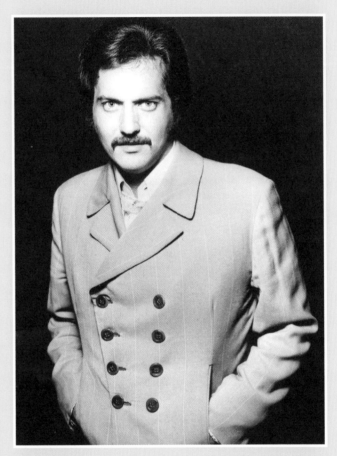

The producer (and drummer) Jimmy Miller began his collaboration with the Stones on *Beggars Banquet*.

reached number 7 and number 10, respectively, in February and May 1967. A friendship developed with Winwood, and when the latter set up Traffic, with Dave Mason on guitar, Chris Wood on flute, sax, and keyboards, and Jim Capaldi on drums, Miller shared in the adventure, producing the superb *Mr. Fantasy* (1967), *Traffic* (1968), and *Last Exit* (1969). In 1969 he then produced the one and only (eponymous) album of Blind Faith, the supergroup made up of Winwood, Eric Clapton, Ric Grech, and Ginger Baker (whose album *Ginger Baker's Air Force* he co-produced the following year), as well as Spooky Tooth's *Spooky Two*.

Phill Brown, who was Miller's assistant, would later say of him: "I loved his approach. Jimmy was a wonderful inspiration to all involved on these albums and probably one of the best two all-around producers I have ever worked with."[71]

The producer in the studio with Keith and Mick in October 1969. This was a partnership that would take the Stones to the peak of their success.

Sympathy for Jimmy Miller

Although an excellent producer, it was for his work with the Stones that Jimmy Miller was to enter the pantheon of rock's great producers. The collaboration between Miller and the band coincides with the Stones' most important creative period. Following "Jumpin' Jack Flash," Miller got together again with the band for the *Beggars Banquet* sessions. "I don't think I could have done Street Fighting Man without him," admits Keith. "Mick would get impatient with my experiments sometimes, but Jimmy gave me a lot of encouragement, saying, 'Let's take this down the line and let's see where it goes.'"[11] And the producer was to play a similarly decisive role in the distinctive atmosphere of "Sympathy for the Devil."

In 1969, Jimmy Miller worked with the Stones again on the single "Honky Tonk Women" / "You Can't Get Always What You Want" and on the album *Let It Bleed*. "When Brian Jones died, Keith took over the musical leadership of the Stones and did it brilliantly," explains Miller. "Keith would suddenly just play something that knocked me out. That was the magic of the Stones."[11] This magic reached its zenith with the next two albums, *Sticky Fingers* (1971) and *Exile on Main St.* (1972), and then *Goats Head Soup*, which was to be the last album the Stones made with Miller. After the Stones, Jimmy Miller continued his career as a producer with Kracker (*Kracker Brand*, 1973), a Florida band who were protégés of the Rolling Stones, and then from 1979, switching genres, with Motörhead, producing their albums *Overkill* and *Bomber*. In 1991 he worked with Primal Scream on *Screamadelica*. Jimmy Miller died on October 22, 1994, in Denver, Colorado. He was only fifty-two years old.

NO EXPECTATIONS

Mick Jagger / Keith Richards / 3:57

Musicians
Mick Jagger: vocals
Keith Richards: rhythm guitar
Brian Jones: slide guitar
Bill Wyman: bass
Charlie Watts: claves
Ian Stewart (?): organ
Nicky Hopkins: piano
Recorded
Olympic Sound Studios, London: March–June 1968
Technical Team
Producer: Jimmy Miller
Sound engineers: Glyn Johns, Eddie Kramer
Assistant sound engineer: Phill Brown

"No Expectations" seems to have been written especially for Brian Jones.

Genesis

Initially called "Slide Doodles," "No Expectations" is a bluesy ballad that is one of the most nostalgic of all Jagger-Richards songs, a return to their roots, in a sense. The narrator is in despair because he no longer has either love or money. In this song, the train, and then the plane, symbolize not a new departure but rather a break with the past. *Our love is like our music/It's here and then it's gone*, sings Mick in a soul-stirring voice, words that would assume tragic connotations a few months later when Brian Jones died. Moreover, it was the founder of the Rolling Stones who imparts this nostalgic feel to "No Expectations" with his slide guitar: "We were sitting around in a circle on the floor, singing and playing, recording with open mikes," explains Mick. "That was the last time I remember Brian really being totally involved in something that was really worth doing. He was there with everyone else. It's funny how you remember—but that was the last moment I remember him doing that, because he had just lost interest in everything."[19]

Production

"No Expectations" is a very pretty blues-tinged folk song. Keith plays rhythm (his Gibson Hummingbird) and Brian accompanies him on slide. The two guitars complement each other magnificently, and Brian seems to have rediscovered an interest in an instrument from which he had been away for too long. Mick: "Brian wasn't really involved on *Beggars Banquet*, apart from some slide on "No Expectations" . . . He wasn't turning up to the sessions and he wasn't very well. In fact we didn't want him to turn up, I don't think."[9] In spite of this distressing observation, Brian delivers a final, dazzling demonstration of his gifts as an instrumentalist on this number. Bill comes in on bass in the fourth line, with a beautiful sonority to his playing. Charlie confines himself to the claves (from 1:29), Nicky plays a very nostalgic piano, while it seems to be Stu on organ between 2:30 and 3:12. Mick is excellent and can even be heard humming in the coda (3:25). It is interesting to note that he talks of recording with "everyone around a mike." This is impossible because in the stereo version, Brian's slide (right-hand channel) would have been picked up by the mics and would be audible over Mick's vocal and Keith's guitar.

1968

DEAR DOCTOR

Mick Jagger / Keith Richards / 3:22

Musicians
Mick Jagger: vocals, harmonica
Keith Richards: acoustic guitars, backing vocals
Bill Wyman: double bass
Charlie Watts: drums, tambourine
Nicky Hopkins: honky-tonk piano
Recorded
Olympic Sound Studios, London: May 13–23, 1968
Technical Team
Producer: Jimmy Miller
Sound engineer: Glyn Johns
Assistant sound engineer: Phill Brown

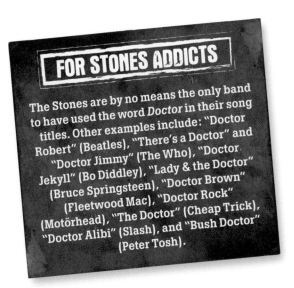

FOR STONES ADDICTS

The Stones are by no means the only band to have used the word *Doctor* in their song titles. Other examples include: "Doctor Robert" (Beatles), "There's a Doctor" and "Doctor Jimmy" (The Who), "Doctor Jekyll" (Bo Diddley), "Lady & the Doctor" (Bruce Springsteen), "Doctor Brown" (Fleetwood Mac), "Doctor Rock" (Motörhead), "The Doctor" (Cheap Trick), "Doctor Alibi" (Slash), and "Bush Doctor" (Peter Tosh).

Genesis

"Dear Doctor" is yet another illustration of Mick Jagger's scathing black humor. The scenario unfolds in all probability in the southern United States, where bourbon is the drink of choice. A boy has to get married—quite definitely against his will, as there is nothing very pleasing about his prospective bride, who is described as a *bow-legged sow.* The groom-to-be is depressed. He appeals to his doctor and to his mother, neither of whom can do much for him. However, this depression turns into relief when he reads a note addressed to him by his fiancée: *Darlin', I'm sorry to hurt you./But I have no courage to speak to your face./But I'm down in Virginia with your cousin Lou.* Outcome: *There be no wedding today.*

This nonmarriage between two people who do not love each other is all the more heartening for the accompanying music in the old hillbilly tradition. Mick Jagger goes as far as to assume a Southern accent in order to lend the tale an air of heavy cynicism. Mick Jagger: "The country songs, like 'Factory Girl' and 'Dear Doctor' on *Beggars Banquet* were really pastiche. There's a sense of humour in country music anyway, a way of looking at life in a humorous kind of way—and I think we were just acknowledging that element of the music."[9]

Production

Musically, "Dear Doctor" is an entirely acoustic country ballad in triple time. Keith Richards plays his Gibson Hummingbird, probably with a "Nashville" tuning that lends it the sound of a 12-string, and it also seems to be Keith on the other acoustic, which is played in more of a lead than a rhythm style. In all likelihood Brian Jones took no part in the recording, as the harmonica part bears Mick Jagger's stamp rather than his. Jagger recalls that Brian's slide guitar on "No Expectations" "was the only thing he played on the whole record," although this is not quite true. On the early takes of this number, Bill Wyman can be heard on electric bass, but switches to double bass for the definitive version. Charlie Watts plays a tambourine (probably attached to his hi-hat) and uses brushes. Finally, Nicky Hopkins delivers a honky-tonk piano part that suits the song perfectly.

PARACHUTE WOMAN

Mick Jagger / Keith Richards / 2:21

Musicians
Mick Jagger: vocals, harmonica (?)
Keith Richards: acoustic guitars, lead guitar
Brian Jones: harmonica (?)
Bill Wyman: bass
Charlie Watts: drums
Recorded
Olympic Sound Studios, London: March–May 1968
Technical Team
Producer: Jimmy Miller
Sound engineers: Glyn Johns, Eddie Kramer
Assistant sound engineer: Phill Brown

Genesis

Following the Stones' controversial incursion (of debatable success) into psychedelic rock, "Parachute Woman" confirms the return of the Stones to what had been their main strength since 1963: an impassioned rereading of the blues. Here there are no half measures from Mick and Keith. The song could even be described as a florid tribute to their sexual exploits—possibly the memory of some erotic experience during a US tour. In this respect the third and final verse could not be any more explicit: *Parachute Woman, will you blow me out?/Well my heavy throbber's itchin' just to lay a solid rhythm down.*

Production

Like "Jumpin' Jack Flash" and "Street Fighting Man," this number confirms Keith's interest in his brand-new cassette recorder, the Philips EL 3302. He used this machine to record a demo with himself on acoustic guitar, Mick on harmonica, and Charlie on drums. The result was then immediately transferred onto the studio multi-track. Keith: "'Parachute Woman,' with that weird sound area like a fly buzzing in your ear or a mosquito or something—that song came so easily. I thought it was going to be difficult because I had that concept of that sound and wasn't sure it would work, but Mick jumped on the idea just like that, and it took little time to record."[2] To arrive at the final result, each musician recorded his own individual part on one of the remaining tracks of the eight-track. Charlie has added bass and probably snare drums, Bill has added a bass part, while Keith has added an intro on his Gibson Hummingbird and a rhythm part, plus some very good licks on his Les Paul Black Beauty with a very short echo. Mick sings with a slight delay on his voice, and probably plays all the harmonica parts, including the coda (Brian having a more technical style of playing). The number had a profound effect on Phill Brown, an assistant sound engineer at the time: "This wonderful, detached feeling took over, for example, while I was listening to 'Parachute Woman', loud, at three in the morning with twenty people in the control room. Then it was everything—romantic, happy, sad, all-powerful—a great 'rush.'"[71]

Mick Jagger in full swing in the studio, being filmed by Jean-Luc Godard for his movie *One + One*.

1968

JIGSAW PUZZLE

Mick Jagger / Keith Richards / 6:06

Musicians
Mick Jagger: vocals
Keith Richards: acoustic guitar, rhythm guitar, slide guitar
Brian Jones: (?): slide guitar (?), electric dulcimer (?)
Bill Wyman: bass
Charlie Watts: drums
Nicky Hopkins: piano
Recorded
Olympic Sound Studios, London: March 1968
Technical Team
Producer: Jimmy Miller
Sound engineers: Glyn Johns, Eddie Kramer
Assistant sound engineer: Phill Brown

Genesis

This is another song that smacks of the influence of the Bob Dylan of *Blonde on Blonde*. When the narrator is not *lying on the floor, trying to do* his *jigsaw puzzle before it rains anymore*, he describes seeing through his window a *tramp* who is *tryin' to waste his time*, the *bishop's daughter* looking a *trifle jealous*, a *gangster* who looks *so frightening with his luger in his hand*. Scenes of everyday life, one might almost say.

However, Mick Jagger, who was responsible for these excellent lyrics, also assumes the role of chronicler of the social realities of the United Kingdom, with the *twenty thousand grandmas* waving *their hankies in the air, all burning up their pensions and shouting "it's not fair,"* the *regiment of soldiers standing looking on* as the *queen is bravely shouting "what the hell is going on?"* before blessing the grandmas. And because he is the singer of the Rolling Stones, he also includes a reference to a rock 'n' roll band: a singer who is *angry at being thrown to the lions*, a bass player who *looks nervous about the girls outside*, guitar players who *look damaged* because *they have been outcasts all their lives*. The images follow one another with all the dazzling rapidity of the writers of the Beat generation.

Production

Keith Richards would later describe "Jigsaw Puzzle" as being a little long. Nevertheless, it is a very well-made country blues, admittedly perhaps somewhat repetitive in form, but possessing a contagious vitality and sung by an inspired-sounding Mick Jagger. Charlie launches the intro with some very good drumming: a highly effective swing with an extraordinary snare drum sound, no doubt the influence of Jimmy Miller. Bill follows with an excellent bass line probably played on his Dallas Tuxedo. Keith plays acoustic, electric rhythm, and slide guitars (both electric parts on his Les Paul). Nicky Hopkins once again demonstrates the value of his contribution to the Stones sound. At 1:50 an instrument enters that is difficult to define. It is not a Mellotron, more like a slide guitar, or possibly an electric dulcimer played with a bottleneck, drenched in reverb and with a delay. Might this be Brian's work? It is difficult to be certain.

Brian and Keith shortly after recording the highly Dylanesque "Jigsaw Puzzle."

STREET FIGHTING MAN

Mick Jagger / Keith Richards / 3:16

Musicians
Mick Jagger: vocals, maracas
Keith Richards: acoustic guitars, bass
Brian Jones: sitar, tambura
Charlie Watts: drums
Nicky Hopkins: piano
Dave Mason: shehnai, bass drum
Jimmy Miller (?): claves

Recorded
Olympic Sound Studios, London: March–May 1968

Technical Team
Producer: Jimmy Miller
Sound engineer: Glyn Johns
Assistant sound engineer: Phill Brown

Keith would later claim that he had based part of the verse tune on the siren of French police cars heard during the riots in Paris in May 1968.[72] John Lennon had also been inspired by a police siren (this time a distinctly British one) when writing "I Am the Walrus," which was released in November 1967.

The student riots in the Latin Quarter of Paris in May 1968, a source of inspiration for the Stones.

Genesis

When Mick Jagger wrote the words to "Street Fighting Man" in the studio in May 1968 (June by some sources), the world was caught up in an infernal spiral of violence. In Southeast Asia, the Tet Offensive had been unleashed (January 1). In the United States, Martin Luther King Jr. had been assassinated (April 4) and then Robert Kennedy was shot dead by a Palestinian extremist (June 6). The situation was also worrying in Europe: in Czechoslovakia, Alexander Dubček's "socialism with a human face" would soon be shattered by Warsaw Pact tanks (August 20–21), while in France, the student revolt highlighted the precarious position of President de Gaulle.

A Revolutionary Song

How true is it to claim that the United Kingdom was spared this tumult? On March 17, Mick Jagger took part in a protest in London against the Vietnam War during the course of which a large number of people were taken to the hospital and another 240 were arrested. However, the anger felt in Britain did not burn with the same intensity as elsewhere. And it is precisely this exceptional situation in the United Kingdom that is the focus of "Street Fighting Man." The refrain leaves no room for doubt on this matter: *Well what can a poor boy do/Except to sing for a rock 'n' roll band. 'Cause in sleepy London town/There's just no place for a street fighting man.* Everywhere else, however, revolution was apparently under way. The narrator, who is also a participant in the generalized revolt, hears the *sound of marching*, thinks *the time is right for a palace revolution*, and will *shout and scream* [that he'll] *kill the King and rail at all his servants*.

Mick Jagger as an instigator of revolution? No, merely an observer of his times. Although inspired to write "Street Fighting Man" by the Trotskyite leader Tariq Ali (himself one of the organizers of the March 17 London demonstration) and allowing the lyrics to be published in the newspaper *Black Dwarf* (to which Ali contributed), he refused to become a spokesperson of the so-called progressive movement—another thing he had in common with Dylan. The Stones' singer never was, and never would be, a "working-class hero."

"Street Fighting Man" was released as a single (with "No Expectations" as the B-side) in various countries, including the United States, France, West Germany, and the Netherlands,

The Stones ritual of throwing a bucket of water over the crowd during live performances of "Street Fighting Man," on this occasion in Rotterdam on October 14, 1973.

in 1968. Banned by many US radio stations because of what was judged to be its subversive message (the single was released in the United States on August 31, just a few days after the Democratic National Convention in Chicago, where the police brutally suppressed a demonstration by the Yippies [Youth International Party]), the song climbed no higher than number 48 on the *Billboard* chart. In the United Kingdom, it was not released until 1971 (with "Surprise Surprise" as the B-side) and reached number 21 on July 24.

Production

"The music came first—before Mick [Jagger] wrote the lyrics," explains Keith Richards to the *Wall Street Journal*. "I had written most of the melody to 'Street Fighting Man' sometime in late 1966 or early '67—before 'Jumpin' Jack Flash'—but I couldn't figure out how to get the sound I wanted."[72] The sound in question turned out to be that of the cassette recorder: "Playing an acoustic, you'd overload the Philips cassette player to the point of distortion so that when it played back it was effectively an electric guitar,"[2] explains Keith. And he would proceed exactly as with "Jumpin' Jack Flash." After sitting down with Charlie and Mick in front of his little cassette player and cheap microphone, they recorded a take of the song together. Keith played his acoustic guitar (Gibson Hummingbird) in open-D tuning, Mick was on maracas, and Charlie played a drum kit of a rather unusual kind: "'Street Fighting Man' was recorded on Keith's cassette with a 1930s toy drum kit called a London Jazz Kit Set, which I bought in an antiques shop, and which I've still got at home,"[9] explains Charlie. The results possess a distorted sonority that appealed to the guitarist: "After we listened to the playback, the sound was perfect,"[72] Keith would confirm. Jimmy Miller and his team then captured the playback of the cassette with a Neumann U67 mic and transferred it

onto one of the tracks on the Ampex eight-track. The overdubs could then begin. Charlie added another drum part with prominent bass tom and a stinging snare. "Actually, I think 'Street Fighting Man' is Charlie's most important record,"[72] explains Keith. It is certainly true that the two drum parts combine to form a fantastic rhythm section. To boost the sound of his first guitar, Keith plays another acoustic part on five strings, this time in open G: "On 'Street Fighting Man' there's one six-string open and one five-string open. They're both open tunings, but then there's a lot of capo work. There are lots of layers of guitars on 'Street Fighting Man.' There's lots of guitars you don't even hear. They're just shadowing. So it's difficult to say what you're hearing on there."[34] Bill was absent on the day of the session and so Keith plays the bass part on his Fender Precision, which is, in fact, the only electric instrument on the track.[2] Nicky is on piano, and Brian adds a sitar and a tambura, a sort of Indian lute that produces a harmonic drone. Dave Mason, the guitarist of Traffic, contributes to the recording on the bass drum and most importantly the shehnai (from 2:28), which is really an Indian oboe. Mick double-tracks his vocal to give it a more substantial sound, and also, it would seem, sings harmonies. Furthermore, he supplements his maracas, as recorded by the cassette player, with a second maracas part that comes in at 2:28. Finally, claves can be heard on all the refrains, in all likelihood played by Jimmy Miller. The production is nothing short of a tour de force, one of the Stones' greatest successes. "'Street Fighting Man' was the first time I had a sound in my head that was bugging me. That would happen again many times, of course, but after that song I knew how to deal with it," says Keith, adding that "When we were completely done recording 'Street Fighting Man' and played back the master, I just smiled. It's the kind of record you love to make—and they don't come that often."[72]

PRODIGAL SON

Robert Wilkins / 2:52

Musicians
Mick Jagger: vocals
Keith Richards: acoustic guitar
Brian Jones (?): harmonica
Charlie Watts: drums
Ry Cooder (?): acoustic guitar
Recorded
Olympic Sound Studios, London: May–June 1968
Technical Team
Producer: Jimmy Miller
Sound engineer: Glyn Johns
Assistant sound engineer: Phill Brown

FOR STONES ADDICTS

On the original bathroom-wall cover of *Beggars Banquet*, "Prodigal Son" credited Robert Wilkins but the released edition credited the song to Jagger-Richards. This mistake was rectified on certain reissues of the album in the early seventies as well as on the CD versions. Reverend Wilkins is said to have thanked the five Rolling Stones in a church service and been applauded by his flock!

Reverend Robert Wilkins, to whom the London quintet owed "Prodigal Son."

Genesis

This was the first time since *Out of Our Heads* (1965) that the Stones had recorded a song written by someone other than the Jagger-Richards duo. "Prodigal Son" is a country blues number by Robert Wilkins. Born in the state of Mississippi, Wilkins had been playing the blues since the twenties, and between 1928 and 1935 had cut numerous records (including "Rolling Stone Parts I & II"—a sign, no doubt!) either alone or accompanied by Sleepy John Estes or Gus Cannon's Jug Stompers. In 1936, he converted to Christianity, becoming a minister. In 1964, Reverend Robert Wilkins recorded eight gospel blues numbers at the Wynwood Recording Studio in Washington, DC. This album was released as *The Original 1964 Recordings*. One of these songs is "Prodigal Son," an adaptation of another country blues number by Wilkins titled "That's No Way to Get Along," recorded in 1929. The title refers, of course, to the parable of the prodigal son as told by Jesus and recounted in the Gospel according to Saint Luke. The symbolism is of the lost sheep and of repentance. In the case of this song, the central character absconds with his father's money. After spending it all and facing starvation, he is forced to work on a farm before returning home to his father, where he hangs his head in shame and cries.

Production

The Stones' version is not so far removed from that of Reverend Robert Wilkins. The style is just as stripped down and the tempo more or less the same, if a little faster than the original. The main difference is Charlie's marking of the beat, initially on the hi-hat and then on the bass drum. Ry Cooder is said to have contributed to the recording, and may be playing the acoustic introduction and accompanying Keith's Hummingbird throughout the number. This is by no means certain, however, and it is even difficult to say for sure that there are two guitars. If Keith is the only guitarist, he deserves credit for his excellent performance, with open-D tuning and a capo on the second fret. There is no bass, but a harmonica can be heard briefly, played by a pretty recessed Brian. Mick chooses to adopt a low voice and a barely recognizable accent, probably in order to adhere closely to the Delta blues atmosphere.

STRAY CAT BLUES

Mick Jagger / Keith Richards / 4:38

Musicians
Mick Jagger: vocals
Keith Richards: rhythm guitar, lead guitar
Brian Jones: Mellotron
Bill Wyman: bass
Charlie Watts: drums
Nicky Hopkins: piano
Rocky Dijon (?): congas
Recorded
Olympic Sound Studios, London: April–May 1968
Technical Team
Producer: Jimmy Miller
Sound engineers: Glyn Johns, Eddie Kramer
Assistant sound engineer: Phill Brown

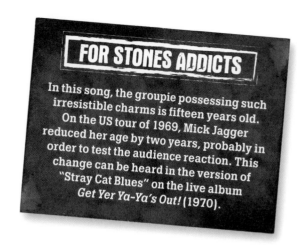

FOR STONES ADDICTS

In this song, the groupie possessing such irresistible charms is fifteen years old. On the US tour of 1969, Mick Jagger reduced her age by two years, probably in order to test the audience reaction. This change can be heard in the version of "Stray Cat Blues" on the live album *Get Yer Ya-Ya's Out!* (1970).

Genesis

Faithful to their bad-boy image, in this song Mick Jagger and Keith Richards describe an unsavory, cynical world as perceived from their elevated status as rock stars. The "stray cat" in question is just fifteen years old but is prepared to do whatever it takes to satisfy the desires of a man one imagines to be far older than she is. This man—a renowned artist, even, perhaps, a rock star?—is no fool. He knows who he is dealing with: *no scare-eyed honey* but a groupie, a teenage girl who is far from home and who clearly possesses a number of trump cards. *Bet your mama don't know you scream like that . . . scratch like that . . . bite like that.* And concerning the nature of this surreptitious relationship, the narrator seeks to reassure the girl by telling her: *It's no capital crime.* And, immediately, to spice things up a bit: *You say you got a friend, that she's wilder than you/Why don't you bring her upstairs?*

The Stones were not the first musicians to show an interest in teenage girls. Chuck Berry sings of the charms of sixteen-year-old girls in "Sweet Little Sixteen," dating from 1958, as does Sam Cooke in "Only Sixteen" from 1959. But the London band brings an air of decadence to the subject that springs directly from real life. Musically, there is a resemblance to the Velvet Underground, whose first album with Nico was released in March 1967. Mick Jagger was to acknowledge this himself in an interview with Nick Kent for the *NME*: "I'll tell you exactly what we pinched from [Lou Reed] too. Y'know 'Stray Cat Blues'? The whole sound and the way it's paced, we pinched from the very first Velvet Underground album. Y'know, the sound on 'Heroin.' Honest to God, we did!"[15]

Production

There is indeed an obvious similarity—right from the intro—with "Heroin" by the Velvet Underground. "Stray Cat Blues" starts with the same guitar quavers over which a second rhythm guitar (tuned to open D) fires off chords, thereby raising the tension. In his quest for sources, Keith has cast his net into the great fishpond of rock 'n' roll and recycles his catch in the characteristic style of the Stones. He is probably using his Gibson Les Paul Black Beauty to obtain this powerful, distinctive sound. Brian is again unable to help

Keith Richards (playing his Les Paul Custom Black Beauty) and Mick Jagger during recording sessions.

The spirit of the Velvet Underground (shown here with Andy Warhol and Nico) hovers over "Stray Cat Blues."

1968

him on guitar, so Keith has to play all the other guitar parts on the track. In addition to the main rhythm part, he adds a second, this time in standard tuning (3:34). He can also be heard playing a first lead part over Mick's vocals and then plays a final solo, here and there with Eastern sonorities, in the coda (3:49). "Stray Cat Blues" also provides an excellent demonstration of the close collaboration of Jimmy Miller and Charlie Watts. Charlie's Ludwig kit has never sounded as good as it does on this album. The sound of his snare drum is magnificent: clear, sharp, and precise, while his use of the hi-hat is excellent, driving the ensemble along with a subtle, intense groove. Bill Wyman is not exactly idle either, providing solid support with a powerful but velvety bass sound. Nicky

Hopkins plays a very good piano part as usual, reasonably compressed but with release on each chord. Mick surfs this libidinous rock number with ease. Each of his lines makes an impact, and his cynical, brutal performance matches Keith's guitar perfectly. It is interesting to note that his voice is pretty recessed in the mix, probably in order to heighten the licentious aspect of the lyrics.

"Stray Cat Blues" is actually made up of two parts: the first consists of the verses and refrains, while the second is instrumental. It is in this second part that Brian can be heard, most likely on the Mellotron with a flute sound (2:48). Finally, it seems that Rocky Dijon is on congas, although the playing is more like that of Mick Jagger.

FACTORY GIRL

Mick Jagger / Keith Richards / 2:09

Musicians
Mick Jagger: vocals
Keith Richards: acoustic guitar
Bill Wyman: bass
Charlie Watts: tabla
Rocky Dijon: congas
Dave Mason: mandolin
Ric Grech: violin
Recorded
Olympic Sound Studios, London: May 1968
Technical Team
Producer: Jimmy Miller
Sound engineer: Glyn Johns
Assistant sound engineer: Phill Brown

Ric Grech of Family plays bluegrass-style
violin on "Factory Girl."

Genesis

The scenario of "Factory Girl" is a man fed up with waiting for his girlfriend, who is getting ready to leave the factory, and paints an unusual picture of her. The tone employed by Mick Jagger is simultaneously ironic and cynical, and there is indeed something caricatural, if not grotesque, about the factory worker he describes. She has *curlers in her hair*, her *knees are much too fat*, and *she wears scarves instead of hats*. Furthermore, she *has no money anywhere* and has a tendency to get *me into fights* and to *get drunk on Friday night*. Musically, "Factory Girl" is a folk song. Keith Richards: "To me 'Factory Girl' felt something like 'Molly Malone,' an Irish jig; one of those ancient Celtic things that emerge from time to time, or an Appalachian song. In those days I would just come up and play something, sitting around the room. I still do that today. If Mick gets interested I'll carry on working on it; if he doesn't look interested. I'll drop it, leave it and say, 'I'll work on it and maybe introduce it later.'"[9]

Production

Keith introduces "Factory Girl" with a very good fingerpicked introduction on his Gibson Hummingbird (with standard tuning). A few plucked violin notes can then be heard, played by Ric Grech, who also plays two distinct (bowed) parts on the instrument in pure bluegrass style. Charlie Watts is conspicuous on this track for having exchanged his drum kit for tabla: "On 'Factory Girl,' I was doing something you shouldn't do, which is playing the tabla with sticks instead of trying to get a sound using your hand, which Indian tabla payers do, though it's an extremely difficult technique and painful if you're not trained."[9] He is supported by the excellent Rocky Dijon on congas. Bill Wyman comes in before the first verse, probably on his Dallas Tuxedo bass. Mick Jagger adapts to the musical style by taking on hillbilly inflections that although exaggerated, suit the lyrics perfectly. Dave Mason accompanies him on bluegrass mandolin, which enhances the Appalachian feel of the song. It is interesting to note that with Brian Jones absent, three outside musicians have been brought in to help with the recording.

SALT OF THE EARTH

Mick Jagger / Keith Richards / 4:47

Musicians
Mick Jagger: vocals
Keith Richards: acoustic guitar, slide guitar, vocals
Bill Wyman: bass
Charlie Watts: drums
Nicky Hopkins: piano
Watts Street Gospel Choir: backing vocals
Recorded
Olympic Sound Studios, London: May 1966
Sunset Sound Studios, Los Angeles: July 1968
Technical Team
Producer: Jimmy Miller
Sound engineer: Glyn Johns
Assistant sound engineer: Phill Brown

Joan Baez and Judy Collins both recorded very good covers of this song, which can be heard on their respective albums, *Blessed Are . . .* (1971) and *Judith* (1975).

FOR STONES ADDICTS

This was not the first time Keith Richards had sung a solo (see "Something Happened to Me Yesterday" on *Between the Buttons*). It was, however, the first time he had sung a complete verse.

Genesis

The *salt of the earth* refers to a passage in the Bible: the Sermon on the Mount as told in the Gospel according to Saint Matthew. "Ye are the salt of the earth: but if the salt have lost his savor, wherewith shall it be salted? It is thenceforth good for nothing, but to be cast out, and to be trodden under foot of men." In other words, people can become the "salt of the earth" by following the precepts of Jesus Christ, which promote a taste for life itself. In this case, the "salt of the earth" represents the "best of humankind," what could be called the elite. Over the course of the centuries, however, the expression has taken on a different meaning, and is now used to denote those who are engaged in a struggle: the workers against the bosses, the exploited against the exploiters, and the weak against the strong.

Mick Jagger raises his glass to the *hardworking people*, to the *lowly of birth*. He prays for the *common foot soldier, for his wife and his children who burn the fires and who still till the earth*. He spares a thought for the wavering millions *who need leading but get gamblers instead*, for the *stay-at-home voter his empty eyes gaze at strange beauty shows and a parade of the gray-suited grafters*. The cynicism of the Rolling Stones' singer is rivaled only by that of society itself.

"'Salt of the Earth,' I think I came up with the title of that and had the basic spur of it, but Mick did all the verses," reveals Keith in *Life*. "This was our thing. I'd spark the idea . . . and after that, Mick, it's all yours. Halfway through he'd say, where do we break it? Where do we go to the middle? Where's the bridge?"[2] It is worth noting that the working title of this song was "Silver Blanket."

Production

Musically, "Salt of the Earth" is one of the most ambitious tracks on the album. The Stones chose to bring *Beggars Banquet* to a close with a mixture of country, blues, and gospel. Keith strums the intro on his Gibson Hummingbird. He also plays slide on a second guitar, his Les Paul Black Beauty (presumably with open-E tuning). Keith can then be heard singing the first verse in a voice that is simultaneously fragile, "rock 'n' roll," and moving. Mick takes up the baton for the second verse, which he sings equally credibly—it is his specialty, after all. Nicky Hopkins accompanies him with

The Rolling Stones performed "Salt of the Earth" on *The Rolling Stones Rock and Roll Circus*. They also sang it with Axl Rose and Izzy Stradlin of Guns N' Roses on the Steel Wheels/Urban Jungle Tour (1989–1990), and Mick Jagger and Keith Richards would subsequently perform it as a tribute to the victims of September 11, 2001, at the Concert for New York City.

Axl Rose accompanies Mick Jagger for a particularly rousing version of "Salt of the Earth" during the 1989–1990 tour.

some excellent piano that is one of the main tones on the track. Indeed, the acoustic guitar/piano combination could be described as one of the key strengths of this album, with the playing of the two musicians complementing each other. Another duo whose work is inseparable from the sound and dynamic of the Stones is that formed by Charlie and Bill, who are absolutely impeccable in their rhythmic support. In the second refrain (2:15), Mick is accompanied by the wonderful Watts Street Gospel Choir. The singers were recorded in July while the Stones were mixing and adding the final overdubs to the album at the famous Sunset Sound Studios in Los Angeles. The choir's contribution is of a high caliber and brings a spiritual dimension to the song. Mick and Keith could occasionally be better in tune on the vocal harmonies, particularly at 2:32, but it does not really matter . . . it is the emotion that counts.

Like "Stray Cat Blues," "Salt of the Earth" is made up of two parts: the first part sung and the second part instrumental. The break between the two occurs at 3:17 and is marked by Keith on his acoustic guitar. The number then develops a totally gospel feel that gradually gathers tempo, generating a spiritual atmosphere in which one expects to hear Mick Jagger launch into a sermon at any moment. Mick remains in the background, however, and the band finishes the number by itself, without choir, led by Charlie's highly effective shuffle and Bill's funky bass.

SIDE A
1968

JUMPIN' JACK FLASH

Mick Jagger / Keith Richards / 3:38

Jumpin' Jack Flash is also the title of a full-length movie directed by Penny Marshall in 1986 and featuring Whoopi Goldberg in the lead role. Alongside the Stones' version of the song, Aretha Franklin's cover can also be heard in the movie.

SINGLE

Jumpin' Jack Flash / Child of the Moon

RELEASE DATE

United Kingdom: May 24, 1968
Record label: Decca
RECORD NUMBER: DECCA F 12782

Musicians

Mick Jagger: vocals
Keith Richards: acoustic guitars, bass, backing vocals, bass tom
Brian Jones: electric rhythm guitar
Bill Wyman: organ, Mellotron (?)
Charlie Watts: drums
Ian Stewart: piano
Jimmy Miller: backing vocal
Rocky Dijon (?): maracas

Recorded

Olympic Sound Studios, London: March 12, 29, 1968

Technical Team

Producer: Jimmy Miller
Sound engineer: Eddie Kramer
Mixing: George Chkiantz, Glyn Johns

Genesis

In *Life*, Keith Richards looks back at the genesis of "Jumpin' Jack Flash": "[The lyrics] came from a gray dawn at Redlands. Mick and I had been up all night, it was raining outside and there was the sound of these heavy stomping rubber boots near the window, belonging to my gardener, Jack Dyer. . . . It woke Mick up. He said, 'What's that?' I said, 'Oh, that's Jack. That's jumping Jack.' . . . Mick said, 'Flash,' and suddenly we had this phrase with a great rhythm and ring to it. So we got to work on it and wrote it."[2]

The main character in the song may have been inspired by Keith's gardener, but the adventures he recounts during the three and a half minutes or so are the fruits of a simultaneously fertile and feverish imagination that was also most likely feeding on distant memories either lived or heard. *I was born in a crossfire hurricane*, sings Mick in the intro. Is this a reference to the bombing of London during the Second World War? What can be said for sure is that the narrator is deeply traumatized and prey to contradictory feelings that may have damaged his mind. He claims to have been *raised by a toothless, bearded hag* and *schooled with a strap right across my back*, then *drowned, washed up*, and *left for dead*, before being *crowned with a spike right through my head*. In short, his life has been a torment, but this does not prevent the Christ-like (?) figure from displaying a furious optimism in the surging refrain: *But it's all right, I'm Jumpin' Jack Flash, it's a gas, gas, gas.*

After two flower-power-tinged albums, were the Stones taking a step back with this number and heralding the end of a dream? The character of Jumpin' Jack Flash seems totally

alien to the countercultural world. On the contrary, this figure scarred forever by his past displays a frenzied individualism that verges on masochism. In 1995, Mick would explain in an interview that this text was all about "having a hard time and getting out. Just a metaphor for getting out of all the acid things."[19] By implication the period of *Their Satanic Majesties Request* . . .

Hats off to Bill. . .

Although credited to Jagger-Richards, the powerful, bewitching music of this number, very much in the image of the "lived" experience of Jumpin' Jack Flash, is partly the work of Bill Wyman: "One night during rehearsals at

Morden," recalls Bill in *Stone Alone*,[6] "I was sitting at the piano waiting for Mick and Keith to arrive. Charlie and Brian came in as I began playing the electric keyboard, messing around with a great riff I've found. Charlie and Brian began jamming with me and it sounded really good and tough." Bill recalls Mick, who arrived at that moment, saying to him: "Keep playing that, it sounds great, don't forget it."[1] "A few weeks later," continues Bill, "when we were in the Olympic studio, out came my riff, the backbone for Mick's terrific lyrics: 'I was born in a crossfire hurricane'. And we all worked on the music. The part I'd composed worked perfectly—but the credit for this, one of our best tracks ever, reads Jagger-Richards."[6]

To date, there have been more than two hundred covers of "Jumpin' Jack Flash," a few of which, such as those by Johnny Winter (1971) and Aretha Franklin (1986), the latter produced by Keith Richards, are almost as good as the original. It is also worth mentioning the versions by Peter Frampton (1972), Terence Trent d'Arby (1987), and Motörhead (1993).

Mick Jagger and Keith Richards hard at work in front of an acoustic panel at Olympic Sound Studios.

Although the riff originally came from Bill Wyman, there can be no mistaking the fact that Keith Richards found the right sound for it and made it the stuff of rock 'n' roll legend: "All my stuff came together and all done on a cassette player. With 'Jumpin' Jack Flash' and 'Street Fighting Man' I'd discovered a new sound I could get out of an acoustic guitar."[2] In terms of its musical qualities, Keith Richards offers the following insight into "Jumpin' Jack Flash": "It's almost Arabic or very old, archaic, classical, the chord setups you could only hear in Gregorian chant or something like that. And it's a weird mixture of your actual rock and roll and at the same time this weird echo of very, very ancient music that you don't even know."[2]

A New Aesthetic

"Jumpin' Jack Flash" was released five and a half months after the album *Their Satanic Majesties Request*. The contrast is more than striking—it is spectacular, breathtaking. Psychedelic rock has given way to a new Rolling Stones aesthetic: a savage, sensual, and untamable blues rock, a music that sounds not so much like a return to the virtues of "(I Can't Get No) Satisfaction" and "19th Nervous Breakdown," but more of a full-blown renaissance. No doubt this new work by the five musicians can be seen as the result of their growing experience, but it is also an expression of the talent of the producer Jimmy Miller, who launched his collaboration with the London quintet with this number.

From the moment of its release in the United Kingdom, on May 24, 1968, "Jumpin' Jack Flash" was a runaway success. It was number 1 in the UK for two weeks from June 25, 1968. In the United States, it peaked at number 3 on the

Billboard chart on July 6 (and was number 1 for a week on the *Cashbox* chart). In the Federal Republic of Germany, the single shot to number 1 on May 28. In France, it reached number 8 just after the student revolt.

Production

"Jumpin' Jack Flash" is the first Stones song to be produced by Jimmy Miller. Eddie Kramer, who had been the Stones' assistant sound engineer since *Between the Buttons*, assumed the role of sound engineer in place of Glyn Johns. "And the first thing Jimmy Miller did was fire me because he'd been using Eddie Kramer as an engineer,"[15] recalls Johns.

When testing his new cassette recorder, a Philips EL 3302, which in 1967 represented a real technical revolution, Keith noticed that by using the basic mic that came with the device, he could saturate the input with his acoustic guitar to obtain a distorted sound not unlike an electric guitar. "You were using the cassette player as a pickup and an amplifier at the same time. You were forcing acoustic guitars through a cassette player, and what came out the other end was electric as hell."[2] Thrilled with the results, he told Jimmy Miller about it, and he and Eddie Kramer set about reproducing the same sound in the studio. Miller placed his own cassette recorder (most probably a Wollensak 4310) on the floor and positioned Richards with his acoustic and Watts with his snare drum around it. "After we cut the track on the cassette machine, we played it back on a little speaker, then rerecorded that on one track of a four-track machine [Olympic Studios was not yet equipped with an eight-track]. That was the guide track, then everybody overdubbed to that,"[73] explains Eddie Kramer.

In 1968, "Jumpin' Jack Flash" became an essential part of any Rolling Stones set list.

And Keith then played the intro on his Gibson Hummingbird, tuned to open D: "Then there was a capo on it [second fret], to get that really tight sound,"[74] (and to enable him to play in open E).

Keith then added a second guitar, this time with "Nashville" tuning (the four lowest strings are replaced with the same four strings of a 12-string guitar [the finer gauge] which are then tuned up an octave). He also plays some excellent bass on his Fender Precision, making an effective contribution to the power of this track. It is interesting to note that in the verses he does not shadow the riff but repeats the same note, a B (the tonality is imprecise, probably because of the guide track recorded on the cassette player, whose speed fluctuates). It is Stu who shadows the riff on the piano. Brian, meanwhile, adds some guitar using Keith's Gibson ES 330TD. Bill is on the organ and is audible mainly in the coda (2:44).

Another keyboard sound can be heard from 2:51, a sustained note somewhere between the harmonica and horns. Is it a Hammond? Is it the Mellotron? Difficult to say. As for Charlie, he has not yet replaced his Ludwig kit with the Gretsch, and contributes some very good, efficient drumming

of a somewhat sober character—bearing Jimmy Miller's signature—that differs considerably from his usual style. Charlie reveals that he is not the one playing the toms: "Keith is playing my floor tom-tom on it to give the 'boom-da, boom-da' sound."[9] Another key rhythmic element is provided by the maracas, played presumably by the excellent Rocky Dijon, a newcomer to the world of the Stones. Finally, Mick, who is responsible for the legendary lyrics, gives a classic performance, quite simply recording one of the best takes of his career. Three voices can be distinguished on backing vocals: Mick, Keith, and Jimmy, the latter probably taking the lowest notes. We have come a long way from the rough and ready harmonies of the early days.

Keith considers the final results to be " . . . the best thing we ever did with Jimmy Miller . . ."[2] and describes the number as a " . . . 'Satisfaction' in reverse"[2] Mick, on the other hand, takes a more qualified view: "I remember the recording session for 'Jumpin' Jack Flash,' and not liking the way it was done very much. It was a bit haphazard—and although the end result was pretty good, it was not quite what I wanted."[9] A difference of opinion between the Glimmer Twins, then?

CHILD OF THE MOON

Mick Jagger / Keith Richards / 3:12

SINGLE

Jumpin' Jack Flash / Child of the Moon

RELEASE DATE

United Kingdom: May 24, 1968

Record label: Decca
RECORD NUMBER: DECCA F 12782

Musicians

Mick Jagger: vocals
Keith Richards: rhythm guitar, backing vocals
Brian Jones: soprano saxophone
Bill Wyman: bass
Charlie Watts: drums
Nicky Hopkins: organ, piano (?)
Jimmy Miller: backing vocals

Recorded

Olympic Sound Studios, London: April 11 and 20, 1968

Technical Team

Producer: Jimmy Miller
Sound engineer: Eddie Kramer
Mixing: George Chkiantz, Glyn Johns

Genesis

"Child of the Moon" can be regarded as the Rolling Stones' farewell to psychedelia. Here Mick Jagger has written some of the most enigmatic lyrics in his career as a songwriter. In the intro to the song, a more or less unintelligible voice can be heard, apparently saying the words: *Lame prick society, I'll be glad I can pay my taxes if I'm stoned*, which may be some kind of private joke. The atmosphere immediately morphs into that of a hazy memory. The story begins at twilight, when *the sun glows at the end of the highway*. In the second verse, the moon appears and her light flickers. Finally, in the third, the Earth's satellite is preparing to give way to a *misty day*. Is this another description of a night with Marianne Faithfull that has evolved into a science fiction tale? Could Marianne be this child of the moon whom the narrator asks for a *wide-awake, crescent-shaped smile*? Or is it a mystical vision of love?

The promotional movie produced by Sanford Lieberson and directed by Michael Lindsay-Hogg perpetuates the mystery. It shows the five Rolling Stones in a forest, looking totally hypnotized, especially Mick Jagger (perched up in the branches, with white horses below) and Brian Jones (who can be seen lurking behind the trunk of a tree). Two women are also present—one young (Eileen Atkins) and one less young—both of whom are gazing at the moon. Watching this promo induces a sense of oppression. This is probably due to the appearance of a furtive-looking Brian, who in all honesty is not looking at his best, and who only exacerbates the feeling of solitude created in the promo. Dan John Miller (leader

The "moon children" pose for posterity.

of the Detroit folk-rock band Blanche) senses Brian's shadow hanging over the song: "I don't think there's another song of theirs that quite captures this perfect blend of country blues with this beautifully sad touch of psychedelia. I'm sure there is a huge chunk of Brian Jones driving this. His spirit really feels a big part of the song."[75]

Production

"Child of the Moon" was developed during the sessions for *Their Majesties Satanic Request*, most probably in July 1967, and worked on again in March–April 1968 during the "Jumpin' Jack Flash" sessions. After the sound of a distorted guitar (with the tape played backward) by way of an intro, Keith immediately launches into a rhythm part, probably on his Black Beauty, and the enigmatic phrase that may be attributable to Jimmy Miller can then be heard, albeit indistinctly. The atmosphere is reminiscent to some degree of the Beatles' "Rain." Bill is on fuzz bass, and indeed so present is the bass sound that it is possible he has been double-tracked by a clear-toned bass. Brian plays the soprano saxophone, but this is not one of his best performances. Nicky Hopkins plays organ and

probably the piano too (very distant in the refrains), as can be heard on a demo dating from October 1967. Mick in turn delivers a very good performance of "Child of the Moon" supported by psychedelic backing vocals.

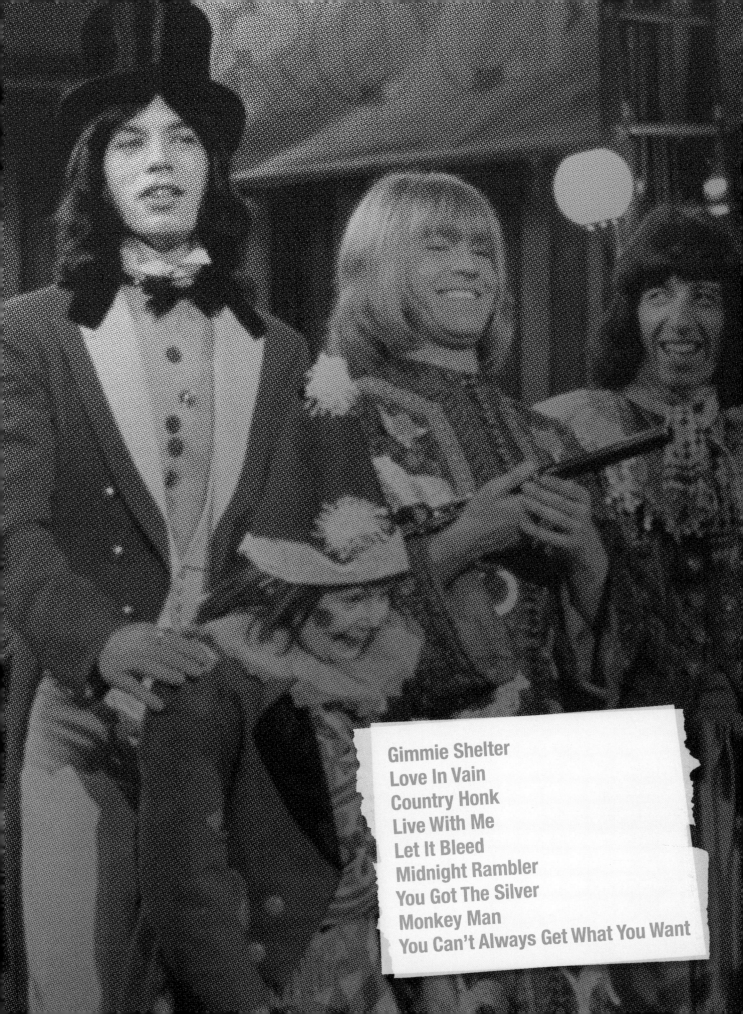

Gimmie Shelter
Love In Vain
Country Honk
Live With Me
Let It Bleed
Midnight Rambler
You Got The Silver
Monkey Man
You Can't Always Get What You Want

ALBUM
RELEASE DATE
United Kingdom:
December 5, 1969
Record label: Decca
RECORD NUMBERS: DECCA LK 5025
(MONO); SKL 5025 (STEREO)
Number 1, on the charts for
29 weeks

LET IT BLEED

LET IT BLEED:
A FAREWELL TO THE SIXTIES

1969. Relations between Brian and the other members of the band had broken down completely. Everything was slipping away from the ill-fated blond angel. All he had built up, or had tried to build up, had collapsed around him like a house of cards: leadership of the Stones had passed to Mick and Keith when they started to write songs, and the ultimate humiliation came when Anita Pallenberg left Brian for Keith. Finally, the abuse of various substances had plunged the founder of the Stones into a state of paranoia that would only intensify as time and events unfolded.

A Painful Decision

While the band was in the process of recording its new album and thinking of going on tour, a painful decision had to be made. At the beginning of June, Mick, Keith, and Charlie went down to Cotchford Farm, the Sussex property newly acquired by Brian, to tell him he could no longer be part of the group. The reasons they gave? His problems with the US immigration authorities and his poor state of health, which was jeopardizing their next world tour; his excessive absences from the recording sessions; and his recurrent dissatisfaction at not playing enough blues. They nevertheless promised him £100,000 (a considerable sum of money) for life and above all gave him the freedom to explain things the way he wished to the media, at the same time suggesting that he cite musical disagreements. Accordingly, on June 8, 1969, the headline "Brian Jones quits the Stones" could be read on the front page. Janie Perrin, a close friend of the guitarist (and

wife of the Stones' PR man Les Perrin), issued an announcement written by Brian himself: "Because I no longer see eye to eye with the other Stones over the discs we are cutting, I have a desire to play my own brand of music. We have agreed that an amicable termination of our relationship is the only answer." What happened next is all too well known: on July 3, Brian Jones was found dead in his swimming pool, and two days later the Stones gave a concert in London's Hyde Park dedicated to his memory—taking the opportunity to introduce their new guitarist, Mick Taylor, to the public. Finally, on September 12, a tribute album was released with a now-famous octagonal sleeve. This is a compilation of twelve songs (from "Jumpin' Jack Flash" to "Honky Tonk Women" through "2000 Light Years from Home" and "Ruby Tuesday") titled *Through the Past, Darkly (Big Hits Vol. 2)* in an allusion to the First Epistle of Paul the Apostle to the Corinthians ("For now we see through a glass, darkly; but then face to face: now I know in part; but then shall I know even as also I am known)."

The Album

The eighth (UK) studio album therefore marks the definitive end of the Brian Jones era (the guitarist plays on only two of the tracks) and sees the Glimmer Twins promoted to joint captaincy of the good ship Rolling Stones. This was a "good writing period," explains Keith Richards. "In those days I used to set up the riffs and the titles and the hook, and Mick would fill it in. That was basically the gig. We didn't really think too much or agonize." Indeed the end of the sixties proved a

Only two of the Rolling Stones, Bill Wyman and Charlie Watts, attended Brian's funeral . . .

virtually inexhaustible source of inspiration. The Vietnam War; communism and its procession of victims in Europe and the People's Republic of China; the assassinations of Martin Luther King Jr. and Robert Kennedy, followed by the murder of Sharon Tate and her friends by members of the Manson Family in the United States—all of this had an apocalyptic feel to it. In 1995, Mick Jagger would describe this period in the following terms: "Well, it's a very rough, very violent era. The Vietnam War. Violence on the screens, pillage and burning. And Vietnam was not war as we knew it in the conventional sense. . . . It was a real nasty war, and people didn't like it. People objected, and people didn't want to fight it."

Playtime Is Over

Ever since taking their first steps under London's foggy skies, the Rolling Stones had enjoyed playing with fire, dancing on the edge of the volcano, demolishing the simple certitudes of the peddlers of morality. With *Let It Bleed*, they continued to apply pressure on the sensitive areas by scoffing at the naïveté of an entire generation. The initial salvos are fired straight after the sublime intro of "Gimme Shelter" and do not let up until the final choral harmonies of "You Can't Always Get What You Want." These two songs chronicle a society in terminal decline. The first is an apocalyptic vision as seen through the prism of Keith Richards's problems and torments—namely his belief that there was a brief, furtive affair between Anita and Mick during the filming of *Performance*; the second in a sense extinguishes the last glowing embers of Swinging London and blows the whistle for the end of playtime. Between these two songs, which respectively open and conclude the album, the undermining is relentless. In "Live with Me," Mick Jagger applies his usual zeal to the decrying of British society: the narrator delights in taking tea at three p.m. and in proposing a ménage à trois to his hypothetical girlfriend; in "Let It Bleed," meanwhile, the narrator speaks of being stabbed in a cellar. Worthy of special mention are "Midnight Rambler," a re-creation in four acts of the diabolical story of the Boston Strangler, and "Monkey Man," Jagger's exhilarating, ironic, and condescending riposte to the hostile media. By comparison with these major numbers in the Stones' catalog, "Love in Vain," "Country Honk," and "You Got the Silver" seem almost like pretty little ditties . . .

A Return to Rock

While their lyrics celebrate the end of the sixties utopia, on a musical level the Rolling Stones remain true to their roots. Printed on the sleeve are the words *This record should be played loud*, and that says it all. Whereas *Beggars Banquet* was largely dominated by acoustic guitar and piano, the guitars have been plugged back in for *Let It Bleed*. And virtually all the parts for this instrument are played by Keith (Brian Jones is credited only with percussion on "Midnight Rambler" and autoharp on "You Got the Silver," while Mick Taylor, the new member, appears on just two tracks: "Country Honk" and "Live with Me"). *Let It Bleed* is therefore an emphatically rock 'n' roll album, as attested by "Gimme Shelter," "Live with Me," and "Monkey Man"—a style of rock 'n' roll born of the encounter between blues and country and western, with songs like "Love in Vain" (an adaptation of a blues number by the legendary Robert Johnson) and "Midnight Rambler" (a supercharged Chicago blues) on the one hand, and "Country Honk," "You Got the Silver," and in a certain sense the title song too, all of which have their roots in the Appalachian tradition, on the other. As for "You Can't Always Get What You Want," the closing song on the album is a ballad with a symphonic dimension.

Let It Bleed was released in the United Kingdom on December 5, 1969. By December 20, it had climbed to number 1 in the charts, knocking the Beatles' *Abbey Road* off the top spot. In the United States, where it had been on sale since November 29, it reached number 3, as in West Germany, and was certified double platinum in both countries. The album was acclaimed by the public and the rock critics alike—and continues to be highly regarded today, for it is currently number 32 in the Rolling Stone list of the 500 Greatest Albums of All Time. Mat Snow writes in Mojo: "'Get real' was not a message you'd expect or wish to hear from The Rolling Stones. Yet their blend of cynicism and hedonism chimed with an era that had lost its innocence."

The Album Cover

This was the second time the Stones had chosen not to put a photograph of themselves on the cover of an album (the first time was *Beggars Banquet*). Instead, the cover image features a vinyl disc bearing the band's name, along with the arm of a phonograph and, suspended above, like a stack of records waiting to be played by an old-fashioned automatic record player, a strange assemblage of objects composed of a tape reel, a clock face, a pizza, and a tire, all of this crowned by a cake on which five statuettes of the Stones (including one representing Brian Jones) take pride of place like candles. On the reverse, the same object is shown in a wrecked state: the disc has been broken, a piece has been cut out of the cake, and a segment of pizza rests on the record, while four out of the five statuettes have toppled over, with Keith the only one still standing. It was also Keith who asked his friend Robert Brownjohn, a graphic designer working in cinema, to design the cover for the band's new album, provisionally titled *Automatic Changer*. Brownjohn contacted the food writer of the *Daily Mirror*, Delia Smith: "I was working then as a jobbing home economist with a food photographer who shot for commercials and magazines. I'd cook anything they needed. One day they said they wanted a cake for a Rolling Stones record cover, it was just another job at the time. They wanted it to be very over-the-top and as gaudy as I could make it." The result certainly lived up to their expectations and inspired a description in *Rolling Stone* magazine as "the crummiest cover art since Flowers."

The album was eventually released with the title *Let It Bleed*, based on an idea by Keith. Some people have wanted to see this as a "dark" response to the Fab Four's *Let It Be*, but the Beatles' latest was only released in the United Kingdom on May 8, 1970, in other words six months later. "Just a coincidence," confirms Keith Richards, while conceding that "maybe there was some influence because *Let It Be* had been kicked around for years for their movie, for that album."

The Recording

The *Let It Bleed* sessions date back to autumn 1968. To November 17, to be precise, when the initial takes of "You Can't Always Get What You Want" (performed by the Rolling Stones on the *Rock and Roll Circus*) were recorded. The bulk of the sessions, however, took place from February 1969 onward, after the band had rehearsed the new tracks in a rehearsal room on Bermondsey Street in southeast London.

That month, work started on the recording of "Midnight Rambler," "You Got the Silver," and "Love in Vain." Next came "Downtown Suzie" (on *Metamorphosis*, 1975), "Gimme Shelter," and various other tracks that were not used on the album, such as the instrumental "And I Was a Country Boy" and "Get a Line" (the future "Shine a Light" on *Exile on Main St.*, 1972). "Monkey Man" was then worked on in April, and from May 12, "Honky Tonk Women" (single), "Live with Me," and "Country Honk." June saw the recording of "Give Me a Drink" (the future "Loving Cup" on *Exile on Main St.*), "Let It Bleed," "I'm Going Down," and "Jiving Sister Fanny" (the last two on *Metamorphosis*).

Leaving aside the initial sessions of November 1968, the recording of *Let It Bleed* extended over a period of six months, from February to July 1969. In October and at the very beginning of November, four months after the death of the much-lamented Brian, the Stones then mixed the album and added some final overdubs. For this they went back to Sunset Sound Studios, as they had for *Beggars Banquet*, and also Elektra Sound Studios (newly founded by Jac Holzman, who had signed the Doors in 1966), both in Los Angeles. Once the disc was finished, the Stones traveled to Fort Collins, Colorado, to launch their new US tour on November 7, having neglected the road since April 1967 (European tour).

New People

Let It Bleed marks the start of the second phase of the Rolling Stones' career. Brian Jones had forced his own band to fire

The Stones, along with their new guitarist Mick Taylor, dedicated their
Hyde Park concert of July 5 to the memory of Brian Jones.

him, and had been replaced by Mick Taylor. For all one could debate the merits of this decision, it has to be acknowledged that the band had few options. Brian was no longer fulfilling his role as a musician and needed to be replaced. It was John Mayall who suggested Mick Taylor to Mick Jagger.

Born in Welwyn Garden City, Hertfordshire, on January 17, 1949, Michael Kevin Taylor discovered the guitar at the age of ten. He left school in 1963 and worked at a number of casual jobs before joining a local band, the Gods, whose members included Greg Lake (later of Emerson, Lake and Palmer) and Ken Hensley (a future member of Uriah Heep). He came across John Mayall and the Bluesbreakers in 1965 and ended up filling the position left vacant by the extraordinary guitarist Peter Green in 1967. He was just seventeen years of age. Finally, at the beginning of 1969, Mayall formed a new band that did not include Taylor, but recommended the guitarist warmly to Mick Jagger: "I just made a phone call to John Mayall. He said, 'I've got this guitar player. You can have him, and he can come down right away.'" Thus Mick Taylor joined the Rolling Stones at the end of May, while Brian was still a member of the band. Keith Richards recalls his first audition: "Mick Taylor turns up and plays like an angel, and I wasn't going to say no." Officially, he replaced Brian Jones on June 13. While making only a modest contribution to *Let It Bleed*, he was to exert a profound influence on the Stones sound over the next five years.

Other musicians also contributed to the album. Ry Cooder, who had played unacknowledged on *Beggars Banquet*, is officially credited for his role on one of the tracks this time. Al Kooper, the extraordinary organist on Bob Dylan's "Like a Rolling Stone," also plays on the album (keyboards and French horn), as do the enormously talented multi-instrumentalist and composer Leon Russell (piano) and the great rock and bluegrass violinist Byron Berline. Merry Clayton (Elvis Presley, Ray Charles, the Supremes) is the fabulous female voice on "Gimme Shelter," while Nanette Workman, Madeline Bell (Donovan, Elton John, Ringo Starr), and Doris Troy (Pink Floyd, Nick Drake, Bob Marley) provide backing vocals on the album, and the female vocal group Reparata & The Delrons contribute to the harmonies on "Honky Tonk Women." As for the horns, saxophonists Steve Gregory (who played with Alan Price and Fleetwood Mac and was responsible for the solo on George Michael's 1984 worldwide hit "Careless Whisper") and Bud Beadle (Ginger Baker, Steve Howe) make contributions, as does the legendary saxophonist Bobby Keys (Buddy Holly, George Harrison, John Lennon, Eric Clapton, Lynyrd Skynyrd), who was to become the traveling companion and close friend of Keith Richards, touring with the band numerous times up to his death in 2014. Meanwhile the old hands include Nicky Hopkins, Jack Nitzsche, and Rocky Dijon.

Let It Bleed was released the day before the tragic concert at Altamont. Both album and concert mark the end of the sixties utopia.

This fine company naturally came under the direction of the highly talented Jimmy Miller, who was producing his second album for the Rolling Stones. Glyn Johns was again the chief sound engineer, assisted this time by George Chkiantz, alias "Irish O'Duffy," who would later work on the albums *Led Zeppelin II* (1969) and *Physical Graffiti* (1975); Vic Smith, who would collaborate with Cat Stevens, Black Sabbath, and the Jam; Bruce Botnick, who went on to record the Doors, most importantly producing *L.A. Woman*, their last album with Jim Morrison, in 1971; and Jerry Hansen (*Uncle Meat* by Mothers of Invention in 1969); and Alan O'Duffy (the Kinks, Deep Purple, Humble Pie, Paul McCartney and others).

Technical Details

In 1969, Olympic Sound Studios modernized its mixing desk, which had been designed by the brilliant Dick Swettenham. It was upgraded from a 16-input/4-output to a 32-input/8-output configuration in order to synchronize with the Ampex eight-track tape recorder, and was equipped with A&D F600 limiters. In parallel with this development, Swettenham was also creating the legendary Helios console, which would be used for the recording of many a legendary rock 'n' roll album over the coming years. Among other places, Helios consoles were installed in the Beatles' Apple Studios on Savile Row, London, in 1969 and later by Richard Branson at The Manor and in Townhouse Studios for Virgin Records (Mike Oldfield's Tubular Bells). They would also be used in the Rolling Stones' first mobile recording studio.

The Instruments

Brian, in his last recording with the Stones, has difficulty finding his niche in the studio. He ends up playing percussion and autoharp, but not the guitar, on the album. The newcomer Mick Taylor plays a Gibson SG Standard. All the others play the same instruments they had used on *Beggars Banquet*, with a few exceptions: Bill had acquired two new basses: a Vox Astro and a Fender Mustang. He also plays vibes and, like Brian, strums the autoharp. Finally, Keith had treated himself to a Gibson Flying V, but favors a semi-acoustic Maton SE777 during the sessions. This was an Australian guitar abandoned by a musician who had had to leave Keith's apartment in a hurry.

Despite its sensational appearance, Keith would use this Gibson Flying V very little in recording sessions.

GIMMIE SHELTER

Mick Jagger / Keith Richards / 4:41

Musicians
Mick Jagger: vocals, harmonica
Keith Richards: rhythm and lead guitar, backing vocals
Bill Wyman: bass
Charlie Watts: drums
Nicky Hopkins: piano
Jimmy Miller: güiro, maracas
Merry Clayton: vocals and backing vocals

Recorded
Olympic Sound Studios, London: February–March 1969
Sunset Sound Studios and/or Elektra Studios,
Los Angeles: October–November 1969

Technical Team
Producer: Jimmy Miller
Sound engineer: Glyn Johns
Assistant sound engineers: George Chkiantz, Bruce Botnick, Jerry Hansen, Vic Smith, Alan O'Duffy

The singer Merry Clayton, whose vocal performance on "Gimme Shelter" remains unsurpassed.

Genesis

Keith Richards wrote "Gimme Shelter" in autumn 1968 in the apartment of his friend Robert Fraser. That day, London was hit by a terrific storm. From the window, the Stones' guitarist watched pedestrians scurrying in all directions for shelter, their faces whipped by torrential rain. At that time, Anita Pallenberg was in the middle of shooting *Performance* with Mick Jagger, directed by Nicolas Roeg and Donald Cammell, whom Keith Richards wholeheartedly detested as a "twister and a manipulator. . . . A razor-sharp mind poisoned with vitriol." The musician did not go to watch the shoot but could not help wondering about it: "God knows what's happening," he would later write in his autobiography. So there was Cammell, but there was also Mick Jagger, who in one scene has to take a bath with the charming Anita.

Keith Richards therefore owes his inspiration for one of the greatest songs in the history of rock 'n' roll to a conjunction of external and internal factors: the natural forces being unleashed outside and the onset of a profound mental anguish.

A storm is threatening my very life today: not only does the first line of "Gimme Shelter" express Keith's feelings, it also describes the situation in the world at large at the end of the sixties: the Vietnam War, the assassination of Martin Luther King Jr., the crushing of the Prague Spring, the murder of Sharon Tate—a torrent of violence that made the lofty ideals of "flower power" seem illusory and absurd. Indeed the verses of the song build up to an apocalyptic vision. *A fire is sweeping the very street,* a *mad bull lost its way,* and the *floods is threatening my very life*: here we are not so far from the territory of Bob Dylan's "A Hard Rain's Gonna Fall" (1963) or "Desolation Row" (1965). "That's a kind of end-of-the-world song, really," Mick Jagger would later claim. "It's apocalypse; the whole record's like that." Nevertheless, "Gimme Shelter" ends on a note of hope with the prospect of redemption through love: *I tell you love, sister, it's just a kiss away.*

And then there is the music—the spellbinding intro with its distinctive rhythm, preparing the ground for Mick Jagger's vocals and harmonica . . . Johnny Marr (former guitarist with the Smiths) would later claim: "I couldn't believe that something could be so perfect," seeing the song as the ultimate proof that rock 'n' roll could be "beautiful and dangerous at

1969

Mick Jagger, Anita Pallenberg, and Michèle Breton on the set of *Performance*.

the same time." For Greil Marcus, "The Stones have never done anything better."

Production

According to Keith, "'Gimme Shelter' and 'You Got the Silver' were the first tracks we recorded in Olympic Studios for what became *Let It Bleed*." And it is "Gimme Shelter," with its extraordinary guitar introduction played unaccompanied by the king of the riff, that opens the album. "That was done on a full-bodied, Australian electric-acoustic, f-hole guitar," he explains. "It kind of looked like an Australian copy of the Gibson model that Chuck Berry used." Keith is referring here to the Maton SE777 that he acquired in an unusual way: "From some guy who stayed at my pad. He crashed out for a couple of days and suddenly left in a hurry, leaving that guitar behind. You know, 'Take care of this for me.' I certainly did!" In order to obtain his special sound, Keith plugged the Maton into his Triumph Silicon 100 amplifier, whose vibrato he particularly liked. He later claimed that the chords were inspired by Jimmy Reed. The influence may not be immediately obvious, but the spirit of the blues is clearly present. Keith also plays lead guitar in the form of short, simple phrases that mesh perfectly with his rhythm playing. The intro continues with Charlie producing a syncopated rhythm on the drums, over which Jimmy Miller's güiro then comes in. And for the first time on the track, we hear Merry Clayton, with her disquieting and truly haunting vocals. The other instruments then enter in turn, first the bass, played by Bill Wyman, and then the piano, played by Nicky Hopkins. This intro continues for a good fifty seconds before Mick Jagger launches into his savage, threatening, aggressive vocals. Mick also plays a distorted-sounding harmonica, for example at 2:04, where he has a solo accompanied by Jimmy Miller on maracas. Keith then follows on lead guitar, and Merry Clayton, whose voice literally transcends the song, has a fabulous solo moment from 2:46.

A Dazzling Vocal Performance

Glyn Johns, who recorded Clayton at Elektra Studios at the very beginning of November, is not going to forget the experience in a hurry: " . . . apparently it was Jack Nitzsche who recommended Merry Clayton to come in and sing with Mick on 'Gimme Shelter' [Mick Jagger would claim that it was Jimmy Miller's idea]. . . . She was called very late at night and, being heavily pregnant and already in bed, was singularly unimpressed at being disturbed at such a late hour. She had no idea who The Rolling Stones were and was reluctant to come. . . . She was absolutely amazing. None of us had ever heard anything quite like what she produced that night. I practically had to stand her in another room, her voice was so powerful. She did three amazing takes, standing there with her hair still in curlers, and went home." The full force of her performance can be felt around 3:03, where her voice stalls under the power of her delivery. Merry Clayton, who had already made numerous recordings, is a fabulous vocalist and backing singer who had been a member of Ray Charles's Raelettes and then a backing singer for Phil Ochs, Burt Bacharach, and Neil Young (on his first album) among many other artists. "Gimme Shelter" is one of the pinnacles of the Stones' catalog. Despite the absence of Brian Jones and his death around the time the song was being finalized, they had succeeded in giving of their very best while at the heart of the storm. And some of the credit for this success can be claimed by the excellent Jimmy Miller and Glyn Johns.

After recording the first verse, everyone in the studio showed their appreciation for Merry Clayton's vocal performance. The singer then insisted on talking about royalties before continuing!

LOVE IN VAIN

Robert Johnson / 4:27

Musicians
Mick Jagger: vocals
Keith Richards: acoustic guitar and slide guitar
Bill Wyman: bass
Charlie Watts: drums
Ry Cooder: mandolin
Recorded
Olympic Sound Studios, London: February–March 1969
Technical Team
Producer: Jimmy Miller
Sound engineer: Glyn Johns
Assistant sound engineers: George Chkiantz, Bruce Botnick, Jerry Hansen, Vic Smith, Alan O'Duffy

Ry Cooder plays mandolin on "Love in Vain," a Delta blues reinterpreted by the Stones.

Genesis

Due to the numerous myths that enshroud his life, for example the story that he signed a pact with the devil in exchange for instant virtuosity on the guitar, Robert Johnson is one of the most legendary of all blues singer-guitarists. The twenty-nine songs he recorded in just two sessions (November 1936 and June 1937) have exerted a phenomenal influence, not only on blues musicians as such, but on every pioneer of rock music from Bob Dylan, to the Rolling Stones, to Jimmy Page.

"Love in Vain Blues" dates from June 20, 1937. For this number, in which the narrator sings of the sadness of losing the love of the woman he describes following to the station with a suitcase in his hand (most likely the bluesman's lover Willie Mae Powell), the songwriter from Mississippi took his inspiration from "In the Evenin' When the Sun Goes Down" by the pianist Leroy Carr. More than thirty years after Robert Johnson wrote this song, the Rolling Stones in turn take up this tale of a breakup. The sadness felt by the narrator endures but is expressed differently. Keith Richards, who heard the song for the first time in 1968, when the second box set dedicated to Robert Johnson was released, recalls: "Mick and I both loved it [the song], and at the time Gram [Parsons] and I started searching around for a different way to present it, because if we were going to record it there was no point in trying to copy the Robert Johnson style or version. So I sat around playing it in all kinds of different ways and styles. We took a little bit more country, a little bit more formalized, and Mick felt comfortable with that." This is confirmed by Mick Jagger: "We changed the arrangement quite a lot from Robert Johnson's. We put in extra chords that aren't there on the Robert Johnson version. Made it more country."

Production

The Stones certainly made "Love in Vain" their own. Their version differs considerably from Robert Johnson's. They have made it more accessible and given it a far wider appeal, but without in any way caricaturing it or doing it a disservice. The great respect they feel for the legendary bluesman is obvious, and, as we have seen, Keith would later acknowledge that the aim was not to try to imitate him. It is a shame that Brian Jones, who so wanted to record the blues, is not present on the track, but unfortunately he lacked the desire, the strength,

The legendary singer and guitarist Robert Johnson (left) photographed around 1935 next to Johnny Shines.

or the opportunity to attend the session. As a result, Keith Richards takes care of all the guitar playing, starting with some superb acoustic, probably his Gibson Hummingbird. His performance is influenced to some degree by country music, a style he was listening to intently around this time. Gram Parsons had something to do with this. Keith's intro is superb and enables Mick to give a nuanced, sincere performance. Then the second guitar, a slide (the Maton? The Les Paul?), makes its entry. Keith plays a very good bottleneck, despite having barely used the technique, which he had always left to Brian. Ry Cooder plays an excellent—credited—bluegrass mandolin part on this track, in contrast with *Beggars Banquet*, where his contribution was never really acknowledged. However, he would later complain of having been misled by the Stones, who, he claims, had got him to come over and then unscrupulously left the tape recorder running in order to exploit the tapes at a later date. Keith would explain: " . . . he was never

brought over for the album, which is the main thing. He came over with Jack Nitzsche to get the music for some movie. He came by and we played together a lot, sure. I mean, he's a gas to play with. He's amazing." The matter at issue was a jam that took place on April 23, 1969, involving Mick Jagger, Charlie Watts, Bill Wyman, Nicky Hopkins, and Ry Cooder. Keith Richards was absent but the tape recorder was running all the same . . . On January 7, 1972, a disc of these recordings was issued with the title *Jamming with Edward*!

As for the rhythm section, Charlie uses brushes on his snare drum, and his hi-hat can hardly be heard. On bass, Bill seems to be playing his Dallas Tuxedo but is pretty recessed in the mix. It would be impossible to discuss "Love in Vain" without mentioning the future live versions with Mick Taylor on slide. Taylor's outstanding playing gives the number an extra dimension (see *Get Yer Ya-Ya's Out!* from 1970). It would seem that his time spent with John Mayall was not in vain . . .

COUNTRY HONK

Mick Jagger / Keith Richards / 3:13

Musicians
Mick Jagger: vocals, car horn (?)
Keith Richards: acoustic guitar, backing vocals
Mick Taylor: slide guitar
Charlie Watts: drums
Byron Berline: violin
Sam Cutler (?): car horn
Nanette Workman: backing vocals
Recorded
Olympic Sound Studios, London: May–July 1969
Sunset Sound Studios / Elektra Studios,
Los Angeles: October 1969
Technical Team
Producer: Jimmy Miller
Sound engineer: Glyn Johns
Assistant sound engineers: George Chkiantz, Bruce
Botnick, Jerry Hansen, Vic Smith, Alan O'Duffy

Genesis

On December 18, 1968, a few days after rehearsals for *The Rolling Stones Rock and Roll Circus*, Mick Jagger and Keith Richards went on vacation for three weeks to Brazil and Peru with their respective partners, Marianne Faithfull and Anita Pallenberg. Keith Richards: "We were headed for the Mato Grosso. We lived for a few days on a ranch, where Mick and I wrote 'Country Honk,' sitting on a veranda like cowboys, boots on the rail, thinking ourselves in Texas." . . . "It was written on an acoustic guitar," he recalls, "and I remember the place because every time you flushed the john these black blind frogs came jumping out—an interesting image."

"Country Honk" is the acoustic, country version of "Honky Tonk Woman." In fact it is an homage to Jimmie Rodgers and Hank Williams, two masters of country blues and the honky-tonk style. The lyrics barely differ from those of the electric version released as a single: the setting is a bar in which alcohol flows like water and hostesses are skilled at making the customers leave their cares behind. There is one small difference, however: in the first verse of "Honky Tonk Women," the bar is located in Memphis, Tennessee, whereas in "Country Honk," it is in Jackson, the Mississippi state capital, perhaps to strike a more Southern, more bluesy note.

Production

In his book *Rolling Stones and the Making of Let It Bleed*, Sean Egan quotes assistant engineer Bruce Botnick's claim that the track was initially recorded in London and then completely redone in Los Angeles. The violin part is played by the bluegrass virtuoso Byron Berline (who would join Gram Parsons and Chris Hillman's Flying Burrito Brothers at the beginning of the seventies and then move to Stephen Stills's Manassas). "We brought Byron Berline and a few other country guys that were in L.A. and I believe Keith played with them," explains Botnick. Mick Jagger was apparently not content simply to have co-written and sung the song, but made another contribution too. Bruce Botnick again: "We took a stereo microphone and put it out in the street and Mick went outside and honked the horn on the car." And it is over this live atmosphere that Keith strums his acoustic Gibson Hummingbird. Mick Taylor, for whom this was one of his very first sessions

In Brazil, Keith Richards and Anita Pallenberg found out they were going to become parents. Their son Marlon was born on August 10, 1969.

Mick Jagger and Marianne Faithfull in Brazil, where "Country Honk" was written.

with the Stones, accompanies him with some very modest slide guitar phrases played on a cheap Hawaiian Selmer. Bill Wyman was one of the members of the Stones unavailable for the recording, while Charlie Watts drums softly on his Gretsch kit, which is recessed in the mix. As for the backing vocals, Keith sings alongside Nanette Workman, who had already contributed to the "Honky Tonk Women" session, but however hard one listens, it is difficult to make out her voice. The track ends the way that it starts, with a street ambiance complete with car horn. According to some accounts, it was not Mick who sounded the horn, but Sam Cutler, the Stones' tour manager. "Country Honk" is more like a demo than a finished song, and in spite of the amusing nature of the concept, it is a shame the Stones did not replace it on the album with "Honky Tonk Women," which is one of their greatest successes.

LIVE WITH ME

Mick Jagger / Keith Richards / 3:41

Musicians
Mick Jagger: vocals
Keith Richards: rhythm guitar, bass, backing vocals
Mick Taylor: rhythm guitar
Charlie Watts: drums
Bobby Keys: tenor saxophone
Nicky Hopkins: piano
Leon Russell: piano, horn arrangement

Recorded
Olympic Sound Studios, London: May 1969
Sunset Sound Studios, Elektra Studios,
Los Angeles: October–November 1969

Technical Team
Producer: Jimmy Miller
Sound engineer: Glyn Johns
Assistant sound engineers: George Chkiantz, Bruce Botnick, Jerry Hansen, Vic Smith, Alan O'Duffy

The American pianist Leon Russell, who wrote the horn arrangements for "Live with Me."

Genesis

Mick Jagger's caustic humor reasserts itself in "Live with Me." The high moral standards inculcated by the best English schools and the various traditions on which British civilization is founded are swept aside by the hurricane that is the Rolling Stones. The narrator, whom the singer clearly delights in embodying, wants his girlfriend to move in with him. However, he does not hide the fact that he has heaps of what he calls *nasty habits*: he takes *tea at three*, which goes against the proprieties of good British society, and demands that the meat he eats for dinner be *hung up for a week*. But worse is to come. His best friend *shoots water rats and feeds them to his geese*. Is it appropriate under these conditions to be envisaging a ménage à trois? *Don'cha think there's a place for you in between the sheets*, asks Jagger in the refrain. The Dantesque descriptions continue in the second verse. This time it is a question of *harebrained children . . . locked in the nursery* with *earphone heads* and *dirty necks*, who *queue up for the bathroom round about 7:35*. As for the staff, they are no more accustomed to high standards of behavior than the narrator: the cook *is a whore, the butler has a place for her behind the pantry door*, and the French maid, who is *wild for Crazy Horse, strips* in front of the chauffeur and causes *the footman's eyes* to *get crossed*.

Production

An intro of twenty or so notes on the bass, stinging electric guitars, a saxophone of considerable erotic power: the music of "Live with Me" is a perfect reflection of the pleasure taken by Mick Jagger in deriding the good old values of prudish Albion. From the very first notes, the listener is grabbed by the heavy, percussive bass playing a rhythmic pattern worthy of James Jamerson or Bootsy Collins. This bass part is taken by Keith Richards and reveals his growing interest in the instrument. He would later explain that Bill Wyman had no problem with him taking his place: "Sometimes I'd say, 'Bill, it goes like this.' And he'd say, 'Why show me? You got it down. Let's make this simple. You do it.'" Charlie Watts then follows with an excellent rhythm on his Gretsch kit, again very "funky" in spirit. And once the guitars join in, the weaving between the two instruments, envisaged by Keith since the earliest days of the band, is immediately apparent, for it is this song that

On June 13, the Stones revealed their new guitarist and Brian's successor, Mick Taylor, on the lawns of Hyde Park.

marks the start of the collaboration between Mick Taylor and the Rolling Stones (of which he is not yet officially a member). "And that was kind of the start of that particular era for the Stones, where Keith and I traded licks," says Mick Taylor, "He'd sometimes play rhythm, I'd sometimes play rhythm, but onstage there'd always be quite a lot of lead guitar playing, which I'd do most of."

On "Live with Me," which was his first real session, he restricts himself to replying to Keith's sharp-edged riffs with highly rhythmic phrases that are nevertheless drenched in the blues. It may be that he did not yet trust himself to really open up on his Gibson SG Standard to his awe-inspiring partner. The two guitars answer one another perfectly, however, and their riffs are like bursts of high-voltage electricity. This track also marks the entrance of saxophonist Bobby Keys into the world of the Stones, having been introduced by Bruce Botnick: "I brought Bobby from Delaney and Bonnie. He's a very sweet man. He's a really fine saxophonist." Bobby Keys recalls this session: "Both the horns and Mick Taylor made their debut on the same album on the same track. At the time a lot of people overlooked the fact that it wasn't just Mick [Taylor] joining the band, that was the whole period where the horns joined too." The tenor sax solo played by Keys at 1:39 is a bravura display for any lover of rock music. Already clearly recognizable in his phrasing is the extraordinary sonority that would light up so many of the band's future tracks. Another new face was Leon Russell. The horn arrangements in the coda are his work, although in truth they are somewhat drowned out in the mix, and other notes from Bobby's sax are difficult to make out. Leon was also responsible for a thunderous piano part that he shares with Nicky Hopkins. The Americans had arrived in force and lent the Stones a new vigor, and there is no mistaking the results! This is far from the world of *Their Satanic Majesties*.

Keith Richards would never forget recording "Let It Bleed" and his bleeding fingers.

LET IT BLEED

Mick Jagger / Keith Richards / 5:38

Musicians
Mick Jagger: vocals
Keith Richards: acoustic guitar and slide guitar
Bill Wyman: bass, autoharp
Charlie Watts: drums
Ian Stewart: piano
Recorded
Olympic Sound Studios, London: March(?), June–July 1969
Technical Team
Producer: Jimmy Miller
Sound engineer: Glyn Johns
Assistant sound engineers: George Chkiantz, Bruce Botnick, Jerry Hansen, Vic Smith, Alan O'Duffy

Coke and sympathy inevitably conjures up associations with *Tea and Sympathy,* the title of the 1956 movie directed by Vincente Minnelli and starring Deborah Kerr and John Kerr.

FOR STONES ADDICTS

Parking lot was an expression used by Marianne Faithfull to refer to her . . . private parts.

Genesis

This song may owe its title to an exclamation made by Keith Richards, when, exhausted after spending hours in the studio playing the same chords over and over, he ended up with bleeding hands and was unable to play. An argument is said to have broken out with Mick Jagger and Jimmy Miller, both of whom were determined to continue the session. However, the Stones guitarist offers a different account: "'Let It Bleed' was just one line in that song Mick wrote. It became the title—we just kicked a line out. We didn't know what to call that song." With "Let It Bleed," the Glimmer Twins continued to rub the conformists the wrong way, all those narrow minds for whom they had always had an aversion. Provocation being a formidable weapon, and one they were very fond of using, insipid compromise has no place here. "Let It Bleed" is clearly a drug song, in which a little coke is snorted and the narrator ends up being knifed in *my dirty filthy basement with that jaded, faded, junky nurse.* The expression "let it bleed" can also be interpreted as a junky looking for a vein.

However, this is also, and most importantly, a song in which sex is no longer merely suggested, but demanded for its therapeutic benefits: *She said "My breasts, they will always be open/Baby, you can rest your weary head right on me/ And there will always be a space in my parking lot."* And a few lines further on: *You can be my rider, you can come all over me.* The lyrics could not be more explicit.

Production

The track opens with what seems to be a scrap of unused take, with Keith Richards on bottleneck, playing alone—or, to be more precise, accompanied by a tape hiss that would horrify Glyn Johns. He then launches into the introduction proper on his Gibson Hummingbird. This reasonably up-tempo track, a kind of country-rock ballad, is jubilant in mood, with Mick Jagger at his very best. Charlie Watts also seems in glorious form and lays down a fantastic rhythm supported by Bill Wyman with some excellent bass playing, despite forgetting to change note at 2:03(!). Ian Stewart proves once more that he is the king of boogie-woogie piano, and Keith Richards gives a wonderful demonstration of slide guitar, taking a solo at 3:44. Finally, Bill can be heard on autoharp at the beginning of the track, creating an almost aquatic sound, drowned in reverb.

MIDNIGHT RAMBLER

Mick Jagger / Keith Richards /6:57

Musicians
Mick Jagger: vocals, harmonica
Keith Richards: rhythm guitar, slide guitar
Brian Jones: percussion
Bill Wyman: bass
Charlie Watts: drums

Recorded
Olympic Sound Studios, London: February, March, May 1969
Sunset Sound Studios and/or Elektra Studios,
Los Angeles: October–November 1969

Technical Team
Producer: Jimmy Miller
Sound engineer: Glyn Johns
Assistant sound engineers: Vic Smith, George Chkiantz, Bruce Botnick, Jerry Hansen, Alan O'Duffy

Keith playing his extraordinary Matton SE777 in the studio. "Midnight Rambler" is one of his most famous riffs.

Genesis

In April 1969, Mick Jagger and Keith Richards took a few days' vacation in southern Italy, at Positano on the Amalfi coast. This charming town is built on a hillside and is bathed in sunshine almost all year round. It was in this delightful setting that various tracks on the album *Let It Bleed*, including "Midnight Rambler," were born. How did the Glimmer Twins come to write one of their darkest songs in such an enchanting place? This is just one more mystery in the long and enthralling history of the Rolling Stones. "Keith and I went to Italy, and Keith had this idea for 'Midnight Rambler,' so we just started changing the tempos within the tune," explains Mick Jagger. "Melodically it remains the same thing, it's just a lot of tempo changes. We worked on it with acoustic guitar and harmonica, just jammed it, went through the tempo changes and had it all organized by the time we had to record it for *Let It Bleed*."

The figure of the "midnight rambler" was inspired by the serial killer Albert DeSalvo, who, between June 1962 and January 1964, raped and strangled thirteen women in Boston, Massachusetts, spreading panic throughout New England. The "Boston Strangler" was eventually arrested in November 1964 and sentenced to life imprisonment. He was killed in jail in 1973.

Mick Jagger made direct use of DeSalvo's confessions when writing his gruesome lyrics. The atmosphere is all the more oppressive as the singer identifies with the serial killer just as he identified with Lucifer in "Sympathy for the Devil." The narrator addresses his wife and ends up confessing that he is the "rambler": *I'm called the hit-and-run raper in anger, the knife-sharpened tippie toe . . . or just the shoot 'em dead brainbell jangler.*

"'Midnight Rambler' is a Chicago blues. The chord sequence isn't, but the sound is pure Chicago," explains Keith Richards in *Life*. "I knew how the rhythm should go. It was in the tightness of the chord sequence, the D's and the A's and the E's. It wasn't a blues sequence, but it came out like heavy-duty blues. That's one of the most original blues you'll hear from the Stones." In an interview with *Guitar World*, he clarifies: "When we did 'Midnight Rambler,' nobody went in there with the idea of doing a blues opera, basically. Or a blues in four parts. That's just the way it turned out. I think that's the

The strange stage ritual of Mick Jagger, the "Midnight Rambler," here at the Empire Pool in Webley, London, in 1973.

strength of the Stones or any good band. You can give them a song half raw and they'll cook it."

Production

"Midnight Rambler" is dominated by Keith, at least on the instrumental level. In order to obtain his extraordinary guitar sound, he is probably using the same combination of guitar and amp as on "Gimme Shelter," in other words the Maton SE 777 through his Triumph Silicon 100. From the very first notes of the riff, Keith's guitar grabs the listener's attention with its semi-distorted blues sonority that conveys all that African American culture he so admires, a Chicago blues sound, to be precise. For that matter, "Midnight Rambler" could almost have been recorded at Chess Studios with Ron Malo at the controls. Respect, however, is due to Jimmy Miller and Glyn Johns for their excellent work on the track. Not to forget the incomparable touch of riff master Keith and his obsession with sound and the perfect note. Vic Smith, one of Glyn Johns's assistants, would later testify to the guitarist's quest for the absolute: "One of my strongest memories is the guitar solo. We spent a whole week doing the guitar solo, which was all done in one take. So it would happen night after night. Just Keith would come in the studio with Jimmy and we'd be doing the 'Midnight Rambler' guitar solo and if that atmosphere wasn't right or the vibe wasn't right for that night, we'd jack it and come back another night. I think it took about five nights to get the final take." Now that Brian Jones had thrown in the towel as far as the

guitar was concerned, and was contributing only percussion to the track, it was Keith, bottleneck on finger, who was taking care of the slide parts. Had it not been for Mick Taylor, a specialist in the technique, he might easily have continued playing slide. Not only is Keith the king of the riff, he is also an excellent and probably much-underrated guitarist. On vocals, Mick Jagger is by no means outdone on this track, however. His performance is nothing short of a lesson in blues rock, and the rambler is a role he inhabits with an incredible intensity. "Midnight Rambler" assumes its full magnitude onstage, one of the high points of any Stones concert, halfway between rock and theater. Mick also underscores the Chicago blues flavor of the track, playing some superb harmonica from the very first bars. It is difficult not to think of Brian, who, just a short time before, had been setting the band's music alight with incendiary, highly inspired harmonica solos.

"Midnight Rambler" also provides Charlie Watts with an opportunity to rhythmically differentiate four different sections, all highly successful and all involving an acceleration of the tempo or impressive drum breaks. The person who can be heard banging the head of a tambourine with a stick between 5:05 and 5:22 seems to be Brian. As for Bill Wyman, his bass part provides unfailing support. With a powerful, though somewhat undermixed sound, he is most probably on his new Vox Astro IV plugged into his Hiwatt amp. Lasting almost seven minutes, "Midnight Rambler" is one of the Stones' longest tracks as well as one of their most successful.

YOU GOT THE SILVER

Mick Jagger / Keith Richards / 2:55

Musicians
Keith Richards: vocals, acoustic guitar, lead guitar
Brian Jones: autoharp
Bill Wyman: bass
Charlie Watts: drums
Nicky Hopkins: piano, organ
Recorded
Olympic Sound Studios, London: February 1969
Technical Team
Producer: Jimmy Miller
Sound engineer: Glyn Johns
Assistant sound engineers: George Chkiantz, Bruce Botnick, Jerry Hansen, Vic Smith, Alan O'Duffy

Michelangelo Antonioni, the Italian director of *Zabriskie Point* (1970) included the song in his film. It is not featured on the soundtrack album, which comprises mainly tracks by Pink Floyd and Jerry Garcia of the Grateful Dead.

Genesis

The song "You Got the Silver" (originally titled "You Got Some Silver Now") is one hundred percent Keith Richards. It bears the stamp of the Stones guitarist all the more emphatically for having been inspired by his girlfriend. *You got my soul/You got the silver, you got the gold/If that's your love, just leave me blind*: these words of love are addressed to Anita Pallenberg, the blond German-Italian beauty who had left Brian Jones for Keith Richards two years before, the Anita whose alluring presence hovers over a number of the band's masterpieces. In his book, Tony Sanchez, Keith's chauffeur and dealer at the time, reveals an interesting facet of Brian, Keith, and Mick's supreme muse: "She was obsessed with black magic and began to carry a string of garlic with her everywhere—even to bed—to ward off vampires. She also had a strange, mysterious old shaker for holy water which she used for some of her rituals. Her ceremonies became increasingly secret, and she would warn me never to interrupt her when she was working on a spell."

Whether he was interested or not in Anita Pallenberg's esotericism, from the very first notes on his acoustic guitar, Keith Richards perfectly conjures up an atmosphere infused with magic and romanticism in "You Got the Silver." Alongside Keith, Brian Jones is still present—on autoharp—on this track. Also worth singling out is the contribution of Nicky Hopkins on piano and organ.

Production

Along with "Gimme Shelter," "You Got the Silver" was one of the first tracks to be recorded in London for *Let It Bleed*. And it is Keith who sings the entire song, a first for the Stones. The reason? During an initial mix, Jimmy Miller asked Glyn Johns to apply a reverse reverb to the lead guitar, the first time the sound engineer had done such a thing. "This is achieved by turning the tape upside down and playing it backward while putting echo on the guitar and recording the return from the chamber on an empty track." When the tape is then played forward, an unusual effect is obtained. Unfortunately, Johns selected the wrong track and erased Mick's voice. To complicate matters, Mick was in Australia at the time, shooting *Ned Kelly* (1970) under the direction of Tony Richardson. Johns recalls "I was mortified, but fortunately there was a positive

Keith and Anita in 1969. "You Got the Silver" is a love song addressed to the Stones' blond muse.

result to my mistake. We asked Keith to sing." The results of this somewhat ghostly effect can be heard at 0:25, just before the first notes on the electric guitar, and elsewhere. Promoted to the position of lead singer, Keith does an admirable job, bringing a new color to the album. His emotion-filled voice exudes sincerity. He also plays some excellent slide acoustic on his Gibson Hummingbird, most likely in open-D or open-E tuning. Another guitar, this time electric lead, probably the Maton SE 777, is also played slide.

What must Brian Jones, who had ruined his own talent, been thinking as he watched his bandmate taking care of the guitar parts as well as singing lead vocals? Whatever might have been going through his mind, it was on "You Got the Silver" that he recorded his very last stringed instrument part for the group he had founded (his other contribution to the album being percussion on "Midnight Rambler"). He plays an auto-harp, which can be heard pretty recessed in the mix, in support of Keith's acoustic. Nicky Hopkins, meanwhile, delivers an organ part that combines extremely well with the effect created by Glyn Johns. He also plays the piano, and his style is perfectly suited to the Stones' ballads. A few years later he would provide further evidence of this on "Angie." As for

Charlie Watts, the drummer can be heard using brushes and maintaining a very good groove throughout the track. Bill is probably playing his Dallas Tuxedo, with its soft, rounded sound that is perfect for country blues.

FOR STONES ADDICTS

A version of this song exists with Mick Jagger singing. Although similar to the final version, it has a more rooted sound, with Jagger giving a very intimate performance and Jones far more present in the mix on his autoharp. In short, an excellent alternative take.

MONKEY MAN

Mick Jagger / Keith Richards / 4:15

Musicians
Mick Jagger: vocals
Keith Richards: rhythm guitar, lead guitar, backing vocals
Bill Wyman: bass, vibraphone
Charlie Watts: drums
Nicky Hopkins: piano
Jimmy Miller: tambourine
Recorded
Olympic Sound Studios, London: April, June–July 1969
Sunset Sound Studios and/or Elektra Studios,
Los Angeles: October–November 1969
Technical Team
Producer: Jimmy Miller
Sound engineer: Glyn Johns
Assistant sound engineers: Vic Smith, George Chkiantz, Bruce Botnick, Jerry Hansen, Alan O'Duffy

FOR STONES ADDICTS

The director Martin Scorsese chose "Monkey Man" for the soundtrack of his gangster film *Goodfellas* (1990).

Genesis

There are many possible interpretations of "Monkey Man." Is Mick Jagger, the author of the lyrics, reflecting on an acid or heroin trip that turned into a nightmare populated by monsters? Or is the song more a case of self-mockery, a response, perhaps, to all those representatives of the media who took pleasure in dragging the London band through the dirt? The singer's stage act was mocked by some: was he now laying it on thick by comparing himself to an ape-man? His private life was maliciously scrutinized, and in this song we see him *bit* and *tossed around by every she-rat in this town*. There is also a nod to the Stones' two previous albums, *Their Satanic Majesties Request* and *Beggars Banquet*: *I hope we're not too messianic or a trifle satanic*, he sings in the second verse, before adding *We love to play the blues*. Is it not also possible, then, that this is another allusion to the forces of evil, insofar as Satan is the monkey of God?

"Monkey Man" was written by Mick Jagger and Keith Richards during their stay on the Amalfi coast, hence the original title "Positano Grande." In terms of its sound world, the song is quite different from anything the Stones had previously recorded. It is evocative of movie music—for a thriller, perhaps, or a science fiction picture.

Production

When the Rolling Stones resumed their recording sessions for *Let It Bleed* on April 17, they moved into Studio 2 at Olympic, which was far smaller than Studio 1: "It really wasn't a good idea. The Stones were like too big to go into number 2," explains George Chkiantz. The bass and drums, in particular, are not as effective as they ought to be. It was Chkiantz who paid the price for this, as he was immediately replaced by Vic Smith: "I was angry about it for ages," Chkiantz would admit. "I felt I wasn't given a chance and what he [Smith] did on that, kind of like forcing the sound through." In spite of these recording problems, the production on "Monkey Man" is of a very high quality, and the track as a whole occupies a special place on the album. The intro is a real success, with its sound world somewhere between Motown and Phil Spector, its repeated bass notes, its arpeggios on the vibes, its hypnotic tambourine, its guitar sound based on

a combination of feedback and violining, the whole developing into a funky groove driven by the superb drumming of Charlie Watts. Bill Wyman plays both bass and vibes, demonstrating that he is also a capable—and all too often underrated—multi-instrumentalist.

Following this long intro, which continues for some thirty seconds, Mick Jagger launches into his vocals with a certain aggressiveness, lending the track a new impetus. The atmosphere changes and the Stones revert to a harder-edged rock sound. It is Keith who electrifies the feel of the number, probably with his Telecaster or Les Paul, obtaining a fantastic rhythm sound that is simultaneously rock 'n' roll and Chicago blues. Moreover, his 6-string has

never sounded as good as it does on this album. It is also Keith on lead guitar and slide, but his licks fail to really take off, giving the impression that he is lacking inspiration. It is something of a shame that Mick Taylor did not take part in the session, given that Keith's playing is based on the interplay between two guitars. For the time being it is Nicky Hopkins who answers him on the piano, before adopting a more lyrical style in the instrumental section that precedes the coda (2:35), where Bill Wyman's vibes restore a more soul flavor to the track. "I'm a monkey," screams Mick Jagger from 3:14 during a final, very funky rock section that provides him with an opportunity to let it rip—just like the rest of the group.

YOU CAN'T ALWAYS GET WHAT YOU WANT

Mick Jagger / Keith Richards / 7:34

Musicians
Mick Jagger: vocals
Keith Richards: acoustic guitar, lead guitar
Bill Wyman: bass
Jimmy Miller: drums
Al Kooper: French horn, piano, organ
Rocky Dijon: percussion
Doris Troy, Nanette Workman,
Madeline Bell: backing vocals
The London Bach Choir: chorus
Choral arrangements: Jack Nitzsche

Recorded
Olympic Sound Studios, London: November 16,
28, 1968; February, April 9, May 28, 1969

Technical Team
Producer: Jimmy Miller
Sound engineer: Glyn Johns
Assistant sound engineers: Bruce Botnick, Jerry Hansen,
George Chkiantz, Vic Smith, Alan O'Duffy, Andy Johns

Genesis
"You Can't Always Get What You Want" is *a* Mick Jagger song. "[It] was something I just played on the acoustic guitar—one of those bedroom songs," he would later explain. Keith Richards recalls perfectly the moment he arrived in the studio and announced that he had a song. "I said, you got any verses? And he said, I have."

That brings us to the words. How should they be interpreted? Five years after "(I Can't Get No) Satisfaction," "You Can't Always Get What You Want" (which, incidentally contains the same number of syllables!) sounds like another slogan. Before, it was the consumer society (against a background of sexual frustration) that was pilloried; now, the end of the sixties utopia was being celebrated. The dream ended when the baby-boomer generation realized that the possibilities were not limitless after all. This seems to be what Jagger is saying. The reception described at the very beginning of the song thus symbolizes Swinging London, and more specifically the curtain that had fallen on the nonstop party that had been going on for several years. In short, the end of innocence.

At the same time, Mick Jagger intersperses a few more personal references into his message. The line *I went down to the demonstration to get my fair share of abuse* probably refers to the Vietnam protest march he joined in London on March 17, 1968, during which various acts of violence were perpetrated. There is also the Chelsea Drugstore, which opened its doors in 1968, and the enigmatic Mr. Jimmy. Is this the producer Jimmy Miller, who played a decisive role in the recording of "You Can't Always Get What You Want"? As for the woman with a glass of wine in her hand, hoping to meet her connection, the peddler of false dreams, this is perhaps Marianne Faithfull. "You Can't Always Get What You Want" remains one of the greatest of all the Stones' songs. It was released as the B-side (in a shorter version than that on the album) of the single "Honky Tonk Women."

Although Mick Jagger wrote the words and came up with the tune of "You Can't Always Get What You Want," Keith Richards played a major part in giving the song its final form. As Richards recounts in *Life*, Mick asked how it was going to sound: "Because he'd written it on guitar, it was like a folk song at the time. I had to come up with a

Keith, Charlie, Mick, Brian, and Bill during *The Rolling Stones Rock and Roll Circus.*

rhythm, an idea . . ." So the band got to work. The sessions for "You Can't Always Get What You Want" were the very first for the album *Let It Bleed.*

Production

Having booked Olympic Sound Studios for two days, November 17 and 28, 1968 (dates courtesy of Bill Wyman) the Stones found themselves in the studio for the first time since the final sessions for *Beggars Banquet,* which had taken place barely five months before. As Nicky Hopkins was unavailable—he was recording with the group Quicksilver Messenger Service—they needed to find a new piano player, and booked Al Kooper. After becoming an organist during the legendary sessions for Bob Dylan's "Like a Rolling Stone" (1965), Al Kooper became a member of the Blues Project and later founded Blood, Sweat & Tears. He happened to be in England for a few days of relaxation.

Having fled the US studios to stroll around London in the company of his friend, the producer Denny Cordell, at whose place he was staying, it was not long before Al Kooper was approached by the Stones' office, requesting his services for a recording session. "How did the Stones know I was coming to town?" he wondered, somewhat puzzled. Not exactly thrilled at the idea of going back into the studio, Kooper bumped into Brian Jones on the Kings Road: "Are you gonna play the session, Al?" "How can you say no to these people?" wondered Kooper. The Stones offered him two sessions, but he agreed to just one before committing himself further.

Once in the studio, all the musicians gathered around Mick and Keith, who played them the song so that they could take note of the rhythm and chord changes. "There was a conga player there who could play congas and roll huge hash joints without missing a lick," recalls Kooper. "It was decided I would play piano on the basic track and overdub organ later."

The Stones benefited from the watchful gaze and sound advice of their producer Jimmy Miller (left).

The roller of joints was none other than the highly talented Rocky Dijon, who, in addition to the congas, would also pick up the maracas, a shaker, and a tambourine—all without interrupting his rhythm. Keith played the main acoustic guitar part in open E, probably on his Gibson Hummingbird, and Bill was on his Vox Wyman bass. Charlie, meanwhile, was trying in vain to reproduce on his Gretsch kit the rhythm Jimmy Miller was suggesting to him, but his playing remained routine and overstiff. Finally, Jimmy, himself a drummer, took his place behind the kit. When Charlie still failed to re-create what his producer was showing him, he reluctantly stepped aside at the insistence of Mick and Keith. Charlie: "[Jimmy Miller] wasn't a great drummer, but he was great at playing drums on records, which is a completely different thing. 'You Can't Always Get What You Want' is a great drum track. Jimmy actually made me stop and think again about the way I played drums in the studio and I became a much better drummer in

the studio thanks to him—together we made some of the best records we've ever made." It is true that Jimmy's funky drumming is a real asset, and he dragged Bill along with him, whose bass in turn became more syncopated, enabling Al Kooper to fit in a piano part inspired by a groove he had heard on the Etta James (!) cover of "I Got You Babe." The only Stone not to participate in the session was Brian Jones. Al Kooper: "Brian Jones lay on his stomach in the corner reading an article on botany through the entire proceedings." Keith later added lead guitar, and Al Kooper his organ part.

A Successful Combination

Then on March 15, 1969, taking up an idea of Mick Jagger's, it was the turn of the London Bach Choir, along with the backing singers Doris Troy, Nanette Workman, and Madeline Bell, to step up to the mic, with arrangements by Jack Nitzsche. Keith Richards: "Let's put on a straight

1969

306   LET IT BLEED

After playing with Bob Dylan, Al Kooper put his talents at the service of the Stones. That farewell to the sixties that is "You Can't Always Get What You Want" reveals a perfect understanding between Kooper and the band.

chorus. In other words, let's try and reach them people up there as well. It was a dare, kind of. Mick and I thought it should go into a choir, a gospel thing, because we'd played with black gospel singers in America. And then, what if we got one of the best choirs in England, all these white, lovely singers, and do it that way, see what we can get out of them? Turn them on a little bit, get them into a little sway and a move, you know?" The idea amused the Stones. "That will be a laugh!" Jagger would later say. The recording required a lot of effort because the choir singers were unable to drop their pronounced English accents, but the result works well. This combination of voices and the mix of folk, gospel, and rock makes "You Can't Always Get What You Want" one of the highlights of *Let It Bleed*.

Production did not finish there, however. During the November 1968 sessions, Al Kooper had suggested to Mick that he could write some horn arrangements if the singer wished. Nine months later, much to his surprise, he received an eight-track master accompanied by a note: "Dear Al, you once mentioned you could put some great horn parts on this. Well, go ahead and do it and send us the tape back. Love, Mick." After recovering from his amazement, Kooper set to work. He recorded a small French horn part, which he played himself, during the introduction, and wrote a score for the rest of the horns, but was not really satisfied with the results. When the disc was released, he realized the Stones had not used his arrangements, other than the brief French horn solo!

With a duration of more than 7:30, this last track on *Let It Bleed* is one of the Rolling Stones' longest songs, and once again it is worth emphasizing the excellent production by Jimmy Miller and the superb recording work by Glyn Johns and his team. For great results, you need great teams at every level, and "You Can't Always Get What You Want" is the proof.

Keith Richards plays a legendary guitar part on "Honky Tonk Women" and launches a fruitful partnership with newcomer Mick Taylor.

SIDE A
1963

HONKY TONK WOMEN

Mick Jagger / Keith Richards / 3:01

SINGLE
Honky Tonk Women / You Can't Always Get What You Want*

RELEASE DATE
United Kingdom: July 4, 1969
Record label: Decca
RECORD NUMBER: DECCA F 12952 * (SEE P. 304)

Musicians
Mick Jagger: vocals
Keith Richards: lead and rhythm guitar, backing vocals
Mick Taylor: solo guitar
Bill Wyman: bass
Charlie Watts: drums
Ian Stewart: piano
Jimmy Miller: cowbell
Steve Gregory, Bud Beadle: saxophones
Johnny Almond: reed arrangements
Reparata & The Delrons, Doris Troy, Nanette Workman: backing vocals
Recorded
Olympic Sound Studios, London: May 12–June 12, 1969
Technical Team
Producer: Jimmy Miller
Sound engineer: Glyn Johns

Genesis
"Honky Tonk Women" is the electric, blues-rock version of "Country Honk," written by the Glimmer Twins during their December 1968 jaunt to Brazil to charge their batteries following months of intense work. They were also hoping to benefit from this period of relaxation to dispel the tension at the heart of the *ménage à quatre* with Anita and Marianne. The Stones' singer was thought to have shared a moment of intimacy with the actress during the shooting of *Performance,* as had Keith with Marianne some time before.

Other than a few small differences, the words of "Honky Tonk Women" are the same as those of "Country Honk." It is only the first verse that differs. The narrator is drinking in a sleazy club when a hostess suggests going upstairs for fun. *She had to heave me right across her shoulder, 'cause I just can't seem to drink you off my mind*, sings Mick immediately before the refrain. The scene then moves to New York, this time with a *divorcee* who *covered me in roses* and who *blew my nose and then she blew my mind*. These words resulted from the process Keith Richards, in *Life*, calls "vowel movement," which involves looking for "the sounds that work."

However, the words count for less than the music, which, a few months after "Jumpin' Jack Flash," confirms the return of the Stones to the hallowed ground of rock 'n' roll. "Honky Tonk Women" (with "You Can't Always Get What You Want" as its B-side) was released in the United Kingdom on July 4, 1969, the day before the Stones' Hyde Park concert in memory of Brian Jones. The song got to number 1 in various countries, including the United

Inflatable dolls dressed to kill come to life during the intro of "Honky Tonk Women" on the 1989 Steel Wheels tour.

Kingdom and the United States, number 2 in the Federal Republic of Germany, and only 13 in France, the country of Johnny Hallyday and Claude François. One thing could be said for sure: the real Stones were back!

Production

The recording of "Honky Tonk Women" marked the start of a new chapter in the history of the Stones, who were embarking on a collaboration with the producer Jimmy Miller and Mick Taylor, the twenty-year-old guitarist recruited on the advice of John Mayall (and supported by Ian Stewart) to succeed Brian Jones. The band took exactly a month to make "Honky Tonk Women," from May 12 to June 12. In his book *Rolling with the Stones*, Bill Wyman provides a perfect summary of the different stages in the recording process. After the initial session on May 12, two more were booked, on May 14 and 25, but aimed at exploring new avenues with Nicky Hopkins on piano and Steve Gregory and Bud Beadle on sax. On May 28, Reparata & The Delrons, Doris Troy, and Nanette Workman recorded the backing vocals. On June 1, Jimmy Miller made a suggestion to Charlie Watts for some drumming and then

came up with the idea for the intro. On the same day, Mick Taylor recorded his guitar part, which significantly transforms the track. Finally on June 4, 8, and 12 came the mixing sessions. It was as simple as that.

In reality, "Honky Tonk Women" gave the Stones more trouble than almost any other track. They spent the period from May 12 to 28 looking for the right formula but without really finding it. It was Jimmy Miller—once again—who broke the stalemate on June 1 after four fruitless sessions. He sat down at the drums and showed Charlie how to play. By contrast with "You Can't Always Get What You Want," however, he let Charlie get hold of the groove and record his own part. And what a part! Moreover, the talented Jimmy picked up a cowbell and with this simple percussion instrument found the right impetus and a rhythmic link between all the musicians.

A Lucky Mistake

The magic formula behind "Honky Tonk Women" is composed of three elements: Charlie's drumming, Jimmy's cowbell, and the fabulous guitar playing of Keith, the human riff. Ironically, this highly effective rhythmic structure was actually

Mick Jagger during a live performance of "Honky Tonk Women."

the result of a timing error. Charlie explains: "We've never played an intro to 'Honky Tonk Women' live the way it is on the record. That's Jimmy playing the cowbell and either he comes in wrong or I come in wrong—but Keith comes in right, which makes the whole thing right . . . It's actually a mistake, but from my point of view, it works." Charlie's Gretsch kit has perhaps never sounded as good as it does on this track. It is heavy, powerful, and has a reasonably long reverb, contrasting with the cowbell, which is shrill and has a short, not particularly prominent reverb. Keith plays his legendary guitar part on a Telecaster, and confesses to not remembering what kind of amp he used. For the very first time, this guitar was in open G and fitted with just five strings. Ry Cooder was clearly the initiator, but little could he have imagined the extent to which this development was to transform the Stones' style and sound over the years to come, with Keith playing and/or composing a string

of impressive songs using this formula ("Start Me Up," "Can't You Hear Me Knockin'," "Brown Sugar," and so on).

Another key element was the presence of Mick Taylor, in his first appearance with the band. His playing (on his Gibson SG Standard) is first-rate, standing out for its fluidity and perfect symbiosis with Keith: "I played the country kind of influence and the rock licks between the verses," he would report in 1980. Mick's initial entry is at 0:46, just before the first refrain. Keith cannot praise him enough: "He was very different to work with than Brian. I really had to refocus things. But Mick Taylor is a brilliant guitar player. Some lovely energy. Sweetly sophisticated playing, way beyond his years. Lovely sense of melody." Comparing the two guitarists, Taylor can be described as fluid, lyrical, and highly sensual, whereas Richards is harder-edged, rawer, more direct. But the two complement each other perfectly.

"Honky Tonk Women" is the first track that Mick Taylor (shown here playing his Gibson SG Standard) recorded with the Stones.

COVERS

"Honky Tonk Women" is one of the Stones' most covered songs. Particularly worthy of mention are the versions by Ike & Tina Turner, Waylon Jennings, Joe Cocker, and Gram Parsons.

"Honky Tonk Women" is also characterized by the incredible performance of Mick Jagger, who is at the peak of his artistry on the track, having perhaps never given a better demonstration of his talent and charisma. As recently as 2007, Ian Hunter (the former singer with Mott The Hoople) went into raptures over Jagger's superlative voice: "Jagger's singing is absolutely masterful—he's a great percussive singer. I think he's underrated. Nobody else can do this."

However, the song is also " . . . just instant move your arse," as Charlie quite rightly points out in 1973. "We've never known why," wonders Keith in turn. The formula is clearly based on the drums/cowbell/riff combination, but Bill Wyman's fearsomely efficient bass playing also has something to do with it. In fact, Bill only comes in on the refrains, like Nicky Hopkins on piano, creating a kind of lacuna in the verses that is particularly effective. No less effective is the instrumental part itself: rather than simply throwing out the same rhythmic patterns, he plays a walking bass, lending the track a feel of acceleration. This is done with great skill. Finally, with the horns of Steve Gregory and Bud Beadle, and the backing vocals of Reparata & The Delrons, Doris Troy, and Nanette Workman, "Honky Tonk Women" is ready for mixing. This was done on June 12. On July 4, the song joined the elite club of hits that have left an indelible impression on the history of rock 'n' roll. Nevertheless, the song's legitimacy as the A-side of the single was bitterly contested by Glyn Johns, who favored "You Can't Always Get What You Want." Jagger was against this, but Johns fought hard. Luckily, a visit to the studio by Eric Clapton brought about a consensus. After being made to listen to both tracks, Clapton was in no doubt: "Eric, telling me I must have a screw loose, chose 'Honky Tonk Women,'" explains Johns!

Jumpin' Jack Flash
Carol
Stray Cat Blues
Love In Vain
Midnight Rambler
Sympathy For The Devil
Live With Me
Little Queenie *
Honky Tonk Women
Street Fighting Man

* Only the released songs will be discussed in this chapter.

ALBUM
RELEASE DATE
United Kingdom:
September 4, 1970
Record label: Decca
RECORD NUMBER: DECCA SKL 5065
Number 1 for 2 weeks, on
the charts for 15 weeks

GET YER YA-YA'S OUT!

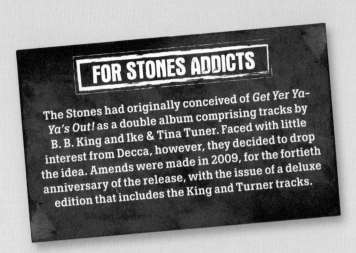
1970 saw the release of *Gimme Shelter*, the celebrated documentary by the Maysles brothers that tells the story of the Stones' 1969 US tour. The poster shows the band on the stage of Madison Square Garden, New York City, in November 1969.

GET YER YA-YA'S OUT!: THE BEST ROCK CONCERT EVER RECORDED

1970

The Album

Four months after the death of Brian Jones and a month before the release of *Let It Bleed*, the Rolling Stones embarked on a twenty-two-date tour of the United States—the first since their July 1966 tour, and, crucially, the first with Mick Taylor. "And the 1969 tour of the States was our first resurrection," explains Keith Richards. "We felt we were a new band; we were starting again. I think we figured that this marked the beginning of a new chapter, and we were wondering whether people would accept the Stones without Brian Jones."[9]

The tour started on November 7 at the Moby Arena in Fort Collins, Colorado, but did not end with the two shows in Boston, Massachusetts, on November 29 as planned. Instead, two further dates were added: November 30 at West Palm Beach, Florida—a festival at which Janis Joplin, Johnny Winter, Spirit, and Grand Funk Railroad also performed—and December 6 at the Altamont Speedway near Livermore, California (not Golden Gate Park, for which the San Francisco City Hall had refused permission). The latter was a free concert during the course of which four people died (including Meredith Hunter, who was killed by the Hells Angels while brandishing a weapon).

On November 26, 1969, a week before Altamont, the Rolling Stones played the Civic Center in Baltimore, Maryland. They then moved to Madison Square Garden in New York for one show on November 27 and two shows on November 28. It was during these four concerts that the Stones' second live album, *Get Yer Ya-Ya's Out!*, unanimously recognized as one of the best in the history of rock music, was recorded. The initial version of the album went on sale on September 4, 1970. It comprises ten songs, mostly from *Beggars Banquet* and *Let It Bleed*, with the remaining two ("Carol" and "Little Queenie") taken from the Chuck Berry catalog. The album was number 1 for two weeks from September 19, 1970, in the United Kingdom, number 2 in Australia and New Zealand, and number 6 in the United States and West Germany.

The second version of *Get Yer Ya-Ya's Out!* was released in 2009. This is a box set in which the original recording is supplemented by five additional Rolling Stones songs from the New York concerts and also five numbers by B. B. King and seven by Ike & Tina Turner, their supporting acts. There is also a DVD that includes the band's performance of "Prodigal Son" and "You Gotta Move" along with archival images. The legendary rock critic Lester Bangs has summed up the album as "The best rock concert ever put on record."[84]

Album Cover

Ethan Russell, a rock photographer par excellence, to whom the Rolling Stones (*Through the Past, Darkly*) (*Big Hits Vol. 2*), the Beatles (*Let It Be,*) and the Who (*Who's Next* and later *Quadrophenia*) all owe record sleeves, followed the London quintet during their 1969 US tour. Chosen to do the covers for *Get Yer Ya-Ya's Out!*, Russell presented a number of shots to Mick Jagger upon his return to London, and these were used on the back of the cover (an exception is the photograph of Keith Richards, which is credited to Dominique Tarlé).

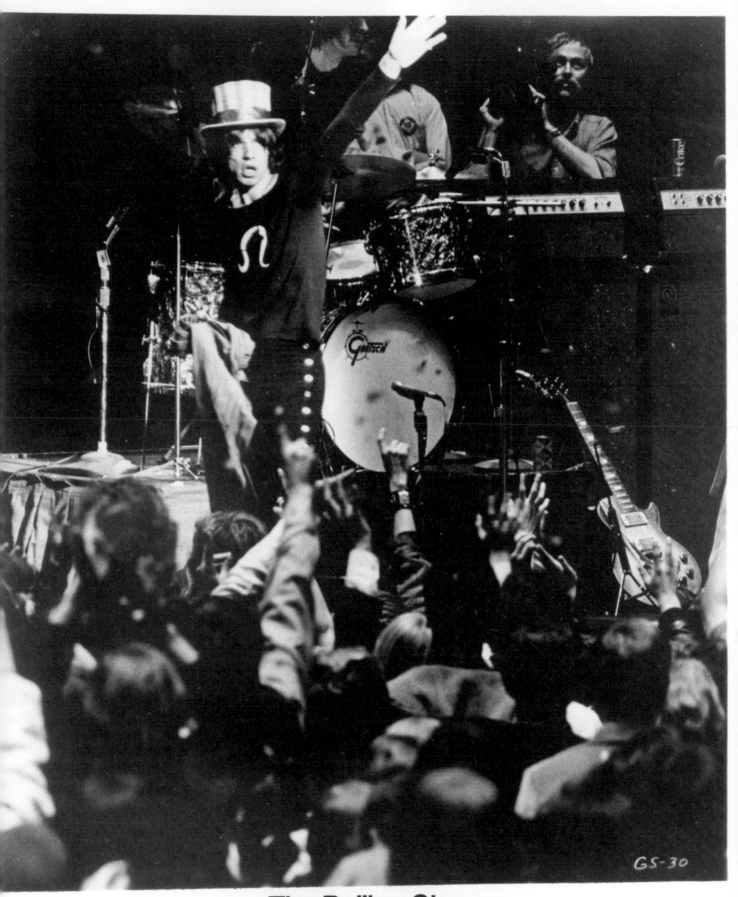

GS-30

THE ROLLING STONES
GIMME SHELTER

Directed by David Maysles, Albert Maysles, Charlotte Zwerin · A Maysles Films, Inc. Production

Mick and Keith (playing his 1930 National Style "O") perform "Prodigal Son" to a New York City audience.

The mood on the front cover is quite different. Here we see Charlie Watts, dressed completely in white, jumping into the air holding a guitar in each hand, with, by his side, a donkey carrying elements of a drum kit and an electric guitar. This photograph was taken by David Bailey on June 7, 1970 (after an initial photo by Michael Berkofsky, dating from February 8, was rejected by the Stones). As for the title of this live album, *Get Yer Ya-Ya's Out!* can be seen as a reference to a blues number by Blind Boy Fuller, "Get Your Yas Yas Out," which dates from October 1938.

What is the true meaning of this somewhat abstruse title? There are a number of hypotheses. The first possibility is "straight from the donkey's ass," but it could equally, according to Jagger himself, refer to the exposing of the male organ. On the other hand, the phrase could be a voodoo expression meaning "to cast out the devil from someone's body."

The Recording

Glyn Johns took on the task of recording the live concert. This he did with the help of the Wally Heider Mobile, the property of the brilliant Wally Heider and his company based in San Francisco. This mobile studio was one of the first to have been made available—from early 1969—to rock musicians. It was an independent studio fitted with the best equipment of the day: an eight-track plus a twenty-four-channel console designed by Frank DeMedio. All the tracks on the album were taken from the Madison Square Garden concerts in New York other than "Love in Vain," which was recorded at the Baltimore concert.

In contrast to *Got Live If You Want It!* (1966), there were very few overdubs. These were probably done at Olympic Sound Studios and Trident Studios in London in December 1969 and then finalized and mixed between January and April 1970. Curiously, in his book *Sound Man*, Glyn Johns tells of having mixed the album in August at the new studios of Chris Blackwell, the founder of Island Records, located at 8–10 Basing Street in London: "The next time I used Basing Street was in August 1970 to mix *Get Yer Ya-Ya's Out!* . . . This was the second occasion that I had mixed a record without the artist being present and the only time I can remember it happening with the Stones . . . Of course, they checked and approved what I had done before we mastered it."[4] With the album's release scheduled for September 4, it seems unlikely that the mixing, mastering, pressing, and distribution would all have been carried out within such a short span of time.

The audience at Madison Square Garden in New York City give the Rolling Stones a triumphant welcome.

On a Gretsch kit like this one, Charlie Watts proved himself to be one of the best drummers in rock music.

Anita Pallenberg: a life as tumultuous as the Rolling Stones' career.

ANITA PALLENBERG: BLOND MUSE, BLACK QUEEN

During their fourth European tour of 1965, which took place between September 11 and 17, the Rolling Stones visited West Germany and Austria. On September 14, they gave two concerts in Munich. One of the shows was attended by a very pretty twenty-one-year-old model. The young woman only had eyes for Brian Jones; she was literally captivated by his stage presence. That woman was Anita Pallenberg. "'That's how I met Brian,' she once revealed. 'He was the only one of the Stones who really bothered to talk to me. He could even speak a little German.'"[10] Mick and Keith "were schoolboys beside him," she adds. At the same time, she discovered Brian to be extremely fragile and at odds with the other members of the group. Anita: "He said, 'Come and spend the night with me. I don't want to be alone.' So I went with him. Almost the whole night he spent crying. Whatever had happened with the other Stones, it had absolutely devastated him."[10] This was the beginning of the romantic idyll between Anita and Brian . . .

From Brian to Keith

Anita Pallenberg was born in Rome on April 6, 1944, two months before the liberation of the city by the Allies. Her father, Arnaldo Pallenberg, was Italian and a lover of classical music who had run a travel agency before the war. Her mother, Paula Wiederhold, was German. As a child, Anita was sent to a German boarding school, which she attended until being expelled in 1960—not before learning to speak four languages fluently. Although she studied medicine for a time, and then picture restoration and graphic design, it was as a model that she earned her living, traveling a great deal. Initially, Brian Jones saw Anita Pallenberg, who, moreover, shared his taste for the exoticism of Morocco, as the ideal woman. Before long, however, the couple embarked on a cycle of self-destruction involving drugs, alcohol, fights, reconciliation, more fighting, and even acts of violence. Furthermore, Anita understood that Keith had fallen secretly in love with her. It was she who made the first move, during a trip to Morocco in February 1967 while Brian was receiving urgent treatment in a French hospital for pneumonia. Keith: "We

realized we were creating 'an unmanageable situation,' maybe threatening the survival of the band. We decided to pull back, to make a strategic retreat."[2] In reality, however, there was no "strategic retreat," and Brian would continue to decline. . .

Anita and Keith is the story of twelve long years marked by the births of Marlon (1969) and Dandelion/Angela (1972), and then the death (just two and a half months after coming into the world) of Tara, but also by a series of narcotics busts, notably at Toronto in 1977. And then there was the Scott Cantrell affair. On July 20, 1979, Cantrell, who worked as a gardener at Keith and Anita's property at South Salem, New York, was found dead. He was only seventeen years old. He was thought to have killed himself while Anita was asleep in the bedroom. The rumor mill went into overdrive: might the young Cantrell, who is supposed to have had an affair with Anita Pallenberg, have killed himself while playing Russian roulette with her . . . ?

The Black Queen

When Keith Richards left Anita Pallenberg for Patti Hansen at the beginning of the eighties, the Rolling Stones also turned a new page. For more than ten years, Anita had played a not inconsiderable role in the history of the London quintet, in part because of her supposed influence on some of the songs ("Sympathy for the Devil," "You Got the Silver," and "Angie," for example). When it is pointed out to Keith Richards what a significant, important influence she has had on the band, he agrees: "It's because she's an amazing lady . . . she's an incredible chick. She found us, through Brian . . ."[11] In parallel to her role in the Stones epic, Anita Pallenberg also acted in many memorable movies, including *A Degree of Murder* (1967) by Volker Schlöndorff, *Barbarella* (1968) by Roger Vadim, in which she plays the part of the Black Queen (otherwise known as the Great Tyrant), *Dillinger is Dead* (1969) by Marco Ferreri, and, of course, *Performance* (1970) by Donald Cammell and Nicolas Roeg. Later, after undergoing a long detox cure, Anita switched from rock 'n' roll and cinema to . . . gardening.

LITTLE QUEENIE

Chuck Berry / 4:33

Musicians
Mick Jagger: vocals
Keith Richards: rhythm and lead guitar, backing vocals
Mick Taylor: rhythm guitar
Bill Wyman: bass
Charlie Watts: drums
Ian Stewart: piano
Recorded
Madison Square Garden, New York:
November 28, 1969 (first concert)
Technical Team
Producers: the Rolling Stones, Glyn Johns
Sound engineer: Glyn Johns
Recording: Wally Heider Mobile

Mick Jagger and Chuck Berry during the Stones' appearance at Madison Square Garden.

Genesis

"Little Queenie" can be regarded as one of Chuck Berry's most famous songs, even if it failed to enter the *Billboard* charts when it was released in 1959. Curiously, it was the other A-side of the single, "Almost Grown," which achieved success on the US hit parade (albeit of a modest kind, reaching number 32). In "Little Queenie," the rock 'n' roll pioneer sticks to his trusty formula of extolling the blessings of youth. The scenario? A teenage girl makes a big impact when she appears: *I got lumps in my throat when I saw her coming down the aisle/I got the wiggles in my knees when she looked at me and sweetly smiled,* sings Berry. But the narrator is too shy to approach this creature of his dreams, particularly when she's *standing over by the record machine.* "Little Queenie" is almost a standard on the British and US rock scene. The Beatles performed it in Hamburg in 1962, after which came Eric Clapton, Savoy Brown, Rod Stewart, the Velvet Underground, and . . . the Rolling Stones.

Production

During the Stones' first concert of November 28 at Madison Square Garden, Keith Richards launched into "Little Queenie" on his Gibson Les Paul Black Beauty (or possibly his new Gibson ES 355) with a pretty heavy rhythm. Charlie Watts follows close behind on his Gretsch kit with more of a swing to his play, and then comes Bill Wyman on his Fender Mustang, with a sound that is unfortunately a little confused and ill-defined. A very good boogie-woogie piano part can also be made out, played by Ian Stewart. The band is on form and it shows as they could play Chuck Berry's songs with their eyes closed. This, at any rate, is the impression given by Mick Jagger, who, from his very first line, sets the number alight with disconcerting ease. Mick Taylor plays the second rhythm guitar (his Gibson SG Standard), although unfortunately he is rather recessed. Keith takes the lead for some nicely felt phrases and a solo. Compared to the original version, the Stones' is significantly more hard-hitting, with a more insistent beat. The recording is decent and the different guitars can be made out reasonably well, the band being sponsored on this US tour by the manufacturer Ampeg (which provided them with amplifiers). In short, "Little Queenie" is a lesson in rock 'n' roll given by the masters.

1970

The slide guitarist virtuoso Ry Cooder plays a key role alongside Mick Jagger on "Memo from Turner."

MEMO FROM TURNER

Mick Jagger / Keith Richards / 4:08

SINGLE
Memo from Turner / Natural Magic
Release date

United Kingdom: October 23, 1970
Record label: Decca
RECORD NUMBER: DECCA F 13067

Musicians (for the *Performance* version)
Mick Jagger: vocals
Ry Cooder: slide guitar
Russ Titelman (?): rhythm guitar
Randy Newman (?): organ
Jerry Scheff (?): fuzz bass
Gene Parsons (?): drums
Unidentified musicians: maracas, claves

Recorded
Olympic Sound Studios, London / Elektra Studios (?),
Los Angeles: September–October 1968, early 1970

Technical Team
Producer: Jack Nitzsche
Sound engineer: Glyn Johns

"Memo from Turner" contains a reference to *The Soft Machine* by William S. Burroughs, a major work by a writer of the Beat generation

Genesis

In 1968, Mick Jagger took his first steps as an actor in *Performance*, directed by Donald Cammell and Nicolas Roeg. He plays the part of Turner, a former rock star. The plot involves a gangster named Chas (James Fox) who has been on the run since killing another hood. He takes refuge with Turner, who lives with two young women, Pherber (Anita Pallenberg) and Lucy (Michèle Breton), in his apartment in Notting Hill, London. A strange relationship develops between the two men from very different milieux, against a background of narcotics and decadence.

With the ambition of attaining the same kind of success that Richard Lester had known with the Beatles, Warner had hoped that the Glimmer Twins would write the music for this full-length movie. However, Anita Pallenberg's intimate relationships during the shoot with Mick Jagger on the one hand and Donald Cammell on the other led Keith Richards to slam the door on the project. As a result, the original soundtrack features only one number, "Memo from Turner," sung by the Stones singer. Although credited to Jagger-Richards, it seems to have been written by Jagger alone (with a modest contribution from Cammell) is typically "Stones" in spirit. Sean Egan rightly calls it the "great lost Rolling Stones classic."[79] In the film, Turner/Jagger performs the song to a group of dumbfounded criminals. And the lyrics are pretty hard-hitting: *I remember you in Hemlock Road in 1956/You're a faggy little leather boy with a smaller piece of stick.*

Mick Jagger, Anita Pallenberg, and Michèle Breton: an iconic scene from the movie *Performance*.

Production

There are three versions of "Memo from Turner." The first was recorded in September and/or October 1968 at Olympic Sound Studios. At this session, Mick Jagger was accompanied by various musicians, including Traffic members Stevie Winwood and Jim Capaldi. Of the three, this is the version that swings the most. In addition to the guitar parts and bass, the talented Winwood seems to have played the Hammond B-3 organ, the sound of which is forever associated with his name. The piano was most likely played by Jack Nitzsche, who was also in charge of the instrumental parts for the film. As for Capaldi, his drumming is excellent in every respect, and he is assisted by Jagger on maracas.

The second version dates from November 17, 1968, and was also recorded at Olympic, with Al Kooper on guitar rather than organ. The day after he had done the session for "You Can't Always Get What You Want," he received a phone call: "It was Mick. He and Keith were down in the lobby. They came to pick me up! That night we cut a track from the film Jagger was currently working on, *Performance*. The song was called 'Memo from Turner,' but was not the version used in the film or on the soundtrack album. I believe it was used on a later album of outtakes. I played guitar with Keith on that one."[82] The other musicians have not been clearly identified. Bill Wyman could be on bass, with Charlie Watts or Jim Capaldi on drums. The funky result eventually found a home on *Metamorphosis* (1975).

The third and final version is the one that can be found on the soundtrack album. This was also released as a single on October 23, 1970, and has been a part of the official Rolling Stones discography ever since. Jagger's voice is taken from the first version, recorded in London. The instruments, on the other hand, were recorded in Los Angeles, most probably at Elektra Studios, with Ry Cooder and possibly Russ Titelman (rhythm guitar), Randy Newman (organ), Jerry Scheff (fuzz bass), and Gene Parsons (drums). The listener is immediately captivated by the slide guitar of the incredible Ry Cooder. This sets the track aglow, lending it an aggressiveness and power that is lacking in the other two versions. Jagger is also exceptional. His performance veers between disdain, provocation, and cynicism, all delivered in a sensual blues-rock voice. The rhythm section, meanwhile, is highly efficient, incorporating Jerry Scheff (?) on fuzz bass. "Memo from Turner" is a real gem, a song that would have merited inclusion on *Let It Bleed*, but Keith, harboring a persistent grudge, would apparently not hear of it . . . It is claimed, incidentally, that faced with Keith's refusal to take part in the song, Mick broke down in tears before Donald Cammell, and the director immediately took advantage of the situation to interfere in the writing of the lyrics. This version was to reach number 32 in the United Kingdom on November 21, 1970.

The songwriter and pianist Randy Newman. He may have taken part in the recording of "Natural Magic."

SIDE B
1963

IN YOUR HEADPHONES

At 1:35, right at the end of the number, two finger snaps can be heard, probably Jack Nitzsche marking time for the musicians.

FOR STONES ADDICTS

The single "Memo from Turner" / "Natural Magic" marks the end of the agreement between Mick Jagger / the Rolling Stones and Decca Records.

NATURAL MAGIC

Jack Nitzsche / 1:39

SINGLE
Memo from Turner / Natural Magic
RELEASE DATE
United Kingdom: October 23, 1970
Record label: Decca
RECORD NUMBER: DECCA F 13067

Musicians
Mick Jagger: maracas (?)
Ry Cooder: slide guitar
Russ Titelman (?): rhythm guitar
Lowell George (?): rhythm guitar
Randy Newman (?): piano
Jerry Scheff (?): bass
Gene Parsons (?): drums
Milt Holland (?): kettledrum
Recorded
Olympic Sound Studios, London / Elektra Studios, Los Angeles: March–September 1968, July–August 1970
Technical Team
Producer: Jack Nitzsche
Sound engineer: Glyn Johns

Genesis
The number chosen for the B-side of the single "Memo from Turner" was "Natural Magic." This was an instrumental composed and produced by Jack Nitzsche, and originally recorded at Olympic between March and September 1968, featuring Ry Cooder in great form playing slide. The track was then reworked and rerecorded in Los Angeles for the soundtrack of *Performance* at the same time that Randy Newman was in the building recording his second album, *12 Songs*, accompanied notably by Ry Cooder, Gene Parsons, and Milt Holland, thereby explaining the possible presence of these musicians on "Natural Magic."

Production
This short instrumental showcases the excellent slide guitar of Ry Cooder. The number in essence hangs on his playing, and it has to be said that he doesn't hold back on the bottleneck. Cooder is accompanied by two other rhythm guitars as well as a very good bass/drum section that provides great support. Among the percussion, an orchestral kettledrum can be heard (Milt Holland?), while Mick Jagger is thought to be on the maracas, which are nevertheless inaudible. Another important element on "Natural Magic" is the piano, drowned in a strong, very short delay with highly pronounced feedback, presumably played by the great Randy Newman. Finally, as this is first and foremost film music, Jack Nitzsche thought it a good idea to add throughout the track a wind effect created on a synthesizer—not a great success.

Look What You've Done
It's All Over Now
Confessin' The Blues
One More Try *
As Tears Go By
The Spider And The Fly
My Girl
Paint It Black
If You Need Me
The Last Time
Blue Turns To Grey
Around And Around

* Only the released songs will be
discussed in this chapter.

COMPILATION ALBUM
RELEASE DATE
United Kingdom: March 6, 1971
Record label: Decca
RECORD NUMBER: DECCA SKL 5084

STONE AGE

1971

STONE AGE:
THE ALBUM THAT SHOULD
NEVER HAVE BEEN RELEASED!

Following the band's split from Decca Records, the Rolling Stones' former record company "took its revenge" by issuing *Stone Age* on March 6, 1971. This compilation had the distinction of bringing together twelve numbers that had been either selected for UK singles or albums destined for the United States and the rest of the world, but not included on any official British album. The album cover is a nod to the photograph of lavatories and graffiti rejected some time before by Decca.

And the track listing and cover were the two specific aspects of the release that provoked such a strong reaction from Mick Jagger, Keith Richards, Bill Wyman, Charlie Watts, and Mick Taylor. At the beginning of 1971, they published an ad in the *Record Mirror* and the *NME* aimed at their fans: "Beware! Message from the Stones Re: Stone Age. We didn't know this record was going to be released. It is, in our opinion, below the standard we try to keep up, both in choice of content and cover design. Signed Mick, Keith, Charlie, Bill, Mick Taylor." As Bill Wyman would later point out, the Stones could not oppose the record release, but neither could Decca prevent them from having their say. He concludes: "Our Decca royalties were so low it hardly mattered if it sold or not."[1]

ONE MORE TRY

Mick Jagger / Keith Richards / 1:58

Musicians
Mick Jagger: vocals
Keith Richards: lead and rhythm guitar, backing vocals
Brian Jones: rhythm guitar (?), harmonica
Bill Wyman: bass
Charlie Watts: drums
Ian Stewart: piano (?)
Recorded
RCA Studios, Hollywood: May 12–13, 1965
Technical Team
Producer: Andrew Loog Oldham
Sound engineer: Dave Hassinger

FOR STONES ADDICTS

"One More Try" can be found on *Stone Age*, as we have seen, but also on another compilation, *The Rest of the Best*, aimed at the German market.

Genesis

There are limits to friendship and love, limits clearly defined in "One More Try." Attempt to borrow a little money and suddenly those who claimed to be your friends will no longer recognize you. Where one's private life is concerned, it's the same story: *You bring her all the things she wants, she don't improve*, sings Jagger in the second verse. The moral of this tale can be summed up in just a few words: *Sit down, shut up, don't dare to cry!*

"One More Try" was recorded at the RCA Studios on May 12–13, 1965, the same session as "The Spider and the Fly," "Good Times," "Cry to Me," and (I Can't Get No) Satisfaction." Why was this song used on the versions of *Out of Our Heads* destined for the United States and continental Europe but not on the British version? It is a mystery (unless explained by the fact that the deadline for the British pressing did not allow for inclusion) because it is a highly successful song (although very short) and is characteristic of the blues-rock the Stones used to play in the middle of the sixties.

Production

"One More Try" is a kind of boogie-woogie-cum-country-blues that brings to the fore Brian Jones's qualities as a harmonica player. Jones plays throughout the track and then takes a short solo around 0:54. It is no discredit to Mick to say that Brian had a far better technique than he did. Although Mick would later shine on numbers like "Midnight Rambler" and "Stop Breaking Down," Brian possessed a feel for, and mastery of, the blues harmonica that were astonishing in a young Englishman one of very few people in the United Kingdom took any interest in such a thing. "One More Try" is also characterized by a very good guitar part from Keith Richards, most likely playing his "reverse" Gibson Firebird VII. It seems to be Brian accompanying him, although it is difficult to be sure. The same goes for Stu's piano: he is presumably present, but is very recessed in the mix. Bill Wyman and Charlie Watts form a very tight rhythm unit, leaving Mick Jagger the task of singing his lyrics, which, based on his somewhat stiff delivery and pacing, he does not seem to have fully mastered. "One More Try" is a good song with harmonies reminiscent of the Beatles, and one can easily imagine it being sung by Ringo Starr.

Brown Sugar
Sway
Wild Horses
Can't You Hear Me Knocking
You Gotta Move
Bitch
I Got The Blues
Sister Morphine
Dead Flowers
Moonlight Mile

ALBUM
RELEASE DATE
United Kingdom: April 23, 1971
Label: Rolling Stones Records
RECORD NUMBER: ROLLING STONES
RECORDS COC 59100
**Number 1 for 5 weeks, on the
charts for 25 weeks**

STICKY
FINGERS

A photo session for the Stones as they were about to record one of the most important albums of their career.

STICKY FINGERS: A MASTERPIECE WITH A TOUCH OF WARHOL

The 1969 US tour, which kicked off in Fort Collins, Colorado, on November 7, 1969, marked the start of a new era for the Rolling Stones, with Mick Taylor taking the place of Brian Jones. Two shows in Boston, Massachusetts, on November 29 should have brought the tour to a close. However, the band decided to travel to the Palm Beach Pop Festival in Florida (November 30) and, having been unable to take part in Woodstock a few months earlier, to give one last concert planned as a celebration of the spirit of the sixties.

Permission was refused for the show to be held in Golden Gate Park in San Francisco, so this "Woodstock of the West Coast" was eventually moved to the Altamont Speedway, near Livermore. Also on the bill were the best of the Californian rock scene: Santana, Jefferson Airplane, the Flying Burrito Brothers, the Grateful Dead, and Crosby, Stills, Nash & Young.

Altamont: The End of the Dream

On December 6, 1969, 300,000 people made their way to the site. The Hells Angels were placed in charge of security (a suggestion from the Grateful Dead). Captured on film by Albert and David Maysles and Charlotte Zwerin (*Gimme Shelter*, 1970), what ensued was the stuff of nightmares. The Jefferson Airplane singer Marty Balin was punched by the Hells Angels for criticizing their violent behavior, Meredith Hunter (a young man, suspected of allegedly intending to shoot Mick Jagger during the band's performance) was murdered, there were three other deaths from different causes, some 850

individuals were treated for overdosing on LSD, and the Stones had to make a quick exit by helicopter. Altamont marked the end of spirit of the sixties and demonstrated that society was intrinsically violent—and not only Vietnam or the ghettos of the major US cities. However, Keith Richards retains a different memory of Altamont: "In actual fact, if it hadn't been for the murder, we'd have thought it a very smooth gig by the skin of its fucking teeth. It was also the first time 'Brown Sugar' was played to a live audience—a baptism from hell, in a confused rumble in the Californian night."[2]

The Album

Sticky Fingers is strongly marked by the Rolling Stones' US experience: the 1969 tour and the tragedy of Altamont on the one hand; the atmosphere of the Southern states, the cradle of the blues and country music, on the other. These were tumultuous times, and it was against this background that the band, now able to benefit from the virtuoso guitar playing of Mick Taylor, created a real masterpiece, "a maelstrom of country licks, blues chords and lines of white powder,"[40] as Andria Lisle has written in *Mojo* magazine.

Mick Jagger and Keith Richards had perhaps never written as well—together or individually—as they did for *Sticky Fingers*. The album opens in grand style with "Brown Sugar," an inflammatory story of slavery, sexual gratification, and drugs, featuring a riff in the finest Stones tradition. "Sway" offers more of the same: sex, drugs, and rock 'n' roll seem to be the watchwords forever colored by the grim drama of

Altamont. "Wild Horses," carried by an inventive and sophisticated melody, expresses Keith Richards's frustration at not being able to see his son Marlon. The epic continues with "Can't You Hear Me Knocking," which develops into a monumental improvisation with a Latin rock feel, led successively by Bobby Keys on saxophone and Mick Taylor on solo guitar. Then there is an homage to the forefathers of the blues in the form of a cover of Mississippi Fred McDowell's "You Gotta Move."

The second side of the LP opens with a salvo of gunfire in the form of "Bitch," based around a demonic riff, in which Mick Jagger draws a parallel between women and sexual pleasure, demonstrating that his talent for provocation is undiminished. The music takes a radical change of direction with "I Got the Blues," which testifies to the influence of Southern soul on the British quintet, and that of Otis Redding in particular. "Sister Morphine" is a macabre ballad that owes a great deal to the bond between Mick Jagger and Marianne Faithfull, and describes the final moments of an accident victim lying on a hospital bed. By comparison, the music of "Dead Flowers," in the country tradition, comes across as far lighter, despite the lyrics describing the breakup of a couple against a backdrop of hard drugs and a rose-pink Cadillac. The album closes with "Moonlight Mile," a song with which Mick Jagger qualifies for inclusion in the ranks of the greatest rock poets.

Sticky Fingers was the first album by the Stones to be released on Rolling Stones Records, the band's own label, officially created on April 6, 1971, following the signing of an agreement with the Kinney group and Atlantic Records (for the United States). The Stones' ninth (British) studio album duly went on sale on April 23. The reception it was given by the rock critics did full justice to the quality of the band's work on the recording. While Lester Bangs crowned it the best rock album of the year, *Rolling Stone* described it as the "latest beautiful chapter in the continuing story of the greatest rock group in the world,"[42] later placing it at number 63 on its list of the 500 Greatest Albums of All Time. The disc rose to number 1 in many countries, including the United Kingdom, the United States, Australia, Canada, West Germany, the Netherlands, Spain, and Norway. In France it peaked at number 3.

The Split with Decca

The contract between the Rolling Stones and Decca expired in July 1970. Relations between the band and Sir Edward Lewis, the chairman, had become increasingly contentious. To make matters worse, despite big record sales and sold-out concerts, the band was on the verge of bankruptcy. On February 4, 1971, in conjunction with their business advisers (an array of accountants and attorneys), the Stones made the decision to become tax exiles in order to get their heads above water, and in early 1971 moved to France for a period of twenty-one months. Meanwhile, on February 19, the band members discovered to their amazement that Allen Klein was now the outright owner of all their master tapes and publishing rights. They immediately decided to break with him, but also to leave Decca and set up their own label instead. Rolling Stones Records was born. The Stones entrusted the task of running it to Marshall Chess, the son of Leonard Chess, one of the founders of Chess Records. They granted the distribution rights in the United States to Atlantic Records, which offered them a contract of $5.7 million for six albums. In the meantime, RCA upped the stakes and offered $7 million, but the band decided to stick with Atlantic, with whom they felt they had a better affinity, thanks not least to the company's charismatic co-founder, Ahmet Ertegun. The deal was concluded on April 1, 1971. Distribution in the United Kingdom and parts of Europe was granted to the Kinney Records Group, while the other regions of the world either came under the responsibility of Warner Bros. Records or were handled locally.

Promotional photo for the release of *Sticky Fingers* on April 23, 1971.

The Album Cover

During a party in New York at the beginning of 1969, Mick Jagger had asked Andy Warhol if he would be willing to design the cover of the next Rolling Stones album, whose title the band had yet to come up with. Sometime later, Warhol showed Mick Jagger and Charlie Watts, while they were on a visit to the Factory, the picture of a pair of jeans with a zipper, and inside, a man's crotch clad in simple cotton undershorts. Mick Jagger liked it, while at the same time insisting that the zipper actually work. The album was initially marketed in this form, but before long it was realized that the zipper was damaging the vinyl disc. For subsequent pressings, it was decided to make the zipper slide to the halfway point only.

The photo shoot of the jeans took place under the aegis of Andy Warhol (who was paid £15,000) and the photographer Billy Name at 33 Union Square, the building that housed the offices of Warhol's magazine *Interview*, which happened to be located next door to an architects' office. Following the release of the album, many names were circulated concerning the identity of the models, starting with those of Mick Jagger himself and the actor and Warhol protégé Joe Dallesandro. In the booklet that accompanies the *Sticky Fingers* anniversary box set, Glenn O'Brien (at that time Warhol's editor at *Interview*) provides some useful clarifications: "Andy shot a bunch of guys—apparently Joe as well as his brother Bobby Dallesandro, who was then

Andy's driver, and Jackie Curtis, an actor and sometimes transvestite mentioned by Lou Reed in 'Walk on the Wild Side.' He shot me in the *Interview* office with his Big Shot Polaroid and while I'm standing there in my underwear with Andy kneeling in front of me, the door opens and a bunch of guys in suits walk in and look stunned. 'Oh, this isn't the architects' office!'"[85] O'Brien continues the account of his adventure in the *New York Post* of June 6, 2015: "I knew it was me because it was my underwear!" he tells the *Post*. "[Warhol] just said it was for a Rolling Stones album cover. I was a huge fan, so I was pleased, and also I got paid $100. Not bad for 20 minutes' work." Again according to O'Brien, the jeans-clad model for the cover photo was Corey Tippin, a makeup artist who was a member of Warhol's circle and who is said to have been paid seventy-five dollars for the session. Andy Warhol's concept was then stylized by Craig Braun.

Sticky Fingers was also the first album to sport the Rolling Stones' famous lolling tongue logo. Its design was entrusted to graphic artist John Pasche, who was recommended by the prestigious Royal College of Art. Initially, he was asked to design a poster for the 1970 European tour. Soon after, Mick Jagger invited Pasche to come and see him at Cheyne Walk. " . . . he presented me with this printed image that he'd got from his local Indian corner shop of Kali, the Hindu Goddess of Time, Change, Power and Destruction. He'd got them to take it off the wall. I just immediately saw the mouth and

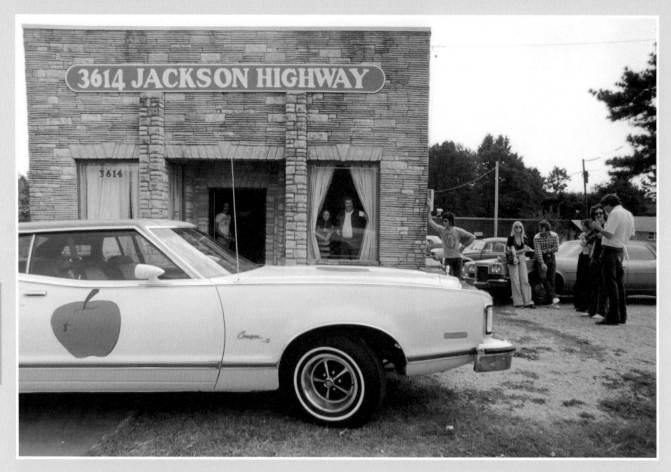

The Muscle Shoals Sound Studios in Alabama, where the story of *Sticky Fingers* began.

tongue."[85] All Pasche needed to do was to refine the look. As for the title, Keith Richards would later claim that the name *Sticky Fingers* was not originally envisioned for the album. "It's just what we called it while we were working on it. Usually though, the working titles stick."[11]

The Recording

The Rolling Stones took from March 1969 to January 1971 to record *Sticky Fingers*. Three studios were used during this relatively extended period: Muscle Shoals Sound Studios in Alabama, Olympic Sound Studios in London, and the Rolling Stones Mobile Studio installed at Stargroves in the English county of Hampshire. They would also use Trident Studios in London for some of the mixing and for the recording of the string arrangements.

At the end of their 1969 US tour, the Rolling Stones decided to record a number of songs in the southern United States. Initially, they chose Memphis, Tennessee, the birthplace of a number of blues musicians, and the home of Sun Records and Stax Records. Although the Stones had been granted permission to tour the United States, for union reasons they were not allowed to record on US soil. This meant they could forget Memphis. What were they to do? Ahmet Ertegun and Jerry Wexler of Atlantic suggested Muscle Shoals Sound Studios in northwest Alabama, where no one was likely to come and stop them from working.

Located at 3614 Jackson Highway, in Sheffield, Muscle Shoals Sound Studios had been founded a few months earlier, in April 1969, by the Swampers, the former rhythm section of Fame Studios, who had decided to spread their wings. They were: Barry Beckett (keyboards), Roger Hawkins (drums), Jimmy Johnson (guitar), and David Hood (bass).

From Muscle Shoals to the Rolling Stones Mobile Studio

The Rolling Stones arrived at the Holiday Inn in Florence on December 2, and quickly set off in the direction of Muscle Shoals Sound Studios. Between December 2 and 4 they laid down the first three tracks of what would eventually become *Sticky Fingers*: "You Gotta Move," "Brown Sugar," and "Wild Horses." Wearing the sound engineer's cap was Jimmy Johnson. The Stones were wholly satisfied with the sound they obtained, to such an extent, in fact, that Keith would later claim their next record, *Exile on Main St.*, would probably have been recorded there had they not been forced to become tax exiles in France in 1971. He also recalls the quality of the place: "It was the crème de la crème, except it was just a shack in the middle of nowhere."[2]

After Altamont, the Stones returned to England. In December, they worked on "Dead Flowers" at Olympic Sound Studios in London. Sessions then resumed in March 1970 and continued until May, now, thanks to their mobile studio, at Mick

Two days after the end of the Muscle Shoals sessions, the Stones were onstage at Altamont. The drama that unfolded there marked the end of flower power.

The Who would record part of "Won't Get Fooled Again," one of their greatest tracks, at Stargroves with Glyn Johns at the controls.

Jagger's home Stargroves. During this phase, "I Got the Blues" and "Can't You Hear Me Knocking" were recorded, plus various other tracks that were not used, and also "Good Time Women," which was to become "Tumbling Dice" (*Exile on Main St.*). In April, Marshall Chess was a little disconcerted by their approach to recording: " . . . at first I was confused by their working methods. I came from the Chess studio tradition—you record three songs in three hours—and the Stones were spending hours, not showing up [in the studio] together."[85]

Finally, between October 21 and the end of November, following a long European tour (August 30–October 9), they recorded "Bitch," "Moonlight Mile," and "Sway," as well as various overdubs for other songs. "Sister Morphine," meanwhile, had been recorded back in May 1968 during the sessions for *Beggars Banquet*.

The resulting album is one of the crowning glories of the Rolling Stones discography, in part due to the producer, Jimmy Miller, even though he had not been present at the Muscle Shoals sessions, " . . . which was equally amazing,"[9] as Charlie Watts would later observe. Among the additional musicians are Rocky Dijon on percussion, plus Bobby Keys, Ry Cooder, Nicky Hopkins, and Jack Nitzsche. Some new instrumentalists also contributed to the sessions, such as Jim Price, a friend and sidekick of Bobby Keys, who would play on many Rolling Stones records and also tour extensively with the band; and the legendary Billy Preston, onetime pianist of

Little Richard and musician on the last two Beatles albums. Another new face was the pianist Jim Dickinson, who would go on to have an outstanding recording career with Bob Dylan, Aretha Franklin, Johnny Cash, and others. For the strings, the Rolling Stones obtained the services of the arranger and composer Paul Buckmaster, who has worked with such names as David Bowie, Elton John, and Miles Davis. As for the sound engineers, Jimmy Johnson (also a producer and guitarist) officiated at Muscle Shoals Sound Studios, while Glyn Johns and his brother Andy were in charge at Olympic Sound Studios and in the Rolling Stones Mobile Studio. Finally, the assistant sound engineers were Chris Kimsey, who would go on to enjoy a career as sound engineer and also produce or co-produce a number of impressive albums, including several for the Rolling Stones, Peter Frampton, and Jimmy Cliff, and Keith Harwood, who would record albums for artists such as David Bowie and Led Zeppelin.

Technical Details

Muscle Shoals Sound Studios was equipped with a Scully 208-8 one-inch eight-track tape recorder, a Universal Audio 610 console, and Altec monitors. As for the reverb, Jimmy Johnson explains: "We just didn't have the room to do a big chamber like they'd had at FAME, which produced some of the best echoes you ever heard."[86] They therefore made do with an (excellent) EMT plate. The result is a recording of

A Gibson ES 355TD-SV like the one added to the Stones' stockpile around this time.

astonishing quality, despite the fact, as Johnson admits, "that one of those Altec monitor speakers was distorting during playback," recalls Johnson, "and the UA console was distorting naturally from lack of headroom! You can hear that on Mick's vocal during 'Wild Horses.'"[86]

The Stones then recorded at Olympic Sound Studios in London, where they had recorded for a number of years. At the end of January 1970, however, they kitted themselves out with a mobile studio along the lines of the Wally Heider Mobile, which they had used to record *Get Yer Ya-Ya's Out!* in November 1969. It was christened, logically, the Rolling Stones Mobile Studio and installed in the courtyard of Mick Jagger's manor house. Glyn Johns: " . . . the Stones truck was fully operational and we used the huge entrance hall of the Victorian pile that was Stargroves to record several tracks that were eventually used on Sticky Fingers."[4] Among other things, the studio was equipped with a sixteen-track 3M tape recorder, an Ampex eight-track, and a twenty-four-channel console designed by the brilliant Dick Swettenham, the creator of the Helios consoles.

The Instruments

Keith Richards made a number of acquisitions around autumn 1969: a prototype Dan Armstrong Plexiglas, a National "O" resonator guitar highly rated by many bluesmen, and a Gibson Martin D12-20. Other guitars would also be added to the collection and would be used by both Keith and Mick T.: a 1959 Gibson Les Paul, a white Fender Telecaster, and a Gibson ES 355. Taylor played mainly a brown Gibson ES 345, but also a 1968 Gibson Les Paul Sunburst that he had bought from Keith Richards via Ian Stewart almost two years before joining the Stones! While remaining faithful to his Dallas Tuxedo, Bill primarily used Fender Mustang basses on the album, and Charlie continued to play his Gretsch kit.

BROWN SUGAR

Mick Jagger / Keith Richards / 3:48

Musicians
Mick Jagger: vocals, maracas, castanets
Keith Richards: lead and rhythm guitar,
acoustic guitar, backing vocals
Mick Taylor: lead and rhythm guitar
Bill Wyman: bass
Charlie Watts: drums
Ian Stewart: piano
Bobby Keys: saxophone

Recorded
Muscle Shoals Sound Studios,
Alabama: December 3–4, 1969
Olympic Sound Studios, London: December
14, 1969; April, December 1970

Technical Team
Producer: Jimmy Miller
Sound engineers: Jimmy Johnson, Andy Johns, Glyn Johns
Assistant sound engineers: Chris Kimsey, Keith Harwood

Pianist Jim Dickinson was moved by the ease
with which Mick wrote "Brown Sugar."

Genesis

It was during the shooting of *Ned Kelly* in Australia, under the direction of Tony Richardson, that Mick Jagger, with a light wound to his hand, wrote the first few lines of "Brown Sugar" and came up with the riff (on the electric guitar) that was destined to become one of the most famous in the Rolling Stones' repertoire. Keith Richards really liked it when he heard it for the first time: "I'm the riff master. The only one I missed and that Mick Jagger got was 'Brown Sugar,' and I'll tip my hat there. There he got me. I did tidy it up a bit, but that was his, words and music."[2] Mick finished writing the lyrics at Muscle Shoals Sound Studios. Jim Dickinson, the pianist who participated in the sessions, recalls with some emotion: "I watched Mick write the lyrics. It took him maybe forty-five minutes; it was disgusting. He wrote it down as fast as he could move his hand. I'd never seen anything like it. He had one of those yellow legal pads, and he'd write a verse a page, just write a verse and then turn the page, and when he had three pages filled, they started to cut it. It was amazing!"[2]

And many more words have been written about these lyrics by other people over the years. At first reading it seems obvious what the song is about: the heinous days of slavery in the United States, when the plantation owners in the Southern states (New Orleans in this instance) used beautiful black women for their sexual gratification. Like the bluesmen before him, however, Mick Jagger plays with a double meaning in this song. "Brown Sugar" certainly refers to the black slaves shipped to America, and more particularly to their private parts (the song's first title being "Black Pussy"). But the term *brown sugar* also refers to heroin, that hardest of hard drugs. "God knows what I'm on about on that song," admits the Stones singer. "It's such a mishmash. All the nasty subjects in one go."[19] It is not impossible that Mick Jagger wrote "Brown Sugar" with the African-American singer and model Marsha Hunt, with whom he had a secret liaison, and who gave him his first child, Karis Jagger (born November 4, 1970), in mind. It is also surely possible that this song was inspired by his friend Claudia Lennear, a backing singer with Ike & Tina Turner. From here it is only a small step to the conclusion that Mick Jagger is insinuating that sex with a black woman is as addictive as heroin . . .

"Brown Sugar," which opens *Sticky Fingers*, was released as a single (with "Bitch" and a live version of "Let It Rock" on

Mick Jagger and Keith Richards at their very best when performing "Brown Sugar."

the B-side) in the United Kingdom on April 16, 1971, and reached number 2 on May 15. The song would get to number 1 in the United States and Switzerland, number 2 in France, and number 4 in West Germany.

Production

"Brown Sugar" is one of the three tracks recorded at Muscle Shoals Sound Studios at the beginning of December 1969, a week after the Palm Beach Pop Festival and two days before the tragic concert at Altamont. The atmosphere of the song evokes the damp and sticky South but is also, at the same time, highly electric. Mick Jagger: "But why it works? I mean, it's a good groove and all that. I mean, the groove is slightly similar to Freddy Cannon, this rather obscure '50s rock performer—'Tallahassee Lassie' or something."[19] In truth, the reason is probably to do with the Stones' particular working method. They tirelessly repeated "Brown Sugar" looking for a magic take, based on the method they had been using since their earliest days. And on that December 3, their second day at Muscle Shoals, the machine was taking a while to get into gear. All of a sudden, however, something sparked in the midst of the sonic confusion and they recorded the base track in a single take. Mick felt tired so the vocals were postponed until the following day.

"Brown Sugar" would not be what it is without the fantastic introductory riff played by Keith in open-G tuning on a 5-string guitar. Which guitar is difficult to say. Keith would later report that he had started to use his Telecaster a lot around this time, and he can also be seen performing the number on his Dan Armstrong Plexiglas on *Top of the Pops* on the BBC in 1971, but it could be a different guitar altogether. The same goes for

Mick Taylor, who can be seen playing his Gibson ES 345 on *Top of the Pops*. Did he use his Gibson SG Standard? Nevertheless, Keith's riff is irresistible, and although Mick may have been responsible for writing the song, the guitarist's distinctive sound is immediately recognizable. He plays with a rich yet subtle distortion (it could also be that the Universal Audio console was responsible for this by distorting at the output stage) and above all with an absolutely brilliant slap-back echo, apparently created by positioning his amp in the bathroom adjacent to the studio (even if it is not exactly in time with the beat). It seems to be Mick Taylor who answers him with a short phrase that is integral to the two-guitar structure, before moving into a rhythm part. Keith also plays acoustic, most likely his Gibson Hummingbird. The number also owes its success to the formidable groove machine of Bill Wyman and Charlie Watts. Bill delivers one of his best-ever bass lines on his Fender Mustang, and Charlie has clearly retained the lessons learned from the master Jimmy Miller (who was nevertheless not present at the sessions). The two of them transform "Brown Sugar" into a blend of funk rock and R&B. It is important to acknowledge Stu's contribution of a superb boogie-woogie piano part, as well as Mick's percussion, particularly the castanets during the instrumental section (1:39) and the maracas from the third refrain (2:07) onward.

All that remained was to record the voices. Jim Dickinson recalls the Glimmer Twins coming together to sing the vocal parts for all three songs in succession ("Brown Sugar," "Wild Horses," and "You Gotta Move") on December 4: "They were unbelievable, the raw vocals. They both stood at the microphone together with the fifth of Bourbon, passing it back and forth, and sang the lead and the harmony into one

Bobby Keys. His solo on "Brown Sugar" single-handedly sums up all the urgency of rock 'n' roll.

There are a number of covers of "Brown Sugar." The most unusual must surely be . . . Bob Dylan's.

microphone on all three songs, pretty much as quick as they could do it on the last night."[2] Dickinson would inform Jagger that he had left out a phrase he had sung in rehearsal the previous day: *Hear him whip the women just around midnight*. It is thanks to him that these few words made it into rock 'n' roll history!

Originally, the instrumental section was earmarked for a solo by Mick Taylor, but one day toward the end of May 1970, Mick Jagger bumped into Bobby Keys and Jim Price, both of whom were in London to play on George Harrison's album *All Things Must Pass*. Mick invited them to come and see the band as soon as they could, and the first song they played on was "I Got the Blues." "Brown Sugar" had to wait another few months. Fast-forward to December 18, to the birthday of Keith Richards and Bobby Keys and the occasion of a small party—and a jam. Al Kooper, one of the guests, recalls: "They cajoled Eric Clapton, myself, and Bobby Keys to join them in

a previously unheard tune called 'Brown Sugar.' George Harrison, who was among the partygoers, was invited to play but declined."[82] Bobby Keys launched into a breathtaking solo (the version that can be heard on CD 2 of the *Sticky Fingers* anniversary box set). A decision was immediately taken to replace Mick Taylor's guitar solo recorded at Muscle Shoals with a solo by Bobby Keys!

The final stage was the mixing. This was taken care of by Glyn Johns under the direction of the Glimmer Twins. Johns based his work on an initial master that had been done by Jimmy Johnson at Muscle Shoals in December 1969. "Glyn called me up from England after they'd done the horn overdub," says Johnson. "He said, 'You know that master you did? Couldn't touch it. Came close once.' That was real nice. I mean, he didn't have to say that."[86] "Brown Sugar," the album's opener, is a brilliant song that was destined to become a Rolling Stones classic.

SWAY

Mick Jagger / Keith Richards / 3:52

Musicians
Mick Jagger: vocals, rhythm guitar
Keith Richards: backing vocals, rhythm guitar (?), acoustic guitar (?)
Mick Taylor: lead guitar
Bill Wyman: bass
Charlie Watts: drums
Nicky Hopkins: piano
Paul Buckmaster: string arrangements

Recorded
**Rolling Stones Mobile Studio, Stargroves, Newbury /
Olympic Sound Studios, London:** October 21–November 1970
Trident Studios, London: January 1971

Technical Team
Producer: Jimmy Miller
Sound engineers: Glyn Johns, Andy Johns
Assistant sound engineers: Chris Kimsey, Keith Harwood

FOR STONES ADDICTS

"Sway" is also the B-side of the "Wild Horses" single released in the United States on June 12, 1971. This version is slightly different in the vocal parts, with Keith more prominent in the harmonies and backing vocals during Mick Taylor's second solo.

Genesis

"Sway" is perhaps the perfect musical manifestation of that morbid triptych of sex, drugs, and rock 'n' roll. Or rather of the price to be paid for a life in their grip. The gaze leveled by Jagger at the world of the rock star is frankly lugubrious. The character in the song wakes up for a spirit-sapping day, a day that is going to destroy any notion he may have of *circular time* because he is in the grip of a *demon life*. The second verse is sung in the first person and its message is even bleaker: *Ain't flinging tears out on the dusty ground for all my friends out on the burial ground*. And nor are the groupies able to restore any sense of hope to the narrator: *One day I woke up to find right in the bed next to mine someone that broke me up with a corner of her smile*.

The bitterness felt by the character in the song is most probably a reflection of what Mick Jagger and the other Rolling Stones were feeling after the tragedy of Altamont. The verdict is a painful one: society is violent—and there is no reason to believe it will ever be any different. "Sway" was the first song to be recorded by the Stones in autumn 1970, when they returned to Stargroves, the Hampshire manor house purchased by Mick Jagger a few months earlier, to use the technical facilities offered by their mobile recording studio.

Production

"Sway," which for all its merits, is not a major track on the album, follows the brilliant "Brown Sugar." The band's desertion by Keith Richards, who did not really like going to Stargroves to make music and traveled down there only rarely, probably had an influence on the quality of this number. His unannounced, repeated absences may also be explained by his increasing addiction to heroin. It was therefore Mick—or rather the two Micks—who took things in hand. As a result, "Sway" is the fruit of a collaboration between Jagger and Taylor (indeed the new guitarist would later claim to be the song's co-writer with the Stones singer). In any case, Taylor plays a major role on the track with his two solos, while Mick Jagger makes his grand debut on electric guitar. In 2002, Keith would tell Alan Di Perna that he liked Mick's acoustic playing but not really his electric: "Yeah . . . Well, like I say, acoustically he's got a nice touch. It doesn't translate electrically. It's not his thing. It's not everybody's cup of tea."[34] Nevertheless,

Mick Taylor and his Gibson Les Paul Sunburst, which plays a decisive role on "Sway."

the (nicely distorted) rhythm part played by Mick in open G provides good support, and considering it is his first time on a Stones disc, he does pretty well. But it is clearly the other Mick who deserves kudos, with his two excellent guitar solos played on his 1968 Gibson Les Paul Sunburst: "I put the slide on my little finger so it would still leave the other three fingers free to play like they would regularly, and I switched from one to the other. That was played in regular tuning,"[83] he would later explain. The two solos were recorded in single takes with no overdubs, the first with a bottleneck (1:37), the second with the fingers (2:40). And there is no denying his talent. Mick Taylor is an outstanding guitarist with an extremely fluid style of playing and a remarkable left-hand vibrato. The rhythm section made up of Bill Wyman and Charlie Watts is also of a high caliber, with Charlie obtaining from his Gretsch

kit a trademark sound that a number of bands would subsequently try to emulate by engaging the services of Glyn Johns at Stargroves, with its exceptional acoustics. It is also important to draw attention to Bill's superbly funky bass part, played on his Mustang. Nicky Hopkins, in his sole contribution to the album, plays a very good piano part characterized by his own peculiar blend of rhythmic and lyrical styles. The string arrangements are by Paul Buckmaster, whose name is associated with the early hits of David Bowie ("Space Oddity") and Elton John ("Your Song"), but their effectiveness is questionable, as they are recessed in the mix and make only a modest contribution. As for the voices, Keith sings the harmonies while Mick delivers a good performance, though perhaps not his best on the album.

WILD HORSES

Mick Jagger / Keith Richards / 5:42

Musicians
Mick Jagger: vocals, percussion
Keith Richards: guitar, backing vocals
Mick Taylor: guitar
Bill Wyman: bass
Charlie Watts: drums
Jim Dickinson: tack piano
Recorded
Muscle Shoals Sound Studios,
Alabama: December 3–4, 1969
Olympic Sound Studios, London:
December 1969, February 1970
Trident Studios, London: August 1970
Technical Team
Producer: Jimmy Miller
Sound engineers: Jimmy Johnson, Andy Johns, Glyn Johns
Assistant sound engineers: Chris Kimsey, Keith Harwood

FOR STONES ADDICTS

In their legal battle with Allen Klein, the Stones had to wrangle over whether the songs written or drafted in 1971, the year the contract between the two parties expired, belonged to them or not. In the end, an agreement was reached whereby they only ceded two songs—"Angie" and "Wild Horses." "He got the publishing of years of our songs and we got a cut of the royalties,"[2] Keith Richards would later report.

Keith Richards wrote "Wild Horses" after having spent weeks at Redlands with Gram Parsons, the member of the Byrds who had introduced him to country music's Bakersfield sound and Nashville sound. Gram Parsons would play guitar and provide vocals on a recording of "Wild Horses" for the Flying Burrito Brothers album *Burrito Deluxe*, which was released in May 1970, a year before *Sticky Fingers* . . .

Genesis

"If there is a classic way of Mick and me working together this is it. I had the riff and the chorus line, Mick got stuck into the verses,"[87] explains Keith Richards in the booklet that accompanies the compilation *Jump Back*, released in 1993. He would later add: "It's like 'Satisfaction.' You just dream it, and suddenly it's all in your hands. Once you've got the vision in your mind of wild horses, I mean, what's the next phrase you're going to use? It's got to be 'couldn't drag me away.' That's one of the great things about songwriting; it's not an intellectual experience. One might have to apply the brain here and there, but basically it's capturing moments."[2]

Originally, Keith wrote "Wild Horses" as a simple lullaby for his son, finding it more and more difficult to part from Marlon to go on tour. Under Mick's pen, however, the song took on a different complexion. Marianne Faithfull has revealed that "Wild horses couldn't drag me away" were the first words she uttered to Mick in the hospital when she came out of a six-day coma caused by an overdose of sleeping pills at the beginning of the summer of 1969. For the Stones singer, however, "Wild Horses" has nothing to do with Marianne Faithfull. Although it is about the breakup of a relationship, this should probably be seen in general, rather than in personal, terms: *I watched you suffer a dull aching pain/Now you decided to show me the same.*

Musically, "Wild Horses" is a little masterpiece—a song that "almost wrote itself,"[2] writes Keith in *Life*. The chords came to him on the 12-string acoustic, which gives the song its forlorn mood. He then played it again using a different tuning, open G, with a blues by Blind Willie McTell in mind. More or less all that remained to do was to record it. Released as a single in the United States on June 12, 1971, "Wild Horses" would reach number 23 on *Billboard* July 24 and would remain on the chart for eight weeks.

Production

The Stones worked on "Wild Horses" at Muscle Shoals Sound Studios on December 3, 1969, just after "You Gotta Move" and "Brown Sugar." When they came to record it, the song was still not quite finished and Keith needed a little more time. He shut himself away in a small bathroom adjacent to the studio, and came back a while later. Reunited with Mick

The Stones perform "Wild Horses" on *Top of the Pops* on April 22, 1971, with Keith Richards playing his Martin D12–20.

Jagger, who had gone off to get something to eat while waiting, the recording could then begin. When Ian Stewart discovered that there were minor chords (which he described as "fucking Chinese music")[2] in the song, he refused to play and began to pack up. Faced with this point-blank refusal, the Stones thought of calling Barry Beckett, the Swampers' pianist. However, Jim Dickinson, a pianist who was present in the studio that day, offered his services and therefore unexpectedly came to be associated with one of the Stones' greatest songs. Before sitting down to play an old tack piano that Keith had spotted in the building, Dickinson asked Keith for the chord chart. Because Keith had his own style of notation, and a limited musical vocabulary, Bill Wyman had to come to his assistance and jot down the right chords. Mick Taylor is said to have then spirited the paper away so that the recording would retain all its spontaneity and freshness. Dickinson would later recall: "I wasn't really a country piano player. Only knew two Floyd Cramer licks. The take they used was mostly me wondering what the next chord might be!"[85] After twenty or so takes, they got the piano down.

"Wild Horses" is a pop ballad with a country accent. It clearly gives pride of place to the guitars—and what guitars! The first to be heard is played by Mick Taylor. He is probably playing Keith's Gibson J-200 in a "Nashville" tuning, that is to say the four lower strings of the guitar strung with the finer-gauge strings of a 12-string set. The sonority created is superb, as is Mick Taylor's playing, which combines strumming, arpeggios, and harmonics, the last blending perfectly with Dickinson's tack piano. Taylor thinks he played a 12-string as well, which is also the instrument Keith plays—or rather, in his case, a 10-string, because it is tuned in open G with the two bottom strings (E) removed. On this instrument he answers Mick Taylor's guitar in perfect consonance. It is also Keith who plays the subtle, finely felt phrases on lead guitar in standard tuning and who has a short, highly inspired solo at 3:05 with a delay similar to that used on "Brown Sugar." Charlie's drumming is highly sophisticated, lending the song extraordinary rhythmic support and also revealing a reinvigorated approach in his playing. Bill accompanies him soberly but efficiently, supporting the harmonies of the two guitars on his Mustang bass. As for Mick Jagger, this is one of his most successful performances on the album, and he comes across as highly attuned to the feel of the song. "I like the song," he would reveal in 1995, and it certainly shows. A certain distortion can be heard in his voice, especially at 2:06 and 2:14. As Jimmy Johnson explains, this came from the mixing desk!

CAN'T YOU HEAR ME KNOCKING

Mick Jagger / Keith Richards / 7:16

Musicians
Mick Jagger: vocals, percussion
Keith Richards: acoustic guitar, lead and
rhythm guitar, backing vocals
Mick Taylor: rhythm and lead guitar
Bill Wyman: bass
Charlie Watts: drums
Bobby Keys: saxophone
Billy Preston: organ, piano (?)
Jimmy Miller: güiro (?)
Rocky Dijon: congas

Recorded
**Rolling Stones Mobile Studio, Stargroves,
Newbury / Olympic Sound Studios, London /
Trident Studios, London:** May, June, July 1970

Technical Team
Producer: Jimmy Miller
Sound engineers: Glyn Johns, Andy Johns, Chris Kimsey
Assistant sound engineer: Keith Harwood

Mick Taylor (shown here in the studio) plays
one of his most beautiful solos on the track.

Genesis

In this song the lyrics count for relatively little. *You got satin shoes/You got plastic boots/Y'all got cocaine eyes/You got speed-freak jive.* Their sole purpose is to match the rhythm. The important thing is the music, which testifies superbly to the urgency of rock 'n' roll. "'Can't You Hear Me Knocking' came out flying—I just found the tuning and the riff and started to swing it and Charlie picked up on it just like that, and we're thinking, hey, this is some groove. So it was smiles all around," recalls Keith Richards in *Life*. The tuning referred to by the Stones guitarist is based on five strings: "Five strings cleared out the clutter. It gave me the licks and laid on textures."[2]

Production

"Can't You Hear Me Knocking" is another title recorded at Stargroves in the Rolling Stones Mobile Studio. It kicks off with a riff in open G fired out by Keith on his Gibson Les Paul Black Beauty (or perhaps his Dan Armstrong?). The stinging guitar has a slight delay on it, or strictly speaking a "Revox echo," obtained using a tape recorder of that name, a very common method in those days, and one of which Jimmy Miller was fond. The riff master is immediately joined by the excellent Charlie Watts and the superb bass of Bill Wyman, the two of them imparting an extremely funky rock groove to the track. Then comes the first verse, sung by a red-hot Mick Jagger supported by Mick Taylor's clear-toned rhythm guitar in standard tuning. "I used the 345, the brown Gibson,"[88] Taylor would explain in 1979. In the refrains, Billy Preston can be heard on organ for the first time, and probably piano too, around 2:06. "Can't You Hear Me Knocking" is a very good rock track that the Stones originally envisioned lasting some two to three minutes. At 2:43, however, there is break, after which the number is relaunched by Rocky Dijon's congas, what seems to be a güiro, most likely played by Jimmy Miller, and Bill on bass. After two bars, Keith sets off on a new rhythmic pattern on the guitar, and the track drifts into a jam. Bobby Keys felt it was okay for him to join in: "So I grabbed my horn and I started playing; I came in something like eight bars after that section started, and I had no idea what I was gonna play. I just stuck my horn in my face and started to blow. That was a first take, a one-time thing."[85] He plays an excellent

Keith Richards communing with Charlie Watts during the 1970 European tour.

solo with a jazz-rock feel, contributing what was more or less a new color on a Stones record. A shaker is added to the rhythm section, now made up of Charlie—happy to play in a style for which he has a strong affinity—on drums, Rocky Dijon on congas, Jimmy Miller on güiro, and Bill on bass. And at 4:41, Mick Taylor plays an absolutely classic, extraordinary solo. His phrasing is highly fluid, with superb vibrato, his inspiration drawn from Latin-rock-blues sources reminiscent of Carlos Santana. Charlie is one of his admirers: "As a lead, virtuoso guitar, Mick was so lyrical on songs like 'Can't You Hear Me Knocking.' . . . He had such a good ear, and I would help push him along. . . . He was a fabulous guitar player."[9] Keith has no less admiration for the guitarist and maintains that "Can't You Hear Me Knocking" is one of two songs (along with "Love in Vain") that represent Mick Taylor's best work for the Stones. As well as being a success, this jam came as a surprise to everyone. Keith: "We didn't even know they were still taping.

We thought we'd finished. We were just rambling and they kept the tape rolling. I figured we'd just fade it off. It was only when we heard the playback that we realized, 'Oh, they kept it going.' Basically we realized we had two bits of music. There's the song and there's the jam."[34]

FOR STONES ADDICTS

There is an alternative take, lacking the saxophone of Bobby Keys, that is now available on the bonus disc (CD 2) of the *Sticky Fingers* box set.

YOU GOTTA MOVE

Mississippi Fred McDowell / 2:34

Musicians
Mick Jagger: vocals
Keith Richards: resonator guitar, backing vocals
Mick Taylor: rhythm guitar, slide guitar
Bill Wyman: electric piano
Charlie Watts: drums
Recorded
Muscle Shoals Sound Studios,
Alabama: December 2, 4, 1969
Rolling Stones Mobile Studio, Stargroves,
Newbury / Olympic Sound Studios, London /
Trident Studios, London: March–May 1970
Technical Team
Producer: Jimmy Miller
Sound engineers: Jimmy Johnson, Andy Johns, Glyn Johns
Assistant sound engineers: Chris Kimsey, Keith Harwood

Mississippi Fred McDowell, who
popularized "You Gotta Move."

Genesis
The message of "You Gotta Move" (also known by the title "You've Got to Move") can be found in the refrain: *Oh when the Lord gets ready, you gotta move.* The earliest recordings of this gospel blues were spread over the end of the forties and the beginning of the fifties: the Two Gospel Keys in 1948, Sister Rosetta Tharpe in 1950, and then the Original Five Blind Boys of Alabama in 1953. In 1962, Reverend Gary Davis recorded a version with a strong gospel feel, then came the turn of Mississippi Fred McDowell in 1965, several years after he had been "discovered" by the ethnomusicologist Alan Lomax. As his name indicates, Mississippi Fred McDowell was a Delta bluesman, the chief proponent of what was called Hill Country Blues (or North Mississippi Blues), a hypnotic form of blues built on just a few chords. The session took place at Berkeley, California, on July 5, 1965. The recording was produced by Chris Strachwitz and the record released on his own label, Arhoolie Records.

Production
Whereas Mick Jagger and Keith Richards performed "You Gotta Move" as a duo at the Stones' second concert at Madison Square Garden, New York City, on November 29 (the recording is included in the fortieth anniversary box set of *Get Yer Ya-Ya's Out!*), it was the whole band that recorded it at Muscle Shoals Sound Studios on December 2. It was actually the first song they got down in Alabama. Finding themselves back with all their bandmates for "You Gotta Move" posed a number of problems, as Keith Richards and Mick Jagger had become used to performing the song as a duo. After ten takes, there was nothing working. It was not until the nineteenth take that the song was cut. Richards plays his National resonator guitar (presumably in open D), and Taylor accompanies him on rhythm electric. As soon as Mick Jagger starts to sing, Taylor switches to slide, playing the melody on a Fender Telecaster with strong distortion. Charlie Watts conserves energy by playing only his bass drum (0:53) and his hi-hat (1:15). Bill Wyman, meanwhile, plays electric piano, around 2:05, with very strong vibrato. Worth noting are Keith's highly successful vocal harmonies, recorded along with the lead vocal on December 4. The Stones' version of "You Gotta Move" is very faithful to McDowell's.

BITCH

Mick Jagger / Keith Richards / 3:38

Musicians
Mick Jagger: vocals
Keith Richards: lead guitar (?), backing vocals
Mick Taylor: rhythm guitar (?)
Bill Wyman: bass
Charlie Watts: drums
Bobby Keys: saxophone
Jim Price: trumpet
Jimmy Miller: percussion
Recorded
Rolling Stones Mobile Studio, Stargroves, Newbury /
Olympic Sound Studios, London: October 21–November, 1970
Technical Team
Producer: Jimmy Miller
Sound engineers: Glyn Johns, Andy Johns
Assistant sound engineers: Chris Kimsey, Keith Harwood

The Stones' groupies would go to any
lengths to get close to their idols!

Genesis

This song sees the Rolling Stones, and Mick Jagger in particular, remaining true to the reputation for misogyny that had led feminists to pillory the band in the sixties. The very title betrays the message of the Stones singer. Woman, here, is synonymous with sexual pleasure and a symbol of sexual fantasy. *When you call my name, I salivate like a Pavlov dog/ When you lay me out, my heart is beating louder than a big bass drum*: the refrain could not be clearer. Jagger goes even further, however. The character in the song needs his dose of sex, just as he needs his drugs or his alcohol. To put it another way, sex and drugs are one of a kind, a theme encountered fairly frequently in Stones songs around this time. Yet Mick Jagger would respond to critics by explaining that the term *bitch* refers to love and not in any way to women, that listeners should understand the lyric as . . . *love, it's a bitch*. Nevertheless, the song would be banned from most of the airwaves, despite having been chosen as the flip side of "Brown Sugar."

Production

According to Jagger, "Bitch" was worked up by himself, Bobby Keys, and Charlie Watts during the course of a jam at Stargroves. Andy Johns also remembers Mick Taylor being there. But Keith's presence was required for the song to find its definitive groove and form, as Andy Johns reveals: "We were doing 'Bitch,' Keith was very late and Jagger and Mick Taylor had been playing the song without him. And it didn't sound very good. I walked out of the kitchen and he [Keith] was sitting on the floor with no shoes, eating a bowl of cereal. Suddenly he said, 'Oi, Andy! Give me that guitar.' He put it on, kicked the song up in tempo and just put the vibe right on it."[85] The recording could then get properly under way. The riff, played simultaneously by Mick Taylor (on his Gibson Les Paul?) and Bill Wyman on his Mustang bass, is rapped out with as much force as Charlie's snare drum rhythm. The sound is aggressive, electric, close to the Led Zeppelin style of hard rock. In all likelihood it is Keith on lead (on his Dan Armstrong?), despite the fact that Mick told Jas Obrecht[88] in 1979 that it had been him. The style and touch and the distinctly "Chuck Berry" licks all point to Keith. He plays throughout the track, and, logically enough, it is also he who takes the final solo, which goes on for almost a minute and a half! Mick Taylor,

Bill Wyman is one of the craftsmen responsible for that gem "Bitch."

meanwhile (if it is actually him), plays a fantastic rhythm guitar, with incredible timing and feel for the groove. It should be pointed out that in this he receives support of the very highest caliber from Charlie Watts, whose playing had become far funkier since Jimmy Miller assumed the role of producer. The same goes for Bill Wyman, whose bass is the real backbone of "Bitch." And for the first time on disc we have a horn section consisting of Bobby Keys and Jim Price. Their contribution is clearly a success. They make an enormous sound, giving the track a resolutely Southern feel in the spirit of the Memphis Horns. Their main role is to double the song's riff and harmonize in certain passages, but Jim Price's trumpet can also be heard wandering off by itself in the coda around 3:20. Jimmy Miller contributes to the percussion but it is not easy to work out what the exact instruments are. He seems to be playing a güiro with plenty of reverb in the opening few bars. Finally,

Mick Jagger delivers a fantastic performance, imbued with a power and aggressiveness that are every bit the equal of the incredible energy expended by his colleagues.

FOR STONES ADDICTS

An extended version of "Bitch" can be found on CD 2 of the *Sticky Fingers* box set: 5:52 of pure Stones rock 'n' roll!

I GOT THE BLUES

Mick Jagger / Keith Richards / 3:53

"I Got the Blues" was covered by Come, an indie rock band from Boston, on its album *11:11* (1992).

Musicians
Mick Jagger: vocals
Keith Richards: rhythm guitar, backing vocals
Mick Taylor: rhythm guitar
Bill Wyman: bass
Charlie Watts: drums
Bobby Keys: saxophone
Jim Price: trumpet
Billy Preston: organ
Recorded
Rolling Stones Mobile Studio, Stargroves,
Newbury / Olympic Sound Studios, London /
Trident Studios, London: March–May 1970
Technical Team
Producer: Jimmy Miller
Sound engineers: Glyn Johns, Andy Johns
Assistant sound engineers: Chris Kimsey, Keith Harwood

Billy Preston, who infuses "I Got the Blues" with a soul vibe.

Genesis

Mick Jagger sings of the despair of a man recalling his time with the woman he loved, who has now abandoned him. *Love is a bed full of blues*, he sings, and very soon the idea of suicide occurs to him as the only way out: *I'll bust my brains out for you.*

Was Jagger thinking of his recent breakup with Marianne Faithfull when he wrote the words to "I Got the Blues"? Perhaps. Alternatively, he may have been merely empathizing, through the song, with all those romantics of a melancholy frame of mind. There is perhaps no better example of the artistic debt the Stones owed the originators of Southern soul than "I Got the Blues." It inevitably recalls the productions of Stax Records, the subtle, pervasive scent of blues and gospel given off by the recordings of Otis Redding, Wilson Pickett, and Sam and Dave. Billy Preston's organ plays a key role in this, as do the horns of Bobby Keys and Jim Price.

Production

"I Got the Blues" is launched by Keith Richards with arpeggios played on a clear-toned guitar with ample reverb. He is immediately joined by Mick Taylor, also playing arpeggios, but with vibrato from the amp. The sound recalls that of Steve Cropper, and the listener expects to hear Otis Redding break into song when the horns strike up. But of course the voice that comes in is that of Mick Jagger, whom Bobby Keys claims wanted to integrate horns more and more into the Stones sound. And it is precisely by adopting a typical Stax configuration that Keys and his partner Jim Price approach the track. "Mick was very much into Otis Redding and Wilson Pickett and the Memphis Horns. And here he had his own Texas Horns. I remember telling him, 'Hey, man, we're the *Longhorns!*'"[89] "I Got the Blues" calls to mind Otis Redding's "I've Been Loving You Too Long," with certain harmonies strangely reminiscent of "Out of Time." Charlie Watts seems ill at ease with the rhythm and does not deliver one of his best drum parts. Bill Wyman nevertheless accompanies him very well on his Dallas Tuxedo. The same goes for Billy Preston, who single-handedly raises the number to a new level with his highly inspired solo, with soul and gospel vibes, on the Hammond organ.

SISTER MORPHINE

Mick Jagger / Keith Richards / Marianne Faithfull / 5:31

Musicians
Mick Jagger: vocals
Keith Richards: acoustic guitar
Bill Wyman: bass
Charlie Watts: drums
Jack Nitzsche: piano
Ry Cooder: slide guitar
Recorded
Olympic Sound Studios, London:
May–June 1968, March 1969
Technical Team
Producer: Jimmy Miller
Sound engineer: Glyn Johns
Assistant sound engineer: Phill Brown

The song "Sister Morphine" is quoted in *The Transmigration of Timothy Archer* (1982), the last book by the great science-fiction author Philip K. Dick.

After *Performance*, Ry Cooder again joined forces with the Stones for "Sister Morphine."

Genesis

Here I lie in my hospital bed/Tell me, Sister Morphine, when are you coming round again? "Sister Morphine" tells of the strange sensory impressions experienced by a man who has suffered an accident and been taken to the hospital. The opium alkaloids are having their effect. The unfortunate accident victim wonders, *Why does the doctor have no face?* and implores the drug with which he has been injected to turn his *nightmares into dreams.* In the fourth and final verse, Cousin Cocaine also gets a look-in during the narrator's very last moments on this earth: *I know in the morning I'll be dead*, sings Mick Jagger in a weary, fatalistic tone.

Mick wrote the music for this song in 1968 during a trip to Rome. Regarding the words, Keith Richards notes in *Life*: "Marianne had a lot to do with 'Sister Morphine.' I know Mick's writing, and he was living with Marianne at the time, and I know from the style of it there were a few Marianne lines in there."[2] While Marianne Faithfull has indeed claimed authorship, Mick Jagger takes a different view: "She wrote a couple of lines; she always says she wrote everything, though. I can't even tell you which ones."[19] The most credible hypothesis could be that Marianne Faithfull rewrote some of Mick's lyrics just before or during the trip to Brazil of the two couples (Marianne and Mick, Anita and Keith), taking her inspiration on the one hand from her hospitalization in Sydney following a suicide attempt, and on the other from Anita's often tempestuous behavior.

Production

The initial takes of "Sister Morphine" were recorded at Elektra Studios in Los Angeles in May 1968, during the sessions for *Beggars Banquet*. Mick Jagger was accompanied by Jack Nitzsche on piano and Ry Cooder on slide guitar. The cut used on the album, however, dates from March 1969, during the recording of the original soundtrack of *Performance* at Olympic Studios, again with Nitzsche and Cooder, Jagger having invited the pair to come and rerecord the song. Brian Jones was still alive at the time, although he was absent from the session. Mick Taylor had not yet joined the Stones.

The power of "Sister Morphine" is already present in the dark and disturbing connotations of the title; this impression is reinforced by the opening notes on the guitar, which plunge the

Mick Jagger and Marianne Faithfull may have written "Sister Morphine" together.

Marianne Faithfull recorded "Sister Morphine" in July 1968 (in reality she laid her voice over Nitzsche and Cooder's backing track). The studio version was released as a single in February 1969, but was withdrawn from sale by Decca two days later. There is also a version on her live album *Blazing Away*, recorded in St. Anne's Cathedral, Brooklyn, in September 1988.

FOR STONES ADDICTS

Marianne Faithfull was not credited as a co-writer of "Sister Morphine" when the album *Sticky Fingers* was originally released, and she brought a lawsuit. The error was rectified when the Stones albums were reissued by Virgin in 1994.

listener into a simultaneously distressing yet entrancing world. Richards strums the initial chords, most probably on his Gibson Hummingbird. When Jagger launches into his lyrics in a fragile, sickly sounding voice, the listener's fears are confirmed and the atmosphere becomes distinctly lugubrious. But what an atmosphere! And how skillfully the band transports us into this world so far removed from Chuck Berry and Muddy Waters. Jagger, as master of ceremonies, inhabits his lyrics utterly and delivers a stunning performance, but "Sister Morphine" only takes on its full magnitude with the entry of Ry Cooder's slide guitar. The phrases he plays on his Fender in open-G tuning with that very present reverb are absolutely stunning. The sonority he obtains with his left-hand vibrato and his expertise with the bottleneck is nothing short of a master class in guitar playing. Mick Taylor is full of admiration: " . . . he played slide guitar on

'Sister Morphine,' which is killer. It's great."[90] The US guitarist plays an incredible improvisation that makes the track literally take off. Another example of brilliant playing is provided by the loyal Jack Nitzsche, who reinforces the already oppressive atmosphere with hallucinatory phrases on a piano totally drenched in short and formidably effective reverb. In order to bring about a change of atmosphere, this effect is suspended from 3:31 and the piano sound suddenly becomes very immediate, before drifting away again into reverb. Bill Wyman also delivers a great performance on his remarkable-sounding Dallas Tuxedo, with a rhythmic pattern played with the fingers, which doesn't hesitate to plumb the depths of the instrument's range. Charlie Watts in turn galvanizes the track with a heavy yet very subtle rhythm. "Sister Morphine," is undoubtedly one of the highlights of *Sticky Fingers*.

DEAD FLOWERS

Mick Jagger / Keith Richards / 4:05

🎧 **IN YOUR HEADPHONES**

Unluckily for Stu, the pianist plays a wrong note on his final lick of the track (3:59).

Musicians
Mick Jagger: vocals, acoustic guitar
Keith Richards: acoustic guitar (?), rhythm and lead guitar, backing vocals
Mick Taylor: lead guitar
Bill Wyman: bass
Charlie Watts: drums
Ian Stewart: piano
Recorded
Olympic Sound Studios, London: December 1969, March–May 1970
Technical Team
Producer: Jimmy Miller
Sound engineers: Glyn Johns, Andy Johns
Assistant sound engineers: Chris Kimsey, Keith Harwood

There have been a number of cover versions of "Dead Flowers." Worthy of special mention is that by the New Riders of the Purple Sage on their album *New Riders* (1976).

FOR STONES ADDICTS

The title "Dead Flowers" could be a reference to "Lay Some Flowers on My Grave" by the blues singer Blind Willie McTell.

Genesis

"Dead Flowers" is one of the most pessimistic songs ever written by Mick Jagger and Keith Richards. In it they describe a relationship in the process of breaking apart between a melancholy man and a woman for whom everything seems to go right, who has become the *queen of the underground*. The final verse leaves no room for doubt: *Well, when you're sitting back in your rose-pink Cadillac . . . I'll be in my basement room with a needle and a spoon and another girl to take my pain away.* The refrain is also utterly bleak, with a good dose of cynicism to boot: *Send me dead flowers to my wedding, and I won't forget to put roses on your grave.* "Maybe this is the first Goth country song,"[91] suggests Rennie Sparks (of The Handsome Family).

As so often in Rolling Stones songs, however, the words and the music are out of sync with each other. Mick Jagger tells this bleak story set to optimistic country and western music. Work started on the recording of "Dead Flowers" on December 15, 1969 at Olympic Sound Studios in London. This was less than ten days after the drama of Altamont. For this reason the tune can perhaps be seen as functioning as a kind of exorcism (while at the same time testifying to the influence of Gram Parsons) . . .

Production

"I'd played it a hundred times at home before we got into the studio,"[85] Mick Jagger explains. And his efforts can be said to have paid off because "Dead Flowers" went on to become a country music standard. Jagger sounds like he is singing the song in cowboy boots, and he is supported by Keith with some very good vocal harmonies. "Keith and I had been playing Johnny Cash records and listening to the Everly Brothers—who were so country—since we were kids. I used to love country music even before I met Keith."[9] Mick Jagger is playing acoustic guitar and is probably doubled on that instrument by Keith, who also plays rhythm on his Telecaster and fires off short phrases in answer to Mick Taylor on his Gibson ES 345. Taylor plays licks that are reminiscent of a pedal steel guitar and then launches into an extremely lyrical solo. Stu plays an excellent piano part in the style of Nashville pianist Floyd Cramer. With Charlie and Bill forming a rhythm section of the first order, "Dead Flowers" is no pastiche but an authentic country number.

MOONLIGHT MILE

Mick Jagger / Keith Richards / 5:52

Musicians
Mick Jagger: vocals, acoustic guitar
Mick Taylor: lead guitar
Bill Wyman: bass
Charlie Watts: drums
Jim Price: piano
Paul Buckmaster: string arrangement
Recorded
**Rolling Stones Mobile Studio, Stargroves,
Newbury:** November 2, 1970
Trident Sound Studios, London: January 1971
Technical Team
Producer: Jimmy Miller
Sound engineers: Glyn Johns, Andy Johns
Assistant sound engineers: Chris Kimsey, Keith Harwood

"Moonlight Mile" has not inspired many covers, but one worth mentioning is the excellent version by the 5th Dimension on their 1975 album *Earthbound*.

Moonlight Mile is also the name of a manga by Yasuo Ohtagaki that was made into a television series in 2007, a novel by Dennis Lehane published in 2010, and a film by Brad Silberling starring Jake Gyllenhaal, Dustin Hoffman, and Susan Sarandon.

Genesis

There are various accounts concerning the genesis of the lyrics to this song. Keith has described "Moonlight Mile" as being entirely Mick Jagger's work: "As far as I can remember, Mick came in with the whole idea of that, and the band just figured out how to play it."[2] In an interview given to Marc Myers of the *Wall Street Journal* of May 28, 2015, the Stones singer had the following to say about the writing of the song: "I wrote some of the early lyrics to 'Moonlight Mile' in a songbook I carried around when we were on tour in the summer of 1970. I was growing road-weary and homesick then. I'm sure the idea for the song first came to me one night while we were on a train and the moon was out." This differs markedly from what he told Tom Donahue in 1971: "I always like to write lyrics to a song before we got into the studio, but the lyrics for 'Moonlight Mile' were not written before we cut the track, it was extemporised."[85]

These lyrics are some of the most poetic the Stones singer has ever written. In them he expresses the solitude felt by a passenger, in all likelihood some kind of performing artist (perhaps a rock star named Jagger?) on a train. The absence of the woman he loves is subtly symbolized by the moonlight, untouchable but enabling him to see more clearly, and the loneliness felt by the narrator is barely eased by the thoughts in which he seeks to take refuge in order to make his nights seem less long. Some people have interpreted the phrase *With a head full of snow* as a reference to narcotics, more specifically cocaine, but there is no guarantee that this is what was intended.

From a musical point of view, "Moonlight Mile" reveals Mick Jagger's desire to explore new avenues: "I also came up with an Oriental-Indian riff on my acoustic guitar. At some point during the tour I played it for Mick Taylor, because I thought he would like it."[85] Mick Taylor confirms that he [Taylor] came up with the riff at the end of the song from which Paul Buckmaster got his inspiration for the string arrangement, and that Mick Jagger "first sang [the song] to me in a first-class railway compartment on the way from London to Bristol."[15]

Production

Bill Wyman recalls the November 1970 sessions at Stargroves: "These were usually held between 9 pm and 7 am. On 2 November we cut 'Moonlight Mile' without Keith—he

In the absence of Keith, the two Micks play a key role in "Moonlight Mile."

never turned up."[1] This was the first time a Stones song would be cut without the band's star guitarist. Whether as a result of toxic substances or bad vibes, Keith was not there. Mick Jagger therefore plays acoustic guitar on the recording. He reveals a sensitive touch and plays a very fine introduction with an emphatically oriental feel. Jim Price is on piano, having abandoned his trumpet for a delicate and entirely unusual keyboard arrangement, here and there resembling a koto. Charlie Watts uses his mallets to create an effect of crashing cymbals and marks the rhythm mainly on his toms. Bill plays a gentle, velvety, and highly lyrical bass part with his fingers, most probably on his Dallas Tuxedo. And Mick Taylor contributes a guitar part of very high caliber, probably on his Gibson ES 345. He alternates harmonics, chords, and solo passages, once more displaying exceptional inspiration and an exceptional touch. Charlie testifies to this: "He was absolutely fantastic on that session. 'Moonlight Mile'—that's when I remember Mick Taylor at his very best."[85] As for Mick

Jagger, his vocal performance is also remarkable, and he switches with ease between a falsetto and a rock voice (and double-tracks himself). According to Andy Johns, his vocal was recorded at "Four or five in the morning with the sun coming up."[85] Finally, the superb strings arranged and conducted by Paul Buckmaster at Trident Studios in January 1971 significantly enrich the track and add to its effectiveness, by contrast with the arrangements on "Sway." It is impossible not to wonder whether John Lennon might have been inspired by them for his album *Imagine*, released in September 1971. It is also worth pointing out that flutes can be heard at around 5:18. Keith, the conspicuous absentee, would also enthuse about the final result: "It was great to hear that because I was very out of it by the end of the album and it was like listening, really listening."[85] "Moonlight Mile" draws the album to a close on a gentle, delicate note, and it is interesting to observe that two Mick Jagger songs, moreover diametrically opposed ones, open and close *Sticky Fingers*.

LET IT ROCK

Chuck Berry / 2:46

SINGLE

Brown Sugar* / Bitch** / Let It Rock

United Kingdom: April 16, 1971

Label: Rolling Stones Records

RECORD NUMBER: ROLLING STONES RECORDS RS 19100 * (SEE P. 339)
** (SEE P. 349)

Musicians
Mick Jagger: vocals
Keith Richards: lead and rhythm guitar
Mick Taylor: lead and rhythm guitar
Bill Wyman: bass
Charlie Watts: drums
Nicky Hopkins: piano
Bobby Keys: saxophone
Jim Price: trumpet

Recorded
Rolling Stones Mobile Studio,
Leeds University: March 13, 1971

Technical Team
Producer: Glyn Johns
Assistant producer: Rod Thear
Technical assistant: Mick McKenna

Genesis

"Let It Rock" is a Chuck Berry hymn to the glory of rock 'n' roll. The guitar hero from St. Louis, Missouri, recorded this number on July 27, 1959. The closing song on the famous album *Rockin' at the Hops* was released as a single in 1960 and reached a modest number 64 on the US *Billboard* chart before attaining sixth place in the British hit parade three years later, on November 20, 1963. Musically, "Let It Rock" bears a close resemblance to "Johnny B. Goode," which dates from 1958. The main character of the song is a railroad worker waiting impatiently for the end of the day, until everyone is panicked by a runaway train. In France, the Rolling Stones gave eighteen concerts in nine British cities between March 4 and 26, 1971. Organized by Marshall Chess, this was christened the "Good-Bye Britain" tour. One of the stopping-off points was Leeds, on March 13, 1971. There the Stones gave an invigorating version of "Let It Rock," which was selected as the B-side of the single "Brown Sugar."

Production

From the moment Keith Richards launches into his introductory riff, the success of the song is a foregone conclusion. However, both the audience and the band judged the concert as a whole to be no more than "average." Only "Let It Rock" stands out, and with it the Stones prove that they are unbeatable when it comes to pure rock 'n' roll. The amazing groove machine of Charlie Watts and Bill Wyman drives the number forward: the former smacking the drums and cymbals of his Gretsch kit with a contagious power and swing; the latter handling his bass like an automatic weapon and playing notes as high up the neck of his Fender Mustang as he possibly can. Mick Jagger is in dazzling form and sings his Chuck Berry lyrics with every bit as much passion as he did in the early days. As for Nicky Hopkins, this was his first tour with the band, and he applies himself to delivering an excellent boogie-woogie piano. On the horns, Jim Price and Bobby Keys huff and puff in vain because they are right at the back of the mix, and do not seem to be in tune. On guitar, Mick Taylor and Keith Richards seem to be sharing roles, although Keith apparently has more of the lead part than Mick Taylor.

"Let It Rock" was on the Stones' set list when they played the Roundhouse in London in March 1971. Bobby Keys can be seen accompanying them on sax.

FOR STONES ADDICTS

This same version would be used as the A-side of a single destined for the German market, which was released in January 1972 and reached number 25 on the charts. It can also be found on the compilations *Rarities 1971–2003* (2005), *The Singles 1971–2006* (2011), and, more recently, on the live CD *Get Yer Leeds Lungs Out*, included in the *Sticky Fingers* anniversary box set (2015; *Get Yer Leeds Lungs Out* having originally been a bootleg).

Rocks Off
Rip This Joint
Shake Your Hips
Casino Boogie
Tumbling Dice
Sweet Virginia
Torn And Frayed
Sweet Black Angel
Loving Cup

Happy
Turd On The Run
Ventilator Blues
I Just Want To See His Face
Let It Loose
All Down The Line
Stop Breaking Down
Shine A Light
Soul Survivor

BONUS TRACKS

Pass The Wine (Sophia Loren)
Plundered My Soul
I'm Not Signifying
Following The River
Dancing In The Light
So Divine (Aladdin Story)

ALBUM
RELEASE DATE
United Kingdom: May 12, 1972
Label: Rolling Stones Records
RECORD NUMBER: ROLLING STONES
RECORDS COC 69100
**Number 1 for 1 week, on the
charts for 16 weeks**

EXILE ON MAIN ST.

1972

EXILE ON MAIN ST.: OUTCASTS IN FRANCE

At the dawn of the seventies, Prince Rupert Loewenstein, an enlightened financier who had taken the Stones' affairs in hand at the band members' request, confirmed what the musicians had been fearing for some time: their former manager Allen Klein had helped himself to what was theirs while failing to represent their best financial interests. It turned out that the founding members of the band, Mick, Keith, Bill, and Charlie, had not paid any income tax for several years. In a country in which the government taxed its fellow citizens at rates of up to 93 percent, this was an utter catastrophe. It had become impossible for the Stones to pay back the Inland Revenue what they owed and, as a result, to remain in Britain. "There was a feeling that you were being edged out of your own country,"[92] Keith Richards would later say.

From March 4 to 26, 1971, the Rolling Stones undertook their Good-Bye Britain tour, during the course of which they gave eighteen concerts in cities from Newcastle to London, capped by a final show at the legendary Marquee Club on March 26. On April 1 they crossed the channel to France. While Mick Jagger checked into the Hotel Plaza Athénée in Paris, the other members of the band and their families headed for the Côte d'Azur. Bill Wyman and Mick Taylor rented villas at Grasse and Le Tignet, and Charlie Watts took a suite in a hotel in Cannes, before settling in Arles. Finally, Keith Richards chose Nellcôte, a property located at Ville-franche-sur-Mer, just outside Nice. The single *Brown Sugar / Bitch / Let It Rock* was released on April 16. To mark the occasion, a party was thrown at the International Yacht Club in Cannes, attended by, among others, Ahmet Ertegun, the head of Atlantic, and the French music producer and record company founder Eddie Barclay. Just under four weeks later, on May 12, Mick Jagger married Bianca Pérez Mora-Macías in the Chapel of Saint Anne in Saint-Tropez.

Nellcôte

With the band "exiled" on the Côte d'Azur, Nellcôte became the nerve center of a dolce vita Rolling Stones–style. Close friends, family, and associates of Keith and Anita and the other band members (Ian Stewart, Jimmy Miller, Bobby Keys, Jim Price, Gram Parsons, Nicky Hopkins, Andy Johns, Marshall Chess, William S. Burroughs . . .) took up residence at the villa, while various shady characters turned up periodically. "Villa Nellcote was a fantastic place, very decadent," recalls Anita Pallenberg. "In the Second World War it used to be the Nazi headquarters—there were swastikas engraved in the heating system—and it was set up for loads of people moving around in it."[30]

While Nellcôte was a place of almost permanent partying it was also a place of music. The Rolling Stones Mobile Studio—first used at Stargroves in 1970 and still equipped with the machinery on which *Sticky Fingers* had been recorded, plus four enormous Tannoy monitors—was brought down from London in four days and became operational (Ian Stewart had the idea of slinging a cable from an overhead line to the villa in order to power it) on June 7, enabling the Stones to play once again. Rehearsals were held from eight o'clock in the

The wedding of Mick and Bianca in Saint-Tropez.

At the concert given by the Stones at the Marquee Club on March 26, 1971, Keith, who arrived four hours late, did not seem to be his normal self. When he saw Harold Pendleton, the manager of the venue, he swung his guitar at Pendleton's head. The reason? An altercation between Pendleton and Jagger shortly beforehand over the club's sign, which had been moved against Mick's wishes. Keith apparently did not take kindly to his mate being crossed . . .

evening to three o'clock in the morning until the end of June. After this, jam sessions were held in the basement and recording started, and nobody counted the hours anymore . . .

The Album

So it was under the azure skies of Villefranche-sur-Mer, or rather in Nellcôte's humid, excessively hot basement, that the Stones recorded the bulk of their tenth (British) album. *Exile on Main St.*, or more accurately the exile on the Côte d'Azur of a group of Englishmen dreaming of the United States, is the most American of all the Stones albums. It is a supercharged odyssey through a rich musical heritage, eighteen songs on four sides. As always, the blues has pride of place, with versions of "Shake Your Hips" by Slim Harpo and "Stop Breaking Down" by Robert Johnson, plus the original compositions "Casino Boogie" and "Ventilator Blues." Soul and gospel, as represented by "I Just Want to See His Face," "Let It Loose," and "Shine a Light," also belong to the Rolling Stones' musical world, as does country music, to which a whole (acoustic) side, consisting of "Sweet Virginia," "Torn and Frayed," "Sweet Black Angel," and "Loving Cup," is devoted. Finally, and perhaps most importantly, there is that abundance of riffs that is unique to the Stones, riffs that could only come to life in the expert hands of Keith Richards, or at least develop out of the collaboration between the Glimmer Twins. Such songs are exemplified by "Rocks Off," "Tumbling Dice," "Happy," "All Down the Line," and "Soul Survivor."

While Keith Richards was experimenting with five strings, Mick Jagger was unleashing his creative powers as a lyricist. As the chronicler of a collapsing world, he no longer set himself any limits. He sings of moral decay in "Rocks Off," flaunts his misogyny in "Tumbling Dice" and "Turd on the Run," turns his attention to the ravages of drug addiction in "Sweet Virginia," and goes in for a torrid eroticism in "Loving Cup." At the same time, he assumes the role of the politically engaged artist in coming to the defense of the militant revolutionary Angela Davis in "Sweet Black Angel" and in poking fun at the US presidential couple Richard and Pat Nixon in "Rip This Joint," and looks back on his ten-year career with the Stones in "Shine a Light," which is largely about Brian Jones, and perhaps also in "Soul Survivor," which could be seen as an allegory of his occasionally stormy relationship with Keith Richards in the Nellcôte basement.

Choosing Freedom

The absence from this album of the type of showcase number on which the Stones had established their cult—"Sympathy for the Devil" and "Street Fighting Man" on *Beggars Banquet*, "Gimme Shelter" and "Midnight Rambler" on *Let It Bleed*, "Brown Sugar" and "Bitch" on *Sticky Fingers*—could be seen as a cause for regret. The truth is that this album (the only double studio album in the history of the Stones) forms a whole, a homogeneous entity, and most importantly makes no concessions to any commercial imperatives. Keith Richards comments: "Around the time that Andrew Oldham left us, we'd done our time, things were changing and I was no longer interested in hitting Number One in the charts every time. What I want to do is good shit—if it's good, they'll get it some time down the road. *Exile* proved that point of view. Also it's the way to sustain a band so that it can expand itself, otherwise you're just trapped into that pop cycle."[9] Mick Jagger expresses a somewhat different view: "'Exile on Main Street is not one of my favourite albums, although I think the record does have a particular feeling. I'm not too sure how great the songs are, but put together it's a nice piece."[9]

Originally given the working title *Tropical Disease*, *Exile on Main St.* was released in the United States on May 22, 1972, and in the United Kingdom and the rest of the world four days later. In Britain it reached number 1 on June 10 and remained on the charts for sixteen weeks. It achieved the top

Keith on the steps of Villa Nellcôte with his son Marlon.

spot in the United States, Canada, the Netherlands, Spain, Norway, and elsewhere. The album was described in *NME* magazine on May 20, 1972, as "A tremendous set which skilfully uses all the accepted musical mechanics of rock 'n' roll."

The Album Cover

While rummaging around in the art bookstores of Los Angeles, Mick Jagger and Charlie Watts conceived the idea of a cover that would capture the spirit of the photographs of Robert Frank, a US artist closely associated with the Beat movement in the fifties. One of Frank's major works, *The Americans*, first published in France in 1958 and in the United States the following year, had a foreword written by Jack Kerouac himself. The book presents a selection of photographs taken in the forty-eight states of the Union on a road trip. One of them was taken in a tattooist's parlor on Route 66 in 1950. This same photograph, of a curious-looking circus performer holding three balls in his mouth, was used on the cover of *Exile on Main St.* Other images from *The Americans* were used on the inside as well as various shots taken by Robert Frank especially for the album—more accurately stills from a Super 8 film in which the Rolling Stones can be seen walking down the street, laughing, yawning, and so on.

All these images were then arranged by John Van Hamersveld, an American graphic artist who also designed album covers for the Beatles (*Magical Mystery Tour*, US version), Bob Dylan (*Pat Garrett & Billy the Kid*), Jefferson Airplane (*Crown of Creation*), and the Grateful Dead (*Skeletons in the Closet*). Inside, among close-ups of mainly Mick Jagger, are a photograph of a terrified-looking Joan Crawford, film noir stills, and some handwritten words by Mick Jagger, including the refrain of "Sweet Virginia": *Got to scrape the shit right off your shoes.* Also attached were twelve postcards by the photographer Norman Seeff.

The Recording

The Stones would remain in the South of France from April to November 1971. They only started to rehearse in June and did not really begin recording until into July. However, the earliest tracks on the album date from 1970, during the sessions for *Sticky Fingers*.

The first chapter in the saga of *Exile on Main St.* therefore begins at Stargroves in March 1970, when the Rolling Stones were recording "Good Time Women," the first version of "Tumbling Dice." That June, and then in the autumn (at Olympic Sound Studios in London), the first takes of "Stop Breaking Down," "Sweet Virginia," "Shine a Light," and "Shake Your Hips" were cut, as well as a version of "All Down the Line" (included as a bonus track on the 2010 release of *Exile on Main St.* for the Japanese market). The band then

The two Micks, Keith, Jimmy Miller, and Bobby Keys in the arms of Jim Price (left to right).

Among the many visitors to Nellcôte was John Lennon. Unfortunately for the Beatle, he began to vomit after gulping down a bottle of wine. Dr. Keith Richards ascribed this to the heat.

returned to Stargroves in October and November 1970, when "Sweet Black Angel" was recorded.

The second chapter unfolds in the basements at Nellcôte from June 7 until October 1971, Ian Stewart having been unable to find a suitable recording studio or movie theater auditorium. He therefore undertook to soundproof a large room situated beneath the kitchen of the villa, covering the floor, walls, and ceiling with thick carpet. Despite this, the acoustics were dreadful. Andy Johns, who, in the absence of his brother Glyn, was at the controls alone in France, asked him to try a different spot. Unfortunately, the layout of the house bore no resemblance to Stargroves, the Victorian manor where a good part of the songs on *Sticky Fingers* had been recorded. The quality of the sound remained problematic for all the sessions, causing a real headache for Andy Johns as well as for Jimmy Miller, who was again producing: "There were a lot of problems with that album, it was the one I was least happy with. I would have been happier if it had been a single album."[92]

The problems to which Miller alludes were due in part to the layout of the basement. "Keith's basement was actually a lot of separate rooms that made up a basement," he explains, "the separation was so poor that we'd have to have the piano in one room and acoustic guitar in the basement kitchen because it had tiles, or had a nice ring. There was another room for the horns, and there was one main studio where the drums and Keith's amp were, and Bill would play in there, but his amp would be out in the hall."[92] There was also the problem of humidity. Andy Johns: "The guitars would go in and out of tune all the time. Mick kept complaining about the sound, and the gear wasn't working properly and the lights would go on and off and there were fires. It was just insane."[92] On top of this came Keith's extreme fatigue, Mick's obligations as a newly married man, and the nervous tension of all the members of the band and those who surrounded them.

Ship of Fools

In truth, the recording of *Exile on Main St.* was an ordeal for everyone concerned. Problems emerged right at the beginning when Keith decided to try go-karting with Tommy Weber, a former race car driver, at a local track. Unfortunately, he lost control of his vehicle and ended up tearing the skin off a good part of his back. Suffering from multiple contusions and injuries, he persuaded himself that there was no better way to stop the pain than to dip into his personal pharmacopoeia . . . Although his consumption of hard drugs had been falling for some time, this incident provided him with a good excuse to re-indulge. From this point on, the atmosphere of the sessions took a completely chaotic turn. Nothing came out of the first two weeks; the band was trying to sort itself out. Jimmy Miller started to get impatient. "Seven weeks went by and we hadn't cut the first track. Every night, I would say, 'Has somebody got a song?'"[92] What Miller did not know was that Mick and Keith had begun to break away from him, having learned what he had to teach in terms of production fundamentals. For the time being, Miller was still in command of the ship and also contributed some drum parts to the recordings.

The real problem, however, was Keith. The guitarist was getting back into heroin with Anita and was only available to record for part of the time. Everyone was spending their time waiting for the moment when he would reemerge. The sessions progressed very slowly, too slowly, and never with the whole band. Bill: "This was, for me, one of the major frustrations of this whole period."[1] Things were exacerbated when Keith's soul mate Gram Parsons, the ex-Byrd and ex–Flying Burrito Brother, came to stay at the villa with his wife Gretchen for a month. As he enjoyed the needle too, Keith would spend more time singing country with Gram than playing with the rest of the band. Mick Jagger, exasperated by the situation and perhaps a little jealous of their friendship, persuaded Keith to ask Parsons to leave Nellcôte. Parsons was

Mick Jagger in the salon at Nellcôte, seeking inspiration on a Gibson Hummingbird.

deeply hurt by this, and, according to his wife, tried to commit suicide by taking an overdose in the bathroom. This was the last time Gram Parsons was to see Keith, for he died of a fatal injection in California on September 19, 1973.

Gram Parsons was not the only one to follow Keith down the slippery white slope. Others around him would acquire a taste for the drug as well. First of all there was the young Andy Johns, barely twenty-one years old, who was initiated by the master himself; there was Jimmy Miller, who before long became completely addicted, as did Bobby Keys; and there was Mick Taylor, who allowed himself to be tempted and gradually sank into a worrying state of depression. Bill, who did not touch hard drugs any more than Charlie or Glyn, observes bitterly: "I felt like I wasn't in the club—not that I wanted to join."[1]

In 2010, Universal, which now manages the Rolling Stones catalog, brought out a remastered *Exile on Main St.* with nine bonus tracks. Alongside alternative takes of "Loving Cup," "Soul Survivor," and "Good Time Women" (the first version of "Tumbling Dice"), this version includes six hitherto unreleased numbers recorded at Nellcôte and subsequently reworked and remixed in November–December 2009: "Pass the Wine (Sophia Loren)," "Plundered My Soul," "I'm Not Signifying," "Following the River," "Dancing in the Light," and "So Divine (Aladdin Story)."

Keith Richards recording in the basement at Nellcôte. He is playing his prototype Dan Armstrong Plexiglas.

Magic Happens

Nevertheless, despite this bleak environment and the difficult recording and acoustic conditions, tracks gradually started to emerge from the chaos, and on the basis of a riff here and a melody or a few words scribbled down on paper there, magic happened. As a result, during the course of the summer and into November, thirty or so songs were cut at Nellcôte, thirteen of which would eventually be included among the eighteen tracks on *Exile on Main St.*: "Loving Cup," "Ventilator Blues," "Torn and Frayed," "All Down the Line," "Turd on the Run," "Tumbling Dice," "I Just Want to See His Face," "Rip This Joint," "Happy," "Soul Survivor," "Rocks Off," "Casino Boogie," and "Let It Loose."

The album was not yet in the bag, however. It remained to make sense of the dozens of tapes, representing countless recording hours. After a short detour to Basing Street Studios in London, with Glyn Johns once again at the controls, the final stage in the making of the double album took place at Sunset Sound Studios in Los Angeles between the end of 1971 and March 1972. Andy Johns took things back in hand just before the Christmas break, organizing the recording of vocal and instrumental overdubs. After going

away for a few days over the holiday, he discovered upon his return that Mick and Keith had replaced him with Joe Zagarino, a sound engineer known for his work with The Band and B. B. King. The results, however, were less than satisfactory, and Andy was brought back in to salvage the situation. After various adventures, a detour to the Wally Heider Studios, and dozens of remixes, all against the backdrop of an inexorably approaching deadline that was causing Marshall Chess and Ahmet Ertegun serious anxiety, the tapes were finally sent for mastering, and the new Stones album was eventually released on May 22 in the United States and four days later in the United Kingdom. Credit for their work should be given to Jimmy Miller and above all Andy Johns, who managed to obtain sound in spite of the somewhat chaotic conditions. Over time, *Exile on Main St.* would come to be recognized as one of the Stones' emblematic albums, not just for the quality of the songs, but also for that of the recording.

The outside musicians were, for the most part, the same ones who had contributed to *Sticky Fingers*, with a few new faces: on upright bass, Bill Plummer (who would play sitar for Henry Mancini and bass for Tom Waits, Byron Berline, and

The exceptional sound of *Exile on Main St.* owes a great deal to Andy Johns (shown here in 2011), recording engineer along with his brother Glyn.

others); on steel guitar, Al Perkins (the Flying Burrito Brothers, Bob Dylan, the Eagles); and on marimba, Richard Washington (alias Amyl Nitrate). For backing vocals, the Stones would call upon the services of a host of singers: Clydie King (Steely Dan, Bob Dylan, Linda Ronstadt), Venetta Fields (Crosby, Stills & Nash, B. B. King), Jesse Kirkland, Tamiya Lynn, Shirley Goodman (a songwriter and a singer with the disco group Shirley & Company, which had a hit with "Shame, Shame, Shame"!), Malcolm Rebennack (alias Dr. John), Joe Green (a songwriter who also sang backing vocals for Billy Preston, Ringo Starr, Quincy Jones, and others), and Kathi McDonald (a singer who provided backing vocals for Freddie King, Leon Russell, and Long John Baldry). Last but not least, the sound engineers: in addition to Andy Johns, Glyn Johns, and Joe Zagarino, a role was also played by Jeremy Gee, who would go on to work with Deep Purple, Thin Lizzy, and Led Zeppelin.

The Instruments

During recording, Mick Taylor used the same guitars that he had played on *Sticky Fingers*, although some new 6-strings also made an appearance. "I was also using the Gibson SG, but I can't remember what I used it on. There's always been three guitars, really, that I've used more than anything else. And that's the Les Paul, the Strat, and for slide I use the Telecaster a lot."[90] Keith bought himself a 1954 butterscotch blond Fender Telecaster and a Harmony Sovereign acoustic. On October 1, 1971 burglars entered the villa and stole a large number of instruments. According to Bill, they took off with nine of Keith's guitars, including his old Gibson Flying V that had once belonged to Albert King, Bill's Fender Mustang bass, and the baritone, alto, and soprano saxophones of Bobby Keys. Keith was devastated, but would build up a new collection, including a Gibson Les Paul Black Beauty with Bigsby vibrato.

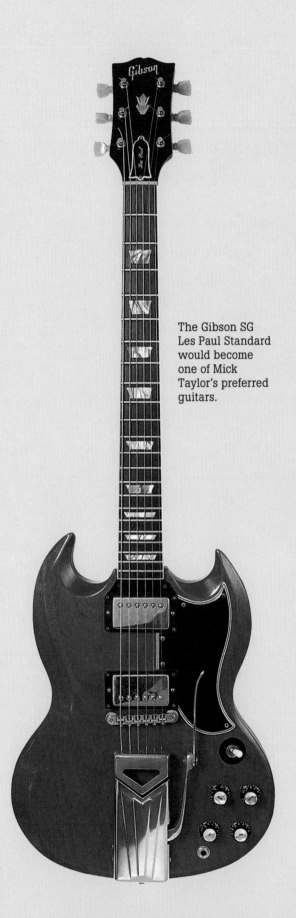

The Gibson SG Les Paul Standard would become one of Mick Taylor's preferred guitars.

1972

ROCKS OFF

Mick Jagger / Keith Richards / 4:32

Musicians
Mick Jagger: vocals, tambourine
Keith Richards: rhythm guitars, backing vocals
Mick Taylor: lead guitar
Bill Wyman: bass
Charlie Watts: drums
Nicky Hopkins: piano
Bobby Keys: saxophone
Jim Price: trumpet, trombone
Recorded
Rolling Stones Mobile Studio, Nellcôte, France: June 7–October 1971
Sunset Sound Studios, Los Angeles: November–December 1971, January–March 1972
Technical Team
Producer: Jimmy Miller
Sound engineers: Andy Johns, Glyn Johns, Joe Zagarino, Jeremy Gee

Jimmy Thackery, the blues singer and guitarist from Pittsburgh, Pennsylvania, made a dazzling version of "Rocks Off." This is included on the album *Exile on Blues Street*, on which a selection of blues musicians (from Lucky Peterson to Joe Louis Walker) present covers of ten songs from *Exile on Main St.*

Genesis

What if "Rocks Off" were a song about physical and moral decline? The main character certainly seems close to sinking into the void. He wants to shout, but can hardly speak, and it is only when he dreams or sleeps that he manages to *get* his *rocks off*—by which is probably meant "satisfies his sexual desire." A character who seems to have stepped out of a novel by Henry Miller seasoned with a dash of rock 'n' roll. A connection readily suggests itself between the lyrics of "Rocks Off" and Keith Richards's heroin addiction. *I'm zipping through the days at lightning speed*; *Heading for the overload, splattered on the dirty road . . .* this bears an uncanny resemblance to a heroin fix. Furthermore the words *feel so hypnotized, can't describe the scene* could be the very Jaggeresque description of a disordering of the senses of the kind beloved by Rimbaud.

As they had got into the habit of doing with *Aftermath*, the Rolling Stones open *Exile on Main St.* with a song that sets the scene perfectly. The introductory riff alone announces that the listener is going to be treated to another of those jamborees to which the Glimmer Twins alone hold the secret. The electric guitars sound the charge, and the piano-bass-drums rhythm section responds with a similar urgency. A new element is also present here: the important role given to the saxophone of Bobby Keys and the trumpet of Jim Price.

Production

"Rocks Off" came into being, and assumed its near-definitive form, in the humid and hot basement at Nellcôte. Keith was cloistered in his cellar recording, while Andy Johns was at the controls outside in the mobile studio. After spending a long time working on "Rocks Off," Keith kept falling asleep during the takes. The intercom wasn't working and Andy couldn't go down to the basement every time to rouse him, so he left the tape running while waiting for the guitarist to wake up. Finally, around three o'clock in the morning, the riff master emerged to join his engineer and listen to the playbacks of what he had managed, despite everything, to record. Barely had he sat down in the mobile studio then he fell asleep again. Thinking that the session was over, Andy set off back to the villa he was sharing with Jim Price, some forty minutes from Nellcôte by car. As soon as he got home, there was a phone

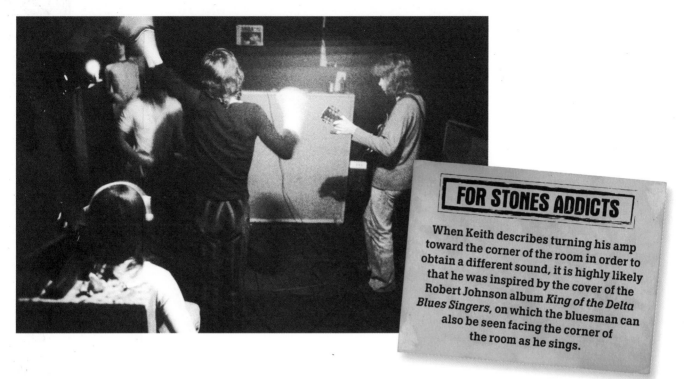

call from a sullen Keith: "Oy! Where the fuck are you? I've got another idea for another guitar part!"[93] And poor Andy had to drive back pronto. Johns recalls that once he had returned, "It was excellent. Like a counter-rhythm part. Two Telecasters, one on each side of the stereo, and it's absolutely brilliant. So I'm glad he got me back there."[93] It should be pointed out that these two rhythm guitar parts are among Keith's best work of this type. Playing his Telecaster (the 1955 or 1956, according to Andy Johns) in open G with the bottom E removed, he obtains a sound that is the ne plus ultra for any self-respecting guitarist, a sort of Holy Grail for any connoisseur of the instrument. Of course, some of this success should be attributed to the Ampeg amps he was using. Andy Johns: "I remember someone saying they were 300 watts, which seemed crazy to me because they were 2x12 combo amps, but they were jolly loud. I thought they were fantastic and I've never seen them anywhere else."[94]

Part of the secret of Keith's sound is his use of reverberation: "You didn't want to add electronic echo unless you had to; you wanted natural echo, and down there you found some really weird ones. I played guitar in a room with tiles, turning the amp round and pointing it at the corner of the room to see what got picked up on the microphone. I remember doing that for 'Rocks Off' and maybe 'Rip This Joint.'"[2]

Another key aspect of the song is Charlie's superb drum part. He obtains a swing and a groove perhaps unlike any he has previously achieved, and really energizes the track. His snare drum playing is particularly good and his pickups are a real treat, as can be gleaned from listening to his lead-in to the verse at the end of the bridge at 2:37. Once Bill's excellent bass part is added, it has to be acknowledged that "Rocks Off" is a real feast. At the time of the album's remastering in 2009, Keith, who had never exactly gone easy on his bassist, could not help harking back to his playing: "And Bill's solid

as a rock, man. What a bass player! I'm actually more and more impressed with him, listening to this. You can get used to a guy, but listening back, going over this stuff to make this record, I'd say, 'Jesus Christ, he's better than I thought!'"[95]

Nicky Hopkins's piano is equally brilliant, as are the horn parts of Bobby Keys and Jim Price. One of the secrets of their sound, moreover, is that Keith made them play with the group, rather than overdubbing their parts later—other than the trombone, which Jim added afterward in order to make up a proper horn section. Mick Taylor's contribution, on the other hand, is reasonably modest; he cannot really be heard until he plays a solo (which is nevertheless too recessed in the mix) at the end of the coda (4:18). Pride of place, of course, is given to Keith's guitar parts. Mick Jagger once again delivers an extraordinary performance. His voice is drawling and lascivious, and at a certain point finds release in an explosion of adrenaline. At his own instigation, he is undermixed, because he wanted people to grasp the full meaning of the track by relistening to it, just as he had in his youth, listening to blues records. "Rocks Off" has a bridge that is every bit as brilliant as the rest of the song. This surreal, dreamlike, somewhat aquatic atmosphere was an idea of Jimmy Miller's. Miller subjected this section (from 2:11 to 2:37) to a phasing effect that is entirely in keeping with Jagger's lyrics, but an important contribution was also made by Andy Johns: " . . . and then I came up with the idea for a lower pitch on Mick's voice with the tremolo on it . . . I used a low-frequency oscillator on it."[15]

"Rocks Off" is an extraordinary Rolling Stones song, underrated despite its status as a key track on *Exile on Main St.* As the overture to the album, it announces the musical flavor of what is to come: an authentic rock sound with no trickery, with the band doing its utmost to deliver the maximum possible pleasure. Exactly as the title of the track suggests, in fact, and who could deny that the Stones have succeeded in this aim?

RIP THIS JOINT

Mick Jagger / Keith Richards / 2:23

Musicians

Mick Jagger: vocals
Keith Richards: rhythm guitar, backing vocals
Mick Taylor: slide guitar
Charlie Watts: drums
Nicky Hopkins: piano
Bobby Keys: saxophone
Jim Price: trombone
Bill Plummer: upright bass

Recorded

Rolling Stones Mobile Studio, Nellcôte, France: June 7–October 1971
Sunset Sound Studios, Los Angeles: November–December 1971, January–March 1972

Technical Team

Producer: Jimmy Miller
Sound engineers: Andy Johns, Glyn Johns, Joe Zagarino, Jeremy Gee

Jimmy Miller inspired some exceptional drumming from Charlie Watts.

Genesis

Mick Jagger was clearly in outstanding form when he wrote the lyrics to "Rip This Joint." While the song lists the names of the cities of the southern United States where the band had given concerts—Tampa, Florida; Memphis, Tennessee; Santa Fe, New Mexico; Dallas, Texas—it also describes the zeal of the customs officers in their treatment of an English rock 'n' roll band with a reputation for consuming illicit substances. The references and plays on words relating to this subject are many and, it has to be said, particularly juicy.

The Deep South is evoked throughout the song. In addition to the aforementioned cities, we encounter the *Butter Queen*, who is simultaneously the Texas beauty queen and, in the colorful jargon of rock 'n' roll, a groupie. The phrase *Dick and Pat in ole D.C.* in the third verse is a derisive reference to Richard Nixon, at that time president of the United States, and his wife Pat. While the presidential couple, logically enough, were based in Washington, *ole D.C.* is phonetically very similar to "Ole Dixie." As for the expression *Wham, bam, Birmingham*, this is another of Mick Jagger's plays on words, clearly having a strong association with the suggestive expression *wham bam thank you, ma'am*.

Production

"Rip This Joint," which is probably the fastest-paced song the Rolling Stones have ever recorded, developed out of a jam session at Nellcôte and pays homage to the timeless masterpieces of the classic rock 'n' roll era, such as "Route 66" and "Back in the USA." Keith Richards would later pride himself on its killer tempo: "That's one of the fastest songs in the world. That really keeps you on your toes."[11] It has to be said that from the very first note, the listener is plunged into a supercharged atmosphere that owes much to Chuck Berry, but a Chuck Berry on amphetamines. The rhythm played by Keith in open G drives the Stones toward an overload of energy that borders heart attack territory. High on adrenaline, Jagger sings in a frenetic voice. Throughout the track he pushes his larynx to the max, exhibiting a truly impressive vitality. It comes as no surprise to learn that he has never really been a fan of the song. "He didn't like 'Rip This Joint,'" says Keith, "it was too fast."[2]

Charlie's drumming is the other key element in this zestful performance. He plays an awesome shuffle, and must have

The phrase *Short, fat Fanny is on the loose* is taken directly from the title of the 1958 Larry Williams song "Short, Fat Fannie," which contains numerous 'n' roll references ("Long Tall Sally," "Heartbreak Hotel," "Tutti Frutti," and so on).

"Rip This Joint" is the fastest-paced song ever to have been performed by the Stones, here onstage in Newcastle, in March, 1971.

worked up a good sweat in the hot and humid Nellcôte basement. Nicky Hopkins's piano part also contributes significantly to making "Rip This Joint" the irresistible number that it is. He whips up a boogie-woogie whirlwind that would have delighted Johnny Johnson. The success of the track can also be attributed in part to the excellent Bobby Keys, who plays two superb saxophone solos, joined in places by Jim Price on trombone, leaving Mick Taylor with just a few short phrases on slide. Only one Rolling Stone, Bill Wyman, is absent from the lineup. Having missed the recording of the number at Nellcôte, Bill then left the task of adding the bass, more specifically the upright bass, to Bill Plummer, a renowned US musician

and friend of the producer Jimmy Miller, at Sunset Sound Studios in Los Angeles. And it has to be acknowledged that Plummer has an extraordinary sense of rhythm, providing Charlie with first-rate support. "Rip This Joint," which follows "Rocks Off," heralds an album that takes its inspiration from the sources of rock 'n' roll and blues. Despite Mick Jagger not retaining the best of memories of *Exile on Main St.*, the double album remains one of the crowning glories in the Stones discography, if only for these two brilliant opening tracks. "Rip This Joint" therefore offers a taste of what is to come . . .

1972

SHAKE YOUR HIPS

James Moore (Slim Harpo) / 2:59

Musicians
Mick Jagger: vocals, harmonica
Keith Richards: rhythm guitar
Mick Taylor: rhythm and lead guitar
Bill Wyman: bass
Charlie Watts: drums
Ian Stewart: piano (?)
Bobby Keys: saxophone

Recorded
Olympic Sound Studios, London: October 1970
Rolling Stones Mobile Studio, Nellcôte, France: June 7–October 1971
Sunset Sound Studios, Los Angeles: November–December 1971, January–March 1972

Technical Team
Producer: Jimmy Miller
Sound engineers: Andy Johns, Glyn Johns, Joe Zagarino, Jeremy Gee
Assistant sound engineers: Chris Kimsey, Keith Harwood

Slim Harpo, one of the masters of swamp blues. The Stones covered his most famous number.

Genesis

Six years after "I'm a King Bee," the Stones covered another number by James Moore, alias Slim Harpo, a bluesman whose name is forever associated with electric Louisiana blues (also known as swamp blues). Harpo recorded "Shake Your Hips" at the J. D. Miller studios in Crowley, Louisiana. The Stones remain faithful to the original spirit of the song and its hypnotic beat, to such an extent, in fact, that it is hard to believe Mick Jagger was not born and raised by the shore of some bayou. In any case, in his best Southern accent, he lures the listener into his sensual dance: *I wanna tell you about a dance that's goin' around . . . Don't move your head, don't move your hands/Don't move your lips, just shake your hips.* Further on, he pays tribute to the bluesman: *Well, I met a girl in a country town. She said "what do you know, there's Slim Harpo!"*

Production

The intro to "Shake Your Hips," which is also known as "Hip Shake" (as the song is styled in the handwritten album notes), immediately recalls the ultra-famous "La Grange" by ZZ Top, dating from 1973. It should be pointed out, however, that the bearded Texans borrowed pretty heavily from the Slim Harpo number. The intro is launched by Keith Richards, most probably on his Telecaster tuned in open G. He is joined almost immediately by Mick Taylor, whose playing interweaves with Keith's to create a rhythm in which the two instruments are utterly indistinguishable. The sound is roots, reinforced by a reasonably strong slap-back echo. Charlie accompanies the guitars on the metal rim of his snare drum in typical rockabilly style, supported by a very good bass line from Bill Wyman, who provides a solid foundation while at the same time getting into a powerful groove. "Shake Your Hips" turns, machine-like, at the same speed from the first note to the last, and Mick Jagger inserts his sensual vocals while playing with the delay that is applied to his voice. In the coda he picks up the harmonica, reproducing the same phrases played by Slim Harpo. Bobby Keys, meanwhile, doubles the counter-rhythms played by Mick Taylor, who then goes into a short solo at 1:27. The album credits indicate that Ian Stewart is on piano, but this part seems to have been eliminated during mixing.

CASINO BOOGIE

Mick Jagger / Keith Richards / 3:34

Musicians
Mick Jagger: vocals, tambourine (?)
Keith Richards: rhythm guitar (?), bass, backing vocals
Mick Taylor: lead guitar, rhythm guitar (?)
Charlie Watts: drums
Nicky Hopkins: electric piano
Bobby Keys: saxophone
Recorded
**Rolling Stones Mobile Studio, Nellcôte,
France:** June 7–October 1971
Sunset Sound Studios, Los Angeles: November–
December 1971, January–March 1972
Technical Team
Producer: Jimmy Miller
Sound engineers: Andy Johns, Glyn Johns,
Joe Zagarino, Jeremy Gee

Bobby Keys, the Stones' saxophonist of choice, delivers a
solo of enormous sensuality on "Casino Boogie."

FOR STONES ADDICTS

Although "Casino Boogie" is a very good song, it has hardly ever been covered, and the Stones themselves have never, to this day, played it in concert.

Genesis

There is no point in looking for a rational explanation for the lyrics of "Casino Boogie," let alone trying to come up with a deeper interpretation. Interviewed by *Uncut* magazine in April 2010, Mick Jagger revealed his modus operandi: "That song was done in cut-ups. It's in the style of William Burroughs, and so on. 'Million Dollar Sad' doesn't mean anything. We did it in LA in the studio. We just wrote phrases on bits of paper and cut them up. The Burroughs style. And then you throw them into a hat, pick them out and assemble them into verses. We did it for one number, but it worked. . . . We probably did it 'cos we couldn't think of anything to write." "Casino Boogie" is nevertheless peppered with allusions to the Rolling Stones' sojourn on the Côte d'Azur, covering such aspects as their day-to-day rock star existence, their problems with the law, and—courtesy of the Cannes Film Festival!—cinema.

Production

"Casino Boogie" is a very well-made blues that could have been recorded in Chicago, so redolent is the song's vibe of Chess Studios. It is probably Keith Richards who launches the track on rhythm guitar (in open G). Nicky Hopkins answers him with a very good electric piano (Wurlitzer?), accompanied immediately by a second rhythm guitar (Mick Taylor?). Bill Wyman was absent for this session so Keith is also on bass, probably his Fender Precision. His playing is good, but bears the stamp of a guitarist rather than a bass player. Charlie Watts works his Gretsch kit powerfully, obtaining a sound that is a model of its kind. Bobby Keys takes the first solo on sax: "And I started to play the solo, but for purposes of song separation, they said 'Hold on till we get it down and then you can do your thing.' Which is what Jim [Price] and I did. We tried a couple things live."[89] Clearly, Jim's part was suppressed during mixing. The second solo is played by Mick Taylor, who delivers a very good improvisation throughout the coda, supported by a number of slide licks from Keith (or possibly overdubbed by Taylor himself). Mick Jagger is joined on the harmonies by Keith, singing, to great effect, in a very high voice.

"Tumbling Dice," originally called "Good Time Women," was written by Mick Jagger.

There are numerous versions of "Tumbling Dice," from Molly Hatchet to Bon Jovi. Linda Ronstadt also recorded it (during the 1977 *Simple Dreams* sessions), getting to number 32 on the *Billboard* chart with her cover.

TUMBLING DICE

Mick Jagger / Keith Richards / 3:46

Musicians

Mick Jagger: vocals, rhythm guitar
Keith Richards: lead and rhythm guitar, backing vocals
Mick Taylor: slide guitar, bass
Charlie Watts: drums
Nicky Hopkins: piano
Bobby Keys: saxophone
Jim Price: trumpet, trombone
Jimmy Miller: drums
Venetta Fields, Clydie King, Sherlie Matthews: backing vocals

Recorded

Rolling Stones Mobile Studio, Nellcôte, France: June 7–October 1971
Sunset Sound Studios, Los Angeles: November–December 1971, January–March 1972

Technical Team

Producer: Jimmy Miller
Sound engineers: Andy Johns, Glyn Johns, Joe Zagarino, Jeremy Gee
Assistant sound engineer: Robin Millar

FOR STONES ADDICTS

The recording of "Good Time Women" is included among the bonus tracks provided on the 2010 rerelease of *Exile on Main St.* This gives listeners an insight into the Rolling Stones' working method. The song's transformation into "Tumbling Dice" is indeed impressive.

Genesis

"Tumbling Dice" started life as a Mick Jagger song titled "Good Time Women." This earlier version deals with the paying relationship between a woman from the red-light district and her client, to whom she ends up saying: *And you know you gonna die with your wife*, a kind of "Honky Tonk Women" revisited . . . Keith then reworked this initial version and Mick provided new words. Keith Richards: "Tumbling Dice may have had something to do with the gambling den that Nellcôte turned into—there were card games and roulette wheels. Monte Carlo was around the corner."[2] And the Stones guitarist continues: "You might have all of the music, a great riff, but sometimes the subject matter is missing. It only takes one guy sitting around a room, saying, 'throwing craps last night . . .' for a song to be born."[2]

Mick Jagger, for his part, has said that *tumbling dice* was an expression used by dice players and also his housekeeper, who was a player too. The lyrics of this second version are, in any case, very different from those of "Good Time Women." The main character is an inveterate charmer and frequenter of casinos. Women find him attractive and take advantage of him—to such an extent that he calls them *low-down gamblers*. They have turned him into a sex beast and above all a *tumblin' dice*—in other words a lover whom they topple onto the bed at will.

"Tumbling Dice" was released as a single (with "Sweet Black Angel" as the flip side) on April 21, 1972 in the United Kingdom, a month before *Exile on Main St.* went on sale. It got to number 5 there on May 13, 1972, number 7 in the United States, and only number 17 in West Germany. As for France, that's another matter . . .

Production

An initial version of "Good Time Women" had been recorded at Stargroves, Mick Jagger's house, using the Rolling Stones Mobile Studio, between March and May 1970. This was a rock track very much in the Stones tradition, carried by Jagger's harmonica, Taylor's guitar, and Ian Stewart's boogie-woogie piano. The transformation took place the following year in the basement at Nellcôte. Keith Richards slowed the tempo and found the groove that gives the song its magic. With his Telecaster tuned in open G, and playing just five strings (the

missing one being the bottom E) with a capo on the fourth fret, he launches into one of his most successful intros. Formed of just a few notes, it nevertheless took a lot of time to get right: "I remember working on that intro for several afternoons."[2] And so did the rest of the song, as Andy Johns attests: "I remember Keith sitting in his chair playing the refrain over and over again for two or three hours without moving. That was in the afternoon before anybody got there. He was trying to lock in the hypnotic part of the vibe."[94] Keith's guitar work is outstanding, and this is one of the main strengths of the song. Curiously enough, it is Jagger who answers him on the second rhythm guitar, as Mick Taylor is fully occupied playing excellent solo slide licks, almost certainly on his Gibson Les Paul. Taylor plays the bass part. "Trying to get everyone in the same room at the same time in a good mood was very tough,"[94] remembers Andy Johns, and Bill Wyman did not play on the definitive recording of "Tumbling Dice": "On 3 August we worked on 'Good Time Woman' [sic] and when I arrived the following day I found Mick Taylor playing bass. I hung around until 3 a.m., then left.'[1] As for the drum part, "Tumbling Dice" was very challenging for Charlie Watts. The rhythm is difficult and demanded a funky style of playing. He did brilliantly until the final break. During this final section, he stumbled: "Charlie had a bit of a mental block about the breakdown and outro section," remembers Andy, "so we did an edit section and Jimmy Miller played the ending."[94] As with "You Can't Always Get What You Want" on *Let It Bleed*, Jimmy

Miller stood in for him. Miller's drumming is absolutely fantastic. He has a highly developed feel for the groove, and succeeds in really getting the outro to swing. "Tumbling Dice" is thus the only Stones track that boasts two drummers. But not just any drummers!

The backing vocals that answer Mick Jagger are another key element. Despite the somewhat licentious lyrics, these backing vocals contribute a gospel color that reinforces the highly individual, indefinable character of the song. Mick's voice is once again undermixed (in keeping with his own aesthetic ideas), and this only helps to bring out the backing singers even more, thereby endowing the song with far more of a soul feel. This was a simple question of balance that was nevertheless very difficult to get right. Andy Johns recalls having had between forty and fifty tapes to mix. Finally, after much equivocation, two very similar mixes were presented to Mick for a verdict. The earlier of the two was used, but many years later the Stones singer is said to have been persuaded that the wrong mix had been chosen for the final version . . . His opinion of the song is pretty negative: "I don't really know what people like about it. I don't think it's our best stuff. I don't think it has good lyrics. But people seem to really like it, so good for them."[19] Keith does not share this view: "I love to play that one on stage. It's not so much the song . . . It's just a great thing to play . . . A lovely riff. It's got such a nice groove and a flow on it."[11]

The influence of Gram Parsons on "Sweet Virginia," is crucial, particularly through Keith Richards, whom the guitarist introduced to the different "schools" of country music.

FOR STONES ADDICTS

It has been said that Gram Parsons contributed to the backing vocals for "Sweet Virginia." This was denied by Mick Taylor in 2002.

SWEET VIRGINIA

Mick Jagger / Keith Richards / 4:27

Musicians
Mick Jagger: vocals, harmonica
Keith Richards: acoustic guitar, backing vocals
Mick Taylor: lead acoustic guitar, backing vocals
Bill Wyman: bass
Charlie Watts: drums
Ian Stewart: piano
Bobby Keys: saxophone
Unidentified musicians: backing vocals, hand claps
Recorded
Olympic Sound Studios, London: June 30–July 1970
Rolling Stones Mobile Studio, Nellcôte, France: June 7–October 1971
Sunset Sound Studios, Los Angeles: November–December 1971, January–March 1972
Technical Team
Producer: Jimmy Miller
Sound engineers: Andy Johns, Glyn Johns, Joe Zagarino, Jeremy Gee
Assistant sound engineer: Chris Kimsey

Gram Parsons reportedly left his mark on the recording of "Sweet Virginia."

Genesis

"Sweet Virginia" is a drug song, or rather a song about the difficulty of giving up an addiction to chemical substances. The person in whom the narrator is interested, a young woman, goes on a trip (in the primary sense of the term), *wadin' through the waste stormy winter* with no friend to help her, but with *speed inside* [her] *shoe*. It seems that she is only able to cope thanks to California wine and its *sweet and bitter fruits*. Then comes the refrain in the form of advice: *Come on down, Sweet Virginia* and *Got to scrape the shit right off your shoes*. Although revisiting the title of a 1926 recording by Mamie Smith ("Sweet Virginia Blues"), the song has a pervasive country feel, not the more commercial Nashville sound, but rather the hillbilly music of country pioneers Jimmie Rodgers and Hank Williams and its modern incarnation, the Bakersfield sound. "Sweet Virginia" was chosen for the B-side of "Rocks Off," a single destined exclusively for Japan in September 1972. Despite not being released elsewhere, the song proved a popular play with radio stations, above all in the United States. The Stones included it in the set list for their 1972 tour.

Production

"Sweet Virginia" may have been worked on as early as 1969, during the sessions for *Sticky Fingers*. However, the first official takes date from June 30, 1970, at Olympic Sound Studios. The sessions continued through March 1972, first of all at Nellcôte, and then at Sunset Sound Studios. Richards plays the intro on his Gibson Hummingbird in pure country style, accompanied by Jagger on harmonica. Taylor plays acoustic lead, coming in with a mandolin sound before launching into excellent, distinctly blues licks, exhibiting an exceptional touch. Watts uses brushes on his drums, while Wyman gives the impression of playing an upright bass. Stewart makes his first proper contribution to the disc, playing a very good boogie-woogie piano. Keys, meanwhile, contributes a decisively more rock color on the sax, and his solo (2:36) is a real success. Mick's voice, which is more prominent in the mix than usual, is enhanced by some very good backing vocals recorded in Los Angeles. It is interesting to note that Mick Taylor can also be heard singing in the refrains. Despite its somewhat pessimistic text, "Sweet Virginia" possesses a contagious energy.

TORN AND FRAYED

Mick Jagger / Keith Richards / 4:17

Musicians
Mick Jagger: vocals
Keith Richards: acoustic guitar, electric
rhythm guitar, backing vocals
Mick Taylor: bass, lead guitar (?)
Charlie Watts: drums
Nicky Hopkins: piano
Jim Price: organ
Al Perkins: pedal steel guitar
Recorded
Rolling Stones Mobile Studio, Nellcôte,
France: June 7–October 1971
Sunset Sound Studios, Los Angeles: November–
December 1971, January–March 1972
Technical Team
Producer: Jimmy Miller
Sound engineers: Andy Johns, Glyn Johns,
Joe Zagarino, Jeremy Gee

Al Perkins, one of the leading players of pedal steel
guitar, gives a brilliant demonstration of his craft.

Genesis

The antihero of "Torn and Frayed" is a Jack Kerouac–style holy hobo. He is a musician who, along with the other members of his band, works the clubs of ill repute of provincial America in order to survive. *The ballrooms and smelly bordellos and dressing rooms filled with parasites* are his lot. *They're a bag of nerves on first nights.* Despite everything, however, and regardless of his *coat . . . torn and frayed,* just as long as the guitar plays, it will *steal your heart away.*

Here too, the references to narcotic substances say it all: *Joe's got a cough, sounds kinda rough/Yeah, and the codeine to fix it/Doctor prescribes, drugstore supplies/Who's gonna help him to kick it?* Should this be seen as an allusion to Keith Richards, or even Gram Parsons, or is the singer poking fun at his own rock star status?

Production

On a musical level, this second song on the acoustic side of *Exile on Main St.* flirts with the Southern rock of the Allman Brothers Band, but also with the country music of the Flying Burrito Brothers. This country-rock-gospel mix works wonderfully well, and it possibly could have been helped by working with a US producer such as Jimmy Miller. Keith plays both acoustic (Hummingbird) and electric (Telecaster) rhythm. Mick Taylor seems to come in on lead with a few solo licks right at the end of the song, around 3:52, but once again it is on bass that he makes his mark. "Torn and Frayed" places a particular emphasis on the keyboards, with Nicky Hopkins on piano and Jim Price—taking a break from his horns—on organ: "I went into that room, picked up the headphones and starting listening, and just started playing organ," he recalls. "It was just for fun. They did a bunch of takes on it, and I never knew they had used it until I saw it on the record."[61] On pedal steel guitar is the excellent Al Perkins, a member of the Flying Burrito Brothers, who plays a very good solo that further accentuates the country aspect of the song. Jagger does not give his best vocal performance, his phrasing occasionally sounding too forced and with his voice somewhere in the middle of the mix, but Keith's harmonies, sung at a higher pitch, lend the lead singer considerable support.

SWEET BLACK ANGEL

Mick Jagger / Keith Richards / 2:58

1972

Musicians
Mick Jagger: vocals, harmonica
Keith Richards: acoustic guitar, backing vocals
Mick Taylor: acoustic guitar (?)
Charlie Watts: woodblock (?)
Jimmy Miller: güiro
Richard Washington: marimba

Recorded
**Rolling Stones Mobile Studio, Stargroves, Newbury /
Olympic Sound Studios, London:** October–November 1970
**Rolling Stones Mobile Studio, Nellcôte,
France:** June 7–October 1971
Sunset Sound Studios, Los Angeles: November–
December 1971, January–March 1972

Technical Team
Producer: Jimmy Miller
Sound engineers: Andy Johns, Glyn Johns,
Joe Zagarino, Jeremy Gee
Assistant sound engineers: Chris Kimsey, Keith Harwood

The African American activist Angela Davis is the subject of "Sweet Black Angel."

Genesis
The "sweet black angel" of this Glimmer Twins song is Angela Davis. An African American activist and member of the Black Panthers and the Communist Party USA, after being fired from her post as a philosophy professor at UCLA, Davis became a staunch defender of three black prisoners (George Jackson, Fleeta Drumgoole, and John Clutchette) accused of killing a prison guard at Soledad, California. On August 7, 1970, during the trial of the Soledad Brothers in the courthouse at Marin County, California, an attempted hostage taking resulted in the deaths of four people. The weapon used to kill Judge Harold Haley had been purchased four days earlier by Angela Davis. Sought by the FBI, the young woman fled but was arrested on October 13, 1970, and was imprisoned pending trial, which began on January 5, 1971. Angela Davis pleaded not guilty, immediately triggering a wave of sympathy that manifested itself in the establishment of committees of support both in the United States and throughout the world. She was finally acquitted and released in 1972.

Mick Jagger and Keith Richards wrote "Sweet Black Angel" before Angela Davis was released, which explains why the lyrics come across as an ardent plea in her defense. Adopting as black-sounding an accent as possible (modeled on the character of Buckwheat in *The Little Rascals*?), Jagger aligns himself with the black US militant, who *ain't no singer* and *ain't no star*, but a *gal in danger*, a *gal in chains*, before launching the heartfelt appeal: *Free the sweet black slave*. "Sweet Black Angel" was chosen as the B-side of the single "Tumbling Dice."

Production
"Sweet Black Angel," initially titled "Bent Green Needle" is a very attractive folk ballad with Caribbean and blues influences, and is an underrated gem in the Rolling Stones canon. It had been worked on in 1970 during the *Sticky Fingers* sessions but was not finalized until a year later. Keith plays his Gibson Hummingbird acoustic, on which he launches the song. His playing combines picking and strumming (with pick). He is immediately joined by Jimmy Miller on güiro with generous reverb, and it is this percussion instrument that lends the song its exotic color. The rhythm he creates is complemented by a woodblock struck most likely by Charlie Watts

(but possibly overdubbed by Jimmy). Keith's Hummingbird is supported by another acoustic guitar, although it is difficult to tell whether it is played by him or by Mick Taylor (who at any rate is not credited by Bill Wyman in his book *Rolling with the Stones*).[1] A marimba, played by Richard "Didymus" Washington, alias Amyl Nitrate, can be heard in the outro at around 2:18. Washington was a percussionist with Dr. John (see the 1972 album *Dr. John's Gumbo*), who contributes to the backing vocals on "Let It Loose." It is difficult not to be reminded here of Brian Jones, who played the marimba for the first time on "Under My Thumb" in 1966. Finally, hats off to Mick Jagger, who delivers his protest with great flair, supported by Keith's harmonies, once again in a high register. Mick also plays some very good harmonica, which is the only blues element on "Sweet Black Angel." This gentle "protest ballad" is one of the best things on the album.

The Rolling Stones have performed "Sweet Black Angel" only once onstage, during the first of the two concerts they gave in Fort Worth, Texas, on June 24, 1972. This performance was dedicated to . . . Angela Davis.

Richard Washington is said not to have particularly appreciated being credited as "Amyl Nitrate" on the album cover. Given that the substance is better known as the vasodilator "poppers," this is perfectly understandable . . .

Mick Jagger was not the only musician to write a song about Angela Davis. Around the same time, John Lennon wrote "Angela" for his album *Some Time in New York City* (1972) with Yoko Ono.

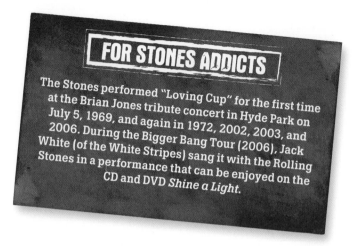

1972

LOVING CUP

Mick Jagger / Keith Richards / 4:24

Musicians
Mick Jagger: vocals
Keith Richards: acoustic guitar, electric rhythm guitar, backing vocals
Bill Wyman: bass
Charlie Watts: drums
Nicky Hopkins: piano
Bobby Keys: saxophone
Jim Price: trumpet, trombone
Jimmy Miller: shaker
Recorded
Rolling Stones Mobile Studio, Nellcôte, France: June 7–October 1971
Sunset Sound Studios, Los Angeles: November–December 1971, January–March 1972
Technical Team
Producer: Jimmy Miller
Sound engineers: Andy Johns, Glyn Johns, Joe Zagarino, Jeremy Gee

Genesis

"Loving Cup" is another example of Mick Jagger's taste for sexual innuendo. The man on the mountain is a *plowman in the valley with a face full of mud*. This humble individual, clearly not the Stones singer, fumbles, knows his *car don't start*, and plays *a bad guitar*; the metaphor seems abundantly clear. In the same vein, the *loving cup*, out of which a toast is drunk by the bride and groom in the Celtic tradition, can be seen as an implicit reference to the female private parts. Jagger's florid language continues throughout the song. Thus, to push and pull and to *spill the beans* are further metaphors for the sexual act and for achieving orgasm.

Production

An initial version of this song, with the title "Give Me a Drink," was recorded during the Olympic Studios sessions for *Let It Bleed* that took place from June 5 to July 3, 1969. During the course of these same sessions, the Jagger-Richards composition was renamed "Loving Cup." This recording is provided as a bonus track on the 2010 rerelease of *Exile on Main St.* It is immediately obvious that the piano intro, played by Nicky Hopkins, is totally different from the final version and that the tempo is slower. There is also far more of a soul vibe than on the definitive version recorded at Nellcôte from June 1971. Nicky became an essential part of the Stones sound, and the new recording brings out the quality of his piano playing. The rhythm section, comprising Bill and Charlie, is a veritable fighting machine, the know-how of these two musicians helping the track to find a dynamism and a groove that were lacking from the 1969 version. Jimmy provides additional support with a shaker, while Keith strums his Hummingbird and is probably on electric rhythm as well. The middle eight of "Loving Cup" comes as a real surprise, taking the form of skillfully implemented rhythmic and harmonic break with high-caliber horn arrangements. Mick records very good vocals accompanied by the loyal Keith on (very high) backing vocals. It is interesting to note that Mick Taylor is not on this recording.

Jimmy Miller was one of the architects of the legendary album *Exile on Main St.*

HAPPY

Mick Jagger / Keith Richards / 3:05

Musicians
Keith Richards: vocals, lead and rhythm guitar, bass
Mick Jagger: backing vocals, tambourine (?)
Bobby Keys: baritone saxophone
Jim Price: trumpet, trombone
Jimmy Miller: drums
Recorded
Rolling Stones Mobile Studio, Nellcôte,
France: September–October 1971
Sunset Sound Studios, Los Angeles: November–
December 1971, January–March 1972
Technical Team
Producer: Jimmy Miller
Sound engineers: Andy Johns, Glyn Johns,
Joe Zagarino, Jeremy Gee

Keith Richards creates the ideal rock 'n' roll riff on "Happy,"
a track on which he also sings lead vocals.

Genesis

In *Life*,[2] Keith Richards recalls the birth of one of his best songs, "Happy": "It just came, tripping off the tongue, then and there. When you're writing this shit, you've got to put your face in front of the microphone, spit it out." It may be that the Stones guitarist found inspiration in his own life: *I never kept a dollar past sunset/It always burned a hole in my pants.* "Happy" is a hymn to the pleasure of the here and now, with a motto that recurs time and again with the Stones: only love can make you happy, certainly not society cocktail parties or private jets. "Happy" is also an outburst of joy from a Keith who had just learned that he was to become a father. Mick Jones, the former singer-guitarist with the Clash, maintains that "Happy stills sounds fucking amazing, especially when all the brass comes in," adding that it is "pure Keef" and that he learned to play everything Richards ever did.[96] "Happy" is, indeed, one hundred percent Keith Richards, words and music alike. The riff alone symbolizes all the energy and magic of rock 'n' roll. Richards: "'Rocks Off,' 'Happy,' 'Ventilator Blues,' 'Tumbling Dice,' 'All Down the Line'—that's five-string, open tuning to the max. I was starting to really fix my trademark; I wrote all that stuff within a few days."[2] An approach the Stones guitarist summed up succinctly as follows: "Five strings, two notes, two fingers, and one asshole."[2]

"Happy" was the A-side of the second single to be taken from *Exile on Main St.* (with "All Down the Line" as the B-side). It peaked at number 22 on the *Billboard* chart on August 19, 1972.

Production

Keith Richards is the only member of the Rolling Stones to have played on the recording of *"Happy"* at Nellcôte. At the beginning of September, Bill Wyman, frustrated by the lack of productivity, rented a yacht and took off for five days. Mick Jagger, Charlie Watts, and Mick Taylor were also absent from this session. It was at this moment that Keith had the idea for a song. Jimmy Miller, who was busy in the mobile studio, putting the previous day's recordings in order, advised him to get the idea down on tape. The guitarist immediately went down to the basement: "So I start laying it down, and suddenly Jimmy's behind me playing the drums. He'd come down from the

A moment of happiness and relaxation for Keith and Marlon in the
Nellcôte gardens between two nocturnal recording sessions.

truck, and I hadn't even noticed. I'm just hammering away, figuring this thing out. Suddenly I hear these great drums behind me, and now it's starting to rock."[95] And then Bobby Keys joined in on sax. He had also been down there testing out the bass of his new baritone. From the first attempt, he and Keith were impressed: "It was a big sound, it was like all of a sudden a foghorn had just come into the room . . . ," says Bobby. "And so he [Keith] said, 'Hey, man, that's a great sound! What else can you do with it?"[89] This is how the three of them, Keith, Jimmy, and Bobby, came to record the basic track of "Happy," a number that would become the guitarist's signature tune. In actual fact, Keith had been thinking of recording a demo. So he told himself he might as well do the vocals as well.

"Happy" is an homage from the guitarist to his guitars. The sound he obtains from his Telecaster with five strings, in open-G tuning, is remarkable. Plugged into an Ampeg amp, it has an exceptional power and warmth. And then there is Keith's playing and touch, which are of equal caliber. He recorded two guitar parts that answer each other and also inserted a number of slide licks, including solos at 1:14 and 2:08. In the absence of Bill, he also plays a very good bass part on his Fender Precision. With Jimmy on drums and Bobby on baritone sax, the song is a real success. According to Andy Johns, an afternoon was all it took to get the track down. That just left the finalizing. Overdubs were added, in particular a horn section with the participation of Jim Price, and a tambourine. Backing vocals were recorded in Los Angeles by Mick Jagger and his favorite guitarist. The success of "Happy," a radiant track brimming with energy, is down to Keith Richards. Despite appearances, however, this emotion is not what the guitarist was experiencing at the time: "I was feeling anything but happy when I wrote 'Happy.' I wrote 'Happy' to make sure there was a word like that and a feeling like that."[11]

FOR STONES ADDICTS

In his book *Every Night's a Saturday Night*,[8] Bobby Keys, considering himself just as responsible for the riff as Keith, expresses regret that he was not included in the credits for "Happy." But he also comments that ultimately all he did was take part in a jam . . .

TURD ON THE RUN

Mick Jagger / Keith Richards / 2:37

"Turd on the Run" was covered by Pussy Galore on their compilation *Corpse Love: The First Year* (1992).

Musicians
Mick Jagger: vocals, harmonica
Keith Richards: rhythm guitar, backing vocals
Mick Taylor: rhythm guitar (?)
Charlie Watts: drums
Nicky Hopkins: piano
Bill Plummer: upright bass
Recorded
Rolling Stones Mobile Studio, Nellcôte, France: June 7–October 1971
Sunset Sound Studios, Los Angeles: November–December 1971, January–March 1972
Technical Team
Producer: Jimmy Miller
Sound engineers: Andy Johns, Glyn Johns, Joe Zagarino, Jeremy Gee

Genesis

Mick Jagger's pen is once again dipped in vitriol to express the resentment he feels toward a woman guilty of a thousand and one betrayals. The second verse is a masterpiece of its kind. Reading between the lines, it seems that the mistress of the unfortunate narrator has taken the diamonds, leaving her ex-lover, as her only parting gift, a dose of venereal disease . . . His desire for somewhat drastic retribution is expressed over a boogie-woogie rock groove on amphetamines. Electric guitar, honky-tonk piano, harmonica in the ancient swamp blues tradition—the Stones alchemy is irresistible.

Production

As was so often the case during the sessions that took place in the humid Nellcôte basement, "Turd on the Run" was recorded in pretty unusual circumstances. As a result of the repeated absences of Keith Richards (to look after his son Marlon) and Mick Jagger (who had just married Bianca), the other members of the group returned to their homes to await developments. This is precisely what Bill Wyman did, which explains why the upright bass that can be heard on "Turd on the Run"—like that on "Rip This Joint"—was recorded later by Bill Plummer at Sunset Sound Studios in Los Angeles. This sonority has the effect of accentuating the Chicago blues/rockabilly vibe of the track already established by Keith's efficient rhythm playing, most probably on his Gibson Les Paul (in open-G tuning). Another guitar can be heard at 1:01, in all likelihood also played by Keith. Charlie Watts maintains an infernal tempo, making excellent use of the brushes, a legacy of his jazz influences. He seems utterly preoccupied with this hypnotic beat, and barely touches the rest of his Gretsch kit. Nicky Hopkins is dazzling, his piano playing demonstrating his incredible ability to embrace every different style. Finally, Mick Jagger divides his attention between his vocal line and the harmonica, revealing the real progress he had made on the instrument since the loss of the late lamented Brian, with a more secure, more inspired style of playing. It would probably be true to say that "Turd on the Run" is an underrated Stones track that deserves to be (re)discovered, if only for the amazing vibe it creates.

As on "Turd on the Run," Mick and Keith share a mic during the Honolulu concert of January 1973.

VENTILATOR BLUES

Mick Jagger / Keith Richards / Mick Taylor / 3:25

Musicians
Mick Jagger: vocals
Keith Richards: acoustic guitar, backing vocals
Mick Taylor: slide guitar
Bill Wyman: bass
Charlie Watts: drums, tambourine
Nicky Hopkins: piano
Bobby Keys: saxophone
Jim Price: trumpet, trombone

Recorded
Rolling Stones Mobile Studio, Nellcôte, France: June–October 1971
Sunset Sound Studios, Los Angeles: November–December 1971, January–March 1972

Technical Team
Producer: Jimmy Miller
Sound engineers: Andy Johns, Glyn Johns, Joe Zagarino, Jeremy Gee

Genesis

The starting point for "Ventilator Blues" was the overwhelming heat and humidity in the basement at Nellcôte and the urgent need for a fan. Andy Johns remembers: "Sometimes, Mick Taylor would stop because he was out of tune. There was this one little tiny fan in the window up in the corner. Which didn't work very well. Therefore, 'Ventilator Blues.' It's one of my favorite tunes."[93] Mick Jagger conquered his claustrophobia by writing a set of feverish, vengeful lyrics. In the first verse, he comes to the defense of a poor guy married to a shrew. In the second, his attack is directed against society as a whole. "Ventilator Blues" is a blues-rock number in the finest Stones tradition, serving as yet another reminder (should one be needed) of the close connection between the British band and the Chess giants, from Muddy Waters to Howlin' Wolf.

Production

"Ventilator Blues" is the only Stones number for which Mick Taylor is credited alongside the Glimmer Twins. Indeed this was to be one of the reasons for his departure in 1974, as he believed he deserved a credit on far more of the band's songs. The slide riff he plays in open G is a real lesson in guitar playing, a riff "made in Chicago" that Keith must have regretted not coming up with himself. He also plays a solo—again slide—at around 2:17, leaving Keith to play acoustic, both strumming and slide (his National "O"?). Bill's bass is heavy and powerful, supporting Charlie's syncopated rhythm, which Bobby Keys had come up with: "Bobby stood next to me clapping the thing and I just followed his timing,"[9] the Stones drummer would later acknowledge. In collaboration with his friend Jim Price, the Texas saxophonist would in turn record a superb horn section that gives the track more of a deep soul feel. Another key element is Nicky Hopkins's piano, which could have come straight out of Chess Studios. "Ventilator Blues" is a lesson in the blues, a blues with multiple influences, such as only the Stones were capable of.

On this track, which he co-wrote, Mick Taylor declares his faith in blues rock.

I JUST WANT TO SEE HIS FACE

Mick Jagger / Keith Richards / 2:53

Musicians
Mick Jagger: vocals, tambourine (?)
Keith Richards: electric piano (?)
Mick Taylor: bass
Charlie Watts: drums
Bobby Whitlock: electric piano (?)
Jimmy Miller: percussion
Bill Plummer: upright bass
Venetta Fields, Clydie King, Jesse Kirkland: backing vocals

Recorded
Rolling Stones Mobile Studio, Nellcôte, France: June–October 1971
Olympic Sound Studios, London: November 1971 (?)
Sunset Sound Studios, Los Angeles: November–December 1971, January–March 1972

Technical Team
Producer: Jimmy Miller
Sound engineers: Andy Johns, Glyn Johns, Joe Zagarino, Jeremy Gee

Bobby Whitlock may be playing electric piano on the atypical "I Just Want to See His Face."

Genesis
"I Just Want to See His Face" begins as a fade-in at the end of "Ventilator Blues," a song with a very different feel. This track was actually the result of a jam session involving Mick Jagger, Mick Taylor, and Charlie Watts in the Nellcôte basement. The Stones singer improvised the words as the number developed: *Sometimes you feel like trouble, sometimes you feel down/ Let this music relax your mind*, he sings in the first verse. During the course of the song, the only remedy for this melancholy seems to reside in the quest for Jesus. Hence the title, which is repeated over and over again at the end of the song: *You just want to see his face.*

This improvisation, which lasts for almost three minutes, has a gospel feel, but is also evocative of some kind of voodoo ritual . . .

Production
The Wurlitzer electric piano—which Mick Jagger would probably have sung to—may originally have been played (improvised) by Keith Richards, before being replaced later by a part performed by Bobby Whitlock, who is nevertheless not credited on the album cover. This, at least, is what Whitlock claims in an interview with Bill Janovitz: "There were two songs I was playing on, one of them was about: (starts singing) 'I don't want to talk about Jesus/I just wanna see his face.' . . . that happened in Olympic Studios . . . I was in England."[97] If this session indeed took place, it can only have been in November, before the Stones flew off to Los Angeles.

"I Just Want to See His Face" is the only number on the album without guitar. It is also the only one to have an electric bass part played by Mick Taylor as well as an upright bass part played by Bill Plummer, who happily incorporates jazz patterns akin to those of the great Charlie Mingus. Charlie Watts plays his toms with restraint while marking the beat on his hi-hat and bass drum. Jimmy Miller, meanwhile, plays an African conga-type percussion instrument. Mick Jagger, who mumbles rather than sings his lyrics, is almost certainly on tambourine, and is surrounded by the superb backing vocals of Venetta Fields, Clydie King, and Jesse Kirkland, who lend the track such a spiritual feel. It is almost certain that Mick did not do any voice overdubs in Los Angeles, as he did for most of the other songs, because his performance sounds very live.

LET IT LOOSE

Mick Jagger / Keith Richards / 5:17

Musicians
Mick Jagger: vocals
Keith Richards: rhythm guitar
Bill Wyman: bass
Charlie Watts: drums
Nicky Hopkins: piano, Mellotron
Bobby Keys: saxophone
Jim Price: trumpet, trombone
Tami Lynn, Sherlie Matthews, Venetta Fields,
Clydie King, Joe Green, Dr. John: backing vocals
Recorded
Rolling Stones Mobile Studio, Nellcôte,
France: June–October 1971
Sunset Sound Studios, Los Angeles: November–
December 1971, January–March 1972
Technical Team
Producer: Jimmy Miller
Sound engineers: Andy Johns, Glyn Johns,
Joe Zagarino, Jeremy Gee

"Let It Loose," a Stones homage to rhythm 'n' blues on which the uncategorizable Dr. John lends a hand in backing vocals.

Genesis

Sadness, solitude, and *sensuality* are three words that immediately come to mind when listening to "Let It Loose." The first verse sounds like a warning from one friend to another: *Who's that woman on your arm, all dressed up to do you harm?* From the second verse, it is the friend who speaks, and what he has to say is perfectly clear-sighted: he is not the dupe of the woman by his side, but she gives him everything he needs (in the bedroom, we are to understand). He adds that he *ain't in love,* . . . and *ain't in luck.* Who wrote the lyrics? Mick Jagger answers this question in an interview with *Uncut* magazine in April 2010: "I think Keith wrote that, actually. That's a very weird, difficult song. I had a whole other set of lyrics to it, but they got lost by the wayside. I don't think that song has any semblance of meaning. It's one of those rambling songs. I didn't really understand what it was about, after the event." Does this mean it would be wrong to see the song as an implicit reference to Keith's feelings following Mick's marriage to Bianca Pérez-Mora?

Production

"Let It Loose" is a song of great emotional power in which Mick Jagger performs a real vocal feat. The song seems to have been recorded mainly in the South of France. What is certain is that the backing vocals were added at Sunset Sound Studios in Los Angeles and have a strong New Orleans feel—thanks to the presence of Dr. John. "He just walked in, Mac Rebennack's like that. If there's music going on, in one way or another, he's gonna get his ass in there. I love the guy."[95] Keith picks arpeggios on his guitar, which he plays through a Leslie speaker with strong vibrato added. Mick Taylor seems not to have been present, unlike Nicky Hopkins, who supports the guitarist with an excellent piano part and chords on the Mellotron. The Charlie-Bill partnership, the "straightest rhythm section" in rock 'n' roll, as they were described at the time, is as efficient as ever. Meanwhile, the horn section, comprising Bobby Keys and Jim Price, contributes a Texas accent that would be closely associated from this point on with the Stones sound. Above all, however, "Let It Loose" is an exceptional dialogue between Mick and the backing singers, a quasi-spiritual dialogue deeply impregnated with gospel and soul.

ALL DOWN THE LINE

Mick Jagger / Keith Richards / 3:49

Musicians
Mick Jagger: vocals
Keith Richards: rhythm guitar, backing vocals
Mick Taylor: slide guitar
Bill Wyman: bass
Charlie Watts: drums
Nicky Hopkins: piano
Bobby Keys: saxophone
Jim Price: trumpet, trombone
Jimmy Miller: tambourine
Kathi McDonald: backing vocals

Recorded
Rolling Stones Mobile Studio, Nellcôte,
France: June–October 1971
Sunset Sound Studios, Los Angeles: November–
December 1971, January–March 1972

Technical Team
Producer: Jimmy Miller
Sound engineers: Andy Johns, Glyn Johns,
Joe Zagarino, Jeremy Gee

Nicky Hopkins rises to the challenge with some
distinctly boogie-woogie piano on "All Down the Line."

Genesis

Following the example of "Rocks Off" on side 1 and "Happy" on side 3, "All Down the Line" opens the fourth side of the LP *Exile on Main St.* with that raw energy possessed by the best rock 'n' roll. "'All Down the Line' came directly out of 'Brown Sugar,' which Mick wrote," recalls Keith Richards. "Most of what I had to do was come up with riffs and ideas that would turn Mick on. To write songs he could handle."[2]

For "All Down the Line," Jagger took his inspiration from one of the great American myths, the railroad, that symbol of travel, speed, and freedom, but also of suffering and disillusion. *Hear the women sighing all down the line/Hear the children crying all down the line*, goes the first verse. And the narrator of the song confides: *I need a sanctified girl with a sanctified mind to help me now*—presumably for his salvation. Clearly a very pious individual, as he adds right away: *We're gonna bust another bottle*, and concludes with a question: *Won't you be my baby for a while?*

Production

"All Down the Line" is one of the oldest Glimmer Twins compositions on *Exile on Main St.* An acoustic demo exists from 1969 and an electric version that was recorded during the *Sticky Fingers* sessions. The track underwent a serious face-lift in the Nellcôte basement, above all through the addition of a typically "Richardsian" riff on his Telecaster in open G, played through the Ampeg amp from which he was able to get such a fantastic sound. Jimmy Miller provides him with first-rate rhythmic support on the tambourine. Charlie Watts is no less effective, delivering a drum part that smacks and swings, joined before long by Bill Wyman's excellent, powerful bass. Neither would "All Down the Line" be what it is without Mick Taylor's Les Paul, on which he delivers a red-hot slide part, a real exhibition of his talents as a guitarist. On top of all this come the spirited horns of the two Texans, Nicky Hopkins's boogie-woogie piano, and Kathi McDonald's backing vocals, making "All Down the Line" one of the best tracks on the album. Andy Johns recalls Jagger's reaction: "That was the first one that actually got finished and Mick said, 'This is a single. This is a single!' And I thought, 'He's out of his fucking mind. This is not a single.' And he went, 'Really? Do ya

Bill Wyman found it hard to adjust to the completely unstructured rhythm of the *Exile* recording sessions.

FOR STONES ADDICTS

Kathi McDonald is the backing singer on "All Down the Line." She had debuted in the music industry as one of Ike & Tina Turner's Ikettes and also sang with Big Brother & the Holding Company.

think so?' And that was the first time I realized, 'Jesus, he'll actually listen to me.'"[93]

After completing some initial mixes of the song in Los Angeles, Andy Johns informed Jagger that he regretted not being able to hear the result played on a local radio station before making a decision. No problem! Jagger immediately sent Stu over to a disc jockey so that the song could be tried out on the air! Shortly after, Johns found himself sitting in the back of a limo in the company of Mick, Keith,

and Charlie, listening to "All Down the Line" on the airwaves. "What do you think?" Mick asked his sound engineer. "I don't know, man,"[93] replied Johns. And so Mick asked Stu to have the song played a second time! In the end it was only released as the B-side of "Happy," the second single from *Exile on Main St.* (in the United States), the first having been "Tumbling Dice."

STOP BREAKING DOWN

Robert Johnson / arrangements Mick Jagger / Keith Richards / 4:35

Musicians
Mick Jagger: vocals, rhythm guitar, harmonica
Mick Taylor: slide guitar
Bill Wyman: bass
Charlie Watts: drums
Ian Stewart: piano

Recorded
Olympic Sound Studios, London: June–July 1970
Rolling Stones Mobile Studio, Nellcôte, France: June–October 1971
Sunset Sound Studios, Los Angeles: November–December 1971, January–March 1972

Technical Team
Producer: Jimmy Miller
Sound engineers: Andy Johns, Glyn Johns, Joe Zagarino, Jeremy Gee
Assistant sound engineers: Chris Kimsey, Keith Harwood

Mick Jagger and Mick Taylor scale the heights on "Stop Breaking Down."

Genesis

"Stop Breaking Down" is one of the blues nuggets recorded by Robert Johnson during his second session (Dallas, Texas, June 19 and 20, 1937). The story is racy, with the twist that is characteristic of the Delta pioneers. A man cannot walk down the street without encountering a woman who starts *breaking down* on him. At first he is conciliatory, but then he starts to tell her a few home truths: *You Saturday night women, now, you just ape and clown* and *You don't do nothing but tear my reputation down.* The only snag is that she is holding a pistol . . .

The Rolling Stones were clearly seduced by the humor, since they incorporated the song into their repertoire during the *Exile on Main St.* sessions. One unusual feature is that Keith Richards is conspicuous by his absence.

Production

" 'Stop Breaking Down' is probably my favorite track," [98] Andy Johns would later claim, and it is certainly true that the Stones have made this cover of a song by the brilliant Robert Johnson one of the highlights of the album. In fact, the rhythm track had been recorded in 1970, during the sessions for *Sticky Fingers,* by Andy's older brother Glyn. Mick's voice and harmonica were then taped at Sunset Sound Studios in Los Angeles by Andy: "I remember getting Mick to play harmonica on that. It did not seem like it was finished. My brother (Glyn) had recorded [the base track] earlier. I said, 'We've got to use this' because Mick Taylor plays some gorgeous lines and I'm very sure that it's Mick Jagger playing the rhythm guitar as well. That's why it's a little choppier."[98]

The Stones singer is indeed playing rhythm guitar, and he does a pretty good job of it too. The main strength of the song, however, is his extraordinary harmonica part. He plays with distortion and an enormous delay, producing an absolutely remarkable effect. Jagger demonstrates a greater mastery of, and talent for, the instrument than ever before. Then there is his voice, which is never as good as when he is singing the blues, and this is borne out once again here. Finally, there is Mick Taylor's sublime slide guitar part, one of his best for the Stones. "Stop Breaking Down" is a little gem of the kind with which the Rolling Stones catalog is peppered.

SHINE A LIGHT

Mick Jagger / Keith Richards / 4:17

Musicians
Mick Jagger: vocals
Mick Taylor: lead guitar
Bill Wyman: bass
Jimmy Miller: drums
Billy Preston: piano, organ
Venetta Fields, Clydie King, Joe Green,
Jesse Kirkland: backing vocals
Unidentified musician: tambourine
Recorded
Olympic Sound Studios, London: June, October 21–31, 1970
Rolling Stones Mobile Studio, Nellcôte,
France: June–October 1971
Sunset Sound Studios, Los Angeles: November–December 1971, January–March 1972
Technical Team
Producer: Jimmy Miller
Sound engineers: Andy Johns, Glyn Johns, Joe Zagarino, Jeremy Gee
Assistant sound engineers: Andy Johns, Chris Kimsey

"Shine a Light" is a gospel number that evokes the decline of Brian Jones, icon and martyr of the rock 'n' roll years.

Genesis

Mick Jagger started to work on this song, which is filled with references to Brian Jones, at the beginning of 1968, when Jones was still a full-fledged member of the band. *A smile on your face and a tear right in your eye, Berber jewelry jangling down the street*—this figure is Brian. *Drunk in the alley, baby, with your clothes all torn* is also Brian. "Shine a Light" is actually a song about the long decline of the musician who was the soul of the Stones, a song in which Jagger himself appeals to the powers above for clemency for his former bandmate: *May the Good Lord shine a light on you/Warm like the evening sun.*

This ode to Brian Jones, recorded without Keith Richards and Charlie Watts, is infused with gospel fervor. "When I was very friendly with Billy [Preston] in the '70s I sometimes used to go to church with him in Los Angeles," recalls Mick Jagger. "It was an interesting experience because we don't have a lot of churches like that in England. I hadn't had a lot of first-hand experience of it." [99]

Production

"Shine a Light" is the final version of "Get a Line on You," recorded on March 31, 1969, during the *Let It Bleed* sessions at London's Olympic Sound Studios. Three main strands can be discerned in this gospel-soul-rock number. First, the excellent performance by Mick Jagger and his fantastic backing singers. "Shine a Light" is a song tinged with solemnity, and all the singers make a heartfelt contribution to this mood. Then there are the keyboard parts played by Billy Preston, a truly inspired musician whose organ playing on this song is astounding. He makes use of all the tricks in the gospel book, while at the same time adapting his playing to the world of the Stones. Finally, there is, once more, the outstanding quality of Mick Taylor's playing, which is imbued with extraordinary grace, inspiration, and feeling. He starts the track with a very light and airy sound (thanks to a looped delay), and closes it with a dazzling solo. "That's one of my favourite tracks on that album," [90] Taylor would later reveal, and it is not difficult to see why. Also worthy of special mention is Jimmy Miller (Charlie being absent), a wonderful drummer with an incredible feel for a groove.

SOUL SURVIVOR

Mick Jagger / Keith Richards / 3:49

Musicians
Mick Jagger: vocals
Keith Richards: rhythm guitar, bass, backing vocals
Mick Taylor: guitar
Charlie Watts: drums
Nicky Hopkins: piano
Bobby Keys: saxophone (?)
Jim Price: trumpet, trombone (?)
Jimmy Miller: tambourine (?)

Recorded
Rolling Stones Mobile Studio, Nellcôte, France: June–October 1971
Sunset Sound Studios, Los Angeles: November–December 1971, January–March 1972

Technical Team
Producer: Jimmy Miller
Sound engineers: Andy Johns, Glyn Johns, Joe Zagarino, Jeremy Gee

Keith Richards, central to "Soul Survivor," whose riff concludes this double album with a flourish.

Genesis

In a literal sense, "Soul Survivor" tells of the final moments of a group of sailors whose frail vessel is heading for the rocks. Metaphorically, the song is evocative of the end of a relationship. That between a man and a woman? Or between two friends? "Soul Survivor" could thus be seen as describing the tensions that rose to the surface during the grueling sessions at Nellcôte between Mick Jagger and Keith Richards, who really established himself as the architect of this album. Hence the innuendo pregnant with meaning: *You've got a cut-throat crew . . . I've taken all of the knocks, you ain't giving me no quarter.* Hence, too, this humility in the guise of derision or provocation: *When you're flying your flags, all my confidence sags.* In other words, the singer is the *soul survivor* and it is the Rolling Stones who are heading toward shipwreck. A crazy interpretation? Perhaps! All the same, it is worth noting that the initial lyrics, most probably written by Keith (it is the guitarist who sings on the alternative cut of "Soul Survivor" on the 2010 rerelease of *Exile on Main St.*), contain no such allusion. What can be said for sure is that *Exile on Main St.* ends the way it began, with an extraordinary riff typical of Keith Richards.

Production

Keith's discovery of open-G tuning significantly influenced his songwriting since *Sticky Fingers*. He seems to have been stimulated by the atmosphere of the Côte d'Azur in particular. The riff of "Soul Survivor," a distant cousin of that of "All Down the Line," announces a rock track very much in the archetypal Stones mold. Pride of place is given to the guitar, whether his own or Mick Taylor's slide. This is confirmed by Keith: "There were endless overdubs . . . There's probably at least six guitars on there, in little pieces, not all the way through. But from the middle eight to the end, there's probably little bits of six overdubs going on, in and out."[11] What sounds like a fuzz guitar can also be heard, although it may be horns in a very recessed mix. As Bill was absent, Keith again plays bass, supported by Charlie's excellent drumming and by Jimmy (probably) on tambourine. Finally, it is worth drawing attention to the superbly rhythmic and funky piano part played by the excellent Nicky Hopkins.

Dancing With Mr. D.
100 Years Ago
Coming Down Again
Doo Doo Doo Doo Doo
   (Heartbreaker)
Angie

Silver Train
Hide Your Love
Winter
Can You Hear The Music
Star Star

ALBUM
RELEASE DATE
United Kingdom: August 31, 1973
Label: Rolling Stones Records
RECORD NUMBER: ROLLING STONES
RECORDS COC 59101
Number 1 for 2 weeks, on the charts for 14 weeks

GOATS HEAD SOUP

Keith and Anita's difficulties with the law (they were under investigation for heroin possession) would have major repercussions for the recording of the new Stones album throughout 1972.

GOATS HEAD SOUP:
JAMAICA FOREVER

In April 1971, the Rolling Stones abandoned the United Kingdom in favor of France for tax reasons. A year and a half later, Keith Richards and Anita Pallenberg found themselves in trouble with the authorities again, this time in their adopted country, and left the Côte d'Azur earlier than planned in order to evade the French justice system. During the recording of *Exile on Main St.* at Nellcôte, the police had been keeping a very close eye on the group and, based on information from disgruntled employees, suspected Keith Richards and Anita Pallenberg of heroin trafficking. At the end of the summer of 1972, Prince Rupert Loewenstein hired a French lawyer, Jean Michard-Pellissier (former member of the French Constitutional Council, Antibes city councillor, and adviser to Prime Minister Jacques Chaban-Delmas), who succeeded in obtaining a guarantee of freedom for the Stones guitarist and his companion on the condition that they continued to rent Nellcôte at a cost of $2,400 per week as a sign of good faith. Thus Keith was able to leave France at the beginning of June 1972.

The "Cocaine and Tequila Sunrise Tour"

The Stones guitarist crossed the Atlantic for the band's North American tour, known as the "STP" (Stones Touring Party) or the "Cocaine and Tequila Sunrise Tour," during the course of which the band gave fifty concerts between June 3 and July 26. Covered by the writer Truman Capote, Princess Lee Radziwill (the younger sister of Jacqueline Kennedy), and the filmmaker and photographer Robert Frank, the tour was punctuated by riots and arrests of all kinds. At the beginning of August 1972,

Keith, having survived the tour, took up residence in a chalet in Villars, Switzerland. Now the father of Dandelion/Angela, born a few months earlier, he was to undergo a detox cure in Vevey. On October 17, 1973, following a search of Nellcôte by French narcotics officers, Keith Richards and Anita Pallenberg were eventually found guilty of possessing heroin. They were given a one-year suspended jail sentence and forbidden to set foot on French soil for a period of two years . . . But for now it is autumn 1972 and the time has come to move on, to write a new chapter in the saga of the Rolling Stones.

The Album

The relationship between the Glimmer Twins had not been great for a while. Nevertheless, Mick and Keith had been working on some new songs and decided to record them as soon as possible. The Stones faced two major problems. First, they had to maintain their tax exile until April 1973. Second, they had to find a country other than France, one where Keith would not be harassed by the authorities, in which to make their next album. They left it to Ahmet Ertegun, the Atlantic Records co-founder, to come up with an ideal location. Thus at the end of November 1972, the five members of the band, along with Jimmy Miller and Andy Johns, found themselves in Jamaica. "I had first gone to Jamaica for a few days off at a place called Frenchman's Cove in 1969," writes Keith Richards. "You could hear the rhythm going around. Free reggae, rock steady and ska."[2] Although not strongly influenced by Jamaican music (unlike some of their future albums),

Mick and Bianca with Ahmet Ertegun, the co-founder of Atlantic Records, the new distributor of Stones records in the United States.

Goats Head Soup nevertheless reveals a change in musical direction in contrast to *Sticky Fingers* and above all *Exile on Main St.* Should this be seen as a result of Keith Richards's recent troubles and a sign of the guitarist distancing himself from Mick Jagger? Keith Richards would later comment wryly that: "I started going my way—which was the downhill road to Dopesville—and Mick ascended to Jetland."[30] In any case, what immediately grabs the attention on *Goats Head Soup* are the ballads. The most famous of these, of course, is "Angie," which—following in the tradition of the illustrious "As Tears Go By," "Lady Jane," and "Ruby Tuesday"—was to top the charts in a number of countries (including France and the United States, but not the United Kingdom). Other good examples are "Coming Down Again" and "Winter." The first is perhaps an evocation of both the relationship between Keith Richards and Anita Pallenberg (around the time he "stole" her from Brian Jones) and the role of junkie that he currently found himself in, while the second is an allegory of winter as the time for sadness and melancholy.

At the same time, however, the Glimmer Twins continued to play their trump card of unrestrained, irreverent rock 'n' roll—and to similar great effect. The album begins with "Dancing with Mr. D." and its typical Richards riff over which Jagger dances with the devil and/or death. "Doo Doo Doo Doo Doo (Heartbreaker)" is a forceful indictment of violence in the United States, and more specifically New York, exemplified by the death of an innocent boy at the hands of the police, and that of a ten-year-old girl (from an overdose) abandoned by all. "Silver Train," which opens the second side of the LP, is another archetypal Rolling Stones number and would not have been out of place on one of the "magic four" albums (*Beggars Banquet, Let It Bleed, Sticky Fingers, Exile on Main St.*). Finally, after the supercharged piano blues of

"Hide Your Love," the Stones bring the curtain down on *Goats Head Soup* with "Star Star" (or "Starfucker" if one prefers), a hymn to groupies in which Steve McQueen and John Wayne are cited by name. Also worth mentioning are "100 Years Ago," which sounds like a return to the heroic fantasy of *Their Satanic Majesties Request*, and "Can You Hear the Music" which stands out above all for its avant-garde orchestration, as if the Rolling Stones had been guided by the spirit of Brian Jones or some Jamaican divinity.

The Rolling Stones' eleventh (British) studio album went out into the world on August 31, 1973. If some critics were initially disappointed, it is because they were judging it against the yardstick of the four previous albums. When critics later compared it to the records that followed, they would come to see *Goats Head Soup* as the final album of the band's golden era. The public, meanwhile, would by and large agree with the judicious comments published in *Sounds* on September 8, 1973: "First impressions, though, at one Saturday morning: too mid-pace, too much balladry, crooning by Mick Jagger . . . But after repeated playings, the groove sits well. On the strength of this album, there seems no more reason to dispute the Stones' title as the Greatest Rock 'n' Roll Band in the World than to dispute the pre-eminence of the Rolls-Royce motor car." As a result, *Goats Head Soup* would achieve the top spot on the album charts in a dozen or so countries, including the United Kingdom, the United States, France, Australia, and the Netherlands, and second place in West Germany and Sweden.

The Album Cover

The design group Hipgnosis, which had already designed a number of record covers for Pink Floyd, was originally chosen to do the cover for *Goats Head Soup.* "The shoot was

The Stones hold a press conference in Munich in September 1973 for the release of their album *Goats Head Soup*.

It was also at Dynamic Sound Studios in Kingston that Serge Gainsbourg would record his legendary album *Aux Armes Et Cætera* in 1979.

organised for 1 p.m.," recalls the designer Aubrey Powell, "and Mick and Keith turned up about 5 p.m. and Keith was in a very bolshy mood. Storm Thorgerson [a photographer and graphic artist] and I had outlined the concept to the Stones and they were all enthusiastic—especially Mick. They were all to be centaurs and minotaurs prancing about in the photo in an Arcadian landscape, like the young bucks they were."[1]

Why was a photo from this shoot not used in the end? It's a mystery. What is known is that Mick Jagger subsequently asked his friend David Bailey to take over the project. Bailey recalls telling Jagger: "'I'm going to make you look like Hepburn.' I think he thought I meant Audrey Hepburn, while I actually meant Katharine Hepburn in *The African Queen*. It was Bianca Jagger who got that one through because she said, 'Oh, it's great, Mick,' while he was saying 'Oh, no, we're going to look like a bunch of poofs.'"[9] In the end, the Stones singer appears on the front cover in isolation. His face can be distinguished wrapped in a scarf in a halo of yellow light. Inside, Bill Wyman, Charlie Watts, and Mick Taylor undergo the same treatment (although Wyman has a green halo). The back cover features the face of Keith Richards in black against a dark background. The photo shoot took place on June 6, 1973, at the London home of David Bailey (Gloucester Avenue). The Stones also wanted to insert a separate photo, taken by John Pasche, of a reddish-colored soup in which the head of an unfortunate billy goat is simmering.

The Recording

Having arrived in Jamaica, the Rolling Stones took up residence at the Terra Nova Hotel, Kingston, once the family home of Chris Blackwell, the founder of Island Records. They had opted for Byron Lee's Dynamic Sound Studios, where, shortly before, Jimmy Cliff and others had recorded

the soundtrack of *The Harder They Come* (1972) and Bob Marley and the Wailers their album *Catch a Fire* (1973). At the Stones' request, Andy Johns had visited Kingston in September. After reconnoitering the place, he asked Byron Lee to make various arrangements (in particular to install soundproofing panels between the musicians and to get hold of a concert grand piano and a Hammond B-3 organ). "Of course, I show up with the band two months later and none of this shit's been done."[61] And neither has Bill Wyman forgotten his first impressions of Dynamic Sound Studios: "We would be driven to Byron Lee's studio through downtown Kingston. Two large, double gates guarded by the man with the shotgun would open and let us in and then close behind us. Studio A was a low building, little bigger than an outhouse. Inside was an eight-track tape recorder and the room where we recorded. Someone described it as 'just this side of claustrophobic,' and they were right."[1] Lee did, however, take the trouble to go to Miami at the beginning of November, bringing back and installing a sixteen-track tape recorder, in keeping with the wishes of his prestigious clients. He also equipped his studio with headphones, as Jamaican musicians generally did not use them. Keith was more impressed than his bandmates: "Dynamic Sounds in Kingston was an amazing place: the drum kits and the amps were nailed to the floor."[9] Moreover, the guitarist was to develop a real affection for Jamaica, and after recording the album, bought a fine villa there from the singer Tommy Steele.

The studio was booked twenty-four hours a day for a month "so that the band could keep the same set-up and develop their songs in their free-form way, starting with a few lyrics and rhythms, jamming and rehearsing while we fixed the sound,"[9] explains Marshall Chess. Between November 23 and December 14, 1972, the band recorded the backing tracks of

The Stones in Jamaica to record their eleventh (British) studio album.

FOR STONES ADDICTS

After mixing the final tracks of *Goats Head Soup* on July 9, 1973, Mick and Keith then recorded an initial take of "It's Only Rock 'n' Roll" in the private studio of a certain Ronnie Wood in Richmond, London. This was a decision that would have consequences for all concerned.

eight of the ten songs on the album: "Coming Down Again," "Winter," "Dancing with Mr. D.," "Can You Hear the Music" "Angie," "100 Years Ago," "Doo Doo Doo Doo Doo (Heartbreaker)," and "Star Star"—plus "Through the Lonely Nights" (the B-side of the single "It's Only Rock 'n' Roll"), "Tops" and "Waiting on a Friend" (both on *Tattoo You*, 1981), "Short and Curlies" (on *It's Only Rock 'n' Roll*, 1974), and other titles that were not used. In total, some thirty songs were cut. "The album itself didn't take that long, but we recorded an awful lot of tracks,"[9] confirms Keith.

A Difficult Return to the Studio

In reality, the Stones were not particularly efficient, and recording proceeded slowly, despite Marshall Chess having been impressed by the ease with which they were able to start playing together again after months of inactivity. They had to interrupt the sessions at the beginning of December to fly back to Nice—Keith excepted—in order to answer a summons from the French judicial authorities, who wanted to question them about the alleged heroin trafficking at Villa Nellcôte. In the end, the authorities adopted a more lenient attitude than anticipated, indicating that if Keith and Anita agreed to undergo a detox cure, the charges against them could be reduced.

Upon their return to Kingston, recording resumed from December 6 to 14, but progress was not as fast as they had hoped. On December 23 there was a dramatic turn of events when Nicaragua, Bianca Jagger's home country, was struck by a major earthquake. Fearing for her mother's life, she traveled there immediately with Mick, taking medical aid. The Stones decided to give a charity concert on January 18, 1973, shortly before leaving to tour the Pacific. As it turned out, the Tokyo

and Hong Kong dates were canceled by the local authorities, who did not much care for the band's provocative image. Instead, the Stones went back into the studio from January 27 to 30, 1973, this time at Village Recorders in Los Angeles, to continue working on the album. Then it was Olympic Sound Studios in London from May 7 to 17; Island Studios, also in the British capital, from May 28 to June 8 (where they cut "Hide Your Love"); and back to Olympic Sound Studios for the final mix-down from July 6 to 9. It should also be pointed out that "Silver Train" had been recorded in October 1970 (again at Olympic) before later being reworked for the album.

An Unsatisfactory Result

Despite working at four studios in three different countries, the large number of recording sessions, and the involvement of three sound engineers, the final result is unconvincing. This, at least, is Mick Taylor's view: "*Goats Head Soup* is not one of my favourite albums, but there's a lot of interesting things on it. I think it's a weak album—it's a bit directionless. I think we all felt that way too."[90] Keith, on the other hand, retains a good memory of cutting the disc: "I enjoyed making it."[2]

Goats Head Soup is not one of the Stones' finest albums. The golden era was well and truly over. Jimmy Miller, who had contributed to the band's renaissance in 1968 and had gone on to produce their best discs, was a mere shadow of his former self. Ravaged by drugs, he was sidelined by the Glimmer Twins, who no longer needed his services. This was to be his last piece of work for the Stones, and at the same time brings to a close one of the most dazzling chapters in their career.

The various sound engineers who worked on the album were Andy Johns, the engineer of the wonderful *Exile on Main St.*, and Rob Fraboni and Baker Bigsby at Village

Bill Wyman wrote that, at the beginning of 1973, Mick Taylor was thinking of leaving the Stones to join the band Free.

The Fender Twin Reverb was one of the amplifiers responsible for the Stones sound during this period.

Keith Richards acquired a 1960 Gibson Les Paul Junior during the *Goats Head Soup* sessions.

Recorders. Fraboni was the brilliant engineer and producer of numerous albums, notably for the Beach Boys, Bob Dylan, and Eric Clapton, while Bigsby manned the controls for the likes of B. B. King, Art Pepper, and John Lee Hooker. The assistant sound engineers were Carlton Lee (Bob Marley, Joe Cocker), Howard Kilgour (Mott The Hoople, the Eagles) and Doug Bennett (the Stranglers, Hawkwind).

Among the musicians who contributed their talents to the album were Nicky Hopkins, Billy Preston, Bobby Keys, and Jim Price, plus a number of new faces: Jim Horn on flute and alto sax (the Beach Boys, George Harrison, Stevie Wonder, Steely Dan), Chuck Findley on trumpet (Ringo Starr, James Brown, Quincy Jones), Anthony Rebop Kwaku Baah, alias Rebop, on congas (Traffic, Steve Winwood, Can), and Nicolas Pascal Raicevic, alias Pascal (a composer of experimental electronic music influenced by the drug culture) on percussion. Not to mention Nicky Harrison, who was responsible for the string arrangements, as he would be for Donovan in 1973 (*Essence to Essence*).

The Instruments

Various new instruments were used during the making of this album. Keith acquired numerous guitars, including a 1959 Fender Stratocaster, a red 1960 Gibson Les Paul Junior, a 1950 Les Paul "Gold Top," a white Gibson SG, a Martin D-45, and a Martin 000-28. Bill used a Gibson EB-3 bass in January 1973, but remained faithful to his Dallas Tuxedo and Fender Mustang in the studio. Mick Jagger, who was starting to play the guitar more and more, used a Gibson Hummingbird and a Gibson Les Paul. As for the amps, the band continued to favor its Ampegs and the Fender Twin Reverbs. Finally, Billy Preston played a Hohner Clavinet and an RMI Electra Piano.

1973

DANCING WITH MR. D.

Mick Jagger / Keith Richards / 4:52

Musicians
Mick Jagger: vocals
Keith Richards: rhythm guitar, backing vocals
Mick Taylor: slide guitar, bass
Charlie Watts: drums
Nicky Hopkins: piano, organ (?)
Unidentified musicians: backing vocals
Recorded
Dynamic Sound Studios, Kingston, Jamaica:
November 23–December 14, 1972
Village Recorders, Los Angeles: January 27–30, 1973
Island Studios, London: May 28–June 8, 1973
Olympic Sound Studios, London: May 7–17, July 6–9, 1973
Technical Team
Producer: Jimmy Miller
Sound engineers: Andy Johns, Rob Fraboni, Baker Bigsby
Assistant sound engineers: Carlton Lee,
Howard Kilgour, Doug Bennett

Genesis

Goats Head Soup begins with a dance macabre. *Lord, keep your hand off me/I'm dancin' with Mr. D.* Might this *D* stand for the devil, whom the Stones singer is so fond of invoking in his songs? And as it is only a short step from the devil to death, *Mr. D.* could equally be a symbol of the grim reaper, hence the lugubrious atmosphere, the cemetery in which the air is simultaneously *sweet* and *sick*. Hence, too, the *lady in black, wearing black silk gloves and a black silk hat.* Whoever Mr. D. may be, the character in the song is approaching his final encounter with him, and lists various ways in which he might meet his end: *poison put in my glass, the bite of a snake, a drink of Belladonna on a Toussaint night,* the settling of scores on *a corner in New York City,* a *forty-four in West Virginia.* "Dancing with Mr. D." was chosen as the flip side of the single "Doo Doo Doo Doo Doo (Heartbreaker)," released in December 1973.

Production

For the opening track on their new album, the Stones chose a number with something of a funk-rock feel that hangs on a Keith Richards riff. The vibe has changed dramatically from *Exile on Main St.* The blues rock of Villa Nellcôte has given way to a more crafted and formatted and less spontaneous sound. Mick Jagger comes across as entirely in his element, although a glance at the 1973 promotional video reveals that he is pretty much the only member of the band who is really having a good time. Charlie Watts ensures a solid rhythm, supported on bass not by Bill Wyman, but by Mick Taylor, who also plays a number of nicely felt phrases on slide guitar. On piano is the unstinting Nicky Hopkins, who also seems to be playing the organ in the intro. What appears to be a fuzz bass can be heard in the refrains (for example, at 2:17), but unfortunately this does not come through clearly in the mix and might even be Billy Preston's clavinet. Mick doubles himself on some of his phrases and is supported by various unidentified backing vocalists. Although a reasonably good track, "Dancing with Mr. D." was perhaps not the best choice to follow immediately after *Exile.*

Keith, shown here with his 1959 Gibson Les Paul Standard, was the catalyst for "Dancing with Mr. D."

100 YEARS AGO

Mick Jagger / Keith Richards / 3:58

Musicians
Mick Jagger: vocals
Keith Richards: bass
Mick Taylor: rhythm guitar and lead guitar
Charlie Watts: drums
Billy Preston: clavinet
Nicky Hopkins: piano
Jimmy Miller: tambourine

Recorded
Dynamic Sound Studios, Kingston, Jamaica:
November 23–December 14, 1972
Island Studios, London: May 28–June 8, 1973
Olympic Sound Studios, London: May 7–17, July 6–9, 1973

Technical Team
Producer: Jimmy Miller
Sound engineer: Andy Johns
Assistant sound engineer: Carlton Lee,
Howard Kilgour, Doug Bennett

FOR STONES ADDICTS

The Stones performed "100 Years Ago" live during their 1973 European tour but have not played it onstage since.

Genesis

"100 Years Ago" was written by Mick Jagger some time before the sessions for *Goats Head Soup* (two years, according to Mick Taylor) and had been worked on during the recording of *Exile on Main St.* In this song, the Stones singer casts his mind back a century or so. The narrator is walking through a forest, where he observes the world as a *carpet laid before* him. He remembers sitting on a gate with his friend Mary *gazin' at some dragon in the sky.* Is this a return to the heroic fantasy world of *Their Satanic Majesties Request?* In any event, we are a long way from the spaced-out, psychedelic atmosphere of the second half of the sixties.

Production

This song opens with an intro from Billy Preston on the clavinet. This is the instrument immortalized by Stevie Wonder on his October 1972 hit "Superstition," released just a few days before the Stones entered the studio. Preston's playing is funky and soulful, and he is joined more or less immediately by Nicky Hopkins with an equally rhythmic, although more lyrical, piano part. This time the bass is played by Keith Richards, as Bill Wyman was still unavailable. Charlie Watts sets a very good groove on his Gretsch kit, particularly bearing in mind that "100 Years Ago" is made up of three different sections with three different tempos, moving from 105 beats per minute in the first section to 70 at 2:09 and then 125 from 2:35. In other words, Charlie is the pivot of the piece and performs this role skillfully, supported on tambourine by Jimmy Miller. As the only guitarist on the track, Mick Taylor also has plenty to do, playing both rhythm and distorted lead. When it comes to his solos (at 1:36 and 2:35), he really lets it rip on his Gibson Les Paul, all the more so as he uses the wah-wah pedal like a machine gun. Playing with the fingers, rather than a bottleneck, he sets the track on fire in a display of breathtaking talent and facility. He would later tell Jas Obrecht: "I like that track,"[90] and it is not difficult to guess why . . . Mick Jagger also gives an excellent performance and joins Keith Richards in the vocal harmonies.

The dominant sound on "100 Years Ago" is the clavinet played by Billy Preston, who can be seen here with Mick Jagger.

COMING DOWN AGAIN

Mick Jagger / Keith Richards / 5:54

🎧 **IN YOUR HEADPHONES**
Throughout the intro, Keith can be heard mumbling and apparently chewing gum.

Musicians
Mick Jagger: vocal harmonies
Keith Richards: vocals, rhythm guitar
Mick Taylor: bass
Charlie Watts: drums
Nicky Hopkins: piano
Bobby Keys: saxophone
Pascal: güiro
Jim Horn: flutes

Recorded
Dynamic Sound Studios, Kingston, Jamaica:
November 23–December 14, 1972
Island Studios, London: May 28–June 8, 1973
Olympic Sound Studios, London: May 7–17, July 6–9, 1973

Technical Team
Producer: Jimmy Miller
Sound engineer: Andy Johns
Assistant sound engineers: Carlton Lee,
Howard Kilgour, Doug Bennett

A stoic Keith Richards, following the fire
that destroyed his home, Redlands.

Genesis

"Coming Down Again" is, in a sense, Keith Richards's response to Mick Jagger's "Shine a Light," recorded by the band during the *Exile on Main St.* sessions. While Jagger sings of friends who *leave you in the cold gray dawn*, Keith Richards wonders *where are all my friends*, before revealing that he is hitting rock bottom. In all likelihood, both songs are about Brian Jones, who faded gradually throughout the second half of the sixties, before eventually being ousted from the band he had formed. *Slipped my tongue in someone else's pie/Tasting better every time*: the breakup with Anita Pallenberg after she had gone off with Keith Richards was probably one of the most painful events ever experienced by Brian Jones.

There are other possible interpretations, however. The song could be a mea culpa from Keith Richards after being unfaithful to Anita Pallenberg, or it could be an expression of his "relationship" with heroin, to which he was addicted at the time, hence the title of the song. In his autobiography *Life*, however, the Stones guitarist casts doubt on this interpretation: "I said not long ago that I wouldn't have written it without heroin. I don't know if it was *about* dope. It was just a mournful song. . . ."[2]

Production

After "Happy" on *Exile on Main St.*, Keith now sings lead vocal on this very pretty ballad, delivering it with sensitivity and gentleness. Mick assists him in the vocal harmonies, and they answer each other to great effect (3:27). Keith also plays rhythm guitar, making considerable use of the wah-wah pedal and Leslie speaker, which gives him that distinctive swirling sound. Mick Taylor is again on bass, and when asked whether Bill Wyman was present, replies in the negative, before elaborating that he "actually played synthesizer on some of the tracks."[90] Charlie Watts does a professional job on the drums, Bobby Keys overdubs two superb, interlocking sax solos, and Jim Horn records two beautiful flute parts that harmonize perfectly with the refrains and the coda (5:06). However, "Coming Down Again" depends most of all on Nicky Hopkins, whose piano playing contributes a lyricism and a melancholy that are in perfect keeping with Keith's words.

DOO DOO DOO DOO DOO (HEARTBREAKER)

Mick Jagger / Keith Richards / 3:27

Musicians
Mick Jagger: vocals
Keith Richards: bass, rhythm guitar (?), backing vocals
Mick Taylor: rhythm and lead guitar, backing vocals
Charlie Watts: drums
Billy Preston: clavinet, electric piano, backing vocals
Rebop: congas
Pascal: tambourine
Bobby Keys: saxophone
Jim Price: horn arrangements, trumpet
Jim Horn: saxophone
Chuck Findley: trumpet

Recorded
Dynamic Sound Studios, Kingston, Jamaica:
November 23–December 14, 1972
Village Recorders, Los Angeles: January 27–30, 1973
Island Studios, London: May 28–June 8, 1973
Olympic Sound Studios, London: May 7–17, July 6–9, 1973

Technical Team
Producer: Jimmy Miller
Sound engineers: Andy Johns, Rob Fraboni, Baker Bigsby
Assistant sound engineers: Carlton Lee,
Howard Kilgour, Doug Bennett

Mick Taylor, probably the only guitarist on the track, once again demonstrates the full extent of his talent.

Genesis

There are two tragic deaths in "Doo Doo Doo Doo Doo (Heartbreaker):" that of a young boy in New York as the result of a police error and that of a ten-year-old girl from an overdose at the corner of a dirty alleyway with no one to help her. It is likely that Mick Jagger found his inspiration for this song in real-life events. In April 1973, while the Stones were recording *Goats Head Soup*, there was a report in the press about a ten-year-old boy shot dead in Queens by police officers who had mistaken him for a fleeing thief, even though he was with his father. Jagger clearly intended to reflect the climate of violence in the United States, and New York in particular. He unambiguously accuses the police officers of being trigger-happy, *heartbreakers* in the literal sense of the term.

"Doo Doo Doo Doo Doo" was released as a single in December 1973 (with "Dancing with Mr. D." as the B-side). It peaked at number 15 in the United States on February 23, 1974, but did not chart anywhere else (either in Europe or the United Kingdom).

Production

Billy Preston gives a brilliant demonstration of his supreme talents as a keyboard player with his raw and gritty intro to "Doo Doo Doo Doo Doo (Heartbreaker)" on the Hohner Clavinet. In the refrains he alters the sound, to brilliant effect, with a wah-wah pedal. He can also be heard providing a softer accompaniment to the verses on an RMI Electra Piano. Charlie Watts delivers an excellent drum part on his Gretsch kit, with a funky style of playing that bears some resemblance to Jimmy Miller's. Rebop supports him on the congas, and Pascal on the tambourine. There is still no Bill Wyman on bass. Keith Richards takes care of that part on his Fender Precision. In 1994, Andy Johns would describe how it took four months to record the track because the guitar and the piano were out of tune and Keith was determined not to recut it. It seems that Keith does not play the guitar on this track, the wah-wah sound emanating instead from Preston's clavinet. That means Mick Taylor is probably the only guitarist. At the start he plays a distorted rhythm guitar with a heavy rock sound, but then moves toward a far more jazz-rock style, playing a superb solo with overtones of Carlos Santana (1:47). His playing is fluid and melodic, with a floating quality, while at the same time

"Heartbreaker" was to become a highlight of Stones concerts from 1973 on.
Performed here at the Empire Pool at Wembley in September 1973.

rooted in rock, and the solo is simple but extremely effective. To obtain the richer, swirling sound, he plugs into the Leslie speaker—as does Keith on "Coming Down Again." Another important element is the horn parts arranged by Jim Price and probably recorded at Olympic Sound Studios. The effect is percussive and significantly peps up the refrains. The horn section consists of Jim Price himself and Findley on trumpet with Bobby Keys and Jim Horn on sax. This was to be Price's last collaboration with the Stones. As for Mick Jagger, it is worth emphasizing the quality of his performance, the singer perhaps enjoying a moment of grace. It is certainly true that he is never as good as he is on aggressive rock tracks, where he gives the impression of starting a blaze with every phrase he utters. Finally, as the title indicates, the backing vocalists' compelling and contagious *doo doo doo*s are an important element in the song.

Despite its disappointing performance as a single, this excellent and underrated song by the Stones deserves a place among the band's classic tracks.

ANGIE

Mick Jagger / Keith Richards / 4:32

Musicians
Mick Jagger: vocals
Keith Richards: acoustic guitar
Mick Taylor: acoustic guitar
Bill Wyman: bass
Charlie Watts: drums
Nicky Hopkins: piano
Nicky Harrison: string arrangement
Recorded
Dynamic Sound Studios, Kingston, Jamaica:
November 23–December 14, 1972
Island Studios, London: May 28–June 8, 1973
Olympic Sound Studios, London: July 6–9, 1973
Technical Team
Producer: Jimmy Miller
Sound engineer: Andy Johns
Assistant sound engineers: Carlton Lee,
Howard Kilgour, Doug Bennett

Declaration or consolation? This superb ballad is thought to have been written by Mick Jagger for Angela Bowie (shown here with her husband David in 1974).

Genesis

In the weeks following the end of recording work on *Exile on Main St.* at Nellcôte, Keith Richards and Anita Pallenberg left the Côte d'Azur to escape the French judiciary, which suspected them of narcotics dealing. After spending time in various places, the couple, along with young Marlon, ended up in Switzerland, where Anita gave birth to Dandelion/Angela on April 17, 1972, while the Stones guitarist was in a clinic in Vevey. This was for a detox cure in the care of a Dr. Denber: "He was American. He looked Swiss, close shaven and rimless glasses, Himmleresque."[2] It was in this improbable place, but evidently inspired by the Swiss landscape, that Keith wrote "Angie."

While the music is by Richards, the lyrics were written by with some input by him, but mostly by Mick Jagger. To whom are the Glimmer Twins referring in the song? Mick Jagger has always categorically denied that the words were addressed to Mary Angela "Angie" Barnett, who had become Mrs. David Bowie on March 20, 1970. The most logical explanation would be that they refer to Keith and Anita's daughter Dandelion/Angela, but Keith has not confirmed this: "While I was in the clinic, Anita was down the road having our daughter, Angela. Once I came out of the usual trauma, I had a guitar with me and I wrote 'Angie' in an afternoon, sitting in bed, because I could finally move my fingers and put them in the right place again. . . ."[2] And he continues: "I just went, 'Angie,' 'Angie.' It was not about any particular person. . . . I didn't know Angela was going to be called Angela when I wrote 'Angie.'"[2]

On the other hand, "Angie" may be addressed to one or another of the Stones' women—those who had previously belonged, or still did, to the circle of their intimate acquaintances. *Ain't it good to be alive? Angie, Angie, they can't say we never tried:* the last lines of the song could refer to the suicide attempt and miscarriage of Marianne Faithfull, but equally, the phrase *All the dreams we held so close seemed to all go up in smoke* could relate to the living hell experienced by Keith Richards and Anita Pallenberg as a result of his heroin addiction.

"Angie" is an irresistible ballad. Released as a single on August 20, 1973 (with "Silver Train" as the flip side), the most romantic song in the Rolling Stones catalog became an international hit. It was number 1 in the United States, France,

🎧 IN YOUR HEADPHONES

Careful listening to the song, on headphones if possible, reveals a faint guide vocal sung by Mick Jagger, which can be heard as an echo on his definitive take (for example, during the instrumental section from 3:06). This is either a badly erased track that has been left on the recording, whether intentionally or accidentally, or leakage picked up by the first acoustic guitar mic, which could not then be erased.

During the 2004 election campaign, the German chancellor Angela "Angie" Merkel chose "Angie" as her party's official campaign song and played it at rallies of the Christian Democratic Union of Germany without seeking permission. Although not happy about it, the Rolling Stones refrained from taking legal action.

Mick Jagger, at his most heartrending, scored a worldwide hit with "Angie."

Canada, Australia, and the Netherlands. In the United Kingdom it only reached number 5, on September 15, 1973.

Production

The first note of "Angie" is a harmonic A. The song is a perennial favorite that every guitarist in the making has, at some point, tried to reproduce. The reason for this is that, although it may be a killer ballad, "Angie" is first and foremost a guitar track. The big question that gnaws at every player of the instrument is: who was responsible for the brilliant intro strummed on a Gibson Hummingbird? In 1979, Mick Taylor would shed some light on the issue in an interview with Jas Obrecht: "Did you play on 'Angie'"? "Yeah, I played on 'Angie'. I played the acoustic guitar." "Was that mainly you?" "Yeah."[90] However, things are not quite as they seem. On the first version of the promotional film shot by Michael Lindsay-Hogg in 1973, Keith can be seen playing the introduction. However, his playing (on the playback) does not correspond precisely to the version on the disc. Moreover, it has to be said that Keith's overall style is not as subtle as Taylor's, although not to say any worse. It would therefore seem more logical to claim that Taylor is responsible for playing the intro on the recording. Let us hope that one or the other of the two guitarists will provide a categorical answer. A similar question can be asked concerning the player of the second rhythm guitar. Necessarily the one who is not playing the intro . . .

In a sense, "Angie" also represents the apotheosis of Nicky Hopkins, whose piano part is one of the key elements in the song. The lyricism of his playing suits the general atmosphere perfectly, and it could probably be claimed that it makes the number more middle of the road than it was at the beginning, when Keith sketched it out in his room in the detox clinic. Then there is the violin arrangement, written by Nicky Harrison and recorded at Island Studios in London, which significantly helped to widen the Stones' audience. This was apparently the idea of Mick Jagger, who was disappointed at the lack of hit singles from *Exile on Main St.* and was eager to reconnect with the charts. The lead singer also makes an important contribution to the success of the song. Although generally giving his best performances in hard-hitting rock numbers, here he finds the perfect balance and tone of voice, delivering what is, for him, somewhat unusual vocals, imbued with fragility and melancholy. Finally, it is also worth emphasizing the quality of the rhythm section, Charlie Watts playing his Gretsch kit with a certain restraint and subtle swing, and Bill Wyman—making his first appearance on the album—resuming his role with a discreet but highly effective and melodious bass line.

Marshall Chess recalls that "Angie" was not immediately regarded as an obvious hit: "Atlantic did not want to take 'Angie' as the single off *Goats Head*—they really wanted another 'Brown Sugar' rather than a ballad—and there were some heated arguments before we all agreed on that choice. . . ."[9] Obviously Atlantic was wrong.

1973

SILVER TRAIN

Mick Jagger / Keith Richards / 4:26

Musicians
Mick Jagger: vocals, rhythm guitar, harmonica
Keith Richards: rhythm guitar, bass (?), backing vocals
Mick Taylor: slide guitar, bass (?), backing vocals
Charlie Watts: drums
Ian Stewart: piano

Recorded
Olympic Sound Studios, London: October 1970
Island Studios, London: May 28–June 8, 1973
Olympic Sound Studios, London: May 7–17, July 6–9, 1973

Technical Team
Producer: Jimmy Miller
Sound engineer: Andy Johns
Assistant sound engineers: Carlton Lee,
Howard Kilgour, Doug Bennett

The Texas guitarist Johnny Winter made a comeback with his version of "Silver Train" on the album *Still Alive and Well*.

Genesis

A man is traveling home on a silver train bound for the southern US. A little while before, he has been enjoying a good time with a girl whose name he does not know. *But I sure love the way that she laughed and took my money* (*. . . and called me "honey"*), sings Jagger. Here we have another Stones song in which the heroine is a prostitute.

"Silver Train" was probably written at the end of the sixties or the beginning of the seventies, around the same time as "All Down the Line," to which it bears a strange resemblance. An initial version was recorded in October 1970 at Olympic Sound Studios in London, and a second in spring 1973. The Texas bluesman Johnny Winter heard the Glimmer Twins' song and liked it so much that he recorded it himself during the sessions for his album *Still Alive and Well*, which was released in March 1973. Furthermore, it was probably Winter's recording of "Silver Train" that led the Rolling Stones to rework their song and ultimately include it on *Goats Head Soup*.

Production

"Silver Train" opens with another Keith Richards riff. It is significant that the song was written before the others on *Goats Head Soup*: it has more of a "roots" *feel*, more of a classic Stones sound; in short, it is more of a rock number. Mick Jagger is literally omnipresent: in addition to his lead vocals, he plays rhythm guitar, apparently a clear-toned Gibson Les Paul, and also harmonica. Although his guitar playing is good, his harmonica is somewhat lackluster and repetitive. He double-tracks it to give it more body, but we are a long way from "Stop Breaking Down," and his interjections fail to electrify the song. Bill Wyman is again absent, his place taken most probably by Mick Taylor, whose bass playing is fairly characteristic, although it has not been possible to confirm this. On the other hand it is definitely Taylor on slide guitar, playing distinctly blues-rock licks as only he can. Ian Stewart, who has so far been quiet on the album, is back at the piano with a furious boogie-woogie that is unfortunately too recessed in the mix. "Silver Train" is a rock number in the Stones tradition, but although a good song, it lacks inspiration and would perhaps have benefited from some reworking. It is not the Stones at their best.

HIDE YOUR LOVE

Mick Jagger / Keith Richards / 4:12

Musicians
Mick Jagger: vocals, piano
Keith Richards: bass (?)
Mick Taylor: lead guitar
Charlie Watts: drums
Jimmy Miller: bass drum (?)
Bobby Keys: saxophone
Rebop (?): congas
Unidentified musicians: hand claps
Recorded
Dynamic Sound Studios, Kingston, Jamaica:
November 23–December 14, 1972
Island Studios, London: May 28–June 8, 1973
Olympic Sound Studios, London: July 6–9, 1973
Technical Team
Producer: Jimmy Miller
Sound engineer: Andy Johns
Assistant sound engineers: Carlton Lee,
Howard Kilgour, Doug Bennett

Rebop, associated primarily with the band Traffic, may
have contributed to the recording of "Hide Your Love."

Genesis

This is a typical Rolling Stones blues that builds on the typical Rolling Stones riff of "Silver Train." Mick Jagger composed it on the piano, in all likelihood sometime before the recording of *Goats Head Soup*. In *The Rolling Stones Complete Recording Sessions 1962–2012*, Martin Elliott[101] suggests that he wrote it in the summer of 1970. What does seem certain is that Andy Johns particularly liked this invigorating piano blues, and encouraged Mick Jagger to finish it and then record it, most probably during the session at Island Studios on May 28, 1973. The story possesses the caustic humor that is so characteristic of both the blues and the Stones. A woman is reluctant to show her boyfriend her love (and even goes so far as to hide it) because he has an unfortunate tendency to drink and is incapable of controlling his recurrent melancholy.

Production

Andy Johns is not the only one who liked this song: Mick Taylor also reveals a positive opinion of it: "Oh, yeah. I like the blues tune, 'Hide Your Love.'"[90] Once again he is absolutely brilliant on lead guitar, delivering a succession of blues licks and solos. Keith Richards apparently accompanies him not on a 6-string but on bass, his playing resembling that of a guitarist more than that of a bass player. On the rhythm side, Charlie Watts plays economically, marking the tempo on his bass drum and making discreet use of the hi-hat and snare drum. Some people say Jimmy Miller is playing the bass drum, but there is no evidence for this, other than a slight timing problem on the track as a whole, which could be attributed to the difficulty of synchronization between him and Charlie. Playing the piano is Mick Jagger—for the very first time on a Stones disc. Obviously he lacks the experience of Ian Stewart and Nicky Hopkins, but he acquits himself pretty well. As for his vocals, a significant delay has been added to his voice in order to reinforce the blues aspect. He gives the impression of singing with the aim not of obtaining a perfect take, but of conveying the spontaneity of a live take. As with "Silver Train," snatches of a guide vocal can be heard very recessed in the mix, but coming forward at certain points (listen between 3:28 and 3:35). Bobby Keys is on sax, but his interjections are undermixed, which is a shame. Finally, congas can be heard, particularly during Mick Taylor's solo parts, in all likelihood played by Rebop.

WINTER

Mick Jagger / Keith Richards / 5:29

Musicians
Mick Jagger: vocals, rhythm guitar
Mick Taylor: lead guitar
Bill Wyman: bass
Charlie Watts: drums
Nicky Hopkins: piano
Nicky Harrison: string arrangement
Recorded
Dynamic Sound Studios, Kingston, Jamaica:
November 23–December 14, 1972
Island Studios, London: May 28–June 8, 1973
Olympic Sound Studios, London: May 7–17, July 6–9, 1973
Technical Team
Producer: Jimmy Miller
Sound engineer: Andy Johns
Assistant sound engineers: Carlton Lee,
Howard Kilgour, Doug Bennett

Mick Taylor and the Texan singer Carla Olson made two versions of "Winter." The first is on the live album *Too Hot for Snakes* (1991), recorded at the Roxy Theatre in Hollywood in 1990, while the second can be heard on Olson's *The Ring of Truth* (2001).

FOR STONES ADDICTS

Several takes (three or four) were recorded of "Winter." The producer, Jimmy Miller, was not entirely satisfied with the vocal part, and is said to have asked Mick Jagger to sing it again. Jagger's response was categorical: he was already on his way back to Bianca.

Genesis

The "Winter" lyricist was Mick Jagger. He draws a parallel between a *cold, cold winter* and the absence of his loved one, and hopes that with the fine days of summer, love will come. There is a sentimental aspect that is not exactly at home in the Stones world. Is the song an expression of nostalgia, under Jamaica's constant sunshine, for England and in particular the Christmas season?

Although "Winter" is credited to Jagger-Richards, the music was born mainly of a collaboration between the Stones singer and Mick Taylor (following the example of "Moonlight Mile" on *Sticky Fingers*), both of whom are playing guitar. This was the first song on *Goats Head Soup* to have been recorded at Dynamic Sound Studios in Kingston.

Production

It is quite likely that Keith had no hand at all in this track, so little does the musical atmosphere resemble his style. Indeed he has confirmed as much himself: "'Winter' had nothing to do with me."[28] It is probably Mick Jagger on guitar in the intro, playing a rhythm part through a Leslie speaker with vibrato. Mick Taylor answers him with some very good licks on lead, again with that highly lyrical mix of blues and rock that is his trademark. For the second time on the album, Bill Wyman is back in his role as bassist, one his fellow guitarists were perhaps a little too inclined to take away from him. Charlie Watts delivers a superb drum part, making ample use of his ride cymbal. At the piano, Nicky Hopkins contributes to the melancholy atmosphere of "Winter" with his own highly lyrical playing, and with the help of Nicky Harrison's very good string arrangements, the song begins to take on a flavor similar to that of "Moonlight Mile." Mick Taylor distinguishes himself once again with excellent solos reminiscent of Santana in his *Caravanserai* (1972) period. His playing is brilliant, and his presence almost forces the Stones to adopt a richer style with jazz-rock inflections. As for Mick Jagger, the lead vocalist seems to drop his rock star mask, assuming a more sensitive and fragile tone than usual. Andy Johns would come to regard "Winter" as one of the band's best numbers.

Mick Jagger and Keith Richards, the Glimmer Twins. One thing is for sure: they knew their music.

CAN YOU HEAR THE MUSIC

Mick Jagger / Keith Richards / 5:32

Musicians
Mick Jagger: vocals
Keith Richards: rhythm guitar, backing vocals
Mick Taylor: lead guitar
Bill Wyman: bass
Charlie Watts: drums
Nicky Hopkins: piano
Jimmy Miller: percussion (?)
Rebop: congas
Pascal: percussion
Jim Horn: flute
Unidentified musicians: backing vocals
Recorded
Dynamic Sound Studios, Kingston, Jamaica:
November 23–December 14, 1972
Island Studios, London: May 28–June 8, 1973
Olympic Sound Studios, London: May 7–17, July 6–9, 1973
Technical Team
Producer: Jimmy Miller
Sound engineer: Andy Johns
Assistant sound engineers: Carlton Lee,
Howard Kilgour, Doug Bennett

FOR STONES ADDICTS

"Can You Hear the Music" does not seem to have convinced any other artists, as it is one of the rare Stones songs not to have been covered at all—at least during the band's career to date.

Genesis

The message conveyed by the Glimmer Twins in this song is universal: music possesses a magic that can soothe the soul, heal many an ill, and even transcend the metaphysical question. *Sometimes I wonder why we're here, but I don't care*, sings Jagger, immediately adding: *When I hear the drummer, get me in the groove/When I hear the guitar, make me wanna move*. In short, *When you hear the music, trouble disappear* . . .

This fine homage to music is also the most complex track on *Goats Head Soup* in terms of its instrumentation. It opens with an atmospheric intro featuring flute, percussion, and bells. This may have been intended as an allusion to the late Brian Jones, who played a leading role in crafting the Stones' sound during the second half of the sixties. But without their multi-instrumentalist "blond angel," the Stones could be said to have lost their way a little on this track.

Production

"Can You Hear the Music" is a strange mix of diverse sonorities reminiscent of the musical arrangements on *Their Satanic Majesties Request*. The Stones' psychedelic frenzy may have been perfectly legitimate in 1967, but in 1973 it fails to make a mark on a disc that has ended up becoming overly heterogeneous. Poor Jimmy Miller has not really succeeded in bringing the Stones back up to scratch as he did on *Beggars Banquet*, and as a result the band lacks direction. In the intro, Pascal creates pleasing tinkling sonorities on the triangle and finger cymbals, while Jim Horn plays an oriental flute that recalls *The Pipes of Pan at Joujouka* (the album recorded by Brian Jones in 1968) against a background of congas with heavy reverb, played by Rebop. Keith Richards then enters with a pretty unmistakable guitar sound, obtained almost certainly using a wah-wah pedal and Leslie speaker. He is followed by Nicky Hopkins, who plays piano arpeggios that sound as if they could have been lifted from a relaxation tape, before being joined by Charlie Watts on drums and Bill Wyman on bass, the only elements on the track that are truly solid and justified. Even Mick Taylor has trouble finding his rightful place, playing a very distorted lead guitar that is recessed in the mix, and if truth be told, not exactly indispensable. As for Mick Jagger, he seems to be the only member of the band who believes in his message.

STAR STAR

Mick Jagger / Keith Richards / 4:24

Musicians
Mick Jagger: vocals
Keith Richards: lead guitar, backing vocals
Mick Taylor: rhythm guitar, lead guitar (?)
Bill Wyman: bass
Charlie Watts: drums
Ian Stewart: piano
Bobby Keys: saxophone
Recorded
Dynamic Sound Studios, Kingston, Jamaica:
November 23–December 14, 1972
Village Recorders, Los Angeles: January 27–30, 1973
Island Studios, London: May 28–June 8, 1973
Olympic Sound Studios, London: May 7–17, July 6–9, 1973
Technical Team
Producer: Jimmy Miller
Sound engineers: Andy Johns, Rob Fraboni, Baker Bigsby
Assistant sound engineers: Carlton Lee,
Howard Kilgour, Doug Bennett

FOR STONES ADDICTS

Although Steve McQueen was, on the whole, amused that his name was mentioned in "Star Star"—the Stones sent him a cassette in order to make sure he was in agreement—this was not the case with John Wayne. In order to pacify the iconic star of many a Western, Andy Johns assured Atlantic that he had put so much echo on the word *Wayne* that it was no longer comprehensible. This was a white lie from the sound engineer!

It is possible that "Star Star" was an implicit response to the song "You're So Vain," Carly Simon's all-out attack on an egocentric lover. Mick Jagger had contributed backing vocals to the track, with the result that when the single came out in November 1972, no one suspected that it might be the Stones singer who was targeted in the song (some people have suggested Warren Beatty as a candidate).

Genesis

A return to Rolling Stones style! *Goats Head Soup* concludes with a highly controversial song. A *rock star* pines for a groupie who has introduced him to an astonishing variety of amorous pleasures, and it is with considerable excitement that he recalls their impassioned embraces, her *legs wrapped around me tight*, her *can of tasty foam*. Indeed the young woman is so gifted that the whole world wants her in their address book, and everyone wants to *get their tongues beneath* [her] *hood* and make her *scream all night*. In short, she's a *starfucker* . . . But this is merely the appetizer. She now has her sights set on movie stars, and in the fourth verse Mick Jagger brings out the big guns. This groupie who lives in New York has not moved to Hollywood for nothing: she has been *givin' head to Steve McQueen*, which made Ali McGraw *mad*, and plans to *get John Wayne before he dies*.

Starfucker is a term commonly used by rock musicians to refer to groupies, and this was the original title of the closing track on the album until Ahmet Ertegun of Atlantic Records put his foot down. The song was therefore renamed "Star Star," both on the album and for the single (with "Doo Doo Doo Doo Doo [Heartbreaker]" as the B-side) that provoked an angry response from feminists upon its release in December 1973. A new affront from the Stones? Mick Jagger would provide an answer in person by straddling an enormous inflatable penis during his performance of the song. The single would achieve only modest success, however, peaking at number 7 in Switzerland and number 32 in West Germany.

Production

From the very first notes of the opening riff, it is clear that the Stones are back in the evergreen territory of Chuck Berry–inspired rock 'n' roll. So how could Keith not launch the closing number on *Goats Head Soup* with a "Johnny B. Goode"–style riff? Nor is it very likely that he would deny himself the pleasure of going through the repertoire, during these four-plus minutes, of everything he learned from the brilliant inventor of the duckwalk. He seems to be coming alive and really getting his kicks on this track, and his pleasure is admittedly contagious. Mick Taylor supports him with some very good rhythm guitar, and also seems to be playing the main solo at 2:09, as the concluding notes are more typical of his style

Mick Jagger and the inflatable penis, the pièce de résistance of "Star Star," also known as "Starfucker."

than of Keith's. It is amusing to observe that throughout the whole duration of this solo, Keith does not stop playing his lead part for a moment, apparently oblivious to everyone else. As a result, it could almost be said that there are two guitar solos going on at the same time! Charlie Watts plays a pretty linear rhythm, only rarely deviating from the same bass drum/hi-hat/snare drum pattern, and, regrettably, there's a certain stiffness to his groove. Bill Wyman, on the other hand, plays an excellent bass line that compensates for this rigidity, and ultimately it may be that Charlie has chosen the right formula after all by provoking a reaction that is the complementary opposite of his own approach. Bill's Fender Mustang bass does not come in until the second verse, which for all intents and purposes relaunches the song—and to great effect. This is a technique the bassist was fond of and employed relatively often. Ian Stewart comes in at the same time with his boogie-woogie piano, of which he was almost certainly the best proponent among the pianists that had played with the Stones to date. His raw, exuberant playing is imbued with irresistible feeling. Of all the piano players, Stu is probably the one to have grasped how best to serve the needs of the band. Bobby Keys makes some short interjections on the saxophone, but unfortunately these are undermixed, with the result that they are not

really worth having at all. Finally, "Star Star" would not be the merry romp it is without Mick Jagger's superb performance. The singer takes delight in leading his troops down politically incorrect avenues. Here he proves once more that he is an exceptional performer of shocking rock 'n' roll numbers! As a result of the topic, the song would have difficulty getting played on certain radio stations, notably the BBC, which boycotted it.

IN YOUR HEADPHONES

Evidence of Andy Johns's attempt to cover up the reference to John Wayne can be heard between 2:58 and 3:01. A horrible echo suddenly invades the whole mix, only to disappear instantly. This begs the question: why didn't Andy apply the echo to Mick's voice alone?

If You Can't Rock Me
Ain't Too Proud To Beg
It's Only Rock'n'Roll (But I Like It)
Till The Next Goodbye
Time Waits For No One

Luxury
Dance Little Sister
If You Really Want To Be My Friend
Short And Curlies
Fingerprint File

ALBUM
RELEASE DATE
United Kingdom: October 18, 1974
Label: Rolling Stones Records
RECORD NUMBER: ROLLING STONES
RECORDS COC 59103
Number 2, on the charts for 9 weeks

IT'S ONLY ROCK' N' ROLL

Just after the *Goats Head Soup* tour, the Glimmer Twins were ready to go back into the studio, this time in Munich.

BRUSSELS AFFAIR

The transporting of French fans to the National Forest by RTL was referred to as the "Brussels Affair." The event lives on in the form of a live album of the same name, officially released in October 2011 (in reality a compilation of the two Brussels shows).

IT'S ONLY ROCK 'N' ROLL: THE END OF AN ERA

On September 1, 1973, the day after the release of *Goats Head Soup*, the Rolling Stones, along with Billy Preston (keyboards), Steve Madaio (trumpet), and Trevor Lawrence (saxophone), embarked on an extensive promotional tour through Europe that would continue until mid-October. Their itinerary took in Austria, West Germany, the United Kingdom, Switzerland, Scandinavia, the Netherlands, and Belgium. There was no question of the band performing in France, as Keith had been prohibited from entering the country for a period of two years after being found guilty of possessing heroin in October 1973. Hence the second concert at the National Forest in Brussels on October 17, given for French fans ferried to the venue on special trains chartered by the radio station RTL.

The Album

The *Goats Head Soup* promotional tour wrapped up with a concert at the Deutschlandhalle in West Berlin on October 19, 1973. Not long after, the Rolling Stones returned to Germany (Munich, to be precise) to record almost all of what would become their twelfth (British) studio album, *It's Only Rock 'n' Roll*. This title only partially reflects the music on the record. Although the title song, "If You Can't Rock Me," "Luxury," and even "Dance Little Sister" follow in the good old Rolling Stones tradition (at least since the band's flamboyant return to blues rock with "Jumpin' Jack Flash" and "Honky Tonk Women"), and although "Short and Curlies" is a blues number that sounds as if it could have been recorded back in the early days of the Stones'

career and "Ain't Too Proud to Beg" is a respectful tribute to Motown soul, some other tracks are imbued with a very different spirit or, to put it more accurately, continue what the songwriters Mick Jagger and Keith Richards had begun on *Goats Head Soup* (even if Munich is a long way from Kingston!). In other words, the Glimmer Twins once again accord an important place to ballads ("Till the Next Goodbye" and "If You Really Want to Be My Friend") and explore new sonorities: Latin American in the case of "Time Waits for No One," and funky in the case of "Fingerprint File."

To a considerable extent, the lyrics to these songs derive from Jagger's personal experience. "If You Can't Rock Me" deals directly with the furtive relationship between a *rock star* and the women who admire him, but could also be seen as a reflection on marriage. Wedlock is again at the center of the narrator's preoccupations in "If You Really Want to Be My Friend," in which he asks the person with whom he is sharing his life for a little more understanding and freedom. As for the title song, "It's Only Rock 'n' Roll" is in a similar spirit to "If You Can't Rock Me": a singer is prepared to go to any lengths to seduce the woman he loves all over again. At the same time, however, the song is a vehement diatribe against journalists and segments of the public who were asking whether the Rolling Stones had any kind of future. On a very different note, "Till the Next Goodbye" is a very pretty love song steeped in the atmosphere of New York, while "Time Waits for No One" is a meditation on nostalgia and the inexorable passing of time, which is as precious as diamonds.

Mick Taylor backstage at the Olympiahalle in Munich on September 28, 1973, with saxophonists Bobby Keys and Trevor Lawrence.

Barely two months before entering the recording studio in Munich, Keith Richards learned of the death of his friend Gram Parsons from a morphine overdose in California on September 19, 1973.

FOR STONES ADDICTS

Guy Peellaert attracted criticism for drawing a small pair of abandoned panties on the last step in his illustration for the back of the *It's Only Rock 'n' Roll* album cover.

Come Hell or High Water

Despite both turning thirty during the sessions for *It's Only Rock 'n' Roll*, the Glimmer Twins had lost none of their inspiration when it came to provoking or castigating conservative attitudes. "Luxury," the story of a disgruntled employee of a Texas oil company who has had enough of working seven days a week simply to enrich his bosses, is nothing short of a social manifesto, while the heroine of "Dance Little Sister" is a teenage girl in a tight-fitting dress who turns heads on the streets of Port of Spain (Trinidad and Tobago). Finally, "Short and Curlies" is an all-out attack on women who emasculate men, in truth a misogynistic tirade.

It's Only Rock 'n' Roll was released in the United States on October 16, 1974, and in the rest of the world two days later. It was a hit in the United States and the United Kingdom, where it was respectively number 1 and number 2 (and certified gold), and also in France. In general, the album was greeted favorably by the music press. Jon Landau, for example, saw it as "one of the most intriguing and mysterious, as well as the darkest, of all Rolling Stones records."[100] Other rock journalists emphasize the major role played by Mick Taylor in the recording sessions. In the columns of the *NME*, Nick Kent wrote: "Mick Taylor was involved in the actual composition of 'Time Waits for No One,' even though the writing credits will go to Jagger and Richards, as ever. It also turns out that Taylor has made creative inserts into other tracks like 'Till the Next Goodbye' and 'If You Really Want to Be My Friend.' Still no credit."[1] Was it this lack of recognition that

would drive Mick Taylor to leave the band? "I had a falling out with Mick Jagger over some songs I should have been credited with co-writing on (the album) 'It's Only Rock 'N' Roll,'" he would reveal in 2007. "I don't get paid for some of the biggest-selling records of all time. Frankly, I was ripped off."[102]

For whatever reason, *It's Only Rock 'n' Roll* turned out to be Taylor's last album with the Rolling Stones. His departure was officially announced on December 12, 1974, just two months after the record went on sale. In the same vein, Bill Wyman's recording between December 1973 and February 1974 of *Monkey Grip* (released May 1974), the first solo album by a member of the Stones (with the exception of the atypical *Brian Jones Presents the Pipes of Pan at Joujouka*, 1971), testifies to the bassist's desire to express himself outside the group, in other words away from the influence of the Jagger-Richards duo. Evidently it was not all smooth sailing on board the good ship Rolling Stones, but although it may not be one of their best, to produce an album like *It's Only Rock 'n' Roll* during such times shows that the band was capable of weathering choppy waters.

The Album Cover

Mick Jagger asked Guy Peellaert to design the cover for *It's Only Rock 'n' Roll*. Peellaert was a Belgian artist and illustrator, influenced by both pop art and psychedelia, who collaborated on the French satirical magazine *Hara-Kiri* during the second half of the sixties. At the beginning of the seventies, he made a name for himself with the publication of *Rock Dreams*,

Mick Jagger onstage in Hawaii. *It's only rock 'n' roll . . .*

a collection of 125 portraits of rock stars that combined painting with photomontage. The portrait of the Stones was particularly provocative, depicting Brian, Keith, and Charlie in SS uniforms with Mick dressed in only a garter belt, surrounded by four young girls, naked, one of whom is playing the piano. Apparently impressed by this image, Jagger decided to commission Peellaert for the cover of the band's new album. The artist produced an illustration in the same spirit as those that had made *Rock Dreams* so successful. It depicts the five Stones, in the guise of the Olympic deities, descending the red-carpeted steps of a colonnaded temple to the acclaim of a crowd of young women clad in Roman togas who are giving the Roman salute. In the foreground is a group of young girls joining hands in a children's dance. The reverse simply shows the steps and the marble columns with the song titles. The cover of *It's Only Rock 'n' Roll* was chosen by the British music magazine *NME* as the best record cover of 1974.

The Recording

With *It's Only Rock 'n' Roll*, one story ends and another begins. It was the first album since the highly atypical *Their Satanic Majesties Request* to be produced by the Rolling Stones, or more precisely the Glimmer Twins, following the exit of Jimmy Miller after six years of good and loyal service. Heroin is not a good mentor, as the brilliant producer

discovered to his detriment. Keith recalls him carving swastikas into the desk at Island Studios: "He had assumed that anybody could adopt my lifestyle after a while, but he hadn't realised that my diet is very, very rare."[9] As a result, Miller was dismissed, permanently and irrevocably, despite all the assistance he had given the band. Keith could not speak highly enough of him after the event, however: "He was one of the warmest guys and an incredible friend. We made our best records with him."[103] Apparently this was not enough . . . Andy Johns, initiated into dope by the master himself in 1970, would meet the same fate. The severity of his addiction meant that he was nearing the end of his collaboration with the Stones, and *It's Only Rock 'n' Roll* would be his swan song. The final firing was that of Bobby Keys, who had also become overdependent on hard drugs. He incurred the wrath of the Glimmer Twins when he decided to take a bath with a young beauty in a tub filled with Dom Pérignon rather than join them onstage with his sax, effectively leaving the band in the lurch. Keith later wrote: "And it took me ten goddamn years or more to get him back in the band, because Mick was implacable, and rightly so."[2]

The Stones' twelfth studio album was recorded at Musicland Studios in Munich, which had been founded at the end of the sixties by Giorgio Moroder, the future master craftsman of disco. Under the supervision of the producer and

It's Only Rock 'N' Roll was to be Mick Taylor's last album with the Stones. Shown here playing his Gibson ES 355TD.

At the end of the Munich sessions in March 1974, Mick Jagger and Bill Wyman joined John Lennon at the Record Plant in New York for an impromptu jam. Among the musicians were Harry Nilsson, Jack Bruce, Jesse Ed Davis, Jim Keltner, Bobby Keys, and Danny Kortchmar. This gave rise to the recording of a Willie Dixon number, "Too Many Cooks (Spoil the Soup)," produced by Lennon and not released until 2007 on *The Very Best of Mick Jagger*. In Bill Wyman's words, "It was actually a fiasco . . ."[1]

sound engineer Reinhold Mack, a succession of big names in rock and pop would come here to work, such as Marc Bolan of T. Rex, Queen, Black Sabbath, ELO, Deep Purple, and Led Zeppelin, to name but a few. Mack recalls his first session with the Stones: "They had a look around the studio, then sat down and one of them began to tinkle away at the piano. Basically, they were like a schoolboy band. Then Mick said: 'That won't do. Let's have a go at something we've done before.' I discovered that there were no rules with them. They always record everything. And at some point it comes together."[104]

Under Control

Between November 14 and 25, 1973, and February 20 and March 3, 1974, the Stones cut eight of the album's ten tracks in Munich with Andy Johns at the controls: "Ain't Too Proud to Beg," "If You Can't Rock Me," "Fingerprint File," "If You Really Want to Be My Friend," "Time Waits for No One," "Luxury," "Dance Little Sister," and "Till the Next Goodbye." Various other songs recorded were not used (an exception being "Waiting for a Friend," which would end up on *Tattoo You* in 1981). Only "Short and Curlies" and the title song predate the Bavarian sessions,

the former having originated during the *Goats Head Soup* sessions at Dynamic Sound Studios in Kingston in late 1972, while the second had taken shape in Ron Wood's studio in his London home, The Wick, in July 1973 before being reworked by Keith at Musicland Studios in Munich at the end of February and the beginning of March 1974. In charge of the overdubs was George Chkiantz. Further sessions would follow at Stargroves, using the Rolling Stones Mobile Studio, with Keith Harwood as the new sound engineer. Harwood went on to work on *Black and Blue* in 1976 and *Love You Live* in 1977. Sadly, he died in a car accident during the sessions for the second of these albums. Finally, *It's Only Rock 'n' Roll* was mixed by Harwood, with Glyn Johns making a brief appearance to work on one track, "Fingerprint File," at Island Studios in London from May 4 to 27. The assistant sound engineers included Tapani Tapanainen (John Mayall, Deep Purple), Rod Thear (Led Zeppelin, King Crimson, Santana), and Howard Kilgour, who had already worked on *Goats Head Soup*.

Mick Taylor was reportedly unable to take part in the November 1973 sessions for *It's Only Rock 'n' Roll* in Munich for medical reasons. He was present at Musicland Studios from

The producer Reinhold Mack (foreground)
with Jeff Lynne of ELO.

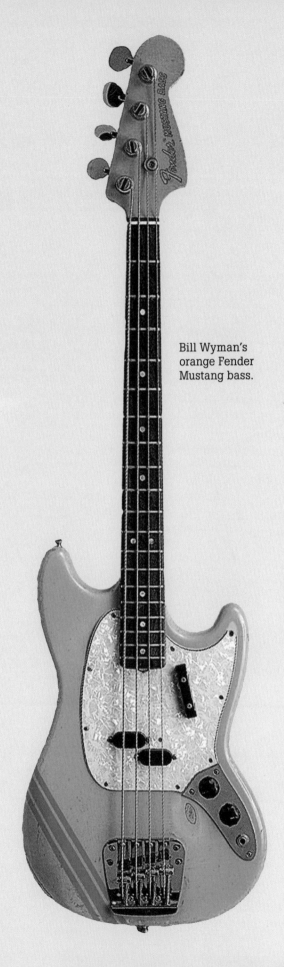

Bill Wyman's
orange Fender
Mustang bass.

the end of February to the beginning of March, but this was to be the last time he would record with the Rolling Stones. As for Mick Jagger, faced with an incapacitated Keith Richards, ravaged by dope, the singer took command of operations, as Mack Reinhold attests: "[Keith] was sitting on a chair with his head resting back and his guitar hanging down. . . . When Mick thought they'd done enough, they simply left." And the engineer elaborated further on Jagger's role: "He was always in control of everything . . . A control freak without appearing to be one."[104]

New musicians made an appearance on the disc, as was to become the norm with each new Stones album: the must-have percussionist Ray Cooper, who played with everyone who was anyone in rock music, including Pink Floyd, Sting, Elton John, George Harrison, Paul McCartney, Eric Clapton, and many others; Jolly Kunjappu (alias Charlie Jolly) on tabla; Ed Leach on cowbell; and the vocal quintet Blue Magic on "If You Really Want to Be My Friend."

Technical Details

When Reinhold Mack took charge of production and recordings at Musicland Studios in Munich, he equipped the control room with a sixteen-channel Helios desk (for which Dick Swettenham, at Mack's request, designed an extension with a further sixteen channels), a Studer A80 sixteen-track tape recorder, and JBL monitors.

The Instruments

For the *It's Only Rock 'n' Roll* sessions, the Stones used more or less the same instruments as they had on the previous album. One big innovation was the use of a multi-effect synthesizer for guitar, the Synthi Hi-Fli, brought to the studio by Mick Taylor with no clear aim in mind.

IF YOU CAN'T ROCK ME

Mick Jagger / Keith Richards / 3:47

Musicians
Mick Jagger: vocals
Keith Richards: rhythm guitars, bass, backing vocals
Mick Taylor: lead guitar
Charlie Watts: drums
Billy Preston: clavinet
Ray Cooper: percussion

Recorded
Musicland Studios, Munich: November 14–25, 1973
Rolling Stones Mobile Studio, Stargroves, Newbury: April 12–May 2, 1974
Island Studios, London: May 5–27, 1974

Technical Team
Producers: The Glimmer Twins
Sound engineers: Andy Johns, Keith Harwood, George Chkiantz
Assistant sound engineers: Tapani Tapanainen, Rod Thear, Howard Kilgour, Reinhold Mack,

Charlie Watts, at his Gretsch kit, sporting a shirt bearing the logo of the Stones.

Genesis

The protagonist in this song, apparently Mick Jagger himself, is onstage and addresses all the women who are looking at him and admiring him, all the *lovely ladies in . . . leather and lace* whose lips he would *love to taste. I'm not so green but I'm feeling so fresh,* claims the singer in the refrain, warning all those who might not be adventurous enough that if they don't succeed in giving him pleasure, others will. In parallel with this " invitation," he claims that he is no longer interested in *some hooker working roughish trade* and that there's nothing like a *perfect mate.* Might this song also be a reflection from Mick Jagger on marriage—which he seems to be saying is not really his cup of tea—three years after his union with Bianca?

Production

Charlie Watts opens the Stones' new album with a triple rap on his snare drum. "If You Can't Rock Me" is essentially a classic rock number with a short incursion, of several bars' duration, into a funkier style. The band cranks itself up, Jagger pushes his vocal cords to the limit, and the guitars are searching for the ultimate riff, but despite all this, the track has difficulty taking off. Keith Richards seems to take care of the two rhythm guitar parts himself, with Mick Taylor playing a number of solo interjections. Billy Preston is on the clavinet, and uses a wah-wah pedal to emphasize the syncopation. On the drums, Charlie is not as effective as he had been in the presence of Jimmy Miller, and his playing is distinctly lacking in groove. This is all the more apparent in the funk-rock bridge (from 1:28), in which Keith performs a solo on distorted bass guitar. Moreover, the listener will notice that there are actually two bass sounds, one "normal" and the other more metallic. It is probably Keith who takes care of both on his Fender Precision, Bill Wyman being either absent or not asked to play. The mixing buries the vocals beneath oversevere compression, eliminating too much expressivity from the performance. The Stones give the impression of doing the job without a great deal of conviction. This is regrettable on an opening track, and doubly so on the first record to bear a Glimmer Twins production credit.

AIN'T TOO PROUD TO BEG

Norman Whitfield / Edward Holland Jr. / 3:31

Musicians
Mick Jagger: vocals
Keith Richards: rhythm guitar, lead guitar, backing vocals
Bill Wyman: bass
Charlie Watts: drums
Billy Preston: piano
Ray Cooper: congas
Ed Leach: cowbell

Recorded
Musicland Studios, Munich: November 14–25, 1973
Rolling Stones Mobile Studio, Stargroves, Newbury: April 12–May 2, 1974
Island Studios, London: May 5–27, 1974

Technical Team
Producers: The Glimmer Twins
Sound engineers: Andy Johns, Keith Harwood, George Chkiantz
Assistant sound engineers: Tapani Tapanainen, Rod Thear, Howard Kilgour, Reinhold Mack,

In 1973, Bill Wyman chose to play a Gibson EB-3 bass in concert, in addition to his other instruments.

Genesis

The composer and producer Norman Whitfield, who had already given the Temptations "Girl (Why You Wanna Make Me Blue)" in 1964, returned to duty two years later following the relative failure for the group of "Get Ready" (composed and produced by Smokey Robinson). After coming up with a catchy melody, Whitfield asked his songwriting partner Eddie Holland to compose the lyrics, and "Ain't Too Proud to Beg" was born. The song is about a man who begs his girlfriend, with whom he is deeply in love, not to leave him—a simple but timeless scenario. Following various improvements made at Berry Gordy's request (and three different recorded versions), "Ain't Too Proud to Beg" was released as a single on March 3, 1966. It climbed to number 1 on the R&B chart (for eight non-consecutive weeks) and number 13 on the pop chart. Seven years after the Temptations, it was the Rolling Stones' turn to record this Motown showcase. Mick Jagger reveals himself to be every bit as persuasive as David Ruffin, and the US public would respond favorably: the Stones version reached number 17 on the *Billboard* chart on December 14, 1974.

Production

Charlie Watts launches into a very good drum part, probably one of his best on the album, with a break on the snare drum. His solid, powerful, and funky playing provides the track with all the verve it needs to rival the "made in Detroit" version. He alternates a distinctly Funk Brothers groove with highly effective playing of his ride cymbal bell. Charlie is impeccably supported by Bill Wyman on bass, and the two alone transform "Ain't Too Proud to Beg" into an invitation to dance. Keith Richards seems to be taking care of all the guitars himself. He plays a rhythm part that stresses the second beat in each of the verses, and a more carefully crafted lead that is funkier and closer in spirit to Motown. He also plays the solo, a characteristically stripped-back one, composed of short phrases, at 1:33. Billy Preston is outstanding as usual on both piano and clavinet, each of these instruments being crucial to the track. On percussion, Ray Cooper distinguishes himself on the congas, while Ed Leach plays the cowbell, which in truth is inaudible. Finally, Mick Jagger delivers an excellent vocal performance, supported by the inimitable Keith, who searches extremely high for his notes, indeed to the verge of the breaking point.

IT'S ONLY ROCK'N'ROLL (BUT I LIKE IT)

Mick Jagger / Keith Richards / 5:07

Musicians
Mick Jagger: vocals
Keith Richards: acoustic guitar, rhythm guitar, lead guitar, backing vocals
Mick Taylor: backing vocals
Ron Wood: 12-string acoustic guitar
Bill Wyman: bass
Kenney Jones: drums
Ian Stewart: piano
Unidentified musician(s): hand claps
Recorded
The Wick home studio, London: July 24, 1973
Musicland Studios, Munich: February 20–March 3, 1974
Rolling Stones Mobile Studio, Stargroves, Newbury: April 12–May 2, 1974
Island Studios, London: May 5–27, 1974
Technical Team
Producers: The Glimmer Twins
Sound engineers: Andy Johns, Keith Harwood, George Chkiantz
Assistant sound engineers: Tapani Tapanainen, Rod Thear, Howard Kilgour, Reinhold Mack

Mick Jagger's inspiration for "It's Only Rock 'n' Roll" may have come from "Rock 'n' Roll Suicide" by David Bowie (on the album *The Rise and Fall of Ziggy Stardust and the Spiders from Mars*, 1972). In this case the suicide is said to reference the stage act of the glam rock star Marc Bolan (T. Rex).

Genesis

In 1973, Ron Wood was not yet a member of the Rolling Stones. He was a friend of Mick Jagger and Keith Richards. At this time he was in the process of recording his first solo album in the studio he had installed in his new home, The Wick, on Richmond Hill in southwest London. This debut album under his own name would be given the jokey title *I've Got My Own Album to Do*. Its tracks include "Act Together" and "Sure the One You Need," two numbers generously donated to Wood, who was still the guitarist of the Faces, by the Glimmer Twins, along with "I Can Feel the Fire," which opens the album. "When I was writing 'I Can Feel the Fire,'" explains Ron Wood in his autobiography, "Mick gave me a hand on the song. I then helped him out on 'It's Only Rock 'N' Roll.'"[105]

Thus the title song of the Rolling Stones' twelfth (British) studio album saw the light of day in Ron Wood's studio. The lyrics bear the imprimatur of Mick Jagger. A singer is prepared to go to any lengths to win back his unfaithful lover: *to stick a pen in* [his] *heart*, to break down and cry, and even to commit *suicide right on stage*. And so what if all this is, in the end, merely rock 'n' roll? Jagger's slogan has the virtue of being as clear as it is effective: *it's only rock 'n' roll, but I like it*. A slogan addressed to the music journalists and segments of their audience who were wondering whether the Stones might be past their prime. "I was getting a bit tired of people having a go, all that, 'oh, it's not as good as their last one' business. The single sleeve had a picture of me with a pen digging into me as if it were a sword. It was a lighthearted, anti-journalistic sort of thing."[87]

"It's Only Rock 'n' Roll" was released as a single (with "Through the Lonely Nights" as the flip side) on July 26, 1974, three months before the album. It got to third place in the French hit parade in September, but only made numbers 10 and 16, respectively, in the United Kingdom and the United States.

Production

"We recorded in my studio at the Wick," explains Ron Wood, "with Mick doing the vocals and both of us on guitar, Willie Weeks on bass and Kenney Jones on drums. David Bowie and I did backup vocals. We're the guys singing 'I like it, I like it'. Mick then got the Stones to overdub on it."[105] When

Five sailors in search of rock 'n' roll in the promotional video by Michael Lindsay–Hogg.

Keith heard the song for the first time, he was pleasantly surprised—"It was damn good,"[2] he would later say—but did not particularly appreciate the participation of the creator of Ziggy Stardust on backing vocals. "Shit, Mick, what are you doing it with Bowie for? Come on, we've got to steal that motherfucker back."[2] And the same went for the guitars: "I took the precaution of removing your guitar parts,"[2] he would tell Ron Wood, although he would do him the favor of retaining his contribution on 12-string, which he would complement with his own acoustic guitar part.

The Stones recorded the overdubs during their second recording session in Munich, at the end of February and the beginning of March. Keith did not want to relinquish his role of electric master and thus recorded two parts, one distorted rhythm, the other distinctly "Chuck Berry," though Jagger reinforces the rhythm part, probably on a Gibson Les Paul. Essentially, Mick Taylor is conspicuous by his absence, although he does contribute to the backing vocals (alongside Mick and Keith), those of Ron Wood and David Bowie having been wiped. Ian Stewart found this return to rock 'n' roll

to his taste and launches into a boogie-woogie piano part (sadly undermixed) as only he can. As for the rhythm section, Keith must, in the end, have made up his mind to retain the talented Kenney Jones's drumming. Charlie Watts tried to reproduce the work of the Faces drummer, who had, in fact, been imitating Charlie on the earlier track, but the results were disappointing. Supported by the excellent bass (Fender Mustang, apparently) of Bill Wyman, who, by the same token, was replacing the bass part recorded by Willie Weeks, he imparts a subtle groove to the track. In all objectivity, however, "It's Only Rock 'n' Roll" owes its strength to Mick Jagger. The singer delivers a superb vocal performance that rocks and is exuberant and more natural than many of the other songs on the album. He sings the second vocal himself. The Stones have succeed in making this number highly dynamic and rousing, despite its medium tempo. Ron Wood has declared that, "With a song like 'It's Only Rock and Roll', you can't really get into who wrote which note."[105] On the album cover, however, he is simply credited as providing "inspiration" for the song.

TILL THE NEXT GOODBYE

Mick Jagger / Keith Richards / 4:37

Musicians
Mick Jagger: vocals, acoustic guitar
Keith Richards: slide guitar (?), backing vocals
Mick Taylor: 12-string acoustic guitar (?)
Bill Wyman: bass
Charlie Watts: drums
Nicky Hopkins: piano

Recorded
Musicland Studios, Munich: November 14–25, 1973
Rolling Stones Mobile Studio, Stargroves, Newbury: April 12–May 2, 1974
Island Studios, London: May 5–27, 1974

Technical Team
Producers: The Glimmer Twins
Sound engineers: Andy Johns, Keith Harwood, George Chkiantz
Assistant sound engineers: Tapani Tapanainen, Rod Thear, Howard Kilgour, Reinhold Mack

The singer Carly Simon is said to have written "Till the Next Goodbye" with Mick Jagger.

Genesis

Like so many Stones songs, "Till the Next Goodbye" tells the story of a couple on the verge of falling apart. A man recalls meeting his lover in a *movie house on Forty-Second Street.* Given that from the early seventies onward, this particular New York thoroughfare was lined mainly with theaters showing porn flicks, it seems a strange place to meet . . . Little matter, time has passed, and having survived one crisis after another, his feelings have become blunted. Nothing can now reawaken the love he once had for his girl, not even her cider-apple-and-elderberry-wine-based miracle cure concocted in New Orleans. He might be arranging to see her in the coffee shop on Fifty-Second Street for a final meeting, and admits that he could do without the tears she will cry when they say good-bye.

Production

The intro is reminiscent of tracks from the *Sticky Fingers* or *Exile on Main St.* era, such as "Wild Horses," featuring two acoustic guitars that answer each other. On "Till the Next Goodbye," a first rhythm part is probably played by Mick Jagger on a Gibson Hummingbird, and a second most likely by Mick Taylor on a (Martin D12-20?) 12-string, his use of harmonics being one of his trademarks. This would leave Keith on electric slide, which is corroborated by the promotional clip shot, as usual, by Michael Lindsay-Hogg in 1974. Furthermore, the phrasing of this slide part is characteristic of Keith, rather than Mick Taylor. Nicky Hopkins, his lyrical style instantly recognizable, makes his first appearance on the album here. Bill Wyman plays a fairly subdued bass line on his Dallas Tuxedo, while Charlie Watts demonstrates a certain inventiveness with an extremely subtle accompaniment that alternates tom and cymbal breaks with a very effective but unobtrusive rhythm. Mick Jagger is perfect, credible in his emotion without being mawkish, and Keith Richards provides valuable support in the vocal harmonies. "Till the Next Goodbye" may not be one of the duo's masterpieces, but it is a good, unpretentious song.

TIME WAITS FOR NO ONE

Mick Jagger / Keith Richards / 6:38

Musicians
Mick Jagger: vocals, rhythm guitar (?)
Keith Richards: rhythm guitar, backing vocals
Mick Taylor: lead guitar, 12-string acoustic guitar
Bill Wyman: bass, synthesizer
Charlie Watts: drums
Nicky Hopkins: piano
Ray Cooper: percussion

Recorded
Musicland Studios, Munich: February 20–March 3, 1974
Rolling Stones Mobile Studio, Stargroves,
Newbury: April 12–May 2, 1974
Island Studios, London: May 5–27, 1974

Technical Team
Producers: The Glimmer Twins
Sound engineers: Andy Johns,
Keith Harwood, George Chkiantz
Assistant sound engineers: Tapani Tapanainen,
Rod Thear, Howard Kilgour, Reinhold Mack

Mick Jagger wrote both the words and the music
of this compelling ballad on *It's Only Rock 'N' Roll*.

Genesis

"Time Waits for No One" is a reflection on the passing years, and the narrator looks back on his life: *Time waits for no one, and he won't wait for me*. He is drowning in nostalgia and regret: *Hours are like diamonds, don't let them waste*. There is a tragic inevitability in his words, for the *dreams of the nighttime have vanished by dawn*. Might Mick Jagger be poking fun at himself after having declared not long before that he could not imagine singing rock 'n' roll after turning thirty?

Production

The music and lyrics may be by Mick Jagger, but the atmosphere of "Time Waits for No One" owes a great deal to Mick Taylor, who suffuses the whole track with a Latin rock flavor that is simultaneously restrained and sensual. Moreover, Taylor would later tell Damian Fanelli of *Guitar World* that this was his favorite Rolling Stones song: "I love that solo. I think it's probably the best thing I did with the Stones. It's not one of their hits; it was an album track. But it's quite lyrical and it's a bit different from a lot of other Stones songs. I'd done something that I'd never done. Because of the structure of the song, it pushed my guitar playing in a slightly different direction."[106] It is difficult to disagree with his view, as the results are both surprising and extraordinary, the solo having been recorded in a single take. By dint of his talent on the guitar, Mick Taylor could be said to have succeeded in laying Brian Jones's ghost to rest, not by replacing him, but by contributing a different color that defies comparison with the Stones' founder. Jones was, and would forever remain, irreplaceable, but Mick Taylor would lead the group toward other sonorities: first of all a return to a more traditional form of blues with his outstanding mastery of the slide guitar, and secondly a jazz-rock fusion with a Latin accent. His highly lyrical solo on this track is clearly reminiscent of Carlos Santana. It is even tempting to wonder whether Santana might have been influenced by some of Taylor's phrasing, notably in his mega hit "Europa (Earth's Cry Heaven's Smile)," dating from 1976. "It's more—I don't like to use the term Carlos Santana-esque because it sounds too pretentious, but I kind of played in a different mode. I was playing over a Cmaj7 to an Fmaj7, which aren't chords the Stones used that much."[106] In order to achieve these results and this sonority, he employed a Synthi

On "Time Waits for No One," Mick Taylor, shown here playing his Fender Stratocaster, was inspired by Carlos Santana.

Ulla Meinecke recorded a good cover of the song in German in 1991—what's more, with accordion. Her version is called "Die Zeit Wartet Auf Niemand."

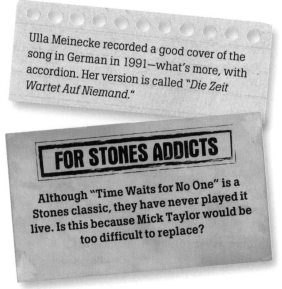

FOR STONES ADDICTS

Although "Time Waits for No One" is a Stones classic, they have never played it live. Is this because Mick Taylor would be too difficult to replace?

Hi-Fli, which is nothing other than a guitar effects synthesizer, and in particular he used the octave shift function to drop the pitch of his main solo by that interval, as can be heard at 3:33. "I just happened to plug into it when we were recording 'Time Waits for No One,'"[28] he would explain. He adds that "I used a Fender Stratocaster on that simply because it was there and it sounded good."[28] This was to be one of the last tracks he would record with the Stones. Keith Richards would regret his departure long afterward: "Why don't Mick Taylor kick himself in the arse and realise what he is? He's a fuckin' great guitar player. If he'd stop pissing about trying to be a songwriter, a producer, a bandleader."[11] One of the reasons for Taylor's departure is closely related to "Time Waits for No One." Convinced that his name would be included among the credits, he was to find out from the journalist Nick Kent how wrong he was: "He went silent for a second before muttering a curt 'We'll see about that!' almost under his breath. Actually he sounded more resigned than anything else . . ."[15] Mick Taylor was aware of his contribution and regarded this injustice as stonewalling. "You know, they had their rock and roll songs and they had their ballads as well, and they were very different. And most of the ballads were usually written by me."[106]

In addition to this fabulous lead, Mick Taylor also plays a (Martin D12-20?) 12-string acoustic. Keith is playing rhythm electric and likewise makes use of the Synthi Hi-Fli, in this case developing a riff with a sound that combines *phasing* and *waa-waa* (the manufacturer's term). Mick Jagger seems to be playing a second rhythm electric part with a degree of distortion. Noticeable right from the intro are sonorities that are pretty unusual for the Stones, for example the synthesizer played by Bill Wyman, who also takes care of the bass. Charlie Watts launches and concludes the track very starkly with rimshots and bass drum, but throughout the course of the song develops an excellent drum part with superb jazz-rock-inspired use of the cymbals. He is accompanied by that magician of the percussion Ray Cooper on congas, tambourine, and a shaker, among other things. Nicky Hopkins delivers one of his best piano parts, with prominent flights of lyricism (listen from 5:23) and a solo that answers Mick Taylor's with equal intensity. Some of the inflections in Mick Jagger's performance are reminiscent of Van Morrison, and although very well crafted, his blues-rock style does not always sit well with the Latin-jazz-rock style developed by Mick Taylor's guitar. Moreover, it is interesting to speculate as to whether Taylor would have changed the Stones' identity over the long term by leading them toward a style that did not really suit the band. We shall never know.

LUXURY

Mick Jagger / Keith Richards / 5:01

Musicians
Mick Jagger: vocals
Keith Richards: rhythm guitars and lead
guitar, bass (?) backing vocals
Bill Wyman: bass
Charlie Watts: drums
Nicky Hopkins: piano
Ray Cooper: percussion
Recorded
Musicland Studios, Munich: November 14–25, 1973
Rolling Stones Mobile Studio, Stargroves,
Newbury: April 12–May 2, 1974
Island Studios, London: May 5–27, 1974
Technical Team
Producers: The Glimmer Twins
Sound engineers: Andy Johns,
Keith Harwood, George Chkiantz
Assistant sound engineers: Tapani Tapanainen,
Rod Thear, Howard Kilgour, Reinhold Mack

Keith Richards. "Luxury" confirms his interest
in the music of the Caribbean.

> Few artists have covered "Luxury," but it is
> worth mentioning the good rock version
> included by the Hammersmith Gorillas on
> their 1999 album *Gorilla Got Me*.

Genesis

The first side of *It's Only Rock 'n' Roll* having concluded with a song shaped largely by the two Micks, Keith Richards takes things back in hand at the beginning of the second. Indeed "Luxury" can be described as a typically "Richardsian" number, with abundant killer guitar. The lyrics can be interpreted as an implacable indictment of man's exploitation of his fellow man. The narrator declares that he has had enough of *working for the company*—which seems to be one of the many oil refineries in Texas—and for bosses who shamelessly grow rich on the back of his hard work and wallow in luxury. *Make a million for the Texans, twenty dollar me*, sings Jagger. The exploited employee, we are told, works seven days a week but can no longer make ends meet. His *woman need a new dress*, while his *daughter got to go to school*.

Production

"Luxury" is the Stones' first incursion into reggae. In truth it is a kind of calypso rock, although Keith Richards would deny this: "Well first off, that is a bona fide reggae 'on-beat' being played there, no matter what anyone may tell you."[28] The idea came to him in Munich while listening to the radio on the way to the studio. When he arrived, he concocted a rock number with a riff played in open G, but the piece did not take off until Charlie Watts gave it its lilting rhythm. Mick Taylor does not seem to have taken part in the recording, leaving Keith to play the second rhythm guitar and solo part. His distinctly "Chuck Berry" style fits perfectly, and the band clearly enjoys playing the number. Bill is probably on bass, although it seems that from the second verse onward (coming in at 0:53), Keith has added a second bass part on his Fender Precision. Nicky Hopkins plays the piano mainly in the refrains and coda, but is somewhat buried in the mix. Ray Cooper distinguishes himself on the timbales, contributing what is the track's only really exotic element. Mick Jagger gives an excellent vocal performance and can be felt thrilling to the music with contagious enthusiasm.

DANCE LITTLE SISTER

Mick Jagger / Keith Richards / 4:12

Musicians
Mick Jagger: vocals
Keith Richards: rhythm guitar, backing vocals
Mick Taylor: lead guitar (?)
Bill Wyman: bass
Charlie Watts: drums
Ian Stewart: piano
Unidentified musician(s): hand claps
Recorded
Musicland Studios, Munich: November 14–25, 1973
Rolling Stones Mobile Studio, Stargroves,
Newbury: April 12–May 2, 1974
Island Studios, London: May 5–27, 1974
Technical Team
Producers: The Glimmer Twins
Sound engineers: Andy Johns,
Keith Harwood, George Chkiantz
Assistant sound engineers: Tapani Tapanainen,
Rod Thear, Howard Kilgour, Reinhold Mack

"Dance Little Sister" is addressed to the girls in the bars of Trinidad and Tobago.

Genesis

The *little sister* who puts curlers in her hair on a Thursday, but cuts a fine figure in her *high-heel shoes* and *dress so tight* the next day is an inhabitant of the Caribbean. In this song, Jagger evokes Frederick Street, the main thoroughfare of Port of Spain, the capital of Trinidad and Tobago, which he had visited with Bianca shortly before. The singer even uses various Trinidadian terms, such as *basodee* and *mamaguy*, meaning, respectively, "intoxicated' and "to tease." In a sense, "Dance Little Sister" is an exotic version of "Honky Tonk Women," or, if one prefers, a song about those who like to frequent clubs. It was chosen as the B-side of the single "Ain't Too Proud to Beg," released on October 25, 1974.

Production

When Jimmy Page was asked in 1977 for his opinion on Keith Richards's brushes with the law, the Led Zeppelin guitarist replied rightly enough: "You only have to put on 'Dance Little Sister' and you forgive the guy for anything."[107] This is a rock number as only Keith could write, featuring heavy, aggressive guitar and every bar imbued with the spirit of Chuck Berry. Rather than a riff, it would be more accurate to talk of a rhythm in which each powerful chord rings out percussively and confidently. Keith seems to be on his Telecaster, and the musical motif develops out of the interplay with Bill Wyman's bass. Charlie Watts provides a perfect beat over which his two partners can interlink, the three of them constituting a top-notch rhythm section. Keith is supported by a second guitar, but the question is, who is playing it? In all likelihood Mick Taylor, as the phrasing is characteristic of him, although at certain points, Keith's distinctive style comes through. However, the guitarist in question possesses a dexterity beyond Keith's grasp. He also uses the whammy bar (listen at 2:30) on his guitar—in all likelihood a Fender Stratocaster—an effect that Keith has never really gone in for. Ian Stewart has deigned to take his place at the piano once more, evidently convinced, and rightly so, by this well-crafted number. Mick Jagger totally immerses himself in this torrent of decibels, brilliantly living up to his reputation. It is just a shame that his voice is slightly undermixed. Listeners will notice that between 3:06 and 3:09 the first voice drops out, leaving only Mick's own doubling. Is this a technical error or a shortness of breath?

IF YOU REALLY WANT TO BE MY FRIEND

Mick Jagger / Keith Richards / 6:16

Musicians
Mick Jagger: vocals
Keith Richards: rhythm guitar, acoustic guitar, backing vocals
Mick Taylor: lead guitar
Bill Wyman: bass
Charlie Watts: drums
Nicky Hopkins: piano
Blue Magic (Ted Mills, Keith Beaton, Wendell Sawyer, Vernon Sawyer): backing vocals
Recorded
Musicland Studios, Munich: February 20–March 3, 1974
Rolling Stones Mobile Studio, Stargroves, Newbury: April 12–May 2, 1974
Island Studios, London: May 5–27, 1974
Technical Team
Producers: The Glimmer Twins
Sound engineers: Andy Johns, Keith Harwood, George Chkiantz
Assistant sound engineers: Tapani Tapanainen, Rod Thear, Howard Kilgour, Reinhold Mack

Genesis

"If You Really Want to Be My Friend" opens with the words: *If you really want to be my friend, let me live it up like I used to do*, followed a few lines later by: *If you really want to understand a man, let him off the lead sometimes, set him free.* Nothing is working for this couple anymore . . . the song's protagonist has realized that his relationship with his wife or girlfriend is becoming more and more onerous to him, and he is asking her to be a little more accommodating. The message sounds like a warning. Is it addressed implicitly to Bianca?

Production

After "Till the Next Goodbye," this is the Stones' second ballad of the album. This time the vocal group Blue Magic has been brought in to provide a touch of gospel. It seems that the English musicians had a genuine fondness for the genre; they had made one of their earliest incursions into it back in 1968 with "Salt of the Earth" on *Beggars Banquet*. Keith Richards opens the song with an augmented fifth chord. To obtain his rich and colorful swirling sound, he is probably plugged into a Leslie speaker, although he might be using the Synthi Hi-Fli as he did on "Time Waits for No One." It is almost certainly Keith on acoustic too (Gibson Hummingbird), and a fuzz guitar can be heard at 1:40 and 2:59 that also bears his signature. Mick Taylor, meanwhile, plays a clear-toned lead, at least in the intro, before delivering a pretty extraordinary solo at 3:32, this time with phasing (on his Gibson Les Paul?). Mick Jagger is not always as comfortable singing ballads as he is in rock or blues numbers, but it has to be acknowledged that he masters this song with ease and flair, perhaps inspired by the presence of Blue Magic. Nicky Hopkins, who joins the others whenever some lyrical piano is required, performs his task with disconcerting facility, demonstrating the importance of his contribution to the Stones sound, especially during this period. As for Bill Wyman and Charlie Watts, their rhythm playing is perfect for this song, the drummer and bassist providing powerful and yet subtle support that shows why, as a unit, they were such a key element in the group.

Backing vocals on this track courtesy of the soul group Blue Magic.

SHORT AND CURLIES

Mick Jagger / Keith Richards / 2:44

Musicians
Mick Jagger: vocals
Keith Richards: rhythm guitar, lead
guitar (?) backing vocals (?)
Mick Taylor: slide guitar, lead guitar (?)
Bill Wyman: bass
Charlie Watts: drums
Ian Stewart: piano
Recorded
Dynamic Sounds, Kingston, Jamaica:
November 23–December 14, 1972
Musicland Studios, Munich: November 14–25, 1973
Rolling Stones Mobile Studio, Stargroves,
Newbury: April 12–May 2, 1974
Island Studios, London: May 5–27, 1974
Technical Team
Producers: The Glimmer Twins
Sound engineers: Andy Johns,
Keith Harwood, George Chkiantz
Assistant sound engineers: Tapani Tapanainen,
Rod Thear, Howard Kilgour, Reinhold Mack

Ian Stewart, still with the Stones, plays the piano on this track on which the band reconnects with its blues-rock roots.

Genesis

The message of this song seems to follow logically from "If You Really Want to Be My Friend." The difference lies in the way the frustration of having a relationship with an interfering woman is expressed. Here it is no longer the male half of the couple who is speaking, but one of his friends, who tells him that he has been *trapped like a rat in a hole* by this woman who knows his name and telephone number. The slang term *short and curlies* refers, of course, to the pubic hair and is used in the expression *to have somebody by the short and curlies* to denote having a person under one's complete control. From the very first line of the song, however, Jagger uses the even blunter equivalent: *Too bad, she's got you by the balls*, before launching into a litany of reproaches: *she crashed your car, she spent your money . . .*

Production

"Short and Curlies" was recorded in Jamaica during the *Goats Head Soup* sessions. This blues-rock number with a strong boogie-woogie accent was reworked in Munich and then at Mick Jagger's house, Stargroves, before being finalized at Island Studios in London. The very good piano intro is played by Ian Stewart, who only played on tracks he liked, leaving Nicky Hopkins or Billy Preston the trouble of recording the ones that did not interest him. "Stu always did what he wanted to do,"[9] confirms Keith. Having set up a boogie-woogie, indeed almost Dixieland, vibe, the pianist is joined almost immediately by Mick Taylor with a brilliant and very clear-toned slide guitar part, probably played on a Telecaster. Keith handles the rhythm guitar, on which he provides unwavering support, apparently leaving Mick Taylor to play lead, now with distortion. Charlie Watts accompanies his bandmates with some excellent drumming, accentuating the shuffle rhythm with the help of Bill Wyman, the two of them very much at ease on this kind of track. As is Mick Jagger, whose performance again lives up to his reputation. He doubles himself in the vocal harmonies and is accompanied presumably by Keith. "Short and Curlies" is a good song that resembles the melody of "Midnight Rambler" (*Let It Bleed*, 1969) in places. It is a shame the Stones do not return to their roots more often.

FINGERPRINT FILE

Mick Jagger / Keith Richards / 6:33

Musicians
Mick Jagger: vocals, rhythm guitar
Keith Richards: rhythm guitar
Mick Taylor: rhythm guitar, bass
Bill Wyman: synthesizer
Charlie Watts: drums
Nicky Hopkins: piano
Billy Preston: clavinet
Jolly Kunjappu: tabla
Recorded
Musicland Studios, Munich: November 14–
25, 1973, February 20–March 3, 1974
**Rolling Stones Mobile Studio, Stargroves,
Newbury:** April 12–May 2, 1974
Island Studios, London: May 5–27, 1974
Technical Team
Producers: The Glimmer Twins
Sound engineers: Andy Johns, Keith Harwood,
George Chkiantz, Glyn Johns
Assistant sound engineers: Tapani Tapanainen,
Rod Thear, Howard Kilgour, Reinhold Mack

"Fingerprint File" was Mick Taylor's farewell to the greatest rock 'n' roll band in the world.

Genesis

Probably under the influence of George Orwell (the author of *1984*), Mick Jagger takes a look at life in a totalitarian society in which the slightest acts and gestures are observed and analyzed. Hence the all-pervading paranoia: the song's hero is depressed because he is being listened in on, followed, and photographed. The Stones wrote this song in 1973, a calamitous year for the United States, thanks to the Watergate affair, which led to the resignation of Richard Nixon. It was also during this troubled time that the Nixon administration refused John Lennon a green card and then tried to deport him. *And there's some little jerk in the FBI a keepin' papers on me six feet high* may indeed be an allusion to the tug-of-war between Nixon's henchmen and the former Beatle.

Production

After reggae, the Stones make an incursion into another new genre with this number, namely funk. And like some sort of premonition, this closing track on the album is the very last on which Mick Taylor would play for the Stones: "'Fingerprint File' I played bass on," he explains. "That's another track that was done with just Charlie, Mick, and myself, and Keith overdubbed later."[90] His guitar is very funky, with jazz accents, and, regrettably, he does not play one last solo on his final track. The main guitar is thus taken care of by Mick Jagger, who plays a very good rhythm part—probably on a Fender strongly colored by a stereo phasing effect—as he does onstage at the LA Forum concert on July 13, 1975. Keith Richards accompanies him on a second rhythm guitar with a wah-wah effect obtained through the Synthi Hi-Fli. Charlie Watts shows that he has learned the lessons of Jimmy Miller and sets an excellent funky beat that unites all the other rhythmic elements. Nicky Hopkins is on piano, Billy Preston on the clavinet (with wah-wah), and Bill Wyman, with a style of play indispensable to the genre, on synthesizer. Jolly Kunjappu, alias Charlie Jolly, is on tabla, unfortunately introducing a different tonality to the song (3:10). Finally, it is worth observing that Mick Jagger has clearly found another musical form—in addition to rock and blues—in which he feels at home.

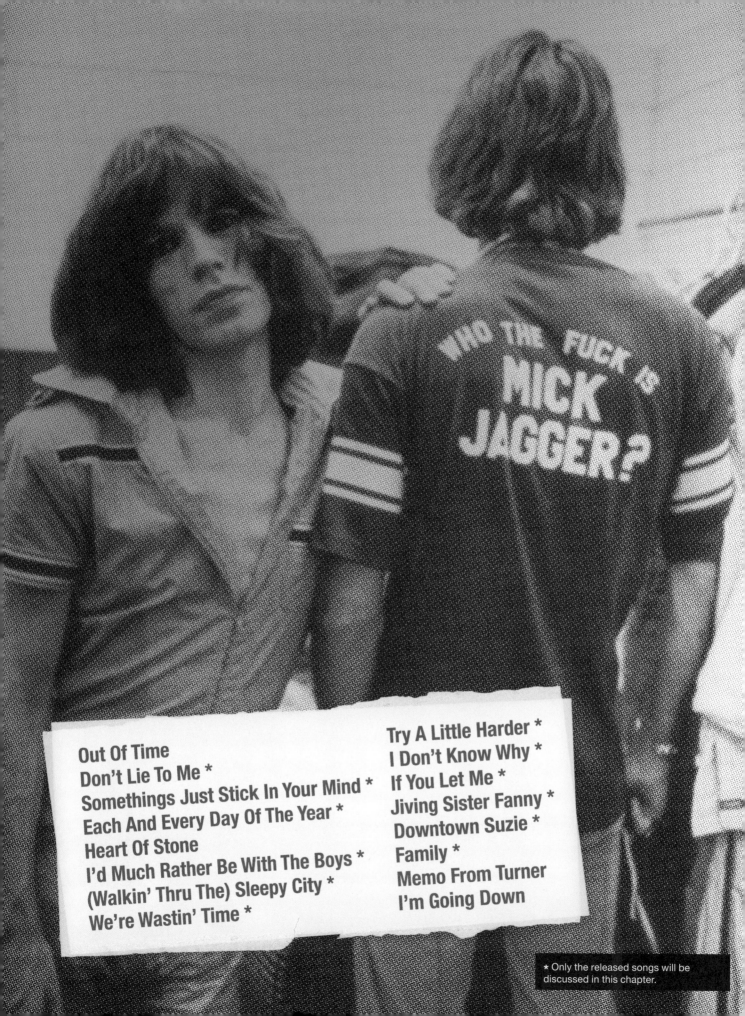

Out Of Time
Don't Lie To Me *
Somethings Just Stick In Your Mind *
Each And Every Day Of The Year *
Heart Of Stone
I'd Much Rather Be With The Boys *
(Walkin' Thru The) Sleepy City *
We're Wastin' Time *

Try A Little Harder *
I Don't Know Why *
If You Let Me *
Jiving Sister Fanny *
Downtown Suzie *
Family *
Memo From Turner
I'm Going Down

* Only the released songs will be discussed in this chapter.

ALBUM
RELEASE DATE
United Kingdom: June 6, 1975
Record label: Decca
RECORD NUMBER: DECCA SKL 5212
Number 45, on the charts for 1 week

META-

MORPHOSIS

The Stones at the Alamo in Texas,
with Ron Wood, who took Mick
Taylor's place for the Tour of the
Americas '75.

FOR STONES ADDICTS

Necrophilia (October 12, 1972), track listing: "Out of Time"; "Don't Lie to Me"; "Have You Seen Your Mother, Baby (Standing in the Shadow)"; "Think"; "Hear It (Instrumental)"; "Somethings Just Stick in Your Mind"; "Aftermath (Instrumental)"; "I'd Much Rather Be with the Boys"; "Andrew's Blues"; "Pay Your Dues"; "Let the Good Times Roll"; "Heart of Stone"; "Each and Every Day of the Year"; "(Walkin' thru the) Sleepy City"; "Try a Little Harder"; "Blue Turns to Grey"; "We're Wastin' Time."

THE APTLY NAMED METAMORPHOSIS

At the end of spring 1975, the Rolling Stones embarked on a long North American tour, with Mick Taylor replaced by Ron Wood. The Tour of the Americas '75 kicked off with two shows in Baton Rouge, Louisiana, on June 1, and concluded in Buffalo, New York, on August 8. A total of forty-six (or forty-five?) concerts were played. To launch this extensive tour, Rolling Stones Records and Atlantic Records released *Made in the Shade*, a compilation of ten songs from the albums *Sticky Fingers* ("Brown Sugar," "Wild Horses," "Bitch"), *Exile on Main St.* ("Tumbling Dice," "Happy," "Rip This Joint"), Goats Head Soup ("Angie," "Doo Doo Doo Doo Doo [Heartbreaker]"), and *It's Only Rock 'n' Roll* (title song and "Dance Little Sister") on May 31 in the United States and June 13 in the United Kingdom. This first "best of" from Rolling Stones Records would reach number 6 in the United States and number 14 in the United Kingdom.

The Metamorphosis of a Compilation

On June 6, 1975, another Rolling Stones compilation went on sale, this time the initiative of ABKCO Records and Allen Klein. *Metamorphosis* was the final outcome of a project originally christened *Necrophilia* that had been launched three years earlier. Conceived in association with Andrew Loog Oldham, the projected album comprised fifteen or so tracks, notably alternative takes of "Have You Seen Your Mother, Baby (Standing in the Shadow)" and "Street Fighting Man" (under the title "Pay Your Dues") as well as various songs that had been left off the track listings up to that point, such as

the highly controversial "Andrew's Blues." Due to a profound disagreement between Oldham and Klein over which tracks should be included, this compilation never officially saw the light of day, and instead was replaced by *More Hot Rocks (Big Hits & Fazed Cookies)*, released on December 11, 1972 (or December 20, 1972, according to some sources), which covered the Stones' Decca period (1963–1969).

The original idea behind *Necrophilia* was not completely shelved, however. It evolved firstly into *Black Box*—a compilation project entrusted to Bill Wyman, which also got no further than draft stage, and then into *Metamorphosis*. The latter brings together no fewer than nine takes initially earmarked for *Necrophilia*: "Out of Time," "Don't Lie to Me," "Somethings Just Stick in Your Mind," "I'd Much Rather Be with the Boys," "Heart of Stone," "Each and Every Day of the Year," "(Walkin' thru the) Sleepy City," "Try a Little Harder," and "We're Wastin' Time." The remaining seven tracks were of more recent vintage. "If You Let Me" dates from 1966 and the sessions for either *Aftermath* or *Between the Buttons*, "Family" was recorded in spring 1968 and was left out of the definitive selection for *Beggars Banquet*, and "Memo from Turner" is an alternative version of the song from the movie *Performance*, dating from November 1968. Finally, "I Don't Know Why," a cover of a Stevie Wonder song, "Jiving Sister Fanny," "Downtown Suzie" (the second song to be credited to Bill Wyman!), and "I'm Going Down" were recorded during sessions in 1969 and 1970.

Although *Metamorphosis* cannot be placed in the same category as the very best of the Stones discs, the compilation

The Stones launch their 1975 tour from a truck on Fifth Avenue in New York City.

Metamorphosis is also the name of an album released in 1970 by the band Iron Butterfly. Curiously, a song titled "Stone Believer" is featured in the track listing.

On the initial pressings of the album, the name Keith Richards was mistakenly spelled without the *s*.

gives listeners a sense of how far Jagger and Richards had come since they first started to write songs. "Family," which has a strong whiff of subversion about it, is worlds apart from the pretty love song "Each and Everyday of the Year," and the alternative versions of "Out of Time," "Heart of Stone," and "Memo from Turner" shed some light on the Rolling Stones' working methods in the studio. *Metamorphosis* would climb to number 8 in the United States and number 45 in the United Kingdom shortly after its release.

The Album Cover

The title of this compilation alludes, of course, to the novella *The Metamorphosis* (published in 1915) by Franz Kafka, in which a traveling salesman (Gregor Samsa) wakes up to find himself transformed into a hideous insect. On the cover, the heads of the five founding members of the Rolling Stones, plus that of Mick Taylor, have accordingly been detached from their bodies and replaced with those of six insects. The concept was developed by Glenn Ross (Al Green, Curtis Mayfield, the Bee Gees), the artistic direction was entrusted to Al Steckler (George Harrison, John Lennon, Royal Philharmonic Orchestra) and Richard Roth (The Moody Blues, Christopher Franke, a member of Tangerine Dream), and the graphic artist was Linda Guymon. Printed on the back cover are long and sincere thanks from the pen of Andrew Loog Oldham.

DON'T LIE TO ME

Hudson Whittaker / 2:02

Musicians
Mick Jagger: vocals
Keith Richards: lead guitar
Brian Jones: rhythm guitar
Bill Wyman: bass
Charlie Watts: drums
Ian Stewart: piano
Recorded
Regent Sound Studios, London: May 12, 1964
Technical Team
Producer: Andrew Loog Oldham
Sound engineer: Bill Farley

FOR STONES ADDICTS

"Don't Lie to Me" is mistakenly credited to Jagger/Richards in the *Metamorphosis* credits.

Brian, Keith, and Charlie on the set of *Thank Your Lucky Stars* in 1964, around the time of "Don't Lie to Me."

Genesis

"Don't You Lie to Me" is a blues number recorded by Tampa Red (also known by the names Hudson Woodbridge and Hudson Whittaker) in 1940 for Lester Melrose's famous Bluebird label. Lying women and cheating men are two types of people the bluesman *just can't stand.* He sings vigorously between playing the odd phrase on the kazoo, and is supported on the piano by Blind John Davis, a boogie-woogie specialist who accompanied Bluebird's leading artists at the end of the thirties and the beginning of the forties (from Tampa Red to Big Bill Broonzy).

A few years after Tampa Red recorded the song, "Don't You Lie to Me" became a favorite with the pioneers of rock 'n' roll, as attested by the versions of Fats Domino and Chuck Berry, which date from 1951 and 1961, respectively. Then came the Rolling Stones' turn to add this classic twelve-bar blues to their repertoire. They recorded an initial version of it at the BBC's Maida Vale Studios in London on February 3, 1964, followed by a second at Regent Sound Studios on May 12 of the same year. It is this second recording that has been pulled out of the drawer for *Metamorphosis*, this time under the title "Don't Lie to Me."

Production

Recorded on the same day as "Congratulations" (the B-side of the US single "Time Is on My Side"), "Don't Lie to Me" is a rock 'n' roll number inspired more by Chuck Berry's version than Tampa Red's. However, the Stones nevertheless manage to differentiate themselves from their predecessor—except in the intro, which attempts to reproduce the saxophone riff. The rhythm is highly dynamic, with Charlie Watts playing his Ludwig kit with verve, the hi-hat half-open, and Bill Wyman flying up and down the neck of his (Framus?) bass. Brian Jones provides a very straightforward rhythm on his Gretsch Anniversary, supported by Keith Richards, who plays the only solo (with plenty of reverb and a rockabilly feel) on his Harmony Meteor H70. Mick Jagger is clearly thoroughly at ease on this rock number, which he sings with an air of studied detachment, but it is Ian Stewart who sets the track on fire with his excellent boogie-woogie piano. Over the coming years he would never deviate from this style, and all one can do is thank him for it!

SOMETHINGS JUST STICK IN YOUR MIND

Mick Jagger / Keith Richards / 2:27

Musicians
Mick Jagger: vocals
Keith Richards (?): guitar
Brian Jones: (?) guitar
Bill Wyman (?): bass
Charlie Watts (?): drums
Ian Stewart (?): piano
Big Jim Sullivan: pedal steel guitar
Jimmy Page (?): guitar
John McLaughlin (?): guitar
Joe Moretti (?): bass
Andy White (?): drums
Mike Leander: arrangements and conducting
Recorded
Regent Sound Studios, London; Decca Studios, West Hampstead, London: February 13 (?), June 29–July 7, 1964 (?)
Technical Team
Producer: Andrew Loog Oldham
Sound engineers (?): Bill Farley, Gus Dudgeon

Genesis

Why does the sky turn gray each evening? What is it that is so entrancing about going on one's first date with a girl? The eternal teenagers Mick Jagger and Keith Richards speculate about these things and others over a pop melody with a somewhat middle-of-the-road arrangement. "Some Things Just Stick in My Mind" was initially recorded at the beginning of 1965 by the American duo Dick and Dee Dee, who had opened for the Rolling Stones on their 1964 tour, and subsequently by Vashti Bunyan, with the help of Nicky Hopkins on piano. In fact, it was the debut single of the folksinger from Newcastle. It is interesting to note that on the *Metamorphosis* cover, both the vinyl and the CD versions, no one seems to have noticed the spelling mistakes in the titles: *Somethings* instead of *Some Things* and *Everyday* instead of *Every Day*.

Production

According to various sources, the Rolling Stones recorded the song either on February 13, 1964, or else during the sessions that extended from June 29 to July 7, 1964. In all probability, the playback was cut during this second phase, because it seems unlikely that any of the Stones other than Mick Jagger actually took part in the recording. Instead, it was probably made by studio musicians recruited by Oldham, because the instrumentation bears no resemblance to that of the London quintet. This is also the backing track Dick and Dee Dee would use for their cover of the song. The only real musical interest lies in the identity of the instrumentalists, such as (very probably) Jimmy Page (but possibly John McLaughlin), who plays the only acoustic guitar part (12-string) with brio, and Big Jim Sullivan on pedal steel guitar, which lends the track a country feel. In addition to these two instruments, Mike Leander's arrangement includes percussion, triangle, bongos, and güiro, a rhythm section consisting of bass and drums, a piano with heavy reverb that calls to mind the sound Jack Nitzsche would achieve with the Stones by the end of that same year, and some slightly uncomfortable backing solos. The results are somewhat reminiscent of Phil Spector, which is not surprising given the admiration the Stones producer had for him.

The Stones are accompanied on this track by the studio musician Big Jim Sullivan (left) and Joe Moretti (right).

EACH AND EVERY DAY OF THE YEAR

Mick Jagger / Keith Richards / 2:48

Musicians
Mick Jagger: vocals
Big Jim Sullivan (?): guitar
Jimmy Page (?): guitar
John McLaughlin (?): guitar
Joe Moretti (?): bass
Andy White (?): drums
Christine Ohlman (?): backing vocals
John Paul Jones (?): arrangements
Mike Leander: arrangements and conducting
Recorded
Regent Sound Studios, London; Decca Studios, West Hampstead, London: August 31–September 1, September 3–4, 1964
Technical Team
Producer: Andrew Loog Oldham
Sound engineers (?): Bill Farley, Gus Dudgeon

FOR STONES ADDICTS

The drummer is probably Andy White, who replaced Ringo Starr for the recording of "Love Me Do," the Beatles' debut single.

Genesis

"Each and Everyday of the Year" is one of the first compositions (1964) by the Jagger-Richards duo, offering no hint of their future misogyny in songs. In fact, it is a thoroughly sad pop song. The story concerns a lovesick man who is forlorn because the woman he passionately loves, for whom he has been waiting every day of the year, has *gone forever.* This song seems to have been recorded by the Rolling Stones several times between January and September 1964. However, the version released first (on November 27, 1964, as the B-side of "All I Want Is My Baby," a composition by Richards and Oldham) was that of the American singer Bobby Jameson (under the title "Each and Everyday") with, what's more, Mick Jagger and Andrew Loog Oldham on backing vocals. One interesting detail: Keith Richards is credited on both sides of the single as "Music Director"!

Production

"Each and Everyday of the Year" is apparently a simple exercise in style by Jagger and Richards, who, spurred on by Oldham, were seeking to form a songwriting duo along the lines of Lennon and McCartney. Their know-how was not yet equal to their aspirations, however, and this slow number with a Spanish flavor is definitely not one of their best songs. The orchestration seems to have been executed and conducted by Mike Leander within the context of the Andrew Oldham Orchestra, and with instruments far removed from the Stones universe: tearful trumpets, a female second voice that seems to have Eurovision ambitions, a heartrending harp, intrusive castanets, and syrupy strings. Mick Jagger, as at ease as a minnow in a shoal of piranhas, does not exactly deliver a memorable performance, and lags far behind Bobby Jameson. Two or three guitars can be heard, including a 12-string, and some sources name the guitarists as Big Jim Sullivan and Jimmy Page or John McLaughlin. It has also been suggested that Joe Moretti is on bass and Andy White on drums (although virtually inaudible). Finally, it is probable that the future Led Zeppelin bassist John Paul Jones joined his guitarist colleague to work on the arrangements. That would help to explain why he didn't continue down this particular path . . .

John Paul Jones (left), the likely arranger of this number, with Andrew Loog Oldham, and an unidentified third man.

I'D MUCH RATHER BE WITH THE BOYS

Andrew Loog Oldham / Keith Richards / 2:11

"I'd Much Rather Be with the Boys" was recorded by the Toggery Five in the sixties and Nikki Sudden in the eighties. More recently, Reigning Sound made a version in 2002.

Musicians
Mick Jagger: vocals
John McLaughlin (?): guitar
Joe Moretti (?): bass
Andy White (?): drums
Christine Ohlman (?): backing vocals
Mike Leander: arrangements and conducting

Recorded
Decca Studios, West Hampstead, London: February 24, 1965

Technical Team
Producer: Andrew Loog Oldham
Sound engineer: Gus Dudgeon (?)

Genesis

"I'd Much Rather Be with the Boys" is one of the very rare songs credited to Andrew Loog Oldham and Keith Richards. There were others in the early days of the Rolling Stones, but with the odd exception, such as "All I Want Is My Baby," (the A-side of "Each and Everyday"), covered by Bobby Jameson in 1964, they either progressed no further than draft stage or disappeared into a drawer at Decca. These lyrics wander off the beaten track a little, at least by comparison with the very first Jagger-Richards compositions. Following a disappointment in love, the song's protagonist prefers to hang out with the other members of his gang rather than embarking on a new affair of the heart.

Production

In composing "I'd Much Rather Be with the Boys," Keith Richards was probably responding to the urgings of Andrew Loog Oldham, who was keen to emulate "Be My Baby," the seminal Ronettes hit produced and co-written by the brilliant Phil Spector. The final outcome had little to do with the Stones, who, with the exception of Mick Jagger, were probably not involved in the recording of the song on February 24. The production was carried out within the context of the Andrew Oldham Orchestra, and responsibility for the arrangements was entrusted to the indispensable Mike Leander and his orchestra. The backing vocals, solo female voice (presumably Christine Ohlman, overdubbed later), flutes, organ, and numerous percussion instruments (woodblock, maracas, hand claps) create a saturated environment in the manner of Phil Spector's wall of sound. The identity of the other musicians can only be guessed at: Andy White is probably on drums, the fantastic John McLaughlin (future guitarist with the Mahavishnu Orchestra) on guitar, and perhaps Joe Moretti, better known as a guitarist (having played with Gene Vincent and Vince Taylor) on bass. Mick Jagger merely lays down a guide vocal, rather than looking for a definitive take.

Keith Richards and Andrew Loog Oldham, collaborated on "I'd Much Rather Be with the Boys."

(WALKIN' THRU THE) SLEEPY CITY

Mick Jagger / Keith Richards / 2:51

Musicians
Mick Jagger: vocals
Big Jim Sullivan (?): guitar
Jimmy Page (?): guitar
John McLaughlin (?): guitar
Doug Schlink (?): guitar
Joe Moretti (?): bass
Reg Guest (?): piano
Andy White (?): drums
Christine Ohlman (?): backing vocals
Mike Leander: arrangements and conducting

Recorded
Regent Sound Studios, London; Decca Studios, West Hampstead, London:
August 31–September 1, September 3–4, 1964

Technical Team
Producer: Andrew Loog Oldham
Sound engineers (?): Bill Farley, Gus Dudgeon

Genesis
This is a song on the theme of solitude in a city at night in which no light burns. Until, that is, a young woman makes her appearance . . . This song, like the majority of those written by Mick Jagger and Keith Richards when they first started out, at Andrew Loog Oldham's urging, is light-years away from those they would later compose. It has a romantic side that comes as something of a surprise on the part of the future Glimmer Twins, who nevertheless capture the spirit of the times very well. This is a pop song with a Spector-like vibe.

This helps to explain why the Rolling Stones were not the first to introduce the number to the general public. That honor fell to the Mighty Avengers—another group managed by Andrew Loog Oldham—who released it as a single in July 1965, albeit unsuccessfully, by contrast with "So Much in Love," another Jagger-Richards song with which the group had reached number 46 on the British hit parade the previous year.

Production
A riff played on electric guitar with heavy reverb opens this new song intended to augment Oldham's publishing catalog and incidentally swell the coffers of Mick Jagger and Keith Richards. In addition to the omnipresent influence of Phil Spector, it is also possible to detect that of the Beach Boys, whose one dream in their early days, amusingly enough, was to rival the master of the wall of sound. This session held at the end of summer 1964 once again took place within the context of the Andrew Oldham Orchestra, of which Mike Leander was the arranger and musical director (at least for this song). Of all the Stones, it is likely that only Mick Jagger took part in the recording, but he does not seem particularly motivated in his performance, which is distinctly lacking in conviction and punch. The drummer (Andy White?) adopts a style similar to that of Hal Blaine, the piano part is very well crafted (by Reg Guest?), and the various guitarists, almost certainly including the excellent Doug Schlink, provide a very good accompaniment. Finally, to reinforce the Spector-like sound world, tubular bells, castanets, and hand claps can be heard.

Mick Jagger, probably the only member of the Stones to have taken part in the recording of this song.

WE'RE WASTIN' TIME

Mick Jagger / Keith Richards / 2:44

Musicians
Mick Jagger: vocals
Big Jim Sullivan: pedal steel guitar
Jimmy Page (?): guitar
John McLaughlin (?): guitar
Doug Schlink (?): guitar
Joe Moretti (?): bass
Reg Guest (?): piano
Andy White (?): drums
Christine Ohlman (?): backing vocals
Mike Leander: arrangements and conducting
Unidentified musician:
Recorded
Regent Sound Studios, London; Decca Studios, West Hampstead, London:
August 31–September 1, September 3–4, 1964
Technical Team
Producer: Andrew Loog Oldham
Sound engineers (?): Bill Farley, Gus Dudgeon

Jimmy Page was probably Mick Jagger's sideman on "We're Wastin' Time."

Genesis

Listening to "We're Wastin' Time," it is not easy to connect this song with the five long-haired musicians who hollered out the words to Willie Dixon's "I Just Want to Make Love to You," recorded by the band at more or less the same time. Another early Jagger-Richards composition, this is the lament, over a waltz rhythm, of a couple who now seem to be killing time. It looks as if the song may have been recorded without any real ambition to include it on a Rolling Stones album. A demo, nothing more . . . It was Jimmy Tarbuck, under the aegis of Andrew Loog Oldham as producer, who released it as a single, albeit without causing a ripple in the hit parades.

Production

Once again, none of the Rolling Stones perform on this country-rock ballad in triple time other than the indispensable Mick Jagger, who delivers a good vocal line with ample reverb. He seems more motivated than on most of the demos recorded during this period. Might this be due to the presence of different guitarists, including one who plays an excellent solo almost thirty seconds long? The touch and phrasing of this soloist are those of a great instrumentalist. Given that Big Jim Sullivan is known to be playing pedal steel guitar, who might it be—Jimmy Page, John McLaughlin, or Doug Schlink? Unfortunately, it is impossible to say. A fiddle, an essential element in reinforcing the country aspect of the track, can also be heard. The rhythm section is very good, as is the piano accompaniment. With hindsight, listening to "We're Wastin' Time" gives the impression that Mick Jagger and Keith Richards were learning their craft as songwriters and that the real masterpieces were not going to be long in coming. Just a little more patience required . . .

TRY A LITTLE HARDER

Mick Jagger / Keith Richards / 2:17

Musicians
Mick Jagger (?): vocals
Keith Richards: backing vocals
Jimmy Page (?): guitar
John McLaughlin (?): guitar
Reg Guest (?): piano
Joe Moretti (?): bass
Andy White (?): drums
Ivy League: backing vocals
Andrew Loog Oldham: backing vocals
Unidentified musicians: horns, percussion
Recorded
Regent Sound Studios, London; Decca Studios, West Hampstead, London: February 13 (?), June 29–July 7, 1964 (?)
Technical Team
Producer: Andrew Loog Oldham
Sound engineers (?): Bill Farley, Gus Dudgeon

Genesis

In helping a friend to seduce the girl who is the object of his desire, Mick Jagger does not stint on his advice. *Try a little harder*; *Don't you see you gotta give her all the lovin' that she needs*: the message is clear. "Try a Little Harder" is the only song among the early compositions of Mick Jagger and Keith Richards collected on *Metamorphosis* that gave rise to no other version. However, it is far from being the weakest from this period, above all thanks to Mick Jagger's performance and Oldham's production, influenced as much by Phil Spector as by Motown. It is for this reason, moreover, that it was chosen as the B-side of "I Don't Know Why," the single taken from *Metamorphosis*.

Production

It is very difficult to say who might have been involved in the recording of "Try a Little Harder." Some sources claim that Mick Jagger was the only member of the Rolling Stones present. Others put Brian Jones on acoustic guitar, Keith Richards on electric, and Bill Wyman on bass. It is also possible that Jimmy Page and/or John McLaughlin played on the song. However Oldham shed a little light on the mystery in 2010: "[It had] a vocal group mixed in with Keith and myself 'bottom humming.' The vocal group would have been the Ivy League, the orchestra were hired hands."[28]

"Try a Little Harder" opens with a bass accompanied by a tambourine. This sound immediately conjures up the Motown signature, albeit, once more, with a hint of the wall of sound. The rhythm section is subdued but effective, and horn arrangements with a predominance of saxes lend the number a reasonably successful coloration. Jagger is provided with perfect support by the backing vocalists, and the result is good in spite of the production, which leaves a little to be desired on a technical level. Uncertainty persists to this day about the recording dates, and sources differ, but it is likely that the February session at Regent Sound Studios in London was the only session dedicated to the song.

The guitarist John McLaughlin, future pioneer of jazz-rock fusion.

I DON'T KNOW WHY

Stevie Wonder / Paul Riser / Don Hunter / Lula Hardaway / 3:01

Musicians
Mick Jagger: vocals
Keith Richards: rhythm guitar, backing vocals
Mick Taylor: rhythm and lead guitar
Bill Wyman: bass
Charlie Watts: drums
Ian Stewart: piano
Unidentified musicians: horn section
Recorded
Olympic Sound Studios, London: June 29–July 3, 1969
Technical Team
Producer: Jimmy Miller
Sound engineer: Glyn Johns

Keith Richards playing his Gibson Flying V, a guitar he adopted in July 1969.

Genesis

You always treat me like a fool, you kick me when I'm down, that's your rule, I don't know why I love you . . . With "I Don't Know Why," the Rolling Stones introduce a change of register relative to the tender love songs on *Metamorphosis*. Here they dip into the catalog of Stevie Wonder, who included the song on his album *For Once in My Life* (1968). Nearly seven months later, the Stones recorded "I Don't Know Why" and give a good rendition of the song during a time when soul was playing an increasingly important role in their musical evolution.

Production

It was during the sessions for *Let It Bleed* that "I Don't Know Why" was cut. The intro, played by Keith Richards, most probably on the brand-new Gibson Flying V he had purchased shortly before the session, inevitably recalls that of "Gimme Shelter": the same silky sound, the same pronounced vibrato and oppressive atmosphere, it has all the ingredients to grab the listener's attention right from the start. And when Mick Taylor answers him on his Gibson SG Standard with more sonorous, more incisive, harder-edged arpeggios, the two complement each other perfectly. The Stones made a shrewd choice of song to cover. They give the number more of a darker, rock vibe, while respecting its soul essence. Mick Jagger delivers a very good performance, exaggerating expressively, and sensibly refraining from trying to compete with Stevie Wonder's vocal prowess. On the rhythm side, Charlie Watts plays an excellent drum part on his Gretsch kit, his snare drum slamming as never before, presumably under the approving eye of Jimmy Miller. Bill Wyman supports each of the song's chords with a very low bass, and Stu accompanies his bandmates on the piano, abandoning the boogie-woogie he so loved for a suitably R&B style. Some very good horns can be heard, heralding the imminent arrival on the scene of Bobby Keys and Jim Price. Finally, it would be impossible to overlook the talent of Mick Taylor, who plays two superb solos exhibiting the exceptional touch and lyricism that would make him an unforgettable Stone. The band may have judged "I Don't Know Why" to be too "soul" for *Let It Bleed*. It is nevertheless a very good cover entirely worthy of its release as a single.

IF YOU LET ME

Mick Jagger / Keith Richards / 3:17

Musicians
Mick Jagger: vocals
Keith Richards: acoustic guitar, rhythm guitar (?), backing vocals
Brian Jones: dulcimer
Bill Wyman: bass
Charlie Watts: drums
Jack Nitzsche (?): Wurlitzer

Recorded
RCA Studios, Los Angeles (?): March 6–9, 1966
Olympic Sound Studios, London (?): November 8–December 6, 1966

Technical Team
Producer: Andrew Loog Oldham
Sound engineer: Dave Hassinger or Glyn Johns

Genesis

"If You Let Me" is one of the most interesting songs on *Metamorphosis*. A new amorous adventure is starting, but who knows where it will lead? *You can get me/If you let me*: the two lines of the refrain can be interpreted a number of ways. Might this also be a plea for free love? Similarly, *It's a brand new thing for me/Loving you so physically* reveals a certain shyness or even naïveté, which is not, strictly speaking, a characteristic of Mick Jagger. Should this be seen as an implicit reference to the—then nascent—relationship between the Stones singer and Marianne Faithfull?

Production

The sources date "If You Let Me" to either the sessions of March 6–9, 1966, or those of November and December of that year, when the Rolling Stones were working on *Aftermath* and *Between the Buttons*. Why did it not make the final selection for one or other of those albums? It is a mystery. The folk-rock vibe is highly successful, once again thanks to Brian Jones, who lends the song a special color with his dulcimer, clearly the electric Vox Bijou. He provides very nice support for the acoustic guitar of Keith Richards, who plays the intro with picked arpeggios on his Gibson Hummingbird. Richards seems to be playing rhythm electric as well. "If You Let Me" also provides Bill Wyman with an opportunity, from the very first bars, to distinguish himself with a highly melodic bass part (on his Framus Humbug?). Taking inspiration from Bill's playing, Mick Jagger vocalizes the melodic bass line before launching into the words. The Stones singer gives a good performance, taking his range of expression a little wider than usual, alternating gentleness and vigor and revealing a sensitivity that would be good to hear more often. The Wurlitzer, which comes in on the first verse, seems to be played by Jack Nitzsche. Finally, Charlie Watts reinforces the folk-rock aspect of the track with more of a country style. Listening to the production, the particular sound quality is closer to that of the English, rather than the US, studios, while the writing and treatment of the song seem closer to *Between the Buttons* than *Aftermath*.

"If You Let Me" is thought to describe the budding relationship between the Stones singer and Marianne Faithfull.

JIVING SISTER FANNY

Mick Jagger / Keith Richards / 2:45

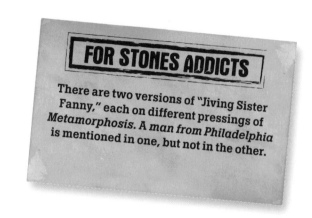

Musicians
Mick Jagger: vocals
Keith Richards: rhythm guitar, lead guitar (?)
Mick Taylor: lead guitar (?)
Bill Wyman: bass
Charlie Watts: drums
Nicky Hopkins: electric piano
Recorded
Olympic Sound Studios, London: June–July 1969
Technical Team
Producer: Jimmy Miller
Sound engineer: Glyn Johns

Mick Taylor and Charlie Watts during a recording session for *Let It Bleed* in 1969.

Genesis

Mick Jagger and Keith Richards—you either love them or love to hate them! In this tale of Fanny with "the brain of a dinosaur," who apparently lives to dance, the Machiavellian duo seem to have rediscovered their taste for provocation. In short, this is a macho diatribe . . . The song was chosen as the B-side of the single "Out of Time," released in August/September 1975.

Production

"Jiving Sister Fanny" was recorded around mid-June/beginning of July 1969 at Olympic Sound Studios in London during the sessions for *Let It Bleed*—shortly before the death of Brian Jones on July 3. The Stones are back in brilliant blues-rock form, and Keith launches the track with a very good riff (probably played on his Gibson Les Paul Black Beauty), a kind of slow variation of "Rip This Joint" on *Exile on Main St*. Charlie Watts immediately takes up the baton, launching a very good drum part with an introductory break in his own inimitable style. It is noticeable that each of the Jimmy Miller–produced albums in turn reveals the sheer quality of Charlie Watts's playing, in all likelihood stimulated by the presence of the talented American producer. Bill Wyman also provides considerable support, with an effective bass line (on the Vox Astro?) that is very prominent in the mix. On electric piano (with vibrato), Nicky Hopkins plays a very rhythmic part that matches Keith's perfectly. Mick Jagger gives a good vocal performance that should not necessarily be regarded as a definitive take, as he does not yet seem to have fully mastered the song. This is a pity, as "Jiving Sister Fanny" has the makings of a good track. At this stage, however, the Stones were probably still working on it. This is borne out by the mixing, which leaves something to be desired and is more like an interim than a final mix. The vocal is buried, the bass too prominent, and above all the guitar solo all of a sudden surges louder (1:13) before Jagger has finished singing, remaining at the same volume until the end of the song. Whether Keith Richards or Mick Taylor is on lead is not clear. But the phrasing points to Keith.

DOWNTOWN SUZIE

Bill Wyman / 3:52

Musicians
Mick Jagger: vocals
Keith Richards: slide and rhythm guitar, backing vocals
Bill Wyman: bass, electric piano (?), backing vocal
Charlie Watts: drums
Ry Cooder: slide guitar
Jimmy Miller: percussion, backing vocals
Unidentified musician(s): hand claps
Recorded
Olympic Sound Studios, London: February (?), April 1969
Technical Team
Producer: Jimmy Miller
Sound engineer: Glyn Johns

Genesis

"Downtown Suzie" is the second Stones number credited to Bill Wyman ("In Another Land" on *Their Satanic Majesties Request* being the first). The lyrics are reasonably entertaining. The unfortunate narrator has a raging hangover and is lying on his bed with an *Alka Seltzer head.* Things do not improve during the next few hours, even when Suzie enters the hotel room. The voluptuous soubrette is not one to show compassion and *kicked him in the hole* (or possibly *hall!*) . . . Presumably the words to "Downtown Suzie" were committed to paper as the musicians in the studio for this *Let It Bleed* session were playing. In any case, they clearly had a lot of fun, starting with Ry Cooder, who is always brilliant on slide.

Production

In his book *Stone Alone,*[6] Bill Wyman dates the first session dedicated to "Downtown Suzie" to the second half of March 1968, when the band was working on "Stray Cat Blues" and "No Expectations" at Olympic Sounds Studios. He seems to be mistaken, however, as the definitive recording took place in April 1969. "At one session we quickly cut my song 'Downtown Suzie' . . . and tried demos of another of my songs. However, I noticed that if my songs did not quite gel in one or two takes, they were rejected and not tried again—whereas with Mick and Keith's songs we would play one for a week if necessary."[9] Nevertheless the results are more than respectable, and the song benefits from the participation of the outstanding Ry Cooder, who plays a superb slide acoustic part. Keith lends a hand on electric, also rendering a few brief phrases on slide, but plays rhythm in the rock sections. Charlie works his Gretsch kit to very good effect, supported by Bill (probably on his Vox Astro), who also seems to be playing electric piano. Jimmy Miller looks after the bongos, and everyone seems to have been involved in overdubbing hand claps and backing vocals. Mick Jagger is excellent, his vocal giving the impression that it has been recorded on a playback slowed down slightly in order to achieve a rise in pitch at normal speed.

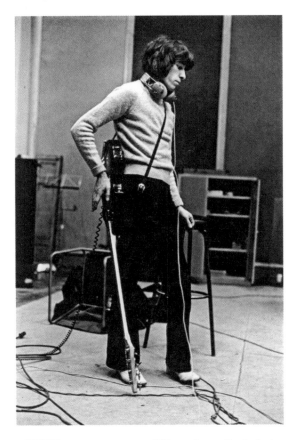

Bill Wyman, composer of "Downtown Suzie," at Olympic Sound Studios in 1969.

FAMILY

Mick Jagger / Keith Richards / 4:06

Musicians
Mick Jagger: vocals, maracas (?)
Keith Richards: acoustic guitar, electric guitar (?), bass (?)
Brian Jones: guitar (?)
Bill Wyman: bass (?)
Charlie Watts: drums
Nicky Hopkins: piano
Jimmy Miller: tambourine (?)
Recorded
Olympic Sound Studios, London: June 28, 1968
Technical Team
Producer: Jimmy Miller
Sound engineer: Glyn Johns
Assistant sound engineer: Phill Brown

IN YOUR HEADPHONES
While the timing leaves something to be desired, there is also an edit at 1:47 that disrupts the rhythm. It never rains, but it pours.

Mick Jagger caught on camera by Jean-Luc Godard during the shooting of *One Plus One*.

Genesis

"Family" is of interest above all for its rather enigmatic words, written in all probability by Mick Jagger, with his caustic, cynical sense of humor. He describes four members of a family who all undergo bizarre adventures. The father has a fatal accident and has had a heart transplant. The daughter dreams of becoming a prostitute and having her father as a customer. The mother has been sucked into a whirlpool, along with her lovers, to see *what the colors of death are all about*. Finally, the son will soon descend into madness upon learning that he will never play the guitar like E. G. Jim and never write like Saint Augustine. Could it be the incestuous dream of the young heroine that prevented the inclusion of "Family" in *Beggars Banquet*?

Production

Before achieving its final form—presumably on June 28, 1968, at Olympic Sound Studios—"Family" was worked on the previous month in a more electric rendition. The version on *Metamorphosis*, by contrast, is mostly acoustic, with Keith providing a strummed rhythm on his Hummingbird. It would seem that "Family" progressed no further than the demo stage. The timing is dubious to say the least (Keith at around 3:12!) and the structure somewhat shaky. Although the song itself is interesting, some additional work would have been needed to bring the track up to scratch. It seems that Keith's acoustic guitar has been captured by a second mic and played back through a Leslie speaker in order to create a phasing and rapid vibrato effect. Or else he double-tracked himself using the same technique. He may also have played the bass part on his Fender Precision, to such an extent that the style resembles that of a guitarist rather than that of a bass player. Charlie provides a rhythm with his brushes, but unfortunately is not strictly in time. Jimmy Miller seems to be on tambourine (with heavy reverb!) and Mick Jagger on maracas. The latter's vocal is reasonably convincing, and it is interesting to note that between 1966 and 1969 he was eager to let the sensitive side of his personality come through. Brian Jones does not seem to have contributed to the cut. Finally, the characteristic lyrical style of Nicky Hopkins is clearly recognizable in what is a good piano part. Nevertheless, in this form, the song was in no way worthy of a place on *Beggars Banquet*.

I'M GOING DOWN

Mick Jagger / Keith Richards / 2:52

Musicians
Mick Jagger: vocals
Keith Richards: rhythm guitar
Mick Taylor: bass
Charlie Watts: drums
Bobby Keys: saxophone
Stephen Stills: guitar (?)
Rocky Dijon: congas
Recorded
Olympic Sound Studios, London: July 14–15, 1970
Technical Team
Producer: Jimmy Miller
Sound engineers: Glyn Johns, Andy Johns

Stephen Stills, who may have contributed as a studio guitarist to the recording of "I'm Going Down."

Genesis

The final track on *Metamorphosis* is also the best—at least for all those who consider Keith Richards's guitar riffs to capture the Rolling Stones magic. The lyrics count for little, even if the image of God ringing someone's doorbell and the notion of an uncontrollable urge to kill a mother-in-law and flee to Mexico have the merit, at least, of being clear. In truth, they are subservient to the rhythm of this irresistible rock number that recalls "Brown Sugar" and "All Down the Line."

Production

There are those who suggest that Keith Richards may not have played on "I'm Going Down," but in that case, Stephen Stills (of Crosby, Stills, Nash & Young) has done an amazing job of imitating him! Is this possible? The handiwork of the master is so distinct, from the very first chord, that it is difficult to believe. He may have contributed more modestly than usual, but there only seems to be one guitar on the entire track. A plausible explanation would be that Stephen Stills did indeed collaborate on the session, but that his guitar has been buried in the mix. Similarly, the name of upright bass player Bill Plummer is mentioned by some (he would later play on a few tracks on *Exile on Main St.*). It has to be recognized, however, that the bass on the track is electric, in all likelihood played—excellently!—by Mick Taylor. Charlie Watts's drumming, combining swing, power, and groove, is of a high caliber, with Jimmy Miller's advice paying dividends. On the other hand, Rocky Dijon's congas do not sit well with the pure, hard rock of this number, as their Latin flavor is out of keeping with the vibe. The same goes for Bobby Keys's sax, which, despite a good performance, is not well-integrated into the track and has little in common with his solo on "Brown Sugar." The problem for both one and the other, however, almost certainly stems from the mixing, which is very mediocre. Mick Jagger does not give one of his best performances. His voice doesn't really take off, and this is a pity, because with a little more work, "I'm Going Down" could have been a great track. And the Stones must have believed this themselves as they seem to have worked on it back in 1969 (Olympic Studios, Sunset Sound Studios, and/or Electra Studios) before returning to it for the final time in July 1970.

Hot Stuff
Hand Of Fate
Cherry Oh Baby
Memory Hotel
Hey Negrita
Melody
Fool To Cry
Crazy Mama

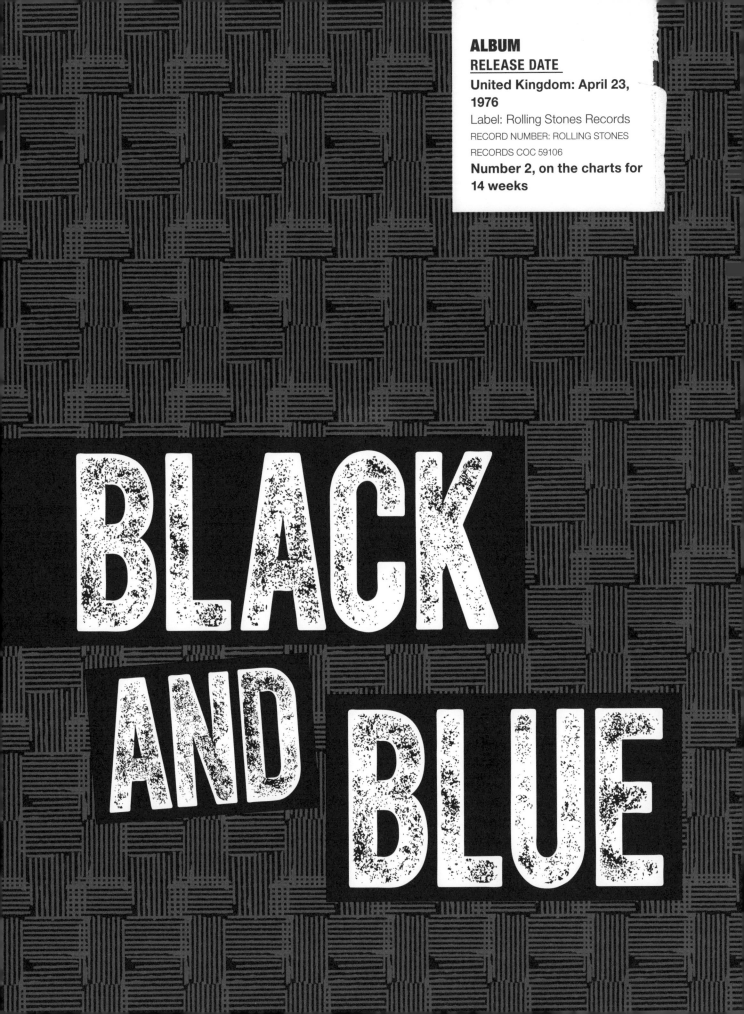

ALBUM
RELEASE DATE
United Kingdom: April 23, 1976
Label: Rolling Stones Records
RECORD NUMBER: ROLLING STONES
RECORDS COC 59106
Number 2, on the charts for 14 weeks

BLACK AND BLUE

AN ADVERTISING SHOCKER

The poster campaign accompanying the release of the album in the United States sparked a bitter controversy. The image featured the top model Anita Russell, tied up with her legs straddling a reproduction of the album cover, and bore the slogan *I'm Black and Blue from the Rolling Stones— and I love it!* The poster provoked the wrath of feminists, and in particular the Women Against Violence Against Women movement, which succeeded in getting the posters withdrawn.

BLACK AND BLUE: THE HOPEFULS' ALBUM

On November 29, 1974, a little over a month after the release of *It's Only Rock 'N' Roll*, Mick Jagger, who was in Nicaragua with Bianca at the time, received a telephone call from Anna Menzies, the Stones' secretary, informing him that Mick Taylor had left the band for good. A few days later, the Rolling Stones were in Munich for the initial recording sessions for their new album. Taylor's departure was officially announced on December 12 by Mick Jagger, who told the newspapers that although he regretted the decision: "No doubt we can find a brilliant six-foot three-inch blond guitarist who can do his own make-up."[35] The next day, Mick Taylor explained: "I'd worked with them in a such a way, and for so long, that I didn't think I could go much further without some different musicians."[27] And on December 21, he was anxious to silence rumors that he had left for financial reasons and as a result of never being credited as a co-writer: "I am very disturbed by those rumours, it had absolutely nothing to do with those things. . . . Whatever I felt about credits on songs has nothing to do with my decision to leave. If Mick Jagger or Keith Richards even want to do solo albums, I'd like to be in on them."[35] No sooner had Mick Taylor left to join Jack Bruce, then various names started to circulate. Ron Wood's cropped up the most, but Chris Spedding, Jeff Beck, Mick Ronson, and Paul Kossoff (among others) were also thought to be in contention . . . On January 18, 1975, *Melody Maker* added Ry Cooder, Dave Clempson, Ollie Halsall, Jorma Kaukonen, and even Steve Hillage to the list. The Stones did not want to rush into anything, however, and would record their thirteenth (British) studio album with the help of various guitarists: Harvey Mandel, who had played with Canned Heat and John Mayall, appears on "Hot Stuff" and "Memory Motel"; Wayne Perkins, whose playing had been enjoyed by every artist who had passed through the doors of Muscle Shoals Sound Studios, contributes to "Hand of Fate," "Memory Hotel," and "Fool to Cry"; Ron Wood, meanwhile, helps the Stones out with guitar and/or backing vocals on "Hey Negrita," "Cherry Oh Baby," "Crazy Mama" (not confirmed), "Hot Stuff," "Hand of Fate," and "Memory Hotel." The other musicians who assisted in the making of the album include Billy Preston on keyboards, Ollie E. Brown (the Temptations, Blondie, Michael Jackson) on percussion, and once again the loyal Ian Stewart and Nicky Hopkins.

The Album

Does this variety of sidemen explain the Rolling Stones' change of musical direction? To a certain extent. Mick Jagger and Keith Richards had been exploring new musical avenues ever since *Goats Head Soup* (1973). "Hot Stuff" exemplifies this development: it is a resolutely funky number that contains the seeds of disco (and indeed looks forward to "Miss You"), a track of which Sly and the Family Stone or the great James Brown would have been proud. The same goes for "Hey Negrita," a kind of Latin funk number that can be seen in retrospect as a kind of joining gift from Ron Wood, and also, in a certain sense, "Melody," which veers—under the influence of Billy Preston—between blues and jazz. As for "Cherry Oh Baby," written by the Jamaican singer Eric Donaldson,

Ron Wood (right), Mick Taylor's successor, shown here with the Jeff Beck Group in 1967 (left to right: Aynsley Dunbar, Jeff Beck, Rod Stewart).

this is the Stones' second love letter to reggae, following their first and somewhat timid incursion into the genre with "Luxury" on the album *It's Only Rock 'N' Roll*.

Alongside these manifestos for funk and reggae, the Glimmer Twins also keep faith with a musical form for which they had been developing more and more of a liking since *Goats Head Soup*. "Memory Motel" and "Fool to Cry" are among the Stones' most penetrating ballads, with brilliant vocal performances from a Mick Jagger who had clearly been spending a lot of time listening to the best soul singers. Finally, no Stones album would be complete without Keith's characteristic riffs. This tradition has been superbly upheld in "Hand of Fate" and "Crazy Mama."

A few months before *Black and Blue* was released in spring 1976 (April 23 in the United Kingdom, April 15 in the United States), the Rolling Stones had completed a long series of concerts in North America—the famous Tour of the Americas '75 (June 1–August 8, 1975). Accompanying them were Ian Stewart (piano), Billy Preston (keyboards), Trevor Lawrence (sax), Ollie E. Brown (percussion), and . . . Ron Wood, despite still being a member of the Faces. "In April [1975], I sat down with Mick and Keith in the Munich Hilton and we had a little meeting. Keith admitted to me that his first choice to replace Mick Taylor had been Steve Marriott, but the Stones agreed that what they really needed was a lead and rhythm guitar player, and eventually settled on three names—Jeff Beck, Eric Clapton and me,"[105] writes Ron Wood. "Keith said to me, 'You're in the band.' I told him, 'Yeah, I know.' Keith added, 'We're not going to tell anyone for years,' and I said, 'That's fine with me.'"[105] Thus at the end of the American tour, when journalists asked the members of the Stones and Ron Wood whether the latter was Mick Taylor's official successor, they all replied in the negative: it was only on December 18, the day Rod Stewart left the Faces, that the mist cleared.

So the Rolling Stones had—quasi-officially—become a quintet again. *Black and Blue* would top the charts in the United States (for four weeks, eventually being certified platinum), as well as in France (where it would be certified gold) and the Netherlands, and would climb to number 2 in the United Kingdom and Norway. On April 23, 1976, Dave Marsh wrote in the columns of *Rolling Stone*: "*Black and Blue* may not be the invincible Rolling Stones of our dreams, but that is also a virtue in its way. *Black and Blue* leaves me remembering the first important lesson I learned from the Stones: 'Empty heart is like an empty life.' This may not be the same band which told us that, but those sullen teenagers would recognize this one, and be proud."[109]

The Album Cover

For the cover of their new album, the Stones turned to Yasuhiro Wakabayashi, a collaborator on *Harper's Bazaar* and *Vogue* and one of the most renowned fashion photographers of his day. Hiro, as he was better known, shot the photos used on the front and back covers and inner sleeve of *Black and Blue* on Sanibel Island, Florida, in February 1976. On the front, the three faces of Mick Jagger, Keith Richards (in almost three-quarter profile), and Bill Wyman (behind, looking more mysterious than ever) are shown in close-up against a sparkling sea and an azure sky. The photo on the reverse depicts the faces of Charlie Watts and Ron Wood (in profile) along with part of Mick Jagger's. Inside, the five Stones, all dressed in white, draw light patterns in the air as the blue of the sky merges with the blue of the sea.

The Recording

The *Black and Blue* sessions began on December 6, 1974, at Musicland Studios in Munich, where the Rolling Stones had recorded their previous album, *It's Only Rock 'N' Roll*. This was the first time since Mick Taylor had walked out that the

The stalwart Charlie Watts at his black Gretsch kit for *Black and Blue*.

Stones found themselves cutting a new record as a foursome: Charlie, Bill, Keith, and Mick. Fortunately, Nicky Hopkins was soon to join them, as were the sound engineers Keith Harwood and Glyn Johns. Glyn, having now returned to the fold, was delighted to be working with a smaller group of musicians: " . . . it was like going back to the beginning, the original team, only without Brian and with the addition of Nicky Hopkins. I must say I took great comfort in this and enjoyed the sessions immensely."[4] The first day they were without Keith and Nicky. The latter made a brief appearance the following day, but managed to take a very serious overdose upon returning to the studio. Once Keith deigned to turn up on day three, the sessions were able to get properly under way. Between December 8 and 15, the basic tracks of "Fool to Cry" and "Cherry Oh Baby" were laid down, as well as those of various songs (such as "Act Together," "Something Good," and "I Got a Letter") that would not be used on the album. Glyn Johns recalls: "We got a huge amount done in the twelve days we were there. In fact, I thought we had very nearly finished the record."[4]

At the beginning of 1975, the Stones were still looking for someone to replace Mick Taylor. They traveled to Rotterdam to record with the Rolling Stones Mobile Studio, again for tax reasons. "Stu had found a concert orchestra rehearsal facility that he felt would be suitable to use as a studio, so we took the Stones Truck,"[4] writes Glyn Johns. Despite its excellent acoustics, which were designed for a symphony orchestra, the place was ill-suited for recording rock music. No matter, the Stones resumed recording and took advantage of the situation to audition a host of guitarists. Among the candidates were Rory Gallagher, Wayne Perkins, and Jeff Beck. The sessions dragged, however, and with the distraction of the auditions, the band was not as focused as they had been in Munich. "A huge amount of recording time was wasted," reports Glyn, "as over the next few days, a steady progression of hopeful guitarists from near and far trooped up and down the stairs and corridors of the building

we were in."[4] Faced with this inefficiency, the sound engineer lost his patience and clashed with Keith for the first and last time. He decided to quit. Having contributed to some of the band's greatest albums, and dedicated himself body and soul to their cause, Glyn walked out in the Netherlands and never saw *Black and Blue* through to completion. Another glorious chapter in the history of the Rolling Stones had drawn to a close.

Having begun around January 22 (21 or 23, according to the sources), the sessions at the De Doelen center in Rotterdam, with the Rolling Stones Mobile Studio, continued through February 9, 1975. "Crazy Mama" and "Melody" were cut, along with "Slave" and "Worried About You" (on *Tattoo You*, 1981) plus various other songs that were subsequently abandoned (such as a cover of "Heat Wave" by Holland-Dozier-Holland, and "Man Eating Woman" with Jeff Beck).

A Hard Act to Follow

While the newspapers were speculating about who would be the lucky individual chosen to replace Mick Taylor, it looked as if the Stones had settled on the American guitarist Wayne Perkins. Yet no official announcement was made. The sessions resumed at Musicland Studios in Munich on March 22 (or 25), still with Wayne Perkins, but also—betraying the Stones' indecision—the guitarist Harvey Mandel, who came along for a trial on March 30. By this time Stones regular Billy Preston was back on keyboards. Then on April 1, Ron Wood came to visit the band and suddenly it seemed obvious: he was the one who would replace Mick Taylor! Although he didn't possess Taylor's virtuosity, his sense of humor, personality, and British background were exactly what Mick and Keith were looking for. Even in his case, however, nothing was official because he did not want to break his commitments to the Faces and Rod Stewart. He did not give his final decision until the end of the year. For the time being, in the days leading up to April 4, the band recorded "Hand of Fate," "Hot

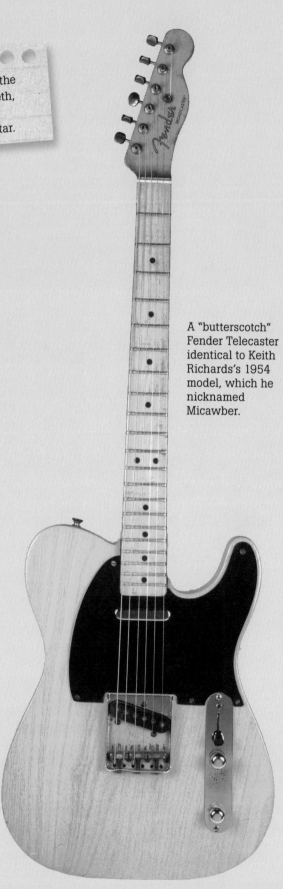

Stuff," "Memory Motel," and "Hey Negrita," as well as various other numbers (including an initial version of "Start Me Up," at that time called "Never Stop"). After the Tour of the Americas '75, the Stones, Ron Wood, Billy Preston, and Ollie E. Brown, along with sound engineers Keith Harwood and Lew Hahn (Bee Gees, Aretha Franklin, Carly Simon), then spent the period from October 19 to November 30 recording overdubs and starting to mix the album at the world-famous Mountain Recording Studios in Montreux, Switzerland, which were owned by the band Queen from 1978 until the middle of the nineties and would see the likes of Yes, David Bowie, AC/DC, Phil Collins, and Sting pass through their doors. Finally, Mick and Keith went to New York in January 1976 to do the final mastering and put the finishing touches on *Black and Blue* at the Atlantic Recording Studios, under the benevolent eye of Ahmet Ertegun.

Another sound engineer who worked on the album was Phil McDonald, who had started his career as an assistant engineer with the Beatles. Among the assistant sound engineers were the old hands Tapani Tapanainen (*It's Only Rock 'N' Roll*) and Jeremy Gee (*Exile on Main St.*), but also new faces, such as Dave Richards (Queen, David Bowie, Yes), Steve Dowd, Gene Paul, and Lee Hulko, who helped with the mastering.

Technical Details

When the Rolling Stones returned to Musicland Studios in Munich, having earlier recorded part of *It's Only Rock 'N' Roll* there, they found a new Harrison 3232 console, Westlake monitors, and almost certainly a 3M 24-track tape recorder. The Rolling Stones Mobile Studio also kept up with technological developments, with the installation of new machinery, including two 3M 24-tracks, a Helios 32/24 console, and Altec 604-8G monitors.

The Instruments

The instruments were essentially the same ones that the Stones had used on their previous album. With the exception of Ron Wood, who began his career with the Rolling Stones with guitars that were individual to him, the main ones being a number of Zemaitis and a 1955 Fender Stratocaster.

A "butterscotch" Fender Telecaster identical to Keith Richards's 1954 model, which he nicknamed Micawber.

1976

HOT STUFF

Mick Jagger / Keith Richards / 5:21

Musicians
Mick Jagger: vocals, percussion
Keith Richards: rhythm guitars, backing vocals
Ron Wood: backing vocals
Bill Wyman: bass, percussion
Charlie Watts: drums, percussion
Ian Stewart: percussion
Billy Preston: piano, backing vocals
Ollie E. Brown: timbales, cowbell
Harvey Mandel: lead guitar
Recorded
Musicland Studios, Munich: March 30, December 1975
Mountain Recording Studios, Montreux:
October–November 1975
Technical Team
Producers: The Glimmer Twins
Sound engineers: Keith Harwood, Phil McDonald, Lew Hahn
Assistant sound engineers: Jeremy Gee, Dave Richards, Tapani Tapanainen, Steve Dowd, Gene Paul, Lee Hulko

Genesis

When Mick Jagger sings *hot stuff, can't get enough*, the first image that springs to mind is of the singer disporting himself with a woman of boundless erotic power, but as the verses progress, it soon becomes apparent the narrator's good vibes are occasioned by music, *'Cause music is what I want to keep my body always moving*, sings Jagger, *music make you forget all your trouble*. The message delivered by the Stones singer to the people of *London, New York*, and *Jamaica* is clear: good music possesses erotic and cathartic powers.

"Hot Stuff," the first song by the Jagger-Richards duo to possess an emphatic funk vibe, also, in a sense, heralds the imminent disco craze that was already starting to invade the world's dance floors. The Stones had not yet replaced Mick Taylor, who had just left the band, and were auditioning various candidates. It was Harvey Mandel, the former guitarist with Canned Heat (the legendary West Coast blues-rock outfit) who got the job for "Hot Stuff." Released as a single, "Hot Stuff" only managed a modest forty-ninth place in the United States, while its B-side, "Fool to Cry," did well on the charts on both sides of the Atlantic, literally stealing the success intended for the other side.

Production

Keith Richards opens "Hot Stuff" with a superbly funky riff, worthy of Nile Rodgers. Played almost certainly on his Fender Telecaster, the sound is percussive, clear-toned, and medium-bodied, with a slight phasing or chorus effect. This is worlds away from the full-on, distorted rhythm parts Keith generally favors. The music of the day was funk, already tending toward disco, and the Stones were by no means immune to it; Mick Jagger even admitted that he had had the band Ohio Players in mind when recording this song. However, the Stones also remain true to themselves, and nothing can stop them from putting their own rock 'n' roll stamp on it. Thus Charlie Watts imparts a wonderful funk drive, while at the same time retaining a heavy beat. He is supported very effectively by Bill Wyman with a superb, insidious groove that transforms the duo into a fearsome swing machine. Furthermore, after the bassist Darryl Jones replaced Bill onstage when the original Stone left in 1993, the number would never move the way this studio version does. Billy Preston contributes

Harvey Mandel, guitarist with Canned Heat and Rolling Stones studio musician, on "Hot Stuff."

Keith Richards backstage during the Tour of the Americas '75, with his "butterscotch" Fender Telecaster.

more of a Latin color, delivering a first-rate piano part with an Afro-Cuban accent. This feel is reinforced by the timbales and cowbell played by Ollie E. Brown, who shares other percussion duties with Bill, Mick, Stu, and Charlie. Mick delivers a very hot lead vocal, adopting a fake Jamaican accent for a section sung in a dub-like style, with heavy delay and radio-style equalization (3:17).

But "Hot Stuff" would not be what it is without the participation of the excellent Harvey Mandel, who takes the lead, first with the hypnotic riff he plays throughout the number, probably on his Gibson Les Paul, then at 2:06 with a very good solo played with distortion and wah-wah. It is interesting to note that for this section the key rises by a tone, a harmonic effect rarely used by the Stones. Harvey recalls his sudden irruption into the world of the Stones: "I was at home. Mick Jagger called me at midnight. At first I thought someone was

goofing on me, but after a while I could tell it was really him. He said, 'I'd like you to fly to Germany tomorrow.' The next day, I'm on my way to Germany."[110] Despite his highly convincing performance, and another on "Memory Motel," Ron Wood would beat him out for the job. Finally, Keith adds a second rhythm part from the second verse, played with the help of a wah-wah pedal.

"Hot Stuff" is a fantastic opening track—the Stones had not had one like it since "Rocks Off" on *Exile on Main St.* If its performance on the charts was disappointing, this is probably due to the fans' surprise at a relatively new style that was, most importantly, far removed from the band's roots. This is a shame, all the more so as the Stones had never played with such solid timing . . .

1976

HAND OF FATE

Mick Jagger / Keith Richards / 4:28

Musicians
Mick Jagger: vocals
Keith Richards: rhythm guitar, backing vocals
Ron Wood: backing vocals
Bill Wyman: bass
Charlie Watts: drums
Billy Preston: piano
Ollie E. Brown: percussion
Wayne Perkins: rhythm and lead guitar
Recorded
Musicland Studios, Munich: March 25, December 1975
Mountain Recording Studios, Montreux:
October–November 1975
Technical Team
Producers: The Glimmer Twins
Sound engineers: Keith Harwood, Phil McDonald, Lew Hahn
Assistant sound engineers: Jeremy Gee, Dave Richards,
Tapani Tapanainen, Steve Dowd, Gene Paul, Lee Hulko

Wayne Perkins (center), who plays on "Hand of Fate," here
with members of the trio Smith Perkins Smith in 1972.

Genesis

"Hand of Fate" tells the story of a man on the run after killing someone out of love for a woman. The ominous *hand of fate is on me now*, he declares. During an interview in 1976, Mick Jagger explained: "It's a narrative, you know, a sort of chopped up narrative about a Southern murder. It's better, you know, than singing about the ordinary things. A lot of people like that one. It's about someone whose woman you take and he decides to take her back."[48]

The use of two different expressions relating to the world of gambling, the *wheel of fortune* and *my chips are down*, is presumably aimed at conveying the idea that the man on the run is simply a pawn in a process that is beyond his control . . .

Production

"Hand of Fate" is first and foremost a celebration by Keith Richards of rock music and his guitar. Riffs he composed all the time, but great riffs he hunted down with as much dedication as a crusader in pursuit of the Holy Grail. Here he has proved it yet again by developing a riff that bears his stamp, with that characteristic sound obtained most likely on his Telecaster in open-G tuning through a Fender Twin Reverb. This track continues where the two previous albums left off, and listeners are given the impression that Mick Taylor is about to join in at any minute. The lead guitar part, though, has been given to Wayne Perkins, a guitarist from Alabama who had already played with many greats of rock, reggae, and the blues, from Albert King to Leon Russell, and Eric Clapton to Bob Marley. In fact, it was via Clapton that Perkins came into contact with the Rolling Stones during the *Black and Blue* sessions (although he had already played on the recording of Bill Wyman's *Monkey Grip* in 1974). Perkins accompanies Keith on rhythm before taking not one but three solos! His phrasing is somewhat reminiscent of Taylor's, at least in terms of its lyricism. The results are excellent and he would no doubt have made a first-rate guitarist with the band. The other members of the gang provide an accompaniment that is faithful to the Stones sound, perhaps even conforming a fraction too much. Similarly, Mick Jagger delivers his rock vocal without doing anything particularly different. Billy Preston comes in on piano during the instrumental bridge at 2:39, and Ollie E. Brown plays cowbell and tambourine.

CHERRY OH BABY

Eric Donaldson / 3:54

Musicians
Mick Jagger: vocals
Keith Richards: rhythm guitar, backing vocals
Ron Wood: rhythm guitar
Bill Wyman: bass
Charlie Watts: drums
Nicky Hopkins: organ

Recorded
Musicland Studios, Munich: December 15, 1974; March 25–April 4; December 1975
Rolling Stones Mobile Studio, Rotterdam: January 22–February 9, 1975 (?)
Mountain Recording Studios, Montreux: October–November 1975

Technical Team
Producers: The Glimmer Twins
Sound engineers: Keith Harwood, Glyn Johns, Phil McDonald, Lew Hahn
Assistant sound engineers: Jeremy Gee, Dave Richards, Tapani Tapanainen, Steve Dowd, Gene Paul, Lee Hulko

The Stones record "Cherry Oh Baby" by Eric Donaldson, a musician they came across during the *Exile* sessions.

Genesis

A native of Jamaica, where he was born in 1947, Eric Donaldson was a pioneering figure in the music scene of the Caribbean island. He formed a vocal group and recorded his first songs in 1964 at Kingston's Studio One. A few years later, he left to pursue a solo career and scored an enormous hit with "Cherry Oh Baby," which he performed at the Festival Song Competition in 1971. It was apparently in the South of France that Jagger discovered Donaldson's album, possibly at the instigation of Charlie Watts, who would later explain that he had had that kind of record with him during their stay in France, or else at Keith's, who, again according to Charlie, listened to "The Harder They Come" during the recording of *Exile on Main St.* Four years later, the Stones tried out the song for their own amusement and decided to use it: " . . . we just did it one day for a laugh and kept it on the album,"[48] explains Jagger. It is with this version of "Cherry Oh Baby" that the band made its first real incursion into reggae.

Production

The third track on the album and the third musical style. Unfortunately, while the Stones are perfectly credible when flirting with disco funk, as in "Hot Stuff," they are much less convincing in reggae. Charlie seems all at sea with his rhythm. He is unable to find a groove in his drumming and fails to accentuate the offbeat as he should. Bill takes care of the bass line as well as he can, given the lack of necessary guidance from his colleague. Keith's guitar playing is limp, his chords noticeably lacking in punch, despite his double-tracking. Ron Wood—whose very first official participation with the band this is—attempts a Jamaican-style palm mute technique (probably on his Zemaitis guitar), but without much conviction, a problem he shares with Nicky Hopkins, who tries to generate some local color with his phrases on the organ. Only Mick gives a thoroughly good performance, his drawling, languorous style being extremely well suited to reggae. Keith lends a hand in the vocal harmonies and backing vocals, which they sing together, first in a high and then in a low register. "Cherry Oh Baby" is not one of the band's better covers, and comparing it with the original version is not advisable.

MEMORY HOTEL

Mick Jagger / Keith Richards / 7:06

Musicians
Mick Jagger: vocals, piano
Keith Richards: electric piano, backing vocals
Ron Wood: backing vocals
Bill Wyman: bass
Charlie Watts: drums
Billy Preston: synthesizer, backing vocals
Harvey Mandel: lead guitar
Wayne Perkins: acoustic guitar
Recorded
Musicland Studios, Munich: March 31, 1975
Mountain Recording Studios, Montreux:
October–November 1975 (?)
Technical Team
Producers: The Glimmer Twins
Sound engineers: Keith Harwood, Phil McDonald, Lew Hahn
Assistant sound engineers: Jeremy Gee, Dave Richards,
Tapani Tapanainen, Steve Dowd, Gene Paul, Lee Hulko

FOR STONES ADDICTS

On July 5, 1998, in Amsterdam, during the Bridges to Babylon Tour, Dave Matthews joined the Stones onstage to sing "Memory Motel" (on the live album *No Security*, 1998).

🎧 **IN YOUR HEADPHONES**
When Mick, Keith, Billy, and Ronnie strike up their *sha la la la* backing vocals, one of them hits a wrong note at 4:12!

Mick Jagger and the photographer Annie Leibovitz at
Niagara Falls in 1975.

Genesis

It was at Andy Warhol's house in Montauk, New York, the Stones' rehearsal venue prior to the 1975 tour, that Mick Jagger started to write "Memory Motel." The title refers to a motel in this village located at the eastern tip of Long Island. He then completed the song during the Tour of the Americas '75. Some of the towns on the tour are mentioned in it (Baton Rouge, San Antonio, Boston. . . .).

The song's heroine, with whom the narrator passes a night at the Memory Motel, is called Hannah. We are told she has hazel eyes and slightly curved teeth. To whom is Mick Jagger referring here? Some have suggested the singer Carly Simon, who is said to have had a brief fling with the Stones singer (and to have targeted him in "You're So Vain"). Others lean more toward Annie Leibovitz, because her first name sounds similar, of course, but most importantly because of her proximity to the Stones, and Mick Jagger in particular, during the Tour of the Americas '75, which she covered for *Rolling Stone* magazine. For his part, Jagger has the following to say: "But actually I don't think that there's any particular . . . it's more about the tour, really, rather than about the girl."[48] This song is about a single night of passion. And the memories that follow . . .

Production

For the first time on a Stones record, Mick Jagger plays the intro himself, on a grand piano. Keith joins him not on the guitar, but on a Fender Rhodes electric piano with a swirling sound (courtesy of a Leslie speaker?). Wayne Perkins is on acoustic guitar and Harvey Mandel on lead, playing in a style not unlike Mick Taylor's. Charlie and Bill provide solid support, while Billy produces a string sound on the synthesizer. Mick sings lead vocals except on the bridges, where Keith takes over. There is a reason for this division of roles, as Keith himself explains: "Yeah, I thought it was beautiful. Mick had nearly all of it planned out, but he had no bridge, no middle part. And it so happened that the other part that I do, I was writing this song that had no other part."[112] The two sections fit together perfectly in a fine example of the Glimmer Twins' alchemy at work. Keith again: "I remember that moment, realizing that we had one song and not two."[112]

HEY NEGRITA

Mick Jagger / Keith Richards / 4:58

Musicians
Mick Jagger: vocals
Keith Richards: rhythm guitar, backing vocals
Ron Wood: lead guitar, backing vocals
Bill Wyman: bass
Charlie Watts: drums
Billy Preston: piano, organ (?), backing vocals
Ollie E. Brown: percussion
Recorded
Musicland Studios, Munich: April 2, 1975
Atlantic Studios, New York: January–February, 1976 (?)
Technical Team
Producers: The Glimmer Twins
Sound engineers: Keith Harwood, Phil McDonald, Lew Hahn
Assistant sound engineers: Jeremy Gee, Dave Richards, Tapani Tapanainen, Steve Dowd, Gene Paul, Lee Hulko

Genesis

"Hey Negrita" was a milestone in the history of the Rolling Stones, as it would seal the union between the four bandmates and the guitarist who was still a member of the Faces at the time. Wood recalls the memorable audition in Munich during which the song saw the light of day: "I walked into the studio, took one look at Mick, Keith, Bill and Charlie and announced, 'I've got a song. I've played it to you before.'"[105] The foursome followed his lead without any difficulty and "Hey Negrita" was born. All that remained was to write the words. And what words! The song would prove extremely controversial. Denounced as sexist, it was also suspected of being racist by all those who saw the word *Negrita*, meaning *little black girl* in Spanish, as a pejorative term. Apparently it was nothing of the sort for Mick, who would deny any racist intent by claiming it was the nickname of his wife, Bianca. For him it was simply "about a South American whore, and the singer, a poor man, is trying to get her price down."[48]

Production

New Stone, new regime: Keith entrusts the introductory riff to Ronnie, and it has be said that the newcomer makes a fine job of it, playing the—more funk than rock—pattern most probably on one of his Zemaitis. Keith then answers with a funk-style palm mute rhythm part with a reggae flavor. Charlie Watts leads in with a very good snare drum break, and he and Bill fall into a highly effective groove. Ollie E. Brown is on cowbell, tambourine, and, probably, maracas (or is it Mick?). Billy Preston plays Afro-Cuban-style piano, which helps make the style of this number somewhat hard to define. He is also indicated as playing the organ, but this is inaudible. Similarly, the instrumental bridge (at 2:34) is rhythmically and harmonically very loose, and its almost jazz-rock feel muddies the water further. But when Ronnie takes a slide solo at around 3:45, everything falls back into place. Mick is in excellent form once again, creating a thoroughly torrid and electric atmosphere. "Hey Negrita" gives the impression of having been improvised in the studio, rather than composed in a calm and collected manner, but the results speak for themselves.

In a sense, "Hey Negrita" marks Ron Wood's elevation to the dizzying status of an official Rolling Stone!

MELODY

Mick Jagger / Keith Richards / 5:48

Musicians
Mick Jagger: vocals, foot stomp
Keith Richards: rhythm guitar
Bill Wyman: bass
Charlie Watts: drums
Billy Preston: piano, organ, backing vocals
Unidentified musician(s): percussion
Arif Mardin: horn arrangements
Recorded
Rolling Stones Mobile Studio, Rotterdam,
Netherlands: January 23, 1975
Mountain Recording Studios, Montreux:
October–November 1975 (?)
Atlantic Studios, New York: January–February 1976
Technical Team
Producers: The Glimmer Twins
Sound engineers: Keith Harwood,
Glyn Johns, Phil McDonald, Lew Hahn
Assistant sound engineers: Jeremy Gee, Dave Richards,
Tapani Tapanainen, Steve Dowd, Gene Paul, Lee Hulko

The Stones singer onstage with Billy Preston, who played a considerable role in the making of "Melody," in 1975.

Genesis

Melody is the second name of a girl from whom, based on the narrator's experience, it is best to keep one's distance. The protagonist has taken her out dancing and she has thanked him by squandering his money and ending up in the arms of his best friend. One day she leaves behind the wheel of his car, taking his *trailer home* and even his *Sunday boots* with her. Since then he has been searching for her relentlessly . . .

"Melody" started life as a melodic line of Billy Preston's. It found its final form with the help of Mick Jagger. "What it is, it sort of came out of something that Billy [Preston] and I were messing around with, just piano and voice. It's got an incredible amount of overdub now, but down in the nitty-gritty it's really just a rhythm section and voice, very simple, sort of four-to-the-bar kind of bass line and drums, sort of old-fashioned rhythm."[48]

Production

For the first time ever on a studio album by the Stones, the musicians on "Melody" are audibly counted in. This is an extremely well-crafted half-jazz, half-soul number. The influence—and even writing—of Billy Preston is clear. The song owes him a great deal, and Ron Wood would attest to this lack of recognition, which was taken badly by the pianist, as it had been by other musicians before him. "There were a number of people who took umbrage, like Billy,"[9] the guitarist would later comment. Furthermore, "Melody" borrows its harmony, beat, and horn color from Preston's own "Do You Love Me?" released in 1973 (*Everybody Likes Some Kind of Music*). Either way, Billy Preston makes a key contribution to this track: he's on piano, B-3 organ, and also sings opposite Mick Jagger. The latter seems to be highly inspired by his presence, as he gives one of his best vocal performances on the album, and, with Preston, delights in improvising vocal sounds resembling a muted trumpet or the meowing of a cat (from 3:16). Charlie plays an appropriate shuffle on his ride cymbal, supported by Bill with a kind of walking bass. Keith is excellent on rhythm guitar, adopting a jazzy style that he carries off extremely well. Finally, the horns, arranged by Arif Mardin, lend the instrumentation a not inconsiderable power. It is interesting to note that Mick has a track reserved entirely for the foot stomp with which he marks the beat!

FOOL TO CRY

Mick Jagger / Keith Richards / 5:02

Musicians
Mick Jagger: vocals, electric piano
Keith Richards: rhythm and lead guitar (?)
Bill Wyman: bass
Charlie Watts: drums
Wayne Perkins: lead guitar
Nicky Hopkins: piano, synthesizer (strings)

Recorded
Musicland Studios, Munich: December 12, 1974;
March 25–April 4, 1975; December 1975
Mountain Recording Studios, Montreux:
October–November 1975

Technical Team
Producers: The Glimmer Twins
Sound engineers: Glyn Johns, Keith Harwood,
Phil McDonald, Lew Hahn
Assistant sound engineers: Jeremy Gee, Dave Richards,
Tapani Tapanainen, Steve Dowd, Gene Paul, Lee Hulko

A dark song performed by an artist who was starting to become aware of the passing years . . .

Genesis

"Fool to Cry" (originally titled "Daddy You're a Fool to Cry") is a sad song, indeed one of the saddest in the Stones catalog. Was Mick Jagger beginning to feel the weight of the passing years more and more? Or were these the sentiments of a rock star who had become a father? The main character in the song is exhausted from working all night, and finds comfort in the company of his daughter, whom he likes to put on his knee. She says: *"Daddy, what's wrong?"/And she whispers in my ear/She says: "Daddy, you're a fool to cry."*

"Fool to Cry" was released as the A-side of a single (with "Crazy Mama" as the B-side) on April 26, 1976. It was in France that it achieved its best chart position: number 2 in July 1976. It peaked at number 6 in the United Kingdom and Canada, number 8 in both the Netherlands and Norway, and only made it to number 10 in the United States.

Production

"Fool to Cry" is a captivating melody performed by a magisterial voice. Even those who prefer Mick Jagger as a rock 'n' roll singer have to admit that his vocal performance in this number is on a par with the greatest soul singers, his falsetto reminiscent of Solomon Burke's. It was around now that he adopted this particular vocal technique, and here he double- and triple-tracks himself, mainly in the refrains, in order to enhance his voice. He also plays the electric piano, probably a Wurlitzer through a Leslie speaker. Nicky Hopkins delivers a wonderful acoustic piano part, again with his characteristic lyrical touch (listen around 2:20). He also creates a reasonably tasteful string accompaniment on synthesizer (ARP Solina?), a hazardous musical initiative that often does not stand the test of time. As for the guitars, Keith Richards is on rhythm with wah-wah and seems to leave the lead to Wayne Perkins. It is something of a shame that the guitar sound is drowned out in a riot of effects (phasing, chorus, stereo, reverb), tending to confuse the musical message. Finally, Charlie provides simultaneously solid and simple support on the drums, while Bill delivers a very good, melodic and rhythmic, bass part. "Fool to Cry" is one of Glyn Johns's favorite songs, and the sound engineer believes he created the definitive mix in Munich in 1974: "I think it eats the version that they finally released a year later,"[4] he would later opine.

CRAZY MAMA

Mick Jagger / Keith Richards / 4:32

Musicians
Mick Jagger: vocals, rhythm guitar
Keith Richards: rhythm guitars, slide and lead guitars (?), bass, piano, backing vocals
Charlie Watts: drums
Ron Wood: lead guitar (?), backing vocals
Billy Preston: piano (?), backing vocals
Ollie E. Brown: percussion

Recorded
Musicland Studios, Munich: March 29, December 1975
Mountain Recording Studios, Montreux: October–November 1975

Technical Team
Producers: The Glimmer Twins
Sound engineers: Keith Harwood, Phil McDonald, Lew Hahn
Assistant sound engineers: Jeremy Gee, Dave Richards, Tapani Tapanainen, Steve Dowd, Gene Paul, Lee Hulko

Genesis
After funk, soul, and ballad, the Rolling Stones wrap up *Black and Blue* with a first-rate rock 'n' roll number featuring a made-to-measure riff in order to go out with a bang. Like almost all the songs on the album, this one saw the light of day in the studio, as Jagger confirms: "We wrote that in the studio, too. All of it, my words and everything. It just 'came' to me."[48] And speaking of words, the lyrics of this song tell of a crazy mama wearing a ball and chain and wielding a sawed-off shotgun. A sort of Ma Barker revisited by the Stones . . . "Crazy Mama" is also the B-side of the single "Fool to Cry."

Production
The band initially worked on this song between January and February 1975 in Rotterdam with the Rolling Stones Mobile Studio, but without achieving a satisfactory outcome. The base track that would be used for the various overdubs was laid down in Munich on March 29. Mick is apparently playing the rhythm guitar that opens the track. He is then answered by the riff master with another, very good guitar part. It also seems to be Keith who plays the exhilarating and highly successful slide guitar. Charlie attacks the beat with loud, chugging drums, his hi-hat half-open, and according to the "track identification chart" reproduced in the album booklet, Keith is on bass. This chart also has him on piano, which is less credible, especially as Billy Preston is present, helping out with the backing vocals. The excellent Ollie E. Brown looks after percussion, notably the cowbells, of which great use is made on this album. Mick is magnificent, as he always is when he sings rock 'n' roll, exhibiting an electrifying dynamism. Finally, there are guitar solos at 2:22 and in the coda from 3:30. These are superb in every way, with a hint of Nashville, but neither the sound (high-pitched, with heavy reverb), nor the playing style is Keith's. In truth, this solo work is closer to Ron Wood's style, although he is not mentioned in the liner notes. Furthermore, it seems possible that the guitar has been recorded at a slower speed in order to obtain its glitzy quality and rapid delivery when sped up. Either way, "Crazy Mama" is an excellent Stones rock track.

The percussionist Ollie E. Brown, a Stones traveling companion during the *Black and Blue* sessions.

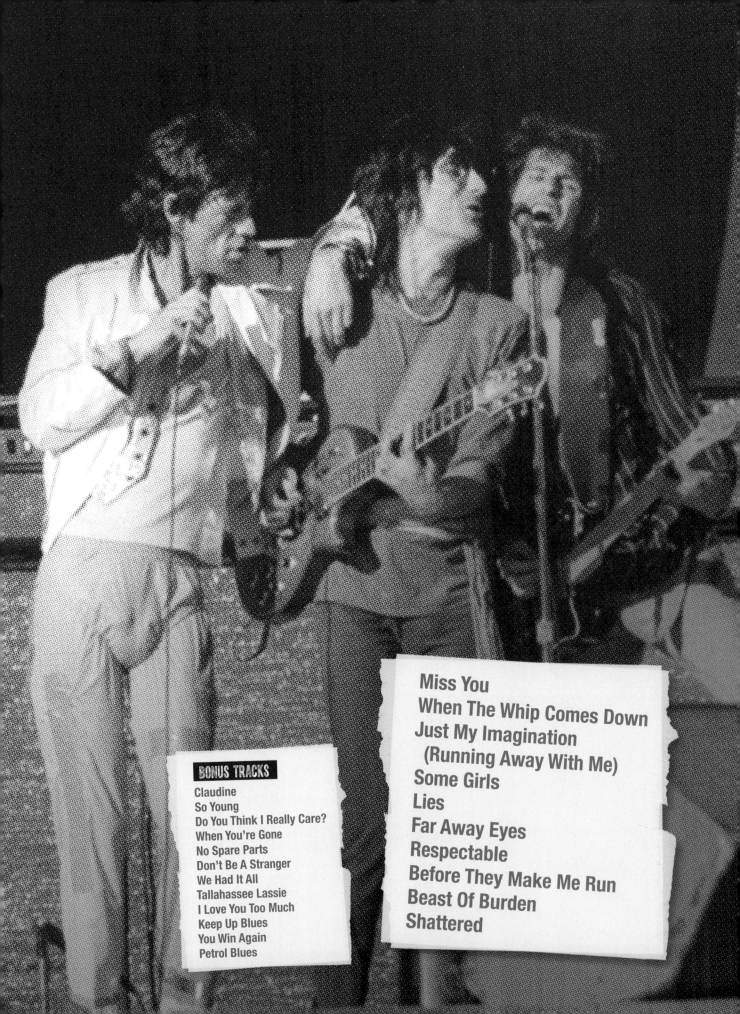

BONUS TRACKS

Claudine
So Young
Do You Think I Really Care?
When You're Gone
No Spare Parts
Don't Be A Stranger
We Had It All
Tallahassee Lassie
I Love You Too Much
Keep Up Blues
You Win Again
Petrol Blues

Miss You
When The Whip Comes Down
Just My Imagination
(Running Away With Me)
Some Girls
Lies
Far Away Eyes
Respectable
Before They Make Me Run
Beast Of Burden
Shattered

ALBUM
RELEASE DATE
United Kingdom: June 9, 1978
Label: Rolling Stones Records
RECORD NUMBER: ROLLING STONES
RECORDS CUN 39108
**Number 2, on the charts for
25 weeks**

SOME

GIRLS

Some Girls, the Glimmer Twins' response to the many who had already written them off.

Like *Exile on Main St., Some Girls* was rereleased, on November 21, 2011, with various bonus tracks recorded during the same period but not used on the album, even though some of them would have merited inclusion: "Claudine," "So Young," "Do You Think I Really Care?," "When You're Gone," "No Spare Parts," "Don't Be a Stranger," "We Had It All," "Tallahassee Lassie," "I Love You Too Much," "Keep Up Blues," "You Win Again," and "Petrol Blues."

SOME GIRLS: THE STONES' LAST GREAT ALBUM?

At the time the Rolling Stones decided to record their fourteenth (British) studio album, the music scene was undergoing a far-reaching transformation. Disco reigned supreme, both on the dance floor and on the charts on both sides of the Atlantic, with Donna Summer ("I Feel Love"), Abba ("Dancing Queen"), KC and the Sunshine Band ("I'm Your Boogie Man"), and the Bee Gees ("How Deep Is Your Love"). At the opposite end of the spectrum, punk had made a twofold rejection—of traditional Western values on the one hand, and of rock music as a flourishing international industry on the other. The Sex Pistols belched out "Anarchy in the UK" and the Ramones stirred up the crowds with "Sheena Is a Punk Rocker," while the Clash sang *I'm so bored with the USA* and *No Elvis, Beatles, or the Rolling Stones* in 1977. These young punks, with their Mohican hairstyles and safety pins, unleashed their frontal attack on the rock establishment at the very moment that the future of the Rolling Stones seemed increasingly uncertain.

The Last Record
before the End of the World

On February 7, 1977, with the five musicians from London booked to play at the El Mocambo club in Toronto, Keith Richards and Anita Pallenberg were arrested in their hotel room for possession of heroin by the Royal Canadian Mounted Police. They were suspected of trafficking and faced the possibility of lengthy prison sentences. Keith and Anita were nevertheless given permission to leave Canada so that the

Stones guitarist could undergo a detox cure in the United States (having obtained a visa thanks to President Jimmy Carter). "It took nineteen months from the bust in March 1977 in Toronto to the trial in October 1978. But at least now I was living in striking distance of New York [South Salem]," writes Keith Richards in *Life*.[2]

Having been granted a visa for France under certain conditions, Keith was able to meet up with the other members of the group in Paris to start work on what was to become the *Some Girls* album. "The sessions for 'Some Girls' always had a following wind from the moment we started rehearsing in the strangely shaped Pathé Marconi Studios in Paris. It was a rejuvenation, surprisingly for such a dark moment, when it was possible that I would go to jail and the Stones would dissolve. But maybe that was part of it. Let's get something down before it happens."[2] This time, the stakes were high, the threat very real. Asked whether the band would break up if Keith went to jail, Mick replied: "We wouldn't if Keith was only in jail for a month or two, but if he were in jail for a long period of time, I suppose we'd have to."[1]

The Album

On February 16, 1977, the Rolling Stones had renewed their contract with Atlantic Records for the United States and Canada, and with the very British EMI for the rest of the world. Mick would make it clear that their choice had been influenced by patriotic feelings: "In this jubilee year I feel it is only fitting that we should sign with a British company."[1] Quite the opposite of

1978

Not only was 1977 the year of disco and punk, it was also the year the King died. Elvis Presley, who went to rockers' heaven in August, was found dead in his bathroom.

Keith Moon (drummer of the Who) and his wife Kim Kerrigan provide Keith Richards with friendly, media-savvy support.

the message delivered by the Sex Pistols in their hit "God Save the Queen," which would be released three months later . . .

The ten songs on the original *Some Girls* album confirm that, contrary to what all the young punks wanted people to believe, the Rolling Stones had lost nothing of their energy or their taste for controversy. As in the glory days of the sixties, Mick Jagger even indulged in a new torrent of invective against women, starting with the title song, which would be considered disgracefully sexist and racist by feminists and the civil rights movements, but also in "Respectable" and "Beast of Burden." As so often, however, the Stones singer was also able to adopt a softer approach, in this case in "Miss You," which could well be his first declaration of love to Jerry Hall, and "Far Away Eyes." His marriage to Bianca had been in a bad way for some time, and the thick-lipped sex symbol had now set his cap for Brian Ferry's girlfriend.

The energy given off by the Rolling Stones throughout the two sides of the LP seems to have been inspired by New York. "And I was noticing that there were a lot of references to New York, so I kept it like that,"[29] Mick Jagger would tell Jonathan Cott. Thus "When the Whip Comes Down" tells the story of a teenage boy from Los Angeles who prostitutes himself in the seedy districts of New York, while "Shattered" transforms the Big Apple into a kind of modern-day Babylon.

And the references to New York are just as striking on a musical level. "Miss You," which takes disco to new heights, is redolent of the torrid atmosphere of Studio 54 (which had opened in April 1977), while "When the Whip Comes Down," "Lies," "Respectable," and "Shattered" are more than a match for the nihilistic manifestos of the punk bands. At the same time, the Stones continue, as ever, to respect their own tradition. "Some Girls" and "Beast of Burden" are ballads, respectively, blues, rock, and soul, that would not have been out of place on *Exile on Main St.*, while "Far Away Eyes," another ballad, has a country feel (the one exception on the album!).

Finally, "Before They Make Me Run," as well as evoking Keith's problems with dope and the Canadian authorities, demonstrates that the Stones magic was as strong as ever.

Is *Some Girls* the Rolling Stones' last great album? Is it their best album with Ron Wood? A lot of fans think so. What is beyond dispute is that from the moment of its release on June 16 in the United Kingdom and the following day in the rest of the world, it would experience a success as vigorous as the energy committed to wax by the five Stones. It topped the album charts in the United States and Canada, and rose to number 2 in the United Kingdom and France, number 3 in Australia, Norway, and Sweden, number 6 in West Germany . . . *Some Girls* would also later rank 269th in *Rolling Stone* magazine's list of the 500 Greatest Albums of All Time.

The Album Cover

This time, Mick Jagger chose Peter Corriston to design the album cover. The graphic designer, based in Greenwich Village, came up with an idea for a distinctly kitsch visual, a kind of retro advertising look (inspired by that of the Valmor Products Company) in which the faces of the Stones would appear alongside those of the twentieth century's most beautiful women. The gag was to deck them out in wigs and to make them up with bright red lipstick. In fact it is a double cover. The outer cover is an illustration in green, yellow, blue, and pink (from top to bottom) pierced by windows adorned with wigs, apertures into which a face would slot. On the reverse there is more retro advertising, this time for bras. On the inner sleeve, the five Rolling Stones found themselves in the glamorous company of icons such as Marilyn Monroe, Judy Garland, Lucille Ball, Jayne Mansfield, Brigitte Bardot, Farrah Fawcett, Raquel Welch, Gina Lollobrigida, and Rita Hayworth (illustrations by Hubert Kretzschmar).

The album was released in this sleeve without it having occurred to the Rolling Stones' attorneys to ask for permission

to reproduce the portraits. Lucille Ball, Farrah Fawcett, Raquel Welch, Liza Minnelli (as the daughter of Judy Garland), and the estate of Marilyn Monroe threatened the Rolling Stones with an enormous lawsuit, as did Valmor Products Company, which was not happy about the copying of its design. This first cover having been censured, *Some Girls* was immediately rereleased with new artwork, the statements *Pardon our appearance* and *cover under reconstruction* replacing the various portraits of the wronged stars.

The Recording

The Rolling Stones chose to record *Some Girls* at the Pathé Marconi EMI Studios on rue de Sèvres in Boulogne-Billancourt, near Paris. This may seem a surprising choice for an album inspired to such an extent by New York, but the British musicians apparently had a strong bond with France, as this was the second time, after *Exile on Main St.*, that they had recorded there. And they would remain faithful to that country for their next four albums. The real reason was that the studios were owned by EMI, with whom they had just signed a worldwide agreement (with the exception of North America). When they turned up, they were presented with three possibilities: there were two large, high-ceilinged studios equipped with 24-tracks, plus a more modest studio equipped with a 16-track. They opted for the latter as a rehearsal room, but Mick wanted to move when it came to recording, in order to

take advantage of the fashionable technology of the day. It should also be pointed out that the control room could not accommodate more than four people at any one time and the two (JBL) playback speakers were not on the same horizontal plane. Chris Kimsey, the sound engineer who had worked as an assistant on *Sticky Fingers* and was now replacing Keith Harwood, who had been killed in a car accident in September 1976, tried to dissuade him, explaining that this technical limitation was actually a blessing: "Well, I think you should stay here—it sounds great in this room . . ."[113] Jagger did not see things the same way, replying: "We can't use that, it's 16-track!"[113] Keith came down on Kimsey's side: "It was a great room to play in. So, despite Mick doing his usual 'Let's move to a proper studio' that's where we stayed, because in a recording session, especially with this kind of music, everything has to feel good."[2]

The Stones Alone

The sessions got under way without the band having an apparent plan of attack. Keith Richards: "Nothing was prepared before we got there. Everything was written in the studio day by day. So it was like the earlier times, at RCA in Los Angeles in the mid-'60s—songs pouring out. Another big difference from recent albums was that we had no other musicians in with us—no horns, no Billy Preston. Extra stuff was dubbed later."[2] The "other musicians" mentioned by the

Stones guitarist were Sugar Blue, an American jazz harmonica player who was living in Paris ("Miss You" and "Some Girls"); Ian McLagan, the former keyboard player with the Faces ("Miss You," "Just My Imagination"); Mel Collins, the saxophonist with King Crimson and the Alan Parsons Project ("Miss You"); and in all likelihood Simon Kirke (Free, Bad Company) on the congas ("Shattered").

The session dates for the individual titles recorded differ considerably from source to source. The Paris sessions took place between October 10 and December 21, 1977. It seems likely that nine of the ten songs on the album ("Lies," "When the Whip Comes Down," "Respectable," "Far Away Eyes," "Shattered," "Beast of Burden," "Some Girls," "Miss You," and "Just My Imagination") were laid down during this period. To these should be added, notably, "I Love You Too Much" and "Claudine" (on the *Some Girls* bonus CD), "Everything Is Turning to Gold" (the B-side of the single "Shattered" and included on the compilation *Sucking in the Seventies*, 1981) as well as an initial version of "Start Me Up" (on *Tattoo You*, 1981). The sessions resumed in January 1978. However, with the exception of "Before They Make Me Run," no track recorded between January 5 and March 2 is on the original *Some Girls*. "Don't Be a Stranger," "Keep Up Blues," "Do You Think I Really Care?" "Petrol Blues," "No Spare Parts," "When You're Gone," "You Win Again," and "So Young"

would all be unearthed for the *Some Girls* bonus CD, "Hang Fire" included on *Tattoo You*, and "Summer Romance" and "Where the Boys Go" on *Emotional Rescue* (1980). Finally, Mick and Keith mixed the album at Atlantic Studios in New York between March 15 and March 31 (mid-April according to some sources). The recording was engineered mainly by Chris Kimsey, although in January 1978, Dave Jordan (the Specials, Bananarama, the Pogues) put in an appearance, mainly to work on "Before They Make Me Run." They were assisted by Barry Sage (Brian Eno, New Order, Pet Shop Boys) and Ben King (Judas Priest, Meat Loaf).

Technical Details

The two large studios at the Pathé Marconi Studios in Boulogne-Billancourt were equipped with 3M 24-track tape recorders and Neve (8048 or 8058?) consoles. The third and smallest studio had a (Studer?) 16-track and an EMI console, probably the famous TG 12345 Mk Q, a model that was a combination of the Mark II and the Mark III. Keith provides a very good description of it: "The primitive mixing desk turned out to be the same kind of soundboard designed by EMI for Abbey Road Studios—very humble and simple, with barely more than a treble and bass button but with a phenomenal sound, which Kimsey fell in love with. . . . The sound it got had clarity but dirtiness, a real funky, club feel to it that suited

Ron Wood, Keith Richards, and Bill
Wyman at Oakland Stadium,
California, in July 1978.

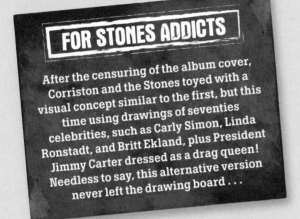

FOR STONES ADDICTS

After the censuring of the album cover,
Corriston and the Stones toyed with a
visual concept similar to the first, but this
time using drawings of seventies
celebrities, such as Carly Simon, Linda
Ronstadt, and Britt Ekland, plus President
Jimmy Carter dressed as a drag queen!
Needless to say, this alternative version
never left the drawing board . . .

A Zemaitis Metal
Front, identical to
Ron Wood's,
which the
guitarist played
on the 1978 North
American tour.

what we were doing."[2] Finally, Mick Jagger's voice was captured using a Neumann U47 mic.

The Instruments

Various new guitars were used during the recording of *Some
Girls*. Keith supplemented his collection with a Zemaitis
5-string given to him by Ron Wood and immediately nicknamed the "Macabre," a 1975 black Fender Telecaster Custom, a blond Gibson L6-S, a Travis Bean TB1000, and a Ted
Newman Jones custom made by his guitar technician. He also
made inordinate use of one guitar effect in particular: "What a
lot of *Some Girls* was down to was this little green box I used,
this MXR pedal, a reverb-echo. For most of the songs on there
I'm using that, and it elevated the band and it gave it a different
sound."[2] He would also use other effects from the same manufacturer, including the MXR Phase 100.

Ron Wood uses the same instruments that he played on
the previous album, with the addition of a Gibson reverse
Firebird, a 1956 Les Paul, a lap steel, a pedal steel guitar,
and various Gibson acoustics, including an "Everly Brothers"
model and a J-200 identical to Keith's. Bill mainly plays a Travis Bean Koa TB 2000, while Charlie remains loyal to his
Gretsch kit. As for the amps, Mesa Boogies (the sound of Carlos Santana!) make an appearance for the guitars, while Bill
remains attached to Ampegs.

MISS YOU

Mick Jagger / Keith Richards / 4:48

Musicians
Mick Jagger: vocals, rhythm guitar
Keith Richards: rhythm guitar, backing vocals
Ron Wood: lead and rhythm guitar, backing vocals
Bill Wyman: bass
Charlie Watts: drums
Mel Collins: saxophone
Ian McLagan: electric piano
Sugar Blue: harmonica

Recorded
EMI Pathé Marconi Studios, Boulogne-Billancourt: October 10–December 21, 1977
Atlantic Studios, New York: March 15–31, 1978

Technical Team
Producers: The Glimmer Twins
Sound engineer: Chris Kimsey
Assistant sound engineers: Barry Sage, Ben King

The bluesman Sugar Blue. His harmonica is featured prominently on "Miss You," an out-and-out disco number.

Genesis

"Mick told me that he wrote 'Miss You' for me but he probably told lots of girls that,"[1] reveals Jerry Hall, who embarked on a relationship with Jagger in 1977, when his marriage with Bianca was on the rocks. The Jagger of "Miss You" is very different from the one responsible for the misogynistic tirades of the sixties. The protagonist in the song is pining for his loved one, and various images are used to convey the mental torment of solitude. Musically, "Miss You" is the Stones' contribution to the tidal wave of disco. "A lot of those songs like 'Miss You' on *Some Girls*, and later 'Undercover' and things like that, were heavily influenced by going to the discos. You can hear it in a lot of those 'four on the floor' rhythms and the Philadelphia-style drumming,"[9] explains Charlie Watts. Mick Jagger would also acknowledge that the song was in the spirit of the times, and ". . . that's what made that record take off."[19]

Released as a single (with "Far Away Eyes" on the flip side), "Miss You" reached number 1 in several countries including one week in the United States (where it remained on the charts for twenty weeks, longer than any of the other Stones songs that had previously entered the *Billboard* chart), France, and Canada, number 2 in the Netherlands, and number 3 in the United Kingdom, Belgium, and Ireland . . .

Production

"Miss You" was born of an improvisation between Mick Jagger and Billy Preston, the former on guitar, the latter on drums. In reality, it was during the band's rehearsals for the concert given by the Stones at the El Mocambo in Toronto in March 1977 that Mick had the idea of turning it into a song. Keith elaborates: "It's a result of all the nights Mick spent at Studio 54 and coming up with that beat, that four on the floor. And he said, add the melody to the beat."[2] Convinced that it was just "some disco shit," Keith acceded to his partner's request. And then, as the number took shape, everyone realized that they had something: "And out of it we got a huge hit," he admits. But in order to get to this end result, the Stones devoted a enormous amount of energy to the song: "'Miss You' took about ten days to get the final master,"[2] notes Chris Kimsey.

In order to soak up this dance music that was invading dance floors all over the world, Mick dragged Charlie into disco

1978

The Stones in New York City in 1978 for the "Miss You" promo, in which powerful Marshall amps get in on the act.

clubs and bought a number of records that they listened to in order to unlock disco's secrets. Bill also spent time hanging out in nightclubs: "The idea for the bass lines came from Billy Preston. We'd cut a rough demo a year earlier after a recording session. I'd already gone home and Billy picked up my old bass when they started running through that song. When we finally came to do the tune the boys said, 'Why don't you work around Billy's idea?' I listened to it, heard that basic run and took it from there. It took some polishing, but the basic idea was Billy's."[1] This bass line turned out to be a real success and one of the keys to "Miss You." Bill plays in octaves and imparts a groove to the track, assisted by some very good drumming from Charlie—the jazz and rock drummer par excellence!—who lays down a dance groove with bass drum on each beat of the bar, playing with an astounding sense of assurance. Ron Wood plays lead on one of his Zemaitis, alternating short licks with a rhythm part. Keith, not particularly well versed in this style of music, acquits himself perfectly credibly, playing the main rhythm part (on his Fender Telecaster?) in a funky style colored with highly emphatic phasing in the bridge (1:55), thanks to one of his MXR pedals. Another key element in the piece is the very good keyboard part played on the Wurlitzer by Ian McLagan in a style reminiscent of Billy Preston's. "Miss You" is also a good opportunity to hear Mel Collins, who plays a very good sax solo, and above all the extraordinary harmonica of Sugar Blue. Ron Wood was deeply impressed: "The thing that blew my mind was what that guy could do, because I play a little harmonica. I know how to suck and bend, blow and bend like Jimmy Reed, but if you gave a harmonica to Sugar Blue, he could play in C, C sharp, C flat, B, A and F, all on the one harmonica. The way he bent it was unreal. . . . What he played was the impossible, and I've never met anyone like him before or since."[9]

On the vocal side, Mick is impeccable in his new role as a singer of dance music, alternating falsetto with a blues voice, and supported by Keith and Ronnie on backing vocals. Although a long way from "Sympathy for the Devil," Mick remains highly credible, and at the same time delivers a good rhythm part on the guitar.

Chris Kimsey was responsible for the "Miss You" mix on the album, cutting down the initial recording from nearly twelve minutes to just under five minutes. But it was Bob Clearmountain, the American sound engineer who made a name for himself working with Bruce Springsteen, David Bowie, Roxy Music, and others, who did the mix for the single as well as for an extended dance version: "That all came about because of the records I'd done with Chic," he would later explain. "They were an incredibly successful act for Atlantic Records, and both Roxy Music and The Stones were on Atlantic and I think they both wanted to get into the dance market more."[114] While a number of fans must have been thoroughly disconcerted by "Miss You," the Stones never lose their identity on the track, despite its disco flavor.

WHEN THE WHIP COMES DOWN

Mick Jagger / Keith Richards / 4:20

Musicians
Mick Jagger: vocals, rhythm guitar
Keith Richards: rhythm guitar, backing vocals
Ron Wood: lead guitar (?), slide guitar (?),
pedal steel guitar (?), backing vocals
Bill Wyman: bass
Charlie Watts: drums

Recorded
**EMI Pathé Marconi Studios, Boulogne-Billancourt,
France:** October 10–December 21, 1977
Atlantic Studios, New York: March 15–31, 1978

Technical Team
Producers: The Glimmer Twins
Sound engineer: Chris Kimsey
Assistant sound engineers: Barry Sage, Ben King

Genesis

After clearing a space for themselves on the dance floor with "Miss You," the Stones then make an equally remarkable and unexpected entry into the world of punk. As often, Keith Richards came up with the riff and Mick wrote the words. "I looked around and said, shit, he's finally written a rock 'n' roll song. By himself!"[2] In the lyrics to "When the Whip Comes Down," Jagger tells the story of a boy, a homosexual, who leaves Los Angeles for New York, where the implication is that he sells his body. "Well, there is one song that's a straight gay song —'When the Whip Comes Down,'" Mick would tell Jonathan Cott some time later, "but I have no idea why I wrote it. It's strange—the Rolling Stones have always attracted a lot of men [laughing]."[29]

Production

The Stones had nothing to learn from the young punks, and they made it clear with this very basic rock number built on the minimum number of chords—two! The sound is raw, and the band feels very closely knit, each musician playing alongside his neighbor, probably without sound screens, in order to promote "leakage," just as Chris Kimsey wanted. A kind of garage band sound. Keith fires off his riff furiously, supported by Mick on rhythm and Ronnie, meshing closely with Keith, on lead. Ronnie also seems to take a solo on the pedal steel guitar at 2:11, albeit one that is not particularly true to the character of the instrument, and in any case somewhat drowned in the mix. It also seems to be Ronnie who plays the very good slide part from 2:35. By contrast with "Miss You," the overall guitar sound is very aggressive. The first two tracks on the album have their sights set fairly and squarely on the two main musical trends of the day: disco and punk. The Stones as opportunists? As for the rhythm section, Charlie is back in rock territory and delivers a ferocious drum part, while Bill plays an excellent bass line on his Travis Bean Koa TB 2000 with its very clean sound. It is interesting to note that the recording is mono, again Kimsey's choice. Meanwhile, Mick seems to have been inspired by Lou Reed—in both his singing and in the lyrics.

Charlie Watts at his black Gretsch kit during the *Black and Blue* sessions.

JUST MY IMAGINATION (RUNNING AWAY WITH ME)

Norman Whitfield / Barrett Strong / 4:38

Musicians
Mick Jagger: vocals, rhythm guitar
Keith Richards: rhythm and lead guitar, backing vocals
Ron Wood: rhythm and lead guitar, backing vocals
Bill Wyman: bass
Charlie Watts: drums
Ian McLagan: organ

Recorded
EMI Pathé Marconi Studios, Boulogne–Billancourt,
France: October 10–December 21, 1977
Atlantic Studios, New York: March 15–31, 1978

Technical Team
Producers: The Glimmer Twins
Sound engineer: Chris Kimsey
Assistant sound engineers: Barry Sage, Ben King

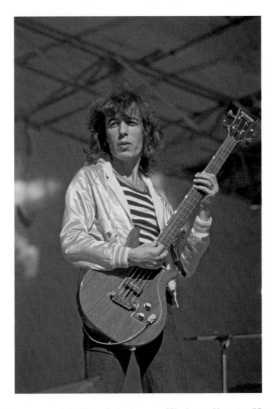

Bill Wyman on his Dan Armstrong. His bass line on "Just My Imagination" comes straight from Motown.

Genesis

At the end of the sixties and the beginning of the seventies, the composer-producer Norman Whitfield and lyricist Barrett Strong helped the Temptations to widen their musical horizons, in particular with "Run Away Child, Running Wild," "Psychedelic Shack," and "Ball of Confusion," which skillfully combine soul and psychedelic rock. In 1971, with "Just My Imagination (Running Away with Me)," the vocal group returned to a more "authentic" form of soul and even greater success, with this new Whitfield-Strong composition topping both the pop and R&B charts in April 1971. In the song, a man tells of his joy at being in love with (and loved in return by) a pretty young New York woman—until he realizes that his feelings are simply a figment of his imagination. Love, fantasy, and an irresistible tune: after "Ain't Too Proud to Beg" on the album *It's Only Rock 'N' Roll*, here the Stones dip into the Temptations' catalog once again. And once again the choice is a shrewd one.

Production

Clearly we are a long way here from the Temptations and the delicate and subtle arrangements of Jerry Long. Instead, the Stones turn what was a very gentle song into a pretty bracing medium-tempo rock number driven by Charlie's drumming. It is nevertheless a success. The British band has made the number utterly its own, to such an extent that it is difficult to make out the original melody. Pride of place once again goes to the guitars, all the more so now that Mick Jagger is making a contribution on rhythm. Keith Richards uses his MXR Phase 100 pedal to obtain a sound strongly colored by phasing, and this time it is the riff master who takes the solo at around 2:01. Ron Wood, who was beginning to exert a major influence on the Stones, plays rhythm guitar and also delivers phrases on lead that mesh perfectly with Keith's playing. Despite clearly not possessing the same facility on the guitar as Mick Taylor, the simplicity and versatility of his playing opened up a space on guitar for Mick Jagger, bringing the band back to more of a rock sound. Bill Wyman clearly seems to be motivated by his presence, and delivers an excellent bass part, especially in the coda, with its backing vocals from Mick, Keith, and Ronnie. Incidentally, it is surprising that the Stones' bassist, a capable singer more than good enough for this kind of thing, almost never joins in.

SOME GIRLS

Mick Jagger / Keith Richards / 4:36

Musicians
Mick Jagger: vocals, rhythm guitar
Keith Richards: rhythm and lead guitar, bass, backing vocals
Ron Wood: rhythm and lead guitar, backing vocals
Bill Wyman: synthesizer
Charlie Watts: drums
Sugar Blue: harmonica

Recorded
EMI Pathé Marconi Studios, Boulogne-Billancourt, France: October 10–December 21, 1977
Atlantic Studios, New York: March 15–31, 1978

Technical Team
Producers: The Glimmer Twins
Sound engineer: Chris Kimsey
Assistant sound engineers: Barry Sage, Ben King

Ron Wood and Mick Jagger. A rock star face designed to win hearts . . .

Genesis

This is one song to be avoided by any sensitive souls! Mick Jagger once again indulges in a settling of scores with women—and does not go in for half measures. Initially in the guise of a gigolo, the narrator describes his relationships with his female clients (*Some girls give me money. . . .*). He then reassumes the role of rock star and turns the spotlight on groupies (*Some girls get the shirt off my back/And leave me with a lethal dose*). All, wherever they hail from, are hauled over the coals. *French girls they want Cartier, Italian girls want cars, American girls want everything in the world.* Having found English girls *so prissy,* he then attacks black girls, who *just wanna get fucked all night.* This explains why the feminist and antiracist organizations were so outraged at the release of the album, a reaction that inspired the following response from Keith Richards: "Well, we've been on the road with a lot of black chicks for many years, and there's quite a few that do. It could have been yellow girls or white girls."[2] One can only imagine the uproar that would have ensued had the most cynical and compromising verses not been cut from the song, which originally lasted nearly twenty-three minutes.

Production

Keith launches "Some Girls" with a riff strongly colored by MXR phasing. The song is a rock ballad with Mick, Ron, and Keith on rhythm guitar. The latter two probably share the various solos, presumably Ron at 1:06, Keith, Chuck Berry–style, at 1:46, and the two together at 2:25. They also play the two acoustic parts in the refrains. Keith is on bass, in perfect symbiosis with Charlie's drumming, while Bill creates layers of synthesizer in the refrains. Sugar Blue is brilliant once again on the harmonica, particularly in his closing solo (4:11). Listeners will notice that the overall sound is mono, with only the acoustic guitars and the synthesizer in stereo in the refrains. Furthermore, Chris Kimsey had to cut down the original recording from twenty-three minutes(!) and remembers the outer face of the master tape being practically continuous Scotch tape! Although his work is highly accurate, two edits remain audible, at 0:51 and 3:40 (small problems with the rhythm).

1978

LIES

Mick Jagger / Keith Richards / 3:11

Musicians
Mick Jagger: vocals, rhythm guitar
Keith Richards: rhythm guitar, backing vocals (?)
Ron Wood: rhythm and lead guitar, backing vocals (?)
Bill Wyman: bass
Charlie Watts: drums
Recorded
EMI Pathé Marconi Studios, Boulogne-Billancourt,
France: October 10–December 21, 1977
Atlantic Studios, New York: March 15–31, 1978
Technical Team
Producers: The Glimmer Twins
Sound engineer: Chris Kimsey
Assistant sound engineers: Barry Sage, Ben King

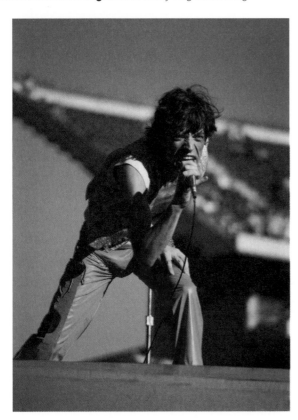

"Lies," a punk-inspired diatribe against those who disseminate falsehood.

FOR STONES ADDICTS

In his lyrics, Mick Jagger refers to Jezebel, a Phoenician princess abhorred by the Jewish people for turning her spouse Ahab, king of Israel, away from the true God.

Genesis

"Lies" is again one hundred percent Mick Jagger. This time, the singer targets liars of all kinds, from the girlfriend who whispers sweetly in the ear of her boyfriend, to the authors of history books, and even to the *lies in my papa's looks*. This builds into a dark, almost nihilistic vision of the world that can be seen as an echo, of sorts, of the "No future" slogan of the "Blank Generation." "Lies" is the Stones' response (over a rhythm Steve Jones, the Sex Pistols' guitarist, would have had difficulty following) to criticisms from bands on the punk rock scene that they were no longer relevant. The song would be included in their set list for the 1978 US tour (beginning at Lakeland, Florida, on June 10, and ending in Oakland, California, on July 26).

Production

It looks as if the Stones meant to prove that they too could play fast, using few chords and making a sound that was distinctly rough around the edges. But they were rich, all were over thirty, they were recording in a sophisticated studio even though the equipment was modest, and they had few worries for the future. This meant their approach was inevitably based on a false premise, however noble the sentiment. But it is difficult to hold this against them. "Lies" is a good, high-energy rock number. It may be somewhat lacking in substance, and not of the same caliber as "Rip This Joint," but the production is excellent. In particular, the guitar sound is perfect, Keith and Ron trading interweaving riffs, and Mick playing a rhythm part that helps to create a deliberate "garage band" feel. Ronnie (probably) plays a well-constructed solo, although without really taking off, because he tends to stick too closely to the other guitars. Charlie is excellent on his Gretsch kit. He pounds away determinedly on his drums and cymbals, and is supported by the majestic Bill, whose bass has a very clear, clean sound. As for Mick, he is obviously completely at ease in rock numbers of this type, but succumbs too much to caricature and overdoes it a little. This is a shame. However, there's no getting away from the fact that the Stones have an advantage over the punk musicians: they really know how to play. As for writing hits, they can do that too. When they're not trying to prove something to themselves.

FAR AWAY EYES

Mick Jagger / Keith Richards / 4:24

Musicians
Mick Jagger: vocals, piano
Keith Richards: electric rhythm guitar, acoustic guitar, piano, backing vocals
Ron Wood: pedal steel guitar, backing vocals
Bill Wyman: bass
Charlie Watts: drums

Recorded
EMI Pathé Marconi Studios, Boulogne-Billancourt, France: October 10–December 21, 1977
Atlantic Studios, New York: March 15–31, 1978

Technical Team
Producers: The Glimmer Twins
Sound engineer: Chris Kimsey
Assistant sound engineers: Barry Sage, Ben King

Keith Richards playing his Ted Newman Jones custom.

Genesis

During his interview with Jonathan Cott in 1978, Mick Jagger claimed to have noticed that "there were a lot of references to New York [on the album]," and that there were connections between the songs, even though "'Some Girls' isn't a 'concept' album, God forbid."[29] The only exception on the album is "Far Away Eyes." The Stones singer elaborates: "You know, when you drive through Bakersfield on a Sunday morning or Sunday evening—I did that about six months ago—all the country-music radio stations start broadcasting live from L.A. black gospel services. And that's what the song refers to. But the song's really about driving alone, listening to the radio."[29] Half-sung, half-spoken, "Far Away Eyes" is thus a song about solitude for which Mick Jagger has taken his inspiration from the preachers on the airwaves. Is salvation perhaps waiting for the driver at the end of the road, when he finds love? What does he mean by the *girl with far away eyes*? Is she someone completely absorbed in her own thoughts, who has cut herself off from the outside world?

Production

The Stones clearly like country music and although Mick would later talk of parody in connection with this song, the results are highly credible. This time, there is no question of giving in to the temptations of disco or punk rock; the target is more Buck Owens and "Together Again." Michael Lindsay-Hogg shot a promo for this number in which Mick can be seen singing his lyrics with heavy irony and tongue-in-cheek humor. However, he is the only one of the five to have a sparkle in his eye. His bandmates seem far less enthusiastic, if not downright lugubrious in the case of Charlie Watts, with his GI haircut. Of course, this does not prevent the drummer from laying down an efficient rhythm, based on a very restrained hi-hat/cross-stick technique. Bill supports him with a bass that respects all the traditions of the genre, while Keith strums his acoustic and also plays electric rhythm, alternating country licks with palm mute in the verses, and using his MXR pedal, this time with an appropriate echo/delay. It is Ronnie, however, who makes the biggest country contribution, with his masterly pedal steel guitar. Finally, Mick accompanies himself on the piano, and Keith lends him a hand from 1:38 with some very good phrases played higher up the keyboard.

1978

RESPECTABLE

Mick Jagger / Keith Richards / 3:06

Musicians
Mick Jagger: vocals, rhythm guitar
Keith Richards: rhythm and lead guitar
Ron Wood: rhythm and lead guitar
Bill Wyman: bass
Charlie Watts: drums

Recorded
EMI Pathé Marconi Studios, Boulogne-Billancourt,
France: October 10–December 21, 1977
Atlantic Studios, New York: March 15–31, 1978

Technical Team
Producers: The Glimmer Twins
Sound engineer: Chris Kimsey
Assistant sound engineers: Barry Sage, Ben King

Bianca, the probable target of Mick Jagger's
invective on "Respectable."

Genesis

"Respectable" is about a young woman who has climbed the social ladder rung by rung and is now reminded where she came from, of her background as a porn queen, by the narrator. Was Mick Jagger indulging in a highly personal interpretation of the very friendly relations between his wife Bianca and Steven Ford, son of the president of the United States? It is not out of the question. The line *We're talking heroin with the President* would be a typically Jaggeresque way of mocking this relationship at the heart of the jet set.

More generally, "Respectable" highlights the hypocrisy of the "high society" that once pilloried the Stones for their bad behavior and now gave them the red-carpet treatment. Mick Jagger confirms that "'Respectable' really started off as a song in my head about how 'respectable' we as a band were supposed to have become."[29]

Mick Jagger has said that he wrote the number over a reasonably slow rhythm. It is apparently Keith Richards who sped it up following a heated discussion. Keith has denied this, claiming that the very opposite was the case. The number reminds Ron Wood of the music he used to play with the Faces. For Mick Jagger, "Respectable" can be interpreted as a "punk meets Chuck Berry number."[87] This "encounter" was released as a single (with "When the Whip Comes Down" as the flip side) on September 22, 1978, climbing to number 16 in Ireland and the Netherlands and number 23 in the United Kingdom.

Production

"Respectable" is one of the Stones' most successful rock numbers. The band was in top form and can be felt trying to attain a sense of urgency in this performance: "Yeah, this is the kind of edgy punk ethos," explains Mick Jagger. "Yeah, the groove of it—and on all of those songs, the whole thing was to play it all fast, fast, fast. I had a lot of problems with Keith about it, but that was the deal at the time."[19] Regardless of who wanted to increase the tempo, the results are exhilarating and the band seems to really enjoy playing together. "In many ways, the album was a celebration of friends,"[105] Ron Wood would later comment. Now that Mick was sharing the guitar playing with his bandmates, he was constantly enriching the overall sound. He can be clearly heard playing rhythm at the center of the

The Rolling Stones during the shooting of the "Respectable" promo.

stereo (and in Michael Lindsay-Hogg's promo he can be seen playing a Fender Jaguar) alongside Ronnie and Keith, who are also on rhythm (respectively, on the left and right of the stereo). It is Keith who takes the first—inevitably very "Chuck Berry"—solo (1:24), while Ronnie plays the second (2:09) in a less clearly definable, but nonetheless effective style. Charlie smacks his drums for all he's worth. He is simultaneously powerful and subtle, without ever losing sight of the groove, which he delivers with pizzazz. Bill is equally effective. His bass line, with the same clean sound and no smudging in the low frequencies (thanks to his superb Travis Bean) is a model of its kind. Mick sings "Respectable" with disconcerting facility, completely at one with this supercharged rock 'n' roll number that he carries to the verge of implosion. He is apparently harmonizing with himself and doubling his vocal throughout the track. Chris Kimsey is helping the Stones to get their soul back after losing their identity in an overly perfect, overly clinical sound on the last few albums. The results are commensurate with his high technical standards.

FOR STONES ADDICTS

When "Respectable" was released as a single in the United Kingdom on September 22, 1978, it only got as far as number 23.

BEFORE THEY MAKE ME RUN

Mick Jagger / Keith Richards / 3:25

Musicians
Keith Richards: vocals, rhythm guitar, acoustic guitar (?), bass
Mick Jagger: backing vocals
Ron Wood: slide guitar, pedal steel guitar, backing vocals (?)
Charlie Watts: drums
Recorded
EMI Pathé Marconi Studios, Boulogne-Billancourt, France: January 5–March 2, 1978
Technical Team
Producers: The Glimmer Twins
Sound engineer: Dave Jordan
Assistant sound engineers: Barry Sage, Ben King

"Before They Make Me Run" deals with Keith's countless brushes with the law . . .

Genesis

"Before They Make Me Run," or the action-packed misadventures of Keith Richards. On February 7, 1977, the Stones guitarist and Anita Pallenberg had been arrested in Toronto for possession of heroin and faced possible life imprisonment. They had been given permission to leave Canada on the one condition that Keith take a detox cure (in New York) prior to his trial, which had been set for October 1978. He therefore composed "Before They Make Me Run" with the sword of Damocles hanging over his head. *Watched my taillights fading*, he sings. And then: *Gonna find my way to heaven, 'cause I did my time in hell.* There is also an allusion in the song to his friend Gram Parsons, who died in September 1973 (probably the consequence of a combination of drugs and alcohol): *another goodbye to another good friend.*

Production

"Before They Make Me Run" was recorded in Paris in the absence of Mick Jagger (who would add his backing vocals later). "That song, which I sang on that record, was a cry from the heart,"[2] Keith would explain in 2010. And this cry can be heard in the vocal performance by the king of the riff, who had not sung sole lead since "Happy" in 1972. Incidentally, Keith, taking pride in his performance, literally wore out poor Dave Jordan, who had replaced Chris Kimsey at the controls, with this song. In his own words, it "burned up the personnel like no other. I was in the studio, without leaving, for five days."[2] Keith may not be the best singer in the world, but there is always a note of sincerity in his voice that makes him terribly human. The same goes for his introductory riff, which is typical of his style. Keith accompanies himself with brio on his 5-string Fender Telecaster in open G, producing a sound that is inimitably his. Ronnie supports him on pedal steel guitar with considerable distortion and even ventures to play some very good slide solos (1:48). As Bill was also absent, Keith takes care of the bass part, supported by Charlie's very good drumming. Another successful aspect of this song, whose working title was "Rotten Roll"(!) are the very good vocal harmonies, reminiscent, for the first time, of the Beatles. The overall sound is excellent, although Keith's vocal is possibly a little undermixed. It is interesting to note that there also seems to be an acoustic guitar playing rhythm.

BEAST OF BURDEN

Mick Jagger / Keith Richards / 4:25

Musicians
Mick Jagger: vocals, rhythm guitar (?)
Keith Richards: rhythm guitar, backing vocals
Ron Wood: rhythm and lead guitar
Bill Wyman: bass
Charlie Watts: drums
Recorded
EMI Pathé Marconi Studios, Boulogne-Billancourt,
France: October 10–December 21, 1977
Atlantic Studios, New York: March 15–31, 1978
Technical Team
Producers: The Glimmer Twins
Sound engineer: Chris Kimsey
Assistant sound engineers: Barry Sage, Ben King

There have been various covers of "Beast of Burden." Of note are those by Buckwheat Zydeco and the Nadas. Bette Midler also recorded the song, with a brief appearance in the video by Mick Jagger.

Genesis

The "burden" in question is Keith Richards himself, whose descent into hell as a result of drugs and arrests almost dealt a fatal blow to the Rolling Stones. "When I returned to the fold after 'closing down the laboratory,'" he explains, using colorful imagery, "I came back into the studio with Mick, around the time of *Emotional Rescue*, to say, 'Thanks, man, for shouldering the burden'—that's why I wrote 'The Beast of Burden' for him, I realise in retrospect."[9] Hence the lines *All your sickness, I can suck it up/Throw it all at me, I can shrug it off.*

Mick Jagger then reworked the song—with Keith claiming to have completed a couple of verses—and, as happened often, transformed it into the expression of a difficult relationship between a man and a woman. Mick explained in an interview: "The song says: I don't need a beast of burden, and I'm not going to be your beast of burden, either. Any woman can see that that's like my saying that I don't want a woman to be on her knees for me."[29] Jared Followill, a member of the alternative rock band Kings of Leon, would later say of this song: "I prefer songs that go to the heart rather than the head, and only few bands can hit the heart with ease, like the Stones. 'Beast of Burden' is one of my absolute favourite songs ever, for the yearning vocal and the great guitar work."[108]

"Beast of Burden" was the A-side of the second single from *Some Girls* (with "When the Whip Comes Down" as the B-side). It rose to number 2 in Scandinavia, number 4 in New Zealand, and number 8 on the *Billboard* chart, but failed to chart in the United Kingdom.

Production

"Beast of Burden" is a somewhat curious track. It gives the impression of being merely a cover by the Stones of a Temptations or an Al Green song. With its feigned calypso or reggae rhythm and distinctly soul groove, it stands out from the other tracks on the album for its nonchalance, offering a moment of respite in the midst of a particularly energetic track listing. The rhythm intro seems to be played by Keith (on the right), although it could be Mick. At any rate, it is Keith who comes in with the second rhythm part, this time in the center of the stereo, with a strong phasing effect obtained using his MXR pedal. On the left, Ronnie contributes another 6-string part, both rhythm and lead, played in his own characteristic style.

Ron Wood playing his Zemaitis Metal Front on "Beast of Burden," a track that could have been written for him . . .

It has to be said that he merges completely with Keith, the two guitars weaving in a natural-sounding way. This was no doubt a risk that Keith Richards considered before making Ronnie the official successor to Mick Taylor. It is very easy to get the two guitarists confused, although Ronnie has more than one trick up his sleeve, and occasionally surprises the listener with an unexpected intervention, such as his very good solo at 1:48.

It is not possible to praise the excellent rhythm section of Bill and Charlie enough. "Beast of Burden" is a fine example of their collaboration, the two of them imparting a very solid soul groove to the track and establishing an unshakable foundation. Ever since the early days, it is these two who have enabled the Stones to roll with complete peace of mind. Their contribution is essential, if always discreet. Mick's take is perfect. His tone is right, displaying palpable emotion, and his voice excellent in every way, even in reaching for the falsetto that he now seems to favor (3:01). He would later claim to have realized after the event that he was probably unconsciously inspired by Buddy Holly's "Peggy Sue" in his singing of the phrase *pretty, pretty, pretty* in the bridge. The use of a delay on his voice can be heard at 2:30.

"Beast of Burden" is one of the album's triumphs, and its groove, which to some extent recalls that of "Tumbling Dice," is largely to thank for this.

SHATTERED

Mick Jagger / Keith Richards / 3:48

Musicians
Mick Jagger: vocals
Keith Richards: rhythm guitar, backing vocals
Ron Wood: rhythm guitar, lead guitar, bass, pedal steel guitar, bass drum (?) backing vocals
Charlie Watts: drums
Simon Kirke (?): congas
Unidentified musician(s): percussion and hand claps
Recorded
EMI Pathé Marconi Studios, Boulogne–Billancourt, France: October 10–December 21, 1977
Atlantic Studios, New York: March 15–31, 1978
Technical Team
Producers: The Glimmer Twins
Sound engineer: Chris Kimsey
Assistant sound engineers: Barry Sage, Ben King

In "Shattered," Mick Jagger uses *Sprechgesang*, a vocal style alternating sung and spoken elements that was inaugurated by Arnold Schoenberg in his melodrama *Pierrot Lunaire* (1912).

FOR STONES ADDICTS

In the fourth verse, Mick Jagger sings *Schmatta, schmatta, schmatta, I can't give it away on Seventh Avenue. Schmatta* is Yiddish slang for *raggedy clothes*, and Seventh Avenue is Manhattan's fashion district.

Genesis

"In 'Shattered,'" explains Mick Jagger to Jonathan Cott, "Keith and Woody [Ron Wood] put a riff down, and all we had was the word *shattered*. So I just made the rest up and thought it would sound better if it were half-talked."[29] This track provides the Stones singer with an opportunity to set out his own vision of New York, a combination of attraction and repulsion, most probably inspired by the famous blackout of the city in July 1977 and the looting that ensued, particularly in the Bronx: *Love and hope and sex and dreams are still surviving on the street*, and later *Pride and joy and greed and sex, that's what makes our town the best*. Thus the Rolling Stones conclude *Some Girls* with an urban rock track worthy of the punk bands. It also affords Mick Jagger an entry, albeit a furtive one, into the world of rap. "Shattered" was released as a single (with "Everything Is Turning to Gold" as the B-side) in the United States, but only made it as far as number 31 (February 1979).

Production

It may be the last track on *Some Girls*, but "Shattered" is nevertheless one of the most interesting. Based on a Keith riff played with ample MXR phasing, the song evolves toward a variety of musical worlds created by a range of instrumental interventions, such as percussion in the bridge (between 1:36 and 1:51) played by musicians who have not been clearly identified (Simon Kirke, Jane Rose [Keith's personal secretary], and a Moroccan percussionist have been muted). Ronnie takes the lion's share of the instrumental parts: in the absence of Bill, he is on bass, takes a second rhythm part around 1:23, plays the main solo, and also gives it some pedal steel guitar (recessed in the mix but nevertheless audible around 1:52). Certain sources also credit him with playing the bass drum, and, if true, this can only be in addition to Charlie's. The latter delivers an excellent drum part, very linear, but with a contagious groove. Mick gives one of his best vocal performances on the album, alternating singing and speaking, while toying exuberantly with his words. In this he is supported by very good backing vocals that take delight in repeating *sha-dooby*, the last remaining vestige of Keith's original lyric.

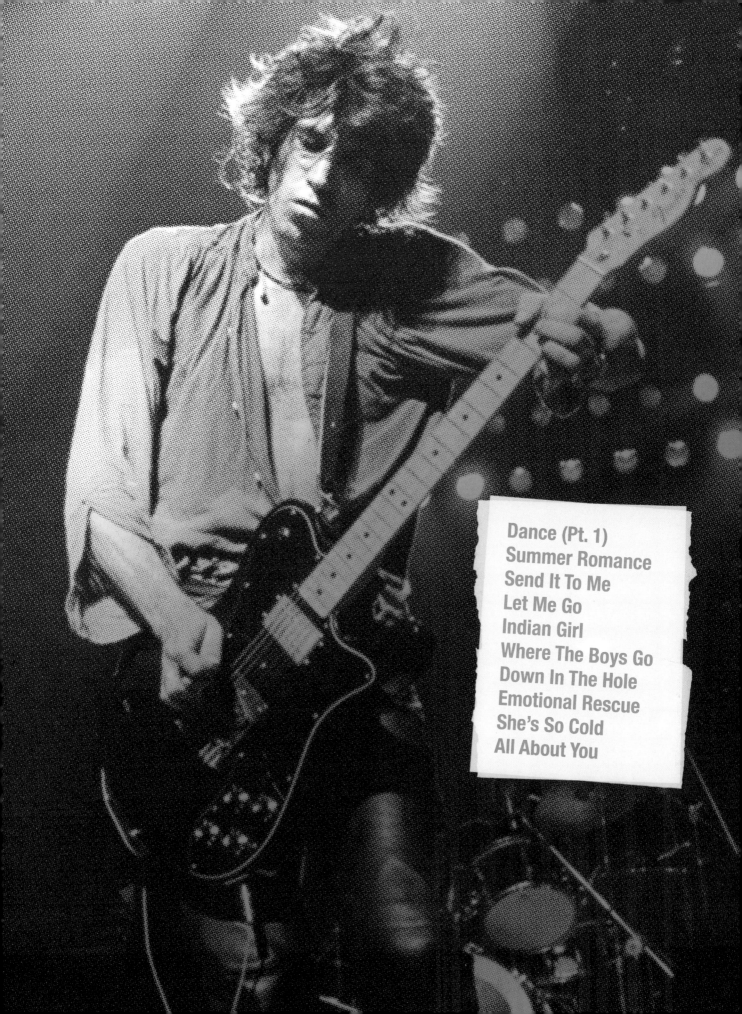

Dance (Pt. 1)
Summer Romance
Send It To Me
Let Me Go
Indian Girl
Where The Boys Go
Down In The Hole
Emotional Rescue
She's So Cold
All About You

ALBUM
RELEASE DATE
United Kingdom: June 20, 1980
Label: Rolling Stones Records
RECORD NUMBER: ROLLING STONES
RECORDS CUN 39111
**Number 1 for 2 weeks, on the
charts for 18 weeks**

EMOTIONAL

RESCUE

EMOTIONAL RESCUE: THE FIRST CRACKS APPEAR

The private lives of the Rolling Stones had never exactly been private. From the earliest days, the tabloids had greedily wallowed in their escapades. The end of the seventies was a period particularly rich in drama and would provide the newspapers with more headlines than ever.

Scandals, a Divorce, and a Trial

Mick Jagger and Bianca divorced on November 2, 1979. The beautiful Nicaraguan had finally had enough, and would tell the *New York Daily News* in 1986: "My marriage ended on my wedding day." For the previous two years, the singer, who had never ceased to make new conquests, had been allowing himself to be seen openly, and more and more frequently, in the company of the Texan Jerry Hall, a top model. The icing on the cake, however, was the Margaret Trudeau scandal of spring 1977. On March 4 the Stones, who had just played their first concert at the El Mocambo Club in Toronto, were invited to a party given in their honor at the Harbour Castle Hotel by Margaret Trudeau, wife of the Canadian prime minister, Pierre Elliott Trudeau. This immediately gave rise to a rumor that the Canadian first lady was having a fling with the singer. But on March 10 the *Daily News* reported that it was Ron Wood who had enjoyed her favors. Charlie Watts would comment dryly, and with a touch of cynicism: "I wouldn't want my wife associating with us."[35]

And most importantly there was the matter of Keith Richards. Almost two years after the start of his difficulties with the Canadian justice system, his trial began in Toronto on October 23, 1978. The Stones guitarist pleaded guilty to heroin possession, and with unusual attention to detail, his attorney, Austin Cooper, proceeded to describe his client's daily struggle to get clean. Judge Lloyd Graburn listened and understood. The verdict was given the next day. Keith Richards was found guilty but, as the guitarist himself explains, " . . . the judge concluded, 'I will not incarcerate him for addiction and wealth.'"[2] The guitarist was allowed to go free on two conditions: that he continue his medical treatment and that he give a charity concert for the blind. On April 22, 1979, two concerts were duly played at the Oshawa Civic Auditorium by Keith and Ronnie's New Barbarians.

The Album

Things therefore looked brighter for the Rolling Stones as they set off once more for the recording studio. "Riding high on the success of *Some Girls* and on the outcome of the court case, we repaired to Nassau in the Bahamas, to Compass Point Studios," writes Keith Richards. "There were ripples of argument between Mick and me that would grow into a rumble soon, but not quite yet."[2] The songs on *Emotional Rescue* hint at the gulf that was beginning to open up between the Glimmer Twins. With "Dance (Pt. 1)" and "Emotional Rescue," which sound like the logical continuation of "Hot Stuff" and "Miss You," Mick Jagger was still displaying a very real interest in disco and funk, whereas Keith Richards's focus was quite different. Having little interest in the still-fashionable music of Donna Summer or KC and the Sunshine Band, he

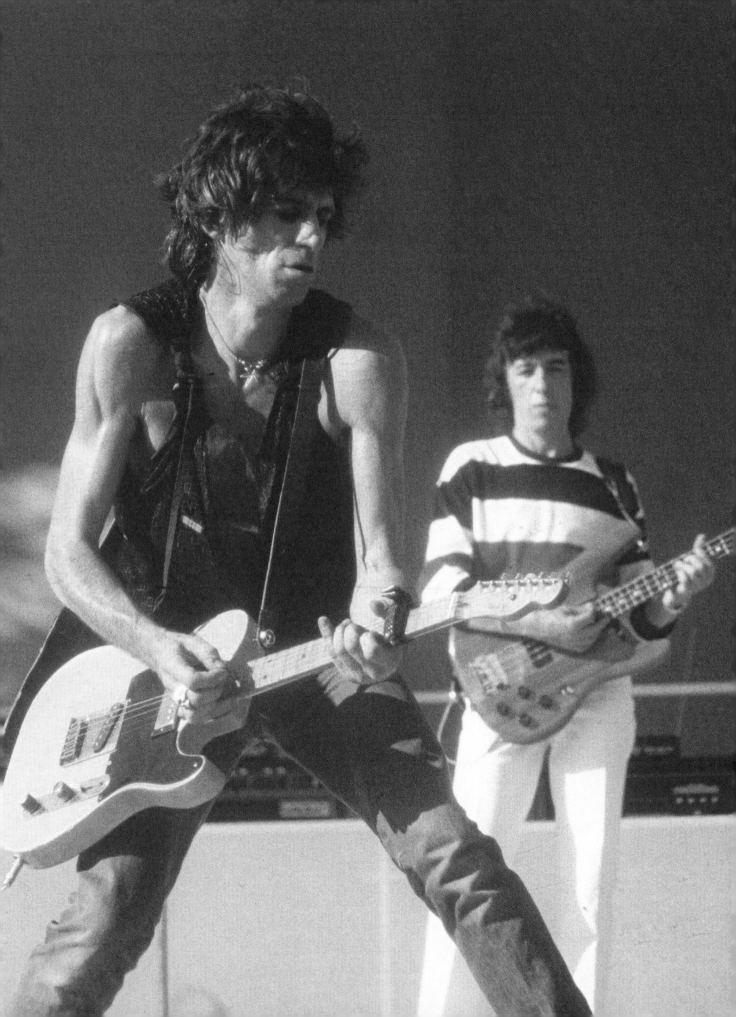

Keith Richards's first solo single, comprising "Run Rudolph, Run" and "The Harder They Come," was released on February 16, 1979, four days after the end of the Bahamas sessions. Rolling Stones Records was planning a solo album by the Stones guitarist, but this never saw the light of day.

Jerry Hall, who played a prominent role in Mick Jagger's life.

was turning to the ballad as a way of exorcising his problems, which did not exclusively have to do with heroin and his detox cures. Thus "All About You" also, most probably, deals with his relationships with Mick and Anita, which in the case of the latter had reached the point of no return.

If "All About You" is the song that is most personal to Keith, Mick pours his own concerns into the other ballad on the album, "Indian Girl," in which he tells of a young Amerindian girl caught up in a deadly civil war in Central America. The other songs on the album nevertheless see the Glimmer Twins coming together and indeed complementing each other: "Send It to Me," for example, which once again reveals the influence of reggae on the band; the blues number "Down in the Hole"; and three numbers brimming with what could perhaps be described as a punk rock energy: "Let Me Go," "Where the Boys Go," and "She's So Cold." As for the lyrics, Jagger has lost nothing of his facility with words. Better to hang out in gay bars than to put up with an intrusive girlfriend—such, essentially, is the message of "Let Me Go," which amounts to nothing less than an appeal for liberty, while "Where the Boys Go" offers a realistic description of what young British men get up to on a Saturday night. Finally, a special mention for "She's So Cold," in which a young man who is as hot as a volcano is attracted to a woman as cold as a tombstone.

The Rolling Stones' fifteenth (British) studio album, and their second with Ron Wood as a fully fledged member of the band, *Emotional Rescue* was given pride of place in the windows of record stores upon its release on June 20, 1980. It would top the charts in various countries, including the United Kingdom, the United States, France, Canada, and the Netherlands, and would make it to number 2 in West Germany and New Zealand. It was the first album since *Goats Head Soup* in 1973 to top the charts on both sides of the Atlantic. The critics were by and large less enthusiastic, especially those who compared the album to *Some Girls*.

The Album Cover

Following his work on *Some Girls*, the artist Peter Corriston was asked back to design the sleeve for *Emotional Rescue*. He in turn commissioned the British-born, Paris-based photographer, painter, engraver, and sculptor Roy Adzak to take photos for the front and back covers and for the interior

poster using a thermal imaging camera. This introduction of an avant-garde element was all very well, but reactions to the end result were mixed. What was the message the Stones wanted to convey? Difficult to say, except, as usual, to transmit a somber and slightly sinister image of themselves.

The Recording

With the exception of "Where the Boys Go" and "Summer Romance," which were originally laid down at the Pathé Marconi Studios in January 1978 and then reworked between August 23 and September 6, 1978, at the Wally Heider Studios in Hollywood—the former RCA Studios where the Stones wrote one of the most glorious chapters in their history—all the songs on *Emotional Rescue* were recorded in 1979, mainly in two studios. Between January 23 and February 12, with the notable addition of saxophonist Bobby Keys—back in favor with the Stones after four years in the wilderness (see *It's Only Rock 'N' Roll*)—and producer Chris Kimsey, the Stones recorded "She's So Cold" and "All About You," plus various other tracks that did not make it to the album, such as "I Think I'm Going Mad" (B-side of the future single "She Was Hot," 1984) and "Lonely at the Top" (which Mick Jagger would later record with Jeff Beck and Pete Townshend for his solo album *She's the Boss*, 1985) at Compass Point Studios in Nassau. Founded in 1977 by Chris Blackwell, the charismatic boss of Island Records, Compass Point Studios would see a procession of celebrated artists pass through their doors, including U2, Roxy Music, Dire Straits, and Bob Marley.

From June 27 to early October, the London quintet returned to the Pathé Marconi Studios in Boulogne-Billancourt in France, still with Bobby Keys and Chris Kimsey, but also with Sugar Blue (harmonica), Michael Shrieve, the extraordinary Santana drummer (now on percussion), and the reggae artist Max Romeo (vocals). Claude Wagner, one of the main sound engineers at the Pathé Marconi Studios

1980

The Stones at a promotional party for the release of the album *Emotional Rescue*.

A little more than a year after the death of Elvis Presley, it was the turn of Keith Moon, drummer of the Who, to pass away (September 7, 1978).

(who did not, however, record the Stones), explains why, in his view, the band liked coming to Boulogne-Billancourt: "If the Stones are so attached to this studio, it's because of its aleatory aspect. If you move Watts's drum kit, the sound you get will be totally different depending on its positioning and the room mics. Similarly, those sound panels that are widely used to prevent the instruments from 'leaking' into one another, the Stones blithely ditch them. Let's say they cultivate a smudging of the sound while directing it. It's a game of chance. They generally work from eleven in the evening to eleven in the morning. They play the whole night through with the tape running. The slightest idea, their laughter, and any moments of rapture are therefore recorded."[116] In this way they successively cut "Dance," the title song, "Down in the Hole," "Indian Girl," "Send It to Me," and "Let Me Go," as well as "No Use in Crying" (the B-side of the 1981 single "Start Me Up"), "Heaven," and "Neighbours" (both on *Tattoo You*).

The atmosphere in the studio was not great, however. Bill Wyman has described sessions beset by tensions, frustrations, health problems, and continual poor timekeeping. According to him, all this shows in the results, preventing the album from featuring among the band's most successful work despite its very good sales. Ron Wood, for his part, remembers the sessions as being exhausting: "I remember that while recording in Paris Keith was very adamant about working above and beyond the call of duty. At about four in the morning, just when everyone was getting really tired, after we'd really done well and cut a couple of basic tracks, Keith would say, 'Right, now we're going to do this', and we'd all go 'Ahhh. . . !' While Bill would be hovering in the doorway. Keith's catchphrase at the time was, 'Nobody sleeps while I'm awake.'"[9]

Mick and Keith would then spend a considerable length of time mixing and adding various overdubs, initially between November and December 1979 at the famous Electric Lady Studios in New York City, which had been opened in 1970 by Jimi Hendrix. For the time being, however, a profound musical disagreement between the Glimmer Twins prevented them from finishing the album. Mixing therefore resumed in April 1980, but relations between the two Stones were not at their best. "According to Keith," Bill would later write, "Mick listened to too many bad records and was too interested in calculating how the 'market' was. Mick wanted hits, Keith couldn't give a . . ."[1] And this difference of opinion would only get worse, with consequences for the future . . .

The sound engineers who assisted Chris Kimsey were Sean Fullan (who would later work with Glyn Johns and produce a number of albums for Lou Reed), Brad Samuelsohn (B. B. King, AC/DC, Foreigner), Ron "Snake" Reynolds (J. J. Cale, Elvis Costello, Merle Haggard), and Jon Smith (Leonard Cohen, the Del-Lords). Finally, among the additional musicians who worked alongside the Stones were Nicky Hopkins, who had been absent from the previous album, and Jack Nitzsche, who resurfaced to do the horn arrangements (conducted by Arif Mardin, himself present on *Some Girls*).

The Instruments

Charlie Watts acquired a new Gretsch drum kit, a 1957 natural wood model. Bill Wyman was still playing his Travis Bean TB 2000 bass, but also brought out his Dallas Tuxedo from time to time. Ronnie took possession of a black Gibson Les Paul Custom, a sunburst Gibson S-1, and a second Metal Front Zemaitis. Finally, Keith, as avid as ever for new things (and all the more so as he had recently lost his Zemaitis "Macabre," given to him by Ronnie, his first Ted Newman Jones custom, and a Martin acoustic in a fire), added to his collection a new 5-string Ted Newman Jones, a 1957 sunburst Gibson Les Paul Junior, and a 1958 Gibson Les Paul TV Junior, all of which he used in the studio. And as on *Some Girls*, he was to make plentiful use of a new MXR pedal with analog delay.

DANCE (PT. 1)

Mick Jagger / Keith Richards / Ron Wood / 4:23

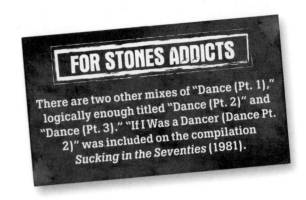

Musicians
Mick Jagger: vocals, percussion (?)
Keith Richards: rhythm and lead guitar, backing vocals
Ron Wood: rhythm and lead guitar, bass (?), saxophone (?), backing vocals
Bill Wyman: bass (?)
Charlie Watts: drums
Bobby Keys: saxophone
Michael Shrieve: percussion
Max Romeo: backing vocals

Recorded
EMI Pathé Marconi Studios, Boulogne-Billancourt, France: June 27–October 8, 1979
Electric Lady Studios, New York City: November–December 1979, April 1980

Technical Team
Producers: The Glimmer Twins
Associate producer: Chris Kimsey
Sound engineer: Chris Kimsey
Assistant sound engineers: Sean Fullan, Brad Samuelsohn, Ron "Snake" Reynolds, Jon Smith

1980

Mick, Keith, and Ron at a benefit concert at the Oshawa Civic Auditorium (Canada).

Genesis

With this opening song, the Rolling Stones make their intentions plain: to lead their fans onto the dance floor. The narrator (Mick Jagger, as it happens) asks himself what he is doing at the corner of West Eighth Street and Sixth Avenue in New York City, and then addresses Keith by name to tell him that the moment has come to *get out* and *get into something new.* From a musical point of view, *this something new* is the logical follow-up to "Hot Stuff" and "Miss You," an irresistible rhythm that owes much to African American funk. Ron Wood came up with the original idea for the song: "'Dance (Pt. 1)' was one strong riff where Mick immediately took the bait, literally got up and danced to it, which was the whole idea of the track: it's a catchy riff."[9] And he continues: "That was an example of a song that originated without words, just a groove with various changes, but never a chorus."[9]

Production

The first-ever number officially co-written by the Glimmer Twins and Ron Wood, "Dance (Pt. 1)" started life as an instrumental, to which Mick then wanted to add words. Keith would regret this: "He did a lot of work on it and he did a good job, but *totally* nullified the track. I said, 'let's make it an instru[mental,' to which he replied], 'I can't waste time on an album with only ten tracks and instrumentals . . .'"[11] "Dance (Pt. 1)" is above all a rhythmic pulse, generated simultaneously by the excellent drumming (Charlie being completely at ease in the world of dance music), Bill's bass (some commentators suggest that it is Ron on bass, which is not impossible), the assortment of percussion instruments played by the outstanding Michael Shrieve, but no doubt shared with Mick (congas, shaker, tambourine, cuíca), and the various funky guitar parts played by Ron and Keith. And all this under the watchful eye of Mick, who seems to take real pleasure in his singing. The voice of reggae singer Max Romeo can be made out in the vocal harmonies, along with those of Keith and Ron. Finally, the former member of the Faces is said by some sources to be playing not only the guitar on this track, but the sax too, accompanying Bobby Keys, who makes his long-awaited return to the band with a few (albeit modest) horn riffs.

SUMMER ROMANCE

Mick Jagger / Keith Richards / 3:16

Musicians
Mick Jagger: vocals, rhythm guitar
Keith Richards: lead guitar, backing vocals
Charlie Watts: drums
Ron Wood: bass, rhythm guitar, backing vocals
Ian Stewart: piano
Recorded
Wally Heider (RCA) Studios, Hollywood:
August 23–September 6, 1978
EMI Pathé Marconi Studios, Boulogne-Billancourt,
France: January–March 1987, June 27–October 8, 1979
Electric Lady Studios, New York City:
November–December 1979, April 1980
Technical Team
Producers: The Glimmer Twins
Associate producer: Chris Kimsey
Sound engineer: Chris Kimsey
Assistant sound engineers: Sean Fullan, Brad
Samuelsohn, Ron "Snake" Reynolds, Jon Smith

Keith Richards, on his Telecaster, commandeers
lead guitar on "Summer Romance."

Genesis

A casual love affair between an adult and a high school student that ends as summer draws to a close . . . The unhappy lover bemoans his situation. He will be going to the pub to drink and play pool while his beloved is studying. While the basic premise of "Summer Romance" may not be the most original ever, the music radiates a redeeming energy. Ron Wood would declare in 1980: "Mick! Before I gave him guitar lessons, we wouldn't have had songs like 'Summer Romance,' because of all that rhythm guitar."[117] This is another Glimmer Twins number that the Stones have never performed live!

Production

The Stones recorded an initial version of "Summer Romance" during the *Some Girls* sessions in January 1978. They then worked on the song at the Wally Heider (formerly RCA) Studios during the summer, before giving it its definitive form at the Pathé Marconi Studios between the end of June and the beginning of October 1979. The early versions reveal a far faster rock track with a distinctly punk feel. The sound is raw and definitely more effective than the album version. Like many of the songs written by Mick Jagger around this time, "Summer Romance" gives prominence to the three guitars: Mick plays an initial rhythm part with a distorted sound (stereo right), Ron answers with a second rhythm guitar played using the palm mute technique (left), and finally Keith takes lead, setting the song on fire with some excellent phrases still very much influenced by the spirit of Chuck Berry (center). He uses his MXR Analog Delay pedal to obtain his vintage sound, enriched with a short, very pronounced reverb. Ian Stewart is on piano, although unfortunately inaudible and buried in the mix except in the coda, where he emerges for a few seconds after 3:06. On some of the working mixes, by contrast, he can be heard throughout the track. Charlie delivers a good drum part, supported by Ronnie's bass, which is excessively guitaristic and as a result not as effective as it could be. "Summer Romance" is a well-made rock track that suffers from overly conventional, overly smooth mixing that eradicates some of its original spirit.

The Jamaican singer Max Romeo is on backing vocals. His earliest releases date from the late sixties, and his major opus, *Revelation Time* (1975), is a concept album dedicated to the glory of the Rastafari movement.

SEND IT TO ME

Mick Jagger / Keith Richards / 3:43

Musicians
Mick Jagger: vocals
Keith Richards: rhythm and lead guitar
Bill Wyman: bass
Charlie Watts: drums
Ron Wood: rhythm, lead, and slide guitar
Nicky Hopkins: synthesizer
Sugar Blue: harmonica
Michael Shrieve: percussion
Max Romeo (?): timbales
Recorded
EMI Pathé Marconi Studios, Boulogne-Billancourt, France: June 27–October 8, 1979
Electric Lady Studios, New York City: November–December 1979, April 1980
Technical Team
Producers: The Glimmer Twins
Associate producer: Chris Kimsey
Sound engineer: Chris Kimsey
Assistant sound engineers: Sean Fullan, Brad Samuelsohn, Ron "Snake" Reynolds, Jon Smith

The Jamaican singer Max Romeo, photographed in Kingston in 2005.

Genesis

"Send It to Me" is predominantly a Mick Jagger song, developed in conjunction with Charlie Watts. The protagonist seeks to overcome his solitude by sending letters to those who are dear to him. It is clear that he is ready to go to any lengths to find romance, to finally be loved by a woman, regardless of whether she is *Romanian, Bulgarian, Albanian, Hungarian, Ukrainian, Australian, or the Alien*, sings Jagger—not without humor—in the last verse. "Send It to Me" attests to the growing influence that Jamaican rhythms had been exerting on the Rolling Stones ever since *Goats Head Soup*.

Production

Although superficially seductive, "Send It to Me" is ultimately disappointing. Despite successful mixing, excellent arrangements, and an appealing melody, it lacks a certain spark. The song's strong point is its locomotive-like rhythm, launched by Charlie Watts with excellent work on his Gretsch kit, and supported by Michael Shrieve's percussion: most likely the shekere, the tambourine, and the timbales, although Max Romeo has been suggested for the latter. Bill Wyman is on bass (although to tell the truth the playing is reminiscent of Ronnie), and Nicky Hopkins marks his return with an organ sound on the synthesizer. Sugar Blue's harmonica is sadly buried in the mix, although it can be made out at various moments, in particular around 1:42. In the intro, Keith and Ronnie play a guitar lick in harmony, which was most probably an idea of Ronnie's. As is his custom, the former Faces man plays a combination of rhythm and lead, and also takes the solo slide parts beginning around 2:03, using the MXR and its analog delay throughout to achieve a more airy sound. Keith answers him with a solid rhythm part very much in the reggae mold (stereo right). Mick, for his part, gives a very good vocal performance with a touch of humor, and a fairly pronounced delay has been added to his voice, probably during mixing. In spite of everything, Keith did not want to include "Send It to Me" on the album: "I thought 'Emotional Rescue' and 'Send It to Me' were just a little too similar—not necessarily musically, just in the sound—that mid-tempo sort of . . ."[11]

LET ME GO

Mick Jagger / Keith Richards / 3:50

Musicians
Mick Jagger: vocals, rhythm guitar
Keith Richards: lead guitar
Bill Wyman: bass
Charlie Watts: drums
Ron Wood: rhythm guitar
Bobby Keys: saxophone
Michael Shrieve: tambourine

Recorded
EMI Pathé Marconi Studios, Boulogne-Billancourt, France: June 27–October 8, 1979
Electric Lady Studios, New York City: November–December 1979, April 1980

Technical Team
Producers: The Glimmer Twins
Associate producer: Chris Kimsey
Sound engineer: Chris Kimsey
Assistant sound engineers: Sean Fullan, Brad Samuelsohn, Ron "Snake" Reynolds, Jon Smith

FOR STONES ADDICTS

Michael Shrieve, the Santana drummer and a key figure at the legendary Woodstock Festival in 1969, would also take part in the sessions for Mick Jagger's first solo album, *She's the Boss*, released in 1985.

Genesis

The party's over, let me go, sings Mick Jagger. The contrast with the previous song is striking, for "Let Me Go" is a song about breaking up, like "Gotta Get Away" and "Out of Time" from a few years before. *You'll never find that perfect love*, continues the Stones singer, referring to the love the girl has read about in books and dreamed of. With the result that the lover is now enamored of the prospect of freedom and even dreams of hanging out in gay bars. This is an example of Jagger at his most cynical! "Let Me Go" may not be a major Rolling Stones song, but it nevertheless went down well onstage during the concerts of 1981–1982.

Production

Compared to the live version, the album cut seems somewhat restrained: the tempo is slower and the band members give the impression of not fully giving themselves up to the song. Although merely an album track, it is a very good one, made by Keith, who, right from the introduction, has no other intention than to lead his pals down the rock 'n' roll path, as he is so adept at doing. He plays an intro that almost brings to mind a less savage Led Zeppelin. His sound is rockabilly, colored by his MXR and its analog delay. He plays an impeccable guitar part with an extremely well-worked solo starting at 1:45, the whole thing supplemented by short but highly prominent reverb. Ron supports him discreetly but highly effectively on rhythm, as does Mick, who has started accompanying his bandmates on the guitar on rock numbers. Charlie works his Gretsch kit with some power, and Bill keeps him on his toes by stressing the beat with his very solid bass line. Michael Shrieve can be heard on tambourine, ultimately a key rhythmic element on the track by virtue of its place in the mix. Bobby Keys contributes on sax, but unfortunately is undermixed and in any case comes in only at the very end of the track, at 3:34. Finally, Mick Jagger is beyond reproach, as on every rock number he sings, harmonizing with and double-tracking himself in the refrains.

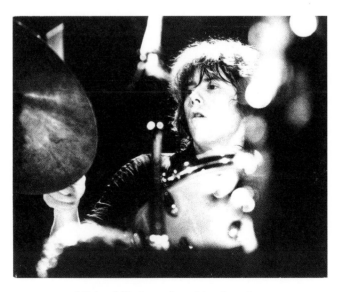

Michael Shrieve played tambourine during the "Let Me Go" session.

INDIAN GIRL

Mick Jagger / Keith Richards / 4:23

Musicians
Mick Jagger: vocals, acoustic guitar (?)
Keith Richards: acoustic guitars (?), piano
Bill Wyman: bass, synthesizer
Charlie Watts: drums
Ron Wood: pedal steel guitar, acoustic guitar (?)
Jack Nitzsche: horn arrangement, marimba (?)
Arif Mardin: horn conducting
Ian Stewart: marimba (?)
Max Romeo: marimba (?)
Unidentified musicians: horns, claves
Recorded
EMI Pathé Marconi Studios, Boulogne-Billancourt, France: June 27–October 8, 1979
Electric Lady Studios, New York City: November–December 1979, April 1980
Technical Team
Producers: The Glimmer Twins
Associate producer: Chris Kimsey
Sound engineer: Chris Kimsey
Assistant sound engineers: Sean Fullan, Brad Samuelsohn, Ron "Snake" Reynolds, Jon Smith

The producer Arif Mardin, to whom the Stones owe the conducting on "Indian Girl."

Genesis

With a few rare exceptions (notably on *Beggars Banquet*), the Rolling Stones seem to have felt that the political events that shook the world during the second half of the twentieth century were no more than indirectly their concern. In "Indian Girl," however, the Glimmer Twins turn the spotlight on the bloody civil wars that had been raging in Central America since the 1960s, in particular in Nicaragua, Bianca Jagger's home country. Like thousands of others, the young Indian girl in the song finds herself alone, her mother having been raped by soldiers and her father fighting in the streets of Masaya, both parents risking their lives for the revolution set in motion years before by Fidel Castro.

Production

Much as they liked to keep up with the musical trends of the day, the Stones retained their fondness for country music, as demonstrated by "Indian Girl"—and, before it, by "Far Away Eyes" on *Some Girls*. Keith is probably responsible for both the acoustic guitar parts, the second not always perfectly in time (listen between 1:49 and 1:54). The marimba, a percussion instrument immortalized by Brian Jones on "Under My Thumb," is played here by Ian Stewart, Jack Nitzsche, or Max Romeo. Charlie plays cross-stick before adopting a heavier beat supported by Bill's very good bass, probably his Dallas Tuxedo. The pianist, meanwhile, is apparently not Nicky Hopkins but Keith Richards: "Indian Girl was [a song by] Mick cos I just played piano on that,"[11] he would reveal in 1980. This would seem to indicate that the two acoustic guitars are played not by him but by Mick and/or Ronnie. The latter plays a good pedal steel guitar, very much in the country style, as are (although belonging to a different national tradition) the mariachi trumpets arranged by Jack Nitzsche (returning to the fold for the first time since *Sticky Fingers*) and conducted by Arif Mardin, who had contributed to "Melody" on *Black and Blue*. Bill is probably the one doubling some of the horn parts and accompanying the track on synthesizer, but this is not always either in tune (2:57) or in good taste. Finally, Mick displays some emotion in his voice in a performance that comes across as relatively refreshing.

WHERE THE BOYS GO

Mick Jagger / Keith Richards / 3:29

Musicians
Mick Jagger: vocals, rhythm guitar
Keith Richards: lead guitar, backing vocals
Charlie Watts: drums
Ron Wood: rhythm guitar, bass (?), backing vocals
Ian Stewart: piano
Jo Karslake, Jerry Hall (?): backing vocals

Recorded
Wally Heider (RCA) Studios, Hollywood:
August 23–September 6, 1978
EMI Pathé Marconi Studios, Boulogne-Billancourt,
France: January–March 1987, June 27–October 8, 1979
Electric Lady Studios, New York City:
November–December 1979, April 1980

Technical Team
Producers: The Glimmer Twins
Associate producer: Chris Kimsey
Sound engineer: Chris Kimsey
Assistant sound engineers: Sean Fullan, Brad
Samuelsohn, Ron "Snake" Reynolds, Jon Smith

Ronnie, Keith, and Mick home in on the punk adolescent
crisis in "Where the Boys Go."

Genesis

Mick Jagger adopts his best cockney accent to evoke the lives of young British working-class men: football on Monday and Tuesday, beer in the pub on Saturday morning. Saturday evening, on the other hand, is party time: the boys are all off to the disco, where they dance and hope to get a nice *piece of ass*. And neither do the girls think about anything other than having a good time. This is another song in the spirit of pub rock (with a nod to Dr. Feelgood and Nick Lowe?) that afforded the Rolling Stones an opportunity to teach the punks a thing or two . . . "Where the Boys Go" was recorded in January 1978 during the *Some Girls* sessions, but was ultimately left off the album. After that it was reworked many times.

Production

In "Where the Boys Go," with its garage band atmosphere and punk rock influences, the Stones' intention is clearly to align themselves with the musical trends of the day. The sound is raw, but lacking any real soul, which is a surprise, given that Chris Kimsey is at the controls. It would seem that "Where the Boys Go" did not come together very easily in the studio, and this is apparent when one listens to the track. The guitar sound of Mick, Ron, and Keith is on the thin side, the different parts do not gel, and by the time Keith plays his very "Chuck Berry" solo at 2:14, the track is still struggling to take off. The bass is most probably taken care of by Ronnie, and although good, the sound is not particularly clean, doing little to support the groove laid down by Charlie, who does his utmost to get this rocker moving. It is presumably Ian Stewart on the piano, but it has to be admitted that he is completely buried in the mix. Even Mick does not seem particularly convinced by what he is singing—and he is usually the one who masters the particular style of a number better than anyone else. The refrains alone—with vocals reminiscent of the Clash—are a success, and the entry of the two female backing singers in the coda at 3:05 introduces a fresh and unexpected note. "Where the Boys Go" is a somewhat over-conventional rock number that holds little real interest. This is a shame because we have become accustomed to better from the Stones.

DOWN IN THE HOLE

Mick Jagger / Keith Richards / 3:57

FOR STONES ADDICTS

Two years after the sessions for *Emotional Rescue*, Sugar Blue would join Willie Dixon and the Chicago Blues All Stars. Forever the blues . . .

Musicians
Mick Jagger: vocals
Keith Richards: rhythm and lead guitar
Bill Wyman: bass
Charlie Watts: drums
Ron Wood: rhythm and lead guitar
Sugar Blue: harmonica
Recorded
EMI Pathé Marconi Studios, Boulogne-Billancourt, France: June 27–October 8, 1979
Electric Lady Studios, New York City: November–December 1979, April 1980
Technical Team
Producers: The Glimmer Twins
Associate producer: Chris Kimsey
Sound engineer: Chris Kimsey
Assistant sound engineers: Sean Fullan, Brad Samuelsohn, Ron "Snake" Reynolds, Jon Smith

Harmonica player Sugar Blue and the Stones recording the blues-infused "Down in the Hole."

Genesis

Can all the money in the world buy forgiveness, keep us in good health, and preserve us from insanity or unhappiness? Such are the questions Mick Jagger asks in this song. Musically, it is a case of the band returning to its origins. And it is probably no exaggeration to claim that "Down in the Hole" proves that the Rolling Stones are unrivaled when it comes to singing the blues. Still at the peak of their glory, the London quintet remained the worthy successors to the founders of modern blues, as embodied in the fifties by Muddy Waters, Howlin' Wolf, and Little Walter. Alongside the Stones, Sugar Blue displays the full extent of his talent and inspiration on the harmonica. The only shame is that the Rolling Stones have never performed "Down in the Hole" live.

Production

Mick Jagger would later claim in an interview that "Down in the Hole" was recorded in barely two takes. And it is tempting to believe him, so strong a sense of spontaneity does the track radiate, unlike "Where the Boys Go," which precedes it on the album. The Stones cannot deny their roots, and their automatic reflexes are still intact. This is also one of the rare occasions when a track on a studio album begins with a fade-in, offering further proof that this recording was made pretty well on the spot. Sugar Blue plays the harmonica intro with extraordinary feeling and produces an extraordinary sound, as befits one of the very best. "He obviously knows he's great, but he doesn't know how valuable he is,"[9] Ron Wood would later comment, full of admiration. Charlie accompanies him with some intense drum work, before each musician in turn then immerses himself in this minor-key blues. Bill provides powerful, weighty support, forming a backbone around which the guitars of Keith and Ron are able to express themselves. Keith chooses to play short, lead-type phrases, while Ron is mainly on rhythm, but they share a solo at 1:57 (and also in the coda), each answering the other with no overlapping. This creates an impression of perfect complementarity, to an even greater extent than during the time of Mick Taylor, who, as an out-and-out soloist, did not necessarily look to engage in interplay with his fellow guitarist. Mick Jagger is perfect. The blues is his preferred genre, and he conveys this through his masterly performance. The Stones are never as good as when they return to their first love.

1980

EMOTIONAL RESCUE

Mick Jagger / Keith Richards / 5:39

Musicians
Mick Jagger: vocals, electric piano
Keith Richards: rhythm and lead guitar
Bill Wyman: synthesizer
Ron Wood: bass
Charlie Watts: drums
Nicky Hopkins (?): electric piano
Bobby Keys: saxophone
Michael Shrieve: percussion
Recorded
EMI Pathé Marconi Studios, Boulogne-Billancourt, France: June 27–October 8, 1979
Electric Lady Studios, New York City: November–December 1979, April 1980
Technical Team
Producers: The Glimmer Twins
Associate producer: Chris Kimsey
Sound engineer: Chris Kimsey
Assistant sound engineers: Sean Fullan, Brad Samuelsohn, Ron "Snake" Reynolds, Jon Smith

Bobby Keys, ever faithful to the Stones, plays sax on "Emotional Rescue."

Genesis

Mick Jagger wrote both the words and the music to "Emotional Rescue," which came into being in a similar fashion to "Miss You." Here, Mick Jagger takes on the role of a man who is deeply in love with a *poor girl in a rich man's house*, and cries over her absence. Initially fatalistic, in the second verse he resolves to rescue her. "You would *never* really write a song like that in *real life*. Comes out in the studio, 'cause it's all ad-libbed, the end part. It was never planned like that,"[117] commented Jagger in 1980.

"Emotional Rescue" is thus a love song and, at the same time, an ode to dance. What never fails to surprise, is the falsetto voice adopted by Mick Jagger, which is completely unlike anything he had done before. It inevitably calls to mind the *Bee Gees* of "Saturday Night Fever" or Marvin Gaye on "Got to Give It Up," certainly not a rock singer, and even less a bluesman. Although atypical of the Stones' output, "Emotional Rescue" would nonetheless perform more than creditably when released as a single (with the very bluesy "Down in the Hole" as its B-side) on June 20, 1980, rising to number 3 on the *Billboard* chart and number 9 in the United Kingdom.

Production

"I wrote that on an electric piano in the studio, then Charlie [Watts] and Woody [Ron Wood] and I cut it immediately, live. It was all done very quickly,"[117] Mick Jagger would later explain. As simple as that. "Emotional Rescue" is not as straightforward a song as it initially seems, however. Charlie Watts opens the number with bass drum on every beat and very effective use of the hi-hat. Chris Kimsey (or one of his assistants) then had the good idea of adding not only a reasonably long delay with generous feedback, but also some phasing and a short reverb. This gives the cymbal an airy, emphatically "dance" quality. And then there's the bass, played by Ron Wood, whose funky style is a triumph in *every* respect. Bill Wyman, who has ceded his place to the guitarist, plays a subtle and highly staccato accompaniment on synthesizer, creating a sonority that is highly unusual for the Stones. And finally, an electric piano, probably a Wurlitzer, is played in symbiosis with the bass, almost certainly by Nicky Hopkins. There is also a second electric piano that does not come in until 0:22, this time played by Mick, and even a third, which

can be heard in the refrains. Each part constitutes another building block in the creation of the whole, and it has to be acknowledged that a good groove is established. The key element in "Emotional Rescue" is, of course, Mick Jagger's voice with its astonishing falsetto: "I think the vocals could've been better,"[117] he would later concede. He would also reveal in an interview that his inspiration came from Don Covay and the Goodtimers, in particular the song "Mercy, Mercy," which the Stones had covered in 1965 on *Out of Our Heads*, and would defend his choice of vocal technique by invoking the king of falsetto, Prince. In truth, it seems strange that one of the greatest of all rock 'n' roll singers should give in to a passing trend, but when all is said and done, "Emotional Rescue" succeeded in winning over more than one fan from the earliest days. Clearly Keith did not care greatly for the number, even though he thought it a good song on the whole. He

would complain that his sidekick was writing songs that were less and less guitaristic. Furthermore, he had had little to do with the song, other than playing some rhythm and a lead part that does not come in until around 3:00. Meanwhile, Bobby Keys has regained a certain legitimacy, delivering some very good phrases on the saxophone that have not been mixed down for a change. Finally, numerous percussion instruments are played throughout the track, probably by Michael Shrieve, such as a bongo, a shaker, a tambourine, and various others that are less easy to identify.

The Stones would shoot two videos for "Emotional Rescue": the first in the traditional way, and the second using the technique of thermography, as on the album cover. For die-hard fans only.

SHE'S SO COLD

Mick Jagger / Keith Richards / 4:12

Musicians
Mick Jagger: vocals, guitar (?)
Keith Richards: rhythm guitar
Bill Wyman: bass
Charlie Watts: drums
Ron Wood: rhythm and slide guitar, pedal steel guitar
Bobby Keys: saxophone
Recorded
Compass Point Studios, Nassau, Bahamas:
January 23–February 12, 1979
Electric Lady Studios, New York City:
November–December 1979, April 1980
Technical Team
Producers: The Glimmer Twins
Associate producer: Chris Kimsey
Sound engineer: Chris Kimsey
Assistant sound engineers: Sean Fullan, Brad
Samuelsohn, Ron "Snake" Reynolds, Jon Smith

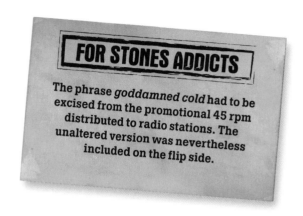

FOR STONES ADDICTS

The phrase *goddamned cold* had to be excised from the promotional 45 rpm distributed to radio stations. The unaltered version was nevertheless included on the flip side.

Genesis

She's so cold . . . The narrator is burning with love for his girl-friend, to the point of likening himself to a *bleeding volcano.* But there is nothing doing. The young woman is cold in the extreme, indeed as glacial as a *tombstone.* Is there some hidden meaning behind this song written by Mick Jagger (in an hour, it has been said)? Probably not. "She's So Cold" was chosen as the A-side of the second single from *Emotional Rescue* (with "Send It to Me" on the flip side). It only made it to number 26 in the United States and number 33 in the United Kingdom.

Production

Evidently Mick Jagger is the real driving force behind "She's So Cold." He invests such energy in the song and exhibits such a desire to communicate his enthusiasm that it seems as if nothing could possibly stand in his way. His performance is brilliant, and it is enough to watch the promotional video shot by Adam Friedman in July 1980 to get an idea of just how much the Stones singer, who has no hesitation in bringing out the innuendo of the lyrics, puts into it. Keith Richards opens the song with a palm mute riff with analog delay, courtesy of his MXR pedal. His sound is rockabilly, and in all likelihood he is using open-G tuning. He delivers a very good guitar part throughout the track, accompanied by a second rhythm part from Ron Wood, who slips in the odd phrase on slide. It is also Ronnie who plays the two solos on pedal steel guitar (1:54 and 3:51). He does not seem to be in great form, however. These two interventions are somewhat anemic and noticeably lacking in energy, especially in comparison to Mick's performance . . . Bill Wyman supports his bandmates with a very prominent bass sound, and avoids the clichés of the genre by seeking out a more inventive melodic line. Charlie Watts takes care of the rhythm, playing an important role in making "She's So Cold" the irresistible number that it is. Finally, poor Bobby Keys's only contribution is an almost surreptitious saxophone effect at 2:01. It would have been good to hear more of him.

Bill Wyman delivers an excellent
bass part on "She's So Cold."

ALL ABOUT YOU

Mick Jagger / Keith Richards / 4:18

Musicians
Keith Richards: vocals, rhythm guitar, piano, acoustic guitar (?), bass
Charlie Watts: drums
Ron Wood: rhythm guitar, backing vocals
Bobby Keys: saxophone

Recorded
Compass Point Studios, Nassau, Bahamas: January 23–February 12, 1979
Electric Lady Studios, New York City: November–December 1979, April 1980

Technical Team
Producers: The Glimmer Twins
Associate producer: Chris Kimsey
Sound engineer: Chris Kimsey
Assistant sound engineers: Sean Fullan, Brad Samuelsohn, Ron "Snake" Reynolds, Jon Smith

Keith and Anita, happy parents following the birth of their first child, Marlon.

Genesis
"All About You" is a song written exclusively by Keith Richards during the period when he was starting to come off heroin: "There's never one thing a song's about, but in this case if it was about anything, it was probably more about Mick."[2] *If the show must go on, let it go on without you/So sick and tired hanging around with jerks like you.* The words are clearly hurtful. Keith apparently had the bitter impression that Mick had taken advantage of his difficulties to keep "me from interfering in day-to-day business."[2] Now the Stones guitarist was back and had to be taken into consideration again. But Mick Jagger is not the only person targeted in "All About You." The song also tackles the relationship between Keith and Anita, which was on its last legs. *You're the first to get blamed, always the last bitch to get paid*: here too, Richards does not beat around the bush. He is probably alluding to the death of Scott Cantrell, with whom Anita was said to have been having an affair.

Production
Following "Before They Make Me Run" on the previous album, here Keith Richards presents us with a new emotional scenario. In "All About You" he has chosen to express himself through a ballad that combines elements of the blues, rock, and jazz. Playing chords strongly colored by MXR phasing, he is joined in the intro by Bobby Keys, who doubles and harmonizes with himself on the sax. Ronnie accompanies on a second guitar, albeit reasonably discreetly. Charlie delivers some restrained drum work, with Keith lending him a hand on the bass. Although perfectly good, this bass playing lacks the special sound and touch that Bill can bring, particularly to this sort of ballad. Curiously, there is no acoustic guitar other than on the very last chord of the track, at 4:13. Keith sings from the soul, and his weariness is all too evident. He also provides some highly successful vocal harmonies alongside Ronnie, and takes care of the piano part as well. He would later claim to have written "All About You" three years earlier, inspired by some other song he had heard. Might this have been the Beatles' "Sexy Sadie," whose harmonies at the beginning of each verse are not dissimilar? No matter. "All About You" is a cry from the heart that stands out strongly from the other songs on this album.

Keith's song about the end of his relationship with Anita Pallenberg, with whom he had three children.

AN ALTERNATIVE EXPLANATION!

In a book published in 2002,[66] Stephen Davis describes an interview in which Keith claims to have been inspired by his Dalmatian dog, which suffered from flatulence, when writing "All About You" . . .

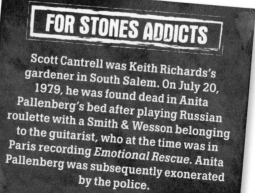

FOR STONES ADDICTS

Scott Cantrell was Keith Richards's gardener in South Salem. On July 20, 1979, he was found dead in Anita Pallenberg's bed after playing Russian roulette with a Smith & Wesson belonging to the guitarist, who at the time was in Paris recording *Emotional Rescue*. Anita Pallenberg was subsequently exonerated by the police.

Start Me Up
Hang Fire
Slave
Little T&A
Black Limousine
Neighbours
Worried About You
Tops
Heaven
No Use In Crying
Waiting On A Friend

ALBUM
RELEASE DATE
United Kingdom: August 24, 1981
Label: Rolling Stones Records
RECORD NUMBER: ROLLING STONES RECORDS COC 16052
Number 2, on the charts for 29 weeks

TATTOO YOU: A HETEROGENEOUS ALBUM

Between the release of *Emotional Rescue* in the United Kingdom on June 27, 1980, and the start of the US tour (September 25–December 19, 1981), the five members of the Rolling Stones took something of a step back. Rumors were rife concerning Bill Wyman's future with the band; Charlie Watts became more and more interested in the modern jazz of Charlie Parker, while Mick Jagger purchased the Château de Fourchette at Pocé-sur-Cisse, near Amboise, France, on September 18, 1980, before flying to Peru in January 1981 for the shooting of Werner Herzog's movie *Fitzcarraldo* (a shoot he would have to abandon because of the Stones' tour). Keith Richards and Ron Wood deliberated over the future of the New Barbarians, the band they had started outside the Stones two years earlier . . . All told, the future of the Rolling Stones was looking uncertain. Keith was putting in less and less of an appearance and no longer seemed inclined to work with his writing partner, while Ronnie's drug addiction was developing into a real problem, Charlie was sinking into alcoholism, and Mick was tending to make decisions alone. It was nevertheless the energy of the Stones singer that prevented the British quintet from going under . . .

The Rolling Stones celebrated the arrival of the eighties with a compilation titled . . . *Sucking in the Seventies* (March 1981). Its track listing comprises "Time Waits for No One" from *It's Only Rock 'N' Roll*; "Hot Stuff," "Fool to Cry," and "Crazy Mama" from *Black and Blue*; "Shattered" and "Beast of Burden" from *Some Girls*, plus "Everything Is Turning to Gold" (the B-side of the single "Shattered"); "If I Was a Dancer

(Dance Pt. 2)," an outtake from *Emotional Rescue*; and live versions of "Mannish Boy" (*Love You Live*) and "When the Whip Comes Down" (recorded in concert in Detroit on July 6, 1978). The band also felt it necessary to release a new album to accompany the tour, which, after drawing to a close in the United States in December, was to resume the following year in Europe (from May 26 to July 25, 1982). "*Tattoo You* really came about because Mick and Keith were going through a period of not getting on," recalls Chris Kimsey. "There was a need to have an album out, and I told everyone I could make an album from what I knew was still there."[118]

The Album

Chris Kimsey, once again in the role of associate producer, and Mick Jagger spent three months selecting recordings made during the sessions for the five preceding albums. "*Tattoo You* is basically an old record," says Jagger. "It's a lot of old tracks that I dug out. They're all from different periods. Then I had to write lyrics and melodies."[118] Keith Richards adds: "The music had to age just like good wine. Sometimes we write our songs in installments—just get the melody and the music, and we'll cut the tracks and write the words later."[118] Whichever way one looks at it, the Rolling Stones' sixteenth (British) studio album constitutes a pretty good summary of the path taken by the band during the second half of the seventies. It opens with a riff that is almost too good to be true for Stones fans—that of "Start Me Up" (which remains to this day the band's last great classic)—and closes with a superb

The Château de Fourchette at Pocé-sur-Cisse, France, acquired by Mick Jagger in September 1980.

While the Stones were working on their future album, John Lennon was murdered by Mark David Chapman on December 8, 1980, in New York City. John was liked by all of the Stones, who were deeply upset at his loss.

ballad titled "Waiting on a Friend," which elevates friendship to the rank of supreme virtue. The space between the two is filled with more great moments: "Hang Fire," an implacable and heavily ironic indictment of Thatcherite Britain; "Slave," which is made by the saxophone playing of Sonny Rollins; the blues number "Black Limousine"; and "Little T&A," one of Keith Richards's best creations since "Happy."

Tattoo You was released in the United States on August 18, 1981, a little more than a month before the opening concert of the US tour (Philadelphia on September 25), and in the United Kingdom on August 28. In spite of its heterogeneous character, it was received warmly by both the press and the public, especially in the United States, where it was number 1 for nine weeks (selling more than four million copies). It also hit the top spot in Australia, Canada, and France, made it to number 2 in the United Kingdom and Spain, and to number 3 in West Germany, Italy, and Norway. The album currently occupies a very honorable 213th place in *Rolling Stone* magazine's list of the 500 Greatest Albums of All Time.

The Album Cover

In an interview given in 1981, Mick Jagger explains how the title of the album came about: "[We called it Tattoo You] because we had these paintings by that guy and we just didn't know what to call it. . . . Some friend of mine from Pharoah [sic] Island did these paintings . . . they're actually photographs but with that tattoo painting on them. I saw him do some other stuff and we liked them so I gave him a couple of pictures and asked him to do them like that. Then we used them for the cover. We had lots of different titles but in the end we decided to call it that."[119] The artistic direction of the cover was once again entrusted to Peter Corriston, who was assisted by the photographer Hubert Kretzschmar and the illustrator Christian Piper. The front cover features Mick Jagger's face, covered in tattoos, against a red background. On the back is Keith Richards against a green background with the track listing printed alongside. No such images of Bill Wyman, Charlie Watts, or Ron Wood. The inner sleeve depicts the hoof of an animal, probably a goat, in the shape of a ladies' pump. Could this be a reference to Beelzebub? This highly original graphic design won Peter Corriston the Grammy Award for the best album cover of 1981.

The Recording

The history of the tracks selected for *Tattoo You* is as follows: "Tops" and "Waiting on a Friend" both date from 1972 and the *Goats Head Soup* sessions held at Dynamic Sound Studios in Kingston, Jamaica, with Mick Taylor on guitar (in the case of "Waiting on a Friend," this part seems to have been wiped by Bob Clearmountain during the final mixing).

"Slave" and "Worried About You" were recorded in Rotterdam, the Netherlands, with the Rolling Stones Mobile Studio during the *Black and Blue* period (1975).

"Start Me Up" and "Hang Fire" date back to the *Some Girls* sessions held at the Pathé Marconi Studios in Boulogne-Billancourt in November 1977. "Black Limousine," which seems to have been recorded originally under the working title "Broken Head Blues," at Musicland Studios in Munich in November 1973, was reworked four years later, also at the Pathé Marconi Studios.

"Little T&A" and "No Use in Crying" originated during the sessions for *Emotional Rescue*—the first at Compass Point Studios, Nassau, Bahamas, from January to February 1979, and the second at the Pathé Marconi Studios between June and October 1979.

Finally, "Neighbours" and "Heaven" were cut at the Pathé Marconi Studios toward the end of 1979 and in autumn 1980, respectively.

Of all the songs that Chris Kimsey gathered together and presented to the band, few would need any overdubs other than the addition of the lead vocal and vocal harmonies, which Mick Jagger would record alone at an (unidentified) location near Paris between April and May 1981. The sound engineer retains a not exactly pleasant memory of this time: "The main thing missing from most of them was Sir Mick's vocal, because he hadn't finished writing the lyrics, so those parts were recorded in Paris in mid-1981. They'd rented a bloody warehouse on the edge of the Peripherique [ring road] in a horrible part of the city—all industrial sites and train sidings . . . no restaurants! I don't know who'd found the warehouse, but it was big and cheap, they put the mobile truck inside there, and it was so cold that, when Mick did the vocals, you could *see* icy breath coming out of his mouth. I remember that place to this day. It was absolutely diabolical."[120] Kimsey explains that the

1981

Bill Wyman was thinking more and more of leaving the Stones.

Bill Wyman, frustrated at not being able to participate in the songwriting for the Stones records, was quietly pursuing a solo career. He had a hit with "(Si Si) Je Suis Un Rock Star," which was released on July 3, 1981, climbing to number 14 on the British charts, number 2 in Australia, and entering the top twenty in many other countries. He would be the only Stone ever to record a solo hit.

vocals could easily have been recorded within a few days at most, but Mick led such an active social life in Paris that the job took six weeks. Nevertheless, the singer's performance is to be applauded, all the more so as it had been necessary to hire an industrial heater to warm the place up: "He'd give it the full performance, moving all over the place . . . " recalls Kimsey. "It was great to watch and equally great to record. He knows how to work a microphone. . . ."[120] The exact opposite of Keith, in fact. "You need a shotgun to get him in front of the mic. He'll wander all over the place while singing, taking an attitude of 'You do your job, you record me.'"[120] Keith did not take part in these sessions, and Mick took care of all the vocals. "He's very good at sounding like Keith on harmonies,"[120] observes Kimsey.

With the vocals in the can, Mick and Keith then got together in New York City to start mixing *Tattoo You* and adding the final touches, probably from mid-May to June 1981. A number of different studios are referred to, such as Atlantic Studios, Electric Lady Studios, the Hit Factory, and the Power Station. Unfortunately, the necessary information to determine which studios were actually used is difficult to find. The Stones singer called in the sound engineer who had been responsible for remixing both the single and extended versions of "Miss You." "And then I took it to [producer] Bob Clearmountain," explains Jagger, "who did this great job of mixing so that it doesn't sound like it's from different periods."[19] Gary Lyons, the sound engineer and producer who went on to work with Aerosmith, Queen, the Grateful Dead, and others, would also do some of the mixing.

Among the many musicians who worked on the different numbers on *Tattoo You* are Mick Taylor; Nicky Hopkins; Wayne Perkins; Pete Townshend, the songwriter and guitarist of the Who, who seems to have contributed to the backing vocals on "Slave," probably Mike Carabello, the talented Santana percussionist; and most likely the sisters Jennifer and Susan McLean in the backing vocals on "Neighbours." The big surprise, however, is the involvement of Sonny Rollins, who was one of Charlie Watts's idols. Mick Jagger got in touch with the great jazz saxophonist after seeing him at the Bottom Line club in New York City in 1981. Charlie Watts was convinced that he would never want to play on a Rolling Stones record. But contrary to all expectations he accepted. Mick Jagger: " . . . he did and he was wonderful. I said, 'Would you like me to stay out there in the studio?' He said, 'Yeah, you tell me where you want me to play and dance the part out.'"[15] His sax parts were overdubbed, to Charlie's regret: " . . . we never played together. Probably just as well. My goodness, I'd sit there and think, 'bloody hell, what am I going to do here?' I'd feel like an impostor, because that's the highest company you can keep."[121]

Technical Details

To record Mick Jagger's vocals, Chris Kimsey used the Rolling Stones Mobile Studio, actually parked inside the Parisian warehouse rented for the occasion. He explains his method: "We put some screens around him, otherwise it would have sounded ridiculous in that giant place, and I recorded all of his vocals with a valve 47. That's what I always used when he was overdubbing without the band."[120]

START ME UP

Mick Jagger / Keith Richards / 3:31

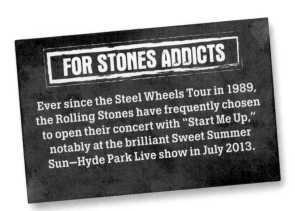

Microsoft decided to use "Start Me Up" as the launch music for Windows 95 in August 1995. The exact fee they paid is not known, but the check no doubt had plenty of zeros in front of the decimal point (the figure of three million dollars has been rumored) . . .

Musicians
Mick Jagger: vocals, hand claps
Keith Richards: lead guitar
Bill Wyman: bass
Charlie Watts: drums
Ron Wood: rhythm guitar
Chris Kimsey, Barry Sage: hand claps
Mike Carabello: congas, cowbell

Recorded
EMI Pathé Marconi Studios, Boulogne-Billancourt, France: October 10–December 21, 1977
Rolling Stones Mobile Studio, Paris (precise location not determined): April–May 1981
Atlantic Studios (?), Power Station, New York City: May–June 1981

Technical Team
Producers: The Glimmer Twins
Associate producer: Chris Kimsey
Sound engineers: Chris Kimsey, Bob Clearmountain, Gary Lyons
Assistant sound engineer: Barry Sage

FOR STONES ADDICTS

Ever since the Steel Wheels Tour in 1989, the Rolling Stones have frequently chosen to open their concert with "Start Me Up," notably at the brilliant Sweet Summer Sun–Hyde Park Live show in July 2013.

Genesis

Before becoming an iconic Stones rock track, "Start Me Up" underwent a long development process. "'Start Me Up' had been a reggae song recorded in Rotterdam three years earlier," explains Chris Kimsey. "When they started playing it this time, it wasn't a reggae song, it was what we know today as the great 'Start Me Up.'"[2] According to Kimsey, it was a Keith song transformed by Mick. Ron Wood offers a different insight, however: "I don't know why 'Start Me Up' was missed off the selection for *Emotional Rescue* or *Some Girls*, because that's when we recorded it. It's strange. I think maybe we were saving it for a single. I have the impression that it was a riff that Mick brought along, like 'Don't Stop' for *Forty Licks*—very much a Mick kind of idea, although in the end 'Start Me Up' became a Mick- and Keith-welded song with contributions from both of them. It was one of those genuine collaborations between the two of them, with a little magic from both sides happening instantly."[9]

The words are highly metaphorical, as so often is the case for the Glimmer Twins. *If you start me up, I'll never stop*; *Kick on the starter, give it all you've got*; *You make a dead man come*: more of a sex symbol than ever, Mick Jagger solicits and stimulates the sexual prowess of his partner in terms that bikers (Hells Angels?) might happily use. And evidently the message was received loud and clear by the fans, who regarded "Start Me Up" as the Stones' great comeback. Released on August 14, 1981, with "No Use in Crying" as its B-side, the single nevertheless topped the charts only in Australia. It climbed to number 2 in the United States, but stalled at number 7 in the United Kingdom.

Production

The production history of "Start Me Up" is not easy to retrace. The initial reggae versions were recorded using the Rolling Stones Mobile Studio in Rotterdam between January and February 1975. The song was then substantially reworked at the Pathé Marconi Studios in Boulogne-Billancourt between October and December 1977. As Chris Kimsey would reveal, "within 24 hours of 'Miss You', 'Start Me Up' was recorded."[120] It was those sessions that saw the emergence of the rock version that would serve as the basis for the later overdubs. The Stones played a huge number of takes

Keith Richards: Telecaster, open tuning, and capo d'astro, for his magical intro to "Start Me Up."

of the song, around seventy, most of them reggae, but Richards was still not happy with the results, as Kimsey explains: "After they cut it, I said, 'That's bloody great! Come and listen.' . . . However, when I played it back, Keith said, 'Nah, it sounds like something I've heard on the radio. Wipe it.' Of course, I didn't, but he really didn't like it, and I'm not sure whether he likes it to this day."[120] The band therefore dropped "Start Me Up" completely. And it was only in 1980, five years after the initial versions recorded in Rotterdam, at the time Chris Kimsey and Mick Jagger were putting together the future Stones album from studio outtakes, that they happened to rediscover the rock version. "Start Me Up" was a " . . . track that was just forgotten about, a reject," recalls Mick Jagger. "The funny thing was that it turned into this reggae song after two takes. And that take on *Tattoo You* was the only take that was a complete rock & roll take. . . . And no one went back to Take 2, which was the one we used, the rock track."[19] The Stones guitarist retains a slightly different memory, claiming that it was after more than thirty reggae takes that he and Charlie Watts gave it a rock makeover, simply as a way of refreshing the atmosphere . . .

What immediately comes to mind when one thinks of "Start Me Up" is the superb intro played by Keith in open G, presumably on one of his Fender Telecasters. And despite the doubts voiced by Ron Wood, Keith was clearly responsible for this, as Jagger would confirm in 1995: "It was Keith's great riff, and I wrote the rest."[19] The reverb that can be heard on his

guitar was probably added by Bob Clearmountain during the mixing of the track at the Power Station in New York City. His technique was to place a mic in the studio bathroom, play back the sound he wanted to treat, and then recapture it, colored by this "bathroom reverb." This is where the unique guitar sound comes from. Ronnie plays the second rhythm guitar, which, with its dryer, more distorted sound, complements Keith's extremely well. Both are plugged into Mesa Boogie amps. There are two short solos at 1:23 and 3:03 that are probably played by Keith. Charlie's drum part is another key element in "Start Me Up," his work being absolutely essential to the groove, and in perfect symbiosis with the main guitar. And with Bill's very good bass playing, most likely on his Travis Bean TB 2000, "Start Me Up" is an invitation to the party. Percussion has been added, including a güiro (on the right) and a cowbell (on the left), played presumably by Mike Carabello, and hand claps most likely from Jagger, Kimsey, and Sage. Mick's performance can be classed as one of the best of his career. He is even more effective than usual, and conveys the innuendo supremely well. For anyone who remains to be convinced, the promo shot by Michael Lindsay-Hogg in June 1981 should clinch it. Most of the vocals on the album were recorded in a rented warehouse close to the Paris beltway between April and mid-May 1981, but if Bob Clearmountain is to be believed, the definitive takes for this particular number, including the backing vocals, were recorded at the Power Station.

HANG FIRE

Mick Jagger / Keith Richards / 2:20

Musicians
Mick Jagger: vocals, rhythm guitar (?)
Keith Richards: lead guitar
Ron Wood: bass (?)
Charlie Watts: drums
Ian Stewart: piano (?)

Recorded
EMI Pathé Marconi Studios, Boulogne-Billancourt, France: October 10–December 21, 1977; June 27–October 8, 1979
Rolling Stones Mobile Studio, Paris (precise location not determined): April–May 1981
Atlantic Studios (?), Power Station (?), New York City: May–June 1981

Technical Team
Producers: The Glimmer Twins
Associate producer: Chris Kimsey
Sound engineers: Chris Kimsey, Bob Clearmountain, Gary Lyons
Assistant sound engineer: Barry Sage

Both onstage and in the studio, Mick Jagger plays guitar on "Hang Fire."

Genesis

The Stones began to record "Hang Fire" during the *Some Girls* sessions between October and December 1977, but Mick Jagger did not add the words until 1979. These lyrics are a scathing indictment of a Britain bogged down in economic crisis, a country in which *nobody ever works* because there is *nowhere to work*. The sardonic humor reaches its climax when Jagger sings *I'm a lazy slob*. His aim was presumably to castigate the policies introduced by Margaret Thatcher in 1979. *We just lost our shirts*, he belches, and, faced with the triumphant employers: *We ain't for hire*. "Hang Fire" was released as a single (with "Neighbours" as the B-side) and reached number 20 on the *Billboard* chart on May 8, 1982.

Production

Musically, "Hang Fire" comes as something of a surprise, particularly from the Stones, as the song is based on the same harmonic structure as ballads like "Blue Moon," the rock version of which was popularized by Elvis Presley in 1956. The British band infuses it with a salutary energy, however: Keith's guitar is in no mood to murmur sweet nothings. On the contrary, the riff master sets the track on fire with short, extremely impassioned solos (using his MXR Analog Delay pedal) with that Chuck Berry feel that is his trademark (0:49). He also plays a very good rhythm part, effectively supporting the other rhythm guitar, played most probably by Mick, who, if it is him (the style of playing bears little resemblance to that of Ron Wood, and it therefore seems safe to attribute it to the singer) has made remarkable progress. Woody in turn seems to be on bass rather than Bill, whose characteristic style is lacking. The guitarist delivers a very good bass line and combines perfectly with Charlie's drumming, which conveys a real sense of pleasure on the part of the drummer. The real surprise on "Hang Fire," however, is its distinctly "pop" backing vocals, hitherto unknown on a Stones track. They work extremely well, however, and it is likely that Mick was solely responsible for them, as his voice can be heard harmonizing with the various vocal parts that had been recorded in the Parisian warehouse. Finally, at the back of the mix, it is just possible to make out a piano, bearing the stamp of Stu's excellent—and all too rarely heard—playing.

SLAVE

Mick Jagger / Keith Richards / 4:59 (6:33 remastered version)

Musicians
Mick Jagger: vocals, tambourine (?)
Keith Richards: lead guitar, backing vocals
Bill Wyman: bass
Charlie Watts: drums
Billy Preston: electric piano (?), organ
Ollie E. Brown: cowbell
Sonny Rollins: saxophone
Mike Carabello: congas (?)
Pete Townshend (?): backing vocals, guitar (?)

Recorded
Rolling Stones Mobile Studio, De Doelen, Rotterdam: January 22–February 9, 1975
EMI Pathé Marconi Studios, Boulogne-Billancourt, France: October 11–November 12, 1980
Rolling Stones Mobile Studio, Paris (precise location not determined): April–May 1981
Atlantic Studios (?), Power Station, New York City: May–June 1981

Technical Team
Producers: The Glimmer Twins
Associate producer: Chris Kimsey
Sound engineers: Keith Harwood, Glyn Johns, Chris Kimsey, Bob Clearmountain, Gary Lyons
Assistant sound engineer: Barry Sage

FOR STONES ADDICTS

One of the working titles for "Slave" was "Black and Blue Jam." Another was "Vagina" . . .

Genesis

"Slave" took shape during a jam session in Rotterdam while the Stones were recording *Black and Blue*. Mick Taylor had left and the band was looking for a suitable replacement. The first version of this song was therefore recorded with the help of guitar hero Jeff Beck, and with Nicky Hopkins on piano and Billy Preston on organ. The words have been stripped back to their minimum form of expression. When the Stones decided to dust this particular tape off, Bob Clearmountain had to make significant changes. Having suppressed Jeff Beck's guitar and Nicky Hopkins's piano, he asked Sonny Rollins to put his stamp on the track and then remixed the whole thing.

Production

"Slave" is another number that is atypical of the Stones. This funky rock jam is an out-and-out triumph that was originally more than eleven minutes long. Charlie gets the ball rolling with some superb work on his Gretsch kit, establishing an incredible groove in which the influence of Jimmy Miller can still be felt all these years later. He is accompanied by Ollie E. Brown on cowbell and (probably) Mick on tambourine. Keith makes his entry with a hard-hitting riff, and is immediately joined by some supportive bass from Bill, who doubles him practically note for note. The effect is awesome and, combined with Charlie's drumming, offers the Stones an opportunity to demonstrate their rhythmic prowess. Keith delivers a number of solo phrases (4:13) and despite the assumption on the part of some commentators that Ron Wood also plays on the track, it has to be acknowledged that there is only one guitar. Billy Preston gives a further demonstration of his talent on electric piano and organ, each of these keyboard parts imbued with the soul that characterizes all his playing. And Sonny Rollins, making his first contribution to the album, lives up to his reputation with an absolutely fantastic sax improvisation, which, although overdubbed, blends perfectly with the Stones' style. Finally, Mick is accompanied on backing vocals by singers who are difficult to identify, although Mick Jagger himself claims that Pete Townshend lent his voice to the track. In his book *Rolling with the Stones*,[1] by contrast, Bill Wyman has Townshend playing the guitar.

LITTLE T&A

Mick Jagger / Keith Richards / 3:23

Musicians
Keith Richards: vocals, lead guitar (?), rhythm guitar, bass (?)
Mick Jagger: backing vocals
Charlie Watts: drums
Ron Wood: lead guitar (?), rhythm guitar
Ian Stewart: piano (?)

Recorded
Compass Point Studios, Nassau, Bahamas:
January 22–February 12, 1979
EMI Pathé Marconi Studios, Boulogne-Billancourt,
France: June 27–October 8, 1979 (?)
Electric Lady Studios, New York City:
November–December 1979
Atlantic Studios (?), Power Station,
New York City: May–June 1981

Technical Team
Producers: The Glimmer Twins
Associate producer: Chris Kimsey
Sound engineers: Chris Kimsey,
Bob Clearmountain, Gary Lyons
Assistant sound engineer: Barry Sage

Keith Richards remains the unrivaled master of the riff with "Little T&A," a song on which he also sings lead vocal.

Genesis

The lyrics of "Little T&A" (standing for *tits and ass*) are about "every good time I've had with somebody I'd met for a night or two and never seen again,"[122] confided the song's author, Keith, to Kurt Loder in 1981. Despite the mind-blowing riff crafted by Keith during the initial recording, the number was left off the final track listing for *Emotional Rescue*, a decision that was regrettable, to say the least. Two years later, the riff master reworked it for *Tattoo You* in a distinctly rockabilly style.

Production

The first sessions dedicated to "Bulldog," the working title of "Little T&A," took place at the beginning of 1979, when the Rolling Stones were recording at Compass Point Studios in Nassau. The Stones would then rework the song in Paris between June and October of that year, and probably a month later at Electric Lady Studios in New York City, where Keith presumably recorded his vocal. The song was finalized at the Power Station, with Bob Clearmountain in charge of the mixing. It is Keith who opens the song with one of the riffs for which he is renowned. He would later claim in an interview that he played it on his 5-string 1957 Telecaster in open G (at that time he was playing through a Mesa Boogie amp). It seems more likely, however, that he stuck to standard tuning for the disc, while using open G in concert. Ron Wood answers him extremely well on rhythm, and it is also most likely Ronnie who plays the solos. It is interesting to note the use made of the MXR pedal, with its characteristic analog delay, by both guitarists. Bill seems to have ceded the bass part to Keith, who plays well enough, but without reaching the standard that Wyman would later set in live performances of this number, as can be seen from the concert at Hampton Coliseum in Virginia on December 18, 1981. Stu is often said to be playing the piano, but if this is the case, his part has been completely buried in the mix. Charlie fails to deliver one of his best accompaniments here, while Mick sings backing vocals with Keith. Were these recorded at Atlantic Studios or at the Power Station between May and June 1981? It remains a mystery.

BLACK LIMOUSINE

Mick Jagger / Keith Richards / Ron Wood / 3:32

Although originally from Mississippi, Johnny "Big Moose" Walker, Ron Wood's other inspiration for the "Black Limousine" riff, spent the best part of his career in Chicago, playing with the likes of Elmore James, Earl Hooker, and Muddy Waters . . .

Musicians
Mick Jagger: vocals, harmonica
Keith Richards: rhythm guitar
Bill Wyman: bass
Charlie Watts: drums
Ron Wood: lead guitar
Ian Stewart: piano

Recorded
EMI Pathé Marconi Studios, Boulogne-Billancourt, France: October 10–December 21, 1977; January 5–March 2, 1978; June 27–October 8, 1979
Rolling Stones Mobile Studio, Paris (precise location not determined): April–May 1981
Atlantic Studios (?), Power Station, New York City: May–June 1981

Technical Team
Producers: The Glimmer Twins
Associate producer: Chris Kimsey
Sound engineers: Chris Kimsey, Bob Clearmountain, Gary Lyons
Assistant sound engineer: Barry Sage

Mick Jagger and Jerry Hall in the back of a limousine in Paris.

Genesis

Pretty girls, limousines, and alcohol flowing like water in fashionable nightspots: all this is part and parcel of being a rock star—and a Rolling Stone, in particular. It is this aspect of the Stones' lives, overplayed by the media, that Mick Jagger evokes in this song, using the past tense, as if describing a crazy dream that has now vanished into thin air. "Black Limousine," for which Ron Wood is credited alongside Mick Jagger and Keith Richards, is a number in the good old Chicago blues tradition. Ronnie would later reveal that he had been inspired by a slide guitar riff he heard on a 45 rpm given to him by Eric Clapton. "And there was another guy called Big Moose, who I've never heard of before or since. I had this one 45 that Eric Clapton gave me which had him on. . . . I thought, 'That's really good, I'm going to apply that.'"[9]

Production

The record from which Ronnie Wood took his inspiration for the exhilarating riff of "Black Limousine" may have been "Rockin' with Hop" by Hop Wilson, which was released in 1958. Ronnie's guitar part is excellent in every respect and he also takes numerous solos, all of which are highly inspired (despite muffing a note at 2:07!). This helps to explain why he insisted on his share of the songwriting credit: "I fought until I was blue in the face to get the credit, going on and on, 'I wrote that, I wrote that.'"[9] Mick lends him a hand by doubling his riff on the harmonica—to great effect. The Stones singer excels on this track as he always does in the blues and boogie, musical styles in which he reveals the full extent of his talent. It seems that he recorded both the lead and backing vocals by himself in the Paris warehouse between April and May 1981. For his part, Keith delivers a very solid rhythm guitar onto which Charlie, who opts to play with brushes, grafts his drum work. Bill supports his bandmates with a very good, inventive bass part with an infectious groove. This time Stu is definitely on the piano, playing in a fitting boogie style, possibly not sufficiently prominent in the mix, but indispensable all the same. Mick Jagger was later astonished by how well this song went down with the fans, and confessed that he had never really cared for it himself.

NEIGHBOURS

Mick Jagger / Keith Richards / 3:31

Musicians
Mick Jagger: vocals, rhythm guitar (?)
Keith Richards: rhythm guitar, backing vocals
Bill Wyman: bass
Charlie Watts: drums
Ron Wood: rhythm and lead guitar
Ian Stewart: piano
Sonny Rollins: saxophone
Jennifer McLean, Susan McLean (?): backing vocals
Recorded
EMI Pathé Marconi Studios, Boulogne-Billancourt,
France: June 27–October 8, 1979, October 11–December 1980
**Rolling Stones Mobile Studio, Paris (precise
location not determined):** April–May 1981
**Atlantic Studios, Power Station (?),
New York City:** May–June 1981
Technical Team
Producers: The Glimmer Twins
Associate producer: Chris Kimsey
Sound engineers: Chris Kimsey,
Bob Clearmountain, Gary Lyons
Assistant sound engineer: Barry Sage

Ian Stewart plays piano on "Neighbours," a song Mick wrote especially for Keith.

Genesis

"Neighbours" is one of the two songs on *Tattoo You* not to have been written or recorded for an earlier album. In it, Mick Jagger, who wrote the lyrics, describes the difficult relations between his friend Keith and his neighbors in the New York City apartment the Stones guitarist was sharing with his new companion, Patti Hansen. Keith: "And these people come up to our door saying, 'We can't even hear Bugs Bunny on our TV, your music's so loud! Turn the kettledrums down!'" And again: "'Neighbours' is the first song I think Mick's ever really written for me. It's one I wish I'd written, that."[122]

Production

Before being recorded at the Pathé Marconi Studios at the end of 1980 and finalized between April and May 1981 at Atlantic Studios in New York City, "Neighbours" seems to have been worked on in Paris in 1979. For this new, high-energy rock number, Mick launches into the intro in an overexcited voice, supported by Charlie, who smacks his Gretsch kit for all he's worth. Shunning his hi-hat, it is mainly his snare drum that comes through, colored by very present reverb. The drummer only deigns to use his cymbals in the coda, around 2:39. The song's real prop is Bill's bass, which, as usual, is powerful, clean, and infused with a terrific swing. Keith is the first to come in on guitar, playing a very solid rhythm part with analog delay courtesy of his MXR, which he no longer seems to be able to do without. Ronnie plays a second rhythm part and delivers an excellent solo, probably one of the best on the album, at 1:13. A third rhythm guitar, probably played by Mick, can be made out from the first refrain onward. Various backing vocals can also be heard in the refrains, and the names of the sisters and models Jennifer and Susan McLean are often mentioned (although in truth they are not very audible). Sonny Rollins again contributes a saxophone solo, with the inimitable phrasing that is the mark of an exceptional musician. Stu is back on piano, but as so often, can only be heard during a short section (from 3:10). "Neighbours" is a typical Stones rock track, lacking any real originality, but led by an incredible Mick Jagger brimming with power and vitality and radiating staggering charisma (see the promo).

WORRIED ABOUT YOU

Mick Jagger / Keith Richards / 5:16

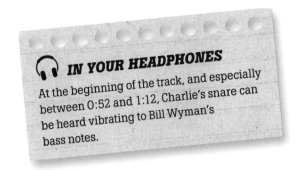
Musicians
Mick Jagger: vocals, electric piano
Keith Richards: rhythm guitar, backing vocals
Bill Wyman: bass
Charlie Watts: drums
Wayne Perkins: lead guitar
Ollie E. Brown (?): tambourine

Recorded
Rolling Stones Mobile Studio, De Doelen, Rotterdam, the Netherlands: January 22–February 9, 1975
EMI Pathé Marconi Studios, Boulogne-Billancourt, France: June 27–October 8, 1979
Rolling Stones Mobile Studio, Paris (precise location not determined): April–May 1981
Atlantic Studios (?), Power Station, New York City: May–June 1981

Technical Team
Producers: The Glimmer Twins
Associate producer: Chris Kimsey
Sound engineers: Keith Harwood, Glyn Johns, Chris Kimsey, Bob Clearmountain, Gary Lyons
Assistant sound engineer: Barry Sage

Ron Wood is absent from the recording of "Worried About You," but was present for the shooting of the video.

Genesis

"Worried About You" is another track on *Tattoo You* that dates back to the *Black and Blue* sessions at the beginning about 1975. Mick Jagger adopts his finest falsetto voice to sing about the life of a couple with its highs and, most importantly, their lows. The narrator ponders his relationship with his lover before declaring: *Lord, I'll find out anyway, sure gonna find myself a girl someday.* To put it in a nutshell, he is eaten away by anxiety, and frets that he cannot seem to find his way. This is a little-known aspect of Mick Jagger's personality, one he does not often divulge . . . The Stones performed "Worried About You" for the first time at the El Mocambo Club in Toronto during the two shows on March 4 and 5, 1977 (more than four years before the release of *Tattoo You*), and again during their 2002–2003, 2006, and 2013–2014 tours.

Production

The electric piano in the introduction is played by Mick. It is probably a Wurlitzer with phasing generated possibly by a Leslie speaker. In Rotterdam, Billy Preston was apparently responsible for the keyboard parts, but his contribution cannot be heard on the final mix. Bill supports Mick with a very prominent bass line, while Charlie marks the beat on his hi-hat. Keith plays a funky rhythm guitar, also colored by phasing and a reasonably short delay. "Worried About You" is far from the best track on *Tattoo You*, but it exudes an engrossing melancholy. Mick Jagger forces his voice a little too much in the falsetto passages, and it comes as a relief when he returns to his normal, hard-edged rock 'n' roll register at 3:22. He is joined in the refrains by Keith, who comes in with a very high voice to harmonize with his bandmate. The excellent solo from 2:46 is played by the talented Wayne Perkins in a style not too different from Mick Taylor's. It is amusing and even a little strange to see Ron Wood imitating Wayne's playing in the mimed promo shot by Michael Lindsay-Hogg in June 1981, Woody who would snatch a place in the band virtually out of Wayne's hands . . . Finally, a tambourine can be heard, played in all likelihood by Ollie E. Brown.

TOPS

Mick Jagger / Keith Richards / 3:45

Musicians
Mick Jagger: vocals, maracas (?)
Keith Richards: rhythm guitar
Mick Taylor: lead guitar
Bill Wyman: bass
Charlie Watts: drums
Nicky Hopkins: piano
Recorded
Dynamic Sounds, Kingston, Jamaica:
November 25–December 21, 1972
**EMI Pathé Marconi Studios, Boulogne-
Billancourt, France:** June 27–October 8, 1979
**Rolling Stones Mobile Studio, Paris (precise
location not determined):** April–May 1981
**Atlantic Studios (?), Power Station,
New York City:** May–June 1981
Technical Team
Producers: The Glimmer Twins
Associate producer: Chris Kimsey
Sound engineers: Andy Johns, Chris Kimsey,
Bob Clearmountain, Gary Lyons
Assistant sound engineer: Barry Sage

"Tops" was recorded while Mick Taylor was
still a member of the Stones.

Genesis

The lyrics of "Tops" sound like a satire of the words a manager might address to a young female singer or actress whose career he wants to take in hand. In essence: I will take you to success, to the very top; I will make you a star. There's no need for acting school or the casting couch . . . These words come across all the more convincingly as they are delivered by Mick Jagger, who was extremely well versed in the cutthroat world of show business.

Production

"Tops" is an extremely well-constructed, soulful rock ballad with touches of Motown, above all in Mick Jagger's highly successful combination of falsetto with a deeper, richer voice. He gives an excellent performance that endows the track with a somewhat unexpected depth. The initial takes date from autumn 1972 and Dynamic Sounds Studios in Kingston, when Mick Taylor was still a full member of the Rolling Stones. Although various sources fail to credit him, it seems highly unlikely that his guitar part would have been wiped when the song was reworked for *Tattoo You*. His very lyrical style, with the left-hand vibrato that neither Keith nor Ronnie possessed, can be identified in the subtle voicing of his chords and above all in the solo at around 2:57, toward the end of the track. Mick Taylor is a musician who contributed a huge amount to the group, and his departure is definitely a cause for regret. Similarly, although he is not credited, Nicky Hopkins, who possessed a distinctive, highly lyrical touch not unlike Taylor's, is almost certainly on the piano. As for the rhythm section, it has to be said that Bill and Charlie are a major asset for the Stones, each of the two developing a groove in his own unique way. Keith delivers a good rhythm guitar part, always on the lookout for the ultimate riff, even in this kind of ballad. Finally, maracas can also be heard, most probably played by Jagger. After Kingston, the band reworked "Tops" in France in 1979, and then in 1981, when Mick was given the task of redoing all the vocals himself, before final mixing by Bob Clearmountain in New York. "Tops" is one of the best things on *Tattoo You*, and despite predating it by more than nine years, the song blends perfectly with the overall color and feel of the album.

HEAVEN

Mick Jagger / Keith Richards / 4:21

Musicians
Mick Jagger: vocals, rhythm guitar
Bill Wyman: bass, synthesizer
Charlie Watts: drums
Chris Kimsey: electric piano
Unidentified musicians: chimes, shaker, claves

Recorded
**EMI Pathé Marconi Studios, Boulogne-Billancourt,
France:** October 11–November 12, 1980
**Rolling Stones Mobile Studio, Paris (precise
location not determined):** April–May 1981
**Atlantic Studios, Power Station (?),
New York City:** May–June 1981

Technical Team
Producers: The Glimmer Twins
Associate producer: Chris Kimsey
Sound engineers: Chris Kimsey,
Bob Clearmountain, Gary Lyons
Assistant sound engineer: Barry Sage

Mick Jagger at the Stadio Comunale
Vittorio Pozzo (Turin) in July 1982.

Genesis

This is the second song (the first being "Neighbours") recorded by the Stones in order to add the finishing touches to *Tattoo You*. The recording took place in October 1980 at the Pathé Marconi Studios during a bitterly cold spell in Paris. In spite of Chris Kimsey getting hold of some radiators, this cold penetrated the studio, hence the particular musical atmosphere of the track, which recalls the psychedelic, spaced-out vibe of *Their Satanic Majesties Request*. Hence also the message Mick Jagger seems to want to convey: paradise and sexual ecstasy are one and the same.

Production

With this somewhat Eastern-sounding vibe, "Heaven" could not contrast more strongly with "Start Me Up." For the recording of this track, the Stones were down to three people, helped out by Chris Kimsey, who recalls his musical contribution: I played alleged piano on 'Heaven.' That was laid down with just Charlie, Mick and I, I think. I don't think anyone else was in the room. But the session was called for like midnight and Mick and Charlie were the first to arrive and Mick started playing the chord sequence and I sat down at the piano and started following along and next thing I knew it sounded really good. So I told the assistant to roll it. . . . "[123] The only guitar on the track is therefore played by Mick Jagger. Some sources also mention Bill Wyman, but there is only one guitar, its sound strongly colored by phasing (by means of a flanger?) and very effective delay. It has to be said that Mick does an exceptional job on guitar, demonstrating a keen sense of rhythm. His various vocals, recorded by him alone in the Paris warehouse between April and May 1981, are excellent, with natural-sounding falsettos, and he immerses himself completely in this dreamlike atmosphere with the help of delay and phasing, the result bearing a certain resemblance to John Lennon's solo work. Charlie Watts delivers a very good beat, calling to mind a drum machine, but with that groove that ensures he could never be mistaken for an automated sound. Bill creates layers of synthesizer with various electronic effects, and also plays the bass part on the synth, reinforcing Charlie's beat. Chris is on electric piano, which he plays with vibrato, and finally a range of percussion instruments can be heard, including chimes, a shaker, and claves.

After several years' service, Ron Wood finally earned his stripes with a co-writing credit for "No Use in Crying."

NO USE IN CRYING

Mick Jagger / Keith Richards / Ron Wood / 3:24

Musicians
Mick Jagger: vocals
Keith Richards: rhythm guitar, backing vocals
Bill Wyman: bass
Charlie Watts: drums
Ron Wood: rhythm guitar, backing vocals (?)
Ian Stewart: piano and/or organ (?)
Nicky Hopkins: piano and/or organ (?)

Recorded
EMI Pathé Marconi Studios, Boulogne-Billancourt, France: June 27–October 8, 1979
Rolling Stones Mobile Studio, Paris (precise location not determined): April–May 1981
Atlantic Studios (?), Power Station, New York City: May–June 1981

Technical Team
Producers: The Glimmer Twins
Associate producer: Chris Kimsey
Sound engineers: Chris Kimsey, Bob Clearmountain, Gary Lyons
Assistant sound engineer: Barry Sage

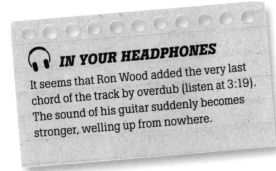

IN YOUR HEADPHONES
It seems that Ron Wood added the very last chord of the track by overdub (listen at 3:19). The sound of his guitar suddenly becomes stronger, welling up from nowhere.

Genesis
"No Use in Crying" is one of the tracks laid down during the second phase of recording for *Emotional Rescue*, which extended from the end of June to the beginning of August 1979. Once again, Ron Wood is credited as co-writer, along with Mick Jagger and Keith Richards. This song is the story of a relationship that has just ended. A young woman abandoned by her lover hopes against hope that he will come back. She sees his face everywhere, but *it's not real*. There is no point in weeping; he is not coming back. The refrain speaks volumes: *It's not me, stay away from me*. This is a subject borrowed directly from the originators of the blues. "No Use in Crying" has never been performed live by the Rolling Stones.

Production
For the penultimate track on *Tattoo You*, the Stones offer up a new blues-rock ballad, this time with a touch of soul. "No Use in Crying" is nothing if not emotional, and Jagger endeavors to give a strong performance while allowing a certain timorous fragility to show through . . . He employs a range of effects, reaching into his bag of "soul man" intonations for, among other things, his falsetto voice, which is far less successful this time than on "Heaven." Although Mick doubles and even triples himself in the refrains, Keith's voice can be heard supporting him. The latter accompanies the track with a very good guitar part, once again colored by his MXR (stereo left). Ronnie, meanwhile, seems to play two rhythm parts, probably on his Fender Stratocaster, unfortunately with less than impeccable tuning and timing, as is evident above all in his arpeggios. He also uses a little too much phasing (flanger?) on his guitars, which ultimately muddies the sound a little. Charlie delivers a good drum part, using his ride cymbal in the verses, which, moreover, display a melodic similarity to "Time Is on My Side" (1965). This track also reserves a nice part for the piano. Although this seems to be the work of Nicky Hopkins (albeit without his usual touch or lyricism), it could equally be Ian Stewart. The same goes for the organ that can be heard at the end of the song, from 2:43.

WAITING ON A FRIEND

Mick Jagger / Keith Richards / 4:34

Musicians
Mick Jagger: vocals
Keith Richards: electric rhythm guitar,
acoustic guitar, backing vocals
Bill Wyman: bass
Charlie Watts: drums
Mick Taylor (?): guitar
Nicky Hopkins: piano
Sonny Rollins: saxophone
Mike Carabello: percussion
Kasper Winding (?): tambourine
Recorded
Dynamic Sounds, Kingston, Jamaica:
November 25–December 21, 1972
**Rolling Stones Mobile Studio, Rotterdam, the
Netherlands:** January 22–February 9, 1975 (?)
**EMI Pathé Marconi Studios, Boulogne-Billancourt,
France:** October 11–November 12, 1980
**Rolling Stones Mobile Studio, Paris (precise
location not determined):** April–May 1981
**Atlantic Studios (?), Power Station,
New York City:** May–June 1981
Technical Team
Producers: The Glimmer Twins
Associate producer: Chris Kimsey
Sound engineers: Andy Johns, Chris Kimsey,
Bob Clearmountain, Gary Lyons
Assistant sound engineer: Barry Sage

An alternative interpretation of "Waiting on
a Friend" is possible: might the friend in
question be Keith's dealer?

FOR STONES ADDICTS

In the video by Michael Lindsay-Hogg, one of the three Rastas sitting on the stoop just below Mick Jagger is none other than Peter Tosh. They are in front of an entrance at 96–98 St. Mark's Place, New York City, the same building that appears on the cover of the extremely famous *Physical Graffiti* by Led Zeppelin in 1975.

Genesis

Keith Richards: "'Waiting on a Friend' is one of those songs that you write sometimes, and when you hear it back you say, 'What was that really about?' At one level it's just a nice song and I don't think there's ever any pointed meanings."[9]

Mick Jagger takes a markedly different view. For him, "Waiting on a Friend," which dates from the *Goats Head Soup* sessions, is a reflection on friendship, as he explains in the booklet to the compilation *Jump Back*: "We all liked it at the time but we didn't have any lyrics, so there we were. As well as the vocal, we stuck on that amazing sax solo at the end by Sonny Rollins. The lyric I added is very gentle and loving, about friendships in the band."[87] The refrain says it all: *I'm not waiting on a lady/I'm just waiting on a friend*. Just like Michael Lindsay-Hogg's video, in fact, which shows Mick Jagger and Keith Richards meeting up outside a New York City apartment building and going to a bar where Bill Wyman, Charlie Watts, and Ron Wood have already congregated.

"Waiting on a Friend" was the A-side of the second single from *Tattoo You*. Released on November 27 and 30, 1981 (coupled with "Little T&A"), it reached number 13 in the United States and the Netherlands, but only made it to number 50 in the United Kingdom.

Production

Chris Kimsey deserves praise for resurrecting this superb ballad, which came out of the band's 1972 sessions in Jamaica, in other words nine years before its official release! Whether an ode to friendship or not, it is imbued with an atmosphere of gentleness and good humor that ensures it is a pleasure to listen to, all the more so as it dates from a time when relations within the band, and above all between the Glimmer Twins, were beginning to sour. Keith strums the intro on electric guitar, with that light phasing that had become ever-present. It also seems to be Keith on acoustic guitar, which can be heard best around 3:52. In the 1972 version, Mick Taylor was also on guitar, as Charlie Watts recalls: "On 'Waiting on a Friend' he went into that Santana style of playing. It was incredible, and it really worked."[9]

However, unlike in "Tops," Taylor's guitar has completely disappeared from the final mix, only to be replaced by the extraordinary Sonny Rollins, who plays two extremely good

Mick Jagger and Keith Richards during the shooting of the "Waiting on a Friend" video.

solos (1:55 and 3:27), with an incredible sound and incredible phrasing, the effectiveness of the whole raised even higher through the addition of delay and strong reverb. To turn to the rhythm section, Charlie establishes a subtle groove that is simple sounding but highly effective. He is accompanied on bass by Bill, whose playing is equally precise and solid. They are supported by various percussion instruments, in all likelihood played by Mike Carabello: bongos, claves, a güiro, and what is probably a cabasa or shaker. The name of Kasper Winding is sometimes put forward for the tambourine, but there is no such instrument on this track, unless it is buried in the mix. Another element that contributes greatly to the charm of "Waiting on a Friend" is the superb piano of Nicky Hopkins, whose playing leaves no doubt about the identity of the pianist. Mick Jagger gives an excellent performance, radiating a freshness and sincerity that lead one to suspect that he was by no means indifferent to what he was singing. "Waiting on a Friend" brings *Tattoo You* to a very fine close.

SIDE A
1982

GOIN' TO A GO-GO (LIVE)

Smokey Robinson, Pete Moore, Bobby Rogers, Marvin Tarplin / 3:23

SINGLE
"Goin' to a Go Go" (live) / "Beast of Burden" (live)
RELEASE DATE
United Kingdom: June 2, 1982
Label: Rolling Stones Records
RECORD NUMBER: ROLLING STONES RECORDS RSR 110

Musicians
Mick Jagger: vocals
Keith Richards: rhythm guitar, backing vocals
Bill Wyman: bass
Charlie Watts: drums
Ron Wood: rhythm guitar
Ian Stewart: piano
Ian McLagan: keyboards, backing vocals
Ernie Watts: saxophone
Recorded
Capital Centre, Largo, Maryland: December 9, 1981
Technical Team
Producers: The Glimmer Twins
Sound engineers: Malcolm Pollack, Barry Bongiovi, Larry Alexander, Phil Gitomer, Kooster McAllister, David Brown, Bob Ludwig
Control room: Bob Clearmountain, David Hewitt

Genesis
"Goin' to a Go-Go" is a song written by Smokey Robinson and the other members of the Miracles: Pete Moore, Bobby Rogers, and Marv Tarplin. It was recorded by Tamla-Motown's flagship act, with Claudette Robinson (Smokey's wife) on backing vocals and the Funk Brothers accompanying, in August 1965. The single was released on December 6 and it hit number 11 on the *Billboard* pop chart on February 12, 1966. The song also gave its name to an album that went on sale in November 1965, the first under the name Smokey Robinson & The Miracles.

"Goin' to a Go-Go" refers to go-go music, a form of soul-derived dance music that was all the rage in the clubs of Washington in the mid-sixties and whose most famous proponent was Chuck Brown. "Goin' to a Go-Go" was added to the Rolling Stones catalog sixteen years after the Miracles' version, more specifically during their 1981 US tour. The London quintet and their sidemen performed the song for the first time at the Freedom Hall in Louisville, Kentucky, on November 3. It was later selected as the A-side of the first single from the live album *Still Life* (released June 1, 1982) with "Beast of Burden" as the flip side. "Goin' to a Go-Go" made it to number 25 on the *Billboard* chart (July 17, 1982) and number 26 in the United Kingdom (June 26, 1982).

Production
When all is said and done, the Stones version is pretty close to that of Smokey Robinson and his Miracles, although the Motown R&B vibe has inevitably given way to a heavier, more rock beat. This is mainly due to Charlie Watts, who smacks

The five Rolling Stones still in Olympic form . . .

his snare drum and toms with considerable force, and Bill Wyman on bass. The two of them steer the band toward a more English, more aggressive interpretation of the song, while still retaining something of a soul feel. Keith Richards attacks the song with a distorted, catchy rhythm guitar that is answered by Ron Wood. The weaving of the two guitars embodies the guitar aesthetic of the king of the riff, a playing style developed in conjunction with Brian Jones during the early days of the band. Mick Jagger assures the success of the live performance as usual, confirming his status as an exceptional rock singer. As for the two keyboards, the sound recording does not really do them justice. This is by no means the case with the talented Ernie Watts, however, who delivers a superb saxophone solo.

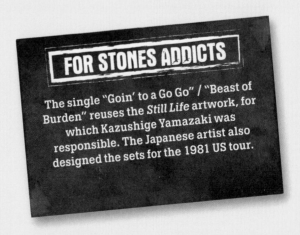

FOR STONES ADDICTS

The single "Goin' to a Go Go" / "Beast of Burden" reuses the *Still Life* artwork, for which Kazushige Yamazaki was responsible. The Japanese artist also designed the sets for the 1981 US tour.

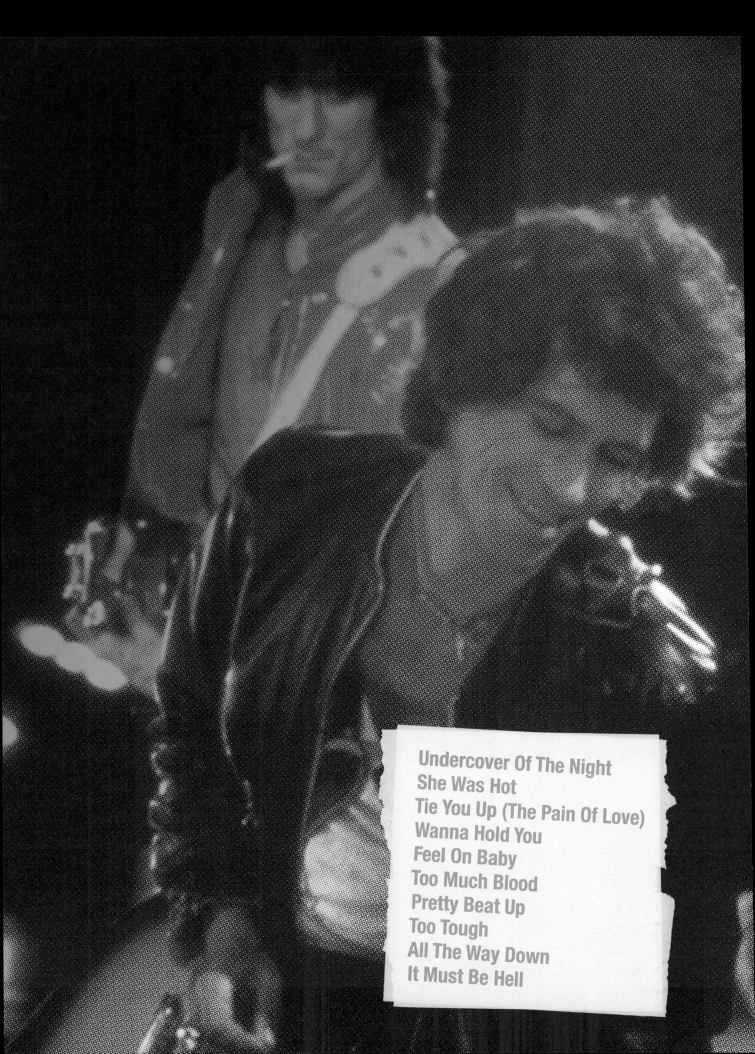

Undercover Of The Night
She Was Hot
Tie You Up (The Pain Of Love)
Wanna Hold You
Feel On Baby
Too Much Blood
Pretty Beat Up
Too Tough
All The Way Down
It Must Be Hell

ALBUM
RELEASE DATE
United Kingdom: November 7, 1983
Label: Rolling Stones Records
RECORD NUMBER: ROLLING STONES
RECORDS CUN 1654361
Number 3, on the charts for 18 weeks

UNDER-
COVER

UNDERCOVER: LET'S DANCE?

1983

The European tour that kicked off in Aberdeen (Scotland) on May 26, 1982, and closed in Leeds (England) on July 25, having passed through West Berlin (June 8), Paris (June 13 and 14), Madrid (July 7 and 9), and Turin (July 11 and 12), was a resounding success. This did not prevent the emergence of musical differences between the Glimmer Twins, however. While Keith Richards wished to return to the Stones' brand of pure, hard blues rock, Mick Jagger wanted to explore in greater depth some of the new paths embarked upon over the previous albums, to embrace the latest trends even more strongly.

The Album

Undercover, the sessions for which started a few months after the end of this European tour, offers a perfect illustration of the gulf that had opened up between the two songwriters. On the one hand, it includes songs that fall into the good old Rolling Stones tradition, such as "She Was Hot," "Too Tough," "All the Way Down," "Wanna Hold You," and "It Must Be Hell." On the other, it comprises numbers that effectively widen the horizons of the London band. "Undercover of the Night" and "Tie You Up (The Pain of Love)" reveal a strong new wave influence, while "Feel on Baby" unfolds to a sensual reggae beat, and "Too Much Blood" provides Mick Jagger with an opportunity to try his hand at rap. "Pretty Beat Up," meanwhile, owes a lot to Ron Wood and sounds a little like "Hot Stuff"—in other words it is one for the dance floor.

In terms of the lyrics, the Stones' view of the world is not especially heartening. The impulse for this comes from Mick Jagger: he is the one who ventures into political terrain. In "Undercover of the Night," for example, written a few months after the Falklands War (April–June 1982), he points an accusatory finger at the military juntas in power in Argentina and Chile, filling their prisons with innocent victims, while in "It Must Be Hell" he has another kind of dictatorial regime in his sights: communism, which continued to hold the USSR and its satellite states beneath a suffocating leaden blanket nearly forty years after the end of the Second World War. The Stones singer also drew inspiration for his lyrics from the notion that modern society had lost its way: while "Too Much Blood" is based on a terrifying news story concerning a Japanese cannibal in Paris, in "Tie You Up (The Pain of Love)" he immerses himself in the equally dark world of sadomasochism. Nor is the message of "All the Way Down," which charts the falling apart of a relationship over the course of the years, exactly cheerful. Fortunately, there is also the occasional flash of humor and self-mockery, as in the scorching "She Was Hot," in which the five musicians are given a hard time by a voluptuous woman of boundless erotic power. On a far more sensitive and emotional level, "Wanna Hold You" is a romantic ballad Keith Richards–style, the guitarist having undergone a thorough transformation since Patti Hansen entered his life.

The Dawning of the MTV Era

Undercover, the first real Stones album of the MTV era, marks a turning point in the career of the band, as indicated by the care they lavished on the production of the videos that

Muddy Waters,
the Stones'
mentor.

accompanied several of the songs on the album. Entrusted to Julien Temple, the director of *The Great Rock 'n' Roll Swindle*, the documentary about the Sex Pistols that had come out two years earlier, these videos conform to the dictates of the television era, which demanded the production of shocking images.

Thus *Undercover* was released into the world on the back of these startling images on November 7, 1983. Number 1 in Sweden and number 2 in Canada and New Zealand, the Stones' seventeenth (British) studio album reached third place in the United Kingdom and Australia and fourth place in the United States (where it would be certified platinum). It was clearly a success, but was it a musical triumph? It has to be acknowledged that some rock critics were disappointed and some fans began to wonder—and worry—about the direction in which their favorite band was going. Kurt Loder provided a spot-on analysis of the situation in the columns of *Rolling Stone*: "If there are disappointments on *Undercover*, they can only be claimed in comparison to past Stones triumphs. If the album lacks the epochal impact of, say, *Sticky Fingers*, then perhaps it's because the mythic years of pop are past—by now, even the Stones have long since bade them goodbye."[124]

The Album Cover

Undercover was the fourth album cover to be designed for the Rolling Stones by Peter Corriston. The cover photo is by Hubert Kretzschmar (as was that of *Tattoo You*). The visuals created by Corriston and Kretzschmar are resolutely pop art. A naked woman whose face cannot be properly made out stands upright in a provocative pose before a blue lamé drape. Her breasts and private parts are covered by superimposed images: the title of the album with a portrait of the five Stones covering the first, and a simple multicolored triangle over the

second. Other images adorn the cover here and there (an eye, another portrait of the five musicians), while the name of the band runs across the top in red letters. The back cover features the same blue drape and the posterior of the top model who took part in the shoot. It is worth mentioning that in the case of the original vinyl album, these superimposed images were stickers that could actually be peeled off!

The Recording

Undercover was the first Rolling Stones album on which a producer was given equal status with the Glimmer Twins, Chris Kimsey up to then having merely been credited as the associate producer. With the exception of "Wanna Hold You" and "She Was Hot," the demos for which seem to have been made in a small eight-track studio in Paris (or the surrounding region) that has not been identified, the sessions for *Undercover* took place at the Pathé Marconi Studios in Boulogne-Billancourt.

The atmosphere was disastrous. "It must have been pretty bad for anyone around us who worked on *Undercover*," admits Keith. "A hostile, discordant atmosphere. We were barely talking or communicating, and if we were, we were bickering and sniping."[2] He goes on to explain that Mick would record between midday and 5 p.m., and he would record between midnight and 5 a.m. so that the two of them could avoid each other. The main reason for this conflict that seemed to be threatening the very existence of the group? Mick Jagger's tendency to dominate everyone. "Mick had developed an overriding desire to control everything. As far as he was concerned, it was Mick Jagger and them,"[2] explains Keith. And then there was a profound musical disagreement, as he noticed in the studio in Paris: "Coming back after a few months apart, I realized that Mick's taste in music had often changed quite drastically.

He wanted to lay on me the latest hit he heard at a disco . . . At the time we were doing *Undercover* in 1983, he was just trying to out-disco everybody."[2] For the king of the riff, this was clearly treason. Relations between the two became so tense that Ron Wood had to calm things down: "There was a terrible tension around and it's where I had to assume my diplomatic role a lot."[9] He also observes that there was a blatant imbalance between the Glimmer Twins: "Keith didn't have many songs on *Undercover*."[9] This left Jagger as much latitude as he wanted to develop his. "On *Undercover* I had been more or less in the hands of Mick, who would come in with his skeleton of a song, which we would then work with."[9]

In spite of this bleak picture, the Stones still found the energy to work, and the record was eventually made in a reasonably satisfactory fashion. Thus from mid-November to mid-December 1982, the following songs (including the two demos) were recorded: "Pretty Beat Up," "All the Way Down," "She Was Hot," "Tie You Up (The Pain of Love)," "Too Tough," "It Must Be Hell," and "Too Much Blood," as well as various other songs that were later abandoned. Finally, "Feel on Baby" and "Undercover of the Night" were cut. The overdubs and mixing were done a little later, between May and the beginning of August at Compass Point Studios in Nassau (Bahamas) and at the Hit Factory in New York City.

As before, the Rolling Stones were joined by a variety of additional musicians, according to the requirements of the song. Robbie Shakespeare (bass) and Sly Dunbar (drums), who had been Jamaica's most effective rhythm section since their collaborations with U-Roy, Max Romeo, Dennis Brown (and also Serge Gainsbourg), contribute to the distinctly reggae "Feel on Baby," while Sly Dunbar lends a hand by himself on "Undercover of the Night" and "Too Much Blood." The pianist Chuck Leavell, who had been a member of the Allman Brothers Band at the beginning of the seventies, plays on every song on the album except "Pretty Beat Up," which has Ian Stewart on piano, and "She Was Hot," while the saxophonist David Sanborn, a herald of closer relations between blues, rock, and jazz musicians, took part in the recording of "Pretty Beat Up." Other musicians can also be heard on the album: Moustapha Cisse (Jean-Luc Ponty), Brahms Coundoul, and Martin Ditcham (Chris Rea, Sade, Roger Daltrey) on percussion, the Stones' technical manager and standby guitarist Jim Barber (who would later play on Mick Jagger's solo albums), and finally the formidable horn section CHOPS (Parliament, Bob Dylan, Jamiroquai).

Helping Chris Kimsey with the engineering was Brian McGee (Brian Ferry, Blue Öyster Cult, Cyndi Lauper). New assistant sound engineers also made an appearance on this album: Rod Thear (who had already worked on *It's Only Rock 'N' Roll*), Steve Lipson (Frankie Goes to Hollywood, Simple Minds, Annie Lennox), John Davenport (a onetime songwriter for Elvis Presley!), Bobby Cohen (Julian Lennon, U2, Foreigner), and Benji Armbrister (AC/DC, Robert Palmer, the B-52s).

The Instruments

For the most part, the same instruments were used on this album as on *Tattoo You*. However, a number of new guitars belonging to Ron Wood seem to have popped up in the studio, notably a 1957 Gretsch White Falcon and a 1958 Mary Kaye Stratocaster (which before long Ronnie would give to Keith). Keith would later report that he used mainly old Telecasters for electric work and old Martins or certain Gibsons, particularly Hummingbirds, for acoustic work.

UNDERCOVER OF THE NIGHT

Mick Jagger / Keith Richards / 4:31

Musicians
Mick Jagger: vocals, rhythm guitar (?)
Keith Richards: rhythm guitar (?)
Bill Wyman: bass (?)
Charlie Watts: drums, timpani (?)
Ron Wood: rhythm and lead guitar
Chuck Leavell: keyboards
Sly Dunbar: Simmons drums, cowbell (?)

Recorded
**EMI Pathé Marconi Studios, Boulogne-Billancourt,
France:** January 31–mid-March 1983
Compass Point Studios, Nassau, Bahamas: May–June 1983
The Hit Factory, New York City: May, end of June–
beginning of August 1983

Technical Team
Producers: the Glimmer Twins, Chris Kimsey
Sound engineers: Chris Kimsey, Brian McGee
Assistant sound engineers: Rod Thear, Steve Lipson,
John Davenport, Bobby Cohen, Benji Armbrister

The dandy of rock 'n' roll was inspired to write this
song by the Beat writer William S. Burroughs.

Genesis

Mick Jagger wrote most of "Undercover of the Night" in Paris in early 1983, at the beginning of the recording sessions for *Undercover*. The singer acknowledges that part of his inspiration came from *Cities of the Red Night* by William S. Burroughs, a freewheeling novel about politics and sexual repression in which the cult writer of the Beat Generation muddles time frames, characters, and places, and asserts that the only way to achieve real liberation is through sex and drugs. In his song, Jagger intersperses references to what was happening at the time in Argentina and Chile, where the military juntas were in power, creating a sinister, realistic depiction of South America. *The opposition's tongue is cut in two; one hundred thousand disparus lost in the jails of South America.* He then turns the spotlight on the military, whether US, Cuban, or Russian, who, after nightfall, take advantage of the *girls painted blue* in the bars, an army rabble attracted by *the smell of sex, the smell of suicide* . . . Jagger appraises his song in the *Jump Back* booklet: "I think it's really good but it wasn't particularly successful at the time because songs that deal overtly with politics never are that successful, for some reason."[87] "Undercover of the Night" (with "All the Way Down" as the B-side) was released as a single on November 1, 1983. Nineteen days later it peaked at number 11 on the British charts, and on December 24 at number 9 on the *Billboard* chart.

Production

Mick Jagger wrote "Undercover of the Night" with the help of Ron Wood. Keith Richards played little part in it: "Mick had this one all mapped out, I just played on it. There were a lot more overlays on this track, because there was a lot more separation in the way we were recording at that time. Mick and I had started to come to loggerheads."[87] In reality, Keith would never really like this song, which is a surprise because it possesses an untamed rock feel that the Stones had not had for a long time. In the early versions, Mick can be heard on acoustic guitar, Charlie on timpani, and Ronnie on electric guitar. The latter retains a good memory of this format: "There was a great percussive and acoustic version, which is the kind of song it should be, really."[9] However, studio work got in the way and the number ended up taking a very different form, a combination of electronic music and pure rock 'n' roll. Sly Dunbar attacks the

The conflict between Mick and Keith seems obvious even onstage, in this case at Feyenoord Stadium (Rotterdam) on June 2, 1982.

intro with an electric drum set that was the height of fashion in 1983, the famous Simmons electronic drums, popularized by bands such as Spandau Ballet and Depeche Mode. He accompanies Charlie Watts throughout the track with breaks and electronic effects, which, surprisingly enough, in no way detract from the final results. Charlie delivers a superb drum part that is a mix of dance music and rock, with bass drum on every beat. It also seems to be Charlie on timpani.

The other powerhouse on this track is Bill Wyman, who plays an excellent, funky bass line with a pronounced swing. Some have suggested that it is not Bill, but Robbie Shakespeare, and it is certainly true that in places the bass is played slap (listen around 1:06), a technique rarely employed by Bill. To this day, however, there is nothing to disprove that it is Bill, and the Stones bassist has shown in the past that he is good at adapting to different styles, as on "Miss You."

Another key element on "Undercover of the Night" are the riffs played most probably by Keith Richards, apparently in standard tuning. His sound is beyond dispute, as is his playing, but some commentators nevertheless maintain that Mick is responsible. This does not seem particularly likely. He was on acoustic guitar in the early versions, and although he plays electric onstage (in open-G tuning), he is far from capable

of achieving this particular sound. There is just one niggling detail: Keith does not play these riffs in concert, but merely supports Mick, so perhaps after all . . . ? There can be no doubt about Ronnie on the second guitar, however, playing both rhythm and solo. His interplay with the first guitar is perfect: this is one of his strong points, indeed the aspect of his work that makes him the ideal partner for Keith. Chuck Leavell, whom we hear for the first time on the album, is on keyboard, notably organ in the intro. Finally, Mick Jagger dominates the track with his aggressive but at the same time subtle rock voice, and although he cannot stop himself from "going falsetto" at times, his performance is one of his best on the album.

"Undercover of the Night" owes a good part of its success to the editing and mixing of the incredible Chris Kimsey, who has added a number of electronic effects (phasing, delay, reverse reverb, etc.) to the voices as well as to the guitars and percussion, but without ever allowing these effects to dominate the music. The proof is that although a lot of the music from this period sounds dated as a result of its excessively artificial and synthetic sonorities, "Undercover of the Night" retains all its original freshness, making it probably the last great Stones song to this day.

SHE WAS HOT

Mick Jagger / Keith Richards / 4:40

Musicians
Mick Jagger: vocals
Keith Richards: rhythm and lead guitar
Bill Wyman: bass
Charlie Watts: drums
Ron Wood: rhythm guitar
Ian Stewart: piano
Chuck Leavell: keyboards
Recorded
**EMI Pathé Marconi Studios, Boulogne-Billancourt,
France:** November 11–December 19, 1982
**Compass Point Studios, Nassau,
Bahamas:** May–June 1983 (?)
The Hit Factory, New York City: May, end of June–
beginning of August 1983
Technical Team
Producers: the Glimmer Twins, Chris Kimsey
Sound engineers: Chris Kimsey, Brian McGee
Assistant sound engineers: Rod Thear, Steve Lipson,
John Davenport, Bobby Cohen, Benji Armbrister

The actress Anita Morris raises the Stones'
temperature in the "She Was Hot" video.

Genesis

Mick Jagger is in his New York City hotel room, bored to death. All of a sudden, a voluptuous, smoldering creature dressed all in red appears before him. *She was hot as she kissed my mouth,* he sings. Next it is Keith Richards's turn to see the woman and be knocked off his feet. Bottle of Jack Daniel's in hand, the guitarist's agitation causes the thermometer to explode . . . Julien Temple's video lives up to the Glimmer Twins' song in every way, combining humor and eroticism against a rock 'n' roll backdrop every bit as hot as the kiss. And Mick Jagger comes out with one of his finest verses: *Down the avenue into the lost bayou/Into the tall bamboo, back to the human zoo/I wish you all the best, I hope we meet again/In a cold Chicago night.*

"She Was Hot" was the A-side of the second single from *Undercover* (with "I Think I'm Going Mad" as the B-side). The song only made it to number 42 in the United Kingdom (in February 1984).

Production

After "She's So Cold" in 1980, the Stones now bring us "She Was Hot," a terrific rock song that represents a return of sorts to the Chuck Berry tradition. Keith opens the track with a guitar intro in rockabilly style, vaguely reminiscent of the Stray Cats, and again with analog delay courtesy of his MXR. The band is in gear and gets off to a flying start, Charlie in the vanguard with some particularly muscular drumming. He smacks his snare drum forcefully and establishes a powerful swing, supported by some excellent bass playing from Bill, who seems to take real pleasure in returning to a simple rock groove. Interestingly, he can be seen holding an upright bass in Julien Temple's video. Ron Wood is on second rhythm guitar, and Chuck Leavell on electric piano. The latter brings a—not exactly indispensable—eighties flavor to each of the refrains with some dubious-sounding digital keyboard that is highly characteristic of this period. Thankfully, the fantastic Stu relights the flame with a superb boogie-woogie piano part from 1:10 on. The one and only solo is played by Keith in his own inimitable style, with tremendous feeling. Mick is excellent, rock 'n' roll and irony becoming a kind of trademark of his, and he can be heard doubling and tripling himself in the refrains.

TIE YOU UP (THE PAIN OF LOVE)

Mick Jagger / Keith Richards / 4:16

Musicians
Mick Jagger: vocals
Keith Richards: rhythm guitar, backing vocals
Charlie Watts: drums
Ron Wood: rhythm and lead guitar (?), bass, backing vocals
Chuck Leavell: electric piano, organ
Moustapha Cisse [?], Brahms Coundoul [?], Martin Ditcham [?], Sly Dunbar [?]): percussion

Recorded
EMI Pathé Marconi Studios, Boulogne-Billancourt, France: November 11–December 19, 1982
Compass Point Studios, Nassau, Bahamas: May–June 1983 (?)
The Hit Factory, New York City: May, end of June–beginning of August 1983

Technical Team
Producers: the Glimmer Twins, Chris Kimsey
Sound engineers: Chris Kimsey, Brian McGee
Assistant sound engineers: Rod Thear, Steve Lipson, John Davenport, Bobby Cohen, Benji Armbrister

Chuck Leavell was a member of the Allman Brothers Band and then Sea Level before working with the Stones.

Genesis

The Rolling Stones raise the curtain on a sadomasochistic stage. *Feel the prickles running up and down your back*: here we are dealing with the *pain of love* . . . And the picture is all the more sexy for being dark and morally taboo. *The old maid is rouging up, applying final touches. Even though she's late for the dance, I tell you tonight she's really gonna have a ball, she's gonna really tie me up*: "Tie You Up (The Pain of Love)" or Mick Jagger ready for the supreme sacrifice . . . Is it possible to see the shadow of Marianne Faithfull, the great-great-niece of the writer Leopold von Sacher-Masoch, who gave his name to masochism, hanging over this song?

As far as its musical ambiance is concerned, the song bears a resemblance to Lowell Fulson's West Coast blues, as Jagger would later corroborate in an interview. To date, "Tie You Up (The Pain of Love)" has never been performed live.

Production

This song does indeed recall the groove of certain Fulson tracks, such as "Tramp," but imbued with the energy of the Rolling Stones, who in no way hold back here. "Tie You Up (The Pain of Love)" is an excellent blues-rock number—with shades of the eighties that do the band's reputation no harm whatsoever. Charlie lays down a good rhythm, supported on bass by Ron Wood, whose playing is nevertheless a touch too guitaristic. Ronnie is also, most probably, on lead guitar, while at the same time providing a high-quality accompaniment combining, as is his custom, rhythm with solo phrases. He can be heard making frequent use of his whammy bar, which Keith rarely touches. Ronnie delivers a wonderful solo at 1:40, and it seems to be him playing the superb lick at the end of the track, at 4:04. This would mean that Keith is playing the second rhythm guitar with the strongly distorted sound. Chuck Leavell is on electric piano, probably a Wurlitzer, but also does some inspired and highly effective work on the organ. Mick relishes his provocative lyrics, which he delivers in a powerful, energetic voice, supported on backing vocals presumably by Keith and Ronnie. From 3:03, however, he is left on his own. The rhythm section is complemented by a number of percussion instruments, notably a tom sound at 2:25, which seems to be produced by a Simmons drum, but also congas and a cowbell, which can be heard toward the end of the track.

WANNA HOLD YOU

Mick Jagger / Keith Richards / 3:52

<u>Musicians</u>
Keith Richards: vocals, rhythm guitar
Charlie Watts: drums
Ron Wood: rhythm and lead guitar, bass, backing vocals
<u>Recorded</u>
Unknown studio, Paris: October 1982
EMI Pathé Marconi Studios, Boulogne-Billancourt,
France: November 11–December 19, 1982
Compass Point Studios, Nassau,
Bahamas: May–June 1983 (?)
The Hit Factory, New York City: May, end of June–
beginning of August 1983
<u>Technical Team</u>
Producers: the Glimmer Twins, Chris Kimsey
Sound engineers: Chris Kimsey, Brian McGee
Assistant sound engineers: Rod Thear, Steve Lipson,
John Davenport, Bobby Cohen, Benji Armbrister

Keith Richards and his new girlfriend, Patti Hansen.
"Wanna Hold You" is dedicated to her.

FOR STONES ADDICTS

"Wanna Hold You" would assume a bigger profile in concert, as, for example, at the December 12, 1997, show at the Trans World Dome in St. Louis, Missouri, where the textures were skillfully enhanced by a horn section (with Bobby Keys) and backing singers.

Genesis

Keith Richards wrote "Wanna Hold You" in Paris, in a little eight-track studio that he rented from a friend around October 1982. Mick Jagger went to visit him on two or three nights, and thus the song was born, with Keith singing and playing guitar, and Mick on drums.

I wanna hold you; I hope you find it funny that I got no money, but if you stick with me, you're gonna get some love for free . . . Keith Richards adopts his finest voice to declare his love to his new beloved. After Anita Pallenberg, with whom he had a relationship that was simultaneously passionate and destructive, Patti Hansen entered the life of the guitarist and Stones songwriter at Studio 54 in March 1979—the seventeenth, to be precise. In January 1980, Keith wrote in his diary: "Incredibly I've found a woman. A miracle! I've pussy at the snap of a finger but I've met a woman!"[2] Patti and Keith would get married on December 18, 1983 (the rock star's fortieth birthday!), a month and a half after the release of *Undercover*.

Production

Keith is in love, and sings about it with great sincerity. He would later explain in an interview that the title of his song references "I Want to Hold Your Hand" by the Beatles, and that its structure resembles that of the early Lennon-McCartney numbers. However, he also provides assurance that his own signature is immediately identifiable and that apart from the harmonies and refrains, his song owes nobody anything. It is probably on one of his Telecaster 5-strings in open G that he launches "Wanna Hold You." He establishes an exhilarating rhythm supported by the excellent and imperturbable Charlie, who discharges his metronomic responsibilities to perfection. Ron Wood is on bass, which is unfortunately a little undermixed. Ronnie also looks after the second rhythm guitar part, which is strongly colored by phasing, and plays a number of solo phases after 2:14, presumably on a Fender Stratocaster. The two guitarists share the backing vocals and it looks as if Mick plays no part at all in this number. Please note: there is no synthesizer on Keith's song . . .

1983

FEEL ON BABY

Mick Jagger / Keith Richards / 5:03

Musicians
Mick Jagger: vocals, harmonica
Keith Richards: rhythm guitar, backing vocals
Charlie Watts: drums
Ron Wood: rhythm guitar
Chuck Leavell: keyboards
Robbie Shakespeare: bass
Sly Dunbar: Simmons drums, percussion (?)
Moustapha Cisse [?], Brahms Coundoul [?],
Martin Ditcham [?]): percussion, backing vocals
Recorded
EMI Pathé Marconi Studios, Boulogne-Billancourt,
France: January 31–mid-March 1983
Compass Point Studios, Nassau, Bahamas: May–June 1983
The Hit Factory, New York City: May, end of June–
beginning of August 1983
Technical Team
Producers: the Glimmer Twins, Chris Kimsey
Sound engineers: Chris Kimsey, Brian McGee
Assistant sound engineers: Rod Thear, Steve Lipson,
John Davenport, Bobby Cohen, Benji Armbrister

FOR STONES ADDICTS

There are two versions of "Feel on Baby":
the one on the album and a 6:31
instrumental dub version originally
released as a 12-inch single.

Genesis

Following some tentative incursions into reggae with "Luxury" (on *It's Only Rock 'N' Roll*) and "Cherry Oh Baby" (on *Black and Blue*), this time the Rolling Stones really get to the heart of the matter. Under the aegis of Keith Richards, who has never tried to conceal the influence an artist like Max Romeo has had on him, "Feel on Baby" is 100 percent Jamaican in spirit. And this influence is legitimized by the presence of bassist Robbie Shakespeare and drummer Sly Dunbar, who, together, constituted the most famous, most acclaimed rhythm section in Jamaica. The lyrics concern a young woman whose sultry charms are redolent of the Caribbean: *From the first time, such a crush, such excitement, such a rush, in the kitchen, in the car, in the ditch on the dirty floor.* "Feel on Baby" has never been performed live.

Production

This Stones-crafted reggae is one of three songs on the album that were not recorded until 1983. As with "Undercover of the Night," Sly Dunbar opens the track on his Simmons drums, with their highly distinctive sound. Various percussion instruments immediately join in, such as a tambourine, bongos, a wood block, and a güiro. Keith plays a rhythm guitar with emphatic phasing, and out of the distance comes the heartfelt cry "Feel on Baby." This is immediately taken up by the backing vocalists, probably Mick, Ronnie, and no doubt various other musicians who happened to be present in the studio. Although not credited on the album, Robbie Shakespeare seems to be on bass, finding an impressive groove that alone encapsulates all the rhythm of the track. Charlie provides support, but in truth reggae is not really his thing. Nevertheless, he acquits himself honorably enough. Ronnie is on second rhythm guitar, Chuck Leavell on keyboards, including a bravura performance on the organ, and Mick makes some excellent interjections on a harmonica boosted by a very long delay that is entirely in keeping with the genre, but with a distorted sound that is more Chicago than Kingston. His voice is perfectly adapted to the steamy atmosphere of the number, and the mixing, which makes liberal use of various effects, such as delays and very long reverbs, makes the whole thing utterly credible. This time the Stones have immersed themselves completely in reggae, and the results speak for themselves.

Sly Dunbar and Robbie Shakespeare, Jamaica's most
impressive rhythm section.

TOO MUCH BLOOD

Mick Jagger / Keith Richards / 6:14

Musicians
Mick Jagger: vocals, guitar (?)
Keith Richards: guitar (?)
Bill Wyman: bass
Charlie Watts: drums
Ron Wood: rhythm guitar
Chuck Leavell: keyboards
Jim Barber: rhythm guitar, lead guitar
The Sugarhill Horn Section CHOPS: horns
Sly Dunbar: Simmons drums, percussion (?)
David Sanborn: saxophone (?)
Moustapha Cisse [?], Brahms Coundoul [?], Martin Ditcham [?]): percussion

Recorded
EMI Pathé Marconi Studios, Boulogne-Billancourt, France: November 11–December 19, 1982
Compass Point Studios, Nassau, Bahamas: May–June 1983
The Hit Factory, New York City: May, end of June–beginning of August 1983

Technical Team
Producers: the Glimmer Twins, Chris Kimsey
Sound engineers: Chris Kimsey, Brian McGee
Assistant sound engineers: Rod Thear, Steve Lipson, John Davenport, Bobby Cohen, Benji Armbrister

In "Too Much Blood," Mick Jagger cites by name the movie *The Texas Chain Saw Massacre*. The movie's scriptwriters, Kim Kenkel and William Tobe Hooper himself, are supposed to have been inspired by one Ed Gein, a serial killer nicknamed the "butcher of Plainfield."

Genesis
"Too Much Blood" was written mainly by Mick Jagger. It tackles the theme of violence, and more precisely the way in which violence is reported by the media, that is to say with an emphasis on the sensational a lot of the time. The Stones singer took his inspiration from a drama that unfolded in Paris in 1981. On June 11, a young Japanese man named Issei Sagawa lured a Dutch student named Renée Hartevelt to his home. After killing her, he engaged in repeated acts of cannibalism with her body. Arrested but judged unfit for trial, he was committed to a psychiatric institution near Paris and then in Japan, which he left in 1986. Sagawa made the front page of the newspapers under the moniker "the Japanese Cannibal."

Production
Mick Jagger found himself in the studio with Bill Wyman and Charlie Watts at the start of the "Too Much Blood" session. In the absence of Keith Richards and Ron Wood, the Stones singer asked Jim Barber, the band's road manager, but also a guitarist, to pick up one of Keith's instruments—a Les Paul Junior—and play in the style of Andy Summers of the Police (using a Boss CE-2 Chorus pedal) in the refrains, and also to execute various licks and distorted effects. At this point, Jagger still only had the riff and the middle section, not even the words. And then he too started to play guitar. Little by little the number took shape, with the Stones singer making his debut as a . . . rapper. In overdub, Ron Wood plays palm-mute-style rhythm guitar from the intro, creating a very funky pulse. Sly Dunbar again plays the Simmons drums, from which he seems to be inseparable, plus numerous percussion instruments, including congas, bongos, and others that are not easy to identify. Charlie lays down a superb rhythm, with bass drum on every beat, supported by a wonderful bass groove from Bill. There is a welcome surprise in the form of the fantastic CHOPS horn section, which sets the track on fire with riffs that would not have disgraced James Brown. At around 5:15 a sax comes in with effects, rather than a solo as such. Is it David Sanborn or one of the members of CHOPS? Chuck Leavell does some discreet but highly effective work on the keyboards. As for Mick, one can only admire the inexhaustible energy he expends on both singing and production, and by imposing songs of this kind on his writing partner, he was

Chuck Leavell and Ron Wood, who play a key role on "Too Much Blood."

showing who was in charge of the Stones. He also reveals himself to be an innovator: following hard on the heels of his falsettos, he now dives into rap.

A video of over seven minutes' duration was shot, again by Julien Temple, in January 1984. In it, Richards, with an evil glint in his eye, attempts to decapitate Jagger with a chain saw.

A Long Way from Rock, a Long Way from the Stones

It is this kind of song that was to create a real gulf between the Glimmer Twins. By all accounts Keith hated it and refused to play on it. And, indeed, how could he be expected to accept a form of music that was so far removed from the one he loved? It has to be said that "Too Much Blood" is a million miles away from the world of the Stones. Essentially, it is dance music, somewhat in the mold of Michael Jackson's "Don't Stop 'Til You Get Enough," released in 1979, with which it has a certain rhythmic similarity. Naturally, fashions change and it is important to evolve. Considered objectively, "Too Much Blood" is a pretty good track. It may not be up to the standard of the specialists of the genre, but the results are fairly good nonetheless. All that remains is to choose which camp one is in, whether to accept or reject.

PRETTY BEAT UP

Mick Jagger / Keith Richards / Ron Wood / 4:03

Musicians
Mick Jagger: vocals, rhythm guitar (?)
Keith Richards: bass, acoustic guitar (?), backing vocals
Bill Wyman: electric piano
Charlie Watts: drums
Ron Wood: rhythm and lead guitar
Ian Stewart: piano
David Sanborn: saxophone
The Sugarhill Horn Section CHOPS: horns
Recorded
EMI Pathé Marconi Studios, Boulogne-Billancourt, France: November 11–December 19, 1982
Compass Point Studios, Nassau, Bahamas: May–June 1983 (?)
The Hit Factory, New York City: May, end of June–beginning of August 1983
Technical Team
Producers: the Glimmer Twins, Chris Kimsey
Sound engineers: Chris Kimsey, Brian McGee
Assistant sound engineers: Rod Thear, Steve Lipson, John Davenport, Bobby Cohen, Benji Armbrister

David Sanborn plays sax on "Pretty Beat Up," another Jagger-Richards-Wood composition.

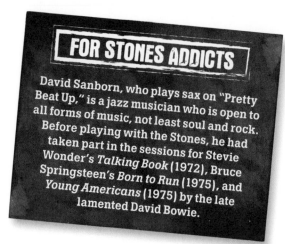

FOR STONES ADDICTS

David Sanborn, who plays sax on "Pretty Beat Up," is a jazz musician who is open to all forms of music, not least soul and rock. Before playing with the Stones, he had taken part in the sessions for Stevie Wonder's *Talking Book* (1972), Bruce Springsteen's *Born to Run* (1975), and *Young Americans* (1975) by the late lamented David Bowie.

Genesis

With a chord sequence by Ron Wood, a song title by Keith Richards, and words by Mick Jagger, this song is a good example of teamwork. The lyrics crack like a whip over the pounding, hypnotic—in short, dance—rhythm. The lyrics are clearly about the breakup of a relationship. "She" has left, and "he," unable to get over it, finds himself in a bad state, like a *battered baby just left on the street* . . . "Pretty Beat Up" is an album track that has never been performed live by the Rolling Stones. Ron Wood, on the other hand, played it on the tour he undertook in the United States and Japan between October 1992 and January 1994. It is also on his first live solo album, *Slide on Live: Plugged In and Standing* (1993).

Production

"Pretty Beat Up" is a well-made blues-rock number with a spellbinding rhythm generated mainly by Charlie's excellent hi-hat work. Keith is on bass, leaving Bill to play the Yamaha electric piano, as stated in the album credits. However hard one listens, though, it is impossible to hear him. The same goes for Stu's piano, which is presumably buried in the mix. On the other hand, Ronnie's excellent guitar, rhythm, and a very good blues lick played slide, comes across loud and clear. It is most probably Mick who accompanies him on electric, and Keith may be on acoustic, although drowned in the mass of sound. The talented David Sanborn (who may also have contributed to "Too Much Blood") has his first proper role on the album. He delivers a superb saxophone part, which helps the track to really take off from 2:00. Incidentally, it is worth pointing out that the Stones had always had outstanding saxophonists with them in the studio, such as Bobby Keys, Mel Collins, and Sonny Rollins. And to remain with the horns for a moment, the CHOPS contingent can be heard playing some very good rhythm 'n' blues riffs in the coda (around 3:43). As for the vocals, Mick does not give one of his best performances. Although reasonably good, his voice is not up to the standard of tracks like "Undercover of the Night."

1983

TOO TOUGH

Mick Jagger / Keith Richards / 3:52

FOR STONES ADDICTS

"Too Tough" was released as a single (with "Miss You" as the B-side) exclusively in the United States in 1984. This is included in the box set *Singles 1971–2006* (2011).

Musicians
Mick Jagger: vocals, rhythm guitar
Keith Richards: rhythm guitar, slide guitar
Bill Wyman: bass
Charlie Watts: drums
Ron Wood: rhythm and lead guitar
Chuck Leavell: synthesizer (?)
Sly Dunbar: percussion (Simmons drums) (?)
Recorded
EMI Pathé Marconi Studios, Boulogne-Billancourt, France: November 11–December 19, 1982
Compass Point Studios, Nassau, Bahamas: May–June 1983 (?)
The Hit Factory, New York City: May, end of June–beginning of August 1983
Technical Team
Producers: the Glimmer Twins, Chris Kimsey
Sound engineers: Chris Kimsey, Brian McGee
Assistant sound engineers: Rod Thear, Steve Lipson, John Davenport, Bobby Cohen, Benji Armbrister

The Rolling Stones drummer, a smile on his lips, laying down a rock-solid rhythm on "Too Tough."

Genesis

I still see you in my dreams with a kitchen knife . . . The narrator, who has just taken a teenage bride, whom he loves *deep inside*, clearly fears that his former lover is going to make life impossible for him. He invites her to go ahead and try, perhaps with poison or drugs. The message speaks for itself.

"Too Tough" has its origins in an instrumental that the Stones recorded in Rotterdam during the *Black and Blue* sessions in January and February 1975 with Wayne Perkins on guitar. Then named "Cellophane Trouser" (or alternatively "Cellophane Y-Fronts," or even "Back to the Country"), it was reworked seven years later in Paris, at Chris Kimsey's instigation, and gradually took shape around this riff, crafted, once again, by Keith Richards.

Production

However, "Too Tough" kicks off with a guitar riff that is most probably not played by Keith, as the sound is less his than Mick's or Ronnie's. These two share the rhythm guitar part, while Keith does not seem to come in with his third rhythm part (stereo left) and various slide phrases until the first refrain (0:43). Ronnie takes care of the solo, probably on one of his Zemaitises with a highly distorted sound, and as Mick would observe in an interview, the result possesses an almost heavy metal quality. Charlie and Bill calmly handle the rhythm section, while Mick pushes his somewhat tired-sounding vocal cords to the limit. He also has difficulty hitting the top notes in the first two lines of the first refrain. The sound recording is no more than average, and Jagger has somewhat overloaded his lead vocal by repeatedly double-tracking himself, thereby stifling any spontaneity. Chuck Leavell seems to come in with layers of synthesizer in the refrains, and at various points on the track (for example 0:56), Charlie (presumably) can be heard playing what sounds like toms—although it may in reality have been produced by Sly Dunbar's Simmons drums. "Too Tough" gives the impression that the Stones are forcing themselves to play rock 'n' roll, rather than genuinely taking pleasure in playing it.

ALL THE WAY DOWN

Mick Jagger / Keith Richards / 3:12

Musicians
Mick Jagger: vocals, rhythm guitar
Keith Richards: lead guitar, acoustic guitar, backing vocals
Bill Wyman: bass
Charlie Watts: drums
Ron Wood: rhythm guitar, backing vocals
Unidentified musician(s): bongos or congas
Recorded
EMI Pathé Marconi Studios, Boulogne-Billancourt, France: November 11–December 19, 1982
Compass Point Studios, Nassau, Bahamas: May–June 1983 (?)
The Hit Factory, New York City: May, end of June– beginning of August 1983
Technical Team
Producers: the Glimmer Twins, Chris Kimsey
Sound engineers: Chris Kimsey, Brian McGee
Assistant sound engineers: Rod Thear, Steve Lipson, John Davenport, Bobby Cohen, Benji Armbrister

Ron Wood and Keith Richards (on piano) in a hotel room. Looking for the perfect riff.

Genesis

Here, Mick Jagger wields his memories with all the skill of a great rock 'n' roll author. There is no mincing of words: he gets straight to the point. The song's protagonist remembers when he was a naïve, eager-to-please twenty-one-year-old, and recalls the woman who entered his life at that time. The years have now passed and there have been *birthdays, kids, and suicides* . . . His verdict is harsh: *But still I play the fool and strut/Still you're a slut.*

The Stones chose "All the Way Down" as the B-side of their single "Undercover of the Night," but have never performed the song live. Maybe they felt it was a little disappointing? This is what Ron Wood suggests: "'All the Way Down' could have been a better song (we didn't explore its full potential)."[9]

Production

The guitarist has a point: "All the Way Down" is not exactly the best song on the album. There is something routine about it . . . The Stones probably needed to get their album finished. The track opens with a slightly sped-up voice (Keith, according to the writer Martin Elliott), picked up on the control room talk-back mic: "Don't wanna hear it from the beginning, just drop us in," the voice seems to be saying. Keith (probably) then launches into a riff strongly colored by phasing, before being joined by the rest of the band. He is answered by two other rhythm guitars, most probably Mick and Ronnie. From 0:56 on, Keith can also be heard strumming an acoustic guitar, an instrument that was sadly becoming something of a rarity in the Stones' universe. Charlie and Bill do what is required of them and are joined by bongos and congas from 1:41 on (at the back of the mix). What can be said about this song? The bridge (1:20) is in poor taste, with Jagger doubling himself in a falsetto. The break at 2:11 recalls that of "Rocks Off" in its general style, but without being remotely as brilliant; it is simply a riot of completely pointless vocal effects. If the performance of the Stones singer is not exactly unforgettable, the sound recording and/or mixing does nothing to help. Ron Wood has made the very fair assessment: "In terms of the musical peaks on that album, there really aren't that many."[9] It is time for Keith to rise from his slumber . . .

IT MUST BE HELL

Mick Jagger / Keith Richards / 5:03

Musicians
Mick Jagger: vocals, rhythm guitar (?)
Keith Richards: rhythm guitar, backing vocals
Bill Wyman: bass
Charlie Watts: drums
Ron Wood: rhythm guitar, slide guitar, backing vocals
Chuck Leavell: piano
Moustapha Cisse [?], Brahms Coundoul [?],
Martin Ditcham [?]): percussion
Recorded
EMI Pathé Marconi Studios, Boulogne-Billancourt, France:
November 11–December 19, 1982
Compass Point Studios, Nassau, Bahamas: May–June 1983 (?)
The Hit Factory, New York City: May, end of June–beginning
of August 1983
Technical Team
Producers: the Glimmer Twins, Chris Kimsey
Sound engineers: Chris Kimsey, Brian McGee
Assistant sound engineers: Rod Thear, Steve Lipson, John
Davenport, Bobby Cohen, Benji Armbrister

Mick Jagger and Jerry Hall at a private showing
at the Mizuno Gallery in Los Angeles.

Genesis

"It Must Be Hell" sees Mick Jagger once again venturing into political territory. This time his target is not South America ("Undercover of the Night"), but presumably the countries that were then (a few years before the fall of the Berlin Wall) in the grip of communism. He paints an apocalyptic picture: millions of people unemployed, hungry children unable to read or write, and prisons and asylums filled with those whose thinking is not in line with the party's; in other words, the politically "incorrect." Mick Jagger seems to have embarked on a crusade against stifling knowledge. His words are carried by another highly typical Stones riff that brings "Soul Survivor" to mind.

Production

And there is a reason for this: good old Keith has simply recycled the riff of the closing track of *Exile on Main St.* for the intro to "It Must Be Hell." He makes a powerful sound, most likely on one of his Telecaster 5-strings in open G, played through a Mesa Boogie amp, again with MXR Analog Delay. The Stones are trying to bring *Undercover* to a close with a rock number of the kind they are renowned for, but the magic is not there. There is too much discord between them. This is a shame because the track is interesting in more than one respect. Charlie's drumming is as brilliant as ever, with plenty of swing in his sticks, if not quite as much power as during the Jimmy Miller era. Bill accompanies him with an excellent bass part, the sound very clean and rounded, played almost certainly on his Travis Bean TB 2000 plugged straight into the console. Keith is supported on rhythm by two other guitars, and Ron plays a very good slide solo at 2:11. Various percussion instruments can be heard, in particular congas (0:44), a cabasa (3:09), and a cowbell (3:21), but we could perhaps be forgiven for wondering what the point is of congas on a track of this type. It is apparently Chuck Leavell on piano at 3:46, playing a boogie-woogie part that could easily be attributed to Stu. Mick gives a good vocal performance, and literally lets go in the coda. "It Must Be Hell" is not the worst track on the album, but it is hard to avoid a comparison with the band's glory years, the period between *Beggars Banquet* and *Exile on Main St.* And all the more so when one relistens to "Soul Survivor" . . .

Ron Wood, who is featured prominently on "I Think I'm Going Mad." Opposite: playing his Zemaitis Metal Front at Wembley Stadium.

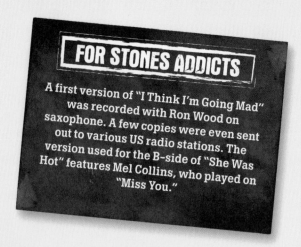

FOR STONES ADDICTS

A first version of "I Think I'm Going Mad" was recorded with Ron Wood on saxophone. A few copies were even sent out to various US radio stations. The version used for the B-side of "She Was Hot" features Mel Collins, who played on "Miss You."

I THINK I'M GOING MAD

Mick Jagger / Keith Richards / 4:20

SINGLE

She Was Hot* / I Think I'm Going Mad

RELEASE DATE

United Kingdom: January 23, 1984

Label: Rolling Stones Records

RECORD NUMBER: ROLLING STONES RECORDS RSR 114 (SEE P. 540)

Musicians

Mick Jagger: vocals, electric piano (?)
Keith Richards: rhythm guitar, backing vocals
Bill Wyman: bass
Charlie Watts: drums
Ron Wood: pedal steel guitar, lead guitar
Ian Stewart (?): piano
Mel Collins (?): saxophone

Recorded

Compass Point Studios, Nassau, Bahamas:
January 22–February 12, 1979
EMI Pathé Marconi Studios, Boulogne-Billancourt, France: November 11–December 19, 1982
The Hit Factory, New York City: May, end of June–beginning of August 1983

Technical Team

Producers: the Glimmer Twins, Chris Kimsey
Sound engineers: Chris Kimsey, Bob Clearmountain (mixing)

Genesis

The least that can be said here is that the protagonist no longer knows where he is. *Life goes by so fast*; *All the women come and go*; *Sometimes I feel so young and sometimes I feel so old*. His hands tremble, his *mind's afloat*. In a nutshell, he thinks he's going insane.

"I Think I'm Going Mad" is a Glimmer Twins composition that dates from the *Emotional Rescue* sessions at Compass Point Studios, Nassau, at the beginning of 1979. Judged inferior to the other ballads, "Indian Girl" and "All About You," it was passed over for the final track listing. It was only four years later, after reworking the song at the Pathé Marconi Studios in Boulogne-Billancourt and then remixing it at the Hit Factory in New York City, that the Rolling Stones decided to release it as the B-side of the single "She Was Hot."

Production

It comes as something of a surprise to discover that this song was not included on any of the albums from *Emotional Rescue* to *Undercover*. B-side status does not do it justice. "I Think I'm Going Mad," in all likelihood written by Mick, is a very good ballad in the spirit of "Fool to Cry" and "Worried About You." Evidently no proper intro had been written, for it opens with a fade-in of Keith's strummed guitar (with emphatic phasing), accompanied by Charlie's bass drum on the offbeat. Bill's weighty-sounding bass is also very prominent. Two pianos can be heard: an electric thought to be played by Mick and an acoustic probably played by Stu. Ronnie comes in on pedal steel guitar in the refrains, and plays some excellent, very clear-toned guitar licks at 2:22, most

likely on his Stratocaster. It seems to be Mel Collins playing the heavily reverbed sax with such skill, although the name of David Sanborn is sometimes mentioned. Mick Jagger rediscovers in his voice a warmth and intonations that are more or less absent from certain tracks on *Undercover*, and that transform "I Think I'm Going Mad" into something rather special. Despite a bad edit at 1:22, the excellent Bob Clearmountain has done a very good job with the mixing.

One Hit (To The Body)
Fight
Harlem Shuffle
Hold Back
Too Rude
Winning Ugly
Back To Zero
Dirty Work
Had It With You
Sleep Tonight

ALBUM
RELEASE DATE
United Kingdom: March 24, 1986
Label: Rolling Stones Records
RECORD NUMBER: ROLLING STONES
RECORDS CBS 86321

DIRTY WORK

In 2005, the famous Chicago–based website Pitchfork included *Dirty Work* in its list of worst covers of all time.

1986

DIRTY WORK:
WAR IS DECLARED

The contract signed by the Rolling Stones and Columbia on August 25, 1983, would drive home the discord that had been brewing for some time between Keith Richards and Mick Jagger. Unknown to Keith, Bill, Charlie, and Ronnie, this contract related not merely to the forthcoming albums of the band; it also covered three solo albums by Mick. Furthermore, the president of CBS, Walter Yetnikoff, went as far as to insist that Jagger's first album be released before the next Stones record. In April 1984, Jagger duly informed Richards and the other members of the band that he was going to devote the period from May through November 1984 to cutting his own record (*She's the Boss*), thereby postponing the recording of the band's album and at the same time destroying a bond that went back some twenty years. Keith later wrote: "It was total disregard for the band. And I'd rather have found out about it before it went down. I was incensed. We didn't build this band up to stab each other in the back."[2]

The Album

By the time the five of them eventually got together again in Paris to begin the delayed sessions for *Dirty Work*, the good ship *Rolling Stones* was listing more than ever. Bill only put in an occasional appearance at the sessions, due partly to the tense atmosphere within the band, and partly to his blossoming relationship with Mandy Smith (who was only fourteen). As for Mick Jagger, all he could think about was *She's the Boss*, and, completely wrapped up in his solo album, had few songs to offer the band. Charlie, meanwhile, was sinking

into drug abuse and alcoholism. He would later acknowledge that during this period he was in such a state that he was not "really aware of the problems between Mick and Keith and the danger these posed to the band's existence."[9] Keith therefore found himself obliged to roll up his shirtsleeves: "So I began writing a lot more on my own for *Dirty Work*, different kinds of songs."[2] Only Ron Wood remained loyally at his post alongside Keith, on whose shoulders now rested the future of the band. Full of bitterness, Richards would make cutting remarks about his writing partner, whom he had nicknamed "Brenda," without compunction: "I went to WHSmith, the English bookshop on the rue de Rivoli [in Paris]. I forget the title of the book, but there it was, some lurid novel by Brenda Jagger. Gotcha, mate! Now you're Brenda whether you know it or not. He certainly didn't like it. It took him ages to find out. We'd be talking about 'that bitch Brenda' with him in the room, and he wouldn't know."[2]

In Memory of Stu

Dirty Work can be divided into three parts. First, there are the covers: "Harlem Shuffle," which had been a hit for Bob & Earl in the sixties, and "Too Rude," written by Half Pint. Then there are two contributions to the album from Mick Jagger: the first-rate blues-rock number "Winning Ugly," in which the singer launches an assault on unscrupulous winners, and "Back to Zero," a song with a funky character over which hovers the specter of imminent nuclear war (unless, that is, the *return to zero* of the title is an implicit reference to the desire

Alexis Korner, a pioneer of British blues, bowed out of this life on January 1, 1984.

The year 1984 started on a sad note for the Stones, with the loss of bluesman Alexis Korner on January 1 at fifty-five years of age. "Without Alexis," writes Bill Wyman, "it is arguable that there would be no Rolling Stones."[1]

of the Stones singer to pursue a solo career). The other six tracks on the album bear Keith's hallmark: "One Hit (to the Body)," one of the best Stones productions of the Ron Wood years; "Fight" and "Had It with You," which, although musically very different from one other, are both eloquent expressions of the guitarist's feelings toward the singer; "Hold Back" and "Dirty Work," which declare war on some people for their certitudes and on others for their exploitation of their fellow human beings; and the closing ballad "Sleep Tonight."

Finally, at the end of the album, there is a hidden track soberly titled "Piano Instrumental" (on the CD, not the album). The Stones wanted to add a 0:33 extract of "Key to the Highway" (by Big Bill Broonzy), a piano blues performed here by Ian Stewart, who died of a heart attack in his cardiologist's waiting room one week after the final mixing of the album. "Very few people realised how important he was to the Stones," said Keith. "He was the glue that held the whole thing together."[1] Stu, the sixth Stone, the one Oldham got rid of because he didn't look the part, the one who always remained calm in the midst of the storm, the one who was the Stones' conscience, had agreed, in spite of everything, to follow his mates through thick and thin. There was only one principle he would not compromise: his refusal to play minor chords! All the band members attended his funeral. Stu, then, had gone to join Brian. *Dirty Work* is dedicated to Ian "Stu" Stewart with gratitude for "25 years of boogie-woogie."

Third World War!

Co-produced by the Glimmer Twins and Steve Lillywhite, the Stones' eighteenth (British) studio album was released on March 24, 1986. It went on to achieve enormous success in the Netherlands and Switzerland (where it hit number 1), and also in Canada, West Germany, and Spain (number 2). It peaked at number 3 in Italy and New Zealand and number 4 in the United Kingdom and the United States. The release

of *Dirty Work* was to have been accompanied by a world tour. In the end, this would not go ahead until 1989. Mick Jagger would later comment: "The band was in no condition to tour . . . the album wasn't that good. The relationships were terrible . . . I wasn't in particularly good shape. The rest of the band, they couldn't walk across the Champs-Élysées, much less go on the road."[35] Keith would react very badly to this decision, and above all to the fact that Jagger sent each of the Stones a letter in which he announced his decision not to tour and to devote himself to his solo career: "I read in one of the English tabloids of Mick saying the Rolling Stones are a millstone around my neck," the guitarist would later write. "He actually said it. Swallow that one, fucker. I had no doubt that some part of his mind was thinking that, but saying it is another thing. That's when World War III was declared."[2]

The Album Cover

Upon close inspection, the cover image says it all. It is a very accurate reflection of the atmosphere of this album, whose title is as revealing as it is unappealing. The photograph depicts five dead-eyed musicians who have been attired in garishly colored suits. Keith, lounging on a greenish sofa, is enthroned at the center of the photo, surrounded by Charlie, Ronnie, Bill, and Mick, who is seated on the ground with one leg negligently resting up on the seat. The photograph was taken by Annie Leibovitz, whose photos had appeared in *Rolling Stone*, *Vanity Fair*, and *Vogue*, and who had followed the Stones' 1975 tour. She had also taken the very last picture of John Lennon just a few hours before he was killed in 1980. With the exception of the illustration for *It's Only Rock 'N' Roll* and the collages for *Some Girls*, *Dirty Work* is the Stones' first proper studio album since *Their Satanic Majesties Request*, whose cover depicts all five members of the Rolling Stones. Was this to reassure all those who feared the band was about to break up due to the dire state of the relationship

Ian Stewart, a member of the Stones before being ousted, passed away soon after: on December 12, 1985.

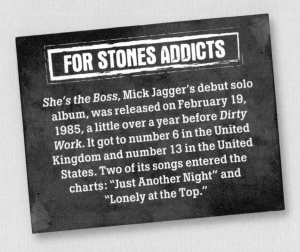

between Mick Jagger and Keith Richards? This is not out of the question. One innovation is that—most probably at the request of CBS, the Stones' new distributor—the lyrics of the ten songs on the album are included, as is a cartoon by Mark Marek, titled *Dirty Workout*. Upon its release, the LP was sold shrink-wrapped in dark red plastic.

The Recording

Following Chris Kimsey's departure, the Rolling Stones called in Steve Lillywhite as co-producer. Lillywhite was an acknowledged master of the new wave, following highly successful collaborations with the Psychedelic Furs, Peter Gabriel, U2, and Simple Minds. But why this change of co-producer? The reason is that Mick was looking for a new way of working and a new sound that was in touch with the market. Ron Wood recalls Keith's reaction: "All right, who's Mick picked this time? He'd better be good!"[9] Despite this inauspicious start, Lillywhite would prove up to the task and would remain friends with the band long after their collaboration had ended, even if he did later admit that he had produced one of the Stones' worst albums . . . Kimsey also relinquished his role as sound engineer. He was replaced by Dave Jerden, the same engineer who would record Mick Jagger's *She's the Boss* and also work with artists of the caliber of Talking Heads, the Red Hot Chili Peppers, and Herbie Hancock.

The tensions that dominated the recording sessions would inevitably have an impact on the quality of the record. Work was impeded by the repeated absences of the band members and the lack of motivation of the majority of them. "It was a hard album to make," Keith would later say, "and usually Stones albums are fun. Everybody was having a bad year."[11] He would also explain that the songs had been written so that they could be performed easily in concert. Which in the end proved to be completely pointless.

The sessions for *Dirty Work* kicked off at the Pathé Marconi Studios in Boulogne-Billancourt in January 1985. In order to get back into the swing of things, and perhaps also to reconnect with their roots, the Stones began by playing a large number of standards and songs of one sort and another. Between mid-January and mid-February/early March, they recorded "One Hit (to the Body)" as well as various numbers that would not, in the end, be used. Between April 5 and June 17, still at the Pathé Marconi Studios, they cut "Had It with You," "Too Rude," "Fight," and "Dirty Work" (plus other tracks that would only appear on bootlegs). According to Bill, by the end of these five months in the studio, they had recorded no fewer than 242 tapes! Despite the tense atmosphere, the Stones were nothing if not productive.

When invited to take part in Live Aid, the band initially declined. In the end, however, three of the Rolling Stones decided to participate, more or less independently, in the spectacular on July 13, 1985: Mick Jagger (having recorded "Dancing in the Street" with David Bowie specially for the humanitarian event organized by Bob Geldof), both solo and with Tina Turner; Keith Richards and Ron Wood alongside Bob Dylan. Sessions resumed from July 16 to August 17, and then from September 10 to October 15, this time at RPM Studios in New York City, where "Harlem Shuffle," "Back to Zero," "Winning Ugly," "Hold Back," and "Sleep Tonight" were cut.

Steve Lillywhite at the mixing desk. He was promoted to Stones co-producer for the *Dirty Work* sessions.

A Fender Stratocaster, identical to Keith Richards's 1959 model.

Finally, most of the mixing was done at Right Track Studios in New York City between November 15 and December 5, 1985.

Dirty Work gave the Stones an opportunity to invite numerous outside musicians along to the studio: Jimmy Page and Bobby Womack on guitar (and vocals in the case of the latter), Don Covay, Steve Jordan (who would also support Keith on his solo projects), Patti Scialfa, Tom Waits, Jimmy Cliff, Ivan Neville (also on bass), Kirsty MacColl, Janice Pendarvis, Beverly D'Angelo (not mentioned in the album credits), and Dolette McDonald on backing vocals, John Regan on bass, Dan Collette on trumpet, and finally Philippe Saisse and, again, Chuck Leavell on keyboards and synthesizers. Dave Jerden, the new sound engineer, was supported by Steve Parker (Virgin Prunes, Wire, Colin Newman), and assistants Tim Crich (Carly Simon, Bon Jovi, Billy Joel) and Mike Krowiak (Herbie Hancock, Lloyd Cole, Buddy Guy).

The Instruments

New album, new guitars. Alan Rogan, who had been Keith's guitar technician since 1981, has revealed that Keith recorded with three custom Jesselli guitars during the early sessions, and then mainly with a blond 1959 Telecaster, but also with Fender Stratocasters, including one from that same year. In terms of acoustic instruments, he used a National Reso-Phonic as well as a Martin D-18 and a Martin 00-21, both from 1967. Woody used Boss pedals, in particular a vibrato one. New Mesa Boogie Simulclass Combo amps made an appearance, and Keith also fell in love with a 1959 Fender Twin. For one particular track, Ron would use an RCA dating from the forties that was capable of running on batteries.

ONE HIT (TO THE BODY)

Mick Jagger / Keith Richards / Ron Wood / 4:44

Musicians
Mick Jagger: vocals
Keith Richards: rhythm guitars, acoustic guitar, backing vocals
Bill Wyman: bass
Charlie Watts: drums
Ron Wood: acoustic guitar, rhythm guitar (?), backing vocals
Jimmy Page: lead guitar
Chuck Leavell: keyboards
John Regan: bass (?)
Bobby Womack, Don Covay, Patti Scialfa, Kirsty MacColl, Beverly D'Angelo: backing vocals

Recorded
EMI Pathé Marconi Studios, Boulogne-Billancourt, France: mid-January–end of February/beginning of March, April 5–June 17, 1985
RPM Studios, New York City: July 16–August 17, September 10–October 15, 1985
Right Track Studios, New York City: November 15–December 5, 1985

Technical Team
Producers: Steve Lillywhite, the Glimmer Twins
Sound engineers: Dave Jerden, Steve Parker
Assistant sound engineers: Tim Crich, Mike Krowiak

Jimmy Page recorded the flamboyant solo on "One Hit" shortly before performing at Live Aid with Led Zeppelin.

Genesis
Your love is just a sweet addiction, I can't clean you out of my veins. It's a lifelong addiction that has damaged my brain. Contrary to what one might believe, particularly in view of Keith Richards's past, "One Hit (to the Body)" is not a drug song. Narcotics are merely used as a metaphor for love, which strikes suddenly, like lightning.

"One Hit (to the Body)" is credited to the Glimmer Twins and Ron Wood. It can be attributed mainly to Keith and Ronnie, however, whose acoustic and electric work reveals a growing synchronicity between the two guitarists. "One Hit (to the Body)" was released as the second single from *Dirty Work* (with the B-side "Fight") on May 9 1986, but only reached number 28 on the US *Billboard* chart, on June 28, and number 80 on the British chart.

Production
The track opens with Charlie on hi-hat and bass drum, sounding curiously like a drum machine. The idea for the acoustic guitar came from Ron Wood, who plays Keith's 1967 Martin D-18. He is immediately joined by Keith with a very good riff, probably played on his newly acquired 1959 Telecaster with its big, aggressive sound. Keith explains how the guitar sonority was achieved: ". . . there's 2 or 3 different electrics all coming in different places. I never, or I very rarely, use an overdub all the way through. I might do 3 different overdubs and 2 of them might be the same thing."[74] He can also be heard playing his National Reso-Phonic guitar in the verses, with a sound described by his guitar technician, Alan Rogan, as resembling the drone of a sitar. After several albums oriented more to dance music, this track marks a return to a guitar-led style, probably due to Mick's loss of interest as a result of his preoccupation with his solo album, and Keith's return to writing. Another guitar hero was to play a key role in "One Hit (to the Body)." Having arrived in New York City for the Live Aid concert, at which he was to appear with Led Zeppelin, which had re-formed specially for the event, Jimmy Page called Ron Wood and asked if he could come to the studio to help out on the album. This is how he came to play two excellent solos, at 2:26 and 4:10, each one bearing the inimitable stamp of the brilliant guitarist. Although his musical approach differs considerably from Keith's, it works well here. The main

Ronnie, Mick, Keith, Bill, and Charlie, ready to do their "Dirty Work."

reservation concerning "One Hit (to the Body)" relates to the rhythm section. Charlie's drumming sounds different than usual: heavy, rigid, cold, and highly impersonal. Although he was going through a difficult time in his personal life, which might explain the difference in style, it is tempting to wonder whether it really is Watts on drums. On the other hand, the actual sound of his Gretsch kit is unmistakable, suggesting that responsibility must lie with Steve Lillywhite's production. Bill's bass, undermixed and uncharacteristic-sounding, is similarly unremarkable. Certain sources suggest that a second bassist, John Regan, had come along to lend a hand. In view of the results, this seems possible. Having contributed to *Undercover*, Chuck Leavell is again on keyboards on this album. His contribution is reasonably discreet, and can be heard mainly in the distinctly eighties digital synth sound in the refrains. As for Mick Jagger, his voice is always good when he sings rock, but around this period he was increasingly slipping into caricature and lacking variety in his performance. He gives the impression of merely doing a job, rather than fully investing himself in the song. Finally, the many backing vocalists add a touch of soul, but are not exactly indispensable. "One Hit (to the Body)" is a very good song, but the production, which is excessively "of its day," and the evident lack of solidarity among the Stones meant the song would perform disappointingly on the charts.

FOR STONES ADDICTS

The Stones turned to the Australian director Russell Mulcahy for the video of "One Hit (to the Body)." In it, the discord between Mick and Keith is so glaringly obvious that they look as if they are about to come to blows.

In addition to Keith Richards and Ron Wood, the backing vocalists include Bobby Womack, Don Covay, Patti Scialfa (a member of the E Street Band and future wife of Bruce Springsteen), Kirsty MacColl (the wife of Steve Lillywhite), and the actress Beverly D'Angelo.

FIGHT

Mick Jagger / Keith Richards / 3:09

Musicians
Mick Jagger: vocals
Keith Richards: rhythm guitar, lead guitar (?), backing vocals
Charlie Watts: drums
Ron Wood: bass guitar, backing vocals
Chuck Leavell: organ
Ivan Neville (?), Steve Jordan (?), Charley Drayton (?), Kirsty MacColl (?), Patti Scialfa (?): backing vocals

Recorded
EMI Pathé Marconi Studios, Boulogne-Billancourt, France: April 5–June 17, 1985
RPM Studios, New York City: July 16–August 17, September 10–October 15, 1985
Right Track Studios, New York City: November 15–December 5, 1985 (?)

Technical Team
Producers: Steve Lillywhite, the Glimmer Twins
Sound engineers: Dave Jerden, Steve Parker
Assistant sound engineers: Tim Crich, Mike Krowiak

A black-eyed Keith playing his Music Man Silhouette.

Genesis
There was nothing doing between the Glimmer Twins. The Stones singer wanted to go off and record his first solo album with musicians such as Jeff Beck, Pete Townshend, and Nile Rodgers. For his part, Keith wanted to stay true to the Stones tradition, and reproached Mick for not putting enough effort into *Dirty Work*.

Gonna pulp you to a mass of bruises; *Gonna blow you to a million pieces*; *What I want is power, more power . . .* if there is one song that embodies the tensions between Mick and Keith in the studio, this is it. "'Fight' gives some idea of the brotherly love between the Glimmer Twins at this juncture," observes Keith wryly in *Life*.

Production
"Fight" is a highly energetic rock song clearly in keeping with the feelings expressed by Keith above. The guitarist would explain that he wrote it in anger after Mick walked out of a session prematurely when the band was struggling to make headway. His inspiration was therefore dictated by a red mist of anger . . . and the results are very good. The intro begins with a succession of chords supported by Ron Wood on bass. Keith then delivers an excellent rhythm guitar part that is solid, aggressive, and in places seems to have something of Pete Townshend about it. In fact, the track as a whole calls to mind the Who—at least as far as the break at 1:56, where the pickup has overtones of Roger Daltrey in "Won't Get Fooled Again" (1971). It seems to be Keith who takes the highly effective and spirited solo at 1:36. According to Alan Rogan, Ron Wood plays a guitar part using a Parsons B-Bender, which is a mechanical device fitted to the guitar that allows pedal steel guitar effects to be obtained. To tell the truth, this cannot be heard, and if it is used, must be buried in the mix. On the other hand, it is definitely Ronnie playing bass in the absence of Bill. Charlie, meanwhile, has rediscovered the touch that was eluding him in "One Hit (to the Body)" and this is nicely enhanced by Steve Lillywhite. Chuck Leavell is excellent on the organ, and Mick delivers a very good, highly inspired vocal performance, presumably goaded into action by the prevailing tension. Keith has even conceded as much himself!

HARLEM SHUFFLE

Bob Relf / Earl Nelson / 3:23

Musicians
Mick Jagger: vocals
Keith Richards: rhythm guitar, backing vocals
Bill Wyman: bass
Charlie Watts: drums
Ron Wood: rhythm guitar, backing vocals
Chuck Leavell: electric piano, organ, synthesizer
Bobby Womack, Don Covay, Ivan Neville (?),
Tom Waits (?): backing vocals
Recorded
EMI Pathé Marconi Studios, Boulogne-Billancourt, France: April 5–June 17, 1985
RPM Studios, New York City: July 16–August 17, September 10–October 15, 1985
Right Track Studios, New York City: November 15–December 5, 1985 (?)
Technical Team
Producers: Steve Lillywhite, the Glimmer Twins
Sound engineers: Dave Jerden, Steve Parker
Assistant sound engineers: Tim Crich, Mike Krowiak

Bob Relf and Ernest Nelson, the writers of "Harlem Shuffle," which was covered by the Stones on *Dirty Work*.

Genesis

With a background in doo-wop, the duo Bob & Earl (Bobby Relf and Earl Nelson) recorded a number of songs at the beginning of the sixties before entering the charts in 1963 with "Harlem Shuffle," arranged by Barry White and Gene Page and produced by Fred Smith. This was a song made for the dance floor, and one that pays tribute to the Harlem Renaissance.

Keith Richards had been a fan of the song for many years, even to the point of recording it on the cassettes he took with him when touring. In 1985, he finally got his way when Mick and the other three members of the band agreed to record it. This turned out to be a very good idea. "Harlem Shuffle" was the first single not signed Jagger-Richards to be released by the Stones since "Ain't Too Proud to Beg" in October 1974 (with the exception of the live version of "Going to a Go Go"). It got to number 1 in New Zealand, number 5 on the *Billboard* 100, number 4 in Belgium, but "only" number 13 in the United Kingdom.

Production

"Harlem Shuffle" felt so natural to the Stones when they came to record it that, according to Ron Wood, only two takes were needed to get it in the can. Steve Lillywhite would later describe how on this occasion he was able to observe just how brilliant the band could be when the magic was working. It seems to be Keith playing mandolin-style in the intro, influenced by a trip to Mexico, where he reports having heard some old fandangos. He and Ronnie take the two excellent, funky rhythm guitar parts, and complement each other perfectly. Charlie and Bill lay down a groove worthy of the kings of R&B, playing in total accord with each other. Chuck Leavell plays electric piano, organ, and also synthesizer, on which he produces some orchestral samples (listen at around 3:00). Jagger is perfect, his performance recalling the one he gives in "Dancing in the Street," recorded with David Bowie. The success of this number is also due in part to the various singers contributing to the backing vocals: "Bobby [Womack] and Don [Covay] helped add a little bit of magic to 'Harlem Shuffle,'"[9] Ron Wood would later recall. It is Bobby Womack who answers Mick from 2:36 on. Tom Waits may also have contributed to the backing vocals, but this has not been confirmed.

HOLD BACK

Mick Jagger / Keith Richards / 3:53

Musicians
Mick Jagger: vocals
Keith Richards: rhythm guitar
Charlie Watts: drums
Ron Wood: rhythm and lead guitar
Ivan Neville: bass
Bobby Womack: rhythm guitar, lead guitar (?)
Chuck Leavell: organ, synthesizer (?)
Recorded
RPM Studios, New York City: July 16–August 17,
September 10–October 15, 1985
Right Track Studios, New York City:
November 15–December 5, 1985 (?)
Technical Team
Producers: Steve Lillywhite, the Glimmer Twins
Sound engineers: Dave Jerden, Steve Parker
Assistant sound engineers: Tim Crich, Mike Krowiak

Bobby Womack plays on "Hold Back," twenty-one years
after the Stones recorded his song "It's All Over Now."

IN YOUR HEADPHONES
Evidently there was a little hiccup during
the production of the master because two
bad (that is to say, out of time) edits can be
heard at 0:54 and 1:23.

Genesis

'Cause if you follow the crowd, 'cause if you act like a cow-
ard, you'll end up yelling out loud: "Hold Back" is a message
of resistance from the Stones to the people. The truth is not
necessarily what is written in the history books, nor what is
spouted all day long by the media: the song's message is you
have to preserve yourself from every influence and come to
your own conclusions about events. In other words, it is only
personal experience that counts . . . As so often in the past,
Mick Jagger wrote the lyrics to "Hold Back" and Keith Richards the music.

Production

This time the bassist is Ivan Neville, son of Aaron Neville, the
extraordinary singer with the Neville Brothers. Keith appreciated Ivan's playing so much that he would involve him in all his
future solo projects. For now he delivers a very good bass part,
at times falling naturally into a slap style (3:07). Keith would
later reveal in an interview that "Hold Back" was actually res-
urrected from the reject pile, mainly on account of Charlie's
drumming (all the track needed was a new bass line). And it
is true that the Stones drummer does a superb job, delivering a heavy rock sound with a ferocious groove. He smacks
his snare drum with considerable power, laying down a rock-
steady foundation for his bandmates. Keith understood this,
and, along with Ron Wood, supports him with some excellent guitar, happily switching between rhythm and licks. Alan
Rogan would reveal that Ronnie overdubbed the solo using an
RCA amp from the forties (1:54). Bobby Womack also lends a
hand on guitar. It is not easy to identify his playing among the
various guitar parts, but he seems to be in action in the coda
from 3:26. Chuck Leavell plays some discreet organ as well
as some phrases on what sounds like a synthesizer at 3:13.
Finally, Mick delivers his lyrics in a strained-sounding voice
with generous delay. "Hold Back" is probably not the band's
best-ever rock track, but it certainly didn't deserve to end up
as an outtake.

TOO RUDE

Lindon Roberts / 3:11

1986

Musicians
Keith Richards: vocals, rhythm guitar, various guitars
Ron Wood: bass, drums, various guitars
Chuck Leavell: keyboards (?)
Jimmy Cliff: vocal harmonies

Recorded
EMI Pathé Marconi Studios, Boulogne-Billancourt, France: April 5–June 17, 1985
RPM Studios, New York City: July 16–August 17, September 10–October 15, 1985
Right Track Studios, New York City: November 15–December 5, 1985 (?)

Technical Team
Producers: Steve Lillywhite, the Glimmer Twins
Sound engineers: Dave Jerden, Steve Parker
Assistant sound engineers: Tim Crich, Mike Krowiak

The reggae pioneer Jimmy Cliff sings backing vocals on "Too Rude."

Genesis

Logically enough, it was during a trip to Jamaica that Keith Richards developed a passion for reggae. He was particularly struck by a song by the Jamaican musician Half Pint (Lindon Andrew Roberts, to give him his real name) titled "Winsome," released as a single in 1983. He decided to record it during the sessions for *Dirty Work* and gave the resulting adaptation the title "Too Rude." The song tells of a pretty girl who turns the heads of all the boys, but turns down the one who loves her more than anything, leading him to predict that she is *bound to fall* . . .

Production

A comparison of the original version of the song with the Stones' take on it reveals that the English outfit has nothing to be ashamed of. Furthermore, this track stands out in the band's history as something of an exception, as neither Mick Jagger, Bill Wyman, nor Charlie Watts play on it. Ron Wood is on drums for a change, revealing, "That was when Charlie was going through a terrible time with Shirley. They were having lots of heavy arguments and so Charlie was often late, or Shirley would come into the studio and forcibly drag him out."[9] And this was one of those occasions when Charlie was late. Keith, growing impatient, pointed Woody in the direction of the drums. After they had been working on the piece for quite a while, Charlie finally turned up. "I stopped playing and said, 'Charlie, here's your sticks', but he said, 'No, come on, let me watch you'."[9] Eventually, having seen what the former member of the Faces was capable of, Charlie willingly relinquished his place, and the results are very good, helped by the superb mixing of Steve Lillywhite, who was well versed in reggae as a result of having produced Steel Pulse in 1978. Every cliché in the book can be heard on this track: extremely rapid delay with abundant feedback, generous reverb, snare drum overdubs (1:49) . . . Ronnie is on bass as well as drums, but also plays 6-string for a range of effects, while Keith takes care of the main rhythm part and lead vocal, supported by one of Jamaica's greatest artists on vocal harmonies. "Too Rude" is the most authentic-sounding reggae number ever recorded by the Stones, and comes as a wonderful surprise.

WINNING UGLY

Mick Jagger / Keith Richards / 4:32

Musicians
Mick Jagger: vocals
Keith Richards: lead guitar, rhythm guitar
Charlie Watts: drums
Ron Wood: lead guitar, rhythm guitar
Chuck Leavell: keyboards, synthesizer
John Regan: bass
Janice Pendarvis, Dolette McDonald: backing vocals
Recorded
RPM Studios, New York City: July 16–August 17,
September 10–October 15, 1985
Right Track Studios, New York City:
November 15–December 5, 1985 (?)
Technical Team
Producers: Steve Lillywhite, the Glimmer Twins
Sound engineers: Dave Jerden, Steve Parker
Assistant sound engineers: Tim Crich, Mike Krowiak

Marvin Gaye (photographed in 1964), whose
influence can be heard on "Winning Ugly."

Genesis

"Winning Ugly" is one of Mick Jagger's main contributions to *Dirty Work*, the other being "Back to Zero." In this song, cynicism is given free rein. The protagonist is prepared to do whatever it takes to win, even if that means fixing the competition. This is a dream opportunity for Mick Jagger to lead a new assault on those who want to rule the world: *I never turn a hair, just like the politicians*, he sings in the first verse. There is cynicism here, then, but at the same time schizophrenia, because back in the dressing room (is the character some sort of artist?), the *other side is weeping* as a result of *winning ugly*. "Winning Ugly" says a great deal about relations between Mick and Keith, which is perhaps why the song has always, to this day, been left off the set list for the Stones' tours!

Production

It is impossible to discern the Stones' roots in this song. Although reasonably well done, it sounds like a second-rate imitation of Duran Duran, some of whose members had in fact visited the Stones during the sessions for *Dirty Work*. Right from the intro, the sound and general vibe announce that this is the eighties, with all the infelicities of that era. Although John Regan plays a very good bass and Charlie's drums really rock, Chuck Leavell's keyboard and synthesizer work, based around Keith's guitar chords, has much in common with the mediocre productions of this period. The resulting sonority is typical of what poured out of FM radio stations all over the world twenty-four hours a day during these years. It is just a pity that the Stones succumbed to it. Although Keith has revealed that the riff of "Winning Ugly" was inspired by Marvin Gaye songs, such as "Stubborn Kind of Fellow," "You're a Wonderful One," and "Can I Get a Witness," it is not easy to hear the Motown spirit in this track. On the other hand, his guitar lick is excellent and, as he himself would admit, has given a lot of trouble to all those who have tried to play it, despite being disconcertingly simple. Alan Rogan explains that Keith plays it on Ron Wood's blond 1959 Fender Telecaster. Ronnie in turn plays another rhythm guitar part, and both guitarists enhance the track through the addition of various other parts. Jagger does what he has to do without any real inspiration, and can be sensed casting around for other paths to pursue solo.

BACK TO ZERO

Mick Jagger / Keith Richards / Chuck Leavell / 4:00

Musicians
Mick Jagger: vocals
Keith Richards: rhythm guitar
Charlie Watts: drums
Ron Wood: rhythm guitar
Chuck Leavell: keyboards, synthesizers
Bobby Womack: rhythm guitar
John Regan (?): bass
Philippe Saisse: keyboards, synthesizers
Dan Collette: trumpet
Anton Fig: percussion

Recorded
EMI Pathé Marconi Studios, Boulogne-Billancourt, France: April 5–June 17, 1985
RPM Studios, New York City: July 16–August 17, September 10–October 15, 1985
Right Track Studios, New York City: November 15–December 5, 1985 (?)

Technical Team
Producers: Steve Lillywhite, the Glimmer Twins
Sound engineers: Dave Jerden, Steve Parker
Assistant sound engineers: Tim Crich, Mike Krowiak

"Back to Zero" has Frenchman Philippe Saisse
(shown above in 2010) on keyboards.

Genesis

Despite the arrival at the head of the Soviet empire of Mikhail Gorbachev, who announced the withdrawal of troops from Afghanistan and spoke of perestroika and glasnost, in the mid-eighties, the world remained divided into two blocs. The Cold War was still a reality. "Back to Zero" can thus be interpreted as a warning about the threat of nuclear war and its potential to wipe out the planet. More than twenty years after Dylan's "A Hard Rain's A-Gonna Fall," now it is Jagger's turn to worry about the world his grandchildren will inherit. Or perhaps the lyrics are a metaphor for his desire to undertake a change of artistic direction. Either way, "Back to Zero" has never been performed live by the Stones.

Production

Everything changes, even in the world of the Stones. Chuck Leavell is credited alongside the Glimmer Twins as co-writer of "Back to Zero." This was a first: no one outside the inner circle had ever been given this honor before. Not even—from within it—Bill Wyman, who, incidentally, does not play bass on this track. Instead, the bass line is played on a Yamaha DX7 synthesizer (as is the timbale part) and doubled by a real bass guitar, played this time not by Ron Wood, but almost certainly by the excellent John Regan, who would also play bass on Mick Jagger and David Bowie's cover of "Dancing in the Street," recorded in June. How could the Stones have released a track like "Back to Zero"? This is a funk track, but well below the standard of the best proponents of the genre, and again with that synth-dominated sound—metallic, cold, soulless—that Keith thoroughly abhorred. The talent of Philippe Saisse, who lends a hand here on synthesizer, with Dan Collette, who plays trumpet in the coda, and Anton Fig, who is most likely responsible for the percussion (tambourine, congas, maracas) is not in doubt, but they add nothing to the music of the Rolling Stones. Theirs is a completely different approach. Fortunately, there is plenty of guitar, all in a very funky style, to provide some reassuring color and relief. This is split between Keith Richards, Ron Wood, and Bobby Womack. As for Mick Jagger, the singer remains in the same register as before, his voice once again sounding extremely strained.

DIRTY WORK

Mick Jagger / Keith Richards / Ron Wood / 3:53

Musicians
Mick Jagger: vocals
Keith Richards: rhythm and lead guitar, backing vocals
Bill Wyman: bass
Charlie Watts: drums
Ron Wood: rhythm guitar, backing vocals
Chuck Leavell: keyboards

Recorded
EMI Pathé Marconi Studios, Boulogne-Billancourt, France: April 5–June 17, 1985
RPM Studios, New York City: July 16–August 17, September 10–October 15, 1985
Right Track Studios, New York City: November 15–December 5, 1985 (?)

Technical Team
Producers: Steve Lillywhite, the Glimmer Twins
Sound engineers: Dave Jerden, Steve Parker
Assistant sound engineers: Tim Crich, Mike Krowiak

Mick Jagger, more of a protest singer than ever on "Dirty Work," a vehement diatribe against exploiters.

Genesis

Once again, Mick Jagger takes a stand. In this song he reveals his deep loathing for all those who exploit others, those who never get their hands dirty, those who make other people do their dirty work. Little by little, the singer shows that anger is brewing. *I'm beginning to hate it. You're a user. I hate ya*, he belches in complete empathy with those who are suffering. A protest song, then, albeit one that has never been performed live. Initially titled "Let Some Fucker Do the Dirty Work," "Dirty Work" can be seen to some extent as a new version of "Salt of the Earth" (on *Beggars Banquet*).

Production

Another rock song that bears the signature of the human riff. The guitars have regained their smile, and Keith would explain in an interview that a base track with just two rhythm parts was originally laid down (Keith on the right; Ronnie on the left), with two more subsequently overdubbed. He would also explain that in order to retain the benefit of interaction, he preferred overdubbing live with his partner, rather than onto separate tracks. It can certainly be said that the two guitars possess a distinctly "rock" sound and display obvious passion. They mark the rhythm with metronomic precision, and Keith lets it rip with an excellent, admirably aggressive solo at 2:03. Charlie smacks his drums vigorously but not without a degree of subtlety, and Bill follows suit, working his strings with some power. Chuck Leavell is on keyboards, notably the organ. Mick's voice once again contains a great deal of passion. This has perhaps become a little rote, but after all, his role is to sing rock music, and he does so to perfection. At 3:06 he launches into a kind of rap, which Steve Lillywhite hastens to subject to a number of effects in varying degrees of good taste during the mixing stage. This is not the Stones' best-ever rock number. Keith can be sensed trying to rediscover some magic within the band, but faced with so much discord, the results are only halfway convincing. "Dirty Work" is no masterpiece, and this is a shame, as the track gives the album its name.

HAD IT WITH YOU

Mick Jagger / Keith Richards / Ron Wood / 3:19

Musicians
Mick Jagger: vocals, harmonica
Keith Richards: rhythm guitar
Charlie Watts: drums
Ron Wood: rhythm guitar, saxophone

Recorded
EMI Pathé Marconi Studios, Boulogne-Billancourt, France: April 5–June 17, 1985
RPM Studios, New York City: July 16–August 17, September 10–October 15, 1985
Right Track Studios, New York City: November 15–December 5, 1985 (?)

Technical Team
Producers: Steve Lillywhite, the Glimmer Twins
Sound engineers: Dave Jerden, Steve Parker
Assistant sound engineers: Tim Crich, Mike Krowiak

Ronnie Wood plays saxophone on "Had It with You"
(shown above onstage with Bobby Keys).

Genesis

In *Life,*[2] Keith Richards reveals how the words to this song came to him: "I wrote 'Had It with You' in Ronnie's front room in Chiswick, right on the banks of the Thames. We were waiting to go back to Paris, but the weather was so dodgy that we were stranded until the Dover ferry started rolling again."

It is such a sad thing to watch a good love die. These words are addressed not to some woman who has walked out, but to Mick Jagger, whose desire for independence from the Stones—made manifest by his recording of *She's the Boss*—was experienced by Keith as a provocation, or, worse, as a betrayal. Did Mick Jagger take the song this way? After all, he is the one who sings it, and persuasively, too . . .

Production

This is the last of the album's four tracks co-written by the Glimmer Twins and Ron Wood, an honor that has never been bestowed on any other member of the band. Furthermore, Ronnie's contribution to the song is pretty unusual in that he provides a saxophone accompaniment, albeit one that is not exactly indispensable and whose phrasing is not in the Bobby Keys league. However, the situation within the band was said to be so explosive, and the musical direction the cause of such friction, that Keith was probably seeking to get back to basics by any means necessary, even if this meant reducing the number of musicians involved. As a result, there is no bass and no keyboards, and Keith would later explain that after a number of attempts, everyone realized that the track sounded better this way. This is certainly a point of view, but the bass is sorely missed. Similarly, the guitars are also reduced to the essentials, the king of the riff taking care of the main rhythm part with a fantastic, very "roots" sound, obtained most likely from his blond 1959 Telecaster plugged into his new Fender Twin amp. Just one overdub, recorded simultaneously with Ronnie, would prove acceptable to Keith. Charlie saves his own skin and delivers a good drum part, while Mick—in addition to a very successful performance that nevertheless leaves the listener wondering why he masochistically agreed to sing such words—makes the best contribution to "Had It with You" with some excellent phrases on the harmonica. Right at the end of the track (3:17) the switch on the control room intercom can be heard clicking on.

SLEEP TONIGHT

Mick Jagger / Keith Richards / 5:10

Musicians
Keith Richards: vocals, acoustic guitar,
rhythm guitar, lead guitar, bass (?)
Ron Wood: drums, bass (?), backing vocals (?)
Chuck Leavell: synthesizer, piano (?)
Tom Waits (?): piano
**Bobby Womack (?), Tom Waits (?), Don Covay (?),
Kirsty MacColl (?), Janice Pendarvis (?),
Dolette McDonald (?):** backing vocals

Recorded
**EMI Pathé Marconi Studios, Boulogne-
Billancourt, France:** April 5–June 17, 1985
RPM Studios, New York City: July 16–August 17,
September 10–October 15, 1985
Right Track Studios, New York City:
November 15–December 5, 1985 (?)

Technical Team
Producers: Steve Lillywhite, the Glimmer Twins
Sound engineers: Dave Jerden, Steve Parker
Assistant sound engineers: Tim Crich, Mike Krowiak

Tom Waits, a friend of Keith Richards, may have
contributed to the recording of "Sleep Tonight."

Genesis
"Sleep Tonight" is a ballad composed on the piano by Keith Richards in the studio. Ron Wood, who was with him and liked the gentle melody, accompanies on drums. Keith later wrote: "The chorus is virtually a doo-wop chorus in C, but then the verses modulate quite naturally into another key. I had to wait for other people to convince me to go ahead with it; for a while I was saying, 'This is all good fun but we're wasting time, because I'm SURE this is somebody else's song' (laughs)."[74]

"Sleep Tonight" is the second song on the album (after "Too Rude") with Keith Richards on lead vocal: *They robbed you of your dignity. They even steal your heart from me. It ain't revenge, you understand . . .*

Production
Thus it is Keith who brings *Dirty Work* to a close, with a ballad that is half-blues and half-gospel. Despite good intentions, however, both melodically and harmonically, the song is weak and sounds like Keith Richards solo, rather than with the Rolling Stones. He and Ron Wood are indeed the only two members of the band present, and they divide up the various roles between them. The pianist seems to be Tom Waits, Keith evidently not possessing this degree of fluidity. Alternatively, it could be Chuck Leavell, who was already present on synthesizers. Keith plays a Martin 00-21 acoustic with Nashville tuning, as on "Wild Horses" in 1971. He is also on electric, and Alan Rogan would point out that this is an ideal opportunity to appreciate his blond 1959 Telecaster. It is certainly true that the instrument has a beautiful sound, and Keith's solo passages are particularly sumptuous (2:18). Keith is also, presumably, playing bass. Ronnie is on drums, as Charlie was incapacitated, but the results do not flatter him. If he had been surprisingly effective on "Too Rude," here he flirts with disaster. However, this can hardly be held against him, as he is a guitarist, not a drummer. What is strange is that Keith wanted to use his take . . . Keith, as we have seen, is on lead vocal. Although this is not one of his best performances, he is helped by some very good backing vocals from the likes of Tom Waits, Don Covay, Kirsty MacColl, Janice Pendarvis, Dolette McDonald, and others.

Sad Sad Sad
Mixed Emotions
Terrifying
Hold On To Your Hat
Hearts For Sale
Blinded By Love
Rock And A Hard Place
Can't Be Seen
Almost Hear You Sigh
Continental Drift
Break The Spell
Slipping Away

ALBUM
RELEASE DATE
United Kingdom: August 29, 1989
Label: Rolling Stones Records
RECORD NUMBER: ROLLING STONES
RECORDS CBS 465752 1
Number 2, on the charts for 18 weeks

STEEL WHEELS

STEEL WHEELS:
AN ELECTROMAGNETIC SPARK

Three years had elapsed since the last Stones album, three years during which Mick Jagger had been preoccupied with his solo career, which was marked by the release of two albums—*She's the Boss* in 1985 and *Primitive Cool* in 1987—and his tour to Japan and the South Pacific in 1988. During this time he seems to have given little thought to the Rolling Stones and Keith Richards, with whom he had fallen out after signing the CBS contract in August 1983, and even more seriously after refusing to go on tour to promote *Dirty Work*. On March 2, 1987, Mick declared in the columns of the *Daily Mirror*: "I love Keith, I admire him, but I don't feel we can really work together anymore."[125] By way of response, Keith released an album the following year titled *Talk Is Cheap*. This was closer to the traditional Stones repertoire than Jagger's two solo offerings, which were designed to win over a new—younger and more pop-oriented—audience.

During the course of autumn 1988, however, just as their fans were beginning to contemplate a future without the Rolling Stones, Mick Jagger—most likely because of the lukewarm reaction to *Primitive Cool*—did a U-turn and got in touch with his former bandmates. Initially surprised, Keith Richards was also wary, especially as he was playing more and more with the X-Pensive Winos (including a US tour from November 24 to December 17, 1988). The idea of getting together again gradually took hold, however, and in mid-January 1989, the Glimmer Twins were reunited under the Barbados sun to begin writing songs for a new album. Mick already had "Hold on to Your Hat" and "Almost Hear

You Sigh" under his belt. "When we meet up again, whatever antagonisms have been whipped up in the meantime, we drop them and start talking about the future. We always come up with something when we're alone together. There's an electromagnetic spark between us. There always has been."[2]

The Album

First of all the title. Why *Steel Wheels*? An image that, despite its ambiguities, evokes the new momentum of the band, which was getting itself moving again with the release of this new record and the announcement of another tour. And then there is the sound of the words, which is always important to the Stones. "I can't remember who came up with the title but it was a working title for a song that's now called 'Between a Rock and a Hard Place,'"[11] explains Keith.

Steel Wheels therefore marks the grand return of the Rolling Stones to the forefront of the music scene. Several of the tracks on the album reconnect with the glory years. While "Sad Sad Sad," "Mixed Emotions," "Hold on to Your Hat," and "Rock and a Hard Place," with its lashings of electric guitar, are perfect symbols of the band's newfound vigor, "Hearts for Sale" represents a return to blues basics. Meanwhile, "Break the Spell," whose atmosphere is reminiscent of Tom Waits, and "Slipping Away" confirm Keith Richards's taste for intimate ballads. Finally, "Continental Drift," recorded with the participation of the Moroccan musicians of Joujouka, and harking back to the album *Brian Jones Presents the Pipes of Pan at Joujouka*, released in 1971, demonstrates a real

The Stones enjoying the inevitable press conference for the release of their new album.

interest in world music, while at the same time paying tribute to the deceased Stone.

Group Therapy!

The recording of *Steel Wheels* would act as a kind of therapy or even exorcism, offering proof that both Keith's and Mick's wounds had healed. "Sad Sad Sad" can therefore be seen as an expression of the Stones' resilience, of their almost supernatural ability to overcome quarrels as well as ego problems, "because the Stones are bigger than any of us when it comes down to the nitty-gritty,"[2] as Keith Richards so rightly observes in *Life*. The notion of therapy is also present in "Mixed Emotions" and "Rock and a Hard Place," in which an afterimage of the disagreement between Keith and Mick can be made out.

The other songs are not directly related to the recent past of the Rolling Stones. In "Terrifying," Mick Jagger sings of the *strange desires* he feels rising within him, whereas in "Blinded by Love," he draws an unusual parallel between the love of Mark Antony and Cleopatra on the one hand and that of Prince Edward and Wallis Simpson, twenty centuries later, on the other. Keith Richards draws on his own experience in "Can't Be Seen," which references his relationship with Anita Pallenberg and Brian Jones's distress, while in "Slipping Away" he ponders happiness, which can only ever be ephemeral, and perhaps his own existence too. As for "Almost Hear You Sigh," this Keith composition for which Mick Jagger rewrote some superb lyrics is all about reconciliation . . .

The Rolling Stones' nineteenth (British) studio album, *Steel Wheels* went on sale planet-wide on August 29, 1989. Its success lived up to fans' expectations, which had built up since *Dirty Work*. The album made it to number 1 in several countries, including Canada and Norway, number 2 in the United Kingdom, Germany, Switzerland, and the Netherlands, number 3 in the United States and New Zealand, number 5 in Italy, and number 6 in France and Spain. *Mojo* had the following to say: "As befits the world's top-selling rock 'n' roll brand, a thoroughly professional job."[30]

A Record-Breaking Tour

On July 11, 1989, a month and a half before the release of *Steel Wheels*, the Rolling Stones were in New York City, where they announced their next tour to some five hundred journalists on a Grand Central Station platform. This unleashed a tidal wave of demand. In Toronto, where the band was due to play on September 3 and 4, 130,000 tickets sold out in under six hours. In Cincinnati, 54,000 tickets for the September 14 show were snapped up in less than an hour and a half, and seats for the October 10 and 11 concerts at Shea Stadium in New York City went just as quickly.

After a surprise gig played to an audience of only seven hundred in New Haven, Connecticut, on August 12, the Steel Wheels Tour kicked off officially on August 31 in Philadelphia. In addition to the five Rolling Stones, the lineup included the Uptown Horns, Bobby Keys on sax, Chuck Leavell and Matt Clifford on keyboards, and Bernard Fowler, Lisa Fischer, and Cindy Mizelle on backing vocals. This tour of the United States and Canada would conclude with concerts in Atlantic City, New Jersey, on December 17, 19, and 20. The Stones then gave ten shows in Tokyo between February 14 and 27, 1990. Next it was Europe's turn to thrill to the beat of the

Mick and Keith at the Rock and Roll Hall of Fame ceremony.

Stones, with forty-five shows in no fewer than fifteen countries (from the Netherlands to the United Kingdom, via Spain, France, Italy, and Germany) between May 18 and August 25. This leg was renamed the Urban Jungle . . .

The Album Cover

The cover artwork was entrusted to John Warwicker, who had already designed a number of covers, including those for the Duran Duran single "Planet Earth" (1981) and the Police compilation *Every Breath You Take: The Singles* (1986). For the new Stones album, Warwicker chose to illustrate the front and rear covers with the same motif: twelve black and gray roundels that could be seen as twelve steel wheels, in reference to the title, or twelve discs simply alluding to the arrival of the CD era. Printed across the top, in blue on a black background, are the name of the band and the title of the album. Inside, photographs of Keith, Charlie, Ronnie, Mick, and Bill alternate with the song lyrics, and a final photograph unites all five members of the band.

The Recording

With the resumption of recording, everyone hoped to rediscover a serenity that had been shattered with the nightmare sessions of *Dirty Work*. "When we got back together for 'Steel Wheels', the atmosphere was kind of kid gloves," recalls Ron Wood, "but there was nevertheless a happy feeling. You could see everybody breathing a sigh of relief that Mick and Keith were getting on again. Thank God!"[11] After recording two songs at Eddy Grant's Blue Wave Studios in Barbados at the beginning of January ("Hang on Tonight" by Mick Jagger and

"Hellhound on My Trail," a Robert Johnson blues—neither used on the album), the Stones then rehearsed at that same venue during the early part of the year with Matt Clifford and Chuck Leavell. The dates vary from mid-January to the beginning of March, depending on the source.

The *Steel Wheels* sessions got properly under way on March 28, this time at AIR Studios (Associated Independent Recording Studios) in Montserrat. AIR was initially a recording complex set up in London in 1969 with the involvement of George Martin. This venture met with rapid success and led the Beatles producer to build another studio on Montserrat, a paradise island in the Caribbean, at the end of the seventies. Some of the biggest names in show business would record there, including the Police, Dire Straits, Elton John, Paul McCartney, Michael Jackson, and Stevie Wonder . . . Sadly, the Rolling Stones would be among the studios' last-ever clients: on September 10, 1989, the island and studios were devastated by the ferocious Hurricane Hugo.

Having tried Steve Lillywhite on *Dirty Work*, the band got back together for this album with Chris Kimsey in the role of co-producer. Christopher Marc Potter (Duran Duran, the Verve, Richard Ashcroft) was called in as sound engineer. One of Montserrat's chief advantages was its lack of distractions, as Keith would confirm: "Working in a city is not always the best thing for a band. On a little island with nowhere to go you get a lot more done, and more quickly."[9] And Mick backs this up: "I was surprised that we got the recording of 'Steel Wheels' done so quickly."[9] To start with, however, the Stones singer was concerned about the prospect of spending weeks in this remote place. "You could always work!"[74] the riff master is said to have amiably retorted!

By May 5, the band had successfully recorded "Wish I'd Never Met You" (the B-side of "Almost Hear You Sigh"), "Mixed Emotions" (both the album version and the 12-inch version), "Rock and a Hard Place" (the album version, dance mix, bonus beats mix, hard dub mix, rock mix edit, and the Michael H. Brauer mix), "Almost Hear You Sigh," "Sad Sad Sad," "Hearts for Sale," "Hold on to Your Hat," "Slipping Away," "Can't Be Seen," "Break the Spell," "Blinded by Love," "Terrifying" (the album version and the 12-inch remix), "Fancyman Blues" (the B-side of "Mixed Emotions"), "Continental Drift" (with supplementary recording in Tangier, Morocco, on June

16 and 17), plus various other numbers that would be left out of the final selection for *Steel Wheels*. The overdubs and mixing took place at Olympic Sound Studios in London between May 15 and the end of June. Michael H. Brauer, who enjoyed a great career mixing Bob Dylan, Paul McCartney, and Aretha Franklin, was responsible for mixing most of the tracks. The one exception is "Mixed Emotions," which was mixed at the Hit Factory in New York City by Chris Kimsey, assisted by Michael Butterworth (Robert Plant, Duran Duran) and Al Stone. Rupert Coulson was the assistant sound engineer working alongside Christopher Marc Potter. He collaborated with artists of the caliber of Queen, the Sparks, and Kate Bush.

An Extensive Lineup

The Stones were supported by a long list of musicians. Chuck Leavell was invited back to share the keyboards with Matt Clifford (Yes, Mick Jagger, Jon Anderson). The horn section was filled by the Kick Horns, comprising Simon Clarke (Oasis, Eric Clapton, David Gilmour), Roddy Lorimer (not Corimer as on the album cover; Suede, the Who, Blur), Tim Sanders (the Who, Rod Stewart, Terence Trent D'Arby), and Paul Spong (Joe Jackson, Eric Clapton, Dr. Feelgood). Responsible for the backing vocals were Bernard Fowler (Yoko Ono, Herbie Hancock, Tackhead), Sara Dash (Patti Labelle & The Bluebelles, Nile Rodgers), and Lisa Fischer (Al Jarreau, George Benson, Aretha Franklin) as well as Sonia Jones Morgan (Mike Oldfield, Simple Minds, Cliff Richard) and Tessa Niles (Tina Turner, Pet Shop Boys, Eric Clapton). Luís Jardim was on percussion (Asia, David Gilmour, Ray Charles), and Phil Beer played fiddle and mandolin (Mike Oldfield, Ashley Hutchings). For "Continental Drift" the Master Musicians of

Joujouka were recorded in Morocco and the ensemble Farafina in London. Finally, a certain Chris Jagger is credited as "literary editor" on two songs. The two Jagger brothers on the same album?

Technical Details

Sound engineer Chris Potter would later reveal that AIR Studios on Montserrat was equipped with a Mitsubishi 32-track tape recorder (believed to be an X-850) and an SSL 4000 E console with a Series G computer and twelve additional channels, each with Focusrite equalization, which were used mainly for Charlie's drum kit.

The Instruments

Alan Rogan was succeeded by a new guitar technician: Pierre de Beauport. The guitars used most by Keith on the album are his three main Telecasters, his 1959 Stratocaster, a white Music Man Silhouette, a Sadowsky Nylon String, and a superb 1956 Velázquez classical. Ronnie, in addition to his usual guitars, plays a white ESP TE fitted with a Parsons B-bender. Meanwhile, Bill branches out by becoming attached to a Wal bass designed by the English instrument maker Ian Waller.

Bill Wyman opened his restaurant in London, which was named *Sticky Fingers*. Its motto was *Good food, good music, good people*.

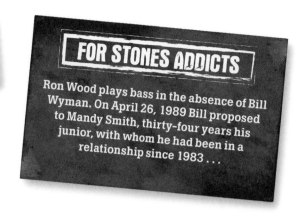

SAD SAD SAD

Mick Jagger / Keith Richards / 3:35

Musicians
Mick Jagger: vocals, rhythm guitar
Keith Richards: rhythm guitars, lead guitar
Charlie Watts: drums
Ron Wood: bass
Chuck Leavell: piano, organ, synthesizer
Bernard Fowler: backing vocals
The Kick Horns: horns

Recorded
AIR Studios, Montserrat: March 29–May 5, 1989
Olympic Sound Studios, London: May 15–June 29, 1989

Technical Team
Producers: Chris Kimsey, the Glimmer Twins
Sound engineer: Christopher Marc Potter
Assistant sound engineer: Rupert Coulson
Mixing: Michael H. Brauer

Charlie Watts, as implacable as ever after playing with the Stones for a quarter of a century.

Genesis

"Sad Sad Sad" is the fanfare that accompanies the Rolling Stones' return to the arena. What is more, the song's riff testifies to an undiminished desire on the part of the Glimmer Twins to enter the fray. A riff is almost certainly from Mick Jagger, who plays electric guitar alongside Keith Richards. *Are you ready for the gilded cage/Are you ready for the tears of rage/Come on baby, don't let them drown you out*: Mick seems to be advising his partner, in a vengeful voice, on how to survive the chaos of her life. Or should the song perhaps be seen as an oblique reference to the indestructibility of the Stones, who had survived the deterioration of relations between Mick and Keith?

Production

"Sad Sad Sad" provides reassurance. Despite the fallings-out and the near breakup of the band, this opening track demonstrates that the Stones are once again enjoying recording together. Mick has rediscovered his ability to sing with emotion; gone are the power plays of *Dirty Work*. A natural, unconstrained energy has flooded back. It is Mick who leads into the song, presumably on one of Keith's 5-string Telecasters in open G, producing a rich, aggressive, distorted sound. Keith would later explain that he devoted a considerable amount of time to adjusting the amp settings, probably on his old Fender Twin or his Mesa Boogie. He joins Mick in the fourth bar, playing a rhythm part that he himself later doubles, and delivers an excellent solo at 1:54 with a sonority and phrasing that he has not had for a long time. He deviates from his usual Chuck Berry–style licks to offer a superb demonstration of rock guitar at its best. Ronnie supports his bandmates ably on a Fender Precision bass, although he is a little undermixed. Charlie lays down a superb rhythm on his Gretsch kit, and is supported in the refrains by hand claps that give the impression of issuing from a drum machine of the Roland TR-707 type. Chuck Leavell, who has been by the Stones' side since *Undercover*, is back at his keyboards and synthesizers, producing sound pads that can be heard particularly well at 2:41. Finally the Kick Horns can be heard making their first contribution, and are convincing, if perhaps somewhat drowned in reverb.

MIXED EMOTIONS

Mick Jagger / Keith Richards / 4:38

Musicians
Mick Jagger: vocals, rhythm guitar, shakers
Keith Richards: rhythm guitar, backing vocals
Bill Wyman: bass
Charlie Watts: drums
Ron Wood: lead guitar
Chuck Leavell: piano, organ
Luis Jardim: percussion
Sarah Dash, Lisa Fischer, Bernard Fowler: backing vocals
The Kick Horns: horns

Recorded
AIR Studios, Montserrat: March 29–May 5, 1989
Olympic Sound Studios, London: May 15–June 29, 1989 (?)
The Hit Factory, New York City: May or June 1989

Technical Team
Producers: Chris Kimsey, the Glimmer Twins
Sound engineer: Christopher Marc Potter
Assistant sound engineer: Rupert Coulson
Mixing: Chris Kimsey
**Assistant sound engineers (the Hit
Factory):** Michael Butterworth, Al Stone

FOR STONES ADDICTS

A comparison of the videos of "One Hit (to
the Body)" and "Mixed Emotions" gives an
idea of the different atmospheres that
prevailed during the production of *Dirty
Work* on the one hand and *Steel Wheels* on
the other. In the first, the Stones display
nothing but friction and hostility; in the
second, they are all smiles . . .

Genesis
Let's bury the hatchet/Wipe out the past . . . Contrary to what the words seem to be saying, Mick Jagger has always maintained that "Mixed Emotions" had nothing to do with his quarrel with Keith Richards, and that it was in no way a response to "You Don't Move Me" (on *Talk Is Cheap*, Keith's first solo album, released in 1988) in which his "twin" accuses him of having *lost the feeling*, and of being *not so appealing*. The Stones singer claims to have been thinking of a girl he used to know when writing this song (but takes care not to mention by name). Hence the refrain, which does indeed seem to be addressed to a former lover: *You're not the only one with mixed emotions/You're not the only ship adrift on this ocean*. For his part, Keith Richards has always believed that "Mixed Emotions" contained a reference to the Glimmer Twins' tempestuous relationship. Others have knowingly and humorously misheard the title as "Mick's Emotions" or even "Mick's Demotion."

"Mixed Emotions" was released on August 17, 1989, as the A-side (with "Fancyman Blues" on the B-side) of the first single to be taken from *Steel Wheels*. Although stalling at number 36 on the British charts on September 16, a week later it had risen to number 5 on the *Billboard* pop chart and number 1 on the *Billboard* Mainstream Rock Tracks on September 2.

Production
A sound engineer at AIR Studios, whose name Keith does not mention, recalls the atmosphere that prevailed during the recording of "Mixed Emotions": "Some bigwig figure in the music business, invited by Mick, came to Montserrat to discuss some contract to do with touring. He obviously fancied himself for his producing abilities, because we're standing in the studio area, playing back "Mixed Emotions." . . . And Keith is standing there with his guitar on and Mick's standing there and we're listening to it. The song finishes, and the guy says, Keith, great song, man, but I tell you, I think if you arranged it a little bit differently it would be so much better. So Keith went to his doctor's bag and pulled out a knife and threw it, and it landed right between the bloke's legs. . . . Keith says, listen, sonny, I was writing songs before you were a glint on your father's dick. Don't you tell me how to write songs. And he walked out."[2]

Mick Jagger and Keith Richards, an indestructible friendship that has survived many a falling-out.

"Mixed Emotions" is a very good song by a band that was rediscovering a cohesion it had not had for a long time. It may not be the best song in their catalog, but it is nevertheless a fine number. From the very first bar, the band is powered by an enormous dose of adrenaline, launching the track with chords that call to mind the intro to the Beatles' "I Want to Hold Your Hand." But that is where the similarity ends, the guitars of Mick (right) and Keith (left), supported by some excellent drumming from Charlie, reminding us that we are dealing with the Stones, who hurtle along with the wind in their sails, not remotely *adrift on the ocean*. Rhythmically, the band is nothing short of explosive, with Charlie and Bill (on one of his last recorded bass lines for the group) at their phenomenal best. Sadly, the Stones would never achieve a comparable drums-bass alchemy again following the departure of Bill Wyman—future restaurateur, photographer, collector, writer, inventor, archaeologist, and blues musician! The two of them are assisted by Luís Jardim on percussion, but other than a tambourine, his work is largely buried in the mix. Mick is credited with playing shakers, but these are no

more audible than the rest of the percussion. The guitars are clearly the central theme of "Mixed Emotions," the Glimmer Twins sharing the two rhythm parts and leaving the lead to Ron Wood, who plays some very good phrases on his clear-toned Stratocaster, notably at 2:27. The other instrumental parts also unfortunately suffer in the mix, including the Kick Horns, whose contribution can be discerned in the refrains and coda (from 3:12), and Chuck Leavell's keyboards, which can hardly be heard at all. On the other hand, the listener is able to discover the incredible voices of the backing vocalists, Sarah Dash, Lisa Fischer, and Bernard Fowler, which are particularly audible in the bridge, at 1:53. Keith joins them in the refrains, his voice clearly recognizable among the others. This song provides Mick Jagger with an opportunity to reconnect with some of his fantastic vocal performances of the past, although he would acknowledge that he found it difficult to reproduce the song live. "Mixed Emotions" is a triumph, but one cannot help feeling that it lacks a certain something that might have raised it to the level of an unforgettable Stones number.

TERRIFYING

Mick Jagger / Keith Richards / 4:53

Musicians
Mick Jagger: vocals, shakers
Keith Richards: rhythm guitar, backing vocals
Bill Wyman: bass
Charlie Watts: drums
Ron Wood: rhythm and lead guitar
Chuck Leavell: organ
Matt Clifford: keyboards
Roddy Lorimer: trumpet
Lisa Fischer: backing vocals

Recorded
AIR Studios, Montserrat: March 29–May 5, 1989
Olympic Sound Studios, London: May 15–June 29, 1989

Technical Team
Producers: Chris Kimsey, the Glimmer Twins
Sound engineer: Christopher Marc Potter
Assistant sound engineer: Rupert Coulson
Mixing: Michael H. Brauer

"Terrifying," a funky rock number of the
kind favored by Ron Wood.

Genesis

I'm rutting like a goat/I'm horny as a hog . . . The Glimmer Twins, and Mick Jagger in particular, resort to animal metaphors to describe the *terrifying love* that has overcome them. *I get these strange strange strange desires*, sings Jagger to a hypnotic, dance-like beat, reminiscent of the "Hot Stuff" era. "Terrifying" was released in Europe (including the United Kingdom) in two main formats: a single (with "Wish I'd Never Met You" as the B-side) and a maxi single (comprising the 12- and 7-inch remixes, the album version, and "Wish I'd Never Met You"). Neither managed to enter the charts.

Production

The Stones give an excellent performance of this highly energetic funk-rock number. In all likelihood, "Terrifying," with its relentless groove, came into being under the influence of Bill Laswell and Nile Rodgers—the producers of Jagger's *She's the Boss*. The rhythm section is fearsomely efficient, with Charlie and Bill each making an outstanding contribution. According to Martin Elliott, Chris Kimsey reports that Michael H. Brauer, the sound engineer in charge of the mixing, was keen to get the best possible sound out of Bill's bass, and he succeeded. It is also interesting to note that Bill is almost certainly playing his English-made Wal bass. The guitarists are no less worthy of praise, Keith and Ronnie each playing a superbly funky rhythm part. It seems to be Woody who takes the one and only solo, which occurs in the intro, on what is most likely his Stratocaster with fairly pronounced chorus/ phasing. Another important element is Matt Clifford's synthesizer. He can be heard producing vibraphone (or celesta) sounds and coming in with numerous percussion effects (including timbales and cowbells), probably on a Yamaha DX7. These can be heard from 4:13. Chuck Leavell, meanwhile, is on organ. Roddy Lorimer of the Kick Horns plays some very jazzy and entirely appropriate phrases on the trumpet. Mick delivers a strong vocal take, singing in a low register that is just right for the song.

HOLD ON TO YOUR HAT

Mick Jagger / Keith Richards / 3:32

Musicians
Mick Jagger: vocals, rhythm guitar
Keith Richards: lead guitar
Charlie Watts: drums
Ron Wood: bass

Recorded
AIR Studios, Montserrat: March 29–May 5, 1989
Olympic Sound Studios, London: May 15–June 29, 1989

Technical Team
Producers: Chris Kimsey, the Glimmer Twins
Sound engineer: Christopher Marc Potter
Assistant sound engineer: Rupert Coulson
Mixing: Michael H. Brauer

Keith Richards referred to the tried-and-true "Rip This Joint" recipe for "Hold on to Your Hat."

Genesis

Despite the passing years, the Stones continued to have faith in Chuck Berry–style rock 'n' roll. "Hold on to Your Hat" exudes an energy not dissimilar to that of "Rip This Joint," recorded seventeen years earlier, during the torrid *Exile on Main St.* sessions. The lyrics also sound like a return to the good old days, taking up the recurrent theme of the jaded lover and the breakup of a relationship. The narrator has had enough of the woman he shares his bed with, and tells her so in no uncertain terms, effectively ordering her to get out of his life and adding: *I've had it up to here with your yackety-yack.* By the way, "Yakety Yak" was the title of one of the Coasters' biggest hits (number 1 on the pop and R&B charts in 1958).

Production

"Hold on to Your Hat" is a curious track that gives the listener a sense of déjà vu (or rather *déjà entendu*), despite what is, for the Stones, an unusual musical color. This impression of a new sound is due mainly to the lead guitar, with Keith playing solo licks of a speed and phrasing never previously heard from him. In doing so, he reveals a hitherto unsuspected hard rock side. One could be forgiven for wondering whether he really did write the song, but the credit in the liner notes leaves no room for doubt. Was he perhaps struck by Guns N' Roses fever, despite not exactly going easy on them around this time? Questions could also be asked about the recording method. Might Keith have recorded his solo on a slowed-down tape recorder? However, the sonority of his guitar does not give this impression. Moving away from Keith, Mick plays the main rhythm guitar part, on an instrument presumably tuned in open G. As Bill was absent, Ronnie is on bass, his playing sadly lacking weight and doing little to support the rhythm. Charlie hammers his drums conscientiously, injecting a dose of high energy that gives the track a significant boost. And while on the subject of power, Jagger falls back into his bad habits of *Dirty Work*, with his voice strained and devoid of nuance, constantly walking a tightrope. From a harmonic point view, "Hold on to Your Hat" is not particularly successful, and despite the best of intentions, it is one of the weaker songs in the track listing. This is a shame, especially after the first three tracks on the album give rise to such hope.

HEARTS FOR SALE

Mick Jagger / Keith Richards / 4:40

Musicians
Mick Jagger: vocals, rhythm guitar, harmonica
Keith Richards: rhythm guitar
Bill Wyman: bass
Charlie Watts: drums
Ron Wood: rhythm and lead guitar
Matt Clifford: keyboards
Bernard Fowler: backing vocals
Recorded
AIR Studios, Montserrat: March 29–May 5, 1989
Olympic Sound Studios, London: May 15–June 29, 1989
Technical Team
Producers: Chris Kimsey, the Glimmer Twins
Sound engineer: Christopher Marc Potter
Assistant sound engineer: Rupert Coulson
Mixing: Michael H. Brauer

Charlie Watts at his Gretsch kit during the
Steel Wheels Tour.

Genesis

On the face of it, "Hearts for Sale" is a harmless enough song, a blues-rock number with a heavy beat, like those the Stones had been recording since their earliest days. Certain phrases merit closer inspection, however, particularly when the narrator, in reality none other than Mick Jagger, claims to be *The voice of conscience/the voice of reason*. Whose are these *Hearts for sale going cheap*? Is this an attack on rock star groupies? Or is it a reflection on the quest for love by any means necessary? It remains a mystery. "Hearts for Sale" has never been performed live.

Production

Mick Jagger plays a very good introductory riff, drenched in the digital reverb that was characteristic of the day. He could almost be Jimi Hendrix warming up! A drier sound then takes over, and "Hearts for Sale" gets into its cruising rhythm. By now, the Stones singer had mastered the art of the rhythm guitar accompaniment, and over the course of just a few albums had developed into a dependable guitarist. Keith supports him on a second rhythm guitar, and Ron Wood on a third. It is worth underscoring the way in which Keith now approaches many of his accompaniments, observing frequent silences in order to allow the song to breathe and all the different elements to interact. And the proof can be heard in the combination of the three guitars, each one finding its natural place. Ronnie is also on lead, and takes a solo at 2:41, most probably on one of his Stratocasters, clear-toned and colored by strong phasing. The only criticism to be made here is that that the reverb is a little too intrusive. Matt Clifford is on keyboards and can be heard creating sound pads to support the harmonies. *Steel Wheels* is an album that places an emphasis on the superb work of Bill and Charlie, their rhythm section constituting one of the undisputed strengths of the band. Their playing never takes the form of a technical demonstration; it is more a question of total harmony between the two of them. Moreover, both drummer and bassist constantly strive to be effective through simplicity—the most difficult thing to achieve. Mick, meanwhile, has returned to a simpler style of delivery and also plays a number of absolutely superb phrases on the harmonica from 4:00. His sound is redolent of the Chicago blues, and it is just a shame he does not reach for the instrument more often.

BLINDED BY LOVE

Mick Jagger / Keith Richards / 4:37

Musicians
Mick Jagger: vocals, acoustic guitar
Keith Richards: acoustic guitar, nylon
string guitar, backing vocals
Bill Wyman: bass
Charlie Watts: drums
Ron Wood: acoustic guitar
Chuck Leavell: organ
Matt Clifford: piano, harmonium
Phil Beer: fiddle, mandolin
Luís Jardim: percussion
Bernard Fowler: backing vocals
Recorded
AIR Studios, Montserrat: March 29–May 5, 1989
Olympic Sound Studios, London: May 15–June 29, 1989
Technical Team
Producers: Chris Kimsey, the Glimmer Twins
Sound engineer: Christopher Marc Potter
Assistant sound engineer: Rupert Coulson
Mixing: Michael H. Brauer

Phil Beer, a member of Show of Hands, plays fiddle (and
mandolin) on this country-style ballad.

FOR STONES ADDICTS

Chris Jagger, Mick's younger brother, is
credited in the liner notes as "literary
editor," possibly for his research into the
historical figures mentioned in the song.
Chris recorded a number of albums
between 1973 (the first being *You Know
the Name but Not the Face*) and 2013, and
also acted in a number of films, including
Kenneth Anger's *Lucifer Rising* (1972).

Genesis

"Blinded by Love" is a ballad with a country and western flavor and exotic Hawaiian accents. In it Mick Jagger invokes a selection of tragic lovers from history in order to warn of the dangers of passionate love, which can divert men from their destiny and lead to their undoing. Hence Mark Antony, ruined by his love for the *Queen of the Nile*, Samson, betrayed by Delilah, and the *poor Prince of Wales* (Edward, Duke of Windsor), forced to abdicate for the sake of the beautiful *eyes of a second-hand* American lady! *You better lock up your soul for safe-keeping*, sings Jagger, against all expectations.

Production

"Blinded by Love" is a steadfastly acoustic track giving pride of place to the stringed instruments. The three guitarists each play acoustic rhythm: Mick in the center, Ronnie most likely on the left, and Keith on the right. The latter seems to be using Nashville tuning and also plays short phrases on a Sadowsky Nylon String guitar, as can be heard at 2:03. This mass of guitars has probably been boosted by various overdubs, but better timing would not have gone amiss in places. Charlie plays cross-stick, Bill tries to do something different to the "pumping" style of bass generally associated with this type of music, and Chuck Leavell comes in with short sequences on the organ (1:52). Matt Clifford plays a very good piano part that is not unlike the style of Nicky Hopkins, and although also credited with the harmonium, it has to be said that he is inaudible on that instrument. Phil Beer, a newcomer to the world of the Stones, plays an effective mandolin part and also a very good fiddle accompaniment, even taking a short solo at 3:27. Mick sings with a certain listlessness, and is supported in the vocal harmonies by Keith and Bernard Fowler. "Blinded by Love" is not the best country track ever written by the Glimmer Twins. It is strangely lacking in imagination and falls away a little after the first few bars. Where is the Stones' craziness? Where is their mockery? Mick Jagger turns himself into a moralizer, and this is a role that does not suit him particularly well—any more than it does his colleagues.

ROCK AND A HARD PLACE

Mick Jagger / Keith Richards / 5:25

Musicians
Mick Jagger: vocals, rhythm guitar
Keith Richards: rhythm guitar
Bill Wyman: bass
Charlie Watts: drums
Ron Wood: rhythm and lead guitar
Chuck Leavell: keyboards
Matt Clifford: keyboards
The Kick Horns: horns
Sarah Dash, Lisa Fischer, Bernard Fowler: backing vocals
Unidentified musician: tambourine

Recorded
AIR Studios, Montserrat: March 29–May 5, 1989
Olympic Sound Studios, London: May 15–June 29, 1989

Technical Team
Producers: Chris Kimsey, the Glimmer Twins
Sound engineer: Christopher Marc Potter
Assistant sound engineer: Rupert Coulson
Mixing: Michael H. Brauer

What better than a boom box to appreciate the very essence of rock music . . .

Genesis

Keith Richards recalls: "This was like going back to the way we worked in the early days, before *Exile*, when we were living around the corner from each other in London. Mick and I hadn't got together in four years since *Dirty Work*, but as soon as we met up in Barbados for a fortnight, with a couple of guitars and a piano, everything was fine."[87]

Between a rock and a hard place: This sums up the frame of mind that Mick Jagger and Keith Richards were in. They had both made solo albums (two in the case of the Mick; one in the case of the Keith), but nevertheless managed to get together for the *Steel Wheels* sessions. *We're in the same boat on the same sea/And we're sailing south on the same breeze*: harmony seems to reign once more between the Glimmer Twins. Looking beyond their personal situation, Mick Jagger (the lyricist) casts a glance at a world of darkness—a world that talks of freedom and human rights while wars proliferate and *peasants* sink further every day into the double spiral of poverty and impotence.

"Rock and a Hard Place" was chosen as the A-side of the second single from *Steel Wheels* (with "Cook Cook Blues" on the flip side). Released on November 4, 1989, it had risen to number 23 on the pop chart and number 1 on the *Billboard* Mainstream Rock Tracks chart within six weeks.

Production

Right from the intro, all the members of the band seem to be on the same wavelength. With Charlie launching the track on his snare drum, "Rock and a Hard Place" blows up like a hurricane, Mick, Keith, and Ronnie playing their guitars in unison to ensure effective delivery of a powerful, untamed riff. Ron Wood then takes care of an excellent rhythm part (on the left) that is the hallmark of the piece. Keith supports him with another, more discreet rhythm part (on the right), subtly combining licks and palm mute, while Mick strums his part, probably on one of Keith's Telecasters in open G. Woody distinguishes himself with two absolutely superb, beautifully phrased solos at 2:38 and 3:56. Charlie supports the groove with a very good drum part that possesses something of a dance drive, with prominent hi-hat and bass drum marking every beat. Bill delivers one of his best bass lines, in a funky rock style, probably on his Wal bass. Chuck Leavell and

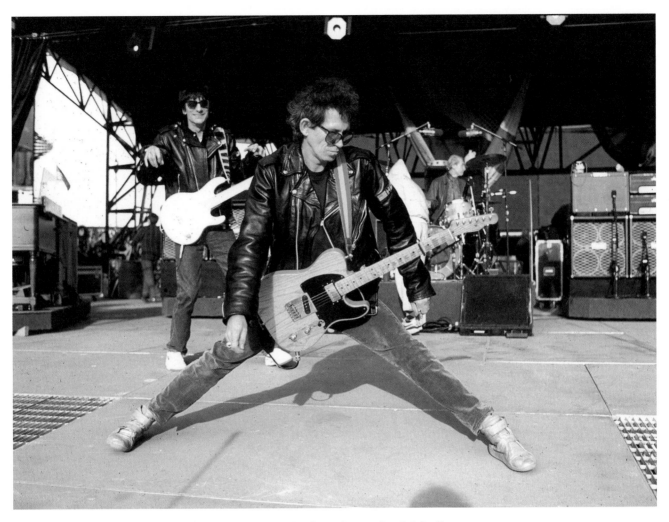

Keith Richards: the epitome of rock 'n' roll.

Matt Clifford share the keyboard work, including organ, pad sounds, and the production of various synthesizer percussion effects, as can be heard in the break at 3:06 (and again at 3:36, 3:40, and 3:44, where a gong sound from a sound bank can be heard). A tambourine is very prominent during this break, as it is throughout the rest of the track; yet it is impossible to identify the musician. The Kick Horns make another appearance in the refrains and coda, but unfortunately are too recessed in the mix. Another important element on "Rock and a Hard Place" is the performance of backing vocalists Sarah Dash, Lisa Fischer, and Bernard Fowler, who bring a soul sonority and color to the song. Mick delivers one of his best vocal takes of the album, literally carried away by his performance. He must have liked this song (which was entirely of his writing, according to Keith), because he would compare it to "Start Me Up," whose first few notes provoke the same irresistible desire to dance. The Stones have succeeded in rediscovering a real cohesion since the *Dirty Work* debacle, even if this is not a classic to compare with those of the past. It certainly bodes well for the future, however.

A promotional video of "Rock and a Hard Place," in which Mick Jagger appears with short hair, was later made by Wayne Isham.

"Rock and a Hard Place" was originally titled . . . "Steel Wheels."

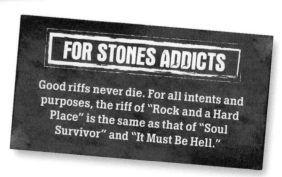

FOR STONES ADDICTS

Good riffs never die. For all intents and purposes, the riff of "Rock and a Hard Place" is the same as that of "Soul Survivor" and "It Must Be Hell."

CAN'T BE SEEN

Mick Jagger / Keith Richards / 4:09

Musicians
Keith Richards: vocals, rhythm and lead guitar
Bill Wyman: bass
Charlie Watts: drums
Ron Wood: rhythm guitar
Chuck Leavell: organ, Wurlitzer
Matt Clifford: clavinet
Luís Jardim: percussion
Bernard Fowler: backing vocals

Recorded
AIR Studios, Montserrat: March 29–May 5, 1989
Olympic Sound Studios, London: May 15–June 29, 1989

Technical Team
Producers: Chris Kimsey, the Glimmer Twins
Sound engineer: Christopher Marc Potter
Assistant sound engineer: Rupert Coulson
Mixing: Michael H. Brauer

Genesis

"Can't Be Seen" is a Keith Richards song performed by . . . Keith Richards. *I just can't be seen with you . . . It's too dangerous, baby . . .* In *Life*,[2] he explains that this song describes the first stirrings of his relationship with Anita Pallenberg, which were kept secret from the unfortunate Brian Jones. Twenty years later, here he is returning to the subject of the famous trip to Morocco, where it all started. Particularly revealing of the consequences of this nascent love affair, "Can't Be Seen" is transformed by Keith into a song not merely about clandestine love, but about forbidden love: *Yeah it was just a dream with you/Yeah because you're married anyway.*

In this song, Keith Richards also almost certainly harks back to the relationship between Bill Wyman and Mandy Smith. When the Stones bassist met Mandy in 1983, she was only thirteen years old. Their liaison remained secret until the tabloids found out about it in 1986 and accused Bill Wyman of being a dangerous corruptor of youth. This new scandal within the Stones universe would come to an end with the marriage of Bill and Mandy (during the mixing of *Steel Wheels*!).

Production

Keith would later reveal that "Can't Been Seen" is one of the two songs written by him (the other being "Before They Make Me Run" on *Some Girls*) that demanded the most time in the studio.[2] The production is polished, with Keith sharing rhythm guitar with Ron Wood. He plays the solo passages himself, introducing some new phrases that are a long way from the Chuck Berry–style licks that had always characterized his solos in the past. He even adopts heavy metal effects, and goes for speed more often than usual in his playing. The real strength of the track, however, lies in his vocal performance, probably one of his most successful to date. He reaches up for the high notes with power and conviction, and always with a certain joyfulness in his voice. Charlie and Bill build a first-rate rhythmic foundation, accompanied by Luís Jardim on percussion, not least a masterful tambourine. Chuck Leavell opens the track on the organ (a B-3?) and also provides support on the Wurlitzer, as does Matt Clifford on the clavinet, although this can hardly be heard.

Despite its evident dynamism, "Can't Be Seen" never really takes off, as a result of its compositional shortcomings.

Bill, happily married to Mandy.

ALMOST HEAR YOU SIGH

Mick Jagger / Keith Richards / Steve Jordan / 4:37

Musicians
Mick Jagger: vocals
Keith Richards: acoustic guitar, rhythm guitar, backing vocals
Bill Wyman: bass
Charlie Watts: drums
Ron Wood: rhythm and lead guitar, backing vocals
Chuck Leavell: keyboards
Matt Clifford: keyboards
Luís Jardim: percussion
Sarah Dash, Lisa Fischer, Bernard Fowler: backing vocals
Recorded
AIR Studios, Montserrat: March 29–May 5, 1989
Olympic Sound Studios, London: May 15–June 29, 1989
Technical Team
Producers: Chris Kimsey, the Glimmer Twins
Sound engineer: Christopher Marc Potter
Assistant sound engineer: Rupert Coulson
Mixing: Michael H. Brauer

Keith Richards with his superb 1956 Velázquez.

Genesis

"Almost Hear You Sigh" is a ballad written by Keith Richards in collaboration with the drummer Steve Jordan for Keith's first solo album *Talk Is Cheap*, although not ultimately used. Keith proposed the song to Mick Jagger when they got together in Barbados. The singer was won over by it, but nevertheless changed some of the words. *I can almost hear you sigh/I can almost hear you cry/On every crowded street/All the places we would meet.* The narrator cannot get over the departure of his loved one, whose kisses were *silky smooth like wine*, and begs her to come back. "Almost Hear You Sigh" was the A-side of the third single from *Steel Wheels*. Released in January 1990 with "Break the Spell" as its B-side, it progressed as far as number 31 on the British charts on July 7 and number 50 in the United States. It was also nominated for a Grammy Award in the category "best vocal rock performance by a duo or group" in 1991.

Production

This is only the second time the Glimmer Twins had shared the writing of a song with a musician from outside the band. After Chuck Leavell with "Back to Zero" on *Dirty Work*, the honor this time goes to Steve Jordan, who was also the co-producer of Keith's solo album. "Almost Hear You Sigh" is one of the triumphs of *Steel Wheels*. This rock number showcases Mick's excellent performance, the singer having rediscovered his full range of vocal expression. It is also an opportunity for Keith to unveil a recent acquisition, his sublime 1956 Velázquez, a classical guitar with an exceptionally beautiful tone recorded by Potter using a Sanken mic. He plays a few solo phrases on it in the intro and again at 2:58. Keith seems a little reserved in his phrasing, as if not yet fully at ease with the instrument. He also plays a rhythm part on his 5-string Telecaster through his vintage Fender Twin amp, doubling this in places with another Telecaster, this time a 6-string one. Ronnie also supports him on rhythm, before in turn playing a very good electric solo, probably on a Strat (3:35). Bill and Charlie are as brilliant as ever, assisted by Luís Jardim on percussion (congas, tambourine). The various keyboards played by Leavell and Clifford contribute to the song's wonderful textures, as do the excellent and indispensable backing vocals.

CONTINENTAL DRIFT

Mick Jagger / Keith Richards / 5:14

Musicians
Mick Jagger: vocals, keyboards, arrangement
Keith Richards: acoustic guitar, bicycle (sound effect)
Charlie Watts: drums
Ron Wood: bass, acoustic guitar
Matt Clifford: percussion programming, arrangement
**Sarah Dash, Lisa Fischer, Tessa Niles, Sonia
Jones Morgan, Bernard Fowler:** backing vocals
**The Master Musicians of Joujouka with
Bachir Attar:** Moroccan instruments
Farafina: African instruments

Recorded
AIR Studios, Montserrat: March 29–May 5, 1989
The Palace of Ben Abbou, Tangier: June 16 and 17, 1989
Olympic Sound Studios, London: May 15–June 29, 1989

Technical Team
Producers: Chris Kimsey, the Glimmer Twins
Sound engineer: Christopher Marc Potter
Assistant sound engineer: Rupert Coulson
Mixing: Christopher Marc Potter, Chris Kimsey

The American percussionist Glen Velez (left) with Bachir Attar, leader of the Master Musicians of Joujouka.

FOR STONES ADDICTS

Starting in the intro (0:05), Keith produces a rather special sound effect by trailing the blade of his knife against the spokes of a spinning bicycle wheel (he is given a "bicycle" credit in the liner notes). This effect recurs a number of times and goes to show that there is more to a rocker's life than Telecaster heroics.

Genesis
With "Continental Drift," were the Stones following along the path pioneered by the Beatles, Led Zeppelin, Peter Gabriel, and Talking Heads, who had been some of the first to combine Eastern and Western musical influences? It may be tempting to think so, but on the other hand it should not be forgotten that, under the aegis of Brian Jones, the London quintet had developed an interest in sonorities from outside Europe as early as the mid-sixties, as can be heard on "Paint It Black" and the albums *Aftermath* and *Their Satanic Majesties Request*.

"Continental Drift" enabled the Stones to go a step further. In an interview with *Rolling Stone* in 1989 with David Fricke, Mick Jagger explained the band's need to move on to something else: "The hard-rock thing just took over, and we lost a little bit of sensitivity and adventure. And it's boring just doing hard rock all the time. You gotta bounce it around a little."[126] Mick Jagger wrote "Continental Drift" in Barbados. "I woke up one morning," says Richards in the same interview, "to find Mick playing this thing on the keyboard. And I thought, 'Ah, that's nice, that reminds me of Morocco.'"[126] A few days later, Mick and Keith were in Tangier to meet the Master Musicians of Joujouka, the Moroccan group recorded by Brian Jones twenty years before. Musically, "Continental Drift" is therefore a stirring homage to Brian Jones! And so too are the words: *Love comes at the speed of light . . . It's as pure as silver/It's as pure as gold . . .*

Production
A long way from "Jumpin' Jack Flash," the Stones are paying tribute to the sonorities of the sixties that were given a new lease on life by the founding of Real World Records in 1989. "Continental Drift" was initially recorded in Montserrat, with drum machine and synthesizer programing by Jagger and Clifford. Richards and Wood are on acoustic guitars, and the latter even plays an acoustic bass. It almost goes without saying that these three instruments are submerged in the mass of sound. Charlie is excellent on drums, accompanied by numerous Moroccan percussion instruments recorded in Tangier in mid-June and African percussion recorded by the Farafina ensemble, from Burkina Faso, between June 18 and 29. Mick gives a good vocal performance supported by the numerous backing vocalists.

BREAK THE SPELL

Mick Jagger / Keith Richards / 3:06

Musicians
Mick Jagger: vocals, rhythm guitar, harmonica
Keith Richards: rhythm guitar
Charlie Watts: drums
Ron Wood: bass, Dobro
Matt Clifford: keyboards
Recorded
AIR Studios, Montserrat: March 29–May 5, 1989
Olympic Sound Studios, London: May 15–June 29, 1989
Technical Team
Producers: Chris Kimsey, the Glimmer Twins
Sound engineer: Christopher Marc Potter
Assistant sound engineer: Rupert Coulson
Mixing: Michael H. Brauer

Mick Jagger with his prototype Kramer Elliot Easton. "Break the Spell" was inspired by the lure of the Old South.

Genesis

Following their detour to Morocco, the Stones stopped off in the southern United States, where they have some of their deepest roots. "Break the Spell" is a real blues, with a spritely rhythm, whose hero is a gypsy *all dressed in white*. When the elements are raging—the glacial winter wind or the floods that accompany the beginning of spring—does the gypsy have the power to ward off bad luck? With this material, we have strayed a long way from the title originally envisioned for this low-down blues: "Call Girl Blues." "Break the Spell" was chosen as the B-side of the single "Almost Hear You Sigh," which was marketed in continental Europe. It has never been performed live, however.

Production

This excellent blues number, of a kind that nobody but the Stones could make (as they had been doing for decades) is apparently launched by Mick Jagger on guitar. Keith joins him straightaway (on the left), and together they construct a fantastic, very Muddy Waters–like intro with a sonority that could almost have been created at Chess Studios with Ron Malo at the helm. Ronnie accompanies them from 1:02 with a Dobro slide part, but is too recessed in the mix. In the absence of Bill, Ronnie is also on bass, but unfortunately he cannot stop himself from trying to play too many notes, coming up with a riff that may be ideal for a rhythm guitar, but is certainly not right for a bass. Charlie chooses to play softly and simply, caressing the skins of his Gretsch kit with brushes. Matt Clifford is credited with keyboards, but his contribution seems to have been buried in the mix. It is Mick who literally dominates "Break the Spell," initially with a surprising, very bass voice closer to Keith's tonalities, before modulating skillfully toward a more familiar style of delivery. He also plays some very good distorted harmonica that is reminiscent of Little Walter, performing a superb solo at 1:21 and helping to make this track one of the triumphs of the album.

Bill Wyman playing a white
Steinberger XM2. "Slipping Away"
marks the end of his decades-long
collaboration with Mick, Keith,
and Charlie.

SLIPPING AWAY

Mick Jagger / Keith Richards / 4:29

1989

Musicians
Keith Richards: rhythm guitar, acoustic guitar, vocals
Bill Wyman: bass
Charlie Watts: drums
Ron Wood: rhythm guitar
Chuck Leavell: piano, organ
Matt Clifford: electric piano, strings
Mick Jagger, Sarah Dash, Lisa Fischer,
Bernard Fowler: backing vocals
The Kick Horns: horns
Unidentified musician: tambourine

Recorded
AIR Studios, Montserrat: March 29–May 5, 1989
Olympic Sound Studios, London: May 15–June 29, 1989

Technical Team
Producers: Chris Kimsey, the Glimmer Twins
Sound engineer: Christopher Marc Potter
Assistant sound engineer: Rupert Coulson
Mixing: Michael H. Brauer

FOR STONES ADDICTS

The Rolling Stones also recorded an
unplugged version of "Slipping Away"
that can be found on the album
Stripped (1995).

Genesis
Keith Richards may be the unsurpassed master of the rock 'n' roll riff, but he is also a fine composer of ballads, a musical form in which he expressed himself more and more as one album followed the next. "I like ballads. Also, you learn about songwriting from slow songs. You get a better rock & roll song by writing it slow to start with, and seeing where it can go. Sometimes it's obvious that it can't go fast, whereas 'Sympathy for the Devil' started out as a Bob Dylan song and ended up as a samba."[127]

"Slipping Away" is a dream that disappears little by little, a love that gradually fades away. Happiness is ephemeral: such is the message Keith Richards seems to be conveying. Does it even exist other than in our imagination and fantasies? *Drifting away . . . Slipping away*, sings Keith Richards. Might he also have been thinking of the ultimate journey to the next world that we all have to make one day?

Production
"Slipping Away" is the very last Stones album track on which Bill Wyman would play (with the exception of the two previously unreleased studio tracks on *Flashpoint*, 1991). The bassist was to bow out in 1993, but for the time being he provides solid support with the same skill and subtlety that he had been bringing to bear since 1963. Charlie responds to his bass line with feeling and a certain swing. This very beautiful Keith ballad provides an opportunity to hear Richards, who was gradually becoming a serious rival to Mick, singing with a certain patina to his voice. Meanwhile, Mick contents himself with singing backing vocals alongside the three talented backing singers who light up the entire track. Chuck Leavell provides a fine accompaniment on organ as well as piano, playing with all the lyricism of Nicky Hopkins, while Matt Clifford plays electric piano and also produces string pads on the synthesizer (1:08). The Kick Horns make a discreet contribution, coloring the harmonies with some good arrangements. As for the guitars, Keith and Ronnie share the rhythm work, playing in a funky rock style. Keith also distinguishes himself by playing a short solo with excellent phrasing on his Sadowsky Nylon String guitar (2:30). Finally, a tambourine can be heard from 3:12. "Slipping Away" brings Steel Wheels to something of an unusual close.

COOK COOK BLUES

Mick Jagger / Keith Richards / 4:11

SINGLE
"Rock and a Hard Place"* / "Cook Cook Blues"
RELEASE DATE
United Kingdom: November 4, 1989
RECORD NUMBER: CBS 655422 7 * (SEE P. 584)

Musicians
Mick Jagger: vocals
Keith Richards: rhythm and lead guitar
Bill Wyman: bass
Charlie Watts: drums
Ron Wood: rhythm guitar, slide guitar
Ian Stewart: piano
Chuck Leavell: organ
Recorded
EMI Pathé Marconi Studios, Boulogne-Billancourt, France: November 11 (?)–December 19, 1982
Olympic Sound Studios, London: May 15–June 29, 1989
Technical Team
Producers: Chris Kimsey, the Glimmer Twins
Sound engineers: Chris Kimsey, Christopher Marc Potter
Assistant sound engineer: Rupert Coulson

Genesis

"Cook Cook Blues" has the air of one of those tracks that were improvised by the Stones over the immortal blues chords by way of preparation for a long session in the studio. It took shape during the recording of *Undercover* at the Pathé Marconi Studios in November and December 1982 (most probably November 11), with Ian Stewart and Chuck Leavell on keyboards. Seven years later, the Stones returned to it when recording the various tracks for *Steel Wheels* at Olympic Sound Studios in London. It was at this point that Mick Jagger is thought to have written the words, which he sings to a rhythm infused with the boogie-woogie of the Old South.

"Cook Cook Blues" is not on any album, but the Rolling Stones decided to make it the B-side of "Rock and a Hard Place" (which is 1:20 shorter than the album version). The single was released on November 4, 1989. "Rock and a Hard Place" peaked at number 23 in the United States and number 63 in the United Kingdom.

Production

This is another twelve-bar blues, like so many played by the Stones. Although there is nothing startlingly new about it, playing the blues is something they did regularly as a way of getting back to their roots. It is true that "Cook Cook Blues" is more of a jam than an original composition, but what room is there for innovation in a genre that has been rehashed over the course of decades? Furthermore, what is not to enjoy about listening to the late lamented Stu playing an impassioned boogie-woogie piano part one more time? The track starts with a fade-in to what turns out to be a veritable feast

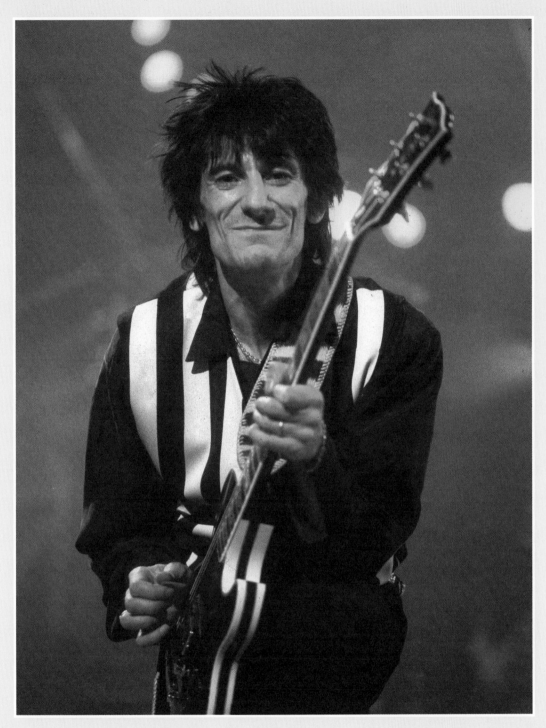

Ron Wood. His heart has always wavered between blues and rock 'n' roll.

of solo guitar offered up by Keith and Ronnie, the former in a very pure style and the latter with slide. The two of them alternate in this fashion all the way to the final note of the track. Chuck Leavell has found a place at the heart of the band, with a very good organ part that sounds as if it could be a Hammond B-3. Charlie and Bill lay down such a well-oiled groove that they could almost be playing with their eyes shut. As for Mick, his inimitable voice is able to glide through this blues with the greatest of ease, and there can be only one regret: that he does not play the harmonica on this track.

IN YOUR HEADPHONES

At 1:44, Ronnie can be heard launching into his slide solo in the belief that his time has come, only to think better of it and wait for Jagger to finish his verse!

Continental Drift
Start Me Up
Sad Sad Sad
Miss You
Rock And A Hard Place
Ruby Tuesday
You Can't Always Get
  What You Want
Factory Girl

Can't Be Seen
Little Red Rooster
Paint It Black
Sympathy For The Devil
Brown Sugar
Jumpin' Jack Flash
(I Can't Get No) Satisfaction
Highwire *
Sex Drive *

★ Only the released songs will be
discussed in this chapter.

ALBUM
RELEASE DATE
United Kingdom: April 2, 1991
Label: Rolling Stones Records
RECORD NUMBER: ROLLING STONES
RECORDS 468135 2
**Number 6, on the charts for 7
weeks**

FLASH-
POINT

The Stones with the members of Living Color, one of the groups that opened the concerts during the Steel Wheels Tour, when *Flashpoint* was recorded.

FLASHPOINT: TESTAMENT TO A RESURRECTION

Flashpoint is a record, in both senses, of the Rolling Stones' 1989 and 1990 world tour, which was christened the Steel Wheels Tour in the United States and Japan and the Urban Jungle Tour in Europe. The fifteen live recordings (including the intro, an extract from "Continental Drift"), were taken from the concerts in Clemson, South Carolina ("Start Me Up," "Can't Be Seen," "[I Can't Get No] Satisfaction"); Atlantic City, New Jersey ("Sad Sad Sad," "Little Red Rooster" [with Eric Clapton]); Jacksonville, Florida ("Miss You," "Rock and a Hard Place," "You Can't Always Get What You Want"); Tokyo ("Ruby Tuesday," "Sympathy for the Devil," "Jumpin' Jack Flash"); London ("Factory Girl"); Barcelona ("Paint It Black"); and Turin ("Brown Sugar").

Two studio recordings, "Highwire" and "Sex Drive," were also added to what was essentially a "best of" collection. These two studio tracks possess symbolic value, as they are the last recordings made with the Rolling Stones by Bill Wyman after some thirty years of good and loyal service. Released on April 2, 1991, *Flashpoint*, the Stones' fifth live album, rose to number 6 on the British charts and number 16 on the *Billboard* album chart. In France, it would eventually be certified double gold (more than 200,000 copies sold).

On the technical side, Chris Kimsey was responsible for putting together and mixing the album at Olympic Sound Studios in London, with the exception, that is, of "Highwire" and "Sex Drive," which were recorded by Mark "Spike" Stent (Björk, U2, Oasis) at the Hit Factory in the British capital.

The bass by British luthier Ian "Wal" Waller, adopted by Bill Wyman, notably for the *Steel Wheels* sessions.

HIGHWIRE

Mick Jagger / Keith Richards / 4:45 (3:41 for the single)

Musicians
Mick Jagger: vocals, rhythm guitar
Keith Richards: rhythm and lead guitar
Bill Wyman: bass
Charlie Watts: drums
Ron Wood: rhythm and lead (?) guitar
Bernard Fowler: backing vocals
Recorded
The Hit Factory, London: January 7–18, 1991
Technical Team
Producers: Chris Kimsey, the Glimmer Twins
Sound engineers: Mark Stent, Charlie Smith

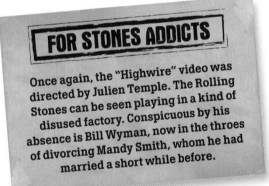

FOR STONES ADDICTS

Once again, the "Highwire" video was directed by Julien Temple. The Rolling Stones can be seen playing in a kind of disused factory. Conspicuous by his absence is Bill Wyman, now in the throes of divorcing Mandy Smith, whom he had married a short while before.

A pyrotechnic effect for Keith Richards during the shooting of the "Highwire" video.

Genesis

In "Highwire," the Stones adopt a political stance. Mick Jagger, who has always taken an interest in the political and social upheavals affecting the world, sings here of the Gulf War, which, between August 1990 and February 1991, brought thirty-four states, supported by the United Nations, into conflict with Saddam Hussein's Iraq. Was it the annexation of Kuwait that triggered the war? The Stones' singer seems to think it was more about oil and arms sales; in other words, a case of business not caring about morality, even if he admits in the same breath that *sometimes dictators need a slap on the wrist* and that *another Munich we just can't afford*. As well as being included on *Flashpoint*, "Highwire" was released as a single in both the United Kingdom and the United States on March 1, 1991 (with the live version of "2000 Light Years from Home" as the B-side). The song made it as far as number 29 in Britain. In continental Europe, it was also released as a maxi single, accompanied by "2000 Light Years from Home," "Sympathy for the Devil," and "I Just Want to Make Love to You."

Production

Mick Jagger plays the introductory riff. He would explain in an interview that he was capable of reproducing more or less all of Keith's riffs on a 5-string guitar in open G . . . And it has to be said that the pupil has learned his lesson well, because it is not at all easy to tell him apart from the master, whether in terms of sound or touch. For his part, Keith accompanies Mick with a very good rhythm part interspersed with some nicely felt licks, and he is probably in turn supported by Ron Wood, who comes in only sporadically, his presence in the studio not having been confirmed after January 12. The main guitar interest of this track lies in the solo section: in truth it is not one but three different, interweaving solos, with Mick on the left, Keith on the right, and Ronnie presumably in the middle. The effect might have been somewhat muddy, but not a bit of it was. The result is highly dynamic and a great success. Charlie and Bill are effective and precise as always. Mick Jagger seems a little less convincing than his bandmates, but this is perhaps due to the song itself, which is a little too self-conscious in its construction and production.

SEX DRIVE

Mick Jagger / Keith Richards / 4:28

Musicians
Mick Jagger: vocals, guitar
Keith Richards: guitar
Bill Wyman: bass
Charlie Watts: drums
Ron Wood: guitar
The Kick Horns: horns
Katie Kissoon, Tessa Niles: backing vocals, tambourine (?)
Recorded
The Hit Factory, London: January 7–18, 1991
Technical Team
Producers: Chris Kimsey, the Glimmer Twins
Sound engineers: Mark Stent, Charlie Smith
Mixing: Chris Kimsey
Additional production and remix: Michael H. Brauer
Assistant sound engineer: Chris Theis

"Sex Drive," a song that gives Keith Richards an opportunity to venture gleefully into James Brown territory.

Genesis

It is to a hypnotic beat somewhere between "Hot Stuff" and "Get Up (I Feel Like Being a) Sex Machine" by James Brown that Mick Jagger reveals his addiction to sex. At any rate, this is the story told by Julien Temple's video, shot in May 1991. In it the Stones singer is shown lying on a couch talking about his problem to a psychoanalyst played by Charlie Watts, while three attractive young women pass before his eyes and then disappear behind a theater curtain, eventually followed by Keith Richards. Is this mere tongue-in-cheek fantasy on the part of Mick Jagger?

"Sex Drive" was released as a single in May 1991 but did not meet with chart success. There are different mixes by Michael H. Brauer: "Sexdrive" the Dirty Hands Mix (B-side of the European single) and "Sexdrive" the Club Version (a maxi single in the Netherlands). In the United States, "Sex Drive" was released as a single with a live version of "Undercover of the Night" on the flip side.

Production

"Sex Drive" clearly has one eye on the "Godfather of Soul" (James Brown). The tone is set with Mick Jagger's opening roar: dance, funk, and rock. Bill and Charlie establish a fabulous groove, and the guitars have some surprises in store. Who would have imagined Keith swinging to a funk beat with quite as much conviction, and playing his astonishing rhythmic lick at 1:41? Or Ronnie, for that matter, or even Mick, who also seems to have a hand in the superb guitar demonstration? The Kick Horns, who had already played on *Steel Wheels*, make a first-rate contribution with some very funky riffs and an excellent sax solo at 2:11. The backing vocalists, meanwhile, are Tessa Niles, who had sung on "Continental Drift" (also on *Steel Wheels*), and Stones newcomer Katie Kissoon. One of the two is presumably playing the tambourine, and both are wonderful in the coda. Finally, Jagger is exceptional, and sets the track on fire with his highly charged performance. It is curious that "Sex Drive" failed to make a mark on the charts. Presumably the fans were disconcerted by what they saw as its excessively funky style.

Love Is Strong
You Got Me Rocking
Sparks Will Fly
The Worst
New Faces
Moon Is Up
Out Of Tears
I Go Wild

Brand New Car
Sweethearts Together
Suck On The Jugular
Blinded By Rainbows
Baby Break It Down
Thru And Thru
Mean Disposition

ALBUM
RELEASE DATE
United Kingdom: July 11, 1994
Label: Virgin
RECORD NUMBER: VIRGIN CDV 2750 (39782 1 UK)
Number 1, on the charts for 34 weeks

VOODOO LOUNGE

Mick Jagger onstage, wearing a T-shirt depicting the mysterious character from the cover of *Voodoo Lounge*.

On August 2, 1993, the Stones found themselves jamming in Ron Wood's studio with Jerry Lee Lewis, who was a neighbor. According to Keith, the results were excellent, but while listening to the playbacks, Jerry made comments about the band's performance. The riff master did not like what he had to say and invited Lewis outside to explain himself . . . Happily, they became good buddies after that.

VOODOO LOUNGE:
THE FIRST ALBUM WITHOUT BILL

After the monster Steel Wheels/Urban Jungle tour, which drew to a close with two concerts at Wembley Stadium in London on August 24 and 25, 1990, Mick, Keith, Bill, Charlie, and Ronnie went their separate ways for a few months. They eventually got together again in January 1991 at the Hit Factory to record "Highwire" and "Sex Drive," the two studio numbers on the album *Flashpoint* (released in April 1991) that were also issued as singles. And then the well-oiled machine that was the Rolling Stones came to a standstill. Keith Richards took advantage of this hiatus to record his second album, *Main Offender*, which went on sale on October 19, 1992. Mick Jagger, who had married Jerry Hall on November 21, 1990, produced his third solo album, *Wandering Spirit*, in conjunction with Rick Rubin. This record hit the stores on February 8, 1993 (a month after the birth of Georgia May Jagger). Ron Wood released *Slide on This* (1992) and *Slide on Live: Plugged In and Standing* (1993), while Charlie Watts temporarily abandoned blues rock for modern jazz with his Charlie Watts Quintet, making the albums *From One Charlie* (1991) and *A Tribute to Charlie Parker with Strings* (1992). As for Bill Wyman, the bassist released the album *Stuff* (which was actually a collection of recordings going back to 1988) in Japan and Argentina in 1992.

Bill Wyman Bows Out

On November 19, 1991, when the Stones signed a contract for $44 million with Virgin Records (for three albums starting in 1993), Bill Wyman refused to add his name. He had

decided to call it a day. Mick and Keith asked him not to say anything to the media. They also asked him to take some time to reconsider his decision, but to no avail. Bill had his mind set on a different kind of life. He was passionate about many different things and the Stones no longer held the same interest for him that they once did. On January 6, 1993, he made his departure official. This was the first time a founding member of the band had quit of his own accord. "When Bill Wyman left in 1991, I got extremely stroppy," admits Keith Richards. "I really did have a go at him. I wasn't very nice. He said he didn't like to fly anymore." It is true that in addition to his desire for a new life, Bill had developed a real fear of flying since the Urban Jungle Tour, but this was not a sufficient argument to calm Keith down: "Nobody leaves this band except in a coffin," he retorted. Bill held firm, and Keith ended up accepting his decision. He would later say of the bassist: "I love Bill dearly. He's a very funny guy, with a very dry wit. . . ."

Bill, along with Charlie, had been integral to the Stones rhythm section. "He had an affinity with Charlie Watts that was quite amazing, and good rhythm sections don't come around that often," says Keith. A replacement had to be found. The band turned to Darryl Jones, a friend of Steve Jordan and Charley Drayton (members of the X-Pensive Winos) and, most importantly, an excellent musician who had played on Miles Davis's *Decoy* (1984) and *You're Under Arrest* (1985) sessions, and also with rock and pop stars, such as Sting, Eric Clapton, and Madonna. Charlie Watts had the final decision: "It felt as though we auditioned

The Stones at a press conference in New York City on May 3, 1994, for the launch of the Voodoo Lounge Tour.

a few thousand players and that I was sitting at my drums for about nine days. It was unbelievable—we had a list of guys to try out, and they were all good. Each of them came with their own recommendations. There was one particular guy who Keith had worked with and liked a lot; there was another Mick liked a lot: Dougie Wimbish, who's a fabulous player." He continues: "Eventually it came down to Dougie Wimbish and Darryl as well as this guy that Keith worked with. It was an extremely close-run thing between the three of them, but Darryl was so easy to work with that in the end he got a unanimous decision." Some people would later comment that his background as a jazzman, a unique quality in Charlie's eyes, helped tip it in his favor . . .

The Album

In April 1993, Mick Jagger and Keith Richards got together again in Barbados to write the bulk of the songs for the next disc. Entitled *Voodoo Lounge*, the first Rolling Stones album without Bill Wyman—and the first at all for five years—would comprise a total of fifteen numbers (only fourteen on the double LP because "Mean Disposition" was left out). Some of these tracks, such as "Love Is Strong" and "You Got Me Rocking," belong to the Stones' tradition of blues rock and brilliant riffs. "Out of Tears," "Sweethearts Together," "Blinded by Rainbows," and "Thru and Thru" reveal the more romantic side of the Glimmer Twins (either together or separately). The glorious past is evoked in the very bluesy "Brand New Car," the distinctly hillbilly "The Worst," and the ballad "New Faces," which is reminiscent of "Lady Jane" on the album *Aftermath*. Meanwhile, the present and future of rock are represented by "Sparks Will Fly" and "I Go Wild," with their grunge accents, "Suck on the Jugular," which seems to have been recorded to keep the night clubbers happy, and the astonishing musical maelstrom that is "Moon Is Up." As for the lyrics, with the exception of "Blinded by Rainbows," which

evokes the conflict in Ulster, they continue to focus on women and love: love at first sight in "Love Is Strong," destructive love in "You Got Me Rocking" and "Sparks Will Fly," romantic love in "New Faces" and "Out of Tears," the femme fatale and sadomasochistic love in "I Go Wild."

This time, the Glimmer Twins co-produced the album with Don Was, the former member of the duo Was (Not Was) who switched to production in the eighties with considerable success, working with Bob Dylan, Iggy Pop, and Carly Simon. He was to produce all the remaining Stones albums.

The Rolling Stones' twentieth (British) studio album hit the record stores on July 11, 1994. *Voodoo Lounge* immediately shot to number 1 in the United Kingdom, which had not happened since *Emotional Rescue* fourteen years before. It would also reach the top spot in various other European countries (the Netherlands, Germany, Austria, Switzerland) as well as in Australia and New Zealand, and would get to number 2 in France, the United States, and Japan, and number 3 in Norway . . . Finally, the album would win a Grammy Award for best rock album. A further illustration of the Stones' indestructibility is the promotional tour that kicked off three weeks after the release of the album. This would take them all over the world once again, from Washington, DC (on August 1, 1994), to Rotterdam (on August 29 and 30, 1995) via Canada, South America, Japan, Australia, and New Zealand.

The Album Cover

The peculiar name of the new album came into being one stormy night. While Barbados was being battered by rain, Keith Richards saved a small cat from certain death. "We called him Voodoo because we were in Barbados and his survival was against the odds—Voodoo luck and charm. And always this little cat followed me everywhere. So the cat became Voodoo and the terrace became Voodoo's Lounge—I put up signs around the perimeter."

Ronnie, Keith, and Charlie in action during the incredible Voodoo Lounge Tour.

The cover design is by Mark Norton. What does it represent? Possibly a voodoo god in a trance or shimmying on the dance floor? Or perhaps an allusion to Andy Warhol's famous banana? On the back, the tracks are listed in red against a grayish background with a prickly Stones' tongue logo underneath. Inside are various photographs of the four Stones taken by Sante D'Orazio and a double-page illustration of a group of skeletons playing cards in a castle room under the jeering eye of a diabolical creature.

The Recording

Demos for *Voodoo Lounge* were recorded at Eddy Grant's studio (which had been used by the Stones for the pre-production of their previous album) in Barbados between April 20 and mid-May 1993. These demos included the first take of "Thru and Thru," on which Pierre de Beauport, a musician and Keith Richards's guitar technician, plays, and various takes of "Suck on the Jugular" (two tracks that were subsequently completed in Ireland). After laying down more tracks between July and September at Ron Wood's studio in Saint Kildare, Ireland, Mick, Keith, Charlie, and Ronnie, along with co-producer Don Was and sound engineer Don Smith (Tom Petty, Bob Dylan, U2), moved to Dublin's Windmill Lane Studios, which had been the stronghold of U2 since 1980 (and, after the Stones, the Cranberries, Mark Knopfler, Elvis Costello, Van Morrison . . .). Between November 3 and December 11, they recorded the rest of the songs on

the album. The chronological order is presumed to be as follows: "Love Is Strong," "Blinded by Rainbows," "Moon Is Up," "The Worst," "Mean Disposition," "You Got Me Rocking," "New Faces," "Sparks Will Fly," "Out of Tears," "Baby Break It Down," "Brand New Car," "Sweethearts Together," and "I Go Wild." In addition to these should be added "The Storm" (the B-side of "Love Is Strong"), "Jump on Top of Me" (the B-side of "You Got Me Rocking"), and "I'm Gonna Drive" (the B-side of the UK single "Out of Tears"), as well as various outtakes. The overdubs and mixing (of the album tracks, not the single remixing) were done at the A&M Studios in Los Angeles between January and April 1994. One track, "I Go Wild," was mixed by Bob Clearmountain at Right Track Studios in New York City.

Back to Basics

Voodoo Lounge can be seen as building on the newfound harmony between the Glimmer Twins. Mick and Keith both wrote a considerable number of songs, but just fifteen were retained. Keith appreciated Don Was as a musician, which made him an interlocutor on a par with Jimmy Miller: "Don Was has incredible diplomacy and great musical insight," he would later comment. Mick would later express some reservations: ". . . [T]here were a lot of things that we wrote for *Voodoo Lounge* that Don [Was, the record's producer] steered us away from: groove songs, African influences and things like that. And he steered us very clear of all that. And I think

Sound engineer Bob Clearmountain (left) and Keith and Ronnie (right) with the producer Don Was.

it was a mistake." In fact, Jagger criticized Don Was, along with his engineer, Don Smith, for wanting to make the band sound as they had during the days of *Exile on Main St*. Nevertheless, the producer's basic intention was commendable. Was explains: "For this project, we wanted to go back to the essence of good band playing, utilising a raw, Chess Records kind of recording technique." In the final analysis, *Voodoo Lounge* is a good, very well-produced album.

Once again, the Stones brought in many outside musicians during the making of their new album. The new faces included Frankie Gavin of Dé Dannan on fiddle and pennywhistle (Elvis Costello), Benmont Tench of Tom Petty and the Heartbreakers on accordion and Hammond B-3 organ (Johnny Cash, Bob Dylan, Roy Orbison), David Campbell arranging the strings (Paul McCartney, Beck, Adele), David McMurray on saxophone (Brian Wilson, Bob Dylan, Khaled), Mark Isham on trumpet (Van Morrison, Joni Mitchell, Marianne Faithfull), Flaco Jiménez on accordion (Ry Cooder, Los Lobos, Linda Ronstadt), Max Baca on bajo sexto (Texas Tornados, Joe Posada), and finally Lenny Castro (B. B. King, the Temptations, Toto) and Phil Jones (Paul McCartney, Tom Petty, Bob Dylan) on percussion.

On the technical side, Dan Bosworth (Bob Dylan, Michael Jackson, Ry Cooder) and Alastair McMillan (Van Morrison, Paul Brady) assisted Don Smith with the recording, while Mike Baumgartner (Billy Idol, Rick Wakeman), Greg Goldman (Bruce Springsteen, Bon Jovi), and Ed Korengo (Miles Davis, Aerosmith) helped with the mixing. Bob Clearmountain was assisted by Jennifer Monnar (Frank Sinatra, Cyndi Lauper) at Right Track Studios in New York City.

The Instruments

The Stones used more or less the same instruments as before, with the exception of a Gibson Robert Johnson L-1 acoustic for Keith and a new harmonica for Mick, a Lee Oskar. Darryl

Jones played a Fender Precision bass most of the time, but would later explain that he also used a Sadowsky bass on forty-five percent of the tracks.

Technical Details

To supplement the equipment at Windmill Lane Studios in Dublin, Don Was and Don Smith added a Neve 10-channel desk and various Neve modules to the existing Amek console. They mainly used a 24-track tape machine with a slave 4-track for specific songs. Apparently Smith was less than enamored with digital technology and did his reductions on a Studer A-27, one of the earliest tape recorders of that brand (which is pretty astonishing). Urei 813C monitors were used, imported from the US especially for this project.

Don Was would explain that in order to record Keith's 1957 Fender Twin, he used an SM57 on one of the loudspeakers and an AKG 451 on the other. In terms of equalization, Smith would use mainly Pultec and API devices. Finally, for Mick Jagger's voice, a range of mics were needed: a Telefunken U47, a Telefunken 251, an RCA ribbon mic, and an Electro-Voice 667. Also a Shure SM7 and an SM58 for live takes with the band.

The year 1994 was a dark one in Stones circles: two months after the release of *Voodoo Lounge*, Nicky Hopkins died in Nashville at the age of fifty, followed by Jimmy Miller in Denver a month later, on October 22, at the age of fifty-two.

LOVE IS STRONG

Mick Jagger / Keith Richards / 3:46

Musicians
Mick Jagger: vocals, harmonica, maracas
Keith Richards: rhythm guitar, acoustic guitar, backing vocals
Charlie Watts: drums
Ron Wood: rhythm guitar, acoustic guitar
Darryl Jones: bass
Chuck Leavell: electric piano (Wurlitzer)
Ivan Neville, Bernard Fowler: backing vocals

Recorded
Ron Wood's Sandymount Studio, Saint Kildare, Ireland: July 9–August 6, September 1993 (?)
Windmill Lane Studios, Dublin, Ireland: November 3–December 11, 1993
A&M Studios, Los Angeles: January 15–April 1994

Technical Team
Producers: Don Was, the Glimmer Twins
Sound engineer: Don Smith
Assistant sound engineers: Dan Bosworth, Alastair McMillan
Assistant sound engineers (mixing): Mike Baumgartner, Greg Goldman, Ed Korengo

FOR STONES ADDICTS

"Love Is Strong" was originally called "Love Is Strange." There is a bootleg recording in existence made by Keith Richards, Ron Wood, Ivan Neville, and Don Was while Mick Jagger was away promoting his album *Wandering Spirit*.

There are a number of alternative versions of "Love Is Strong." These were remixed by Teddy Riley (the Extended Remix, Radio Remix, Extended Rock Remix, Dub Remix, Instrumental), Bob Clearmountain (the Remix), and Joe Nicolo (the Joe The Butcher Club Remix).

Genesis

The music for "Love Is Strong" came from Keith Richards, who took his inspiration from the excellent "Wicked as It Seems" on his solo album *Main Offender*. Mick Jagger then made various changes and wrote some new lyrics. Once again, this is a song is about love at first sight. A glimpse of an unknown woman in the street is all it takes to bewitch the narrator. *I followed you across the stars, I looked for you in seedy bars*, sings Mick Jagger. Or maybe this is a metaphor for the indestructible bond between the Glimmer Twins?

"Love Is Strong" was the A-side of the first single from *Voodoo Lounge*, released with "The Storm" as the flip side, on July 4, 1994. It peaked at number 14 in the United Kingdom on July 16. The video, a model of its kind, was made by David Fincher (who had just shot his first full-length movie, *Alien 3*, in 1992) and edited by Robert Duffy at his Spot Welders studio in Venice, California. Shot in black and white, it shows Mick, Keith, Ronnie, Charlie, and a number of intriguing young women stalking the streets of Manhattan as giants.

Production

This was the first opportunity for fans to hear Bill Wyman's replacement on bass. Darryl Jones is a jazz giant and an extraordinary musician who was able to adapt very quickly to the world of rock. And this he proves beyond all doubt on "Love Is Strong." His playing is discreet but with an ever-present groove, somewhat in the style of Bill, only with his own, inevitably different vision of the instrument. He is presumably playing his Fender Precision, on which he produces a rich, velvety sound. This is the bass on which he auditioned and was offered the job. Charlie applies himself to responding to the quality of his playing with a very good drum part, supported by Mick on maracas. The Stones singer excels in his vocal performance, adroitly varying his timbre and also making some superb interjections on the harmonica, in all likelihood a Lee Oskar, the brand he had just discovered and now favored over his Hohner. The introductory riff is by the master himself, and is accompanied by Ronnie's very good rhythm guitar. Each guitarist then adds an acoustic part whose sonority provides the whole with effective support.

YOU GOT ME ROCKING

Mick Jagger / Keith Richards / 3:34

Musicians
Mick Jagger: vocals, maracas
Keith Richards: rhythm guitar, "mystery guitar," backing vocals
Charlie Watts: drums
Ron Wood: slide guitar
Darryl Jones: bass
Chuck Leavell: piano
Ivan Neville, Bernard Fowler: backing vocals
Recorded
Ron Wood's Sandymount Studio, Kildare County, Ireland: July 9–August 6, September 1993 (?)
Windmill Lane Studios, Dublin, Ireland: November 3–December 11, 1993
A&M Studios, Los Angeles: January 15–April 1994
Technical Team
Producers: Don Was, the Glimmer Twins
Sound engineer: Don Smith
Assistant sound engineers: Dan Bosworth, Alastair McMillan
Assistant sound engineers (mixing): Mike Baumgartner, Greg Goldman, Ed Korengo

Keith playing the killer riff of "You Got Me Rocking" on the inevitable Telecaster.

Genesis

"You Got Me Rocking" was originally written by Keith for the piano and then transposed to guitar in order to transform it into a typical Stones rock number. "I was playing the guitar, Keith is playing piano and singing," Mick Jagger tells David Fricke. "And then I started playing slide guitar, and it started to sound like Elmore James. And then back to something else. Finally I said, 'Keith, you've got to come off the piano and play guitar. I can't hear what's going on, there's too much racket!' Then the song had to take on the band thing, with everybody playing, so you start to codify it a bit, where the chorus is and so on."

Jagger then wrote the words, adopting in the song the role of a man taking what proves to be rather bleak stock of his life. He felt like a *boxer who can't get in the ring*, a *hooker losing her looks*, a writer who *can't write another book*. In short, his life was utterly grim until he met the woman who has him *rocking now*.

Like "Love Is Strong," "You Got Me Rocking" was released as a single (on September 26, 1994). It climbed to number 23 on the UK charts on October 8. The song spawned a number of different versions, including the Perfecto Mix, the Sexy Disco Dub Mix, and the Trance Mix.

Production

What, then, is the "mystery guitar" the liner notes describe Keith as playing on this track? He would explain that it was simply a Dobro solid body strummed with a piece of wood he picked up in Ronnie's garden. He was struck by the particular sonority and percussive effect this produced, and retained it on the track (where it can be heard most clearly after 3:26). He also plays a riff of his own devising on rhythm guitar, with Ronnie answering on a second guitar, which he plays slide. The two also share a number of solos between them. Charlie smacks his Gretsch kit with vigor, mainly working his toms. The enormous sound of his drum kit is explained by its positioning in the stairwell of the studio, where it had been installed by the sound engineer in order to try to achieve a live effect. Jagger plays the maracas and delivers a very good vocal performance, his voice enveloped in a reasonably short delay. The mixing preserves a roots feel without sacrificing any definition or clarity. Hats off to Don Smith.

SPARKS WILL FLY

Mick Jagger / Keith Richards / 3:14

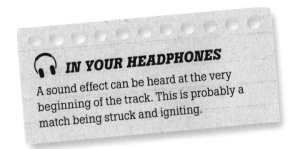

🎧 **IN YOUR HEADPHONES**
A sound effect can be heard at the very beginning of the track. This is probably a match being struck and igniting.

Musicians
Mick Jagger: vocals
Keith Richards: rhythm guitar, acoustic guitar, backing vocals
Charlie Watts: drums
Ron Wood: B-bender guitar
Darryl Jones: bass
Bernard Fowler: backing vocals

Recorded
Ron Wood's Sandymount Studio, Kildare County, Ireland: July 9–August 6, September 1993
Windmill Lane Studios, Dublin, Ireland: November 3–December 11, 1993
A&M Studios, Los Angeles: January 15–April 1994

Technical Team
Producers: Don Was, the Glimmer Twins
Sound engineer: Don Smith
Assistant sound engineers: Dan Bosworth, Alastair McMillan
Assistant sound engineers (mixing): Mike Baumgartner, Greg Goldman, Ed Korengo

Charlie was by Keith's side when ideas for "Sparks Will Fly" were flowing.

Genesis

"Sparks will fly" presumably refers to what is going to happen upon the return of the narrator (a strong and handsome stud?), who is planning to transmit his passion to his partner, to make her scream with pleasure, which is apparently not too difficult a task. *I have never found a woman so hot*, sings Jagger, who also claims to be in *total chaos*. The Stones singer would reveal with some amusement that Keith and Charlie were a little surprised by the tenor of the words, not least by the phrase *I want to fuck your sweet ass*. "Did he really say that?" Mick said Keith asked. "Did he?"

Production

The idea for the song came to Keith while he was lighting a wood fire on the grounds of Ron Wood's home. He was immediately inspired by the sight of the jumping sparks, and rushed to Ronnie's home studio. Only Charlie was in attendance and this shows, for the song is built around an absolute understanding between Keith Richards and Charlie Watts. "'Sparks Will Fly' was actually eyeball-to-eyeball with Charlie Watts more than anybody to start with," Richards tells Jas Obrecht, "because we wouldn't let anybody else play on it until we'd honed down that rhythm track thing dead right. You know, it was like, three's a crowd [laughs] for a minute, until we'd worked it out." And it has to be acknowledged that the rhythm part is absolutely impeccable, the two musicians complementing each other perfectly and acting totally in sync. Charlie's part is magnificent and possesses an exceptional sound, as does Keith's guitar, which roars out from beginning to end of the track. Of particular note is a very good rhythm passage at 1:47 that is typical of open-G playing. Keith can also be heard on an acoustic, presumably one of his Martins, while Ronnie takes the solo most likely on his ESP TE fitted with a B-bender (2:02). Darryl Jones delivers an efficient and discreet bass part, and Mick succeeds in setting the song alight with his highly flammable lyrics. It is worth emphasizing the quality not only of his performance but also of the sound recording.

THE WORST

Mick Jagger / Keith Richards / 2:24

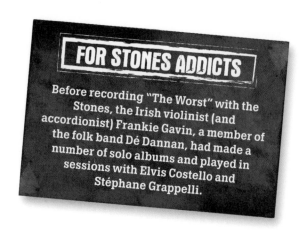

FOR STONES ADDICTS

Before recording "The Worst" with the Stones, the Irish violinist (and accordionist) Frankie Gavin, a member of the folk band Dé Dannan, had made a number of solo albums and played in sessions with Elvis Costello and Stéphane Grappelli.

Musicians
Keith Richards: vocals, acoustic guitar, backing vocals
Mick Jagger: backing vocals
Charlie Watts: drums
Ron Wood: pedal steel guitar
Darryl Jones: bass
Chuck Leavell: piano
Frankie Gavin: fiddle
Recorded
Ron Wood's Sandymount Studio, Saint Kildare,
Ireland: July 9–August 6, September 1993 (?)
Windmill Lane Studios, Dublin, Ireland:
November 3–December 11, 1993
A&M Studios, Los Angeles: January 15–April 1994
Technical Team
Producers: Don Was, the Glimmer Twins
Sound engineer: Don Smith
Assistant sound engineers: Dan Bosworth, Alastair McMillan
Assistant sound engineers (mixing): Mike Baumgartner, Greg Goldman, Ed Korengo

Irish fiddler Frankie Gavin, co-founder
of the folk group Dé Dannan.

Genesis

In the second half of the sixties, the Stones started to make repeated incursions into the world of country and western, the most striking examples being the acoustic version of "Honky Tonk Women," which was renamed "Country Honk," and the second side of the LP *Exile on Main St.* In the case of "The Worst," it is more a tribute to Irish music by the Glimmer Twins—and in particular Keith Richards, the main songwriter and singer. A singer, moreover, who does not have a very high opinion of himself, going as far as advising his girlfriend to walk away: *I said from the first, I am the worst kind of guy.* Do warnings come any clearer than this?

Production

Curiously, this song recorded under Dublin's damp skies was actually written by Keith in the kitchen of Blue Wave Studios in Barbados. Yet this very pretty ballad retains no hint of Caribbean sunshine. On the contrary, the song quite definitely conjures up the melancholy atmosphere of the Irish landscape, a color reinforced by Frank Gavin's fiddle, which is infused with the spirit of Irish traditional music. Then there is the country element dispensed by Ron Wood on pedal steel guitar, his highly successful solo at 1:50 providing yet another demonstration of his skill on the instrument. Keith plays his Gibson Robert Johnson L-1 acoustic, on which he launches the track with a very gentle intro. He also sings, demonstrating a striking assurance of timbre informed by the experience of working on his two solo albums to date. Keith sings in a low register quite different from the very high vocal harmonies he used to provide during the Mick Taylor years. Mick Jagger, meanwhile, sings second voice, adopting such an unusual timbre that he would later admit to not being able to recognize himself! "The Worst" is admirably served by Charlie's drumming, which possesses a subtlety of feeling and an incredible sonority, his snare (or brushes) permeating the stereo field without any hint of aggression, yet at the same time supporting the rhythm to great effect (thanks, not least, to Don Smith and his extraordinary work). Darryl Jones does a good enough job, although Bill Wyman would probably have suited this musical style better. Finally, Chuck Leavell's piano part makes an important contribution to the lyricism of the song, despite being recessed in the mix.

NEW FACES

Mick Jagger / Keith Richards / 2:50

It is amusing to note the absence of Ron Wood on a track titled "New Faces"!

Musicians
Mick Jagger: vocals, acoustic guitar
Keith Richards: acoustic guitar, backing vocals
Charlie Watts: tambourine
Darryl Jones: bass
Chuck Leavell: harpsichord, harmonium
Frankie Gavin: pennywhistle
Luís Jardim: shaker
Recorded
Ron Wood's Sandymount Studio, Saint Kildare,
Ireland: July 9–August 6, September 1993 (?)
Windmill Lane Studios, Dublin, Ireland:
November 3–December 11, 1993
A&M Studios, Los Angeles: January 15–April 1994
Technical Team
Producers: Don Was, the Glimmer Twins
Sound engineer: Don Smith
Assistant sound engineers: Dan Bosworth, Alastair McMillan
Assistant sound engineers (mixing): Mike Baumgartner, Greg Goldman, Ed Korengo

Darryl Jones. After playing jazz with Miles Davis, the bassist adapted seamlessly to the needs of the Stones.

Genesis

With "New Faces," the Stones send us back to the mid-sixties. In particular, the song calls to mind the atmosphere of the album *Aftermath* and the ballad "Lady Jane." The main difference lies in the lyrics. *There's a new guy in town . . . He's the figure of youth/His eyes are so blue and they're looking at you*: the years have passed and the narrator no longer embodies the insolence of youth. He cannot be sure anymore of the feelings of the woman he loves, who may well allow herself to be seduced by another.

The Stones singer wrote this ballad on the guitar. ". . . [W]hen we were in Barbados, Keith started playing keyboards on it," recalls Mick. "And then I switched to play keyboards, and he played guitar and I played harpsichord. So it gave it a slightly different feel, but it always was a sort of 16th century form. And I was trying to take it away from there a little bit, but then I brought it back." The bridge, on the other hand, could easily have been written by Keith Richards . . .

Production

In the Elizabethan atmosphere of this new ballad, Mick Jagger adopts a vocal timbre that we rarely get to hear: lowish, well rounded, serene . . . perhaps reflecting a more fulfilling period in his life. The improved relations with Keith are probably not unconnected with this. Mick also plays acoustic guitar (on the left), and apparently whispers the count-in at the beginning of the track. Keith plays second acoustic guitar with an excellent touch, as can be heard in his solo at 1:49. For one of the very few times since he officially joined the band, Ron Wood plays no part in the recording. Charlie's contribution is limited to the tambourine, assisted by Luís Jardim on the shaker (from 1:33). After having played fiddle on the "The Worst," Frankie Gavin now picks up the pennywhistle, which is not greatly in evidence, to tell the truth, although it can be heard from 1:33. Darryl Jones plays a solid bass line, but with a sound that is not particularly well adapted to this musical style. Finally, Chuck Leavell delivers a good harpsichord part, probably on a synthesizer. This was Mick's idea (also claimed by Keith!), but in all honesty the success of this choice of instrument and its highly prominent place in the mix is questionable.

MOON IS UP

Mick Jagger / Keith Richards / 3:41

Musicians
Mick Jagger: vocals, harmonica, castanets
Keith Richards: acoustic guitars, rhythm guitars, tambourine
Charlie Watts: "mystery drum"
Ron Wood: pedal steel guitar
Darryl Jones: bass
Chuck Leavell: harmonium
Benmont Tench: accordion
Bernard Fowler, Bobby Womack: backing vocals

Recorded
Ron Wood's Sandymount Studio, Saint Kildare, Ireland: July 9–August 6, September 1993 (?)
Windmill Lane Studios, Dublin, Ireland: November 3–December 11, 1993
A&M Studios, Los Angeles: January 15–April 1994

Technical Team
Producers: Don Was, the Glimmer Twins
Sound engineer: Don Smith
Assistant sound engineers: Dan Bosworth, Alastair McMillan
Assistant sound engineers (mixing): Mike Baumgartner, Greg Goldman, Ed Korengo

Benmont Tench (second from left) with the members of Tom Petty and the Heartbreakers in 1976.

Genesis

"Moon Is Up" is a song recorded by the Rolling Stones in Ireland at the beginning of the *Voodoo Lounge* sessions. *The moon is up, the sky is black/I'll sail away and won't come back/The sun goes down, the stars will rise and dance across the darkened skies*: the atmosphere is supremely well established in the lyrics. But this is not the most important aspect of the track: "Moon Is Up" is of note first and foremost for its special musical color.

Production

"If Charlie Watts is willing to experiment in the studio, then I'm the happiest man in the world," Keith Richards is reported to have said. In effect, the musical approach taken by the Stones in putting together this song is one of experimentation. Don Smith would later explain that "Moon Is Up" included every means of altering the sound that he, the band, and Don Was could come up with, "from Charlie banging on a garbage can with brushes to Ronnie playing his pedal steel through a Mutron [most likely the Mu-tron wah-wah pedal], Keith playing his acoustic guitar through the Hammond organ's Leslie cabinet, and Mick singing through his harmonica mic which had phasing on it." The results are in keeping with their efforts, and "Moon Is Up" is one of the band's most inventive pieces since the sixties. The culmination of all this experimentation has to be Charlie's drumming, on what is credited in the liner notes as a "mystery drum." "Don [Was] wanted to find something else for Charlie to bang on," says Don Smith, "so I found this trash can sitting on a flightcase and we placed it and Charlie out on the third floor." He used a stereo mic to record it, with one side close to the trash can and the other facing into the stairwell in order to capture the resonance. And the results are superb, as can be heard right from the intro. Apart from the various effects described above, the remaining instruments, such as Darryl Jones's bass and Keith's other rhythm guitars, seem to have been tampered with less, although nevertheless enhanced with phasing. The same goes for Benmont Tench's accordion, whose sound is altered to a degree, and Chuck Leavell's harmonium. Mick Jagger, who is not fond of returning to the past, has said that he would have eliminated "Moon Is Up" had it been necessary to reduce the number of tracks from fifteen to ten. That would have been a mistake . . .

OUT OF TEARS

Mick Jagger / Keith Richards / 5:25

Musicians
Mick Jagger: vocals, acoustic guitar
Keith Richards: rhythm guitar
Charlie Watts: drums
Ron Wood: slide guitar
Darryl Jones: bass
Chuck Leavell: piano
Benmont Tench: organ
Lenny Castro: percussion
David Campbell: string arrangement
Recorded
Ron Wood's Sandymount Studio, Saint Kildare,
Ireland: July 9–August 6, September 1993
Windmill Lane Studios, Dublin, Ireland:
November 3–December 11, 1993
A&M Studios, Los Angeles: January 15–April 1994
Technical Team
Producers: Don Was, the Glimmer Twins
Sound engineer: Don Smith
Assistant sound engineers: Dan Bosworth, Alastair McMillan
Assistant sound engineers (mixing): Mike Baumgartner,
Greg Goldman, Ed Korengo

Ron Wood gives a dazzling demonstration of his mastery of the slide guitar on "Out of Tears."

Genesis

Mick Jagger wrote "Out of Tears" on the piano in Ron Wood's studio. Over the course of the years, the singer had toned down his misogyny, which had proved more than a tad provocative, in favor of a fairly romantic vision of male-female relationships. And indeed here, in a voice filled with emotion, he describes the end of a beautiful romance: *I won't cry when you say goodbye/I'm out of tears*, expressing the inner torment of the narrator. This song follows in direct succession from "Let It Loose," "Angie," and "Fool to Cry."

"Out of Tears" was the A-side of the third single from *Voodoo Lounge*. Released on November 1, 1994, it peaked at number 36 on the UK charts on December 10. This single also included the same song remixed by Bob Clearmountain at Right Track Studios in New York City in April 1994 (the Bob Clearmountain Remix Edit) and "I'm Gonna Drive."

Production

Don Smith explains that while mixing the album at the A&M Studios in Los Angeles, it was to "Out of Tears" that he applied the biggest effects, seeking to achieve a result both more direct and more appealing: "I actually tried to imitate the John Lennon 'Imagine' feel by putting 15 ips tape slap on the drums to start with, and then I wondered what it would sound like if I put it on the piano too. I ended up putting it on everything, the whole track, just like the old Phil Spector way of doing things—and it worked." The mixing is of astonishing clarity and evident depth, and has delivered superb results, even if the echo is actually pretty modest. We are a long way here from Spector's later work—apart from Ronnie's excellent slide part with a solo at 3:00 that is reminiscent of George Harrison.

The rest of this very beautiful ballad shows us the Stones singer adopting a rather different approach to his singing, searching for new inflections and letting his sensitivity show through as he already has on "New Faces." Chuck Leavell delivers a good piano part, and Benmont Tench skillfully blends his organ with the magnificent strings arranged by David Campbell. Charlie and Darryl provide good rhythmic support, while Mick is on acoustic guitar and Keith provides a subtle accompaniment on electric. "Out of Tears" is one of the triumphs of the album.

I GO WILD

Mick Jagger / Keith Richards / 4:23

Musicians
Mick Jagger: vocals, rhythm guitar
Keith Richards: rhythm guitar, backing vocals
Charlie Watts: drums
Ron Wood: B-bender guitar, lead guitar
Darryl Jones: bass
Chuck Leavell: organ
Phil Jones: percussion
Ivan Neville, Bernard Fowler: backing vocals
Recorded
Ron Wood's Sandymount Studio, Kildare County,
Ireland: July 9–August 6, September 1993 (?)
Windmill Lane Studios, Dublin, Ireland:
November 3–December 11, 1993
A&M Studios, Los Angeles: January 15–April 1994 (?)
Right Track Studios, New York City: January 15–April 1994
Technical Team
Producers: Don Was, the Glimmer Twins
Sound engineer: Don Smith
Assistant sound engineers: Dan Bosworth, Alastair McMillan
Sound engineer (mixing): Bob Clearmountain
Assistant sound engineers (mixing): Jennifer Monnar

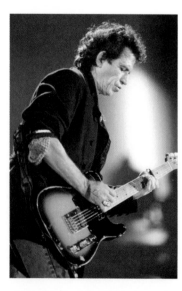

Keith Richards on his 5-string Telecaster for "I Go Wild."

FOR STONES ADDICTS

The waitresses with broken noses in "I Go Wild" are a nod to Ron Wood, who "knew every waitress in Dublin," as Mick Jagger would later reveal with a little smile.

Genesis

In "I Go Wild," the main songwriter, Mick Jagger, once again turns the spotlight on those strange creatures that have haunted him ever since he achieved rock star status. Moreover, the doctor has told the protagonist: *You'd be okay and if you'd only stay away from femmes fatales and dirty bitches . . .* , *working girls and blue stockings, waitresses with broken noses* and *politicians' garish wives.* He has not taken any notice, however, because he knows that the woman he is mad about has a *poison kiss* and that without her he is *dead meat.*

This song, which points the finger at the demonic power of femmes fatales with a certain taste for sadomasochism, was the A-side of the fourth single taken from *Voodoo Lounge.* Released on July 3, 1995, it rose to number 29 in prim and proper Albion some 14 days later.

Production

"I Go Wild" is a typical example of a Rolling Stones rock number of the kind the band had regularly been delighting its fans with since *Some Girls.* This type of track is generally constructed around Charlie's drumming, which, fifty percent of the time, launches the song on the snare drum (as is the case here) and with a Keith riff played more often than not on a 5-string Telecaster in open G. This style of rock music, which is not always highly inspired in terms of its melody, derives its power from a singer brimming with energy, who goads his bandmates into displaying the same degree of motivation as himself. However, "I Go Wild" is the exception that proves the rule, because although Charlie does indeed launch the song on his snare drum, it is Jagger, not Richards, who takes the first rhythm guitar part, and instead of abandoning himself to an adrenaline-fired vocal performance as in the past, the singer adopts a more nuanced style that serves the song extremely well. Keith supports him on another rhythm guitar, in open G, and Ronnie alternates between phrases on the B-bender (listen between 3:02 and 3:19) and a solo part played simultaneously fingerstyle and slide (2:18). Darryl Jones follows with some bass playing that is a little too static, while Chuck Leavell plays an excellent Hammond B-3 organ part. As for the mixing, Bob Clearmountain does not do as well for the band with this track as he has with others in the past.

BRAND NEW CAR

Mick Jagger / Keith Richards / 4:13

Musicians
Mick Jagger: vocals, rhythm guitar
Keith Richards: rhythm guitar, lead guitar, bass, backing vocals
Charlie Watts: drums
Chuck Leavell: piano
David McMurray: saxophone
Mark Isham: trumpet
Lenny Castro, Luis Jardim: percussion
Ivan Neville: backing vocals
Recorded
Ron Wood's Sandymount Studio, Kildare County, Ireland: July 9–August 6, September 1993 (?)
Windmill Lane Studios, Dublin, Ireland: November 3–December 11, 1993
A&M Studios, Los Angeles: January 15–April 1994
Technical Team
Producers: Don Was, the Glimmer Twins
Sound engineer: Don Smith
Assistant sound engineers: Dan Bosworth, Alastair McMillan
Assistant sound engineers (mixing): Mike Baumgartner, Greg Goldman, Ed Korengo

Mick Jagger at the wheel of a brand-new car . . .

Genesis
Although recorded during the *Voodoo Lounge* sessions, "Brand New Car" could have been cut at any point during the Stones' career. Like a new "Terraplane Blues" (Robert Johnson) or "Me and My Chauffeur Blues" (Memphis Minnie), the song effectively reaffirms the link between the London band and the blues. As befits a bluesman with a great deal of experience under his belt, Mick Jagger carves out a number of well-chosen metaphors. He clearly wants us to see this brand-new automobile as resembling a woman who is *slinky like a panther*, who can be heard purring, and who is like fur to the touch. This beast of a song has since roared into life onstage during the 1994–1995, 1999, and 2002 tours.

Production
It is sufficiently rare to merit a mention: Mick Jagger employs vibrato in his singing voice! Indeed, *Voodoo Lounge* would mark nothing short of a new vocal approach on Jagger's part, one in which he explores new singing techniques with considerable success. "Brand New Car" is the proof: his more restrained delivery is excellent, and with the support of Mark Isham's trumpet and David McMurray's saxophone, the effect obtained at 1:30 and 2:50 is a real masterstroke that has something of *Exile on Main St.* about it, whether Mick Jagger likes it or not. In addition to singing, Mick also plays a clear-toned rhythm guitar, as does Keith, who shadows him supportively. The latter also uses a wah-wah pedal and can be heard playing some solo passages in a style that differs considerably from his normal approach. Ronnie does not play any part in the recording and neither does Darryl Jones, who is replaced by Keith. The king of the riff plays a very good bass line, delaying his entry until 0:42 in order to increase the instrument's impact. For the same reason, he refrains from playing between 1:30 and 2:50. This produces a powerful effect. Chuck is credited on piano, but it is difficult to confirm his presence. By contrast, the percussionists Lenny Castro and Luís Jardim can be heard playing a güiro from the intro, and later a shaker. Darryl Jones has subsequently claimed that "Brand New Car" is one of his favorite tracks on the album, and it is not difficult to see why that might be.

SWEETHEARTS TOGETHER

Mick Jagger / Keith Richards / 4:46

Mick Jagger: vocals, acoustic guitar
Keith Richards: vocals, acoustic guitar, rhythm guitar
Charlie Watts: drums
Ron Wood: pedal steel guitar, lap steel
Chuck Leavell: organ
Flaco Jiménez: accordion
Max Baca: bajo sexto
Luís Jardim: percussion (triangle, bongos, claves)
Ivan Neville, Bernard Fowler: backing vocals
Recorded
Ron Wood's Sandymount Studio, Saint Kildare,
Ireland: July 9–August 6, September 1993 (?)
Windmill Lane Studios, Dublin, Ireland:
November 3–December 11, 1993
A&M Studios, Los Angeles: January 15–April 1994
Technical Team
Producers: Don Was, the Glimmer Twins
Sound engineer: Don Smith
Assistant sound engineers: Dan Bosworth, Alastair McMillan
Assistant sound engineers (mixing): Mike Baumgartner,
Greg Goldman, Ed Korengo

FOR STONES ADDICTS

The bass played by Max Baca is a bajo sexto, a 6-string acoustic guitar that is the bass instrument used in Mexican music.

Genesis

At the risk of surprising their fans, if not provoking complete and utter incomprehension on their part, the Stones venture on this track into the realm of a particularly exotic strain of pop. Just as disconcertingly, Mick Jagger sings of the benefits of harmonious coupledom. Love is all about sharing troubles and pain with one's partner; it is about healing one's wounds; it is two hearts beating as one . . . and this from the singer of the Stones!

The Tex-Mex vibe of "Sweethearts Together" derives from the presence alongside the Stones of the Texan accordionist Flaco Jiménez, of Max Baca (founder of Los Texmaniacs, a leading Tex-Mex group), and of the Portuguese percussionist Luís Jardim. Flaco Jiménez recalls: "I was on tour playing in San Francisco three months ago while they were recording in Hollywood, and at the gig I get a message in the dressing room from Don Was. I said, 'Who in the hell is Don Was?' Then they said he was producing the Stones and they wanted me to go record with them. I almost flipped, man. Wowee, good news. The next day I was in the studio with them—didn't have time to listen to the song or do homework at all."

Production

If there is one track that symbolizes the atmosphere of this album and at the same time seals the reconciliation between the Glimmer Twins, "Sweethearts Together" is it. Don Was: "They were standing eyeball-to-eyeball, about 18 inches apart. . . . They did this incredible Everly Brothers–type harmony all the way through the song. I thought it was very cool, but the people in the control room who had worked with them for 10 or 15 years were like, 'I can't believe this is happening!'" And so it was on a Tex-Mex ballad that the miracle occurred . . . Similarly, Mick and Keith play the two acoustic guitars together. Keith then switches to electric rhythm guitar with a fairly pronounced vibrato, while Ronnie is on pedal steel guitar and also lap steel, on which he plays some very good solo breaks (2:48). The bass is played by Max Baca and the accordion by Flaco Jiménez, who was surprised to see his employers expressing their satisfaction at his warm-up take. For the closing chorus, the backing vocalists can be heard singing *Chihuahua* with some emotion . . .

The Tejano accordionist Flaco Jiménez and his Tex-Mex sound are essential to "Sweethearts Together."

SUCK ON THE JUGULAR

Mick Jagger / Keith Richards / 4:26

Musicians
Mick Jagger: vocals, rhythm guitar, harmonica
Keith Richards: rhythm guitar, lead guitar, bass, backing vocals
Charlie Watts: drums
Ron Wood: rhythm guitar, backing vocals
Darryl Jones: bass
David McMurray: saxophone
Mark Isham: trumpet
Lenny Castro, Luis Jardim: percussion
Ivan Neville: organ, backing vocals
Bernard Fowler: backing vocals

Recorded
Ron Wood's Sandymount Studio, Kildare County, Ireland: July 9–August 6, September 1993 (?)
Windmill Lane Studios, Dublin, Ireland: November 3–December 11, 1993
A&M Studios, Los Angeles: January 15–April 1994

Technical Team
Producers: Don Was, the Glimmer Twins
Sound engineer: Don Smith
Assistant sound engineers: Dan Bosworth, Alastair McMillan
Assistant sound engineers (mixing): Mike Baumgartner, Greg Goldman, Ed Korengo

FOR STONES ADDICTS

"Suck on the Jugular" was initially titled "Holetown Prison" for the simple reason that the Blue Wave Studios were located close to that particular facility, Holetown being a town in Barbados.

Genesis
After the wide and sweltering expanses of Texas, the Stones now find themselves back in an atmosphere that, although very different, is every bit as torrid—that of the dance floor. Indeed, this song, which came into being during the sessions at Blue Wave Studios in Barbados at the beginning of 1993 (the lyrics were written later), was intended from the very beginning as an out-and-out dance track, and is perhaps the most successful example of its type since "Hot Stuff" eighteen years before. This is a success in which Darryl Jones, David McMurray, and Mark Isham play a full part. The Stones have never performed the number live, but it would no doubt have made quite an impact . . .

Production
Here, then, is the one and only concession to funk (of which Mick was so fond) on *Voodoo Lounge*, and right from the intro, there is no mistaking the territory. Charlie Watts's funky groove is unstoppable and Darryl Jones's superb bass significantly boosts the dance vibe of this track, the sound he makes being just as impressive as his actual playing. Darryl would later confess that he had wanted to pay tribute to the legendary bassist Jaco Pastorius with a bass line inspired by "River People" on the album *Mr. Gone.* (1978). "Suck on the Jugular" is a Mick Jagger track of which James Brown would have been proud. The harmonic shift at 0:52 inevitably calls to mind "Get Up (I Feel Like Being a) Sex Machine," but the Stones remain the Stones, and it is quite definitely their own sound that prevails. No melody as such emerges; instead, Mick uses the band as a vehicle for his lyrics, to which the backing singers respond intermittently with great enthusiasm. Mick also plays a very good rhythm guitar part, making free use of the wah-wah pedal. Keith plays various licks, rhythm patterns, and solos (listen at 3:43), as does Ronnie, who adds to the different guitar effects by playing palm mute. The horns of McMurray and Isham contribute to the groove of this track with their crisp, highly effective riffs. The other major surprise of "Suck on the Jugular" is Mick's excellent harmonica solo, which would later occur to him as strange, reminding him, he would claim, of the phrasing of a trumpet rather than that of a harmonica.

BLINDED BY RAINBOWS

Mick Jagger / Keith Richards / 4:33

Musicians
Mick Jagger: vocals, rhythm guitar
Keith Richards: acoustic guitars, rhythm guitar (?), backing vocals
Charlie Watts: drums
Ron Wood: lead guitar
Darryl Jones: bass
Benmont Tench: piano, organ, harpsichord (?)
Lenny Castro: percussion
Recorded
Ron Wood's Sandymount Studio, Kildare County, Ireland: July 9–August 6, September 1993
Windmill Lane Studios, Dublin, Ireland: November 3–December 11, 1993
A&M Studios, Los Angeles: January 15–April 1994
Technical Team
Producers: Don Was, the Glimmer Twins
Sound engineer: Don Smith
Assistant sound engineers: Dan Bosworth, Alastair McMillan
Assistant sound engineers (mixing): Mike Baumgartner, Greg Goldman, Ed Korengo

Benmont Tench (shown here in 2014) plays on several *Voodoo Lounge* tracks, including "Blinded by Rainbows."

Genesis

Mick Jagger wrote "Blinded by Rainbows" in September 1992, at the end of the sessions for his solo album *Wandering Spirit*. The Stones later recorded it in Ireland, a bastion of Celtic culture, whose northern provinces were under the rule of the British Crown.

Do you ever hear the screams as the limbs are all torn off/Did you ever kiss the child who just saw his father shot? These words, like those of the other verses of this song, are about the conflict in Northern Ireland and the anti-Catholic discrimination, hence the reference to Christ and his suffering on the cross. *Blinded by rainbows . . .* the rainbows in question could symbolize the two causes, political and religious, that have the power to blind and can never be reconciled.

Production

The arpeggiated guitar in the intro, with its pronounced tremolo, is played by Mick Jagger. He is immediately joined by the harpsichord. The atmosphere is melancholy and the message could not be more serious. The singer would later explain that he had wanted to re-create the spirit of the Staple Singers, with its gospel and R&B sound and its tremolo guitar characteristic of the founder of the group, Roebuck "Pops" Staples. Although intending the song for his third solo album, he discovered in the end that it suited the Stones better than it did himself as a solo artist. It is also interesting to speculate that U2 might have made a terrific version of the song had they covered it, as the harmonies and message seem to be tailor-made for them. Mick Jagger adopts a somber-sounding voice that unfailingly hits the mark in terms of intent and emotion. He is joined in the vocal harmonies by Keith. Benmont Tench plays the Hammond C-3, using a Leslie speaker to create a flute-like sound. Keith strums an acoustic guitar and seems to add a second acoustic part as well as an electric rhythm part. Ron Wood's involvement is limited to the track's one solo (2:55), which is excellent. Charlie lays down a superb rhythm part and smacks his snare drum with considerable power. Attention should also be drawn to the excellent recording of his drums. Darryl Jones finds himself in a supporting role, although the sound of his bass is a little too big for this kind of song. "Blinded by Rainbows" is a very attractive ballad with folk accents, and stands out strongly from the rest of the album.

BABY BREAK IT DOWN

Mick Jagger / Keith Richards / 4:07

Musicians
Mick Jagger: vocals
Keith Richards: acoustic guitars, rhythm
guitars, piano, backing vocals
Charlie Watts: drums
Ron Wood: pedal steel guitar
Darryl Jones: bass
Ivan Neville: organ, backing vocals
Bernard Fowler: backing vocals
Recorded
Ron Wood's Sandymount Studio, Saint Kildare,
Ireland: July 9–August 6, September 1993
Windmill Lane Studios, Dublin, Ireland:
November 3–December 11, 1993
A&M Studios, Los Angeles: January 15–April 1994
Technical Team
Producers: Don Was, the Glimmer Twins
Sound engineer: Don Smith
Assistant sound engineers: Dan Bosworth, Alastair McMillan
Assistant sound engineers (mixing): Mike Baumgartner,
Greg Goldman, Ed Korengo

Mick Jagger and Charlie Watts en route
to the voodoo ceremony . . .

Genesis

You're standing on your side, I'm standing on mine: this song by Keith Richards tells of the difficulty of communication within a couple. This should not be seen as alluding specifically to the stormy relationship between Jagger and Richards, which lasted for a good part of the eighties, but rather as a reflection on the difficulties of overcoming the adversities of that *long, long way to go* that is life. It is also a message of hope. There's *no river running that we can't cross*, sings Jagger, accompanied by the voices of Keith Richards, Bernard Fowler, and Ivan Neville. "Baby Break It Down" has never been performed live.

Production

Mid-tempo rock tracks are few and far between on Rolling Stones albums, but "Baby Break It Down," with its moderate pace and insidious charm, is one of them. Charlie's drumming reins in the tempo, preventing any unwarranted acceleration, and Darryl Jones's very good bass is sufficiently weighty to help him in this task. Keith opens the track with a riff in open G that is accompanied by a second rhythm guitar. Although this example of his playing holds no great surprises, it is always a pleasure to hear him on the 5-string, presumably one of his Telecasters plugged into his 1957 Fender Twin. He can also be heard strumming two acoustic parts from 1:44, as well as playing the piano, which can be made out in the intro. As a multitasking Stone, Keith also contributes to the vocal harmonies, and his voice, which was getting deeper around this time, emerges in a very distinctive fashion during the verses. Ron Wood is on pedal steel, proving his mastery of the instrument once again with a highly successful solo at 2:12. The Hammond B-3 organ is played by Ivan Neville, the style and color of his work recalling those of Steve Winwood in places. Mick seems to have left behind for good the strained voice, forever on a knife-edge, that had characterized his singing for so long, especially on the last three albums. His timbre is now lower, more assured, and less aggressive. Might this be a sign of growing wisdom on the part of the Stones singer?

THRU AND THRU

Mick Jagger / Keith Richards / 6:15

Musicians
Keith Richards: vocals, rhythm and lead guitar, piano
Mick Jagger: backing vocals
Charlie Watts: drums
Darryl Jones: bass
Pierre de Beauport: acoustic guitar
Ivan Neville, Bernard Fowler: backing vocals
Unidentified musicians: synthesizer, organ

Recorded
Blue Wave Studios, Barbados: April–May 1993
**Ron Wood's Sandymount Studio, Saint Kildare,
Ireland:** July 9–August 6, September 1993
Windmill Lane Studios, Dublin, Ireland:
November 3–December 11, 1993
A&M Studios, Los Angeles: January 15–April 1994

Technical Team
Producers: Don Was, the Glimmer Twins
Sound engineer: Don Smith
Assistant sound engineers: Dan Bosworth, Alastair McMillan
Assistant sound engineers (mixing): Mike Baumgartner,
Greg Goldman, Ed Korengo

Keith Richards. The idea for "Thru and Thru" came
to him late at night . . . or early in the morning.

On the CD, the initial duration of "Thru and
Thru" was 6:15, whereas the track actually
ends at 5:59 with sixteen seconds of silence
at the end. This is probably due to the extra
song on the CD, "Mean Disposition," that
does not appear on the LP.

Genesis

Keith Richards wrote "Thru and Thru" when he was with
Mick Jagger and Pierre de Beauport in Barbados. It came as a
sudden stroke of inspiration one morning, he explains to Jas
Obrecht. ". . . [W]e'd been out to a club in Bridgetown. Tropical night. We had a night off, you know. And we get back to
Eddy Grant's studio, which is where we were living and working, at five in the morning and get out of the car. And I start
staggering in, and suddenly I turn around to Pierre. I said,
'Switch the stuff on, man. Incoming, incoming.' I guess maybe
in the car. . . . But I just went into the studio and laid it all down
in one take." So this is a song inspired by a sultry, starry Bar-
badian night of a kind that favors introspection. The solitary
individual waiting for his loved one to call seems to be Keith.
But there is no happy ending, for: *I only found out yester-
day/I heard it on the news/What I heard really pissed me off*,
he sings in a voice both tortured and disillusioned, suggesting
that his beloved has left him.

Production

"Thru and Thru" is one of the most ambitious tracks on *Voodoo Lounge*. Keith reveals a rich vocal palette of astonishing
sensitivity. The emotional charge in his performance and the
harmonic structure of his chords are far superior to his lyrics,
whose meaning comes across as pretty bland by comparison.
He is most probably playing this superb ballad, which swings
between rock, blues, and folk, on one of his Telecasters. The
sonority of his guitar playing is truly splendid, with each note
imbued with feeling) and he also uses his voice, with its rug-
ged timbre, to deliver a performance that is fragile and highly
nuanced. The song has two distinct sections: a first with an
almost dreamlike atmosphere (making use of reverse reverb)
in which a synthesizer can be heard emitting crystalline sound
pads, and a second from 3:48 on that is all-out rock, with a
fantastic drum part from Charlie recorded in the stairwell of
the studio, its sound recalling that of John Bonham. "The
stairwell was concrete and it had tremendous echo," confirms Don Was. With some very good bass from Darryl Jones,
the acoustic guitar of Pierre de Beauport, superb backing
vocals from Mick, Ivan, and Bernard, and a highly successful
sound collage in the coda (5:06), "Thru and Thru" is one of
the key tracks on the album.

MEAN DISPOSITION

Mick Jagger / Keith Richards / 4:09

It is interesting to note that Muddy Waters, the Stones' ultimate point of reference, wrote a blues called "Mean Disposition" (1949). Dave Davies of the Kinks also recorded a song by the same name for his solo album *Chosen People* (1983).

Musicians
Mick Jagger: vocals
Keith Richards: lead guitar
Charlie Watts: drums
Ron Wood: rhythm guitar
Darryl Jones: acoustic bass
Chuck Leavell: piano
Recorded
Ron Wood's Sandymount Studio, Kildare County, Ireland: July 9–August 6, September 1993 (?)
Windmill Lane Studios, Dublin, Ireland: November 3–December 11, 1993
A&M Studios, Los Angeles: January 15–April 1994
Technical Team
Producers: Don Was, the Glimmer Twins
Sound engineer: Don Smith
Assistant sound engineers: Dan Bosworth, Alastair McMillan

Genesis

The tempo picks up considerably for the last song on *Voodoo Lounge*. Originally a simple rockabilly-style instrumental, Mick Jagger then added the lyrics, which deal once again with the tempestuous story of a man and a woman: *I never close my eyes, I never sleep*; *I never trusted you and you never trusted me*. Humor is never very far away, however: *She's got a mean disposition/Got a big shooter too . . .* to such an extent that the unfortunate narrator feels like Davy Crockett at the Battle of the Alamo.

Production

"Mean Disposition" is a good old-fashioned boogie-woogie with a rock 'n' roll feel that provides the perfect conclusion to the Rolling Stones' twentieth album. The machine is running smoothly and the musicians give the impression of jamming, rather than recording a definitive take, but they nevertheless play with spirit and an infectious energy. Mick Jagger is excellent, his voice relaxed and under control and when, like any self-respecting rock singer, he needs to force his vocal cords, he is clearly up to the task. The rhythm section is impeccable, with Charlie laying down a fast and furious groove on his 1957 Gretsch kit and Darryl Jones keeping up with him effortlessly on Ronnie's fretless Zemaitis acoustic bass. It is just a pity that the bassist is slightly recessed in the mix. Chuck Leavell plays a very good boogie-woogie piano part that to some extent recalls the style of Stu, who had died years nine years before. Ronnie is on the distorted-sounding rhythm guitar, while Keith plays lead, split between a rhythm part on what sounds like Woody's 1957 Gretsch White Falcon, and two solo passages, the first at 1:51 and the second throughout the coda, in other words continuing for 1:15. The style is deliberately Chuck Berry–like, and Keith gives the impression of enjoying his instrument. "Mean Disposition" may not be the best track on *Voodoo Lounge*, but the sense of spontaneity it exudes makes for a very enjoyable conclusion to the album.

Charlie Watts at his Gretsch kit, imbuing "Mean Disposition" with a boogie-woogie groove.

Mick Jagger onstage. "When the wind blows . . ."

SINGLE

CD 1994

THE STORM

Mick Jagger / Keith Richards / 2:50

SINGLE (CD)

Love Is Strong* / The Storm / So Young / Love Is Strong**

RELEASE DATE

United Kingdom: July 4, 1994
Record number: Virgin Records VSCDT 1503
* LOVE IS STRONG
** BOB CLEARMOUNTAIN REMIX

Musicians

Mick Jagger: vocals, harmonica, Dobro
Keith Richards: rhythm guitar
Charlie Watts: drums
Ron Wood: slide guitar
Darryl Jones: bass (?)
Chuck Leavell: piano
Don Was: bass (?)

Recorded

Windmill Lane Studios, Dublin, Ireland:
November 3–December 11, 1993
A&M Studios, Los Angeles: January 15–April 1994

Technical Team

Producers: Don Was, the Glimmer Twins
Sound engineer: Don Smith
Assistant sound engineers: Dan Bosworth, Alastair McMillan
Assistant sound engineers (mixing): Mike Baumgartner, Greg Goldman, Ed Korengo

Genesis

The storm in question seems to have broken mainly inside the head of Mick Jagger, who is unsurpassed when he adopts the guise of an old bluesman of the Deep South. *The storm started howlin', I'm out of my brain*, he sings, *Felt a mighty rumble, comin' from the ground*. Once again, Mick Jagger delivers a spellbinding harmonica part. Although not included on *Voodoo Lounge*, a place was found for this excellent blues alongside "Love Is Strong" and "So Young" on the first single to be taken from the album.

Production

Mick Jagger would explain that on the last day dedicated to *Voodoo Lounge*—when everybody was getting ready to wrap up the sessions at Windmill Lane Studios in Dublin—Don Was reminded him that they still needed three B-sides for the forthcoming singles. Jagger, who had never intentionally written a B-side, told the producer he was tired and would not have time to write the tracks. Was, a pragmatist, suggested that the singer install himself in a corner of the cafeteria and come up with something on the spot. Jagger duly returned a short while later with "The Storm," "Jump on Top of Me," and "I'm Gonna Drive"! He went straight into the studio with the rest of the group, recorded the backing tracks in a single take, and announced that he would finish the lyrics later. After doing so, he recorded them at the A&M Studios in Los Angeles at the beginning of 1994. It is remarkable to think that in 1964, he and Keith really had to rack their brains to come up with some songs of their own under pressure from Andrew Loog Oldham . . . "The Storm" is an electric blues that might have come straight out of Chicago. Ron Wood is on slide, most probably his Zemaitis, and shadows the main vocal line in the finest tradition of the genre. Jagger's singing, with vibrato, is excellent. He also plays a Dobro part on Ronnie's "Uncle Harvey," and delivers some superb phrases on the harmonica. Keith plays electric rhythm, while the bass seems to be played by someone other than Darryl Jones (possibly Don Was?). Chuck's piano is buried in the mix, and Charlie offers support with brushes.

CD 1994

SO YOUNG

Mick Jagger / Keith Richards / 3:20

SINGLE (CD)
Love Is Strong* / The Storm / So Young / Love Is Strong**
RELEASE DATE
United Kingdom: July 4, 1994
Record number: Virgin Records VSCDT 1503
* LOVE IS STRONG
** BOB CLEARMOUNTAIN REMIX

Musicians
Mick Jagger: vocals, Dobro, harmonica
Keith Richards: rhythm and lead (?) guitar, backing vocals
Bill Wyman: bass
Charlie Watts: drums
Ian Stewart: piano
Ron Wood: rhythm guitar
Chuck Leavell: piano solo
Recorded
EMI Pathé Marconi Studios, Boulogne-Billancourt, France: January 5–March 2, 1978
A&M Studios, Los Angeles: January 15–April 1994
Technical Team
Producers: Chris Kimsey, the Glimmer Twins
Sound engineers: Bobby Sage, Don Smith (?)

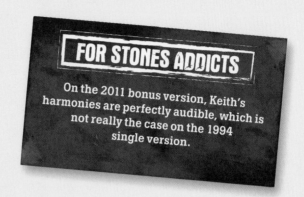

FOR STONES ADDICTS

On the 2011 bonus version, Keith's harmonies are perfectly audible, which is not really the case on the 1994 single version.

Genesis
The narrator has met a girl in a movie theater who is so young that he appeals to the Lord for help not give in to temptation. At first glance, however, she is not particularly seductive: she has zits on her face, and is incapable of walking straight. Everything changes rapidly, however, when the narrator buys her a pair of boots. He has to calm his excitement and prepare to *beat a quick retreat*. "So Young" dates back to the *Some Girls* sessions at the Pathé Marconi Studios in Boulogne-Billancourt, in the suburbs of Paris, at the beginning of 1978. There are a number of versions. The one used for the single "Love Is Strong" and later included in the box set *The Singles 1971—2006* (2011), is the 1978 recording produced by Chris Kimsey and enhanced in 1994 with some piano from Chuck Leavell. There is also the 2011 version on the *Some Girls* bonus disc, which has vocal additions from Mick Jagger. Finally, there is a piano version that was made available as a download in the United Kingdom and the United States in 2011.

Production
When the Stones stop trying to keep up with the latest musical trends, they revert to their natural inclination for rock 'n' roll. This fabulous rock number resuscitated some sixteen years after it was originally cut, in Boulogne-Billancourt, proves the point. When the British band is cruising—there is no way anything can overtake it! Mick Jagger sings with a passion and sensuality that make him a one-off in the genre. Keith and Ronnie are well coordinated on the guitar, each of them playing a killer rhythm part, and it seems to be Keith who takes the solo at 1:53. Charlie smacks his skins with power, and Bill, whom we encounter once again on this track, reminds us what a fantastic bassist he was and what an extraordinary rhythm section he formed with Charlie. Similarly, the late lamented Stu is also to be heard on "So Young," although it has to be said that the high point on the track is Chuck Leavell's superb boogie-woogie piano solo added at the A&M Studios in Los Angeles.

JUMP ON TOP OF ME

Mick Jagger / Keith Richards / 4:24

SINGLE
You Got Me Rocking* / Jump on Top of Me
RELEASE DATE
United Kingdom: September 26, 1994
RECORD NUMBER: VIRGIN RECORDS VSCDG1518
"YOU GOT ME ROCKING"*

Musicians
Mick Jagger: vocals, rhythm guitar, harmonica
Keith Richards: rhythm and lead guitar
Charlie Watts: drums
Ron Wood: slide guitar
Darryl Jones: bass (?)
Don Was: bass (?)
Frankie Gavin: fiddle (?)
Recorded
Windmill Lane Studios, Dublin, Ireland:
November 3–December 11, 1993
A&M Studios, Los Angeles: January 15–April 1994
Technical Team
Producers: Don Was, the Glimmer Twins
Sound engineer: Don Smith
Assistant sound engineers: Dan Bosworth, Alastair McMillan
Assistant sound engineers (mixing): Mike Baumgartner, Greg Goldman, Ed Korengo

Genesis
Blues rock is a genre in which the Stones' faithful disciples by far outnumber their worthy rivals. "Jump on Top of Me" is a prime example of the supremacy in this field, combining as it does all the different elements of the band's timeless aesthetic, starting with the harmonica that sounds as if it is straight out of Chess Studios, and the guitars of Keith and Ronnie. As for the song's lyrics, they conform to the hedonist philosophy of their author, Mick Jagger. After working excessively hard and feeling the pain, the last thing one needs is to be subjected to noise and cursing, and the only solution is to indulge in a good bout of lovemaking. "Jump on Top of Me" dates from the *Voodoo Lounge* sessions. It was worked up at Windmill Lane Studios in Dublin and then finalized and mixed in Los Angeles. This song was chosen as the B-side of the single "You Got Me Rocking."

Production
Along with "The Storm" and "I'm Gonna Drive," "Jump on Top of Me" is one of the three songs written by Mick Jagger in a corner of the cafeteria at Windmill Studios in Dublin so that they could be laid down as quickly as possible during the *Voodoo Lounge* sessions. Listening to the results, one can only admire the quality of all three, each, according to Mick, recorded in a single take. "Jump on Top of Me," an irresistible blues rock tinged with boogie-woogie, is perhaps the best of the bunch. Charlie once again proves his worth as a swing machine. The albeit modest bass (whether it is played by Don Was or Darryl Jones) provides his beat with significant support, and the three guitars set the track on fire. Mick

Mick Jagger in mid-levitation, onstage at Longchamp Racecourse, Paris, on July 1, 1995!

is responsible for the rhythm guitar intro, although until he is joined by the drums, his timing is not great. Keith takes care of the second rhythm part, while Ron is once again on slide. Each of them takes a short solo, and each one is highly effective. The first is played by Keith in more of a country than a rock style (1:17), the second by Mick not on guitar but on harmonica, with excellent vibrato (2:17), and the third by Ronnie on slide (3:44). "Jump on Top of Me" is a brilliant demonstration of the outstanding talent that continued to drive the Stones, and it is only a shame that it was not included on *Voodoo Lounge*.

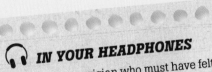

IN YOUR HEADPHONES

There is one musician who must have felt a little frustrated upon listening to the final mix: the violinist (presumably Frankie Gavin), who can be heard only between 3:16 and 3:23 and then on only one note!

I'M GONNA DRIVE

Mick Jagger / Keith Richards / 3:44

SINGLE
"Out of Tears"* / "I'm Gonna Drive"

Release date
United Kingdom: October 17, 1994
RECORD NUMBER (US): VIRGIN RECORDS NR-38459
"OUT OF TEARS"*

Musicians
Mick Jagger: vocals, Dobro (?)
Keith Richards: rhythm and lead guitar
Charlie Watts: drums
Ron Wood: slide guitar, backing vocals (?)
Darryl Jones: bass (?)
Don Was: bass (?)

Recorded
Windmill Lane Studios, Dublin, Ireland:
November 3–December 11, 1993
A&M Studios, Los Angeles: January 15–April 1994

Technical Team
Producers: Don Was, the Glimmer Twins
Sound engineer: Don Smith
Assistant sound engineers: Dan Bosworth, Alastair McMillan
Assistant sound engineers (mixing): Mike Baumgartner, Greg Goldman, Ed Korengo

Ron Wood and his beloved black Zemaitis.

Genesis

I've got itchy fingers, I've got muddy feet/And my mind is wanderin' in the steamy heat. The protagonist of this song has had enough of the world in which he lives. He therefore plans to escape at the wheel of his car—with a tank full of gasoline, with the oil topped up, and with the air-conditioning switched on—in order to discover the exhilaration of wide-open spaces. He does not want to see any more fires, disasters, hurricanes, or sad eyes, or to have any more bad dreams.

"I'm Gonna Drive" was left off the track listing for *Voodoo Lounge*, but is on the "Out of Tears" single and maxi single and is also included in the box set *The Singles 1971–2006* (2011).

Production

"I'm Gonna Drive" has an emphatic blues-rock and almost J. J. Cale vibe, with a superb vocal from Mick Jagger. This song, although occupying a relatively minor place in the Stones' catalog when all is said and done, also confirms Ron Wood's brilliance on slide guitar (stereo left). "I've always used the black Zemaitis 6-string for slide,"   he would later explain. He plays

Mick, Keith, Charlie, and Ronnie on tour again in the US.

a very good accompaniment, perfectly complementing Keith's guitar without either guitarist interfering with the playing of the other. Ronnie may be no Mick Taylor, but he certainly knows how to shape a phrase, and this can be heard in the solo he shares with Keith (2:02). Meanwhile, the riff master delivers a fantastic rhythm part, encouraging the track to breathe with a series of well-judged, loosely woven interventions (stereo right). Mick seems to be playing the Dobro, as he was on "The Storm," and given that the two tracks were laid down during the same session (most probably during the weekend of December 10–11), there is every reason to suppose that he would have picked it up again. The snare drum roll in the intro heralds a superb contribution from Charlie from the beginning to the end of "I'm Gonna Drive." He plays with a very pronounced swing and lays down a fearsomely efficient groove. The bass playing and sonority are not easily attributable to Darryl Jones and it is quite possible that Don Was, himself a bassist, is responsible for them. Finally, it is most likely Ronnie's husky voice, rivaling Keith's as an illustration of the ill effects of tobacco on the vocal cords, that can be heard in the backing vocals . . .

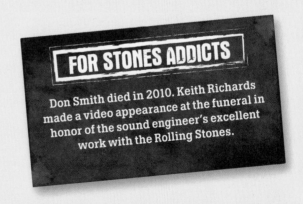

FOR STONES ADDICTS

Don Smith died in 2010. Keith Richards made a video appearance at the funeral in honor of the sound engineer's excellent work with the Rolling Stones.

Flip The Switch
Anybody Seen My Baby?
Low Down
Already Over Me
Gunface
You Don't Have To Mean It
Out Of Control

Saint Of Me
Might As Well Get Juiced
Always Suffering
Too Tight
Thief In The Night
How Can I Stop

ALBUM
RELEASE DATE
United Kingdom: September 29, 1997
Label: Virgin
RECORD NUMBER: VIRGIN CDV 2840
Number 6, on the charts for 10 weeks

BRIDGES TO BABYLON

BRIDGES TO BABYLON: A PRODUCTION TOUR DE FORCE

Following their world tour (the Voodoo Lounge Tour), which wound up in Rotterdam on August 30, 1995, and the release on November 13 of *Stripped*, the live acoustic album recorded at the Olympia in Paris and the Paradiso in Amsterdam, among other studios, the Stones began thinking about a follow-up to *Voodoo Lounge*. Despite Keith Richards becoming a grandfather on May 29, 1996, and Mick Jagger having launched his own movie production company, Jagged Films, the Glimmer Twins have always needed their shot of adrenaline from the studio—and so too have Charlie Watts and Ron Wood.

At the beginning of November 1996, the four Rolling Stones met up in New York City for a planning session. By November 21, they were already working on new songs at Dangerous Music Studios, in that same city, with the producer Don Was, who had worked with the band on the *Voodoo Lounge* sessions. Keith Richards then retreated to his Connecticut house in order to do some more writing and hold some auditions. Rehearsals resumed in mid-January 1997, again at Dangerous Music Studios. The Glimmer Twins then traveled to Barbados in mid-February, again to write. Finally, various sessions were held in London, at Westside Studios and at Trevor Horn's Sarm West Studios, before moving back across the Atlantic to Ocean Way Recording Studios in Los Angeles.

The Album

From the outset, Keith Richards and Mick Jagger wanted to pursue the blues-rock path (in the spirit of the remarkable *Sticky Fingers* and *Exile on Main St.*), while at the same time experimenting with new sounds in order to appeal to contemporary taste. "Mick and I agreed that instead of us coming together, he would cut some tracks his way and I'd cut some tracks my way," Keith would later explain. Although this new approach sounds promising, the reality was by no means smooth sailing. "I wanted to see how Mick would take that idea and he took it a lot further than I expected," continues Keith. "I had no idea that Mick thought that meant he had a licence to have a different producer for every song. Which was not quite what I had in mind." The Stones singer thus turned to a number of different producers (nevertheless working under the Glimmer Twins and Don Was). These included the Dust Brothers (John King and Mike Simpson), specialists in electronic music who played an important part in the success of Beck (*Odelay*, 1996); Danny Saber, a producer, remixer, and DJ totally immersed in cutting-edge rock; Rob Fraboni (at the insistence of Keith Richards!), who had worked with the Beach Boys, Bob Dylan, Joe Cocker, and Eric Clapton; and Pierre de Beauport, a guitar technician who was to turn his hand to production, mixing, keyboards, bass, and even contribute to the writing of a song! "So with all these producers and musicians, including a total of eight bass players, it got out of hand," explains Keith Richards. "We actually ended up for the first time almost making separate records—mine and Mick's." But according to Keith, it was not long before the Stones singer became

Charlie Watts, whose drumming guarantees the smooth running of the Rolling Stones rock 'n' roll machine.

disenchanted: "Then Mick realized his mistake and said get me out of here."

While relations between the Glimmer Twins once again proved difficult, *Bridges to Babylon* is a success—despite the heterogeneity that becomes all too apparent upon listening to the album. The traditional Stones aesthetic, is evident in a number of highly invigorating tracks featuring some killer guitar, such as "Flip the Switch," "Low Down," and "Too Tight," as well as in the ballads "Always Suffering," "Thief in the Night," "How Can I Stop," and "You Don't Have to Mean It," a number that fluctuates between Tex-Mex and reggae. However, there is also a more modern side to the album, which is exemplified by "Already Over Me" (a Babyface-style ballad), "Gunface" (strongly influenced by alternative and "noisy" rock), and "Might as Well Get Juiced" (a blues reworked by the Dust Brothers). Finally, the track listing includes three out-and-out hits: "Anybody Seen My Baby?" "Out of Control," and "Saint of Me."

The lyrics, on the other hand, vary little. With the exception of "Flip the Switch," which deals with death (and implicitly with the collective suicide of the Heaven's Gate sect in 1997), and the apocalyptic "Might as Well Get Juiced," the subjects all center on the life of the couple: truth and lies between lovers in "Low Down," "You Don't Have to Mean It," and "Too Tight"; infidelity in "Saint of Me"; revenge in "Gunface"; breaking up in "Already Over Me"; an evocation of passing time in "Out of Control," "Always Suffering," "Thief in the Night," and "How Can I Stop"; the search for a vanished loved one in "Anybody Seen My Baby?"

Bridges to Babylon is the Rolling Stones' twenty-first (British) studio album. It went out into the world on September 29, 1997, and was immediately acclaimed by a public that had been waiting since *Voodoo Lounge*. Although reaching only number 3 in the United States (but still selling more than a million copies!) and climbing no higher than number 6 in the United Kingdom (100,000 copies), it reached the top spot in

Germany (500,000 copies and platinum status), Austria, and Scandinavia, and number 2 in France (200,000 copies and double gold), Belgium, the Netherlands, and Canada. In spite of presenting a disparate collection of music, something the critics did not fail to notice, the album was a commercial success, and also gave rise to another world tour.

The Album Cover

For the *Bridges to Babylon* artwork, Mick Jagger had a very specific concept in mind. To implement it he chose Stefan Sagmeister, an Austrian graphic designer who had been nominated for a Grammy Award with his cover for H.P. Zinker's album *Mountains of Madness* (1995). The Stones singer suggested that Sagmeister visit the British Museum to view its collection of Assyrian sculpture. This inspired the majestic, roaring lion that rears up on its hind legs on the cover. Inside, there is a photograph of the four Stones dressed completely in black, a wide-angle view of a desert (specifically the Plain of Shinar) on which the Tower of Babel is depicted, the lyrics to the thirteen songs, and the credits. Stefan Sagmeister was responsible for the artistic direction, Hjalti Karlsson for the design, and Max Vadukul for the photography. The title derives in part from the British playwright Tom Stoppard, who, after seeing the maquette of a bridge intended as an element of the set for the Stones' next tour, came up with various Babylon-related ideas. One of these was abbreviated by Mick Jagger to *Bridges to Babylon*.

The Recording

After several days of rehearsing and recording at Dangerous Music Studios in New York City, and then in London, the Stones took off for Los Angeles. Their destination was Ocean Way Recording Studios, in view of its history as one of the most prestigious recording venues on the West Coast. Originally founded by Bill Putnam as United Western Studios (Frank Sinatra, Sam Cooke, the Beach Boys, Phil Spector),

Ron, Mick, Keith, and Charlie Watts bidding farewell to the
Wembley crowds at the end of the concert on June 11, 1999.

the studios were renamed when Allen Sides bought the complex in 1984.

From March 13, 1997 through July, the studios were occupied by the four Stones and Don Was, along with the various other producers and additional musicians who contributed to the album. During that period, they recorded "Low Down," "Anybody Seen My Baby?" (various versions), "Flip the Switch," "Always Suffering," "Thief in the Night," "Saint of Me" (various versions), "You Don't Have to Mean It," "Already Over Me," "Too Tight," "Gunface," "Out of Control" (various versions), and "How Can I Stop," plus "Paying the Cost to Be the Boss" (included on the B. B. King album *Deuces Wild*, 1997), "Anyway You Look at It" (the B-side of the single "Saint of Me" [Radio Edit], 1998, included on the 2005 CD *Rarities* and in the box set *The Singles 1971–2006*, 2011) as well as four other songs that were not used.

The Stones have never, before or since, employed as many technicians and musicians as they did on *Bridges to Babylon*. There were no fewer than four producers (in addition to the Glimmer Twins and Don Was), twelve sound engineers with nine assistants, nine bassists (if Pierre de Beauport is included), nine keyboard players, two guitarists, three singers (for the backing vocals), three percussionists, one trumpeter, and two saxophonists; in other words, more than fifty individuals, and that is without including the mastering technicians and other sundry roles related to the album—or the Stones themselves! Keith describes the new producers as a bunch of "people who had won Grammys and were all cutting-edge," and Charlie would attest to the difficulties

experienced by himself and Keith in adapting to their methods: "You'd sit down, Keith would play a song, you'd wait until you got the right tempo and then you'd play it three or four times. These tracks are made late at night with nobody around." He would complain that once it had been recorded, the taped part could be totally wiped or manipulated by a producer guided by his own wishes alone. "In fact, I enjoyed doing it," continues Charlie, "because I had never worked like that before. But although I found it really interesting, I knew that I would hate to make records like that on a permanent basis, because then it becomes a producer's game—it's got nothing to do with the musicians at all." Keith would report that none of the band members were particularly thrilled at hearing Charlie's drumming put on a loop like a common drum machine. In the end, though, the guitarist was pleased with the results: "It was an interesting experiment and I like the album—you can sense the diversity and the division—but it did create a bit of a rickety bridge between us."

The Bridges to Babylon Tour

The Bridges to Babylon Tour kicked off in Chicago on September 23, 1997, six days before the release of the album. It eventually drew to a close with the Istanbul concert on September 19, 1998. Between these two dates, the Stones gave nearly one hundred concerts, in the United States, Japan, South America, and Europe, with some prestigious first-half acts, including the Foo Fighters, Sheryl Crow, the Smashing Pumpkins, the Dave Matthews Band, Pearl Jam, Santana, Buddy Guy, the Corrs, and, last but by no means least, Bob Dylan.

FLIP THE SWITCH

Mick Jagger / Keith Richards / 3:28

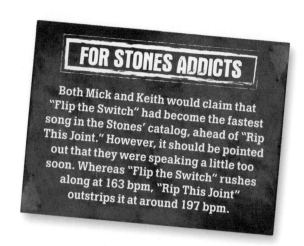

Musicians
Mick Jagger: vocals
Keith Richards: rhythm and lead guitar, backing vocals, hand claps
Charlie Watts: drums
Ron Wood: rhythm guitar
Waddy Wachtel: rhythm guitar
Jeff Sarli: upright bass
Jim Keltner: percussion
Joe Sublett: baritone saxophone
Bernard Fowler: backing vocals
Blondie Chaplin: tambourine, backing vocals
Recorded
Ocean Way Recording Studios, Hollywood: March 13–July 1997
Technical Team
Producers: Don Was, the Glimmer Twins
Sound engineers: Rob Fraboni, Dan Bosworth
Assistant sound engineers: Alan Sanderson, John Sorenson
Mixing: Tom Lord-Alge, assisted by Mauricio Riagorri

Genesis

"Flip the Switch" is a song about death and the death sentence as the ultimate sanction . . . *Pick me up—baby, I'm ready to go/Yeah, take me up—baby I'm ready to blow* . . . Keith Richards tells of the great shock he had a few days after writing the first few verses of this song upon hearing of the mass suicide of thirty-nine members of Heaven's Gate, a sect founded in San Diego by Marshall Applewhite and Bonnie Nettles. The drama occurred between March 24 and 26, 1997, just as Comet Hale-Bopp was passing. He writes in *Life* that he then "jauntily" added another verse: *Lethal injection is a luxury/I wanna give it/To the whole jury/I'm just dying/For one more squeeze*. The fatal cocktail in question, mixed by Marshall Applewhite, was a blend of barbiturates and vodka. Might Keith have been one to appreciate this ultimate beverage?

Production

Bridges to Babylon's furious opening number is launched with a hurtling train of a beat by Charlie Watts, assisted by Jim Keltner on percussion. The sound is almost live and the vibe far removed from that of a drum machine, as the Stones had all feared. The melodic impulse comes from Jeff Sarli's rockabilly upright bass, which the various guitars then latch onto. Keith Richards initially takes care of a made-to-measure riff (with a wrong note at 1:57!), supported on rhythm by Ron Wood and also Waddy Wachtel, a guitarist who had already had a varied career (Linda Ronstadt, James Taylor) and who would play a part in all of Keith's projects. Keith plays the one and only solo on the track, demonstrating that he has lost nothing of his Chuck Berry–like touch (1:44). Joe Sublett contributes a very good R&B flavor with his rhythmic riffs on baritone sax. Keith Richards, Bernard Fowler, and Blondie Chaplin (who also plays tambourine) provide dynamic, indeed jubilant backing vocals in support of an excellent performance by Mick Jagger, who is utterly at ease in this adrenaline-fueled rock number. Attention should also be drawn to the presence of Rob Fraboni in the role of sound engineer. Fraboni had been brought in at Keith's express request in order to counterbalance Mick's production choices, the name of the game being self-assertion . . . Incidentally, it is interesting to note that "Flip the Switch" was initially more than twenty-five minutes long.

Waddy Wachtel, guitarist with the X-Pensive Winos, accompanies Keith Richards on "Flip the Switch."

ANYBODY SEEN MY BABY?

Mick Jagger / Keith Richards / k.d. lang / Ben Mink / 4:31

Musicians
Mick Jagger: vocals, rhythm guitar
Keith Richards: rhythm guitar, backing vocals
Charlie Watts: drums
Ron Wood: rhythm guitar
Waddy Wachtel: lead guitar, acoustic guitar
Jamie Muhoberac: bass, keyboards
Don Was: keyboards
Bernard Fowler: backing vocals
Blondie Chaplin: backing vocals, shaker

Recorded
Ocean Way Recording Studios, Hollywood: March 13–July 1997

Technical Team
Producers: Don Was, the Dust Brothers, the Glimmer Twins
Sound engineers: the Dust Brothers, Dan Bosworth
Assistant sound engineers: Alan Sanderson, Charles Gooden
Mixing: Tom Lord-Alge, assisted by Mauricio Riagorri

Angelina Jolie, the beautiful crop-haired stranger in the "Anybody Seen My Baby?" video.

Genesis

The narrator is a rock singer who has fallen in love with a woman who has *vanished on the breeze*. He has been looking for her ever since. Has she run away? His anxiety increases from second to second until eventually the rock star asks himself whether this woman, whom he has called *a thousand times*, exists only in his imagination.

"Anybody Seen My Baby?" is mainly the work of Mick Jagger, who may have written it in memory of the actress Mary Badham (whom he met while he was married to Bianca). The word *mainly* is used because the refrain bears an uncanny resemblance to "Constant Craving" by k.d. lang, while the rap section is borrowed from "A One Two" by the hip-hop artist Biz Markie. As the A-side of a single released on September 22, 1997, the song hit number 1 in Canada, but got no further than number 22 in the United Kingdom, and failed to enter the charts in the United States. The title may be an allusion, for "Has Anybody Seen My Baby?" was also the name of a song Brian Jones is thought to have written after being ousted from the Rolling Stones!

Production

This song is clearly influenced by R&B. This tone is announced right from the intro by Charlie Watts's incredible groove supported by Jamie Muhoberac's superb bass, which almost sounds as if it could have been produced by a sequencer. Mick was in command for this track, and he wanted a contemporary sound. The number has a catchy tune, and the way the singer's voice combines with the backing vocalists in the refrains is highly successful, as indeed is all his vocal work on the track. There are two raps: a first at 2:49, which samples Biz Markie, and a second, very short, rap by Jagger himself at 4:06. In terms of guitars, the Stones do it in style: Keith and Mick are on rhythm (with phasing), Ronnie seems to be playing a highly Richardsesque riff at 1:28, and Waddy Wachtel plays acoustic as well as some excellent solo passages with very pronounced sustain, notably at 2:50 and toward the end of the track, from 3:48. Keyboard duties are shared by Jamie Muhoberac, by no means only a bassist, and the producer Don Was. Finally, note the excellent shaker part played by Blondie Chaplin (the Beach Boys, the Band), who appeared on Keith's *Crosseyed Heart* in 2015.

LOW DOWN

Mick Jagger / Keith Richards / 4:26

Musicians
Mick Jagger: vocals
Keith Richards: rhythm guitar, backing vocals
Charlie Watts: drums
Ron Wood: rhythm guitar, slide guitar
Blondie Chaplin: bass, maracas, backing vocals
Waddy Wachtel: rhythm guitar, lead guitar (?)
Jim Keltner: shaker
Joe Sublett: saxophone
Darrell Leonard: trumpet
Bernard Fowler: backing vocals

Recorded
Ocean Way Recording Studios, Hollywood: March 13–July 1997

Technical Team
Producers: Don Was, the Glimmer Twins
Sound engineers: Rob Fraboni, Dan Bosworth
Assistant sound engineers: Alan Sanderson, John Sorenson
Mixing: Tom Lord-Alge, assisted by Mauricio Riagorri

The saxophonist Joe Sublett lent the Stones a hand on the "Low Down" sessions in Hollywood.

Genesis

"Low Down" is the first song written by Mick Jagger and Keith Richards for *Bridges to Babylon* in the studio, with the Stones singer demoing the drums, and Keith, naturally enough, picking up the guitar. Although denoting the strand of blues that has remained most faithful to its Mississippi Delta roots, the term *low down* is used here in the sense of just give me the truth. A man asks his partner not to give him the sports or political news, nor to pass on the gossip, but to tell him the truth about the state of their relationship, to reveal a future that cannot be gleaned from any horoscope . . . The Rolling Stones only performed "Low Down" during their 1997–1998 tour.

Production

And to think that the Stones were afraid of losing their soul as a result of the new production methods unwisely solicited by Mick! "Low Down" is a rock number with an impressive sound and groove that takes the Stones back to a level of quality they had not attained for quite a while. Once again, Keith Richards, the eternal riff master, opens this track, most likely on a 5-string Telecaster in open G. His guitar sound is fabulous, with an impact like an instant uppercut. Charlie Watts joins him with an excellent drum part in which he rediscovers a feel, derived from the late Jimmy Miller, that he seemed to have forgotten over the last few albums. Worth emphasizing is the support provided on the shaker by Jim Keltner, a talented drummer and percussionist who had recorded with John Lennon, George Harrison, Eric Clapton, and Bob Dylan. Another important factor is the enormous and highly impressive bass of Blondie Chaplin. And then there is Mick's voice, which is absolutely impeccable, and far removed from its perpetually strained timbre of the eighties. In the melody of its refrains, "Low Down" is reminiscent of Led Zeppelin, and it has to be said that this impression is boosted by the guitar playing of Keith, Ronnie (on rhythm and slide), and Waddy. The three share an excellent break at 2:08, with Wachtel apparently on lead. This is highly effective and makes for a powerful pickup back into the track. The horns of Darrell Leonard and Joe Sublett are difficult to make out, although they can be heard in the refrains. Meanwhile, the backing vocalists contribute a very appealing pop flavor to the track.

ALREADY OVER ME

Mick Jagger / Keith Richards / 5:24

Musicians
Mick Jagger: vocals, acoustic guitar
Keith Richards: rhythm and lead guitar, backing vocals
Charlie Watts: drums
Ron Wood: baritone guitar, Dobro
Blondie Chaplin: piano, backing vocals
Benmont Tench: organ, keyboards
Don Was: bass
Kenny Aronoff: bucket
Jim Keltner: percussion
Bernard Fowler: backing vocals
Recorded
Ocean Way Recording Studios, Hollywood: March 13–
July 1997
Technical Team
Producers: Don Was, the Glimmer Twins
Sound engineers: John X. Volaitis, Dan Bosworth
Assistant sound engineers: Alan Sanderson, John Sorenson
Mixing: Bob Clearmountain, assisted by Ryan Freeland

Genesis

This is another meditation from the Stones on the breakup of a couple. *You're so cold/You're so cruel/I'm your man/ Not your fool*: the words speak for themselves. The originality of the song resides above all in its atmosphere: "It was like a Babyface ballad put on top of 'Wild Horses,'" explains the producer Don Was. In a 1997 interview, the Stones singer describes the genesis of this song that he had initially begun working on with Babyface (Kenneth Edmonds): "'It was really my fault—I threw the wrong song at him," Jagger says of Babyface. "We went in and wrote the loops and the programs. We got Charlie to play on it. And in the end, I didn't like the way it was looped. I said, 'Kenny, leave it. I'm gonna do it another way.'" "Already Over Me" was cut live in the studio. The band would perform the song onstage during the 1997–1998 tour.

Production

In the end, as we have seen, the band adopted a more traditional approach to the album version of "Already Over Me." Right from the intro, Mick Jagger plunges us into a mellow, although somewhat somber, atmosphere, his strummed guitar accompanied by Blondie Chaplin's piano and Benmont Tench's keyboard pads. Charlie Watts taps his cymbals before attacking the rhythm more forcefully at 0:40, underpinned by Don Was's bass. The producer would later report that it took him a while to understand the unusual way in which Charlie operated, the way he infused a number with an inimitable groove by taking his cue from and constructing his drumming around the singer. Keith plays a rhythm accompaniment as well as two very good solos, at 1:59 and 3:41. Meanwhile, Ron Wood innovates by playing a superb Dobro part with bottleneck, before switching to a rhythm part with pronounced vibrato on a baritone guitar, most probably a Fender Jaguar or a Danelectro, a guitar that was very popular with the surf music bands of the early sixties. Benmont Tench also plays the Hammond C-3 organ, which can be heard from 1:10. Kenny Aronoff is credited as playing the bucket, the vessel in question being diverted from its primary function and used as a percussion instrument, although it should be pointed out that it is impossible to hear. The mixing is by Bob Clearmountain and is his only contribution to the album.

Blondie Chaplin. After the Beach Boys and the Band, the South African singer (and guitarist) hooked up with the Stones.

GUNFACE

Mick Jagger / Keith Richards / 5:02

Musicians
Mick Jagger: vocals, rhythm guitar
Keith Richards: rhythm guitar, backing vocals
Charlie Watts: drums
Ron Wood: lead and slide guitar
Danny Saber: bass, keyboards, rhythm guitar
Jim Keltner: percussion

Recorded
Ocean Way Recording Studios, Hollywood: March 13–July 1997

Technical Team
Producers: Danny Saber, the Glimmer Twins
Sound engineer: John X. Volaitis
Assistant sound engineers: John Sorenson, Alan Sanderson
Mixing: John X. Volaitis

"Gunface" is one of Charlie Watts's best performances on the album *Bridges to Babylon*.

Genesis

I taught her everything/I taught her how to dream/I'm gonna teach her how to scream. The narrator is clearly motivated by a desire for revenge on his ex-girlfriend, and it is with a gun in his hand that he intends to satisfy this desire. The situation could not be clearer. The lover feels betrayed and plans to let his weapon do the talking, and then quit town without a trace. "Gunface" exemplifies the Stones' new approach. It is simultaneously rock and funk, and bears the stamp of Danny Saber, a California producer and remixer, and onetime member of Black Grape. The producer and sound engineer of this Manchester-based alternative rock group was none other than the excellent John X. Volaitis, who was responsible for much of the technical work on *Bridges to Babylon*. "Gunface" has never been performed onstage.

Production

The opening drums are reminiscent of "Superstition" by Stevie Wonder, but there the resemblance ends. This is not to take anything away from the extraordinary drum work, for Charlie is at the top of his game on this album. Jim Keltner's contribution is also prominent, driving home the rhythm with his shaker before turning his attention to the congas, the maracas, and various other percussion instruments. Danny Saber, a veritable one-man band, plays a very effective low and funky bass line, and also throws in some guitar. And it is over this superb rhythm section that Keith (or possibly even Mick?) adds his own guitar and some masterfully crafted riffs, enhanced by a delay of the kind he had a tendency to overuse in the eighties (thanks to his MXR pedal). Ronnie then answers him, initially with a series of short solo phrases, some played with the fingers and some played slide (he does not come in until the twenty-fourth bar), and then with a heavily distorted solo at 2:54, almost certainly on his black Zemaitis. In the refrains, Danny Saber is also on keyboards, with synth pads and electronic effects that are frankly out of keeping with the musical world of the Stones and therefore not in the best of taste. Mick, meanwhile, gives a very good vocal performance, as at ease in R&B as he is in rock and blues.

YOU DON'T HAVE TO MEAN IT

Mick Jagger / Keith Richards / 3:44

Musicians
Keith Richards: vocals, rhythm guitar
Charlie Watts: drums
Ron Wood: rhythm guitar
Darryl Jones: bass
Jim Keltner: percussion
Joe Sublett: saxophone
Darrell Leonard: trumpet
Clinton Clifford: electric piano, organ
Blondie Chaplin, Bernard Fowler: backing vocals

Recorded
Ocean Way Recording Studios, Hollywood: March 13–July 1997

Technical Team
Producers: Don Was, Rob Fraboni, the Glimmer Twins
Sound engineers: Rob Fraboni, Dan Bosworth
Assistant sound engineer: Alan Sanderson
Mixing: Rob Fraboni
Mixing engineer: John Sorenson, assisted by Robi Banerji

Bernard Fowler, a backing vocalist for Mick Jagger and, from 1985, for the Stones, sings on "You Don't Have to Mean It."

Genesis
Keith Richards had the idea for "You Don't Have to Mean It" after renting a room for the night in an old brothel in Jamaica. After engaging in conversation with two residents (hand-picked by the proprietor), he ends up asking them what they generally say to their clients. The girls' answer? "Anything—don't have to mean it." Based on this experience, Keith comes up with a story as old as time: a man asks his girlfriend to tell him not what she thinks, but what he wants to hear, even if she does not mean a word of it!

After listening to the definitive version of this song, with the exception of the melody, perhaps, it is difficult to believe that it was originally a Buddy Holly–style rock 'n' roll number. Little by little, the song developed more exotic rhythms and took on a Tex-Mex vibe tinged with reggae, a genre Keith Richards, in particular, has liked since the seventies. And it is Keith who sings the lead vocal, supported by the voices of Bernard Fowler and Blondie Chaplin. Although Mick Jagger had worked up "You Don't Have to Mean It" on the drums with Keith on guitar, he had no hand in the recording.

Production
It is on a Hammond B-3 that Clinton Clifford, right from the intro, gives a demonstration of his skills as a keyboard player. He also plays electric piano with that extraordinary delay that is one of the characteristic reggae sounds. Keith, in addition to singing, plays palm mute rhythm guitar, very much in the Jamaican spirit, supported on second guitar by Ronnie, who marks the rhythm with chords that are in sync with the snare drum. Charlie had never shown a particular aptitude for reggae, but proves the opposite on this track, with some excellent drum work. He is supported to good effect by Jim Keltner on percussion, notably the maracas. The very good bass part is played by Darryl Jones, making his first appearance on the album. On the horns are Joe Sublett and Darrell Leonard, whose arrangements are indispensable to this genre of music.

OUT OF CONTROL

Mick Jagger / Keith Richards / 4:43

Musicians
Mick Jagger: vocals, wah–wah guitar, harmonica, shaker
Keith Richards: rhythm guitar, backing vocals
Charlie Watts: drums
Ron Wood: rhythm guitar
Waddy Wachtel: rhythm and lead (?) guitar
Jamie Muhoberac: keyboards
Don Was: Wurlitzer, keyboards
Danny Saber: bass, clavinet
Jim Keltner: percussion
Bernard Fowler, Blondie Chaplin: backing vocals

Recorded
Ocean Way Recording Studios, Hollywood: March 13–July 1997

Technical Team
Producers: Don Was, the Glimmer Twins
Sound engineers: John X. Volaitis, Dan Bosworth
Assistant sound engineers: John Sorenson, Alan Sanderson
Mixing: Wally Gagel, assisted by Alan Sanderson

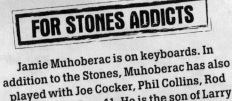

FOR STONES ADDICTS

Jamie Muhoberac is on keyboards. In addition to the Stones, Muhoberac has also played with Joe Cocker, Phil Collins, Rod Stewart, and Sum 41. He is the son of Larry Muhoberac, himself the former keyboard player of Elvis Presley's famous TCB Band.

Genesis

"Out of Control" was largely inspired by the bass line of "Papa Was a Rollin' Stone," a composition by Norman Whitfield and Barrett Strong for the Temptations. It is also one of the best tracks on *Bridges to Babylon*. Who is the character embodied by Mick Jagger in the song? The solitary individual is strolling by a bridge spanning dark waters and talking to a stranger about times gone by. And he remembers: *I was young/I was foolish*. Now he describes himself as out of control, and appeals for help . . . So who is he? A rock star fallen from grace? A condemned man? (This seems possible in view of the police pointing him to his *final destination*.) Just like the lyrics, the musical atmosphere of "Out of Control" is strange and oppressive, with a harmonica part that recalls the best passage on "Gimme Shelter." This song was chosen as the A-side of the third single from *Bridges to Babylon*. It peaked at number 51 on the British charts in August 1998 (with the Radio Edit as the B-side).

Production

The bass is not the only aspect of "Papa Was a Rollin' Stone" to have inspired the Glimmer Twins in the verses of "Out of Control." Jagger is on wah-wah guitar, and flings out disembodied chords just like those in the Temptations number. Furthermore, in addition to the rhythm, which is also similar, the Stones singer goes as far as to reproduce the beginning of the trumpet theme on the harmonica, at precisely 2:47 (0:32 on "Papa Was a Rollin' Stone"). This is a witty allusion that demonstrates how much Mick must have liked the Motown hit. Moving beyond this pastiche, the rest of his harmonica part is also superb, especially the closing solo (4:06), with a sound and phrasing that mark Jagger as one of the best harmonica players in all of rock. The refrains, meanwhile, bear the stamp of the Stones, and the entire band pulls out all the stops to support Jagger as he howls *Now I'm out of control*, with Keith, Ronnie, and Waddy Wachtel on distorted, ill-tempered guitars, the latter apparently also playing a number of solo passages. With an excellent rhythm section, keyboards that are very prominent without being intrusive, and effective support from the backing vocals, "Out of Control" is one of the triumphs of the album.

SAINT OF ME

Mick Jagger / Keith Richards / 5:15

Musicians
Mick Jagger: vocals, acoustic guitar, keyboards
Charlie Watts: drums
Ron Wood: rhythm guitar
Waddy Wachtel: rhythm and lead guitar
Jamie Muhoberac: keyboards
Billy Preston: organ
Pierre de Beauport: 6-string bass
MeShell Ndegeocello: bass
Bernard Fowler, Blondie Chaplin: backing vocals
Recorded
Ocean Way Recording Studios, Hollywood: March 13–
July 1997
Technical Team
Producers: the Dust Brothers, the Glimmer Twins
Sound engineers: the Dust Brothers, Dan Bosworth
Assistant sound engineers: Alan Sanderson, Charles Gooden
Mixing: Tom Lord-Alge, assisted by Mauricio Riagorri

On "Saint of Me," Billy Preston joins the Stones for the first time since *Goats Head Soup* (1973).

Genesis

In an interview given to Paul Du Noyer in 2001, Mick Jagger revealed: "I like using religious themes in songs. There's quite a few, whether they're gospel things like the one on *Exile* ['Just Wanna See His Face'] or 'Sympathy for the Devil,' or 'Saint of Me' on the last album. If it's part of your life then it should be part of your expression. But it's very hard to write a song about spirituality—as opposed to a car, for instance."
In "Saint of Me," Jagger refers to a number of symbolic figures from Christianity: Saint Paul, prior to his conversion a persecutor of the early disciples of Jesus; Saint Augustine, a devotee of the pleasures of the flesh before repenting for his sins; John the Baptist, who paid with his life for denouncing the sinful marriage of Herod and his sister-in-law Herodias. The Stones singer calls them as witnesses to plead his cause. *I do believe in miracles/And I want to save my soul/And I know that I'm a sinner/I'm gonna die here in the cold*, he sings. No doubt he was alluding here to his recurrent transgressions, in particular with the actress Uma Thurman and the Czech model Jana Rajlich, which led to his divorce from Jerry Hall.

Released as a single with "Anyway You Look at It" as the B-side, "Saint of Me" peaked at number 26 in the United Kingdom and number 94 in the United States (although it also reached number 13 on the *Billboard* Mainstream Rock Tracks chart).

Production

Musically, "Saint of Me" is like a happy encounter between "Shine a Light" (for its gospel vibe) and "Sympathy for the Devil" (for the chords in the refrain). The song came into being on a Roland TR-808 drum machine and a digital keyboard in the Dust Brothers' Silver Lake studio (Los Angeles). Mick Jagger struggled to put together a demo, with the help of Charlie on drums, which he sent to Ocean Way Recording Studios. And by contrast with the spiritual atmosphere of the verses, the refrains are explosions of funk, with Charlie grooving like a madman on the TR-808, supported by MeShell Ndegeocello's extraordinary electric bass. (It is most likely Pierre de Beauport on 6-string bass in the verses.) With Keith absent, the guitars are played by Ronnie and Waddy, the latter delivering a superb solo at 3:53. Mick Jagger is dazzling, and "Saint of Me" is one of the highlights of the album.

MIGHT AS WELL GET JUICED

Mick Jagger / Keith Richards / 5:23

Musicians
Mick Jagger: vocals, keyboards, harmonica
Keith Richards: rhythm guitar
Charlie Watts: drums
Ron Wood: slide guitar
Waddy Wachtel: rhythm guitar
Doug Wimbish: bass
Recorded
Ocean Way Recording Studios, Hollywood: March 13–
July 1997
Technical Team
Producers: the Dust Brothers, the Glimmer Twins
Sound engineers: the Dust Brothers,
Ed Cherney, Dan Bosworth
Assistant sound engineers: Alan Sanderson, Charles Gooden
Mixing: Danny Saber, Rich Lowe

Doug Wimbish, a member of Living Colour, plays bass on "Might as Well Get Juiced."

> **FOR STONES ADDICTS**
>
> "Might as Well Get Juiced" was the first demo played by Mick Jagger to the Dust Brothers with a view to their co-producing *Bridges to Babylon*. "I was really impressed," recalls Mike Simpson. "I said, 'Wow, it sounds like we already worked on this.'"

Genesis

Wolves howling at the door, vultures waiting for their chance, children who kick their parents out of their home. What could possibly be the link between all these elements, other than a desire on the part of Mick Jagger to create an apocalyptic atmosphere? Or perhaps the singer simply had fun picking words at random from a rhyming dictionary: *sump* and *hump* (of a camel in this case), *abused* and *juiced*. As so often in Stones songs, the lyrics to "Might as Well Get Juiced" are subservient to the music, and more precisely, in this instance, to the beat laid down by Charlie Watts. This does not alter the fact that the song is one of the most original on the album. A "fake blues for the '90s," is how Mick Jagger has described it. Or, if one prefers, the fruit of an encounter between the Stones, servants of the twelve-bar blues since the beginning of the sixties, and the Dust Brothers (John King and Mike Simpson), who were catalysts not merely of alternative rock, but of hip-hop and electronic music as well.

Production

The start of this track is somewhat reminiscent of the VCS-3 on "Won't Get Fooled Again" by the Who. Mick Jagger would later describe how, surrounded by synthesizers, he amused himself by producing a multitude of sounds that led to the composition of "Might as Well Get Juiced." With this sonority, generated right from the intro by a kind of arpeggiator, which dominates the entire track, one could be forgiven for fearing an incursion from the Stones into the world of electronic rock. But this song has a big surprise in store: it is actually a blues revisited to great effect by the Dust Brothers. Charlie's drumming, which has clearly been put on a loop, is superbly hypnotic and radiates a murky atmosphere in which Mick happily immerses himself, his voice presumably distorted by a sound effect such as a flanger or phasing. Another key element on this track is the bass. The house sound produced by Doug Wimbish, bassist with the Sugarhill Gang and Grandmaster Flash, is powerful and gives the impression of having been realized on a sequencer. (It is interesting to note that the bass falls away on the bridges.) Ronnie excels with some good phrases on slide, and Keith plays some effective rhythm, while Waddy is also on guitar, in a supporting role. Finally, Mick plays another excellent harmonica solo at 2:21.

ALWAYS SUFFERING

Mick Jagger / Keith Richards / 4:43

For the first time in the history of the Stones, a guitar technician, Pierre de Beauport to be precise, finds himself in the role of co-producer with the Glimmer Twins.

Musicians

Mick Jagger: vocals, rhythm guitar
Keith Richards: rhythm and lead guitar, backing vocals
Charlie Watts: drums, backing vocals
Ron Wood: pedal steel guitar
Darryl Jones: bass, backing vocals
Waddy Wachtel: acoustic guitar, backing vocals
Jim Keltner: percussion, backing vocals
Benmont Tench: organ, piano
Blondie Chaplin: tambourine, backing vocals
Bernard Fowler, Doug Wimbish: backing vocals

Recorded

Ocean Way Recording Studios, Hollywood: March 13–July 1997

Technical Team

Producers: Don Was, Pierre de Beauport, the Glimmer Twins
Sound engineers: Ed Cherney, Dan Bosworth
Assistant sound engineer: Alan Sanderson
Mixing: Ed Cherney, assisted by Stewart Brawley

Jim Keltner, possibly rock music's most famous session drummer and Stones sideman on "Always Suffering."

Genesis

"Always Suffering" is a beautiful love song. A man and a woman are taking a stroll and remembering the difficult years they have been through. *When all our friends were wavering, we kept on trying*, sings Mick Jagger. But this is not to say they haven't suffered. *Now the rain is falling slow and the nights grow long.* All the same, the Stones singer wants to send out a message of hope, and concludes with the words: *For life is but a chance on a windswept hill and the seeds of love are swirling above.* This song can be seen as an expression of the Stones singer's own torments. "Always Suffering" has never been performed live.

Production

Waddy Wachtel opens this gentle ballad on acoustic guitar, enabling Mick Jagger to adopt an unusually intimate tone. His voice is devoid of any trace of aggression; on the contrary, the rocker of "Midnight Rambler" gives the impression of having quieted down over the years. He accompanies Wachtel on electric, playing arpeggios with a fairly strong tremolo. Keith contributes with the other, clear-toned rhythm part, played most probably on a Telecaster. He takes two solos, a first at 2:57 and a second, with a slightly more distorted sound, in the coda (4:08). Ronnie is on pedal steel guitar, playing some good phrases that are sadly undermixed (3:08). Darryl Jones makes his second contribution to the album with a bass line that, in the refrains, recalls Bill Wyman. He seems to be playing his 1966 white Jazz Bass. Charlie Watts is again supported by Jim Keltner on percussion (shaker, maracas), continuing their highly successful collaboration. And if the album credits are to be believed, something unprecedented occurs involving the Stones drummer: Charlie has come out from behind his kit to add his voice to the backing vocals, which he shares with Keith, Darryl, Waddy, Jim, Blondie, Bernard, and Doug. Finally, "Always Suffering" owes part of its lyricism to Benmont Tench's very good work on both the Hammond B-3 and piano.

TOO TIGHT

Mick Jagger / Keith Richards / 3:37

Musicians
Mick Jagger: vocals
Keith Richards: rhythm and lead (?) guitar, backing vocals
Charlie Watts: drums
Ron Wood: rhythm and lead (?) guitar, pedal steel guitar (?)
Waddy Wachtel: rhythm guitar
Jeff Sarli: acoustic bass
Jim Keltner: percussion
Blondie Chaplin: piano, tambourine (?), backing vocals
Bernard Fowler: backing vocals

Recorded
Ocean Way Recording Studios, Hollywood: March 13–July 1997

Technical Team
Producers: Don Was, the Glimmer Twins
Sound engineers: Rob Fraboni, Dan Bosworth, Jim Scott
Assistant sound engineers: Alan Sanderson, John Sorenson
Mixing: Tom Lord-Alge, assisted by Mauricio Riagorri

Alongside Keith and Ronnie, Waddy Wachtel is the third guitarist on "Too Tight.

Genesis

"Too Tight" is a song written mainly by Keith Richards and then reworked by Mick Jagger. *Don't try to reel me in/with all those charm school looks/I've seen it all a thousand times/I sung that song . . .* Are these words addressed to the groupies who hang around backstage at the end of every Stones concert? Perhaps not. A phrase such as: *Baby, don't get too tight with me/Yes, you're far too tight for me* seems to relate more to the private sphere—and more specifically to the singer's by now stormy relationship with Jerry Hall (even before his affair with the Brazilian top model Luciana Morad and the birth of their son). In 2010, Jerry Hall would reveal in her memoir excerpted in the *Daily Mail*: "Over ten years, the Stones staged five world tours. Mick started to miss important family events—children's birthdays and our anniversary. I was heartbroken that he wasn't home in time for the birth of our fourth child, Gabriel, in December 1997. . . . Mick called while I was in labour to say he was so sorry he could not be there. He arrived home a week later. Then, after a holiday, he went back to the band's Bridges to Babylon tour."

Production

Keith's name is written all over this somewhat too predictable rock number, the umpteenth incarnation of a prototype devised in the sixties and subsequently recycled to greater or lesser effect in a number of variants. "Too Tight" nevertheless falls into the category of "good songs," that is to say those one enjoys listening to in spite of an overwhelming feeling of déjà vu. The intro takes the form of a cleverly worked out Richards/Wood/Wachtel combination with Keith playing rhythm on his 5-string Telecaster in open G. He is doubled by Waddy, while Ronnie, on what is most likely a Stratocaster, plays licks that interlink with the other two guitars. The riff then comes in at the same time as the rest of the band surges into action. Charlie smacks his drums heavily, supported on acoustic bass by Jeff Sarli, who, to tell the truth, is lacking a certain vigor, his instrument ill suited to a rock number as punchy as this. It is worth drawing attention to Blondie Chaplin's very good piano part and Mick Jagger's strong performance. Ronnie is given a credit for pedal steel guitar but cannot be heard on this instrument.

THIEF IN THE NIGHT

Mick Jagger / Keith Richards / Pierre de Beauport / 5:15

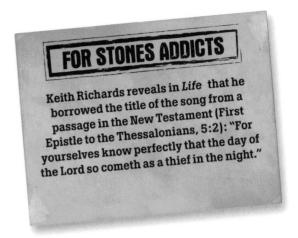

Musicians

Keith Richards: vocals, rhythm and acoustic guitar, piano
Charlie Watts: drums
Ron Wood: rhythm guitar
Darryl Jones: bass
Waddy Wachtel: rhythm guitar
Pierre de Beauport: Fender Rhodes piano, Wurlitzer
Jim Keltner: percussion
Joe Sublett: saxophone
Darrell Leonard: trumpet
Blondie Chaplin: tambourine, backing vocals
Bernard Fowler: backing vocals

Recorded

Ocean Way Recording Studios, Hollywood: March 13–July 1997
Unidentified studio, Long Island: June–July 1997

Technical Team

Producers: Don Was, the Glimmer Twins
Sound engineers: Rob Fraboni, Dan Bosworth
Assistant sound engineer: Alan Sanderson
Mixing: Rob Fraboni and Pierre de Beauport, assisted by George Fullan

Keith took his inspiration from the holy scriptures, but seems to be pointing the way with a provocative finger!

Genesis

The lyrics of "Thief in the Night" evoke a number of women who have come into Keith Richards's life at one moment or another. "It's a song about several women and actually starts when I was a teenager. I knew where she lived and I knew where her boyfriend lived, and I would stand outside a semi-detached house in Dartford. Basically the story goes on from there. Then it was about Ronnie Spector, then it was about Patti and it was also about Anita."

Production

On a musical level, "Thief in the Night" started life as a guitar riff by Pierre de Beauport. While the guitar technician was playing it with Charlie in the studio, Keith, who had just arrived, became very interested in what he was hearing and joined them, adding his own personal touch. This led to Pierre's consecration as a songwriter in the form of a share of the credits. Keith eventually decided to sing the song himself: "Mick put a vocal on the song, but he couldn't feel it, he couldn't get it, and the track sounded terrible." To tell the truth, Mick Jagger seems to have been less than enthralled by the song, because after Keith had worked away all night, to the point of exhaustion, redoing the vocals with Blondie and Bernard, he discovered the next day that his tape had been sabotaged. He therefore grabbed the master and shut himself away for two days and two nights in a studio at the northern shore of Long Island to complete and mix the song. However, Don Was was quick to see that he would come up against a refusal from Mick, who would not tolerate Keith singing three songs on a record. The producer therefore suggested diplomatically that the last two tracks on the album (sung by Keith) be linked together in the style of a medley. Lo and behold, the subterfuge worked! The result is a blues-tinged R&B ballad that opens with some reversed sounds over which Pierre de Beauport's riff can be heard. Beauport himself plays a Fender Rhodes and a Wurlitzer. Charlie goes for a mellow rhythm with very prominent ride cymbal, and the various guitar parts color the harmony with highly expressive little touches here and there. When all is said and done, "Thief in the Night" sounds more like a Keith Richards song, very much in keeping with the tracks on his two solo albums, than a Stones song.

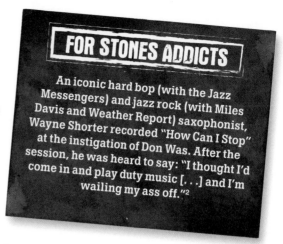

HOW CAN I STOP

Mick Jagger / Keith Richards / 6:54

Musicians
Keith Richards: vocals, rhythm guitar
Charlie Watts: drums
Ron Wood: rhythm guitar
Don Was: Wurlitzer
Blondie Chaplin: piano, backing vocals
Waddy Wachtel: rhythm guitar
Jeff Sarli: acoustic bass
Jim Keltner: percussion
Wayne Shorter: soprano saxophone
Bernard Fowler: backing vocals
Recorded
Ocean Way Recording Studios, Hollywood: March 13–July 1997
Technical Team
Producers: Don Was, the Glimmer Twins
Sound engineers: Rob Fraboni
Assistant sound engineers: Alan Sanderson, John Sorenson
Mixing: John Sorenson, assisted by Robi Banerji

Jazz great Wayne Shorter played sax on "How Can I Stop."

Genesis

Another Keith Richards love song . . . *You offer me/All your love and sympathy/Sweet affection baby/It's killing me.* "How Can I Stop" is not about one specific woman any more than his other love songs, which are mostly "about imaginary loves, a compilation of women you've known," writes Keith, adding that "'How Can I Stop' is a real song from the heart. Perhaps everyone's getting old." This would explain why there is no reference to Anita Pallenberg or Patti Hansen . . . The closing track on *Bridges to Babylon* was also the last to be recorded. Don Was recalls that a car was even waiting outside the studio to whisk Charlie Watts to the airport. The ensemble is superb. The atmosphere is not so very far from the gentle soul harmonies of the vocal group the Chi-Lites ("A Lonely Man"), with, as a bonus, a majestic soprano sax solo from the great Wayne Shorter at the end.

Production

Don Was has explained that the recording of "How Can I Stop" would completely change his life. Repeating the final four chords of the song over and over again like a mantra, Don on a Wurlitzer electric piano (with tremolo) and Keith at the other end of the studio on guitar gave him an insight into the power and magic of being in the moment: "This is what I've been searching for. I've just never played with a master musician before." After finishing the take, he rushed into the control room to listen to the playback, imagining they had cut about five minutes of music: "The engineers said, 'which reel?'—we'd been playing for over an hour." It is true that "How Can I Stop" possesses a certain luminous force. There are no overdubs on it, just ten or so musicians playing together in the same room until they get the ultimate take. The guitars of Keith, Ronnie, and Waddy complement one another perfectly. Charlie Watts delivers his beat mainly cross-stick, supported by Jeff Sarli's very good bass part and Jim Keltner on what sound like steel drums (only audible at 6:38). The harmonies are subtly colored by Blondie Chaplin's piano. Keith delivers a delicate performance, laying bare his heart, which is that of a rocker with, in the final analysis, more than a little of the romantic in him. He is supported by the superb backing vocals of Bernard and Blondie, who bring a touch of soul to the track.

Street Fighting Man
Gimmie Shelter
(I Can't Get No) Satisfaction
The Last Time
Jumpin' Jack Flash
You Can't Always Get What You Want
19th Nervous Breakdown
Under My Thumb
Not Fade Away
Have You Seen Your Mother Baby?

Sympathy For The Devil
Mother's Little Helper
She's A Rainbow
Get Off Of My Cloud
Wild Horses
Ruby Tuesday
Paint It Black
Honky Tonk Women
It's All Over Now
Let's Spend The Night Together

Start Me Up
Brown Sugar
Miss You
Beast Of Burden
Don't Stop *
Happy
Angie
You Got Me Rocking
Shattered
Fool To Cry

Love Is Strong
Mixed Emotions
Keys To Your Love *
Anybody Seen My Baby?
Stealing My Heart *
Tumbling Dice
Undercover Of The Night
Emotional Rescue
It's Only Rock'n'roll (But I Like It)
Losing My Touch *

★ Only the released songs will be discussed in this chapter.

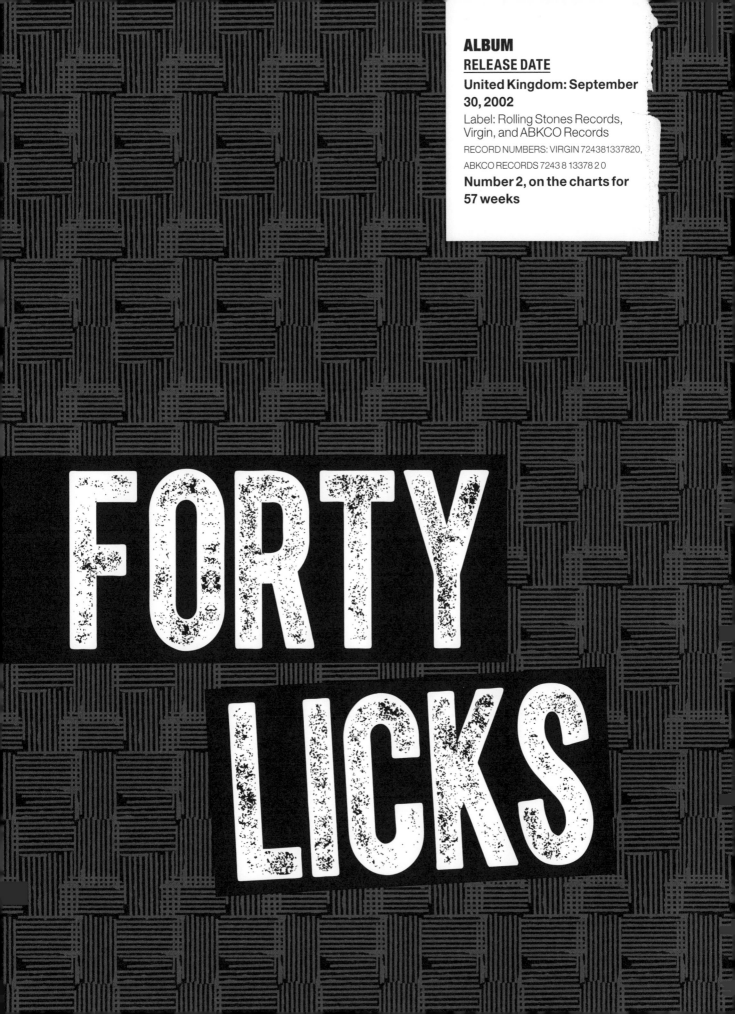

ALBUM
RELEASE DATE
United Kingdom: September 30, 2002
Label: Rolling Stones Records, Virgin, and ABKCO Records
RECORD NUMBERS: VIRGIN 724381337820,
ABKCO RECORDS 7243 8 13378 2 0
Number 2, on the charts for 57 weeks

FORTY
LICKS

The Licks World Tour kicked off in Toronto on August 16, 2002. By the time it drew to a close in Hong Kong on November 9, 2003, the Stones would have played 117 shows all over the world.

FORTY LICKS:
FORTY YEARS OF ROCK 'N' ROLL

The Album

On September 30, 2002, Virgin released a double CD titled *Forty Licks* in order to celebrate the forty-year anniversary of the Rolling Stones' career. Of the forty songs in the compilation, thirty-six are classics from the albums recorded by the band since 1964. All were remastered, but those recorded prior to 1968 were left in mono. "(I Can't Get No) Satisfaction," "19th Nervous Breakdown," "Jumpin' Jack Flash," "Honky Tonk Women," "Sympathy for the Devil," "Brown Sugar," "It's Only Rock 'n' Roll" . . . the party goes on and on . . .

A Fine Retrospective
with Four Brand-New Tracks

For many fans, however, the album's interest lay not in its retrospective aspect, but in the four new tracks the Rolling Stones had decided to add to the set. These four songs, "Don't Stop," "Keys to Your Love," "Stealing My Heart," and "Losing My Touch," were recorded at Studio Guillaume Tell in Suresnes, a suburb of Paris, between May 13 and June 8, 2002, the Pathé Marconi Studios having closed their doors for good at the end of the nineties.

Boosted by the four new tracks, *Forty Licks* was a great success throughout the world. It was number 1 in France, Belgium, and Italy, and number 2 in the United Kingdom, the United States, Canada, Germany, and the Netherlands. The cover design features the Stones tongue restyled by Tom Hingston, a graphic designer who had collaborated with Massive Attack, Nick Cave, and Robbie Williams as well as with various famous brands, including Christian Dior. Inside, there is an essay by David Wild (a rock critic for *Rolling Stone* and host of a music show on the television station Bravo) plus some very good photographs of the band.

2002

DON'T STOP

Mick Jagger / Keith Richards / 3:58

Musicians
Mick Jagger: vocals, rhythm guitar
Keith Richards: rhythm guitar, acoustic guitar
Charlie Watts: drums
Ron Wood: lead guitar, acoustic guitar
Darryl Jones: bass
Chuck Leavell: keyboards
Unidentified musician(s): hand claps
Recorded
Studio Guillaume Tell, Suresnes,
France: May 13–June 8, 2002
Technical Team
Producers: Don Was, the Glimmer Twins
Sound engineer: Ed Cherney
Mixing: Bob Clearmountain

Ron Wood, seen here in Boston in 2002, plays
an incisive solo on "Don't Stop."

Genesis

Mick Jagger started to write "Don't Stop" just before or during
the sessions for his fourth solo album, *Goddess in the Doorway* (2001), but chose to record the song with the Stones.
"I could see that Mick had designed it to come across well in
large venues, a 'Start Me Up'–style crowd song, with a simple
kind of message and a straightforward structure," explains
Ron Wood. In terms of the lyrics, the Stones singer has cut
straight to the chase by once again presenting a couple who
get their thrills from dangerous sadomasochistic games: *Well
you bit my lip and drew first blood and warmed my cold,
cold heart/And you wrote your name right on my back . . .*
In spite of everything, however, love underlies this disturbing
relationship, a love that motivates the narrator to lament: *I'm
losing you, I know your heart is miles away.* "Don't Stop"
(the *Forty Licks* version) was released as a single on December 16, 2002, along with a New Rock Mix version and a remix
of "Miss You." It reached number 36 on the British charts on
December 28, 2002, and achieved a very honorable seventh
place in Germany. The song was performed live during the
Licks World Tour of 2002–2003.

Production

It was therefore once again at a studio in Paris that the Stones
got together to record their new songs. "Don't Stop" is a
Stones rock track par excellence, featuring a good tune, a contagious rhythm, and a band that is in full cry from beginning
to end. Mick Jagger is on electric guitar, possibly the superb
vintage Gibson ES-175 that was on hand during the sessions,
and plays a rhythm part with some good riffs. Keith, despite
being the first to play on the intro, does not have pride of place
on this track. This is confirmed by Ron Wood: "Because Mick
is playing guitar, there isn't so much room for Keith, but he
did manage to find a way of stabbing away at it, so that he
was semi-happy with the result." Ronnie, on the other hand,
plays lead guitar and delivers a very good solo (1:47) exactly
as Mick had hoped for, a "trademark Woody guitar solo," in
the words of the guitarist. Supported by Darryl Jones, Charlie
has no problem getting his bandmates to groove, with snare
drum on every beat. Finally, Mick sings with no less enthusiasm and energy than he had forty years before . . .

2002

KEYS TO YOUR LOVE

Mick Jagger / Keith Richards / 4:12

Musicians
Mick Jagger: vocals, rhythm guitar (?)
Keith Richards: acoustic guitar (?)
Charlie Watts: drums
Ron Wood: lead guitar (?)
Darryl Jones: bass
Chuck Leavell: keyboards
Blondie Chaplin: tambourine
Recorded
Studio Guillaume Tell, Suresnes, France:
May 13–June 8, 2002
Technical Team
Producers: Don Was, the Glimmer Twins
Sound engineer: Ed Cherney
Mixing: Bob Clearmountain

Genesis

"Keys to Your Love" is another of the songs recorded by the Stones during the May–June 2002 sessions at the Guillaume Tell Studios in France. This track reveals another important facet of the Glimmer Twins' career—their work as composers of soul ballads. *I've got the keys to your love/I've got the secret of your heart*: Mick Jagger plays the part of a lover whose love is so intense that he has put a spell on the object of his affections, a woman whose *every code and every pin* he claims to know . . .

"Keys to Your Love" is a love song whose music recalls the sophisticated, romantic soul of Curtis Mayfield's Impressions. Hence the falsetto voice adopted by Mick here and there . . . Remarkable as it may seem, this song has never been performed live . . .

Production

Listening to "Keys to Your Love," one could be forgiven for wondering whether the song may have been written during the *Black and Blue* period. Mick Jagger's falsetto is reminiscent of "Fool to Cry," although not as good. The Stones had taken five years to get back into the studio, and despite its virtues, this song does not quite live up to the occasion—especially as a new track on an album celebrating forty years of the Rolling Stones. The song features three guitars, but their roles are poorly defined. Mick seems to be on electric rhythm guitar, which can be heard on the left, with Keith on acoustic and Ronnie on lead, playing some very good licks and a clear-toned solo at 2:36 (on a Stratocaster?). Charlie Watts lays down an effective rhythm as always, with Darryl Jones on bass, and the talented instrumentalist and backing vocalist Blondie Chaplin, who had contributed so brilliantly to the 1997 album *Bridges to Babylon*, back with the band on tambourine. Another excellent musician, Chuck Leavell, is on electric piano, adding that special sonority that is so characteristic of the Stones ballads. Inspired by the soul of Curtis Mayfield, Mick Jagger delivers a mixed performance. His vocal is split between a falsetto on the one hand and rich, mellow tones on the other, but he never really convinces as he had on the band's two previous albums. An agreeable enough song, but hardly unforgettable.

"Keys to Your Love," a soul number directly inspired by Curtis Mayfield (above).

STEALING MY HEART

Mick Jagger / Keith Richards / 3:42

Musicians
Mick Jagger: vocals, rhythm guitar
Keith Richards: rhythm guitar, acoustic guitar
Charlie Watts: drums
Ron Wood: rhythm guitar, slide guitar, acoustic guitar
Darryl Jones: bass
Chuck Leavell: organ
Unidentified musician(s): hand claps
Recorded
Studio Guillaume Tell, Suresnes,
France: May 13–June 8, 2002
Technical Team
Producers: Don Was, the Glimmer Twins
Sound engineer: Ed Cherney
Mixing: Bob Clearmountain

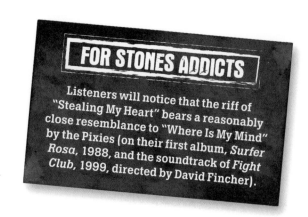

FOR STONES ADDICTS

Listeners will notice that the riff of "Stealing My Heart" bears a reasonably close resemblance to "Where Is My Mind" by the Pixies (on their first album, *Surfer Rosa*, 1988, and the soundtrack of *Fight Club*, 1999, directed by David Fincher).

Genesis

What did Mick Jagger mean with the lyrics to "Stealing My Heart"? The line *Well I was out there, chaste as a nun, but it's easier said than done* seems to be saying that it is difficult to resist love when it comes along. But when Mick sings *I can't seem to stop it now, it grows and it grows, and it grows*, is he singing, as ever, of love? Or, on the contrary, of not being loved? Is this another meditation on the nature of love and chance? Or a reflection on a sudden passion that becomes all-consuming? An enigmatic song in terms of its words, "Stealing My Heart" is nevertheless more or less classic Stones in terms of its music, and Ron Wood seems to agree, judging the number to be a "really good blended effort by Mick and Keith." This is another song that has never been performed live.

Production

Although reasonably effective, on the basis of the evidence, "Stealing My Heart" is not of sufficient stature to rub shoulders with numbers like "Start Me Up" or "Tumbling Dice," which follows it on the album. The idea of offering fans some new tracks may have been fundamentally sound, but it is a dangerous thing to attempt on a compilation a strong as *Forty Licks*. The musical atmosphere of "Stealing My Heart" is dominated by electric guitar, the three guitarists having a highly distorted, somewhat "garage band" sound. Mick plays the first rhythm guitar, Keith responds with some licks, and Ronnie reinforces the overall sound with a third rhythm guitar. He also delivers a slide solo, most likely on his black Zemaitis, at 1:40, and his playing in the instrumental bridge creates a very effective atmosphere that is somewhat reminiscent of U2's The Edge (between 1:57 and 2:14). He also shares some acoustic guitar work with Keith. Chuck Leavell is on the organ, which can be heard above all in the coda from 3:02. As for the rhythm section, Darryl Jones's bass line is a little too linear and ends up becoming monotonous. Sir Mick's vocal performance is reasonably good, although one senses that, like Keith, he is no more than moderately invested in the recording.

Darryl Jones. From jazz to blues rock, he has never really recognized any boundaries.

LOSING MY TOUCH

Mick Jagger / Keith Richards / 5:06

Musicians
Keith Richards: vocals, acoustic guitar
Charlie Watts: drums
Ron Wood: pedal steel guitar
Darryl Jones: acoustic bass
Chuck Leavell: piano

Recorded
Studio Guillaume Tell, Suresnes,
France: May 13–June 8, 2002

Technical Team
Producers: Don Was, the Glimmer Twins
Sound engineer: Ed Cherney
Mixing: Bob Clearmountain

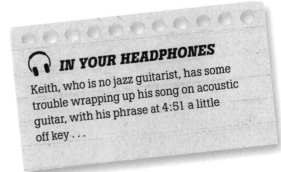

Genesis

Keith Richards wrote "Losing My Touch" at his house in Jamaica with the help of Mick Jagger. "It's about a guy on the run who's gotta say goodbye, and he doesn't really know how to say it," explains Keith in a 2002 interview. Some people have seen this story of a man on the run, who claims he has lost his touch and says that it *seems things are in a lockdown*, as a metaphor with which Keith evokes his sense of losing faith in what he was doing. The music is a sentimental ballad, an end-of-evening song for when the glasses are empty, the ashtrays full, and the exhausted pianist is playing his last few notes on the piano.

Production

The task of bringing *Forty Licks* to a close therefore falls to Keith, with what sounds like an intimate confession. While he has no more than a discreet presence on the other three new tracks on the album, without even singing backing vocals, here he whispers his lyrics in a voice that reveals the patina of age, and with all the emotion and sincerity that characterize his style. Listeners might also wonder whether he was influenced by *Come Away with Me*, the Norah Jones album that has sold twenty million copies since its release in February 2002, a few months before the session at the studios. It shares the same hushed atmosphere, breathy voice, and pared-down instrumentation, not to mention the jazzy harmonies accentuated by the superb beat played with the brushes by Charlie, who is very much at home in this world. Darryl Jones, Miles Davis's former bassist, seems here to be playing acoustic bass, and is also very much in his element. Chuck Leavell's piano part is sumptuous, but at the same time light and nuanced, combining blues and jazz with great finesse. Keith accompanies him with well-spaced phrases on the acoustic guitar, and also plays a short solo at 2:51. At Keith's request, Ron Wood comes in with pedal steel at 2:03. According to Woody, Keith had a precise idea of what he wanted him to play: "'Ronnie please play a pedal steel line. Imagine you're playing pedal steel on it.'" The resulting sonority reinforces the connection with Norah Jones, who, some years later, would sing a duo with Keith Richards on "Illusion," a number on his 2015 solo album *Crosseyed Heart*.

Keith Richards, composer of the introspective ballad "Losing My Touch."

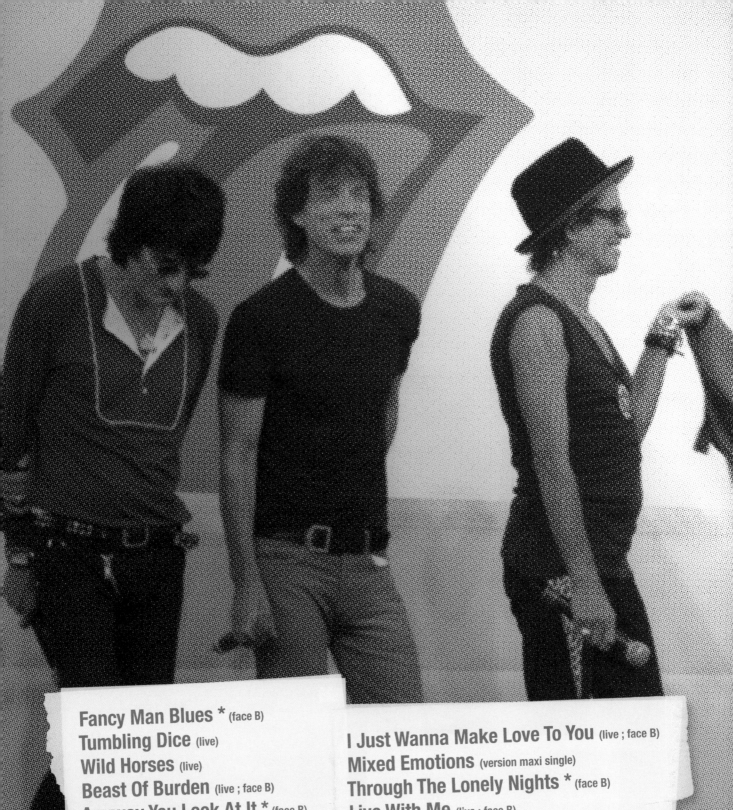

Fancy Man Blues * (face B)
Tumbling Dice (live)
Wild Horses (live)
Beast Of Burden (live ; face B)
Anyway You Look At It * (face B)
If I Was A Dancer (Dance Pt.2)
Miss You (Dance Version)
Wish I'd Never Met You * (face B)

I Just Wanna Make Love To You (live ; face B)
Mixed Emotions (version maxi single)
Through The Lonely Nights * (face B)
Live With Me (live ; face B)
Let It Rock (live ; face B)
Harlem Shuffle (Extended Mix)
Mannish Boy (live)
Thru And Thru (live)

* Only the released songs will be discussed in this chapter.

ALBUM
RELEASE DATE
United Kingdom: November 22, 2005
Label: Virgin
RECORD NUMBER: VIRGIN CDVX 3015

RARITIES
1971 - 2003

RARITIES 1971–2003: A COMPILATION FOR HARDCORE FANS

The Album

This album does not actually contain that many "rarities," contrary to Ron Wood's comments in the liner notes, in which he deplores the fact that certain outtakes have fallen into oblivion: "There are songs we've done for albums in the past that I've thought, oh, it's a shame that song didn't make the album. Then you get carried away with promoting it and you forget about it." So what is actually on this compilation, which came out three years after *Forty Licks*? It comprises sixteen songs, of which eight are live recordings and the other eight are studio recordings, five of them having already been used as the B-sides of singles, while the others are remixes and an outtake.

The eight live recordings are: "Tumbling Dice" (recorded during a rehearsal and left off the final selection for *Stripped*, 1995), "Wild Horses" (recorded in Tokyo on March 3 and 5, 1995, and taken from *Stripped*), "Beast of Burden" (recorded at the Los Angeles Memorial Coliseum on October or 11, 1981, and the B-side of the single "Going to a Go-Go," 1982), "I Just Wanna Make Love to You" (recorded at Wembley Stadium on July 6, 1990, and the B-side of the 12-inch single "Highwire," 1991), "Live with Me" (recorded at Brixton Academy in London on July 19, 1995 and the B-side of the single "Wild Horses," rereleased in 1996), "Let It Rock" (recorded at the University of Leeds on March 13, 1971, and the B-side of the single "Brown Sugar," 1971), "Mannish Boy" (recorded at the El Mocambo Club in Toronto in March 1977 and taken from "Love You Live," 1977), and "Thru and Thru" (recorded at Madison Square Garden in New York City in January 2003 and taken from the DVD *Four Flicks*, 2003).

The eight studio recordings are: "Fancy Man Blues" (the B-side of the single "Mixed Emotions," 1989), "Anyway You Look at It" (the B-side of the single "Saint of Me," 1998),"If I Was a Dancer (Dance Pt. 2)" (an outtake from *Emotional Rescue* taken from "Sucking in the Seventies," 1981), "Miss You" (Dance Version, 1978), "Wish I'd Never Met You" (the B-side of the singles "Almost Hear You Sigh" and "Terrifying," 1990), "Mixed Emotions" (12-inch single version, 1989), "Through the Lonely Nights" (the B-side of the single "It's Only Rock 'n' Roll [But I Like It"], 1974), and "Harlem Shuffle" (Extended Remix).

Here we review those four songs recorded in the studio that had never previously been released on an album.

Rarities 1971–2003 went on sale on November 21, 2005. It went on to achieve an honorable seventy-sixth place on the *Billboard* chart. On the other side of the Atlantic, however, the compilation sank more or less without a trace. The cover features a photograph (black and white except for the red tongue on Mick Jagger's T-shirt) taken during the shooting of the video for "Respectable" by Michael Lindsay-Hogg. Highly symbolically, this same photograph had been used in the *Forty Licks* box set, only there it was in color and included Bill Wyman on bass, whereas he is absent from the *Rarities* cover!

FANCY MAN BLUES

Mick Jagger / Keith Richards / 4:49

Musicians
Mick Jagger: vocals, harmonica
Keith Richards: rhythm and lead (?) guitar
Bill Wyman: bass
Charlie Watts: drums
Ron Wood: rhythm and lead (?) guitar
Chuck Leavell: piano
Recorded
AIR Studios, Montserrat: March 29–May 5, 1989
Olympic Sound Studios, London: May 15–June 29, 1989
Technical Team
Producers: Chris Kimsey, the Glimmer Twins
Sound engineer: Christopher Marc Potter
Assistant sound engineer: Rupert Coulson
Mixing: Michael H. Brauer

IN YOUR HEADPHONES

Mick can be heard singing into his harmonica mic for a few seconds, and therefore making a distorted sound, at 3:12, just after his first solo. This confirms that the track was recorded "live" in the studio.

Jagger, the archetypal fancy man, at the Live Aid concert in Philadelphia on July 13, 1985.

Genesis

In "Fancy Man Blues," the narrator claims to be head over heels in love with a women for whose smile he has fallen and with whom he loves to *while away the time.* The only problem is that she seems to have another man in her life . . . "Fancy Man Blues" can be seen as a further demonstration of the Stones' passion for the blues, a passion that had never deserted them since their very first gigs in the clubs of London. In this number, it is the sensual swamp blues of Jimmy Reed and Slim Harpo that they bring out, rather than the more strident Chicago blues of Muddy Waters and Howlin' Wolf. This recording dates from the *Steel Wheels* sessions held at AIR Studios in Montserrat in spring 1989, with Chuck Leavell on piano, playing a part apparently influenced by the late lamented Ian Stewart. It was then chosen as the B-side of the single "Mixed Emotions," released the following August 17, before eventually being included on *Rarities 1971–2003.*

Production

This song demonstrates why the Stones were still at the very pinnacle of their art even after they had been going for more than a quarter of a century. They always sound authentic when playing the blues, and this is precisely why they are so admired. In this case, the spontaneity of the ensemble playing attests to the fact that "Fancy Man Blues" was recorded "live" in the studio. Keith and Ronnie share the two guitars: one an excellent rhythm part with a lumbering, distorted sound very much in keeping with the characteristic style of the genre; the other playing a lead accompaniment with a solo at 1:37—most likely Keith, even if some of its phrases sound like Ronnie. We are reunited here with the band's original rhythm section, consisting of Charlie on his Gretsch kit and Bill on bass, unfortunately somewhat recessed in the mix. Chuck Leavell plays a superb piano part, delivering licks capable of winning over even those fans who cannot see past Billy Preston. Mick is clearly in his best vocal form in this blues number, but it is once again on harmonica that he takes the track to another level, delivering two solos of dazzling phrasing and sonority (2:42 and 3:46).

2005

ANYWAY YOU LOOK AT IT

Mick Jagger / Keith Richards / 4:21

Musicians
Mick Jagger: vocals
Keith Richards: acoustic guitar, vocals
Charlie Watts: drums
Ron Wood: acoustic guitar
Darryl Jones (?): bass
Unidentified musician: cello
Recorded
Ocean Way Recording Studios,
Hollywood: March 13–July 1997
Technical Team
Producers: Chris Kimsey, the Glimmer Twins

Charlie Watts picks up his brushes for "Anyway You Look at It," a new soul ballad.

Genesis

"Anyway You Look at It" is a ballad recorded during the *Bridges to Babylon* sessions. Rarely had the Glimmer Twins revealed themselves to be this romantic. The protagonist in the song tells his girlfriend that he has been very lucky to fall in love with her and that whatever he does and wherever he goes, he will always come to the same conclusion: she is the one he loves.

Although it dates from the second half of the 1990s, this tender declaration of love would not have looked out of place in the Stones' sixties catalog—the period of *Aftermath* and *Between the Buttons*—in terms of the writing, if not the form. "Anyway You Look at It" was released as the B-side of the single "Saint of Me" (Radio Edit) in January 1998. It was subsequently included in the *Rarities* compilation and the box set *The Singles Collection 1971–2006*.

Production

"Anyway You Look at It" comes as something of a surprise from the Stones. Jazzy in terms of musical color, it is melancholy in atmosphere. This superb song bears a certain resemblance to "Losing My Touch" on *Forty Licks*, not least because of Charlie's use of the brushes, which is absolutely perfect. This time, however, the bass is not acoustic, although it does seem to be played again by Darryl Jones, his phrasing simultaneously melodic and rhythmic. The influence of Jaco Pastorius, the bassist so admired by Darryl Jones, can be detected in the lick he plays at 3:50 and in the harmonics he adds at the very end of the track (4:11). Keith plays an acoustic part full of nuance, and Ronnie supports him on acoustic. A cello reinforces the nostalgic side and lends a romantic air to the whole song. It is most likely a live musician playing rather than a sample, although it has not been possible to confirm this. Mick sings with abundant emotion, almost as if in confidence, and Keith takes over from him on lead vocal in the bridge (2:33). They complement each other perfectly. It is understandable that the Stones only reserved a B-side for this—excessively atypical—ballad, even if it did deserve better.

WISH I'D NEVER MET YOU

Mick Jagger / Keith Richards / 4:42

Musicians
Mick Jagger: vocals
Keith Richards: rhythm guitar
Bill Wyman: bass
Charlie Watts: drums
Ron Wood: slide guitar
Chuck Leavell: piano
Recorded
AIR Studios, Montserrat: March 29–May 5, 1989
Olympic Sound Studios, London: May 15–June 29, 1989
Technical Team
Producers: Chris Kimsey, the Glimmer Twins
Sound engineer: Christopher Marc Potter
Assistant sound engineer: Rupert Coulson
Mixing: Michael H. Brauer

Ron was in on the act for this 1989 blues that would later serve as the B-side of two singles.

Genesis

The hero of this song does not pull his punches. He wishes he had never met the woman who has thrown his life into disarray, but he is so much in love that he has become a slave to his passion. He has tried to forget her but to no avail, and the time has come for regrets . . . "Wish I'd Never Met You" seems to date back to the *Dirty Work* sessions and 1985. It was during the recording of *Steel Wheels* (1989), however, that the number was finally cut, with Chuck Leavell on the piano. This is a Chicago-style blues in the spirit of the timeless music of Howlin' Wolf. Left off the track listing of *Steel Wheels*, "Wish I'd Never Met You" was chosen as the B-side for two singles: "Almost Hear You Sigh" and "Terrifying." It is also on the album *Flashpoint*, released in 1991.

Production

There are B-sides that the Stones tossed out as quickly as possible and others, such as "Anyway You Look at It" (the B-side of "Saint of Me," 1998) that they carefully honed. Unfortunately, "Wish I'd Never Met You" belongs in the first category. The track is badly constructed, there was no time to write a melody for the bridge (2:35), and none of the musicians seem motivated (to say the least). Mick sings with little enthusiasm. He swallows his words, seems unsure of the tune, and gives the impression of not being particularly convinced by the results. The same goes for Charlie, whose playing is totally lacking in groove. The drummer also botches snare drum rolls (4:14) and slows down and speeds up the tempo. Bill, in turn, seems listless. Ronnie plays slide but is in no better form than the others. He gives the impression of rehearsing the song rather than recording it, and his solos at 1:38 and 2:20 are hardly unforgettable. Keith, who is on rhythm guitar, forgets to stop playing his chord on the break at 0:55, and the remainder of his accompaniment is pretty unconvincing. The only one who seems rather more focused is Chuck Leavell, who delivers a strong piano part. When all is said and done, however, it is difficult to hold this mediocre performance against the Stones. They were perhaps planning to rework "Wish I'd Never Met You," but in the end, no doubt for some reason or another, left it as it was. It is a drop in the ocean and matters not a jot.

THROUGH THE LONELY NIGHTS

Mick Jagger / Keith Richards / 4:13

Musicians
Mick Jagger: vocals
Keith Richards: rhythm guitar, acoustic
guitar (?), backing vocals
Bill Wyman: bass (?)
Charlie Watts: drums
Mick Taylor: rhythm and lead guitar, backing vocals
Nicky Hopkins: piano
Recorded
Dynamic Sounds Studios, Kingston, Jamaica:
November 25–December 21, 1972
Island Studios, London: May 28–June 8, 1973 (?),
May 4–27, 1974 (?)
Technical Team
Producer: Jimmy Miller
Sound engineers: Andy Johns, Keith Harwood

Mick Taylor was still a member of the Stones when
the band recorded this song of heartbreak.

For many years, rumors have been circulating that Jimmy Page plays on the recording of "Through the Lonely Nights." These rumors are based mainly on the fact that Keith Harwood (then the sound engineer for Led Zeppelin) was in attendance at the overdub sessions at Island Studios. More fantasy than fact, it would seem . . .

Genesis

Another heartache. *Through the lonely nights I think of you/ Through the lonely hours I dream of you.* There seems to be no hope for this lover who finds it difficult to be separated from the woman he loves. He does not want to crack, however, or to give in to tears. "Through the Lonely Nights" goes back to the *Goats Head Soup* sessions, most probably those held at Dynamic Sounds Studios in Kingston in November and December 1972. This ballad with its predominantly acoustic sound was eventually left off the track listing for the album, but was chosen as the B-side of the single "It's Only Rock 'n' Roll," released on July 26, 1974. It was included on *Rarities 1971–2003*, and again in the box set *The Singles Collection 1971–2006*.

Production

This song takes us straight back to the atmosphere of *Goats Head Soup*. Keith plays arpeggios on his guitar, which is most likely plugged into a Leslie speaker before then being played rhythm, with very prominent wah-wah. He also seems to be strumming the acoustic guitar that can be heard on this track. Mick Taylor, here at his very best, supports him on a second rhythm guitar (at 0:54), before playing a solo, which, although short, is of stunning quality, with absolutely exceptional melodic motif and phrasing. Once again, this gives a sense of just how much Taylor contributed to the Stones. It seems to be Bill on bass, although his playing is not particularly characteristic. We can be certain, on the other hand, that the drummer is Charlie, who is betrayed by his signature groove and nonchalant, yet extremely effective, style of playing. On piano, Nicky Hopkins is also instantly recognizable. Mick Jagger gives a good vocal performance and is supported exceptionally well on backing vocals by Keith Richards and Mick Taylor, the latter having confirmed this in an interview. As we have seen, "Through the Lonely Nights" was recorded in Kingston at the end of 1972, with the overdubs, at least Nicky Hopkins's piano, added either between May and June 1973 or else in May 1974.

Rough Justice
Let Me Down Slow
It Won't Take Long
Rain Fall Down
Streets Of Love
Back Of My Hand
She Saw Me Coming
Biggest Mistake
This Place Is Empty
Oh No, Not You Again
Dangerous Beauty
Laugh, I Nearly Died
Sweet Neo Con
Look What The Cat
  Dragged In
Driving Too Fast
Infamy

ALBUM
RELEASE DATE
United Kingdom: September 5, 2005
Label: Virgin
RECORD NUMBER: VIRGIN CDV3012
Number 2, on the charts for 5 weeks

A BIGGER BANG

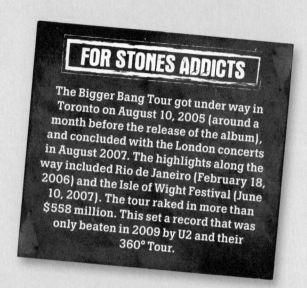

FOR STONES ADDICTS

The Bigger Bang Tour got under way in Toronto on August 10, 2005 (around a month before the release of the album), and concluded with the London concerts in August 2007. The highlights along the way included Rio de Janeiro (February 18, 2006) and the Isle of Wight Festival (June 10, 2007). The tour raked in more than $558 million. This set a record that was only beaten in 2009 by U2 and their 360° Tour.

A BIGGER BANG: A STORMING COMEBACK

On August 14, 2004, two months after Charlie Watts's jazz band canceled its dates in continental Europe (but not at Ronnie Scott's in London), the news was announced that the Stones drummer was suffering from throat cancer and had already been undergoing radiotherapy. "I didn't even want my family to come in and see me," he would later say. "The best way for me at any rate, was to be left alone. Totally alone. Like a dog that's been hurt . . . You go in there and you're terrified. All the machines, it's like space age stuff. The surgeons and nurses literally have your life in their hands. I didn't think of the Rolling Stones at all."   Would the Stones be able to carry on without their legendary drummer? For many of their fans, this was inconceivable. While waiting to hear the outcome of Charlie's treatment, Mick Jagger and Keith Richards continued to work as planned on the preparation of their new album. They also took part in the ceremony of March 15, 2004, at the Rock 'n' Roll Hall of Fame at which Jann S. Wenner (the publisher of *Rolling Stone*) and the blues-rock band ZZ Top were inducted, and Mick Jagger recorded the soundtrack of *Alfie*, the remake of the Lewis Gilbert comedy drama, with Dave Stewart at Abbey Road Studios. At the end of September 2004 there was good news when Shirley Watts announced at a press conference that her husband had recovered.

The Album

By the time Charlie Watts was finally ready to pick up his drumsticks again, Mick Jagger and Keith Richards had been working on preproduction of the next album at La Fourchette, the château owned by the Stones singer (who had been ennobled in 2003) at Pocé-sur-Cisse, not far from Amboise, France, and also on Saint Vincent in the Caribbean, for more than a year. "We were tight together, got some good stuff working," writes Keith. "There was less of the moodiness." Thus the two of them got together to write and make demos for the new album in Mick's home studio, face-to-face just as they had done in the good old days of the sixties. It was probably this intimacy that encouraged them to write and play in a simpler, almost purified way. And the place evidently fostered creativity, for when Charlie returned, no fewer than sixteen songs had been earmarked for the album.

A Bigger Bang is a multifaceted album. It embraces the dazzling guitar of the glory days ("Rough Justice," "It Won't Take Long," "She Saw Me Coming"), low-down blues ("Back to My Hand"), and soul ("Biggest Mistake"), and also reveals a certain fondness for the ballad ("Streets of Love," "This Place Is Empty"). However, a conscious decision has also been made to sound modern ("Dangerous Beauty," "Laugh, I Nearly Died") and to play the dance card ("Rain Fall Down," "Look What the Cat Dragged In").

As for the lyrics, there is an obvious desire on the part of the Stones—or more precisely Mick Jagger—to take sides, to do battle against the warmongers with their inappropriately clean consciences. "Sweet Neo Con" is a virulent indictment of the Bush administration and its neoconservative advisers, who are judged responsible for the clash of civilizations. A

Photo shoot with the four Stones in Milan, July 11, 2006.

similar accusation is made in "Dangerous Beauty," inspired by the hair-raising scandal of Abu Ghraib prison, while "Rain Fall Down" is a bleak description of London. The Rolling Stones have not completely broken with tradition, however: women get hauled over the coals once again in "Rough Justice," "It Won't Take Long," "She Saw Me Coming," "Laugh, I Nearly Died," "Look What the Cat Dragged In," and also to a certain extent in "Oh No, Not You Again." At the same time, however, Mick Jagger and Keith Richards, respectively, reveal their vulnerability and fear of solitude in "Biggest Mistake" and "This Place Is Empty." In short, *A Bigger Bang* has something of both *Exile on Main St.* and *Some Girls* about it.

Produced by the Glimmer Twins and Don Was, the Stones' twenty-second (British) studio album was released on September 5, 2005, eight years after *Bridges to Babylon*. Its success was in proportion to the significance of the event. Number 1 in Canada, the Netherlands, Denmark, Germany, and Italy, number 2 in the United Kingdom and Spain, and number 3 in the United States and France, sales would eventually reach more than two million copies. The critics, meanwhile, were generally favorable. Alan Light, in the columns of *Rolling Stone*, wrote that Mick Jagger and Keith Richards "are still standing—grumpy old men, full of piss and vinegar, spite and blues chords, and they wear it well." In *NME*, Dan Martin wrote that although *A Bigger Bang* "is no masterpiece . . . a world with the Stones is better than one without them."

The Album Cover

The cover picture is by Nick Knight, a London fashion photographer known mainly for his work in magazines such as *Vogue*, *The Face*, and for prestigious brands including Saint Laurent, Calvin Klein, and Mercedes. The cover returns to the original spirit of the group, with neither the band's name nor the title showing on the front, and featuring a dark cover image such as the band had started to cultivate in the sixties. Mick, Keith, Charlie, and Ronnie form a circle in the dark, illuminated only by white light that irradiates their faces.

The whole thing evokes a supernova, inviting a play of words on *A Bigger Bang* and *A Bigger Band* (or is this a fanciful interpretation?).

The Recording

The birth of *A Bigger Bang* goes back to June 2004, when Keith Richards joined Mick Jagger at his château in France. It was there that he learned of Charlie Watts's health worries. Should everything be put on hold? ". . . I thought for a minute," recalls Keith, "and said, no, let's start. We're starting to write songs, so we don't need Charlie right now . . . Let's write a few, send Charlie the tapes so he can have a listen to where we're at." Initially, it was Mick Jagger who sat down at the drums. Although only one of his drum parts would survive once Charlie had rerecorded them, each of the tracks would retain the beat he himself had laid down. Mick and Keith would also share the bass and guitar parts between them, and some of these would survive on the album. Charlie joined his two bandmates around September 20 and played with renewed vigor. The sessions would get properly under way in November and December, with the producer Don Was but without Ron Wood, who was undergoing detox. With fewer distractions at Pocé-sur-Cisse, the Stones were able to focus on their work.

Mick's idea for the recording was that the three of them would play in one of the château's smaller rooms, with Don Was and the sound engineer alongside them and without any of the conventional separation. This was made possible by the technology of the day, and the resulting sound quality is nothing less than professional. This simplicity, combined with a newfound intimacy, would enable them to obtain a more direct and immediate sound and style of playing, not unlike that of the *Exile* period. However, Mick Jagger was still planning to go into a "real" studio afterward. When he revealed this to the other members of the group, their reaction was one of irritation: "Don Was and I looked at each other," recalls Keith, "and Charlie looked at me . . . Fuck this shit. We've already got it down right here. Why do you want to spring for

Mick Jagger in the front line of the impressively staged Bigger Bang World Tour.

all that bread? So you can say it was cut in so-and-so studio, the glass wall and the control room? We ain't going nowhere, pal. So finally he relented." The sessions then resumed in March 2005, again at La Fourchette, and continued until the end of April, still without Ron Wood, but now with Darryl Jones and Chuck Leavell. Finally, between June 6 and 28, the Stones (without Charlie) were in Los Angeles (Ocean Way Recording Studios, Henson Recording Studios, the Village Recorder, and Mix This!) for the overdubs and mixing. Ronnie, who was finally present, plays on only ten of the sixteen songs, having recorded his overdubs in barely four days due to time constraints!

Thus, between November 2004 and June 2005, on the banks of the Loire and then in Los Angeles, the following tracks were recorded: "Rain Fall Down," "Let Me Down Slow," "Streets of Love," "It Won't Take Long," "Back of My Hand," "She Saw Me Coming," "Dangerous Beauty," "Oh No, Not You Again," "This Place Is Empty," "Driving Too Fast," "Biggest Mistake," "Laugh, I Nearly Died," "Infamy," "Look What the Cat Dragged In," "Sweet Neo Con," and "Rough Justice," plus the outtakes "Don't Wanna Go Home" and "Under the Radar" (on the UK and US DVD *A Bigger Bang*).

The sound engineer on this project was Krish Sharma, an old acquaintance of Don Was who had recorded the albums of Was (Not Was), the producer's former band. There was also Ryan Castle (Primal Scream, Oasis), who was in charge of the technical side of things on one song, "Rough Justice." Responsible for the mixing were Jack Joseph Puig (Amy Grant, Black Crowes, Eric Clapton) and Dave Sardy (Marilyn Manson, Oasis). The assistant sound engineers were Germán Villacorta (Ozzy Osbourne, Alice Cooper), Dean Nelson (Charlotte Gainsbourg, the Pussycat Dolls), and Andy Brohard (Oasis, Rickie Lee Jones).

Unlike the preceding albums, there is no plethora of additional musicians on *A Bigger Bang*. Matt Clifford (*Steel Wheels*, 1989) is back on keyboards, Lenny Castro (*Voodoo Lounge*, 1994) is back on percussion, and the multi-instrumentalist Blondie Chaplin (*Bridges to Babylon*, 1997) also returns to the fold.

The Instruments

Charlie remains loyal to his 1957 Gretsch kit, while the other members of the band draw on the phenomenal collection of guitars accumulated over the course of forty-plus years. Mick, however, has acquired a new model, a red Sears Silvertone 1457. Keith plays his black Gibson ES-355, his Telecasters, and a Martin acoustic. Ronnie, meanwhile, favors his black Zemaitis and his 1955 Fender Stratocaster.

France clearly agrees with the Stones, as they have recorded a large part of their discography there. Even better: *Exile on Main St.* was recorded at Keith's villa in the South of France, and *A Bigger Bang* at Sir Mick's château on the banks of the Loire. Does this make France the equal of Memphis or Chicago?

ROUGH JUSTICE

Mick Jagger / Keith Richards / 3:12

Musicians

Mick Jagger: vocals, rhythm guitar
Keith Richards: rhythm guitar
Charlie Watts: drums
Ron Wood: slide guitar
Darryl Jones: bass
Chuck Leavell: piano

Recorded

La Fourchette Home Studio, Pocé-sur-Cisse, France: November–December 2004, March–April 2005
The Village Recorder, Los Angeles: June 6–28, 2005

Technical Team

Producers: Don Was, the Glimmer Twins
Sound engineer: Ryan Castle, Krish Sharma (?)
Assistant sound engineer: Andy Brohard
Mixing (the Village Recorder): Dave Sardy

The grand master of the riff, seen here playing his black Gibson ES-355, opens the album with "Rough Justice."

Genesis

In an interview in 2005, Keith Richards recalled how "Rough Justice" had come into being: "That came to me in my sleep. It's almost like 'Satisfaction,' Yeah, I almost sort of woke up and said, 'Where's my guitar?' Sometimes you do dream a riff, you know? I had to get up, and it's really hard to get me up. Once I go down, I go down, you know?"   And it is clearly a very Stones-sounding riff (even if Ron Wood was to detect a certain Faces influence in it).

The words *rough justice* are addressed to a former girlfriend or wife, who, within the space of a few years, has developed from the status of caring and considerate lover into a woman of voracious appetites: *One time you were my baby chicken/Now you've grown into a fox*. In spite of everything, the narrator wishes to remain magnanimous: *But you know I'll never break your heart*, sings Mick Jagger in the refrain.

The opening song on the album was recorded at La Fourchette, Mick Jagger's château at Pocé-sur-Cisse, France, before being mixed at the Village Recorder in Los Angeles. It was chosen as one of the two A-sides (the other being "Streets of Love") of a single released on August 22, 2005, that climbed to number 15 in the United Kingdom and, in the United States, to number 25 on the *Billboard* Mainstream Rock Tracks chart.

Production

Here then, after eight years of silence, are the Rolling Stones exploding back onto the scene. "Rough Justice" is a very well-made rock track capable of reassuring any Stones fan that the Englishmen still had some fire in their bellies! It is clearly Keith who opens hostilities, with a riff from his own workshop—a good, if not exactly trailblazing, example. No matter, he is the one his bandmates all follow. Starting with Charlie, whose drumming displays a power and weight of rare and reassuring intensity, and the bass of Darryl Jones—efficient and energetic, but just a little too predictable. The honor of setting a spark to the whole thing goes to Ronnie, with a great slide part played on his black Zemaitis (nicknamed "Stay with Me") and a solo, at 1:27, that is one of his best ever for the Stones. Mick is on rhythm guitar and, of course, lead vocal, giving an excellent performance with a lightly distorted sound that creates something of a garage band feel.

2005

LET ME DOWN SLOW

Mick Jagger / Keith Richards / 4:16

Musicians
Mick Jagger: vocals, rhythm guitar
Keith Richards: acoustic guitar (?), rhythm
guitar, lead guitar, backing vocals
Charlie Watts: drums
Ron Wood: slide guitar
Darryl Jones: bass
Recorded
La Fourchette Home Studio, Pocé-sur-Cisse, France:
November–December 2004, March–April 2005
Ocean Way Recording Studios, Hollywood: June 6–28, 2005
Technical Team
Producers: Don Was, the Glimmer Twins
Sound engineer: Krish Sharma
Assistant sound engineer: Dean Nelson
Mixing (Ocean Way Recording Studios): Jack Joseph Puig

"Let Me Down Slow" winds the clock back more than thirty
years, to the brief fling between Keith and Marianne Faithfull.

Genesis

"Let Me Down Slow" is a Mick Jagger song. Other than the
refrain, that is, which bears the signature of Keith Richards.
The lyrics are somewhat atypical of the Glimmer Twins. They
tell of a *fragile* lover who begs his girlfriend to let him down
easy. *If you've something to say/Don't be too direct; I don't
want a confrontation/I got my back to the wall*: we almost
need to pinch ourselves to believe that it actually is Mick Jagger singing these words. In fact, "Let Me Down Slow" relates
to a colorful episode in the life of the Stones. At the end of the
sixties, Keith spent the night with Marianne Faithfull in order
to get his revenge on Mick for succumbing to the charms of
Anita Pallenberg on the set of *Performance*. The Stones guitarist gives his own account of it in *Life*: "In fact, I had to leave
the premises rather abruptly when the cat [Mick Jagger] came
back. Hey, it was our only time, hot and sweaty. We were just
there in, as Mick calls it in 'Let Me Down Slow,' the afterglow,
my head nestled between those two beautiful jugs. And we
heard his car drive up, and there was a big flurry, and I did one
out the window, got my shoes, out the window through the
garden, and I realized I'd left my socks."

Production

On "Let Me Down Slow," the most important quality once
again is energy. From the very first notes, Mick and Keith
each play a sustained rhythm guitar part, each with distortion
from the amp. Another guitar is also present, a Martin acoustic strummed most probably by Keith. The latter would reveal
in an interview that the effective descending melody of the
refrain was his work, which is further enhanced by the harmonization of the voices and guitars of the Glimmer Twins. It is
also used skillfully in the second half of Keith's solo, after 2:31.
Ron Wood again plays slide on his black Zemaitis, and inserts
some good licks before playing solo phrases from 3:20. On
the drums, Charlie pulsates with a fierce energy, and is supported on bass by a very powerful-sounding Darryl Jones,
who seems to be playing his Sadowsky. Mick sings without
overdoing it, with inflections in his voice (in the refrains) that
are reminiscent of the sixties!

IT WON'T TAKE LONG

Mick Jagger / Keith Richards / 3:54

Musicians
Mick Jagger: vocals, rhythm guitar
Keith Richards: rhythm guitar, backing vocals
Charlie Watts: drums
Ron Wood: rhythm and lead guitar
Darryl Jones: bass
Chuck Leavell: organ

Recorded
La Fourchette Home Studio, Pocé-sur-Cisse, France:
November–December 2004, March–April 2005
Ocean Way Recording Studios, Hollywood: June 6–28, 2005

Technical Team
Producers: Don Was, the Glimmer Twins
Sound engineer: Krish Sharma
Assistant sound engineer: Dean Nelson
Mixing (Ocean Way Recording Studios): Jack Joseph Puig

Genesis

This is another track in the great Stones rock 'n' roll tradition. At more than sixty years of age, the Glimmer Twins still kept the faith, and "It Won't Take Long" is the proof. Keith even pulls off the feat of going down a new path and introducing a little variation to the riff we thought we had heard a thousand times. Once again the lyrics are directed against women, or more accurately certain women: those who can gain a fortune or lose their soul in an instant. To an even greater extent than the (presumably ungrateful!) woman in question here, time is at the center of the Stones singer's preoccupations in this song. *And it won't take long to forget you/Time it passes fast*, he sings.

Production

It is no surprise that on this album, written by Mick and Keith without the presence of any other band member, the Glimmer Twins give pride of place to the guitars—and, of course, riffs. Thus Keith cannot keep himself from launching "It Won't Take Long" with his much-loved signature guitar style, and the track then takes off at quite a pace, thanks to Charlie's superb drum part, featuring a resplendent snare drum. Mick is on rhythm guitar, and it is regrettable that he confines himself to such a sober style of playing, having demonstrated, notably on *Bridges to Babylon*, that he now possessed a sufficient level of skill to be able to respond more elaborately to his two fellow guitarists. For the time being, this task falls to Ronnie, who plays both rhythm and solo. It is tempting to wonder about the impact his detox has had, because here, as on the two preceding tracks, his playing is brilliant: inventive and melodic, with an ideal sonority, qualities he has not consistently had on previous recordings. Darryl Jones is on bass, but gives the impression that he is holding back: his playing has become static by dint of trying to keep things simple. As for Chuck Leavell, who could only be heard at the very end of "Rough Justice," this time his organ part is completely inaudible! "It Won't Take Long" is a good enough rock track, but it lacks any real soul. It is merely filler.

Ron Wood plays both rhythm and lead on "It Won't Take Long."

RAIN FALL DOWN

Mick Jagger / Keith Richards / 4:54

Musicians
Mick Jagger: vocals, rhythm guitar, keyboards, vibes
Keith Richards: rhythm and lead guitar
Charlie Watts: drums
Ron Wood: rhythm and lead guitar
Darryl Jones: bass
Matt Clifford: keyboards, vibes, programming
Recorded
La Fourchette Home Studio, Pocé-sur-Cisse, France:
November–December 2004, March–April 2005
Henson Recording Studios, Hollywood: June 6–28, 2005
Technical Team
Producers: Don Was, the Glimmer Twins
Sound engineer: Krish Sharma
Assistant sound engineer: Dean Nelson
Mixing (Henson Recording Studios): Krish Sharma
Assistant sound engineer (Henson Recording Studios):
Germán Villacorta
Preproduction: Matt Clifford:

will.i.am, a member of the Black Eyed Peas,
who did a remix of "Rain Fall Down."

will.i.am, who remixed "Rain Fall Down," is the famous rapper William James Adams Jr., a member of the Black Eyed Peas and producer of Michael Jackson, U2, and Lady Gaga. Ashley Beedle, who made his own version of the track, is a British DJ who co-founded the Ballistic Brothers and X-Press 2.

Genesis

Mick Jagger wrote "Rain Fall Down" thinking of his own fair city of London, where it had all begun for the Stones forty-five years before. The song describes a young couple living in an apocalyptic setting of gray and decrepit apartments strewn with garbage and abandoned even by those who built them (the politicians, presumably). Through the prism of this couple, Mick Jagger would himself acknowledge, in an interview given to *L'Express* in 2005, that "'Rain Fall Down' is a song about London. It has a line, 'Feel like we're living in a battleground, everyone's jazzed.' That was in my head already. There were so many armed police in the streets. Walking around, seeing machine guns, is not how you imagine London to be."

"Rain Fall Down" was the second single taken from *A Bigger Bang* (coupled, moreover, with a will.i.am remix version and another version named Ashley Beedle's "Heavy Disco" Vocal Re-Edit). The single climbed to number 33 in the United Kingdom and number 21 on the *Billboard* Dance Club Play chart.

Production

"Rain Fall Down" is a return to dance music, a genre with which the Stones had been flirting since *Black and Blue*. This is clearly a song composed by Mick Jagger, with a very good funky riff he plays himself (on a Fender Stratocaster?). Keith answers him on guitar, as does Ronnie, and it can be pretty difficult to work out who is who, particularly since a muted guitar loop has also been programmed and added by Matt Clifford. Some of the licks, however, reveal Ronnie's handiwork (2:24), while other more rock ones can be attributed to Keith (4:04). Various keyboard sounds can also be discerned, all played by Mick or Matt. As for Charlie, it is over a drum loop (hi-hat, bass drum, snare drum), programmed by the Stones singer, that Charlie Watts superimposes his own funky drumming. This is underpinned by an excellent bass part from Darryl Jones, who gives a master class in groove. "Rain Fall Down" also features an excellent vocal performance by Mick Jagger, who reveals himself on this track to be a veritable one-man band. As well as lead vocal, keyboards, and guitars, he also provides some superb backing vocals that he most likely sings alone (overdubbed). It is worth noting the tambourine part that does not seem to have been programmed.

STREETS OF LOVE

Mick Jagger / Keith Richards / 5:10

Musicians
Mick Jagger: vocals, rhythm guitar
Keith Richards: acoustic guitar (?), rhythm guitar
Charlie Watts: drums
Ron Wood: rhythm and lead guitar
Darryl Jones: bass
Chuck Leavell: piano, organ
Matt Clifford: piano, organ, strings, programming
Unidentified musician: tambourine
Recorded
La Fourchette Home Studio, Pocé-sur-Cisse, France:
November–December 2004, March–April 2005
Ocean Way Recording Studios, Hollywood: June 6–28, 2005
Technical Team
Producers: Don Was, the Glimmer Twins, Matt Clifford
Sound engineer: Krish Sharma
Assistant sound engineer: Dean Nelson
Mixing (Ocean Way Recording Studios): Jack Joseph Puig

Genesis

Mick Jagger may have written "Streets of Love" at the same time as "Wicked Time," which appears on the soundtrack to the Charles Shyer movie *Alfie* (2004). *I must admit you broke my heart/The awful truth, it's really sad/I must admit I was awful bad.* It is apparent from the very first verse that this superb ballad is a mea culpa from a former lover to a woman he has mistreated. Now he walks *the streets of love*, which are *full of tears* and *full of fears*. When Mick Jagger wrote these lyrics, he may have had in mind his relationship with Jerry Hall, which ended in 1999 on account of his repeated infidelities. In any case, the song is filled with regret, above all when he sings: *A band just played the wedding march/And the corner store/Mends broken hearts.* And memories too, including, presumably, those of their Hindu wedding in Bali in 1990 (declared by Jagger at the time of the divorce to have been invalid). "Streets of Love" was released as a single on August 22, 2005. Although it only reached number 15 in the United Kingdom, this Mick-penned ballad made it to number 1 in Spain and entered the top ten in several other European countries (the Netherlands, Belgium, Denmark . . .).

Production

Mick Jagger would later say that he did not particularly like writing ballads unless they were of real quality. "Streets of Love" is definitely one of those, as described by Keith. "It's a Mick tour de force, in a way. But we all really enjoyed playing it. When we first knocked it out on acoustic, we felt, Oh, that's nice, but it sounded kind of standard."   In actual fact, the song has hit quality. The refrain is very catchy, Mick Jagger sings with emotion, his falsettos and vocal harmonies work extremely well, and the arrangements are on a par with the quality of the composition. "Streets of Love" starts with an acoustic guitar, played in arpeggios with phasing that makes it sound like a 12-string. This is doubled by an electric guitar and piano. Other, distorted, guitars enter in the refrain, as do Clifford's strings and Charlie's drums. Ronnie plays a very airy solo at 2:38, doubled by violins that are not in especially good taste. However, with a very good bass line from Darryl Jones, Chuck Leavell's organ, and Mick Jagger's very good vocals, "Streets of Love" is a real triumph. The song was co-produced, incidentally, with Matt Clifford.

Far from the madding crowd, Mick Jagger and Jerry Hall set out on the path to love.

BACK OF MY HAND

Mick Jagger / Keith Richards / 3:33

Musicians
Mick Jagger: vocals, slide guitar, harmonica, maracas, bass
Keith Richards: rhythm guitar
Charlie Watts: drums
Recorded
La Fourchette Home Studio, Pocé-sur-Cisse, France: November–December 2004, March–April 2005
Henson Recording Studios, Hollywood: June 6–28, 2005
Technical Team
Producers: Don Was, the Glimmer Twins
Sound engineer: Krish Sharma
Assistant sound engineer: Dean Nelson
Mixing (Henson Recording Studios): Krish Sharma
Assistant sound engineer (Henson Recording Studios): Germán Villacorta

Mick Jagger starts to play the guitar more and more, notably his Sears Silvertone 1457 on the Bigger Bang Tour.

Genesis

"Back of My Hand" is a blues by Mick Jagger that came to him during the recording of *A Bigger Bang.* Keith remembers, "I sleep downstairs and the studio is upstairs. One night I thought I was hearing this old Muddy Waters track I didn't know, but it turned out to be Mick working on a slide part for 'Back of My Hand.'" In actual fact, "Back of My Hand" belongs to a blues tradition that goes back way beyond Muddy Waters or Willie Dixon. It has the heavy, sluggish atmosphere of founding fathers, such as Leadbelly and Bukka White, who had felt the iron discipline of the penitentiaries. It also contains one of the stock blues characters: the preacher man, in this case a street-corner preacher who announces that *trouble's a comin'* and who hears a mournful melody that he can read like the back of his hand.

Production

This is the first time Mick Jagger has played slide, and the results are surprising. He would later say that he used a Sears Silvertone 1457 bought for barely $44 and tuned in open G. Keith Richards's confusion becomes more comprehensible when one realizes, listening to this track, that Jagger sounds almost like Muddy Waters. "He's always been a good, smooth acoustic player, but the electric seemed like an untamed beast for him until this year. When I heard him this time I thought, 'My God! The boy's finally got it.'" This album, and above all the exceptional state of affairs with the Glimmer Twins recording as a duo, forced Mick to reveal his hand as a talented multi-instrumentalist. For he also, on this track, plays bass—although that's not particularly audible—maracas (doubled), sings, and plays the blues harmonica, whose sonority calls to mind Little Walter. Keith would later regret that they did not record him at Chess Studios in Chicago in 1964! Here, Keith accompanies him on rhythm, playing with considerable subtlety and beauty, and Charlie keeps it as simple as possible by confining himself to the bass drum.

SHE SAW ME COMING

Mick Jagger / Keith Richards / 3:12

Musicians
Mick Jagger: vocals, bass, percussion
Keith Richards: rhythm guitar, backing vocals, piano
Charlie Watts: drums
Ron Wood: rhythm and lead guitar
Blondie Chaplin: backing vocals
Recorded
La Fourchette Home Studio, Pocé-sur-Cisse, France: November–December 2004, March–April 2005
Ocean Way Recording Studios, Hollywood: June 6–28, 2005
Technical Team
Producers: Don Was, the Glimmer Twins
Sound engineer: Krish Sharma
Assistant sound engineer: Dean Nelson
Mixing (Ocean Way Recording Studios): Jack Joseph Puig

Blondie Chaplin lends Mick Jagger considerable support on "She Saw Me Coming."

Genesis

Mick Jagger wrote "She Saw Me Coming" either at his château in Pocé-sur-Cisse, France, or else at his luxurious property on Mustique. Did the Stones singer find himself in a position of weakness? One way or the other, the woman he describes in the song puts him through a tough time. She makes him feel like a *stupid jerk*, screwed him over, and *burglarized [his] soul*. And the worst thing is that she saw him coming but he did not see her . . .

Production

"She Saw Me Coming" is a mid-tempo rock number that could easily have been given a reggae makeover. It is a good song, melodious and catchy. The track's title is chanted so often that it sticks in the memory. Mick Jagger's voice, supported by the excellent Blondie Chaplin, back with the band again after having previously worked on *Bridges to Babylon*, sounds just right: rock-infused and not without a touch of humor. It is also Mick on bass, and it has to be said that he does a good job of it, his straightforward playing providing ideal support for the drums. Charlie Watts gives a superb demonstration of groove, with unfailingly efficient pickups on the snare drum. The Stones singer also seems to be supporting Charlie on percussion, playing what is probably a shaker or the maracas, but this is not really audible. The main riff of the track is clearly played by Keith, probably on his 5-string Telecaster tuned in open G, and it is important to underscore the extent to which his contribution respects the phrasing and pacing that is essential to the groove of this track. This is a refinement that not all rhythm guitarists have managed to incorporate into their playing . . . The other guitar is taken care of by Ronnie, who accompanies his bandmates with some excellent half-rock, half-funk rhythm playing into which he inserts some very good licks. This is one of the main strengths of "She Saw Me Coming." At 1:39 two very brief slide interjections can be heard that could be the work of either guitarist. Finally, Keith is indicated as playing the piano, but it is impossible to hear him.

2005

BIGGEST MISTAKE

Mick Jagger / Keith Richards / 4:06

Musicians
Mick Jagger: vocals, acoustic guitar (?)
Keith Richards: acoustic guitar (?), rhythm guitar, backing vocals
Charlie Watts: drums
Ron Wood: acoustic guitar (?), rhythm guitar
Darryl Jones: bass
Chuck Leavell: organ

Recorded
La Fourchette Home Studio, Pocé-sur-Cisse, France: November–December 2004, March–April 2005
Ocean Way Recording Studios, Hollywood: June 6–28, 2005

Technical Team
Producers: Don Was, the Glimmer Twins
Sound engineers: Krish Sharma, Jack Joseph Puig, Dean Nelson
Assistant sound engineer: Dean Nelson
Mixing (Ocean Way Recording Studios): Jack Joseph Puig

By cheating on Jerry Hall to such an extent that she left him, was Mick Jagger making his biggest mistake?

Genesis

Mick Jagger was responsible for both the words and the music of "Biggest Mistake." He wrote the song in order to remove a weight from his shoulders—presumably his final breakup with Jerry Hall—and perhaps also to banish his demons as an inveterate Don Juan. One thing is for sure: he was feeling vulnerable. "It's crazy to think someone can't be hurt just because he's famous or he struts across a stage," explains Jagger. "If you go back through Stones albums, I'm sure you'll find vulnerability along with the swagger."

In "Biggest Mistake," this fragility is expressed through the story of a love affair between a man of a certain age and a young woman. The story ends a year later, when the harmony they once enjoyed has dissipated and the man's thoughts turn to the past and to rebellion. Ultimately he realizes that he has made the biggest mistake of his life. The consequences are dire: the narrator finds himself *down in a slump*. He's *eating alone*, not going out, and spending his time watching television and drinking on his couch. A grim state of affairs, then, which is intensified by Mick Jagger's vocals, inspired by the great voices of soul, from Solomon Burke to Don Covay. The third single from *A Bigger Bang*, "Biggest Mistake" was released on August 21, 2006, and reached number 51 on the British charts on September 2.

Production

Sir Mick Jagger may let something of his fragility show through in his lyrics, but he uses the music to dampen the intensity of his revelations. "Biggest Mistake" is an attractive ballad with a vague country flavor, but the atmosphere remains light, rather than at any point overwhelming or excessively intimate. The song's opening phrases are sung falsetto, a technique Jagger seems to take pleasure in rediscovering on this album. A number of guitars can be heard on the track: a typical Keith Richards rhythm guitar, another rhythm with licks characteristic of Ron Wood, and two or three acoustics (in the refrains), presumably played by one of these two guitarists and perhaps also by Mick. The bass/drums section functions without a hitch, and this time Chuck Leavell's organ rings out loud and clear, particularly in the sections sung by Mick with his head voice (2:17). As for the lead singer, his vocal is excellent, even if he works hard not to sink into poignancy.

THIS PLACE IS EMPTY

Mick Jagger / Keith Richards / 3:17

Musicians
Keith Richards: vocals, acoustic guitar, piano, bass
Mick Jagger: acoustic slide guitar, backing vocals
Charlie Watts: drums
Don Was: piano
Recorded
La Fourchette Home Studio, Pocé-sur-Cisse, France:
November–December 2004, March–April 2005
Ocean Way Recording Studios, Hollywood: June 6–28, 2005
Technical Team
Producers: Don Was, the Glimmer Twins
Sound engineer: Krish Sharma
Assistant sound engineer: Dean Nelson
Mixing (Ocean Way Recording Studios): Jack Joseph Puig

The composer and singer Hoagy Carmichael influenced
Keith Richards in the writing of "This Place Is Empty."

FOR STONES ADDICTS

The fact that the Stones performed "The
Nearness of You" (a standard dating from
1938) at their concert at the Olympia in
Paris on July 11, 2003, with Keith Richards
on lead vocal, can perhaps be seen as proof
of the Hoagy Carmichael influence.

Genesis

"This Place Is Empty" is a love song written by Keith Richards for his wife Patti Hansen. One evening when the young woman was away, the Stones guitarist, alone in his house in Weston, Connecticut, found himself overcome by a kind of melancholy that inspired in him this melancholy tune and the words: *This place is empty without you; You and me we're just like all the rest/And we don't want to be alone.*

Keith Richards was probably thinking of popular songs by the Broadway composers when he carved out the delicate notes of "This Place Is Empty." "I like to surprise people," he would later tell Alan Di Perna in an interview. "Hey, I grew up with [that Hoagy Carmichael/Cole Porter] thing, man! My mother played me jazz and all the standards. That stuff just drips off of me." He composed the song on acoustic guitar, before recording it on piano.

Production

The harmonies on this tender ballad by Keith are fairly unusual, lying somewhere between blues, jazz, and country. His voice bears a dangerous resemblance to that of Tom Waits, the atmosphere is hushed, and it is in the same confidential tone that he tells of his love. Mick doubles him in the vocal harmonies with a high voice, providing a contrast with his sidekick's. It is probably Don Was who opens the track on the piano, Keith Richards coming in only sporadically on a second piano to complement his playing. The riff master strums and plays arpeggios as well as licks on an acoustic guitar (probably one of his Martins). Charlie accompanies the first two verses on the cymbals, before playing a more sustained beat, accompanied by a bass played this time by Keith himself. After having tasted slide electric on "Back of My Hand," the Stones singer could not resist having another go at it, but this time on an acoustic guitar (from 1:24). Mostly he uses the bottleneck to underscore Keith's tune, to very successful effect.

OH NO, NOT YOU AGAIN

Mick Jagger / Keith Richards / 3:46

Musicians
Mick Jagger: vocals, rhythm guitar
Keith Richards: rhythm and lead guitar, bass (?)
Charlie Watts: drums
Ron Wood: rhythm guitar
Darryl Jones: bass
Recorded
La Fourchette Home Studio, Pocé-sur-Cisse, France:
November–December 2004, March–April 2005
Ocean Way Recording Studios, Hollywood: June 6–28, 2005
Technical Team
Producers: Don Was, the Glimmer Twins
Sound engineer: Krish Sharma
Assistant sound engineer: Dean Nelson
Mixing (Ocean Way Recording Studios): Jack Joseph Puig

Darryl Jones may have been doubled by Keith
(likewise on bass) on "Oh No, Not You Again."

Genesis

Another riff that came to Keith Richards during his evidently troubled sleep. The lyrics, on the other hand, were inspired by a real-life experience. Memories of a beautiful woman waiting to be kissed. *How could I resist?* sings Mick Jagger with impeccable logic. The woman in question makes another appearance in his life some time later. We are told that she has now *got daughters*, which does not exactly support her cause. In fact, the narrator now sees in her every fault under the sun, and in telling her so, deploys his humor in all its misogynistic glory!

"Oh No, Not You Again," which at certain moments calls to mind the punkier offerings on *Some Girls*, was never released as a single. "Biggest Mistake" was chosen in its place. It was, however, given plenty of airplay by US radio stations, and on the back of that made it to number 34 on the *Billboard* Mainstream Rock Tracks chart (December 2005).

Production

The fifth rock nugget on the album, "Oh No, Not You Again" opens, like so many Stones tracks, with a snare drum break from Charlie. As there is nothing new under the sun, Mick then delivers a very good distorted rhythm part and is immediately joined by Keith, possibly a little loud in the mix, but with his characteristic sound and immediately identifiable licks. Ronnie joins them at around 1:31 on a third rhythm guitar, which he probably also uses for his slide part. Incidentally his bottleneck can be heard sliding by itself at the very end of the track at exactly 3:43 (center). The king of the riff looks after the solo (2:04), demonstrating that Chuck Berry still has a hold over him. Charlie smacks his drums heavily, their sonority taking on a strong garage band feel. He is supported by Darryl Jones with some powerful, rhythmic bass-playing. Curiously, Keith is also credited in the liner notes with bass. Is this a mistake, or are the two of them really playing together? Finally, Mick has absolutely no trouble in assuming his role of lead singer—with the energy and enthusiasm that never fail him. It may not be a Stones masterpiece, but "Oh No, Not You Again" is a good rock track that really works, and this is demonstrated by the place it carved out for itself on the charts.

DANGEROUS BEAUTY

Mick Jagger / Keith Richards / 3:48

Musicians
Mick Jagger: vocals, rhythm guitar, bass
Keith Richards: rhythm and lead guitar
Charlie Watts: drums
Unidentified musician: organ
Recorded
La Fourchette Home Studio, Pocé-sur-Cisse, France: November–December 2004, March–April 2005
Ocean Way Recording Studios, Hollywood: June 6–28, 2005
Technical Team
Producers: Don Was, the Glimmer Twins
Sound engineer: Krish Sharma
Assistant sound engineer: Dean Nelson
Mixing (Ocean Way Recording Studios): Jack Joseph Puig

2005

Genesis
"Dangerous Beauty" turns the spotlight on one of the most resounding scandals perpetrated by the US Army in Iraq. In 2003, the former penitentiary complex of Abu Ghraib, a detention center of fearsome repute under the regime of Saddam Hussein, was reopened by the United States and converted into a prison for soldiers of the Iraq Army. The dissemination all over the world a year later of photographs showing tortured solders forced to submit to the sexual whims of their American jailers provoked an outcry. One picture had a particular impact on spectators and incensed the international community. It showed a woman holding a prisoner on a leash. Her name? Lynndie England. She is the *dangerous beauty* referred to by Mick Jagger, the one nicknamed *the lady with the leash. You look so fancy in those photographs/With your rubber gloves on/You're a favorite with the Chiefs of Staff*, he sings, castigating US imperialism in passing.

Production
Another rock track, this time recorded with smaller forces. Only the three original Stones play on this song, with the possible exception of the two organ parts that can be heard at 2:06 and 3:00. These are not credited in the liner notes, but could have been played by Mick Jagger, Chuck Leavell, or Don Was. The track opens with a catchy riff that is apparently played by Mick and Keith at the same time. The two guitars are opposite each other in the stereo image, and the sound is aggressive and powerful. Keith plays a second guitar (in the center), and of course the solo too. Although his style is unmistakable, there is a relatively rare hint of B. B. King to his playing (2:19). Turning to the drums, Charlie assures a steady beat with the same energy and with a heavy, stinging snare drum. The Stones singer is once again on bass, and the results are surprising, given that he is playing the instrument for the first time on this album. There is a certain lack of precision in the sound, but otherwise he seems to have the instrument perfectly under control. As for his singing, Mick stands out for the phrasing that is his alone, in which humor, derision, and chastisement are combined. Which is not to overlook the extraordinary rock feel he projects.

The Stones playing under the gaze of Brian and Charlie. How symbolic . . .

LAUGH, I NEARLY DIED

Mick Jagger / Keith Richards /4:54

Musicians
Mick Jagger: vocals, rhythm guitar, keyboards, percussion
Keith Richards: rhythm guitar
Charlie Watts: drums
Darryl Jones: bass
Recorded
La Fourchette Home Studio, Pocé-sur-Cisse, France: November–December 2004, March–April 2005
Henson Recording Studios, Hollywood: June 6–28, 2005
Technical Team
Producers: Don Was, the Glimmer Twins
Sound engineer: Krish Sharma
Assistant sound engineer: Dean Nelson
Mixing (Henson Recording Studios): Krish Sharma
Assistant sound engineer (Henson Recording Studios): Germán Villacorta

Genesis

"Laugh, I Nearly Died" was probably written by Mick Jagger during the recording of the *Alfie* soundtrack. The end of a love affair has driven the unfortunate narrator to cast himself adrift on the world. He has wandered from Rome to Greece, and then to Africa, Arabia (where he has *seen a million stars* and *been sipping champagne on the boulevards!*), and eventually India (which *froze [his] bones*). But this diversity of landscapes and sensations has not enabled him to overcome his solitude or made him forget the woman he loves. *Laugh, laugh, I nearly died*: not only is his journey to these magnificent vistas unforgiving, he continues to be eaten away by bitterness. Another possible interpretation suggests itself: this journey around the world could be a quest for the truth rather than for forgetting, a way for the narrator to attribute some meaning to his existence . . .

The accompanying music was the fruit of studio work at Mick's home at Pocé-sur-Cisse. Overall, the song possesses a gospel vibe.

Production

Charlie launches the track at a reasonably slow tempo (75 bpm). Mick and Keith then come in on guitar, with Ronnie once again absent. Mick plays a bluesy sort of rhythm part with a degree of distortion and reasonably discreet delay. Keith delivers a second rhythm part with a more funky feel, favoring the higher reaches of the neck and interspersing licks and muted picking. Darryl Jones's bass seems to flirt with groove, so low and muffled is the sound he makes. Charlie, probably taking his cue from a drum machine preprogrammed by Jagger, gives an impression of metronomic rigor, thereby reinforcing the somewhat harrowing atmosphere of the song. With his newfound eagerness to express himself, the Stones singer takes to the keyboards: pads can be made out, as can an electric piano drenched in a kind of swirly phasing resembling a Leslie effect. He also takes charge of a number of percussion instruments, such as the tambourine and the maracas. It is also Mick who sings the different backing vocal parts, which have a distinctly gospel flavor. He can be heard singing simultaneously in a lowish voice and a falsetto. The track has an a cappella ending, with backing vocals, hand claps, and floor tom. The Stones singer is simply brilliant and "Laugh, I Nearly Died" is a triumph.

Charlie Watts, more of a dandy than ever on this number, which seems to reflect his victory over his illness.

SWEET NEO CON

Mick Jagger / Keith Richards / 4:33

Musicians
Mick Jagger: vocals, rhythm guitar, acoustic guitar (?), harmonica, bass, keyboards
Keith Richards: rhythm guitar, acoustic guitar (?)
Charlie Watts: drums

Recorded
La Fourchette Home Studio, Pocé-sur-Cisse, France: November–December 2004, March–April 2005
Henson Recording Studios, Hollywood: June 6–28, 2005

Technical Team
Producers: Don Was, the Glimmer Twins
Sound engineer: Krish Sharma
Assistant sound engineer: Dean Nelson
Mixing (Henson Recording Studios): Krish Sharma
Assistant sound engineer (Henson Recording Studios): Germán Villacorta

Genesis

"Sweet Neo Con" follows in a direct line from "Dangerous Beauty." This time, the target is not the US Army, but the Bush administration. *You call yourself a Christian/I think that you're a hypocrite/You say you are a patriot/I think that you're a crock of shit*: these words seem to be addressed to George W. Bush, although Mick Jagger has since denied it. More generally, the Stones singer has the president's neoconservative advisers in his sights. These include Vice President Dick Cheney, Secretary of Defense Donald Rumsfeld, and Deputy Secretary of Defense Paul Wolfowitz, who, following the September 11 attacks, threw themselves into a relentless war on terrorism and transformed the Afghanistan and Iraq conflicts into a battle of the civilizations. The neoconservatives present themselves as the defenders of democracy, but, sings Jagger, if you're not with them, *it's prison without trial.* What motivates them in reality is petroleum, money, and world domination—the notion of a unipolar world. They have no need of *foolish friendships* (by which we are to understand old Europe and the UN). And the Stones singer grinds his point home: *How come you're so wrong?/My sweet neocon.* Keith Richards, who has no great interest in political matters, initially wondered about the appropriateness of this frontal attack on Bush's politics on the album: "I said to Mick, 'Are you sure these guys are worth a Rolling Stones song?' But he felt strongly about it. . . . I said, 'If you feel like that about it and you feel it needs to be said, then I'm backing you up, pal.'" The act of a gentleman!

Production

The Little Walter–like intro leads us to expect a blues. But instead, the Stones choose to play a kind of mid-tempo rock number with touches of funk, resulting in a vibe that is reminiscent of the Clash. Charlie is the central pivot of the song, around which Mick hangs his bass, his rhythm guitar, and his keyboards. Keith boosts the sound with a more muscular, distorted accompaniment, before coming in with another electric part (with phasing) and an acoustic in the refrains. Although good overall, "Sweet Neo Con" is guilty of a certain melodic weakness, which is a pity.

In "Sweet Neo Con," Mick Jagger points an accusatory finger at George W. Bush and his merry crew.

2005

LOOK WHAT THE CAT DRAGGED IN

Mick Jagger / Keith Richards / 3:57

FOR STONES ADDICTS

At the end of the song, Mick Jagger sings: *You look like a leper dressed as Sergeant Pepper.* Is he deliberately lobbing a stone at the Beatles?

Musicians
Mick Jagger: vocals, rhythm guitar, bass, backing vocals
Keith Richards: rhythm guitar
Charlie Watts: drums
Ron Wood: rhythm and lead guitar
Darryl Jones: bass
Lenny Castro: percussion
Unidentified musician: organ

Recorded
La Fourchette Home Studio, Pocé-sur-Cisse, France: November–December 2004, March–April 2005
Henson Recording Studios, Hollywood: June 6–28, 2005

Technical Team
Producers: Don Was, the Glimmer Twins
Sound engineer: Krish Sharma
Assistant sound engineer: Dean Nelson
Mixing (Henson Recording Studios): Krish Sharma
Assistant sound engineer (Henson Recording Studios): Germán Villacorta

Michael Hutchence, the singer of INXS, whose hit "Need You Tonight" bears a curious resemblance to the riff played by Ron.

Genesis

"Look What the Cat Dragged In" is the reproach used by the narrator of this song to his girlfriend, who evidently has a strong inclination toward independence. We are told that she likes *to go out drinking*, and loves *to have a good time* . . . The spurned lover then launches into a litany of criticisms of his partner. Her *hair's all over the place* and her *breath's got a horrible taste* after she has spent the weekend partying. He is alone in the morning reading the paper about what was happening *in Syria and Lebanon.* Mick Jagger seems to be venting a great deal of bitterness here. Unless it is simply an example of his irony: the woman out having a good time while the man stays at home, which would perhaps be something out of the ordinary in the world of the Stones . . .

Production

"Look What the Cat Dragged In" is halfway between dance and rock. It is probably Ronnie who attacks the intro with an initial, cantankerous riff strongly inspired by the 1987 INXS hit "Need You Tonight." Even the beat is similar, though more spirited in the hands of the Stones. This does not detract in the slightest from the quality of the song, which is an absolute rocket. The second riff (0:06), which introduces the verse melody, possesses an effective oriental color. Mick is on rhythm, and so too is Keith, who gives the impression of crouching in the shadows in order to come to Mick's assistance when his guitar sound needs bolstering. It is Woody, however, who blows the track apart with his dazzling playing, and his two solos (2:34 and 3:07) are both outstanding. Could *A Bigger Bang* be said to mark a rebirth of the ex-Face? Charlie also seems to be on an adrenaline drip, such is the power and fury with which he smacks his drums. He is apparently supported on bass by both Mick and Darryl. This is a strange configuration, and it is very difficult to work out who plays what. Lenny Castro is back on percussion (congas and tambourine) and Sir Mick Jagger excels with a supercharged vocal performance, doubling his voice and harmonizing with himself in the backing vocals. It is worth pointing out that there is also an organ part (0:31) that is not credited in the liner notes (0:31).

DRIVING TOO FAST

Mick Jagger / Keith Richards / 3:56

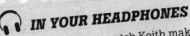

🎧 **IN YOUR HEADPHONES**

It is rare to be able to catch Keith making a timing error, but this is the case at 0:45, where he seems to be in too much of a hurry.

Musicians
Mick Jagger: vocals, rhythm guitar, maracas
Keith Richards: rhythm guitar
Charlie Watts: drums
Ron Wood: slide guitar
Darryl Jones: bass
Chuck Leavell: piano

Recorded
La Fourchette Home Studio, Pocé-sur-Cisse, France:
November–December 2004, March–April 2005
Ocean Way Recording Studios, Hollywood: June 6–28, 2005

Technical Team
Producers: Don Was, the Glimmer Twins
Sound engineer: Krish Sharma
Assistant sound engineer: Dean Nelson
Mixing (Ocean Way Recording Studios): Jack Joseph Puig

Genesis

A car is being driven at breakneck speed while the elements rage all around. The occupants, a couple, are risking a fatal accident at any moment. Rain lashes the windshield, the headlights cannot *pierce through the night* . . . there is a sense of doom about the situation. *Driving too fast/Hang on to the wheel/I think you're gonna crash*: the words are unambiguous. Going beyond the tale of an impending accident, however, it is possible to sense another message when Jagger sings: *Too many roads lead to nowhere*. Can this be interpreted as an admission of the impasse the couple has strayed into, an acknowledgment that the relationship has reached the point of no return? With the apparently inevitable accident as the breakup? "Driving Too Fast" is a rock number that does not add a great deal to the Stones' catalog, other, perhaps, than the chaotic rhythm that makes us feel that an accident could occur on Keith Richards's very next chord. One thing is for certain: the Stones have never performed "Driving Too Fast" live.

Production

It could perhaps be claimed that *A Bigger Bang* commits the sin of having too many songs, that it might have been advisable to cut the track listing down. "Driving Too Fast" is a good rock track, but by this stage of the disc, the formula seems to have grown a little repetitive. Charlie once again launches into a vigorous tempo. Mick and Keith play the main riff together, before splitting off into their respective rhythm parts. Mick then launches into his lyrics over a drum-dominated accompaniment, his impressive phrasing merely punctuated by the interjections of the two guitarists and Darryl Jones on bass. And finally we get to the refrain, where everyone joins in— Mick picking up the maracas and Chuck pounding the piano keyboard. This is all very well, but there is not a big enough element of surprise about the track, which is a shame. "Driving Too Fast" is good, but from the Stones, we have come to expect excellence. Ronnie gives another very fine demonstration of distorted slide (from 1:35), probably on his black Zemaitis, and plays a superb solo that deserves to be more prominent in the mix. In the coda (3:24), he also doubles the main riff on slide; it is a shame he doesn't do this right from the intro.

The Stones pianist Chuck Leavell shares a passion for blues rock with the band.

2005

INFAMY

Mick Jagger / Keith Richards / 3:47

Musicians
Keith Richards: vocals, acoustic guitar, rhythm guitar, lead guitar, keyboards, bass, percussion
Mick Jagger: acoustic guitar (?), rhythm guitar, backing vocals, harmonica, keyboards, percussion
Charlie Watts: drums
Blondie Chaplin: backing vocals
Recorded
La Fourchette Home Studio, Pocé-sur-Cisse, France: November–December 2004, March–April 2005
Henson Recording Studios, Hollywood: June 6–28, 2005
Technical Team
Producers: Don Was, the Glimmer Twins
Sound engineer: Krish Sharma
Assistant sound engineer: Dean Nelson
Mixing (Henson Recording Studios): Krish Sharma
Assistant sound engineer (Henson Recording Studios): Germán Villacorta

Genesis

A Bigger Bang concludes with a song in which the complicity between Mick Jagger and Keith Richards is absolute. *It's you that write the song baby/But it's me who's got to sing.* Furthermore they recorded it by themselves, with support only from Charlie Watts on drums and Blondie Chaplin on backing vocals. All in all, the lyrics are pretty enigmatic. *Things they are not what they seem/You're living in a nightmare, baby/But I mistook it for a dream*: is it the couple in the hot seat once again? Are relationships at home being seen as the source of infamy? One hardly dares think the song could be about the relationship between the Glimmer Twins!

Production

Other than the instrumental bridge, "Infamy" is based on a sequence of three main chords, and the track has a home studio ring to it from beginning to end. There is nothing pejorative about this; it simply implies a different way of working, with the use of sequencer programming and more of a do-it-yourself mentality. Charlie's drumming, which is almost certainly on a rhythm loop, contributes the necessary groove that would be virtually impossible to obtain from a programmed machine. Mick and Keith are apparently both playing tambourine, one of them entering later on in the track (3:11). The track opens with the sound of an organ, before Keith, on a loop, launches into a riff whose sound is marked by phasing or flanging. The structure of "Infamy" calls to mind some of the early work by the Cure, although admittedly somewhat less glacial. Acoustic and electric guitars plus other keyboards figure in the instrumentation, and Keith also plays bass, although not terribly effectively and without enough volume. Mick plays some good phrases on the harmonica, and sings backing vocals alongside Blondie. Keith, meanwhile, is on lead vocals and gives a good performance, his timbre on the hoarse side—as is only proper. But what are we to make of this last track? The Glimmer Twins are now able to take care of virtually all the instrumental parts themselves, we discover. But is this really the Rolling Stones?

"Infamy," a track that reflects the deep bond between Mick and Keith.

SIDE A
2010

PLUNDERED MY SOUL

Mick Jagger / Keith Richards / 3:59

SINGLE
Plundered My Soul / All Down the Line
RELEASE DATE
United Kingdom: April 17, 2010
RECORD NUMBER: UNIVERSAL MUSIC 273 547-7

<u>Musicians</u>
Mick Jagger: vocals, acoustic guitar (?), tambourine
Keith Richards: rhythm guitar
Mick Taylor: lead guitar
Bill Wyman: bass
Charlie Watts: drums
Nicky Hopkins: piano, organ (?)
Bobby Keys: saxophone
Lisa Fischer, Cindy Mizelle: backing vocals
<u>Recorded</u>
Rolling Stones Mobile Studio, Nellcôte,
France: June 7–October 1971
One East Studio, New York City: Autumn 2009
Henson Recording Studios / The Village Recorder /
Mix This!, Los Angeles: Autumn 2009
Unidentified London studio: Autumn 2009
<u>Technical Team</u>
Producers: Jimmy Miller, Don Was, the Glimmer Twins
Sound engineer: Glyn Johns
Additional recording and mixing: Krish Sharma
Mixing: Bob Clearmountain

Genesis

Universal's rerelease of *Exile on Main St.*, remastered and in new packaging, was accompanied by a number of supplementary recordings. The producer Don Was and the Stones unearthed what would become "Plundered My Soul" in a vast warehouse where dozens of tapes recorded over the years were stored. This particular song dates back to the *Exile on Main St.* sessions held in the basement at Nellcôte during the torrid summer of 1971. What they found was the backing tape containing rhythm guitars, bass, drums, and piano. The song now needed to be reworked and, of course, words had to be added.

Mick Jagger set to work straightaway. "Plundered My Soul" is a story of resentment. An ex-lover admits to being a bad loser because the woman he loved stole his heart. He adds: *I thought you wanted my money, but you plundered my soul.* A song of wounded love, "Plundered My Soul" was released as a limited-edition single on April 17, 2010 (with "All Down the Line" as the B-side), accompanied by a video made by the Swede Jonas Odell ("Make Me Smile [Come Up and See Me]" by Erasure, "Take Me Out" by Franz Ferdinand). This was the first single by the Stones since "Biggest Mistake" four years earlier (with the exception of the digital reissues of "Paint It Black," "She's a Rainbow," "Sympathy for the Devil," and "Wild Horses"). "Plundered My Soul" performed modestly in the United Kingdom (number 200) and the United States (number 42 on *Billboard's* Rock Songs Airplay), but climbed to an unexpected fifteenth place in France.

The Stones recording *Exile on Main St.* in an improvised studio in the Nellcôte basement.

Production

Mick Jagger began to work on the base track, consisting of Keith Richards's rhythm guitar, Bill Wyman's bass, Charlie Watts's drums, and Nicky Hopkins's piano, and called upon Mick Taylor for help. "But this particular song didn't have a vocal on it and it didn't have any lead guitar," explains Taylor. "It just had Keith Richards, Bill Wyman and Charlie Watts playing on it. So he [Jagger] asked me to step into the studio one afternoon, and I did some guitar in about three or four passes. I thought it turned out well."   Listening to the track, one cannot help but think that the idea of resuscitating a nugget from Villa Nellcôte may not have been such a good idea after all. The first issue Don Was came up against was the difference in timbre between Mick Jagger's voice as it was in 1971 and as it was in 2010. What could be done to soften the contrast? There is no miracle solution: the voice of the Stones singer has matured and the difference is obvious. The same goes for Mick Taylor's lead guitar. The results are, on the whole, satisfactory—the listener is able to rediscover the guitarist's touch and lyricism, which made such a mark on the band's recordings from that

period, but to try to recapture the same exact spirit and sound that he had in that sweltering basement in the South of France would be futile. It was Keith who took the most sensible view on the production approach: "You don't have to make it sound like 'Exile'. It IS 'Exile,'"   he would comment to Don Was.

From the very first chords, Keith's distorted rhythm guitar, Charlie's drumming, Bill's bass, and the piano playing of the late Nick Hopkins bring back that special atmosphere of the early seventies. As soon as Mick Taylor comes in on lead, however, we immediately feel that we are in a different room and period. The same applies to Mick Jagger. The problem lies not so much with his voice, as perhaps with Bob Clearmountain's mix, which has buried his vocal in keeping with the custom of the day—but a little too deeply. The way it comes across is not really satisfactory. And despite Bobby Keys's sax, an acoustic guitar probably added by Mick Jagger, and superb backing vocals from Lisa Fischer and Cindy Mizelle, "Plundered My Soul" lacks a certain something. The fact of having been completed and mixed in 1971 perhaps?

NO SPARE PARTS

Mick Jagger / Keith Richards / 4:31

SINGLE
No Spare Parts / Before They Make Me Run
RELEASE DATE
United Kingdom: November 13, 2011
RECORD NUMBER: ROLLING STONES RECORDS A&M 278 806-8

Musicians
Mick Jagger: vocals, electric piano, acoustic guitar, tambourine
Keith Richards: piano
Ron Wood: rhythm guitar, slide guitar (?), pedal steel guitar
Bill Wyman: bass
Charlie Watts: drums
Recorded
EMI Pathé Marconi Studios, Boulogne-Billancourt, France: mid-January–March 2, 1978
La Fourchette Home Studio, Pocé-sur-Cisse, France: August 2011
Electric Lady Studios, New York City: August–September 2011
Mix This!, Los Angeles: August–September 2011
Technical Team
Producers: the Glimmer Twins, Chris Kimsey, Don Was
Sound engineers: Chris Kimsey, Krish Sharma, Matt Clifford
Assistant sound engineers: Barry Sage, Ben King, Phil Joly
Mixing: Bob Clearmountain

Genesis

"No Spare Parts" is one of the twelve bonus tracks that accompanied the release of the two-CD deluxe edition of *Some Girls* in November 2011. It is a song by Mick Jagger. "The idea for the song began at the *Some Girls* sessions," he explains, "but I finished the idea and turned it into a complete piece. It's all about driving from San Antonio to Los Angeles to meet a woman, which I did once, so it's based on my own experience." A road song, then, in which the feelings of the narrator unfold as he crosses the country and finds himself confronted by mechanical problems.

"No Spare Parts" is also a song about solitude sublimated by the big open spaces of the United States . . . It is in the spirit of country and western, a genre the Glimmer Twins had appreciated for many years and to whose pioneers they had paid regular homage, starting with "Country Honk" on *Let It Bleed*. This *Some Girls* bonus track was released as a single a year and a half after "Plundered My Soul," on November 13, 2011, to be exact (with "Before They Make Me Run" as the B-side), and reached number 2 on the *Billboard* Hot Singles Sales in the United States.

Production

Starting in the intro, it seems that Ron Wood plays a number of phrases with the bottleneck on his guitar, rather than on pedal steel, as indicated in the credits. He does use this instrument later on the track, however, from 1:30 on. Mick is on acoustic guitar and electric piano, whose sonority calls to mind "Fool to Cry" on *Black and Blue* (1976). By contrast, Keith chooses to play a discreet accompaniment on acoustic

Charlie Watts and Ron Wood publicizing the reissue of *Some Girls* in autumn 2011.

FOR STONES ADDICTS

The video of "No Spare Parts" was shot by Mat Whitecross, the director of *Spike Island* (2012) and a number of videos for Coldplay ("Christmas Lights," "Every Teardrop Is a Waterfall," "Charlie Brown").

piano that he does not, however, bring in until 2:58. He is therefore replaced by Ronnie, who plays a rhythm part colored by a strong tremolo (0:40). Charlie lays down a simple but effective beat, supported by Bill, who plays his bass with a Zen attitude that is entirely in keeping with the mood of the song. Mick Jagger, as a true country fan, sings with conviction, and it is not surprising that the track met with such favor in the United States. "No Spare Parts" is a good song, but at the same time it is not difficult to see why the Stones did not include it on *Some Girls*.

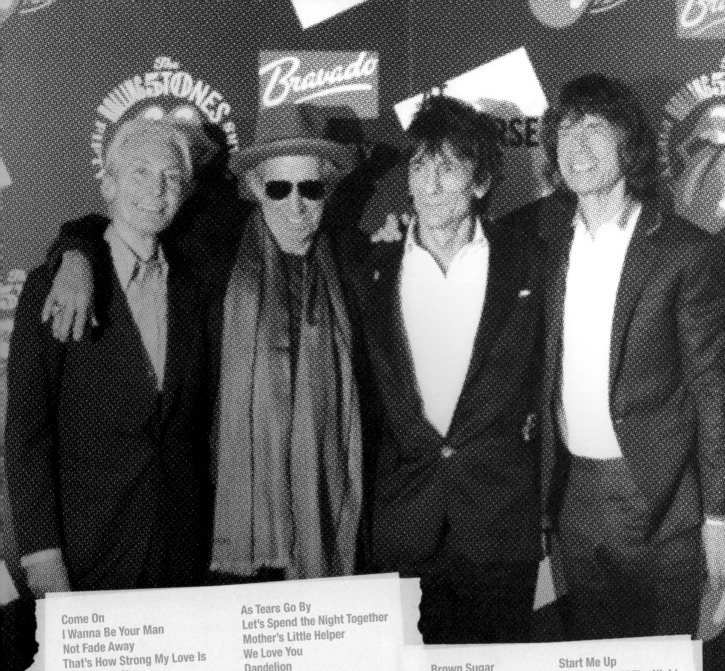

Come On
I Wanna Be Your Man
Not Fade Away
That's How Strong My Love Is
It's All Over Now
Little Red Rooster
The Last Time
(I Can't Get No) Satisfaction
Heart Of Stone
Get Off Of My Cloud
She Said Yeah
I'm Free
Play With Fire
Time Is On My Side
19th Nervous Breakdown
Paint It Black
Have You Seen Your Mother, Baby,
   Standing In The Shadow ?
She's A Rainbow
Under My Thumb
Out Of Time

As Tears Go By
Let's Spend the Night Together
Mother's Little Helper
We Love You
Dandelion
Lady Jane
Flight 505
2000 Light Years From Home
Ruby Tuesday
Jumpin' Jack Flash
Sympathy For The Devil
Child Of The Moon
Salt Of The Earth
Honky Tonk Women
Midnight Rambler
Gimmie Shelter
You Got The Silver
You Can't Always Get
   What You Want
Street Fighting Man
Wild Horses

Brown Sugar
Bitch
Tumbling Dice
Rocks Off
Happy
Doo Doo Doo Doo Doo
   (Heartbreaker)
Angie
It's Only Rock 'N' Roll
Dance Little Sister
Fool To Cry
Respectable
Miss You
Shattered
Far Away Eyes
Beast Of Burden
Emotional Rescue
Dance Pt. 1
She's So Cold
Waiting On A Friend
Neighbours

Start Me Up
Undercover Of The Night
She Was Hot
Harlem Shuffle
Mixed Emotions
Highwire
Almost Hear You Sigh
You Got Me Rocking
Love Is Strong
I Go Wild
Like A Rolling Stone
Anybody Seen My Baby?
Saint Of Me
Don't Stop
Rough Justice
Rain Fall Down
Streets Of Love
Plundered My Soul
Doom and Gloom *
One More Shot *

* Only the released songs will be
discussed in this chapter.

ALBUM

<u>**RELEASE DATE**</u>

United Kingdom: November 12, 2012

Label: Interscope Records; Polydor; Universal Music; ABKCO

RECORD NUMBERS: INTERSCOPE RECORDS 3711006; POLYDOR 3711006; UNIVERSAL MUSIC 3711006; ABKCO RECORDS 3711006

Number 3, on the charts for 38 weeks

ALBUM

<u>**RELEASE DATE**</u>

United Kingdom: November 12, 2012

Mick Jagger onstage at London's 02
on November 29, 2012, to celebrate
fifty years of the Rolling Stones.

GRRR!
THE DEFINITIVE COMPILATION?

The Album

In 2012, the Rolling Stones celebrated their fiftieth anniversary. Who can top that? The event was commemorated with the issue on November 12 (November 13 in North America), of a box set retracing the extraordinary career of the London quintet. The compilation includes two songs recorded at Studio Guillaume Tell in Suresnes in the suburbs of Paris, in August 2012: "Doom and Gloom" and "One More Shot." These were the same studios where the four new tracks for *Forty Licks* ("Don't Stop," "Keys to Your Love," "Stealing My Heart," and "Losing My Touch") had been recorded exactly ten years before, between May and June 2002. Named *GRRR!*, this new compilation was available in various editions:

- A set of four CDs with a bonus CD comprising five demos recorded at the IBC Studios in 1963 ("Diddley Daddy," "Road Runner," "Bright Lights Big City," "Honey What's Wrong" [real title: "Baby, What's Wrong"], and "I Want to Be Loved"), a vinyl EP containing four songs recorded during a BBC session in 1964 ("Route 66," "Cops and Robbers," "You Better Move On," and "Mona [I Need You Baby])," plus a book, a poster, and a set of postcards.
- A set of three CDs with a twelve-page booklet. Fifty songs.
- A set of three CDs with a thirty-six-page book and five postcards. Fifty songs.
- A set of five vinyl discs. Fifty songs.
- A Blu-ray audio disc with a twelve-page booklet (Europe and Mexico only). Fifty songs.

This anniversary compilation was a success all over the world. It made number 1 in Germany, Austria, and Croatia; number 3 in the United Kingdom, Ireland, and Greece; number 4 in Belgium and the Netherlands; and number 5 in France. In the United States it only progressed as far as number 129.

The Album Cover

For the cover of the new CD, the Stones called upon the services of Walton Ford, an artist from the state of New York who was profoundly influenced by the American naturalist and painter John James Audubon. Ford is also directly involved in the environmental protection movement. He chose to depict the head of a gorilla, a sort of King Kong for the twenty-first century, with a voluptuous red mouth and protruding tongue. A new and original way of recontextualizing the famous logo by John Pasche, by agreement with the Stones, of course.

DOOM AND GLOOM

Mick Jagger / Keith Richards / 4:07

Musicians
Mick Jagger: vocals, rhythm guitar, maracas, hand claps
Keith Richards: rhythm guitar
Charlie Watts: drums
Ron Wood: rhythm and lead guitar
Darryl Jones: bass
Chuck Leavell: organ
Jeff Bhasker: synthesizers
Emile Haynie: drum programming
Recorded
Studio Guillaume Tell, Suresnes: August 20–23, 2012
Technical Team
Producers: Don Was, the Glimmer Twins, Jeff Bhasker
Co-producer: Emile Haynie
Sound engineer: Krish Sharma

Has Mick, then, got nothing more to declare?

Genesis

For the studio reunion of Mick, Keith, Charlie, and Ronnie, their first for seven years (since *A Bigger Bang*), the Glimmer Twins appear not to have been in the best of spirits. Or, more accurately, it was Mick Jagger who was out of sorts, for after all he was the main songwriter (words and music) behind "Doom and Gloom." The scenario is bleak, if not downright terrifying. The Stones singer has had a bad dream in which he is at the controls of an airplane, whose passengers are drunk and insane. The plane crashes in a Louisiana swamp and is attacked by a horde of zombies. *All I hear is doom and gloom*, sings Mick Jagger. In this song, another example of an apocalyptic tableau in a Stones number, the only glimmer of hope is the face of a beautiful stranger glimpsed in the night . . . Producer Jeff Bhasker recalls the day when Mick wrote the words to the song: "Watching Mick come up with the lyrics to that song, I thought he just killed it; the lines are so good. There's social references, it's ballsy, he's talking about zombies and planes crashing. It's crazy."

"Doom and Gloom" was the first original composition to be released by the Stones (on October 11, 2012, one month before the compilation *GRRR!*) since "Biggest Mistake" in August 2006. It peaked at number 61 in the United Kingdom and at number 30 on the *Billboard* Rock Songs chart.

Production

"So we banged out a couple of tracks in the autumn in Paris, 'Doom and Gloom' and 'One More Shot,'" explains Keith Richards in an interview with Mark Ellen. "I don't think the Stones have ever cut a track so fast. It was like three takes and—boom ! We were like looking at each other and going, 'Got anything else?' It was amazingly quick." Carried by a typical Rolling Stones riff, created by Mick Jagger rather than Keith Richards, this song is an adrenaline-fired rock number, with Jagger on the verge of apoplexy but as outstanding as ever. Keith Richards plays a reasonably discreet accompaniment, Ron Wood delivers a number of solo phrases, Charlie Watts lays down a beat that combines with Emile Haynie's drum programming, Darryl Jones's bass lurks in the depths, Chuck Leavell is on the Hammond, and Jeff Bhasker's synthesizers add the kind of contemporary touch beloved of rappers. The return of the Stones is an out-and-out triumph!

2012

ONE MORE SHOT

Mick Jagger / Keith Richards / 3:10

Musicians
Mick Jagger: vocals
Keith Richards: rhythm guitar, backing vocals
Charlie Watts: drums
Ron Wood: rhythm and lead guitar
Darryl Jones: bass
Chuck Leavell: piano, organ
Recorded
Studio Guillaume Tell, Suresnes: August 20–23, 2012
Technical Team
Producers: Don Was, the Glimmer Twins, Jeff Bhasker
Co-producer: Emile Haynie
Sound engineer: Krish Sharma (?)

The riff master's long-suffering fingers, 2012.
Still serving rock 'n' roll.

Genesis

Keith Richards recorded a demo of "One More Shot" in New York City in 2011, not with a future solo number in mind, but in hopes of including it in the program of future reunions with Mick, Charlie, and Ronnie. He told *Q* magazine: "I thought, if we get the Stones back in the studio, this is made for Mick. He and I have a very tight partnership. One that's had to survive several knocks, but that strengthens the bond, in a way."

Give me one more shot/Baby it's all I got: an ex-lover is ready to do whatever it takes to win back the woman he loves. There is no particular subliminal message in "One More Shot" other than the one the Glimmer Twins had been conveying since the sixties: that rock 'n' roll and the Stones are one and the same. "One More Shot" is a typical Keith Richards riff in the tradition of "Street Fighting Man" (while the melody is akin to that of "Mixed Emotions").

Production

Don Was would report that everyone in the studio was wearing a smile once "One More Shot" was in the can. And it has to be said that the track is a very lively rock number with a vitality that, at the very least, is reassuring with regard to the band's state of health. The intro takes the form of a Keith riff delivered with that special touch and sound that are undeniably his. He may be using the same formula over and over again, but it is a formula that still works. Ronnie answers him with a very good phrase redolent of the sixties (and specifically the Byrds), clear-toned and medium power (0:08). Darryl Jones plays a very good bass line in the spirit of Bill Wyman, before delving into a more personal style. Ronnie takes a solo at 1:58, presumably slide. Despite the passing years, Charlie has changed nothing about the way he approaches a rock track. He is imperturbable, combining a special swing and a highly individual touch that make him one of the best rock drummers around. On keyboards, Chuck Leavell divides his attention between a piano and a Hammond B-3. Mick Jagger does a good job on lead vocal, and yet "One More Shot" leaves the listener with the sense of having heard it (too many times) before. Moreover, the *na na na*s in the backing vocals are not exactly in the best of taste, hinting at a certain complacency. Shame.

GLOSSARY

Appalachian music: see *Hillbilly*.

Blues shouter: a term applied to vocalists with powerful voices, mainly from Kansas City, Missouri, who would sing the blues at the head of big bands.

Bottleneck: a tube of glass (or metal) that guitarists place on one finger and then slide along the strings to produce a metallic sound. This style of playing originated with the pioneers of the blues, who indeed used the neck of a glass bottle. The bottleneck is generally used in *open tuning*, in other words when the instrument's six open strings form a chord (G or D, for example).

Break: an instrumental interlude that interrupts the development of a song. A hiatus, in other words, that eventually reintroduces the main musical material.

Bridge: a musical passage connecting two parts of a song. The bridge generally links the verse to the refrain.

British blues boom: a movement that developed in England in the mid-sixties, led by the Rolling Stones and other British rock groups strongly influenced by their African-American elders, such as Muddy Waters and Howlin' Wolf.

Chicago blues: there are several different types of Chicago blues. Ele   ctric Chicago blues, an amplified version of Delta blues, is embodied mainly by the artists of Chess Records, from Willie Dixon to Howlin' Wolf via Muddy Waters and Sonny Boy Williamson II.

Coda: this Italian term denotes an additional section, of varying length, that concludes a song or track.

Compressor: an electronic circuit that serves to amplify low-volume sounds or, conversely, to reduce high-volume sounds during recording or mixing.

Cover: a recording or performance of a pre-existing song or track, usually in an arrangement that differs from the original version.

Cowbell: a percussion instrument used in popular music (such as rhythm 'n' blues) as well as in classical music (Gustav Mahler, Richard Strauss) and avant-garde music (Karlheinz Stockhausen, Olivier Messiaen) in the European tradition.

Delta blues: a form of blues played in the Mississippi Delta from Memphis to the Yazoo River. Performed with the bottleneck, its most prominent proponents include Charley Patton, Robert Johnson, Bukka White, Skip James, and Big Joe Williams.

Effects pedal: a small electronic device whereby the sound of an instrument is subjected to a particular effect. Generally operated by foot, as in the case of the fuzz box, there are also wah-wah, distortion, chorus, delay, and flanger pedals, among others.

Fade-in: the process of gradually increasing the sound (generally at the beginning of a song).

Fade-out: the process of gradually reducing the sound (generally at the end of a song).

Finger-picking: a guitar technique, used mainly in folk music and the blues, whereby certain chords are played with the fingers of the right hand (in the case of a right-handed musician), plucking the strings independently of one another (the opposite of *strumming*). This generally allows the performer to bring out the bass line and melody of the song.

Flanging: a sound effect obtained by supplementing the original signal with the same signal delayed by a few milliseconds.

FM Rock: eighties rock, characterized by the use of synthesizers and designed to be played on FM radio. In the United States, the expression *album-oriented rock* (AOR) is also used.

Fretless (bass): a (generally electric) bass guitar whose frets have been removed in order to approximate the sound of the upright bass. One of the masters of the fretless bass was Rick Danko of The Band.

Fuzz: a distorted sound effect obtained by saturating the sound signal, mainly by means of a foot-pedal known as the fuzz box. The Rolling Stones, along with the Beatles ("Think for Yourself") and Jimi Hendrix ("Purple Haze"), were pioneers of the fuzz box. This effect is used mainly on guitars.

Gimmick: a succession of notes whose purpose is to grab the listener's attention. This technique was developed by jazz musicians before making the logical progression into rock music.

Groove: the moment when musicians, in total communion with one another, imbue a song or track with its own special atmosphere, an alchemical process that takes in both rhythm and harmony and is felt by all the musicians as one.

Hillbilly: a synonym of *yokel*. In music, the term denotes the popular music that developed among the white communities of the Appalachians, based (in the main) on Celtic ballads. The terms *Appalachian* and *old time* music are also used.

Honky-tonk: a type of bar in the United States that gave rise to a style of music in the country and western tradition. An important aspect of this music is a form of piano playing inspired by both ragtime and boogie-woogie.

Jam: a generally informal and improvised gathering of musicians motivated as a rule by the mere pleasure of playing together.

Kazoo: a device with a membrane that modifies the sound of the voice. Originally from Africa, it was adopted by blues, folk, and subsequently rock musicians.

Laid back: a relaxed style of guitar-playing raised to an art by J. J. Cale and later Mark Knopfler.

Larsen: a physical phenomenon that occurs when an amplified output (the speakers of an amp, for example) is located too close to an input device (especially the pickup of an electric guitar or a singer's mic). This results in a hissing noise or a strong buzz. Since the sixties, this feedback effect has been much used by rock guitarists. The best example can be heard in the guitar intro to the Beatles' "I Feel

Fine," which is often cited as the very first Larsen effect recorded on disc.

Lead: a term that denotes the principal voice or instrument on a song or track (*lead* vocal or *lead* guitar, for example).

Leslie speaker: a cabinet housing a rotating loudspeaker, typically used with Hammond organs. The swirling acoustic effect can be adjusted as required.

Lick: a short musical phrase within a well-defined musical style (blues, rock, country, jazz, etc.), played to complement or accompany the arrangement and/or melodic line of a song.

Low-down: in music, this term is used to describe a rural and authentic form of blues, unadulterated by any outside influence.

Mute: a technique to turn off the sound on a channel strip. Alternatively, the term is used to mean deadening a string on a guitar.

Nashville sound: a branch of country and western music that developed in the Tennessee city in the fifties, characterized by the use of string sections and backing vocalists, and representing a clear break with authentic hillbilly.

Old time music: see *Hillbilly*.

Open tuning: an alternative method of tuning a guitar to obtain a chord made up generally of the six open strings. This technique (for example, open G, D, and A tunings) is commonly used in the blues.

Overdubbing/overdub: a procedure by means of which additional sounds (for example, a guitar part or a second voice) are added to a recording. (See also *Rerecording*.)

Palm mute: a guitar technique that involves stopping the strings with the right hand (in the case of right-handed guitarists), while simultaneously playing the notes with a pick.

Pattern: a sequence that recurs throughout a track and that can be repeated indefinitely to form a loop.

Phasing: an electronic effect that subjects the audio signal to various filters and oscillators, allowing a more rich and powerful sound to be obtained, especially on distorted guitars.

Playback: the partially or fully formed instrumental part of a song that provides the singer or instrumentalist with an adequate musical basis over which to record his or her performance.

Power chord: this type of guitar chord is made up of two notes, the tonic and the fifth, and is highly effective in rock music, above all when combined with distortion.

Premix: a rough mix or stage in the recording process that consists in mixing the various tracks of a multitrack tape recorder to gain an idea of the progress made so far.

Rerecording: a technique for recording one or more tracks while listening to a previously recorded track or tracks.

Reverb: an effect created in the studio, either electronically or using a natural echo chamber, in order to provide certain sounds (particularly voices) with a sense of space and acoustic relief during the recording or mixing process.

Riff: a riff is a short phrase that recurs regularly throughout a song or track.

Rimshot: a drumming technique that involves striking the rim and head of the snare drum (or tom) at the same time. This produces an accented, attacking sound.

Roadhouse: a drinking establishment in the rural United States where blues, hillbilly, and honky-tonk are played.

Roots: this term, used as both a noun and an adjective, denotes a return to the origins of popular music, from blues to Appalachian music.

Score: a notated musical arrangement.

Shuffle: a musical style that originated in Jamaica in the fifties, a kind of rhythm 'n'

blues that can be seen as a forerunner of ska. Also, a slow rhythm practiced by slaves.

Slap-back echo: an echo typically employed by the pioneers of rock 'n' roll, such as Elvis Presley, Gene Vincent, and Buddy Holly.

Songster: heir to the oral tradition, the songster collected stories of various kinds and related them in the style of the work song, the ballad, the spiritual, and the blues. The term is used above all to describe the Texas bluesmen, such as Henry "Ragtime" Thomas and Leadbelly.

Songwriter: a term used in the United States to denote a single individual who writes both the words and the music of a song.

Strumming: a guitar technique that involves brushing the right hand (in the case of right-handed guitarists) across the strings, with or without a pick. This is one of the most widespread techniques employed on the instrument.

Sustain: the ability of an instrument to maintain a note over time. This is a property not least of electric guitars, on which it is frequently extended by various artificial means, such as distortion, sustainer pedals, etc.

Topical song: a song prompted by a politically or socially conscious movement and dealing with a specific event; for example, the Stones' "Dangerous Beauty," about the torture at Abu Ghraib Prison in Iraq.

Track listing: the list of songs on an album.

Walking bass: a style of bass guitar accompaniment (and left hand on the piano) that involves playing a single note on each beat of the bar. This style of playing was made their own by the boogie-woogie pianists in the honky-tonks of the southern United States during the early years of the twentieth century.

INDEX

The Rolling Stones' albums and songs that are subject to an analysis are in bold. Songs written by other composers are not in bold. The page numbers in bold refer to the analyses and portraits.

"100 Years Ago," 394, 398, **399**, 403
13th Floor Elevators (The), 76
"19th Nervous Breakdown," 140, 160-161, 166, 176, 178, 276, 648, 650, 692
"2000 Light Years from Home," 212, 217–219, 228, **234-235**, 282
"2000 Man," 217, **226**
"2120 South Michigan Avenue," 53, 56, **60**, 68

A Bigger Bang, 195, **664–685**, 694
Abner, Ewart, 32
Abramson, Herb, 97
AC/DC, 460, 496, 497, 537
Adams Jr., William James, 673
Adele, 606
Adler, Lou, 19, 193, 206
Adzak, Roy, 496
Aerosmith, 515, 606
Aftermath, 113, **134–159**, 370, 438, 449, 588, 604, 611, 661
"Ain't Too Proud to Beg," 416, 418, 422, **425**, 432, 481, 562
AIR Studios, 575–578, 580–590, 660, 662
Åkerlund, Jonas, 694
Aldon Music, 122
Alexander, Arthur, 48
Alexander, James W., 101, 109
Alexander, Larry, 530
Ali, Tariq, 266
"All About You," 492, 496, **508–509**, 550
"All Down the Line," 360, 364, 365, 368, 383, **389–390**, 393, 409, 453, 686
"All Sold Out," 184, **198**
"All the Way Down," 532, 534, 537, 538, **548**
Allen Klein and Company, 122
Allison, Gene, 41,
Allman Brothers Band, 107, 379, 537, 541
Allman, Gregg, 101
Almond, Johnny, 308
"Almost Hear You Sigh," 570, 572, 574, 575, **587**, 589, 658, 662, 690
"Already over Me," 628, 632, 633, **637**
Altman, Keith, 139
"Always Suffering," 628, 632, 633, **644**
Ammons, Albert, 13
Anderson, Jon,
Anderson, Lindsay, 18
Anderson, Wes, 112, 156
Andrew Oldham Orchestra (The), 28, 110, 443–445
Andrew Sisters (The), 84
"Andrew's Blues," 28–29, 438
Andrews, Pat, 8
"Angie," 230, 613, 648, 690, 692
Animals (The), 59
"Anybody Seen My Baby?," 628, 632, 633, **635**, 648
"Anyway You Look at It," 633, 642, 656, 658, **661**, 662
Applewhite, Marshall, 634
Arcade Fire, 228
Arlen, Harold, 236
Armbrister, Benji,
Arnold, Eddy, 116
Aronoff, Kenny, 637
"Around and Around," 10, 56, **62**, 68, 624
"As Tears Go By," 101, 110, 128, 130, **160–165**, 173, 188, 196, 210, 398, 692
Ashby, Hal, 534
Ashcroft, Richard, 111, 575
Asher, Jane, 164
Asher, Tony, 193
Atkins, Eileen, 278
Atlantic Studios, 466, 467, 476, 478, 480–485, 488, 490, 515–526, 528
Attar, Bachir, 588
Avory, Mick, 10
Axton, Estelle, 42
A&M Studios, Los Angeles 605–626

B-52s (The), 537
Babiuk, Andy, 209, 235
"Baby Break It Down," 605, **619**
Babyface, 632, 637
Baca, Max, 606, 616
Bach, Johann Sebastian, 210
Bacharach, Burt, 289
"Back of My Hand," 666, 669, **675**, 678
"Back Street Girl," 184, 188–189, **194**, 204, 206
"Back to Zero," 554, 557, 565, **566**, 587
Bad Company, 476
Badham, Mary, 635
Baez, Joan, 147, 164, 272
Baez, Margarita Mimi, 147
Bailey, David, 72, 94, 139, 316, 399
Baker, Ginger, 253, 260, 286
Bakshi, Ralph, 562
Baldry, Long John, 8, 369
Balin, Marty, 216, 332
Ball, Lucille, 474, 475
Ballard, Hank, 41
Band (The), 368, 401, 635
Banerji, Robi, 639, 647
Bangs, Lester, 334, 314
Barber, Chris, 8
Barber, Jim, 537, 544
Barclay, Eddie, 362
Barclay, Michael, 49, 183
Bardot, Brigitte, 474
Baring, James, 26
Barnett, Mary Angela, see Bowie, Angela
Barrett, Syd, 225, 460
Bart, Lionel, 162–163
Bartók, Béla, 229
Bateman, Robert, 58
Baudelaire, Charles, 256
Baumgartner, Mike, 606–613, 615–620, 622, 624, 626
Bayer, Samuel, 635
Beach Boys (The), 62, 85, 138–140, 151, 159, 186, 192–193, 199, 630, 633, 635, 637, 400, 401, 445
Beach, Sandy, see Loog Oldham, Andrew
Beadle, Bud, 286, 308, 309, 311
"Beast of Burden," 309, 470, 474, 476, **488–489**, 512, 512, 530, 531, 648, 656, 658, 690
Beatles (The), 11–12, 18–21, 26, 31, 39–40, 47, 49, 52, 79, 88, 92, 94, 96, 101–103, 109, 119, 123, 126–127, 214, 216–219, 222, 227, 229–231, 233, 236, 243–244, 252–254, 279
Beaton, Keith, 433
Beatty, Warren,
Beauport, Pierre (de), 576, 605, 620, 630, 633, 642, 644, 646
Beck, 606, 630
Beck, Jeff, 456, 458, 459, 496, 519, 561
Beckett, Barry, 336, 345
Beckwith, Bob, 9–10, 62
Bee Gees (The), 440, 460, 467, 472, 505
Beedle, Ashley, 673
Beer, Phil, 576, 583
"Before They Make Me Run," 470, 474, 476, **487**, 508, 586, 677, 688
Beggars Banquet, 13, 67, 136, 206, 228, 230, **246–273**, 284–287, 291, 302, 305, 314, 337, 352, 364, 398, 412, 433, 438, 452, 456, 502, 534, 549, 657, 622
Bell, Madeline, 286, 304, 306
Below, Fred, 31
Bennett, Doug, 401–414
Benson, George, 194, 576
Berkofsky, Michael, 316
Berline, Byron, 286, 292, 368
Berns, Bert, 76, 103
Berry, Chuck, 9–10, 14–16, 26, 30, 37–38, 46, 53, 60–62, 70, 72–73, 79, 84, 88, 92, 102, 104, 118, 138, 161, 164, 202, 210, 229–230, 269, 289, 314, 319, 350, 353, 358, 372, 414, 427, 431, 432, 441, 432, 441, 482, 485, 486, 499, 518, 540, 577, 581, 586, 621, 634, 679
Best, Pete, 88
Between the Buttons, 104, 136, 138, 178, **184–203**, 206, 216, 220, 230, 236, 250, 276, 438, 449, 661
Bhasker, Jeff, 694, 695
Bienstock, Freddy, 40
Big Bopper (The), 152
Big Brother & the Holding Company, 206, 390
"Biggest Mistake," 664, 666, 668, 669, **677**, 679, 686, 694
Billy Boy Arnold, 10
"Bitch," 330, 334, 337, 339, **349**, 350, 358, 362, 364, 438, 690
Björk, 596
Black and Blue, **454–469**, 502, 512, 514, 519, 543, 547, 653, 673, 688
Black Crowes (The), 669
Black Eyed Peas (The), 673
Black Grape, 638
Black Keys (The), 101
"Black Limousine," 510, 514, **521**
Black Sabbath, 28, 38, 287, 422
Black, Cilla, 18
Black, Ludella, 171
Blackwell, Chris, 260, 316, 399, 496
Blaine, Hal, 445
Blake, William, 162, 165
Blind Faith, 253, 260
"Blinded by Love," 570, 574, 575, **583**
"Blinded by Rainbows," 600, 604, 605, **618**
Block, Leslie, 214
Blondie, 193, 456, 565
Blood, Sweat & Tears, 305
Bloomfield, Mike, 200
Blue Magic, 423, 433
Blue Öyster Cult, 155, 537
"Blue Turns to Grey," 94, 128, 130, **133**, 324
Blue Wave Studios, 610,617,620
Blues Brothers (The), 76
Blues By Six, 9–10
Blues Incorporated, 8–10, 181
Blues Project, 305
Bob & Earl, 554
Bob Marley and the Wailers, 399
Bobby Blue Band, 106
Bolan, Marc, 422
Bon Jovi, 558, 606
Bongiovi, Barry, 530
Bonham, John, 54, 229, 620
Bono, Sonny, 96, 144
Booker T. & The M.G.'s, 22–23, 182
Boss Hog, 175
Bosworth, Dan, 606–621, 622, 624, 626, 634–640, 642–646
Botnick, Bruce, 287, 288, 290, 292, 294, 295, 296, 298, 300, 302, 304
Boulgakov, Mikhaïl, 165, 256
Bourguignon, Serge, 141
Bowie, Angela, 407
Bowie, David, 230, 238, 254, 337, 343, 407, 426, 427, 460, 467, 479, 497, 557, 562, 565, 566
Boyd, Reggie, 102
Bradbury, Ray, 234
Bradford, Geoff, 9–10
Bradford, Janie, 47
Brady, Paul, 606
Bragg, Billy, 196
"Brand New Car," 600, 604, 605, **615**
Branson, Richard, 287
Brauer, Michael H., 660, 662, 575–577, 580–584, 586, 587, 589, 590, 599
"Break the Spell," 570, 572, 575, 587, **589**
Breton, Michèle, 289, 321
Bridges to Babylon, 465, **628–647**, 653, 661, 668, 669, 672, 676
British Invasion, 26, 30, 40, 52, 92, 96
Broadwater, Eleanor, 89
Brohard, Andy, 669–670
Broonzy, Big Bill, 441, 556
"Brown Sugar," 255, 309, 310, 330, 332, 336, **339–341**, 342, 344, 345, 349, 358, 362, 364, 399, 408, 438, 453, 594, 596, 648, 650, 658, 679, 690,
Brown, Buster, 108
Brown, Chuck, 530
Brown, David, 530
Brown, Dennis, 537
Brown, James, 62, 94, 537, 401, 456, 544, 599, 617
Brown, Ollie E., 456, 458, 460, 461, 462, 463, 466, 469, 519, 523
Brown, Phill, 254, 256, 260, 262–266, 268–269, 271–272, 352
Brown, Rick, 230
Brown, Ruth, 41
Brown, Walter, 61
Browne, Tara, 190, 259
Brownjohn, Robert, 285
Bruce, Jack, 8, 422, 456
Buckingham, Lindsey, 196
Buckmaster, Paul, 337, 342, 343, 356, 357
Buddy Holly & The Crickets, 50, 155
Bunyan, Vashti, 442
Burke, Solomon, 58, 76–77, 97, 103, 171, 468, 677
Burroughs, William S., 362, 375, 538
Burton, James, 89
Bush, Kate, 576
Butler, Arthur, 78
Butler, Jerry, 182
Butterworth, Michael, 576, 578
"Bye Bye Johnny," 28, 44, 46
Byrds (The), 73, 101, 109, 133, 186, 216, 234, 344, 695

Cage, John, 87, 235
Calder, Tony, 164
Cale, J.-J., 497, 626
Cammell, Donald, 288, 318, 320, 321
Campbell, David, 606, 613
"Can I Get a Witness," 24, 28–29, 34, **40**, 98, 565
"Can You Hear the Music," 394, **398**, 399, **412**
"Can't Be Seen," 570, 574, 575, 586, 594, 596
"Can't You Hear Me Knocking," 330, 334, 336, **346–347**
Canned Heat, 456, 461
Cannon, Freddy, 340
Cantrell, Scott, 318, 508, 509
Capaldi, Jim, 260, 321
Capital Center, 530
Capitol, 79
Capote, Truman, 396
Captain Beefheart & His Magic Band, 199
Carabello, Mike, 515, 516, 517, 519, 528, 529
Cardiff, Jack, 164–165
Carmichael, Hoagy, 678
"Carol," 24, 28, **37**, 102, 312, 314
Carr, Leroy, 290
Carr, Roy, 48, 189
Carter, Jimmy, 472, 476
Cash, Johnny, 337, 354, 606, 612
"Casino Boogie," 360, 364, 368, **375**
Castle, Ryan, 669, 670
Castro, Lenny, 606, 613, 615, 617, 618, 669, 670, 683
Cattini, Clem, 106
Chabrol, Claude, 18
Chaplin, Blondie, 634–640, 642, 644–647, 653, 669, 676, 685
Chapman, Mark David, 514
Chapman, Tony, 9–10
Charles, Ray, 40, 102, 116, 263, 286, 289, 576
Chaucer, Geoffrey, 146–147
Cheap Trick, 263
Checker, Chubby, 97
Chenail, Bill, 240
Cheney, Dick, 682
Cherry Keys (The), 97
"Cherry Oh Baby," 454, 456, 459, **464**, 543
Chess, Leonard, 60, 334
Chess, Marshall, 334, 337, 358, 362, 368, 399, 400, 408
Chess Studios, 52, 58–62, 80, 82, 84, 86, 94, 97, 99, 108, 132
Chi-Lites (The), 647
"Child of the Moon," 220, 248, 260, 274, **278–279**, 690
Childish, Billy, 228
Chkiantz, George, 243, 274, 278, 287, 288, 290, 292, 294, 298, 300, 302, 304, 422, 425, 424, 426, 428, 429, 431, 432–435
CHOPS, 537, 544, 546
"Citadel," 212, 217, 220, **223**
Clapton, Eric, 173, 260, 286, 311, 319, 341, 362, 401, 423, 458, 463, 467, 521, 576, 596, 602, 630, 636, 669
Clark, Dick, 319
Clark, Gene, 379
Clarke, Allan, 28–29, 35
Clarke, Kenny, 259
Clarke, Simon, 576
Clarke, Stanley, 499
Clash (The), 159, 383, 472, 502, 682
"Claudine," 470, 476
Claunch, Quinton, 99
Clayton, Merry, 286, 288, 289
Clearmountain, Bob, 479, 514, 515–526, 528, 530, 550, 551, 605, 606, 607, 613, 614, 622, 623, 637, 652–655, 686, 687, 688
Clempson, David "Clem," 456
Cliff, Jimmy, 337, 399, 558, 564, 574
Clifford, Clinton, 639
Clifford, Matt, 688, 574–576, 580, 582–590, 669, 673, 674
Cliftons (The), 10
Coasters (The), 20, 49, 78, 581
Cocker, Joe, 144, 231, 311, 401, 630, 640
Cohen, Bobby, 537, 538, 540–544, 546, 547, 548, 549
Cohen, Leonard, 497
Cole, Lloyd, 558
Cole, Nat King, 30
Cole, Natalie, 30
Collette, Dan, 558, 566
Collins, Judy, 272
Collins, Mel, 476, 478, 479, 546, 550, 551
Collins, Phil, 640, 460
"Come On," **14–16**, 20–21, 29–30, 37, 46, 486, 690
"Coming Down Again," 394, 398, 399, **404**, 406
Compass Point Studios, 496, 507, 508, 514, 520, 537–550
"Complicated," 184, 188, **201**
"Confessin' the Blues," 56, 61, 68, 324
"Congratulations," **64–65**, 68, 83, 441
"Connection," 184, 188, **195**
"Continental Drift," 570, 572, 574–576, **588**, 594, 596, 599
Cooder, Ry, 253, 255, 268, 286, 290, 291, 310, 320–322, 352, 353, 440, 451, 456, 606
"Cook Cook Blues," 584, **592–593**
Cooke, Sam, 52, 66, 73, 100–101, 122, 269, 633
"Cool, Calm and Collected," 184, 188–189, **197**–198, 203, 230
Cooper, Alice, 161, 669
Cooper, Michael, 190, 195, 219
Cooper, Ray, 423, 424–425, 429–431
Cordell, Denny, 305
Corliss, Richard, 217
Corriston, Peter, 474, 477, 496, 514, 536
Corrs (The), 633
Corso, Gregory, 164
Costello, Elvis, 497, 605, 606
Costner, Kevin, 101
Cott, Jonathan, 146, 474, 480, 484, 488, 490
Coulson, Rupert, 576–578, 580–584, 586–590, 592, 660, 662
"Country Honk," 280, 284, 285, **292–293**, 308, 610, 688
Covay, Don, 76, 92, 97, 109, 506, 558, 559, 560, 562, 569, 677
Cramer, Floyd, 345, 354
Cramps (The), 30
Cranberries (The), 605
Crawford, Joan, 365
"Crazy Mama," 454, 456, 458, 459, 468, **469**, 512
Cream, 8, 198, 460
Creedence Clearwater Revival, 89
Crich, Tim, 558, 559, 561, 569
Cropper, Steve, 22, 351
Crosby, Stills, Nash & Young, 332, 453
Crosland, Alan, 236
Crow, Sheryl, 633
Cry to Me, 90, 94, **103**, 328
Crystals (The), 144
Cullum, Jamie, 153
Curtis, Jackie, 335
Cutler, Sam, 292, 293
Cyril Davies R&B All-Stars, 8, 230

D'Angelo, Beverly, 558, 560
D'Arby, Terence Trent, 276, 432, 576
D'Orazio, Sante, 605
Dalí, Salvador, 202
Dallesandro, Bobby, 335
Dallesandro, Joe, 335
Daltrey, Roger, 537, 561
"Dance (Pt. 1)," 492, 494, **498**, 690
"Dance Little Sister," 416, 418, 420, 422, **432**, 438, 690
"Dancing in the Light," 360, 367
"Dancing with Mr D.," 394, 398–399, **402**, 405
"Dandelion," 189, **242–245**, 690
"Dangerous Beauty," 664, 666, 669, **680**, 682
Darin, Bobby, 122
Darling, Candy, 223
Dash, Sarah, 576, 578–579, 584–585, 587–588, 590
Dave Berry & The Crusaders, 49
Dave Clark Five (The), 39
Dave Matthews Band, 633
Davenport, John, 537–538, 540–544, 546–549
Davies, Cyril, 8–9, 230
Davies, Dave, 621
Davies, Ray, 150, 197
Davis, Angela, 364, 380–381
Davis, Blind John, 441
Davis, Gary (Reverend), 348
Davis, Jesse Ed, 422
Davis, Miles, 337, 602, 606, 611, 655
Dayne, Taylor, 468
De Caro, Nick, 194
Dé Dannan, 606, 610
De Lane Lea Studios, 20, 22
"Dead Flowers," 330, 334, 336, **354**
Dean, James, 18
"Dear Doctor," 250, 253, **263**
Decca: 12, 15,18, 29, 32, 35, 46–49, 64, 72, 92, 94, 113, 116, **123**, 178, 229, 252, 253, 326, **334**, 353, 438
Decca Recording Studios, 46–49, 180, 183
December's Children (and Everybody's), 48, 95, **128–133**, 140, 163
Deep Purple, 168, 287, 338, 369, 422, 460
Del-Lords (The), 497
Delon, Nathalie, 362
DeMedio, Frank, 316
Depeche Mode, 539
Derek and The Dominos, 460
DeSalvo, Albert, 298
DeShannon, Jackie, 144
DeVille, Willy, 144
Devo, 118
Di Perna, Alan, 143, 342, 678
Dick and Dee Dee, 133, 442
Dick, Philip K., 352
Dickinson, Jim, 337, 339–340, 344–345
Diddley, Bo, 10–11, 31, 33, 38, 50–51, 53, 59, 73, 117, 161, 199, 210, 263
Dijon, Rocky, 253–254, 256, 259, 269–271, 274, 277, 286, 304–305, 337, 346–347, 453
Dire Straits, 496, 575
Dirty Work, 97, **552–569**, 572, 574–575, 577, 581, 584–585, 587, 662
"Dirty Work," 556–557, **567**
Ditcham, Martin, 537, 541, 543–544, 549

Dixon, Willie, 11, 16–17, 31, 52, 60, 72–73, 82, 422, 446, 504, 675
"Do You Think I Really Care?," 470, 472, 476
Domino, Fats, 441
Don Covay & the Goodtimers, 97, 506
Donahue, Tom, 356
Donaldson, Eric, 456, 464
"Doncha Bother Me," 134, 138, 140, **150**, 209
Donovan, 194, 230, 286, 401
"Don't Be a Stranger," 470, 472, 476
"Don't Lie to Me," 436, 438, **441**
"Don't Stop," 648, 650, **652**, 690, 692
"Don't Wanna Go Home," 669
"Doo Doo Doo Doo Doo (Heartbreaker)," 394, 398–399, 402, **405–406**, 414, 438, 690
Doobie Brothers (The), 194
Dooley, Tom, 162
Doors (The), 36, 108–109, 113, 132, 139, 193, 285, 287
Dorsey, Lee, 87, 125
Douglas, Alfred "Bosie" Lord, 245
Dowd, Steve, 460–461, 463–469
Dowland, Thomas, 240
"Down Home Girl," 68, 73, **78**, 84, 98
"Down in the Hole," 492, 496–497, **504**–505
"Down the Road Apiece," 10, 68, 72, **84**
"Downtown Suzie," 225, 285, 436, 438, **451**
Dozier, Lamont, 26, 40
Dr. Feelgood, 503, 576
Dr. John, 104, 369, 381, 388
Dragonaires (The), 396
Drake, Nick, 253, 286
Drayton, Charley, 561, 602
Drifters (The), 48, 78, 85
"Driving Too Fast," 664, 669, **684**
Drumgoole, Fleeta, 380
Du Noyer, Paul, 642
Dudgeon, Gus, 442–447
Duffy, Robert, 607
Dunbar, Aynsley, 458
Dunbar, John, 164–165
Dunbar, Robert, 164
Dunbar, Sly, 537–539, 541, 543–544, 547
Dunn, Donald, 22
Duran Duran, 565, 575–576
Dust Brothers (The), 630, 632, 635, 642–643
Dyer, Jack, 274
Dylan, Bob, 18, 108, 118, 138–139, 142, 151–152, 156, 186, 196, 200, 203, 223, 240, 248, 250, 252, 254, 256, 265–266, 286, 288, 290–291, 305, 307, 337, 365, 368–369, 379, 400–401, 440, 482, 537, 557, 566, 576, 590, 604–606, 612, 630, 633, 636, 668
Dynamic Sounds Studios, 410–412, 414, 422, 434, 524, 528, 663

E Street Band, 560
"Each and Everyday of the Year," 436, 438, 440, 443
Eagles (The), 368, 379, 401
Easton, Edward D., 123
Easton, Eric, 12, 14–16, 18, 20, 22–23, 47, 49, 70, 108, 122–123, 170
Edge (The), 654
Edmonds, Kenneth, 637
Egan, Sean, 292, 320
Electric Lady Studios, 497–508, 515, 520, 688
Electric Prunes (The), 73, 173
Elektra Sound Studios, 285, 288, 289, 292, 294, 296, 302, 320–322, 352
Ellen, Mark, 694
Elliott, Martin, 410, 548, 580
Ellison, Harlan, 402
Elman, Ralph, 26
ELO, 422–423
Emerson, Lake and Palmer, 286, 337
EMI, Pathé-Marconi Studios, 478, 480–488, 490, 498–505, 516, 518–528, 538, 540–550, 559–569, 592, 688
Emotional Rescue, 476, 488, **492–509**, 512, 514, 516, 520, 550, 604, 658
"Emotional Rescue," 494, 500, **505–506**, 648, 690
"Empty Heart," 56, **59**, 68
England, Lynndie, 680
Eno, Brian, 476
Epstein, Brian, 12, 18, 94, 123
Erasure, 686
Eric Burdon & The New Animals, 168
Errington, F. C., 178
Ertegün, Ahmet, 165, 334–336, 362, 368, 396, 398, 414, 460
Estes, Sleepy John, 268
Etherington, Allen, 9, 62
Evans, Bill, 103
Everly Brothers (The), 116, 354, 477, 616
Everly, Don, 255
"Everybody Needs Somebody to Love," 68, 70, 73, **76–77**, 98, 103, 114
Exile on Main St., 136, 150, 230, 261, 285, 336–337, **360–393**, 396, 398, 400, 402–404, 407–408, 412, 428, 438, 450, 453, 456, 460, 462, 464, 472, 474–475, 520, 549, 581, 584, 606, 610, 615, 630, 642, 668, 686–687

Fab Four (The), 12, 21, 31, 285, 316
Faces (The), 426–427, 458–459, 466, 476, 485, 564, 670, 683
"Factory Girl," 246, 250, 253, 263, **271**, 594, 596
Faithfull, Glynn, 164
Faithfull, Marianne, 145, 155, 158, 163–**165**, 168, 188, 190, 192, 196, 201, 214, 238, 240–241, 245, 248, 256, 259, 278, 292–293, 296, 304, 334, 344, 351–352, 407, 449, 541, 606
Family, 260, 271
"Family," 436, 438, 440, **452**
"Fancy Man Blues," 656, 658, **660**
Fanelli, Damian, 429
"Far Away Eyes," 470, 474, 476, 478, **484**, 502, 690
Fariña, Richard, 146–147
Farley, Bill, 28, 30–38, 40–42, 50, 54, 64, 66–67, 73–74, 79, 83, 85, 88–89, 106, 441–443, 445–447
Farlowe, Chris, 19, 109, 154, 158, 192, 209
Fawcett, Farrah, 474–475
"Feel on Baby," 532, 534, 537, **543**
Feinstein, Barry, 252
Feliciano, José, 89
Fenton, Joe, 122
Ferlinghetti, Lawrence, 164
Ferry, Brian, 474, 537
Fields, Venetta, 369, 376, 387–388, 392
Fig, Anton, 566
"Fight," 552, 556–557, 559, **561**
Fincher, David, 607, 654
Findley, Chuck, 401, 405–406
"Fingerprint File," 416, 418, 422, **435**
Firth, Dixon (Dr), 214
Fischer, Lisa, 574, 578–580, 584–585, 587–588, 590, 686–687
Five by Five (EP), **56–67**
Flashpoint, 271, 590, **594–599**, 602, 662
Fleetwood Mac, 263, 286, 338
Fleetwood, Mike, 319
"Flight 505," 134, 140, **152**, 155, 690
"Flip the Switch," 628, 632–**634**
Flowers, 140, 154, **204–211**, 285
Flying Burrito Brothers (The), 292, 332, 344, 366, 368, 378–379
Followill, Jared, 488
"Following the River," 360
Foo Fighters, 633
"Fool to Cry," 454, 456, 458–459, 461, **468–469**, 512, 550, 613, 648, 653, 688, 690
Fools (The), 254
Ford, Eric, 163
Ford, Steven, 485
Ford, Walton, 692
"Fortune Teller," 49, 176, 180, **183**,
Forty Licks, **648–655**, 658, 661, 692
Fowler, Bernard, 574, 576–579, 582–588, 590, 598, 607–609, 612, 614, 616–617, 619–620, 634–637, 639–640, 642, 644–647
Fox, James, 320
Foxx, John, 121
Fraboni, Rob, 400, 402, 405, 414, 630, 634, 636, 639, 645–647
Frampton, Peter, 276, 337
Frank, Robert, 365, 396
Franke, Christopher, 440
Frankie Goes to Hollywood, 537
Franklin, Aretha, 97, 104, 118, 274, 291, 337, 460, 576
Franklin, Bertha, 100
Fraser, Robert, 164, 214, 288
Free, 476
Freeland, Ryan, 637
Fricke, David, 590, 608
Friedman, Adam, 507
Fullan, George, 646
Fullan, Sean, 497–505, 507–508
Fuller, Blind Boy, 316
Fulson, Lowell, 541
Funk Brothers (The), 425, 530, 599
Fuqua, Harvey, 47

Gabriel, Peter, 557, 588
Gagel, Wally, 640
Gainsbourg, Charlotte, 669
Gainsbourg, Serge, 537
Gallagher, Rory, 459
Garcia, Jerry, 231
Garfunkel, Art, 231
Garland, Judy, 475
Gavin, Frankie, 606, 610–611, 624–625
Gaye, Marvin, 40, 47, 92, 97–98, 100, 154, 505, 565
Gee, Jeremy, 369–370, 372, 374–376, 378–380, 382–383, 385–389, 391–393, 460–461, 463–469
Gein, Ed, 544
Geldof, Bob, 557
Genesis, 234
Gentry, Bobbie, 78
George Thorogood & The Destroyers, 60
George, Boy, 660
George, Lowell, 322
Gerry & the Pacemakers, 18
"Get Off of My Cloud," 92, 94, 109, **124–126**, 128, 130, 136, 174, 176, 178, 241, 648, 690
Get Yer Ya-Ya's Out!, 37, 269, 291, **312–319**, 338, 348
"(Get Your Kicks on) Route 66," 24, 28, **30**, 37, 128, 130, 372, 692
Gibbs, Christopher, 252
Gilbert, Lewis, 666
Gilmour, David, 576
"Gimme Shelter," 280, 284–286, **288–289**, 299–300, 364, 448, 640, 648, 690
Ginsberg, Allen, 164–165, 243, 248
Gitomer, Phil, 530
Goats Head Soup, 230, 261, **394–415**, 418, 422, 434, 438, 456, 458, 496, 500, 514, 528, 576, 642, 663
Godard, Jean-Luc, 18, 165, 253–254, 258–259, 264, 452
Goffin, Gerry, 122
"Goin' Home," 134, 138, **151**, 166, 209
"Goin' to a Go-Go (live)," **530–531**
Goldman, Greg, 606–613, 615–620, 622, 624, 626
Gomelsky, Giorgio, 10–11, 18
"Gomper," 212, 216–217, 220, **233**
"Good Times," 94–95, 100, 328
"Good Times, Bad Times," 28, **54**, 68, 90
Gooden, Charles, 635, 642–643
Goodman, Shirley, 369
Goodtimers (The), 97
Gordy, Berry, 40, 47, 67, 425
Gospelaires (The), 80
Got Live If You Want It! (EP), 94, **114–117**, 130
Got Live If You Want It!, **176–183**, 316
"Gotta Get Away," 90, 92, 94–95, **101**, 109, 128, 130, 163, 501
Graburn, Lloyd, 494
Grand Funk Railroad, 314
Grandmaster Flash, 643
Grant, Amy, 669
Grant, Eddy, 575, 605, 620
Grateful Dead, 36, 59, 73, 222, 300, 332, 365, 515
Gray, John, 252
Grech, Ric, 253–254, 260, 271
Green, Al, 440, 488
Green, Jerome, 33
Green, Joe, 369, 388, 392
Green, Peter, 286
Greenfield, Robert, 112, 125
Greenhornes (The), 167
Greenslade, Arthur, 154
Gregory, Steve, 286, 308–309, 311
"Grown Up Wrong," 12, 65, 68, 70, 73, **83**
GRRR!, 20, **690–695**
Guest, Reg, 445–447
Guitar Slim, 104
"Gunface," 628, 632–633, **638**
Guns'N'Roses, 256, 273, 581
Gus Cannon's Jug Stompers, 268
Guthrie, Woody, 200
Guy, Buddy, 67, 72, 558, 633
Guymon, Linda, 440

H.P. Zinker, 632
Hackford, Taylor, 144
"Had It with You," 552, 556–557, **568**
Haggard, Merle, 484, 497
Haglund, Kalle, 652
Hahn, Lew, 460–461, 463–469
Haley, Harold, 380
Hall, Jerry, 474, 478, 494, 496, 503, 521, 549, 602, 642, 645, 674, 677
Hall, Rick, 48, 336
Halsall, Ollie, 456
Hammond, John, 291
Hancock, Herbie, 557–558, 576
"Hand of Fate," 454, 456, 458, 460, **463**
Handsome Family (The), 354
"Hang Fire," 476, 510, 514, **518**
Hansen, Jerry, 287, 288, 290, 292, 294, 296, 298, 300, 302, 304
Hansen, Patti, 318, 522, 534, 542, 647, 678
"Happy," 202, 360, 364, 368, **383–384**, 389–390, 404, 438, 487, 514, 648, 690
Hardaway, Lula, 448
Hardin, Charles, 50
Hardy, Françoise, 163
"Harlem Shuffle," 97, 552, 554, 557, **562**, 656, 658, 690
Harpo, Slim, 26, 36, 89, 364, 374, 660
Harris, Betty, 103
Harris, Emmylou, 379
Harrison, George, 12, 123, 140, 158, 169–170, 214, 231, 252, 286, 341, 401, 423, 426, 440, 599, 613, 636
Harrison, Nicky, 401, 407–408, 411
Harrison, Pattie, 214
Hartevelt, Renée, 544
Harwood, Keith, 337, 339, 342, 344, 346, 348–349, 351, 354, 356, 374, 380, 391, 422, 424–426, 428–429, 431, 432–435, 458–461, 463–469, 475, 519, 523, 663
Hassinger, Dave, 76, 78, 87, 94–96, 98, 100–104, 106–107, 109–112, 118–121, 124, 126, 133, 140, 142, 144–160, 166, 168, 171–174, 182, 189, 192–195, 197–203, 208–210, 328, 449
Hassinger, Marie, 142
Hatchet, Molly, 376
"Have You Seen Your Mother, Baby, Standing in the Shadow?," **172–174**, 176, 178, 180, 189, 204, 206, 208, 245, 438, 648, 690
Havers, Michael, 214
Hawkins, Dale, 89
Hawkins, Roger, 336
Hawkins, Screamin' Jay, 653
Haynie, Emile, 694–695
Head, Murray, 141
"Heart of Stone," 68, 82, 90, 92, 94, **106–107**, 436, 438, 440, 690
"Hearts for Sale," 570, 572, 575, **582**
"Heaven," 497, 510, 514, **525**–526
Heckstall-Smith, Dick, 8
Hells Angels, 149, 314, 332, 516
Hendrix, Jimi, 97, 173, 189, 233, 248, 254, 497, 582
Henry, Pierre, 235
Hensley, Ken, 286
Henson Recording Studios, 669, 673, 675, 681–685
Hit Factory (The), 537, 538, 540–550, 578, 598, 599
Herzog, Werner, 512
Hewitt, David, 530
"Hey Negrita," 454, 456, 458, 460, **466**
"Hide Your Love," 394, 398, 400, **410**
"High and Dry," 134, 138, 140, **153**
"Highwire," 594, 596, **598**, 602, 658, 690
Hillage, Steve, 456
Hillman, Chris, 292
Hingston, Tom, 650
Hiro, 458
"Hitch Hike," 90, 92, 94, **98**
Hoffman, Dustin, 356
"Hold Back," 552, 556–557, **563**
"Hold on to Your Hat," 570, 572, 575, **581**
Holiday, Billie, 103, 291
Holland-Dozier-Holland, 26, 40, 459
Holland, Brian, 40
Holland, Eddie, 425
Holland, Milt, 322
Hollies (The), 28, 35, 39, 48, 159
Holly, Buddy, 33, 50–51, 152, 286, 489, 639
"Honest I Do," 26, 28, **32**
Honeymoon Killers (The), 175
"Honky Tonk Women," 255, 261, 292–293, 304, **308–311**, 312, 376, 418, 432, 505, 610, 648, 650, 690
Hood, David, 336
Hooker, Earl, 35, 521
Hooker, John Lee, 83, 374, 401
Hopkins, Freda and Alfred, 230
Hopkins, Nicky, 191, 197, 200, 218, 222, 224, 226–229, **230–231**, 232–236, 242–244, 250, 255–256, 259, 262–263, 265–266, 269–270, 272–273, 278–279, 286, 288–289, 291, 294–295, 300–303, 305, 309, 311, 337, 342–343, 358, 362, 370–376, 379, 382, 385–389, 393, 401–404, 407–408, 410–412, 428–431, 433–435, 442, 450, 452, 456, 459, 464, 468, 497, 500, 502, 505–506, 515, 519, 524, 526, 528–529, 583, 590, 606, 663, 686–687
Horn, Jim, 401, 404–406, 412
Horn, Trevor, 630
Horton, Big Walter, 16, 88
"Hot Stuff," 454, 456 458, 460–**462**, 464, 494, 498, 512, 534, 580, 599, 617
Houston, Cissy, 80
Houston, Thelma, 472
"How Can I Stop," 628, 632–633, **647**
Howard, Robert E., 223
Howe, Deering, 316
Howe, Steve, 286
Howitt, Mary, 121
Howlin' Wolf, 13, 52–53, 60, 66–67, 82–83, 386, 504, 660, 662
Hulko, Lee, 460–461, 463–469
Humble Pie, 287
Hunt, Marsha, 339
Hunter, Don, 448
Hunter, Ian, 311
Hunter, Meredith, 149, 314, 332
Hussein, Saddam, 598, 680
Hutchings, Ashley, 576
Hutmaker, Jimmy, 307

"I Am Waiting," 134, 138, 140, **156**
IBC Studios, 11, 16, 132, 162, 163, 172, 174, 182, 183, 208
"I Can't Be Satisfied," 68, 72, **86**
"(I Can't Get No) Satisfaction," 92, 94, 100, 108, **118**–122, 124, 136, 152, 154, 156, 158, 163, 176, 180, 189, 241, 253, 276, 304, 328, 344, 463, 594, 596, 648, 650, 670, 690
"I Don't Know Why (Don't Know Why I Love You)," 436, 438, 447–**448**
"I Go Wild," 600, 604–605, **614**
"I Got the Blues," 330, 334, 336, 341, **351**
"I Just Want to Make Love to You," 24, 26, 28, **31**, 38–39, 598, 658
"I Just Want to See His Face," 360, 364, 368, **387**
"I Love You Too Much," 470, 472, 476
"I Need You Baby (Mona)," 24, **33**, 68
"I Think I'm Going Mad," 496, 540, **550–551**
"I Wanna Be Your Man," **20**–22, 29, 46, 690
"I Want to Be Loved," 14, **16–17**, 692
"I'd Much Rather Be with the Boys," 436, 438, **444**
"I'm a King Bee," 24, 28, **36**, 374
"I'm Alright," 94, 114, **117**, 176, 180
"I'm Free," 90, 92, 94–95, **109**, 128, 130 690
"I'm Going Down," 285, 436, 438, **453**
"I'm Gonna Drive," 605, 613, 622, 624, **626–627**
"I'm Moving On," 114, **116**, 128, 130
"I'm Not Signifying," 360
"I've Been Loving You Too Long," 94, 176, 180, **182**–183, 351
Idol, Billy, 606
"If I Was a Dancer (Dance Pt. 2)," 498, 512, 656, 658
"If You Can't Rock Me," 416, 418, 422, **424**
"If You Let Me," 190, 436, 438, **449**
"If You Need Me," 56, **58**–59, 68, 324
"If You Really Want to Be My Friend," 416, 418, 420, 422–423, **433**–434
Ike & Tina Turner, 144, 311, 314, 339
Impressions (The), 78, 653
"In Another Land," 212, 217, 220, **224–225**, 232, 451
"Indian Girl," 492, 496–497, **502**, 550
"Infamy," 664, 669, **685**
INXS, 683
Iron Butterfly, 440
Isham, Mark, 606, 615, 617
Isham, Wayne, 585
Island Studios, 400, 402–405, 407, 409–412, 414, 421, 422, 424–435, 663
Isley Brothers (The), 103, 125
"It Must Be Hell," 532, 534, 537, **549**, 585
"It Won't Take Long," 664, 666, 668–669, **672**
"It's All Over Now," **52–53**, 54, 59, 66–68, 72, 217, 324, 648, 690
"It's Not Easy," 134, 138, 140, **155**
It's Only Rock'N'Roll, 400, **416–435**, 438, 456, 458–460, 481, 496, 512, 537, 543, 556
"It's Only Rock'N'Roll (But I Like It)," 400, 416, 421, **426–427**, 648, 650, 658, 663

Jackson, Al, 22
Jackson, George, 380
Jackson, Jesse, 482
Jackson, Joe, 576
Jackson, Laura, 14, 160
Jackson, Melvin "Lil' Son," 36
Jackson, Michael, 456, 545, 575, 606, 673
Jackson, Roddy, 96
Jagger, Basil "Joe," 9
Jagger, Bianca, see Pérez Morena Macías, Bianca,
Jagger, Brenda, 554
Jagger, Christopher, 9
Jagger, Eva, 9
Jagger, Gabriel, 645
Jagger, Georgia May, 602
Jagger, Karis, 339
Jagger, Mick, 8–695
Jam (The), 287
Jamal, Ahmad, 73
James, Elmore, 8, 14, 150, 608
James, Etta, 31, 53, 306, 548
James, Skip, 240
Jameson, Bobby, 294, 443–444
Jamiroquai, 537
Jamison, Roosevelt, 99
Janovitz, Bill, 108
Jardim, Luís, 576, 578–579, 583, 586–587, 611, 615–617
Jarreau, Al, 576
Jarrett, Ted, 41
Jeff Beck Group, 230, 458
Jefferson Airplane, 73, 186, 216, 222, 230, 234, 332, 365
Jefferson, Blind Lemon, 66
Jennings, Will, 144
Jerden, Dave, 557–559, 561–567
Jerry Garcia Band, 76
Jet Harris & Tony Meehan, 49
"Jigsaw Puzzle," 246, 250, 253, **265**
Jiménez, Flaco, 606, 616
"Jiving Sister Fanny," 285, 436, 438, **450**
Jobim, Antônio Carlos, 103
Joel, Billy, 73, 558
John Mayall and the Bluesbreakers, 286
John Mellencamp Band, 85, 637
John, Elton, 286, 337, 343, 423, 575
Johns, Andy, 219, 304, 337, 339, 342, 344, 346, 348–349, 351, 354, 356–357, 362, 366–372, 374–380, 382–393, 396, 399–400, 402–405, 407, 409–412, 414–415, 421–422, 424–426, 428–429, 431–435, 453, 524
Johns, Glyn, 11, 16–17, 116–117, 162–163, 172–173, 180, 182–183, 189–197, 203, 208, 219–220, 222–224, 226–228, 230, 232–234, 236, 238–240, 242, 253–254, 256, 260, 262–266, 268–269, 271–272, 274, 276, 278, 287–292, 294, 296, 298–302, 304, 307–308, 311–316, 319–320, 322, 337–339, 341–344, 346, 348–349, 351–352, 354, 356–358, 368–372, 374–376, 378–380, 382–383, 385–389, 391–393, 422, 435, 440, 448–453, 459, 464, 467–468, 497, 519, 523, 686
Johnson, Jimmy, 336–337, 339, 341, 344–345, 348
Johnson, Johnny, 373
Johnson, Robert, 210, 284, 290–291, 339, 364, 371, 391, 575, 615
Jolie, Angelina, 635
Jolly, Charlie, 423, 435
Joly, Phil, 688
Jones Morgan, Sonia, 576, 588
Jones, Booker T., 23
Jones, Brian, 8–695
Jones, Darryl, 461, 602, 604, 606–615, 617–622, 624, 626–627, 639, 644, 646, 652–655, 661, 669–674, 677, 679, 681, 683–684, 694–695
Jones, John Paul, 228–229, 440, 443
Jones, Johnny, 66
Jones, Kenney, 426–427
Jones, Mick, 383
Jones, Norah, 655
Jones, Pete, 18
Jones, Phil, 606, 614
Jones, Quincy, 369, 401
Jones, Rickie Lee, 85, 119, 669
Jones, Steve, 483
Joplin, Janis, 108, 206, 252, 314
Jordan, Dave, 476, 487
Jordan, Neil, 256
Jordan, Steve, 558, 561, 587, 602
Joseph, Michael, 252
"Jump on Top of Me," 605, 622, **624–625**
"Jumpin' Jack Flash," 220, 228, 248, 253, 255–256, 260–261, 264, 267, **274**–279, 282, 308, 312, 418, 463, 505, 588, 594, 596, 648, 650, 690
"Just My Imagination (Running Away with Me)," 470, 476, **481**

K-Doe, Ernie, 87
Karslake, Jo, 503
Kaukonen, Jorma, 456
KC and the Sunshine Band, 472, 494
"Keep Up Blues," 470, 472, 476
Keith, Linda, 240–241
Keltner, Jim, 422, 634, 636–640, 644–647
Kendrick, Eddie, 208
Kenkel, Kim, 544
Kennedy, Jacqueline, 396
Kennedy, John F., 250, 256
Kennedy, Robert, 248, 250, 256, 266, 284
Kent, Nick, 269, 420, 430
Kerouac, Jack, 365, 379
Kerr, John, 296
Kesler, Stanley, 10
"Keys to Your Love," 650, **653**, 692
Keys, Bobby, 72, 286, 294–295, 334, 337, 339, 341, 346–347, 349–351, 358–359, 362, 366–367, 369–376, 378, 382–384, 386, 388–389, 393, 401, 404–406, 410, 414–415, 420–422, 448, 453, 496, 498, 501, 505–508, 529, 542, 546, 568, 574, 648, 686–687
Kick Horns (The), 576–580, 584–585, 590, 599

Kilgour, Howard, 401–405, 407, 409–412, 414, 422, 424–426, 428–429, 431–435
Kimsey, Chris, 337, 339, 342, 344, 346, 348–349, 351, 354, 356, 374, 378, 380, 391–392, 475–476, 478–488, 490, 496–505, 507–508, 512, 514–526, 528, 536–544, 546–550, 557, 575–578, 580–584, 586–590, 592, 596, 598–599, 623, 660–662, 688
King Crimson, 234, 422, 476
King, Albert, 369, 463
King, B. B., 314, 368–369, 401, 497, 606, 633, 680
King, Ben, 476, 478, 480–485, 487–488, 490, 688
King, Carole, 122
King, Clydie, 369, 376, 387–388, 392
King, Freddie, 369
King, John, 630, 643
King Jr., Martin Luther, 248, 266, 284, 288
Kings of Leon, 488
Kingsmen (The), 125
Kinks (The), 10, 28, 142, 150, 188, 197, 203, 230, 287
Kirke, Simon, 476, 490
Kirshner, Don, 122
Kiss, 226
Kissoon, Katie, 599
Klein, Allen, 23, 92, 94, 100, 108, 120, **122–123**, 136, 316, 334, 362, 438
Klossowski De Rola, Stanislas (Stash), 214
Knight, Brian, 9
Knight, Nick, 668
Knopfler, Mark, 605
Kooper, Al, 286, 304–307, 321, 341, 440
Korengo, Ed, 606–613, 615–620, 622, 624, 626
Korner, Alexis, 8–9, 13, 62, 556
Kossoff, Paul, 456
Kracker, 261
Krall, Diana, 103
Kramer, Billy J., 18
Kramer, Eddie, 189, 192–203, 219, 222–224, 226–228, 232–234, 236, 238, 240, 242, 244, 254, 262, 264–265, 269, 274, 276–278
Kretzschmar, Hubert, 474, 514, 536
Kricfalusi, John, 562
Krieger, Robbie, 113
Kroes, Doutzen, 677
Krowiak, Mike, 558–559, 561–569
Kubrick, Stanley, 234
Kunjappu, Jolly, see Jolly, Charlie
Kwaku Baah, Anthony (Reebop), 401

La Fourchette home studio, 670–685, 688
"Lady Jane," 64, 113, 134, 138–140, 143, **146–147**, 149, 156, 176, 180, 197, 204, 206, 210, 228, 245, 398, 604, 611, 690
Lake, Greg, 286
Landau, John, 420
Lane, Ronnie, 224–225, 568
lang, k.d., 635
Laswell, Bill, 580
"Laugh, I Nearly Died," 664, 666, 668–669, **681**
Lawrence, D. H., 146
Lawrence, Trevor, 418, 420, 458
Lawson, Janet, 448
Lay, Sam, 66
Leach, Ed, 423, 425
Leadbelly, 54, 153, 675
Leander, Mike, 28, 162–163, 172–173, 208, 241, 440, 442–446
Lear, Amanda, 202
Leary, Timothy, 186, 216, 234
Leavell, Chuck, 537–541, 543–545, 547, 549, 558–567, 569, 574–580, 583–587, 590, 592–593, 607–608, 610–616, 621–623, 652–655, 660, 662, 669–670, 672, 674, 677, 680, 684, 694–695
Led Zeppelin, 36, 116, 189, 219, 228–230, 254, 287, 337–338, 349, 369, 422, 432, 440, 443, 497, 501, 528, 559, 588, 636, 663
Lee, Brenda, 104
Lee, Byron, 396, 399
Lee, Carlton, 401–405, 407, 409–412, 414
Lehane, Dennis, 356
Leiber, Jerry, 17, 49, 78, 122
Leibovitz, Annie, 465, 556
Lennear, Claudia, 339
Lennon, John, 15, 19–21, 53, 76, 79, 94, 123, 190, 218, 231–232, 242–244, 258, 266 286, 357, 422, 435, 440, 479, 514, 556, 613, 636
Lennon, Julian, 537
Lennox, Annie, 537
Leonard, Darrell, 636, 639, 646
Lester, Richard, 320
Let It Bleed, 136, 191, 261, 273, **280–307**, 314, 321, 364, 377, 382, 392, 398, 434, 448, 450–451, 456, 622, 688
"Let It Bleed," 280, 284–285, **296**,
"Let It Loose," 360, 364, 368, 381, **388**, 613
"Let It Rock," 339, **358–359**, 362, 656, 658
"Let Me Down Slow," 664, 669, **671**, 677
"Let Me Go," 492, 496–497, **501**
"Let's Spend the Night Together," 144, 189, 191, 204, 206, **238**–241, 648, 690
Leven, Jackie, 145
Levi, Eliphas, 165
Levy, Morris, 79
Lewis, Edouard (Sir), 122–123, 252, 334
Lewis, Elmo, see Jones, Brian
Lewis, Jerry Lee, 230, 602
Lewis, Rudy, 85
Lewis, Stan, 89
Lieberson, Sanford, 278
"Lies," 470, 474, 476, **483**
Light, Alan, 668
Lightfoot, Gordon, 101, 194
Lightnin' Slim, 89
Lillywhite, Steve, 556–569, 575
Lindsay-Hogg, Michael, 278, 408, 427–428, 469, 484, 486, 517, 523, 528, 658
Lipson, Steve, 537–538, 540–544, 546–549
Lisle, Andria, 332
Little Boy Blue and the Blue Boys, 9, 62
"Little by Little," 24, 26, 28, **35**, 50
"Little Queenie," 312, 314, **319**
"Little Red Rooster," **66**–68, 73, 88, 594, 596, 690
Little Richard, 18, 97, 337
"Little T&A," 510, 514, **520**
Little Walter, 31, 61, 88, 504, 589, 675, 682
Little, Carlo, 230
"Live with Me," 280, 284–285, **294–295**, 312, 656, 658
Living Colour, 596, 643
Lobos (Los), 606
Loder, Kurt, 520, 536
Loewenstein, Rupert Prince, 123, 165, 362, 396
Lofgren, Nils, 231
Lomax, Alan, 348
London Bach Choir (The), 294, 304, 306
London, Julie, 30
Long John Baldry, 8, 181, 369
Long, Jerry, 481
"Long Long While," 140, 168, **171**
Loog Oldham, Andrew, 12–16, **18–19**, 20–23, 26, 28–42, 46–52, 54, 58–62, 64, 66–67, 70, 72–73, 76, 78–80, 82–89, 92, 94, 96–104, 106–112, 116–118, 120–127, 130, 132–133, 139, 142, 145–146, 148, 150–160, 162, 164, 166, 168, 170–174, 178, 181–183, 186, 188, 192–203, 208–210, 217, 219, 238–240, 242, 244–245, 253, 328, 364, 438, 440–447, 449, 556, 622
"Look What the Cat Dragged In," 664, 666, 668–669, **683**
"Look What You've Done,"128, 130, **132**, 324
Lord-Alge, Tom, 634, 636, 642, 645
Lorimer, Roddy, 576, 580
"Losing My Touch," 648, 650, **655**, 661, 692
Louis Brooks and his Hi-Toppers, 41
"Love in Vain," 280, 284–285, **290–291**, 312, 316, 347
"Love Is Strong," 600, 604–605, **607**–608, 622–623, 648, 690
Love, 82
"Loving Cup," 230, 285, 360, 364, 367–368, **382**
"Low Down," 628, 632–633, **636**
Lowe, Nick, 503
Ludwig, Bob, 530
Luft, Eric V. D., 193
Lulu, 336
Lündstrom, Astrid, 224
"Luxury," 416, 418, 420, 422, **431**, 458, 543
Lynn, Tami, 369, 388
Lynne, Jeff, 423
Lynyrd Skynyrd, 286
Lyons, Gary, 515–516, 518–526, 528

MacColl, Kirsty, 558–559, 561, 569
Machat, Marty, 122
Mack, Reinhold, 421, 423–426, 428–429, 431–435
Madaio, Steve, 418
Madonna, 602, 694
Mahavishnu Orchestra, 444
Major, John, 618
Malo, Ron, 52–53, 58–62, 73–74, 80, 82, 84, 86, 94, 97, 99, 108, 121, 132, 299, 589
Mamas & the Papas (The), 208
Manassas, 292, 379
Mancini, Henry, 84, 368
Mandel, Harvey, 456, 459, 461–462, 465
Mankowitz, Gered, 94, 130, 138, 180, 189
Mann, Manfred, 84
"Mannish Boy," 512, 656, 658
Mansfield, Jayne, 474
Manzarek, Ray, 132
Mar-Keys (The), 182
Marcus, Greil, 288
Mardin, Arif, 467, 497, 502
Marek, Mark, 557
Markie, Biz, 635
Marley, Bob, 286, 401, 463, 496
Marr, Johnny, 98, 288
Marriott, Steve, 224–225, 458
Marsh, Dave, 458
Marshall, Penny, 274
Martha and the Vandellas, 98
Martin, Dan, 668
Martin, Dean, 70
Martin, George, 144, 163, 575, 660
Martinez, Cristina, 175
Marvelettes (The), 58
Mason, Dave, 253–254, 260, 266–267, 271
Mason, Nick, 243
Masonics (The), 171
Massive Attack, 650
Master Musicians of Jajouka (The), 576, 588
Matassa, Cosimo, 104
Matthew, Brian, 18
Matthews, Dave, 465
Matthews, Gwen, 72
Matthews, Sherlie, 376, 388
May, Phil, 103
Mayall, John, 286, 291, 309, 422, 456
Mayfield, Curtis, 78, 101, 440, 653
Maysles, Albert and David, 314, 332
MC5, 59
McAllister, Kooster, 530
McCartney, Linda, 362
McCartney, Paul, 20–21, 26, 51, 102, 123, 138, 152, 163–164, 218, 231, 236, 242–244, 287, 362, 423, 443, 542, 575–576, 606, 613, 660
McDaniel, Ellas, see Diddley, Bo
McDonald, Dolette, 558, 565, 569
McDonald, Kathi, 369, 389
McDonald, Phil, 460–461, 463–469
McDowell, Mississippi Fred, 334, 348
McGee, Brian, 537–538, 540–544, 546–549
McGowan, Cathy, 136
McGuinn, Roger, 141
McKenna, Mick, 358, 458
McLagan, Ian, 474, 476, 478–479, 481, 530
McLaughlin, John, 440, 442–447
McLean, Jennifer, 522
McLean, Susan, 515, 522
McMillan, Alastair, 606–622, 624, 626
McMurray, David, 606, 615, 617
McPhatter, Clyde, 37
McQueen, Steve, 398, 414
McShann, Jay, 61
McTell, Blind Willie, 54, 344
Meade Lux Lewis, 13
Meade, Norman, 80
Meaden, Peter, 18
"Mean Disposition," 600, 604–605, **621**
Meat Puppets (The), 159
Meaux, Huey P., 104
Meevowiffen, Tony, 219
Meinecke, Ulla, 430
"Melody," 454, 456, 459, **467**, 502
Melrose, Lester, 441
"Memo from Turner," **320**–322, 436, 438, 440
"Memory Hotel," 454, 456, 458, 460, 462, **465**
Memphis Horns (The), 182, 350–351
Memphis Minnie, 66, 615
Menzies, Anna, 456
Mercury Rev, 199
"Mercy Mercy," 90, 92, 94, **97**, 133, 506
Merkel, Angela, 408
Metamorphosis, 106, 154, 190, 285, 321, **436–453**
Meters (The), 499
Michael, George, 286
"Midnight Rambler," 191, 280, 284–285, **298–299**, 301, 312, 328, 364, 434, 644, 690
"Might as Well Get Juiced," 628, 632, **643**
Mighty Avengers (The), 133, 445
Mike Leander Orchestra (The), 172–173, 208
Milburn, Amos, 84
Millar, Robin, 376
Miller, Dan John, 278–279
Miller, Frankie, 231
Miller, Henry, 370
Miller, J. D., 36
Miller, Jimmy, **260–261**, 287–290, 292, 294, 296, 298–300, 302, 304, 306–309, 337, 339–340, 342, 344, 346–352, 354, 356, 362, 366–368, 370–380, 382–383, 385, 387–389, 391–393, 396, 400, 402–405, 407, 409–412, 414, 421, 424, 435, 448, 450–453, 519, 549, 605, 626, 663, 686
Miller, Rice, see Williamson II, Sonny Boy
Miller, Ronald Dean, 97
Milligan, Spike, 242
Mills, Ted, 433
Mingus, Charlie, 387, 460
Mink, Ben, 635
Minnelli, Liza, 475
"Miss Amanda Jones," 184, 189, **202**
"Miss You," 456, 470, 474, 476, **478**–480, 494, 498, 505, 515–516, 539, 547, 550, 594, 596, 648, 652, 656, 658, 690
Mitchell, Joni, 606
Mix This!, 686, 688
"Mixed Emotions," 570, 572, 574–576, **578–579**, 648, 656, 658, 660, 690, 695
Mizelle, Cindy, 574, 686–687
Moby, 104, 694
Modeliste, Joseph Zigaboo, 499
"Money," 28, 44, **47**, 49
Monkeys (The), 140
"Monkey Man," 280, 284–285, **302–303**
Monnar, Jennifer, 606, 614
Monroe, Marilyn, 474–475
Montague, Nathaniel "Magnificent," 97
Montez, Chris, 18
Montgomery, Wes, 103
Moody Blues (The), 234, 440
"Moon Is Up," 600, 604–605, **612**
Moon, Keith, 474
"Moonlight Mile," 330, 334, 337, **356–357**, 411
Moore, James, see Harpo, Slim
Moore, Johnny, 85
Moore, Lovell, 36
Moore, Pete, 530
Moore, Scotty, 89
Morad, Luciana, 645
Moretti, Joe, 440, 442–447
Morganfield, McKinley, see Waters, Muddy
Moroder, Giorgio, 421
Morris, Anita, 540
Morrison, Jim, 109, 287
Morrison, Van, 430, 599, 605–606
Morrissey, Dick, 13
Morrissey, Paul, 223
"Mother's Little Helper," 134, 136, 138–140, **142–143**, 146, 158, 166, 204, 206, 209, 648, 690
Motörhead, 261, 263, 276
Mott The Hoople, 311, 401
Mountain Recording Studios, 460, 461, 463–465, 467–469
Mozart, Wolfgang Amadeus, 229
Muhoberac, Jamie, 635, 640, 642
Muhoberac, Larry, 640
Murray the K, 52
Muse, 613
Muscle Shoals Sound Studios, 336, 337, 339, 340, 344, 348
Musicland Studios, 421–426, 429–435, 459–466, 468, 469, 514
"My Girl," 94, 204, 206, **208**, 324
"My Obsession," 184, **193**
Myers, Marc, 356

Nadas, 488
Name, Billy, 335
Nanker Phelge, 22–23, 34–35, 59–60, 108, 112, 117, 170
Nash, Graham, 28–29, 35, 440
"Natural Magic," 253, 320, **322**
"Neighbours," 497, 510, 514–515, 518, **522**, 525, 690
Nelson, Dean, 669, 671–685
Nelson, Earl, 669
Nelson, Ernest, 562
Nelson, Ricky, 89
Nettles, Bonnie, 634
Neville Brothers (The), 563
Neville, Aaron, 563
Neville, Ivan, 558, 561–563, 607–608, 614–617, 619–620
Neville, Naomi, see Toussaint, Allen
Nevins, Al, 122
New Barbarians (The), 487, 494, 499, 512
"New Faces," 602, 604–605, **611**, 613
New Order, 476
New Riders of the Purple Sage (The), 354
Newman, Colin, 558
Newman, Randy, 320–322
Nice (The), 19
Nico, 269–270
Nicolo, Joe, 607
Niles, Tessa, 576, 588, 599
Nitrate, Amyl, see Washington, Richard
Nitzsche, Jack, 73, 78, 87, 102–103, 106–107, 110–113, 118, 120, 126, 142, **144**–147, 149, 151, 154, 156–157, 166–168, 170–175, 182, 189, 191–192, 194, 196, 198, 201–203, 208–210, 238, 240–241, 244, 286, 289, 291, 304, 306, 320–322, 337, 352–353, 440, 442, 449, 497, 502
Nixon, Pat, 364
Nixon, Richard, 364, 372, 435
"No Expectations," 246, 251, 253, **262**–263, 266, 451
"No Spare Parts," 470, 472, 476, **688–689**
"No Use in Crying," 497, **526**
Norton, Mark, 604
"Not Fade Away," 28, 33, 35, **50–51**, 176, 180, 648, 690
"Now I've Got a Witness (Like Uncle Phil and Uncle Gene)," 24, 26, **34**

O'Brien, Glenn, 335
O'Dell, Chris, 520
O'Duffy, Alan, 287–288, 290, 292, 294, 296, 298, 300, 302, 304
Oasis, 576, 596, 669
Obrecht, Jas, 349, 403, 408, 609, 620
Ocean Way Recording Studios, 630, 634–647
Ochs, Phil, 289
Odell, Jonas, 686
"Off the Hook," 66–68, 70, 73, **88**
Offspring (The), 101
"Oh, Baby (We Got a Good Thing Going)," 68, 90, 94, **104**
Ogerman, Claus, 103
"Oh No, Not You Again," 664, 668–669, **679**
Ohio Players (The), 461
Ohlman, Christine, 443–446
Oldfield, Mike, 287, 576
Oldham, Celia, 18
Olson, Carla, 411
Olympic Sound Studios, 14, 16, 17, 189, 192–197, 204, 220–228, 232–244, 252–256, 262–269, 271–278
"On with the Show," 212, 220, **236**
"One Hit (to the Body)," 552, 554, 556–557, **559**–561, 578
"One More Try," 94, 324, **328**
Ono, Yoko, 94, 381, 576
Orbison, Roy, 120, 606
Original Five Blind Boys of Alabama (The), 348
Ormsby-Gore, David, 146, 251
Orwell, George, 435
Osbourne, Ozzy, 669
Ōtagaki, Yasuo, 356
"Out of Control," 628, 632–633, **640**
Out of Our Heads, **90–109**, 130, 133, 268, 328, 506
"Out of Tears," 600, 604–605, **613**, 626
"Out of Time," **154**, 351, 436, 438, 440, 450, 501, 690
Owens, Buck, 484
Ozen, Barbara Lynn, 104

Pachelbel, Johann, 209
Page, Gene, 562
Page, Jimmy, 37, 54, 106–107, 154, 199, 210, 229, 290, 432, 440, 442–443, 445–447, 558–559, 663
"Pain in My Heart," 68, 70, 73, **87**, 114, 182
"Paint It Black," 139, 140–141, 143–144, 149, 158, **168**–171, 178, 186, 241, 324, 588, 594, 596, 648, 686, 690
Palace of Ben Abbou (The), 588
Palladin, Patti, 127
Pallenberg, Anita, 95 138, 164, 202, 240–241, 244, 248, 256, 259, 282, 288–289, 292, 300, **318**, 320, 362, 396, 398, 404, 407, 472, 487, 509, 542, 574, 586, 647
Palmer, Robert, 537
"Parachute Woman," 246, 250, 253, **264**
Parker, Charlie, 61, 512, 602
Parker, Graham, 144
Parker, Steve, 558–559, 561–569,
Parliament, 537
Parsons, Gene, 320–322
Parsons, Gram, 255, 290–292, 354, 362, 366–367, 378–380, 484, 487
Parsons, Gretchen, 366
Pasche, John, 335, 399, 692
Pass, Joe, 143
Pastorius, Jaco, 617, 661
Patterson, Meg, 472
Patti Labelle & The Bluebelles, 576
Patton, Charley, 66
Paul Ray and the Cobras, 636
Paul, Clarence, 98
Paul, Gene, 460–461, 463–469
Pearl Jam, 633
Peellaert, Guy, 420–421
Pendarvis, Janice, 558, 565, 569
Pendleton, Brian, 103
Pendleton, Harold, 364
Pepper, Art, 401
Pepusch, Johann Christoph, 252
Pérez Morena Macías, Bianca, 362, 364, 385, 388, 398–400, 411, 424, 432–433, 456, 466, 474, 478, 485, 494, 502, 635
Perkins, Al, 368, 379
Perkins, Wayne, 456, 459, 463, 465, 468, 515, 523, 547
Perks, Molly, 10
Perks, William, 10
Perks, William George, see Wyman, Bill
Perrin, Janie, 282
Perrin, Les, 282
Pet Shop Boys, 476, 576
Peterson, Lucky, 370
"Petrol Blues," 470, 472, 476
Petty, Norman, 50
Petty, Tom, 605–606, 612
Phelge, James, 10, 22
Phillips, John, 19
Phillips, Sam, 42
Pickett, Wilson, 58, 76, 97, 171, 351
Pierce, Webb, 41, 116
Pink Floyd, 36, 108, 225, 234, 250, 286, 398, 423
Pint, Half, see Roberts, Lindon
Pitney, Gene, 28–29, 34–35, 38, 51
Plant, Robert, 576
"Play with Fire," 64, 94, 110, **112–113**, 690
"Please Go Home," 184, 189, **199**, 204, 206
Plummer, Bill, 368, 372–373, 385, 387, 453
"Plundered My Soul," 360, 367, 686–687, 688, 690
Poe, Edgar Allan, 217, 232
Pogues (The), 476
"Poison Ivy," 20, 28, 44, **49**, 183
Police (The), 544, 575, 660
Pollack, Malcolm, 530
Ponty, Jean-Luc, 537
Pop, Iggy, 604, 694
Pope, Alexander, 214
Porter, Cole, 678
Portishead, 199
Posada, Joe, 606
Posta, Adrienne, 164
Potier, Suki, 251, 256, 259
Potter, Christopher Mark, 575–584, 586–590, 592, 660, 662
Powell, Aubrey, 398
Powell, Willie Mae, 290
Power Station, 515–528
Presley, Elvis, 26, 49, 78, 89, 260, 286, 336, 474, 497, 518, 537, 545, 640
Preston, Billy, 197, 337, 346, 351, 369, 392, 401–403, 405, 418, 424–425, 434–435, 456, 458–463, 465–467, 469, 476, 478–479, 519, 523, 642, 660
"Pretty Beat Up," 532, 534, 537, **546**
Pretty Things (The), 33, 103, 337
Price, Alan, 286
Price, Jim, 337, 341, 349–351, 356–358, 362, 366, 370–373, 375–376, 379, 382–384, 386, 388–389, 393, 401, 403, 405–406, 448
Price, Lloyd, 58
Price, Will, 79
Priest, Judas, 476
Primal Scream, 261, 669
Prince, 506
Prince, Viv, 103
"Prodigal Son," 246, 250, 253, **268**, 314, 316
Professor Longhair, 87
Psychedelic Furs (The), 557
Puig, Jack Joseph, 669, 671–672, 674, 676–680, 684
Pussy Galore, 385
Pussycat Dolls (The), 669
Putnam, Bill, 633

Quant, Mary, 18, 136
Quatro, Suzi, 89
Queen, 422, 460, 515, 576
Quicksilver Messenger Service, 231, 305

Radiohead, 153, 613
Radziwill, Lee Princess, 396
Raelettes (The), 289
Ragovoy, Jordan "Jerry," see Meade, Norman
Raicevic, Nik Pascal, 401
"Rain Fall Down," 664, 666, 669, **673**, 690
Rainbows (The), 97
Raitt, Bonnie, 633
Rajlich, Jana, 642
Ramones (The), 472, 480
Ramrods (The), 8
Rapace, Noomi, 694
Rarities 1971–2003, 31, 633, **656–663**
Raye, Don, 84
Raye, Tony, 10
RCA Studios, 72, 73, 76, 78, 87, 94, 96, 98, 100–104, 106, 110–112, 118–121, 124, 126, 133, 139, 140, 142, 145, 146, 148, 150–160, 166, 168, 171, 172, 174, 180, 182, 189–203, 208, 209, 210, 239
Rea, Chris, 537
Rebennack, Malcom, see Dr. John
Rebop, 401, 405, 410, 412
Redding, Otis, 87, 99–100, 103, 106, 119–120, 136, 159, 171, 182, 208, 334, 351
Reed, Jimmy, 10–12, 26, 32, 35, 104, 121, 289, 479, 660
Reed, Lou, 223, 269, 335, 480, 497, 632
Rees-Mogg, William, 214
Regan, John, 558–560, 565–566
Regent Sound Studios, 17, 26, 28–42, 50, 51, 54, 64, 66, 72, 73, 76, 79, 83, 85, 88, 89, 106, 132
Relf, Bob "Bobby," 562
Reparata and The Delrons, 286, 308–309, 311
Resnick, Arthur, 85
"Respectable," 470, 474, 476, **485–486**, 658, 690
Reynolds, Ron "Snake," 497–505, 507–508
Riagorri, Mauricio, 634–636, 642, 645
Rich, Buddy, 73
Richard, Cliff, 133, 576
Richards, Angela (Dandelion), 244, 318, 396, 407
Richards, Dave, 460–461, 463–467
Richards, Doris, 9
Richards, Herbert William, 9
Richards, Keith, 10–695
Richards, Marlon, 244, 293, 318, 334, 344, 365, 384–385, 393, 407, 508
Richards, Tara, 318

Richardson, Tony, 18, 165, 300, 339, 540
"Ride On, Baby," 140, 204, 206, **209**
Right Track Studios, 557, 559, 561–569, 605, 606, 613, 614
Rimbaud, Arthur, 165, 370
"Rip This Joint," 202, 360, 364, 368, 371–**373**, 385, 438, 450, 483, 581, 634
Riser, Paul, 448
Ritz, Martin, 49
Rivers, Johnny, 89
Roberts, Lindon, 554, 564
Robey, Don, 10
Robinson, Alvin, 78
Robinson, Claudette, 530
Robinson, Eric, 11
Robinson, Smokey, 47, 97, 136, 161, 170–171, 208, 425, 530
"Rock and a Hard Place," 570, 572, 574–575, **584–585**, 592, 594, 596
Rocket 88, 13
"Rocks Off," 360, 364, 368, **370–371**, 373, 378, 383, 389, 462, 548, 690
Rodgers, Jimmie, 292, 378
Rodgers, Nile, 461, 561, 576, 580
Roeg, Nicolas, 279, 318, 320
Rogan, Alan, 558–559, 561, 563, 565, 569, 576
Rogers, Bobby, 530
Rogers, Jimmy, 31, 66
Rolling Stones Mobile Studio, 336, 338, 342, 346–351, 356–358, 362, 370, 374–393, 380, 422, 425–435, 459, 460, 464, 467, 469, 514–528, 686
Rolling Stones Records, 334, 438, 496
Rollin' Stones (The), 10–12, 18
Rollins, Sonny, 514–515, 519, 522, 528, 546
Romeo, Max, 496, 498, 500, 502, 537, 543
Ronettes (The), 144, 444
Ronson, Mick, 456
Ronstadt, Linda, 369, 606, 634
Rose, Axl, 273
Rose, Jane, 490
Ross, Diana, 467
Ross, Glenn, 440
Ross, Scott, 119
Roth, Richard, 440
"Rough Justice," 664, 666, 668–**670**, 671–672, 690
Rowe, Dick, 12, 15, 49
Roxy Music, 223, 254, 479, 496
Royal Philharmonic Orchestra (The), 440
RPM Studios, 557, 559, 561–563, 569
Rubin, Rick, 602
"Ruby Tuesday," 189, 204, 206, 228, 238, **240–241**, 282, 398, 594, 596, 648, 690
Ruffin, David, 208, 425
Rumsfeld, Donald, 682
Russell, Anita, 456
Russell, Bert, see Berns, Bert
Russell, Ethan, 314
Russell, Leon, 294–295, 369, 463

Saber, Danny, 630, 638, 640, 643
Sacher-Masoch, Eva von, 164
Sacher-Masoch, Leopold von, 164, 541
"Sad Day," 140, 161, **166–167**
"Sad Sad Sad," 570, 572, 575, **577**, 594, 596
Sagmeister, Stefan, 632
"Saint of Me," 628, 632–633, **642**, 658, 661–662, 690
Sainte-Marie, Buffy, 144
Saisse, Philippe, 558, 566
"Salt of the Earth," 246, 250, 253, **272–273**, 433, 567, 690
Sam and Dave, 351
Samson, 583
Samuelsohn, Brad, 497–505, 507–508
Sanborn, David, 537, 544, 546, 551
Sanchez, Tony, 295, 300
Sanders, Sonny, 58
Sanders, Tim, 576
Sanderson, Alan, 634–640, 642–647
Sandymount Studio, 607–621
Santana, 332, 411, 422, 496, 515, 528, 633
Santana, Carlos, 347, 405, 429–430, 477
Sardy, Dave, 669–670
Sarli, Jeff, 634, 645, 647
Savage, Roger, 14–17
Sawyer, Vernon, 433
Sawyer, Wendell, 433
Scaggs, Boz, 336
Schatzberg, Jerry, 139
Scheff, Jerry, 320–322
Schifrin, Lalo, 153
Schlink, Doug, 445–446
Schlöndorff, Volker, 241, 318
Schönberg, Arnold, 490
Scialfa, Patti, 558–559, 561
Scorsese, Martin, 96, 109
Scott, Jim, 645
Scott, Keith, 8
Screaming Lord Sutch, 125
Screaming Lord Sutch and the Savages, 230
Seaga, Edward, 396
Seahorn, Marshall, 87
Sea Level, 541
Searchers (The), 144, 159
Secombe, Harry, 242
Seeff, Norman, 365
Segovia, Andrés, 210
Sellers, Peter, 242, 279
"Send It to Me," 492, 496–497, **500**, 507
Setzer, Brian, 30
"Sex Drive," 594, 596, **599**, 602
Sex Pistols (The), 159, 472, 483, 534
Shadows (The), 103, 133
"Shake Your Hips," 360, 364–365, **374**
Shakespeare, Robbie, 537, 539, 543
Shankar, Ravi, 170
Sharma, Krish, 669, 671–686, 688, 694–695
"Shattered," 470, 474, 476, **490**, 512, 648, 690
"She Said Yeah," 90, 92, 94–**96**, 128, 130, 690
"She Saw Me Coming," 664, 666, 668–669, **676**
"She Smiled Sweetly," 184, 188, **196**
"She Was Hot," 496, 532, 534, 536–537, **540**, 550, 690
"She's a Rainbow," 212, 216–219, **228**–230, 232, 234–235, 686, 690
"She's So Cold," 492, 496, **507**, 540, 690
Sherlock, George Raymond, 108
Sherman, Garry, 80
Sherrill, Billy, 336
Shiloh, 379
"Shine a Light," 285, 360, 364–365, 382, **392**, 404, 642
Shines, Johnny, 291
Shirelles (The), 20
Shirley & Company, 369
"Short and Curlies," 400, 416, 418, 420, 422, **434**
Shorter, Wayne, 647
Show of Hands, 583
Shrieve, Michael, 496, 498, 500–501, 505–506
Shrimpton, Chrissie, 113, 136, 138, 145, 148, 161, 164, 168, 188, 192, 201
Shrimpton, Jean, 136, 145
Shyer, Charles, 674
Sides, Allen, 633
Silberling, Brad, 356
"Silver Train," 394, 398, 400, 407, **409**–410
Simon, Carly, 414, 428, 460, 465, 477, 558, 604
Simons, Judith, 19
Simple Minds, 537, 557, 576
Simpson, Mike, 630, 643
Simpson, Wallis, 574
Sinatra, Frank, 103 606, 633
"Sing This All Together," 212, 216, 220, **222**, 223, 227
"Sing This All Together (See What Happens)," 212, 216, 220, **227**, 233
"Sister Morphine," 165, 253, 330, 334, 337, **352–353**
"Slave," 459, 510, 514–515, **519**
"Sleep Tonight," 552, 556–557, **569**
"Slipping Away," 570, 572, 574–575, **590**
Sly and the Family Stone, 456
Small Faces (The), 19, 198, 217, 225
Smashing Pumpkins (The), 633
Smith Perkins Smith, 463
Smith, Charlie, 598–599
Smith, Delia, 285
Smith, Don, 605–624, 626–627
Smith, Fred, 562
Smith, Harry, 165
Smith, Jon, 497–505, 507–508
Smith, Mamie, 378
Smith, Mandy, 554, 577, 586, 598
Smith, Patti, 497
Smith, Vic, 287–288, 290, 292, 294, 296, 298–300, 302, 304
Smiths (The), 98, 288
Smokey Robinson & The Miracles, 47, 97, 170–171, 208, 530
Snow, Hank, 116
Snow, Mat, 284
"So Divine (Aladdin Story)," 360
"So Young," 470, 476, 622–**623**,
Soft Machine, 250
Some Girls, **470–491**, 494, 496–497, 499, 502–503, 512, 514, 516, 518, 556, 586, 614, 623, 668, 679, 688–689
"Some Girls," 470, 474, 476, **482**
"Something Happened to Me Yesterday," 186, 188, **203**, 230, 272
"Somethings Just Stick in Your Mind," 436, 438, **442**
Sonny & Cher, 96
Sorenson, John, 634, 636–640, 645, 647
Soul Stirrers (The), 101
"Soul Survivor," 360, 364, 367–368, **393**, 549, 585
Spandau Ballet, 539
Spann, Otis, 31, 230
Sparks (The), 576
"Sparks Will Fly," 600, 604–605, **609**,
Sparks, Rennie, 354
Specials (The), 476
Spector, Phil, 26, 28, 34–35, 51, 73, 78, 96, 112–113, 136, 144, 157, 173, 188, 193–194, 302, 440, 442, 444–445, 447, 613, 633
Spector, Ronnie, 646
Spedding, Chris, 456
Spellman, Benny, 183
Spencer Davis Group, 260
Spirit, 314
Spitz, Marc, 428
Spong, Paul, 576
Spooky Tooth, 260
Springfield, Dusty, 76
Springsteen, Bruce, 263, 291, 479, 546, 606
Squeeze, 460
St. Louis Jimmy, 10
Stafford, Tom, 336
Staple Singers (The), 110–111, 618
Staples, Roebuck "Pops," 618
"Star Star," 394, 398–399, **414–415**
Stardust, Ziggy, see Bowie, David
Starr, Ringo, 21, 29, 109, 123, 144, 231, 286, 328, 369, 401, 443, 612
"Start Me Up," 255, 310, 460, 476, 497, 510, 512, 514, **516–517**, 525, 585, 594, 596, 648, 652, 654, 679, 690
"Stealing My Heart," 648, 650, **654**, 692
Steckler, Al, 440
Steel Pulse, 564
Steel Wheels, **570–591**, 592, 596, 599, 605, 660, 662, 669
Steele, Tommy, 399
Steely Dan, 369, 401
Stent, Mark "Spike," 596, 598–599
Stephen, John, 18
Steve Miller Band, 230
Stevens, Cat, 287
Stevenson, William "Mickey," 47, 98
Stewart Dillane, Cynthia, 13
Stewart, Billy, 97
Stewart, Dave, 666
Stewart, Ian (Stu), 9–10, 12–**13**, 15–16, 18–23, 28–29, 34, 37–38, 40–41, 48, 58–62, 124, 139, 145, 148–152, 154–155, 159–160, 171, 174–175, 182, 191, 193, 195, 198, 202, 220, 222, 230, 255, 262, 274, 296, 308–309, 319, 328, 338–339, 345, 354, 362, 364, 366, 374, 376, 378, 391, 409–410, 414–415, 426, 432, 434, 441–442, 448, 456, 458, 461, 499, 502–503, 518, 520–522, 526, 530, 537, 540, 546, 550, 556–**557**, 569, 592, 623, 660
Stewart, Jim, 42
Stewart, Johnnie, 245
Stewart, Rod, 319, 426, 458–459, 576
Sticky Fingers, 136, 219, 230, 253, 261, **330–357**, 359, 362, 364–366, 368–369, 378, 380, 389, 391–393, 396, 398, 411, 428, 438, 456, 475, 502, 536, 630
Stills, Stephen, 292, 379, 453
Sting, 423, 460, 565, 602
Stoller, Mike, 17, 49, 78, 122
Stone, Al, 576, 578
Stone Age, 95, **324–329**
"Stoned," 20, **22–23**, 29
"Stop Breaking Down," 328, 360, 364–365, **391**, 409
Stoppard, Tom, 632
Strachwitz, Chris, 348
Stranglers (The), 401
"Stray Cat Blues," 246, 250, 253, **269**–270, 273, 312, 451
Stray Cats (The), 540
"Street Fighting Man," 246, 250, 253, 261, 264, **266–267**, 276, 312, 364, 438, 648, 690, 695
"Streets of Love," 664, 666, 669–670, **674**, 690
Strong, Barrett, 47, 481, 640
Studio Guillaume Tell, 650–655, 692–695
"Stupid Girl," 134, 138, 140, **145**, 150, 168
Sublett, Joe, 634, 636, 639, 646
"Suck on the Jugular," 600, 604–605, **617**
Sudden, Nikki, 444
Sugar Blue, 476, 478–479, 482, 496, 500, 504
Sugarhill Gang (The), 643
Sullivan, Big Jim, 440, 442–443, 445–446
Sullivan, Ed, 81, 238
Sullivan, Jim, 163
Sum 41, 640
Sumlin, Hubert, 66
"Summer Romance," 476, 492, 496, **499**
Summer, Donna, 461, 472, 494
Summers, Andy, 544
Sunset Sound Studios, 253, 272, 273
Supremes (The), 40, 62, 154, 286
"Susie Q," 68, 70, 73, **89**
Sutch, David Edward, 125
Swampers (The), 336, 345
"Sway," 330, 332, 337, **342–343**, 357
"Sweet Black Angel," 360, 364, 366, 376, **380–381**
"Sweet Neo Con," 664, 666, 669, **682**
"Sweet Virginia," 360, 364–365, **378**
"Sweethearts Together," 600, 604–605, **616**
Swettenham, Dick, 287, 338, 423
Sylvestre, Cleo, 28
"Sympathy for the Devil," 165, 230, 246, 250, 253, **256**–259, 261, 298, 312, 318, 364, 479, 590, 594, 596, 598, 642, 648, 650, 686, 690

T. Rex, 422
Tackhead, 576
"Take It or Leave It," 134, 138–140, **157**, 166, 204, 206
"Talkin' About You," **102**–103
Talking Heads, 557, 565, 588
"Tallahassee Lassie," 340, 470
Talmy, Shel, 230
Tampa Red, 441
Tangerine Dream, 440
Tapanainen, Tapani, 422, 424–426, 428–429, 431–435, 460–461, 463–469
Tarbuck, Jimmy, 446
Tarplin, Marvin "Marv," 530
Tate, Sharon, 284, 288
Tattoo You, 230, 400, 422, 459, 476, 497, **510–529**, 536–537
Taylor, Dick, 8–10, 62, 103
Taylor, James, 379, 634
Taylor, Mick, 37–695
Taylor, Vince, 444
Taylor, William, 10
TCB Band, 640
Teel, Jerry, 175
"Tell Me (You're Coming Back)," 24, 26, 28, **38–39**, 41, 66, 83, 106, 133,
Temple, Julien, 534, 539–540, 545, 599
Temptations (The), 208, 425, 456, 481, 488, 606, 640
Ten Years After, 337
Tench, Benmont, 606, 612–613, 618, 637, 644
"Terrifying," 570, 574–575, **580**, 658, 662
Tex, Joe, 76
Texas Tornados, 606
Texmaniacs (Los), 616
Thackery, Jimmy, 370
Tharpe, Rosetta (Sister), 348
"That's How Strong My Love Is," 92, 94, **99**, 690
Thatcher, Margaret, 214, 514, 518
"The Lantern," 212, 217, 220, 224, **232**
"The Last Time," **110**–112, 176, 178, 324, 648, 690
The Rolling Stones, **24–43**
The Rolling Stones (EP), **44–49**
The Rolling Stones No. 2, **68–89**
Their Satanic Majesties Request, 13–19, 136, 138, 186, **212–237**, 238–245, 248, 250, 275–276, 279, 302, 398, 403, 412, 421, 451, 525, 556, 588
"The Singer Not the Song," 95, 124, **126**–128, 130
"The Spider and the Fly," 94, 118–119, **121**, 324, 328
"The Storm," 605, 607, **622**–624, 627
"The Under Assistant West Coast Promotion Man," 83, 90, 92, 94, **108**, 119
"The Worst," 600, 604–605, **610**–611
Thear, Rod, 358, 422, 424–426, 428–429, 431–435, 537–538, 540–544, 546–549
Theis, Chris, 599
Them, 30
Thérémin, Léon, 199
"Thief in the Night," 628, 632–633, **646**
Thin Lizzy, 369
"Think," 134, 138, 140, **158**, 438
"This Place Is Empty," 664, 666, 668–669, **678**
Thomas, Irma, 80, 87
Thomas, Rufus, 42
Thorgerson, Storm, 398
Thorogood, Frank, 448
"Through the Lonely Nights," 400, 426, 656, 658, **663**
"Thru and Thru," 600, 604–605, **620**, 656, 658
Thunders, Johnny, 127
"Tie You Up (The Pain of Love)," 532, 534, 537, **541**
"Till the Next Goodbye," 416, 418, 420, 422, **428**, 433
"Time Is on My Side," 64–65, 68, 70, 73, **80–81**, 441, 526, 690
"Time Waits for No One," 416, 418, 422–423, **429–430**, 433, 512
Tippin, Corey, 335
Titelman, Russ, 320–322
Tom Petty and the Heartbreakers, 612
"Too Much Blood," 532, 534, 537, **544**–546
"Too Rude," 552, 554, 557, **564**, 569
"Too Tight," 628, 632–633, **645**
"Too Tough," 532, 534, 537, **547**
"Tops," 400, 510, 514, **524**, 528
"Torn and Frayed," 360, 364, 368, **379**
Tornados (The), 49, 606
Tosh, Peter, 528
Toto, 606
Toussaint, Allen, 28, 87, 183, 194
Townshend, Pete, 117, 426, 496, 515, 519, 561, 575
Traffic, 253, 260, 267, 321, 401, 410
Troup, Bobby, 30
Troy, Doris, 286, 304, 306, 308–309, 311
Trudeau, Margaret, 494
Trudeau, Pierre Elliott, 494
Truffaut, François, 18
Truman, Harry, 402
"Try a Little Harder," 436, 438, **447**
"Tumbling Dice," 337, 360, 364–365, 367–368, **376–377**, 380, 383, 390, 438, 489, 648, 654, 656, 658, 690
"Turd on the Run," 360, 368, **385**
Turner, Tina, 557, 576
Twice as Much, 210
Twiggy, 136
Two Gospel Keys (The), 348

U Roy, 537
U2, 496, 537, 557, 596, 605, 618, 633, 654, 666, 673
"Under My Thumb," 134, 138, 140, **148–149**, 150, 154–155, 176, 178, 209, 217, 259, 332, 381, 502, 648, 690
"Under the Boardwalk," 42, 65, 68, 73, **85**
Undercover, 478, **532–549**, 550–551, 560, 577, 592
"Undercover of the Night," 532, 534, 536–**539**, 599, 648, 690
Uptown Horns (The), 574

Vadim, Roger, 318
Vadukul, Max, 632
Valens, Ritchie, 10, 125, 152
Valentinos (The), 52–53
Van Dyke, Earl, 40
Van Hamersveld, John, 365
Velez, Glen, 588
Velvet Underground (The), 98, 108, 223, 269–270, 319
"Ventilator Blues," 360, 364, 368, 383, **386**–387, 453
Verve (The), 111, 575
Villacorta, Germán, 669, 673, 675, 681–683, 685
Village Recorder (The), 400, 402, 405, 414, 669, 670, 686
Vincent, Gene, 444
Virgin Prunes, 558
Vivaldi, Antonio, 210
Volaitis, John X., 637–638, 640
Voodoo Lounge, **600–621**, 622–626, 630, 632, 669

Wagner, Claude, 496
"Waiting on a Friend," 400, 510, 514, **528–529**, 690
Waits, Tom, 368, 558, 562, 569, 572, 678
Wakabayashi, Yasuhiro, see Hiro
Wakeman, Rick, 606
Walker, Joe Louis, 370
Walker, Johnny "Big Moose," 521
"(Walkin' Thru the) Sleepy City," 436, 438, **445**
"Walking the Dog," 24, 28, **42**, 85
Waller, Ian "Wal," 576, 596
Wally Heider (RCA) Studios, 499, 503
Walsh, Joe, 231
Walter, Little, 31, 88, 504, 589, 675, 682
"Wanna Hold You," 532, 534, 536, **542**, 579
Ward Baker, Roy, 126
Warhol, Andy, 217, 223, 270, 332, 334–335, 465, 605
Warnes, Jennifer, 144
Warwick, Dee Dee, 80
Warwick, Dionne,
Warwicker, John, 575
Was (Not Was), 604, 669
Was, Don, 604–622, 624, 626–627, 630, 633–637, 639–640, 644–647, 652–655, 668–688, 694–695
Washington, Richard, 368, 380–381
Watchel, Waddy, 634–636, 640, 642–647
Waters, Ethel, 236
Waters, Muddy, 31, 46, 52–53, 60, 70, 72, 74, 82, 86, 132, 228–229, 238, 353, 386, 504, 521, 536, 589, 621, 660, 675
Watts Street Gospel Choir, 253, 272–273
Watts, Charlie, 10–695
Watts, Ernie, 530–531
Watts, Seraphina, 248
Watts, Shirley, 564, 666
Wayne, Isham, 585
Wayne, John, 398, 414–415
"We Had It All," 470, 472
"We Love You," 189, 218–220, 230, **242**–245, 690
"We Want the Stones," 114
"We're Wastin' Time," 436, 438, **446**
Weber, Tommy, 366
Webster, Guy, 139, 206
Weedon, Bert, 18
Welch, Raquel, 474–475
Wells, Junior, 35
Wenner, Jann S., 190, 666
West Five, 65
Wexler, Jerry, 58, 76, 85, 336, 388
"What a Shame," 68, 70, 73, **82**–83, 107
"What to Do," 134, 136, 138–140, **159**
"When the Whip Comes Down," 470, 474, 476, **480**, 485, 488, 512
"When You're Gone," 470, 476
"Where the Boys Go," 476, 492, 496, **503**–504
White Stripes (The), 382
White, Andy, 440, 442–447
White, Barry, 562
White, Bukka, 675
White, Jack, 382
White, Ronald, 208
Whitecross, Mat, 689
Whitehead, Peter, 244–245
Whitelaw, Sandy, 478
Whitfield, Norman, 425, 481, 640
Whiting, James, see Sugar Blue
Whitlock, Bobby, 387
Whittaker, Hudson, see Tampa Red
Who (The), 161, 189, 217, 230, 263, 314, 337–338, 423, 447, 474, 515, 561, 576, 643
"Who's Been Sleeping Here?," 184, 188, **200**
"Who's Driving Your Plane?," 172, **174–175**
Wick Home Studios (The), 426
Wiederhold, Paula, 318
Wiig, Kristen, 228
"Wild Horses," 165, 330, 332, 336, 338, 340, 342, **344–345**, 428, 438, 569, 637, 648, 656, 658, 686, 690
Wild, David, 650
Wilde, Oscar, 138, 245
Wilkes, Tom, 206
Wilkins, Robert, 268
Will Bradley Trio, 84
Will Bradley/Ray McKinley Orchestra, 84
will.i.am., 673
Williams, Hank, 292, 378
Williams, Larry, 92, 96
Williams, Lucinda, 391
Williams, Paul, 208
Williams, Robbie, 650
Williams, Tennessee, 354
Williamson II, Sonny Boy, 59, 82
Wilson, Brian, 140, 151, 193, 606
Wilson, Dennis, 101
Wilson, Harold, 362
Wilson, Hop, 521
Wilson, Tom, 118
Wimbish, Doug "Dougie," 604, 643–644
Winding, Kai, 80
Winding, Kasper, 528–529
Windmill Lane Studios, 605–626
Winehouse, Amy, 338
"Winning Ugly," 552, 554, 557, **565**
"Winter," 394, 398–399, **411**
Winter, Johnny, 270, 314, 409
Winwood, Steve (Stevie), 260, 321, 401, 619
Wire, 558
"Wish I'd Never Met You," 575, 580, 656, **662**
Wolf, Peter, 76
Wolfowitz, Paul, 682
Womack, Bobby, 52–53, 97, 558–560, 562–563, 566, 569, 612
Womack, Shirley, 53
Wonder, Stevie, 97, 120, 145, 253, 401, 403, 438, 448, 497, 546, 575, 638, 660
Wood, Chris, 260
Wood, Ron, 362–695
Woodbridge, Hudson, see Tampa Red
Workman, Nanette, 286, 292–293, 304, 306, 308–309, 311
"Worried About You," 459, 510, 514, **523**, 550
Wright, Gary, 286
Wright, Nicholas, 29
Wright, O. V., 99
Wyman, Bill, 10–695

X-Pensive Winos, 572, 602, 634
X-Press 2, 673

Yamazaki, Kazushige, 531
Yardbirds (The), 59, 116
Yes, 234, 460, 576
"Yesterday's Paper," 184, 186, 188, **192**–193, 196
Yetnikoff, Walter, 554
"You Better Move On," 28, 44, **48**, 128, 130, 692
"You Can Make It If You Try," 24, 28, **41**
"You Can't Always Get What You Want," 144, 165, 261, 273, 280, 284–285, 294, **304**–309, 311, 377, 594, 596, 648, 690
"You Can't Catch Me," 68, 73, **79**
"You Can't Judge a Book," 9–10
"You Don't Have to Mean It," 628, 632–633, **639**
"You Got Me Rocking," 600, 604–605, **608**, 624, 648, 690
"You Got the Silver," 280, 284–285, 289, **300–301**, 318, 690,
"You Gotta Move," 314, 330, 334, 336, 340, 344, **348**
"You Win Again," 470, 472, 476
Young, Kenny, 85
Young, Neil, 144–146, 289

Zagarino, Joe, 368–370, 372, 374–376, 378–380, 382–383, 385–389, 391–393
Zappa, Frank, 118, 186, 190, 287
Zydeco, Buckwheat, 488
ZZ Top, 374, 666

BIBLIOGRAPHY

The works here have served as references for the analysis of the songs.

1 Wyman, Bill. *Rolling with the Stones*. London: Dorling Kindersley Ltd., 2002.

2 Richards, Keith, and James Fox. *Life*. New York: Little, Brown & Company, 2010.

3 Phelge, James. *Phelge's Stones*. Kingswood, Surrey, England: Buncha Asshole Books, 1998.

4 Johns, Glyn. *Sound Man: A Life Recording Hits with the Rolling Stones, the Who, Led Zeppelin, the Eagles, Eric Clapton, The Faces . . .* New York: Penguin Group, 2014.

5 Loog Oldham, Andrew. *Stoned*. London: Secker & Warburg, 2000.

6 Wyman, Bill. *Stone Alone: The Story of a Rock 'n' Roll Band*. Boston: Da Capo Press Inc., 1997.

7 The Beatles. *The Beatles Anthology*. Apple Corps Ltd., London: 2000.

8 Booth, Stanley. *The True Adventures of the Rolling Stones*. London: Sphere Books Ltd., 1989.

9 Jagger, Mick, Keith Richards, Charlie Watts, and Ronnie Wood. *According to the Rolling Stones*. San Francisco: Chronicle Books, 2009.

10 Jackson, Laura. *Golden Stone: The Untold Life and Mysterious Death of Brian Jones*. London: Smith Gryphon Publishers, 1992.

11 Richards, Keith. *Keith Richards on Keith Richards: Interviews and Encounters*. London: Omnibus Press, 2014.

12 Salewicz, Chris. *Mick & Keith: Parallel Lines*. London: Orion, 2002.

13 Sheff, David. *The Playboy Interviews with John and Yoko: The Final Testament*. New York: Playboy Press/A division of PEI Books, Inc., 1982.

14 Richards, Keith. *In His Own Words*. London: Omnibus Press, 1994.

15 Janovitz, Bill. *Rocks Off: 50 Tracks That Tell the Story of the Rolling Stones*. Edinburgh: Polygon, 2014.

16 Berry, Chuck. *The Autobiography*. New York: Simon & Schuster Inc., 1987.

17 *Mojo*, Interview with Jimmy Page (September 2007).

18 Cott, Jonathan. "Mick Jagger: The Rolling Stone Interview." *Rolling Stone Magazine* (October 12, 1968).

19 Wenner, Jann S. "Jagger Remembers." *Rolling Stone Magazine* (December 14, 1995).

20 Musician Magazine. Interview with Andrew Loog Oldham (April 1987).

21 *Boyfriend*. Interview with Keith Richards (April 11, 1964).

22 Leiber, Jerry, Mike Stoller, and David Ritz. *Hound Dog: The Leiber & Stoller Autobiography*. New York: Simon & Schuster, 2009.

23 Norman, Philip. *The Stones: The Definitive Biography*. London: Pan Books, 2002.

24 *CREEM: America's Only Rock 'n' Roll Magazine*. Interview with Mick Jagger (July 1974)

25 Goodall, Nigel. *Jump Up*. Chessington, UK: Castle Communications Plc, 1995.

26 *CREEM: America's Only Rock 'n' Roll Magazine*. Interview with Bill Wyman (November 1978).

27 Paytress, Mark. *The Rolling Stone: Off the Record*. London: Omnibus Press, 2003.

28 Babiuk, Andy, and Greg Prevost. *Rolling Stones Gear: All the Stones' Instruments from Stage to Studio*. Milwaukee: Backbeat Books, 2013.

29 *Rolling Stone Magazine*. Interview with Jonathan Cott (June 29, 1978).

30 *Mojo Special Edition. The Rolling Stones: Inside the World's Greatest Rock 'n' Roll Band—40th Anniversary Collector's Edition*. Interview with Andrew Loog Oldham by Pat Gilbert (2003).

31 *New Musical Express (NME)*. Interview with Brian Jones. (January 22, 1965).

32 " 'Out Of Our Heads'/'December's Children': An All Time Stone Cold Classic in Our Gered Mankowitz Exhibition." Snap Galleries, 2013 (snapgalleries.com).

33 Interview with Dave Hassinger, Steve Hoffman Music. http://forums.stevehoffman.tv/threads/rolling-stones-mofi-box-dave-hassinger-interview-and-question.78620

34 Di Perna, Alan. "From The Archive: The Rolling Stones' Keith Richards Looks Back on 40 Years of Making Music." *Guitar World* (October 2002).

35 Bonanno, Massimo. *The Rolling Stones: The First 50 Years*. New York: Simon & Schuster, 2012.

36 *Circus*, no. 165. Interview with Keith Richards. (September 29, 1977).

37 Dalton, David, and Mick Farren. *The Rolling Stones in Their Own Words*. New York: Delilah/Putnam, 1983.

38 Bockris, Victor. *Keith Richards: The Biography*. London: Random House UK, 1992.

39 *CREEM: America's Only Rock 'n' Roll Magazine*. Interview with Keith Richards (December 1973).

40 *Mojo Special Edition. The Rolling Stones Inside the World's Greatest Rock 'n' Roll Band: 40th Anniversary Collector's Edition*. Interview with Andria Lisle (2003).

41 *Mojo*. Interview with Rickie Lee Jones (September 2007).

42 *Rolling Stone Magazine* (May 1971).

43 *Mojo*. Interview with John Foxx (September 2007).

44 *New Musical Express (NME)*. Interview with Keith Altham (January 14, 1967).

45 Hassinger, Dave. Cover notes for the album *Aftermath*.

46 Sandford, Christopher. *The Rolling Stones: Fifty Years*. New York: Simon & Schuster, 2012.

47 *Mojo*. Interview with Jackie Leven (September 2007).

48 *Rolling Stone Magazine*. Interview with Chet Flippo (May 6, 1976).

49 Greenfield, Robert. Interview with Keith Richards. *Rolling Stone Magazine* (August 19, 1971).

50 *Mojo*. Interview with Alice Cooper (September 2007).

51 Townshend, Pete. *Who I Am: A Memoir*. Paris: Michel Lafont, 2012.

52 Faithfull, Marianne. *An Autobiography*. New York: First Cooper Square Press, 2000.

53 *New Musical Express (NME)*. "Stones Reveal Secrets," (September 22, 1966).

54 *Record Mirror*. "At Home," (September 24, 1966).

55 *Melody Maker*. Interview with Mick Jagger (January 7, 1967).

56 Official website of the Rolling Stones: http://www.rollingstones.com/.

57 Whiteley, Sheila., *Sexing the Groove: Popular Music and Gender*. London: Routledge, 1997.

58 Luft, Eric V. D. *Die at the Right Time!: A Subjective Cultural History of the American Sixties*. North Syracuse, N.Y.: Gegensatz Press, 2009.

59 Wilson, Brian. *Wouldn't It Be Nice*. New York: HarperCollins Publishers, 1991.

60 Perkins, Jeff, and Michael Heatley. *The Rolling Stones Uncensored on the Record*. Wootton Wawen, Warwickshire, England: Coda Books Ltd., 2011.

61 Appleford, Steve. *The Rolling Stones: It's Only Rock 'n' Roll*. London: Carlton Books, 1997.

62 *Esquire*. Interview with Scott Raab (September 2015).

63 *Mojo*. Interview with Billy Childish (September 2007).

64 *Hit Parader*. Interview with Valerie Wilmar (December 1968).

65 Beatles Bible. http://www.beatlesbible.com/.

66 Davis, Stephen. *Old Gods Almost Dead: The 40-Year Odyssey of the Rolling Stones*. New York: Broadway Books, 2002.

67 *Sunday Mirror*. "Beggar's Banquet," (December 1, 1968).

68 *Chicago Sun Times*. (January 26, 1969).

69 Dawson, Julian. *And on Piano . . . Nicky Hopkins*. San Francisco: Plus One Press, 2011.

70 *The Independent*. Interview with Jimmy Miller (October 25, 1994).

71 Brown, Phill. "Are We Still Rolling?" Tape Op Books, 2010 (www.tapeop.com/ books@tapeop.com).

72 *Wall Street Journal.* Interview with Marc Myers (December 11, 2013).

73 Interview with Eddie Kramer. https://50licks. wordpress.com/.

74 http://www. timeisonourside.com/.

75 *Mojo.* Interview with Dan John Miller (September 2007).

76 *Mojo.* Interview with Mat Snow (September 2007).

77 *Mojo.* Interview with Johnny Marr (September 2007).

78 *Rolling Stone Magazine.* Interview with Greil Marcus (December 27, 1969).

79 Egan, Sean. *Rolling Stones and the Making of Let It Bleed.* London: Unanimous Ltd., 2007.

80 *Rolling Stone Magazine.* Interview with Robert Greenfield (January 23, 2015).

81 Sanchez, Tony. *Up and Down with the Rolling Stones: My Rollercoaster Ride with Keith Richards.* London: John Blake Publishing Ltd., 2010.

82 Kooper, Al. *Backstage Passes & Backstabbing Bastards.* New York: Billboard Books, 2008.

83 *Guitar Player.* Interview with Jas Obrecht (February 1980).

84 Bangs, Lester. *Rolling Stone Magazine* (September 4, 1970).

85 Booklet by Nick Kent in the June 2015 deluxe reissue of *Sticky Fingers.*

86 Simons, Dave. "Mark Neill: Recording the Black Keys at Muscle Shoals" (August 2011), http://www. soundonsound.com/.

87 Liner notes of *Jump Back,* 2004.

88 Interview with Jas Obrecht (June 22, 1979), jasobrecht.com.

89 Keys, Bobby. *Every Night's a Saturday Night.* London: Omnibus Press, 2012.

90 Interview with Jas Obrecht (June 22, 1979), jasobrecht.com

91 *Mojo.* Interview with Rennie Sparks (September 2007).

92 *Stones in Exile.* DVD. New York: Eagle Rock Entertainment, 2010.

93 Greenfield, Robert. *Exile on Main St.* New York: Da Capo Press, 2006.

94 *Guitar Player.* Interview with Matt Blackett (May 20, 2010).

95 *Guitar Player.* Interview with Alan Di Perna (December 18, 2014).

96 *Mojo.* Interview with Mick Jones (September 2007).

97 Janovitz, Bill. *Exile on Main Street.* London: Bloomsbury, 2005.

98 *Goldmine Magazine.* Interview with Harvey Kubernik (May 8, 2010).

99 Flanagan, Bill. *Written in My Soul: Conversations with Rock's Great Songwriters.* London: Music Sales, 1990.

100 *Rolling Stone Magazine.* Interview with John Landau (October 16, 1974).

101 Elliott, Martin. *The Rolling Stones Complete Recording Sessions 1962–2012.* London: Cherry Red Books, 2006.

102 Interview with Mick Taylor by Kristina Pedersen. *Daily Mail Online* (January 28, 2007).

103 *Wall Street Journal.* Interview with Keith Richards by Marc Myers. (December 11, 2013).

104 *Abendzeitung.* Interview with Reinhold Mack by Christian Jooss (July 25, 2013).

105 Wood, Ron. *Ronnie.* London: Macmillan, 2007.

106 *Guitar World.* Interview with Damian Fanelli (March 5, 2012).

107 *Circus Weekly,* "Led Zeppelin Plays It for Fun," by Wesley Strick (February 1977).

108 *Mojo.* Interview with Jared Followill (September 2007).

109 *Rolling Stone Magazine.* Interview with Dave Marsh (April 23, 1976).

110 *Examiner.com.* Interview with Harvey Mandel by Harold Lepidus (2011).

111 "100 Greatest Rolling Stones Songs." (October 15, 2013), http://www.rollingstone.com/.

112 *Rolling Stone Magazine.* Interview with Patrick Doyle (October 2015).

113 *Modern Recording and Music Magazine.* Interview with Rob Patterson (October 1983).

114 *Sound on Sound* website (June 1999), http://www. soundonsound.com/.

115 Sheff, David. *All We Are Saying: The Last Major Interview with John Lennon and Yoko Ono.* New York: St. Martin's/Griffin, 2000.

116 *Best.* Interview with Gérard Bar-David (April 1985).

117 *Rolling Stone Magazine.* Interview with Chet Flippo (August 21, 1980).

118 Interview with Dylan Jones (July 12, 2011), GQMagazine.com.

119 *Rock & Folk,* no. 179. Interview with Mick Jagger (December 1981).

120 Buskin, Richard. *Sound on Sound.* Interview with Chris Kimsey (April 2004).

121 *The Guardian.* (January 24, 2010).

122 *Rolling Stone Magazine.* Interview with Kurt Loder (November 12, 1981).

123 Quotation from Chris Kimsey (1982), www. timeisonourside.com/.

124 *Rolling Stone Magazine.* Interview with Kurt Loder (November 7, 1983).

125 *Daily Mirror.* Interview with Mick Jagger (March 2, 1987).

126 Fricke, David. "The Rolling Stones: Mick Jagger and Keith Richards' Uneasy Truce." *Rolling Stone Magazine* (September 7, 1989).

127 Fricke, David. "Will Keith Richards Bury Us All?" *Rolling Stone Magazine* (October 17, 2002).

128 Buskin, Richard. *Sound on Sound.* Interview with Don Was (December 2004).

129 Fricke, David. "Rolling Stones Push Back the Clock with 'Voodoo Lounge' Album and Tour." *Rolling Stone Magazine* (July 14, 1994).

130 Interview with Jas Obrecht, jasobrecht.com (July 14, 1994).

131 Buskin, Richard. *Sound on Sound.* Interview with Don Was (December 1994).

132 *Los Angeles Times.* Interview with Jim Washburn (July 19, 1994).

133 Interview with Ron Wood by Jas Obrecht (July 14, 1994), jasobrecht.com.

134 Fricke, David. "The Rhythm Twins: Mick Jagger and Keith Richards Lead a March toward Babylon." *Rolling Stone Magazine* (September 4, 1997).

135 Interview with Paul Du Noyer, http://www.pauldunoyer.com.

136 *Daily Mail.* Interview with Jerry Hall (September 26, 2010).

137 *The Washington Post* "Jeff Sarli: Bassist Played on Rolling Stones Album," (September 2, 2006).

138 *Billboard.* Interview with Keith Richards (September 14, 2002).

139 *Rolling Stone Magazine.* Interview with Alan Light (September 5, 2005).

140 *New Musical Express (NME).* Interview with Dan Martin (September 19, 2005).

141 *Billboard.* "Stones Dust off Cobwebs with Toronto Show" (August 17, 2005).

142 www.songfacts.com.

143 *Guitar World.* Interview with Alan Di Perna (August 12, 2008).

144 Bhasker, Jeff. americansongwriter. com (July 10, 2013).

145 *Esquire.* Interview with Keith Richards by Mark Ellen (July 26, 2015).

146 *Q Magazine,* cited by Adam Bychawski in *NME.* "The Rolling Stones' Mick Jagger: "I'll be Camping Out at Glastonbury for the Whole Weekend." (October 9, 2012).

147 *Yahoo Music* "Some Girls, Some 33 Years Later" (November 28, 2011).

148 *Guitar World.* Interview with Mick Taylor by Damian Fanelli (March 5, 2012).

149 Booklet of the compilation *Rarities 1971–2003* (2005).

Black Dog & Leventhal Publishers
Hachette Book Group
1290 Avenue of the Americas
New York, NY 10104

www.hachettebookgroup.com
www.blackdogandleventhal.com

First English Edition: October 2016

Black Dog & Leventhal Publishers is an imprint of Hachette Books, a division of Hachette Book Group. The
Black Dog & Leventhal Publishers name and logo are trademarks of Hachette Book Group, Inc.

The publisher is not responsible for websites (or their content) that are not owned by the publisher.

The Hachette Speakers Bureau provides a wide range of authors for speaking events. To find
out more, go to www.HachetteSpeakersBureau.com or call (866) 376-6591.

Library of Congress Cataloging-in-Publication Data has been applied for.

ISBNs: 978-0-316-31774-0 (hardcover); 978-0-316-31773-3 (ebook)

Printed in China

1010

10 9 8 7 6 5 4 3 2 1